Poetry of the English Renaissance
1509-1660

*Selected from early editions and
manuscripts and edited by*

J. WILLIAM HEBEL
Late of Cornell University

and

HOYT H. HUDSON
Late of Princeton University

APPLETON-CENTURY-CROFTS, INC.

NEW YORK

PREFACE

The lyrical poetry of the period drawn upon by this volume has been well presented in a number of anthologies; but so far as we are aware, no previous anthology has given an adequate representation of the rich store of non-dramatic poetry in its wide variety. This we have attempted to do. In order that we might have sufficient space for the inclusion of a number of long poems we have omitted Spenser, Shakespeare, and Milton. We have been willing to do so because we believe that all readers and students desire to have complete editions of these poets. For the most part, the authors represented herein are accessible, if at all, only in scarce or expensive editions. A very few poems we have reprinted for the first time; many others have seen but one previous reprinting. We have not, however, aimed at novelty; we have attempted to give from the English Renaissance such poems as a lover of poetry might wish to have at his command. We have made poetic merit the principal test for inclusion. Yet in presenting poetry of the past one must yield something to the necessity for historical background, without which the full significance, or even the full beauty, of the cherished poetic legacy cannot appear. We have therefore added a few poems of historical or biographical interest, illustrating the literary life of Tudor-Stuart England. We have amplified the material of this nature by the inclusion of some noteworthy prefaces and dedications, and by extracts from the critical works of Sidney and Jonson.

Having begun with the purpose of illustrating English poetry from the beginning of Henry VIII's reign to the Restoration, in the progress of our work we found a continuous tradition which unified this body of poetry. The animating impulses of this tradition appear to be those which flow from the Renaissance. Thus the title for the volume at which we arrived seems to us exact and adequate. As might have been expected, the exact limits of 1509–1660 have been transgressed. Some particular poems early in the book were composed before 1509; and we have deliberately gone beyond 1660 by the inclusion of Traherne, who obviously belongs with his fellows, Herbert, Crashaw, and Vaughan, rather than with poets of the Restoration.

We have thought that the text of poetry for the reader and student should be prepared as carefully as that in definitive editions for the scholar. Hence our text is taken from the original editions and manuscripts, with a few exceptions made necessary when the desired volume or manuscript was in private hands and inaccessible to us. Except for correcting obvious printer's errors, such as turned or omitted letters, we have found emendation almost unnecessary, for usually the passage which at first seems corrupt proves merely to be one of obscure or unexpected meaning. Where change from the basic text seemed unavoidable, we have in almost every instance drawn upon another equally authoritative early text. Every such deviation has been noted, with the authority for our reading. In the notes we have also added a few interesting variant readings from other early editions or manuscripts.

With reluctance we have modernized the spelling. Although the original spelling, often the product of the printer's caprice or necessity, cannot be taken, in most cases, to represent the author's intent, yet some flavor departs when the Renaissance exuberance is curbed by standardization even in such a detail. In modernizing we had in mind the reader who is not a specialist and who may not be of antiquarian tastes. For the further convenience of the modern reader we have punctuated the text in accordance with the logical pointing of our day. Frequently the original punctuation has left the meaning ambiguous; we have been forced to settle upon the interpretation which seemed to us closest to the author's meaning. Exceptions to modernization of spelling will be found where rhythm or rhyme demands the original form of a word. When the suffix *ed* is to be pronounced as a syllable, we have marked it with a diæresis except in the case of words, such as *yielded*, where the pronunciation is unmistakable. We have also indicated by a diæresis the dissyllabic *ion* where necessary for rhyme. We have sometimes indicated accentuation which varies from modern usage. Wherever necessary for rhythm, we have retained the elision of the text, marking it with an apostrophe. Pronouns referring to the deity we print without capitals except where there is possibility of a mistaken reference.

Our principle has been to include whole poems; but in order to represent such works as Surrey's Virgil, Warner's *Albion's England*, Daniel's *Musophilus*, Drayton's *Poly-Olbion*, and Chapman's Homer, we have given extracts of a unified nature. All omissions are indicated. By the saving of space so effected we have been able to give complete such notable longer poems as Sackville's *Induction*, Marlowe's *Hero and Leander*, Davies's *Orchestra*, Drayton's *Nymphidia*, and whole cantos of Giles Fletcher's *Christ's Victory and Triumph* and Phineas Fletcher's *Locusts, or Apollyonists*.

Anonymous material and poems by authors not given separate headings are grouped in sections, as follows: 'Minor "Courtly Makers" of Henry VIII's Reign,' 'Elizabethan Miscellanies,' 'Sonnet-Sequences,' 'Songs from Plays,' 'Broadside Ballads,' 'Lyrics from Song-Books,' 'Epigrams,' and 'Stuart and Commonwealth Miscellanies.' Poems of known authorship in these sections we have signed with the author's name. To make these divisions more valuable, particularly to the teacher who wishes to discuss types of poetry, we have, in the introductions to each section, given cross-references to all other poems in our volume which relate to that group.

Titles of poems stand as in the source used. When the poem had no title, and one could not be supplied from another early edition, we have raised the first line or a part of it, in brackets, to serve as a title. We have not given titles to sonnets in sequence or to poems in the section, 'Songs from Plays.'

We have supplied an introduction and notes to each author or section of poems. These will be found at the end of the volume, so that the reader who desires to avoid any interruption need not be disturbed by them. The introductions give the minimum of biographical information necessary to the understanding of the poems; anecdotes which throw light upon the character of the subject have been given preference over a recital of dates and events. Critical comment has been directed toward showing a given author's place with relation to the general course of Tudor-Stuart poetry. To each introduction we have appended a selected bibliography of the best modern editions and critical comment, and a statement of the location of the exemplar used as basic text. In order fully to identify the edition used by us, we have given in parentheses after the title the entry-number of the Bibliographical Society's *Short-Title Catalogue* . . . *of English Books, 1475–1640*, compiled by Pollard and Redgrave.

In preparing the notes we have not thought it necessary to replace the desk dictionary; nor have we wished to rob the student of the pleasure of finding for himself echoes of one poet in another or borrowings from well-known classics. Words and meanings of words now unfamiliar but common in the sixteenth and seventeenth centuries we have annotated once or twice, upon their first appearances in the volume.

It seemed most convenient to supply only a single index, in which authors, titles, and first lines of poems are all given in alphabetical arrangement. Our Table of Contents is by authors and sections only.

We wish to acknowledge our indebtedness to Mr. Norman Ault's *Elizabethan Lyrics* and *Seventeenth Century Lyrics*, which enabled us to locate the printed and manuscript sources of a few poems which we had not been able to find elsewhere. For the use of rare books and manuscripts we are indebted to the librarians of the British Museum, the Bodleian, Cambridge University, the Huntington Library, Harvard University, Cornell University, Princeton University, and the Elizabethan Club of Yale University. We feel a special debt to Messrs. A. M. and H. T. White of Brooklyn for their generous permission to use the collection made by their father, Mr. W. A. White. Mr. Leon Mandel, II, of Chicago, kindly placed at our disposal several volumes from his library. For aid in collating texts we wish to thank Miss Gertrude Sibley, Associate Professor of English, College of the Pacific; Mr. Charles T. Phillips, Librarian of Chetham's Library, Manchester; Mr. R. F. Treharne, of the Department of History, the University, Manchester; Mr. John C. Adams, of King's College, Cambridge; Mr. Chilson Leonard, Instructor in English, Yale University; Miss Mary Potter, the Huntington Library; Miss Ethel Stokes, London; and Miss E. G. Parker, Oxford. We wish to acknowledge the secretarial aid of Mr. Raymond W. Short. To Mr. Woodford Patterson we are indebted for the lay-out of the title-page and for advice on typography. The design of the Tudor rose and the Stuart thistle, used on the binding and the title-page, we owe to Mr. Christian Midjo. Aside from these specific debts, the editors wish to acknowledge their obligation to Professor J. Q. Adams, Jr., of Cornell University, under whom both of them pursued studies in Elizabethan literature.

J. W. H.
H. H. H.

Princeton, February 28, 1929

Note: For this printing the text (pages 13–27) and the Introduction and Notes (pages 912–14) for Sir Thomas Wyatt's poems have been revised.

Francis R. Johnson

Stanford University

TABLE OF CONTENTS

POETRY OF THE ENGLISH
RENAISSANCE
1509–1660

JOHN SKELTON

The Introduction and Notes are at page 908

FROM *Pithy, Pleasant, and Profitable Works*, 1568

Philip Sparrow

Pla ce bo,
Who is there? Who?
Di le xi,
Dame Margery.
Fa, re, mi, mi,
Wherefore and why, why?
For the soul of Philip Sparrow,
That was late slain at Carow
Among the Nunnës Blake,
For that sweet soul's sake   10
And for all sparrows' souls
Set in our beadrolls,
Pater noster qui
With an *Ave Mari,*
And with the corner of a Creed,
The more shall be your meed.

When I remember again
How my Philip was slain,
Never half the pain
Was between you twain,   20
Pyramus and Thisbe,
As then befell to me:
I wept and I wailed,
The tearës down hailed,—
But nothing it availed
To call Philip again,
Whom Gib, our cat, hath slain.

Gib, I say, our cat
Worrowëd her on that
Which I loved best.   30
It cannot be expressed—
My sorrowful heaviness,
But all without redress;

For within that stound,
Half slumb'ring, in a swound,
I fell down to the ground.
Unneth I cast mine eyes
Toward the cloudy skies,
But when I did behold
My sparrow dead and cold,   40
No creature but that wold
Have rued upon me,
To behold and see
What heaviness did me pang;
Wherewith my hands I wrang,
That my sinews cracked
As though I had been racked;
So pained and so strained
That no life well-nigh remained.
I sighed and I sobbed   50
For that I was robbed
Of my sparrow's life.
O maiden, widow, and wife,
Of what estate ye be,
Of high or low degree,
Great sorrow then ye might see,
And learn to weep at me!
Such pains did me fret
That mine heart did beat,
My visage pale and dead,   60
Wan and blue as lead,
The pangs of hateful death
Well-nigh stopped my breath.
Heu, heu, me,
That I am woe for thee!
Ad Dominum, cum tribularer,
         clamavi:
Of God nothing else crave I

3

But Philip's soul to keep
From the marees deep
Of Acheronte's well,   70
That is a flood of hell,
And from the great Pluto,
The prince of endless woe;
And from foul Alecto
With visage black and blo;
And from Medusa, that mare,
That like a fiend doth stare;
And from Megera's adders,
For ruffling of Philip's feathers,
And from her fiery sparklings   80
For burning of his wings;
And from the smokës sour
Of Proserpina's bower;
And from the dennës dark
Where Cerberus doth bark,
Whom Theseus did affray,
Whom Hercules did outray,
As famous poets say;
From that hell-hound
That lieth in chainës bound,   90
With ghastly headës three,
To Jupiter pray we
That Philip preserved may be!
Amen, say ye with me!
    Do mi nus,
Help now, sweet Jesus!

. . . .

It was so pretty a fool,
It would sit on a stool
And learned after my school
For to keep his cut,   100
With, Philip, keep your cut!
    It had a velvet cap,
And would sit upon my lap
And seek after small worms
And sometime white bread
    crumbs;
And many times and oft
Between my brestës soft
It would lie and rest;
It was propre and prest.
    Sometime he would gasp   110

When he saw a wasp;
A fly or a gnat—
He would fly at that;
And prettily he would pant
When he saw an ant;
Lord, how he would pry
After the butterfly!
Lord, how he would hop
After the gressop!
And when I said, Phip! Phip!   120
Then he would leap and skip,
And take me by the lip.
Alas, it will me slo
That Philip is gone me fro!
    Si in i qui ta tes,
Alas, I was evil at ease!
De pro fun dis cla ma vi,
When I saw my sparrow die!

. . . .

    That vengeance I ask and cry,
By way of exclamation,   130
On all the whole nation
Of cattës wild and tame:
God send them sorrow and shame!
That cat specially
That slew so cruelly
My little pretty sparrow
That I brought up at Carow.
    O cat of churlish kind,
The fiend was in thy mind
When thou my bird un-
    twined,—   140
I would thou hadst been blind!
The leopardës savage,
The lions in their rage,
Might catch thee in their paws
And gnaw thee in their jaws!
These serpents of Lybany
Might sting thee venomously!
The dragons with their tongues
Might poison thy liver and lungs!
The mantycors of the moun-
    tains   150
Might feed them on thy brains!
    Melanchates, that hound

That plucked Acteon to the
    ground,
Gave him his mortal wound,
Changed to a deer;
The story doth appear
Was changed to an hart:
So thou, foul cat that thou art,
The self-same hound
Might thee confound   160
That his own lord bote,
Might bite asunder thy throat!
    Of Ind the greedy gripes
Might tear out all thy tripes!
Of Arcady the bears
Might pluck away thine ears!
The wild wolf Lycaon
Bite asunder thy back-bone!
Of Ætna the brenning hill
That day and night brenneth
    still,   170
Set in thy tail a blaze,
That all the world may gaze
And wonder upon thee,
From Ocean, the great sea,
Unto the isles of Orchady;
From Tilbury ferry
To the plain of Salisbury!
So traitorously my bird to kill,
That never ought thee evil will!
    Was never bird in cage   180
More gentle of corage
In doing his homage
Unto his soveraine.
Alas, I say again,
Death hath departed us twain!
The false cat hath thee slain,—
Farewell, Philip, adieu!
Our Lord thy soul rescue!
Farewell without restore,
Farewell for evermore!   190

. . . .

Colin Clout

What can it avail
To drive forth a snail,
Or to make a sail

Of an herring's tail?
To rhyme or to rail,
To write or to indite,
Either for delight
Or else for despite?
Or books to compile
Of divers manner style,   10
Vice to revile
And sin to exile?
To teach or to preach
As reason will reach?
Say this, and say that:
His head is so fat
He wotteth never what
Nor whereof he speaketh;
He crieth and he creaketh,
He prieth and he peeketh,   20
He chides and he chatters,
He prates and he patters,
He clitters and he clatters,
He meddles and he smatters,
He glozes and he flatters!
Or if he speak plain,
Then he lacketh brain,
He is but a fool;
Let him go to school.
A three-footed stool!   30
That he may down sit,
For he lacketh wit!
And if that he hit
The nail on the head,
It standeth in no stead;
The devil, they say, is dead,
The devil is dead.
    It may well so be,
Or else they would see
Otherwise, and flee   40
From worldly vanity,
And foul covetousness
And other wretchedness,
Fickle falseness,
Variableness
With unstableness.
    And if ye stand in doubt
Who brought this rhyme about,
My name is Colin Clout.

I purpose to shake out 50
All my cunning bag
Like a clerkly hag;
For though my rhyme be ragged,
Tattered and jagged,
Rudely rain-beaten,
Rusty and moth-eaten,
If ye take well therewith
It hath in it some pith.
For, as far as I can see,
It is wrong with each degree: 60
For the temporalty
Accuseth the spiritualty;
The spiritual again
Doth grudge and complain
Upon temporal men;
Thus each of other blother,
The t'one against the t'other,—
Alas, they make me shudder!
For in hudder-mudder
The church is put in faute; 70
The prelates been so haut,
They say, and look so high
As though they would fly
Above the starry sky.
 Laymen say indeed
How they take no heed
Their seely sheep to feed,
But pluck away and pull
The fleeces of their wool;
Unnethes they leave a lock 80
Of wool amongst their flock;
And as for their cunning,
A glomming and a mumming,
And make thereof a jape;
They gasp and they gape
All to have promotion,
There is their whole devotion,
With money, if it will hap,
To catch the forkèd cap;
Forsooth, they are too lewd 90
To say so,—all beshrewed!

. . . . . .

 Thus I, Colin Clout,
As I go about,

And wand'ring as I walk,
I hear the people talk.
Men say, for silver and gold
Mitres are bought and sold;
There shall no clergy appose
A mitre nor a crose,
But a full purse; 100
A straw for Goddès curse!
What are they the worse?
For a simoniac
Is but a harmoniac;
And no more ye make
Of simony, men say,
But a child's play.
 Over this, the foresaid lay
Report how the Pope may
A holy anker call 110
Out of the stony wall
And him a bishop make,
If he on him dare take
To keep so hard a rule—
To ride upon a mule
With gold all betrapped,
In purple and pall belapped;
Some hatted and some capped,
Richèly bewrapped,
God wot to their great pains, 120
In rotchets of fine Raynes,
White as morrow's milk;
Their tabards of fine silk,
Their stirrups of mixed gold be-
 garred;
There may no cost be spared;
Their mulès gold doth eat,
Their neighbors die for meat.
 What care they though Gil
 sweat,
Or Jack of the Noke?
The poor people they yoke 130
With summons and citations
And excommunications,
About churches and market;
The bishop on his carpet
At home full soft doth sit.
This is a fearful fit,
To hear the people jangle,

How warily they wrangle,—
Alas, why do ye not handle
And them all mangle?   140
Full falsely on you they lie,
And shamefully you ascry,
And say as untruly
As the butterfly
A man might say in mock
Were the weathercock
Of the steeple of Poules;
And thus they hurt their souls
In slandering you, for truth:
Alas, it is great ruth!   150

. . . . . .

To Mistress Isabel Pennell

By Saint Mary, my lady,
Your mammy and your dady
Brought forth a goodly baby!
    My maiden Isabel,
Reflaring rosabell,
The flagrant camamell, ·
    The ruddy rosary,
The sovereign rosemary,
The pretty strawberry,
    The columbine, the nepte,   10
The jeloffer well set,
The proper violet;
    Ennewèd your colowre
Is like the daisy flower
After the April shower;
    Star of the morrow gray,
The blossom on the spray,
The freshest flower of May:
    Maidenly demure,
Of womanhood the lure;   20
Wherefore I make you sure
    It were an heavenly health,
It were an endless wealth,
A life for God himself,
    To hear this nightingale

Among the birdès smale
Warbeling in the vale,—
Dug, dug, jug, jug,
Good year and good luck,   29
With chuck, chuck, chuck, chuck!

To Mistress Margaret Hussey

Merry Margaret,
As midsummer flower,
Gentil as falcon
Or hawk of the tower;
    With solace and gladness,
Much mirth and no madness,
All good and no badness,
So joyously,
So maidenly,
So womanly   10
Her demeaning
In every thing,—
Far, far passing
That I can endite
Or suffice to write
Of merry Margaret,
As midsummer flower,
Gentil as falcon
Or hawk of the tower.
    As patient and as still   20
And as full of good will
As fair Isiphill,
Coliander,
Sweet pomander,
Good Cassaunder;
Steadfast of thought,
Well made, well wrought;
Far may be sought
Erst that ye can find
So curteise, so kind   30
As merry Margaret,
This midsummer flower,
Gentil as falcon
Or hawk of the tower. ·

A prayer to the Father of heaven

O radiant luminary of light interminable,
    Celestial Father, potential God of might,

Of heaven and earth O Lord incomparable,
    Of all perfections the essential most perfite!
    O maker of mankind, that forméd day and night,
Whose power imperial comprehendeth every place:
    Mine heart, my mind, my thought, my whole delight
Is after this life to see thy glorious face.

Whose magnificence is incomprehensible,
    All arguments of reason which far doth exceed,   10
Whose deity doubtless is indivisible,
    From whom all goodness and virtue doth proceed;
    Of thy support all creätures have need:
Assist me, good Lord, and grant me of thy grace
    To live to thy pleasure in word, thought, and deed,
And after this life to see thy glorious face.

HENRY VIII

The Introduction and Notes are at page 910

From *Additional Ms.* 31922

[*Pastime with good company*]

Pastime with good company
I love, and shall until I die.
Grutch who lust, but none deny,
So God be pleased, thus live will I.
For my pastance,
Hunt, sing, and dance,
My heart is set;
All goodly sport
For my comfort,
Who shall me let?   10

Youth must have some dalliance,
Of good or ill some pastance;
Company methinks then best,
All thoughts and fancies to digest.
For idleness is chief mistress
Of vices all; then who can say
But mirth and play
Is best of all?

Company with honesty
Is virtue, vices to flee;   20
Company is good and ill,
But every man hath his free will.
The best ensue,
The worst eschew;
My mind shall be,—
Virtue to use,
Vice to refuse,
Thus shall I use me.

[*Whereto should I express*]

Whereto should I express
My inward heaviness?
No mirth can make me fain
Till that we meet again.

Do 'way, dear heart, not so!
Let no thought you dismay;
Though ye now part me fro,
We shall meet when we may.

When I remember me
Of your most gentil mind, 10
It may in no wise agree
That I should be unkind.

The daisy delectable,
The violet wan and blo—
Ye are not variable,
I love you and no mo.

I make you fast and sure;
It is to me great pain
Thus longë to endure
Till that we meet again. 20

[Whoso that will]

Whoso that will for gracë sue
His intent must needs be true,
And lovë her in heart and deed,
Else it were pity that he should
    speed.
Many one saith that love is ill,
But those be they which can no
    skill.

Or else because they may not ob-
    tain,
They would that other should it
    disdain.
But love is a thing given by God,
In that therefore can be none
    odd; 10
But perfect indeed and between
    two,
Wherefore then should we it
    eschew?

[Green groweth the holly]

Green groweth the holly, so doth
    the ivy.
Though winter blasts blow never
    so high,
Green groweth the holly.

As the holly groweth green
    And never changeth hue,
So I am, and ever hath been,
    Unto my lady true.
        Green groweth . . . etc.

As the holly groweth green,
    With ivy all alone, 10
When flowerys cannot be seen
    And green-wood leaves be gone,
        ut supra

Now unto my lady
    Promise to her I make:
From all other only
    To her I me betake.
        ut supra

Adieu, mine own lady,
    Adieu, my specïal, 20
Who hath my heart truly,
    Be sure, and ever shall.

Green groweth the holly, so doth
    the ivy.
Though winter blasts blow never
    so high,
Green groweth the holly.

SIR THOMAS MORE

The Introduction and Notes are at page 911

From Works, 1557

Childhood

I am called Childhood: in play is all my mind,
To cast a quoit, a cockstele, and a ball.

A top can I set, and drive it in his kind;
But would to God these hateful bookës all
Were in a fire brent to powder small!
Then might I lead my life always in play,
Which life God send me to mine ending day.

Manhood

Manhood I am: therefore I me delight
To hunt and hawk, to nourish up and feed
The greyhound to the course, the hawk to the flight,
And to bestride a good and lusty steed.
These things become a very man indeed.
Yet thinketh this boy his peevish game swetter,
But what! no force, his reason is no better.

Age

Old Age am I, with lockës thin and hoar:
Of our short life the last and best part,
Wise and discreet; the public weal therefore
I help to rule, to my labor and smart.
Therefore, Cupid, withdraw thy fiery dart,
Chargeable matters shall of love oppress
Thy childish game and idle business.

Two short ballettes . . .
Made for his pastime while he was prisoner in the Tower of London

Lewis, the lost lover

Eye-flattering fortune, look thou never so fair,
Or never so pleasantly begin to smile,
As though thou wouldst my ruin all repair;
During my life thou shalt me not beguile.
Trust shall I God, to enter in a while
His haven of heaven, sure and uniform;
Ever after thy calm look I for a storm.

Davy, the dicer

Long was I, Lady Luck, your serving-man,
And now have lost again all that I gat;
Wherefore, when I think on you now and than
And in my mind remember this and that,
Ye may not blame me though I beshrew your cat.
But, in faith, I bless you again, a thousand times,
For lending me now some leisure to make rhymes.

JOHN HEYWOOD

The Introduction and Notes are at page 911

FROM RICHARD TOTTEL'S *Songs and Sonnets*, 1557

A praise of his lady

Give place, you ladies, and be
    gone,
Boast not yourselves at all,
For here at hand approacheth one
Whose face will stain you all.

The virtue of her lively looks
Excels the precious stone,
I wish to have none other books
To read or look upon!

In each of her two crystal eyes
Smileth a naked boy;   10
It would you all in heart suffice
To see that lamp of joy.

I think nature hath lost the
    mould
Where she her shape did take,
Or else I doubt if nature could
So fair a creature make.

She may be well compared
Unto the phœnix kind,
Whose like was never seen nor
    heard,
That any man can find.   20

In life she is Diana chast,
In truth, Penelope;
In word and eke in deed stead-
    fast—
What will you more we say?

If all the world were sought so
    far,
Who could find such a wight?

Her beauty twinkleth like a star
Within the frosty night.

Her rosial color comes and goes
With such a comely grace,   30
More redier too than doth the
    rose
Within her lively face.

At Bacchus' feast none shall
    her meet,
Ne at no wanton play;
Nor gazing in an open street
Nor gadding as a stray.

The modest mirth that she doth
    use
Is mixed with shamefastness.
All vice she doth wholly refuse,
And hateth idleness.   40

O Lord, it is a world to see
How virtue can repair
And deck her in such honesty,
Whom nature made so fair.

Truly, she doth as far exceed
Our women nowadays
As doth the gillyflower a weed,
And more, a thousand ways.

How might I do to get a graff
Of this unspotted tree,   50
For all the rest are plain but chaff,
Which seem good corn to be.

This gift alone I shall her give
When death doth what he can:
Her honest fame shall ever live
Within the mouth of man.

FROM *Works*, 1562
Jack and his father

Jack (quoth his father) how shall I ease take?
If I stand, my legs ache; and if I kneel

My knees ache; if I go, then my feet ache;
If I lie, my back ach'th; if I sit, I feel
My hips ache; and lean I never so weel,
My elbows ache. Sir (quoth Jack) pain to exile,
Since all these ease not, best ye hang awhile.

Of loving a dog

Love me, love my dog: by love to agree
I love thy dog as well as I love thee.

Of a sheep's eye

He cast a sheep's eye at her: a strange eye-spread
To see a sheep's eye look out of a calf's head.

Of enough and a feast

As good enough as a feast: yea, God save it!
Enough were even as good if we might have it.

Of late and never

Better late than never: yea, mate,
But as good never as too late.

Of a cat's look

A cat may look on a king: and what of that?
When a cat so looketh, a cat is but a cat.

Of Heywood

Art thou Heywood, with the mad merry wit?
Yea, forsooth, master! that same is even hit.
Art thou Heywood that applieth mirth more than thrift?
Yea, sir, I take merry mirth a golden gift.
Art thou Heywood that hath made many mad plays?
Yea, many plays; few good works in all my days.
Art thou Heywood that hath made men merry long?
Yea, and will, if I be made merry among.
Art thou Heywood that would be made merry now?
Yea, sir, help me to it now, I beseech yow.

SIR THOMAS WYATT

The Introduction and Notes are at page 912

FROM *Egerton Ms.* 2711

[*The lover compareth his state to a ship in perilous storm tossed on the sea*]

My galley chargèd with forgetfulness
Thorrough sharp seas, in winter nights, doth pass
'Tween rock and rock; and eke mine enemy, alas,
That is my lord, steereth with cruelness;
And every oar a thought in readiness,
As though that death were light in such a case.
An endless wind doth tear the sail apace,
Of forcèd sighs and trusty fearfulness;
A rain of tears, a cloud of dark disdain,
Have done the wearied cords great hinderance;   10
Wreathèd with error and eke with ignorance,
The stars be hid that led me to this pain;
Drownèd is reason, that should me consort,
And I remain despairing of the port.

[*The lover's life compared to the Alps*]

Like to these unmeasurable mountains,
Is my painful life, the burden of ire,
For of great height be they, and high is my desire,
And I of tears, and they be full of fountains;
Under craggy rocks they have full barren plains,
Hard thoughts in me my woeful mind doth tire;
Small fruit and many leaves their toppès do attire,
Small effect with great trust in me remains.
The boistous windès oft their high boughs do blast,
Hot sighs from me continually be shed;   10
Cattle in them, and in me love is fed;
Immovable am I, and they are full steadfast.
Of the restless birds they have the tune and note,
And I always plaints that pass thorough my throat.

[*Description of the contrarious passions in a lover*]

I find no peace, and all my war is done;
I fear and hope; I burn, and freeze like ice;

I fly above the wind, yet can I not arise;
And nought I have, and all the world I season.
That looseth nor locketh holdeth me in prison,
And holdeth me not, yet can I 'scape no wise;
Nor letteth me live, nor die, at my devise,
And yet of death it giveth none occasion.
Without eyen, I see; and without tongue, I plain;
I desire to perish, and yet I askë health;   10
I love another, and thus I hate myself;
I feed me in sorrow, and laugh in all my pain.
Likewise displeaseth me both death and life,
And my delight is causer of this strife.

[*The lover for shamefastness hideth his desire within his faithful heart*]

The long love that in my thought doth harbor,
And in mine heart doth keep his residence,
Into my face presseth with bold pretense
And therein campeth, spreading his banner.
She that me learneth to love and suffer
And wills that my trust and lust's negligence
Be reined by reason, shame, and reverence,
With his hardiness taketh displeasure.
Wherewithall unto the heart's forest he fleeth,
Leaving his enterprise with pain and cry,   10
And there him hideth, and not appeareth:
What may I do when my master feareth
But in the field with him to live and die?
For good is the life ending faithfully.

[*A renouncing of love*]

Farewell, love, and all thy laws for ever,
Thy baited hooks shall tangle me no more;
Senec and Plato call me from thy lore
To perfect wealth, my wit for to endeavor;
In blindë error when I did perséver,
Thy sharp repulse that pricketh aye so sore
Hath taught me to set in trifles no store,
And scape forth, since liberty is lever.
Therefore, farewell! Go trouble younger hearts,
And in me claim no more authority;   10
With idle youth go use thy property,
And thereon spend thy many brittle darts.
For hitherto though I have lost all my time,
Me lusteth no longer rotten boughs to climb.

[*Whoso list to hunt*]

Whoso list to hunt, I know where is an hind,
　But as for me——alas, I may no more.
　The vain travail hath wearied me so sore,
　I am of them that farthest cometh behind.
Yet may I, by no means, my wearied mind
　Draw from the deer; but as she fleeth afore
　Fainting I follow. I leave off therefore,
　Since in a net I seek to hold the wind.
Who list her hunt, I put him out of doubt,
　As well as I, may spend his time in vain.
　And graven with diamonds in letters plain
There is written, her fair neck round about:
　Noli me tangere, for Cæsar's I am,
　And wild for to hold, though I seem tame.

From *Additional Ms.* 17492

[*Divers doth use*]

Divers doth use, as I have heard and know,
　(When that to change their ladies do begin),
　To mourn and wail, and never for to lin,
　Hoping thereby to pease their painful woe.
And some there be, that when it chanceth so
　That women change, and hate where love hath been,
　They call them false, and think with words to win
　The hearts of them which otherwhere doth grow.
But as for me, though that by chance indeed
　Change hath outworn the favor that I had,
　I will not wail, lament, nor yet be sad,
Nor call her false that falsely did me feed;
　But let it pass, and think it is of kind
　That often change doth please a woman's mind.

From Richard Tottel's *Songs and Sonnets,* 1557

Of his return from Spain

Tagus, farewell, that westward with thy streams
Turns up the grains of gold already tried;
For I with spur and sail go seek the Temes,
Gainward the sun, that showeth her wealthy pride;
And to the town that Brutus sought by dreams,
Like bended moon that leans her lusty side,

My king, my country, I seek, for whom I live—
O mighty Jove, the winds for this me give!

Of such as had forsaken him

Lux, my fair falcon, and thy fellows all,
How well pleasant it were, your liberty!
Ye not forsake me that fair might you fall;
But they that sometime liked my company
Like lice away from dead bodies they crawl—
Lo, what a proof in light adversity!
But ye, my birds, I swear by all your bells,
Ye be my friends, and very few else.

A description of such a one as he would love

A face that should content me wondrous well
Should not be fair, but lovely to behold,
Of lively look, all grief for to repel,
With right good grace, so would I that it should
Speak without word such words as none can tell;
The tress also should be of crispèd gold.
With wit, and these, perchance I might be tied,
And knit again with knot that should not slide.

That speaking or proffering brings alway speeding

Speak thou and speed, where will or power aught help'th,
Where power doth want, will must be won by wealth;
For need will speed where will works not his kind,
And gain, thy foes thy friends shall cause thee find:
For suit and gold—what do not they obtain?
Of good and bad the triers are these twain.

Description of a gun

Vulcan begat me; Minerva me taught;
Nature, my mother; craft nourished me year by year;
Three bodies are my food, my strength is in nought;
Anger, wrath, waste, and noise are my children dear:
Guess, friend, what I am and how I am wrought,
Monster of sea, or of land, or of elsewhere?
Know me, and use me, and I may thee defend,
And if I be thine enemy, I may thy life end.

FROM *Harleian Ms.* 78

[Wyatt being in prison, to Bryan]

Sighs are my food, drink are my tears;
Clinking of fetters such music would crave;

Stink and close air, away my life wears;
Innocency is all the hope I have.
Rain, wind, or weather I judge by mine ears;
Malice assaulted that righteousness should have.
Sure I am, Bryan, this wound shall heal again,
But yet, alas, the scar shall still remain.

FROM *Egerton Ms.* 2711

[*Of his love called Anna*]

What word is that, that changeth not
Though it be turned, and made in twain?
It is mine answer, God it wot,
And eke the causer of my pain.
A love rewardeth with disdain,
Yet is it loved—what would ye more?
It is my health, and eke my sore.

[*To a lady, to answer directly with yea or nay*]

Madam, withouten many words,
Once I am sure, ye will or no;
And if ye will, then leave your bordes,
And use your wit, and shew it so;
And with a beck ye shall me call.
And if of one that burneth alway
Ye have any pity at all,
Answer him fair, with yea or nay:
If it be yea, I shall be fain;
If it be nay, friends as before;   10
Ye shall another man obtain,
And I mine own, and yours no more.

FROM *Additional Ms.* 17492

[*The lover to his bed, with describing of his unquiet state*]

The restful place, reviver of my smart,
The labor's salve, increasing my sorrów,
The body's ease, and troubler of my heart,
Quieter of mind, and mine unquiet foe,
Forgetter of pain, remembering my woe,
The place of sleep wherein I do but wake,—
Besprent with tears, my bed, I thee forsake.
   The frost, the snow, may ..ot redress my heat,
Nor yet no heat abate my fervent cold.
I know nothing to ease my painës meet;   10
Each care causeth increase by twenty fold,

Reviving cares upon my sorrows old;
Such overthwart affects they do me make,
Besprent with tears, my bed for to forsake.
  Yet helpeth it not. I find no better ease
In bed, or out. This most causeth my pain,
Where most I seek how best that I may please,
My lost labor, alas, is all in vain.
Yet that I gave I cannot call again;
No place from me my grief away can take,   20
Wherefore with tears, my bed, I thee forsake.

FROM *Egerton Ms.* 2711

*[The lover showeth how he is forsaken of such as he
sometime enjoyed]*

  They flee from me, that sometime did me seek,
With naked foot stalking in my chamber.
I have seen them gentle, tame, and meek,
That now are wild, and do not remember
That sometime they have put themselves in danger
To take bread at my hand; and now they range,
Busily seeking with a continual change.
  Thanked be fortune it hath been otherwise,
Twenty times better; but once, in special,
In thin array, after a pleasant guise,   10
When her loose gown from her shoulders did fall,
And she me caught in her arms long and small;
Therewithal sweetly did me kiss
And softly said, 'Dear heart, how like you this?'
  It was no dream; I lay broad waking.
But all is turned thorough my gentleness,
Into a strange fashion of forsaking;
And I have leave to go, of her goodëness,
And she also to use newfangleness.
But since that I so kindëly am served,
I would fain know what she hath deserved?

[Help me to seek]

Help me to seek—for I lost it
  there,
And if that ye have found it, ye
  that be here,
And seek to convey it secretly,
Handle it soft and treat it tenderly

Or else it will plain, and then appear.
But rather restore it mannerly,
Since that I do ask it thus hon-
  estly,
For to lese it, it sitteth me too
  near:
                Help me to seek!

Alas, and is there no remedy? [10]
But have I thus lost it wilfully?
I wis it was a thing all too dear
To be bestowed, and wist not
  where:
It was mine heart! I pray you
  heartily
        Help me to seek.

FROM *Additional Ms.* 17492

[*Forget not yet*]

Forget not yet the tried intent
Of such a truth as I have meant,
My great travail, so gladly spent,
    Forget not yet.

Forget not yet when first began
The weary life ye know, since
  whan
The suit, the service none tell can,
    Forget not yet.

Forget not yet the great assays,
The cruel wrong, the scornful
  ways; [10]
The painful patience in denays,
    Forget not yet.

Forget not yet, forget not this,
How long ago hath been, and is,
The mind that never meant
  amiss,—
    Forget not yet.

Forget not, then, thine own approved,
The which so long hath thee so
  loved,
Whose steadfast faith yet never
  moved,
    Forget not this. [20]

[*And wilt thou leave me
  thus?*]

And wilt thou leave me thus?
Say nay, say nay! For shame,

To save thee from the blame
Of all my grief and grame.
And wilt thou leave me thus?
Say nay, say nay.

And wilt thou leave me thus,
That hath loved thee so long
In wealth and woe among?
And is thy heart so strong [10]
As for to leave me thus?
Say nay, say nay.

And wilt thou leave me thus,
That hath given thee my heart,
Never for to depart
Neither for pain nor smart;
And wilt thou leave me thus?
Say nay, say nay.

And wilt thou leave me thus,
And have no more pity [20]
Of him that loveth thee?
Alas, thy cruelty!
And wilt thou leave me thus?
Say nay, say nay!

[*Blame not my lute*]

Blame not my lute, for he must
  sound
Of this or that as liketh me;
For lack of wit the lute is bound
To give such tunes as pleaseth
  me.
Though my songs be somewhat
  strange,
And speaks such words as touch
  thy change,
        Blame not my lute.

My lute, alas, doth not offend,
Though that perforce he must
  agree
To sound such tunes as I intend [10]
To sing to them that heareth me;
Then though my songs be some-
  what plain

And toucheth some that use to
    feign,
      Blame not my lute.

My lute and strings may not deny,
But as I strike they must obey;
Break not them, then, so wrong-
    fully,
But wreak thyself some wiser
    way;
And though the songs which I
    indite
Do quit thy change with right-
    ful spite,   20
      Blame not my lute.

Spite asketh spite, and changing
    change,
And falsëd faith must needs be
    known;
The fault so great, the case so
    strange,
Of right it must abroad be blown.
Then since that by thine own
    desart
My songs do tell how true thou
    art,
      Blame not my lute.

Blame but the self that hast mis-
    done
And well deservëd to have
    blame;   30
Change thou thy way so evil be-
    gun
And then my lute shall sound
    that same;
But if till then my fingers play,
By thy desert, their wonted way,
      Blame not my lute.

Farewell, unknown, for though
    thou break
My strings in spite, with great dis-
    dain,
Yet have I found out for thy sake

Strings for to string my lute
    again.
And if perchance this foolish
    rhyme   40
Do make thee blush at any time,
      Blame not my lute.

[*Since you will needs*]

Since you will needs that I shall
    sing,
Take it in worth, such as I have,
Plenty of plaint, moan, and
    mourning
In deep despair and deadly pain,
Bootless for boot, crying to crave,
      To crave in vain.

Such hammers work within my
    head
That sound nought else unto my
    ears
But fast at board, and wake abed;
Such tune the temper to my song 10
To wail my wrong, that I want
    tears
      To wail my wrong.

Death and despair afore my face,
My days decays, my grief doth
    grow;
The cause thereof is in this place,
Whom cruelty doth still con-
    strain
For to rejoice, though it be woe
      To hear me plain.

A broken lute, untunëd strings
With such a song may well bear
    part,   20
That neither pleaseth him that
    sings
Nor them that hear, but her alone
That with her heart would strain
    my heart,
      To hear it groan.

If it grieve you to hear this same
That you do feel but in my voice,
Consider then what pleasant game
I do sustain in every part,
To cause me sing or to rejoice
      Within my heart. 30

[Tangled I was]

Tangled I was in love's snare,
Oppressed with pain, torment with
   care,
Of grief right sure, of joy full
   bare,
Clean in despair by cruelty,—
But ha! ha! ha! full well is me,
For I am now at liberty.

The woeful days so full of pain,
The weary night all spent in vain,
The labor lost for so small gain,
To write them all it will not
   be. 10
But ha! ha! ha! full well is me,
For I am now at liberty.

Everything that fair doth show,
When proof is made it proveth
   not so,
But turneth mirth to bitter woe;
Which in this case full well I see.
But ha! ha! ha! full well is me,
For I am now at liberty.

Too great desire was my guide
And wanton will went by my
   side; 20

Hope rulëd still, and made me
   bide
Of love's craft th' extremity.
But ha! ha! ha! full well is me,
For I am now at liberty.

With feignëd words that were
   but wind
To long delays I was assigned;
Her wily looks my wits did blind;
Thus as she would I did agree.
But ha! ha! ha! full well is me,
For I am now at liberty. 30

Was never bird tangled in lime
That brake away in better time
Than I, that rotten boughs did
   climb,
And had no hurt, but scapëd free.
Now ha! ha! ha! full well is me,
For I am now at liberty.

[Hate whom ye list]

Hate whom ye list, for I care not,
Love whom ye list and spare not,
Do what ye list and dread not,
Think what ye list, I fear not,
For, as for me, I am not
But even as one that recks not
Whether ye hate or hate not;
For in your love I dote not,
Wherefore I pray you forget not,
But love whom ye list, for I care
   not. 10

From Richard Tottel's *Songs and Sonnets,* 1557

Of the mean and sure estate

Written to John Poins

My mother's maids when they do sew and spin,
They sing a song made of the fieldish mouse;
That forbecause her livelihood was but thin,
Would needs go see her townish sister's house.

She thought herself endured to grievous pain;
The stormy blasts her cave so sore did souse,
That when the furrows swimmëd with the rain,
She must lie cold and wet, in sorry plight.
And worse than that, bare meat there did remain
To comfort her when she her house had dight: 10
Sometime a barley corn, sometime a bean,
For which she labored hard both day and night
In harvest time, while she might go and glean.
And when her store was 'stroyëd with the flood,
Then wellaway, for she undone was clean.
Then was she fain to take instead of food
Sleep, if she might, her hunger to beguile.
My sister, quoth she, hath a living good,
And hence from me she dwelleth not a mile.
In cold and storm she lieth warm and dry   20
In bed of down, the dirt doth not defile
Her tender foot, she labors not as I;
Richly she feeds, and at the richman's cost,
And for her meat she needs not crave nor cry.
By sea, by land, of delicates the most
Her cater seeks, and spareth for no peril;
She feeds on boil meat, bake meat, and on roast,
And hath therefore no whit of charge nor travail.
And when she list, the liquor of the grape
Doth glad her heart, till that her belly swell.   30
And at this journey makes she but a jape;
So forth she goes, trusting of all this wealth
With her sister her part so for to shape
That if she might there keep herself in health,
To live a lady while her life doth last.
And to the door now is she come by stealth,
And with her foot anon she scrapes full fast.
T' other for fear durst not well scarce appear,
Of every noise so was the wretch aghast.
At last she askëd softly who was there.   40
And in her language as well as she could,
Peep, quoth the other, sister, I am here.
Peace, quoth the town mouse, why speakest thou so loud?
And by the hand she took her fair and well,
Welcome, quoth she, my sister, by the rood.
She feasted her that joy it was to tell
The fare they had, they drank the wine so clear;
And as to purpose, now and then it fell
She cheerëd her with, How, sister, what cheer?
Amid this joy befell a sorry chance,   50

That, wellaway, the stranger bought full dear
The fare she had. For as she looked askance,
Under a stool she spied two stemming eyes
In a round head, with sharp ears; in France
Was never mouse so feared, for the unwise
Had not yseën such a beast before;
Yet had nature taught her, after her guise,
To know her foe and dread him evermore.
The town mouse fled, she knew whither to go;
The other had no shift, but wonders sore,   60
Fear'd of her life; at home she wished her though!
And to the door, alas, as she did skip,
The heaven it would, lo, and eke her chance was so,
At the threshold her seely foot did trip,
And ere she might recover it again,
The traitor cat had caught her by the hip,
And made her there against her will remain,
That had forgot her power, surety, and rest,
For seeming wealth, wherein she thought to reign.
Alas, my Poins, how men do seek the best   70
And find the worst, by error as they stray.
And no marvel, when sight is so oppressed,
And blinds the guide; anon out of the way
Goeth guide and all in seeking quiet life.
O wretched minds, there is no gold that may
Grant that you seek, no war, no peace, no strife.
No, no, although thy head were hooped with gold,
Sergeant with mace, with hauberk, sword, nor knife,
Cannot repulse the care that follow should.
Each kind of life hath with him his disease.   80
Live in delight, even as thy lust would,
And thou shalt find when lust doth most thee please,
It irketh straight, and by itself doth fade.
A small thing is it that may thy mind appease;
None of you all there is that is so mad
To seek for grapes on brambles or on briars;
For none I trow that hath his wit so bad
To set his hay for conies over rivers,
Nor ye set not a dragnet for a hare;
And yet the thing that most is your desire   90
You do misseek with more travail and care.
Make plain thine heart, that it be not knotted
With hope of dread, and see thy will be bare
From all affects, whom vice hath ever spotted.
Thyself content with that is thee assigned,
And use it well that is to thee allotted.

Then seek no more out of thyself to find
The thing that thou hast sought so long before,
For thou shalt feel it sticking in thy mind,
Mad, if ye list to continue your sore,   100
Let present pass, and gape on time to come,
And deep yourself in travail more and more.
Henceforth, my Poins, this shall be all and sum;
These wretched fools shall have nought else of me;
But to the great God and to his high doom,
None other pain pray I for them to be,
But when the rage doth lead them from the right,
That looking backward, virtue they may see
Even as she is, so goodly fair and bright.
And whilst they clasp their lusts in arms across,   110
Grant them, good Lord, as thou mayst of thy might,
To fret inward for losing such a loss.

Of the courtier's life
Written to John Poins

Mine own John Poins, since ye delight to know
The causes why that homeward I me draw,
And flee the press of courts, whereso they go,
Rather than to live thrall, under the awe
Of lordly looks, wrappèd within my cloak,
To will and lust learning to set a law;
It is not for because I scorn or mock
The power of them, whom fortune here hath lent
Charge over us, of right to strike the stroke.
But true it is that I have always meant   10
Less to esteem them than the common sort,
Of outward things that judge in their intent
Without regard what doth inward resort.
I grant sometime that of glory the fire
Doth touch my heart. Me list not to report
Blame by honor, and honor to desire.
But how may I this honor now attain,
That cannot dye the color black a liar?
My Poins, I cannot frame my tune to feign,
To cloak the truth, for praise without desert,   20
Of them that list all vice for to retain.
I cannot honor them that set their part
With Venus and Bacchus all their life long;
Nor hold my peace of them, although I smart.
I cannot crouch nor kneel to such a wrong,
To worship them like God on earth alone,

That are as wolves these seely lambs among.
I cannot with my words complain and moan
And suffer nought, nor smart without complaint,
Nor turn the word that from my mouth is gone;   30
I cannot speak and look like as a saint,
Use wiles for wit, and make deceit a pleasure;
Call craft counsel, for lucre still to paint;
I cannot wrest the law to fill the coffer
With innocent blood to feed myself fat,
And do most hurt where that most help I offer.
I am not he that can allow the state
Of high Cæsar, and damn Cato to die;
That with his death did scape out of the gate
From Cæsar's hands, if Livy doth not lie,   40
And would not live where liberty was lost,
So did his heart the commonwealth apply.
I am not he, such eloquence to boast,
To make the crow in singing as the swan,
Nor call the lion of coward beasts the most,
That cannot take a mouse as the cat can;
And he that dieth for hunger of the gold,
Call him Alexander, and say that Pan
Passeth Apollo in music manifold;
Praise Sir Thopas for a noble tale,   50
And scorn the story that the Knight told;
Praise him for counsel that is drunk of ale;
Grin when he laughs that beareth all the sway,
Frown when he frowns, and groan when he is pale;
On others' lust to hang both night and day.
None of these points would ever frame in me;
My wit is nought, I cannot learn the way.
And much the less of things that greater be,
That asken help of colors of device
To join the mean with each extremity;   60
With nearest virtue aye to cloak the vice.
And as to purpose likewise it shall fall,
To press the virtue that it may not rise;
As drunkenness good fellowship to call;
The friendly foe, with his fair double face,
Say he is gentle and courteous therewithal;
Affirm that favel hath a goodly grace
In eloquence; and cruelty to name
Zeal of justice, and change in time and place;
And he that suff'reth offence without blame,   70
Call him pitiful, and him true and plain
That raileth reckless unto each man's shame;

Say he is rude that cannot lie and feign;
The lecher a lover, and tyranny
To be the right of a prince's reign.
I cannot, I; no, no, it will not be.
This is the cause that I could never yet
Hang on their sleeves, that weigh, as thou mayst see,
A chip of chance more than a pound of wit.
This maketh me at home to hunt and hawk,   80
And in foul weather at my book to sit,
In frost and snow then with my bow to stalk.
No man doth mark whereso I ride or go.
In lusty leas at liberty I walk,
And of these news I feel nor weal nor woe,
Save that a clog doth hang yet at my heel.
No force for that, for it is ordered so
That I may leap both hedge and dike full well;
I am not now in France, to judge the wine,
With sav'ry sauce those delicates to feel.   90
Nor yet in Spain where one must him incline,
Rather than to be, outwardly to seem.
I meddle not with wits that be so fine,
Nor Flanders' cheer lets not my sight to deem
Of black and white, nor takes my wit away
With beastliness; they beasts do so esteem.
Nor I am not where Christ is given in prey
For money, poison, and treason; at Rome
A common practice, used night and day.
But here I am in Kent and Christendom,   100
Among the Muses, where I read and rhyme;
Where if thou list, my Poins, for to come,
Thou shalt be judge how I do spend my time.

FROM *Egerton Ms.* 2711

[*The lover complaineth the unkindness of his love*]

My lute, awake, perform the last
Labor that thou and I shall waste,
And end that I have now begun;
For when this song is sung and
    past,
My lute, be still, for I have done.
  As to be heard where ear is none,
As lead to grave in marble stone,
My song may pierce her heart as
    soon.
Should we then sigh, or sing, or
    moan?

No, no, my lute, for I have done. 10
  The rocks do not so cruelly
Repulse the waves continually,
As she my suit and affection;
So that I am past remedy,
Whereby my lute and I have done.
  Proud of the spoil that thou hast
    got
Of simple hearts, thorough love's
    shot;
By whom, unkind, thou hast them
    won,

Think not he hath his bow forgot,
Although my lute and I have
  done.   20
  Vengeance shall fall on thy dis-
    dain,
That makest but game on earnest
  pain;
Think not alone under the sun
Unquit to cause thy lovers plain,
Although my lute and I have done.
  Perchance thee lie withered and
    old,
In winter nights that are so cold,
Plaining in vain unto the moon;
Thy wishes then dare not be told.
Care then who list, for I have
  done.   30

And then may chance thee to
  repent
The time that thou hast lost and
  spent
To cause thy lovers sigh and
  swoon;
Then shalt thou know beauty but
  lent,
And wish and want as I have done.
  Now cease, my lute, this is the
  last
Labor that thou and I shall waste,
And ended is that we begun.
Now is this song both sung and
  past,
My lute, be still, for I have done.   40

HENRY HOWARD, EARL OF SURREY

The Introduction and Notes are at page 915

From Richard Tottel's *Songs and Sonnets*, 1557

Description of spring, wherein each thing renews save only the lover

The soote season that bud and bloom forth brings
With green hath clad the hill and eke the vale,
The nightingale with feathers new she sings,
The turtle to her make hath told her tale.
Summer is come, for every spray now springs,
The hart hath hung his old head on the pale,
The buck in brake his winter coat he flings,
The fishes float with new repairèd scale,
The adder all her slough away she slings,
The swift swallow pursueth the flyës smale,   10
The busy bee her honey now she mings,—
Winter is worn, that was the flowers' bale:
And thus I see, among these pleasant things
Each care decays—and yet my sorrow springs.

The frailty and hurtfulness of beauty

Brittle beauty that nature made so frail,
Whereof the gift is small, and short the season,

Flow'ring to-day, to-morrow apt to fail,
Tickle treasure, abhorred of reason,
Dangerous to deal with, vain, of none avail,
Costly in keeping, passed not worth two peason,
Slipper in sliding as is an eelë's tail,
Hard to attain, once gotten not geason,
Jewel of jeopardy that peril doth assail,
False and untrue, enticëd oft to treason,   10
En'my to youth (that most may I bewail!),
Ah, bitter sweet! infecting as the poison,
Thou farest as fruit that with the frost is taken:
To-day ready ripe, to-morrow all to-shaken.

Description and praise of his love Geraldine

From Tuscan came my lady's worthy race,
Fair Florence was sometime her ancient seat,
The western isle whose pleasant shore doth face
Wild Camber's cliffs did give her lively heat;
Fostered she was with milk of Irish breast,
Her sire an earl, her dame of princes' blood;
From tender years in Britain she doth rest
With king's child, where she tasteth costly food.
Hunsdon did first present her to mine eyne;
Bright is her hue, and Geraldine she hight;   10
Hampton me taught to wish her first for mine,
And Windsor, alas, doth chase me from her sight.
Her beauty, of kind; her virtues, from above;
Happy is he that can obtain her love.

A complaint by night of the lover not beloved

Alas, so all things now do hold their peace,
Heaven and earth disturbëd in nothing;
The beasts, the air, the birds their song do cease.
The nightë's chair the stars about doth bring;
Calm is the sea, the waves work less and less.
So am not I, whom love, alas, doth wring,
Bringing before my face the great increase
Of my desires, whereat I weep and sing
In joy and woe, as in a doubtful ease.
For my sweet thoughts sometime do pleasure bring,   10
But by and by the cause of my disease
Gives me a pang that inwardly doth sting,
When that I think what grief it is again
To live and lack the thing should rid my pain.

Complaint of a lover rebuked

Love that liveth and reigneth in my thought,
That built his seat within my captive breast,
Clad in the arms wherein with me he fought,
Oft in my face he doth his banner rest.
She that me taught to love and suffer pain,
My doubtful hope and eke my hot desire
With shamefast cloak to shadow and refrain,
Her smiling grace converteth straight to ire;
And coward love then to the heart apace
Taketh his flight, whereas he lurks and plains
His purpose lost, and dare not show his face.
For my lord's guilt thus faultless bide I pains;
Yet from my lord shall not my foot remove,—
Sweet is his death that takes his end by love.

Vow to love faithfully, howsoever he be rewarded

Set me whereas the sun doth parch the green,
Or where his beams do not dissolve the ice,
In temperate heat where he is felt and seen;
In presence prest of people, mad or wise;
Set me in high or yet in low degree,
In longest night or in the shortest day,
In clearest sky or where clouds thickest be,
In lusty youth or when my hairs are gray.
Set me in heaven, in earth, or else in hell;
In hill, or dale, or in the foaming flood;
Thrall or at large, alive whereso I dwell,
Sick or in health, in evil fame or good:
Hers will I be, and only with this thought
Content myself although my chance be nought.

The lover comforteth himself with the worthiness of his love

When raging love with extreme pain
Most cruelly distrains my heart,
When that my tears, as floods of rain,
Bear witness of my woeful smart;
When sighs have wasted so my breath
That I lie at the point of death,
I call to mind the navy great
That the Greeks brought to Troyë town,
And how the boysteous winds did beat
Their ships, and rent their sails adown;

Till Agamemnon's daughter's blood
Appeased the gods that them withstood.
　　And how that in those ten years' war
Full many a bloody deed was done,
And many a lord that came full far
There caught his bane, alas, too soon;
And many a good knight overrun,
Before the Greeks had Helen won.
　　Then think I thus: sith such repair,
So long time war of valiant men,　　　　　　20
Was all to win a lady fair,
Shall I not learn to suffer then,
And think my life well spent to be,
Serving a worthier wight than she?
　　Therefore I never will repent,
But pains contented still endure;
For like as when, rough winter spent,
The pleasant spring straight draweth in ure,
So, after raging storms of care,
Joyful at length may be my fare.　　　　　　30

A praise of his love, wherein he reproveth them that compare their ladies with his

Give place, ye lovers here before
That spent your boasts and brags
　　in vain,
My lady's beauty passeth more
The best of yours, I dare well sayn,
Than doth the sun the candle-light,
Or brightest day the darkest night;
　　And thereto hath a troth as just
As had Penelope the fair;
For what she saith, ye may it trust
As it by writing sealèd were.　　10
And virtues hath she many mo
Than I with pen have skill to show.
　　I could rehearse, if that I wold,
The whole effect of nature's plaint
When she had lost the perfect
　　mould,
The like to whom she could not
　　paint;
With wringing hands how she did
　　cry,

And what she said, I know it, I.
　　I know she swore with raging
　　mind,
Her kingdom only set apart,　　20
There was no loss, by law of kind,
That could have gone so near her
　　heart.
And this was chiefly all her
　　pain,—
She could not make the like again.
　　Sith nature thus gave her the
　　praise,
To be the chiefest work she
　　wrought,
In faith, methink some better ways
On your behalf might well be
　　sought
Than to compare, as ye have
　　done,
To match the candle with the
　　sun.　　30

How no age is content with his own estate, and how the age
of children is the happiest, if they had skill to understand it

Laid in my quiet bed, in study as I were,
I saw within my troubled head a heap of thoughts appear,
And every thought did show so lively in mine eyes
That now I sighed, and then I smiled, as cause of thought did rise.
I saw the little boy, in thought, how oft that he
Did wish of God to scape the rod, a tall young man to be;
The young man eke that feels his bones with pains oppressed,
How he would be a rich old man, to live and lie at rest;
The rich old man that sees his end draw on so sore,
How he would be a boy again, to live so much the more.   10
Whereat full oft I smiled, to see how all these three,
From boy to man, from man to boy, would chop and change degree;
And musing thus, I think the case is very strange
That man from wealth to live in woe doth ever seek to change.
Thus thoughtful as I lay, I saw my withered skin,
How it doth show my dented jaws, the flesh was worn so thin;
And eke my toothless chaps, the gates of my right way,
That opes and shuts as I do speak, do thus unto me say:
Thy white and hoarish hairs, the messengers of age,
That show like lines of true belief that this life doth assuage,   20
Bids thee lay hand and feel them hanging on thy chin,
The which do write two ages past, the third now coming in.
Hang up, therefore, the bit of thy young wanton time,
And thou that therein beaten art, the happiest life define.
Whereat I sighed and said: Farewell, my wonted joy,
Truss up thy pack and trudge from me to every little boy,
And tell them thus from me, Their time most happy is,
If to their time they reason had to know the truth of this.

Of the death of Sir T. W. the elder

W. [yatt] resteth here, that quick could never rest;
Whose heavenly gifts increasèd by disdain,
And virtue sank the deeper in his breast,
Such profit he by envy could obtain.
A head where wisdom mysteries did frame,
Whose hammers beat still in that lively brain
As on a stithy, where that some work of fame
Was daily wrought, to turn to Britain's gain.
A visage stern and mild, where both did grow
Vice to contemn, in virtue to rejoice;   10
Amid great storms whom grace assurèd so
To live upright and smile at fortune's choice.

A hand that taught what might be said in rhyme,
That reft Chaucer the glory of his wit,
A mark the which (unparfited, for time)
Some may approach, but never none shall hit.

A tongue that served in foreign realms his king;
Whose courteous talk to virtue did inflame
Each noble heart; a worthy guide to bring
Our English youth by travail unto fame.   20

An eye whose judgment none affect could blind,
Friends to allure and foes to reconcile;
Whose piercing look did represent a mind
With virtue fraught, reposèd, void of guile.

A heart where dread was never so impressed,
To hide the thought that might the truth advance;
In neither fortune lost nor yet repressed,
To swell in wealth or yield unto mischance.

A valiant corps where force and beauty met,
Happy—alas, too happy, but for foes!   30
Lived, and ran the race that nature set,
Of manhood's shape where she the mould did lose.

But to the heavens that simple soul is fled,
Which left with such as covet Christ to know
Witness of faith that never shall be dead;
Sent for our health, but not receivèd so.
Thus for our guilt this jewel have we lost:
The earth, his bones; the heavens possess his ghost.

Prisoned in Windsor, he recounteth his pleasure there passed

So cruel prison how could betide, alas,
As proud Windsor? Where I in lust and joy
With a king's son my childish years did pass
In greater feast than Priam's sons of Troy;
Where each sweet place returns a taste full sour:
The large green courts where we were wont to hove
With eyes cast up into the maidens' tower,
And easy sighs, such as folk draw in love;
The stately seats, the ladies bright of hue,
The dances short, long tales of great delight;   10
With words and looks that tigers could but rue,
Where each of us did plead the other's right;
The palm play where, despoilèd for the game,
With dazèd eyes oft we by gleams of love
Have missed the ball and got sight of our dame,
To bait her eyes, which kept the leads above;

The gravel ground, with sleeves tied on the helm,
On foaming horse, with swords and friendly hearts,
With cheer, as though one should another whelm,
Where we have fought, and chasëd oft with darts;   2c
With silver drops the mead yet spread for ruth,
In active games of nimbleness and strength,
Where we did strain, trainëd with swarms of youth,
Our tender limbs that yet shot up in length;
The secret groves which oft we made resound
Of pleasant plaint and of our ladies' praise,
Recording oft what grace each one had found,
What hope of speed, what dread of long delays;
The wild forest, the clothëd holts with green,   30
With reins avaled, and swift ybreathëd horse,
With cry of hounds and merry blasts between,
Where we did chase the fearful hart of force;
The wide vales eke that harbored us each night,
Wherewith, alas, reviveth in my breast
The sweet accord; such sleeps as yet delight,
The pleasant dreams, the quiet bed of rest;
The secret thoughts imparted with such trust,
The wanton talk, the divers change of play,
The friendship sworn, each promise kept so just,
Wherewith we passed the winter night away.   40
And with this thought the blood forsakes the face,
The tears berain my cheeks of deadly huė,
The which as soon as sobbing sighs, alas,
Upsuppëd have, thus I my plaint renew:
O place of bliss, renewer of my woes,
Give me account—where is my noble fere?
Whom in thy walls thou dost each night enclose,
To other lief, but unto me most dear!
Echo, alas, that doth my sorrow rue,
Returns thereto a hollow sound of plaint.   50
Thus I alone, where all my freedom grew,
In prison pine with bondage and restraint;
And with remembrance of the greater grief
To banish the less, I find my chief relief.

Exhortation to learn by others' trouble

My Ratcliffe, when thy reckless youth offends,
Receive thy scourge by others' chastisement;
For such calling, when it works none amends,
Then plagues are sent without advertisement.
Yet Solomon said, The wrongëd shall recure;
But Wyatt said true, The scar doth aye endure.

36869

FROM WILLIAM BALDWIN's *Treatise of Moral Philosophy*, 1547

The things that cause a quiet life
Written by Martial

My friend, the things that do
attain
The happy life be these, I find:
The riches left, not got with pain,
The fruitful ground, the quiet
mind.

The mean diet, no dainty fare;
Wisdom joined with simpleness; 10
The night dischargëd of all care,
Where wine the wit may not op-
press.

The equal friend—no grudge,
no strife;
No charge of rule, nor governance;
Without disease, the healthy life,
The household of continuance;

The faithful wife, without debate;
Such sleeps as may beguile the
night:
Content thyself with thine estate,
Neither wish death, nor fear his
might.

FROM *Additional Ms.* 36529

[*London, hast thou accusëd me?*]

London, hast thou accusëd me
Of breach of laws, the root of
strife?
Within whose breast did boil to see,
So fervent hot, thy dissolute life,
That even the hate of sins that
grow
Within thy wicked walls so rife,
For to break forth did convert so
That terror could not it repress.
The which, by words since
preachers know
What hope is left for to redress, 10
By unknown means it likëd me
My hidden burden to express,
Whereby it might appear to thee
That secret sin hath secret spite,
From justice' rod no fault is free;
But that all such as works unright
In most quiet are next ill rest.
In secret silence of the night
This made me, with a reckless
breast,

To wake thy sluggards with my
bow— 20
A figure of the Lord's behest,
Whose scourge for sin the Scrip-
tures show.
That, as the fearful thunder-clap
By sudden flame at hand we know,
Of pebble-stones the soundless rap
The dreadful plague might make
thee see
Of God's wrath that doth thee en-
wrap;
That pride might know, from con-
science free
How lofty works may her defend;
And envy find, as he hath sought 30
How other seek him to offend;
And wrath taste of each cruel
thought,
The just shapp higher in the end;
And idle sloth, that never wrought,
To heaven his spirit lift may begin;
And greedy lucre live in dread

To see what hate ill-got goods win;
The lechers, ye that lusts do feed,
Perceive what secrecy is in sin;
And gluttons' hearts for sorrow
    bleed,   40
Awakèd, when their fault they
    find:
In loathsome vice each drunken
    wight
To stir to God, this was my mind.
Thy windows had done me no spite,
But proud people that dread no
    fall,
Clothèd with falsehood and un-
    right,
Bred in the closures of thy wall;
But wrested to wrath in fervent
    zeal,
Thou haste to strife, my secret
    call.
Endurèd hearts no warning feel; 50
O shameless whore, is dread then
    gone
By such thy foes as meant thy weal?

O member of false Babylon!
The shop of craft, the den of ire!
Thy dreadful doom draws fast
    upon;
Thy martyrs' blood, by sword and
    fire,
In heaven and earth for justice
    call.
The Lord shall hear their just de-
    sire,
The flame of wrath shall on thee
    fall,
With famine and pest lamentably
Stricken shall be thy lechers all; 61
Thy proud towers and turrets high,
En'mies to God, beat stone from
    stone,
Thine idols burnt that wrought in-
    iquity;
When none thy ruin shall bemoan,
But render unto the right wise
    Lord
That so hath judgèd Babylon,
Immortal praise with one accord.

FROM *Certain Books of Virgil's Æneis*, 1557

Book II

They whisted all, with fixèd face attent,
When prince Æneas from the royal seat
Thus gan to speak: O Queen, it is thy will
I should renew a woe cannot be told!
How that the Greeks did spoil and overthrow
The Phrygian wealth and wailful realm of Troy.
Those ruthful things that I myself beheld
And whereof no small part fell to my share,
Which to express, who could refrain from tears?
What Myrmidon? or yet what Dolopes?   10
What stern Ulysses' wagèd soldïer?
And lo, moist night now from the welkin falls,
And stars, declining, counsel us to rest.
But since so great is thy delight to hear
Of our mishaps and Troyë's last decay,
Though to record the same my mind abhors
And plaint eschews, yet thus will I begin.
    The Greeks' chieftains, all irkèd with the war

Wherein they wasted had so many years,
And oft repulsed by fatal destiny, 20
A huge horse made, high raisëd like a hill,
By the divine science of Minerva,
(Of cloven fir compacted were his ribs)
For their return a feignëd sacrifice;
The fame whereof so wandered it at point.
In the dark bulk they closed bodies of men,
Chosen by lot, and did enstuff by stealth
The hollow womb with armëd soldïers.
    There stands in sight an isle hight Tenedon,
Rich and of fame while Priam's kingdom stood, 30
Now but a bay, and road unsure for ship.
Hither them secretly the Greeks withdrew,
Shrouding themselves under the desert shore.
And, weening we they had been fled and gone,
And with that wind had fet the land of Greece,
Troyë discharged her long-continued dole.
    The gates cast up, we issued out to play,
The Greekish camp desirous to behold,
The places void, and the forsaken coasts.
Here Pyrrhus' band, there fierce Achilles', pight; 40
Here rode their ships; there did their battles join.
Astonied, some the scatheful gift beheld,
Behight by vow unto the chaste Minerve,
All wond'ring at the hugeness of the horse.
    And first of all Timœtes gan advise
Within the walls to lead and draw the same,
And place it eke amid the palace court,—
Whether of guile or Troyë's fate it would—
Capys, with some of judgment more discreet,
Willed it to drown, or underset with flame, 50
The suspect present of the Greeks' deceit,
Or bore and gauge the hollow caves uncouth.
So diverse ran the giddy people's mind.
    Lo, foremost of a rout that followed him,
Kindled Laocoon hasted from the tower,
Crying far off, O wretched citizens,
What so great kind of frenzy fretteth you?
Deem ye the Greeks, our enemies, to be gone?
Or any Greekish gifts can you suppose
Devoid of guile? Is so Ulysses known? 60
Either the Greeks are in this timber hid
Or this an engine is to annoy our walls,
To view our towers and overwhelm our town.
Here lurks some craft. Good Trojans, give no trust

Unto this horse, for, whatsoever it be,
I dread the Greeks—yea, when they offer gifts!
And with that word with all his force a dart
He lancèd then into that crooked womb;
Which trembling stuck, and shook within the side,
Wherewith the caves gan hollowly resound.　　70
And but for fates, and for our blind forecast,
The Greeks' device and guile had he descried,
Troy yet had stand, and Priam's towers so high.

．　　．　　．　　．　　．　　．

Us caitiffs then a far more dreadful chance
Befell, that troubled our unarmèd breasts.
Whiles Laocoon, that chosen was by lot
Neptunus' priest, did sacrifice a bull
Before the holy altar, suddenly
From Tenedon, behold, in circles great
By the calm seas came fleeting adders twain,　　80
Which plied towards the shore—I loathe to tell—
With rearèd breast lift up above the seas;
Whose bloody crests aloft the waves were seen.
The hinder part swam hidden in the flood,
Their grisly backs were linkèd manifold;
With sound of broken waves they gat the strand,
With glowing eyne, tainted with blood and fire;
Whose walt'ring tongues did lick their hissing mouths.
We fled away, our face the blood forsook;
But they, with gait direct, to Lacoon ran.　　90
And first of all each serpent doth enwrap
The bodies small of his two tender sons,
Whose wretched limbs they bit, and fed thereon.
Then raught they him, who had his weapon caught
To rescue them. Twice winding him about,
With folded knots and circled tails his waist,
Their scalèd backs did compass twice his neck,
With rearèd heads aloft and stretchèd throats.
He with his hands strave to unloose the knots,
Whose sacred fillets all besprinkled were　　100
With filth of gory blood and venom rank,
And to the stars such dreadful shouts he sent,
Like to the sound the roaring bull forth lows
Which from the altar wounded doth astart,
The swerving axe when he shakes from his neck.
The serpents twain with hasted trail they glide
To Pallas' temple and her towers of height;
Under the feet of which, the goddess stern,

Hidden behind her target's boss they crept.
New gripes of dread then pierce our trembling breasts.   110
They said Lacoon's deserts had dearly bought
His heinous deed, that piercèd had with steel
The sacred bulk, and thrown the wicked lance.
The people cried, with sundry greeing shouts,
To bring the horse to Pallas' temple blive,
In hope thereby the goddess' wrath t'appease.
We cleft the walls and closures of the town,
Whereto all help, and underset the feet
With sliding rolls and bound his neck with ropes.
This fatal gin thus overclamb our walls,   120
Stuffed with armed men; about the which there ran
Children and maids that holy carols sang,
And well were they whose hands might touch the cords.
With threatening cheer thus slided through our town
The subtle tree, to Pallas' temple-ward.
O native land! Ilion! And of the gods
The mansion place! O warlike walls of Troy!
Four times it stopped in th' entry of our gate;
Four times the harness clattered in the womb.
But we go on, unsound of memory,   130
And, blinded eke by rage, perséver still.
This fatal monster in the fane we place.

·   ·   ·   ·   ·   ·   ·   ·   ·   ·

THOMAS, LORD VAUX

The Introduction and Notes are at page 918

FROM RICHARD TOTTEL'S *Songs and Sonnets,* 1557

The aged lover renounceth love

   I loathe that I did love;
In youth that I thought sweet,
As time requires for my behove,
Me thinks they are not meet.
   My lusts they do me leave,
My fancies all be fled,
And tract of time begins to weave
Gray hairs upon my head.
   For age, with stealing steps,
Hath clawed me with his crutch;   10
And lusty life away she leaps
As there had been none such.
   My muse doth not delight
Me as she did before,
My hand and pen are not in plight
As they have been of yore.
   For reason me denies
This youthly idle rhyme,
And day by day to me she cries,

Leave off these toys in time! [20]
 The wrinkles in my brow,
The furrows in my face,
Say limping age will hedge him
 now
Where youth must give him
 place.
 The harbinger of death,
To me I see him ride;
The cough, the cold, the gasping
 breath,
Doth bid me to provide
 A pickaxe and a spade,
And eke a shrouding sheet; [30]
A house of clay for to be made
For such a guest most meet.
 Me thinks I hear the clerk
That knolls the careful knell,
And bids me leave my woeful
 work
Ere nature me compel.

My keepers knit the knot
That youth did laugh to scorn;
Of me that clean shall be forgot
As I had not been born. [40]
 Thus must I youth give up,
Whose badge I long did wear;
To them I yield the wanton cup
That better may it bear.
 Lo, here the barëd skull
By whose bald sign I know
That stooping age away shall pull
Which youthful years did sow.
 For beauty, with her band,
These crooked cares hath
 wrought, [50]
And shippëd me into the land
From whence I first was brought.
 And ye that bide behind,
Have ye none other trust;
As ye of clay were cast by kind,
So shall ye waste to dust.

From Richard Edwards's *Paradise of Dainty Devices*, 1576
A lover, disdained, complaineth

If ever man had love too dearly bought,
Lo, I am he, that plays within her maze,
And finds no way to get the same I sought;
But as the deer are driven unto the gaze.
And to augment the grief of my desire,
Myself to burn, I blow the fire.
But shall I come nigh you,
Of force I must fly you.

What death, alas, may be compared to this? [10]
I play within the maze of my sweet foe,
And when I would of her but crave a kiss,
Disdain enforceth her away to go.
Myself I check, yet do I twist the twine;
The pleasure hers, the pain is mine.
But shall I come nigh you,
Of force I must fly you.

You courtly wights that wants your pleasant choice,
Lend me a flood of tears to wail my chance!
Happy are they in love that can rejoice,

To their great pains, where fortune doth advance. 20
For sith my suit, alas, can not prevail,
Full fraught with care in grief still will I wail,
Sith you will needs fly me,
I may not come nigh you.

No pleasure without some pain

How can the tree but waste and wither away
That hath not some time comfort of the sun?
How can that flower but fade and soon decay
That always is with dark clouds over-run?
Is this a life? Nay, death you may it call,
That feels each pain and knoweth no joy at all.

What foodless beast can live long in good plight?
Or is it life where senses there be none?
Or what availeth eyes without their light?
Or else a tongue to him that is alone? 10
Is this a life? Nay, death you may it call,
That feels each pain and knows no joy at all.

Whereto serve ears if that there be no sound?
Or such a head where no device doth grow?
But all of plaints, since sorrow is the ground,
Whereby the heart doth pine in deadly woe.
Is this a life? Nay, death you may it call,
That feels each pain and knows no joy at all.

Of a contented mind

When all is done and said, in the end thus shall you find,
He most of all doth bathe in bliss that hath a quiet mind;
And, clear from worldly cares, to deem can be content
The sweetest time in all his life in thinking to be spent.

The body subject is to fickle fortune's power,
And to a million of mishaps is casual every hour.
And death in time doth change it to a clod of clay,
Whenas the mind, which is divine, runs never to decay.

Companion none is like unto the mind alone,
For many have been harmed by speech, through thinking few or
 none. 10
Few oftentimes restraineth words, but makes not thoughts to cease,
And he speaks best that hath the skill when for to hold his peace.

Our wealth leaves us at death, our kinsmen at the grave,
But virtues of the mind unto the heavens with us we have:
Wherefore, for virtue's sake, I can be well content
The sweetest time in all my life to deem in thinking spent.

MINOR 'COURTLY MAKERS' OF HENRY VIII'S REIGN

The Introduction and Notes are at page 918

FROM *Additional Ms.* 5465

[*That was my woe*]

That was my woe is now my
 most gladness,
That was my pain is now my joyous chance;
That was my fear is now my sik-
 erness,
That was my grief is now my al-
 legiance.
Thus hath now grace enrichëd
 my pleasance,
Wherefore I am, and shall be
 till I die,
Your true servant with thought,
 heart, and body.
 [*Robert Fairfax*]

FROM WYNKYN DE WORDE'S
 Christmas Carols, 1521

*A carol, bringing in the boar's
 head*

Caput apri differo,
Reddens laudes domino.
The boar's head in hand bring I,
With garlands gay and rosemary;
I pray you all sing merrily,
 Qui estis in convivio.

The boar's head, I understand,
Is the chief service in this land;
Look wherever it be fand,
 Servite cum cantico. 10

Be glad, lords both more and less,
For this hath ordained our stew-
 ard
To cheer you all this Christmas,
The boar's head with mustard.

FROM *XX Songs*, 1530

[*In youth, in age*]

In youth, in age,
Both in wealth and woe,
Auxilium meum a domino.

Though poets feign that fortune,
 by her chance
And her free will, doth oppress
 and advance,
Fortune doth miss her will and
 liberty.
Then trust to virtue; let fortune
 go,
Auxilium meum a domino.

Of grace divine, with heavenly assistance,

If virtue do remain, virtue alway [10]
When she list may call fortune's
    chance again.
What force I then though for-
    tune be my foe?
Auxilium meum a domino.

[*Robert Cooper*]

[*Pleasure it is*]

Pleasure it is
To hear, I wis,
The birds sing;
The deer in the dale,
The sheep in the vale,
The corn springing;
God's purveyance
For sustenance
It is, for man.
Then we always   [10]
To him give praise
And thank him than,
And thank him than.

[*William Cornish*]

From *Royal Ms. Appendix* 58

[*Ah! the sighs*]

Ah! the sighs that come from my
    heart,
    They grieve me passing sore;
Sith I must from my love depart,
    Farewell, my joy, for ever-
        more.

Oft to me with her goodly face
    She was wont to cast an eye,
And now absence to me in place—
    Alas, for woe I die, I die!

I was wont her to behold,
    And taken in armës twain; [10]
And now with sighës manifold,
    Farewell, my joy, and wel-
        come, pain.

Ah! methink that I see her yet,
    As would to God that I might!
There might no joys compare with
    it
    Unto my heart, to make it
        light.

[*William Cornish*]

[*Western wind*]

Western wind, when will thou
    blow?
The small rain down can rain,—
Christ, if my love were in my
    arms
And I in my bed again!

[*My little fool*]

My little fool
Is gone to play,
She will tarry no longer with me.
    Hey ho, frisk-a jolly,
Under the greenwood tree!
    Hey ho, frisk-a jolly,
Under the greenwood tree!
    Hey ho, frisk-a jolly.

From *Additional Ms.* 31922

[*England, be glad*]

England, be glad, pluck up thy
    lusty heart!
Help now the king, the king, and
    take his part.

Against the Frenchmen in the
    field to fight
In the quarrel of the church, and
    in the right,
With spears and shields on goodly
    horses light,
Bows and arrows to put them all
    to flight,
To put them all to flight. Help
    now the king!

FROM *Harleian Ms.* 7578

[*These women all*]

These women all
Both great and small
  Are wavering to and fro,
Now here, now there,
Now everywhere,—
  But I will not say so.

So they love to range,
Their minds doth change
  And makes their friend their
      foe;
As lovers true   10
Each day they choose new,—
  But I will not say so.

They laugh, they smile,
They do beguile

As dice that men doth throw.
Who useth them much
Shall never be rich,—
  But I will not say so.

Some hot, some cold,
There is no hold
  But as the wind doth blow;
When all is done,
They change like the moon,—
  But I will not say so.

So thus one and other
Taketh after their mother
  As cock by kind doth crow.
My song is ended,
The best may be amended,—
  But I will not say so.   30
            [*Heath*]

FROM *Additional Ms.* 26737

[*O death, rock me asleep*]

O death, O death, rock me
    asleep,
Bring me to quiet rest;
Let pass my weary guiltless ghost
Out of my careful breast.
  Toll on your passing bell,
  Ring out my doleful knell;
  Thy sound my death abroad will
    tell,
    For I must die,
    There is no remedy.

My pains, my pains, who can
    express?   10
Alas, they are so strong!
My dolors will not suffer strength
My life for to prolong.
  Toll on . . .

Alone, alone in prison strong
I wail my destiny.
Woe worth the cruel hap that I
Must taste this misery!
  Toll on . . .

Farewell, farewell, my pleas-
    ures past!   20
Welcome, my present pain!
I feel my torment so increase
That life can not remain.
  Cease now, then, passing bell,
  Ring out my doleful knoll;
  For thou my death dost tell.
  Lord, pity thou my soul!
    Death doth draw nigh,
    Sound dolefully!
    For now I die,   30
    I die, I die!

[*George Boleyn, Viscount Rochford?*]

FROM *Ashmole Ms.* 48

To his posterity
Written over a chamber door where he was wont to lie at Hallingbury

Never was I less alone than being alone
Here in this chamber. Evil thought had I none,
But always I thought to bring the mind to rest,
And that thought of all thoughts I judge it the best.
For if my coffers had been full of pearl and gold
And fortune had favored me even as that I wold,
The mind out of quiet, so sage Senec saith,
It had been no felicity, but a painful death.
Love then who love will to stand in high degree;
I blame him not a whit so that he follow me   10
And take his loss as quietly as when that he doth win.
Then fortune hath no mast'ry of that state he is in;
But rules, and is not ruled, and takes the better part.
Oh, that man is blessed that learns this gentle art!
This was my felicity, my pastime, and my game:
I wish all my posterity they would ensue the same.

                     [*Henry Parker, Lord Morley*]

FROM RICHARD TOTTEL's *Songs and Sonnets,* 1557

The poor estate to be holden for best

Experience now doth show what God us taught before,
Desired pomp is vain and seldom doth it last;
Who climbs to reign with kings may rue his fate full sore,—
Alas, the woeful end that comes with care full fast!
Reject him doth renown; his pomp full low is cast;
Deceivèd is the bird by sweetness of the call;
Expel that pleasant taste wherein is bitter gall.
    Such as with oaten cakes in poor estate abides,
Of care have they no cure; the crab with mirth they roast.
More ease feel they than those that from their height down slides;   10
Excess doth breed their woe, they sail in Scylla's coast,
Remaining in the storms till ship and all be lost.
Serve God, therefore, thou poor; for lo, thou lives in rest;
Eschew the golden hall, thy thatchèd house is besT.

                 [*Edward Seymour, Duke of Somerset?*]

The lover showeth his woeful state and prayeth pity

Like as the lark within the marlian's foot
With piteous tunes doth chirp her yelden lay,

So sing I now, seeing none other boot,
My rendering song, and to your will obey.
Your virtue mounts above my force so high,
And with your beauty seized I am so sure,
That there avails resistance none in me,
But patiently your pleasure to endure.
For on your will my fancy shall attend;
My life, my death,—I put both in your choice;
And rather had this life by you to end,
Than live by other always to rejoice.
And if your cruelty do thirst my blood,
Then let it forth, if it may do you good.

Upon consideration of the state of this life he wisheth death

The longer life, the more of-
fence;
The more offence, the greater
pain;
The greater pain, the less de-
fence;
The less defence, the lesser gain.
The loss of gain long ill doth try,
Wherefore come death, and let me
die.
  The shorter life, less count I
find;
The less account, the sooner
made;
The count soon made, the mer-
rier mind;
The merry mind doth thought
evade.   10
Short life in truth this thing doth
try,
Wherefore come death, and let
me die.
  Come, gentle death, the ebb of
care,
The ebb of care, the flood of life;
The flood of life, the joyful fare;
The joyful fare, the end of strife;

The end of strife, that thing wish
I,
Wherefore come death, and let
me die.

Of a new-married student

A student, at his book so placed
That wealth he might have won,
From book to wife did fleet in
haste,
From wealth to woe to run.
Now, who hath played a feater
cast
Since juggling first begun?
In knitting of himself so fast
Himself he hath undone.

Harpalus' complaint of Phil-lida's love bestowed on Corin, who loved her not, and denied him that loved her

  Phillida was a fayer maid
And fresh as any flower,
Whom Harpalus, the herdman,
prayed
To be his paramour.
  Harpalus and eke Corin
Were herdmen both yfere;

And Phillida could twist and spin,
And thereto sing full clear.
   But Phillida was all too coy
For Harpalus to win;   10
For Corin was her only joy,
Who forced her not a pin.
   How often would she flowers
     twine,
How often garlands make
Of cowslips and of columbine,
And all for Corin's sake.
   But Corin he had hawks to
     lure,
And forcëd more the field;
Of lovers' law he took no cure,
For once he was beguiled.   20
   Harpalus prevailëd nought,
His labor all was lost;
For he was farthest from her
     thought,
And yet he loved her most.
   Therefore waxed he both pale
     and lean,
And dry as clot of clay;
His flesh it was consumëd clean,
His color gone away.
   His beard it had not long be
     shave,
His hair hung all unkempt;   30
A man most fit even for the grave,
Whom spiteful love had spent.
   His eyes were red and all for-
     watched,
His face besprent with tears;
It seemed unhap had him long
     hatched
In mids of his despairs.
   His clothes were black and also
     bare,
As one forlorn was he;
Upon his head always he ware
A wreath of willow tree.   40
   His beasts he kept upon the hill,
And he sate in the dale;
And thus, with sighs and sorrows
     shrill,

He gan to tell his tale:
   O Harpalus, thus would he say,
Unhappiest under sun,
The cause of thine unhappy day
By love was first begun;
   For thou wentest first by suit
     to seek
A tiger to make tame,   50
That sets not by thy love a leek,
But makes thy grief her game.
   As easy it were for to convert
The frost into the flame
As for to turn a froward heart
Whom thou so fain wouldst
     frame.
   Corin he liveth carëless,
He leaps among the leaves;
He eats the fruits of thy redress;
Thou reaps, he takes the sheaves. 60
   My beasts, awhile your food re-
     frain,
And hearken your herdman's
     sound,
Whom spiteful love, alas, hath
     slain,
Through-girt with many a wound.
   Oh, happy be ye, beastës wild,
That here your pasture takes;
I see that ye be not beguiled
Of these, your faithful makes.
   The hart he feedeth by the
     hind,
The buck hard by the doe;   70
The turtle-dove is not unkind
To him that loves her so;
   The ewe she hath by her the
     ram,
The young cow hath the bull;
The calf, with many a lusty lamb,
Do feed their hunger full.
   But, wellaway! that nature
     wrought
Thee, Phillida, so fair;
For I may say that I have bought
Thy beauty all too dear.   80
   What reason is it that cruelty

With beauty should have part?
Or else that such great tyranny
Should dwell in woman's heart?
I see therefore to shape my
    death
She cruelly is prest;
To th' end that I may want my
    breath,
My days been at the best.
O Cupid, grant this my request
And do not stop thine ears,   90
That she may feel within her
    breast
The pains of my despairs;
Of Corin that is careless
That she may crave her fee
As I have done, in great distress,
That loved her faithfully.
But since that I shall die her
    slave,
Her slave and eke her thrall,
Write you, my friends, upon my
    grave
This chance that is befall: 100
Here lieth unhappy Harpalus
Whom cruel love hath slain,
By Phillida unjustly thus
Murdered with false disdain.

FROM RICHARD TOTTEL's *Songs
and Sonnets*, 1557 (second
edition)

Totus mundus in maligno positus

Complain we may, much is
    amiss:
Hope is nigh gone to have re-
    dress;
These days been ill, nothing sure
    is,
Kind heart is wrapped in heavi-
    ness.
The stern is broke, the sail is
    rent,

The ship is given to wind and
    wave,
All help is gone, the rock pres-
    ent;
That will be lost, what man can
    save?
Things hard therefore are now
    refused,
Labor in youth is thought but
    vain,   10
Duty by 'will not' is excused;
Remove the stop, the way is plain.
Learning is lewd and held a
    fool,
Wisdom is shent, counted to rail,
Reason is banished out of school,
The blind is bold, and words pre-
    vail.
Power, without care, sleepeth at
    ease;
Will, without law, runn'th where
    he list;
Might, without mercy, cannot
    please.   19
A wise man saith not, had I wist.
When power lacks care and
    forceth not,
When care is feeble and may
    not,
When might is slothful and will
    not,
Weeds may grow where good
    herbs cannot.
Take wrong away, law needeth
    not,
For law to wrong is bridle and
    pain;
Take fear away, law booteth not.
To strive 'gainst stream, it is but
    vain.
Wily is witty, brainsick is wise,
Truth is folly, and might is
    right;   30
Words are reason, and reason is
    lies,
The bad is good, darkness is light.

Wrong to redress, wisdom dare
 not.
Hardy is happy, and ruleth most;
Wilful is witless, and careth not
Which end go first, till all be
 lost.
 Few right do love and wrong
  refuse;
Pleasure is sought in every state;
Liking is lust; there is no choose;
The low give to the high check-
 mate.   40
 Order is broke in things of
  weight,—
Measure and mean, who doth not
 flee?
Two things prevail, money and
 sleight;
To seem is better than to be.
 The bowl is round and doth
  down slide;
Each one thrusteth, none doth up-
 hold.
A fall fails not where blind is
 guide;
The stay is gone,—who can him
 hold?
 Folly and falsehood prayeth
  apace;
Truth under bushel is fain to
 creep;   50
Flatt'ry is treble, pride sings the
 bass;
The mean the best part scant doth
 peep.
 This fiery plague the world in-
  fects;
To virtue and truth it gives no
 rest.
Men's hearts are burned with sun-
 dry sects,
And to each man his way is best.
 With floods and storms thus be
  we tossed,
Awake, good Lord, to thee we
 cry:

Our ship is almost sunk and lost,
Thy mercy help our misery! 60
 Man's strength is weak, man's
  wit is dull,
Man's reason is blind. These
 things t' amend,
Thy hand, O Lord, of might is
 full,
Awake betime and help us fend.
 In thee we trust, and in no
  wight.
Save us as chickens under the hen.
Our crookedness thou canst make
 right;
Glory to thee for aye! Amen.

An old lover to a young gentlewoman

Ye are too young to bring me in,
And I too old to gape for flies;
I have too long a lover been,
If such young babes should blear
 mine eyes.
But trill the ball before my face,
I am content to make you play;
I will not see, I hide my face,
And turn my back and run away.
 But if you follow on so fast,
And cross the ways where I should
 go,   10
Ye may wax weary at the last,
And then at length your self
 o'erthrow.
I mean where you and all your
 flock
Devise to pen men in the pound,
I know a key can pick your lock
And make you run yourselves on
 ground.
 Some birds can eat the strawy
  corn
And flee the lime the fowlers set,
And some are 'feard of every
 thorn

And so thereby they scape the net. [20]
But some do light and never look
And seeth not who doth stand in wait,
As fish that swallow up the hook
And is beguilèd through the bait.
 But men can look before they leap
And be at price for every ware,
And pennyworths cast, to buy good cheap,
And in each thing hath eye and care;
But he that bluntly runs on head
And seeth not what the race shall be, [30]
Is like to bring a fool to bed,—
And thus ye get no more of me.

Of the vanity of man's life

Vain is the fleeting wealth
Whereon the world stays,
Sith stalking time by privy stealth
Encroacheth on our days.
 And eld, which creepeth fast
To taint us with her wound,
Will turn each bliss unto a blast,
Which lasteth but a stound.
 Of youth the lusty flower
Which whilom stood in price [10]
Shall vanish quite within an hour,
As fire consumes the ice.
 Where is become that wight
For whose sake Troy town
Withstood the Greeks till ten years' fight
Had razed the walls adown?
 Did not the worms consume
Her carrion to the dust?
Did dreadful death forbear his fume
For beauty, pride, or lust? [20]

NICHOLAS GRIMALD

The Introduction and Notes are at page 921

From Richard Tottel's *Songs and Sonnets*, 1557

A true love

What sweet relief the showers to thirsty plants we see,
What dear delight the blooms to bees, my true love is to me.
As fresh and lusty Ver foul winter doth exceed,
As morning bright, with scarlet sky, doth pass the evening's weed,
As mellow pears above the crabs esteemèd be,
So doth my love surmount them all, whom yet I hap to see.
The oak shall olives bear, the lamb the lion fray,
The owl shall match the nightingale in tuning of her lay,
Or I my love let slip out of mine entire heart,
So deep reposèd in my breast is she, for her desert. [10]
For many blessèd gifts, O happy, happy land,
Where Mars and Pallas strive to make their glory most to stand,
Yet, land, more is thy bliss that in this cruel age
A Venus' imp thou hast brought forth, so steadfast and so sage.

Among the Muses nine, a tenth, if Jove would make,
And to the Graces three, a fourth, her would Apollo take.
   Let some for honor hunt, and hoard the massy gold,
With her so I may live and die, my weal cannot be told.

Man's life, after Posidonius or Crates

What path list you to tread? what trade will you assay?
The courts of plea, by brawl and bate, drive gentle peace away.
In house, for wife and child, there is but cark and care;
With travail and with toil enough in fields we use to fare.
Upon the seas lieth dread; the rich, in foreign land,
Do fear the loss; and there the poor like misers poorly stand.
Strife, with a wife; without, your thrift full hard to see;
Young brats a trouble; none at all, a maim it seems to be;
Youth, fond; age hath no heart, and pincheth all too nigh.
Choose then the liefer of these two: no life, or soon to die.

Metrodorus' mind to the contrary

What race of life run you? what trade will you assay?
In courts is glory got and wit increasèd, day by day.
At home we take our ease, and beek ourselves in rest;
The fields our nature do refresh with pleasures of the best.
On seas is gain to get; the stranger, he shall be
Esteemèd, having much; if not, none knoweth his lack but he.
A wife will trim thy house; no wife? then art thou free.
Brood is a lovely thing; without, thy life is loose to thee.
Young bloods be strong; old sires in double honor dwell.
Do 'way that choice, no life, or soon to die; for all is well.

Description of virtue

What one art thou, thus in torn weed yclad?
Virtue, in price whom ancient sages had.
Why poorly 'rayed? For fading goods past care.
Why double-faced? I mark each fortune's fare.
This bridle, what? Mind's rages to restrain.
Tools why bear you? I love to take great pain.
Why wings? I teach above the stars to fly.
Why tread you death? I only cannot die.

To his familiar friend

No image carved with cunning hand, no cloth of purple dye,
No precious weight of metal bright, no silver plate give I.
Such gear allures not heavenly hearts; such gifts no grace they bring;
I, lo, that know your mind, will send none such. What then? Nothing.

A funeral song, upon the decease of Annes, his mother

Yea, and a good cause why thus should I plain,
For what is he can quietly sustain
So great a grief with mouth as still as stone?
My love, my life, of joy my jewel, is gone.
This hearty zeal if any wight disprove
As woman's work, whom feeble mind doth move,
He neither knows the mighty nature's laws
Nor, touching elders' deeds, hath seen old saws.
Martius to vanquish Rome was set on fire,
But vanquished fell, at mother's boon, his ire.   10
Into Hesperian land Sertorius, fled,
Of parent aye chief care had in his head.
Dear weight on shoulders Sicil brethren bore
While Ætna's giant spouted flames full sore.
Not more of Tyndar's imps hath Sparta spoke
Than Arge of chargèd necks with parent's yoke.
Nor only them thus did foretime entreat;
Then was the nurse also in honor great,
Caiet, the Phrygian, from amid fire-flame
Rescued, who gave to Latin strands the name;   20
Acca, in double sense Lupa ycleped,
To Roman calendars a feast hath heaped.
His Capra Jove among the stars hath pight,
In welkin clear yet, lo, she shineth bright.
Hyades as gratefully Lyai did place,
Whom, in prime-tide, supports the Bull's fair face.
And should not I express my inward woe
When you, most loving dam, so soon hence go?
I, in your fruitful womb conceived, borne was
While wandering moon ten months did overpass.   30
Me, brought to light, your tender arms sustained,
And with my lips your milky paps I strained.
You me embraced, in bosom soft you me
Cherished, as I your only child had be.
Of issue fair with numbers were you blest,
Yet I the best-beloved of all the rest.
Good luck certain fore-reading mothers have,
And you of me a special judgment gave.
Then, when firm pace I fixèd on the ground,
When tongue can cease to break the lisping sound,   40
You me straightway did to the Muses send,
Ne suffered long a loitering life to spend;
What gain the wool, what gain the web had brought,

It was his meed that me there daily taught.
When with Minerve I had acquaintance won,
And Phœbus seemed to love me as his son,
Brownshold I bade, at parents' hest, farewell;
And gladly there in schools I gan to dwell
Where Granta gives the ladies nine such place
That they rejoice to see their blissful case.   50
With joys at heart in this Parnasse I bode
While through his signs five times great Titan glode;
And twice as long by that fair ford whereas
Swan-feeder Thames no further course can pass.
Oh, what desire had you, therewhile, of me!
Mid doubtful dreads what joys were wont to be!
Now linen clothes, wrought with those fingers fine,
Now other things of yours did you make mine;
Till your last threads gan Clotho to untwine,
And of your days the date extreme assign.   60
Hearing the chance, your neighbors made much moan;
A dear-worth dame, they thought, their comfort gone.
Kinswomen wept; your charge, the maidens, wept;
Your daughters wept, whom you so well had kept.
But my good sire gave, with soft words, relief,
And cloaks with outward cheer his inward grief,
Lest by his care your sickness should augment,
And on his case your thoughtful heart be bent.
You, not forgetting yet a mother's mood,
When at the door dart-thirling death there stood,   70
Did say: Adieu, dear spouse, my race is run;
Whereso he be, I have left you a son.
And Nicholas you named and named again,
With other speech, aspiring heavenly reign,
When into air your sprite departed fled
And left the corpse a-cold in lukewarm bed.
Ah, could you thus, dear mother, leave us all?
Now should you live, that yet, before your fall,
My songs you might have sung, have heard my voice,
And in commodities of your own rejoice.   80
My sisters, yet unwedded, who shall guide?
With whose good lessons shall they be applied?
Have, mother, monuments of our sore smart:
No costly tomb, areared with curious art,
Nor Mausolean mass, hung in the air,
Nor lofty steeples that will once appair;
But wailful verse and doleful song accept.
By verse the names of ancient peers be kept:

By verse lives Hercules; by verse, Achil;
Hector, Ene, by verse be famous still.   90
Such former years, such death hath chancëd thee,
Closed with good end good life is wont to be.
But now, my sacred parent, fare you well.
God shall cause us again together dwell,
What time this universal globe shall hear
Of the last trump the ringing voice, great fear
To some, to such as you a heavenly cheer.
Till then, reposed rest you in gentle sleep,
While He whom-to you are bequeathed, you keep.

Marcus Tullius Cicero's death

Now have I lived, O Rome, enough for me;
My passëd life nought suffereth me to doubt
Noisome oblivion of the loathsome death.
Slay me, yet all th' offspring to come shall know
And this decease shall bring eternal life.
Yea, and unless I fail and all in vain,
Rome, I sometime thy augur chosen was,
Not evermore shall friendly fortune thee
Favor, Antonius; once the day shall come
When her dear wights, by cruel spite thus slain,   10
Victorious Rome shall at thy hands require.
Me likes, therewhile, go see the hopëd heaven.
Speech had he left, and therewith he, good man,
His throat prepared, and held his head unmoved;
His hasting to those fates the very knights
Be loath to see, and rage rebated when
They his bare neck beheld, and his hoar hairs;
Scant could they hold the tears that forth gan burst,
And almost fell from bloody hands the swords.
Only the stern Herennius, with grim look,   20
Dastards, why stand you still, he saith, and straight
Swaps off the head with his presumptuous iron.
Ne with that slaughter yet is he not filled:
Foul shame on shame to heap is his delight.
Wherefore the hands also doth he off smite,
Which durst Antonius' life so lively paint.
Him, yielding strainëd ghost, from welkin high
With loathly cheer lord Phœbus gan behold,
And in black cloud, they say, long hid his head.

The Latin Muses, and the Grayes, they wept,
And for his fall eternally shall weep.
And lo, heart-piercing Pytho, strange to tell,
Who had to him sufficed both sense and words
When so he spake, and dressed with nectar soote
That flowing tongue; when his windpipe disclosed,
Fled with her fleeing friend, and, out alas,
Hath left the earth, ne will no more return.
Popilius flyeth, therewhile, and leaving there
The senseless stock, a grisly sight doth bear
Unto Antonius' board, with mischief fed.

ELIZABETH

The Introduction and Notes are at page 922

From *Rawlinson Poetry Ms.* 85

[When I was fair and young]

When I was fair and young, and favor gracèd me,
   Of many was I sought, their mistress for to be;
But I did scorn them all, and answered them therefore,
     Go, go, go, seek some otherwhere,
       Impórtune me no more!

How many weeping eyes I made to pine with woe,
   How many sighing hearts, I have no skill to show;
Yet I the prouder grew, and answered them therefore,
     Go, go, go, seek some otherwhere,
      Impórtune me no more!

10

Then spake fair Venus' son, that proud victorious boy,
   And said: Fine dame, since that you be so coy,
I will so pluck your plumes that you shall say no more,
     Go, go, go, seek some otherwhere,
      Impórtune me no more!

When he had spake these words, such change grew in my breast
   That neither night nor day since that, I could take any rest.
Then lo! I did repent that I had said before,
     Go, go, go, seek some otherwhere,
      Impórtune me no more!

20

FROM *The Art of English Poesy*, 1589

[*The doubt of future foes*]

The doubt of future foes exiles my present joy,
And wit me warns to shun such snares as threaten mine annoy.
For falsehood now doth flow and subject faith doth ebb,
Which would not be if reason ruled or wisdom weaved the web.
But clouds of toys untried do cloak aspiring minds,
Which turn to rain of late repent by course of changëd winds.
The top of hope supposed, the root of ruth will be,
And fruitless all their graffëd guiles, as shortly ye shall see.
The dazzled eyes with pride, which great ambition blinds,
Shall be unseeled by worthy wights whose foresight falsehood finds.   10
The daughter of debate that eke discord doth sow
Shall reap no gain where former rule hath taught still peace to grow.
No foreign banished wight shall anchor in this port;
Our realm it brooks no stranger's force, let them elsewhere resort.
Our rusty sword with rest shall first his edge employ
To poll the tops that seek such change and gape for joy.

JOHN HARINGTON, THE ELDER

The Introduction and Notes are at page 923

FROM *Nugæ Antiquæ*, 1769

*A sonnet made on Isabella Markham, when I first thought
her fair as she stood at the Princess's window in goodly
attire and talked to divers in the court-yard*

Whence comes my love? O heart, disclose!
'Twas from cheeks that shame the rose,
From lips that spoil the ruby's praise,
From eyes that mock the diamond's blaze.
Whence comes my woe? As freely own,
Ah me, 'twas from a heart like stone!

The blushing cheek speaks modest mind,
The lips, befitting words most kind;
The eye does tempt to love's desire,
And seems to say 'tis Cupid's fire.   10
Yet all so fair but speak my moan,
Since nought doth say the heart of stone.

Why thus, my love, so kind bespeak
Sweet lip, sweet eye, sweet blushing cheek,
Yet not a heart to save my pain?
O Venus, take thy gifts again;
Make not so fair to cause our moan,
Or make a heart that's like our own!

THOMAS SACKVILLE, EARL OF DORSET

The Introduction and Notes are at page 923

FROM *A Mirror for Magistrates,* 1563

The induction

The wrathful winter, 'proaching on apace,
With blustering blasts had all ybared the treen,
And old Saturnus, with his frosty face,
With chilling cold had pierced the tender green;
The mantles rent, wherein enwrappéd been
    The gladsome groves that now lay overthrown,
    The tapets torn, and every bloom down blown.

The soil, that erst so seemly was to seen,
Was all despoiléd of her beauty's hue;
And soote fresh flowers, wherewith the summer's queen   10
Had clad the earth, now Boreas' blasts down blew;
And small fowls flocking, in their song did rue
    The winter's wrath, wherewith each thing defaced
    In woeful wise bewailed the summer past.

Hawthorn had lost his motley livery,
The naked twigs were shivering all for cold,
And dropping down the tears abundantly;
Each thing, methought, with weeping eye me told
The cruel season, bidding me withhold
    Myself within; for I was gotten out   20
    Into the fields, whereas I walked about.

When lo, the night with misty mantles spread,
Gan dark the day and dim the azure skies;
And Venus in her message Hermes sped
To bloody Mars, to will him not to rise,
Which she herself approached in speedy wise;

And Virgo, hiding her disdainful breast,
With Thetis now had laid her down to rest.

Whiles Scorpio, dreading Sagittarius' dart,
Whose bow prest bent in fight, the string had slipped,   30
Down slid into the ocean flood apart;
The Bear, that in the Irish seas had dipped
His grisly feet, with speed from thence he whipped;
    For Thetis, hasting from the Virgin's bed,
    Pursued the Bear, that ere she came was fled.

And Phaethon now, near reaching to his race
With glist'ring beams, gold streaming where they bent,
Was prest to enter in his resting place;
Erythius, that in the cart first went,
Had even now attained his journey's stent;   40
    And, fast declining, hid away his head,
    While Titan couched him in his purple bed.

And pale Cynthia, with her borrowed light,
Beginning to supply her brother's place,
Was past the noonstead six degrees in sight,
When sparkling stars amid the heaven's face
With twinkling light shone on the earth apace,
    That, while they brought about the nightë's chair,
    The dark had dimmed the day ere I was ware.

And sorrowing I to see the summer flowers,   50
The lively green, the lusty leas forlorn,
The sturdy trees so shattered with the showers,
The fields so fade that flourished so beforn,
It taught me well all earthly things be born
    To die the death, for nought long time may last;
    The summer's beauty yields to winter's blast.

Then looking upward to the heaven's leams,
With nightë's stars thick powdered everywhere,
Which erst so glistened with the golden streams
That cheerful Phœbus spread down from his sphere,   60
Beholding dark oppressing day so near;
    The sudden sight reducëd to my mind
    The sundry changes that in earth we find.

That musing on this worldly wealth in thought,
Which comes and goes more faster than we see
The flickering flame that with the fire is wrought,

My busy mind presented unto me
Such fall of peers as in this realm had be,
    That oft I wished some would their woes descrive,
    To warn the rest whom fortune left alive.   70

And straight forth stalking with redoubled pace,
For that I saw the night drew on so fast,
In black all clad there fell before my face
A piteous wight, whom woe had all forwaste;
Forth from her eyne the crystal tears out brast,
    And sighing sore, her hands she wrung and fold,
    Tare all her hair, that ruth was to behold.

Her body small, forwithered and forspent,
As is the stalk that summer's drought oppressed;
Her welkëd face with woeful tears besprent,   80
Her color pale, and, as it seemed her best,
In woe and plaint reposëd was her rest;
    And as the stone that drops of water wears,
    So dented were her cheeks with fall of tears.

Her eyes swollen with flowing streams afloat;
Wherewith, her looks thrown up full piteously,
Her forceless hands together oft she smote,
With doleful shrieks that echoed in the sky;
Whose plaint such sighs did straight accompany,
    That, in my doom, was never man did see   90
    A wight but half so woebegone as she.

I stood aghast, beholding all her plight,
'Tween dread and dolor, so distrained in heart
That, while my hairs upstarted with the sight,
The tears outstreamed for sorrow of her smart;
But when I saw no end that could apart
    The deadly deule which she so sore did make,
    With doleful voice then thus to her I spake:

Unwrap thy woes, whatever wight thou be,
And stint betime to spill thyself with plaint;   100
Tell what thou art, and whence, for well I see
Thou canst not dure, with sorrow thus attaint.
And with that word of sorrow, all forfaint
    She lookëd up, and prostrate as she lay,
    With piteous sound, lo, thus she gan to say:

Alas, I, wretch whom thus thou seest distrained
With wasting woes that never shall aslake,
Sorrow I am, in endless torments pained
Among the Furies in the infernal lake
Where Pluto, god of Hell, so grisly black,   110
    Doth hold his throne, and Lethe's deadly taste
    Doth reave remembrance of each thing forepast.

Whence come I am, the dreary destiny
And luckless lot for to bemoan of those
Whom fortune, in this maze of misery,
Of wretched chance, most woeful mirrors chose;
That when thou seest how lightly they did lose
    Their pomp, their power, and that they thought most sure,
    Thou mayst soon deem no earthly joy may dure.

Whose rueful voice no sooner had out brayed   120
Those woeful words wherewith she sorrowed so,
But out, alas, she shright and never stayed,
Fell down, and all to-dashed herself for woe;
The cold pale dread my limbs gan overgo,
    And I so sorrowed at her sorrows eft
    That, what with grief and fear, my wits were reft.

I stretched myself and straight my heart revives,
That dread and dolor erst did so appall;
Like him that with the fervent fever strives,
When sickness seeks his castle health to scale,   130
With gathered spirits so forced I fear to avale;
    And rearing her with anguish all fordone,
    My spirits returned and then I thus begun:

O Sorrow, alas, sith Sorrow is thy name,
And that to thee this drear doth well pertain,
In vain it were to seek to cease the same;
But as a man himself with sorrow slain,
So I, alas, do comfort thee in pain,
    That here in sorrow art forsunk so deep
    That at thy sight I can but sigh and weep.   140

I had no sooner spoken of a sike,
But that the storm so rumbled in her breast
As Æolus could never roar the like;
And showers down rainèd from her eyne so fast
That all bedrent the place, till at the last

Well easëd they the dolor of her mind,
As rage of rain doth swage the stormy wind.

For forth she pacëd in her fearful tale:
Come, come, quoth she, and see what I shall show;
Come hear the plaining and the bitter bale   150
Of worthy men by fortune overthrow;
Come thou and see them rueing all in row;
    They were but shades that erst in mind thou rolled;
    Come, come with me, thine eyes shall them behold.

What could these words but make me more aghast,
To hear her tell whereon I mused whilere?
So was I mazed therewith, till at the last,
Musing upon her words, and what they were,
All suddenly well-lessoned was my fear;
    For to my mind returnëd how she telled   160
    Both what she was and where her wone she held.

Whereby I knew that she a goddess was,
And therewithal resorted to my mind
My thought, that late presented me the glass
Of brittle state, of cares that here we find,
Of thousand woes to silly men assigned;
    And how she now bid me come and behold,
    To see with eye that erst in thought I rolled.

Flat down I fell, and with all reverence
Adored her, perceiving now that she,   170
A goddess sent by godly providence,
In earthly shape thus showed herself to me,
To wail and rue this world's uncertainty;
    And while I honored thus her godhead's might,
    With plaining voice these words to me she shright:

I shall guide thee first to the grisly lake
And thence unto the blissful place of rest
Where thou shalt see and hear the plaint they make
That whilom here bare swing among the best;
This shalt thou see, but great is the unrest   180
    That thou must bide before thou canst attain
    Unto the dreadful place where these remain.

And with these words, as I upraisëd stood,
And gan to follow her that straight forth paced,
Ere I was ware, into a desert wood

We now were come, where, hand in hand embraced,
She led the way and through the thick so traced
  As, but I had been guided by her might,
  It was no way for any mortal wight.

But lo, while thus amid the desert dark   190
We passèd on with steps and pace unmeet,
A rumbling roar, confused with howl and bark
Of dogs, shook all the ground under our feet,
And struck the din within our ears so deep
  As, half distraught, unto the ground I fell,
  Besought return, and not to visit hell.

But she, forthwith, uplifting me apace,
Removed my dread, and with a steadfast mind
Bade me come on; for here was now the place,
The place where we our travail end should find;   200
Wherewith I arose, and to the place assigned
  Astoined I stalk, when straight we approached near
  The dreadful place that you will dread to hear.

An hideous hole all vast, withouten shape,
Of endless depth, o'erwhelmed with ragged stone,
With ugly mouth and grisly jaws doth gape,
And to our sight confounds itself in one;
Here entered we, and yeding forth, anon
  An horrible loathly lake we might discern,
  As black as pitch, that clepèd is Avern.   210

A deadly gulf where nought but rubbish grows,
With foul black swelth in thickened lumps that lies,
Which up in the air such stinking vapors throws
That over there may fly no fowl but dies,
Choked with the pestilent savors that arise;
  Hither we come, whence forth we still did pace,
  In dreadful fear amid the dreadful place.

And first, within the porch and jaws of hell,
Sat deep Remorse of Conscience, all besprent
With tears, and to herself oft would she tell   220
Her wretchedness, and cursing never stent
To sob and sigh, but ever thus lament
  With thoughtful care as she that, all in vain,
  Would wear and waste continually in pain.

Her eyes unsteadfast, rolling here and there,
Whirled on each place, as place that vengeance brought,
So was her mind continually in fear,
Tossed and tormented with the tedious thought
Of those detested crimes which she had wrought;
    With dreadful cheer and looks thrown to the sky,   230
    Wishing for death, and yet she could not die.

Next saw we Dread, all trembling how he shook,
With foot uncertain, proffered here and there,
Benumbed of speech, and with a ghastly look,
Searched every place, all pale and dead for fear,
His cap borne up with staring of his hair,
    'Stoined and amazed at his own shade for dread,
    And fearing greater dangers than was need.

And next, within the entry of this lake,
Sat fell Revenge, gnashing her teeth for ire,   240
Devising means how she may vengeance take,
Never in rest till she have her desire;
But frets within so far forth with the fire
    Of wreaking flames, that now determines she
    To die by death, or venged by death to be.

When fell Revenge, with bloody foul pretense
Had showed herself as next in order set,
With trembling limbs we softly parted thence,
Till in our eyes another sight we met,
When from my heart a sigh forthwith I fet,   250
    Rueing, alas, upon the woeful plight
    Of Misery, that next appeared in sight.

His face was lean and somedeal pined away,
And eke his hands consumèd to the bone,
But what his body was I cannot say,
For on his carcass raiment had he none,
Save clouts and patches, piecèd one by one;
    With staff in hand and scrip on shoulders cast,
    His chief defence against the winter's blast.

His food, for most, was wild fruits of the tree,   260
Unless sometimes some crumbs fell to his share,
Which in his wallet long, God wot, kept he,
As on the which full daint'ly would he fare;
His drink, the running stream; his cup, the bare

Of his palm closed; his bed, the hard cold ground;
To this poor life was Misery ybound.

Whose wretched state when we had well beheld,
With tender ruth on him and on his fears,
In thoughtful cares forth then our pace we held;
And by and by another shape appears, 270
Of greedy Care, still brushing up the breres,
    His knuckles knobbed, his flesh deep dented in,
    With tawëd hands and hard ytannëd skin.

The morrow grey no sooner had begun
To spread his light, even peeping in our eyes,
When he is up and to his work yrun;
But let the night's black misty mantles rise,
And with foul dark never so much disguise
    The fair bright day, yet ceaseth he no while, 280
    But hath his candles to prolong his toil.

By him lay heavy Sleep, the cousin of Death,
Flat on the ground and still as any stone,
A very corpse, save yielding forth a breath;
Small keep took he whom fortune frownëd on
Or whom she lifted up into the throne
    Of high renown; but as a living death,
    So, dead alive, of life he drew the breath.

The body's rest, the quiet of the heart,
The travail's ease, the still night's fere was he,
And of our life in earth the better part; 290
Reaver of sight, and yet in whom we see
Things oft that tide, and oft that never be;
    Without respect, esteeming equally
    King Crœsus' pomp, and Irus' poverty.

And next in order sad Old Age we found,
His beard all hoar, his eyes hollow and blind,
With drooping cheer still poring on the ground,
As on the place where nature him assigned
To rest, when that the sisters had untwined
    His vital thread and ended with their knife 300
    The fleeting course of fast declining life.

There heard we him with broken and hollow plaint
Rue with himself his end approaching fast,
And all for nought his wretched mind torment

With sweet remembrance of his pleasures past,
And fresh delights of lusty youth forewaste;
　　Recounting which, how would he sob and shriek,
　　And to be young again of Jove beseek!

But, and the cruel fates so fixëd be
That time forepast cannot return again,　　　　　　　　310
This one request of Jove yet prayëd he,
That in such withered plight and wretched pain
As eld, accompanied with his loathsome train,
　　Had brought on him, all were it woe and grief,
　　He might a while yet linger forth his life,

And not so soon descend into the pit
Where Death, when he the mortal corpse hath slain,
With reckless hand in grave doth cover it,
Thereafter never to enjoy again
The gladsome light, but in the ground ylain,　　　　　320
　　In depth of darkness waste and wear to nought,
　　As he had never into the world been brought.

But who had seen him sobbing, how he stood
Unto himself and how he would bemoan
His youth forepast, as though it wrought him good
To talk of youth, all were his youth foregone,
He would have mused and marvelled much, whereon
　　This wretched Age should life desire so fain,
　　And knows full well life doth but length his pain.

Crookbacked he was, tooth-shaken, and blear-eyed,　　330
Went on three feet, and sometimes crept on four,
With old lame bones that rattled by his side,
His scalp all pilled and he with eld forlore;
His withered fist still knocking at Death's door,
　　Fumbling and drivelling as he draws his breath;
　　For brief, the shape and messenger of Death.

And fast by him pale Malady was placed,
Sore sick in bed, her color all foregone,
Bereft of stomach, savor, and of taste,
Ne could she brook no meat, but broths alone;　　　340
Her breath corrupt, her keepers every one
　　Abhorring her, her sickness past recure,
　　Detesting physic and all physic's cure.

But oh, the doleful sight that then we see!
We turned our look and on the other side
A grisly shape of Famine might we see,
With greedy looks and gaping mouth that cried
And roared for meat, as she should there have died;
    Her body thin and bare as any bone,
    Whereto was left nought but the case alone.   350

And that, alas, was gnawn on everywhere,
All full of holes that I ne mought refrain
From tears to see how she her arms could tear,
And with her teeth gnash on the bones in vain,
When all for nought, she fain would so sustain
    Her starven corpse, that rather seemed a shade
    Than any substance of a creature made.

Great was her force, whom stone wall could not stay,
Her tearing nails snatching at all she saw;
With gaping jaws that by no means ymay   360
Be satisfied from hunger of her maw,
But eats herself as she that hath no law;
    Gnawing, alas, her carcass all in vain,
    Where you may count each sinew, bone, and vein.

On her while we thus firmly fixed our eyes,
That bled for ruth of such a dreary sight,
Lo, suddenly she shrieked in so huge wise
As made hell gates to shiver with the might;
Wherewith a dart we saw, how it did light
    Right on her breast, and therewithal, pale Death   370
    Enthrilling it, to reave her of her breath.

And by and by a dumb dead corpse we saw,
Heavy and cold, the shape of Death aright,
That daunts all earthly creatures to his law;
Against whose force in vain it is to fight;
Ne peers, ne princes, nor no mortal wight,
    No towns, ne realms, cities, ne strongest tower,
    But all, perforce, must yield unto his power.

His dart, anon, out of the corpse he took,
And in his hand, a dreadful sight to see,   380
With great triumph eftsoons the same he shook,
That most of all my fears affrayèd me;
His body dight with nought but bones, perdy,
    The naked shape of man there saw I plain,
    All save the flesh, the sinew, and the vein.

Lastly, stood War, in glittering arms yclad,
With visage grim, stern looks, and blackly hued;
In his right hand a naked sword he had,
That to the hilts was all with blood imbrued;
And in his left, that kings and kingdoms rued,   390
   Famine and fire he held, and therewithal
   He razëd towns and threw down towers and all.

Cities he sacked and realms that whilom flowered
In honor, glory, and rule above the best,
He overwhelmed and all their fame devoured,
Consumed, destroyed, wasted, and never ceased
Till he their wealth, their name, and all oppressed;
   His face forhewed with wounds, and by his side
   There hung his targe, with gashes deep and wide.

In midst of which, depainted there, we found   400
Deadly Debate, all full of snaky hair,
That with a bloody fillet was ybound,
Out-breathing nought but discord everywhere,
And round about were portrayed, here and there,
   The hugy hosts, Darius and his power,
   His kings, princes, his peers, and all his flower.

Whom great Macedo vanquished there in sight
With deep slaughter, despoiling all his pride,
Pierced through his realms and daunted all his might;
Duke Hannibal beheld I there beside,   410
In Canna's field victor how he did ride,
   And woeful Romans that in vain withstood,
   And consul Paulus covered all in blood.

Yet saw I more: the fight at Thrasimene,
And Treby field, and eke when Hannibal
And worthy Scipio last in arms were seen
Before Carthago gate, to try for all
The world's empire, to whom it should befall;
   There saw I Pompey and Cæsar clad in arms,
   Their hosts allied and all their civil harms.   420

With conquerors' hands, forbathed in their own blood,
And Cæsar weeping over Pompey's head;
Yet saw I Sulla and Marius where they stood,
Their great cruelty and the deep bloodshed
Of friends; Cyrus I saw and his host dead,
   And how the queen with great despite hath flung
   His head in blood of them she overcome.

Xerxes, the Persian king, yet saw I there
With his huge host that drank the rivers dry,
Dismounted hills, and made the vales uprear, 430
His host and all yet saw I plain, perdy;
Thebes I saw, all razed how it did lie
    In heaps of stones, and Tyrus put to spoil,
    With walls and towers flat evened with the soil.

But Troy, alas, methought above them all,
It made mine eyes in very tears consume,
When I beheld the woeful word befall,
That by the wrathful will of gods was come;
And Jove's unmovèd sentence and foredoom 440
    On Priam king, and on his town so bent,
    I could not lin, but I must there lament.

And that the more, sith destiny was so stern
As, force perforce, there might no force avail,
But she must fall, and by her fall we learn
That cities, towers, wealth, world, and all shall quail;
No manhood, might, nor nothing mought prevail;
    All were there prest, full many a prince and peer,
    And many a knight that sold his death full dear.

Not worthy Hector, worthiest of them all,
Her hope, her joy, his force is now for nought; 450
O Troy, Troy, Troy, there is no boot but bale,
The hugy horse within thy walls is brought;
Thy turrets fall, thy knights, that whilom fought
    In arms amid the field, are slain in bed,
    Thy gods defiled and all thy honor dead.

The flames upspring and cruelly they creep
From wall to roof till all to cinders waste;
Some fire the houses where the wretches sleep,
Some rush in here, some run in there as fast;
In everywhere or sword or fire they taste; 460
    The walls are torn, the towers whirled to the ground;
    There is no mischief but may there be found.

Cassandra yet there saw I how they haled
From Pallas' house, with spercled tress undone,
Her wrists fast bound and with Greeks' rout empaled;
And Priam eke, in vain how did he run
To arms, whom Pyrrhus with despite hath done
    To cruel death, and bathed him in the baign
    Of his son's blood, before the altar slain.

But how can I descrive the doleful sight   470
That in the shield so livelike fair did shine?
Sith in this world I think was never wight
Could have set forth the half, not half so fine;
I can no more but tell how there is seen
    Fair Ilium fall in burning red gledes down,
    And from the soil great Troy, Neptunus' town.

Herefrom when scarce I could mine eyes withdraw,
That filled with tears as doth the springing well,
We passëd on so far forth till we saw
Rude Acheron, a loathsome lake to tell,   480
That boils and bubs up swelth as black as hell;
    Where grisly Charon, at their fixëd tide,
    Still ferries ghosts unto the farther side.

The aged god no sooner Sorrow spied,
But hasting straight unto the bank apace,
With hollow call unto the rout he cried
To swerve apart and give the goddess place;
Straight it was done, when to the shore we pace,
    Where, hand in hand as we then linkëd fast,
    Within the boat we are together placed.   490

And forth we launch full fraughted to the brink,
When with the unwonted weight, the rusty keel
Began to crack as if the same should sink;
We hoise up mast and sail, that in a while
We fetched the shore, where scarcely we had while
    For to arrive, but that we heard anon
    A three-sound bark confounded all in one.

We had not long forth passed but that we saw
Black Cerberus, the hideous hound of hell,
With bristles reared and with a three-mouthed jaw   500
Fordinning the air with his horrible yell,
Out of the deep dark cave where he did dwell;
    The goddess straight he knew, and by and by,
    He peased and couched while that we passëd by.

Thence come we to the horror and the hell,
The large great kingdoms and the dreadful reign
Of Pluto in his throne where he did dwell,
The wide waste places and the hugy plain,
The wailings, shrieks, and sundry sorts of pain,
    The sighs, the sobs, the deep and deadly groan,   510
    Earth, air, and all, resounding plaint and moan.

Here puled the babes, and here the maids unwed
With folded hands their sorry chance bewailed,
Here wept the guiltless slain, and lovers dead,
That slew themselves when nothing else availed;
A thousand sorts of sorrows here, that wailed
   With sighs and tears, sobs, shrieks, and all yfear,
   That oh, alas, it was a hell to hear.

We stayed us straight, and with a rueful fear,
Beheld this heavy sight, while from mine eyes   520
The vapored tears down stillëd here and there,
And Sorrow eke, in far more woeful wise,
Took on with plaint, upheaving to the skies
   Her wretched hands, that with her cry the rout
   Gan all in heaps to swarm us round about.

Lo here, quoth Sorrow, princes of renown,
That whilom sat on top of fortune's wheel,
Now laid full low, like wretches whirlëd down,
Even with one frown, that stayed but with a smile;
And now behold the thing that thou, erewhile,   530
   Saw only in thought, and what thou now shalt hear,
   Recount the same to kesar, king, and peer.

Then first came Henry, Duke of Buckingham,
His cloak of black all pilled and quite forworn,
Wringing his hands, and fortune oft doth blame,
Which of a duke hath made him now her scorn;
With ghastly looks, as one in manner lorn,
   Oft spread his arms, stretched hands he joins as fast
   With rueful cheer and vapored eyes upcast.

His cloak he rent, his manly breast he beat,   540
His hair all torn, about the place it lay;
My heart so molt to see his grief so great,
As feelingly methought it dropped away;
His eyes they whirled about withouten stay,
   With stormy sighs the place did so complain,
   As if his heart at each had burst in twain.

Thrice he began to tell his doleful tale,
And thrice with sighs did swallow up his voice,
At each of which he shriekëd so withal,
As though the heavens rivëd with the noise;   550
Till at the last, recovering his voice,
   Supping the tears that all his breast berained,
   On cruel fortune, weeping, thus he plained.

THOMAS TUSSER

The Introduction and Notes are at page 924

FROM *Five Hundred Points of Good Husbandry*, 1580

A preface to the buyer of this book

What lookest thou herein to have?
   Fine verses thy fancy to please?
Of many my betters that crave;
   Look nothing but rudeness in
      these.

What other thing lookest thou
   then?
   Grave sentences many to find?
Such, poets have, twenty and ten—
   Yea, thousands—contenting thy
      mind.

What look ye, I pray you, show
   what?
   Terms painted with rhetoric
      fine?   10

Good husbandry seeketh not
   that,
   Nor is't any meaning of mine.

What lookest thou? Speak at the
   last.
   Good lessons for thee and thy
      wife?
Then keep them in memory fast
   To help as a comfort to life.

What look ye for more in my book?
   Points needful and meet to be
      known?
Then daily be sure to look,
   To save, to be sure, thine own. 20

[*The praise of husbandry*]
As true as thy faith,
This riddle thus saith.

I seem but a drudge, yet I pass any king;
To such as can use me great wealth I do bring.
Since Adam first livëd I never did die,
When Noe was a shipman there also was I.
The earth to sustain me, the sea for my fish,
Be ready to pleasure me as I would wish.
What hath any life but I help to preserve?
What wight without me but is ready to starve?
In woodland, in champian, city, or town,
If long I be absent, what falleth not down?   10
If long I be present, what goodness can want?
Though things at my coming were never so scant.
So many as love me and use me aright
With treasure and pleasure I richly acquite.
Great kings I do succor, else wrong it would go;
The King of all kings hath appointed it so.

A description of the properties of winds at all times of the year

In winter	North winds send hail, South winds bring rain,
	East winds we bewail, West winds blow amain;
	North-east is too cold, South-east not too warm,
	North-west is too bold, South-west doth no harm.
At the spring	The North is a noyer to grass of all suits,
	The East a destroyer to herb and all fruits,
Summer	The South with his showers refresheth the corn,
	The West to all flowers may not be forborne.
Autumn	The West, as a father, all goodness doth bring,
	The East, a forbearer no manner of thing,
	The South, as unkind, draweth sickness too near,
	The North, as a friend, maketh all again clear.
God is the	With temperate wind we be blessed of God,
Governor of	With tempest we find we are beat with his rod;
wind and	All power, we know to remain in his hand,
weather	However wind blow, by sea or by land.

10

.   .   .   .

Christmas husbandly fare

Good husband and housewife now chiefly be glad
    Things handsome to have, as they ought to be had.
They both do provide, against Christmas do come,
    To welcome good neighbor, good cheer to have some.

Good bread and good drink, a good fire in the hall,
    Brawn, pudding, and souse, and good mustard withal.

Beef, mutton, and pork, shred pies of the best,
    Pig, veal, goose, and capon, and turkey well dressed,
Cheese, apples, and nuts; jolly carols to hear,
    As then in the country is counted good cheer.

10

What cost to good husband is any of this?
    Good household provision only it is.
Of other the like I leave out a many
    That costeth the husbandman never a penny.

A sonnet upon the author's first seven years service

Seven times hath Janus ta'en new year by hand,
Seven times hath blust'ring March blown forth his power,

To drive out April's buds, by sea and land,
For minion May to deck most trim with flower.
  Seven times hath temperate Ver like pageant played,
And pleasant Æstas eke her flowers told,
  Seven times Autumnë's heat hath been delayed
With Hiems' boisterous blasts and bitter cold.
  Seven times the thirteen moons have changëd hue,
Seven times the sun his course hath gone about,   10
  Seven times each bird her nest hath built anew,
Since first time you to serve I choosëd out.
  Still yours am I, though thus the time hath passed,
And trust to be, as long as life shall last.

BARNABE GOOGE

The Introduction and Notes are at page 925

From *Eclogues, Epitaphs, and Sonnets,* 1563

To the right worshipful M. William Lovelace, Esquire, Reader of Gray's Inn, Barnabe Googe wisheth health.

How loath I have been, being of long time earnestly required to suffer these trifles of mine to come to light, it is not unknown to a great number of my familiar acquaintance, who both daily and hourly moved me thereunto, and little of long time prevailed therein. For I both considered and weighed with myself the grossness of my style, which thus committed to the gazing show of every eye should forthwith disclose the manifest folly of the writer, and also I feared and mistrusted the disdainful minds of a number both scornful and carping correctors, whose heads are ever busied in taunting judgments, lest they should otherwise interpret my doings than indeed I meant them. These two so great mischiefs utterly dissuaded me from the following of my friends' persuasions, and willed me rather to condemn them to continual darkness, whereby no inconvenience could happen, than to endanger myself in giving them to light, to the disdainful doom of any offended mind. Notwithstanding, all the diligence that I could use in the suppression thereof could not suffice; for I myself being at that time out of the realm, little fearing any such thing to happen, a very friend of mine, bearing, as it seemed, better will to my doings than respecting the hazard of my name, committed them altogether unpolished to the hands of the printer. In whose hands, during his absence from the city till his return of late, they remained. At which time he declared the matter wholly unto me, showing me that being so far passed, and paper provided for the impression thereof, it could not without great hindrance of the poor printer be now revoked. His sudden tale made me at the first utterly amazed; and doubting a great while what was best to be done, at the length agreeing both with necessity and his counsel, I said with Martial, iam sed poteras tutior esse domi. *And calling to mind to whom I might chiefly commit the fruits of my smiling muse, suddenly was cast before my eyes the perfect view of your friendly mind, gentle Master Lovelace; unto whom, for the numbered heaps of sundry friendships accounting myself as bound, I have thought best to give them, not doubting but that they shall be as well taken as I do presently mean them.*

Desiring you herein, as all such as shall read them, especially to bear with the unpleasant form of my too hastily finished Dream, *the greater part whereof with little advice I lately ended, because the beginning of it, as a senseless head separated from the body, was given with the rest to be printed. And thus desiring but for recompense the friendly receiving of my slender gift, I end; wishing unto you, good Master Lovelace, in this life the happy enjoying of prosperous years, and hereafter the blessed estate of never-ceasing joy.*

Yours assuredly,
Barnabe Googe.

Coming homeward out of Spain

O raging seas, and mighty Neptune's reign,
In monstrous hills that throwest
thyself so high,
That with thy floods dost beat the
shores of Spain,
And break the cliffs that dare thy
force envý;
Cease now thy rage and lay thine
ire aside.
And thou that hast the governance of all,
O mighty God! grant weather,
wind, and tide,
Till in my country coast our anchor fall.

Out of sight, out of mind

The oftener seen, the more I lust,
The more I lust, the more I
smart,
The more I smart, the more I
trust,
The more I trust, the heavier
heart;
The heavy heart breeds mine unrest,
Thy absence, therefore, like I best.

The rarer seen, the less in mind,
The less in mind, the lesser pain,
The lesser pain, less grief I find,
The lesser grief, the greater
gain,   10
The greater gain, the merrier I,
Therefore I wish thy sight to fly.

The further off, the more I joy,
The more I joy, the happier life,
The happier life, less hurts annoy,
The lesser hurts, pleasure most
rife:
Such pleasures rife shall I obtain
When distance doth depart us
twain.

[*Once musing as I sat*]

Once musing as I sat,
  and candle burning by,
When all were hushed, I might
    discern
  a simple silly fly,
That flew before mine eyes
  with free rejoicing heart,
And here and there with wings
    did play,
  as void of pain and smart.
Sometime by me she sat,
  when she had played her fill, 10
And ever when she rested had,
  about she flittered still.
When I perceived her well,
  rejoicing in her place,
O happy fly, quoth I, and eke

O worm in happy case,
  Which two of us is best?
  I that have reason? No;
But thou that reason art without
  and therewith void of woe. 20
I live, and so dost thou,
  but I live all in pain,
And subject am to her, alas,
  that makes my grief her gain.
Thou livest, but feelst no grief,
  no love doth thee torment;
A happy thing for me it were,
  if God were so content,
That thou with pen wert placëd
    here
  and I sat in thy place, 30
Then I should joy, as thou dost
    now,
  and thou shouldst wail thy case.

To Doctor Bale

Good aged Bale, that with thy hoary hairs
Dost yet persist to turn the painful book,
O happy man, that hast obtained such years,
And leav'st not yet on papers pale to look,
Give over now to beat thy wearied brain,
And rest thy pen that long hath labored sore;
For aged men unfit sure is such pain,
And thee beseems to labor now no more.
But thou, I think, Don Plato's part will play,
With book in hand to have thy dying day. 10

An epitaph of the death of Nicholas Grimald

Behold this fleeting world, how all things fade,
How every thing doth pass and wear away;
Each state of life, by common course and trade,
Abides no time, but hath a passing day.
For look, as Life, that pleasant dame, hath brought
The pleasant years and days of lustiness,
So Death, our foe, consumeth all to nought;
Envýing thief, with dart doth us oppress.
And that which is the greatest grief of all,
The greedy gripe doth no estate respect, 10
But where he comes he makes them down to fall;

Nor stays he at the high sharp-witted sect.
For if that wit or worthy eloquence
Or learning deep could move him to forbear,
O Grimald, then thou hadst not yet gone hence,
But here hadst seen full many an aged year;
Nor had the Muses lost so fine a flower,
Nor had Minerva wept to leave thee so;
If wisdom might have fled the fatal hour,
Thou hadst not yet been suffered for to go.   20
A thousand doltish geese we might have spared,
A thousand witless heads death might have found,
And taken them for whom no man had cared,
And laid them low in deep oblivious ground:
But fortune favors fools, as old men say,
And lets them live, and takes the wise away.

GEORGE TURBERVILLE

The Introduction and Notes are at page 926

FROM *Epitaphs, Epigrams, Songs and Sonnets,* 1567

To his love
That sent him a ring wherein was graved
'Let reason rule'

Shall reason rule where reason hath no right
Nor never had? Shall Cupid lose his lands?
His claim? his crown? his kingdom? name of might?
And yield himself to be in reason's bands?
No, friend, thy ring doth will me thus in vain.
Reason and love have ever yet been twain.
They are by kind of such contrary mould
As one mislikes the other's lewd device;
What reason wills, Cupido never would;
Love never yet thought reason to be wise.   10
To Cupid I my homage erst have done,
Let reason rule the hearts that she hath won.

Verse in praise of Lord Henry Howard, Earl of Surrey

What should I speak in praise of Surrey's skill
Unless I had a thousand tongues at will?
No one is able to depaint at full
The flowing fountain of his sacred skull,

Whose pen approved what wit he had in mew,
Where such a skill in making sonnets grew.
Each word in place with such a sleight is couched,
Each thing whereof he treats so firmly touched,
As Pallas seemed within his noble breast
To have sojourned and been a daily guest.   10
Our mother tongue by him hath got such light
As ruder speech thereby is banished quite.
Reprove him not for fancies that he wrought,
For fame thereby, and nothing else, he sought.
What though his verse with pleasant toys are fright?
Yet was his honor's life a lamp of light.
A mirror he, the simple sort to train,
That ever beat his brain for Britain's gain.
By him the nobles had their virtues blazed,
When spiteful death their honors' lives had razed;   20
Each that in life had well deservëd aught,
By Surrey's means an endless fame hath caught.
To quite his boon and aye well-meaning mind,
Whereby he did his sequel seem to bind,
Though want of skill to silence me procures,
I write of him whose fame for aye endures;
A worthy wight, a noble for his race,
A learned lord that had an earl's place.

Of drunkenness

At night when ale is in,
    Like friends we part to bed;
In morrow grey, when ale is out,
    Then hatred is in head.

The lover to his lady
That gazed much up to the skies

My girl, thou gazest much
    Upon the golden skies:
Would I were heaven! I would behold
    Thee then with all mine eyes.

FROM *Tragical Tales*, 1587

To a fair gentlewoman, false to her friend

Within the garden-plot of thy fair face
Doth grow a graff of divers qualities:
A matter rare, within so little space

A man to find such sundry properties;
For commonly the root in every tree,
Bark, body, boughs, bud, leaf, and fruit agree.
  First, for the root, is rigor in the breast,
Treason the tree that springeth of the same,
Beauty the bark that overspreads the rest,
The boughs are brave, and climbing up to fame;   10
Brawls be the buds that hang on every bough,
A blossom fit for such roots to allow.
  Love is the leaf that little time endures,
Flatt'ry the fruit which treason's tree doth bear;
Though beauty's bark at first the eye allure,
Yet at the last ill will, the worm, doth wear
Away the leaf, the blossoms, boughs, and all,
And rigor's root makes beauty's buds to fall.

*He declares that albeit he were imprisoned in Russia, yet his
mind was at liberty and did daily repair to his friend*

  Now find I true that hath been often told,
No man may reave the freedom of the mind.
Though keeper's charge in chains the captive hold,
Yet can he not the soul in bondage bind;
That this is true, I find the proof in me,
Who captive am, and yet at liberty.
  Though at my heel a cruel clog they tie,
And ranging out by rigor be restrained,
Yet maugre might, my mind doth freely fly
Home to my friend,—it will not be enchained.   10
No churlë's check, no tyrant's threat can stay
A lover's heart that longs to be away.
  I do desire no aid of Dædalus,
By feat to forge such waxen wings anew
As erst he gave his son, young Icarus,
When they from Crete for fear of Minos flew;
Dame Fancy hath such feathers still in store
For me to fly, as I desire no more.

*Unable by long and hard travel to banish love, returns her
friend*

  Wounded with love and piercing deep desire
Of your fair face, I left my native land
With Russia snow to slack mine English fire;
But well I see no cold can quench the brand
That Cupid's coals enkindle in the breast,

Frost hath no force where friendship is possessed.
The ocean sea, for all his fearful flood,
The perils great of passage, not prevail,
To banish love the rivers do no good,
The mountains high cause Cupid not to quail,   10
Wight are his wings, and fancy flies as fast
As any ship, for all his sails and mast.
The river Dwina cannot wash away
With all his waves the love I bear to thee,
Nor Suchan swift love's raging heat delay,—
Good will was graffed upon so sure a tree.
Sith travel then, nor frost, can cool this fire,
From Moscow I thy friend will home retire.

That he finds others as fair, but not so faithful as his friend

I sundry see, for beauty's gloss,
    That with my mistress may compare,
But few I find for true good will
    That to their friends so friendly are.
Look what she says, I may assure
    Myself thereof—she will not feign;
What others speak is hard to trust,
    They measure all their words by gain.
Her looks declare her loving mind,
    Her count'nance and her heart agree;   10
When others laugh they look as smooth
    But love not half so well as she.
The grief is hers when I am griped,
    My finger's ache is her disease;
With me though others mourn to sight,
    Yet are their hearts at quiet ease.
So that I mark, in Cupid's court
    Are many fair and fresh to see,
Each where is sown Dame Beauty's seed,
    But fair and faithful few there be.   20

To his friend, promising that though her beauty fade, yet his love shall last

I wot full well that beauty cannot last;
No rose that springs but lightly doth decay,
And feature like a lily leaf doth waste,
Or as the cowslip in the midst of May;
I know that tract of time doth conquer all,
And beauty's buds like fading flowers do fall.

That famous dame, fair Helen, lost her hue
When withered age with wrinkles changed her cheeks,
Her lovely looks did loathsomeness ensue
That was the *A per se* of all the Greeks.
And sundry mo that were as fair as she,
Yet Helen was as fresh as fresh might be.

No force for that, I price your beauty light
If so I find you steadfast in good will.
Though few there are that do in age delight,
I was your friend, and so do purpose still;
No change of looks shall breed my change of love,
Nor beauty's want my first good will remove.

THOMAS HOWELL

The Introduction and Notes are at page 927

From *The Arbor of Amity*, 1568

When he thought himself contemned

O heart, why dost thou sigh, and wilt not break?
O doleful chance, thou hast a cause thereto;
For thy reward in love and kindness eke
Is recompensed by hate and deadly woe.

Have I so plight my heart and mind to thee?
Have I been bent so whole unto thy hand,
And others now obtain the fruit from me?
Thou art unkind, forsooth, such foe to stand.

O doleful heart, thus plunged in pinching pain,
Lament no more, but break, thy truth to try;
For where thy comfort was and joy did reign,
Now hate returns no news, O heart, now die!

Lo, thus the breeding birds their nests do build,
But others take the gains and fruits of them;
The crooked clown so ear'th the toiling field,
But oft the crop remains to other men.

Well, time may come wherein my fruitless part,
So ill bestowed, some others may bewail,
And wish they had received my yielding heart
Whose loving root took ground to small avail.

Of misery

Corpse, clad with carefulness,
Heart, heaped with heaviness,
Purse, poor and penniless,
Back, bare in bitterness,
Lips, laide with loathsomeness;
Oh, get my grave in readiness,
Fain would I die to end this stress,
    Remédiless.

The rose

Whenas the mildest month
  Of jolly June doth spring,
And gardens green with happy
      hue
    Their famous fruits do bring;
When eke the lustiest time
    Reviveth youthly blood,
Then springs the finest featured
      flower
    In border fair that stood;
Which moveth me to say,
    In time of pleasant year   10
Of all the pleasant flowers in
      June
    The red rose hath no peer.

To one who after death would leave his lively picture

To leave behind a picture, fine to see,
It may small time well stand in stead for thee;
But picture fair of noble acts of mind—
That far excels to learn to leave behind,
Which will maintain a noble name for aye
As Tully's tongue and Cæsar's acts can say;
As Chaucer shows, and eke our moral Gower,
With thousands more whose fame shall still endure.

Jack shows his qualities and great good will to Jone

Mine own zweet Jone, let me not
      moan,
    no more I thee require,
But as I crave, so let me have
    the thing I do desire.
And ich shall still even at thy will
    be ready at thy hand,
To fling, to spring, and run at ring
    whilst ich am able stand.
With cap and knee ich will serve
      thee,
    what should ich more de-
      clare?   10
Thy mind to please and body ease
    is only all my care.
Though ich am not zo seemly,
      'chwot,
    as been the courtnoles gay,
Yet 'ch'ave a flail that will not
      fail
    to thrash both night and
      day.
And vor manhood 'cham zure
      'cham good,
    vor all our town can zay
How stout ich stood with Robart
      Whood
    when Baldoone volk vetcht
      May;   20
And eke ich pass both more and lass

in dancing Downtoone's round:
To trip, to skip, and handle a whip
    'cham zure my peer's not vound.
To clout a shoe, ich may tell you,
    veow cunnigare there be;
And eke to thatch, where can ye vetch
    another like to me?
In husbandry ich am truly
    ycounted to excel;   30
Yea, and ich can, if need be than,
    wait at the table well.
For once ich went up into Kent
    with the head man of our town,
Where ich did wait at every bait,
    chee vore the 'cham no clown.
Why, for my manor, ich bear the banner
    before my Lord of May;
No country man there is that can
    teach me, though I do zay. 40
And furthermore thou knowest gay store
    of good will fall to me;
Vor vather zed, when he is dead
    that all mine own shall be:
Both calf and cow and our great zow
    that vifteen pigs did varrow
Even at one time, shall then be mine,
    and eke our new wheelbarrow.
Beside all this, ich shall not miss
    of red ones to have store, 50
That zaw no zun, nor yet the moon,
    of years 'cham zure a score.
And all, my Jone, shalt thou alone
    at thy commandment have,
If thou wilt let me friscals vet
    in place where ich do crave.

FROM *H. His Devices*, 1581

Of the golden world

The golden world is past, saith some,
But now, say I, that world is come:
Now all things may for gold be had,
For gain of gold, both good and bad.
Now honor high for gold is bought,
That erst of greater price was thought.
For gold the fool aloft doth rise,
And oft is placed above the wise.
For gold the subtile show their skill,
For gold the wicked win their will. 10
For gold who shuns to wrest a wrong,
And make it seem as right and strong?
Who spares to plead as pleaseth thee
If bring thou do a golden fee?
The fatherless is quite forgot
Where golden gifts do fall to lot;
For gold the widow is oppressed,
And rightful heirs are dispossessed.
Poor Irus' cause at door doth stand,
If Crœsus come with gold in hand. 20
What mischief may almost be thought
That now for gold not daily wrought?
A heap of ills for gold are cloaked,
Yea, vice for gold hath virtue choked.

For gain of gold the flatterer
    smiles
And on thee fawns with sundry
    wiles.
I will not, here, through golden
    traps
Say lovers light in ladies' laps.
But, brief to be, what can you
    crave
That now for gold you may not
    have?   30
Then truth to tell, and not to
    feign,
Right now the golden world doth
    reign.

To his lady, of her doubtful answer

'Twixt death and doubtfulness,
'Twixt pain and pensiveness,
'Twixt hell and heaviness,
Rests all my carefulness.

Oh, vain security,
That will not liberty,
Fie on that fantasy
That brings captivity!

My life is loathsomeness,
My pleasure pastimeless,   10
My end your doubtfulness
If you be merciless.

In doubt is jealousy,
Hope helpeth misery;
Most women commonly
Have answers readily.

THOMAS CHURCHYARD

The Introduction and Notes are at page 927

FROM *The First Part of Churchyard's Chips,* 1575

The praise of our soldiers

Would God my pen might be your trump of fame,
To sound the praise that you deservèd there!
O martial men, that seeks but noble name,
Ye ought of right be honored ev'rywhere.
To you I speak, on whom the burthen lies
Of wars, and doth by sword and service rise,
Who spares no charge nor pain in prince's right,
When state must stand by stout and manly fight.

Your hearts are such you hate at home to bide
When any bruit or voice of wars is heard;   10

Ashamed in street on foot-cloth here to ride,
When forward minds in field should be preferred.
And scorning pomp and peevish pleasures vain
For true renown, ye trudge and toil amain
Where danger dwells and heaps of hazards are,
And hardness great you find, with hungry fare.

You ward the day and watch the winter's night,
In frost, in cold, in sun and heat also;
You are so bent that labor seemeth light
And in the stead of joy you welcome woe.   20
For wealth you take such want as doth befall,
Not shunning grief, but tasting sorrows all;
More glad to die than live with blame or blot,
Most ready still where least is to be got.

And least esteemed of all the men that lives
(Like hackney horse cast off when turn is served),
Yet are you those that greatest honor gives,
If world may judge what soldiers have deserved,
Unto your prince; for you are pale and park
To keep the deer, and lanterns in the dark   30
To show them light, that else at plain noon-day
Might stumble down, or slyly shrink away.

Who bides the brunt, or who bears off the blows
But you alone? Yea, who doth show his face
In time of need, among our foreign foes,
Or boldly saith, Let me supply your place?
Tush! that's a tale was never heard nor seen,—
That anyone, to serve a king or queen,
Did strive with you, or offered half so much
For fame as they who now these verses touch.   40

Wherefore step out, and bear a branch of bays
In sign of world the victors sure you are;
For this I know, in right respect of praise
And worthy laud, may none with you compare.
You may be called the awful martial band,
The jewels gay and garland of the land,
The buds of fame and blossoms of renown,
The country's hope, and beauty of the crown.

Now must you mark: I mean not hirelings here,
Nor summer birds and swallows for the time,   50
That wages takes and serves but once a year,
And sprouts a while as flowers do in their prime;
But those whose minds and noble manners shows
In peace or war, Lo! there a soldier goes,
Of life most clear, of deed and word full just,
In trial still a man of special trust.

FROM THOMAS PROCTER's *Gorgeous Gallery of Gallant
Inventions*, 1578

*The lover deceived by his lady's unconstancy writeth unto her
as followeth*

The heat is past that did me fret,
The fire is out that nature
  wrought;
The plants of youth that I did set
Are dry and dead within my
  thought;
The frost hath slain the kindly sap
That kept the heart in lively state;
The sudden storm and thunder-
  clap
Hath turnëd love to mortal hate.

The mist is gone that bleared mine
  eyes,
The low'ring clouds I see appear;
Though that the blind eat many
  flies,   11
I would you knew my sight is clear.
Your sweet deceiving flatt'ring
  face
Did make me think that you were
  white;
I muse how you had such a grace
To seem a hawk, and be a kite.

Where precious ware is to be sold
They shall it have that giveth
  most;
All things we see are won with
  gold,
Few things is had where is no
  cost.   20
And so it fareth now by me,
Because I press to give no gifts
She takes my suit unthankfully,
And drives me off with many
  drifts.

Is this th' end of all my suit,
For my good will to have a scorn?
Is this of all my pains the fruit,
To have the chaff instead of corn?
Let them that list possess such
  dross,
For I deserve a better gain;   30
Yet had I rather leave with loss
Than serve and sue, and all in
  vain.

GEORGE GASCOIGNE

The Introduction and Notes are at page 928

FROM *A Hundreth Sundry Flowers*, [1573]

Gascoigne's good morrow

You that have spent the silent
    night
In sleep and quiet rest,
And joy to see the cheerful light
That riseth in the east,
Now clear your voice, now cheer
    your heart,
Come help me now to sing,
Each willing wight come bear a
    part,
To praise the heavenly King.

And you whom care in prison
    keeps,
Or sickness doth suppress,   10
Or secret sorrow breaks your
    sleeps,
Or dolors do distress,
Yet bear a part in doleful wise,
Yea, think it good accord
And acceptáble sacrifice
Each sprite to praise the Lord.

The dreadful night with dark-
    some storms
Had overspread the light,
And sluggish sleep with drowsi-
    ness
Had over-pressed our might;   20
A glass wherein we may behold
Each storm that stops our breath,
Our bed the grave, our clothes
    like mold,
And sleep like dreadful death.

Yet, as this deadly night did
    last

But for a little space,
And heavenly day, now night is
    past,
Doth show his pleasant face,
So must we hope to see God's
    face
At last in heaven on high,   30
When we have changed this mor-
    tal place
For immortality.

And of such haps and heavenly
    joys
As then we hope to hold,
All earthly sights, all worldly toys
Are tokens to behold.
The day is like the day of doom,
The sun, the Son of Man,
The skies the heavens, the earth
    the tomb
Wherein we rest till than.   40

The rainbow bending in the
    sky,
Bedecked with sundry hues,
Is like the seat of God on high
And seems to tell these news:
That, as thereby he promisëd
To drown the world no more,
So by the blood which Christ hath
    shed
He will our health restore.

The misty clouds that fall some-
    time
And overcast the skies   50
Are like to troubles of our time,
Which do but dim our eyes;

But as such dews are dried up
    quite
When Phœbus shows his face,
So are such fancies put to flight
Where God doth guide by grace.

The carrion crow, that loath-
    some beast,
Which cries against the rain,
Both for her hue and for the rest
The devil resembleth plain;   60
And as with guns we kill the
    crow
For spoiling our relief,
The devil so must we overthrow
With gunshot of belief.

The little birds which sing so
    sweet
Are like the angels' voice,
Which render God his praises
    meet
And teach us to rejoice;
And as they more esteem that
    mirth
Than dread the night's annoy,   70
So must we deem our days on
    earth
But hell to heavenly joy.

Unto which joys for to attain
God grant us all his grace,
And send us after worldly pain
In heaven to have a place,
Where we may still enjoy that
    light
Which never shall decay;
Lord, for thy mercy, lend us
    might
To see that joyful day!   80

Gascoigne's arraignment

At Beauty's bar as I did stand,
When False Suspect accusëd me,

George (quoth the judge), hold
    up thy hand.
Thou art arraigned of flattery;
Tell therefore how thou wilt be
    tried?
Whose judgment here wilt thou
    abide?

My lord (quoth I), this lady
    here,
Whom I esteem above the rest,
Doth know my guilt, if any were;
Wherefore her doom shall please
    me best.   10
Let her be judge and juror both,
To try me, guiltless by mine oath.

Quoth Beauty, No, it fitteth
    not,
A prince herself to judge the
    cause.
Here is our justice, well you wot,
Appointed to discuss our laws;
If you will guiltless seem to go,
God and your country quit you
    so.

Then Craft, the crier, called a
    quest,
Of whom was Falsehood fore-
    most fere;   20
A pack of pickthanks were the rest
Which came false witness for to
    bear.
The jury such, the judge unjust,
Sentence was said I should be
    trussed.

Jealous, the jailer, bound me
    fast,
To hear the verdict of the bill;
George (quoth the judge), now
    thou art cast,
Thou must go hence to Heavy
    Hill

And there be hanged, all but the
   head:
God rest thy soul when thou art
   dead.   30

Down fell I then upon my
   knee,
All flat before Dame Beauty's
   face,
And cried: Good lady, pardon
   me,
Which here appeal unto your
   grace!
You know if I have been untrue
It was in too much praising you.

And though this judge do make
   such haste
To shed with shame my guiltless
   blood,
Yet let your pity first be placed,
To save the man that meant you
   good.   40
So shall you show yourself a
   queen,
And I may be your servant seen.

Quoth Beauty, Well; because
   I guess
What thou dost mean henceforth
   to be.
Although thy faults deserve no
   less
Than justice here hath judgëd
   thee,
Wilt thou be bound to stint all
   strife
And be true prisoner all thy life?

Yea, madam (quoth I), that I
   shall.
Lo, Faith and Truth my sureties.   50
Why then (quoth she), come
   when I call;
I ask no better warrantise.

Thus am I Beauty's bounden
   thrall,
At her command when she doth
   call.

Gascoigne's lullaby

Sing lullaby, as women do,
Wherewith they bring their babes
   to rest,
And lullaby can I sing too
As womanly as can the best.
With lullaby they still the child,
And if I be not much beguiled,
Full many wanton babes have I
Which must be stilled with lul-
   laby.

First, lullaby my youthful years,
It is now time to go to bed,   10
For crooked age and hoary hairs
Have won the haven within my
   head;
With lullaby, then, youth be still,
With lullaby, content thy will,
Since courage quails and comes be-
   hind,
Go sleep, and so beguile thy mind.

Next, lullaby my gazing eyes,
Which wonted were to glance
   apace.
For every glass may now suf-
   fice
To show the furrows in my face;   20
With lullaby, then, wink awhile,
With lullaby, your looks beguile,
Let no fair face nor beauty bright
Entice you eft with vain delight.

And lullaby, my wanton will,
Let reason's rule now reign thy
   thought,
Since all too late I find by skill
How dear I have thy fancies
   bought;

With lullaby, now take thine ease,
With lullaby, thy doubts appease;
For trust to this, if thou be still,   31
My body shall obey thy will.

Eke, lullaby my loving boy,
My little Robin, take thy rest;
Since age is cold and nothing coy,
Keep close thy coin, for so is best;
With lullaby, be thou content,
With lullaby, thy lusts relent,
Let others pay which have mo
    pence,
Thou art too poor for such ex-
    pense.   40

Thus lullaby, my youth, mine
    eyes,
My will, my ware, and all that
    was!
I can no mo delays devise,
But welcome pain, let pleasure
    pass;
With lullaby, now take your
    leave,
With lullaby, your dreams de-
    ceive,
And when you rise with waking
    eye,
Remember Gascoigne's lullaby.

Gascoigne's De profundis

*The occasion of the writing here-
of (as I have heard Master
Gascoigne say) was this: riding
alone between Chelmsford and
London, his mind mused upon
the days past, and therewithal
he gan accuse his own conscience of much time misspent,
when a great shower of rain
did overtake him; and he being
unprepared for the same, as in
a jerkin without a cloak, the
weather being very fair and un-
likely to have changed so, he
began to accuse himself of his
carelessness; and thereupon in
his good disposition compiled
first this sonnet, and afterwards
the translated Psalm of De
profundis. . . .*

The skies gan scowl, o'ercast
    with misty clouds,
When (as I rode alone by Lon-
    don way,
Cloakless, unclad) thus did I sing
    and say:
Behold, quoth I, bright Titan—
    how he shrouds
His head aback, and yields the
    rain his reach,
Till in his wrath Dan Jove have
    soused the soil
And washed me, wretch which in
    his travail toil.
But holla! here doth rudeness me
    apeach.
Since Jove is Lord and King of
    mighty power,
Which can command the sun to
    show his face,   10
And, when him list, to give the
    rain his place,
Why do not I my weary muses
    frame
(Although I be well soused in
    this shower)
To write some verse in honor of
    his name?

[Inscription in his garden]

If any flower that there is grown,
Or any herb, may ease your pain,
Take, and accompt it as your
    own,
But recompense the like again:
For some and some is honest play,
And so my wife taught me to say.

If here to walk you take de-
      light,
Why, come and welcome, when
      you will;
If I bid you sup here this night,
Bid me another time, and still   10
Think some and some is honest
      play,
For so my wife taught me to say.

Thus if you sup or dine with
      me,
If you walk here or sit at ease,
If you desire the thing you see,
And have the same, your mind to
      please,
Think some and some is honest
      play,
And so my wife taught me to say.

FROM *The Whole Works of George Gascoigne*, 1587

Deep Desire sung this song

Come, Muses, come, and help me to lament,
      Come woods, come waves, come hills, come doleful dales!
Since life and death are both against me bent,
      Come gods, come men, bear witness of my bales.
O heavenly nymphs, come help my heavy heart,
      With sighs to see Dame Pleasure thus depart.

If death or dole could daunt a deep desire,
      If privy pangs could counterpeise my plaint,
If tract of time a true intent could tire,
      Or cramps of care a constant mind could taint;   10
Oh then might I at will here live and starve,
      Although my deeds did more delight deserve.

But out, alas, no gripes of grief suffice
      To break in twain this harmless heart of mine;
For though delight be banished from mine eyes,
      Yet lives Desire, whom pains can never pine.
Oh strange affects! I live, which seem to die,
      Yet die to see my dear delight go by.

Then farewell, sweet, for whom I taste such sour,
      Farewell, delight, for whom I dwell in dole!   20
Free will, farewell, farewell my fancy's flower,
      Farewell, content, whom cruel cares control.
Oh farewell, life; delightful death, farewell!
      I die in heaven, yet live in darksome hell.

FROM *The Steel Glass*, [1576]

The steel glass

.   .   .   .

For whiles I mark this weak and wretched world,
Wherein I see how every kind of man

Can flatter still, and yet deceives himself,
I seem to muse, from whence such error springs,
Such gross conceits, such mists of dark mistake,
Such surquedry, such weening over-well
(And yet, indeed, such dealings too, too bad),
And as I stretch my weary wits, to weigh
The cause thereof, and whence it should proceed,
My battered brains (which now be shrewdly bruised   10
With cannon shot of much misgovernment)
Can spy no cause but only one conceit
Which makes me think the world goeth still awry.

I see and sigh (because it makes me sad)
That peevish pride doth all the world possess;
And every wight will have a looking-glass
To see himself, yet so he seeth him not.
Yea, shall I say, a glass of common glass,
Which glist'reth bright and shows a seemly show,
Is not enough: the days are past and gone   20
That beryl glass, with foils of lovely brown,
Might serve to show a seemly favored face.
That age is dead, and vanished long ago,
Which thought that steel both trusty was and true,
And needed not a foil of contraries,
But showed all things even as they were indeed.
Instead whereof, our curious years can find
The crystal glass, which glimpseth brave and bright,
And shows the thing much better than it is,
Beguiled with foils of sundry subtile sights,   30
So that they seem, and covet not to be.

This is the cause (believe me now, my lord)
That realms do rue from high prosperity,
That kings decline from princely government,
That lords do lack their ancestors' good will,
That knights consume their patrimony still,
That gentlemen do make the merchant rise,
That plowmen beg, and craftsmen cannot thrive,
That clergy quails and hath small reverence,
That laymen live by moving mischief still,   40
That courtiers thrive at latter Lammas Day,
That officers can scarce enrich their heirs,
That soldiers starve, or preach at Tyburn cross,
That lawyers buy, and purchase deadly hate,
That merchants climb, and fall again as fast,
That roisters brag above their betters' room,

That sycophants are counted jolly guests,
That Lais leads a lady's life aloft,
And Lucrece lurks with sober bashful grace.

This is the cause (or else my muse mistakes)   50
That things are thought which never yet were wrought,
And castles built above in lofty skies
Which never yet had good foundation.
And that the same may seem no feignëd dream,
But words of worth, and worthy to be weighed,
I have presumed my lord for to present
With this poor glass, which is of trusty steel,
And came to me by will and testament
Of one that was a glass-maker indeed.

Lucilius this worthy man was named,   60
Who at his death bequeathed the crystal glass
To such as love to seem but not to be;
And unto those that love to see themselves,
How foul or fair soever that they are,
He gan bequeath a glass of trusty steel,
Wherein they may be bold always to look,
Because it shows all things in their degree.
And since myself (now pride of youth is past)
Do love to be, and let all seeming pass;
Since I desire to see myself indeed—   70
Not what I would, but what I am, or should—
Therefore I like this trusty glass of steel.

.   .   .   .

But holla! here I see a wondrous sight,
I see a swarm of saints within my glass.
Behold, behold! I see a swarm indeed
Of holy saints, which walk in comely wise,
Not decked in robes nor garnishëd with gold,
But some unshod, yea, some full thinly clothed;
And yet they seem so heavenly for to see
As if their eyes were all of diamonds,   80
Their face of rubies, sapphires, and jacinths,
Their comely beards and hair of silver wires,—
And to be short, they seem angelical.
What should they be, my lord, what should they be?

O gracious God, I see now what they be.
These be my priests, which pray for ev'ry state;
These be my priests, divorcëd from the world,

And wedded yet to heaven and holiness;
Which are not proud nor covet to be rich,
Which go not gay nor feed on dainty food,   90
Which envy not nor know what malice means,
Which loathe all lust, disdaining drunkenness,
Which cannot feign, which hate hypocrisy,
Which never saw Sir Simony's deceits,
Which preach of peace, which carp contentions,
Which loiter not, but labor all the year,
Which thunder threats of God's most grievous wrath,
And yet do teach that mercy is in store.

Lo, these, my lord, be my good praying priests,
Descended from Melchizedek by line,   100
Cousins to Paul, to Peter, James, and John;
These be my priests, the seas'ning of the earth,
Which will not leese their sav'riness, I trow.

Not one of these, for twenty hundred groats,
Will teach the text that bids him take a wife,
And yet be cumbered with a concubine.

Not one of these will read the holy writ
Which doth forbid all greedy usury,
And yet receive a shilling for a pound.

Not one of these will preach of patience   110
And yet be found as angry as a wasp.

Not one of these can be content to sit
In taverns, inns, and alehouses all day,
But spends his time devoutly at his book.

Not one of these will rail at rulers' wrongs
And yet be blotted with extortion.

Not one of these will paint out worldly pride,
And he himself as gallant as he dare.

Not one of these rebuketh avarice
And yet procureth proud pluralities.   120

Not one of these reproveth vanity
Whiles he himself, with hawk upon his fist
And hounds at heel, doth quite forget his text.

Not one of these corrects contentions
For trifling things, and yet will sue for tithes.

Not one of these, not one of these, my lord,
Will be ashamed to do even as he teacheth.

My priests have learnt to pray unto the Lord,
And yet they trust not in their lip-labor.

My priests can fast, and use all abstinence 130
From vice and sin, and yet refuse no meats.

My priests can give in charitable wise
And love also to do good almës deeds,
Although they trust not in their own deserts.

My priests can place all penance in the heart
Without regard of outward ceremonies.

My priests can keep their temples undefiled
And yet defy all superstition.

Lo now, my lord, what think you by my priests,
Although they were the last that showed themselves? 140
I said at first their office was to pray;
And since the time is such, even nowadays,
As hath great need of prayers truly prayed,
Come forth, my priests, and I will bid your beads.
I will presume, although I be no priest,
To bid you pray as Paul and Peter prayed.

Then pray, my priests, yea, pray to God himself *The Poet's*
That he vouchsafe, even for his Christë's sake, *Beads:*
To give his word free passage here on earth,
And that his church, which now is militant, 150
May soon be seen triumphant over all;
And that he deign to end this wicked world
Which walloweth still in sinks of filthy sin.

Eke pray, my priests, for princes and for kings, *For*
Emperors, monarchs, dukes, and all estates *Princes;*
Which sway the sword of royal government
(Of whom our Queen, which lives without compare,
Must be the chief, in bidding of my beads,
Else I deserve to leese both beads and bones);
That God give light unto their noble minds, 160

To maintain truth, and therewith still to weigh
That here they reign not only for themselves,
And that they be but slaves to common wealth;
Since all their toils and all their broken sleeps
Shall scant suffice to hold it still upright.

Tell some (in Spain) how close they keep their closets,
How seld the wind doth blow upon their cheeks,
While as, meanwhile, their sunburnt suitors starve
And pine before their process be preferred.
Then pray, my priests, that God will give his grace   170
To such a prince, his fault in time to mend.

Tell some (in France) how much they love to dance,
While suitors dance—attendance at the door.
Yet pray, my priests, for prayers princes mend.

Tell some (in Portugal) how cold they be
In setting forth of right religion;
Which more esteem the present pleasures here
Than stablishing of God his holy word.
And pray, my priests, lest God such princes spit
And vomit them out of his angry mouth.   180

Tell some (Italian) princes how they wink
At stinking stews, and say they are, forsooth,
A remedy to quench foul, filthy lust;
Whenas in deed they be the sinks of sin.
And pray, my priests, that God will not impute
Such willful facts unto such princes' charge,
When he himself commandeth every man
To do none ill that good may grow thereby.

And pray likewise for all that rulers be   *For All*   190
By kings' commands, as their lieutenants here,   *Nobility*
All magistrates, all councillors, and all   *and Council-*
That sit in office or authority.   *lors;*
Pray, pray, my priests, that neither love nor meed
Do sway their minds from furthering of right,
That they be not too saintish nor too sour,
But bear the bridle evenly between both;
That still they stop one ear, to hear him speak
Which is accusèd, absent as he is;
That evermore they mark what mood doth move
The mouth which makes the information;   200
That faults forepast (so that they be not huge

Nor do exceed the bonds of loyalty)
Do never quench their charitable mind
Whenas they see repentance hold the reins
Of heady youth, which wont to run astray;
That malice make no mansion in their minds,
Nor envy fret to see how virtue climbs.
The greater birth the greater glory, sure,
If deeds maintain their ancestors' degree.

Eke pray, my priests, for them and for yourselves,   *For the*   210
For bishops, prelates, arch-deans, deans, and priests,   *Clergy;*
And all that preach, or otherwise profess
God's holy word, and take the cure of souls.
Pray, pray, that you, and every one of you,
May walk upright in your vocation;
And that you shine like lamps of perfect life,
To lend a light and lantern to our feet.

Say therewithal that some (I see them, I,
Whereas they fling in Flanders all afar,
For why my glass will show them as they be)   220
Do neither care for God nor yet for devil,
So liberty may launch about at large.

And some, again, (I see them well enough,
And note their names, in Liegeland where they lurk)
Under pretense of holy humble hearts,
Would pluck adown all princely diadem.
Pray, pray, my priests for these; they touch you near.

Shrink not to say that some do, Roman-like,
Esteem their pall and habit over-much.
And therefore pray, my priests, lest pride prevail.   230

Pray that the souls of sundry damnëd ghosts
Do not come in, and bring good evidence
Before the God which judgeth all men's thoughts
Of some whose wealth made them neglect their charge,
Till secret sins, untouched, infect their flocks
And bred a scab which brought the sheep to bane.

Some other ran before the greedy wolf,
And left the fold unfended from the fox,
Which durst nor bark nor bawl for both their ears.
Then pray, my priests, that such no more do so.   240

Pray for the nurses of our noble realm,
I mean the worthy Universities,
(And Cantabridge shall have the dignity,
Whereof I was unworthy member once)
That they bring up their babes in decent wise: *For All*
That Philosophy smell no secret smoke   *Learned;*
Which Magic makes, in wicked mysteries;
That Logic leap not over every stile
Before he come a furlong near the hedge,
With curious *quids* to maintain argument;   250
That Sophistry do not deceive itself;
That Cosmography keep his compass well;
And such as be historiographers
Trust not too much in every tattling tongue,
Nor blinded be by partiality;
That Physic thrive not over-fast by murder;
That numb'ring men, in all their evens and odds,
Do not forget that only Unity
Unmeasurable, infinite, and one;
That Geometry measure not so long   260
Till all their measures out of measure be;
That Music with his heavenly harmony
Do not allure a heavenly mind from heaven,
Nor set men's thoughts in worldly melody
Till heavenly hierarchies be quite forgot;
That Rhetoric learn not to over-reach;
That Poetry presume not for to preach,
And bite men's faults with satire's corrosives,
Yet pamper up her own with poultices,
Or that she dote not upon Erato,   270
Which should invoke the good Calliope;
That Astrology look not over-high
And light, meanwhile, in every puddled pit;
That Grammar grudge not at our English tongue
Because it stands by *monosyllaba*
And cannot be declined, as others are.
Pray thus, my priests, for Universities.
And if I have forgotten any art
Which hath been taught or exercisèd there,
Pray you to God the good be not abused   280
With glorious show of overloading skill.

Now these be past, my priests, yet shall you pray   *For the*
For common people, each in his degree,   *Common-*
That God vouchsafe to grant them all his grace.   *alty.*
Where should I now begin to bid my beads?

Or who shall first be put in common place?
My wits be weary and my eyes are dim,
I cannot see who best deserves the room;
Stand forth, good Piers, thou plowman, by thy name,—
Yet so, the sailor saith I do him wrong.   290
That one contends his pains are without peer;
That other saith that none be like to his;
Indeed they labor both exceedingly.
But since I see no shipman that can live
Without the plow, and yet I many see
Which live by land that never saw the seas,
Therefore I say, stand forth, Piers plowman, first;
Thou win'st the room by very worthiness.

Behold him, priests, and though he stink of sweat   *The*
Disdain him not. For, shall I tell you what?   *Plowman.*300
Such climb to heaven before the shaven crowns.
But how? Forsooth, with true humility.
Not that they hoard their grain when it is cheap,
Nor that they kill the calf to have the milk,
Nor that they set debate between their lords
By earing up the balks that part their bounds;
Nor for because they can both crouch and creep
(The guileful'st men that ever God yet made)
Whenas they mean most mischief and deceit;
Nor that they can cry out on landlords loud,   310
And say they rack their rents an ace too high,
When they themselves do sell their landlord's lamb
For greater price than ewe was wont be worth.
(I see you, Piers; my glass was lately scoured.)
But for they feed with fruits of their great pains
Both king and knight, and priests in cloister pent,
Therefore, I say, that sooner some of them
Shall scale the walls which lead us up to heaven
Than corn-fed beasts whose belly is their god,
Although they preach of more perfection.   320

And yet, my priests, pray you to God for Piers,
As Piers can pinch it out for him and you.
And if you have a paternoster spare,
Then shall you pray for sailors (God them send
More mind of him whenas they come to land—
For toward shipwreck many men can pray),
That they once learn to speak without a lie,
And mean good faith without blaspheming oaths;
That they forget to steal from every freight,

And for to forge false cockets, free to pass;   330
That manners make them give their betters place,
And use good words, though deeds be nothing gay.

But here methinks my priests begin to frown
And say that thus they shall be overcharged,
To pray for all which seem to do amiss;
And one I hear, more saucy than the rest,
Which asketh me, When shall our prayers end?

I tell thee, priest: when shoemakers make shoes
That are well sewed, with never a stitch amiss,
And use no craft in utt'ring of the same;   340
When tailors steal no stuff from gentlemen;
When tanners are with curriers well agreed,
And both so dress their hides that we go dry;
When cutlers leave to sell old rusty blades,
And hide no cracks with solder nor deceit;
When tinkers make no more holes than they found,
When thatchers think their wages worth their work,
When colliers put no dust into their sacks,
When maltmen make us drink no firmentie,
When Davie Diker digs, and dallies not,   350
When smiths shoe horses as they would be shod,
When millers toll not with a golden thumb,
When bakers make not barm bear price of wheat,
When brewers put no baggage in their beer,
When butchers blow not over all their flesh,
When horse-coursers beguile no friends with jades,
When weavers' weight is found in housewives' web.
(But why dwell I so long among these louts?)

When mercers make more bones to swear and lie,
When vintners mix no water with their wine,   360
When printers pass none errors in their books,
When hatters use to buy none old cast robes,
When goldsmiths get no gain by soldered crowns,
When upholsters sell feathers without dust,
When pewterers infect no tin with lead,
When drapers draw no gains by giving day,
When parchmenters put in no ferret silk,
When surgeons heal all wounds without delay.
(Tush! these are toys, but yet my glass showeth all.)

When purveyors provide not for themselves,   370
When takers take no bribes nor use no brags,

When customers conceal no covin used,
When searchers see all corners in a ship
(And spy no pence by any sight they see),
When shrieves do serve all process as they ought,
When bailiffs strain none other thing but strays,
When auditors their counters cannot change,
When proud surveyors take no parting pence,
When silver sticks not on the teller's fingers,   380
And when receivers pay as they receive,
When all these folk have quite forgotten fraud.

(Again, my priests, a little, by your leave)
When sycophants can find no place in court
But are espied for echoes, as they are;
When roisters ruffle not above their rule,
Nor color craft by swearing precious coals;
When fencers' fees are like to apes' rewards—
A piece of bread, and therewithal a bob;
When Lais lives not like a lady's peer,   390
Nor useth art in dyeing of her hair:
When all these things are ordered as they ought,
And see themselves within my glass of steel,
Even then, my priests, may you make holiday
And pray no more but ordinary prayers.

And yet therein I pray you, my good priests,
Pray still for me, and for my glass of steel,
That it (nor I) do any mind offend
Because we show all colors in their kind.
And pray for me, that since my hap is such   400
To see men so, I may perceive myself.
Oh, worthy words to end my worthless verse—
Pray for me, priests, I pray you pray for me.

Tam Marti, quam Mercurio

GEORGE WHETSTONE

The Introduction and Notes are at page 930

FROM *The Rock of Regard,* 1576

Description of cozeners

A lawyer's head to draw a crafty deed,
A harlot's look to witch with wanton sight,

A flatterer's tongue with sugared words to feed,
A tyrant's heart to wound the harmless wight,
To toll with cheer a greedy glutton's gorge,
A merchant's mouth of falsehood truth to forge,

A scrivener's fist by nimbleness to race,
To scrape, to forge, to counterfeit a name,
A lackey's leg to trudge in every place,
A desperate mind which dreads no kind of shame,—   10
These limbs, well linked, and set on cozener's soil,
A work were sure of all the devils the toil!

For each of them a fiend in force can bind;
Yet some, I grant, by virtue guides their place;
But seldom 'tis that kit ne follows kind,
If one be good, a score doth want the grace.
But all in league, their dealings lewd beware,
For then they do the devil and all off scare!

Epilogus

Lo, ladies, here (if you can use it well)
An arbor fenced from burning fire and frost;
A place it is where pride shall never dwell,
Nor fortune work a maze, do she her worst;
A place wherein the worthy dame should live,
Whom no extreme may change from virtuous thought:
Even such a place my muse, fair dames, doth give
To you, the which with double toil is wrought.
Here may you see, by lamps of others' lives,
A president to live in worthy name;   10
Here may you see, when death your days deprives,
In spite of death remembrance of your fame.

HUMPHREY GIFFORD

The Introduction and Notes are at page 930

FROM *A Posy of Gillyflowers*, 1580

For soldiers

Ye buds of Brutus' land, courageous youths, now play your parts,
Unto your tackle stand, abide the brunt with valiant hearts!
For news is carried to and fro that we must forth to warfare go,
Men muster now in every place, and soldiers are pressed forth apace.

Faint not, spend blood, to do your Queen and country good!
Fair words, good pay, will make men cast all care away.

The time of war is come: prepare your corslet, spear, and shield.
Methinks I hear the drum strike doleful marches to the field,
Tantara, tantara! the trumpets sound, which makes our hearts with
    joy abound;
The roaring guns are heard afar, and every thing denounceth war.   10
Serve God, stand stout, bold courage brings this gear about;
Fear not, forth run, faint heart fair lady never won.

Ye curious carpet knights, that spend the time in sport and play,
Abroad, and see new sights! your country's cause calls you away.
Do not, to make your ladies game, bring blemish to your worthy name,
Away to field and win renown! with courage beat your enemies down!
Stout hearts gain praise when dastards sail in slander's seas.
Hap what hap shall, we sure shall die but once for all.

Alarm methinks they cry. Be packing, mates, be gone with speed!
Our foes are very nigh,—shame have that man that shrinks at need!   20
Unto it boldly let us stand, God will give right the upper hand;
Our cause is good, we need not doubt. In sign of courage give a
    shout!
March forth, be strong, good hap will come ere it be long;
Shrink not, fight well, for lusty lads must bear the bell.

All you that will shun evil must dwell in warfare every day,
The world, the flesh, and devil always do seek our souls' decay:
Strive with these foes with all your might, so shall you fight a worthy
    fight.
That conquest doth deserve most praise where vice do yield to virtue's
    ways.
Beat down foul sin! a worthy crown then shall ye win!
If we live well, in heaven with Christ our souls shall dwell.   30

A delectable dream

A woman's face is full of wiles,
  Her tears are like the crocodile;
With outward cheer on thee she
    smiles
When in her heart she thinks
    thee ill.
Her tongue still chats of this and
    that,
Than aspen leaf it wags more
    fast;
And as she talks she knows not
    what,
There issues many a truthless
    blast.
Thou far dost take thy mark
    amiss

If thou think faith in them to
    find.   10
The weathercock more constant is,
    Which turns about with every
    wind.
Oh, how in pity they abound!
    Their heart is mild like marble
    stone;
If in thyself no hope be found,
    Be sure of them thou gettest
    none.
I know some pepper-nosëd dame

Will term me fool and saucy
    jack,
That dare their credit so defame
    And lay such slanders on their
    back.   20
What though on me they pour their
    spite?
I may not use the glozer's trade:
I cannot say the crow is white,
    But needs must call a spade a
    spade.
.   .   .   .   .

RICHARD STANYHURST

The Introduction and Notes are at page 931

FROM *The First Four Books of Virgil*, 1582

A prayer to the Trinity

Trinity blessed, deity co-equal,
Unity sacred, God one eke in essence,
Yield to thy servant, pitifully calling,
    Merciful hearing.
Virtuous living did I long relinquish,
Thy will and precepts miserably scorning.
Grant to me, sinful, patïent repenting,
    Healthful amendment.
Blessed I judge him that in heart is healëd;
Cursëd I know him that in health is harmëd: 10
Thy physic therefore to me, wretch unhappy,
    Send, my redeemer!
Glory to God, the father, and his only
Son, the protector of us earthly sinners,
The sacred spirit, laborers refreshing,
    Still be renownëd!
                Amen.

EDWARD DE VERE, EARL OF OXFORD

The Introduction and Notes are at page 931

FROM RICHARD EDWARDS's *Paradise of Dainty Devices*, 1576

Of the mighty power of love

My meaning is to work what woundës love hath wrought,
Wherewith I muse why men of wit have love so dearly bought.

For love is worse than hate, and eke more harm hath done;
Record I take of those that rede of Paris, Priam's son.

It seemed the god of sleep had mazed so much his wits
When he refusëd wit for love, which cometh but by fits.
But why accuse I him whom earth hath covered long?
There be of his posterity alive; I do him wrong.

Whom I might well condemn, to be a cruel judge
Unto myself, who hath that crime in others that I grudge.   10

From *Rawlinson Poetry Ms.* 85

[*Who taught thee first to sigh?*]

Who taught thee first to sigh, alas, my heart?
Who taught thy tongue the woeful words of plaint?
Who filled your eyes with tears of bitter smart?
Who gave thee grief, and made thy joys to faint?

Who first did paint with colors pale thy face?
Who first did break thy sleeps of quiet rest?
Above the rest in court who gave thee grace?
Who made thee strive, in honor to be best?

In constant truth to bide so firm and sure?
To scorn the world, regarding but thy friends?   10
With patient mind each passion to endure?
In one desire to settle to the end?

  Love then thy choice, wherein such choice thou bind
  As nought but death may ever change thy mind.

[*If women could be fair*]

If women could be fair and yet not fond,
Or that their love were firm, not fickle, still,
I would not marvel that they make men bond,
By service long to purchase their good will.
  But when I see how frail those creatures are,
  I muse that men forget themselves so far.

To mark the choice they make and how they change,
How oft from Phœbus they do fly to Pan,
Unsettled still, like haggards wild they range,
These gentle birds that fly from man to man;   10

Who would not scorn, and shake them from the fist,
And let them fly, fair fools, which way they list?

Yet for disport we fawn and flatter both,
To pass the time when nothing else can please;
And train them to our lure with subtle oath
Till, weary of their wiles, ourselves we ease;
And then we say, when we their fancy try,
To play with fools, oh, what a fool was I!

FROM *Breton's Bower of Delights,* 1591

Of the birth and bringing up of Desire

When wert thou born, Desire? In pomp and prime of May.
By whom, sweet boy, wert thou begot? By Good Conceit, men say.
Tell me, who was thy nurse? Fresh Youth, in sugared joy.
What was thy meat and daily food? Sad sighs, with great annoy.
What had you then to drink? Unfeignëd lovers' tears.
What cradle were you rockëd in? In hope devoid of fears.
What brought you then asleep? Sweet Speech, which likes men best.
And where is now your dwelling-place? In gentle hearts I rest.
Doth company displease? It doth, in many one.
Where would Desire then choose to be? He likes to muse alone.   10
What feedeth most your sight? To gaze on favor still.
Who find you most to be your foe? Disdain of my good will.
Will ever age or death bring you unto decay?
No, no! Desire both lives and dies a thousand times a day.

FROM R. S.'s *Phœnix Nest,* 1593

[*What cunning can express?*]

What cunning can express
The favor of her face
To whom in this distress
I do appeal for grace?
　A thousand Cupids fly
　About her gentle eye.

From whence each throws a dart
That kindleth soft sweet fire
Within my sighing heart,
Possessëd by desire.   10
　No sweeter life I try
　Than in her love to die.

The lily in the field
That glories in his white,
For pureness now must yield
And render up his right.
　Heav'n pictured in her face
　Doth promise joy and grace.

Fair Cynthia's silver light
That beats on running streams   20
Compares not with her white,
Whose hairs are all sun-beams.
　Her virtues so do shine
　As day unto mine eyne.

With this there is a red
Exceeds the damask rose,
Which in her cheeks is spread,
Whence every favor grows.
  In sky there is no star
  That she surmounts not far. ³⁰

When Phœbus from the bed
Of Thetis doth arise,
The morning blushing red

In fair carnation wise,
  He shows it in her face
  As queen of every grace.

This pleasant lily-white,
This taint of roseate red,
This Cynthia's silver light,
This sweet fair Dea spread,   ⁴⁰
  These sun-beams in mine eye,
  These beauties make me die!

SIR PHILIP SIDNEY

The Introduction and Notes are at page 932

From *Sir P. S. his Astrophel and Stella*, 1591

To the worshipful and his very good friend, Ma. Francis
Flower, Esquire, increase of all content.

*It was my fortune (right worshipful) not many days since, to light
upon the famous device of* Astrophel and Stella, *which carrying the
general commendation of all men of judgment, and being reported
to be one of the rarest things that ever any Englishman set abroach, I
have thought good to publish it under your name, both for I know the
excellency of your worship's conceit, above all other to be such as is
only fit to discern of all matters of wit, as also for the credit and
countenance your patronage may give to such a work. Accept of it,
I beseech you, as the first fruits of my affection, which desires to
approve itself in all duty unto you; and though the argument perhaps
may seem too light for your grave view, yet considering the worthiness of the author, I hope you will entertain it accordingly. For my
part, I have been very careful in the printing of it, and whereas, being
spread abroad in written copies it had gathered much corruption by
ill writers, I have used their help and advice in correcting and re-
storing it to his first dignity, that I know were of skill and experience
in those matters. And the rather was I moved to set it forth because I
thought it pity anything proceeding from so rare a man should be obscured, or that his fame should not still be nourished in his works,
whom the works with one united grief bewailed. Thus craving pardon
for my bold attempt, and desiring the continuance of your worship's
favor unto me, I end.*

Yours always to be commanded,

Tho. Newman.

FROM *The Countess of Pembroke's Arcadia,* 1598

To the reader.

The disfigured face, gentle reader, wherewith this work not long since appeared to the common view, moved that noble lady, to whose honor consecrated, to whose protection it was committed, to take in hand the wiping away those spots wherewith the beauties thereof were unworthily blemished. But as often in repairing a ruinous house, the mending of some old part occasioneth the making of some new, so here her honorable labor, begun in correcting the faults, ended in supplying the defects; by the view of what was ill done guided to the consideration of what was not done. Which part with what advice entered into, with what success it hath been passed through, most by her doing, all by her directing, if they may be entreated not to define, which are unfurnished of means to discern, the rest, it is hoped, will favorably censure. . . .

H. S.

Astrophel and Stella

Loving in truth, and fain in verse my love to show,
   That she, dear she, might take some pleasure of my pain,
   Pleasure might cause her read, reading might make her know,
   Knowledge might pity win, and pity grace obtain,—
I sought fit words to paint the blackest face of woe;
   Studying inventions fine, her wits to entertain,
   Oft turning others' leaves to see if thence would flow
   Some fresh and fruitful showers upon my sun-burned brain.
But words came halting forth, wanting invention's stay;
   Invention, nature's child, fled step-dame Study's blows,   10
   And others' feet still seemed but strangers in my way.
Thus, great with child to speak, and helpless in my throes,
   Biting my truant pen, beating myself for spite,
   Fool, said my muse to me, look in thy heart and write.

Not at the first sight, nor with a dribbed shot,
   Love gave the wound, which, while I breathe, will bleed;
   But known worth did in mine of time proceed,
   Till by degrees it had full conquest got.
I saw and liked; I liked but lovèd not;
   I loved, but straight did not what love decreed;
   At length to love's decrees I, forced, agreed,
   Yet with repining at so partial lot.
Now even that footstep of lost liberty
   Is gone, and now, like slave-born Muscovite,   10
   I call it praise to suffer tyranny;

And now employ the remnant of my wit
 To make me self believe that all is well,
 While, with a feeling skill, I paint my hell.

Let dainty wits cry on the sisters nine,
 That, bravely masked, their fancies may be told;
 Or Pindar's apes flaunt they in phrases fine,
 Enam'ling with pied flowers their thoughts of gold;
Or else let them in statelier glory shine,
 Ennobling new-found tropes with problems old;
 Or with strange similes enrich each line,
 Of herbs or beasts which Ind or Afric hold.
For me, in sooth, no Muse but one I know;
 Phrases and problems from my reach do grow,
 And strange things cost too dear for my poor sprites.
How then? even thus,—in Stella's face I read
 What love and beauty be, then all my deed
 But copying is, what in her Nature writes.

It is most true that eyes are formed to serve
 The inward light, and that the heavenly part
 Ought to be king, from whose rules who do swerve,
 Rebels to nature, strive for their own smart.
It is most true what we call Cupid's dart
 An image is which for ourselves we carve,
 And, fools, adore in temple of our heart
 Till that good god make church and churchman starve.
True, that true beauty virtue is indeed,
 Whereof this beauty can be but a shade,
 Which elements with mortal mixture breed.
True, that on earth we are but pilgrims made,
 And should in soul up to our country move;
 True, and yet true that I must Stella love.

Some lovers speak, when they their muses entertain,
 Of hopes begot by fear, of wot not what desires,
 Of force of heav'nly beams infusing hellish pain,
 Of living deaths, dear wounds, fair storms, and freezing fires;
Someone his song in Jove and Jove's strange tales attires,
 Bordered with bulls and swans, powdered with golden rain;
 Another humbler wit to shepherd's pipe retires,
 Yet hiding royal blood full oft in rural vein;

To some a sweetest plaint a sweetest style affords,
  While tears pour out his ink, and sighs breathe out his words,   10
  His paper pale despair, and pain his pen doth move.
I can speak what I feel, and feel as much as they,
  But think that all the map of my state I display
  When trembling voice brings forth that I do Stella love.

When nature made her chief work, Stella's eyes,
  In color black why wrapped she beams so bright?
  Would she in beamy black, like painter wise,
  Frame daintiest luster mixed of shades and light?
Or did she else that sober hue devise
  In object best to knit and strength our sight,
  Lest, if no veil these brave gleams did disguise,
  They, sunlike, should more dazzle than delight?
Or would she her miraculous power show,
  That, whereas black seems beauty's contrary,   10
  She even in black doth make all beauties flow?
Both so, and thus,—she, minding Love should be
  Placed ever there, gave him this mourning weed
  To honor all their deaths who for her bleed.

Alas, have I not pain enough, my friend,
  Upon whose breast a fiercer gripe doth tire
  Than did on him who first stole down the fire,
  While Love on me doth all his quiver spend,—
But with your rhubarb words ye must contend,
  To grieve me worse, in saying that desire
  Doth plunge my well-formed soul even in the mire
  Of sinful thoughts which do in ruin end?
If that be sin which doth the manners frame,
  Well stayed with truth in word and faith of deed,   10
  Ready of wit and fearing nought but shame;
If that be sin which in fixed hearts doth breed
  A loathing of all loose unchastity,
  Then love is sin, and let me sinful be.

You that do search for every purling spring
  Which from the ribs of old Parnassus flows,
  And every flower, not sweet perhaps, which grows
  Near thereabouts into your poesy wring;
You that do dictionary's method bring
  Into your rhymes, running in rattling rows;
  You that poor Petrarch's long-deceasèd woes
  With new-born sighs and denizened wit do sing;

You take wrong ways, those far-fet helps be such
 As do bewray a want of inward touch,   10
 And sure at length stol'n goods do come to light.
But if, both for your love and skill, your name
 You seek to nurse at fullest breasts of Fame,
 Stella behold, and then begin to endite.

Fly, fly, my friends, I have my death wound, fly;
 See there that boy, that murth'ring boy, I say,
 Who, like a thief, hid in dark bush doth lie
Till bloody bullet get him wrongful prey.
So tyrant he no fitter place could spy,
 Nor so fair level in so secret stay,
 As that sweet black which veils the heav'nly eye:
There himself with his shot he close doth lay.
Poor passenger, pass now thereby I did,
 And stayed, pleased with the prospect of the place, 10
 While that black hue from me the bad guest hid;
But straight I saw motions of lightning grace,
 And then descried the glist'ring of his dart;
 But ere I could fly thence, it pierced my heart.

Your words, my friend, (right healthful caustics) blame
 My young mind marred, whom love doth windlass so
 That mine own writings, like bad servants, show
 My wits quick in vain thoughts, in virtue lame;
That Plato I read for nought but if he tame
 Such coltish years; that to my birth I owe
 Nobler desires, lest else that friendly foe,
 Great expectation, wear a train of shame.
For since mad March great promise made of me,
 If now the May of my years much decline,   10
 What can be hoped my harvest time will be?
Sure, you say well, Your wisdom's golden mine
 Dig deep with learning's spade. Now tell me this,
 Hath this world aught so fair as Stella is?

Rich fools there be whose base and filthy heart
 Lies hatching still the goods wherein they flow,
 And damning their own selves to Tantal's smart,
 Wealth breeding want, more blest, more wretched grow.
Yet to those fools heaven such wit doth impart,
 As what their hands do hold, their heads do know;
 And knowing, love; and loving, lay apart
 As sacred things, far from all danger's show.

But that rich fool, who by blind fortune's lot
   The richest gem of love and life enjoys,   10
   And can with foul abuse such beauties blot,
Let him, deprived of sweet but unfelt joys,
   Exiled for aye from those high treasures which
   He knows not, grow in only folly rich!

You that with allegory's curious frame
   Of others' children changelings use to make,
   With me those pains, for God's sake, do not take;
I list not dig so deep for brazen fame.
When I say Stella, I do mean the same
   Princess of beauty for whose only sake
   The reins of love I love, though never slake,
And joy therein, though nations count it shame.
I beg no subject to use eloquence,
   Nor in hid ways do guide philosophy;   10
   Look at my hands for no such quintessence,
But know that I in pure simplicity
   Breathe out the flames which burn within my heart,
   Love only reading unto me this art.

Whether the Turkish new-moon minded be
   To fill his horns this year on Christian coast;
   How Poles' right king means without leave of host
To warm with ill-made fire cold Muscovy;
If French can yet three parts in one agree;
   What now the Dutch in their full diets boast;
   How Holland hearts, now so good towns be lost,
Trust in the shade of pleasing Orange-tree;
How Ulster likes of that same golden bit
   Wherewith my father once made it half tame;   10
   If in the Scotch Court be no welt'ring yet:
These questions busy wits to me do frame.
   I, cumbered with good manners, answer do,
   But know not how, for still I think of you.

With how sad steps, O moon, thou climb'st the skies!
   How silently, and with how wan a face!
   What! may it be that even in heav'nly place
That busy archer his sharp arrows tries?
Sure, if that long-with-love-acquainted eyes
   Can judge of love, thou feel'st a lover's case;
   I read it in thy looks,—thy languished grace
To me, that feel the like, thy state descries.

Then, ev'n of fellowship, O moon, tell me,
  Is constant love deemed there but want of wit?
  Are beauties there as proud as here they be?
Do they above love to be loved, and yet
  Those lovers scorn whom that love doth possess?
  Do they call virtue there ungratefulness?

I might—unhappy word!—oh me, I might,
  And then would not, or could not, see my bliss;
Till now, wrapped in a most infernal night,
  I find how heav'nly day, wretch, I did miss.
Heart, rent thyself, thou dost thyself but right;
  No lovely Paris made thy Helen his,
  No force, no fraud, robbed thee of thy delight,
  Nor fortune of thy fortune author is;
But to myself myself did give the blow,
  While too much wit, forsooth, so troubled me
  That I respects for both our sakes must show,
And yet could not by rising morn foresee
  How fair a day was near; oh, punished eyes,
  That I had been more foolish—or more wise!

Come, let me write. And to what end? To ease
  A burthened heart. How can words ease, which are
  The glasses of thy daily vexing care?
Oft cruel fights well pictured forth do please.
Art not ashamed to publish thy disease?
  Nay, that may breed my fame, it is so rare.
  But will not wise men think thy words fond ware?
Then be they close, and so none shall displease.
What idler thing than speak and not be heard?
  What harder thing than smart and not to speak?
  Peace, foolish wit! with wit my wit is marred.
Thus write I, while I doubt to write, and wreak
  My harms on ink's poor loss. Perhaps some find
  Stella's great powers, that so confuse my mind.

What may words say, or what may words not say,
  Where truth itself must speak like flattery?
  Within what bounds can one his liking stay,
  Where nature doth with infinite agree?
What Nestor's counsel can my flames allay,
  Since reason's self doth blow the coal in me?
  And ah, what hope that hope should once see day,
  Where Cupid is sworn page to chastity?

Honor is honored, that thou dost possess
　　Him as thy slave, and now long-needy Fame
　　Doth even grow rich, naming my Stella's name.
Wit learns in thee perfection to express,
　　Not thou by praise, but praise in thee is raised;
　　It is a praise to praise, when thou art praised.

My mouth doth water, and my breast doth swell,
　　My tongue doth itch, my thoughts in labor be;
　　Listen then, lordings, with good ear to me,
　　For of my life I must a riddle tell.
Toward Aurora's court a nymph doth dwell,
　　Rich in all beauties which man's eye can see;
　　Beauties so far from reach of words that we
　　Abase her praise saying she doth excel;
Rich in the treasure of deserved renown,
　　Rich in the riches of a royal heart,
　　Rich in those gifts which give th' eternal crown;
Who, though most rich in these and every part
　　Which make the patents of true worldly bliss,
　　Hath no misfortune but that Rich she is.

Come sleep! O sleep, the certain knot of peace,
　　The baiting place of wit, the balm of woe,
　　The poor man's wealth, the prisoner's release,
　　Th' indifferent judge between the high and low;
With shield of proof shield me from out the prease
　　Of those fierce darts despair at me doth throw;
　　O make in me those civil wars to cease;
　　I will good tribute pay, if thou do so.
Take thou of me smooth pillows, sweetest bed,
　　A chamber deaf to noise and blind to light,
　　A rosy garland and a weary head;
And if these things, as being thine by right,
　　Move not thy heavy grace, thou shalt in me,
　　Livelier than elsewhere, Stella's image see.

As good to write as for to lie and groan.
　　O Stella dear, how much thy power hath wrought,
　　That hast my mind, none of the basest, brought
　　My still-kept course, while other sleep, to moan;
Alas, if from the height of virtue's throne
　　Thou canst vouchsafe the influence of a thought
　　Upon a wretch that long thy grace hath sought,
　　Weigh then how I by thee am overthrown;

And then think thus—although thy beauty be
  Made manifest by such a victory,   10
  Yet noblest conquerors do wrecks avoid.
Since then thou hast so far subduëd me,
  That in my heart I offer still to thee,
  Oh, do not let thy temple be destroyed.

Having this day my horse, my hand, my lance
  Guided so well that I obtained the prize,
  Both by the judgment of the English eyes
  And of some sent from that sweet enemy, France;
Horsemen my skill in horsemanship advance,
  Town-folks my strength; a daintier judge applies
  His praise to sleight which from good use doth rise;
  Some lucky wits impute it but to chance;
Others, because of both sides I do take
  My blood from them who did excel in this,   10
  Think nature me a man of arms did make.
How far they shot awry! The true cause is,
  Stella looked on, and from her heav'nly face
  Sent forth the beams which made so fair my race.

Stella oft sees the very face of woe
  Painted in my beclouded stormy face,
  But cannot skill to pity my disgrace,
  Not though thereof the cause herself she know;
Yet hearing late a fable, which did show
  Of lovers never known a grievous case,
  Pity thereof gat in her breast such place
  That, from the sea derived, tears' spring did flow.
Alas, if fancy, drawn by imaged things
  Though false, yet with free scope, more grace doth breed   10
  Than servant's wrack, where new doubts honor brings;
Then think, my dear, that you in me do read
  Of lovers' ruin some sad tragedy.
  I am not I; pity the tale of me.

Because I breathe not love to every one,
  Nor do not use set colors for to wear,
  Nor nourish special locks of vowëd hair,
  Nor give each speech a full point of a groan,
The courtly nymphs, acquainted with the moan
  Of them who in their lips Love's standard bear,
  What, he! say they of me, Now I dare swear
  He cannot love; no, no, let him alone.

And think so still, so Stella know my mind;
    Profess indeed I do not Cupid's art;   10
    But you, fair maids, at length this true shall find,
That his right badge is but worn in the heart;
    Dumb swans, not chatt'ring pies, do lovers prove;
    They love indeed who quake to say they love.

Muses, I oft invoked your holy aid,
    With choicest flowers my speech t' engarland so
    That it, despised in true but naked show,
    Might win some grace in your sweet grace arrayed;
And oft whole troops of saddest words I stayed,
    Striving abroad a-foraging to go,
    Until by your inspiring I might know
    How their black banner might be best displayed.
But now I mean no more your help to try,
    Nor other sug'ring of my speech to prove,   10
    But on her name incessantly to cry;
For let me but name her whom I do love,
    So sweet sounds straight mine ear and heart do hit,
    That I well find no eloquence like it.

O grammar-rules, O now your virtues show;
    So children still read you with awful eyes,
    As my young dove may, in your precepts wise,
    Her grant to me by her own virtue know;
For late, with heart most high, with eyes most low,
    I craved the thing which ever she denies;
    She, lightning Love displaying Venus' skies,
    Lest once should not be heard, twice said, No, No!
Sing then, my muse, now Io Pæan sing;
    Heav'ns envy not at my high triumphing,   10
    But grammar's force with sweet success confirm;
For grammar says,—oh this, dear Stella, weigh,—
    For grammar says,—to grammar who says nay?—
    That in one speech two negatives affirm!

First song

Doubt you to whom my muse these notes intendeth,
Which now my breast, o'ercharged, to music lendeth?
To you, to you, all song of praise is due;
Only in you my song begins and endeth.

Who hath the eyes which marry state with pleasure?
Who keeps the key of nature's chiefest treasure?

To you, to you, all song of praise is due;
Only for you the heaven forgat all measure.

Who hath the lips where wit in fairness reigneth?
Who womankind at once both decks and staineth?   10
To you, to you, all song of praise is due;
Only by you Cupid his crown maintaineth.

Who hath the feet whose step of sweetness planteth?
Who else, for whom fame worthy trumpets wanteth?
To you, to you, all song of praise is due;
Only to you her scepter Venus granteth.

Who hath the breast whose milk doth passions nourish?
Whose grace is such that when it chides doth cherish?
To you, to you, all song of praise is due;
Only through you the tree of life doth flourish.   20

Who hath the hand which without stroke subdueth?
Who long dead beauty with increase reneweth?
To you, to you, all song of praise is due;
Only at you all envy hopeless rueth.

Who hath the hair which, loosest, fastest tieth?
Who makes a man live then glad, when he dieth?
To you, to you, all song of praise is due;
Only of you the flatterer never lieth.

Who hath the voice which soul from senses sunders?
Whose force but yours the bolts of beauty thunders?   30
To you, to you, all song of praise is due;
Only with you not miracles are wonders.

Doubt you to whom my muse these notes intendeth,
Which now my breast, o'ercharged, to music lendeth?
To you, to you, all song of praise is due;
Only in you my song begins and endeth.

No more, my dear, no more these counsels try;
  Oh, give my passions leave to run their race;
  Let fortune lay on me her worst disgrace;
  Let folk o'ercharged with brain against me cry;
Let clouds bedim my face, break in mine eye;
  Let me no steps but of lost labor trace;
  Let all the earth with scorn recount my case,
  But do not will me from my love to fly.

I do not envy Aristotle's wit,
  Nor do aspire to Cæsar's bleeding fame;   10
  Nor aught do care though some above me sit;
Nor hope nor wish another course to frame,
  But that which once may win thy cruel heart;
  Thou art my wit, and thou my virtue art.

Oh, joy too high for my low style to show!
  Oh, bliss fit for a nobler state than me!
  Envy, put out thine eyes, lest thou do see
What oceans of delight in me do flow!
My friend, that oft saw, through all masks, my woe,
  Come, come, and let me pour myself on thee.
  Gone is the winter of my misery!
My spring appears, oh see what here doth grow;
For Stella hath, with words where faith doth shine,
  Of her high heart giv'n me the monarchy;   10
  I, I, oh I may say that she is mine!
And though she give but thus conditionly
  This realm of bliss, while virtuous course I take,
  No kings be crowned but they some covenants make.

I never drank of Aganippe well,
  Nor ever did in shade of Tempe sit,
  And Muses scorn with vulgar brains to dwell;
Poor layman I, for sacred rites unfit.
Some do I hear of poets' fury tell,
  But, God wot, wot not what they mean by it;
  And this I swear by blackest brook of hell,
I am no pick-purse of another's wit.
How falls it then, that with so smooth an ease
  My thoughts I speak, and what I speak doth flow   10
  In verse, and that my verse best wits doth please?
Guess we the cause? What, is it thus? Fie, no.
  Or so? Much less. How then? Sure thus it is:
  My lips are sweet, inspired with Stella's kiss.

Fourth song

Only joy, now here you are,
Fit to hear and ease my care;
Let my whispering voice obtain
Sweet reward for sharpest pain;
Take me to thee, and thee to me—
'No, no, no, no, my dear, let be.'

Night hath closed all in her cloak,
Twinkling stars love-thoughts pro-
  voke,
Danger hence, good care doth
  keep,
Jealousy itself doth sleep;   10

Take me to thee, and thee to me—
'No, no, no, no, my dear, let be.'

Better place no wit can find,
Cupid's yoke to loose or bind;
These sweet flowers on fine bed
        too,
Us in their best language woo;
Take me to thee, and thee to me—
'No, no, no, no, my dear, let be.'

This small light the moon bestows
Serves thy beams but to disclose;   20
So to raise my hap more high,
Fear not else, none can us spy;
Take me to thee, and thee to me—
'No, no, no, no, my dear, let be.'

That you heard was but a mouse,
Dumb sleep holdeth all the house;
Yet asleep, methinks they say,
Young folks, take time while you
        may;
Take me to thee, and thee to me—
'No, no, no, no, my dear, let be.'

Niggard time threats, if we miss
This large offer of our bliss,   32

Long stay ere he grant the same;
Sweet, then, while each thing doth
        frame,
Take me to thee, and thee to me—
'No, no, no, no, my dear, let be.'

Your fair mother is a-bed,
Candles out and curtains spread;
She thinks you do letters write;
Write, but let me first endite;   40
Take me to thee, and thee to me—
'No, no, no, no, my dear, let be.'

Sweet, alas, why strive you thus?
Concord better fitteth us;
Leave to Mars the force of hands,
Your power in your beauty stands;
Take thee to me, and me to thee—
'No, no, no, no, my dear, let be.'

Woe to me, and do you swear
Me to hate? but I forbear;   50
Cursèd be my destines all,
That brought me so high to fall;
Soon with my death I will please
        thee—
'No, no, no, no, my dear, let be.'

Stella, think not that I by verse seek fame,
    Who seek, who hope, who love, who live but thee;
    Thine eyes my pride, thy lips mine history;
    If thou praise not, all other praise is shame.
Nor so ambitious am I as to frame
    A nest for my young praise in laurel tree;
    In truth, I swear I wish not there should be
    Graved in mine epitaph a poet's name.
Ne, if I would, I could just title make,
    That any laud to me thereof should grow,   10
    Without my plumes from others' wings I take;
For nothing from my wit or will doth flow,
    Since all my words thy beauty doth endite,
    And love doth hold my hand and makes me write.

Envious wits, what hath been mine offence,
That with such poisonous care my looks you mark,
That to each word, nay sigh of mine, you hark,
As grudging me my sorrow's eloquence?
Ah, is it not enough that I am thence,
Thence, so far thence, that scarcely any spark
Of comfort dare come to this dungeon dark,
Where rigor's exile locks up all my sense?
But if I by a happy window pass,
If I but stars upon mine armor bear—   10
Sick, thirsty, glad, though but of empty glass—
Your moral notes straight my hid meaning tear
From out my ribs, and, puffing, proves that I
Do Stella love; fools, who doth it deny?

Eleventh song

Who is it that this dark night
Underneath my window plaineth?
  It is one who from thy sight
  Being, ah, exiled, disdaineth
Every other vulgar light.

Why, alas, and are you he?
Be not yet those fancies changëd?
  Dear, when you find change in me,
  Though from me you be estrangëd,
Let my change to ruin be.   10

Well, in absence this will die;
Leave to see and leave to wonder.
  Absence sure will help, if I
  Can learn how myself to sunder
From what in my heart doth lie.

But time will these thoughts remove;
Time doth work what no man knoweth.
  Time doth as the subject prove;
  With time still the affection groweth
In the faithful turtle dove.   20

What if you new beauties see,
Will not they stir new affection?

I will think they pictures be,
Image-like, of saint's perfection,
Poorly counterfeiting thee.

But your reason's purest light
Bids you leave such minds to nourish.
  Dear, do reason no such spite;
  Never doth thy beauty flourish
More than in my reason's sight.

But the wrongs love bears will make   31
Love at length leave undertaking.
  No, the more fools it do shake,
  In a ground of so firm making
Deeper still they drive the stake.

Peace, I think that some give ear;
Come no more lest I get anger.
  Bliss, I will my bliss forbear;
  Fearing, sweet, you to endanger;
But my soul shall harbor there.   40

Well, begone, begone, I say,
Lest that Argus' eyes perceive you.
  Oh, unjust fortune's sway,
  Which can make me thus to leave you,
And from louts to run away.

CERTAIN SONNETS
[The nightingale]

The nightingale, as soon as April bringeth
  Unto her rested sense a perfect waking,
While late bare earth, proud of new clothing, springeth,
  Sings out her woes, a thorn her song-book making,
    And mournfully bewailing,
  Her throat in tunes expresseth
  What grief her breast oppresseth
    For Tereus' force on her chaste will prevailing.
O Philomela fair, O take some gladness,
That here is juster cause of plaintful sadness: 10
Thine earth now springs, mine fadeth;
Thy thorn without, my thorn my heart invadeth.

Alas, she hath no other cause of anguish
  But Tereus' love, on her by strong hand wroken,
Wherein she suffering, all her spirits languish;
  Full womanlike complains her will was broken.
    But I, who daily craving,
  Cannot have to content me,
  Have more cause to lament me,
    Since wanting is more woe than too much having.   20
O Philomela fair, O take some gladness,
That here is juster cause of plaintful sadness:
Thine earth now springs, mine fadeth;
Thy thorn without, my thorn my heart invadeth.

[Ring out your bells]

Ring out your bells, let mourning
    shows be spread;
For Love is dead—
  All Love is dead, infected
With plague of deep disdain;
  Worth, as nought worth, re-
    jected,
And Faith fair scorn doth gain.
  From so ungrateful fancy,
  From such a female franzy,
  From them that use men thus,
Good Lord, deliver us!   10

Weep, neighbors, weep; do you
    not hear it said
That Love is dead?
  His death-bed, peacock's folly;
His winding-sheet is shame;
  His will, false-seeming holy;
His sole exec'tor, blame.
  From so ungrateful, &c.

Let dirge be sung and trentals
    rightly read,
For Love is dead;   19

Sir Wrong his tomb ordaineth
My mistress Marble-heart,
  Which epitaph containeth,
Her eyes were once his dart.
    From so ungrateful, &c.

Alas, I lie, rage hath this error
    bred;
Love is not dead;

Love is not dead, but sleepeth
In her unmatchèd mind,
  Where she his counsel keepeth,
Till due desert she find.   30
  Therefore from so vile fancy,
  To call such wit a franzy,
  Who Love can temper thus,
  Good Lord, deliver us!

[*Thou blind man's mark*]

Thou blind man's mark, thou fool's self-chosen snare,
Fond fancy's scum, and dregs of scattered thought;
Band of all evils, cradle of causeless care;
Thou web of will, whose end is never wrought;
Desire, desire! I have too dearly bought,
With price of mangled mind, thy worthless ware;
Too long, too long, asleep thou hast me brought,
Who should my mind to higher things prepare.
But yet in vain thou hast my ruin sought;
In vain thou madest me to vain things aspire;   10
In vain thou kindlest all thy smoky fire;
For virtue hath this better lesson taught,—
Within myself to seek my only hire,
Desiring nought but how to kill desire.

[*Leave me, O love*]

Leave me, O love which reachest but to dust;
And thou, my mind, aspire to higher things;
Grow rich in that which never taketh rust,
Whatever fades but fading pleasure brings.
Draw in thy beams, and humble all thy might
To that sweet yoke where lasting freedoms be;
Which breaks the clouds and opens forth the light,
That doth both shine and give us sight to see.
O take fast hold; let that light be thy guide
In this small course which birth draws out to death,   10
And think how evil becometh him to slide,
Who seeketh heav'n, and comes of heav'nly breath.
    Then farewell, world; thy uttermost I see;
    Eternal Love, maintain thy life in me.

Splendidis longum valedico nugis.

FROM *The Countess of Pembroke's Arcadia*, 1593

[*O sweet woods*]

O sweet woods, the delight of solitariness!
Oh, how much I do like your solitariness!
Where man's mind hath a freed consideration,
Of goodness to receive lovely direction.
Where senses do behold th' order of heav'nly host,
And wise thoughts do behold what the creator is;
Contemplation here holdeth his only seat,
Bounded with no limits, born with a wing of hope,
Climbs even unto the stars, nature is under it.
Nought disturbs thy quiet, all to thy service yields,　10
Each sight draws on a thought (thought, mother of science)
Sweet birds kindly do grant harmony unto thee,
Fair trees' shade is enough fortification,
Nor danger to thyself if 't be not in thyself.

O sweet woods, the delight of solitariness!
Oh, how much I do like your solitariness!
Here nor treason is hid, veilèd in innocence,
Nor envy's snaky eye finds any harbor here,
Nor flatterers' venomous insinuations,
Nor coming humorists' puddled opinions,　20
Nor courteous ruin of proffered usury,
Nor time prattled away, cradle of ignorance,
Nor causeless duty, nor cumber of arrogance,
Nor trifling title of vanity dazzleth us,
Nor golden manacles stand for a paradise,
Here wrong's name is unheard, slander a monster is;
Keep thy sprite from abuse, here no abuse doth haunt.
What man grafts in a tree dissimulation?

O sweet woods, the delight of solitariness!
Oh, how well I do like your solitariness!　30
Yet, dear soil, if a soul closed in a mansion
As sweet as violets, fair as lily is,
Straight as cedar, a voice stains the canary birds,
Whose shade safety doth hold, danger avoideth her;
Such wisdom that in her lives speculation;
Such goodness that in her simplicity triumphs;
Where envy's snaky eye winketh or else dieth;

Slander wants a pretext, flattery gone beyond;
Oh! if such a one have bent to a lonely life,
Her steps glad we receive, glad we receive her eyes,   40
And think not she doth hurt our solitariness,
For such company decks such solitariness.

FROM FRANCIS DAVISON'S *Poetical Rhapsody*, 1602

Two pastorals

*Made by Sir Philip Sidney, never yet published, upon his meeting with
his two worthy friends and fellow-poets, Sir Edward Dyer
and Master Fulke Greville*

Join mates in mirth to me,
  Grant pleasure to our meeting;
Let Pan, our good god, see
  How grateful is our greeting.
    *Join hearts and hands, so let
      it be,
    Make but one mind in bodies
      three.*

Ye hymns and singing skill
  Of god Apollo's giving,
Be prest our reeds to fill
  With sound of music living.   10
    Join hearts and hands, &c.

Sweet Orpheus' harp, whose sound
  The steadfast mountains movèd,
Let here thy skill abound
  To join sweet friends belovèd.
    Join hearts and hands, &c.

My two and I be met,
  A happy blessed trinity,
As three most jointly set
  In firmest band of unity.   20
    Join hands, &c.

Welcome, my two, to me,   *E. D.*
The number best belovèd, *F. G.*
             P. S.
Within my heart you be
  In friendship unremovèd.
    Join hands, &c.

Give leave your flocks to range,
  Let us the while be playing;
Within the elmy grange   29
  Your flocks will not be straying.
    Join hands, &c.

Cause all the mirth you can,
  Since I am now come hether,
Who never joy but when
  I am with you together.
    Join hands, &c.

Like lovers do their love,
  So joy I you in seeing;
Let nothing me remove
  From always with you being.   40
    Join hands, &c.

And as the turtle dove
  To mate with whom he liveth,
Such comfort fervent love
  Of you to my heart giveth.
    Join hands, &c.

Now joinèd be our hands,
  Let them be ne'er asunder,
But linked in binding bands
  By metamorphosed wonder.   50
    *So should our severed bodies
      three
    As one for ever joinèd be.*

SIR EDWARD DYER

The Introduction and Notes are at page 936

FROM WILLIAM BYRD'S *Psalms, Sonnets, and Songs,* 1588

[*My mind to me a kingdom is*]

My mind to me a kingdom is;
  Such perfect joy therein I find
That it excels all other bliss
  Which God or nature hath as-
    signed.
Though much I want that most
    would have,
Yet still my mind forbids to crave.

No princely port, nor wealthy
    store,
  No force to win a victory,
No wily wit to salve a sore,
  No shape to win a loving eye; [10]
To none of these I yield as thrall,—
For why? my mind despise them
    all.

I see that plenty surfeit oft,
  And hasty climbers soonest fall;
I see that such as are aloft
  Mishap doth threaten most of
    all.
These get with toil and keep with
    fear;
Such cares my mind can never bear.

I press to bear no haughty sway,
  I wish no more than may suf-
    fice, [20]
I do no more than well I may,
  Look, what I want my mind
    supplies.
Lo! thus I triumph like a king,
My mind content with anything.

I laugh not at another's loss,
  Nor grudge not at another's
    gain;
No worldly waves my mind can
    toss;
  I brook that is another's bane.
I fear no foe, nor fawn on friend,
I loathe not life, nor dread mine
    end. [30]

My wealth is health and perfect
    ease,
  And conscience clear my chief
    defence;
I never seek by bribes to please,
  Nor by desert to give offence.
Thus do I live, thus will I die,—
Would all did so as well as I!

FROM *Rawlinson Poetry Ms.* 85

[*The man whose thoughts*]

The man whose thoughts against him do conspire,
On whom mishap her story doth depaint,
The man of woe, the matter of mishap,
Free of the dead, that lives in endless pain,—
  His spirit am I, which in this desert lie,
  To rue his case whose cause I cannot fly.

Despair my name, who never finds relief,
Friended of none, but to myself a foe;
An idle care, maintained by firm belief
That praise of faith shall through my torments grow;   10
    And count those hopes that others' hearts do ease
    But base conceits the common sense to please.

For sure I am I never shall attain
The happy good from whence my joys arise;
Nor have I power my sorrows to refrain,
But wail the want, when nought else may suffice;
    Whereby my life the shape of death must bear,
    That death which feels the worst that life doth fear.

But what avails, with tragical complaint,
Not hoping help, the furies to awake?   20
Or why should I the happy minds acquaint
With doleful tunes, their settled peace to shake?
    All ye that here behold infortune's fare
    May judge no woe may with my grief compare.

FROM SIR PHILIP SIDNEY's *The Countess of Pembroke's
Arcadia,* 1598

[*Prometheus when first from heaven*]

Prometheus when first from heaven high
    He brought down fire, ere then on earth not seen,
Fond of delight, a satyr, standing by,
    Gave it a kiss, as it like sweet had been.

Feeling forthwith the other burning power,
    Wood with the smart, with shouts and shrieking shrill
He sought his ease in river, field, and bower,
    But for the time his grief went with him still.

So silly I, with that unwonted sight,
    In human shape an angel from above,   10
Feeding mine eyes, the impression there did light,
    That since I run and rest as pleaseth love.
    The difference is, the satyr's lips, my heart,
    He for a while, I evermore, have smart.

FULKE GREVILLE, LORD BROOKE

The Introduction and Notes are at page 937

FROM R. S.'s *Phœnix Nest*, 1593

An epitaph upon the Right Honorable Sir Philip Sidney

Silence augmenteth grief, writing increaseth rage,
Staled are my thoughts, which loved and lost the wonder of our age;
Yet quickened now with fire, though dead with frost ere now,
Enraged I write I know not what; dead, quick, I know not how.

Hard-hearted minds relent and rigor's tears abound,
And envy strangely rues his end, in whom no fault was found.
Knowledge her light hath lost, valor hath slain her knight,
Sidney is dead, dead is my friend, dead is the world's delight.

Place, pensive, wails his fall whose presence was her pride;
Time crieth out, My ebb is come; his life was my spring tide.   10
Fame mourns in that she lost the ground of her reports;
Each living wight laments his lack, and all in sundry sorts.

He was (woe worth that word!) to each well-thinking mind
A spotless friend, a matchless man, whose virtue ever shined;
Declaring in his thoughts, his life, and that he writ,
Highest conceits, longest foresights, and deepest works of wit.

He, only like himself, was second unto none,
Whose death (though life) we rue, and wrong, and all in vain do
    moan;
Their loss, not him, wail they that fill the world with cries,
Death slew not him, but he made death his ladder to the skies.   20

Now sink of sorrow I who live—the more the wrong!
Who wishing death, whom death denies, whose thread is all too long;
Who tied to wretched life, who looks for no relief,
Must spend my ever dying days in never ending grief.

Heart's ease and only I, like parallels, run on,
Whose equal length keep equal breadth and never meet in one;
Yet for not wronging him, my thoughts, my sorrow's cell,
Shall not run out, though leak they will for liking him so well.

Farewell to you, my hopes, my wonted waking dreams,
Farewell, sometimes enjoyëd joy, eclipsëd are thy beams.
Farewell, self-pleasing thoughts which quietness brings forth,
And farewell, friendship's sacred league, uniting minds of worth.

And farewell, merry heart, the gift of guiltless minds,
And all sports which for life's restore variety assigns;
Let all that sweet is, void; in me no mirth may dwell:
Philip, the cause of all this woe, my life's content, farewell!

Now rhyme, the son of rage, which art no kin to skill,
And endless grief, which deads my life, yet knows not how to kill,
Go, seek that hapless tomb, which if ye hap to find
Salute the stones that keep the limbs that held so good a mind.   40

From John Bodenham's (?) *England's Helicon*, 1600

Another, of his Cynthia

Away with these self-loving lads,
Whom Cupid's arrow never glads.
Away, poor souls that sigh and
    weep,
In love of them that lie and sleep;
    For Cupid is a meadow god,
    And forceth none to kiss the
        rod.

God Cupid's shaft, like destiny,
Doth either good or ill decree.
Desert is born out of his bow,
Reward upon his feet doth go.   10
    What fools are they that have
        not known
    That Love likes no laws but his
        own?

My songs they be of Cynthia's
    praise,
I wear her rings on holy-days,
On every tree I write her name,

And every day I read the same.
    Where Honor, Cupid's rival, is,
    There miracles are seen of his.

If Cynthia crave her ring of me,
I blot her name out of the tree.
If doubt do darken things held
    dear,   21
Then welfare nothing once a year.
    For many run, but one must win;
    Fools only hedge the cuckoo in.

The worth that worthiness should
    move
Is love, which is the due of love.
And love as well the shepherd can
As can the mighty nobleman.
    Sweet nymph, 'tis true you
        worthy be,
    Yet without love, nought worth
        to me.   30

From *Mustapha*, 1609

Chorus sacerdotum

Oh, wearisome condition of humanity,
Born under one law, to another bound;

Vainly begot, and yet forbidden vanity,
Created sick, commanded to be sound.
What meaneth nature by these diverse laws?
Passion and reason self-division cause.
It is the mark or majesty of power
To make offences that it may forgive.
Nature herself doth her own self deflower,
To hate those errors she herself doth give. 10
For how should man think that he may not do,
If nature did not fail and punish too?
Tyrant to others, to herself unjust,
Only commands things difficult and hard,
Forbids us all things which it knows is lust,
Makes easy pains, unpossible reward.
If nature did not take delight in blood,
She would have made more easy ways to good.
We that are bound by vows and by promotion,
With pomp of holy sacrifice and rites, 20
To teach belief in God and still devotion,
To preach of heaven's wonders and delights,—
Yet when each of us in his own heart looks
He finds the God there far unlike his books.

FROM *Certain Learned and Elegant Works*, 1633

Cælica

You little stars that live in skies
And glory in Apollo's glory,
In whose aspects conjoinëd lies
The heaven's will and nature's story,
Joy to be likened to those eyes,
Which eyes make all eyes glad or sorry;
  For when you force thoughts from above,
  These overrule your force by love.

And thou, O love, which in these eyes
Hast married reason with affection, 10
And made them saints of beauty's skies,
Where joys are shadows of perfection,
Lend me thy wings that I may rise
Up, not by worth, but thy election;
  For I have vowed in strangest fashion,
  To love, and never seek compassion.

The world, that all contains, is ever moving;
The stars within their spheres for ever turned;

Nature, the queen of change, to change is loving,
And form to matter new is still adjourned.

Fortune, our fancy-god, to vary liketh;
Place is not bound to things within it placed;
The present time upon time passèd striketh;
With Phœbus' wand'ring course the earth is graced.

The air still moves, and by its moving cleareth;
The fire up ascends and planets feedeth;
The water passeth on and all lets weareth;
The earth stands still, yet change of changes breedeth.

Her plants, which summer ripes, in winter fade;
Each creature in unconstant mother lieth;
Man made of earth, and for whom earth is made,
Still dying lives and living ever dieth;
   Only, like fate, sweet Myra never varies,
   Yet in her eyes the doom of all change carries.

Cupid, thou naughty boy, when thou wert loathèd,
Naked and blind, for vagabonding noted,
Thy nakedness I in my reason clothèd,
Mine eyes I gave thee, so was I devoted.

Fie, wanton, fie! who would show children kindness?
No sooner he into mine eyes was gotten
But straight he clouds them with a seeing blindness,
Makes reason wish that reason were forgotten.

From thence to Myra's eyes the wanton strayeth,
Where while I charge him with ungrateful measure,
So with fair wonders he mine eyes betrayeth,
That my wounds and his wrongs become my pleasure;
   Till for more spite to Myra's heart he flyeth,
   Where living to the world, to me he dieth.

Fie, foolish earth, think you the heaven wants glory
Because your shadows do yourself benight?
All's dark unto the blind, let them be sorry;
The heavens in themselves are ever bright.

Fie, fond desire, think you that love wants glory
Because your shadows do yourself benight?
The hopes and fears of lust may make men sorry,
But love still in herself finds her delight.

Then earth, stand fast, the sky that you benight
Will turn again and so restore your glory;
Desire, be steady, hope is your delight,
An orb wherein no creature can be sorry,
    Love being placed above these middle regions
    Where every passion wars itself with legions.

10

Cælica, I overnight was finely used,
Lodged in the midst of paradise, your heart;
Kind thoughts had charge I might not be refused,
Of every fruit and flower I had part.

But curious knowledge, blown with busy flame,
The sweetest fruits had in down shadows hidden,
And for it found mine eyes had seen the same,
I from my paradise was straight forbidden.

Where that cur, rumor, runs in every place,
Barking with care, begotten out of fear;
And glassy honor, tender of disgrace,
Stand seraphim to see I come not there;
    While that fine soil which all these joys did yield,
    By broken fence is proved a common field.

10

Under a throne I saw a virgin sit,
The red and white rose quartered in her face;
Star of the north! and for true guards to it,
Princes, church, states, all pointing out her grace;
The homage done her was not born of wit;
Wisdom admired, zeal took ambition's place,
State in her eyes taught order how to fit
And fix confusion's unobserving race.
    Fortune can here claim nothing truly great,
    But that this princely creature is her seat.

10

The earth with thunder torn, with fire blasted,
With waters drowned, with windy palsy shaken,
Cannot for this with heaven be distasted,
Since thunder, rain, and winds from earth are taken;
Man torn with love, with inward furies blasted,
Drowned with despair, with fleshly lustings shaken,
Cannot for this with heaven be distasted;
Love, fury, lustings out of man are taken.
Then, man, endure thyself, those clouds will vanish;
Life is a top which whipping sorrow driveth;
Wisdom must bear what our flesh cannot banish.
The humble lead, the stubborn bootless striveth.

10

Or, man, forsake thyself, to heaven turn thee,
Her flames enlighten nature, never burn thee.

[Sion lies waste]

Sion lies waste, and thy Jerusalem,
O Lord, is fallen to utter desolation;
Against thy prophets and thy holy men
The sin hath wrought a fatal combination;
　　Profaned thy name, thy worship overthrown,
　　And made thee, living Lord, a God unknown.

Thy powerful laws, thy wonders of creation,
Thy word incarnate, glorious heaven, dark hell,
Lie shadowed under man's degeneration;
Thy Christ still crucified for doing well;　　　　10
　　Impiety, O Lord, sits on thy throne,
　　Which makes thee, living light, a God unknown.

Man's superstition hath thy truths entombed,
His atheism again her pomps defaceth;
That sensual unsatiable vast womb
Of thy seen church thy unseen church disgraceth.
　　There lives no truth with them that seem thine own,
　　Which makes thee, living Lord, a God unknown.

Yet unto thee, Lord, mirror of transgression,
We who for earthly idols have forsaken　　　　20
Thy heavenly image, sinless, pure impression,
And so in nets of vanity lie taken,
　　All desolate implore that to thine own,
　　Lord, thou no longer live a God unknown.

Yet, Lord, let Israel's plagues not be eternal,
Nor sin forever cloud thy sacred mountains,
Nor with false flames, spiritual but infernal,
Dry up thy mercy's ever springing fountains.
　　Rather, sweet Jesus, fill up time and come
　　To yield the sin her everlasting doom.　　　　30

ROBERT DEVEREUX, EARL OF ESSEX

The Introduction and Notes are at page 938
FROM ROBERT DOWLAND's *Musical Banquet*, 1610

[Change thy mind]

Change thy mind, since she doth change!
Let not fancy still abuse thee.

Thy untruth can not seem strange
When her falsehood doth excuse thee.
    Love is dead and thou art free,
    She doth live, but dead to thee.

Whilst she loved thee best a while,
See how she hath still delayed thee,
Using shows for to beguile
Those vain hopes that have deceived thee.   10
    Now thou seest, although too late,
    Love loves truth, which women hate.

Love no more, since she is gone—
She is gone, and loves another.
Being once deceived by one,
Leave her love, but love none other.
    She was false—bid her adieu;
    She was best, but yet untrue.

Love, farewell, more dear to me
Than my life, which thou preservest.   20
Life, all joys are gone from thee,
Others have what thou deservest.
    Oh, my death doth spring from hence,
    I must die for her offence.

Die, but yet before thou die,
Make her know what she hath gotten;
She, in whom my hopes did lie,
Now is changed—I, quite forgotten.
    She is changed, but changëd base,
    Baser in so vild a place.   30

[*To plead my faith*]

To plead my faith where faith had no reward,
To move remorse where favor is not borne,
To heap complaints where she doth not regard,—
Were fruitless, bootless, vain, and yield but scorn.

I lovëd her whom all the world admired,
I was refused of her that can love none;
And my vain hopes, which far too high aspired,
Is dead, and buried, and for ever gone.

Forget my name, since you have scorned my love,
And woman-like do not too late lament;   10
Since for your sake I do all mischief prove,
I none accuse nor nothing do repent.

I was as fond as ever she was fair,
Yet loved I not more than I now despair.

FROM *Chetham Ms.* 8012

A passion

Happy were he could finish forth his fate
In some unhaunted desert, more obscure
From all society, from love and hate
Of worldly folk; there might he sleep secure,
There wake again and give God ever praise;
Content with hips and haws and bramble-berry;
In contemplation passing still his days,
And change of holy thoughts to make him merry:
  That when he dies his tomb might be a bush
  Where harmless robin dwelleth with the thrush.   10

SIR WALTER RALEGH

The Introduction and Notes are at page 938

FROM *Rawlinson Poetry Ms.* 160

To Queen Elizabeth

Our passions are most like to floods and streams,
  The shallow murmur, but the deep are dumb;
So, when affections yield discourse, it seems
  The bottom is but shallow whence they come.
They that are rich in words must needs discover
That they are poor in that which makes a lover.

Wrong not, dear empress of my heart,
  The merit of true passion
With thinking that he feels no smart
  That sues for no compassion;   10
Since, if my plaints serve not to prove
  The conquest of your beauty,
They come not from defect of love
  But from access of duty.

For knowing that I sue to serve
  A saint of such perfection
As all desire (yet none deserve)
  A place in her affection,
I rather choose to want relief
  Than venture the revealing;   20
When glory recommends the grief,
  Despair distrusts the healing.

Thus those desires that aim too high
  For any mortal lover,
When reason cannot make them die
  Discretion doth them cover.
Yet, when discretion doth bereave
  The plaints that they should utter,
Then your discretion may perceive
  That silence is a suitor.   30

Silence in love bewrays more woe
  Than words, though ne'er so witty;
A beggar that is dumb, you know,
  Deserveth double pity.
Then misconceive not, dearest heart,
  My true though secret passion;
He smarteth most that hides his smart
  And sues for no compassion.

FROM R. S.'s *Phœnix Nest,* 1593

[*Praised be Diana's fair and harmless light*]

Praised be Diana's fair and harmless light,
Praised be the dews wherewith she moists the ground;
Praised be her beams, the glory of the night;
Praised be her power, by which all powers abound.

Praised be her nymphs, with whom she decks the woods;
Praised be her knights, in whom true honor lives;
Praised be that force by which she moves the floods;
Let that Diana shine, which all these gives.

In heaven queen she is among the spheres;
In aye she mistress-like makes all things pure;   10
Eternity in her oft change she bears;
She beauty is; by her the fair endure.

Time wears her not—she doth his chariot guide;
Mortality below her orb is placed.
By her the virtue of the stars down slide,
In her is virtue's perfect image cast.

A knowledge pure it is her worth to know;
With Circes let them dwell that think not so.

[*Like truthless dreams*]

Like truthless dreams, so are my joys expired,
And past return are all my dandled days;
My love misled, and fancy quite retired—
Of all which passed the sorrow only stays.

My lost delights, now clean from sight of land,
Have left me all alone in unknown ways;
My mind to woe, my life in fortune's hand—
Of all which passed the sorrow only stays.

As in a country strange, without companion,   10
I only wail the wrong of death's delays,
Whose sweet spring spent, whose summer well-nigh done—
Of all which passed the sorrow only stays.

Whom care forewarns, ere age and winter cold,
To haste me hence to find my fortune's fold.

[*Like to a hermit*]

Like to a hermit poor in place obscure
I mean to spend my days of endless doubt,
To wail such woes as time cannot recure,
Where none but love shall ever find me out.

My food shall be of care and sorrow made,
My drink nought else but tears fall'n from mine eyes;
And for my light in such obscurèd shade
The flames shall serve which from my heart arise.

A gown of gray my body shall attire,
My staff of broken hope whereon I'll stay;   10
Of late repentance linked with long desire
The couch is framed whereon my limbs I'll lay;

And at my gate despair shall linger still
To let in death when love and fortune will.

A description of love

Now what is love? I pray thee,
    tell.
It is that fountain and that well
Where pleasure and repentance
    dwell.
It is perhaps that saucing bell
That tolls all into heaven or hell:
And this is love, as I hear tell.

Yet what is love? I pray thee say.
It is a work on holy-day;
It is December matched with
    May;   9
When lusty bloods, in fresh array,
Hear ten months after of the play:
And this is love, as I hear say.

Yet what is love? I pray thee sain.
It is a sunshine mixed with rain;
It is a tooth-ache, or like pain;

It is a game where none doth gain;
The lass saith no, and would full
    fain:
And this is love, as I hear sain.

Yet what is love? I pray thee say.
It is a yea, it is a nay,   20
A pretty kind of sporting fray;
It is a thing will soon away;
Then take the vantage while you
    may:
And this is love, as I hear say.

Yet what is love, I pray thee show.
A thing that creeps, it cannot go;
A prize that passeth to and fro;
A thing for one, a thing for mo;
And he that proves must find it so:
And this is love, sweet friend, I
    trow.   30

An epitaph upon the Right Honorable Sir Philip Sidney, Knight, Lord Governor of Flushing

To praise thy life or wail thy worthy death,
And want thy wit, thy wit high, pure, divine,
Is far beyond the power of mortal line;
Nor any one hath worth that draweth breath.

Yet rich in zeal, though poor in learning's lore,
And friendly care obscured in secret breast,
And love that envy in thy life suppressed,—
Thy dear life done, and death, hath doubled more.

And I, that in thy time and living state
Did only praise thy virtues in my thought,   10
As one that, seeled, the rising sun hath sought,
With words and tears now wail thy timeless fate.

Drawn was thy race aright from princely line,
Nor less than such, by gifts that nature gave
(The common mother that all creatures have),
Doth virtue show, and princely lineage shine.

A king gave thee thy name; a kingly mind,
That God thee gave, who found it now too dear
For this base world, and hath resumed it near
To sit in skies, and sort with powers divine.   20

Kent thy birth days, and Oxford held thy youth;
The heavens made haste and stayed nor years nor time;
The fruits of age grew ripe in thy first prime,
Thy will, thy words—thy words, the seals of truth.

Great gifts and wisdom rare employed thee thence
To treat from kings with those more great than kings,
Such hope men had to lay the highest things
On thy wise youth, to be transported hence.

Whence to sharp wars sweet honor did thee call,
Thy country's love, religion, and thy friends;   30
Of worthy men the marks, the lives, and ends,
And her defence for whom we labor all.

There didst thou vanquish shame and tedious age,
Grief, sorrow, sickness, and base fortune's might.
Thy rising day saw never woeful night,
But passed with praise from off this worldly stage.

Back to the camp by thee that day was brought
First, thine own death; and after, thy long fame;
Tears to the soldiers; the proud Castilian's shame;
Virtue expressed, and honor truly taught.   40

What hath he lost that such great grace hath won?
Young years for endless years, and hope unsure
Of fortune's gifts for wealth that still shall dure—
Oh, happy race, with so great praises run!

England doth hold thy limbs, that bred the same,
Flanders thy valor, where it last was tried,
The camp thy sorrow, where thy body died,
Thy friends thy want, the world thy virtue's fame.

Nations thy wit, our minds lay up thy love;
Letters thy learning; thy loss, years long to come;   50
In worthy hearts sorrow hath made thy tomb,
Thy soul and sprite enrich the heavens above.

Thy liberal heart embalmed in grateful tears,
Young sighs, sweet sighs, sage sighs bewail thy fall;
Envy her sting, and spite hath left her gall,
Malice herself a mourning garment wears.

That day their Hannibal died, our Scipio fell,
Scipio, Cicero, and Petrarch of our time,
Whose virtues, wounded by my worthless rhyme,
Let angels speak, and heavens thy praises tell.   60

From Edmund Spenser's *Fairy Queen*, 1590

A vision upon this conceit of the Fairy Queen

Methought I saw the grave where Laura lay,
Within that temple where the vestal flame
Was wont to burn; and passing by that way
To see that buried dust of living fame,
Whose tomb fair Love and fairer Virtue kept,
All suddenly I saw the Fairy Queen;
At whose approach the soul of Petrarch wept,
And from thenceforth those graces were not seen,
For they this Queen attended; in whose stead
Oblivion laid him down on Laura's hearse.   10
Hereat the hardest stones were seen to bleed,
And groans of buried ghosts the heavens did pierce;
    Where Homer's sprite did tremble all for grief,
    And cursed th' access of that celestial thief.

From John Bodenham's (?) *England's Helicon*, 1600

The nymph's reply to the shepherd

If all the world and love were young,
And truth in every shepherd's tongue,
These pretty pleasures might me move
To live with thee and be thy love.

Time drives the flocks from field to fold
When rivers rage and rocks grow cold,
And Philomel becometh dumb;
The rest complains of cares to come.

The flowers do fade, and wanton fields
To wayward winter reckoning yields;   10
A honey tongue, a heart of gall,
Is fancy's spring, but sorrow's fall.

Thy gowns, thy shoes, thy beds of roses,
Thy cap, thy kirtle, and thy posies
Soon break, soon wither, soon forgotten,—
In folly ripe, in reason rotten.

Thy belt of straw and ivy buds,
Thy coral clasps and amber studs,
All these in me no means can move
To come to thee and be thy love.   20

But could youth last and love still breed,
Had joys no date nor age no need,
Then these delights my mind might move
To live with thee and be thy love.

From *Malone Ms.* 19

To his son

Three things there be that prosper all apace
And flourish, while they are asunder far;
But on a day they meet all in a place,
And when they meet, they one another mar.
And they be these: the wood, the weed, the wag.
The wood is that that makes the gallows tree;
The weed is that that strings the hangman's bag;
The wag, my pretty knave, betokens thee.
Now mark, dear boy: while these assemble not,
Green springs the tree, hemp grows, the wag is wild;   10
But when they meet, it makes the timber rot,
It frets the halter, and it chokes the child.
       God bless the child!

From *Harleian Ms.* 6917

[*Nature, that washed her hands*]

Nature, that washed her hands in milk,
    And had forgot to dry them,
Instead of earth took snow and silk,
    At love's request to try them,
If she a mistress could compose
    To please love's fancy out of those.

Her eyes he would should be of light,
    A violet breath, and lips of jelly;
Her hair not black, nor over-bright,
    And of the softest down her belly;   10
As for her inside he 'ld have it
Only of wantonness and wit.

At love's entreaty such a one
  Nature made, but with her
    beauty
She hath framed a heart of stone;
  So as love, by ill destiny,
Must die for her whom nature
    gave him,
Because her darling would not
    save him.

But time (which nature doth
    despise
  And rudely gives her love the
    lie,   20
Makes hope a fool, and sorrow
    wise)
  His hands do neither wash nor
    dry;
But being made of steel and rust,
Turns snow and silk and milk to
    dust.

The light, the belly, lips, and
    breath,
  He dims, discolors, and de-
    stroys;
With those he feeds but fills not
    death,
  Which sometimes were the food
    of joys.
Yea, time doth dull each lively
    wit,
And dries all wantonness with it. 30

Oh, cruel time! which takes in
    trust
  Our youth, our joys, and all
    we have,
And pays us but with age and
    dust;
  Who in the dark and silent
    grave
When we have wandered all our
    ways
Shuts up the story of our days.

FROM FRANCIS DAVISON'S
Poetical Rhapsody, 1608

The lie

Go, soul, the body's guest,
Upon a thankless arrant.
Fear not to touch the best;
The truth shall be thy warrant.
  Go, since I needs must die,
  And give the world the lie.

Say to the court, it glows
And shines like rotten wood;
Say to the church, it shows
What's good, and doth no good: 10
  If church and court reply,
  Then give them both the lie.

Tell potentates, they live
Acting by others' action,
Not loved unless they give,
Not strong but by affection:
  If potentates reply,
  Give potentates the lie.

Tell men of high condition
That manage the estate,   20
Their purpose is ambition,
Their practice only hate:
  And if they once reply,
  Then give them all the lie.

Tell them that brave it most,
They beg for more by spending,
Who, in their greatest cost,
Like nothing but commending:
  And if they make reply,
  Then give them all the lie. 30

Tell zeal it wants devotion;
Tell love it is but lust;
Tell time it meets but motion;
Tell flesh it is but dust:
  And wish them not reply,
  For thou must give the lie.

Tell age it daily wasteth;
Tell honor how it alters;
Tell beauty how she blasteth;
Tell favor how it falters: 40
 And as they shall reply,
 Give every one the lie.

Tell wit how much it wrangles
In tickle points of niceness;
Tell wisdom she entangles
Herself in over-wiseness:
 And when they do reply,
 Straight give them both the lie.

Tell physic of her boldness;
Tell skill it is prevention;   50
Tell charity of coldness;
Tell law it is contention:
 And as they do reply,
 So give them still the lie.

Tell fortune of her blindness;
Tell nature of decay;
Tell friendship of unkindness;

Tell justice of delay:
 And if they will reply,
 Then give them all the lie.   60

Tell arts they have no soundness,
But vary by esteeming;
Tell schools they want profound-
    ness,
And stand too much on seeming:
 If arts and schools reply,
 Give arts and schools the lie.

Tell faith it's fled the city;
Tell how the country erreth;
Tell, manhood shakes off pity,
Tell, virtue least preferrëd: 70
 And if they do reply,
 Spare not to give the lie.

So when thou hast, as I
Commanded thee, done blabbing,
Because to give the lie
Deserves no less than stabbing,
 Stab at thee he that will—
 No stab thy soul can kill.

FROM J. HANNAH's *Courtly Poets from Raleigh to Montrose*, 1870

The Ocean to Cynthia

Book XI

. . . .

But stay, my thoughts, make end, give fortune way;
 Harsh is the voice of woe and sorrow's sound;
Complaints cure not, and tears do but allay
 Griefs for a time, which after more abound.

To seek for moisture in the Arabian sand
 Is but a loss of labor and of rest;
The links which time did break of hearty bands

Words cannot knit, or wailings make anew.
 Seek not the sun in clouds when it is set.
On highest mountains, where those cedars grew,   10
 Against whose banks the troubled ocean beat,

And were the marks to find thy hopëd port,
   Into a soil far off themselves remove;
On Sestos' shore, Leander's late resort,
   Hero hath left no lamp to guide her love.

Thou lookest for light in vain, and storms arise;
   She sleeps thy death that erst thy danger sighed;
Strive then no more, bow down thy weary eyes,
   Eyes which to all these woes thy heart have guided.

She is gone, she is lost, she is found, she is ever fair;   20
   Sorrow draws weakly where love draws not too;
Woe's cries sound nothing, but only in love's ear.
   Do then by dying what life cannot do.

Unfold thy flocks and leave them to the fields,
   To feed on hills or dales, where likes them best,
Of what the summer or the springtime yields,
   For love and time hath given thee leave to rest.

Thy heart which was their fold, now in decay
   By often storms and winter's many blasts,
All torn and rent becomes misfortune's prey;   30
   False hope, my shepherd's staff, now age hath brast.

My pipe, which love's own hand gave my desire
   To sing her praises and my woe upon,
Despair hath often threatened to the fire,
   As vain to keep now all the rest are gone.

Thus home I draw, as death's long night draws on;
   Yet every foot, old thoughts turn back mine eyes;
Constraint me guides, as old age draws a stone
   Against the hill, which over-weighty lies

For feeble arms or wasted strength to move;   40
   My steps are backward, gazing on my loss,
My mind's affection and my soul's sole love,
   Not mixed with fancy's chaff or fortune's dross.

To God I leave it, who first gave it me,
   And I her gave, and she returned again,
As it was hers; so let His mercies be
   Of my last comforts the essential mean.

But be it so or not, the effects are past;
   Her love hath end, my woe must ever last.

FROM ANTHONY SCOLOKER'S *Daiphantus*, 1604

*The passionate man's pilgrimage, supposed to be written by
one at the point of death*

Give me my scallop-shell of quiet,
My staff of faith to walk upon,
My scrip of joy, immortal diet,
My bottle of salvation,
My gown of glory, hope's true gage,
And thus I'll take my pilgrimage.

Blood must be my body's balmer,
No other balm will there be given,
Whilst my soul like a white palmer
Travels to the land of heaven,　　　　10
Over the silver mountains,
Where spring the nectar fountains;
And there I'll kiss
The bowl of bliss,
And drink my eternal fill
On every milken hill.
My soul will be a-dry before,
But after it will ne'er thirst more;
And by the happy blissful way
More peaceful pilgrims I shall see,　　　20
That have shook off their gowns of clay
And go appareled fresh like me.
I'll bring them first
To slake their thirst,
And then to taste those nectar suckets,
At the clear wells
Where sweetness dwells,
Drawn up by saints in crystal buckets.

And when our bottles and all we
Are filled with immortality,　　　　30
Then the holy paths we'll travel,
Strewed with rubies thick as gravel,
Ceilings of diamonds, sapphire floors,
High walls of coral, and pearl bowers.

From thence to heaven's bribeless hall
Where no corrupted voices brawl,
No conscience molten into gold,
Nor forged accusers bought and sold,

No cause deferred, nor vain-spent journey,
For there Christ is the king's attorney,⁴⁰
Who pleads for all without degrees,
And he hath angels, but no fees.
When the grand twelve million jury
Of our sins and sinful fury,
'Gainst our souls black verdicts give,
Christ pleads his death, and then we live.
Be thou my speaker, taintless pleader,
Unblotted lawyer, true proceeder,
Thou movest salvation even for alms,⁵⁰
Not with a bribèd lawyer's palms.

And this is my eternal plea
To him that made heaven, earth, and sea,
Seeing my flesh must die so soon,
And want a head to dine next noon,
Just at the stroke when my veins start and spread,
Set on my soul an everlasting head.
Then am I ready, like a palmer fit,
To tread those blest paths which before I writ.

MARY HERBERT, COUNTESS OF PEMBROKE

The Introduction and Notes are at page 941

FROM *Antonius*, 1592
Chorus

Alas, with what tormenting fire
Us martyreth this blind desire
  To stay our life from flying;
How ceaselessly our minds doth
    rack,
How heavy lies upon our back
  This dastard fear of dying!
Death rather healthful succor
    gives,
Death rather all mishaps relieves
  That life upon us throweth;
And ever to us doth unclose   ¹⁰
The door whereby from cureless
  woes

Our weary soul out goeth.
What goddess else more mild than
    she
To bury all our pain can be?
  What remedy more pleasing?
Our painèd hearts, when dolor
    stings
And nothing rest or respite brings,
  What help have we more eas-
    ing?
Hope, which to us doth comfort
    give
And doth our fainting hearts re-   ²⁰
    vive,
  Hath not such force in anguish;
For, promising a vain relief,
She oft us fails in midst of grief

And helpless lets us languish.
But death, who call on her at
    need,
Doth never with vain semblant
    feed,
    But, when them sorrow pain-
        eth,
So rids their souls of all distress
Whose heavy weight did them op-
    press,
    That not one grief remain-
        eth.   30

.   .   .   .   .

How abject him, how base! think
    I,
Who, wanting courage, cannot
    die
    When need him thereto call-
        eth;
From whom the dagger, drawn
    to kill
The cureless griefs that vex him
    still,
    For fear and faintness fall-
        eth.

O Antony, with thy dear mate,
Both in misfortunes fortunate,
    Whose thoughts, to death aspir-
        ing,
Shall you protect from victor's
    rage,   40
Who on each side doth you en-
    cage,
    To triumph much desiring.
That Cæsar may you not offend
Nought else but death can you de-
    fend,
    Which his weak force derid-
        eth;
And all in this round earth con-
    tained
Powerless on them whom, once
    enchained,
    Avernus' prison hideth
Where great Psammetic's ghost
    doth rest,
Not with infernal pain possessed   50
    But in sweet fields detainëd;
And old Amasis' soul likewise
And all our famous Ptolemies
    That whilom on us reignëd.

WILLIAM WARNER

The Introduction and Notes are at page 941

FROM *Albion's England,* 1592

Chapter XXXVIII

Eight Henry, heir indubitate of York and Lancaster,
Succeeded and with kingly rites his father did inter;
His mind, his words, his looks, his gait, his lineaments, and stature,
Were such for majesty as showed a king composed by nature.
All subjects now of civil strife, all counter-minds for reign,
All envious of his empire now were rid, were pleased, or slain.
Rich were his sundry triumphs, but his cost had foison then
When Terwin and strong Turnay in resisting France he won;
When Maximilian, emperor, did under Henry fight;
When English ships did often put the French sea-power to flight;   10

And that the French king was enforced to crave and buy his peace,
Who, wiving lovely Mary, so the wars for then did cease.
    This sister to our King, and then the French king's goodly queen,
Was welcomèd with triumphs such as erst in France unseen.
Jousts, barriers, tilts, and tourneys were proclaimed eachwhere for all;
Wherefore to Paris at the time flocked cavaliers full tall,
With princes brave and ladies fair of every realm about,
And hence, with mo, Charles Brandon, in fine chivalry most stout,
Whose body fitted to his mind, whose mind was puissant, and
Whose puissance yielded not to Mars; this Mars in France did land, 20
With whom encountered valiant knights, but none might him with-
        stand.
The English-French queen standing there, admired for beauty rare,
Beheld the triumphs, in the which high feats performèd were.
But Brandon, yet not duked, was the knight above the rest,
That in her eye (nor did she err) acquitted him the best.
For whether that he trots, or turns, or bounds his barded steed,
Did run at tilt at random, or did cast a spear with heed,
Or fight at barriers, he in all did most her fancy feed.
Weak on a couch her King lay there, whom though she lovèd well,
Yet liked she Brandon, and the same loved her ere this befell;   30
For chastely had they fancied long before she came to France,
Or that from mean estate to duke Henry did him advance.
    The days of triumph were expired and English peers with praise
Come home, and Louis, King of France, deceased within few days.
Charles Brandon, Duke of Suffolk then, with honor furnished hence,
Was sent to France for to return the widow queen from thence;
She had been wed scarce thrice three weeks unto a sickly king;
To her, a fair young queen, therefore small time might solace bring.
Yet less did time than brave Duke Charles assuage fair Mary's grief;
He chats, she cheers, he courts, she coys, he woos, she yields in brief.   40
No winds, thought she, assist those sails that seek no certain shore,
Nor find they constant lives that, but they live, respect no more.
Let each one's life aim some one end, as, if it be to marry,
Then see, hear, love, and soon conclude, it betters not to tarry.
To cast too many doubts, thought she, were oft to err no less
Than to be rash. And thus, no doubt, the gentle queen did guess,
That seeing this or that at first or last had likelihood,
A man so much a manly man were dastardly withstood.
Then kisses reveled on their lips to either's equal good,
And lest King Henry should dissent, they secretly did wed,   50
And then solicit his good will, and of their wishes speed.
The perjured valiant Scotch King James, slain at brave Flodden's
        slaughter,
Had also left in widowhood England's fair elder daughter.
She also weds a Scottish earl, unlicensed of her brother,

And was to her son's daughter's son, now sixth James, great-grand-
    mother.
    A scruple, after twenty years, did enter Henry's mind,
For wedding of Queen Catherine, a lady fair and kind,
Spain's daughter, then the Emperor's aunt, and for her virtuous life
Well worthy Henry; but for she had been his brother's wife,
And also of their coiture surmise directed laws,   60
He seemed in conscience touched and sought to rid him of the cause.
Then was the matter of divorce through Christendom disputed,
The match of all adjudgëd void, and so the Queen non-suited;
Who, after tears to him from whom she was to be divorced,
Did humbly say, And am I not, my lord, to be remorsed,
That twenty years have been your wife and borne your children, and
Have loved and lived obediently, and unsuspected stand?
I am (ah, too too sweetly erred), I was, poor soul, the same
Whom once you did prefer, nor now of me you need to shame;
The blossoms of my beauty were your booty, nor my favor   70
Now alters so to alter so from me your late behavior.
But conscience is the color of this quarrel, well I wot;
I also have a conscience that in this accuseth not;
But as the same, perhaps, might say that me succeeds, say I
That for the pleasure of a prince go many things awry.
    Which her foredooms seemed to effect in her that her succeeded;
In Queen Anne Bullen, who, for she in Lutherism proceeded,
Was hated of the Papists and envied because preferred,
And through the King's too light belief (for kings have sometimes
    erred)
She lost her head, and might have said, some thought, ere she did die, 80
That for the pleasure of a prince go many things awry.
So died the gracious mother of our now most glorious Queen,
Whose zeal in reverent Foxe his works authentical is seen.
The King's four other queens (for why he died a sexamus)
Shall pass, though Jane did bear a son to him, a king to us,
Edward the sixth, and of the same we shall deliver thus.

THOMAS WATSON

The Introduction and Notes are at page 942

From *Hecatompathia, or Passionate Century of Love*, [1582]

[Some that report]

The author still pursuing his invention upon the song of his mistress,
in the last staff of this sonnet he falleth into this fiction: that whilst he

*greedily laid open his ears to the hearing of his lady's voice, as one
more than half in a doubt that Apollo himself had been at hand, Love,
espying a time of advantage, transformed himself into the substance
of air and so deceitfully entered into him with his own great good-will
and desire, and now by main force still holdeth his possession.*

Some that report great Alexander's life,
They say that harmony so moved his mind
That oft he rose from meat to warlike strife
At sound of trump or noise of battle kind;
 And then that music's force of softer vein
 Caused him return from strokes to meat again.
And as for me, I think it nothing strange
That music having birth from heav'ns above
By divers tunes can make the mind to change;
For I myself, in hearing my sweet love,
 By virtue of her song both tasted grief
 And such delight as yielded some relief.
When first I gan to give attentive ear,
Thinking Apollo's voice did haunt the place,
I little thought my lady had been there;
But whilst mine ears lay open in this case,
 Transformed to air love entered with my will
 And now perforce doth keep possession still.

10

[If Cupid were a child]

 *The author in this passion reproveth the usual description of love
which old poets have so long time embraced, and proveth by proba-
bilities that he neither is a child (as they say) nor blind nor winged
like a bird nor armed archer-like with bow and arrows, neither frantic
nor wise nor yet unclothed nor, to conclude, any god at all. And yet
when he hath said all he can to this end, he crieth out upon the secret
nature and quality of love as being that whereunto he can by no means
attain, although he have spent a long and tedious course of time in his
service.*

If Cupid were a child, as poets feign,
How comes it then that Mars doth fear his might?
If blind, how chance so many to their pain
Whom he hath hit can witness of his sight?
 If he have wings to fly where thinks him best,
 How haps he lurketh still within my breast?
If bow and shafts should be his chiefest tools,
Why doth he set so many hearts on fire?
If he were mad, how could he further fools

To whet their wits as place and time require?　10
If wise, how could so many leese their wits
Or dote through love and die in frantic fits?
If naked still he wander to and fro,
How doth not sun or frost offend his skin?
If that a god he be, how falls it so
That all wants end which he doth once begin?
　　Oh wondrous thing, that I whom love hath spent
　　Can scarcely know himself or his intent.

My love is past

The author feigneth here that Love, essaying with his brand to fire the heart of some such lady on whom it would not work, immediately, to try whether the old virtue of it were extinguished or no, applied it unto his own breast and thereby foolishly consumed himself. His invention hath some relation unto the Epitaph of Love *written by M. Girolimo Parabosco:*

> *In cenere giace qui sepolto Amore,*
> *Colpa di quella, che morir mi face, &c.*

Resolved to dust, entombed here lieth Love
Through faults of her who here herself should lie;
He struck her breast, but all in vain did prove
To fire the ice; and doubting by and by
　　His brand had lost his force, he gan to try
　　Upon himself, which trial made him die.
In sooth, no force; let those lament that lust,
I'll sing a carol song for obsequy,
For towards me his dealings were unjust
And cause of all my passèd misery.　10
　　The Fates, I think, seeing what I had passed,
　　In my behalf wrought this revenge at last.
But somewhat more to pacify my mind
By illing him through whom I lived a slave,
I'll cast his ashes to the open wind
Or write this epitaph upon his grave:
　　Here lieth Love, of Mars the bastard son,
　　Whose foolish fault to death himself hath done.

FROM *The first set of Italian Madrigals Englished,* 1590

Vezzosi augelli

Ev'ry singing bird that in the wood rejoices,
Come and assist me with your charming voices.
Zephirus, come too, and make the leaves and the fountains

Gently to send a whisp'ring sound unto the mountains.
And from thence pleasant Echo sweetly replying,
Stay here playing, where my Phillis now is lying.
And lovely graces with wanton satyrs come and play,
Dancing and singing a horn-pipe or a roundelay.

Questo di verde

How long with vain complaining,
How long with dreary tears and joys refraining,
Shall we renew his dying?
Whose happy soul is flying
Not in a place of sadness,
But of eternal gladness.
Sweet Sidney lives in heav'n, oh, therefore let our weeping
Be turned to hymns and songs of pleasant greeting.

FROM *The Tears of Fancy*, 1593

I saw the object of my pining thought
Within a garden of sweet nature's placing,
Wherein an arbor, artificial wrought
By workman's wondrous skill, the garden gracing,
Did boast his glory, glory far renowned,
For in his shady boughs my mistress slept;
And with a garland of his branches crowned,
Her dainty forehead from the sun ykept.
Imperious love upon her eyelids tending,
Playing his wanton sports at every beck
And into every finest limb descending
From eyes to lips, from lips to ivory neck,
And every limb supplied, and t'every part
Had free access, but durst not touch her heart.

Each tree did boast the wishèd spring-time's pride
When solitary in the vale of love
I hid myself, so from the world to hide
The uncouth passions which my heart did prove.
No tree whose branches did not bravely spring,
No branch whereon a fine bird did not sit,
No bird but did her shrill notes sweetly sing,
No song but did contain a lovely dit.
Trees, branches, birds, and songs were framèd fair,
Fit to allure frail mind to careless ease;
But careful was my thought, yet in despair
I dwelt, for brittle hope me cannot please.

For when I view my love's fair eyes' reflecting
I entertain despair, vain hope rejecting.

In clouds she shines, and so obscurely shineth
That like a mastless ship at seas I wander,
For want of her to guide my heart that pineth,
Yet can I not entreat ne yet command her.
So am I tied in labyrinths of fancy,
In dark and obscure labyrinths of love,
That every one may plain behold that can see
How I am fettered and what pains I prove.
The lamp whose light should lead my ship about
Is placed upon my mistress' heavenly face;   10
Her hand doth hold the clew must lead me out
And free my heart from thraldom's loathèd place.
But clew to lead me out, or lamp to light me,
She scornfully denied—the more to spite me.

ROBERT GREENE

The Introduction and Notes are at page 943

FROM *Menaphon*, 1589

Doron's description of Samela

Like to Diana in her summer weed,
Girt with a crimson robe of brightest dye,
            Goes fair Samela.
Whiter than be the flocks that straggling feed,
When washed by Arethusa faint they lie,
            Is fair Samela.
As fair Aurora in her morning-grey,
Decked with the ruddy glister of her love,
            Is fair Samela.
Like lovely Thetis on a calmèd day,   10
Whenas her brightness Neptune's fancy move,
            Shines fair Samela.
Her tresses gold, her eyes like glassy streams,
Her teeth are pearl, the breasts are ivory
            Of fair Samela;
Her cheeks, like rose and lily, yield forth gleams,
Her brows, bright arches framed of ebony.
            Thus fair Samela

Passeth fair Venus in her bravest hue,
And Juno in the show of majesty   20
         (For she's Samela),

Pallas in wit. All three, if you well view,
For beauty, wit, and matchless dignity,
         Yield to Samela.

Doron's jig

Through the shrubs as I can crack
  For my lambs' little ones,
  'Mongst many pretty ones—
Nymphs, I mean,—whose hair
    was black
    As the crow,
    Like the snow
Her face and brows shined, I
    ween;
  I saw a little one,
  A bonny pretty one,
As bright, buxom, and as sheen[10]
    As was she
    On her knee
That lulled the god whose arrows
    warms
  Such merry little ones,

Such fair-faced pretty ones,
As dally in love's chiefest harms.
    Such was mine,
    Whose gay eyne
Made me love. I gan to woo
  This sweet little one,   20
  This bonny pretty one;
I wooed hard, a day or two,
    Till she bade,
    Be not sad,
Woo no more, I am thine own,
  Thy dearest little one,
  Thy truest pretty one.
Thus was faith and firm love
    shown
    As behoves
  Shepherds' loves.   30

Sephestia's song to her child

Weep not, my wanton, smile upon my knee,
When thou art old there's grief enough for thee.
  Mother's wag, pretty boy,
  Father's sorrow, father's joy,
  When thy father first did see
  Such a boy by him and me,
  He was glad, I was woe;
  Fortune changed made him so,
  When he left his pretty boy,
  Last his sorrow, first his joy.   10

Weep not, my wanton, smile upon my knee,
When thou art old there's grief enough for thee.
  Streaming tears that never stint,
  Like pearl-drops from a flint,
  Fell by course from his eyes,

That one another's place supplies.
Thus he grieved in every part;
Tears of blood fell from his heart,
When he left his pretty boy,
Father's sorrow, father's joy.   20

Weep not, my wanton, smile upon my knee,
When thou art old there's grief enough for thee.
    The wanton smiled, father wept,
    Mother cried, baby leapt;
    More he crowed, more we cried,
    Nature could not sorrow hide.
    He must go, he must kiss
    Child and mother, baby bliss,
    For he left his pretty boy,
    Father's sorrow, father's joy.   30
Weep not, my wanton, smile upon my knee,
When thou art old there's grief enough for thee.

FROM *Greene's Mourning Garment*, 1590

The shepherd's wife's song

Ah, what is love? It is a pretty thing,
As sweet unto a shepherd as a king—
    And sweeter too,
For kings have cares that wait upon a crown,
And cares can make the sweetest love to frown.
    Ah then, ah then,
If country loves such sweet desires do gain,
What lady would not love a shepherd swain?

His flocks once folded, he comes home at night
As merry as a king in his delight—   10
    And merrier too,
For kings bethink them what the state require,
Where shepherds careless carol by the fire.
    Ah then, ah then,
If country loves such sweet desires gain,
What lady would not love a shepherd swain?

He kisseth first, then sits as blithe to eat
His cream and curds as doth the king his meat—
    And blither too,
For kings have often fears when they do sup,   20
Where shepherds dread no poison in their cup.
    Ah then, ah then,

If country loves such sweet desires gain,
What lady would not love a shepherd swain?

To bed he goes, as wanton then, I ween,
As is a king in dalliance with a queen—
    More wanton too,
For kings have many griefs, affects to move,
Where shepherds have no greater grief than love.
    Ah then, ah then,   30
If country loves such sweet desires gain,
What lady would not love a shepherd swain?

Upon his couch of straw he sleeps as sound
As doth the king upon his beds of down—
    More sounder too,
For cares cause kings full oft their sleep to spill,
Where weary shepherds lie and snort their fill.
    Ah then, ah then,
If country loves such sweet desires gain,
What lady would not love a shepherd swain?   40

Thus with his wife he spends the year, as blithe
As doth the king, at every tide or sithe—
    And blither too,
For kings have wars and broils to take in hand,
Where shepherds laugh and love upon the land.
    Ah then, ah then,
If country loves such sweet desires gain,
What lady would not love a shepherd swain?

Hexametra Alexis in laudem Rosamundi

Oft have I heard my lief Corydon report on a love-day,
When bonny maids do meet with the swains in the valley by Tempe,
How bright-eyed his Phillis was, how lovely they glancëd
When fro th'arches ebon black flew looks as a lightning
That set afire with piercing flames even hearts adamantine.
Face rose-hued, cherry-red, with a silver taint like a lily,
Venus' pride might abate, might abash with a blush to behold her.
Phœbus' wires, compared to her hairs, unworthy the praising;
Juno's state, and Pallas' wit, disgraced with the graces
That graced her whom poor Corydon did choose for a love-mate.   10
Ah! but had Corydon now seen the star that Alexis
Likes and loves so dear that he melts to sighs when he sees her;
Did Corydon but see those eyes, those amorous eyelids,
From whence fly holy flames of death or life in a moment;

Ah! did he see that face, those hairs that Venus, Apollo,
'Bashed to behold,—and both, disgraced, did grieve that a creature
Should exceed in hue, compare both a god and a goddess;
Ah! had he seen my sweet paramour, the saint of Alexis:
Then had he said, Phillis, sit down surpassèd in all points,
For there is one more fair than thou, beloved of Alexis.   20

From *Greene's Never too Late*, 1590

The palmer's ode

Old Menalcas on a day
As in field this shepherd lay,
Tuning of his oaten pipe,
Which he hit with many a stripe,
Said to Coridon that he
Once was young and full of glee.
Blithe and wanton was I then,—
Such desires follow men.
As I lay and kept my sheep,
Came the god that hateth sleep,   10
Clad in armor all of fire,
Hand in hand with queen desire;
And with a dart that wounded me
Pierced my heart as I did lie;
That when I woke I gan swear
Phillis' beauty palm did bear.
Up I start, forth went I
With her face to feed mine eye.
There I saw desire sit,
That my heart with love did hit,   20
Laying forth bright beauty's hooks
To entrap my gazing looks.
Love I did, and gan to woo,
Pray, and sigh; all would not do;
Women, when they take the toy,
Covet to be counted coy.
Coy was she that I gan court;
She thought love was but a sport;
Profound hell was in my thought,
Such a pain desire had wrought   30
That I sued with sighs and tears.
Still ingrate she stopped her ears
Till my youth I had spent.
Last, a passion of repent
Told me flat, that desire

Was a brand of love's fire,
Which consumeth men in thrall,
Virtue, youth, wit, and all.
At this saw, back I start,
Beat desire from my heart,   40
Shook off love, and made an oath
To be enemy to both.
Old I was when thus I fled
Such fond toys as cloyed my head;
But this I learned at virtue's gate,
The way to good is never late.

From *Greene's Farewell to Folly*, 1591

[*Sweet are the thoughts*]

Sweet are the thoughts that savor
    of content,
    The quiet mind is richer than
        a crown;
Sweet are the nights in careless
    slumber spent,
    The poor estate scorns fortune's
        angry frown:
Such sweet content, such minds,
    such sleep, such bliss,
Beggars enjoy, when princes oft
    do miss.

The homely house that harbors
    quiet rest,
    The cottage that affords no
        pride nor care,
The mean that grees with coun-
    try music best,
    The sweet consort of mirth and
        music's fare,   10

Obscurëd life sets down a type of
  bliss;
A mind content both crown and
  kingdom is.

FROM *Philomela, the Lady Fitz-*
  water's Nightingale, 1592

Philomela's ode that she sung
  in her arbor

Sitting by a river side
Where a silent stream did glide,
Muse I did of many things
That the mind in quiet brings.
I gan think how some men deem
Gold their god; and some esteem
Honor is the chief content
That to man in life is lent;
And some others do contend
Quiet none like to a friend;   10
Others hold there is no wealth
Compared to a perfect health;
Some man's mind in quiet stands
When he is lord of many lands:
But I did sigh, and said all this
Was but a shade of perfect bliss;

And in my thoughts I did approve
Nought so sweet as is true love.
Love 'twixt lovers passeth these,
When mouth kisseth and heart
  grees,   20
With folded arms and lippës meet-
  ing,
Each soul another sweetly greet-
  ing;
For by the breath the soul fleet-
  eth
And soul with soul in kissing
  meeteth.
If love be so sweet a thing,
That such happy bliss doth bring,
Happy is love's sugared thrall;
But unhappy maidens all,
Who esteem your virgin's blisses
Sweeter than a wife's sweet kisses.
No such quiet to the mind   31
As true love with kisses kind;
But if a kiss prove unchaste,
Then is true love quite disgraced.
Though love be sweet, learn this
  of me:
No love sweet but honesty.

FROM *Greene's Orpharion,* 1599

[*Cupid abroad was lated*]

Cupid abroad was lated in the night,
  His wings were wet with ranging in the rain;
Harbor he sought, to me he took his flight
  To dry his plumes. I heard the boy complain;
    I oped the door and granted his desire,
    I rose myself, and made the wag a fire.

Looking more narrow by the fire's flame,
  I spied his quiver hanging by his back.
Doubting the boy might my misfortune frame,
  I would have gone, for fear of further wrack;   10
    But what I drad did me, poor wretch, betide,
    For forth he drew an arrow from his side.

He pierced the quick, and I began to start,
  A pleasing wound but that it was too high;

His shaft procured a sharp yet sugared smart.
Away he flew, for why his wings were dry;
But left the arrow sticking in my breast,
That sore I grieved I welcomed such a guest.

THOMAS LODGE

The Introduction and Notes are at page 943

FROM *Scilla's Metamorphosis*, 1589

Sonnet

The earth, late choked with showers,
Is now arrayed in green;
Her bosom springs with flowers,
The air dissolves her teen.
  The heavens laugh at her glory,
  Yet bide I sad and sorry.
The woods are decked with leaves
And trees are clothëd gay,
And Flora, crowned with sheaves,
With oaken boughs doth play; 10
  Where I am clad in black,
  The token of my wrack.

The birds upon the trees
Do sing with pleasant voices,
And chant in their degrees
Their loves and lucky choices;
  When I, whilst they are sing-
    ing,
  With sighs mine arms am
    wringing.
The thrushes seek the shade,
And I my fatal grave; .   20
Their flight to heaven is made,
My walk on earth I have.
  They free, I thrall; they jolly,
  I sad and pensive wholly.

FROM *Rosalind*, 1592

Rosalind's madrigal

Love in my bosom like a bee
  Doth suck his sweet;
Now with his wings he plays with
    me,
  Now with his feet.
Within mine eyes he makes his
    nest,
His bed amidst my tender breast,
My kisses are his daily feast,
And yet he robs me of my rest—
  Ah, wanton, will ye?

And if I sleep, then percheth he 10
  With pretty flight,
And makes his pillow of my knee
  The livelong night.
Strike I my lute, he tunes the
    string,

He music plays if so I sing,
He lends me every lovely thing,
Yet cruel he my heart doth
    sting—
  Whist, wanton, still ye!

Else I with roses every day
  Will whip you hence,   20
And bind you, when you long to
    play,
  For your offence.
I'll shut mine eyes to keep you
    in,
I'll make you fast it for your
    sin,
I'll count your power not worth a
    pin;
Alas! what hereby shall I win
  If he gainsay me?

What if I beat the wanton boy
  With many a rod?
He will repay me with annoy, 30
  Because a god.
Then sit thou safely on my knee,

And let thy bower my bosom be,
Lurk in mine eyes, I like of
  thee.
O Cupid, so thou pity me,
Spare not, but play thee!

Montanus' sonnet

Phœbe sat,
Sweet she sat,
  Sweet sat Phœbe when I saw her;
White her brow,
Coy her eye,
  Brow and eye how much you please me!
Words I spent,
Sighs I sent,
  Sighs and words could never draw her.
O my love,   10
Thou art lost,
  Since no sight could ever ease thee. ˙

Phœbe sat
By a fount,
  Sitting by a fount I spied her;
Sweet her touch,
Rare her voice,
  Touch and voice, what may distain you?
As she sang,
I did sigh,   20
  And by sighs whilst that I tried her,
O mine eyes,
You did lose
  Her first sight, whose want did pain you.

Phœbe's flocks
White as wool,
  Yet were Phœbe's locks more whiter;
Phœbe's eyes
Dovelike mild,
  Dovelike eyes, both mild and cruel;   30
Montan swears,
In your lamps
  He will die for to delight her.
Phœbe, yield,
Or I die—
  Shall true hearts be fancy's fuel?

Rosader's second sonetto

Turn I my looks unto the skies,
Love with his arrows wounds mine eyes;
If so I gaze upon the ground,
Love then in every flower is found;
Search I the shade, to fly my pain,
He meets me in the shade again;
Wend I to walk in secret grove,
Ev'n there I meet with sacred love;
If so I bain me in the spring,
Ev'n on the brink I hear him sing;   10
If so I meditate alone,
He will be partner of my moan;
If so I mourn, he weeps with me,
And where I am there will he be.
Whenas I talk of Rosalind
The god from coyness waxeth kind,
And seems in self-same flames to fry
Because he loves as well as I.
Sweet Rosalind, for pity rue!
For why than love I am more true.   20
He, if he speed, will quickly fly,
But in thy love I live and die.

From *The Life and Death of William Longbeard*, 1593

[*My mistress when she goes*]

My mistress when she goes
To pull the pink and rose
Along the river bounds,
And trippeth on the grounds,
And runs from rocks to rocks
With lovely scattered locks,
Whilst amorous wind doth play
With hairs so golden gay;
The water waxeth clear,
The fishes draw her near,   10
The sirens sing her praise,
Sweet flowers perfume her ways,
And Neptune, glad and fain,
Yields up to her his reign.

From R. S.'s *Phœnix Nest*, 1593

[*Strive no more*]

Strive no more,
Forspoken joys, to spring!
Since care hath clipt thy wing;
But stoop those lamps before
That nursed thee up at first with
friendly smiles
And now through scorns thy trust
beguiles.
Pine away,
That pining you may please,
For death betides you ease;

Oh, sweet and kind decay, [10]
To pine and die whilst love gives
      looking on
And pines to see your pining moan.

    Dying joys,
Your shrine is constant heart

That glories in his smart,
    Your trophies are annoys;
And on your tomb by love these
      lines are placed,
Lo, here they lie whom scorn de-
    faced.

[The fatal star]

The fatal star that at my birthday shinëd,
   Were it of Jove, or Venus in her brightness,
All sad effects, sour fruits of love divinëd
          In my love's lightness.

Light was my love, that all too light believëd
   Heaven's ruth to dwell in fair alluring faces,
That love, that hope that damnëd and reprievëd
          To all disgraces!

Love that misled, hope that deceived my seeing;
   Love, hope no more, mocked with deluding object;   10
Sight full of sorrow that denies the being
          Unto the subject.

Soul, leave the seat where thoughts with endless swelling
   Change into tears and words of no persuasion;
Tears, turn to tongues and spend your tunes in telling
          Sorrow's invasion.

Wonder, vain world, at beauty's proud refusal;
   Wonder in vain at love's unkind denial,
Why love thus lofty is, that doth abuse all
          And makes no trial.   20

Tears, words, and tunes, all, signify my sadness!
   My speechless grief, look pale without dissembling.
Sorrow, sit mute and tell thy torment's madness
          With true heart's trembling.

And if pure vows, or hands heaved up to heaven,
   May move the gods to rue my wretched blindness,
My plaints shall make my joys in measure even
          With her unkindness.

That she whom my true heart hath found so cruel,
Mourning all mirthless, may pursue the pleasure   30
That scorns her labors, poor in her joy's jewel
And earthly treasure.

[Like desert woods]

Like desert woods with darksome shades obscured
Where dreadful beasts, where hateful horror reigneth,
Such is my wounded heart, whom sorrow paineth.

The trees are fatal shafts, to death inured,
That cruel love within my breast maintaineth
To whet my grief whenas my sorrow waneth.

The ghastly beasts, my thoughts in cares assured,
Which wage me war (whilst heart no succor gaineth)
With false suspect, and fear that still remaineth.

The horrors, burning sighs by cares procured,   10
Which forth I send whilst weeping eye complaineth,
To cool the heat the helpless heart containeth.

But shafts, but cares, sighs, horrors unrecured,
Were nought esteemed if, for these pains awarded,
My faithful love by you might be rewarded.

FROM *Phillis honored with Pastoral Sonnets, Elegies, and Amorous Delights,* 1593

O pleasing thoughts, apprentices of love,
Forerunners of desire, sweet mithridates
The poison of my sorrows to remove,
With whom my hopes and fear full oft debates,—
    Enrich yourselves and me by your self riches
Which are the thoughts you spend on heaven-bred beauty,
Rouse you my muse beyond our poets' pitches,
And working wonders, yet say all is duty;
    Use you no eaglets' eyes nor phœnix' feathers
To tower the heaven from whence heaven's wonder sallies,   10
For why, your sun sings sweetly to her weathers,
Making a spring of winter in the valleys.
    Show to the world, though poor and scant my skill is,
    How sweet thoughts be that are but thought on Phillis.

No stars her eyes, to clear the wandering night,
But shining suns of true divinity,

That make the soul conceive her perfect light;
No wanton beauties of humanity
        Her pretty brows, but beams that clear the sight
Of him that seeks the true philosophy;
No coral is her lip, no rose her fair,
But even that crimson that adorns the sun;
        No nymph is she, but mistress of the air,
By whom my glories are but new begun.   10
        But when I touch and taste as others do,
        I then shall write and you shall wonder too.

        Love guides the roses of thy lips
And flies about them like a bee;
        If I approach he forward skips,
And if I kiss he stingeth me.
        Love in thine eyes doth build his bower
And sleeps within their pretty shine;
        And if I look, the boy will lour
And from their orbs shoot shafts divine.
        Love works thy heart within his fire,
And in my tears doth firm the same;   10
        And if I tempt it will retire,
And of my plaints doth make a game.
        Love, let me cull her choicest flowers,
And pity me, and calm her eye,
        Make soft her heart, dissolve her lours,
Then will I praise thy deity.
        But if thou do not, Love, I'll truly serve her
        In spite of thee, and by firm faith deserve her.

My Phillis hath the morning sun
        At first to look upon her,
And Phillis hath morn-waking birds
        Her risings for to honor.
My Phillis hath prime-feathered flowers
        That smile when she treads on them,
And Phillis hath a gallant flock
        That leaps since she doth own them.
But Phillis hath so hard a heart
        (Alas, that she should have it!)   10
As yields no mercy to desert
        Nor grace to those that crave it.
Sweet sun, when thou lookest on,
        Pray her regard my moan;

Sweet birds, when you sing to her,
To yield some pity woo her;
Sweet flowers, whenas she treads on,
Tell her, her beauty deads one;
And if in life her love she nill agree me,
Pray her, before I die she will come see me.   20

I'll teach thee, lovely Phillis, what love is:
It is a vision, seeming such as thou,
That flies as fast as it assaults mine eyes;
It is affection that doth reason miss;
  It is a shape of pleasure like to you,
Which meets the eye, and seen on sudden dies;
It is a doubled grief, a spark of pleasure
Begot by vain desire. And this is love,
  Whom in our youth we count our chiefest treasure,
In age, for want of power, we do reprove.   10
  Yea, such a power is love, whose loss is pain,
  And having got him, we repent our gain.

An ode

Now I find thy looks were feignëd,
Quickly lost and quickly gainëd;
Soft thy skin like wool of wethers,
Heart unstable, light as feathers;
Tongue untrusty, subtle-sighted,
Wanton will, with change delighted.
  Siren pleasant, foe to reason,
  Cupid plague thee for this treason.

Feigned acceptance when I askëd,
Lovely words, with cunning maskëd;
Holy vows but heart unholy,—
Wretched man, my trust was folly;   20
Lily white, and pretty winking,
Solemn vows, but sorry thinking.
  Siren pleasant, foe to reason,
  Cupid plague thee for this treason.

Of thine eyes I made my mirror;
From thy beauty came mine error;   10
All thy words I counted witty;
All thy smiles I deemëd pity;
Thy false tears that me aggrievëd
First of all my trust deceivëd.
  Siren pleasant, foe to reason,
  Cupid plague thee for this treason.

Now I see (O seemly cruel!)
Others warm them at my fuel.
Wit shall guide me in this durance,
Since in love is no assurance.
Change thy pasture, take thy pleasure,
Beauty is a fading treasure.   30
  Siren pleasant, foe to reason,
  Cupid plague thee for this treason.

Prime youth lasts not, age will fol-
low,
And make white these tresses yel-
low;
Wrinkled face for looks delightful
Shall acquaint the dame despiteful;

And when time shall eat thy
glory,
Then too late thou wilt be sorry.
Siren pleasant, foe to reason,
Cupid plague thee for this trea-
son.

NICHOLAS BRETON

The Introduction and Notes are at page 944

From *The Arbor of Amorous Devices*, 1597

A pastoral of Phillis and Coridon

On a hill there grows a flower,
  Fair befall the dainty sweet!
By that flower there is a bower
  Where the heavenly Muses
    meet.

In that bower there is a chair
  Fringëd all about with gold,
Where doth sit the fairest fair
  That did ever eye behold.

It is Phillis fair and bright,
  She that is the shepherds' joy, ¹⁰
She that Venus did despite
  And did blind her little boy.

This is she, the wise, the rich,
  And the world desires to see;
This is *ipsa quæ* the which
  There is none but only she.

Who would not this face admire?
  Who would not this saint
    adore?
Who would not this sight desire,
  Though he thought to see no
    more? ²⁰

O fair eyes, yet let me see!
  One good look, and I am gone,

Look on me, for I am he—
  Thy poor silly Coridon.

Thou that art the shepherds'
    queen,
  Look upon thy silly swain;
By thy comfort have been seen
  Dead men brought to life
    again.

A sweet lullaby

Come, little babe; come, silly
    soul,
Thy father's shame, thy mother's
    grief,
Born, as I doubt, to all our dole
And to thyself unhappy chief:
  Sing lullaby, and lap it warm,
  Poor soul that thinks no crea-
    ture harm.

Thou little think'st and less dost
    know
The cause of this thy mother's
    moan,
Thou want'st the wit to wail her
    woe,
And I myself am all alone. ¹⁰
  Why dost thou weep? why dost
    thou wail?
  And knowest not yet what thou
    dost ail.

Come, little wretch—ah, silly
    heart,
Mine only joy, what can I more?
If there be any wrong thy smart,
That may the destinies implore,
    'Twas I, I say, against my
      will;
    I wail the time, but be thou
      still.

And dost thou smile? Oh, thy
    sweet face,
Would God himself he might
    thee see;   20
No doubt thou wouldst soon pur-
    chase grace,
I know right well, for thee and
    me.
    But come to mother, babe, and
      play,
    For father false is fled away.

Sweet boy, if it by fortune chance
Thy father home again to send,
If death do strike me with his
    lance,
Yet mayst thou me to him com-
    mend;
    If any ask thy mother's name,
    Tell how by love she purchased
      blame.   30

Then will his gentle heart soon
    yield;
I know him of a noble mind.
Although a lion in the field,
A lamb in town thou shalt him
    find.
    Ask blessing, babe, be not
      afraid;
    His sugared words hath me be-
      trayed.

Then mayst thou joy and be right
    glad,
Although in woe I seem to moan.
Thy father is no rascal lad,

A noble youth of blood and
    bone;   40
    His glancing looks, if he once
      smile,
    Right honest women may be-
      guile.

Come, little boy, and rock asleep,
Sing lullaby, and be thou still;
I that can do nought else but
    weep
Will sit by thee and wail my fill.
    God bless my babe, and lul-
      laby,
    From this thy father's quality.

FROM JOHN BODENHAM's (?)
    England's Helicon, 1600

[*Say that I should say*]

Say that I should say I love ye,
    Would you say 'tis but a say-
      ing?
But if love in prayers move ye,
    Will you not be moved with
      praying?

Think I think that love should
    know ye,
    Will you think 'tis but a think-
      ing?
But if love the thought do show
    ye,
    Will ye lose your eyes with
      winking?

Write that I do write you blessed,
    Will you write 'tis but a writ-
      ing?   10
But if truth and love confess it,
    Will ye doubt the true indit-
      ing?

No: I say, and think, and write
    it,—

Write, and think, and say your
 pleasure.
Love and truth and I indite it,
 You are blessed out of measure.

Phillida and Coridon

In the merry month of May,
In a morn by break of day
Forth I walked by the wood-side,
Whenas May was in his pride.
There I spiëd, all alone,
Phillida and Coridon.
Much ado there was, God wot,
He would love and she would
  not.
She said, Never man was true;
He said, None was false to you. 10
He said he had loved her long.
She said, Love should have no
  wrong.
Coridon would kiss her then;
She said maids must kiss no men
Till they did for good and all.
Then she made the shepherd call
All the heavens to witness truth,
Never loved a truer youth.
Thus, with many a pretty oath,
Yea and nay, and faith and
  troth,   20
Such as silly shepherds use
When they will not love abuse,
Love which had been long de-
 luded
Was with kisses sweet concluded.
And Phillida with garlands gay
Was made the lady of the May.

Song of Phillida and Coridon

Fair in a morn (O fairest morn,
 Was never morn so fair)
There shone a sun, though not the
  sun
  That shineth in the air.
For the earth and from the earth,
 (Was never such a creature)

Did come this face; (was never
  face
  That carried such a feature).
Upon a hill (O blessed hill,
 Was never hill so blessed)   10
There stood a man; (was never
  man
  For woman so distressëd).
This man beheld a heavenly view
 Which did such virtue give
As clears the blind and helps the
  lame,
 And makes the dead man live.
This man had hap (O happy
  man,
 More happy none than he),
For he had hap to see the hap
 That none had hap to see.   20
This silly swain (and silly swains
 Are men of meanest grace)
Had yet the grace (O gracious
  guest)
 To hap on such a face.
He pity cried, and pity came,
 And pitied so his pain,
As dying, would not let him die,
 But gave him life again.
For joy whereof he made such
  mirth
 As all the woods did ring; 30
And Pan with all his swains came
  forth
 To hear the shepherd sing.
But such a song sung never was,
 Nor shall be sung again,
Of Phillida, the shepherds' queen,
 And Coridon, the swain.
Fair Phillis is the shepherds'
  queen
 (Was never such a queen as
  she),
And Coridon her only swain
 (Was never such a swain as
  he).   40
Fair Phillis hath the fairest face
 That ever eye did yet behold,

And Coridon the constants' faith
    That ever yet kept flock in fold.
Sweet Phillis is the sweetest sweet
    That ever yet the earth did
        yield,
And Coridon the kindest swain
    That ever yet kept lambs in
        field.
Sweet Philomel is Phillis' bird,
    Though Coridon be he that
        caught her;   50
And Coridon doth hear her sing,
    Though Phillida be she that
        taught her.
Poor Coridon doth keep the fields,
    Though Phillida be she that
        owes them;
And Phillida doth walk the
        meads,
    Though Coridon be he that
        mows them.
The little lambs are Phillis' love,
    Though Coridon is he that
        feeds them;
The gardens fair are Phillis'
        ground,
    Though Coridon be he that
        weeds them.   60
Since then that Phillis only is
    The only shepherd's only queen,
And Coridon the only swain
    That only hath her shepherd
        been;
Though Phillis keep her bower of
        state,
    Shall Coridon consume away?
No, shepherd, no, work out the
        week,
    And Sunday shall be holy-day.

FROM *Melancholic Humors,* 1600

An odd conceit

Lovely kind, and kindly loving,
Such a mind were worth the mov-
    ing;

Truly fair, and fairly true,
Where are all these but in you?

Wisely kind, and kindly wise—
Blessed life, where such love lies!
Wise, and kind, and fair, and
    true,
Lovely live all these in you.

Sweetly dear, and dearly sweet—
Blessed, where these blessings
    meet!   10
Sweet, fair, wise, kind, blessed,
    true,
Blessed be all these in you!

FROM *The Passionate Shepherd,*
1604

Pastoral [1]

Flora hath been all about
And hath brought her wardrobe
    out,
With her fairest, sweetest flowers,
All to trim up all your bowers.
Bid the shepherds and their
    swains
See the beauty of their plains,
And command them, with their
    flocks,
To do reverence on the rocks,
Where they may so happy be
As her shadow but to see.   10
Bid the birds in every bush
Not a bird to be at hush,
But to sit, chirrup, and sing
To the beauty of the spring.
Call the sylvan nymphs together,
Bid them bring their music
    hither.
Trees their barky silence break,
Crack, yet though they cannot
    speak.
Bid the purest, whitest swan
Of her feathers make her fan.   20
Let the hound the hare go chase,

Lambs and rabbits run at base,
Flies be dancing in the sun,
While the silk-worm's webs are
    spun;
Hang a fish on every hook
As she goes along the brook:
So with all your sweetest powers
Entertain her in your bowers,
Where her ear may joy to hear
How ye make your sweetest
    choir;   30
And in all your sweetest vein,
Still, Aglaia! strike the strain.
But when she her walk doth turn,
Then begin as fast to mourn,
All your flowers and garlands
    wither,
Put up all your pipes together;
Never strike a pleasing strain
Till she come abroad again!

Pastoral [2]

Who can live in heart so glad
As the merry country lad?
Who upon a fair green balk
May at pleasure sit and walk,
And amid the azure skies
See the morning sun arise;
While he hears in every spring
How the birds do chirp and sing;
Or before the hounds in cry
See the hare go stealing by;   10
Or along the shallow brook
Angling with a baited hook,
See the fishes leap and play
In a blessed sunny day;
Or to hear the partridge call
Till she have her covey all;
Or to see the subtle fox,
How the villain plies the box,
After feeding on his prey
How he closely sneaks away   20
Through the hedge and down the
    furrow,
Till he gets into his burrow;

Then the bee to gather honey,
And the little black-haired coney
On a bank for sunny place
With her forefeet wash her face:
Are not these, with thousands
    mo
Than the courts of kings do
    know,
The true pleasing-spirits sights
That may breed true love's de-
    lights?   30
But with all this happiness
To behold that shepherdess
To whose eyes all shepherds yield,
All the fairest of the field,
Fair Aglaia, in whose face
Lives the shepherds' highest
    grace,
In whose worthy-wonder praise
See what her true shepherd says:
She is neither proud nor fine,
But in spirit more divine;   40
She can neither lour nor leer,
But a sweeter smiling cheer;
She had never painted face,
But a sweeter smiling grace;
She can never love dissemble,
Truth doth so her thoughts as-
    semble
That where wisdom guides her
    will
She is kind and constant still.
All in sum, she is that creature
Of that truest comfort's nature,   50
That doth show (but in exceed-
    ings)
How their praises had their breed-
    ings.
Let, then, poets feign their pleas-
    ure
In their fictions of love's treasure,
Proud high spirits seek their
    graces
In their idol-painted faces;
My love's spirit's lowliness
In affection's humbleness

Under heav'n no happiness
Seeks but in this shepherdess.   60
For whose sake I say and swear
By the passions that I bear,
Had I got a kingly grace
I would leave my kingly place
And in heart be truly glad
To become a country lad,

Hard to lie, and go full bare,
And to feed on hungry fare,
So I might but live to be
Where I might but sit to see   70
Once a day, or all day long,
The sweet subject of my song—
In Aglaia's only eyes
All my worldly paradise.

CHRISTOPHER MARLOWE

The Introduction and Notes are at page 945

FROM JOHN BODENHAM's (?) *England's Helicon*, 1600

The passionate shepherd to his love

Come live with me and be my love,
And we will all the pleasures prove
That valleys, groves, hills, and
    fields,
Woods, or steepy mountain yields.

And we will sit upon the rocks,
Seeing the shepherds feed their
    flocks,
By shallow rivers to whose falls
Melodious birds sings madrigals.

And I will make thee beds of roses
And a thousand fragrant posies,   10
A cap of flowers, and a kirtle
Embroidered all with leaves of
    myrtle;

A gown made of the finest wool
Which from our pretty lambs we
    pull;
Fair linëd slippers for the cold,
With buckles of the purest gold;

A belt of straw and ivy buds,
With coral clasps and amber studs:
And if these pleasures may thee
    move,
Come live with me, and be my
    love.   20

The shepherds' swains shall dance
    and sing
For thy delight each May morning:
If these delights thy mind may
    move,
Then live with me and be my love.

FROM *Hero and Leander* . . . *for Edward Blunt*, 1598

To the Right Worshipful Sir Thomas Walsingham, Knight.

Sir, we think not ourselves discharged of the duty we owe to our friend when we have brought the breathless body to the earth; for albeit the eye there taketh his ever farewell of that beloved object, yet the impression of the man that hath been dear unto us, living an after life in our memory, there putteth us in mind of farther obsequies due unto the deceased. And namely of the performance of whatsoever we may judge shall make to his living credit, and to the effecting of his determinations prevented by the stroke of death. By these meditations, as by an intellectual will, I suppose myself executor to the unhappily deceased author of this poem, upon whom knowing that in his life-time you bestowed many kind favors, entertaining the parts of reckon-ing and worth which you found in him, with good countenance and liberal affection, I cannot but see so far into the will of him dead, that whatsoever issue of his brain should chance to come abroad, that the first breath it should take might be the gentle air of your liking; for since his self had been accustomed thereunto, it would prove more agreeable and thriving to his right children than any other foster countenance whatsoever. At this time seeing that this unfinished tragedy happens under my hands to be imprinted, of a double duty, the one to yourself, the other to the deceased, I present the same to your most favorable allowance, offering my utmost self now and ever to be ready at your Worship's disposing.

Edward Blunt.

Hero and Leander

[First sestiad]

On Hellespont, guilty of true love's blood,
In view, and opposite, two cities stood,
Sea-borderers, disjoined by Neptune's might;
The one Abydos, the other Sestos hight.
At Sestos, Hero dwelt; Hero the fair,
Whom young Apollo courted for her hair,
And offered as a dower his burning throne,
Where she should sit for men to gaze upon.
The outside of her garments were of lawn,
The lining purple silk, with gilt stars drawn; 10
Her wide sleeves green, and bordered with a grove
Where Venus in her naked glory strove
To please the careless and disdainful eyes
Of proud Adonis, that before her lies;
Her kirtle blue, whereon was many a stain,
Made with the blood of wretched lovers slain.
Upon her head she ware a myrtle wreath,
From whence her veil reached to the ground beneath.
Her veil was artificial flowers and leaves,
Whose workmanship both man and beast deceives; 20
Many would praise the sweet smell as she passed,
When 'twas the odor which her breath forth cast;
And there for honey bees have sought in vain,

And, beat from thence, have lighted there again.
About her neck hung chains of pebble-stone,
Which, lightened by her neck, like diamonds shone.
She ware no gloves, for neither sun nor wind
Would burn or parch her hands, but to her mind,
Or warm or cool them, for they took delight
To play upon those hands, they were so white.   10
Buskins of shells all silvered, uséd she,
And branched with blushing coral to the knee,
Where sparrows perched, of hollow pearl and gold,
Such as the world would wonder to behold;
Those with sweet water oft her handmaid fills,
Which, as she went, would chirrup through the bills.
Some say, for her the fairest Cupid pined,
And, looking in her face, was strooken blind.
But this is true: so like was one the other,
As he imagined Hero was his mother;   40
And oftentimes into her bosom flew,
About her naked neck his bare arms threw,
And laid his childish head upon her breast,
And with still panting rocked, there took his rest.
So lovely fair was Hero, Venus' nun,
As nature wept, thinking she was undone,
Because she took more from her than she left
And of such wondrous beauty her bereft;
Therefore, in sign her treasure suffered wrack,
Since Hero's time hath half the world been black.   50
Amorous Leander, beautiful and young,
(Whose tragedy divine Musæus sung)
Dwelt at Abydos; since him dwelt there none
For whom succeeding times make greater moan.
His dangling tresses that were never shorn,
Had they been cut and unto Colchis borne,
Would have allured the vent'rous youth of Greece
To hazard more than for the Golden Fleece.
Fair Cynthia wished his arms might be her sphere;
Grief makes her pale, because she moves not there.   60
His body was as straight as Circe's wand;
Jove might have sipped out nectar from his hand.
Even as delicious meat is to the taste,
So was his neck in touching, and surpassed
The white of Pelops' shoulder. I could tell ye
How smooth his breast was, and how white his belly,
And whose immortal fingers did imprint
That heavenly path, with many a curious dint,
That runs along his back; but my rude pen

Can hardly blazon forth the loves of men,
Much less of powerful gods; let it suffice
That my slack muse sings of Leander's eyes,
Those orient cheeks and lips, exceeding his
That leapt into the water for a kiss
Of his own shadow, and despising many,
Died ere he could enjoy the love of any.
Had wild Hippolytus Leander seen,
Enamoured of his beauty had he been;
His presence made the rudest peasant melt,
That in the vast uplandish country dwelt;
The barbarous Thracian soldier, moved with nought,
Was moved with him, and for his favor sought.
Some swore he was a maid in man's attire,
For in his looks were all that men desire:
A pleasant smiling cheek, a speaking eye,
A brow for love to banquet royally;
And such as knew he was a man, would say,
Leander, thou art made for amorous play;
Why art thou not in love, and loved of all?
Though thou be fair, yet be not thine own thrall.

    The men of wealthy Sestos every year,
For his sake whom their goddess held so dear,
Rose-cheeked Adonis, kept a solemn feast.
Thither resorted many a wand'ring guest
To meet their loves; such as had none at all,
Came lovers home from this great festival.
For every street, like to a firmament,
Glistered with breathing stars, who, where they went,
Frighted the melancholy earth, which deemed
Eternal heaven to burn, for so it seemed
As if another Phaeton had got
The guidance of the sun's rich chariot.
But, far above the loveliest, Hero shined,
And stole away th' enchanted gazer's mind;
For like sea-nymphs' inveigling harmony,
So was her beauty to the standers by.
Nor that night-wand'ring pale and wat'ry star
(When yawning dragons draw her thirling car
From Latmos' mount up to the gloomy sky,
Where, crowned with blazing light and majesty,
She proudly sits) more over-rules the flood,
Than she the hearts of those that near her stood.
Even as when gaudy nymphs pursue the chase,
Wretched Ixion's shaggy-footed race,
Incensed with savage heat, gallop amain

From steep pine-bearing mountains to the plain,
So ran the people forth to gaze upon her,
And all that viewed her were enamoured on her.
And as in fury of a dreadful fight,
Their fellows being slain or put to flight,   120
Poor soldiers stand with fear of death dead-strooken,
So at her presence all, surprised and tooken,
Await the sentence of her scornful eyes;
He whom she favors lives, the other dies.
There might you see one sigh, another rage,
And some, their violent passions to assuage,
Compile sharp satires; but alas, too late,
For faithful love will never turn to hate.
And many, seeing great princes were denied,
Pined as they went, and thinking on her, died.   130
On this feast day, oh, cursed day and hour!,
Went Hero thorough Sestos, from her tower
To Venus' temple, where unhappily,
As after chanced, they did each other spy.
So fair a church as this had Venus none;
The walls were of discolored jasper stone,
Wherein was Proteus carvëd, and o'erhead
A lively vine of green sea-agate spread,
Where by one hand light-headed Bacchus hung,
And with the other wine from grapes out-wrung.   140
Of crystal shining fair the pavement was;
The town of Sestos called it Venus' glass;
There might you see the gods in sundry shapes,
Committing heady riots, incest, rapes;
For know that underneath this radiant floor
Was Danaë's statue in a brazen tower;
Jove slyly stealing from his sister's bed
To dally with Idalian Ganymed,
And for his love Europa bellowing loud,
And tumbling with the rainbow in a cloud;   150
Blood-quaffing Mars heaving the iron net
Which limping Vulcan and his Cyclops set;
Love kindling fire to burn such towns as Troy;
Silvanus weeping for the lovely boy
That now is turned into a cypress tree,
Under whose shade the wood-gods love to be.
And in the midst a silver altar stood;
There Hero sacrificing turtles' blood,
Veiled to the ground, veiling her eyelids close,
And modestly they opened as she rose;   160
Thence flew love's arrow with the golden head,

And thus Leander was enamourëd.
Stone still he stood, and evermore he gazed,
Till with the fire that from his count'nance blazed,
Relenting Hero's gentle heart was strook;
Such force and virtue hath an amorous look.

   It lies not in our power to love or hate,
For will in us is over-ruled by fate.
When two are stripped, long ere the course begin
We wish that one should lose, the other win;
And one especially do we affect
Of two gold ingots, like in each respect.
The reason no man knows, let it suffice,
What we behold is censured by our eyes.
Where both deliberate, the love is slight;
Who ever loved, that loved not at first sight?

   He kneeled, but unto her devoutly prayed;
Chaste Hero to herself thus softly said:
Were I the saint he worships, I would hear him;
And as she spake these words, came somewhat near him.
He started up; she blushed as one ashamed;
Wherewith Leander much more was inflamed.
He touched her hand; in touching it she trembled;
Love deeply grounded hardly is dissembled.
These lovers parlëd by the touch of hands;
True love is mute, and oft amazëd stands.
Thus while dumb signs their yielding hearts entangled,
The air with sparks of living fire was spangled,
And night, deep drenched in misty Acheron,
Heaved up her head, and half the world upon
Breathed darkness forth (dark night is Cupid's day).
And now begins Leander to display
Love's holy fire with words, with sighs, and tears,
Which like sweet music entered Hero's ears;
And yet at every word she turned aside,
And always cut him off as he replied.
At last, like to a bold sharp sophister,
With cheerful hope thus he accosted her:

   Fair creature, let me speak without offence;
I would my rude words had the influence
To lead thy thoughts as thy fair looks do mine!
Then shouldst thou be his prisoner who is thine.
Be not unkind and fair; misshapen stuff
Are of behavior boisterous and rough.
Oh, shun me not, but hear me ere you go,
God knows I cannot force love, as you do.
My words shall be as spotless as my youth,

Full of simplicity and naked truth.
This sacrifice, whose sweet perfume descending
From Venus' altar to your footsteps bending, 210
Doth testify that you exceed her far,
To whom you offer, and whose nun you are.
Why should you worship her? her you surpass
As much as sparkling diamonds flaring glass.
A diamond set in lead his worth retains;
A heavenly nymph, beloved of human swains,
Receives no blemish, but ofttimes more grace;
Which makes me hope, although I am but base,
Base in respect of thee, divine and pure,
Dutiful service may thy love procure, 220
And I in duty will excel all other,
As thou in beauty dost exceed Love's mother.
Nor heaven, nor thou, were made to gaze upon;
As heaven preserves all things, so save thou one.
A stately builded ship, well rigged and tall,
The ocean maketh more majestical;
Why vowest thou then to live in Sestos here,
Who on love's seas more glorious would appear?
Like untuned golden strings all women are,
Which long time lie untouched, will harshly jar. 230
Vessels of brass, oft handled, brightly shine;
What difference betwixt the richest mine
And basest mold, but use? for both, not used,
Are of like worth. Then treasure is abused,
When misers keep it; being put to loan,
In time it will return us two for one.
Rich robes themselves and others do adorn;
Neither themselves nor others, if not worn.
Who builds a palace, and rams up the gate,
Shall see it ruinous and desolate. 240
Ah, simple Hero, learn thyself to cherish!
Lone women, like to empty houses, perish.
Less sins the poor rich man that starves himself
In heaping up a mass of drossy pelf,
Than such as you; his golden earth remains,
Which after his decease some other gains;
But this fair gem, sweet in the loss alone,
When you fleet hence, can be bequeathed to none.
Or if it could, down from th' enamelled sky
All heaven would come to claim this legacy, 250
And with intestine broils the world destroy,
And quite confound nature's sweet harmony.
Well! therefore by the gods decreed it is

We human creatures should enjoy that bliss.
One is no number; maids are nothing, then,
Without the sweet society of men.
Wilt thou live single still? one shalt thou be
Though never-singling Hymen couple thee.
Wild savages, that drink of running springs,
Think water far excels all earthly things,   260
But they that daily taste neat wine, despise it;
Virginity, albeit some highly prize it,
Compared with marriage, had you tried them both,
Differs as much as wine and water doth.
Base bullion for the stamp's sake we allow;
Even so for men's impression do we you,
By which alone, our reverend fathers say,
Women receive perfection every way.
This idol which you term virginity   270
Is neither essence subject to the eye,
No, nor to any one exterior sense,
Nor hath it any place of residence,
Nor is 't of earth or mould celestial,
Or capable of any form at all.
Of that which hath no being, do not boast;
Things that are not at all, are never lost.
Men foolishly do call it virtuous;
What virtue is it, that is born with us?
Much less can honor be ascribed thereto;   280
Honor is purchased by the deeds we do.
Believe me, Hero, honor is not won
Until some honorable deed be done.
Seek you, for chastity, immortal fame,
And know that some have wronged Diana's name?
Whose name is it, if she be false or not,
So she be fair, but some vile tongues will blot?
But you are fair, ay me, so wondrous fair,
So young, so gentle, and so debonair,
As Greece will think, if thus you live alone,   290
Some one or other keeps you as his own.
Then, Hero, hate me not, nor from me fly
To follow swiftly blasting infamy.
Perhaps thy sacred priesthood makes thee loath;
Tell me, to whom mad'st thou that heedless oath?
    To Venus, answered she, and as she spake,
Forth from those two tralucent cisterns brake
A stream of liquid pearl, which down her face
Made milk-white paths, whereon the gods might trace
To Jove's high court. He thus replied: The rites

In which love's beauteous empress most delights   300
Are banquets, Doric music, midnight revel,
Plays, masks, and all that stern age counteth evil.
Thee as a holy idiot doth she scorn,
For thou, in vowing chastity, hast sworn
To rob her name and honor, and thereby
Commit'st a sin far worse than perjury,
Even sacrilege against her deity,
Through regular and formal purity.
To expiate which sin, kiss and shake hands;
Such sacrifice as this Venus demands.   310

   Thereat she smiled, and did deny him so
As, put thereby, yet might he hope for mo.
Which makes him quickly reinforce his speech,
And her in humble manner thus beseech:

   Though neither gods nor men may thee deserve,
Yet for her sake whom you have vowed to serve,
Abandon fruitless cold virginity,
The gentle queen of love's sole enemy.
Then shall you most resemble Venus' nun,
When Venus' sweet rites are performed and done.   320
Flint-breasted Pallas joys in single life,
But Pallas and your mistress are at strife.
Love, Hero, then, and be not tyrannous,
But heal the heart that thou hast wounded thus;
Nor stain thy youthful years with avarice;
Fair fools delight to be accounted nice.
The richest corn dies if it be not reaped;
Beauty alone is lost, too warily kept.
These arguments he used, and many more,
Wherewith she yielded, that was won before.   330
Hero's looks yielded, but her words made war;
Women are won when they begin to jar.
Thus having swallowed Cupid's golden hook,
The more she strived, the deeper was she strook;
Yet, evilly feigning anger, strove she still,
And would be thought to grant against her will.
So having paused a while, at last she said:
Who taught thee rhetoric to deceive a maid?
Ay me! such words as these should I abhor,
And yet I like them for the orator.   340

   With that Leander stooped to have embraced her,
But from his spreading arms away she cast her,
And thus bespake him: Gentle youth, forbear
To touch the sacred garments which I wear.
   Upon a rock, and underneath a hill,

Far from the town, where all is whist and still
Save that the sea playing on yellow sand
Sends forth a rattling murmur to the land,
Whose sound allures the golden Morpheus
In silence of the night to visit us,   350
My turret stands; and there, God knows, I play
With Venus' swans and sparrows all the day.
A dwarfish beldame bears me company,
That hops about the chamber where I lie,
And spends the night, that might be better spent,
In vain discourse and apish merriment.
Come thither. As she spake this, her tongue tripped,
For unawares, Come thither, from her slipped;
And suddenly her former color changed,
And here and there her eyes through anger ranged.   360
And like a planet moving several ways
At one self instant, she, poor soul, assays,
Loving, not to love at all, and every part
Strove to resist the motions of her heart;
And hands so pure, so innocent, nay such
As might have made heaven stoop to have a touch,
Did she uphold to Venus, and again
Vowed spotless chastity, but all in vain.
Cupid beats down her prayers with his wings;
Her vows above the empty air he flings;   370
All deep enraged, his sinewy bow he bent,
And shot a shaft that burning from him went;
Wherewith she, strooken, looked so dolefully,
As made Love sigh to see his tyranny.
And as she wept, her tears to pearl he turned,
And wound them on his arm, and for her mourned.
Then towards the palace of the Destinies,
Laden with languishment and grief, he flies,
And to those stern nymphs humbly made request,
Both might enjoy each other, and be blest.   380
But with a ghastly dreadful countenance,
Threat'ning a thousand deaths at every glance,
They answered Love, nor would vouchsafe so much
As one poor word, their hate to him was such.
Hearken awhile, and I will tell you why:
Heaven's wingèd herald, Jove-born Mercury,
The self-same day that he asleep had laid
Enchanted Argus, spied a country maid,
Whose careless hair, instead of pearl t' adorn it,
Glistered with dew, as one that seemed to scorn it;   390
Her breath as fragrant as the morning rose,

Her mind pure, and her tongue untaught to gloze;
Yet proud she was, for lofty pride that dwells
In towered courts is oft in shepherds' cells,
And too too well the fair vermilion knew,
And silver tincture of her cheeks, that drew
The love of every swain. On her this god
Enamoured was, and with his snaky rod
Did charm her nimble feet, and made her stay,
The while upon a hillock down he lay,   400
And sweetly on his pipe began to play,
And with smooth speech her fancy to assay;
Till in his twining arms he locked her fast,
And then he wooed with kisses, and at last,
As shepherds do, her on the ground he laid,
And tumbling in the grass, he often strayed
Beyond the bounds of shame, in being bold
To eye those parts which no eye should behold.
And like an insolent commanding lover,
Boasting his parentage, would needs discover   410
The way to new Elysium; but she,
Whose only dower was her chastity,
Having striv'n in vain, was now about to cry,
And crave the help of shepherds that were nigh.
Herewith he stayed his fury, and began
To give her leave to rise; away she ran;
After went Mercury, who used such cunning,
As she, to hear his tale, left off her running;
Maids are not won by brutish force and might,
But speeches full of pleasure and delight;   420
And knowing Hermes courted her, was glad
That she such loveliness and beauty had
As could provoke his liking, yet was mute,
And neither would deny nor grant his suit.
Still vowed he love, she wanting no excuse
To feed him with delays, as women use,
Or thirsting after immortality—
All women are ambitious naturally—
Imposed upon her lover such a task
As he ought not perform, nor yet she ask.   430
A draught of flowing nectar she requested,
Wherewith the king of gods and men is feasted.
He, ready to accomplish what she willed,
Stole some from Hebe (Hebe Jove's cup filled)
And gave it to his simple rustic love;
Which being known (as what is hid from Jove?)

He inly stormed, and waxed more furious
Than for the fire filched by Prometheus,
And thrusts him down from heaven; he wand'ring here
In mournful terms, with sad and heavy cheer,   440
Complained to Cupid. Cupid, for his sake,
To be revenged on Jove did undertake;
And those on whom heaven, earth, and hell relies,
I mean the adamantine Destinies,
He wounds with love, and forced them equally
To dote upon deceitful Mercury.
They offered him the deadly fatal knife
That shears the slender threads of human life;
At his fair-feathered feet the engines laid
Which th' earth from ugly Chaos' den upweighed;   450
These he regarded not, but did entreat
That Jove, usurper of his father's seat,
Might presently be banished into hell,
And aged Saturn in Olympus dwell.
They granted what he craved, and once again
Saturn and Ops began their golden reign.
Murder, rape, war, lust, and treachery
Were with Jove closed in Stygian empery.
But long this blessed time continued not;
As soon as he his wishèd purpose got,   460
He, reckless of his promise, did despise
The love of th' everlasting Destinies.
They seeing it, both Love and him abhorred,
And Jupiter unto his place restored.
And but that Learning, in despite of Fate,
Will mount aloft, and enter heaven gate,
And to the seat of Jove itself advance,
Hermes had slept in hell with Ignorance;
Yet as a punishment they added this,
That he and Poverty should always kiss.   470
And to this day is every scholar poor;
Gross gold from them runs headlong to the boor.
Likewise, the angry sisters thus deluded,
To venge themselves on Hermes, have concluded
That Midas' brood shall sit in Honor's chair,
To which the Muses' sons are only heir;
And fruitful wits that inspiring are,
Shall, discontent, run into regions far;
And few great lords in virtuous deeds shall joy,
But be surprised with every garish toy;   480
And still enrich the lofty servile clown,

Who with encroaching guile keeps learning down.
Then muse not Cupid's suit no better sped,
Seeing in their loves the Fates were injurëd.

[Second sestiad]

By this, sad Hero, with love unacquainted,
Viewing Leander's face, fell down and fainted.
He kissed her and breathed life into her lips,
Wherewith, as one displeased, away she trips.
Yet as she went, full often looked behind,
And many poor excuses did she find
To linger by the way, and once she stayed
And would have turned again, but was afraid,
In off'ring parley, to be counted light.
So on she goes, and in her idle flight,   10
Her painted fan of curlëd plumes let fall,
Thinking to train Leander therewithal.
He, being a novice, knew not what she meant,
But stayed, and after her a letter sent,
Which joyful Hero answered in such sort
As he had hope to scale the beauteous fort
Wherein the liberal graces locked their wealth,
And therefore to her tower he got by stealth.
Wide open stood the door, he need not climb;
And she herself, before the 'pointed time,   20
Had spread the board, with roses strewed the room,
And oft looked out, and mused he did not come.
At last he came; oh, who can tell the greeting
These greedy lovers had at their first meeting.
He asked, she gave, and nothing was denied;
Both to each other quickly were affied.
Look how their hands, so were their hearts united,
And what he did she willingly requited.
Sweet are the kisses, the embracements sweet,
When like desires and affections meet;   30
For from the earth to heaven is Cupid raised,
Where fancy is in equal balance peised.
Yet she this rashness suddenly repented,
And turned aside, and to herself lamented,
As if her name and honor had been wronged
By being possessed of him for whom she longed;
Ay, and she wished, albeit not from her heart,
That he would leave her turret and depart.
The mirthful god of amorous pleasure smiled
To see how he this captive nymph beguiled;   40

For hitherto he did but fan the fire,
And kept it down that it might mount the higher.
Now waxed she jealous lest his love abated,
Fearing her own thoughts made her to be hated.
Therefore unto him hastily she goes,
And like light Salmacis, her body throws
Upon his bosom, where with yielding eyes
She offers up herself, a sacrifice
To slake his anger if he were displeased.
Oh, what god would not therewith be appeased?   50
Like Æsop's cock, this jewel he enjoyed,
And as a brother with his sister toyed,
Supposing nothing else was to be done,
Now he her favor and goodwill had won.
But know you not that creatures wanting sense
By nature have a mutual appetence,
And wanting organs to advance a step,
Moved by love's force, unto each other lep?
Much more in subjects having intellect,
Some hidden influence breeds like effect.   60
Albeit Leander, rude in love and raw,
Long dallying with Hero, nothing saw
That might delight him more, yet he suspected
Some amorous rites or other were neglected.
Therefore unto his body hers he clung;
She, fearing on the rushes to be flung,
Strived with redoubled strength; the more she strived,
The more a gentle pleasing heat revived,
Which taught him all that elder lovers know;
And now the same gan so to scorch and glow,   70
As in plain terms, yet cunningly, he craved it;
Love always makes those eloquent that have it.
She, with a kind of granting, put him by it,
And ever as he thought himself most nigh it,
Like to the tree of Tantalus she fled,
And, seeming lavish, saved her maidenhead.
Ne'er king more sought to keep his diadem,
Than Hero this inestimable gem.
Above our life we love a steadfast friend,
Yet when a token of great worth we send,   80
We often kiss it, often look thereon,
And stay the messenger that would be gone;
No marvel then though Hero would not yield
So soon to part from that she dearly held;
Jewels being lost are found again, this never;
'Tis lost but once, and once lost, lost forever.

Now had the morn espied her lover's steeds,
Whereat she starts, puts on her purple weeds,
And, red for anger that he stayed so long,
All headlong throws herself the clouds among.   90
And now Leander, fearing to be missed,
Embraced her suddenly, took leave, and kissed.
Long was he taking leave, and loath to go,
And kissed again, as lovers use to do.
Sad Hero wrung him by the hand and wept,
Saying, Let your vows and promises be kept.
Then, standing at the door, she turned about,
As loath to see Leander going out.
And now the sun that through th' horizon peeps,
As pitying these lovers, downward creeps,   100
So that in silence of the cloudy night,
Though it was morning, did he take his flight.
But what the secret trusty night concealed,
Leander's amorous habit soon revealed;
With Cupid's myrtle was his bonnet crowned,
About his arms the purple riband wound
Wherewith she wreathed her largely-spreading hair;
Nor could the youth abstain, but he must wear
The sacred ring wherewith she was endowed,
When first religious chastity she vowed;   110
Which made his love through Sestos to be known,
And thence unto Abydos sooner blown
Than he could sail, for incorporeal Fame,
Whose weight consists in nothing but her name,
Is swifter than the wind, whose tardy plumes
Are reeking water and dull earthly fumes.
Home, when he came, he seemed not to be there,
But like exilèd air thrust from his sphere,
Set in a foreign place; and straight from thence,
Alcides like, by mighty violence   120
He would have chased away the swelling main
That him from her unjustly did detain.
Like as the sun in a diameter
Fires and inflames objects removèd far,
And heateth kindly, shining lat'rally,
So beauty sweetly quickens when 'tis nigh,
But being separated and removed,
Burns where it cherished, murders where it loved.
Therefore even as an index to a book,
So to his mind was young Leander's look.   130
Oh, none but gods have power their love to hide;
Affection by the count'nance is described.

The light of hidden fire itself discovers,
And love that is concealed betrays poor lovers.
His secret flame apparently was seen;
Leander's father knew where he had been,
And for the same mildly rebuked his son,
Thinking to quench the sparkles new begun.
But love, resisted once, grows passionate,
And nothing more than counsel lovers hate;   140
For as a hot proud horse highly disdains
To have his head controlled, but breaks the reins,
Spits forth the ringled bit, and with his hooves
Checks the submissive ground, so he that loves,
The more he is restrained, the worse he fares.
What is it now but mad Leander dares?
O Hero, Hero! thus he cried full oft,
And then he got him to a rock aloft,
Where having spied her tower, long stared he on 't,
And prayed the narrow toiling Hellespont   150
To part in twain, that he might come and go;
But still the rising billows answered no.
With that he stripped him to the iv'ry skin,
And crying, Love, I come, leaped lively in.
Whereat the sapphire-visaged god grew proud,
And made his cap'ring Triton sound aloud,
Imagining that Ganymede, displeased,
Had left the heavens; therefore on him he seized.
Leander strived; the waves about him wound,
And pulled him to the bottom, where the ground   160
Was strewed with pearl, and in low coral groves
Sweet singing mermaids sported with their loves
On heaps of heavy gold, and took great pleasure
To spurn in careless sort the shipwreck treasure.
For here the stately azure palace stood,
Where kingly Neptune and his train abode.
The lusty god embraced him, called him love,
And swore he never should return to Jove.
But when he knew it was not Ganymed,
For under water he was almost dead,   170
He heaved him up, and looking on his face,
Beat down the bold waves with his triple mace,
Which mounted up, intending to have kissed him,
And fell in drops like tears, because they missed him.
Leander, being up, began to swim,
And looking back, saw Neptune follow him;
Whereat aghast, the poor soul gan to cry:
Oh, let me visit Hero ere I die!

The god put Helle's bracelet on his arm,
And swore the sea should never do him harm. 180
He clapped his plump cheeks, with his tresses played,
And smiling wantonly, his love bewrayed.
He watched his arms, and as they opened wide,
At every stroke betwixt them would he slide,
And steal a kiss, and then run out and dance,
And as he turned, cast many a lustful glance,
And threw him gaudy toys to please his eye,
And dive into the water, and there pry
Upon his breast, his thighs, and every limb,
And up again, and close beside him swim, 190
And talk of love. Leander made reply:
You are deceived, I am no woman, I.
Thereat smiled Neptune, and then told a tale
How that a shepherd, sitting in a vale,
Played with a boy so fair and kind,
As for his love both earth and heaven pined;
That of the cooling river durst not drink
Lest water-nymphs should pull him from the brink;
And when he sported in the fragrant lawns,
Goat-footed satyrs and up-staring fauns 200
Would steal him thence. Ere half this tale was done,
Ay me, Leander cried, th' enamoured sun,
That now should shine on Thetis' glassy bower,
Descends upon my radiant Hero's tower.
Oh, that these tardy arms of mine were wings!
And as he spake, upon the waves he springs.
Neptune was angry that he gave no ear,
And in his heart revenging malice bear;
He flung at him his mace, but as it went
He called it in, for love made him repent. 210
The mace returning back, his own hand hit,
As meaning to be venged for darting it.
When this fresh bleeding wound Leander viewed,
His color went and came, as if he rued
The grief which Neptune felt. In gentle breasts
Relenting thoughts, remorse, and pity rests;
And who have hard hearts and obdurate minds
But vicious, hare-brained, and illit'rate hinds?
The god, seeing him with pity to be moved,
Thereon concluded that he was beloved. 220
(Love is too full of faith, too credulous,
With folly and false hope deluding us.)
Wherefore, Leander's fancy to surprise,
To the rich oceän for gifts he flies.

'Tis wisdom to give much; a gift prevails
When deep persuading oratory fails.
By this, Leander being near the land,
Cast down his weary feet, and felt the sand.
Breathless albeit he were, he rested not
Till to the solitary tower he got, 230
And knocked and called, at which celestial noise
The longing heart of Hero much more joys
Than nymphs or shepherds when the timbrel rings,
Or crooked dolphin when the sailor sings;
She stayed not for her robes, but straight arose,
And drunk with gladness, to the door she goes;
Where seeing a naked man, she screeched for fear,
(Such sights as this to tender maids are rare)
And ran into the dark herself to hide.
Rich jewels in the dark are soonest spied; 240
Unto her was he led, or rather drawn,
By those white limbs which sparkled through the lawn.
The nearer that he came, the more she fled,
And seeking refuge, slipped into her bed.
Whereon Leander sitting, thus began,
Through numbing cold all feeble, faint, and wan:
    If not for love, yet, love, for pity sake,
Me in thy bed and maiden bosom take;
At least vouchsafe these arms some little room,
Who, hoping to embrace thee, cheerly swoom; 250
This head was beat with many a churlish billow,
And therefore let it rest upon thy pillow.
Herewith affrighted Hero shrunk away,
And in her lukewarm place Leander lay,
Whose lively heat like fire from heaven fet,
Would animate gross clay, and higher set
The drooping thoughts of base declining souls,
Than dreary Mars carousing nectar bowls.
His hands he cast upon her like a snare;
She, overcome with shame and sallow fear, 260
Like chaste Diana, when Actæon spied her,
Being suddenly betrayed, dived down to hide her;
And as her silver body downward went,
With both her hands she made the bed a tent,
And in her own mind thought herself secure,
O'ercast with dim and darksome coverture.
And now she lets him whisper in her ear,
Flatter, entreat, promise, protest, and swear;
Yet ever as he greedily assayed
To touch those dainties, she the harpy played, 270

And every limb did, as a soldier stout,
Defend the fort and keep the foeman out;
For though the rising iv'ry mount he scaled,
Which is with azure circling lines empaled,
Much like a globe (a globe may I term this,
By which love sails to regions full of bliss)
Yet there with Sisyphus he toiled in vain,
Till gentle parley did the truce obtain.
Wherein Leander on her quivering breast,
Breathless spoke something, and sighed out the rest;   280
Which so prevailed, as he with small ado
Enclosed her in his arms and kissed her too.
And every kiss to her was as a charm,
And to Leander as a fresh alarm,
So that the truce was broke, and she, alas,
Poor silly maiden, at his mercy was.
Love is not full of pity, as men say,
But deaf and cruel where he means to prey.
Even as a bird, which in our hands we wring,
Forth plunges and oft flutters with her wing,   290
She trembling strove; this strife of hers, like that
Which made the world, another world begat
Of unknown joy. Treason was in her thought,
And cunningly to yield herself she sought.
Seeming not won, yet won she was at length;
In such wars women use but half their strength.
Leander now, like Theban Hercules,
Entered the orchard of th' Hesperides,
Whose fruit none rightly can describe but he
That pulls or shakes it from the golden tree.   300
And now she wished this night were never done,
And sighed to think upon th' approaching sun;
For much it grieved her that the bright daylight
Should know the pleasure of this blessed night,
And them like Mars and Erycine displayed,
Both in each other's arms chained as they laid.
Again she knew not how to frame her look,
Or speak to him who in a moment took
That which so long so charily she kept;
And fain by stealth away she would have crept,   310
And to some corner secretly have gone,
Leaving Leander in the bed alone.
But as her naked feet were whipping out,
He on the sudden clinged her so about,
That mermaid-like unto the floor she slid,
One half appeared, the other half was hid.

Thus near the bed she blushing stood upright,
And from her countenance behold ye might
A kind of twilight break, which through the hair,
As from an orient cloud, glimpse here and there;   320
And round about the chamber this false morn
Brought forth the day before the day was born.
So Hero's ruddy cheek Hero betrayed,
And her all naked to his sight displayed;
Whence his admiring eyes more pleasure took
Than Dis on heaps of gold fixing his look.
By this, Apollo's golden harp began
To sound forth music to the oceän;
Which watchful Hesperus no sooner heard,
But he the day-bright-bearing car prepared,   330
And ran before, as harbinger of light,
And with his flaring beams mocked ugly night
Till she, o'ercome with anguish, shame, and rage,
Danged down to hell her loathsome carriage.
        Desunt nonnulla.

ELIZABETHAN MISCELLANIES

The Introduction and Notes are at page 947

FROM GEORGE GASCOIGNE'S *Hundreth Sundry Flowers,* [1573]

A strange passion of a lover

Amid my bale I bathe in bliss,
I swim in heaven, I sink in hell;
I find amends for every miss,
And yet my moan no tongue can
        tell.
I live and love (what would you
        more?)
As never lover lived before.

I laugh sometimes with little lust;
So jest I oft and feel no joy;
Mine ease is builded all on trust,
And yet mistrust breeds mine
        annoy.   10
I live and lack, I lack and have,
I have and miss the thing I crave.

These things seem strange, yet are
        they true.

Believe me, sweet, my state is such,
One pleasure which I would es-
        chew
Both slakes my grief and breeds my
        grutch.
So doth one pain which I would
        shun
Renew my joys where grief begun.

Then like the lark, that passed the
        night
In heavy sleep, with cares op-
        pressed,   20
Yet when she spies the pleasant
        light,
She sends sweet notes from out her
        breast,
So sing I now because I think

How joys approach when sorrows
    shrink.

And as fair Philomene, again,
Can watch and sing when other
    sleep,
And taketh pleasure in her
    pain,
To wray the woe that makes her
    weep,

So sing I now for to bewray
The loathsome life I lead alway. 30

The which to thee, dear wench, I
    write,
That know'st my mirth but not my
    moan.
I pray God grant thee deep delight
To live in joys when I am gone.
I cannot live—it will not be:
I die to think to part from thee.

The lover declareth his affection, together with the cause thereof

When first I thee beheld, in colors black and white,
Thy face in form well framed, with favor blooming still,
My burning breast in cares did choose his chief delight
With pen to paint thy praise, contrary to my skill;
Whose worthiness compared with this my rude devise,
I blush, and am abashed this work to enterprise.

But when I call to mind thy sundry gifts of grace,
Full fraught with manners meek, in happy quiet mind,
My hasty hand forthwith doth scribble on apace,
Lest willing heart might think it meant to come behind.   10
Thus do both hand and heart these careful meters use,
'Twixt hope and trembling fear, my duty to excuse.

Wherefore accept these lines, and banish dark disdain.
Be sure they come from one that loveth thee in chief;
And guerdon me, thy friend, in like with love again.
So shalt thou well be sure to yield me such relief
As only may redress my sorrows and my smart.
For proof whereof I pledge, dear dame, to thee my heart.

FROM RICHARD EDWARDS's *Paradise of Dainty Devices*, 1576

Amantium iræ amoris redintegratio est

In going to my naked bed as one that would have slept,
I heard a wife sing to her child, that long before had wept.
She sighëd sore and sang full sweet to bring the babe to rest,
That would not rest, but criëd still, in sucking at her breast.
She was full weary of her watch and grievëd with her child,
She rockëd it and rated it until on her it smiled.
Then did she say, Now have I found the proverb true to prove,
The falling out of faithful friends is the renewing of love.

Then took I paper, pen, and ink, this proverb for to write,
In register for to remain of such a worthy wight.   10
As she proceeded thus in song unto her little brat,
Much matter uttered she of weight, in place whereas she sat;
And provëd plain there was no beast, nor creature bearing life,
Could well be known to live in love without discord and strife.
Then kissëd she her little babe and sware, by God above,
The falling out of faithful friends is the renewing of love.

She said that neither king, ne prince, ne lord could live aright
Until their puissance they did prove, their manhood, and their might;
When manhood shall be matchëd so that fear can take no place,
Then weary works makes warriors each other to embrace,   20
And leave their force that failëd them, which did consume the rout,
That might before have lived their time and nature out.
Then did she sing as one that thought no man could her reprove,
The falling out of faithful friends is the renewing of love.

She said she saw no fish, ne fowl, nor beast within her haunt
That met a stranger in their kind, but could give it a taunt.
Since flesh might not endure, but rest must wrath succeed,
And force the fight to fall to play in pasture where they feed,
So noble nature can well end the works she hath begun,
And bridle well that will not cease her tragedy in some.   30
Thus in her song she oft rehearsed, as did her well behove,
The falling out of faithful friends is the renewing of love.

I marvel much, perdy, (quoth she) for to behold the rout,
To see man, woman, boy, and beast, to toss the world about.
Some kneel, some crouch, some beck, some check, and some can
    smoothly smile,
And some embrace others in arms, and there think many a wile.
Some stand aloof at cap and knee, some humble and some stout,
Yet are they never friends indeed until they once fall out!
Thus ended she her song, and said, before she did remove,
The falling out of faithful friends is the renewing of love.
                                            [*Richard Edwards*]

M. Edwards' May

When May is in his prime, then may each heart rejoice;
When May bedecks each branch with green, each bird strains forth
    his voice.
The lively sap creeps up into the blooming thorn;
The flowers which cold in prison kept now laughs the frost to scorn.
All nature's imps triumphs whiles joyful May doth last;
When May is gone, of all the year the pleasant time is past.

May makes the cheerful hue, May breeds and brings new blood;
May marcheth throughout every limb, May makes the merry mood.
May pricketh tender hearts their warbling notes to tune,—
Full strange it is, yet some we see do make their May in June.
Thus things are strangely wrought whiles joyful May doth last;
Take May in time, when May is gone the pleasant time is past.

All ye that live on earth, and have your May at will,
Rejoice in May, as I do now, and use your May with skill.
Use May while that you may, for May hath but his time,
When all the fruit is gone, it is too late the tree to climb.
Your liking and your lust is fresh whiles May doth last;
When May is gone, of all the year the pleasant time is past.

[Richard Edwards]

Being importunate, at the length he obtaineth

A. Shall I no way win you to grant my desire?
B. What woman will grant you the thing you require?
A. You only to love me is all that I crave.
B. You only to leave me is all I would have.
A. My dear, alas, now say not so!
B. To love you best I must say no.
A. Yet will I not flit. *B*. Then play on the bit.
A. I will. *B*. Do still. *A*. Yet kill not. *B*. I will not.
A. Make me your man! *B*. Beshrew me than!

A. The swifter I follow, then you fly away.
B. Swift hawks in their flying oft times miss their prey.
A. Yet some killeth deadly that fly to the mark.
B. You shall touch no feather thereof, take no cark!
A. Yet hope shall further my desire.
B. You blow the coals and raise no fire.
A. Yet will I not flit. *B*. Then play on the bit.
A. I will. *B*. Do still. *A*. Yet kill not. *B*. I will not.
A. Make me your man! *B*. Beshrew me than!

A. To love is no danger where true love is meant.
B. I will love no ranger lest that I repent.
A. My love is no ranger, I make God a vow.
B. To trust your smooth sayings I sure know not how.
A. Most truth I mean, as time shall well try.
B. No truth in men I oft espy.
A. Yet will I not flit. *B*. Then play on the bit.
A. I will. *B*. Do still. *A*. Yet kill not. *B*. I will not.
A. Make me your man! *B*. Beshrew me than!

A. Some women may say nay, and mean love most true.
B. Some women can make fools of as wise men as you.
A. In time I shall catch you, I know when and where.   20
B. I will soon dispatch you, you shall not come there.
A. Some speeds at length that oft have missed.
B. I am well armed, come when you list.
A. Yet will I not flit. *B.* Then play on the bit.
A. I will. *B.* Do still. *A.* Yet kill not. *B.* I will not.
A. Make me your man! *B.* Beshrew me than!

A. Yet work your kind kindly, grant me love for love.
B. I will use you friendly, as I shall you prove.
A. Most close you shall find me, I this do protest.
B. Then sure you shall bind me to grant your request.   40
A. Oh, happy thread now have I spun!
B. You sing before the conquest won!
A. Why, then, will you swerve? *B.* Even as you deserve.
A. Love still. *B.* I will. *A.* Yet kill not. *B.* I will not.
A. Make me your man! *B.* Come to me than!

[Richard Edwards?]

No pains comparable to his attempt

What watch, what woe, what want, what wrack,
Is due to those that toil the seas!
Life led with loss, of pains no lack,
In storms to win much restless ease;
A bedless board in sea's unrest
May hap to him that chanceth best.

How sundry sounds with lead and line
Unto the deep the shipman throws;
'No foot to spare,' he cries oft times,
'No near!' when 'How?' the master blows.   10
If Neptune frown, all be undone,
Straightway the ship the wrack hath won.

These dangers great do oft befall
On those that sheer upon the sand,—
Judge of their lives, the best who shall?
How vile it is, few understand.
Alack, who then may judge their game?
Not they which have not felt the same.

But they that fall in storms and wind,
And days and years have spent therein,   20

Such well may judge, since proof they find,
In rage no rest till calm begin.
No more, then, those that love do feign
Give judgment of true lovers' pain.

[*William Hunnis*]

Look or you leap

If thou in surety safe wilt sit,
If thou delight at rest to dwell,
Spend no more words than shall
    seem fit,
Let tongue in silence talk expel;
In all things that thou seest men
    bent,
See all, say nought, hold thee con-
    tent.

The doers doubt of praise or
    shame;
The lookers-on find surest ground,
They have the fruit, yet free from
    blame:
This doth persuade in all here
    meant,
See all, say nought, hold thee con-
    tent.

In worldly works degrees are
    three,
Makers, doers, and lookers-on:
The lookers-on have liberty
Both the others to judge upon;   10
Wherefore, in all, as men are bent,
See all, say nought, hold thee con-
    tent.

The proverb is not south and
    west
Which hath been said long time
    ago: 20
Of little meddling cometh rest,
The busy man ne'er wanted
    woe.
The best way is in all worlds
    sent,
See all, say nought, hold thee con-
    tent.

The makers oft are in fault
    found,

[*Jasper Heywood*]

FROM THOMAS PROCTER'S *Gorgeous Gallery of Gallant Inventions,*
1578

Respice finem

Lo, here the state of every mortal wight,
See here the fine of all their gallant joys;
Behold their pomp, their beauty, and delight,
Whereof they vaunt as safe from all annoys.
To earth the stout, the proud, the rich shall yield,
The weak, the meek, the poor shall shrouded lie
In dampish mold; the stout with spear and shield
Cannot defend himself when he shall die.
The proudest wight, for all his lively shows,
Shall leave his pomp, cut off by dreadful death;   10
The rich, whose hutch with golden ruddocks flows,

At length shall rest uncoined in dampish earth.
By nature's law we all are born to die,
But where or when, the best uncertain be;
No time prefixed, no goods our life shall buy,
Of dreadful death no friends shall set us free.
We subject be a thousand ways to death:
Small sickness moves the valiant's heart to fear;
A little push bereaves your breathing breath
Of brave delights, whereto you subject are.
Your world is vain; no trust in earth you find;
Your valiant'st prime is but a brittle glass;
Your pleasures vade, your thoughts a puff of wind;
Your ancient years are but a withered grass.

[*Thomas Procter*]

A proper sonnet, how time consumeth all earthly things

Ay me, ay me, I sigh to see the scythe afield,
Down goeth the grass, soon wrought to withered hay.
Ay me, alas! ay me, alas, that beauty needs must yield,
And princes pass, as grass doth fade away.

Ay me, ay me, that life cannot have lasting leave,
Nor gold take hold of everlasting joy.
Ay me, alas! ay me, alas, that time hath talents to receive,
And yet no time can make a sure stay.

Ay me, ay me, that wit cannot have wishëd choice,
Nor wish can win that will desires to see.
Ay me, alas! ay me, alas, that mirth can promise no rejoice,
Nor study tell what afterward shall be.

Ay me, ay me, that no sure staff is given to age,
Nor age can give sure wit that youth will take.
Ay me, alas! ay me, alas, that no counsel wise and sage
Will shun the show that all doth mar and make.

Ay me, ay me, come time, shear on and shake thy hay,
It is no boot to balk thy bitter blows.
Ay me, alas! ay me, alas, come time, take every thing away,
For all is thine, be it good or bad that grows.

A true description of love

Ask what love is? It is a passïon
Begun with rest and pampered up in play,
Planted on sight, and nourished day by day,
With talk at large, for hope to graze upon.
It is a short joy, long sought and soon gone;
An endless maze wherein our wills do stray;

A guileful gain, repentance is the pay;
A great fire bred of small occasïon;
A plague to make our frailty to us known,
Where we thereby are subject to their lay   10
Whose frailty ought to lean until our stay,
In case ourselves this custom had not known,
Of hope and health, such creatures for to pray
Whose glory resteth chiefly on denay.

The lover in the praise of his beloved and comparison of her beauty

Not she for whom proud Troy did fall and burn,
The Greeks eke slain, that bloody race did run;
Nor she for spite that did Acteon turn
Into an hart her beauty coy did shun;
Nor she whose blood upon Achilles' tomb,
Whose face would tame a tiger's heart;
Nor she that won by wise of Paris' doom
Th' apple of gold for beauty to her part;
Nor she whose eyes did pierce true Troilus' breast,
And made him yield that knew in love no law,—   10
Might be compared to the fairest and the best,
Whom nature made to keep the rest in awe,
For beauty's sake sent down from Jove above.
Thrice happy is he that can attain her love!

The lover exhorteth his lady to be constant
To the tune of, *Attend thee, go play thee*

Not light of love, lady!
Though fancy do prick thee,
Let constancy possess thy heart.
Well worthy of blaming
They be, and defaming,
From plighted troth which back do
    start.
    Dear dame,
Then fickleness banish
And folly extinguish,
Be skillful in guiding   10
    And stay thee from sliding,
    And stay thee, &c.

The constant are praisëd,
Their fame high is raisëd,

Their worthiness doth pierce the
    sky.
The fickle are blamëd,
Their lightilove shamëd,
Their foolishness doth make them
    die.
    As well
Can Cressid bear witness,   20
Forge of her own distress,
Whom leprosy painted
    And penury tainted,
    And penury, &c.

Still muses are busy
To tell us of Thisbe,

Whom steadfastness doth much
    commend.
And Camma is placëd
To blame the defacëd,
That light of love do send.   30
    Phedra
Is checked most duly
Because that untruly,
Forced thereto by love light,
    She slayeth Hippolite,
    She slayeth, &c.

A spring of annoyance
And well of disturbance
New-fangleness in love hath been:
It killeth the master,   40
It poisons the taster,
No worldly wight by it doth win.
    Therefore,
Good lady, be constant,
So shall you not be shent
But worthily praisëd
    As you have deservëd,
    As you have, &c.

FROM H. C.'s *Forest of Fancy*, 1579

A plain description of perfect friendship

True friendship unfeignëd
Doth rest unrestrainëd,
    No terror can tame it.
Not gaining nor losing
Nor gallant gay glozing
    Can ever reclaim it.

In pain and in pleasure
The most truest measure
    That may be desirëd
Is loyal love deemëd,   10
Of wisdom esteemëd,
    And chiefly requirëd.

The strange pangs of a poor passionate lover

Not as I am, nor as I wish to be,
But as false fortune frames my froward fate,
Even so I am not bound nor fully free,
Not quite forlorn, nor yet in quiet state.
I wish for death, and yet the death I hate,
This life lead I, which life is wondrous strange,
Yet for no life would I my life exchange.
I seek the sight of that I sigh to see,
I joy in that which breeds my great unrest,—
Such contraries do daily cumber me   10
As in one thing I find both joy and rest,
Which gain he gets that is Cupido's guest;
For whom he catcheth in his cursed snare
He gives great hope, yet kills his heart with care.

FROM *Chetham Ms.* 8012

Epigram

Were I a king, I could command content;
Were I obscure, hidden should be my cares;
Or were I dead, no cares should me torment,

Nor hopes, nor hates, nor loves, nor griefs, nor fears.
A doubtful choice, of these three which to crave—
A kingdom, or a cottage, or a grave.

[*Edward de Vere, Earl of Oxford*]

Answered thus by Sir P. S.

Wert thou a king, yet not command content,
Sith empire none thy mind could yet suffice;
Wert thou obscure, still cares would thee torment;
But wert thou dead, all care and sorrow dies.
An easy choice, of these three which to crave:
No kingdom, nor a cottage, but a grave.

[*Sir Philip Sidney*]

Another, of another mind [1]

A king, oh boon for my aspiring mind!
A cottage makes a country swad rejoice;
And as for death, I like him in his kind,
But God forbid that he should be my choice!
A kingdom or a cottage or a grave,—
Nor last, nor next, but first and best I crave;
The rest I can whenas I list enjoy,
Till then salute me thus, *Vive le Roy!*

[*F. M.*]

Another, of another mind [2]

The greatest kings do least command content,
For greatest cares do still attend a crown;
A grave all happy fortunes do prevent,
Making the noble equal with the clown;
A quiet country life to lead I crave,—
A cottage then; no kingdom nor a grave.

FROM *Verses of Praise and Joy written upon Her Majesty's
Preservation,* 1586

Tichborne's elegy, written with his own hand in the Tower before his execution

My prime of youth is but a frost of cares,
My feast of joy is but a dish of pain,
My crop of corn is but a field of tares,
And all my good is but vain hope of gain;
The day is past, and yet I saw no sun,
And now I live, and now my life is done.

My tale was heard and yet it was not told,
My fruit is fall'n and yet my leaves are green,
My youth is spent and yet I am not old,
I saw the world and yet I was not seen;   10
My thread is cut and yet it is not spun,
And now I live, and now my life is done.

I sought my death and found it in my womb,
I looked for life and saw it was a shade,
I trod the earth and knew it was my tomb,
And now I die, and now I was but made;
My glass is full, and now my glass is run,
And now I live, and now my life is done.

[Chidiock Tichborne]

FROM R. S.'s Phœnix Nest, 1593

[The time when first]

The time when first I fell in love,
  Which now I must lament;
The year wherein I lost such time
  To compass my content;

The day wherein I saw too late
  The follies of a lover;
The hour wherein I found such
    loss
As care cannot recover;

And last, the minute of mishap,   9
  Which makes me thus to plain
The doleful fruits of lovers' suits,
  Which labor lose in vain:

Doth make me solemnly protest,
  As I with pain do prove,
There is no time, year, day, nor
    hour,
Nor minute, good to love.

[O night, O jealous night]

O night, O jealous night, repugnant to my pleasures,
  O night so long desired yet cross to my content,
There's none but only thou that can perform my pleasures,
  Yet none but only thou that hindereth my intent.

Thy beams, thy spiteful beams, thy lamps that burn too brightly,
  Discover all my trains, and naked lay my drifts;
That night by night I hope, yet fail my purpose nightly,
  Thy envious glaring gleam defeateth so my shifts.

Sweet night, withhold thy beams, withhold them till to-morrow,
  Whose joys, in lack so long, a hell of torments breeds;   10
Sweet night, sweet gentle night, do not prolong my sorrow,
  Desire is guide to me, and love no lode-star needs.

Let sailors gaze on stars and moon so freshly shining,
  Let them that miss the way be guided by the light;
I know my lady's bower, there needs no more divining,
  Affection sees in dark, and love hath eyes by night.

Dame Cynthia, couch awhile, hold in thy horns for shining,
  And glad not low'ring night with thy too glorious rays;
But be she dim and dark, tempestuous and repining,
  That in her spite my sport may work thy endless praise.   20

And when my will is wrought, then, Cynthia, shine, good lady,
  All other nights and days in honor of that night,
That happy, heavenly night, that night so dark and shady,
  Wherein my love had eyes that lighted my delight.

[*Set me where Phœbus' heat*]

Set me where Phœbus' heat the flowers slayeth
  Or where continual snow withstands his forces;
Set me where he his temp'rate rays displayeth,
  Or where he comes, or where he never courses;

Set me in fortune's grace, or else dischargëd,
  In sweet and pleasant air, or dark and glooming,
Where days and nights are lesser or enlargëd,
  In years of strength, in failing age or blooming;

Set me in heaven or earth, or in the center;
  Low in a vale, or on a mountain placëd;   10
Set me to danger, peril, and adventure,
  Gracëd by fame, or infamy disgracëd:
    Set me to these, or any other trial,
    Except my mistress' anger and denial.

[*Sought by the world*]

Sought by the world, and hath the world disdained,
  Is she, my heart, for whom thou dost endure;
Unto whose grace, sith kings have not obtained,
  Sweet is thy choice, though loss of life be sour;
    Yet to the man whose youth such pains must prove
    No better end than that which comes by love.

Steer then thy course unto the port of death
  (Sith thy hard hap no better hap may find)
Where, when thou shalt unlade thy latest breath,
  Envy herself shall swim, to save thy mind   10
    Whose body sunk in search to gain that shore
    Where many a prince had perishëd before.

And yet, my heart, it might have been foreseen,
  Sith skillful med'cines mends each kind of grief,
Then in my breast full safely hadst thou been;
  But thou, my heart, wouldst never me believe
    Who told thee true when first thou didst aspire,
    Death was the end of every such desire.

FROM JOHN BODENHAM'S (?) *England's Helicon*, 1600

A nymph's disdain of love

  Hey down, a down, did Dian sing,
    Amongst her virgins sitting,
  Than love there is no vainer thing,
    For maidens most unfitting.
  And so think I, with a down, down, derry.

  When women knew no woe,
    But lived themselves to please,
  Men's feigning guiles they did not know,
    The ground of their disease.
  Unborn was false suspect,
    No thought of jealousy;
  From wanton toys and fond affect
    The virgin's life was free.
      Hey down, a down, did Dian sing, &c.

  At length men usèd charms;
    To which what maids gave ear,
  Embracing gladly endless harms,
    Anon enthrallèd were.
  Thus women welcomed woe
    Disguised in name of love;
  A jealous hell, a painted show,
    So shall they find that prove.

  Hey down, a down, did Dian sing,
    Amongst her virgins sitting,
  Than love there is no vainer thing,
    For virgins most unfitting.
  And so think I, with a down, down, derry.

Phillida's love-call to her Corydon, and his replying

Phil. Corydon, arise my Corydon,
      Titan shineth clear.
Cor. Who is it that calleth Corydon?
      Who is it that I hear?

Phil. Phillida, thy true love, calleth thee.
     Arise then, arise then,
          Arise and keep thy flock with me.
Cor. Phillida, my true love, is it she?
     I come then, I come then,
          I come and keep my flock with thee.   10

Phil. Here are cherries ripe, my Corydon,
     Eat them for my sake.
Cor. Here's my oaten pipe, my lovely one,
     Sport for thee to make.
Phil. Here are threads, my true love, fine as silk,
     To knit thee, to knit thee
          A pair of stockings white as milk.
Cor. Here are reeds, my true love, fine and neat,
     To make thee, to make thee
          A bonnet to withstand the heat.   20

Phil. I will gather flowers, my Corydon,
     To set in thy cap.
Cor. I will gather pears, my lovely one,
     To put in thy lap.
Phil. I will buy my true love garters gay
     For Sundays, for Sundays,
          To wear about his legs so tall.
Cor. I will buy my true love yellow say
     For Sundays, for Sundays,
          To wear about her middle small.   30

Phil. When my Corydon sits on a hill,
     Making melody,—
Cor. When my lovely one goes to her wheel,
     Singing cheerily,—
Phil. Sure methinks my true love doth excel
     For sweetness, for sweetness,
          Our Pan, that old Arcadian knight.
Cor. And methinks my true love bears the bell
     For clearness, for clearness,
          Beyond the nymphs that be so bright.   40

Phil. Had my Corydon, my Corydon,
     Been, alack, my swain,—
Cor. Had my lovely one, my lovely one,
     Been in Ida plain,—
Phil. Cynthia Endymion had refused,
     Preferring, preferring
          My Corydon to play withal;

Cor. The queen of love had been excused,
        Bequeathing, bequeathing
            My Phillida the golden ball.   50

Phil. Yonder comes my mother, Corydon,
        Whither shall I fly?
Cor. Under yonder beech, my lovely one,
        While she passeth by.
Phil. Say to her thy true love was not here.
        Remember, remember,
            To-morrow is another day.
Cor. Doubt me not, my true love. Do not fear.
        Farewell then, farewell then,
            Heaven keep our loves alway.   60

The nymph Selvagia, her song

Shepherd, who can pass such wrong,
    And a life in woes so deep?
Which to live is too too long,
    As it is too short to weep.

Grievous sighs in vain I waste,
    Leesing my affiance, and
I perceive my hope at last
    With a candle in the hand.

What time then to hope among
Bitter hopes that never sleep? 10

When this life is too too long,
    As it is too short to weep.

This grief which I feel so rife,
    Wretch, I do deserve as hire,
Since I came to put my life
    In the hands of my desire.

Then cease not my complaints so strong,
    For, though life her course doth keep,
It is not to live so long,
    As it is too short to weep.   20
                    [*Bartholomew Young*]

Melisea, her song in scorn of her shepherd Narcissus

Young shepherd, turn aside and move
    Me not to follow thee;
For I will neither kill with love,
    Nor love shall not kill me.

Since I will live and never show,
    Then die not, for my love I will not give,
For I will never have thee love me so,
    As I do mean to hate thee while I live.

That since the lover so doth prove
  His death, as thou dost see,
Be bold, I will not kill with love,   10
  Nor love shall not kill me.

[Bartholomew Young]

A palinode

As withereth the primrose by the river,
As fadeth summer's sun from gliding fountains,
As vanisheth the light-blown bubble ever,
As melteth snow upon the mossy mountains:
So melts, so vanisheth, so fades, so withers
The rose, the shine, the bubble, and the snow,
Of praise, pomp, glory, joy, which short life gathers,
Fair praise, vain pomp, sweet glory, brittle joy.
The withered primrose by the mourning river,
The faded summer's sun from weeping fountains,   10
The light-blown bubble, vanishëd for ever,
The molten snow upon the naked mountains,
  Are emblems that the treasures we uplay
  Soon wither, vanish, fade, and melt away.

For as the snow, whose lawn did overspread
Th' ambitious hills which giant-like did threat
To pierce the heaven with their aspiring head,
Naked and bare doth leave their craggy seat;
Whenas the bubble, which did empty fly
The dalliance of the undiscernëd wind   20
On whose calm rolling waves it did rely,
Hath shipwreck made where it did dalliance find;
And when the sunshine which dissolved the snow,
Colored the bubble with a pleasant vary,
And made the rathe and timely primrose grow,
Swarth clouds withdrawn, which longer time do tarry:
  Oh, what is praise, pomp, glory, joy, but so
  As shine by fountains, bubbles, flowers, or snow?

[Edmund Bolton]

A canzon pastoral in honor of Her Majesty

Alas, what pleasure, now the pleasant spring
  Hath given place
To harsh black frosts the sad ground covering,
  Can we, poor we, embrace?
When every bird on every branch can sing

Nought but this note of woe, alas!
Alas, this note of woe why should we sound?
With us, as May, September hath a prime;
Then, birds and branches, your *alas* is fond,
Which call upon the absent summer-time.   10
     For did flowers make our May
     Or the sun-beams your day,
When night and winter did the world embrace,
Well might you wail your ill, and sing, alas!

Lo, matron-like the earth herself attires
    In habit grave;
Naked the fields are, bloomless are the briers,
    Yet we a summer have,
Who in our clime kindleth these living fires,
    Which blooms can on the briers save.   20
No ice doth crystallize the running brook,
No blast deflowers the flower-adornëd field;
Crystal is clear, but clearer is the look
Which to our climes these living fires doth yield;
    Winter, though everywhere,
    Hath no abiding here,
On brooks and briers she doth rule alone,—
The sun which lights our world is always one.
                  [*Edmund Bolton*]

To Colin Clout

Beauty sat bathing by a spring
  Where fairest shades did hide
    her;
The winds blew calm, the birds
    did sing,
  The cool streams ran beside her.
My wanton thoughts enticed mine
    eye
  To see what was forbidden,
But better memory said fie!
  So vain desire was chidden.
    Hey nonny, nonny, &c.

Into a slumber then I fell,   10
  When fond imagination
Seemed to see, but could not tell
  Her feature or her fashion.
But even as babes in dreams do
    smile
  And sometime fall a-weep-
    ing,
So I awaked, as wise this while
  As when I fell a-sleeping.
    Hey nonny, nonny, &c.
       [*Anthony Munday*]

FROM FRANCIS DAVISON's *Poetical Rhapsody*, 1602

Ode

Absence, hear thou my protestation
    Against thy strength,
    Distance, and length;

Do what thou canst for alteration,
　　For hearts of truest mettle
　　Absence doth join, and time doth settle.

Who loves a mistress of such quality,
　　He soon hath found
　　Affection's ground
Beyond time, place, and all mortality.   10
　　To hearts that cannot vary
　　Absence is present, time doth tarry.

My senses want their outward motions,
　　Which now within
　　Reason doth win,
Redoubled in her secret notions;
　　Like rich men that take pleasure
　　In hiding, more than handling, treasure.

By absence this good means I gain,
　　That I can catch her   20
　　Where none can watch her,
In some close corner of my brain;
　　There I embrace and kiss her,
　　And so I both enjoy and miss her.

　　　　　　　　　　　　　　[John Hoskins?]

Madrigal

My love in her attire doth show her wit,
　　It doth so well become her;
For every season she hath dressings fit,
　　For winter, spring, and summer.
　　No beauty she doth miss
　　When all her robes are on;
　　But beauty's self she is
　　When all her robes are gone.

To time

Eternal time, that wastest without waste,
　　That art and art not, diest and livest still;
Most slow of all and yet of greatest haste,
　　Both ill and good, and neither good nor ill:
　　How can I justly praise thee or dispraise?
　　Dark are thy nights, but bright and clear thy days.

Both free and scarce, thou giv'st and tak'st again;
  Thy womb, that all doth breed, is tomb to all;
What so by thee hath life by thee is slain;
  From thee do all things rise, by thee they fall;   10
    Constant, inconstant, moving, standing still.
    Was, Is, Shall be, do thee both breed and kill.

I lose thee while I seek to find thee out.
  The farther off, the more I follow thee;
The faster hold, the greater cause of doubt;
  Was, Is, I know; but *Shall* I cannot see.
    All things by thee are measured; thou, by none;
    All are in thee; thou, in thyself alone.

                                            [*A. W.*]

Upon visiting his lady by moonlight

The night, say all, was made for rest;
  And so say I, but not for all:
To them the darkest nights are best,
  Which give them leave asleep to fall;
    But I that seek my rest by light
    Hate sleep, and praise the clearest night.

Bright was the moon, as bright as day,
  And Venus glistered in the west,
Whose light did lead the ready way
  That brought me to my wishëd rest;   10
    Then each of them increased their light
    While I enjoyed her heavenly sight.

Say, gentle dames, what moved your mind
  To shine so bright above your wont?
Would Phœbe fair Endymion find?
  Would Venus see Adonis hunt?
    No, no, you fearëd by her sight
    To lose the praise of beauty bright.

At last for shame you shrunk away,
  And thought to reave the world of light;   20
Then shone my dame with brighter ray
  Than that which comes from Phœbus' sight:
    None other light but hers I praise
    Whose nights are clearer than the days.

                                            [*A. W.*]

A fiction

How Cupid made a nymph wound herself with his arrows

It chanced of late, a shepherd's swain,
That went to seek a strayëd sheep,
Within a thicket on the plain
Espied a dainty nymph asleep.

Her golden hair o'erspread her face,
Her careless arms abroad were cast,
Her quiver had her pillow's place,
Her breast lay bare to every blast.

The shepherd stood and gazed his fill;
Nought durst he do, nought durst he say,   10
When chance, or else perhaps his will,
Did guide the god of love that way.

The crafty boy that sees her sleep—
Whom, if she waked, he durst not see—
Behind her closely seeks to creep,
Before her nap should ended be.

There come, he steals her shafts away
And puts his own into their place;
Ne dares he any longer stay,
But ere she wakes hies thence apace.   20

Scarce was he gone when she awakes
And spies the shepherd standing by.
Her bended bow in haste she takes,
And at the simple swain let fly.

Forth flew the shaft and pierced his heart,
That to the ground he fell with pain;
Yet up again forthwith he start,
And to the nymph he ran amain.

Amazed to see so strange a sight,
She shot, and shot, but all in vain;   30
The more his wounds, the more his might;
Love yieldeth strength in midst of pain.

Her angry eyes are great with tears;
She blames her hands, she blames her skill;

The bluntness of her shafts she fears,
And try them on herself she will.

Take heed, sweet nymph, try not the shaft,
Each little touch will prick the heart.
Alas, thou knowest not Cupid's craft,—
Revenge is joy, the end is smart.   40

Yet try she will, and prick some bare;
Her hands were gloved, and next to hand
Was that fair breast, that breast so rare,
That made the shepherd senseless stand.

That breast she pricked, and through that breast
Love finds an entry to her heart;
At feeling of this new-come guest,
Lord, how the gentle nymph doth start!

She runs not now, she shoots no more.
Away she throws both shafts and bow;   50
She seeks for that she shunned before,
She thinks the shepherd's haste too slow.

Though mountains meet not, lovers may;
So others do, and so do they.
The god of love sits on a tree
And laughs that pleasant sight to see.

                                        [*A. W.*]

Sonnet

Were I as base as is the lowly plain,
And you, my love, as high as heav'n above,
Yet should the thoughts of me, your humble swain,
Ascend to heaven in honor of my love.
Were I as high as heav'n above the plain,
And you, my love, as humble and as low
As are the deepest bottoms of the main,
Wheresoe'er you were, with you my love should go.
Were you the earth, dear love, and I the skies,
My love should shine on you like to the sun,   10
And look upon you with ten thousand eyes,
Till heaven waxed blind and till the world were dun.
    Wheresoe'er I am, below, or else above you,
    Wheresoe'er you are, my heart shall truly love you.
                                [*Joshua Sylvester?*]

Commendation of her beauty, stature, behavior, and wit

Some there are as fair to see to,
But by art and not by nature;
Some as tall and goodly be, too,
But want beauty to their stature;
Some have gracious kind behavior,
But are foul or simple creatures;
Some have wit, but want sweet favor,
Or are proud of their good features.
    Only you in court or city
    Are both fair, tall, kind, and witty.   10

[Francis Davison]

Upon his timorous silence in her presence

Are lovers full of fire?
How comes it then my verses are so cold?
    And how, when I am nigh her,
And fit occasion wills me to be bold,
The more I burn, the more I do desire,
    The less I dare require.
Ah, love, this is thy wondrous art,
To freeze the tongue, and fire the heart.

[Francis Davison]

To Cupid

Love, if a god thou art,
    Then evermore thou must
    Be merciful and just.
If thou be just, oh, wherefore doth thy dart
Wound mine alone, and not my lady's heart?

If merciful, then why
    Am I to pain reserved
    Who have thee truly served?
While she that by thy power sets not a fly
Laughs thee to scorn and lives in liberty?   10

Then if a god thou wouldst accounted be,
Heal me like her, or else wound her like me.

[Francis Davison]

From Francis Davison's *Poetical Rhapsody*, 1608

[*The sound of thy sweet name*]

The sound of thy sweet name, my dearest treasure,
  Delights me more than sight of other faces;
A glimpse of thy sweet face breeds me more pleasure
  Than any other's kindest words and graces.

One gracious word that from thy lips proceedeth
  I value more than others' dove-like kisses,
And thy chaste kiss in my conceit exceedeth
  Others' embraces, and love's chiefest blisses.

[Francis Davison]

A sonnet of the moon

Look how the pale queen of the silent night
Doth cause the ocean to attend upon her,
And he, as long as she is in his sight,
With her full tide is ready her to honor.
But when the silver waggon of the moon
Is mounted up so high he cannot follow,
The sea calls home his crystal waves to moan,
And with low ebb doth manifest his sorrow.
So you that are the sovereign of my heart
Have all my joys attending on your will;
My joys low-ebbing when you do depart,
When you return their tide my heart doth fill.
  So as you come and as you do depart,
  Joys ebb and flow within my tender heart.

[Charles Best]

10

SONNET-SEQUENCES

The Introduction and Notes are at page 952

From Giles Fletcher's *Licia*, [1593]

To the Reader.

*I had thought, courteous and gentle reader, not to have troubled
thy patience with these lines; but that, in the neglect thereof, I should
either scorn thee, as careless of thine opinion, a thing savoring of a*

proud humor; or despair to obtain thy favor, which I am loath to conceive of thy good nature.

If I were known, I would entreat in the best manner; and speak for him whom thou knewest. But being not known, thou speakest not against me; and therefore I much care not. For this kind of poetry wherein I wrote, I did it only to try my humor. And for the matter of love, it may be I am so devoted to some one into whose hands these may light by chance that she may say (which thou now sayest) that surely he is in love; which if she do, then have I the full recompense of my labor, and the poems have dealt sufficiently for the discharge of their own duty. . . .

If thou muse what my Licia is: take her to be some Diana, at the least chaste; or some Minerva; no Venus—fairer far. It may be she is learning's image, or some heavenly wonder, which the precisest may not mislike. Perhaps under that name I have shadowed Discipline. It may be I mean that kind courtesy which I found at the patroness of these poems; it may be some college. It may be my conceit, and portend nothing. . . .

Licia

Sad, all alone, not long I musing sat,
But that my thoughts compelled me to aspire;
A laurel garland in my hand I gat,
So the Muses I approached the nigher.
My suit was this, a poet to become,
To drink with them, and from the heavens be fed.
Phœbus denied, and sware there was no room,
Such to be poets as fond fancy led.
With that I mourned and sat me down to weep;
Venus she smiled, and smiling to me said,   10
Come drink with me, and sit thee still, and sleep.
This voice I heard; and Venus I obeyed.
That poison sweet hath done me all this wrong,
For now of love must needs be all my song.

———

First did I fear, when first my love began,
Possessed in fits by watchful jealousy;
I sought to keep what I by favor wan,
And brooked no partner in my love to be.
But tyrant sickness fed upon my love,
And spread his ensigns, dyed with color white;
Then was suspicion glad for to remove,
And, loving much, did fear to lose her quite.
Erect, fair sweet, the colors thou didst wear;
Dislodge thy griefs, the short'ners of content;   10

For now of life, not love, is all my fear,
Lest life and love be both together spent.
 Live but, fair love, and banish thy disease,
 And love, kind heart, both when and whom thou please.

Seven are the lights that wander in the skies,
And at these seven I wonder in my love:
So see the moon, how pale she doth arise,
Standing amazed as though she durst not move;
So is my sweet much paler than the snow,
Constant her looks, those looks that cannot change.
Mercury the next, a god sweet-tongued we know,
But her sweet voice doth wonders speak more strange.
The rising sun doth boast him of his pride,
And yet my love is far more fair than he.
The warlike Mars can wieldless weapons guide,
But yet that god is far more weak than she.
The lovely Venus seemeth to be fair,
But at her best, my love is far more bright.
Saturn for age with groans doth dim the air,
Whereas my love with smiles doth give it light.
 Gaze at her brows, where heaven ingrafted is;
 Then sigh, and swear, there is no heaven but this.

I live, sweet love, whereas the gentle wind
Murmurs with sport in midst of thickest boughs,
Where loving woodbine doth the harbor bind,
And chirping birds do echo forth my vows;
Where strongest elm can scarce support the vine,
And sweetest flowers enameled have the ground;
Where Muses dwell; and yet hereat repine
That on the earth so rare a place was found.
But winds delight, I wish to be content;
I praise the woodbine, but I take no joy;
I moan the birds that music thus have spent;
As for the rest, they breed but mine annoy.
 Live then, fair Licia, in this place alone;
 Then shall I joy though all of these were gone.

In time the strong and stately turrets fall,
In time the rose and silver lilies die,
In time the monarchs captive are, and thrall,
In time the sea and rivers are made dry;
The hardest flint in time doth melt asunder;
Still-living fame in time doth fade away;
The mountains proud we see in time come under;

And earth, for age, we see in time decay.
The sun in time forgets for to retire
From out the east where he was wont to rise;
The basest thoughts we see in time aspire,
And greedy minds in time do wealth despise.
 Thus all, sweet fair, in time must have an end,
 Except thy beauty, virtues, and thy friend.

10

Whenas her lute is tunëd to her voice,
The air grows proud for honor of that sound,
And rocks do leap to show how they rejoice
That in the earth such music should be found.
Whenas her hair, more worth, more pale, than gold,
Like silver thread lies wafting in the air,
Diana-like she looks, but yet more bold,
Cruel in chase, more chaste and yet more fair.
Whenas she smiles, the clouds for envy breaks;
She Jove, in pride, encounters with a check;
The sun doth shine for joy whenas she speaks;
Thus heaven and earth do homage at her beck.
 Yet all these graces blots, not graces, are,
 If you, my love, of love do take no care.

10

Like Memnon's rock, touched with the rising sun,
Which yields a sound and echoes forth a voice,
But when it's drowned in western seas is done,
And drowsy-like leaves off to make a noise;
So I, my love, enlightened with your shine,
A poet's skill within my soul I shroud—
Not rude, like that which finer wits decline,
But such as Muses to the best allowed.
But when your figure and your shape is gone,
I speechless am, like as I was before;
Or if I write, my verse is filled with moan,
And blurred with tears by falling in such store;
 Then muse not, Licia, if my muse be slack,
 For when I wrote I did thy beauty lack.

10

If sad complaint would show a lover's pain,
Or tears express the torments of my heart,
If melting sighs would ruth and pity gain,
Or true laments but ease a lover's smart;

Then should my plaints the thunder's noise surmount,
And tears like seas should flow from out my eyes;

Then sighs like air should far exceed all count,
And true laments with sorrow dim the skies.

But plaints and tears, laments and sighs I spend,
Yet greater torments do my heart destroy;
I could all these from out my heart still send,
If after these I might my love enjoy.

But heavens conspire, and heavens I must obey,
That seeking love I still must want my ease;
For greatest joys are tempered with delay,
Things soon obtained do least of all us please.

My thoughts repine and think the time too long;
My love, impatient, wisheth to obtain;
I blame the heavens that do me all this wrong,
To make me loved, and will not ease my pain.

No pain like this, to love and not enjoy;
No grief like this, to mourn and not be heard;
No time so long as that which breeds annoy;
No hell like this, to love and be deferred.

But heaven shall stand, and earth inconstant fly,
The sun shall freeze, and ice inconstant burn,
The mountains flow and all the earth be dry,
Ere time shall force my loving thoughts to turn.

Do you resolve, sweet love, to do the same;
Say that you do, and seal it with a kiss.
Then shall our truths the heavens' unkindness blame,
That can not hurt, yet shows their spite in this.

The silly prentice, bound for many years,
Doth hope that time his service will release;
The town besieged that lives in midst of fears
Doth hope in time the cruel wars will cease.

The toiling plowman sings in hope to reap,
The tossèd bark expecteth for a shore;
The boy at school to be at play doth leap
And straight forgets the fear he had before.

If those by hope do joy in their distress,
And constant are in hope to conquer time,

Then let not hope in us, sweet friend, be less,
And cause our love to wither in the prime.

Let me conspire, and time will have an end,
So both of us in time shall have a friend.

FROM BARNABE BARNES's *Parthenophil and Parthenophe*, [1593]

Mistress, behold in this true-speaking glass
    Thy beauty's graces, of all women rarest,
      Where thou mayst find how largely they surpass
    And stain in glorious loveliness the fairest.
But read, sweet mistress, and behold it nearer,
    Pond'ring my sorrow's outrage with some pity;
    Then shalt thou find no worldly creature dearer
    Than thou to me, thyself in each love ditty.
But in this mirror equally compare
    Thy matchless beauty with mine endless grief;   10
    There like thyself none can be found so fair,
Of chiefest pains there, are my pains the chief.
    Betwixt these both, this one doubt shalt thou find:
    Whether are here extremest in their kind?

Madrigal

Once in an arbor was my mistress sleeping,
    With rose and woodbine woven,
    Whose person thousand graces had in keeping;
    Where for mine heart her heart's hard flint was cloven
To keep him safe. Behind stood, pertly peeping,
    Poor Cupid, softly creeping,
    And drave small birds out of the myrtle bushes,
    Scared with his arrows; who sate cheeping
On every sprig; whom Cupid calls and hushes
    From branch to branch; whiles I, poor soul, sate weeping   16
    To see her breathe (not knowing)
Incense into the clouds, and bless with breath
The winds and air; whiles Cupid underneath
With birds, with songs, nor any posies throwing,
    Could her awake—
Each noise sweet lullaby was, for her sake.

Ah, sweet content, where is thy mild abode?
    Is it with shepherds and light-hearted swains
    Which sing upon the downs and pipe abroad,
    Tending their flocks and cattle on the plains?
Ah, sweet content, where dost thou safely rest?

In heaven, with angels? which the praises sing
Of him that made, and rules at his behest,
The minds and hearts of every living thing.
Ah, sweet content, where doth thine harbor hold?
    Is it in churches, with religious men
    Which please the gods with prayers manifold,
    And in their studies meditate it then?
Whether thou dost in heaven or earth appear,
Be where thou wilt, thou wilt not harbor here!

Burn on, sweet fire, for I live by that fuel
    Whose smoke is as an incense to my soul.
Each sigh prolongs my smart. Be fierce and cruel,
    My fair Parthenophe. Frown and control,
Vex, torture, scald, disgrace me. Do thy will!
    Stop up thine ears; with flint immure thine heart,
And kill me with thy looks, if they would kill.
Thine eyes, those crystal phials which impart
The perfect balm to my dead-wounded breast,
    Thine eyes, the quivers whence those darts were drawn
Which me to thy love's bondage have addressed;
    Thy smile and frown, night-star and daylight's dawn,
Burn on, frown on, vex, stop thine ears, torment me!
    More, for thy beauty borne, would not repent me.

This careful head, with divers thoughts distressed,
    My fancy's chronicler, my sorrow's muse;
    These watchful eyes, whose heedless aim I curse,
    Love's sentinels, and fountains of unrest;
This tongue still trembling, herald fit addressed
    To my love's grief (than any torment worse);
    This heart, true fortress of my spotless love,
    And rageous furnace of my long desire:
Of these, by nature, am I not possessed,
    Though nature their first means in me did move.
    But thou, dear sweet, with thy love's holy fire,
    My head grief's anvil made, with cares oppressed;
Mine eyes, a spring; my tongue, a leaf, wind-shaken;
    My heart, a wasteful wilderness forsaken.

Ode

When I walk forth into the woods,
With heavy passion to complain,
I view the trees with blushing buds
Ashamed, or grievèd at my pain.
There amaranth, with rosy stain,
Me pitying, doth his leaves ingrain.

When I pass pensive to the shore,
The water-birds about me fly,
As if they mourned; when rivers roar,
Chiding thy wrathful cruelty,   10
Halcyon watcheth warily
To chide thee when thou comest by.

If to the city I repair,
Mine eyes thy cruelty betray;
And those which view me find my care—
Swoll'n eyes and sorrows it betray,
Whose figures in my forehead are.
These curse the cause of mine ill fare.

When I go forth to feed my flocks,

As I, so they, hang down their heads.   20
If I complain to ruthless rocks,
(For that it seems hard rocks her bred)
Rocks' ruth in rivers may be read,
Which from those rocks down tricklëd.

When shepherds would know how I fare,
And ask, How doth Parthenophil?
Ill, Echo answers in void air,
And with these news each place doth fill.
Poor herd-grooms from each cottage will
Sing my complaints on every hill.   30

FROM BARNABE BARNES's *Divine Century of Spiritual Sonnets*, 1595

No more lewd lays of lighter loves I sing,
    Nor teach my lustful muse abused to fly
    With sparrows' plumes, and for compassion cry
    To mortal beauties which no succor bring.
But my muse, feathered with an angel's wing,
    Divinely mounts aloft unto the sky,
    Where her love's subjects, with my hopes, do lie.
For Cupid's darts prefigurate hell's sting;
His quenchless torch foreshows hell's quenchless fire,
    Kindling men's wits with lustful lays of sin—   10
    Thy wounds my cure, dear Savior! I desire,
To pierce my thoughts, thy fiery cherubin,
    By kindling my desires true zeal t'infuse,
    Thy love my theme, and Holy Ghost my muse!

———

Fortress of hope, anchor of faithful zeal,
    Rock of affiance, bulwark of sure trust,
    In whom all nations for salvation must
    Put certain confidence of their souls' weal:
Those sacred mysteries, dear Lord, reveal
    Of that large volume, righteous and just.
    From me, though blinded with this earthly dust,

Do not those gracious mysteries conceal;
That I by them, as from some beamsome lamp,
   May find the bright and right direction   10
   To my soul, blinded, marching to that camp
Of sacred soldiers whose protection
   He that victorious on a white horse rideth
   Taketh, and evermore triumphant guideth.

A blast of wind, a momentary breath,
   A wat'ry bubble symbolized with air,
   A sun-blown rose, but for a season fair,
   A ghostly glance, a skeleton of death;
A morning dew, pearling the grass beneath,
   Whose moisture sun's appearance doth impair;
   A lightning glimpse, a muse of thought and care,
   A planet's shot, a shade which followeth,
A voice which vanisheth so soon as heard,
   The thriftless heir of time, a rolling wave,   10
   A show, no more in action than regard,
A mass of dust, world's momentary slave,—
   Is man, in state of our old Adam made,
   Soon born to die, soon flourishing to fade.

FROM WILLIAM PERCY's *Cælia*, 1594

Judged by my goddess' doom to endless pain,
Lo, here I ope my sorrow's passion,
That every silly eye may view most plain
   A sentence given on no occasion.
   If that by chance they fall (most fortunate)
Within those cruel hands that did enact it,
Say but, Alas, he was too passionate,
   My doom is passed, nor can be now unactit.
   So mayst thou see I was a spotless lover,
And grieve withal that e'er thou dealt so sore;   10
Unto remorse who goes about to move her,
   Pursues the wingèd winds, and tills the shore.
     Lovely is her semblance, hard is her heart,
     Wavering is her mind, sure is her dart.

Relent, my dear yet unkind Cœlia,
At length relent, and give my sorrows end.
So shall I keep my long-wished holiday,
   And set a trophy on a froward friend.
   Nor tributes, nor imposts, nor other duties
Demand I will, as lawful conqueror;

Duties, tributes, imposts unto thy beauties
Myself will pay as yielded servitor.
   Then quick relent, thyself surrender us.
Brave sir, and why (quoth she) must I relent?   10
Relent (cried I), thyself doth conquer us.
When eftsoons with my proper instrument
   She cut me off, ay me, and answerëd,
   You cannot conquer, and be conquerëd.

It shall be said I died for Cœlia;
Then quick, thou grisly man of Erebus,
Transport me hence unto Proserpina,
To be adjudged as—wilful amorous;
   To be hung up within the liquid air,
For all the sighs which I in vain have wasted;
To be through Lethe's waters cleansëd fair,
For those dark clouds which have my looks o'ercasted;
   To be condemned to everlasting fire,
Because at Cupid's fire I wilful brent me;   10
And to be clad for deadly dumps in mire.
Among so many plagues which shall torment me
   One solace I shall find, when I am over,—
   It will be known I died a constant lover.

From *Zepheria*, 1594

Alli veri figlioli delle Muse

Ye modern laureates, famoused for your writ,
Who for your pregnance may in Delos dwell,
On your sweet lines eternity doth sit,
Their brows ennobling with applause and laurel.
Triumph and honor aye invest your writ!
Ye fet your pens from wing of singing swan,
When (sweetly warbling to herself) she floats
Adown Meander streams, and like to organ
Imparts into her quills melodious notes.
   Ye from the father of delicious phrases
Borrow such hymns as make your mistress live
When time is dead; nay, Hermes tunes the praises
Which ye in sonnets to your mistress give.
   Report throughout our western isle doth ring
The sweet-tuned accents of your Delian sonnetry,
Which to Apollo's violin ye sing,—
Oh then, your high strains drown his melody.
   From forth dead sleep of everlasting dark.

Fame, with her trump's shrill summon, hath awaked
The Roman Naso and the Tuscan Petrarch, 20
Your spirit-ravishing lines to wonder at.
    Oh, theme befitting high-mused Astrophil,
He to your silvery songs lent sweetest touch,
Your songs, the immortal spirit of your quill!
Oh pardon, for my artless pen too much
Doth dim your glories through his infant skill.
    Though may I not with you the spoils divide
(Ye sacred offspring of Mnemosyne)
Of endless praise, which have your pens achieved
(Your pens the trumps to immortality); 30
Yet be it lawful that like maims I bide,
Like brunts and scars in your love's warfare,
And here, though in my homespun verse, of them declare.

<hr>

Proud in thy love, how many have I cited
Impartial thee to view, whose eyes have lavished
Sweet beauteous objects oft have men delighted;
But thou above delight their sense hast ravished.
    They, amorous artists, thee pronounced love's queen,
And unto thy supremacy did swear;
(Venus, at Paphos keep, no more be seen!)
Now Cupid after thee his shafts shall bear.
    How have I spent my spirit of invention
In penning amorous stanzas to thy beauty, 10
But heavenly graces may not brook dimension;
Nor more may thine, for infinite they be.
    But now in harsh tune I of amours sing,
My pipe for them grows hoarse, but shrill to plaining.

<hr>

When we, in kind embracements, had agreed
To keep a royal banquet on our lips,
How soon have we another feast decreed,
And how, at parting, have we mourned by fits!
    Eftsoons, in absence have we wailed much more
Till those void hours of intermission
Were spent, that we might revel as before.
How have we bribèd time for expedition!
    And when remitted to our former love-plays,
How have we, overweening in delight, 10
Accused the father sexton of the days
That then with eagle's wings he took his flight.
    But now, old man, fly on as swift as thought,
Sith eyes from love, and hope from heart, is wrought.

<hr>

What? Shall I ne'er more see those halcyon days,
Those sunny Sabbaths, days of jubilee,
Wherein I caroled merry roundelays,
Odes, and love songs? which, being viewed by thee,
    Received allowance worthy better writ.
When we on shepherds' holy-days have hied
Down to the flow'ry pastures (flowers for thy treading fit)
Holy the day, when thou it sanctified!
    When thou, Zepheria, wouldst but deign to bless it,
How have I, jealous over Phœbus' rays,   10
Clouded thy fair; then, fearing he would guess it
By thy white brow, it have I cinct with bays.
    But woe is me, that I have fenced thy beauty,
    Sith other must enjoy it, and not I!

From E. C.'s *Emaricdulfe*, 1595

Within her hair Venus and Cupid sport them;
    Some time they twist it, amber-like, in gold,
To which the whistling winds do oft resort them,
    As if they strove to have the knots unrolled;
Some time they let their golden tresses dangle,
    And therewith nets and amorous gins they make
Wherewith the hearts of lovers to entangle,
    Which once enthralled, no ransom they will take.
But as two tyrants sitting in their thrones
    Look on their slaves with tyrannizing eyes;   10
So they, no whit regarding lovers' moans,
    Doom worlds of hearts to endless slaveries
Unless they subject-like swear to adore
And serve Emaricdulfe forevermore.

I am enchanted with thy snow-white hands
    That maze me with their quaint dexterity,
And with their touch tie in a thousand bands
    My yielding heart ever to honor thee;
Thought of thy dainty fingers long and small,
    For pretty action that exceed compare,
Sufficient is to bless me, and withal
    To free my chainèd thoughts from sorrow's snare.
But that which crowns my soul with heavenly bliss,
    And gives my heart fruition of all joys,   10
Their dainty concord and sweet music is,
    That poisons grief and cureth all annoys.

Those eyes that see, those ears are blest that hear
These heavenly gifts of nature in my dear.

My heart is like a ship on Neptune's back;
   Thy beauty is the sea where my ship saileth;
Thy frowns the surges are that threat my wrack,
   Thy smiles the winds that on my sails soft galeth.
Long tossed betwixt fair hope and foul despair,
   My sea-sick heart, arrivëd on thy shore—
Thy love, I mean—begs that he may repair
   His broken vessel with thy bounteous store.
Dido relieved Æneas in distress,
   And lent him love, and gave to him her heart;   10
If half such bounty thou to me express,
   From thy fair shore I never will depart,
But thank kind fortune that my course did sort
To suffer shipwreck on so sweet a port.

From Richard Lynche's *Diella*, 1596

Soon as the azure-colored gates of th' east
   Were set wide open by the watchful morn,
I walked abroad, as having took no rest
   (For nights are tedious to a man forlorn);
And viewing well each pearl-bedewëd flower,
   Then waxing dry by splendor of the sun,
All scarlet-hued I saw him 'gin to lour
   And blush, as though some heinous act were done.
At this amazed, I hied me home amain,
   Thinking that I his anger causëd had.   10
And at his set, abroad I walked again;
   When lo, the moon looked wondrous pale and sad:
Anger the one, and envy moved the other,
To see my love more fair than Love's fair mother.

What sugared terms, what all-persuading art,
   What sweet mellifluous words, what wounding looks
Love used for his admittance to my heart!
   Such eloquence was never read in books.
He promised pleasure, rest, and endless joy,
   Fruition of the fairest she alive.
His pleasure, pain; rest, trouble; joy, annoy,
   Have I since found, which me of bliss deprive.
The Trojan horse thus have I now let in,
   Wherein enclosed these armëd men were placed—   10
Bright eyes, fair cheeks, sweet lips, and milk-white skin;

These foes my life have overthrown and razed.
Fair outward shows prove inwardly the worst,
Love looketh fair, but lovers are accurst.

Weary with serving where I nought could get,
    I thought to cross great Neptune's greatest seas,
To live in exile; but my drift was let
    By cruel fortune, spiteful of such ease.
The ship I had to pass in was my mind,
    Greedy desire was topsail of the same,
My tears were surges, sighs did serve for wind,
    Of all my ship despair was chiefest frame;
Sorrow was master; care, the cable rope;
    Grief was the mainmast; love, the captain of it;   10
He that did rule the helm was foolish hope;
    But beauty was the rock that my ship split,
Which since hath made such shipwreck of my joy
That still I swim in th' ocean of annoy.

End this enchantment, love, of my desires,
    Let me no longer languish for thy love.
Joy not to see me thus consume in fires,
    But let my cruel pains thy hard heart move.
And now, at last with pitiful regard
    Eye me, thy lover, lorn for lack of thee,
Which, dying, lives in hope of sweet reward
    Which hate hath hitherto withheld from me.
Constant have I been, still in fancy fast,
    Ordained by heavens to dote upon thy fair;   10
Nor will I e'er, so long as life shall last,
    Say any's fairer, breathing vital air.
But when the ocean sands shall lie unwet,
Then shall my soul to love thee, dear, forget.

From William Smith's *Chloris*, 1596

To the most excellent and learned shepherd, Colin Clout

Colin, my dear and most entire beloved,
    My muse audacious stoops her pitch to thee,
Desiring that thy patience be not moved
    By these rude lines, written here you see;
Fain would my muse, whom cruel love hath wronged,
    Shroud her love-labors under thy protection,
And I myself with ardent zeal have longed
    That thou mightst know to thee my true affection.

Therefore, good Colin, graciously accept
  A few sad sonnets which my muse hath framed;   10
  Though they but newly from the shell are crept,
  Suffer them not by envy to be blamed.
But underneath the shadow of thy wings
Give warmth to these young-hatchëd orphan things.

Feed, silly sheep, although your keeper pineth,
  Yet like to Tantalus doth see his food.
  Skip you and leap, no bright Apollo shineth,
  Whilst I bewail my sorrows in yon wood
Where woeful Philomela doth record,
  And sings with notes of sad and dire lament
  The tragedy wrought by her sister's lord;
  I'll bear a part in her black discontent.
That pipe which erst was wont to make you glee,   10
  Upon these downs whereon you careless graze,
  Shall to her mournful music tunëd be.
  Let not my plaints, poor lambkins, you amaze;
There underneath that dark and dusky bower
Whole showers of tears to Chloris I will pour.

Whole showers of tears to Chloris I will pour
  As true oblations of my sincere love;
  If that will not suffice, most fairest flower,
  Then shall my sighs thee unto pity move.
If neither tears nor sighs can aught prevail,
  My streaming blood thine anger shall appease;
  This hand of mine by vigor shall assail
  To tear my heart asunder thee to please.
Celestial powers, on you I invocate: 10
  You know the chaste affections of my mind,
  I never did my faith yet violate,
  Why should my Chloris then be so unkind?
That neither tears, nor sighs, nor streaming blood
Can unto mercy move her cruel mood.

When I more large thy praises forth shall show,
  That all the world thy beauty shall admire,
  Desiring that most sacred nymph to know
  Which hath the shepherd's fancy set on fire;
Till then, my dear, let these thine eyes content;
  Till then, fair love, think if I merit favor;
  Till then, oh, let thy merciful assent
  Relish my hopes with some comforting savor.
So shall you add such courage to my muse

That she shall climb the steep Parnassus hill,
   That learned poets shall my deeds peruse
   When I from thence obtainëd have more skill.
And what I sing shall always be of thee
As long as life or breath remains in me!

From Bartholomew Griffin's *Fidessa, More Chaste than Kind*, 1596

Arraigned, poor captive at the bar I stand,
   The bar of beauty, bar to all my joys;
And up I hold my ever-trembling hand,
   Wishing or life or death to end annoys.
And when the judge doth question of the guilt
   And bids me speak, then sorrow shuts up words.
   Yea, though he say, Speak boldly what thou wilt,
   Yet my confused affects no speech affords.
For why, alas, my passions have no bound,
   For fear of death that penetrates so near;   10
   And still one grief another doth confound,
   Yet doth at length a way to speech appear.
Then, for I speak too late, the judge doth give
His sentence that in prison I shall live.

      ————————

Compare me to the child that plays with fire,
   Or to the fly that dieth in the flame,
   Or to the foolish boy that did aspire
   To touch the glory of high heaven's frame;
Compare me to Leander struggling in the waves,
   Not able to attain his safety's shore,
   Or to the sick that do expect their graves,
   Or to the captive crying evermore;
Compare me to the weeping wounded hart,
   Moaning with tears the period of his life,   10
   Or to the boar that will not feel his smart
   When he is stricken with the butcher's knife:
No man to these can fitly me compare;
These live to die, I die to live in care.

      ————————

Care-charmer sleep, sweet ease in restless misery,
   The captive's liberty, and his freedom's song,
Balm of the bruisëd heart, man's chief felicity,
   Brother of quiet death, when life is too, too long!
A comedy it is, and now an history—
   What is not sleep unto the feeble mind!
   It easeth him that toils and him that's sorry,
   It makes the deaf to hear, to see the blind.

Ungentle sleep, thou helpest all but me,
  For when I sleep my soul is vexëd most.   10
  It is Fidessa that doth master thee;
  If she approach, alas, thy power is lost.
But here she is. See, how he runs amain!
I fear at night he will not come again.

  Fly to her heart, hover about her heart,
  With dainty kisses mollify her heart,
  Pierce with thy arrows her obdurate heart,
  With sweet allurements ever move her heart,
  At mid-day and at midnight touch her heart,
  Be lurking closely, nestle about her heart,
  With power (thou art a god) command her heart,
  Kindle thy coals of love about her heart,
  Yea, even into thyself transform her heart.
  Ah, she must love! Be sure thou have her heart,   10
  And I must die if thou have not her heart,
  Thy bed, if thou rest well, must be her heart,
  He hath the best part sure that hath the heart.
  What have I not, if I have but her heart!

I have not spent the April of my time,
  The sweet of youth, in plotting in the air,
  But do at first adventure seek to climb,
  Whilst flowers of blooming years are green and fair.
I am no leaving of all-withering age,
  I have not suffered many winter lours;
  I feel no storm unless my love do rage,
  And then in grief I spend both days and hours.
This yet doth comfort, that my flower lasted
  Until it did approach my sun too near,   10
  And then, alas, untimely was it blasted,
  So soon as once thy beauty did appear.
But after all, my comfort rests in this,
That for thy sake my youth decayëd is.

Fair is my love that feeds among the lilies,
  The lilies growing in that pleasant garden
  Where Cupid's mount, that well belovëd hill is,
  And where that little god himself is warden.
See where my love sits in the beds of spices,
  Beset all round with camphor, myrrh, and roses,
  And interlaced with curious devices,
  Which her from all the world apart incloses.

There doth she tune her lute for her delight,
  And with sweet music makes the ground to move,   10
Whilst I, poor I, do sit in heavy plight,
  Wailing alone my unrespected love;
Not daring rush into so rare a place,
That gives to her, and she to it, a grace.

Tell me of love, sweet Love, who is thy sire?
  Or if thou mortal or immortal be?
Some say thou art begotten by desire,
  Nourished with hope, and fed with fantasy,
Engendered by a heavenly goddess' eye,
  Lurking most sweetly in an angel's face;
Others, that beauty thee doth deify—
  O sovereign beauty, full of power and grace!
But I must be absurd all this denying,
  Because the fairest fair alive ne'er knew thee.   10
Now, Cupid, comes thy godhead to the trying:
  'Twas she alone (such is her power) that slew me.
She shall be love, and thou a foolish boy,
Whose virtue proves thy power but a toy.

Work, work apace, you blessed sisters three,
  In restless twining of my fatal thread.
O let your nimble hands at once agree
  To weave it out and cut it off with speed.
Then shall my vexëd and tormented ghost
  Have quiet passage to the Elysian rest,
And sweetly over death and fortune boast
  In everlasting triumphs with the blest.
But ah, too well I know you have conspired
  A lingering death for him that loatheth life,   10
As if with woes he never could be tired;
  For this you hide your all-dividing knife.
One comfort yet the heavens have assigned me,
That I must die and leave my griefs behind me.

If great Apollo offered as a dower
  His burning throne to beauty's excellence;
If Jove himself came in a golden shower
  Down to the earth, to fetch fair Io thence;
If Venus in the curlëd locks were tied
  Of proud Adonis not of gentle kind;
If Tellus for a shepherd's favor died,
  The favor cruel love to her assigned;

If heaven's wingëd herald, Hermes, had
   His heart enchanted with a country maid;
   If poor Pygmalion were for beauty mad;
   If gods and men have all for beauty strayed:
I am not then ashamed to be included
'Mongst those that love, and be with love deluded.

From Robert Tofte's *Laura*, 1597

Unto thy favor, which when nature formed
She went beyond herself with cunning hand,
I may compare what is in world adorned
With beauty most and with most grace doth stand.
But every mortal whiteness ne'er so white
The ivory white of thy white hand exceeds,
So that my soul, which doth fair whiteness like,
Rests on fair whiteness and on whiteness feeds.
   For this is thought and hopëd of from thee:
   White as thy hands, so white thy faith shall be.

When she was born she came with smiling eye
Laughing into the world, a sign of glee;
When I was born, to her quite contrary,
Wailing I came into the world to see.
   Then mark this wonder strange: what nature gave,
   From first to th' last this fashion kept we have.
She in my sad laments doth take great joy;
I through her laughing die, and languish must
Unless that love, to save me from this 'noy,
Do unto me, unworthy, show so just
   As for to change her laughter into pain,
   And my complaints into her joy again.

In love his kingdom great, two fools there be:
My lady's one, myself the other am.
The fond behavior of both which to see,
Whoso but nicely marks will say the same.
Foolish our thoughts are; foolish our desire;
Foolish our hearts in fancy's flame to fry;
Foolish to burn in love's hot scorching fire,—
But what! Fools are we none. My tongue doth lie.
   For who most foolish is and fond, in love,
   More wiser far than others oft doth prove.

Strange is this thing! My horse I cannot make
With spur, with speech, nor yet with rod in hand
Force him to go, although great pains I take.

Do what I can, he still as tired doth stand.
No doubt he feels an heavy weight of me,
Which is the cause he standeth still as stone;
Nor is he ware that now he carrieth three—
He thinks, poor jade, I am on's back alone.
    But three we are: with mine own self, I prove,
    Laura is in my heart, in soul is love.   10

FROM HENRY LOK's *Sonnets of Christian Passions*,
      published with *Ecclesiastes*, 1597

It is not, Lord, the sound of many words,
  The bowëd knee, or abstinence of man,
  The filëd phrase that eloquence affords,
  Or poet's pen, that heavens do pierce, or can;
By heavy cheer of color pale and wan,
  By pinëd body of the Pharisay,
  A mortal eye repentance oft doth scan,
  Whose judgment doth on outward shadows stay.
But thou, O God, dost heart's intent bewray
  For from thy sight, Lord, nothing is concealed,   10
  Thou formedst the frame fro out the very clay,
  To thee the thoughts of hearts are all revealed.
    To thee, therefore, with heart and mind prostrate,
    With tears I thus deplore my sinful state.

Words may well want, both ink and paper fail,
  Wits may grow dull, and will may weary grow,
  And world's affairs may make my pen more slow,
  But yet my heart and courage shall not quail.
Though cares and troubles do my peace assail
  And drive me to delay thy praise awhile,
  Yet all the world shall not from thoughts exile
  Thy mercies, Lord, by which my plaints prevail.
And though the world with face should grateful smile
  And me her peddler's pack of pleasures show,   10
  No hearty love on her I would bestow,
  Because I know she seeks me to beguile;
    Ne will defile my happy peace of mind
    For all the solace I in earth may find.

FROM ALEXANDER CRAIG's *Amorous Songs, Sonnets, and
      Elegies*, 1606

To Pandora

Go you, O winds that blow from north to south,
Convey my secret sighs unto my sweet;

Deliver them from mine unto her mouth,
And make my commendations till we meet.
But if perhaps her proud aspiring sprite
Will not accept nor yet receive the same,
The breast and bulwark of her bosom beat,
Knock at her heart, and tell from whence you came;
Importune her, nor cease nor shrink for shame.
Sport with her curls of amber-colored hair,   10
And when she sighs, immix yourselves with thame,
Give her her own, and thus beguile the fair.
    Blow winds, fly sighs, whereas my heart doth haunt,
    And secretly commend me to my saunt.

To his Pandora, from England

Now, while amid those dainty downs and dales
With shepherd swains I sit, unknown to me,
We sweetly sing and tell pastoral tales,
But my discourse and song's theme is of thee.
For otherways, alas, how can it be?
Let Venus leave her blest abode above
To tempt my love, yet thou, sweet soul, shalt see
That I thy man and thou shalt die my love.
No tract of time nor sad eclipse of place
Nor absence long, which sometime were due cures   10
To my disease, shall make thy slave to cease
From serving thee till life or breath endures;
    And till we meet, my rustic mates and I
    Through woods and plains Pandora's praise shall cry.

HENRY CONSTABLE

The Introduction and Notes are at page 958

From *Diana*, 1592

Mine eye with all the deadly sins is fraught.
    First *proud*, sith it presumed to look so high;
    A watchman being made, stood gazing by,
And *idle*, took no heed till I was caught;
And *envious* bears envy that my thought
    Should in his absence be to her so nigh;
    To kill my heart, mine eye let in her eye,
And so consent gave to a *murder* wrought;
    And *covetous*, it never would remove

From her fair hair, gold so doth please his sight;   10
   Unchaste, a bawd between my heart and love;
A *glutton* eye, with tears drunk every night:
   These sins procurëd have a goddess' ire,
   Wherefore my heart is damned in love's sweet fire.

From *Diana,* [1594]

Dear to my soul, then leave me not forsaken!
   Fly not, my heart within thy bosom sleepeth.
   Even from myself and sense I have betaken
   Me unto thee for whom my spirit weepeth,
And on the shore of that salt teary sea,
   Couched in a bed of unseen seeming pleasure,
   Where in imaginary thoughts thy fair self lay;
   But being waked, robbed of my life's best treasure,
I call the heavens, air, earth, and seas to hear
My love, my truth, and black disdained estate;   10
   Beating the rocks with bellowings of despair,
   Which still with plaints my words reverberate;
Sighing, Alas, what shall become of me?
Whilst echo cries, What shall become of me?

Whilst echo cries, What shall become of me?
   And desolate, my desolations pity,
   Thou in thy beauty's carrack sit'st to see
   My tragic downfall, and my funeral ditty.
No timbrel, but my heart thou play'st upon,
   Whose strings are stretched unto the highest key;
   The diapason, love; love is the unison;
   In love my life and labors waste away.
Only regardless to the world thou leav'st me,
   Whilst slain hopes, turning from the feast of sorrow   10
   Unto despair, their king which ne'er deceives me,
   Captives my heart, whose black night hates the morrow;
And he in ruth of my distressëd cry
Plants me a weeping star within my eye.

To live in hell and heaven to behold;
   To welcome life and die a living death;
   To sweat with heat, and yet be freezing cold;
   To grasp at stars and lie the earth beneath;
To tread a maze that never shall have end;
   To burn in sighs and starve in daily tears;
   To climb a hill and never to descend;
   Giants to kill, and quake at childish fears;

To pine for food, and watch th' Hesperian tree;
   To thirst for drink, and nectar still to draw;   10
   To live accursed, whom men hold blest to be,
   And weep those wrongs which never creature saw:
If this be love, if love in these be founded,
My heart is love, for these in it are grounded.

Fair grace of graces, muse of muses all,
   Thou paradise, thou only heaven I know,
   What influence hath bred my hateful woe,
That I from thee and them am forced to fall?
Thou fall'n from me, from thee I never shall;
   Although my fortunes thou hast brought so low,
   Yet shall my faith and service with thee go,
For live I do on heaven and thee to call.
Banished all grace, no graces with me dwell;   10
   Compelled to muse, my muses from me fly;
   Excluded heaven, what can remain but hell?
   Exiled from paradise, in hate I lie
Cursing my stars; albeit I find it true,
I lost all these when I lost love and you.

FROM THOMAS PARK's *Harleian Miscellany*, vol. ix, 1812

To his mistress

Upon occasion of a Petrarch he gave her, showing her the reason why the Italian commenters dissent so much in the exposition thereof

Miracle of the world, I never will deny
That former poets praise the beauty of their days,
But all those beauties were but figures of thy praise
And all those poets did of thee but prophesy.

Thy coming to the world hath taught us to descry
What Petrarch's Laura meant, for truth the lip bewrays.
Lo, why th' Italians, yet which never saw thy rays,
To find out Petrarch's sense such forgëd glosses try:

The beauties which he in a veil enclosed beheld   10
But revelations were within his secret heart,
By which in parables thy coming he foretold.
His songs were hymns of thee, which only now before
   Thy image should be sung; for thou that goddess art
   Which only we without idolatry adore.

FROM *Harleian Ms.* 7553

To St. Peter and St. Paul

He that for fear his Master did deny,
    And at a maiden's voice amazèd stood,
    The mightiest monarch of the earth withstood,
And on his Master's cross rejoiced to die.
He whose blind zeal did rage with cruelty
    And helped to shed the first of martyrs' blood,
    By light from heaven his blindness understood,
And with the chief apostle slain doth lie.
O three times happy two! O golden pair!
    Who with your blood did lay the church's ground   10
    Within the fatal town which twins did found,
And settled there the Hebrew fisher's chair
    Where first the Latin shepherd raised his throne,
    And since, the world and church were ruled by one.

To St. Mary Magdalen

Such as, retired from sight of men, like thee
    By penance seek the joys of heaven to win,
    In deserts make their paradise begin
And even among wild beasts do angels see.
In such a place my soul doth seem to be,
    When in my body she laments her sin
    And none but brutal passions finds therein,
Except they be sent down from heaven to me.
Yet if those graces God to me impart
    Which he inspired thy blessed breast withal,   10
    I may find heaven in my retired heart;
And if thou change the object of my love,
    The winged affection which men Cupid call
    May get his sight, and like an angel prove.

FROM JOHN BODENHAM'S (?) *England's Helicon*, 1600

Damelus' song to his Diaphenia

Diaphenia, like the daffadown-
    dilly,
White as the sun, fair as the lily,
    Heigh ho, how I do love
    thee!
I do love thee as my lambs
Are belovèd of their dams—

How blest were I if thou
    wouldst prove me!

Diaphenia, like the spreading roses,
That in thy sweets all sweets in-
    closes,
Fair sweet, how I do love thee!

I do love thee as each flower   10
Loves the sun's life-giving power,
   For, dead, thy breath to life
      might move me.

Diaphenia, like to all things
   blessed,

When all thy praises are ex-
   pressëd,
   Dear joy, how I do love
     thee!
As the birds do love the spring,
Or the bees their careful king,—
   Then in requite, sweet virgin,
     love me!

The shepherd's song of Venus and Adonis

Venus fair did ride,
   Silver doves they drew her
By the pleasant lawns,
   Ere the sun did rise;
Vesta's beauty rich
   Opened wide to view her,
Philomel records
   Pleasing harmonies;
Every bird of spring
   Cheerfully did sing,   10
     Paphos' goddess they sa-
      lute.
Now love's queen so fair
   Had of mirth no care,
     For her son had made her
      mute.
In her breast so tender
He a shaft did enter,
     When her eyes beheld a
      boy,
Adonis was he named,
By his mother shamed,
     Yet he now is Venus'
      joy.   20

Him alone she met,
   Ready bound for hunting;
Him she kindly greets,
   And his journey stays;
Him she seeks to kiss,
   No devices wanting,
Him her eyes still woo,
   Him her tongue still prays.
He with blushing red
Hangeth down the head,   30
   Not a kiss can he afford;

His face is turned away,
Silence said her nay,
     Still she wooed him for a
      word.
Speak, she said, thou fairest,
Beauty thou impairest;
     See me, I am pale and wan;
Lovers all adore me,
I for love implore thee.
     Crystal tears with that ran
      down.   40

Him herewith she forced
   To come sit down by her;
She his neck embraced,
   Gazing in his face;
He, like one transformed,
   Stirred no look to eye her.
Every herb did woo him,
   Growing in that place;
     Each bird with a ditty
      Prayëd him for pity   50
       In behalf of beauty's
       queen;
Waters' gentle murmur
   Cravëd him to love her,
     Yet no liking could be
      seen.
Boy, she said, look on me,
Still I gaze upon thee,
     Speak, I pray thee, my de-
      light.
Coldly he replied,
And, in brief, denied
     To bestow on her a sight.   60

I am now too young
　To be won by beauty;
Tender are my years,
　I am yet a bud.
Fair thou art, she said,
　Then it is thy duty,
Wert thou but a blossom,
　To effect my good.
　　Every beauteous flower
　　　Boasteth in my power,　70
　　Birds and beasts my laws ef-
　　　fect.
Myrrha, thy fair mother,
　Most of any other
　　Did my lovely hests re-
　　　spect.
Be with me delighted,
Thou shalt be requited,
　　Every nymph on thee shall
　　　tend;
　All the gods shall love thee,
Man shall not reprove thee,
　　Love himself shall be thy
　　　friend.　　80

Wend thee from me, Venus,
　I am not disposed;
Thou wring'st me too hard,
　Prithee, let me go;
Fie, what a pain it is
　Thus to be enclosed;
If love begin with labor,
　It will end in woe.
　　Kiss me, I will leave.
　　Here a kiss receive.　90
　　　A short kiss I do it find,
Wilt thou leave me so?
　Yet thou shalt not go;
　　Breathe once more thy
　　　balmy wind,
It smelleth of the myrrh tree
That to the world did bring
　thee,
　　Never was perfume so
　　　sweet.
When she had thus spoken,

She gave him a token,
　And their naked bosoms
　　meet.　100

Now, he said, let's go,
　Hark, the hounds are crying,
Grisly boar is up,
　Huntsmen follow fast.
At the name of boar
　Venus seemèd dying,
Deadly-colored pale,
　Roses overcast.
　　Speak, said she, no more
　　　Of following the boar;　110
　　　　Thou, unfit for such a
　　　　　chase,
　　Course the fearful hare,
　　　Venison do not spare,
　　　　If thou wilt yield Venus
　　　　　grace.
Shun the boar, I pray thee,
Else I still will stay thee.
　　Herein he vowed to
　　　please her mind;
Then her arms enlarged,
Loath she him discharged,
　　Forth he went as swift
　　　as wind.　120

Thetis Phœbus' steeds
　In the west retained;
Hunting sport was past,
　Love her love did seek;
Sight of him too soon,
　Gentle queen she gained.
On the ground he lay;
　Blood had left his cheek,
　　For an orpèd swine
　　　Smit him in the groin,　130
　　　Deadly wound his death
　　　　did bring.
Which when Venus found
　She fell in a swound,
　　And awaked, her hands
　　　did wring.

Nymphs and satyrs skipping
Came together tripping,
   Echo every cry **ex-**
     pressed.

Venus by her power
Turned him to a flower,
   Which she weareth in her
     crest.   140

ROBERT SOUTHWELL

The Introduction and Notes are at page 959

FROM *Mœoniæ*, 1595

Upon the image of death

Before my face the picture hangs
   That daily should put me in
     mind
Of those cold names and bitter
     pangs
   That shortly I am like to find;
But yet, alas, full little I
   Do think hereon that I must
     die.
I often look upon a face
   Most ugly, grisly, bare, and
     thin;
I often view the hollow place
   Where eyes and nose had some-
     times been;   10
I see the bones across that lie,
   Yet little think that I must die.
I read the label underneath,
   That telleth me whereto I
     must;
I see the sentence eke that saith
   Remember, man, that thou art
     dust!
But yet, alas, but seldom I
   Do think indeed that I must
     die.
Continually at my bed's head
   A hearse doth hang, which doth
     me tell   20
That I ere morning may be dead,
   Though now I feel myself full
     well;
But yet, alas, for all this, I

Have little mind that I must
   die.
The gown which I do use to wear,
   The knife wherewith I cut my
     meat,
And eke that old and ancient chair
   Which is my only usual seat,—
All those do tell me I must die,
   And yet my life amend not I.   30
My ancestors are turned to clay,
   And many of my mates are
     gone;
My youngers daily drop away,
   And can I think to 'scape
     alone?
No, no, I know that I must die,
   And yet my life amend not I.
Not Solomon for all his wit,
   Nor Samson, though he were so
     strong,
No king nor person ever yet
   Could 'scape but death laid him
     along;   40
Wherefore I know that I must
   die,
   And yet my life amend not I.
Though all the East did quake to
     hear
   Of Alexander's dreadful name,
And all the West did likewise fear
   To hear of Julius Cæsar's fame,
Yet both by death in dust now lie;

Who then can 'scape but he
    must die?
If none can 'scape death's dread-
    ful dart,
  If rich and poor his beck obey, 50
If strong, if wise, if all do smart,

Then I to 'scape shall have no
    way.
Oh, grant me grace, O God, that
    I
My life may mend, sith I must
    die.

FROM *St. Peter's Complaint . . . for J. Wolfe*, 1595

Look home

Retirëd thoughts enjoy their own delights,
As beauty doth in self-beholding eye;
Man's mind a mirror is of heavenly sights,
A brief wherein all marvels summëd lie,
Of fairest forms and sweetest shapes the store,
Most graceful all, yet thought may grace them more.

The mind a creature is, yet can create,
To nature's patterns adding higher skill;
Of finest works wit better could the state
If force of wit had equal power of will. 10
Device of man in working hath no end,
What thought can think, another thought can mend.

Man's soul of endless beauty image is,
Drawn by the work of endless skill and might;
This skillful might gave many sparks of bliss
And, to discern this bliss, a native light;
To frame God's image as his worths required
His might, his skill, his word and will conspired.

All that he had his image should present,
All that it should present it could afford, 20
To that he could afford his will was bent,
His will was followed with performing word.
Let this suffice, by this conceive the rest,—
He should, he could, he would, he did, the best.

Love's servile lot

Love mistress is of many minds
  Yet few know whom they
    serve;
They reckon least how little love
  Their service doth deserve.

The will she robbeth from the wit,

The sense from reason's lore;
She is delightful in the rind,
  Corrupted in the core.

She shroudeth vice in virtue's
    veil,
  Pretending much good will, 10

She off'reth joy, affordeth grief,
 A kiss where she doth kill.

A honey-shower rains from her lips,
 Sweet lights shine in her face;
She hath the blush of virgin mild,
 The mind of viper's race.

She makes thee seek yet fear to find,
 To find but not enjoy;
In many frowns some gliding smiles
 She yields—to more annoy.   20

She woos thee to come near the fire
 Yet doth she draw it from thee;
Far off she makes thy heart to fry
 And yet to freeze within thee.

She letteth fall some luring baits
 For fools to gather up;
To sweet, to sour, to every taste,
 She tempereth her cup.

Soft souls she binds in tender twist,
 Small flies in spinner's web; 30
She sets afloat some luring streams
 But makes them soon to ebb.

Her watery eyes have burning force,
 Her floods and flames conspire;
Tears kindle sparks, sobs fuel are,
 And sighs do blow her fire.

May never was the month of love
 For May is full of flowers,
But rather April, wet by kind,
 For love is full of showers.   40

Like tyrant cruel wounds she gives,

Like surgeon salve she lends,
But salve and sore have equal force,
 For death is both their ends.

With soothing words enthrallèd souls
 She chains in servile bands;
Her eye in silence hath a speech
 Which eye best understands.

Her little sweet hath many sours;
 Short hap, immortal harms; 50
Her loving looks are murd'ring darts,
 Her songs, bewitching charms.

Like winter rose and summer ice
 Her joys are still untimely;
Before her, hope; behind, remorse;
 Fair first, in fine unseemly.

Moods, passions, fancies, jealous fits
 Attend upon her train;
She yieldeth rest without repose,
 A heaven in hellish pain.   60

Her house is sloth, her door deceit,
 And slippery hope her stairs;
Unbashful boldness bids her guests
 And every vice repairs.

Her diet is of such delights
 As please till they be past,
But then the poison kills the heart
 That did entice the taste.

Her sleep in sin doth end in wrath,
 Remorse rings her awake; 70
Death calls her up, shame drives her out,
 Despairs her upshot make.

Plow not the seas, sow not the
    sands,
Leave off your idle pain;

Seek other mistress for your
    minds,
Love's service is in vain.

FROM *St. Peter's Complaint, newly augmented,* [*c.* 1605]

New prince, new pomp

Behold, a seely tender babe
    In freezing winter night
In homely manger trembling
    lies,—
    Alas, a piteous sight!
The inns are full, no man will
    yield
    This little pilgrim bed,
But forced he is with seely beasts
    In crib to shroud his head.
Despise him not for lying there,
    First, what he is enquire,   10
An orient pearl is often found
    In depth of dirty mire.
Weigh not his crib, his wooden
    dish,
    Nor beasts that by him feed;

Weigh not his mother's poor at-
    tire
    Nor Joseph's simple weed.
This stable is a prince's court,
    This crib his chair of state,
The beasts are parcel of his pomp,
    The wooden dish his plate.   20
The persons in that poor attire
    His royal liveries wear;
The prince himself is come from
    heaven—
    This pomp is prizèd there.
With joy approach, O Christian
    wight,
    Do homage to thy king;
And highly prize his humble
    pomp
    Which he from heaven doth
    bring.

The burning babe

As I in hoary winter's night stood shivering in the snow,
Surprised I was with sudden heat which made my heart to glow;
And lifting up a fearful eye to view what fire was near,
A pretty babe all burning bright did in the air appear;
Who, scorchèd with excessive heat, such floods of tears did shed
As though his floods should quench his flames which with his tears were
    fed.
Alas, quoth he, but newly born in fiery heats I fry,
Yet none approach to warm their hearts or feel my fire but I!
My faultless breast the furnace is, the fuel wounding thorns,
Love is the fire, and sighs the smoke, the ashes shame and scorns;   10
The fuel justice layeth on, and mercy blows the coals,
The metal in this furnace wrought are men's defilèd souls,
For which, as now on fire I am to work them to their good,
So will I melt into a bath to wash them in my blood.
With this he vanished out of sight and swiftly shrunk away,
And straight I callèd unto mind that it was Christmas day.

RICHARD BARNFIELD

The Introduction and Notes are at page 959

FROM *Cynthia,* 1595

To his mistress

Bright star of beauty, fairest fair alive,
Rare president of peerless chastity,
(In whom the Muses and the Graces strive,
Which shall possess the chiefest part of thee)
O let these simple lines accepted be,
    Which here I offer at thy sacred shrine,
    Sacred, because sweet beauty is divine.

And though I cannot please each curious ear
With sugared notes of heavenly harmony,
Yet if my love shall to thy self appear,   10
No other muse I will invoke but thee;
And if thou wilt my fair Thalia be,
    I'll sing sweet hymns and praises to thy name
    In that clear temple of eternal fame.

But ah, alas, how can mine infant muse,
That never heard of Helicon before,
Perform my promise past, when they refuse
Poor shepherds' plaints? Yet will I still adore
Thy sacred name, although I write no more;
    Yet hope I shall, if this accepted be,   20
    If not, in silence sleep eternally.

FROM *Poems in Divers Humors,* published with *The Encomion of
Lady Pecunia,* 1598

To his friend Master R. L., in praise of music and poetry

If music and sweet poetry agree,
As they must needs (the sister and the brother),
Then must the love be great 'twixt thee and me,
    Because thou lov'st the one, and I the other.
    Dowland to thee is dear, whose heavenly touch
Upon the lute doth ravish human sense;
Spenser to me, whose deep conceit is such
    As, passing all conceit, needs no defence.
    Thou lov'st to hear the sweet melodious sound

That Phœbus' lute (the queen of music) makes;   10
And I in deep delight am chiefly drowned
  Whenas himself to singing he betakes.
    One god is god of both (as poets feign),
    One knight loves both, and both in thee remain.

Against the dispraisers of poetry

Chaucer is dead; and Gower lies in grave;
The Earl of Surrey long ago is gone;
Sir Philip Sidney's soul the heavens have;
George Gascoigne him before was tombed in stone.
  Yet, though their bodies lie full low in ground,
As every thing must die that erst was born,
Their living fame no fortune can confound,
Nor ever shall their labors be forlorn.
  And you, that discommend sweet poetry,
(So that the subject of the same be good)   10
Here may you see your fond simplicity,
Sith kings have favored it, of royal blood.
  The King of Scots (now living) is a poet,
  As his *Lepanto* and his *Furies* show it.

A remembrance of some English poets

Live, Spenser, ever in thy *Fairy Queen*,
Whose like, for deep conceit, was never seen.
Crowned mayst thou be, unto thy more renown,
As king of poets, with a laurel crown.

And Daniel, praisèd for thy sweet-chaste verse,
Whose fame is graved on Rosamond's black hearse,
Still mayst thou live; and still be honorèd
For that rare work, *The White Rose and the Red*.

And Drayton, whose well-written tragedies   10
And sweet epistles soar thy fame to skies,
Thy learned name is equal with the rest,
Whose stately numbers are so well addressed.

And Shakespeare, thou whose honey-flowing vein,
Pleasing the world, thy praises doth obtain;
Whose *Venus* and whose *Lucrece*, sweet and chaste,
Thy name in fame's immortal book have placed:
  Live ever you, at least in fame live ever;
  Well may the body die, but fame dies never.

An ode

As it fell upon a day
In the merry month of May,
Sitting in a pleasant shade
Which a grove of myrtles made,
Beasts did leap and birds did sing,
Trees did grow and plants did spring;
Every thing did banish moan,
Save the nightingale alone.
She, poor bird, as all forlorn,
Leaned her breast up-till a thorn   10
And there sung the doleful'st ditty,
That to hear it was great pity.
Fie, fie, fie, now would she cry,
Teru, teru, by and by;
That to hear her so complain,
Scarce I could from tears refrain;
For her griefs so lively shown
Made me think upon mine own.
Ah, thought I, thou mourn'st in vain;
None takes pity on thy pain;   20
Senseless trees, they cannot hear thee;
Ruthless bears, they will not cheer thee.
King Pandion, he is dead,
All thy friends are lapped in lead.
All thy fellow birds do sing,
Careless of thy sorrowing.

Whilst as fickle fortune smiled,
Thou and I were both beguiled.
Every one that flatters thee
Is no friend in misery: 30
Words are easy, like the wind,
Faithful friends are hard to find;
Every man will be thy friend
Whilst thou hast wherewith to spend,
But if store of crowns be scant,
No man will supply thy want.
If that one be prodigal,
Bountiful they will him call;
And with such-like flattering
Pity but he were a king.   40
If he be addict to vice,
Quickly him they will entice;
If to women he be bent,
They have at commandëment;
But if fortune once do frown,
Then farewell his great renown;
They that fawned on him before
Use his company no more.
He that is thy friend indeed
He will help thee in thy need: 50
If thou sorrow, he will weep;
If thou wake, he cannot sleep;
Thus of every grief, in heart,
He with thee doth bear a part.
These are certain signs to know
Faithful friend from flatt'ring foe.

FROM JOHN BODENHAM'S (?) *England's Helicon*, 1600
The unknown shepherd's complaint

My flocks feed not, my ewes breed not,
My rams speed not, all is amiss;
Love is denying, faith is defying,
Heart's renying, causer of this.
All my merry jigs are quite forgot,
All my lady's love is lost, God wot;
Where her faith was firmly fixed in love,
There a nay is placed without remove.

One silly cross wrought all my loss,
O frowning fortune, cursed fickle dame,   10
For now I see inconstancy
More in women than in men remain.

In black mourn I, all fears scorn I,
Love hath forlorn me, living in thrall;
Heart is bleeding, all help needing,
Oh, cruel speeding, fraughted with gall.
My shepherd's pipe can sound no deal,
My wether's bell rings doleful knell.
My curtail dog that wont to have played
Plays not at all, but seems afraid;   20
    With sighs so deep, procures to weep
    In howling wise to see my doleful plight:
    How sighs resound through heartless ground
    Like a thousand vanquished men in bloody fight.

Clear wells spring not, sweet birds sing not,
Green plants bring not forth their dye;
Herds stand weeping, flocks all sleeping,
Nymphs back peeping fearfully.
All our pleasure known to us poor swains,
All our merry meeting on the plains,   30
All our evening sports from us are fled,
All our love is lost, for love is dead.
    Farewell, sweet love, thy like ne'er was
    For sweet content, the cause of all my moan.
    Poor Coridon must live alone,—
    Other help for him I see that there is none.

SAMUEL DANIEL

The Introduction and Notes are at page 960

From *Delia*, 1594

To the Right Honorable, the Lady Mary, Countess of Pembroke

Wonder of these! glory of other times!
    O thou whom envy ev'n is forced t' admire!
Great patroness of these my humble rhymes,
    Which thou from out thy greatness dost inspire!
Sith only thou hast deigned to raise them higher,

Vouchsafe now to accept them as thine own,
Begotten by thy hand and my desire,
Wherein my zeal and thy great might is shown;
And seeing this unto the world is known,
    O leave not still to grace thy work in me.   10
Let not the quick'ning seed be overthrown,
Of that which may be born to honor thee;
Whereof the travail I may challenge mine,
But yet the glory, madam, must be thine.

From *The Whole Works*, 1623

To Delia

Fair is my love, and cruel as she's fair:
    Her brow shades frowns, although her eyes are sunny,
    Her smiles are lightning, though her pride despair,
    And her disdains are gall, her favors honey.
A modest maid, decked with a blush of honor,
    Whose feet do tread green paths of youth and love;
    The wonder of all eyes that look upon her,
    Sacred on earth, designed a saint above.
Chastity and beauty, which were deadly foes,
    Live reconcilèd friends within her brow;   10
    And had she pity to conjoin with those,
    Then who had heard the plaints I utter now?
For had she not been fair and thus unkind,
My muse had slept, and none had known my mind.

———————

Why should I sing in verse, why should I frame
    These sad neglected notes for her dear sake?
    Why should I offer up unto her name
    The sweetest sacrifice my youth can make?
Why should I strive to make her live forever,
    That never deigns to give me joy to live?
    Why should m' afflicted muse so much endeavor
    Such honor unto cruelty to give?
If her defects have purchased her this fame,
    What should her virtues do, her smiles, her love?   10
    If this her worst, how should her best inflame?
    What passions would her milder favors move?
Favors, I think, would sense quite overcome,
And that makes happy lovers ever dumb.

———————

Look, Delia, how w' esteem the half-blown rose,
    The image of thy blush and summer's honor,
    Whilst yet her tender bud doth undisclose

That full of beauty time bestows upon her.
No sooner spreads her glory in the air
   But straight her wide-blown pomp comes to decline;
   She then is scorned that late adorned the fair;
   So fade the roses of those cheeks of thine.
No April can revive thy withered flowers,
   Whose springing grace adorns the glory now;   10
   Swift speedy time, feathered with flying hours,
   Dissolves the beauty of the fairest brow.
Then do not thou such treasure waste in vain,
But love now whilst thou mayst be loved again.

But love whilst that thou mayst be loved again,
   Now whilst thy May hath filled thy lap with flowers,
   Now whilst thy beauty bears without a stain;
   Now use the summer smiles ere winter lours.
And whilst thou spread'st unto the rising sun
   The fairest flower that ever saw the light,
   Now joy thy time before thy sweet be done;
   And, Delia, think thy morning must have night,
And that thy brightness sets at length to west,
   When thou wilt close up that which now thou show'st,   10
   And think the same becomes thy fading best,
   Which then shall most inveil and shadow most.
Men do not weigh the stalk for that it was,
When once they find her flower, her glory, pass.

When men shall find thy flower, thy glory, pass,
   And thou with careful brow sitting alone,
   Receivèd hast this message from thy glass,
   That tells the truth and says that all is gone;
Fresh shalt thou see in me the wounds thou mad'st,
   Though spent thy flame, in me the heat remaining;
   I that have loved thee thus before thou fad'st,
   My faith shall wax when thou art in thy waning.
The world shall find this miracle in me,
   That fire can burn when all the matter's spent;   10
   Then what my faith hath been, thyself shall see,
   And that thou wast unkind, thou mayst repent.
Thou mayst repent that thou hast scorned my tears,
When winter snows upon thy sable hairs.

When winter snows upon thy sable hairs,
   And frost of age hath nipped thy beauties near,
   When dark shall seem thy day that never clears,
   And all lies withered that was held so dear,

Then take this picture which I here present thee,
　Limned with a pencil not all unworthy;
　Here see the gifts that God and nature lent thee,
　Here read thyself and what I suffered for thee.
This may remain thy lasting monument,
　Which happily posterity may cherish;
　These colors with thy fading are not spent,
　These may remain when thou and I shall perish.
If they remain, then thou shalt live thereby;
They will remain, and so thou canst not die.

Thou canst not die whilst any zeal abound
　In feeling hearts that can conceive these lines;
　Though thou, a Laura, hast no Petrarch found,
　In base attire yet clearly beauty shines.
And I, though born within a colder clime,
　Do feel mine inward heat as great (I know it),
　He never had more faith, although more rhyme;
　I love as well, though he could better show it.
But I may add one feather to thy fame,
　To help her flight throughout the fairest isle,
　And if my pen could more enlarge thy name,
　Then shouldst thou live in an immortal style.
For though that Laura better limnëd be,
Suffice, thou shalt be loved as well as she.

Most fair and lovely maid, look from the shore,
　See thy Leander striving in these waves,
　Poor soul, quite spent, whose force can do no more;
　Now send forth hope, for now calm pity saves,
And waft him to thee with these lovely eyes,
　A happy convoy to a holy land.
　Now show thy power and where thy virtue lies;
　To save thine own, stretch out the fairest hand.
Stretch out the fairest hand, a pledge of peace,
　That hand that darts so right and never misses;
　I shall forget old wrongs, my griefs shall cease;
　And that which gave me wounds, I'll give it kisses,
Once let the ocean of my cares find shore,
That thou be pleased, and I may sigh no more.

Beauty, sweet love, is like the morning dew,
　Whose short refresh upon the tender green
　Cheers for a time, but till the sun doth shew,
　And straight 'tis gone as it had never been.
Soon doth it fade that makes the fairest flourish,

Short is the glory of the blushing rose;
　　The hue which thou so carefully dost nourish,
　　Yet which at length thou must be forced to lose,
When thou, surcharged with the burthen of thy years,
　　Shalt bend thy wrinkles homeward to the earth, 10
　　And that in beauty's lease expired appears
　　The date of age, the kalends of our death.
But ah! no more, this must not be foretold,
For women grieve to think they must be old.

————

Care-charmer sleep, son of the sable night,
　　Brother to death, in silent darkness born,
　　Relieve my languish and restore the light;
　　With dark forgetting of my care, return.
And let the day be time enough to mourn
　　The shipwreck of my ill-adventured youth;
　　Let waking eyes suffice to wail their scorn
　　Without the torment of the night's untruth.
Cease, dreams, th' images of day-desires,
　　To model forth the passions of the morrow; 10
　　Never let rising sun approve you liars,
　　To add more grief to aggravate my sorrow.
Still let me sleep, embracing clouds in vain,
And never wake to feel the day's disdain.

————

Let others sing of knights and paladins
　　In agèd accents and untimely words,
　　Paint shadows in imaginary lines
　　Which well the reach of their high wits records;
But I must sing of thee, and those fair eyes
　　Authentic shall my verse in time to come,
　　When yet th' unborn shall say, Lo where she lies,
　　Whose beauty made him speak that else was dumb.
These are the arks, the trophies I erect,
　　That fortify thy name against old age; 10
　　And these thy sacred virtues must protect
　　Against the dark and time's consuming rage.
Though th' error of my youth in them appear,
Suffice, they show I lived and loved thee dear.

————

None other fame mine unambitious muse
　　Affected ever but t' eternize thee;
　　All other honors do my hopes refuse,
　　Which meaner prized and momentary be.
For God forbid I should my papers blot
　　With mercenary lines, with servile pen,

Praising virtues in them that have them not,
    Basely attending on the hopes of men.
No, no, my verse respects nor Thames nor theaters,
    Nor seeks it to be known unto the great;   10
But Avon, poor in fame and poor in waters,
    Shall have my song, where Delia hath her seat.
Avon shall be my Thames and she my song;
No other prouder brooks shall hear my wrong.

Lo, here the impost of a faith entire,
    Which love doth pay and her disdain extorts;
Behold the message of a chaste desire
    Which tells the world how much my grief imports.
These tributary passions, beauty's due,
    I send those eyes, the cabinets of love,
That cruelty herself might grieve to view
    Th' affliction her unkind disdain doth move,
And how I live, cast down from off all mirth,
    Pensive, alone, only but with despair;   10
My joys, abortive, perish in their birth;
    My griefs long lived, and care succeeding care.
This is my state, and Delia's heart is such;
I say no more, I fear I said too much.

An ode

Now each creature joys the other,
    Passing happy days and hours;
One bird reports unto another
    In the fall of silver showers,
Whilst the earth, our common
        mother,
    Hath her bosom decked with
        flowers.

Whilst the greatest torch of heaven
    With bright rays warms Flora's
        lap,
Making nights and days both even,
    Cheering plants with fresher
        sap;   10
My field of flowers quite bereaven
    Wants refresh of better hap.

Echo, daughter of the air,
    Babbling guest of rocks and
        hills,
Knows the name of my fierce fair,
    And sounds the accents of my
        ills.
Each thing pities my despair,
    Whilst that she her lover kills;

Whilst that she, oh, cruel maid!
    Doth me and my love de-
        spise;   20
My life's flourish is decayed,
    That depended on her eyes.
But her will must be obeyed,
    And well he ends for love who
        dies.

The complaint of Rosamond

Out from the horror of infernal deeps
My poor afflicted ghost comes here to plain it,

Attended with my shame that never sleeps,
The spot wherewith my kind and youth did stain it;
My body found a grave where to contain it,
　　A sheet could hide my face, but not my sin,
　　For fame finds never tomb t' inclose it in.

And which is worse, my soul is now denied
Her transport to the sweet Elysian rest,
The joyful bliss for ghosts repurified,　　　　　　　　　10
The ever-springing gardens of the blest;
Charon denies me waftage with the rest,
　　And says my soul can never pass the river,
　　Till lovers' sighs on earth shall it deliver.

So shall I never pass, for how should I
Procure this sacrifice amongst the living?
Time hath long since worn out the memory
Both of my life and life's unjust depriving;
Sorrow for me is dead for aye reviving.
　　Rosamond hath little left her but her name,　　　　20
　　And that disgraced, for time hath wronged the same.

No muse suggests the pity of my case;
Each pen doth overpass my just complaint,
Whilst others are preferred, though far more base;
Shore's wife is graced, and passes for a saint;
Her legend justifies her foul attaint.
　　Her well-told tale did such compassion find
　　That she is passed, and I am left behind.

Which seen with grief, my miserable ghost
(Whilom invested in so fair a veil,　　　　　　　　　30
Which whilst it lived was honored of the most,
And being dead, gives matter to bewail)
Comes to solicit thee, whilst others fail,
　　To take this task and in thy woeful song
　　To form my case and register my wrong.

Although I know thy just lamenting muse,
Toiled in th' affection of thine own distress,
In others' cares hath little time to use,
And therefore mayst esteem of mine the less;
Yet as thy hopes attend happy redress,　　　　　　　40
　　The joys depending on a woman's grace,
　　So move thy mind a woeful woman's case.

Delia may hap to deign to read our story,
And offer up her sighs among the rest,
Whose merit would suffice for both our glory,
Whereby thou mightst be graced and I be blest;
That indulgence would profit me the best.
  Such power she hath by whom thy youth is led,
  To joy the living and to bless the dead.

So I, through beauty made the woeful'st wight, 50
By beauty might have comfort after death;
That dying fairest, by the fairest might
Find life above on earth, and rest beneath.
She that can bless us with one happy breath,
  Give comfort to thy muse to do her best,
  That thereby thou mayst joy and I might rest.

Thus said, forthwith moved with a tender care
And pity, which myself could never find,
What she desired my muse deigned to declare,
And therefore willed her boldly tell her mind; 60
And I, more willing, took this charge assigned
  Because her griefs were worthy to be known,
  And telling hers, might hap forget mine own.

Then write, quoth she, the ruin of my youth,
Report the downfall of my slipp'ry state;
Of all my life reveal the simple truth,
To teach to others what I learnt too late.
Exemplify my frailty, tell how fate
  Keeps in eternal dark our fortunes hidden,
  And ere they come, to know them 'tis forbidden. 70

For whilst the sunshine of my fortune lasted,
I joyed the happiest warmth, the sweetest heat
That ever yet imperious beauty tasted;
I had what glory ever flesh could get,
But this fair morning had a shameful set.
  Disgrace darked honor, sin did cloud my brow,
  As note the sequel, and I'll tell thee how.

The blood I stained was good and of the best,
My birth had honor and my beauty fame;
Nature and fortune joined to make me blest, 80
Had I had grace t' have known to use the same.
My education showed from whence I came,
  And all concurred to make me happy first,
  That so great hope might make me more accursed.

Happy lived I whilst parents' eye did guide
The indiscretion of my feeble ways,
And country home kept me from being eyed,
Where best unknown I spent my sweetest days;
Till that my friends mine honor sought to raise
    To higher place, which greater credit yields, 90
    Deeming such beauty was unfit for fields.

From country then to court I was preferred,
From calm to storms, from shore into the deeps;
There where I perished, where my youth first erred;
There where I lost the flower which honor keeps;
There where the worser thrives, the better weeps.
    Ah me, poor wench, on this unhappy shelf
    I grounded me and cast away myself.

There whereas frail and tender beauty stands
With all assaulting powers environëd; 100
Having but prayers and weak feeble hands
To hold their honor's fort unvanquishëd;
There where to stand and be unconquerëd
    Is to b' above the nature of our kind,
    That cannot long for pity be unkind.

For thither comed (when years had armed my youth
With rarest proof of beauty ever seen,
When my reviving eye had learnt the truth
That it had power to make the winter green,
And flower affections whereas none had been), 110
    Soon could I teach my brow to tyrannize,
    And make the world do homage to mine eyes.

For age, I saw (though years with cold conceit
Congealed their thoughts against a warm desire)
Yet sigh their want, and look at such a bait;
I saw how youth was wax before the fire;
I saw by stealth, I framed my look a liar,
    Yet well perceived how fortune made me then
    The envy of my sex, and wonder unto men.

Look how a comet at the first appearing 120
Draws all men's eyes with wonder to behold it;
Or as the saddest tale at sudden hearing
Makes silent list'ning unto him that told it;
So did my speech when rubies did unfold it,
    So did the blazing of my blush appear
    T' amaze the world, that holds such sights so dear.

Ah, beauty! siren! fair enchanting good!
Sweet silent rhetoric of persuading eyes!
Dumb eloquence, whose power doth move the blood
More than the words or wisdom of the wise!   130
Still harmony, whose diapason lies
   Within a brow, the key which passions move
   To ravish sense and play a world in love!

What might I then not do whose power was such?
What cannot women do that know their power?
What woman knows it not (I fear too much)
How bliss or bale lies in their laugh or lour,
Whilst they enjoy their happy blooming flower,
   Whilst nature decks them in their best attires
   Of youth and beauty, which the world admires?   140

Such one was I, my beauty was mine own,
No borrowed blush which bankrupt beauties seek;
That new-found shame, a sin to us unknown,
Th' adulterate beauty of a falsèd cheek,
Vile stain to honor and to women eke,
   Seeing that time our fading must detect,
   Thus with defect to cover our defect.

Impiety of times, chastity's abater,
Falsehood, wherein thyself thyself deniest,
Treason to counterfeit the seal of nature,   150
The stamp of heaven, impressed by the highest,
Disgrace unto the world, to whom thou liest,
   Idol unto thyself, shame to the wise,
   And all that honor thee idolatrize.

Far was that sin from us whose age was pure,
When simple beauty was accounted best,
The time when women had no other lure
But modesty, pure cheeks, a virtuous breast,
This was the pomp wherewith my youth was blest;
   These were the weapons which mine honor won   160
   In all the conflicts which my eyes begun;

Which were not small—I wrought on no mean object;
A crown was at my feet, scepters obeyed me;
Whom fortune made my king, love made my subject;
Who did command the land most humbly prayed me;
Henry the second, that so highly weighed me,
   Found well, by proof, the privilege of beauty,
   That it had power to countermand all duty.

For after all his victories in France,
And all the triumphs of his honor won,   170
Unmatched by sword, was vanquished by a glance,
And hotter wars within his breast begun—
Wars whom whole legions of desires drew on,
    Against all which my chastity contends
    With force of honor, which my shame defends.

.   .   .   .   .   .

And safe mine honor stood, till that in truth
One of my sex, of place and nature bad,
Was set in ambush to entrap my youth,
One in the habit of like frailty clad,
One who the liv'ry of like weakness had,   180
    A seeming matron, yet a sinful monster,
    As by her words the chaster sort may conster.

She set upon me with the smoothest speech
That court and age could cunningly devise;
Th' one authentic made her fit to teach,
The other learned her how to subtilize.
Both were enough to circumvent the wise,
    A document that well might teach the sage
    That there's no trust in youth, nor hope in age.

.   .   .   .   .   .

So well the golden balls cast down before me   190
Could entertain my course, hinder my way;
Whereat my wretchless youth, stooping to store me,
Lost me the goal, the glory, and the day.
Pleasure had set my well-schooled thoughts to play,
    And bade me use the virtue of mine eyes,
    For sweetly it fits the fair to wantonize.

Thus wrought to sin, soon was I trained from court
T' a solitary grange, there to attend
The time the king should thither make resort,
Where he love's long-desirèd work should end.   200
Thither he daily messages doth send,
    With costly jewels, orators of love,
    Which (ah, too well men know) do women move.

The day before the night of my defeature
He greets me with a casket richly wrought,
So rare that art did seem to strive with nature
T' express the cunning workman's curious thought;
The mystery whereof I prying sought,

And found engraven on the lid above
Amymone, how she with Neptune strove.   210

Amymone, old Danaus' fairest daughter,
As she was fetching water all alone
At Lerna, whereas Neptune came and caught her,
From whom she strived and struggled to be gone,
Bathing the air with cries and piteous moan;
    But all in vain, with him she's forced to go.
    'Tis shame that men should use poor maidens so.

There might I see describëd how she lay,
At those proud feet not satisfied with prayer;
Wailing her heavy hap, cursing the day,   220
In act so piteous to express despair.
And by how much more grieved, so much more fair;
    Her tears upon her cheeks, poor careful girl,
    Did seem, against the sun, crystal and pearl;

Whose pure clear streams, which lo, so fair appears,
Wrought hotter flames (oh, miracle of love)
That kindles fire in water, heat in tears,
And makes neglected beauty mightier prove,
Teaching afflicted eyes affects to move;
    To show that nothing ill becomes the fair,   230
    But cruelty, which yields unto no prayer.

This having viewed, and therewith something moved,
Figured I find within the other squares
Transformëd Io, Jovë's dearly loved;
In her affliction how she strangely fares,
Strangely distressed (oh beauty, born to cares),
    Turned to a heifer, kept with jealous eyes,
    Always in danger of her hateful spies.

These precedents presented to my view,
Wherein the presage of my fall was shown,   240
Might have forewarned me well what would ensue,
And others' harms have made me shun mine own;
But fate is not prevented, though foreknown,
    For that must hap, decreed by heavenly powers
    Who work our fall yet make the fault still ours.

Witness the world, wherein is nothing rifer
Than miseries unkenned before they come.
Who can the characters of chance decipher,

Written in clouds of our concealëd dome?
Which though perhaps have been revealed to some,   *250*
   Yet that so doubtful (as success did prove them)
   That men must know they have the heav'ns above them.

I saw the sin wherein my foot was ent'ring,
I saw how that dishonor did attend it,
I saw the shame whereon my flesh was vent'ring,
Yet had I not the power for to defend it.
So weak is sense, when error hath condemned it;
   We see what's good, and thereto we consent,
   But yet we choose the worst, and soon repent.

   .   .   .   .   .

What greater torment ever could have been,   *260*
Than to enforce the fair to live retired?
For what is beauty if it be not seen?
Or what is 't to be seen if not admired,
And though admired, unless in love desired?
   Never were cheeks of roses, locks of amber,
   Ordained to live imprisoned in a chamber.

Nature created beauty for the view,
Like as the fire for heat, the sun for light;
The fair do hold this privilege as due
By ancient charter, to live most in sight,   *270*
And she that is debarred it, hath not right.
   In vain our friends from this do us dehort,
   For beauty will be where is most resort.

Witness the fairest streets that Thames doth visit,
The wondrous concourse of the glitt'ring fair;
For what rare woman decked with beauty is it
That thither covets not to make repair?
The solitary country may not stay her;
   Here is the center of all beauties best,
   Excepting Delia, left t' adorn the west.   *280*

Here doth the curious with judicial eyes
Contemplate beauty gloriously attired;
And herein all our chiefest glory lies,
To live where we are praised and most desired.
Oh, how we joy to see ourselves admired,
   Whilst niggardly our favors we discover;
   We love to be beloved, yet scorn the lover.

Yet would to God my foot had never moved
From country safety, from the fields of rest,
To know the danger to be highly loved,
And live in pomp to brave among the best;
Happy for me, better had I been blest,
   If I unluckily had never strayed,
   But lived at home a happy country maid,

Whose unaffected innocency thinks
No guileful fraud, as doth the courtly liver;
She's decked with truth; the river where she drinks
Doth serve her for her glass, her counsel-giver;
She loves sincerely, and is lovéd ever;
   Her days are peace, and so she ends her breath—
   True life, that knows not what's to die till death.

So should I never have been regist'red
In the black book of the unfortunate,
Nor had my name enrolled with maids misled,
Which bought their pleasures at so high a rate;
Nor had I taught, through my unhappy fate,
   This lesson, which myself learnt with expense,
   How most it hurts that most delights the sense.

Shame follows sin, disgrace is duly given,
Impiety will out, never so closely done;
No walls can hide us from the eye of heaven,
For shame must end what wickedness begun;
Forth breaks reproach when we least think thereon,
   And this is ever proper unto courts,
   That nothing can be done but fame reports.

Fame doth explore what lies most secret hidden,
Ent'ring the closet of the palace dweller,
Abroad revealing what is most forbidden;
Of truth and falsehood both an equal teller,
'Tis not a guard can serve for to expel her.
   The sword of justice cannot cut her wings,
   Nor stop her mouth from utt'ring secret things.

And this our stealth she could not long conceal
From her whom such a forfeit most concerned,
The wrongéd queen, who could so closely deal
That she the whole of all our practice learned,
And watched a time when least it was discerned,

290

300

310

320

In absence of the king, to wreak her wrong
With such revenge as she desirëd long.

The labyrinth she entered by that thread 330
That served a conduct to my absent lord,
Left there by chance, reserved for such a deed,
Where she surprised me whom she so abhorred.
Enraged with madness, scarce she speaks a word,
  But flies with eager fury to my face,
  Off'ring me most unwomanly disgrace.

Look how a tigress that hath lost her whelp
Runs fiercely ranging through the woods astray,
And seeing herself deprived of hope or help,
Furiously assaults what's in her way, 340
To satisfy her wrath, not for a prey;
  So fell she on me in outrageous wise,
  As could disdain and jealousy devise.

And after all her vile reproaches used,
She forced me take the poison she had brought
To end the life that had her so abused,
And free her fears and ease her jealous thought.
No cruelty her wrath could leave unwrought,
  No spiteful act that to revenge is common,
  No beast being fiercer than a jealous woman. 350

Here take, saith she, thou impudent, unclean,
Base, graceless strumpet, take this next your heart;
Your love-sick heart, that overcharged hath been
With pleasure's surfeit, must be purged with art.
This potion hath a power that will convert
  To nought those humors that oppress you so;
  And, girl, I'll see you take it ere I go.

What, stand you now amazed, retire you back?
Tremble you, minion? Come, dispatch with speed;
There is no help, your champion now you lack, 360
And all these tears you shed will nothing stead;
Those dainty fingers needs must do the deed.
  Take it, or I will drench you else by force,
  And trifle not, lest that I use you worse.

Having this bloody doom from hellish breath,
My woeful eyes on every side I cast,
Rigor about me, in my hand my death,

Presenting me the horror of my last,
All hope of pity and of comfort past.
　　No means, no power, no forces to contend,   370
　　My trembling hands must give myself my end.

Those hands that beauty's ministers had been,
They must give death, that me adorned of late;
That mouth that newly gave consent to sin,
Must now receive destruction in thereat;
That body which my lust did violate,
　　Must sacrifice itself t' appease the wrong:
　　So short is pleasure, glory lasts not long.

And she no sooner saw I had it taken,
But forth she rushes, proud with victory,   380
And leaves m' alone, of all the world forsaken,
Except of death, which she had left with me;
Death and myself alone together be,
　　To whom she did her full revenge refer;
　　Oh, poor weak conquest, both for him and her.

Then straight my conscience summons up my sin
T' appear before me in a hideous face;
Now doth the terror of my soul begin,
When ev'ry corner of that hateful place
Dictates mine error and reveals disgrace;   390
　　Whilst I remain oppressed in every part,
　　Death in my body, horror at my heart.

Down on my bed my loathsome self I cast,
The bed that likewise gives in evidence
Against my soul, and tells I was unchaste,
Tells I was wanton, tells I followed sense;
And therefore cast by guilt of mine offence,
　　Must here the right of heaven needs satisfy,
　　And where I wanton lay, must wretched die.

Here I began to wail my hard mishap,   400
My sudden, strange, unlooked-for misery;
Accusing them that did my youth entrap,
To give me such a fall of infamy.
And, Poor distressèd Rosamond, said I,
　　Is this thy glory got, to die forlorn
　　In deserts where no ear can hear thee mourn?

Nor any eye of pity to behold
The woeful end of my sad tragedy?
But that thy wrongs unseen, thy tale untold,
Must here in secret silence buried lie,   410
And with thee thine, excuse together die.
    Thy sin revealed, but thy repentance hid,
    Thy shame alive, but dead what thy death did.

This, and much more, I would have uttered then,
A testament to be recorded still,
Signed with my blood, subscribed with conscience' pen,
To warn the fair and beautiful from ill.
Though I could wish, by th' example of my will,
    I had not left this note unto the fair,
    But died intestate to have had no heir.   420

But now the poison spread through all my veins
Gan dispossess my living senses quite,
And nought-respecting death, the last of pains,
Placed his pale colors, th' ensign of his might,
Upon his new-got spoil before his right;
    Thence chased my soul, setting my day ere noon,
    When I least thought my joys could end so soon.

And as conveyed t' untimely funerals,
My scarce-cold corpse not suffered longer stay,
Behold, the king, by chance returning, falls   430
T' encounter with the same upon the way,
As he repaired to see his dearest joy;
    Not thinking such a meeting could have been,
    To see his love, and seeing been unseen.

Judge those whom chance deprives of sweetest treasure,
What 'tis to lose a thing we hold so dear,
The best delight wherein our soul takes pleasure,
The sweet of life, that penetrates so near.
What passions feels that heart, enforced to bear
    The deep impression of so strange a sight   440
    That overwhelms us, or confounds us quite?

Amazed he stands, nor voice nor body steers,
Words had no passage, tears no issue found,
For sorrow shut up words, wrath kept in tears;
Confused affects each other do confound,
Oppressed with grief his passions had no bound.

Striving to tell his woes, words would not come,
For light cares speak, when mighty griefs are dumb.

At length extremity breaks out a way,
Through which th' imprisoned voice with tears attended   450
Wails out a sound that sorrows do bewray,
With arms a-cross and eyes to heaven bended,
Vaporing out sighs that to the skies ascended—
  Sighs, the poor ease calamity affords,
  Which serve for speech when sorrow wanteth words.

O heavens, quoth he, why do mine eyes behold
The hateful rays of this unhappy sun?
Why have I light to see my sins controlled,
With blood of mine own shame thus vilely done?
How can my sight endure to look thereon?   460
  Why doth not black eternal darkness hide
  That from mine eyes my heart cannot abide?

What saw my life wherein my soul might joy?
What had my days, whom troubles still afflicted,
But only this to counterpoise annoy?
This joy, this hope, which death hath interdicted;
This sweet, whose loss hath all distress inflicted;
  This, that did season all my sour of life,
  Vexed still at home with broils, abroad in strife.

Vexed still at home with broils, abroad in strife,   470
Dissension in my blood, jars in my bed,
Distrust at board, suspecting still my life,
Spending the night in horror, days in dread:
Such life hath tyrants, and this life I led.
  These miseries go masked in glittering shows,
  Which wise men see, the vulgar little knows.

Thus as these passions do him overwhelm,
He draws him near my body to behold it;
And as the vine married unto the elm
With strict embraces, so doth he enfold it;   480
And as he in his careful arms doth hold it,
  Viewing the face that even death commends,
  On senseless lips millions of kisses spends.

Pitiful mouth, saith he, that living gavest
The sweetest comfort that my soul could wish,
Oh, be it lawful now, that dead thou havest

This sorrowful farewell of a dying kiss;
And you, fair eyes, containers of my bliss,
    Motives of love, born to be matchèd never,
    Entombed in your sweet circles, sleep forever.   490

Ah, how methinks I see death dallying seeks
To entertain itself in love's sweet place;
Decayèd roses of discolored cheeks
Do yet retain dear notes of former grace,
And ugly death sits fair within her face;
    Sweet remnants resting of vermilion red,
    That death itself doubts whether she be dead.

Wonder of beauty, O receive these plaints,
These obsequies, the last that I shall make thee;
For lo, my soul that now already faints,   500
That loved thee living, dead will not forsake thee,
Hastens her speedy course to overtake thee.
    I'll meet my death, and free myself thereby,
    For, ah, what can he do that cannot die?

Yet ere I die, this much my soul doth vow,
Revenge shall sweeten death with ease of mind,
And I will cause posterity shall know
How fair thou wert above all women-kind,
And after-ages monuments shall find
    Showing thy beauty's title, not thy name,   510
    Rose of the world, that sweetened so the same.

This said, though more desirous yet to say,
For sorrow is unwilling to give over,
He doth repress what grief would else bewray,
Lest he too much his passions should discover;
And yet respect scarce bridles such a lover,
    So far transported that he knows not whither,
    For love and majesty dwell ill together.

Then were my funerals not long deferred,
But done with all the rites pomp could devise,   520
At Godstow, where my body was interred,
And richly tombed in honorable wise,
Where yet as now scarce any note descries
    Unto these times the memory of me,
    Marble and brass so little lasting be.

.   .   .   .   .   .

But here an end, I may no longer stay,
I must return t' attend at Stygian flood;
Yet ere I go, this one word more I pray,
Tell Delia now her sigh may do me good,
And will her note the frailty of our blood;   530
   And if I pass unto those happy banks,
   Then she must have her praise, thy pen her thanks.

So vanished she, and left me to return
To prosecute the tenor of my woes,
Eternal matter for my muse to mourn;
But yet the world hath heard too much of those,
My youth such errors must no more disclose.
   I'll hide the rest, and grieve for what hath been;
   Who made me known must make me live unseen.

To the Lady Margaret, Countess of Cumberland

He that of such a height hath built his mind,
And reared the dwelling of his thoughts so strong
As neither fear nor hope can shake the frame
Of his resolvëd powers, nor all the wind
Of vanity or malice pierce to wrong
His settled peace, or to disturb the same,
What a fair seat hath he, from whence he may
The boundless wastes and wilds of man survey.

And with how free an eye doth he look down
Upon these lower regions of turmoil   10
Where all the storms of passions mainly beat
On flesh and blood; where honor, power, renown,
Are only gay afflictions, golden toil,
Where greatness stands upon as feeble feet
As frailty doth, and only great doth seem
To little minds, who do it so esteem.

He looks upon the mightiest monarchs' wars
But only as on stately robberies,
Where evermore the fortune that prevails
Must be the right, the ill-succeeding mars   20
The fairest and the best-faced enterprise;
The great pirate, Pompey, lesser pirates quails.
Justice, he sees, as if seducëd, still
Conspires with power, whose cause must not be ill.

He sees the face of right t' appear as manifold
As are the passions of uncertain man,

Who puts it in all colors, all attires,
To serve his ends and make his courses hold;
He sees that let deceit work what it can,
Plot and contrive base ways to high desires,   30
That the all-guiding Providence doth yet
All disappoint, and mocks this smoke of wit.

Nor is he moved with all the thunder-cracks
Of tyrants' threats, or with the surly brow
Of power, that proudly sits on others' crimes,
Charged with more crying sins than those he checks;
The storms of sad confusion that may grow
Up in the present, for the coming times,
Appal not him, that hath no side at all
But of himself, and knows the worst can fall.   40

Although his heart, so near allied to earth,
Cannot but pity the perplexëd state
Of troublous and distressed mortality,
That thus make way unto the ugly birth
Of their own sorrows, and do still beget
Affliction upon imbecility;
Yet seeing thus the course of things must run,
He looks thereon, not strange, but as foredone.

And whilst distraught ambition compasses
And is encompassed, whilst as craft deceives   50
And is deceived, whilst man doth ransack man,
And builds on blood, and rises by distress,
And th' inheritance of desolation leaves
To great-expecting hopes, he looks thereon
As from the shore of peace with unwet eye,
And bears no venture in impiety.

Thus, madam, fares that man that hath prepared
A rest for his desires, and sees all things
Beneath him, and hath learned this book of man,
Full of the notes of frailty, and compared   60
The best of glory with her sufferings,
By whom I see you labor all you can
To plant your heart, and set your thoughts as near
His glorious mansion as your powers can bear;

Which, madam, are so soundly fashionëd
By that clear judgment that hath carried you
Beyond the feeble limits of your kind,

As they can stand against the strongest head
Passion can make, inured to any hue
The world can cast, that cannot cast that mind   70
Out of her form of goodness, that doth see
Both what the best and worst of earth can be.

Which makes that, whatsoever here befalls,
You in the region of yourself remain,
Where no vain breath of th' impudent molests;
That hath secured within the brazen walls
Of a clear conscience that without all stain
Rises in peace, in innocency rests,
Whilst all what malice from without procures   80
Shows her own ugly heart, but hurts not yours.

And whereas none rejoice more in revenge
Than women use to do, yet you well know
That wrong is better checked by being contemned
Than being pursued, leaving to him t' avenge
To whom it appertains; wherein you show
How worthily your clearness hath condemned
Base malediction, living in the dark,
That at the rays of goodness still doth bark.

Knowing the heart of man is set to be
The center of this world, about the which   90
These revolutions of disturbances
Still roll, where all th' aspects of misery
Predominate, whose strong effects are such
As he must bear, being powerless to redress;
And that unless above himself he can
Erect himself, how poor a thing is man!

And how turmoiled they are that level lie
With earth, and cannot lift themselves from thence;
That never are at peace with their desires,
But work beyond their years, and even deny   100
Dotage her rest, and hardly will dispense
With death; that when ability expires,
Desire lives still, so much delight they have
To carry toil and travail to the grave.

Whose ends you see, and, what can be the best
They reach unto, when they have cast the sum
And reckonings of their glory, and you know
This floating life hath but this port of rest—

A heart prepared, that fears no ill to come.
And that man's greatness rests but in his show,   110
The best of all whose days consumèd are
Either in war, or peace conceiving war.

This concord, madam, of a well-tuned mind
Hath been so set by that all-working hand
Of heaven, that though the world hath done his worst
To put it out by discords most unkind,
Yet doth it still in perfect union stand
With God and man, nor ever will be forced
From that most sweet accord, but still agree,
Equal in fortunes in equality.   120

And this note, madam, of your worthiness
Remains recorded in so many hearts,
As time nor malice cannot wrong your right
In th' inheritance of fame you must possess;
You that have built you by your great deserts,
Out of small means, a far more exquisite
And glorious dwelling for your honored name
Than all the gold that leaden minds can frame.

To the Lady Lucy, Countess of Bedford

Though virtue be the same when low she stands
    In th' humble shadows of obscurity,
    As when she either sweats in martial bands
Or sits in court clad with authority,
    Yet, madam, doth the strictness of her room
    Greatly detract from her ability;
For, as in-walled within a living tomb
    Her hands and arms of action labor not,
    Her thoughts, as if abortive from the womb,
Come never born, though happily begot.   10
But where she hath mounted in open sight,
    An eminent and spacious dwelling got,
    Where she may stir at will and use her might,
There is she more herself, and more her own;
    There in the fair attire of honor dight
    She sits at ease and makes her glory known;
Applause attends her hands, her deeds have grace;
    Her worth, new-born, is straight as if full grown.
    With such a godly and respected face
Doth virtue look, that's set to look from high,   20
    And such a fair advantage by her place

Hath state and greatness to do worthily.
And therefore well did your high fortunes meet
    With her, that gracing you, comes graced thereby;
    And well was let into a house so sweet,
So good, so fair, so fair, so good a guest,
    Who now remains as blessed in her seat,
    As you are with her residency blest.
And this fair course of knowledge whereunto
    Your studies, learned lady, are addressed,   30
    Is th' only certain way that you can go
Unto true glory, to true happiness;
    All passages on earth besides are so
    Encumbered with such vain disturbances
As still we lose our rest in seeking it,
    Being but deluded with appearances;
    And no key had you else that was so fit
T' unlock that prison of your sex as this,
    To let you out of weakness, and admit
    Your powers into the freedom of that bliss   40
That sets you there where you may oversee
    This rolling world, and view it as it is,
    And apprehend how th' outsides do agree
With th' inward, being of the things we deem
    And hold in our ill-cast accounts to be
    Of highest value and of best esteem;
Since all the good we have rests in the mind,
    By whose proportions only we redeem
    Our thoughts from out confusion, and do find
The measure of ourselves and of our powers;   50
    And that all happiness remains confined
    Within the kingdom of this breast of ours,
Without whose bounds all that we look on lies
    In others' jurisdictions, others' powers,
    Out of the circuit of our liberties.
All glory, honor, fame, applause, renown,
    Are not belonging to our royalties,
    But t' others' wills, wherein they're only grown;
And that unless we find us all within,
    We never can without us be our own,   60
    Nor call it right our life that we live in,
But a possession held for others' use,
    That seem to have most interest therein;
    Which we do so dissever, part, traduce,
Let out to custom, fashion, and to show,
    As we enjoy but only the abuse
    And have no other deed at all to show.

How oft are we constrainëd to appear
   With other countenance than that we owe,
   And be ourselves far off, when we are near!   70
How oft are we forced on a cloudy heart
   To set a shining face and make it clear,
   Seeming content to put ourselves apart
To bear a part of others' weaknesses!
   As if we only were composed by art,
   Not nature, and did all our deeds address
T' opinion, not t' a conscience, what is right;
   As framed b' example, not advisedness,
   Into those forms that entertain our sight.
And though books, madam, cannot make this mind   80
   Which we must bring apt to be set aright,
   Yet do they rectify it in that kind,
And touch it so as that it turns that way
   Where judgment lies; and though we cannot find
   The certain place of truth, yet do they stay
And entertain us near about the same,
   And give the soul the best delight that may
   Encheer it most, and most our spirits inflame
To thoughts of glory, and to worthy ends;
   And therefore in a course that best became   90
   The clearness of your heart, and best commends
Your worthy powers, you run the rightest way
   That is on earth, that can true glory give,
   By which, when all consumes, your fame shall live.

Musophilus
Containing a general defence of all learning

Philocosmus.

Fond man, Musophilus, that thus dost spend
In an ungainful art thy dearest days,
Tiring thy wits and toiling to no end
But to attain that idle smoke of praise,
Now when this busy world cannot attend
Th' untimely music of neglected lays:
   Other delights than these, other desires,
   This wiser profit-seeking age requires.

Musophilus.

Friend Philocosmus, I confess indeed
   I love this sacred art thou set'st so light,   10
   And though it never stand my life in steed,

It is enough it gives myself delight
   The whiles my unafflicted mind doth feed
   On no unholy thoughts for benefit.
Be it that my unseasonable song
   Come out of time, that fault is in the time,
   And I must not do virtue so much wrong
   As love her aught the worse for other's crime;
   And yet I find some blessed spirits among
   That cherish me, and like and grace my rhyme.   20
Again, that I do more in soul esteem
   Than all the gain of dust the world doth crave;
   And if I may attain but to redeem
   My name from dissolution and the grave,
   I shall have done enough, and better deem
   T' have lived to be, than to have died to have.
Short-breathed mortality would yet extend
   That span of life so far forth as it may,
   And rob her fate, seek to beguile her end
   Of some few ling'ring days of after-stay,   30
   That all this little all might not descend
   Into the dark a universal prey;
   And give our labors yet this poor delight,
   That when our days do end they are not done;
   And though we die, we shall not perish quite,
   But live two lives, where other have but one.

Philocosmus.

Silly desires of self-abusing man,
   Striving to gain th' inheritance of air,
   That having done the uttermost he can,
   Leaves yet, perhaps, but beggary to his heir.   40
   All that great purchase of the breath he wan
   Feeds not his race or makes his house more fair.
And what art thou the better, thus to leave
   A multitude of words to small effect,
   Which other times may scorn, and so deceive
   Thy promised name of what thou dost expect?
   Besides, some viperous critic may bereave
   Th' opinion of thy worth for some defect,
And get more reputation of his wit
   By but controlling of some word or sense,   50
   Than thou shalt honor for contriving it,
   With all thy travail, care, and diligence,
   Being learning now enough to contradict
   And censure others with bold insolence.

Besides, so many so confusedly sing,
 Whose diverse discords have the music marred,
 And in contempt that mystery doth bring,
 That he must sing aloud that will be heard;
 And the received opinion of the thing,
 For some unhallowed string that vilely jarred, 60
Hath so unseasoned now the ears of men
 That who doth touch the tenor of that vein
 Is held but vain, and his unreckoned pen
 The title but of levity doth gain—
 A poor, light gain, to recompense their toil
 That thought to get eternity the while.
And therefore, leave the left and outworn course
 Of unregarded ways, and labor how
 To fit the times with what is most in force;
 Be new with men's affections that are new; 70
 Strive not to run an idle counter-course
 Out from the scent of humors men allow.
For, not discreetly to compose our parts
 Unto the frame of men, which we must be,
 Is to put off ourselves, and make our arts
 Rebels to nature and society;
 Whereby we come to bury our deserts
 In th' obscure grave of singularity.

Musophilus.

Do not profane the work of doing well,
 Seducëd man, that canst not look so high 80
 From out that mist of earth, as thou canst tell
 The ways of right which virtue doth descry,
 That overlooks the base contemptibly,
 And low-laid follies of mortality;
Nor mete out truth and right-discerning praise
 By that wrong measure of confusïon,
 The vulgar foot that never takes his ways
 By reason, but by imitatïon,
 Rolling on with the rest, and never weighs
 The course which he should go, but what is gone. 90
Well were it with mankind if what the most
 Did like were best; but ignorance will live
 By others' square, as by example lost,
 And man to man must th' hand of error give
 That none can fall alone, at their own cost,
 And all because men judge not, but believe.
For what poor bounds have they whom but th' earth bounds?

What is their end whereto their care attains,
  When the thing got relieves not, but confounds,
  Having but travail to succeed their pains? 100
What joy hath he of living, that propounds
  Affliction but his end, and grief his gains?
Gath'ring, encroaching, wresting, joining to,
  Destroying, building, decking, furnishing,
  Repairing, alt'ring, and so much ado
To his soul's toil and body's travailing,—
  And all this doth he, little knowing who
  Fortune ordains to have th' inheriting.
And his fair house raised high in envy's eye,
  Whose pillars reared, perhaps, on blood and wrong, 110
  The spoils and pillage of iniquity,
Who can assure it to continue long?
  If rage spared not the walls of piety,
  Shall the profanest piles of sin keep strong?
How many proud aspiring palaces
  Have we known made the prey of wrath and pride,
  Leveled with th' earth, left to forgetfulness
Whilst titlers their pretended rights decide,
  Or civil tumults, or an orderless
  Order, pretending change of some strong side? 120
Then where is that proud title of thy name?
  Written in ice of melting vanity.
  Where is thine heir left to possess the same?
Perhaps not so well as in beggary.
  Something may rise to be beyond the shame
  Of vile and unregarded poverty,
Which I confess, although I often strive
  To clothe in the best habit of my skill,
  In all the fairest colors I can give,
Yet for all that methinks she looks but ill; 130
  I cannot brook that face, which dead-alive
  Shows a quick body but a buried will.
Yet oft we see the bars of this restraint
  Holds goodness in, which loose wealth would let fly,
  And fruitless riches, barrener than want,
Brings forth small worth from idle liberty,
  Which when disorders shall again make scant,
  It must refetch her state from poverty.
But yet in all this interchange of all,
  Virtue, we see, with her fair grace stands fast; 140
  For what high races hath there come to fall
With low disgrace, quite vanishèd and past,
  Since Chaucer lived, who yet lives, and yet shall,

Though (which I grieve to say) but in his last.
Yet what a time hath he wrested from time
    And won upon the mighty waste of days,
    Unto th' immortal honor of our clime
    That by his means came first adorned with bays;
    Unto the sacred relics of whose rhyme
    We yet are bound in zeal to offer praise.   150
And could our lines, begotten in this age,
    Obtain but such a blessed hand of years,
    And scape the fury of that threat'ning rage
    Which in confusëd clouds ghastly appears,
    Who would not strain his travails to engage
    When such true glory should succeed his cares?
But whereas he came planted in the spring,
    And had the sun before him of respect,
    We, set in th' autumn, in the withering
    And sullen season of a cold defect,   160
    Must taste those sour distastes the times do bring
    Upon the fullness of a cloyed neglect;
Although the stronger constitutions shall
    Wear out th' infection of distempered days,
    And come with glory to outlive this fall,
    Recov'ring of another springing of praise,
    Cleared from th' oppressing humors wherewithal
    The idle multitude surcharge their lays.
Whenas, perhaps, the words thou scornest now
    May live, the speaking picture of the mind,   170
    The extract of the soul that labored how
    To leave the image of herself behind,
    Wherein posterity, that love to know,
    The just proportion of our spirits may find.
For these lines are the veins, the arteries,
    And undecaying life-strings of those hearts
    That still shall pant, and still shall exercise
    The motion, spirit and nature both imparts;
    And shall with those alive so sympathize
    As, nourished with their powers, enjoy their parts.   180
O blessed letters, that combine in one
    All ages past, and make one live with all,
    By you we do confer with who are gone,
    And the dead-living unto council call;
    By you th' unborn shall have communïon
    Of what we feel and what doth us befall.
Soul of the world, knowledge, without thee
    What hath the earth that truly glorious is?
    Why should our pride make such a stir to be,

To be forgot? What good is like to this,
To do worthy the writing, and to write
Worthy the reading, and the world's delight?
And let th' unnatural and wayward race,
    Born of one womb with us, but to our shame,
    That never read t' observe, but to disgrace,
    Raise all the tempest of their power to blame;
    That puff of folly never can deface
    The work a happy genius took to frame.
Yet why should civil learning seek to wound
    And mangle her own members with despite?
    Prodigious wits that study to confound
    The life of wit, to seem to know aright,
    As if themselves had fortunately found
    Some stand from off the earth beyond our sight,
    Whence, overlooking all as from above,
    Their grace is not to work, but to reprove—
But how came they placed in so high degree,
    Above the reach and compass of the rest?
    Who hath admitted them only to be
    Free denizens of skill, to judge the best?
    From whom the world as yet could never see
    The warrant of their wit soundly expressed.
T' acquaint our times with that perfection
    Of high conceit, which only they possess,
    That we might have things exquisitely done,
    Measured with all their strict observances,
    Such would, I know, scorn a translation,
    Or bring but others' labors to the press;
    Yet, oft these monster-breeding mountains will
    Bring forth small mice of great expected skill.
Presumption, ever fullest of defects,
    Fails in the doing to perform her part;
    And I have known proud words and poor effects
    Of such indeed as do condemn this art;
    But let them rest, it ever hath been known,
    They others' virtues scorn that doubt their own.
And for the divers disagreeing chords
    Of inter-jangling ignorance that fill
    The dainty ears and leave no room for words,
    The worthier minds neglect, or pardon will;
    Knowing the best he hath, he frankly 'fords,
    And scorns to be a niggard of his skill.
And that the rather, since this short-lived race,
    Being fatally the sons of but one day,
    That now with all their power ply it apace,

To hold out with the greatest might they may
Against confusion, that hath all in chase,
To make of all an universal prey.
For now great nature hath laid down at last
  That mighty birth wherewith so long she went, 240
And overwent the times of ages past,
  Here to lie in, upon our soft content,
Where fruitful she hath multiplied so fast
  That all she hath on these times seemed t' have spent.
All that which might have many ages graced
  Is born in one, to make one cloyed with all,
Where plenty hath impressed a deep distaste
  Of best and worst, and all in general,
That goodness seems goodness to have defaced,
  And virtue hath to virtue given the fall. 250
For emulation, that proud nurse of wit,
  Scorning to stay below or come behind,
Labors upon that narrow top to sit
  Of sole perfection in the highest kind;
Envy and wonder, looking after it,
  Thrust likewise on the selfsame bliss to find,
And so, long striving till they can no more,
  Do stuff the place, or others' hopes shut out,
Who, doubting to overtake those gone before,
  Give up their care and cast no more about; 260
And so in scorn leave all as fore-possessed,
  And will be none where they may not be best.
Ev'n like some empty creek that long hath lain
  Left or neglected of the river by,
Whose searching sides, pleased with a wand'ring vein,
  Finding some little way that close did lie,
Steal in at first, then other streams again
  Second the first, then more than all supply,
Till all the mighty main hath borne, at last,
  The glory of his chiefest power that way, 270
Plying this new-found pleasant room so fast,
  Till all be full, and all be at a stay;
And then about and back again doth cast,
  Leaving that, full, to fall another way:
So fares this hum'rous world, that evermore
  Rapt with the current of a present course,
Runs into that which lay contemned before,
  Then, glutted, leaves the same and falls t' a worse.
Now zeal holds all, no life but to adore,
  Then cold in spirit, and faith is of no force; 280
Straight, all that holy was unhallowed lies,

The scattered carcasses of ruined vows;
Then truth is false, and now hath blindness eyes,
Then zeal trusts all, now scarcely what it knows,
That evermore, too foolish or too wise,
It fatal is to be seduced with shows.
Sacred religion, mother of form and fear,
How gorgeously sometimes dost thou sit decked!
What pompous vestures do we make thee wear!
What stately piles we prodigal erect! 290
How sweet perfumed thou art, how shining clear!
How solemnly observed, with what respect!
Another time, all plain, all quite threadbare,
Thou must have all within and nought without,
Sit poorly without light, disrobed, no care
Of outward grace to amuse the poor devout,
Powerless, unfollowed, scarcely men can spare
The necessary rites to set thee out.
Either truth, goodness, virtue, are not still
The selfsame which they are, and always one, 300
But alter to the project of our will;
Or we our actions make them wait upon,
Putting them in the livery of our skill,
And cast them off again when we have done.
You mighty lords that with respected grace
Do at the stern of fair example stand,
And all the body of this populace
Guide with the turning of your hand,
Keep a right course, bear up from all disgrace,
Observe the point of glory to our land, 310
Hold up disgracèd knowledge from the ground,
Keep virtue in request, give worth her due,
Let not neglect with barbarous means confound
So fair a good to bring in night anew:
Be not, oh, be not accessory found
Unto her death, that must give life to you.
Where will you have your virtuous name safe laid?
In gorgeous tombs, in sacred cells secure?
Do you not see those prostrate heaps betrayed
Your fathers' bones, and could not keep them sure? 320
And will you trust deceitful stones fair laid,
And think they will be to your honor truer?
No, no, unsparing time will proudly send
A warrant unto wrath, that with one frown
Will all these mock'ries of vain glory rend,
And make them as before, ungraced, unknown,
Poor idle honors that can ill defend

Your memories that cannot keep their own.
And whereto serve that wondrous trophy now,
　That on the goodly plain near Wilton stands?　330
　That huge dumb heap that cannot tell us how,
　Nor what, nor whence it is, nor with whose hands,
　Nor for whose glory, it was set to show
　How much our pride mocks that of other lands.
Whereon, when as the gazing passenger
　Hath greedy looked with admiratïon,
　And fain would know his birth, and what he were,
　How there erected, and how long agone,
　Inquires, and asks his fellow traveller
　What he hath heard, and his opinïon,　340
And he knows nothing; then he turns again
　And looks, and sighs, and then admires afresh,
　And in himself with sorrow doth complain
　The misery of dark forgetfulness,
　Angry with time that nothing should remain
　Our greatest wonder's wonder to express.
Then ignorance, with fabulous discourse,
　Robbing fair art and cunning of their right,
　Tells how those stones were by the devil's force
　From Afric brought to Ireland in a night,　350
　And thence to Britainy by magic course,
　From giants' hands redeemed by Merlin's sleight,
And then near Ambri placed, in memory
　Of all those noble Britons murthered there
　By Hengist and his Saxon treachery,
　Coming to parle in peace at unaware.
　With this old legend then credulity
　Holds her content, and closes up her care.
But is antiquity so great a liar?
　Or do her younger sons her age abuse,　360
　Seeing after-comers still so apt t' admire
　The grave authority that she doth use,
　That reverence and respect dares not require
　Proof of her deeds, or once her words refuse?
Yet wrong they did us to presume so far
　Upon our easy credit and delight;
　For, once found false, they straight became to mar
　Our faith and their own reputation quite,
　That now her truths hardly believëd are,
　And though sh' avouch the right, she scarce hath right.　370
And as for thee, thou huge and mighty frame
　That stands corrupted so with time's despite,
　And giv'st false evidence against their fame

That set thee there to testify their right,
And art become a traitor to their name
That trusted thee with all the best they might,
Thou shalt stand still belied and slanderëd,
The only gazing-stock of ignorance,
And by thy guile the wise, admonishëd,
Shall never more desire such heaps t' advance,   380
Nor trust their living glory with the dead
That cannot speak; but leave their fame to chance,
Considering in how small a room do lie,
And yet lie safe, as fresh as if alive,
All those great worthies of antiquity
Which long forelived thee and shall long survive,
Who stronger tombs found for eternity
Than could the powers of all the earth contrive;
Where they remain these trifles to upbraid,
Out of the reach of spoil and way of rage,   390
Though time with all his power of years hath laid
Long battery, backed with undermining age;
Yet they make head only with their own aid,
And war with his all-conquering forces wage,
Pleading the heav'ns prescription to be free,
And t' have a grant t' endure as long as he.

Philocosmus.

Behold how every man, drawn with delight
Of what he doth, flatters him in his way,
Striving to make his course seem only right,
Doth his own rest and his own thoughts betray;   400
Imagination bringing, bravely dight,
Her pleasing images in best array,
With flattering glasses that must show him fair
And others foul; his skill and wit best,
Others seduced, deceived, and wrong in their;
His knowledge right, all ignorant the rest;
Not feeling how these minions in the air
Present a face of things falsely expressed,
And that the glimmering of these errors shown
Are but a light to let him see his own.   410
Alas, poor fame, in what a narrow room,
As an encagëd parrot, art thou pent
Here amongst us, where even as good be dumb
As speak and to be heard with no attent!
How can you promise of the time to come,
Whenas the present are so negligent?

Is this the walk of all your wide renown,
  This little point, this scarce-discernëd isle,
  Thrust from the world, with whom our speech unknown
  Made never any traffic of our style?   420
  And in this all, where all this care is shown,
  T' enchant your fame to last so long a while,
  And for that happier tongues have won so much,
  Think you to make your barbarous language such?
Poor narrow limits for so mighty pains,
  That cannot promise any foreign vent;
  And yet if here to all your wondrous veins
  Were generally known, it might content;
  But lo, how many reads not, or disdains,
  The labor of the chief and excellent?   430
How many thousands never heard the name
  Of Sidney, or of Spenser, or of their books?
  And yet brave fellows, and presume of fame,
  And seem to bear down all the world with looks.
  What then shall they expect of meaner frame,
  On whose endeavors few or none scarce looks?
Do you not see these pamphlets, libels, and rhymes,
  These strange confusëd tumults of the mind,
  Are grown to be the sickness of these times,
  The great disease inflicted on mankind?   440
  Your virtues, by your follies made your crimes,
  Have issue with your indiscretion joined.
Schools, arts, professions, all in so great store,
  Pass the proportion of the present state,
  Where, being as great a number as before,
  And fewer rooms them to accommodate,
  It cannot be but they must throng the more,
  And kick, and thrust, and shoulder with debate.
For when the greater wits cannot attain
  Th' expected good which they account their right,   450
  And yet perceive others to reap that gain
  Of far inferior virtues in their sight,
  They, present with the sharp of envy, strain
  To wound them with reproaches and despite;
  And for these cannot have as well as they,
  They scorn their faith should deign to look that way.
Hence discontented sects and schisms arise,
  Hence interwounding controversies spring,
  That feed the simple and offend the wise,
  Who know the consequence of cavilling   460
  Disgrace, that these to others do devise.
  Contempt and scorn on all in th' end doth bring,

Like scolding wives, reck'ning each other's fault,
Make standers-by imagine both are naught.
For when to these rare dainties time admits
All comers, all complexions, all that will,
Where none should be let in but choicest wits,
Whose mild discretion could comport with skill,
For when the place their humor neither fits,
Nor they the place, who can expect but ill? 470
For being unapt for what they took in hand,
And for aught else whereto they shall b' addressed,
They ev'n become th' encumbrance of the land,
As out of rank, disord'ring all the rest.
This grace of theirs, to seem to understand,
Mars all their grace to do without their rest.
Men find that action is another thing
Than what they in discoursing papers read:
The world's affairs require in managing
More arts than those wherein you clerks proceed; 480
Whilst timorous knowledge stands considering,
Audacious ignorance hath done the deed;
For who knows most, the more he knows to doubt,
The least discourse is commonly most stout.
This sweet enchanting knowledge turns you clean
Out from the fields of natural delight,
And makes you hide, unwilling to be seen
In th' open concourse of a public sight;
This skill, wherewith you have so cunning been,
Unsinews all your powers, unmans you quite. 490
Public society and commerce of men
Requires another grace, another port;
This eloquence, these rhymes, these phrases then,
Begot in shades, do serve us in no sort;
Th' unmaterial swelling of your pen
Touch not the spirit that action doth import.
A manly style, fitted to manly ears,
Best grees with wit, not that which goes so gay,
And commonly the gaudy liv'ry wears
Of nice corruptions, which the times do sway, 500
And waits on th' humor of his pulse that bears
His passions set to such a pleasing kay.
Such dainties serve only for stomachs weak,
For men do foulest when they finest speak.
Yet do I not dislike that in some wise
Be sung the great heroical deserts
Of brave renownèd spirits, whose exercise
Of worthy deeds may call up others' hearts,

And serve a model for posterities,
To fashion them fit for like glorious parts;   510
But so that all our spirits may tend hereto,
To make it not our grace to say, but do.

Musophilus.
Much thou hast said, and willingly I hear,
    As one that am not so possessed with love
    Of what I do, but that I rather bear
    An ear to learn than a tongue to disprove;
    I know men must, as carried in their sphere,
    According to their proper motions, move,
    And that course likes them best which they are on,
    Yet truth hath certain bounds, but falsehood none.   520
I do confess our limits are but small,
    Compared with all the whole vast earth beside,
    All which, again rated to that great all,
    Is likewise as a point, scarcely descried;
    So that in these respects we may this call
    A point but of a point, where we abide.
But if we shall descend from that high stand
    Of over-looking contemplation,
    And cast our thoughts but to, and not beyond
    This spacious circuit which we tread upon,   530
    We then may estimate our mighty land
    A world within a world, standing alone;
Where if our fame, confined, cannot get out,
    What, shall we imagine it is penned
    That hath so great a world to walk about,
    Whose bounds with her reports have both one end?
    Why shall we not rather esteem her stout
    That farther than her own scorn to extend?
Where being so large a room, both to do well
    And eke to hear th' applause of things well done,   540
    That farther, if men shall our virtues tell,
    We have more mouths but not more merit won;
    It doth not greater make that which is laudable,
    The flame is bigger blown, the fire all one.
And for the few that only lend their ear,
    That few is all the world, which with a few
    Do ever live, and move, and work, and stir.
This is the heart doth feel and only know;
    The rest of all that only bodies bear,
    Roll up and down, and fill up but the row,   550
And serves as others' members, not their own,

The instruments of those that do direct.
Then, what disgrace is this, not to be known
To those know not to give themselves respect?
And though they swell, with pomp of folly blown,
They live ungraced and die but in neglect.
And for my part, if only one allow
The care my laboring spirits take in this,
He is to me a theater large enow,
And his applause only sufficient is,　　　　560
All my respect is bent but to his brow;
That is my all, and all I am is his.
And if some worthy spirits be pleasëd too,
It shall more comfort breed, but not more will.
But what if none? It cannot yet undo
The love I bear unto this holy skill;
This is the thing that I was born to do,
This is my scene, this part must I fulfil.

　　　　·　　　·　　　·

Power above powers, O heavenly eloquence,
That with the strong rein of commanding words　　　　570
Dost manage, guide, and master th' eminence
Of men's affections more than all their swords,—
Shall we not offer to thy excellence
The richest treasure that our wit affords?
Thou that canst do much more with one poor pen
Than all the powers of princes can effect,
And draw, divert, dispose, and fashion men
Better than force or rigor can direct,—
Should we this ornament of glory then,
As th' unmaterial fruits of shades, neglect?　　　　580
Or should we, careless, come behind the rest
In power of words, that go before in worth?
Whenas our accents, equal to the best,
Is able greater wonders to bring forth;
When all that ever hotter spirits expressed,
Comes bettered by the patience of the north.
And who, in time, knows whither we may vent
The treasure of our tongue, to what strange shores
This gain of our best glory shall be sent
T' enrich unknowing nations with our stores?　　　　590
What worlds in th' yet unformëd occident
May come refined with th' accents that are ours?
Or who can tell for what great work in hand
The greatness of our style is now ordained?
What powers it shall bring in, what spirits command,

What thoughts let out, what humors keep restrained,
What mischief it may powerfully withstand,
And what fair ends may thereby be attained?

·　·　·　·　·

[*Love is a sickness*]

Love is a sickness full of woes,
　All remedies refusing;
A plant that with most cutting
　　grows,
　Most barren with best using.
　　　Why so?
　More we enjoy it, more it dies;
If not enjoyed it sighing cries,
　　　Hey ho.

Love is a torment of the mind,
　A tempest everlasting;　　　　10
And Jove hath made it of a kind,
　Not well, nor full, nor fasting.
　　　Why so?
　More we enjoy it, more it dies;
If not enjoyed it sighing cries,
　　　Hey ho.
　　　　　From *Hymen's Triumph*

FROM *Certain Small Poems*, 1605

Ulysses and the Siren

Sir. Come, worthy Greek, Ulys-
　　　ses, come,
Possess these shores with me;
The winds and seas are trouble-
　　　some,
And here we may be free.
　Here may we sit and view
　　　their toil
That travail on the deep,
And joy the day in mirth the
　　　while,
And spend the night in sleep.

Ulys. Fair nymph, if fame or
　　　honor were
To be attained with ease,　　10
Then would I come and rest
　　　with thee,
And leave such toils as these.
　But here it dwells, and here
　　　must I
With danger seek it forth;
To spend the time luxuriously
Becomes not men of worth.

Sir. Ulysses, O be not deceived
With that unreal name;
This honor is a thing conceived,

And rests on others' fame.　　20
　Begotten only to molest
Our peace, and to beguile
The best thing of our life, our
　　　rest,
And give us up to toil.

Ulys. Delicious nymph, suppose
　　　there were
Nor honor nor report,
Yet manliness would scorn to
　　　wear
The time in idle sport.
　For toil doth give a better
　　　touch,
To make us feel our joy;　　30
And ease finds tediousness, as
　　　much
As labor, yields annoy.

Sir. Then pleasure likewise seems
　　　the shore
Whereto tends all your toil,
Which you forgo to make it
　　　more,
And perish oft the while.
　Who may disport them di-
　　　versly,
Find never tedious day,

And ease may have variety
As well as action may. 40

Ulys. But natures of the noblest
    frame
These toils and dangers please,
And they take comfort in the
    same
As much as you in ease,
    And with the thoughts of ac-
      tions past
Are recreated still;
When pleasure leaves a touch at
    last
To show that it was ill.

Sir. That doth opinion only cause
That's out of custom bred, 50
Which makes us many other
    laws
Than ever nature did.
    No widows wail for our de-
      lights,
Our sports are without blood;
The world, we see, by warlike
    wights

Receives more hurt than good.

Ulys. But yet the state of things
    require
These motions of unrest,
And these great spirits of high
    desire
Seem born to turn them best, 60
    To purge the mischiefs that
      increase
And all good order mar;
For oft we see a wicked peace
To be well changed for war.

Sir. Well, well, Ulysses, then I
    see
I shall not have thee here,
And therefore I will come to
    thee,
And take my fortunes there.
    I must be won that cannot
      win,
Yet lost were I not won; 70
For beauty hath created been
T' undo, or be undone.

FROM *Tethys' Festival*, 1610

[*Are they shadows?*]

Are they shadows that we see?
And can shadows pleasure give?
Pleasures only shadows be
Cast by bodies we conceive,
    And are made the things we
      deem
    In those figures which they
      seem.
But these pleasures vanish fast,
Which by shadows are expressed.
Pleasures are not, if they last;

In their passing is their best. 10
Glory is most bright and gay
In a flash, and so away.
Feed apace then, greedy eyes,
On the wonder you behold.
    Take it sudden as it flies,
    Though you take it not to hold;
    When your eyes have done their
      part,
    Thought must length it in the
      heart.

MICHAEL DRAYTON

The Introduction and Notes are at page 962

FROM *Idea, the Shepherd's Garland*, 1593

The eighth eclogue

Far in the country of Arden
There wonned a knight hight
    Cassemen,
    As bold as Isenbras;
Fell was he and eager bent
In battle and in tournament,
    As was the good Sir Thopas.
He had, as antique stories tell,
A daughter clepëd Dowsabell,
    A maiden fair and free;
And for she was her father's
    heir,   10
Full well she was yconned the
    lere
    Of mickle courtesy.
The silk well couth she twist and
    twine,
And make the fine marchpine,
    And with the needle work;
And she couth help the priest to
    say
His matins on a holy-day,
    And sing a psalm in kirk.
She ware a frock of frolic green
Might well beseem a maiden
    queen,   20
    Which seemly was to see;
A hood to that so neat and fine,
In color like the columbine,
    Ywrought full featously.
Her feature all as fresh above
As is the grass that grows by
    Dove,
    As lithe as lass of Kent;
Her skin as soft as Lemster wool,
As white as snow on Peakish
    hull,

Or swan that swims in
    Trent.   30
This maiden in a morn betime
Went forth when May was in her
    prime
    To get sweet cetywall,
The honeysuckle, the harlock,
The lily, and the lady-smock,
    To deck her summer hall.
Thus as she wandered here and
    there,
Ypicking of the bloomëd breer,
    She chancëd to espy
A shepherd sitting on a bank;   40
Like chanticleer he crowëd crank,
    And piped with merry glee.
He leared his sheep as he him
    list,
When he would whistle in his
    fist,
    To feed about him round,
Whilst he full many a carol
    sung,
Until the fields and meadows
    rung,
    And that the woods did sound.
In favor this same shepherd's
    swain
Was like the bedlam Tambur-
    laine,   50
    Which held proud kings in
    awe.
But meek he was as lamb mought
    be,
Ylike that gentle Abel he,
    Whom his lewd brother slaw.
This shepherd ware a sheep-grey
    cloak,
Which was of the finest loke

That could be cut with shear;
His mittens were of bauzens' skin,
His cockers were of cordiwin,
  His hood of meniveere; 60
His awl and lingel in a thong,
His tar-box on his broad belt
    hung,
  His breech of cointrie blue.
Full crisp and curlëd were his
    locks,
His brows as white as Albion
    rocks,
  So like a lover true.
And piping still he spent the day,
So merry as the popinjay;
  Which likëd Dowsabell,
That would she aught or would
    she nought, 70
This lad would never from her
    thought,
  She in love-longing fell.
At length she tuckëd up her
    frock,
White as the lily was her smock,
  She drew the shepherd nigh.
But then the shepherd piped a
    good
That all his sheep forsook their
    food
  To hear his melody.
Thy sheep, quoth she, cannot be
    lean,
That have a jolly shepherd's
    swain 80
  The which can pipe so well.
Yea but, saith he, their shepherd
    may,
If piping thus he pine away
  In love of Dowsabell.
Of love, fond boy, take thou no
    keep,
Quoth she, look well unto thy
    sheep
  Lest they should hap to stray.
Quoth he, So had I done full
    well,

Had I not seen fair Dowsabell
  Come forth to gather May. 90
With that she gan to vail her
    head;
Her cheeks were like the roses
    red,
  But not a word she said.
With that the shepherd gan to
    frown;
He threw his pretty pipes adown,
  And on the ground him laid.
Saith she, I may not stay till
    night
And leave my summer hall un-
    dight,
  And all for long of thee.
My cote, saith he, nor yet my
    fold, 100
Shall neither sheep nor shepherd
    hold,
  Except thou favor me.
Saith she, Yet liefer I were
    dead,
Than I should lose my maiden-
    head,
  And all for love of men.
Saith he, Yet are you too un-
    kind,
If in your heart you cannot find
  To love us now and then;
And I to thee will be as kind
As Colin was to Rosalind, 110
  Of courtesy the flower.
Then will I be as true, quoth she,
As ever maiden yet might be
  Unto her paramour.
With that she bent her snow-
    white knee;
Down by the shepherd kneelëd
    she,
  And him she sweetly kissed.
With that the shepherd whooped
    for joy;
Quoth he, There's never shep-
    herd's boy
  That ever was so blist. 120

FROM *Idea's Mirror*, 1594

To the dear child of the Muses, and his ever kind Mæcenas, Ma. Anthony Cooke, Esquire

Vouchsafe to grace these rude unpolished rhymes,
    Which long, dear friend, have slept in sable night,
And come abroad now in these glorious times,
    Can hardly brook the pureness of the light.
But sith you see their destiny is such
    That in the world their fortune they must try,
Perhaps they better shall abide the touch
    Wearing your name, their gracious livery.
Yet these mine own, I wrong not other men,
    Nor traffic further than this happy clime,   10
Nor filch from Portes' nor from Petrarch's pen,
    A fault too common in this latter time.
Divine Sir Philip, I avouch thy writ,
I am no pickpurse of another's wit.

Black pitchy night, companion of my woe,
    The inn of care, the nurse of dreary sorrow,
Why length'nest thou thy darkest hours so,
    Still to prolong my long-time-looked-for morrow?
Thou sable shadow, image of despair,
    Portrait of hell, the air's black mourning weed,
Recorder of revenge, remembrancer of care,
    The shadow and the veil of every sinful deed,
Death like to thee, so live thou still in death,
    The grave of joy, prison of day's delight.   10
    Let heavens withdraw their sweet ambrosian breath,
    Nor moon nor stars lend thee their shining light,
For thou alone renew'st that old desire
Which still torments me in day's burning fire.

FROM *England's Heroical Epistles*, 1599

Many there be excelling in this kind,
Whose well-tricked rhymes with all invention swell;
Let each commend as best shall like his mind,
Some Sidney, Constable, some Daniel.
That thus their names familiarly I sing,
Let none think them disparagèd to be;
Poor men with reverence may speak of a king,
And so may these be spoken of by me.
My wanton verse ne'er keeps one certain stay,

But now at hand, then seeks invention far,   10
And with each little motion runs astray,
Wild, madding, jocund, and irregular;
   Like me that lust, my honest merry rhymes
   Nor care for critic, nor regard the times.

From *Poems*, 1619

Idea

To the reader of these sonnets

Into these loves who but for passion looks,
At this first sight here let him lay them by,
And seek elsewhere, in turning other books
Which better may his labor satisfy.
No far-fetched sigh shall ever wound my breast,
Love from mine eye a tear shall never wring,
Nor in *Ah me's* my whining sonnets dressed.
A libertine, fantastically I sing;
My verse is the true image of my mind,
Ever in motion, still desiring change.   10
And as thus to variety inclined,
So in all humors sportively I range;
   My muse is rightly of the English strain,
   That cannot long one fashion entertain.

Like an adventurous seafarer am I,
Who hath some long and dang'rous voyage been,
And called to tell of his discovery,
How far he sailed, what countries he had seen;
Proceeding from the port whence he put forth,
Shows by his compass how his course he steered,
When east, when west, when south, and when by north,
As how the pole to ev'ry place was reared,
What capes he doubled, of what continent,
The gulfs and straits that strangely he had passed,   10
Where most becalmed, where with foul weather spent,
And on what rocks in peril to be cast:
   Thus in my love, time calls me to relate
   My tedious travels and oft-varying fate.

How many paltry, foolish, painted things,
That now in coaches trouble ev'ry street,
Shall be forgotten, whom no poet sings,
Ere they be well wrapped in their winding sheet!
Where I to thee eternity shall give,

When nothing else remaineth of these days,
And queens hereafter shall be glad to live
Upon the alms of thy superfluous praise;
Virgins and matrons reading these my rhymes
Shall be so much delighted with thy story   10
That they shall grieve they lived not in these times,
To have seen thee, their sex's only glory.
    So shalt thou fly above the vulgar throng,
    Still to survive in my immortal song.

As other men, so I myself do muse
Why in this sort I wrest invention so,
And why these giddy metaphors I use,
Leaving the path the greater part do go.
I will resolve you: I am lunatic,
And ever this in madmen you shall find—
What they last thought of, when the brain grew sick,
In most distraction they keep that in mind.
Thus talking idly in this bedlam fit,
Reason and I, you must conceive, are twain;   10
'Tis nine years now since first I lost my wit,
Bear with me, then, though troubled be my brain.
    With diet and correction, men distraught
    (Not too far past) may to their wits be brought.

To nothing fitter can I thee compare
Than to the son of some rich penny-father,
Who having now brought on his end with care,
Leaves to his son all he had heaped together;
This new-rich novice, lavish of his chest,
To one man gives, doth on another spend,
Then here he riots; yet amongst the rest
Haps to lend some to one true honest friend.
Thy gifts thou in obscurity dost waste,
False friends thy kindness, born but to deceive thee;   10
Thy love, that is on the unworthy placed;
Time hath thy beauty, which with age will leave thee;
    Only that little which to me was lent,
    I give thee back, when all the rest is spent.

An evil spirit, your beauty, haunts me still,
Wherewith, alas, I have been long possessed,
Which ceaseth not to tempt me to each ill,
Nor gives me once but one poor minute's rest;
In me it speaks, whether I sleep or wake,
And when by means to drive it out I try.

With greater torments then it me doth take,
And tortures me in most extremity;
Before my face it lays down my despairs,
And hastes me on unto a sudden death,   10
Now tempting me to drown myself in tears,
And then in sighing to give up my breath.
 Thus am I still provoked to every evil
 By this good wicked spirit, sweet angel devil.

A witless gallant, a young wench that wooed
(Yet his dull spirit her not one jot could move),
Entreated me, as e'er I wished his good
To write him but one sonnet to his love;
When I, as fast as e'er my pen could trot,
Poured out what first from quick invention came,
Nor never stood one word thereof to blot,
Much like his wit, that was to use the same;
But with my verses he his mistress won,
Who doted on the dolt beyond all measure.   10
But see, for you to heav'n for phrase I run,
And ransack all Apollo's golden treasure;
 Yet by my froth this fool his love obtains,
 And I lose you for all my wit and pains.

Methinks I see some crooked mimic jeer,
And tax my muse with this fantastic grace;
Turning my papers, asks, What have we here?
Making withal some filthy antic face.
I fear no censure, nor what thou canst say,
Nor shall my spirit one jot of vigor lose.
Think'st thou my wit shall keep the pack-horse way
That ev'ry dudgeon low invention goes?
Since sonnets thus in bundles are impressed,
And ev'ry drudge doth dull our satiate ear,   10
Think'st thou my love shall in those rags be dressed
That ev'ry dowdy, ev'ry trull doth wear?
 Up to my pitch no common judgment flies,
 I scorn all earthly dung-bred scarabies.

Our floods' queen, Thames, for ships and swans is crowned,
And stately Severn for her shore is praised;
The crystal Trent for fords and fish renowned,
And Avon's fame to Albion's cliffs is raised;
Carlegion Chester vaunts her holy Dee;
York many wonders of her Ouse can tell,
The Peak her Dove, whose banks so fertile be,

And Kent will say her Medway doth excel;
Cotswold commends her Isis to the Tame;
Our northern borders boast of Tweed's fair flood;   10
Our western parts extol their Wylye's fame,
And the old Lea brags of the Danish blood;
    Arden's sweet Anker, let thy glory be
    That fair Idea only lives by thee.

Some misbelieving and profane in love,
When I do speak of miracles by thee,
May say that thou art flatterëd by me
Who only write my skill in verse to prove;
See miracles, ye unbelieving, see
A dumb-born muse made to express the mind,
A cripple hand to write, yet lame by kind,
One by thy name, the other touching thee;
Blind were mine eyes till they were seen of thine,   10
And mine ears deaf by thy fame healëd be,
My vices cured by virtues sprung from thee,
My hopes revived, which long in grave had lyne;
    All unclean thoughts foul spirits cast out in me
    Only by virtue that proceeds from thee.

Dear, why should you command me to my rest,
When now the night doth summon all to sleep?
Methinks this time becometh lovers best;
Night was ordained together friends to keep.
How happy are all other living things,
Which though the day disjoin by sev'ral flight,
The quiet evening yet together brings,
And each returns unto his love at night!
O thou that art so courteous else to all,
Why shouldst thou, Night, abuse me only thus,   10
That ev'ry creature to his kind dost call,
And yet 'tis thou dost only sever us?
    Well could I wish it would be ever day,
    If when night comes you bid me go away.

Some men there be which like my method well,
And much commend the strangeness of my vein;
Some say I have a passing pleasing strain,
Some say that in my humor I excel;
Some, who not kindly relish my conceit,
They say, as poets do, I use to feign,
And in bare words paint out my passion's pain.
Thus sundry men their sundry minds repeat.

I pass not, I, how men affected be,
Nor who commends or discommends my verse;
It pleaseth me if I my woes rehearse,
And in my lines if she my love may see.
    Only my comfort still consists in this,
    Writing her praise I cannot write amiss.

10

Whilst thus my pen strives to eternize thee,
Age rules my lines with wrinkles in my face,
Where, in the map of all my misery,
Is modeled out the world of my disgrace;
Whilst in despite of tyrannizing times,
Medea-like I make thee young again.
Proudly thou scorn'st my world-outwearing rhymes,
And murther'st virtue with thy coy disdain;
And though in youth my youth untimely perish
To keep thee from oblivion and the grave,
Ensuing ages yet my rhymes shall cherish,
Where I, entombed, my better part shall save;
    And though this earthly body fade and die,
    My name shall mount upon eternity.

10

In pride of wit, when high desire of fame
Gave life and courage to my lab'ring pen,
And first the sound and virtue of my name
Won grace and credit in the ears of men;
With those the throngèd theaters that press
I in the circuit for the laurel strove,
Where the full praise, I freely must confess,
In heat of blood, a modest mind might move.
With shouts and claps at ev'ry little pause,
When the proud round on ev'ry side hath rung,
Sadly I sit, unmoved with the applause,
As though to me it nothing did belong.
    No public glory vainly I pursue,
    All that I seek is to eternize you.

10

Clear Anker, on whose silver-sanded shore
My soul-shrined saint, my fair Idea lies,
O blessed brook, whose milk-white swans adore
Thy crystal stream, refinèd by her eyes,
Where sweet myrrh-breathing Zephyr in the spring
Gently distils his nectar-dropping showers,
Where nightingales in Arden sit and sing
Amongst the dainty dew-empearlèd flowers;
Say thus, fair brook, when thou shalt see thy queen:

Lo, here thy shepherd spent his wand'ring years,
And in these shades, dear nymph, he oft hath been,
And here to thee he sacrificed his tears. 10

    Fair Arden, thou my Tempe art alone,
    And thou, sweet Anker, art my Helicon.

Since there's no help, come let us kiss and part;
Nay, I have done, you get no more of me,
And I am glad, yea glad with all my heart
That thus so cleanly I myself can free;
Shake hands forever, cancel all our vows,
And when we meet at any time again,
Be it not seen in either of our brows
That we one jot of former love retain.
Now at the last gasp of love's latest breath,
When, his pulse failing, passion speechless lies, 10
When faith is kneeling by his bed of death,
And innocence is closing up his eyes,
    Now if thou wouldst, when all have given him over,
    From death to life thou mightst him yet recover.

Truce, gentle love, a parley now I crave;
Methinks 'tis long since first these wars begun,
Nor thou, nor I, the better yet can have;
Bad is the match where neither party won.
I offer free conditions of fair peace,
My heart for hostage that it shall remain;
Discharge our forces, here let malice cease,
So for my pledge thou give me pledge again;
Or if no thing but death will serve thy turn,
Still thirsting for subversion of my state, 10
Do what thou canst, raze, massacre, and burn,
Let the world see the utmost of thy hate;
    I send defiance, since if overthrown,
    Thou vanquishing, the conquest is mine own.

England's Heroical Epistles

Henry Howard, Earl of Surrey, to the Lady Geraldine

THE ARGUMENT

The Earl of Surrey, that renownèd lord,
Th' old English glory bravely that restored,
That prince and poet (a name more divine),
Falling in love with beauteous Geraldine

Of the Geraldi, which derive their name
From Florence, whither, to advance her fame,
He travels, and in public jousts maintained
Her beauty peerless, which by arms he gained;
But staying long, fair Italy to see,
To let her know him constant still to be,
From Tuscany this letter to her writes,
Which her rescription instantly invites.

From learned Florence, long time rich in fame,
From whence thy race, thy noble grandsires, came
To famous England, that kind nurse of mine,
Thy Surrey sends to heav'nly Geraldine;
Yet let not Tuscan think I do it wrong,
That I from thence write in my native tongue,
That in these harsh-tuned cadences I sing,
Sitting so near the Muses' sacred spring;
But rather think itself adorned thereby,
That England reads the praise of Italy.   10
Though to the Tuscans I the smoothness grant,
Our dialect no majesty doth want
To set thy praises in as high a key
As France, or Spain, or Germany, or they.
    What day I quit the foreland of fair Kent,
And that my ship her course for Flanders bent,
Yet think I with how many a heavy look
My leave of England and of thee I took,
And did entreat the tide, if it might be,
But to convey me one sigh back to thee.   20
Up to the deck a billow lightly skips,
Taking my sigh, and down again it slips;
Into the gulf itself it headlong throws,
And as a post to England-ward it goes.
As I sat wond'ring how the rough seas stirred,
I might far off perceive a little bird,
Which, as she fain from shore to shore would fly,
Had lost herself in the broad vasty sky,
Her feeble wing beginning to deceive her,
The seas of life still gaping to bereave her;   30
Unto the ship she makes, which she discovers,
And there, poor fool, a while for refuge hovers.
And when at length her flagging pinion fails,
Panting she hangs upon the rattling sails,
And being forced to loose her hold with pain,
Yet beaten off, she straight lights on again,
And tossed with flaws, with storms, with wind, with weather,

Yet still departing thence, still turneth thither;
Now with the poop, now with the prow doth bear,
Now on this side, now that, now here, now there.   40
Methinks these storms should be my sad depart,
The silly helpless bird is my poor heart,
The ship to which for succor it repairs,
That is yourself, regardless of my cares.
Of every surge doth fall, or waves doth rise,
To some one thing I sit and moralize.
  When for thy love I left the Belgic shore,
Divine Erasmus and our famous More,
Whose happy presence gave me such delight
As made a minute of a winter's night,   50
With whom a while I stayed at Rotterdam,
Now so renownèd by Erasmus' name;
Yet every hour did seem a world of time
Till I had seen that soul-reviving clime,
And thought the foggy Netherlands unfit,
A wat'ry soil to clog a fiery wit.
And as that wealthy Germany I passed,
Coming unto the Emperor's court at last,
Great learn'd Agrippa, so profound in art,
Who the infernal secrets doth impart,   60
When of thy health I did desire to know,
Me in a glass my Geraldine did show,
Sick in thy bed and, for thou couldst not sleep,
By a wax taper set the light to keep;
I do remember thou didst read that ode
Sent back whilst I in Thanet made abode,
Where when thou cam'st unto that word of love,
Even in thine eyes I saw how passion strove;
That snowy lawn which coverèd thy bed,
Methought looked white, to see thy cheek so red,   70
Thy rosy cheek, oft changing in my sight,
Yet still was red, to see the lawn so white;
The little taper which should give thee light,
Methought waxed dim to see thine eye so bright;
Thine eye again supplied the taper's turn,
And with his beams more brightly made it burn;
The shrugging air about thy temples hurls
And wrapped thy breath in little clouded curls,
And as it did ascend, it straight did seize it,
And as it sunk, it presently did raise it.   80
Canst thou by sickness banish beauty so?
Which if put from thee knows not where to go,
To make her shift and for her succor seek

To every riveled face, each bankrupt cheek.
If health preserved, thou beauty still dost cherish,
If that neglected, beauty soon doth perish.
Care draws on care, woe comforts woe again,
Sorrow breeds sorrow, one grief brings forth twain;
If live or die, as thou dost so do I,
If live, I live, and if thou die, I die: 90
One heart, one love, one joy, one grief, one troth,
One good, one ill, one life, one death to both.

    If Howard's blood thou hold'st as but too vile,
Or not esteem'st of Norfolk's princely style,
If Scotland's coat no mark of fame can lend,
That lion placed in our bright silver bend,
(Which as a trophy beautifies our shield
Since Scottish blood discolored Flodden field,
When the proud Cheviot our brave ensign bare
As a rich jewel in a lady's hair,   100
And did fair Bramston's neighboring valleys choke
With clouds of cannons, fire-disgorgèd smoke),
Or Surrey's earldom insufficient be
And not a dower so well contenting thee,
Yet am I one of great Apollo's heirs,
The sacred Muses challenge me for theirs.
By princes my immortal lines are sung,
My flowing verses graced with ev'ry tongue;
The little children, when they learn to go,
By painful mothers daded to and fro,   110
Are taught my sugared numbers to rehearse,
And have their sweet lips seasoned with my verse.

    When heav'n would strive to do the best it can,
And put an angel's spirit into a man,
The utmost power it hath it then doth spend
When to the world a poet it doth intend;
That little diff'rence 'twixt the gods and us,
By them confirmed, distinguished only thus:
Whom they, in birth, ordain to happy days,
The gods commit their glory to our praise;   120
T' eternal life when they dissolve their breath,
We likewise share a second power by death.

    When time shall turn those amber locks to gray,
My verse again shall gild and make them gay,
And trick them up in knotted curls anew,
And to thy autumn give a summer's hue;
That sacred power that in my ink remains
Shall put fresh blood into thy withered veins,
And on thy red decayed, thy whiteness dead,

Shall set a white more white, a red more red;   130
When thy dim sight thy glass cannot descry,
Nor thy crazed mirror can discern thine eye,
My verse, to tell th' one what the other was,
Shall represent them both, thine eye and glass,
Where both thy mirror and thine eye shall see
What once thou saw'st in that, that saw in thee,
And to them both shall tell the simple truth,
What that in pureness was, what thou in youth.

   If Florence once should lose her old renown,
As famous Athens, now a fisher town,   140
My lines for thee a Florence shall erect
Which great Apollo ever shall protect,
And with the numbers from my pen that falls
Bring marble mines to re-erect those walls.
Nor beauteous Stanhope, whom all tongues report
To be the glory of the English court,
Shall by our nation be so much admired,
If ever Surrey truly were inspired.
And famous Wyatt, who in numbers sings
To that enchanting Thracian harper's strings,   150
To whom Phœbus, the poets' god, did drink
A bowl of nectar filled up to the brink,
And sweet-tongued Bryan, whom the Muses kept
And in his cradle rocked him whilst he slept,
In sacred verses most divinely penned,
Upon thy praises ever shall attend.

   What time I came into this famous town
And made the cause of my arrival known,
Great Medici a list for triumphs built;
Within the which, upon a tree of gilt,   160
Which was with sundry rare devices set,
I did erect thy lovely counterfeit
To answer those Italian dames' desire,
Which daily came thy beauty to admire;
By which my lion, in his gaping jaws,
Held up my lance, and in his dreadful paws
Reacheth my gauntlet unto him that dare
A beauty with my Geraldine's compare.
Which, when each manly valiant arm assays,
After so many brave triumphant days   170
The glorious prize upon my lance I bare,
By herald's voice proclaimed to be thy share.
The shivered staves, here for thy beauty broke,
With fierce encounters passed at ev'ry shock,
When stormy courses answered cuff for cuff,

Denting proud beavers with the counter-buff,
Upon an altar, burnt with holy flame,
I sacrificed as incense to thy fame;
Where, as the phœnix from her spicëd fume
Renews herself in that she doth consume,   180
So from these sacred ashes live we both,
Ev'n as that one Arabian wonder doth.

    When to my chamber I myself retire,
Burnt with the sparks that kindled all this fire,
Thinking of England, which my hope contains,
The happy isle where Geraldine remains,
Of Hunsdon, where those sweet celestial eyne
At first did pierce this tender breast of mine,
Of Hampton Court and Windsor, where abound
All pleasures that in paradise were found;   190
Near that fair castle is a little grove,
With hanging rocks all covered from above,
Which on the bank of goodly Thames doth stand,
Clipped by the water from the other land,
Whose bushy top doth bid the sun forbear
And checks his proud beams that would enter there;
Whose leaves still mutt'ring as the air doth breathe,
With the sweet bubbling of the stream beneath,
Doth rock the senses, whilst the small birds sing,
Lullëd asleep with gentle murmuring;   200
Where light-foot fairies sport at prison-base
(No doubt there is some power frequents the place),
There the soft poplar and smooth beech do bear
Our names together carvëd ev'rywhere,
And Gordian knots do curiously entwine
The names of Henry and of Geraldine.
Oh, let this grove in happy times to come
Be called the lovers' blest Elysium;
Whither my mistress wonted to resort,
In summer's heat in those sweet shades to sport;   210
A thousand sundry names I have it given,
And called it Wonder-hider, Cover-heaven,
The roof where beauty her rich court doth keep,
Under whose compass all the stars do sleep.
There is one tree which now I call to mind,
Doth bear these verses carvëd in his rind:
When Geraldine shall sit in thy fair shade,
Fan her sweet tresses with perfumëd air,
Let thy large boughs a canopy be made
To keep the sun from gazing on my fair;   220
And when thy spreading branchëd arms be sunk,

And thou no sap nor pith shalt more retain,
Ev'n from the dust of thy unwieldy trunk
I will renew thee, phœnix-like, again,
And from thy dry decayèd root will bring
A new-born stem, another Æson's spring.

I find no cause, nor judge I reason why
My country should give place to Lombardy;
As goodly flowers on Thamesis do grow
As beautify the banks of wanton Po;   230
As many nymphs as haunt rich Arno's strand,
By silver Severn tripping hand in hand;
Our shade's as sweet, though not to us so dear,
Because the sun hath greater power there;
This distant place doth give me greater woe,
Far off, my sighs the farther have to go.
Ah absence! why shouldst thou seem so long?
Or wherefore shouldst thou offer time such wrong,
Summer so soon to steal on winter's cold,
Or winter's blasts so soon make summer old?   240
Love did us both with one self arrow strike,
Our wound's both one, our cure should be the like,
Except thou hast found out some mean by art,
Some powerful med'cine to withdraw the dart;
But mine is fixed, and absence being proved,
It sticks too fast, it cannot be removed.
   Adieu, adieu, from Florence when I go
By my next letters Geraldine shall know,
Which if good fortune shall by course direct,
From Venice by some messenger expect;   250
Till when, I leave thee to thy heart's desire:
By him that lives thy virtues to admire.

ODES

To the Virginian voyage

You brave heroic minds
Worthy your country's name,
  That honor still pursue,
  Go, and subdue,
Whilst loit'ring hinds
Lurk here at home, with shame.

Britons, you stay too long;
Quickly aboard bestow you,
  And with a merry gale

Swell your stretched sail,   10
  With vows as strong
  As the winds that blow you.

Your course securely steer,
West and by south forth keep,
  Rocks, lee-shores, nor shoals,
  When Æolus scowls,
You need not fear,
So absolute the deep.

And cheerfully at sea,
Success you still entice,   20

To get the pearl and gold,
    And ours to hold,
Virginia,
Earth's only paradise,

Where nature hath in store
Fowl, venison, and fish,
    And the fruitful'st soil
    Without your toil
Three harvests more,
All greater than your wish.   30

And the ambitious vine
Crowns with his purple mass,
    The cedar reaching high
    To kiss the sky,
The cypress, pine,
And useful sassafras.

To whose the golden age
Still nature's laws doth give,
    No other cares that tend,
    But them to defend   40
From winter's age,
That long there doth not live.

Whenas the luscious smell
Of that delicious land,
    Above the seas that flows,
    The clear wind throws,
Your hearts to swell
Approaching the dear strand,

In kenning of the shore,
Thanks to God first given,   50
    O you, the happi'st men,
    Be frolic then,
Let cannons roar,
Frighting the wide heaven.

And in regions far
Such heroes bring ye forth
    As those from whom we came,
    And plant our name
Under that star
Not known unto our north.   60

And as there plenty grows
Of laurel everywhere,
    Apollo's sacred tree,
    You it may see
A poet's brows
To crown, that may sing there.

Thy voyages attend,
Industrious Hakluÿt,
    Whose reading shall enflame
    Men to seek fame,   70
And much commend
To after times thy wit.

The crier

Good folk, for gold or hire,
But help me to a crier;
For my poor heart is run astray
After two eyes that passed this
            way.
        Oyes, oyes, oyes,
        If there be any man
        In town or country can
        Bring me my heart again,
        I'll please him for his pain;
And by these marks I will you
            show   10
That only I this heart do owe.
        It is a wounded heart,
        Wherein yet sticks the dart;
Ev'ry piece sore hurt throughout
            it,
Faith and troth writ round about
            it;
It was a tame heart, and a dear,
        And never used to roam;
But having got this haunt, I
            fear
'Twill hardly stay at home.
For God's sake, walking by the
            way,   20
        If you my heart do see,
Either impound it for a stray,
        Or send it back to me.

*To the Cambro-Britons and
their harp, his ballad of
Agincourt*

Fair stood the wind for France,
When we our sails advance,
Nor now to prove our chance,
    Longer will tarry;
But putting to the main
At Kaux, the mouth of Seine,
With all his martial train,
    Landed King Harry.

And taking many a fort,
Furnished in warlike sort,   10
Marcheth towards Agincourt,
    In happy hour;
Skirmishing day by day
With those that stopped his way,
Where the French gen'ral lay
    With all his power.

Which in his height of pride,
King Henry to deride,
His ransom to provide
    To the King sending;   20
Which he neglects the while
As from a nation vile,
Yet with an angry smile
    Their fall portending.

And turning to his men,
Quoth our brave Henry then:
Though they to one be ten,
    Be not amazèd.
Yet have we well begun,
Battles so bravely won   30
Have ever to the sun
    By fame been raisèd.

And for myself, quoth he,
This my full rest shall be,
England ne'er mourn for me,
    Nor more esteem me;
Victor I will remain,
Or on this earth lie slain,

Never shall she sustain
    Loss to redeem me.   40

Poitiers and Crécy tell,
When most their pride did swell,
Under our swords they fell;
    No less our skill is
Than when our grandsire great,
Claiming the regal seat
By many a warlike feat,
    Lopped the French lilies.

The Duke of York so dread
The eager vaward led;   50
With the main Henry sped
    Amongst his henchmen.
Excester had the rear,
A braver man not there,
O Lord, how hot they were
    On the false Frenchmen!

They now to fight are gone,
Armor on armor shone,
Drum now to drum did groan,
    To hear was wonder,   60
That with cries they make
The very earth did shake,
Trumpet to trumpet spake,
    Thunder to thunder.

Well it thine age became,
O noble Erpingham,
Which didst the signal aim
    To our hid forces;
When from a meadow by,
Like a storm suddenly,   70
The English archery
    Stuck the French horses.

With Spanish yew so strong,
Arrows a cloth-yard long,
That like to serpents stung,
    Piercing the weather;
None from his fellow starts,
But playing manly parts,

And like true English hearts,
  Stuck close together.   80

When down their bows they
      threw,
And forth their bilboes drew,
And on the French they flew,
  Not one was tardy;
Arms were from shoulders sent,
Scalps to the teeth were rent,
Down the French peasants went;
  Our men were hardy.

This while our noble King,
His broad sword brandishing,   90
Down the French host did ding,
  As to o'erwhelm it;
And many a deep wound lent,
His arms with blood besprent,
And many a cruel dent
  Bruisèd his helmet.

Gloster, that Duke so good,
Next of the royal blood,

For famous England stood
  With his brave brother;   100
Clarence, in steel so bright,
Though but a maiden knight,
Yet in that furious fight,
  Scarce such another.

Warwick in blood did wade,
Oxford the foe invade,
And cruel slaughter made,
  Still as they ran up;
Suffolk his axe did ply,
Beaumont and Willoughby   110
Bare them right doughtily,
  Ferrers and Fanhope.

Upon Saint Crispin's day
Fought was this noble fray,
Which fame did not delay
  To England to carry;
Oh, when shall English men
With such acts fill a pen,
Or England breed again
  Such a King Harry?   120

ECLOGUES
The ninth eclogue

Batt. Gorbo, as thou cam'st this
      way
By yonder little hill,
Or as thou through the fields
      didst stray,
Saw'st thou my Daffodil?

She's in a frock of Lincoln
      green,
Which color likes her sight,
And never hath her beauty seen
But through a veil of white;

Than roses, richer to behold,
That trim up lovers' bowers,   10
The pansy and the marigold,
Though Phœbus' paramours.

Gorbo. Thou well describ'st the
      daffodil;

It is not full an hour
Since by the spring, near yonder
      hill,
I saw that lovely flower.

Batt. Yet my fair flower thou
      didst not meet,
Nor news of her didst bring,
And yet my Daffodil's more
      sweet
Than that by yonder spring.   20

Gorbo. I saw a shepherd that doth
      keep
In yonder field of lilies,
Was making, as he fed his sheep,
A wreath of daffodillies.

Batt. Yet, Gorbo, thou delud'st
      me still,

My flower thou didst not see,
For know, my pretty Daffodil
Is worn of none but me.

To show itself but near her seat
No lily is so bold,   30
Except to shade her from the
    heat,
Or keep her from the cold.

Gorbo. Through yonder vale as I
    did pass,
Descending from the hill,
I met a smirking bonny lass,
They call her Daffodil;

Whose presence, as along she
    went,

The pretty flowers did greet,
As though their heads they
    downward bent
With homage to her feet.   40

And all the shepherds that were
    nigh,
From top of every hill,
Unto the valleys loud did cry,
There goes sweet Daffodil.

Batt. Ay, gentle shepherd, now
    with joy
Thou all my flocks dost fill,
That's she alone, kind shep-
    herd's boy,
Let us to Daffodil.

. . . . .

From *Poly-Olbion*, [1612]

The thirteenth song

Upon the midlands now th' industrious muse doth fall,
That shire which we the heart of England well may call,
As she herself extends (the midst which is decreed)
Betwixt St. Michael's Mount and Berwick-bord'ring Tweed,
Brave Warwick, that abroad so long advanced her bear,
By her illustrious earls renownèd everywhere,
Above her neighboring shires which always bore her head.
    My native country then, which so brave spirits hast bred,
If there be virtue yet remaining in thy earth,
Or any good of thine thou breath'dst into my birth,   10
Accept it as thine own whilst now I sing of thee,
Of all thy later brood th' unworthiest though I be.
    Muse, first of Arden tell, whose footsteps yet are found
In her rough woodlands, more than any other ground
That mighty Arden held even in her height of pride,
Her one hand touching Trent, the other Severn's side.
    The very sound of these the wood-nymphs doth awake,
When thus of her own self the ancient forest spake:
    My many goodly sites when first I came to show,
Here opened I the way to mine own overthrow;   20
For when the world found out the fitness of my soil,
The gripple wretch began immediately to spoil
My tall and goodly woods, and did my grounds inclose,
By which in little time my bounds I came to lose.
    When Britain first her fields with villages had filled,

Her people waxing still and wanting where to build,
They oft dislodged the hart and set their houses where
He in the broom and brakes had long time made his lair.
Of all the forests here within this mighty isle,
If those old Britons then me sovereign did instyle, 30
I needs must be the great'st, for greatness 'tis alone
That gives our kind the place, else were there many a one
For pleasantness of shade that far doth me excel.
But of our forests' kind the quality to tell,
We equally partake with woodland as with plain,
Alike with hill and dale, and every day maintain
The sundry kinds of beasts upon our copious wastes
That men for profit breed, as well as those of chase.
　　Here Arden of herself ceased any more to show, 40
And with her sylvan joys the muse along doth go.
　　When Phœbus lifts his head out of the winter's wave,
No sooner doth the earth her flowery bosom brave,
At such time as the year brings on the pleasant spring,
But Hunts-up to the morn the feathered sylvans sing,
And in the lower grove, as on the rising knoll,
Upon the highest spray of every mounting pole,
Those quiristers are perched with many a speckled breast.
Then from her burnished gate the goodly glitt'ring east
Gilds every lofty top, which late the humorous night
Bespangled had with pearl to please the morning's sight; 50
On which the mirthful choirs with their clear open throats
Unto the joyful morn so strain their warbling notes
That hills and valleys ring, and even the echoing air
Seems all composed of sounds, about them everywhere.
The throstle, with shrill sharps, as purposely he song
T' awake the lustless sun, or chiding that so long
He was in coming forth that should the thickets thrill;
The woosell near at hand, that hath a golden bill,
As nature him had marked of purpose t' let us see
That from all other birds his tunes should different be; 60
For with their vocal sounds they sing to pleasant May.
Upon his dulcet pipe the merle doth only play;
When in the lower brake the nightingale hard by
In such lamenting strains the joyful hours doth ply,
As though the other birds she to her tunes would draw;
And but that nature, by her all-constraining law,
Each bird to her own kind this season doth invite,
They else, alone to hear that charmer of the night
(The more to use their ears) their voices sure would spare,
That moduleth her tunes so admirably rare, 70
As man to set in parts at first had learned of her.

To Philomel the next the linnet we prefer,
And by that warbling bird the wood-lark place we then,
The red sparrow, the nope, the redbreast, and the wren,
The yellowpate, which though she hurt the blooming tree,
Yet scarce hath any bird a finer pipe than she;
And of these chanting fowls the goldfinch not behind,
That hath so many sorts descending from her kind.
The tydie for her notes as delicate as they,
The laughing hecco, then the counterfeiting jay,   80
The softer with the shrill (some hid among the leaves,
Some in the taller trees, some in the lower greaves),
Thus sing away the morn, until the mounting sun
Through thick exhalèd fogs his golden head hath run,
And through the twisted tops of our close covert creeps
To kiss the gentle shade, this while that sweetly sleeps.
   And near to these our thicks, the wild and frightful herds,
Not hearing other noise but this of chattering birds,
Feed fairly on the lands; both sorts of seasoned deer,
Here walk the stately red, the freckled fallow there;   90
The bucks and lusty stags amongst the rascals strewed,
As sometime gallant spirits amongst the multitude.

. . . .

   To forests that belongs, but yet this is not all:
With solitude what sorts that here's not wondrous rife?
Whereas the hermit leads a sweet retirèd life,
From villages replete with ragg'd and sweating clowns,
And from the loathsome airs of smoky citied towns.
Suppose 'twixt noon and night the sun his halfway wrought,
The shadows to be large by his descending brought,
Who with a fervent eye looks through the twiring glades   100
And his dispersèd rays commixeth with the shades,
Exhaling the milch dew, which there had tarried long
And on the ranker grass till past the noon-stead hong,
Whenas the hermit comes out of his homely cell,
Where from all rude resort he happily doth dwell;
Who in the strength of youth a man-at-arms hath been,
Or one who of this world the vileness having seen,
Retires him from it quite, and with a constant mind
Man's beastliness so loathes, that flying human kind,
The black and darksome nights, the bright and gladsome days   110
Indifferent are to him, his hope on God that stays.
Each little village yields his short and homely fare;
To gather wind-fall'n sticks his great'st and only care,
Which every aged tree still yieldeth to his fire.
   This man that is alone a king in his desire,

By no proud ignorant lord is basely overawed,
Nor his false praise affects who, grossly being clawed,
Stands like an itchy moil; nor of a pin he weighs
What fools abusèd kings and humorous ladies raise.
His free and noble thought ne'er envies at the grace   120
That oftentimes is given unto a bawd most base,
Nor stirs it him to think on the impostor vile
Who seeming what he's not, doth sensually beguile
The sottish purblind world; but absolutely free,
His happy time he spends the works of God to see
In those so sundry herbs which there in plenty grow,
Whose sundry strange effects he only seeks to know.
And in a little maund, being made of osiers small,
Which serveth him to do full many a thing withal,
He very choicely sorts his simples got abroad.   130

.   .   .   .

But from our hermit here the muse we must enforce,
And zealously proceed in our intended course:
How Arden of her rills and riverets doth dispose;
By Alcester how Alne to Arrow eas'ly flows,
And mildly being mixed, to Avon hold their way;
And likewise toward the north, how lovely tripping Rhea
T' attend the lustier Tame is from her fountain sent;
So little Cole and Blythe go on with him to Trent;
His Tamworth at the last he in his way doth win,
There playing him awhile till Anker should come in,   140
Which trifleth 'twixt her banks, observing state, so slow
As though into his arms she scorned herself to throw;
Yet Arden willed her Tame to serve her on his knee,
For by that nymph alone they both should honored be.
The forest so much fall'n from what she was before,
That to her former height fate could her not restore,
Though oft in her behalf the genius of the land
Importunèd the heavens with an auspicious hand.
Yet granted at the last, the aged nymph to grace,
They by a lady's birth would more renown that place   150
Than if her woods their heads above the hills should seat;
And for that purpose first made Coventry so great,
(A poor thatched village then, or scarcely none at all,
That could not once have dreamed of her now stately wall)
And thither wisely brought that goodly virgin band,
Th' eleven thousand maids, chaste Ursula's command,
Whom then the Briton kings gave her full power to press,
For matches to their friends in Brittany the less.
At whose departure thence, each by her just bequest

Some special virtue gave, ordaining it to rest 160
With one of their own sex, that there her birth should have,
Till fullness of the time which fate did choicely save
Until the Saxons' reign, when Coventry at length
From her small mean regard recovered state and strength,
By Leofric, her lord, yet in base bondage held,
The people from her marts by tollage who expelled;
Whose duchess, which desired this tribute to release,
Their freedom often begged. The duke, to make her cease,
Told her that if she would his loss so far enforce,
His will was she should ride stark nak'd upon a horse 170
By daylight through the street; which certainly he thought
In her heroic breast so deeply would have wrought,
That in her former suit she would have left to deal.
But that most princely dame, as one devoured with zeal,
Went on, and by that mean the city clearly freed.

· · · · · · ·

But whilst about this tale smooth Anker trifling stays,
Unto the lustier Tame as loath to come her ways,
The flood entreats her thus: Dear brook, why dost thou wrong
Our mutual love so much, and tediously prolong
Our mirthful marriage hour, for which I still prepare? 180
Haste to my broader banks, my joy and only care.
For as of all my floods thou art the first in fame,
When frankly thou shalt yield thine honor to my name,
I will protect thy state; then do not wrong thy kind.
What pleasure hath the world that here thou mayst not find?

· · · · · ·

From *The Battle of Agincourt*, 1627

To my most dearly loved friend, Henry Reynolds, Esquire Of poets and poesy

My dearly lovëd friend, how oft have we
In winter evenings, meaning to be free,
To some well-chosen place used to retire,
And there with moderate meat, and wine, and fire,
Have passed the hours contentedly with chat;
Now talked of this, and then discoursed of that,
Spoke our own verses 'twixt ourselves; if not,
Other men's lines which we by chance had got,
Or some stage pieces famous long before,
Of which your happy memory had store; 10
And I remember you much pleasëd were
Of those who livëd long ago to hear,

As well as of those of these latter times
Who have enriched our language with their rhymes,
And in succession how still up they grew,
Which is the subject that I now pursue.
For from my cradle you must know that I
Was still inclined to noble poesy,
And when that once *Pueriles* I had read,
And newly had my Cato construëd,   20
In my small self I greatly marveled then,
Amongst all other, what strange kind of men
These poets were; and pleasëd with the name,
To my mild tutor merrily I came,
(For I was then a proper goodly page,
Much like a pigmy, scarce ten years of age)
Clasping my slender arms about his thigh,
O my dear master! cannot you, quoth I,
Make me a poet? Do it if you can,
And you shall see I'll quickly be a man.   30
Who me thus answered smiling: Boy, quoth he,
If you'll not play the wag, but I may see
You ply your learning, I will shortly read
Some poets to you. Phœbus be my speed,
To 't hard went I, when shortly he began
And first read to me honest Mantuan,
Then Virgil's *Eclogues*; being entered thus,
Methought I straight had mounted Pegasus,
And in his full career could make him stop
And bound upon Parnassus' bi-clift top.   40
I scorned your ballad then, though it were done
And had for finis, William Elderton.
But soft, in sporting with this childish jest
I from my subject have too long digressed;
Then to the matter that we took in hand,
Jove and Apollo for the Muses stand.
  Then noble Chaucer, in those former times
The first enriched our English with his rhymes,
And was the first of ours that ever brake
Into the Muses' treasure, and first spake   50
In weighty numbers, delving in the mine
Of perfect knowledge, which he could refine
And coin for current; and as much as then
The English language could express to men,
He made it do, and by his wondrous skill,
Gave us much light from his abundant quill.
  And honest Gower, who in respect of him
Had only sipped at Aganippe's brim,

And though in years this last was him before,
Yet fell he far short of the other's store. 60
    When after those, four ages very near,
They with the Muses which conversëd were:
That princely Surrey, early in the time
Of the eight Henry, who was then the prime
Of England's noble youth; with him there came
Wyatt, with reverence whom we still do name
Amongst our poets; Bryan had a share
With the two former, which accompted are
That time's best makers, and the authors were
Of those small poems which the title bear 70
Of *Songs and Sonnets,* wherein oft they hit
On many dainty passages of wit.
    Gascoigne and Churchyard after them again
In the beginning of Eliza's reign,
Accompted were great meterers many a day,
But not inspirëd with brave fire; had they
Lived but a little longer they had seen
Their works before them to have buried been.
    Grave moral Spenser after these came on,
Than whom I am persuaded there was none 80
Since the blind bard his *Iliads* up did make
Fitter a task like that to undertake,
To set down boldly, bravely to invent,
In all high knowledge surely excellent.
    The noble Sidney with this last arose,
That heroë for numbers and for prose,
That throughly paced our language as to show
The plenteous English hand in hand might go
With Greek or Latin; and did first reduce
Our tongue from Lyly's writing, then in use: 90
Talking of stones, stars, plants, of fishes, flies,
Playing with words and idle similes;
As th' English apes and very zanies be,
Of everything that they do hear and see,
So imitating his ridiculous tricks,
They spake and writ all like mere lunatics.
    Then Warner, though his lines were not so trimmed,
Nor yet his poem so exactly limned
And neatly jointed, but the critic may
Easily reprove him, yet thus let me say 100
For my old friend: some passages there be
In him which I protest have taken me
With almost wonder, so fine, clear, and new
As yet they have been equallëd by few.

Neat Marlowe, bathëd in the Thespian springs,
Had in him those brave translunary things
That the first poets had; his raptures were
All air and fire, which made his verses clear,
For that fine madness still he did retain
Which rightly should possess a poet's brain. 110

And surely Nashe, though he a proser were,
A branch of laurel yet deserves to bear;
Sharply satiric was he, and that way
He went, since that his being to this day
Few have attempted, and I surely think
Those words shall hardly be set down with ink,
Shall scorch and blast so as his could, where he
Would inflict vengeance. And be it said of thee,
Shakespeare, thou hadst as smooth a comic vein,
Fitting the sock, and in thy natural brain 120
As strong conception and as clear a rage
As anyone that trafficked with the stage.

Amongst these, Samuel Daniel, whom if I
May speak of, but to censure do deny,
Only have heard some wise men him rehearse
To be too much historian in verse;
His rhymes were smooth, his meters well did close,
But yet his manner better fitted prose.
Next these, learn'd Jonson in this list I bring,
Who had drunk deep of the Pierian spring, 130
Whose knowledge did him worthily prefer,
And long was lord here of the theater;
Who in opinion made our learn'st to stick,
Whether in poems rightly dramatic,
Strong Seneca or Plautus, he or they
Should bear the buskin or the sock away.
Others again here livëd in my days
That have of us deservëd no less praise
For their translations than the daintiest wit
That on Parnassus thinks he high'st doth sit, 140
And for a chair may 'mongst the muses call
As the most curious maker of them all;
As reverent Chapman, who hath brought to us
Musæus, Homer, and Hesiodus
Out of the Greek, and by his skill hath reared
Them to that height, and to our tongues endeared,
That were those poets at this day alive
To see their books thus with us to survive,
They would think, having neglected them so long,
They had been written in the English tongue. 150

And Sylvester, who from the French more weak
Made Bartas of his six days' labor speak
In natural English; who, had he there stayed
He had done well, and never had bewrayed
His own invention to have been so poor,
Who still wrote less in striving to write more.

Then dainty Sandys, that hath to English done
Smooth sliding Ovid, and hath made him run
With so much sweetness and unusual grace,
As though the neatness of the English pace   160
Should tell the jetting Latin that it came
But slowly after, as though stiff and lame.

So Scotland sent us hither, for our own,
That man whose name I ever would have known
To stand by mine, that most ingenious knight,
My Alexander, to whom in his right
I want extremely, yet in speaking thus
I do but show the love that was 'twixt us,
And not his numbers which were brave and high,
So like his mind was his clear poesy;   170
And my dear Drummond, to whom much I owe
For his much love, and proud I was to know
His poesy; for which two worthy men,
I Menstry still shall love, and Hawthornden.

Then the two Beaumonts and my Browne arose,
My dear companions whom I freely chose
My bosom friends, and in their several ways
Rightly born poets, and in these last days
Men of much note and no less nobler parts,
Such as have freely told to me their hearts,   180
As I have mine to them; but if you shall
Say in your knowledge that these be not all
Have writ in numbers, be informed that I
Only myself to these few men do tie,
Whose works oft printed, set on every post,
To public censure subject have been most;
For such whose poems, be they ne'er so rare,
In private chambers that encloistered are,
And by transcription daintily must go,
As though the world unworthy were to know   190
Their rich composures, let those men that keep
These wonderous relics in their judgment deep,
And cry them up so, let such pieces be
Spoke of by those that shall come after me;
I pass not for them, nor do mean to run
In quest of these that them applause have won

Upon our stages in these latter days,
That are so many—let them have their bays
That do deserve it; let those wits that haunt
Those public circuits, let them freely chant   200
Their fine composures, and their praise pursue;
And so, my dear friend, for this time, adieu.

Nymphidia, the court of fairy

Old Chaucer doth of Thopas tell,
Mad Rab'lais of Pantagruel,
A latter third of Dowsabell,
    With such poor trifles playing;
Others the like have labored at,
Some of this thing and some of
    that,
And many of they know not
    what,
    But that they must be saying.

Another sort there be that will
Be talking of the fairies still,   10
Nor never can they have their
    fill,
    As they were wedded to them;
No tales of them their thirst can
    slake,
So much delight therein they take,
And some strange thing they fain
    would make,
    Knew they the way to do them.

Then since no muse hath been so
    bold,
Or of the later, or the old,
Those elvish secrets to unfold,
    Which lie from others' read-
        ing,   20
My active muse to light shall
    bring
The court of that proud fairy
    king,
And tell there of the reveling;
    Jove prosper my proceeding.

And thou, Nymphidia, gentle fay,
Which meeting me upon the way
These secrets didst to me bewray,
    Which now I am in telling,
My pretty light fantastic maid,
I here invoke thee to my aid   30
That I may speak what thou hast
    said,
    In numbers smoothly swelling.

This palace standeth in the air,
By necromancy placéd there,
That it no tempests needs to fear,
    Which way soe'er it blow it.
And somewhat southward toward
    the noon,
Whence lies a way up to the
    moon,
And thence the fairy can as soon
    Pass to the earth below it.   40

The walls of spiders' legs are
    made,
Well mortiséd and finely laid;
He was the master of his trade,
    It curiously that builded;
The windows of the eyes of cats,
And for the roof, instead of slats,
Is covered with the skins of bats,
    With moonshine that are
        gilded.

Hence Oberon him sport to make,
Their rest when weary mortals
    take,   50
And none but only fairies wake,
    Descendeth for his pleasure.

And Mab, his merry queen, by
    night
Bestrides young folks that lie up-
    right,
(In elder times the Mare that
    hight)
    Which plagues them out of
      measure.

Hence shadows, seeming idle
    shapes,
Of little frisking elves and apes,
To earth do make their wanton
    scapes,
    As hope of pastime hastes
      them;   60
Which maids think on the hearth
    they see
When fires well ne'er consumèd
    be,
There dancing hays by two and
    three,
    Just as their fancy casts them.

These make our girls their slut-
    tery rue
By pinching them both black and
    blue,
And put a penny in their shoe,
    The house for cleanly sweep-
      ing;
And in their courses make that
    round,
In meadows and in marshes
    found,   70
Of them so called the fairy
    ground,
    Of which they have the keep-
      ing.

These, when a child haps to be
    got
Which after proves an idiot,
When folk perceive it thriveth
    not,
    The fault therein to smother,

Some silly doting brainless calf
That understands things by the
    half,
Say that the fairy left this auf
    And took away the other.   80

But listen and I shall you tell
A chance in fairy that befell,
Which certainly may please some
    well,
    In love and arms delighting:
Of Oberon that jealous grew
Of one of his own fairy crew,
Too well, he feared, his queen
    that knew,
    His love but ill requiting.

Pigwiggen was this fairy knight,
One wondrous gracious in the
    sight   90
Of fair Queen Mab, which day
    and night
    He amorously observèd;
Which made King Oberon sus-
    pect
His service took too good effect,
His sauciness and often checked,
    And could have wished him
      starvèd.

Pigwiggen gladly would com-
    mend
Some token to Queen Mab to
    send,
If sea or land him aught could
    lend,
    Were worthy of her wear-
      ing;   100
At length this lover doth devise
A bracelet made of emmets' eyes,
A thing he thought that she
    would prize,
    No whit her state impairing.

And to the queen a letter writes,
Which he most curiously indites,

Conjuring her by all the rites
  Of love, she would be pleasëd
To meet him, her true servant,
    where
They might without suspect or
    fear   110
Themselves to one another clear,
  And have their poor hearts
    easëd.

At midnight the appointed hour,
And for the queen a fitting bower,
Quoth he, is that fair cowslip
    flower
  On Hipcut hill that groweth;
In all your train there's not a fay
That ever went to gather May
But she hath made it in her way,
  The tallest there that grow-
    eth.   120

When by Tom Thumb, a fairy
    page,
He sent it, and doth him engage,
By promise of a mighty wage,
  It secretly to carry;
Which done, the queen her maids
    doth call,
And bids them to be ready all;
She would go see her summer
    hall,
  She could no longer tarry.

Her chariot ready straight is
    made,
Each thing therein is fitting
    laid   130
That she by nothing might be
    stayed,
  For nought must her be let-
    ting;
Four nimble gnats the horses
    were,
Their harnesses of gossamer,
Fly Cranion, her charioteer,
  Upon the coach-box getting.

Her chariot of a snail's fine shell,
Which for the colors did excel,
The fair Queen Mab becoming
    well,
  So lively was the limning;   140
The seat the soft wool of the bee;
The cover, gallantly to see,
The wing of a pied butterflee,
  I trow, 'twas simple trimming.

The wheels composed of crickets'
    bones,
And daintily made for the nonce;
For fear of rattling on the stones
  With thistle-down they shod
    it;
For all her maidens much did
    fear,
If Oberon had chanced to hear   150
That Mab his queen should have
    been there,
  He would not have abode it.

She mounts her chariot with a
    trice,
Nor would she stay for no advice,
Until her maids, that were so
    nice,
  To wait on her were fitted,
But ran herself away alone;
Which when they heard, there
    was not one
But hasted after to be gone,
  As she had been diswitted.   160

Hop and Mop and Drop so clear,
Pip and Trip and Skip that were
To Mab, their sovereign, ever
    dear,
  Her special maids of honor;
Fib and Tib and Pink and Pin,
Tick and Quick and Jill and Jin,
Tit and Nit and Wap and Win,
  The train that wait upon her.

Upon a grasshopper they got,
And what with amble and with
trot, 170
For hedge nor ditch they sparëd
not,
But after her they hie them.
A cobweb over them they throw,
To shield the wind if it should
blow;
Themselves they wisely could be-
stow,
Lest any should espy them.

But let us leave Queen Mab a
while,
Through many a gate, o'er many
a stile,
That now had gotten by this
wile,
Her dear Pigwiggen kissing, 180
And tell how Oberon doth fare,
Who grew as mad as any hare,
When he had sought each place
with care
And found his queen was miss-
ing.

By grisly Pluto he doth swear,
He rent his clothes and tore his
hair,
And as he runneth here and there
An acorn cup he greeteth;
Which soon he taketh by the
stalk,
About his head he lets it walk, 190
Nor doth he any creature balk,
But lays on all he meeteth.

The Tuscan poet doth advance
The frantic Paladin of France,
And those more ancient do en-
hance
Alcides in his fury;
And others, Ajax, Telamon;
But to this time there hath been
none

So bedlam as our Oberon,
Of which I dare assure you. 200

And first encount'ring with a
wasp,
He in his arms the fly doth clasp
As though his breath he forth
would grasp,
Him for Pigwiggen taking.
Where is my wife, thou rogue?
quoth he,
Pigwiggen, she is come to thee,
Restore her or thou di'st by me.
Whereat the poor wasp quak-
ing,

Cries, Oberon, great Fairy King,
Content thee I am no such
thing; 210
I am a wasp, behold my sting.
At which the fairy started;
When soon away the wasp doth
go,
Poor wretch was never frighted
so,
He thought his wings were much
too slow,
O'erjoyed they so were parted.

He next upon a glow-worm light,
(You must suppose it now was
night),
Which for her hinder part was
bright,
He took to be a devil. 220
And furiously doth her assail
For carrying fire in her tail;
He thrashed her rough coat with
his flail,
The mad king feared no evil.

O, quoth the glow-worm, hold
thy hand,
Thou puissant King of Fairyland,
Thy mighty strokes who may
withstand;

Hold, or of life despair I!
Together then herself doth roll,
And tumbling down into a
    hole,   230
She seemed as black as any coal,
  Which vexed away the fairy.

From thence he ran into a hive,
Amongst the bees he letteth drive,
And down their combs begins to
    rive,
  All likely to have spoilëd;
Which with their wax his face be-
    smeared,
And with their honey daubed his
    beard;
It would have made a man
    afeard
  To see how he was moilëd. 240

A new adventure him betides,
He met an ant, which he be-
    strides,
And post thereon away he rides,
  Which with his haste doth
    stumble
And came full over on her snout,
Her heels so threw the dirt about,
For she by no means could get
    out,
  But over him doth tumble.

And being in this piteous case,
And all beslurried, head and
    face,   250
On runs he in this wild-goose
    chase;
  As here and there he rambles
Half blind, against a molehill hit,
And for a mountain taking it,
For all he was out of his wit,
  Yet to the top he scrambles.

And being gotten to the top,
Yet there himself he could not
    stop,

But down on th' other side doth
    chop,
  And to the foot came rum-
    bling,   260
So that the grubs therein that
    bred,
Hearing such turmoil overhead,
Thought surely they had all been
    dead,
  So fearful was the jumbling.

And falling down into a lake,
Which him up to the neck doth
    take,
His fury somewhat it doth slake,
  He calleth for a ferry;
Where you may some recovery
    note,
What was his club he made his
    boat,   270
And in his oaken cup doth float
  As safe as in a wherry.

Men talk of the adventures
    strange
Of Don Quishott, and of their
    change
Through which he armëd oft did
    range,
  Of Sancho Pancha's travel;
But should a man tell everything
Done by this frantic fairy king,
And them in lofty numbers sing,
  It well his wits might
    gravel.   280

Scarce set on shore, but there-
    withal
He meeteth Puck, which most
    men call
Hobgoblin, and on him doth fall
  With words from frenzy
    spoken.
Ho, ho, quoth Hob, God save thy
    grace,

Who dressed thee in this piteous
    case?
He thus that spoiled my sover-
    eign's face
    I would his neck were broken.

This Puck seems but a dreaming
    dolt,
Still walking like a ragged colt, 290
And oft out of a bush doth bolt,
    Of purpose to deceive us.
And leading us, makes us to stray,
Long winter's nights, out of the
    way,
And when we stick in mire and
    clay,
    Hob doth with laughter leave
    us.

Dear Puck, quoth he, my wife is
    gone;
As e'er thou lov'st King Oberon,
Let everything but this alone,
    With vengeance and pursue
    her;   300
Bring her to me alive or dead,
Or that vile thief Pigwiggen's
    head.
That villain hath defiled my bed,
    He to this folly drew her.

Quoth Puck, My liege, I'll never
    lin,
But I will thorough thick and
    thin
Until at length I bring her in,
    My dearest lord, ne'er doubt it.
Thorough brake, thorough brier,
Thorough muck, thorough mire,
Thorough water, thorough fire, 311
    And thus goes Puck about it.

This thing Nymphidia overheard,
That on this mad king had a
    guard,
Not doubting of a great reward

For first this business broach-
    ing;
And through the air away doth
    go,
Swift as an arrow from the bow,
To let her sovereign Mab to
    know
    What peril was approach-
    ing.   320

The queen, bound with love's
    powerful'st charm,
Sat with Pigwiggen, arm in arm;
Her merry maids that thought no
    harm
    About the room were skipping.
A humble-bee, their minstrel,
    played
Upon his hautboy; ev'ry maid
Fit for this revels was arrayed,
    The hornpipe neatly tripping.

In comes Nymphidia and doth
    cry:
My sovereign, for your safety
    fly,   330
For there is danger but too nigh,
    I posted to forewarn you;
The king hath sent Hobgoblin
    out
To seek you all the fields about,
And of your safety you may
    doubt,
    If he but once discern you.

When like an uproar in a town,
Before them everything went
    down;
Some tore a ruff and some a
    gown,
    'Gainst one another just-
    ling.   340
They flew about like chaff i' th'
    wind,
For haste some left their masks
    behind,

Some could not stay their gloves
    to find,
  There never was such bustling.

Forth ran they by a secret way
Into a brake that near them lay,
Yet much they doubted there to
    stay
  Lest Hob should hap to find
    them;
He had a sharp and piercing sight,
All one to him the day and night,
And therefore were resolved by
    flight   351
  To leave this place behind
    them.

At length one chanced to find a
    nut
In th' end of which a hole was
    cut,
Which lay upon a hazel root,
  There scattered by a squirrel
Which out the kernel gotten had;
When quoth this fay, Dear
    Queen, be glad,
Let Oberon be ne'er so mad,
  I'll set you safe from peril.   360

Come all into this nut, quoth she,
Come closely in, be ruled by me,
Each one may here a chooser be,
  For room ye need not wrastle,
Nor need ye be together heaped.
So one by one therein they crept,
And lying down they soundly
    slept,
  As safe as in a castle.

Nymphidia, that this while doth
    watch,
Perceived if Puck the queen should
    catch,   370
That he would be her over-match,
  Of which she well bethought
    her.

Found it must be some powerful
    charm,
The queen against him that must
    arm,
Or surely he would do her harm,
  For throughly he had sought
    her.

And list'ning if she aught could
    hear
That her might hinder, or might
    fear,
But finding still the coast was
    clear,   379
  Nor creature had descried her;
Each circumstance and having
    scanned,
She came thereby to understand
Puck would be with them out of
    hand,
  When to her charms she hied
    her.

And first her fern seed doth be-
    stow,
The kernel of the mistletoe,
And here and there as Puck should
    go,
  With terror to affright him,
She nightshade straws to work
    him ill,
Therewith her vervain and her
    dill,   390
That hind'reth witches of their
    will,
  Of purpose to despite him.

Then sprinkles she the juice of
    rue
That groweth underneath the
    yew,
With nine drops of the midnight
    dew,
  From lunary distilling;
The molewarp's brain mixed
    therewithal,

And with the same the pismire's
    gall,
For she in nothing short would
    fall,
   The fairy was so willing.   400

Then thrice under a brier doth
    creep,
Which at both ends was rooted
    deep,
And over it three times she leap,
   Her magic much availing;
Then on Proserpina doth call,
And so upon her spell doth fall,
Which here to you repeat I shall,
   Not in one tittle failing:

By the croaking of the frog,
By the howling of the dog,   410
By the crying of the hog,
   Against the storm arising;
By the evening curfew bell,
By the doleful dying knell,
Oh, let this my direful spell,
   Hob, hinder thy surprising.

By the mandrake's dreadful
    groans,
By the lubrican's sad moans,
By the noise of dead men's bones
   In charnel houses rattling;   420
By the hissing of the snake,
The rustling of the fire-drake,
I charge thee thou this place for-
    sake,
   Nor of Queen Mab be prat-
    tling.

By the whirlwind's hollow sound,
By the thunder's dreadful stound,
Yells of spirits under ground,
   I charge thee not to fear us;
By the screech-owl's dismal note,
By the black night-raven's throat,
I charge thee, Hob, to tear thy
    coat   431

With thorns, if thou come near
   us.

Her spell thus spoke, she stepped
    aside,
And in a chink herself doth hide
To see thereof what would betide,
   For she doth only mind him;
When presently she Puck espies,
And well she marked his gloating
    eyes,
How under every leaf he pries,
   In seeking still to find them.   440

But once the circle got within,
The charms to work do straight
    begin,
And he was caught as in a gin;
   For as he thus was busy,
A pain he in his head-piece feels,
Against a stubbèd tree he reels,
And up went poor Hobgoblin's
    heels,
   Alas, his brain was dizzy.

At length upon his feet he gets,
Hobgoblin fumes, Hobgoblin
    frets,   450
And as again he forward sets,
   And through the bushes scram-
   bles,
A stump doth trip him in his pace,
Down comes poor Hob upon his
    face,
And lamentably tore his case
   Amongst the briers and bram-
   bles.

A plague upon Queen Mab, quoth
    he,
And all her maids, where'er they
    be,
I think the devil guided me
   To seek her so provokèd.   460
Where stumbling at a piece of
   wood

He fell into a ditch of mud,
Where to the very chin he stood
    In danger to be chokèd.

Now worse than e'er he was be-
    fore,
Poor Puck doth yell, poor Puck
    doth roar,
That waked Queen Mab, what
    doubted sore
    Some treason had been wrought
        her,
Until Nymphidia told the queen
What she had done, what she had
    seen,   470
Who then had well-near cracked
    her spleen
    With very extreme laughter.

But leave we Hob to clamber out,
Queen Mab and all her fairy
    rout,
And come again to have about
    With Oberon, yet madding;
And with Pigwiggen now dis-
    traught,
Who much was troubled in his
    thought,
That he so long the queen had
    sought,
    And through the fields was gad-
        ding.   480

And as he runs he still doth cry:
King Oberon, I thee defy,
And dare thee here in arms to try
    For my dear lady's honor;
For that she is a queen right good,
In whose defence I'll shed my
    blood,
And that thou in this jealous mood
    Hast laid this slander on her.

And quickly arms him for the
    field,
A little cockle-shell his shield, 490

Which he could very bravely
    wield,
    Yet could it not be piercèd;
His spear, a bent both stiff and
    strong,
And well near of two inches long;
The pile was of a horsefly's
    tongue,
    Whose sharpness nought re-
        versèd.

And puts him on a coat of mail,
Which was of a fish's scale,
That when his foe should him as-
    sail,
    No point should be prevail-
        ing;   500
His rapier was a hornet's sting,
It was a very dangerous thing,
For if he chanced to hurt the king
    It would be long in healing.

His helmet was a beetle's head,
Most horrible and full of dread,
That able was to strike one dead,
    Yet did it well become him;
And for a plume a horse's hair,
Which being tossèd with the air
Had force to strike his foe with
    fear,   511
    And turn his weapon from
        him.

Himself he on an earwig set,
Yet scarce he on his back could
    get,
So oft and high he did curvet
    Ere he himself could settle;
He made him turn, and stop, and
    bound,
To gallop, and to trot the round,
He scarce could stand on any
    ground,
    He was so full of mettle. 520

When soon he met with Tomalin,
One that a valiant knight had
    been,
And to King Oberon of kin;
    Quoth he, Thou manly fairy,
Tell Oberon I come prepared,
Then bid him stand upon his
    guard,
This hand his baseness shall re-
    ward,
    Let him be ne'er so wary.

Say to him thus, that I defy
His slanders and his infamy,   530
And as a mortal enemy
    Do publicly proclaim him;
Withal, that if I had mine own
He should not wear the fairy
    crown,
But with a vengeance should come
    down,
    Nor we a king should name
    him.

This Tomalin could not abide
To hear his sovereign vilified,
But to the fairy court him hied,
    Full furiously he posted,   540
With ev'rything Pigwiggen said:
How title to the crown he laid,
And in what arms he was arrayed,
    And how himself he boasted.

'Twixt head and foot, from point
    to point,
He told th' arming of each joint,
In every piece how neat and
    quaint,
    For Tomalin could do it;
How fair he sat, how sure he rid,
As of the courser he bestrid,   550
How managed, and how well he
    did.
    · The king which listened to it,

Quoth he, Go, Tomalin, with
    speed,
Provide me arms, provide my
    steed,
And everything that I shall need,
    By thee I will be guided.
To strait account call thou thy
    wit,
See there be wanting not a whit,
In everything see thou me fit,
    Just as my foe's provided.   560

Soon flew this news through fairy-
    land,
Which gave Queen Mab to under-
    stand
The combat that was then in hand
    Betwixt those men so mighty;
Which greatly she began to rue,
Perceiving that all fairy knew
The first occasion from her grew,
    Of these affairs so weighty.

Wherefore, attended with her
    maids,
Through fogs and mists and
    damps she wades,   570
To Proserpine, the Queen of
    Shades,
    To treat that it would please
    her
The cause into her hands to take,
For ancient love and friendship's
    sake,
And soon thereof an end to make,
    Which of much care would ease
    her.

A while there let we Mab alone,
And come we to King Oberon,
Who armed to meet his foe is
    gone,   579
    For proud Pigwiggen crying;
Who sought the fairy king as fast,
And had so well his journeys cast
That he arrivèd at the last,
    His puissant foe espying.

Stout Tomalin came with the
    king,
Tom Thumb doth on Pigwiggen
    bring,
That perfect were in everything
    To single fights belonging.
And therefore they themselves
    engage
To see them exercise their rage 590
With fair and comely equipage,
    Not one the other wronging.

So like in arms these champions
    were
As they had been a very pair,
So that a man would almost swear
    That either had been either;
Their furious steeds began to
    neigh,
That they were heard a mighty
    way;
Their staves upon their rests they
    lay,
    Yet ere they flew together   600

Their seconds minister an oath,
Which was indifferent to them
    both,
That on their knightly faith and
    troth
    No magic them suppliëd;
And sought them that they had no
    charms
Wherewith to work each other's
    harms,
But came with simple open arms
    To have their causes triëd.

Together furiously they ran,
That to the ground came horse
    and man,   610
The blood out of their helmets
    span,
    So sharp were their encounters;
And though they to the earth were
    thrown

Yet quickly they regained their
    own,
Such nimbleness was never shown,
    They were two gallant mount-
    ers.

When in a second course again
They forward came with might
    and main,
Yet which had better of the twain
    The seconds could not judge
    yet;   620
Their shields were into pieces
    cleft,
Their helmets from their heads
    were reft,
And to defend them nothing left,
    These champions would not
    budge yet.

Away from them their staves they
    threw,
Their cruel swords they quickly
    drew,
And freshly they the fight renew,
    They every stroke redoubled;
Which made Proserpina take
    heed,
And make to them the greater
    speed,   630
For fear lest they too much should
    bleed,
    Which wondrously her trou-
    bled.

When to th' infernal Styx she
    goes,
She takes the fogs from thence
    that rose
And in a bag doth them enclose;
    When well she had them
    blended,
She hies her then to Lethe spring,
A bottle and thereof doth bring,
Wherewith she meant to work the
    thing
    Which only she intended. 640

Now Proserpine with Mab is gone
Unto the place where Oberon
And proud Pigwiggen, one to one,
    Both to be slain were likely;
And there themselves they closely
    hide,
Because they would not be espied,
For Proserpine meant to decide
    The matter very quickly.

And suddenly unties the poke,
Which out of it sent such a smoke
As ready was them all to choke,   651
    So grievous was the pother;
So that the knights each other
    lost,
And stood as still as any post,
Tom Thumb nor Tomalin could
    boast
    Themselves of any other.

But when the mist gan somewhat
    cease,
Proserpina commandeth peace,
And that awhile they should re-
    lease
    Each other of their peril;   660
Which here, quoth she, I do pro-
    claim
To all, in dreadful Pluto's name,
That as ye will eschew his blame,
    You let me hear the quarrel.

But here yourselves you must en-
    gage,
Somewhat to cool your spleenish
    rage,
Your grievous thirst and to as-
    suage,
    That first you drink this liquor,
Which shall your understanding
    clear,
As plainly shall to you appear,   670
Those things from me that you
    shall hear
    Conceiving much the quicker.

This Lethe water, you must know,
The memory destroyeth so,
That of our weal or of our woe
    It all remembrance blotted;
Of it nor can you ever think,
For they no sooner took this drink,
But nought into their brains could
    sink
    Of what had them besotted.   680

King Oberon forgotten had
That he for jealousy ran mad;
But of his queen was wondrous
    glad,
    And asked how they came
        thither.
Pigwiggen likewise doth forget
That he Queen Mab had ever
    met,
Or that they were so hard beset
    When they were found to-
        gether.

Nor neither of them both had
    thought
That e'er they had each other
    sought,   690
Much less that they a combat
    fought,
    But such a dream were loath-
        ing.
Tom Thumb had got a little sup,
And Tomalin scarce kissed the
    cup,
Yet had their brains so sure locked
    up
    That they remembered noth-
        ing.

Queen Mab and her light maids
    the while
Amongst themselves do closely
    smile
To see the king caught with this
    wile,
    With one another jesting.   700

And to the fairy court they
   went,
With mickle joy and merriment,

Which thing was done with good
   intent,
  And thus I left them feasting.

The Shepherd's Sirena

Near to the silver Trent
  Sirena dwelleth,
She to whom nature lent
  All that excelleth;
By which the Muses late,
  And the neat Graces,
Have for their greater state
  Taken their places;
Twisting an anadem,
  Wherewith to crown her,   10
As it belonged to them
  Most to renown her.
    On thy bank,
    In a rank,
Let the swans sing her,
  And with their music
Along let them bring her.

Tagus and Pactolus
  Are to thee debtor,
Nor for their gold to us   20
  Are they the better;
Henceforth of all the rest
  Be thou the river,
Which as the daintiest
  Puts them down ever.
For as my precious one
  O'er thee doth travel,
She to pearl paragon
  Turneth thy gravel.
    On thy bank,
    In a rank,   30
Let thy swans sing her,
  And with their music
Along let them bring her.

Our mournful Philomel,
  That rarest tuner,
Henceforth in Aperil

Shall wake the sooner,
And to her shall complain
  From the thick cover,   40
Redoubling every strain
  Over and over;
For when my love too long
  Her chamber keepeth,
As though it suffered wrong
  The morning weepeth.
    On thy bank,
    In a rank,
Let thy swans sing her,
  And with their music   50
Along let them bring her.

Oft have I seen the sun,
  To do her honor,
Fix himself at his noon
  To look upon her;
And hath gilt every grove,
  Every hill near her,
With his flames from above
  Striving to cheer her,
And when she from his sight   60
  Hath herself turnëd,
He, as it had been night,
  In clouds hath mournëd.
    On thy bank,
    In a rank,
Let thy swans sing her,
  And with their music
Along let them bring her.

The verdant meads are seen,
  When she doth view them,   70
In fresh and gallant green
  Straight to renew them;
And every little grass
  Broad itself spreadeth,
Proud that this bonny lass
  Upon it treadeth;

Nor flower is so sweet
  In this large cincture,
But it upon her feet
  Leaveth some tincture.   80
    On thy bank,
    In a rank,
  Let thy swans sing her,
    And with their music
  Along let them bring her.

The fishes in the flood,
  When she doth angle,
For the hook strive a good
  Them to entangle,
And leaping on the land   90
  From the clear water,
Their scales upon the sand
  Lavishly scatter;
Therewith to pave the mold
  Whereon she passes,
So herself to behold
  As in her glasses.
    On thy bank,
    In a rank,
  Let thy swans sing her,   100
    And with their music
  Along let them bring her.

When she looks out by night
  The stars stand gazing,
Like comets to our sight
  Fearfully blazing,
As wond'ring at her eyes
  With their much brightness,
Which to amaze the skies,
  Dimming their lightness;   110
The raging tempests are calm
  When she speaketh,
Such most delightsome balm
  From her lips breaketh.
    On thy bank,
    In a rank,
  Let thy swans sing her,
    And with their music
  Along let them bring her.

In all our Britainy   120
  There's not a fairer,
Nor can you fit any
  Should you compare her.
Angels her eyelids keep,
  All hearts surprising,
Which look whilst she doth sleep
  Like the sun's rising;
She alone of her kind
  Knoweth true measure,
And her unmatchèd mind   130
  Is heaven's treasure.
    On thy bank,
    In a rank,
  Let thy swans sing her,
    And with their music
  Along let them bring her.

Fair Dove and Darwin clear,
  Boast ye your beauties,
To Trent, your mistress, here
  Yet pay your duties;   140
My love was higher born
  Towards the full fountains,
Yet she doth moorland scorn
  And the Peak mountains;
Nor would she none should dream
  Where she abideth,
Humble as is the stream
  Which by her slideth.
    On thy bank,
    In a rank,   150
  Let thy swans sing her,
    And with their music
  Along let them bring her.

Yet my poor rustic muse
  Nothing can move her,
Nor the means I can use,
  Though her true lover;
Many a long winter's night
  Have I waked for her,
Yet this my piteous plight   160
  Nothing can stir her.
All thy sands, silver Trent,
  Down to the Humber,

The sighs that I have spent
  Never can number.
    On thy bank,
    In a rank,

Let thy swans sing her,
  And with their music
Along let them bring her.   ¹⁷⁰

.   .   .   .   .

FROM *The Muses' Elysium*, 1630

The description of Elysium

A paradise on earth is found,
Though far from vulgar sight,
Which with those pleasures doth
    abound
That it Elysium hight.

Where in delights that never fade
The Muses lullëd be,
And sit at pleasure in the shade
Of many a stately tree,

Which no rough tempest makes to
    reel
Nor their straight bodies bows;   ¹⁰
Their lofty tops do never feel
The weight of winter's snows.

In groves that evermore are green,
No falling leaf is there,
But Philomel, of birds the queen,
In music spends the year.

The merle upon her myrtle perch,
There to the mavis sings,
Who from the top of some curled
    birch
Those notes redoubled rings.   ²⁰

There daisies damask every place,
Nor once their beauties lose,
That when proud Phœbus hides
    his face
Themselves they scorn to close.

The pansy and the violet here,
As seeming to descend
Both from one root, a very pair,
For sweetness yet contend.

And pointing to a pink, to tell
Which bears it, it is loath   ³⁰
To judge it; but replies, for smell
That it excels them both.

Wherewith displeased they hang
    their heads,
So angry soon they grow,
And from their odoriferous beds
Their sweets at it they throw.

The winter here a summer is,
No waste is made by time,
Nor doth the autumn ever miss
The blossoms of the prime.   ⁴⁰

The flower that July forth doth
    bring,
In April here is seen;
The primrose that puts on the
    spring,
In July decks each green.

The sweets for sovereignty con-
    tend,
And so abundant be
That to the very earth they lend
And bark of every tree.

Rills rising out of every bank
In wild meanders strain,   ⁵⁰
And playing many a wanton prank
Upon the speckled plain,

In gambols and lascivious gyres
Their time they still bestow,
Nor to their fountains none retires,
Nor on their course will go.

Those brooks with lilies bravely
   decked,
So proud and wanton made
That they their courses quite neg-
   lect,
And seem as though they stayed [60]

Fair Flora in her state to view,
Which through those lilies looks;
Or as those lilies leaned to shew
Their beauties to the brooks,

That Phœbus in his lofty race
Oft lays aside his beams
And comes to cool his glowing face
In these delicious streams.

Oft spreading vines climb up the
   clives,
Whose ripened clusters there [70]
Their liquid purple drop, which
   drives
A vintage through the year,

Those clives whose craggy sides
   are clad
With trees of sundry suits,
Which make continual summer
   glad,
Even bending with their fruits,

Some ripening, ready some to fall,
Some blossomed, some to bloom,
Like gorgeous hangings on the
   wall
Of some rich princely room. [80]

Pomegranates, lemons, citrons, so
Their laded branches bow,
Their leaves in number that outgo
Nor roomth will them allow.

There in perpetual summer's shade
Apollo's prophets sit
Among the flowers that never fade,
But flourish like their wit;

To whom the nymphs upon their
   lyres
Tune many a curious lay, [90]
And with their most melodious
   choirs
Make short the longest day.

The thrice three virgins heavenly
   clear
Their trembling timbrels sound,
Whilst the three comely Graces
   there
Dance many a dainty round.

Decay nor age there nothing
   knows,
There is continual youth,
As time on plant or creatures
   grows,
So still their strength renew'th. [100]

The poets' paradise this is,
To which but few can come,
The Muses' only bower of bliss,
Their dear Elysium;

Here happy souls, their blessed
   bowers
Free from the rude resort
Of beastly people, spend the hours
In harmless mirth and sport.

Then on to the Elysian plains
Apollo doth invite you, [110]
Where he provides with pastoral
   strains
In nymphals to delight you.

The sixth nymphal

Silvius, Halcius, Melanthus.

A woodman, fisher, and a swain
This nymphal through with mirth maintain,
Whose pleadings so the nymphs do please
That presently they give them bays.

Clear had the day been from the dawn,
All checkered was the sky,
Thin clouds like scarfs of cobweb lawn
Veiled heaven's most glorious eye.
The wind had no more strength than this,
That leisurely it blew
To make one leaf the next to kiss
That closely by it grew.
The rills that on the pebbles played
Might now be heard at will;   10
This world they only music made,
Else everything was still.
The flowers like brave embroidered girls
Looked as they much desired
To see whose head with orient pearls
Most curiously was tired;
And to itself the subtle air
Such sovereignty assumes,
That it received too large a share
From nature's rich perfumes.   20
When the Elysian youth were met
That were of most account,
And to disport themselves were set
Upon an easy mount;
Near which of stately fir and pine
There grew abundant store,
The tree that weepeth turpentine,
And shady sycamore.
Amongst this merry youthful train
A forester they had,   30
A fisher, and a shepherd's swain,
A lively country lad;
Betwixt which three a question grew
Who should the worthiest be,
Which violently they pursue
Nor stickled would they be;
That it the company doth please

This civil strife to stay,
Freely to hear what each of these
For his brave self could say.   40
When first this forester of all,
That Silvius had to name,
To whom the lot being cast doth fall,
Doth thus begin the game.

Silvius. For my profession, then, and for the life I lead,
All others to excel, thus for myself I plead:
I am the prince of sports, the forest is my fee,
He's not upon the earth for pleasure lives like me;
The morn no sooner puts her rosy mantle on,
But from my quiet lodge I instantly am gone,   50
When the melodious birds from every bush and brier
Of the wild spacious wastes make a continual choir;
The motlied meadows then, new varnished with the sun,
Shut up their spicy sweets upon the winds that run
In eas'ly ambling gales, and softly seem to pace,
That it the longer might their lusciousness embrace.
I am clad in youthful green, I other color scorn;
My silken baldrick bears my bugle or my horn,
Which setting to my lips I wind so loud and shrill,
As makes the echoes shout from every neighboring hill. 60
My doghook at my belt, to which my lyam's tied,
My sheaf of arrows by, my woodknife at my side,
My crossbow in my hand, my gaffle, or my rack
To bend it when I please or it I list to slack;
My hound then in my lyam, I by the woodman's art
Forecast where I may lodge the goodly high-palmed hart;
To view the grazing herds, so sundry times I use,
Where by the loftiest head I know my deer to choose,
And to unherd him then I gallop o'er the ground
Upon my well-breathed nag to cheer my earning hound.   70
Sometime I pitch my toils the deer alive to take,
Sometime I like the cry the deep-mouthed kennel make;
Then underneath my horse I stalk my game to strike,
And with a single dog to hunt him, hurt, I like.
The sylvans are to me true subjects, I their king;
The stately hart his hind doth to my presence bring,
The buck his lovèd doe, the roe his tripping mate,
Before me to my bower, whereas I sit in state.
The dryads, hamadryads, the satyrs and the fauns
Oft play at hide and seek before me on the lawns;   80
The frisking fairy oft when hornèd Cynthia shines
Before me as I walk dance wanton matachines;

The numerous feathered flocks that the wild forests haunt
Their sylvan songs to me in cheerful ditties chaunt;
The shades, like ample shields, defend me from the sun,
Through which me to refresh the gentle rivulets run;
No little bubbling brook from any spring that falls
But on the pebbles plays me pretty madrigals.
I' th' morn I climb the hills, where wholesome winds do blow,
At noontide to the vales and shady groves below,   90
Towards evening I again the crystal floods frequent,
In pleasure thus my life continually is spent.
As princes and great lords have palaces, so I
Have in the forests here my hall and gallery;
The tall and stately woods, which underneath are plain,
The groves my gardens are; the heath and downs again
My wide and spacious walks; then say all what ye can,
The forester is still your only gallant man.

He of his speech scarce made an end
But him they load with praise;   100
The nymphs most highly him commend,
And vow to give him bays.
He's now cried up of everyone,
And who but only he?
The forester's the man alone,
The worthiest of the three.
When some, than th' other far more staid,
Willed them a while to pause,
For there was more yet to be said
That might deserve applause.   110
When Halcius his turn next plies,
And silence having won,
Room for the fisherman, he cries,
And thus his plea begun.

Halcius. No, forester, it so must not be borne away,
But hear what for himself the fisher first can say:
The crystal-current streams continually I keep,
Where every pearl-paved ford, and every blue-eyed deep,
With me familiar are; when in my boat being set
My oar I take in hand, my angle and my net   120
About me; like a prince myself in state I steer,
Now up, now down the stream, now am I here, now there;
The pilot and the fraught myself, and at my ease
Can land me when I list, or in what place I please;
The silver-scalèd shoals about me in the streams,
As thick as ye discern the atoms in the beams,

Near to the shady bank where slender sallows grow
And willows their shag'd tops down towards the waters bow,
I shove in with my boat to shield me from the heat,
Where choosing from my bag some proved especial bait,   130
The goodly well-grown trout I with my angle strike,
And with my bearded wire I take the ravenous pike,
Of whom when I have hold he seldom breaks away,
Though at my line's full length so long I let him play
Till by my hand I find him well-near wearied be,
When softly by degrees I draw him up to me.
The lusty salmon too I oft with angling take,
Which me above the rest most lordly sport doth make,
Who feeling he is caught, such frisks and bounds doth fetch,
And by his very strength my line so far doth stretch   140
As draws my floating cork down to the very ground,
And wresting of my rod doth make my boat turn round.
I never idle am: sometime I bait my weels,
With which by night I take the dainty silver eels,
And with my draught-net then I sweep the streaming flood;
And to my trammel next and cast-net, from the mud
I beat the scaly brood; no hour I idly spend,
But wearied with my work I bring the day to end.
The naiades and nymphs that in the rivers keep,
Which take into their care the store of every deep,   150
Amongst the flowery flags, the bulrushes and reed,
That of the spawn have charge, abundantly to breed,
Well mounted upon swans, their naked bodies lend
To my discerning eye, and on my boat attend;
And dance upon the waves before me, for my sake,
To th' music the soft wind upon the reeds doth make;
And for my pleasure more, the rougher gods of seas
From Neptune's court send in the blue Nereides,
Which from his bracky realm upon the billows ride
And bear the rivers back with every streaming tide;   160
Those billows 'gainst my boat, borne with delightful gales,
Oft seeming as I row to tell me pretty tales,
Whilst ropes of liquid pearl still load my laboring oars,
As stretched upon the stream they strike me to the shores;
The silent meadows seem delighted with my lays,
As sitting in my boat I sing my lass's praise;
Then let them that like the forester up-cry,
Your noble fisher is your only man, say I.

This speech of Halcius turned the tide,
And brought it so about   170

That all upon the fisher cried
That he would bear it out;
Him for the speech he made, to clap
Who lent him not a hand,
And said 'twould be the water's hap
Quite to put down the land?
This while Melanthus silent sits,
For so the shepherd hight,
And having heard these dainty wits   180
Each pleading for his right,
To hear them honored in this wise
His patience doth provoke;
When, For a shepherd, room, he cries,
And for himself thus spoke.

Melanthus. Well, fisher, you have done, and forester, for you,
Your tale is neatly told—s' are both's, to give you due,
And now my turn comes next, then hear a shepherd speak:
My watchfulness and care gives day scarce leave to break
But to the fields I haste, my folded flock to see,
Where, when I find nor wolf nor fox hath injured me,   190
I to my bottle straight, and soundly baste my throat;
Which done, some country song or roundelay I rote
So merrily that to the music that I make
I force the lark to sing ere she be well awake;
Then Baull, my cut-tailed cur, and I begin to play,
He o'er my sheephook leaps, now th' one, now th' other way,
Then on his hinder feet he doth himself advance,
I tune, and to my note my lively dog doth dance;
Then whistle in my fist, my fellow swains to call,
Down go our hooks and scrips, and we to nine-holes fall,   200
At dust-point or at quoits else are we at it hard,
All false and cheating games we shepherds are debarred.
Surveying of my sheep, if ewe or wether look
As though it were amiss, or with my cur or crook
I take it, and when once I find what it doth ail,
It hardly hath that hurt but that my skill can heal;
And when my careful eye I cast upon my sheep,
I sort them in my pens, and sorted so I keep;
Those that are big'st of bone I still reserve for breed,
My cullings I put off, or for the chapman feed.   210
When the evening doth approach I to my bagpipe take,
And to my grazing flocks such music then I make
That they forbear to feed; then me a king you see,

I playing go before, my subjects follow me.
My bell-wether most brave before the rest doth stalk,
The father of the flock, and after him doth walk
My writhen-headed ram with posies crowned in pride,
Fast to his crooked horns with ribands neatly tied.
And at our shepherds' board that's cut out of the ground,
My fellow swains and I together at it round,   220
With green-cheese, clouted cream, with flawns and custards stored,
Whig, cider, and with whey, I domineer, a lord.
When shearing time is come I to the river drive
My goodly well-fleeced flocks (by pleasure thus I thrive)
Which being washed at will, upon the shearing day
My wool I forth in lokes fit for the winder lay,
Which upon lusty heaps into my cote I heave,
That in the handling feels as soft as any sleave;
When every ewe two lambs that yeanëd hath that year,
About her new-shorn neck a chaplet then doth wear.   230
My tarbox and my scrip, my bagpipe at my back,
My sheephook in my hand, what can I say I lack?
He that a scepter swayed, a sheephook in his hand
Hath not disdained to have, for shepherds then I stand;
Then forester, and you, my fisher, cease your strife,
I say your shepherd leads your only merry life.

They had not cried the forester
And fisher up before
So much, but now the nymphs prefer
The shepherd ten times more,   240
And all the ging goes on his side,
Their minion him they make,
To him themselves they all apply,
And all his party take;
Till some in their discretion cast,
Since first the strife begun,
In all that from them there had passed,
None absolutely won;
That equal honor they should share
And their deserts to show,   25^
For each a garland they prepare,
Which they on them bestow,
Of all the choicest flowers that were,
Which purposely they gather,
With which they crown them, parting there
As they came first together.

SIR JOHN DAVIES

The Introduction and Notes are at page 965

FROM *Epigrams and Elegies,* [*c.* 1595]

Of a gull

Oft in my laughing rhymes I name a gull,
But this new term will many questions breed;
Therefore at first I will express at full
Who is a true and perfect gull indeed:
A gull is he who fears a velvet gown,
And when a wench is brave dares not speak to her;
A gull is he which traverseth the town,
And is for marriage known a common wooer;
A gull is he which while he proudly wears
A silver-hilted rapier by his side   10
Endures the lies and knocks about the ears,
Whilst in his sheath his sleeping sword doth bide;
A gull is he which wears good handsome clothes,
And stands in presence stroking up his hair,
And fills up his unperfect speech with oaths,
But speaks not one wise word throughout the year.
    But to define a gull in terms precise,
    A gull is he which seems, and is not, wise.

In Ciprium

The fine youth Ciprius is more terse and neat
Than the new garden of the Old Temple is,
And still the newest fashion he doth get
And with the time doth change from that to this.
He wears a hat now of the flat-crown block,
The treble ruffs, long cloak, and doublet French;
He takes tobacco, and doth wear a lock,
And wastes more time in dressing than a wench:
    Yet this new-fangled youth, made for these times,
    Doth above all praise old Gascoigne's rhymes!   10

In Haywodum

Heywood, which did in epigrams excel,
Is now put down since my light muse arose—
    As buckets are put down into a well
    Or as a school-boy putteth down his hose.

In Dacum

Dacus, with some good color and pretense,
Terms his love's beauty *silent eloquence*,—
 For she doth lay more colors on her face
 Than ever Tully used his speech to grace.

In Titum

Titus, the brave and valorous young gallant,
Three years together in this town hath been;
Yet my Lord Chancellor's tomb he hath not seen,
Nor the new water-work, nor the elephant.
 I cannot tell the cause without a smile,—
 He hath been in the Counter all this while.

In Flaccum

The false knave Flaccus once a bribe I gave;
The more fool I to bribe so false a knave.
But he gave back my bribe; the more fool he
That for my folly did not cozen me.

In Decium

Audacious painters have nine worthies made,
But poet Decius, more audacious far,
Making his mistress march with men of war,
With title of Tenth Worthy doth her lade.
 Methinks that gull did use his terms as fit
 Which termed his love *a giant for her wit*.

From *Chetham Ms.* 8012

To his good friend, Sir Anthony Cooke

Here my chameleon muse herself doth change
To divers shapes of gross absurdities,
And like an antic mocks with fashion strange
The fond admirers of lewd gulleries.
Your judgment sees with pity and with scorn
The bastard sonnets of these rhymers base,
Which in this whisking age are daily born,
To their own shames and poetry's disgrace.
Yet some praise those—and some perhaps will praise
Even these of mine; and therefore these I send   10
To you, that pass in court your glorious days;

That if some rich rash gull these rhymes commend,
Thus you may set this formal wit to school,
Use your own grace, and beg him for a fool.

Gulling Sonnets

The lover, under burthen of his mistress' love
Which like to Ætna did his heart oppress,
Did give such piteous groans that he did move
The heav'ns at length to pity his distress.
But for the Fates, in their high court above,
Forbade to make the grievous burthen less,
The gracious powers did all conspire to prove
If miracle this mischief might redress.
Therefore, regarding that the load was such
As no man might with one man's might sustain,   10
And that mild patïence imported much
To him that should endure an endless pain,
By their decree he soon transformëd was
Into a patient burden-bearing ass.

The hardness of her heart and truth of mine
When the all-seeing eyes of heaven did see,
They straight concluded that by power divine
To other forms our hearts should turnëd be.
Then hers, as hard as flint, a flint became,
And mine, as true as steel, to steel was turned;
And then between our hearts sprang forth the flame
Of kindest love, which unextinguished burned.
And long the sacred lamp of mutual love
Incessantly did burn in glory bright,   10
Until my folly did her fury move
To recompense my service with despite;
And to put out with snuffers of her pride
The lamp of love which else had never died.

The sacred muse that first made love divine
Hath made him naked and without attire;
But I will clothe him with this pen of mine,
That all the world his fashion shall admire:
His hat of hope, his band of beauty fine,
His cloak of craft, his doublet of desire,
Grief, for a girdle, shall about him twine,
His points of pride, his eyelet-holes of ire,
His hose of hate, his codpiece of conceit,
His stockings of stern strife, his shirt of shame.   10

His garters of vain-glory gay and slight,
His pantofles of passions I will frame;
Pumps of presumption shall adorn his feet,
And socks of sullenness exceeding sweet.

My case is this: I love Zepheria bright;
Of her I hold my heart by fealty,
Which I discharge to her perpetually;
Yet she thereof will never me acquite.
For now, supposing I withhold her right,
She hath distrained my heart to satisfy
The duty which I never did deny,
And far away impounds it with despite.
I labor therefore justly to repleve   10
My heart, which she unjustly doth impound;
But quick conceit, which now is love's high shrieve
Returns; it is esloigned, not to be found.
Then, which the law affords, I only crave
Her heart for mine in withernam to have

From *Orchestra*, 1596

Orchestra, or a poem of dancing

Where lives the man that never yet did hear
Of chaste Penelope, Ulysses' queen?
Who kept her faith unspotted twenty year,
Till he returned, that far away had been,
And many men and many towns had seen;
   Ten year at siege of Troy he lingering lay,
   And ten year in the midland sea did stray.

Homer, to whom the Muses did carouse
A great deep cup with heavenly nectar filled;
The greatest deepest cup in Jove's great house,   10
(For Jove himself had so expressly willed),
He drank of all, ne let one drop be spilled;
   Since when his brain, that had before been dry,
   Became the wellspring of all poetry,—

Homer doth tell, in his abundant verse,
The long laborious travails of the man,
And of his lady too he doth rehearse,
How she illudes, with all the art she can,
Th' ungrateful love which other lords began;
   For of her lord false fame long since had sworn   20
   That Neptune's monsters had his carcass torn.

All this he tells, but one thing he forgot,
One thing most worthy his eternal song;
But he was old and blind and saw it not,
Or else he thought he should Ulysses wrong,
To mingle it his tragic acts among;
    Yet was there not, in all the world of things,
    A sweeter burden for his muse's wings.

The courtly love Antinous did make,
Antinous, that fresh and jolly knight,   30
Which of the gallants that did undertake
To win the widow, had most wealth and might,
Wit to persuade, and beauty to delight;
    The courtly love he made unto the queen,
    Homer forgot, as if it had not been.

Sing then, Terpsichore, my light Muse, sing
His gentle art and cunning courtesy!
You, lady, can remember everything,
For you are daughter of queen Memory;
But sing a plain and easy melody,   40
    For the soft mean that warbleth but the ground
    To my rude ear doth yield the sweetest sound.

Only one night's discourse I can report:
When the great torchbearer of heaven was gone
Down, in a mask, unto the Ocean's court,
To revel it with Tethys, all alone
Antinous, disguisèd and unknown,
    Like to the spring in gaudy ornament,
    Unto the castle of the princess went.

The sovereign castle of the rocky isle,   50
Wherein Penelope the princess lay,
Shone with a thousand lamps, which did exile
The dim dark shades, and turned the night to day.
Not Jove's blue tent, what time the sunny ray
    Behind the bulwark of the earth retires,
    Is seen to sparkle with more twinkling fires.

That night the queen came forth from far within,
And in the presence of her court was seen.
For the sweet singer Phœmius did begin
To praise the worthies that at Troy had been;   60
Somewhat of her Ulysses she did ween
    In his grave hymn the heav'nly man would sing,
    Or of his wars, or of his wandering.

Pallas that hour, with her sweet breath divine,
Inspired immortal beauty in her eyes,
That with celestial glory she did shine
Brighter than Venus, when she doth arise
Out of the waters to adorn the skies.
　　The wooers, all amazèd, do admire
　　And check their own presumptuous desire.　　70

Only Antinous, when at first he viewed
Her star-bright eyes that with new honor shined,
Was not dismayed; but therewithal renewed
The noblesse and the splendor of his mind;
And as he did fit circumstances find,
　　Unto the throne he boldly gan advance,
　　And with fair manners, wooed the queen to dance:

Goddess of women! sith your heav'nliness
Hath now vouchsafed itself to represent
To our dim eyes, which though they see the less,　　80
Yet are they blest in their astonishment;
Imitate heav'n, whose beauties excellent
　　Are in continual motion day and night,
　　And move thereby more wonder and delight.

Let me the mover be, to turn about
Those glorious ornaments that youth and love
Have fixèd in you, every part throughout;
Which if you will in timely measure move,
Not all those precious gems in heaven above
　　Shall yield a sight more pleasing to behold　　90
　　With all their turns and tracings manifold.

With this the modest princess blushed and smiled
Like to a clear and rosy eventide,
And softly did return this answer mild:
Fair sir! you needs must fairly be denied,
Where your demand cannot be satisfied.
　　My feet, which only nature taught to go,
　　Did never yet the art of footing know.

But why persuade you me to this new rage?
For all disorder and misrule is new,　　100
For such misgovernment in former age
Our old divine forefathers never knew;
Who if they lived, and did the follies view
　　Which their fond nephews make their chief affairs,
　　Would hate themselves, that had begot such heirs.

Sole heir of virtue, and of beauty both!
Whence cometh it, Antinous replies,
That your imperious virtue is so loath
To grant your beauty her chief exercise?
Or from what spring doth your opinion rise   110
   That dancing is a frenzy and a rage,
     First known and used in this new-fangled age?

Dancing, bright lady, then began to be
When the first seeds whereof the world did spring,
The fire, air, earth, and water did agree
By Love's persuasion, nature's mighty king,
To leave their first disordered combating,
   And in a dance such measure to observe
     As all the world their motion should preserve.

Since when they still are carried in a round,   120
And changing come one in another's place;
Yet do they neither mingle nor confound,
But every one doth keep the bounded space
Wherein the dance doth bid it turn or trace.
   This wondrous miracle did Love devise,
     For dancing is love's proper exercise.

Like this he framed the gods' eternal bower,
And of a shapeless and confusèd mass,
By his through-piercing and digesting power,
The turning vault of heaven formèd was,   130
Whose starry wheels he hath so made to pass
   As that their movings do a music frame,
     And they themselves still dance unto the same.

Or if this all, which round about we see,
As idle Morpheus some sick brains hath taught,
Of undivided motes compacted be,
How was this goodly architecture wrought?
Or by what means were they together brought?
   They err that say they did concur by chance;
     Love made them meet in a well-ordered dance!   140

As when Amphion with his charming lyre
Begot so sweet a siren of the air,
That, with her rhetoric, made the stones conspire
The ruins of a city to repair,
A work of wit and reason's wise affair;
   So Love's smooth tongue the motes such measure taught
     That they joined hands, and so the world was wrought!

How justly then is dancing termëd new,
Which with the world in point of time began?
Yea, Time itself, whose birth Jove never knew,   150
And which is far more ancient than the sun,
Had not one moment of his age outrun,
    When out leaped Dancing from the heap of things
    And lightly rode upon his nimble wings.

Reason hath both their pictures in her treasure:
Where Time the measure of all moving is,
And Dancing is a moving all in measure.
Now, if you do resemble that to this,
And think both one, I think you think amiss;   160
    But if you judge them twins, together got,
    And Time first born, your judgment erreth not.

Thus doth it equal age with Age enjoy,
And yet in lusty youth forever flowers;
Like Love, his sire, whom painters make a boy,
Yet is he eldest of the heav'nly powers;
Or like his brother Time, whose wingëd hours,
    Going and coming, will not let him die,
    But still preserve him in his infancy.

This said, the queen, with her sweet lips divine,
Gently began to move the subtle air,   170
Which gladly yielding, did itself incline
To take a shape between those rubies fair;
And being formed, softly did repair,
    With twenty doublings in the empty way,
    Unto Antinous' ears, and thus did say:

What eye doth see the heav'n, but doth admire
When it the movings of the heav'ns doth see?
Myself, if I to heav'n may once aspire,
If that be dancing, will a dancer be;
But as for this, your frantic jollity,   180
    How it began, or whence you did it learn,
    I never could with reason's eye discern.

Antinous answered: Jewel of the earth!
Worthy you are that heav'nly dance to lead;
But for you think our Dancing base of birth,
And newly born but of a brain-sick head,
I will forthwith his antique gentry read,
    And, for I love him, will his herald be,
    And blaze his arms, and draw his pedigree.

When Love had shaped this world, this great fair wight,   ¹⁹⁰
That all wights else in this wide womb contains,
And had instructed it to dance aright
A thousand measures, with a thousand strains,
Which it should practise with delightful pains
   Until that fatal instant should revolve,
   When all to nothing should again resolve;

The comely order and proportion fair
On every side did please his wand'ring eye;
Till, glancing through the thin transparent air,
A rude disordered rout he did espy   200
Of men and women, that most spitefully
   Did one another throng and crowd so sore
   That his kind eye, in pity, wept therefor.

And swifter than the lightning down he came,
Another shapeless chaos to digest;
He will begin another world to frame,
For Love, till all be well, will never rest.
Then with such words as cannot be expressed
   He cuts the troops, that all asunder fling,
   And ere they wist he casts them in a ring.   210

Then did he rarefy the element,
And in the center of the ring appear;
The beams that from his forehead shining went
Begot a horror and religious fear
In all the souls that round about him were,
   Which in their ears attentiveness procures,
   While he, with such like sounds, their minds allures:

How doth Confusion's mother, headlong Chance,
Put Reason's noble squadron to the rout?
Or how should you, that have the governance   220
Of Nature's children, heaven and earth throughout,
Prescribe them rules, and live yourselves without?
   Why should your fellowship a trouble be,
   Since man's chief pleasure is society?

If sense hath not yet taught you, learn of me
A comely moderation and discreet,
That your assemblies may well ordered be;
When my uniting power shall make you meet,
With heav'nly tunes it shall be tempered sweet,
   And be the model of the world's great frame,   230
   And you, earth's children, dancing shall it name.

Behold the world, how it is whirlëd round!
And for it is so whirled, is namëd so;
In whose large volume many rules are found
Of this new art, which it doth fairly show.
For your quick eyes in wand'ring to and fro,
    From east to west, on no one thing can glance,
    But, if you mark it well, it seems to dance.

First you see fixed in this huge mirror blue
Of trembling lights a number numberless;   240
Fixed, they are named, but with a name untrue;
For they are moved and in a dance express
The great long year that doth contain no less
    Than threescore hundreds of those years in all,
    Which the sun makes with his course natural.

What if to you these sparks disordered seem,
As if by chance they had been scattered there?
The gods a solemn measure do it deem
And see a just proportion everywhere,
And know the points whence first their movings were,   250
    To which first points, when all return again,
    The axletree of heav'n shall break in twain.

Under that spangled sky five wand'ring flames,
Besides the king of day and queen of night,
Are wheeled around, all in their sundry frames,
And all in sundry measures do delight;
Yet altogether keep no measure right;
    For by itself each doth itself advance,
    And by itself each doth a galliard dance.

Venus, the mother of that bastard Love,   260
Which doth usurp the world's great marshal's name,
Just with the sun her dainty feet doth move;
And unto him doth all her gestures frame,
Now after, now afore, the flattering dame
    With divers cunning passages doth err,
    Still him respecting that respects not her.

For that brave sun, the father of the day,
Doth love this earth, the mother of the night;
And, like a reveler in rich array,
Doth dance his galliard in his leman's sight,   270
Both back and forth and sideways passing light.
    His gallant grace doth so the gods amaze
    That all stand still and at his beauty gaze.

But see the earth when she approacheth near,
How she for joy doth spring and sweetly smile;
But see again her sad and heavy cheer,
When changing places, he retires a while;
But those black clouds he shortly will exile,
    And make them all before his presence fly,
    As mists consumed before his cheerful eye.   280

Who doth not see the measure of the moon?
Which thirteen times she danceth every year,
And ends her pavan thirteen times as soon
As doth her brother, of whose golden hair
She borroweth part, and proudly doth it wear.
    Then doth she coyly turn her face aside
    That half her cheek is scarce sometimes descried.

Next her, the pure, subtile, and cleansing fire
Is swiftly carried in a circle even,
Though Vulcan be pronounced by many a liar   290
The only halting god that dwells in heaven;
But that foul name may be more fitly given
    To your false fire, that far from heaven is fall,
    And doth consume, waste, spoil, disorder all.

And now behold your tender nurse, the air,
And common neighbor that aye runs around;
How many pictures and impressions fair
Within her empty regions are there found,
Which to your senses dancing do propound?
    For what are breath, speech, echoes, music, winds,   300
    But dancings of the air, in sundry kinds?

For when you breathe the air in order moves,
Now in, now out, in time and measure true,
And when you speak, so well the dancing loves
That doubling oft and oft redoubling new,
With thousand forms she doth herself endue.
    For all the words that from your lips repair
    Are nought but tricks and turnings of the air.

Hence is her prattling daughter, Echo, born,
That dances to all voices she can hear.   310
There is no sound so harsh that she doth scorn,
Nor any time wherein she will forbear
The airy pavement with her feet to wear;
    And yet her hearing sense is nothing quick,
    For after time she endeth every trick.

And thou, sweet music, dancing's only life,
The ear's sole happiness, the air's best speech,
Lodestone of fellowship, charming rod of strife,
The soft mind's paradise, the sick mind's leech,
With thine own tongue thou trees and stones canst teach,   320
   That when the air doth dance her finest measure,
   Then art thou born, the gods' and men's sweet pleasure.

Lastly, where keep the winds their revelry,
Their violent turnings and wild whirling hays,
But in the air's tralucent gallery?
Where she herself is turned a hundred ways,
While with those maskers wantonly she plays.
   Yet in this misrule they such rule embrace
   As two, at once, encumber not the place.

If then fire, air, wand'ring and fixëd lights,   330
In every province of th' imperial sky,
Yield perfect forms of dancing to your sights,
In vain I teach the ear that which the eye,
With certain view, already doth descry;
   But for your eyes perceive not all they see,
   In this I will your senses' master be.

For lo, the sea that fleets about the land,
And like a girdle clips her solid waist,
Music and measure both doth understand;
For his great crystal eye is always cast   340
Up to the moon, and on her fixëd fast;
   And as she danceth in her pallid sphere,
   So danceth he about the center here.

Sometimes his proud green waves in order set,
One after other, flow unto the shore;
Which when they have with many kisses wet,
They ebb away in order, as before;
And to make known his courtly love the more,
   He oft doth lay aside his three-forked mace,
   And with his arms the timorous earth embrace.   350

Only the earth doth stand forever still:
Her rocks remove not, nor her mountains meet,
Although some wits enriched with learning's skill
Say heav'n stands firm and that the earth doth fleet,
And swiftly turneth underneath their feet;
   Yet, though the earth is ever steadfast seen,
   On her broad breast hath dancing ever been.

For those blue veins that through her body spread,
Those sapphire streams which from great hills do spring,
The earth's great dugs, for every wight is fed
With sweet fresh moisture from them issuing,
Observe a dance in their wild wandering;
    And still their dance begets a murmur sweet,
    And still the murmur with the dance doth meet.

Of all their ways, I love Meander's path,
Which, to the tunes of dying swans, doth dance
Such winding sleights. Such turns and tricks he hath,
Such creeks, such wrenches, and such dalliance
That, whether it be hap or heedless chance,
    In his indented course and wringling play,
    He seems to dance a perfect cunning hay.

But wherefore do these streams forever run?
To keep themselves forever sweet and clear;
For let their everlasting course be done,
They straight corrupt and foul with mud appear.
O ye sweet nymphs, that beauty's loss do fear,
    Contemn the drugs that physic doth devise,
    And learn of Love this dainty exercise.

See how those flowers, that have sweet beauty too,
The only jewels that the earth doth wear
When the young sun in bravery her doth woo,
As oft as they the whistling wind do hear,
Do wave their tender bodies here and there;
    And though their dance no perfect measure is,
    Yet oftentimes their music makes them kiss.

What makes the vine about the elm to dance
With turnings, windings, and embracements round?
What makes the lodestone to the north advance
His subtile point, as if from thence he found
His chief attractive virtue to redound?
    Kind nature first doth cause all things to love;
    Love makes them dance, and in just order move.

Hark how the birds do sing! and mark then how,
Jump with the modulation of their lays,
They lightly leap and skip from bough to bough;
Yet do the cranes deserve a greater praise,
Which keep such measure in their airy ways,
    As when they all in order rankèd are,
    They make a perfect form triangular.

360

370

380

390

In the chief angle flies the watchful guide;
And all the followers their heads do lay
On their foregoers' backs, on either side;
But, for the captain hath no rest to stay
His head, forwearied with the windy way,
    He back retires; and then the next behind,
    As his lieutenant, leads them through the wind.

But why relate I every singular?
Since all the world's great fortunes and affairs
Forward and backward rapt and whirlëd are,
According to the music of the spheres;   410
And Chance herself her nimble feet upbears
    On a round slippery wheel, that rolleth aye,
    And turns all states with her impetuous sway;

Learn then to dance, you that are princes born,
And lawful lords of earthly creatures all;
Imitate them, and thereof take no scorn,
For this new art to them is natural.
And imitate the stars celestïal;
    For when pale death your vital twist shall sever,
    Your better parts must dance with them forever.   420

Thus Love persuades, and all the crowd of men
That stands around, doth make a murmuring,
As when the wind, loosed from his hollow den,
Among the trees a gentle bass doth sing,
Or as a brook, through pebbles wandering;
    But in their looks they uttered this plain speech:
    That they would learn to dance, if Love would teach.

Then, first of all, he doth demonstrate plain
The motions seven that are in nature found;
Upward and downward, forth and back again,   430
To this side and to that, and turning round;
Whereof a thousand brawls he doth compound,
    Which he doth teach unto the multitude,
    And ever with a turn they must conclude.

As when a nymph arising from the land,
Leadeth a dance with her long watery train,
Down to the sea she wries to every hand,
And every way doth cross the fertile plain;
But when, at last, she falls into the main,
    Then all her traverses concluded are,
    And with the sea her course is circular.   440

Thus when at first Love had them marshallëd,
As erst he did the shapeless mass of things,
He taught them rounds and winding hays to tread,
And about trees to cast themselves in rings;
As the two Bears, whom the first mover flings
  With a short turn about heaven's axletree,
  In a round dance forever wheeling be.

But after these, as men more civil grew,
He did more grave and solemn measures frame; 450
With such fair order and proportion true,
And correspondence every way the same,
That no fault-finding eye did ever blame;
  For every eye was movëd at the sight
  With sober wond'ring and with sweet delight.

Not those old students of the heavenly book,
Atlas the great, Prometheus the wise,
Which on the stars did all their lifetime look,
Could ever find such measures in the skies,
So full of change and rare varieties; 460
  Yet all the feet whereon these measures go
  Are only spondees, solemn, grave, and slow.

But for more divers and more pleasing show,
A swift and wand'ring dance she did invent,
With passages uncertain, to and fro,
Yet with a certain answer and consent
To the quick music of the instrument.
  Five was the number of the music's feet,
  Which still the dance did with five paces meet.

A gallant dance! that lively doth bewray 470
A spirit and a virtue masculine;
Impatient that her house on earth should stay,
Since she herself is fiery and divine.
Oft doth she make her body upward flyne
  With lofty turns and caprioles in the air,
  Which with the lusty tunes accordeth fair.

What shall I name those current traverses,
That on a triple dactyl foot do run,
Close by the ground, with sliding passages?
Wherein that dancer greatest praise hath won, 480
Which with best order can all orders shun;
  For everywhere he wantonly must range,
  And turn, and wind, with unexpected change.

Yet is there one, the most delightful kind,
A lofty jumping, or a leaping round,
When, arm in arm, two dancers are entwined,
And whirl themselves with strict embracements bound,
And still their feet an anapest do sound;
    An anapest is all their music's song,
    Whose first two feet are short, and third is long.   490

As the victorious twins of Leda and Jove,
That taught the Spartans dancing on the sands
Of swift Eurotas, dance in heav'n above,
Knit and united with eternal bands,
Among the stars their double image stands,
    Where both are carried with an equal pace,
    Together jumping in their turning race.

This is the net wherein the sun's bright eye
Venus and Mars entangled did behold;
For in this dance their arms they so imply,   500
As each doth seem the other to enfold.
What if lewd wits another tale have told,
    Of jealous Vulcan, and of iron chains?
    Yet this true sense that forgëd lie contains.

These various forms of dancing Love did frame,
And besides these, a hundred million mo;
And as he did invent, he taught the same,
With goodly gesture and with comely show,
Now keeping state, now humbly honoring low.
    And ever for the persons and the place,   510
    He taught most fit, and best according grace.

For Love, within his fertile working brain,
Did then conceive those gracious virgins three,
Whose civil moderation did maintain
All decent order and conveniency,
And fair respect, and seemly modesty;
    And then he thought it fit they should be born,
    That their sweet presence dancing might adorn.

Hence is it that these Graces painted are
With hand in hand, dancing an endless round;   520
And with regarding eyes, that still beware
That there be no disgrace amongst them found,
With equal foot they beat the flow'ry ground,
    Laughing or singing, as their passions will;
    Yet nothing that they do becomes them ill.

Thus Love taught men! and men thus learned of Love
Sweet music's sound with feet to counterfeit;
Which was long time before high-thundering Jove
Was lifted up to heav'n's imperial seat.
For though by birth he were the prince of Crete,   530
    Nor Crete nor heav'n should that young prince have seen,
    If dancers with their timbrels had not been.

Since when all ceremonious mysteries,
All sacred orgies and religious rites,
All pomps and triumphs and solemnities,
All funerals, nuptials, and like public sights,
All parliaments of peace, and warlike fights,
    All learned arts, and every great affair,
    A lively shape of dancing seems to bear.

For what did he, who with his ten-tongued lute   540
Gave beasts and blocks an understanding ear,
Or rather into bestial minds and brutes
Shed and infused the beams of reason clear?
Doubtless, for men that rude and savage were,
    A civil form of dancing he devised,
    Wherewith unto their gods they sacrificed.

So did Musæus, so Amphion did,
And Linus with his sweet enchanting song,
And he whose hand the earth of monsters rid,
And had men's ears fast chainëd to his tongue,   550
And Theseus to his wood-born slaves among,
    Used dancing as the finest policy
    To plant religion and society.

And therefore, now, the Thracian Orpheus' lyre
And Hercules himself are stellified,
And in high heaven, amidst the starry choir,
Dancing their parts, continually do slide;
So, on the zodiac, Ganymede doth ride,
    And so is Hebe with the Muses nine,
    For pleasing Jove with dancing, made divine.   560

Wherefore was Proteus said himself to change
Into a stream, a lion, and a tree,
And many other forms fantastic strange,
As in his fickle thought he wished to be?
But that he danced with such facility,
    As like a lion he could pace with pride,
    Ply like a plant, and like a river slide.

And how was Cæneus made at first a man,
And then a woman, then a man again,
But in a dance? which when he first began,   570
He the man's part in measure did sustain;
But when he changed into a second strain,
    He danced the woman's part another space,
    And then returned unto his former place.

Hence sprang the fable of Tiresias,
That he the pleasure of both sexes tried;
For in a dance he man and woman was,
By often change of place, from side to side;
But for the woman easily did slide,
    And smoothly swim with cunning hidden art,   580
    He took more pleasure in a woman's part.

So to a fish Venus herself did change,
And swimming through the soft and yielding wave,
With gentle motions did so smoothly range
As none might see where she the water drave;
But this plain truth that falsèd fable gave,
    That she did dance with sliding easiness,
    Pliant and quick in wand'ring passages.

And merry Bacchus practised dancing too,
And to the Lydian numbers rounds did make;   590
The like he did in th' eastern India do,
And taught them all, when Phœbus did awake,
And when at night he did his coach forsake,
    To honor heav'n, and heav'n's great rolling eye,
    With turning dances and with melody.

Thus they who first did found a commonweal,
And they who first religion did ordain,
By dancing first the people's hearts did steal;
Of whom we now a thousand tales do feign.
Yet do we now their perfect rules retain,   600
    And use them still in such devices new,
    As in the world, long since, their withering grew.

For after towns and kingdoms founded were,
Between great states arose well-ordered war,
Wherein most perfect measure doth appear;
Whether their well-set ranks respected are
In quadrant forms or semicircular,
    Or else the march, when all the troops advance
    And to the drum in gallant order dance.

And after wars, when white-winged victory
Is with a glorious triumph beautified,
And everyone doth Io, Io! cry,
While all in gold the conqueror doth ride,
The solemn pomp that fills the city wide
    Observes such rank and measure everywhere,
    As if they all together dancing were.

The like just order mourners do observe,
But with unlike affection and attire,
When some great man that nobly did deserve,
And whom his friends impatiently desire,
Is brought with honor to his latest fire.
    The dead corpse too in that sad dance is moved,
    As if both dead and living, dancing loved.

A diverse cause, but like solemnity,
Unto the temple leads the bashful bride,
Which blusheth like the Indian ivory
Which is with dip of Tyrian purple dyed;
A golden troop doth pass on every side
    Of flourishing young men and virgins gay,
    Which keep fair measure all the flow'ry way.

And not alone the general multitude,
But those choice Nestors, which in council grave
Of cities and of kingdoms do conclude,
Most comely order in their sessions have;
Wherefore the wise Thessalians ever gave
    The name of leader of their country's dance
    To him that had their country's governance.

And those great masters of the liberal arts
In all their several schools do dancing teach;
For humble grammar first doth set the parts
Of congruent and well-according speech,
Which rhetoric, whose state the clouds doth reach,
    And heavenly poetry do forward lead,
    And divers measures diversly do tread.

For rhetoric, clothing speech in rich array,
The looser numbers teacheth her to range
With twenty tropes, and turnings every way,
And various figures, and licentious change;
But poetry, with rule and order strange,
    So curiously doth move each single pace
    As all is marred if she one foot misplace.

610

620

630

640

650

These arts of speech the guides and marshals are,
But logic leadeth reason in a dance,
Reason, the cynosure and bright lodestar
In this world's sea, t' avoid the rocks of chance,
For with close following and continuance,
 One reason doth another so ensue
 As, in conclusion, still the dance is true.

So music to her own sweet tunes doth trip,
With tricks of 3, 5, 8, 15, and more;   660
So doth the art of numb'ring seem to skip
From ev'n to odd, in her proportioned score;
So do those skills, whose quick eyes do explore
 The just dimension both of earth and heav'n,
 In all their rules observe a measure ev'n.

Lo, this is Dancing's true nobility:
Dancing, the child of Music and of Love;
Dancing itself, both love and harmony,
Where all agree and all in order move;
Dancing, the art that all arts do approve; 670
 The fair chäracter of the world's consent,
 The heav'n's true figure, and th' earth's ornament.

The queen, whose dainty ears had borne too long
The tedious praise of that she did despise,
Adding once more the music of the tongue
To the sweet speech of her alluring eyes,
Began to answer in such winning wise
 As that forthwith Antinous' tongue was tied,
 His eyes fast fixed, his ears were open wide.

Forsooth, quoth she, great glory you have won 680
To your trim minion, Dancing, all this while,
By blazing him Love's first begotten son,
Of every ill the hateful father vile,
That doth the world with sorceries beguile,
 Cunningly mad, religiously profane,
 Wit's monster, reason's canker, sense's bane.

Love taught the mother that unkind desire
To wash her hands in her own infant's blood;
Love taught the daughter to betray her sire
Into most base unworthy servitude; 690
Love taught the brother to prepare such food
 To feast his brothers that the all-seeing sun,
 Wrapped in a cloud, the wicked sight did shun.

And even this self-same Love hath dancing taught,
An art that showeth th' idea of his mind
With vainness, frenzy, and misorder fraught;
Sometimes with blood and cruelties unkind,
For in a dance Tereus' mad wife did find
    Fit time and place, by murdering her son,
      T' avenge the wrong his traitorous sire had done.   700

What mean the mermaids when they dance and sing,
But certain death unto the mariner?
What tidings do the dancing dolphins bring,
But that some dangerous storm approacheth near?
Then sith both Love and Dancing liveries bear
    Of such ill hap, unhappy may they prove
      That, sitting free, will either dance or love!

Yet once again Antinous did reply:
Great Queen! condemn not Love the innocent,
For this mischievous Lust, which traitorously   710
Usurps his name and steals his ornament;
For that true Love, which dancing did invent,
    Is he that tuned the world's whole harmony,
      And linked all men in sweet society.

He first extracted from th' earth-mingled mind
That heav'nly fire, or quintessence divine,
Which doth such sympathy in beauty find
As is between the elm and fruitful vine,
And so to beauty ever doth incline;
    Life's life it is, and cordial to the heart,   720
      And of our better part the better part.

This is true Love, by that true Cupid got,
Which danceth galliards in your amorous eyes,
But to your frozen heart approacheth not;
Only your heart he dares not enterprise,
And yet through every other part he flies,
    And everywhere he nimbly danceth now,
      That in yourself yourself perceive not how.

For your sweet beauty daintily transfused
With due proportion throughout every part,   730
What is it but a dance where Love hath used
His finer cunning and more curious art?
Where all the elements themselves impart,
    And turn, and wind, and mingle with such measure
      That th' eye that sees it surfeits with the pleasure.

Love in the twinkling of your eyelids danceth,
Love danceth in your pulses and your veins,
Love, when you sew, your needle's point advanceth,
And makes it dance a thousand curious strains
Of winding rounds, whereof the form remains   740
  To show that your fair hands can dance the hay,
  Which your fine feet would learn as well as they.

And when your ivory fingers touch the strings
Of any silver-sounding instrument,
Love makes them dance to those sweet murmurings
With busy skill and cunning excellent.
Oh, that your feet those tunes would represent
  With artificial motions to and fro,
  That Love this art in ev'ry part might show!

Yet your fair soul, which came from heav'n above   750
To rule this house (another heav'n below)
With divers powers in harmony doth move;
And all the virtues that from her do flow
In a round measure, hand in hand do go;
  Could I now see, as I conceive this dance,
  Wonder and love would cast me in a trance.

The richest jewel in all the heav'nly treasure,
That ever yet unto the earth was shown,
Is perfect concord, th' only perfect pleasure
That wretched earth-born men have ever known;   760
For many hearts it doth compound in one,
  That whatso one doth will, or speak, or do,
  With one consent they all agree thereto.

Concord's true picture shineth in this art,
Where divers men and women rankèd be,
And everyone doth dance a several part,
Yet all as one in measure do agree,
Observing perfect uniformity;
  All turn together, all together trace,
  And all together honor and embrace.   770

If they whom sacred Love hath linked in one
Do as they dance, in all their course of life,
Never shall burning grief nor bitter moan
Nor factious difference nor unkind strife
Arise between the husband and the wife;
  For whether forth, or back, or round he go,
  As doth the man, so must the woman do.

woman's place

What if by often interchange of place
Sometime the woman gets the upper hand?
That is but done for more delightful grace,   780
For on that part she doth not ever stand;
But as the measure's law doth her command,
    She wheels about, and ere the dance doth end,
    Into her former place she doth transcend.

But not alone this correspondence meet
And uniform consent doth dancing praise;
For Comeliness, the child of Order sweet,
Enamels it with her eye-pleasing rays;
Fair Comeliness ten hundred thousand ways
    Through dancing sheds itself, and makes it shine   790
    With glorious beauty and with grace divine.

For comeliness is a disposing fair
Of things and actions in fit time and place,
Which doth in dancing show itself most clear
When troops confused, which here and there do trace
Without distinguishment or bounded space,
    By dancing rule into such ranks are brought
    As glads the eye and ravisheth the thought.

Then why should reason judge that reasonless
Which is wit's offspring, and the work of art,   800
Image of concord and of comeliness?
Who sees a clock moving in every part,
A sailing pinnace, or a wheeling cart,
    But thinks that reason, ere it came to pass,
    The first impulsive cause and mover was?

Who sees an army all in rank advance,
But deems a wise commander is in place,
Which leadeth on that brave victorious dance?
Much more in dancing's art, in dancing's grace,
Blindness itself may reason's footsteps trace;   810
    For of love's maze it is the curious plot,
    And of man's fellowship the true-love knot.

But if these eyes of yours, lodestars of love,
Showing the world's great dance to your mind's eye,
Cannot, with all their demonstrations, move
Kind apprehension in your fantasy
Of dancing's virtue and nobility,
    How can my barbarous tongue win you thereto,
    Which heav'n and earth's fair speech could never do?

O Love, my king! if all my wit and power   820
Have done you all the service that they can,
O be you present in this present hour
And help your servant and your true liegeman!
End that persuasion which I erst began!
     For who in praise of dancing can persuade
     With such sweet force as Love, which dancing made?

Love heard his prayer, and swifter than the wind,
Like to a page in habit, face, and speech,
He came, and stood Antinous behind,
And many secrets of his thoughts did teach.   830
At last a crystal mirror he did reach
     Unto his hands, that he with one rash view
     All forms therein by Love's revealing knew.

And humbly honoring, gave it to the queen
With this fair speech: See, fairest queen, quoth he,
The fairest sight that ever shall be seen,
And th' only wonder of posterity!
The richest work in nature's treasury!
     Which she disdains to show on this world's stage,
     And thinks it far too good for our rude age.   840

But in another world, divided far,
In the great fortunate triangled isle,
Thrice twelve degrees removed from the North Star,
She will this glorious workmanship compile,
Which she hath been conceiving all this while
     Since the world's birth; and will bring forth at last,
     When six and twenty hundred years are past.

Penelope the queen, when she had viewed
The strange eye-dazzling admirable sight,
Fain would have praised the state and pulchritude;   850
But she was stroken dumb with wonder quite,
Yet her sweet mind retained her thinking might.
     Her ravished mind in heav'nly thoughts did dwell;
     But what she thought no mortal tongue can tell.

You, lady Muse, whom Jove the counsellor
Begot of Memory, Wisdom's treasuress,
To your divining tongue is given a power
Of uttering secrets, large and limitless;
You can Penelope's strange thoughts express,
     Which she conceived, and then would fain have told,   860
     When she the wondrous crystal did behold.

Her wingéd thoughts bore up her mind so high
As that she weened she saw the glorious throne
Where the bright moon doth sit in majesty;
A thousand sparkling stars about her shone,
But she herself did sparkle more alone
    Than all those thousand beauties would have done
    If they had been confounded all in one.

And yet she thought those stars moved in such measure
To do their sovereign honor and delight,   870
As soothed her mind with sweet enchanting pleasure,
Although the various change amazed her sight,
And her weak judgment did entangle quite;
    Beside, their moving made them shine more clear,
    As diamonds moved more sparkling do appear.

This was the picture of her wondrous thought!
But who can wonder that her thought was so,
Sith Vulcan, king of fire, that mirror wrought,
Which things to come, present, and past doth know,
And there did represent in lively show   880
    Our glorious English court's divine imáge,
    As it should be in this our golden age?

Away, Terpsichore, light Muse, away!
And come, Urania, prophetess divine!
Come, Muse of heav'n, my burning thirst allay!
Even now for want of sacred drink I tine;
In heav'nly moisture dip this pen of mine,
    And let my mouth with nectar overflow,
    For I must more than mortal glory show!

Oh, that I had Homer's abundant vein,   890
I would hereof another *Ilias* make!
Or else the man of Mantua's charméd brain,
In whose large throat great Jove the thunder spake!
Oh, that I could old Geoffrey's muse awake,
    Or borrow Colin's fair heroic style,
    Or smooth my rhymes with Delia's servant's file!

Oh, could I, sweet companion, sing like you,
Which of a shadow, under a shadow sing!
Or like fair Salve's sad lover true!
Or like the bay, the marigold's darling,   900
Whose sudden verse Love covers with his wing!
    Oh, that your brains were mingled all with mine,
    T' enlarge my wit for this great work divine!

Yet Astrophel might one for all suffice,
Whose supple muse chameleon-like doth change
Into all forms of excellent device;
So might the swallow, whose swift muse doth range
Through rare Idæas and inventions strange,
    And ever doth enjoy her joyful spring,
    And sweeter than the nightingale doth sing.

Oh, that I might that singing swallow hear,
To whom I owe my service and my love!
His sugared tunes would so enchant mine ear,
And in my mind such sacred fury move,
As I should knock at heav'n's great gate above
    With my proud rhymes; while of this heav'nly state
    I do aspire the shadow to relate.

FROM *Hymns of Astræa*, 1599

Of Astræa

E arly before the day doth spring
L et us awake, my muse, and sing,
I t is no time to slumber;
S o many joys this time doth bring
A s time will fail to number.

B ut whereto shall we bend our lays?
E ven up to heaven, again to raise
T he maid which thence descended,
H ath brought again the golden days
A nd all the world amended.

R udeness itself she doth refine,
E ven like an alchemist divine,
G ross times of iron turning
I nto the purest form of gold,
N ot to corrupt till heaven wax old,
A nd be refined with burning.

To the spring

E arth now is green and heaven is blue,
L ively spring which makes all new,
I olly spring, doth enter;
S weet young sun-beams do subdue
A ngry, aged winter.

B lasts are mild and seas are calm,
E very meadow flows with balm,
T he earth wears all her riches;
H armonious birds sing such a psalm
A s ear and heart bewitches.   10

R eserve, sweet spring, this nymph of ours
E ternal garlands of thy flowers,
G reen garlands never wasting;
I n her shall last our state's fair spring
N ow and forever flourishing
A s long as heaven is lasting.

To the rose

E ye of the garden, queen of flowers,
L ove's cup wherein he nectar pours,
I ngendered first of nectar;
S weet nurse-child of the spring's young hours,
A nd beauty's fair chárácter.

B lest jewel that the earth doth wear
E ven when the brave young sun draws near,
T o her hot love pretending,
H imself likewise like form doth bear
A t rising and descending.   10

R ose of the queen of love beloved,—
E ngland's great kings, divinely moved,
G ave roses in their banner;
I t showed that beauty's rose indeed
N ow in this age should them succeed,
A nd reign in more sweet manner.

FROM *Nosce Teipsum*, 1599
Of human knowledge

Why did my parents send me to the schools
  That I with knowledge might enrich my mind?
Since the desire to know first made men fools,
  And did corrupt the root of all mankind.

For when God's hand had written in the hearts
  Of the first parents all the rules of good,
So that their skill infused did pass all arts
  That ever were, before or since the flood,

And when their reason's eye was sharp and clear,
   And, as an eagle can behold the sun,
   Could have approached th' eternal light as near
   As the intellectual angels could have done,
                                     10

Even then to them the spirit of lies suggests
   That they were blind, because they saw not ill,
   And breathes into their incorrupted breasts
   A curious wish, which did corrupt their will.

For that same ill they straight desired to know;
   Which ill, being nought but a defect of good,
   And all God's works the devil could not show
   While man their lord in his perfection stood.
                                     20

So that themselves were first to do the ill,
   Ere they thereof the knowledge could attain;
   Like him that knew not poison's power to kill,
   Until, by tasting it, himself was slain.

Even so by tasting of that fruit forbid,
   Where they sought knowledge, they did error find;
   Ill they desired to know, and ill they did,
   And to give passion eyes, made reason blind.

For then their minds did first in passion see
   Those wretched shapes of misery and woe,
   Of nakedness, of shame, of poverty,
   Which then their own experience made them know.
                                     30

But then grew reason dark, that she no more
   Could the fair forms of good and truth discern;
   Bats they became, that eagles were before,
   And this they got by their desire to learn.

But we, their wretched offspring, what do we?
   Do not we still taste of the fruit forbid,
   Whiles with fond fruitless curiosity
   In books profane we seek for knowledge hid?
                                     40

What is this knowledge but the sky-stolen fire
   For which the thief still chained in ice doth sit,
   And which the poor rude satyr did admire,
   And needs would kiss, but burnt his lips with it.

What is it but the cloud of empty rain,
 Which when Jove's guest embraced, he monsters got?
 Or the false pails which oft being filled with pain,
 Received the water, but retained it not?

Shortly, what is it but the fiery coach
 Which the youth sought, and sought his death withal?   50
 Or the boy's wings, which when he did approach
 The sun's hot beams, did melt and let him fall?

And yet, alas, when all our lamps are burned,
 Our bodies wasted, and our spirits spent,
 When we have all the learned volumes turned,
 Which yield men's wits both help and ornament,

What can we know, or what can we discern,
 When error chokes the windows of the mind,
 The diverse forms of things, how can we learn,
 That have been ever from our birthday blind?   60

When reason's lamp, which like the sun in sky,
 Throughout man's little world her beams did spread,
 Is now become a sparkle which doth lie
 Under the ashes, half extinct and dead;

How can we hope that through the eye and ear
 This dying sparkle, in this cloudy place,
 Can recollect these beams of knowledge clear,
 Which were infused in the first minds by grace?

So might the heir whose father hath in play
 Wasted a thousand pound of ancient rent,   70
 By painful earning of a groat a day
 Hope to restore the patrimony spent.

The wits that dived most deep and soared most high,
 Seeking man's powers, have found his weakness such;
 Skill comes so slow and life so fast doth fly,
 We learn so little and forget so much.

For this the wisest of all mortal men
 Said, He knew nought but that he nought did know;
 And the great mocking master mocked not then,
 When he said, Truth was buried deep below.   80

For how may we to others' things attain,
  When none of us his own soul understands?
For which the devil mocks our curious brain,
  When, Know thyself, his oracle commands.

For why should we the busy soul believe,
  When boldly she concludes of that and this;
When of herself she can no judgment give,
  Nor how, nor whence, nor where, nor what she is?

All things without, which round about we see,
  We seek to know, and how therewith to do;   90
But that whereby we reason, live, and be,
  Within ourselves we strangers are thereto.

We seek to know the moving of each sphere,
  And the strange cause of th' ebbs and floods of Nile;
But of that clock within our breasts we bear,
  The subtle motions we forget the while.

We that acquaint ourselves with every zone,
  And pass both tropics and behold the poles,
When we come home, are to ourselves unknown,
  And unacquainted still with our own souls.   100

We study speech, but others we persuade;
  We leech-craft learn, but others cure with it;
We interpret laws, which other men have made,
  But read not those which in our hearts are writ.

Is it because the mind is like the eye,
  Through which it gathers knowledge by degrees—
Whose rays reflect not, but spread outwardly—
  Not seeing itself when other things it sees?

No, doubtless, for the mind can backward cast
  Upon herself her understanding light;   110
But she is so corrupt and so defaced,
  As her own image doth herself affright.

As in the fable of the lady fair,
  Which for her lust was turned into a cow:
When thirsty to a stream she did repair,
  And saw herself transformed, she wist not how,

At first she startles, then she stands amazed,
    At last with terror she from thence doth fly,
    And loathes the wat'ry glass wherein she gazed,
    And shuns it still, though she for thirst do die.   120

Even so man's soul, which did God's image bear,
    And was at first fair, good, and spotless pure,
    Since with her sins her beauties blotted were,
    Doth of all sights her own sight least endure.

For even at first reflection she espies
    Such strange chimeras and such monsters there,
    Such toys, such antics, and such vanities,
    As she retires and shrinks for shame and fear.

And as the man loves least at home to be,
    That hath a sluttish house haunted with sprites,   130
    So she, impatient her own faults to see,
    Turns from herself and in strange things delights.

For this, few know themselves; for merchants broke
    View their estate with discontent and pain,
    And seas are troubled when they do revoke
    Their flowing waves into themselves again.

And while the face of outward things we find
    Pleasing and fair, agreeable and sweet,
    These things transport and carry out the mind,
    That with herself herself can never meet.   140

Yet if affliction once her wars begin,
    And threat the feebler sense with sword and fire,
    The mind contracts herself and shrinketh in,
    And to herself she gladly doth retire,

As spiders touched seek their webs' inmost part,
    As bees in storms unto their hives return,
    As blood in danger gathers to the heart,
    As men seek towns when foes the country burn.

If aught can teach us aught, affliction's looks,
    Making us look into ourselves so near,   150
    Teach us to know ourselves beyond all books,
    Or all the learned schools that ever were.

This mistress lately plucked me by the ear,
   And many a golden lesson hath me taught;
   Hath made my senses quick and reason clear,
   Reformed my will and rectified my thought.

So do the winds and thunders cleanse the air;
   So working lees settle and purge the wine;
   So lopped and prunëd trees do flourish fair;
   So doth the fire the drossy gold refine.   160

Neither Minerva nor the learned muse,
   Nor rules of art, nor precepts of the wise,
   Could in my brain those beams of skill infuse,
   As but the glance of this dame's angry eyes.

She within lists my ranging mind hath brought,
   That now beyond myself I list not go;
   Myself am center of my circling thought,
   Only myself I study, learn, and know.

I know my body's of so frail a kind
   As force without, fevers within, can kill;   170
   I know the heavenly nature of my mind,
   But 'tis corrupted both in wit and will;

I know my soul hath power to know all things,
   Yet is she blind and ignorant in all;
   I know I am one of nature's little kings,
   Yet to the least and vilest things am thrall.

I know my life's a pain and but a span,
   I know my sense is mocked with everything;
   And to conclude, I know myself a man,
   Which is a proud and yet a wretched thing.   180

That the soul is immortal, and cannot die

Nor hath He given these blessings for a day,
   Nor made them on the body's life depend;
   The soul, though made in time, survives for aye,
   And though it hath beginning, sees no end.

Her only end is never-ending bliss,
   Which is, th' eternal face of God to see,
   Who last of ends and first of causes is;
   And to do this she must eternal be.

How senseless, then, and dead a soul hath he   10
  Which thinks his soul doth with his body die!
Or thinks not so, but so would have it be,
  That he might sin with more security.

For though these light and vicious persons say,
  Our soul is but a smoke or airy blast,
Which during life doth in our nostrils play,
  And when we die doth turn to wind at last;

Although they say, Come, let us eat and drink,
  Our life is but a spark which quickly dies;
Though thus they say, they know not what to think,   20
  But in their minds ten thousand doubts arise.

Therefore no heretics desire to spread
  Their light opinions like these Epicures;
For so the staggering thoughts are comforted,
  And other men's assent their doubt assures.

Yet though these men against their conscience strive,
  There are some sparkles in their flinty breasts
Which cannot be extinct, but still revive,
  That though they would, they cannot quite be beasts.

But whoso makes a mirror of his mind
  And doth with patience view himself therein,   30
His soul's eternity shall clearly find,
  Though th' other beauties be defaced with sin.

An acclamation

O ignorant poor man, what dost thou bear
  Locked up within the casket of thy breast?
What jewels and what riches hast thou there?
  What heavenly treasure in so weak a chest?

Look in thy soul and thou shalt beauties find
  Like those which drowned Narcissus in the flood;
Honor and pleasure both are in thy mind,
  And all that in the world is counted good.

Think of her worth, and think that God did mean   10
  This worthy mind should worthy things embrace;
Blot not her beauties with thy thoughts unclean,
  Nor her dishonor with thy passions base.

Kill not her quick'ning power with surfeitings,
   Mar not her sense with sensuality,
Cast not her serious wit on idle things,
   Make not her free-will slave to vanity.

And when thou think'st of her eternity,
   Think not that death against her nature is;
Think it a birth, and when thou goest to die,
   Sing like a swan, as if thou went'st to bliss.   20

And if thou, like a child, didst fear before,
   Being in the dark where thou didst nothing see,
Now I have brought the torchlight, fear no more,
   Now when thou diest, thou canst not hoodwinked be.

And thou, my soul, which turn'st thy curious eye
   To view the beams of thine own form divine,
Know that thou canst know nothing perfectly
   While thou art clouded with this flesh of mine.

Take heed of overweening, and compare
   Thy peacock's feet with thy gay peacock's train;   30
Study the best and highest things that are,
   But of thyself an humble thought retain.

Cast down thyself, and only strive to raise
   The glory of thy maker's sacred name;
Use all thy powers that blessed power to praise,
   Which gives thee power to be, and use the same.

JOSEPH HALL, BISHOP OF NORWICH

The Introduction and Notes are at page 968

From *Virgidemiarum*, 1597

Satire I

Nor lady's wanton love, nor wand'ring knight
Legend I out in rhymes all richly dight;
Nor fright the reader with the pagan vaunt
Of mighty Mahound and great Termagaunt.
Nor list I sonnet of my mistress' face,
To paint some blowess with a borrowed grace;
Nor can I bide to pen some hungry scene

For thick-skin ears, and undiscerning eyne.
Nor ever could my scornful muse abide
With tragic shoes her ankles for to hide.   10
Nor can I crouch, and writhe my fawning tail
To some great patron, for my best avail.
Such hunger-starven trencher-poetry,
Or let it never live, or timely die;
Nor under every bank and every tree,
Speak rhymes unto my oaten minstrelsy;
Nor carol out so pleasing lively lays
As mought the Graces move my mirth to praise.
Trumpet, and reeds, and socks, and buskins fine,
I them bequeath whose statues wand'ring twine   20
Of ivy, mixed with bays, circlen around,
Their living temples likewise laurel-bound.
Rather had I, albe in careless rhymes,
Check the mis-ordered world and lawless times;
Nor need I crave the muse's midwifery
To bring to light so worthless poetry.
Or, if we list, what baser muse can bide
To sit and sing by Granta's naked side?
They haunt the tided Thames and salt Medway
E'er since the fame of their late bridal day.   30
Nought have we here but willow-shaded shore
To tell our Grant his banks are left forlore.

Satire VI

Another scorns the homespun thread of rhymes
Matched with the lofty feet of elder times.
Give me the numbered verse that Virgil sung
And Virgil self shall speak the English tongue:
Manhood and garboils shall he chant, with changëd feet,
And headstrong dactyls making music meet;
The nimble dactyls striving to outgo
The drawling spondees pacing it below;
The ling'ring spondees, laboring to delay
The breathless dactyls with a sudden stay.   10
Whoever saw a colt, wanton and wild,
Yoked with a slow-foot ox on fallow field,
Can right areed how handsomely besets
Dull spondees with the English dactylets.
If Jove speak English in a thund'ring cloud,
Thwick thwack, and riff raff, roars he out aloud.
Fie on the forgëd mint that did create
New coin of words never articulate!

Satire VI (Book II)

A gentle squire would gladly entertain
Into his house some trencher-chaplain,
Some willing man that might instruct his sons
And that would stand to good conditïons.
First, that he lie upon the truckle-bed
Whiles his young master lieth o'er his head.
Second, that he do on no default
Ever presume to sit above the salt.
Third, that he never change his trencher twice.
Fourth, that he use all common courtesies,   10
Sit bare at meals, and one half rise and wait.
Last, that he never his young master beat
But he must ask his mother to define
How many jerks she would his breech should line.
All these observed, he could contented be
To give five marks and winter livery.

JOHN MARSTON

The Introduction and Notes are at page 969

From *The Scourge of Villainy*, 1598

To Detraction I present my poesy

Foul canker of fair virtuous action,
Vile blaster of the freshest blooms on earth,
Envy's abhorrëd child, Detraction,
I here expose to thy all-tainting breath
   The issue of my brain; snarl, rail, bark, bite,
   Know that my spirit scorns Detraction's spite.

Know that the genius which attendeth on
And guides my powers intellectual,
Holds in all vile repute Detractïon;
My soul, an essence metaphysical   10
   That in the basest sort scorns critics' rage,
   Because he knows his sacred parentage.

My spirit is not huffed up with fat fume
Of slimy ale, nor Bacchus' heating grape.
My mind disdains the dungy muddy scum

Of abject thoughts, and envy's raging hate.
   True judgment slight regards opinïon;
   A sprightly wit disdains Detractïon.

A partial praise shall never elevate
My settled censure of mine own esteem.   20
A cankered verdict of malignant hate
Shall ne'er provoke me worse myself to deem.
   Spite of despite and rancor's villainy,
   I am myself, so is my poesy.

Satire X

Humors

Sleep, grim reproof, my jocund muse doth sing
In other keys, to nimbler fingering.
Dull-sprited Melancholy, leave my brain!
To hell, Cimmerian night! in lively vein
I strive to paint; then hence, all dark intent
And sullen frowns! Come, sporting merriment,
Cheek-dimpling laughter, crown my very soul
With jouissance, whilst mirthful jests control
The gouty humors of these pride-swollen days,
Which I do long until my pen displays.   10
Oh, I am great with mirth; some midwifery,
Or I shall break my sides at vanity!
   Room for a capering mouth, whose lips ne'er stir
But in discoursing of the graceful slur;
Who ever heard spruce skipping Curio
E'er prate of aught but of the whirl on toe,
The turn above ground, Robrus' sprawling kicks,
Fabius' caper, Harry's tossing tricks?
Did ever any ear e'er hear him speak
Unless his tongue of cross-points did entreat?   20
His teeth do caper whilst he eats his meat,
His heels do caper whilst he takes his seat,
His very soul, his intellectual,
Is nothing but a mincing capreal.
He dreams of toe-turns, each gallant he doth meet
He fronts him with a traverse in the street;
Praise but *Orchestra* and the skipping art,
You shall command him; faith, you have his heart
Even cap'ring in your fist. A hall, a hall,
Room for the spheres, the orbs celestial   30
Will dance Kemp's jig. They'll revel with neat jumps;
A worthy poet hath put on their pumps! . . .

Luscus, what's played to-day? Faith, now I know
I set thy lips abroach, from whence doth flow
Nought but pure Juliet and Romeo.
Say, who acts best, Drusus or Roscio?
Now I have him, that ne'er of aught did speak
But when of plays or players he did treat.
H' hath made a commonplace book out of plays
And speaks in print; at least, whate'er he says   40
Is warranted by Curtain plaudities;
If e'er you heard him courting Lesbia's eyes,
Say, courteous sir, speaks he not movingly
From out some new pathetic tragedy?
He writes, he rails, he jests, he courts, what not,
And all from out his huge, long-scrapèd stock
Of well-penned plays. . . .
    But room for Tuscus, that jest-monging youth,
Who ne'er did ope his apish gerning mouth
But to retail and broke another's wit.   50
Discourse of what you will, he straight can fit
Your present talk with, Sir, I'll tell a jest,
(Of some sweet lady or grand lord, at least)
Then on he goes; and ne'er his tongue shall lie
Till his engrossèd jests are all drawn dry;
But then as dumb as Maurus, when at play
H' hath lost his crowns and pawned his trim array.
He doth nought but retail jests; break but one,
Out flies his table-book, let him alone,
He'll have 't, i' faith. Lad, hast an epigram,   60
Wilt have it put into the chaps of fame?
Give Tuscus copies; sooth, as his own wit,
His proper issue he will father it.
Oh, that this echo, that doth speak, spit, write,
Nought but the excrements of others' sprite,
This ill-stuffed trunk of jests, whose very soul
Is but a heap of gibes, should once enroll
His name 'mong creatures termèd rational,
Whose chief repute, whose sense, whose soul and all
Are fed with offal scraps that sometimes fall   70
From liberal wits, in their large festival.

To everlasting Oblivion

Thou mighty gulf, insatiate cormorant,
Deride me not, though I seem petulant
To fall into thy chops. Let others pray
Forever their fair poems flourish may;
But as for me, hungry Oblivion,

Devour me quick, accept my orison,
　My earnest prayers, which do impórtune thee
With gloomy shade of thy still empery,
　To veil both me and my rude poesy.

Far worthier lines in silence of thy state   10
Do sleep securely, free from love or hate,
From which this, living, ne'er can be exempt,
But whilst it breathes will hate and fury tempt.
Then close his eyes with thy all-dimming hand,
Which not right glorious actions can withstand.
Peace, hateful tongues, I now in silence pace;
Unless some hound do wake me from my place,
　I with this sharp, yet well-meant poesy,
　Will sleep secure, right free from injury
Of cankered hate or rankest villainy.   20

FROM *The Dutch Courtezan*, 1605

[*O love, how strangely sweet*]

O love, how strangely sweet
　Are thy weak passions,
That love and joy should meet
　In self-same fashions.
Oh, who can tell
　The cause why this should move?
But only this:
　No reason ask of love.

GEORGE CHAPMAN

The Introduction and Notes are at page 970

FROM *The Shadow of Night*, 1594

Hymnus in Noctem

All you possessed with indepressed spírits,
Indued with nimble and aspiring wits,
Come consecrate with me to sacred night
Your whole endeavors, and detest the light.
Sweet peace's richest crown is made of stars,
Most certain guides of honored marinars.
No pen can anything eternal write

That is not steeped in humor of the night.
  Hence, beasts and birds, to caves and bushes, then,
And welcome night, ye noblest heirs of men.   10
Hence, Phœbus, to thy glassy strumpet's bed
And nevermore let Themis' daughters spread
Thy golden harness on thy rosy horse,
But in close thickets run thy oblique course.
  See, now ascends the glorious bride of brides,
Nuptials and triumphs glitt'ring by her sides;
Juno and Hymen do her train adorn,
Ten thousand torches round about them borne.
Dumb Silence, mounted on the Cyprian star,
With becks rebukes the winds before his car,   20
Where she, advanced, beats down with cloudy mace
The feeble light to black Saturnius' paláce.
Behind her, with a brace of silver hinds,
In ivory chariot swifter than the winds,
Is great Hyperion's horned daughter drawn,
Enchantress-like, decked in disparent lawn,
Circled with charms and incantations
That ride huge spirits and outrageous passions.
Music and mood she loves, but love she hates
(As curious ladies do their public cates).   30
This train, with meteors, comets, lightenings,
The dreadful presence of our empress sings:
Which grant for ever, O eternal night,
Till virtue flourish in the light of light!

FROM *Ovid's Banquet of Sense*, 1595

A coronet for his mistress Philosophy

Muses that sing love's sensual empery,
    And lovers kindling your enragëd fires
At Cupid's bonfires burning in the eye,
    Blown with the empty breath of vain desires;
You that prefer the painted cabinet
    Before the wealthy jewels it doth store ye,
That all your joys in dying figures set,
    And stain the living substance of your glory:
Abjure those joys, abhor their memory,
    And let my love the honored subject be   10
Of love, and honor's complete history;
    Your eyes were never yet let in to see
The majesty and riches of the mind,
But dwell in darkness; for your god is blind.

From *The Mask of the Middle Temple and Lincoln's Inn,* 1613

[*Descend, fair sun*]

One alone.

Descend, fair sun, and sweetly rest
   In Tethys' crystal arms thy toil.
Fall burning on her marble breast
   And make with love her billows boil.

Another alone.

Blow, blow, sweet winds. Oh, blow away
   All vapors from the finëd air,
That to this golden head no ray
   May languish with the least impair.

Cho.

Dance, Tethys, and thy love's red beams
   Embrace with joy; he now descends,   10
Burns, burns with love to drink thy streams,
   And on him endless youth attends.

[*Now, sleep, bind fast*]

Now, sleep, bind fast the flood of air,
   Strike all things dumb and deaf,
And to disturb our nuptial pair
   Let stir no aspen leaf.
Send flocks of golden dreams
   That all true joys presage,
Bring, in thy oily streams,
   The milk and honey age.
Now close the world-round sphere of bliss
And fill it with a heavenly kiss.   10

From *The Whole Works of Homer,* [*c.* 1616]

Iliad

Book XVIII

.   .   .   .

This said, he left her there, and forth did to his bellows go,
Apposed them to the fire again, commanding them to blow.
Through twenty holes made to his hearth at once blew twenty pair
That fired his coals, sometimes with soft, sometimes with vehement
   air,

As he willed and his work required. Amids the flame he cast
Tin, silver, precious gold, and brass; and in the stock he placed
A mighty anvil; his right hand a weighty hammer held,
His left his tongs. And first he forged a strong and spacious shield,
Adorned with twenty several hues; about whose verge he beat
A ring, three-fold and radiant, and on the back he set   10
A silver handle. Five-fold were the equal lines he drew
About the whole circumference, in which his hand did shew
(Directed with a knowing mind) a rare variety:
For in it he presented earth; in it the sea and sky;
In it the never-wearied sun, the moon exactly round,
And all those stars with which the brows of ample heaven are crowned,
Orion, all the Pleiades, and those sev'n Atlas got,
The close-beamed Hyades, the Bear, surnamed the Chariot,
That turns about heav'n's axle-tree, holds ope a constant eye
Upon Orion; and, of all the cressets in the sky,   20
His golden forehead never bows to th' ocean empery.
   Two cities in the spacious shield he built, with 'goodly state
Of divers-languaged men. The one did nuptials celebrate,
Observing at them solemn feasts, the brides from forth their bowers
With torches ushered through the streets, a world of paramours
Excited by them; youths and maids in lovely circles danced,
To whom the merry pipe and harp the spritely sounds advanced,
The matrons standing in the doors admiring. Otherwhere
A solemn court of law was kept, where throngs of people were.

.   .   .   .

   The other city other wars employed as busily: 30
Two armies glittering in arms of one confederacy
Besieged it; and a parley had with those within the town.
Two ways they stood resolved,—to see the city overthrown,
Or that the citizens should heap in two parts all their wealth
And give them half. They neither liked, but armed themselves by
     stealth,
Left all their old men, wives, and boys behind to man their walls,
And stole out to their enemy's town. The queen of martïals
And Mars himself conducted them,—both which being forged of gold
Must needs have golden furniture, and men might so behold
They were presented deities; the people Vulcan forged   40
Of meaner metal. When they came where that was to be urged
For which they went, within a vale close to a flood whose stream
Used to give all their cattle drink, they were enambushed them;
And sent two scouts out to descry when th' enemy's herds and sheep
Were setting out. They straight came forth, with two that used to
     keep
Their passage always, both which piped and went on merrily,

Nor dreamed of ambuscadoes there. The ambush then let fly,
Slew all their white-fleeced sheep, and neat, and by them laid their
 guard.
When those in siege before the town so strange an uproar heard
Behind, amongst their flocks and herds—being then in council set— 50
They then start up, took horse, and soon their subtle enemy met,
Fought with them on the river's shore, where both gave mutual blows
With well-piled darts. Amongst them all perverse Contention rose,
Amongst them Tumult was enraged, amongst them ruinous Fate
Had her red finger; some they took in an unhurt estate,
Some hurt, yet living; some quite slain, and those they tugged to them
By both the feet, stripped off and took their weeds, with all the stream
Of blood upon them that their steels had manfully let out;
They fared as men alive indeed drew dead indeed about.

To these the fiery artisan did add a new-eared field, 60
Larged and thrice plowed, the soil being soft and of a wealthy yield;
And many men at plow he made, that drave earth here and there,
And turned up stitches orderly,—at whose end when they were
A fellow ever gave their hands full cups of luscious wine,
Which emptied, for another stitch the earth they undermine,
And long till th' utmost bound be reached of all the ample close.
The soil turned up behind the plow all black like earth arose,
Though forged of nothing else but gold; and lay in show as light
As if it had been plowed indeed, miraculous to sight.

There grew by this a field of corn, high, ripe, where reapers
 wrought, 70
And let thick handfuls fall to earth, for which some other brought
Bands and made sheaves. Three binders stood and took the handfuls
 reaped
From boys that gathered quickly up, and by them armfuls heaped.
Amongst these, at a furrow's end, the king stood pleased at heart,
Said no word, but his scepter showed. And from him much apart
His harvest-bailiffs underneath an oak a feast prepared,
And having killed a mighty ox, stood there to see him shared,
Which women for their harvest-folks (then come to sup) had dressed,
And many white wheat-cakes bestowed, to make it up a feast.

He set near this a vine of gold that cracked beneath the weight 80
Of bunches black with being ripe, to keep which at the height
A silver rail ran all along, and round about it flowed
An azure moat, and to this guard a quick-set was bestowed,
Of tin,—one only path to all, by which the pressmen came
In time of vintage. Youths, and maids that bore not yet the flame
Of manly Hymen, baskets bore of grapes and mellow fruit.
A lad that sweetly touched a harp to which his voice did suit
Centered the circles of that youth, all whose skill could not do
The wantons' pleasure to their minds, that danced, sung, whistled too.

A herd of oxen then he carved, with high raised heads, forged all 90
Of gold and tin for color mixed, and bellowing from their stall
Rushed to their pastures at a flood, that echoed all their throats,
Exceeding swift and full of reeds; and all in yellow coats
Four herdsmen followed; after whom nine mastiffs went. In head
Of all the herd, upon a bull that deadly bellowëd
Two horrid lions ramped and seized and tugged off, bellowing still.
Both men and dogs came; yet they tore the hide, and lapped their fill
Of black blood, and the entrails ate. In vain the men assayed
To set their dogs on; none durst pinch, but cur-like stood and bayed
In both the faces of their kings, and all their onsets fled.   100

Then in a passing pleasant vale the famous artsman fed
Upon a goodly pasture-ground rich flocks of white-fleeced sheep,
Built stables, cottages, and cotes, that did the shepherds keep
From wind and weather. Next to these he cut a dancing-place
All full of turnings, that was like the admirable maze
For fair-haired Ariadne made by cunning Dædalus;
And in it youths and virgins danced, all young and beauteous,
And gluëd in another's palms. Weeds that the wind did toss
The virgins wore; the youths, woven coats that cast a faint dim gloss
Like that of oil. Fresh garlands, too, the virgins' temples crowned.   110
The youths gilt swords wore at their thighs, with silver baldrics bound.
Sometimes all wound close in a ring, to which as fast they spun
As any wheel a turner makes, being tried how it will run,
While he is set; and out again as full of speed they wound,
Not one left fast, or breaking hands. A multitude stood round,
Delighted with their nimble sport; to end which, two begun
Mids all a song, and turning sung the sport's conclusïon.
All this he circled in the shield, with pouring round about
In all his rage the ocëan, that it might never out.

.   .   .   .

FROM *Homer's Odysseys*, [*c.* 1614]

Odyssey

Book XII

.   .   .   .

In mean time flew our ships, and straight we fetched
The sirens' isle; a spleenless wind so stretched
Her wings to waft us, and so urged our keel.
But having reached this isle, we could not feel
The least gasp of it; it was stricken dead,
And all the sea in prostrate slumber spread,—
The sirens' devil charmed all. Up then flew
My friends to work, struck sail, together drew

And under hatches stowed them, sat, and plied
Their polished oars; and did in curls divide
The white-head waters. My part then came on:
A mighty waxen cake I set upon,
Chopped it in fragments with my sword, and wrought
With strong hand every piece till all were soft;
The great power of the sun, in such a beam
As then flew burning from his diadem,
To liquefaction helped us. Orderly
I stopped their ears; and they as fair did ply
My feet and hands with cords, and to the mast
With other halsers made me soundly fast.

   Then took they seat, and forth our passage strook;
The foamy sea beneath their labor shook.

   Rowed on, in reach of an erected voice,
The sirens soon took note, without our noise,
Tuned those sweet accents that made charms so strong,
And these learn'd numbers made the sirens' song:

   Come here, thou, worthy of a world of praise,
That dost so high the Grecian glory raise!
Ulysses, stay thy ship! and that song hear
That none passed ever but it bent his ear,
But left him ravished, and instructed more
By us than any ever heard before.
For we know all things whatsoever were
In wide Troy labored; whatsoever there
The Grecians and the Trojans both sustained
By those high issues that the gods ordained.
And whatsoever all the earth can show
T' inform a knowledge of desert, we know.

   This they gave accent in the sweetest strain
That ever opened an enamoured vein.

. . . . . .

EDWARD FAIRFAX

The Introduction and Notes are at page 971

FROM *Godfrey of Bulloigne*, 1600

Book XVI

. . . . .

When they had passëd all those troubled ways,
The garden sweet spread forth her green to show,
The moving crystal from the fountains plays,

Fair trees, high plants, strange herbs and flowerets new,
Sunshiny hills, dales hid from Phœbus' rays,
Groves, arbors, mossy caves, at once they view,
    And that which beauty most, most wonder brought,
    Nowhere appeared the art which all this wrought.

So with the rude the polished mingled was
That natural seemed all and every part,
Nature would craft in counterfeiting pass,
And imitate her imitator art;
Mild was the air, the skies were clear as glass,
The trees no whirlwind felt, nor tempest smart;
    But ere their fruit drop off, the blossom comes,
    This springs, that falls, that ripeneth and this blooms.

The leaves upon the self-same bough did hide
Beside the young the old and ripened fig,
Here fruit was green, there ripe with vermeil side,
The apples new and old grew on one twig,
The fruitful vine her arms spread high and wide
That bended underneath their clusters big,
    The grapes were tender here, hard, young, and sour,
    There purple ripe, and nectar sweet forth pour.

The joyous birds, hid under greenwood shade,
Sung merry notes on every branch and bough,
The wind that in the leaves and waters played
With murmur sweet, now sung, and whistled now;
Ceasëd the birds, the wind loud answer made,
And while they sung, it rumbled soft and low;
    Thus were it hap or cunning, chance or art,
    The wind in this strange music bore his part.

With parti-colored plumes and purple bill,
A wondrous bird among the rest there flew,
That in plain speech sung love-lays loud and shrill,
Her leden was like human language true;
So much she talked, and with such wit and skill,
That strange it seemëd how much good she knew,
    Her feathered fellows all stood hush to hear,
    Dumb was the wind, the waters silent were.

The gently budding rose, quoth she, behold,
That first scant peeping forth with virgin beams,
Half ope, half shut, her beauties doth upfold
In their dear leaves, and less seen, fairer seems,

And after spreads them forth more broad and bold,
Then languisheth and dies in last extremes;
    Nor seems the same that deckëd bed and bower
    Of many a lady late, and paramour;

So, in the passing of a day, doth pass
The bud and blossom of the life of man,   50
Nor e'er doth flourish more, but like the grass
Cut down, becometh withered, pale and wan.
Oh, gather then the rose while time thou hast,
Short is the day, done when it scant began,
    Gather the rose of love, while yet thou mayest,
    Loving, be loved; embracing, be embraced.

He ceased, and as approving all he spoke,
The choir of birds their heavenly tunes renew,
The turtles sighed, and sighs with kisses broke,
The fowls to shades unseen by pairs withdrew;   60
It seemed the laurel chaste, and stubborn oak,
And all the gentle trees on earth that grew,
    It seemed the land, the sea, and heaven above,
    All breathed out fancy sweet, and sighed out love.

.   .   .   .

SONGS FROM PLAYS

The Introduction and Notes are at page 972

FROM JOHN BALE's *King John, Devonshire Ms.,* [*c.* 1538]

    Wassail, wassail, out of the milk-pail,
    Wassail, wassail, as white as my nail,
    Wassail, wassail, in snow, frost, and hail,
    Wassail, wassail, with partridge and rail,
    Wassail, wassail, that much doth avail,
    Wassail, wassail, that never will fail.

FROM R. WEVER's *Lusty Juventus,* [*c.* 1560]

In a herber green, asleep whereas I lay,
The birds sang sweet in the middës of the day;
I dreamëd fast of mirth and play,
    In youth is pleasure, in youth is pleasure.

Methought as I walked still to and fro,
And from her company I could not go;

But when I waked it was not so,
  In youth is pleasure, in youth is pleasure.

Therefore my heart is surely pight
Of her alone to have a sight,   10
Which is my joy and heart's delight,
  In youth is pleasure, in youth is pleasure.

FROM WILLIAM STEVENSON'S *Gammer Gurton's Needle*, 1575

Back and side go bare, go bare,
  Both foot and hand go cold;
But, belly, God send thee good ale
    enough,
  Whether it be new or old.

I cannot eat but little meat,
  My stomach is not good;
But sure I think that I can drink
  With him that wears a hood.
Though I go bare, take ye no care,
  I am nothing a-cold;   10
I stuff my skin so full within
  Of jolly good ale and old.

Back and side go bare, go bare,
  Both foot and hand go cold;
But, belly, God send thee good ale
    enough,
  Whether it be new or old.

I love no roast but a nutbrown
    toast,
  And a crab laid in the fire;
A little bread shall do me stead,
  Much bread I not desire.   20
No frost nor snow, no wind, I
    trow,
  Can hurt me if I would,

I am so wrapped, and throughly
    lapped
  Of jolly good ale and old.

Back and side go bare, &c.

And Tib my wife, that as her life
  Loveth well good ale to seek,
Full oft drinks she, till ye may see
  The tears run down her cheeks.
Then doth she troll to me the bowl,
  Even as a maltworm should,   31
And saith, Sweetheart, I took my
    part
  Of this jolly good ale and old.

Back and side go bare, &c.

Now let them drink, till they nod
    and wink,
  Even as good fellows should do;
They shall not miss to have the
    bliss
  Good ale doth bring men to;
And all poor souls that have
    scoured bowls
  Or have them lustily trolled,   40
God save the lives of them and
    their wives,
  Whether they be young or old.

Back and side go bare, &c.

FROM *Tom Tyler and His Wife*, 1661

The proverb reporteth, no man can deny,
  That wedding and hanging is destiny.

I am a poor tiler in simple array,
And get a poor living, but eightpence a day,

My wife as I get it, doth spend it away;
   And I cannot help it, she saith; wot ye why?
   For wedding and hanging is destiny.

I thought when I wed her, she had been a sheep,
At board to be friendly, to sleep when I sleep.
She loves so unkindly, she makes me to weep;   10
   But I dare say nothing, God wot, wot ye why?
   For wedding and hanging is destiny.

Besides this unkindness whereof my grief grows,
I think few tilers are matched with such shrows;
Before she leaves brawling, she falls to deal blows
   Which early and late doth cause me cry
   That wedding and hanging is destiny.

The more that I please her, the worse she doth like me,
The more I forbear her, the more she doth strike me,
The more that I get her, the more she doth glike me;   20
   Woe worth this ill fortune that maketh me cry
   That wedding and hanging is destiny.

If I had been hangèd when I had been married,
My torments had ended, though I had miscarried;
If I had been warnèd, then would I have tarried;
   But now all too lately I feel and cry
   That wedding and hanging is destiny.

FROM *Misogonus, Devonshire Ms.,* [1560–1577]

A song to the tune of Heart's Ease

Sing care away with sport and play,
   Pastime is all our pleasure;
If well we fare for nought we care,
   In mirth consist our treasure.

Let snudges lurk and drudges work,
   We do defy their slavery;
He is but a fool that goes to school,
   All we delight in bravery.

What doth avail far hence to sail
   And lead our life in toiling;   10
Or to what end should we here spend
   Our days in irksome moiling?

It is the best to live at rest,
   And take 't as God doth send it,
To haunt each wake and mirth to make,
   And with good fellows spend it.

Nothing is worse than a full purse
   To niggards and to pinchers;
They always spare and live in care,
   There's no man loves such flinchers.   20

The merry man with cup and can
   Lives longer than doth twenty;
The miser's wealth doth hurt his health,
   Examples we have plenty.

'Tis a beastly thing to lie mus-
ing
With pensiveness and sorrow,
For who can tell that he shall
well
Live here until the morrow?

We will therefore for evermore,
  While this our life is lasting,   30
Eat, drink, and sleep, and lemans
keep;
  It's popery to use fasting.

In cards and dice our comfort lies,
  In sporting and in dancing,
Our minds to please and live at
ease,
  And sometimes to use prancing.

With Bess and Nell we love to
dwell,
  In kissing and in haking;
But whoop ho holly, with trolly
lolly,
  To them we'll now be walking.   40

FROM JOHN PHILLIPS'S *Comedy of Patient and Meek Grissell*
[*c.* 1566]

Lulla by baby, lulla by baby,
Thy nurse will tend thee, as duly as may be.

Be still, my sweet sweeting, no longer do cry,
  Sing lulla by baby, lulla by baby.
Let dolors be fleeting, I fancy thee, I,
  To rock and to lull thee, I will not delay me.
Lulla by baby, &c.

What creature now living would hasten thy woe?
  Sing lulla by, lulla by, lulla by baby.
See for thy relieving, the time I bestow,   10
  To dance, and to prance thee, as prett'ly as may be.
Lulla by baby, &c.

The gods be thy shield and comfort in need,
  Sing lulla by, lulla by, lulla by baby;
They give thee good fortune and well for to speed,
  And this to desire, I will not delay me.

FROM JOHN PICKERING'S *New Interlude of Vice, containing the
History of Horestes*, 1567

Farewell, adieu, that courtly life,
To war we tend to go;
It is good sport to see the strife
Of soldiers in a row.
  How merrily they forward
  march

These enemies to slay,
With hey, trim, and trixie too,
Their banners they display.

Now shall we have the golden
cheats,

When others want the same;   10
And soldiers have full many
     feats
Their enemies to tame;
     With cocking here, and boom-
          ing there,
     They break their foe's array;
     And lusty lads amid the
          fields
     Their ensigns do display.

The drum and flute play lustily,
The trumpet blows amain,
And venturous knights coura-
     geously
Do march before their train   20
     With spears in rest, so lively
          dressed
     In armor bright and gay;
     With hey, trim, and trixie too,
     Their banners they display.

FROM *The Trial of Treasure*, 1567

Hey ho, care away, let the world pass,
For I am as lusty as ever I was,
In flowers I flourish as blossoms in May,
Hey ho, care away; hey ho, care away.

————

Am not I in blessed case,
Treasure and pleasure to possess?
I would not wish no better place,
If I may still have wealthiness,
And to enjoy in perfect peace
     My lady, lady.
My pleasant pleasure shall increase,
     My dear lady.

Helen may not comparëd be,
Nor Cressida that was so bright,   10
These cannot stain the shine of thee,
Nor yet Minerva of great might.
Thou passest Venus far away,
     Lady, lady;
Love thee I will both night and day,
     My dear lady.

My mouse, my nobs, my coney sweet,
My hope and joy, my whole delight,
Dame Nature may fall at thy feet,
And may yield to thee her crown of right.   20
I will thy body now embrace,
     Lady, lady,
And kiss thy sweet and pleasant face,
     My dear lady.

FROM *The Marriage of Wit and Science,* [*c.* 1570]

Idleness singeth

Come, come, lie down, and thou shalt see
None like to me to entertain
Thy bones and thee oppressed with pain.
Come, come and ease thee in my lap,
And if it please thee, take a nap;
A nap that shall delight thee so
That fancies all will thee forgo.
By musing still, what canst thou find
But wants of will and restless mind?
A mind that mars and mangles all,   10
And breedeth jars to work thy fall;
Come, gentle Wit, I thee require,
And thou shalt hit thy chief desire,
Thy chief desire, thy hopëd prey,
First ease thee here, and then away!

FROM *Common Conditions,* [*c.* 1576]

Lustily, lustily, lustily let us sail forth,
The wind trim doth serve us, it blows at the north.

All things we have ready, and nothing we want,
To furnish our ship that rideth hereby:
Victuals and weapons, they be nothing scant,
Like worthy mariners ourselves we will try.
    Lustily, lustily, &c.

Her flags be new trimmed set flaunting aloft,
Our ship for swift swimming, oh, she doth excel;
We fear no enemies, we have escaped them oft;   10
Of all ships that swimmeth, she beareth the bell.
    Lustily, lustily, &c.

And here is a master excelleth in skill,
And our master's mate, he is not to seek;
And here is a boatswain will do his good will,
And here is a shipboy, we never had his leek.
    Lustily, lustily, &c.

If fortune then fail not, and our next voyage prove,
We will return merrily, and make good cheer,
And hold all together as friends linked in love;   20
The cans shall be filled with wine, ale, and beer.
    Lustily, lustily, &c.

FROM *Fedele and Fortunio, or the Two Italian Gentlemen,* 1585

If love be like the flower that in the night,
When darkness drowns the glory of the skies,
Smells sweet, and glitters in the gazer's sight,
But when the gladsome sun begins to rise,
    And he that views it would the same embrace,
    It withereth and loseth all his grace;

Why do I love and like the cursed tree,
Whose buds appear, but fruit will not be seen?
Why do I languish for the flower I see,
Whose root is rot, when all the leaves be green?
    In such a case it is a point of skill
    To follow chance, and love against my will.

FROM JOHN LYLY's *Six Court Comedies,* 1632

Cupid and my Campaspe played
At cards for kisses; Cupid paid.
He stakes his quiver, bow, and arrows,
His mother's doves and team of sparrows,
Loses them too; then down he throws
The coral of his lip, the rose
Growing on's cheek (but none knows how),
With these the crystal of his brow,
And then the dimple of his chin:
All these did my Campaspe win.
At last he set her both his eyes;
She won, and Cupid blind did rise.
    O Love! has she done this to thee?
    What shall, alas, become of me?

From Alexander and Campaspe

What bird so sings, yet so does wail?
Oh, 'tis the ravished nightingale.
Jug, jug, jug, jug, tereu, she cries,
And still her woes at midnight rise.
Brave prick-song! who is't now we hear?
None but the lark so shrill and clear;
How at heaven's gates she claps her wings,
The morn not waking till she sings.
Hark, hark, with what a pretty throat
Poor robin redbreast tunes his note;
Hark how the jolly cuckoos sing
Cuckoo, to welcome in the spring,
Cuckoo, to welcome in the spring.

From Alexander and Campaspe

A song in making of the arrows

My shag-hair Cyclops, come, let's
    ply
Our Lemnian hammers lustily.
By my wife's sparrows,
I swear these arrows
Shall singing fly
Through many a wanton's eye.
These headed are with golden
    blisses,
These silver ones feathered with
    kisses;

But this of lead
Strikes a clown dead,   10
When in a dance
He falls in a trance,
To see his black-brow lass not buss
    him,
And then whines out for death t'
    untruss him.
So, so, our work being done, let's
    play,
Holiday, boys, cry holiday.

From Sapho and Phao

Song by fairies

Omnes. Pinch him, pinch him, black and blue,
    Saucy mortals must not view
    What the queen of stars is doing,
    Nor pry into our fairy wooing.
1 *Fairy.*   Pinch him blue.
2 *Fairy.*   And pinch him black.
3 *Fairy.*   Let him not lack
    Sharp nails to pinch him blue and red,
    Till sleep has rocked his addlehead.
4 *Fairy.* For the trespass he hath done,   10
    Spots o'er all his flesh shall run.
    Kiss Endymion, kiss his eyes,
    Then to our midnight haydegyes.

From Endymion

FROM GEORGE PEELE's *Arraignment of Paris*, 1584

Œnone. Fair and fair and twice
    so fair,
    As fair as any may be;
    The fairest shepherd on our
    green,
    A love for any lady.

Paris. Fair and fair and twice so
    fair,
    As fair as any may be;
    Thy love is fair for thee alone,
    And for no other lady.

Œnone. My love is fair, my love
    is gay,
    As fresh as been the flowers in
    May,   10
    And of my love my rounde-
    lay,
    My merry, merry, merry
    roundelay
    Concludes with Cupid's curse:
    They that do change old love
    for new,
    Pray gods they change for worse.

Ambo simul. They that do change,
&c.

Œnone. Fair and fair, &c.

Paris. Fair and fair, &c. Thy love
is fair, &c.

Œnone. My love can pipe, my
love can sing,

My love can many a pretty
thing, 20
And of his lovely praises ring
My merry, merry roundelays.
  Amen to Cupid's curse:
They that do change, &c.

Paris. They that do change, &c.

Ambo. Fair and fair, &c.

From George Peele's *Polyhymnia*, 1590

His golden locks time hath to silver turned;
  Oh, time too swift, oh, swiftness never ceasing!
His youth 'gainst time and age hath ever spurned,
  But spurned in vain; youth waneth by increasing.
Beauty, strength, youth, are flowers but fading seen;
Duty, faith, love, are roots, and ever green.

His helmet now shall make a hive for bees,
  And lover's sonnets turned to holy psalms,
A man-at-arms must now serve on his knees,
  And feed on prayers, which are age his alms; 10
But though from court to cottage he depart,
His saint is sure of his unspotted heart.

And when he saddest sits in homely cell,
  He'll teach his swains this carol for a song:
Blest be the hearts that wish my sovereign well,
  Cursed be the souls that think her any wrong!
Goddess, allow this aged man his right,
To be your beadsman now, that was your knight.

From George Peele's *Hunting of Cupid*, [c. 1591]

What thing is love? for, well I wot, love is a thing.
It is a prick, it is a sting,
It is a pretty, pretty thing;
It is a fire, it is a coal,
Whose flame creeps in at ev'ry hole;
And as my wit doth best devise,
Love's dwelling is in ladies' eyes,
From whence do glance love's piercing darts
That make such holes into our hearts;
And all the world herein accord 10
Love is a great and mighty lord;
And when he list to mount so high,
With Venus he in heaven doth lie,

And evermore hath been a god
Since Mars and she played even and odd.

Coridon and Melampus' song

Cor. Melampus, when will love be void of fears?
Mel. When jealousy hath neither eyes nor ears.
Cor. Melampus, when will love be thoroughly shrieved?
Mel. When it is hard to speak, and not believed.
Cor. Melampus, when is love most malcontent?
Mel. When lovers range and bear their bows unbent.
Cor. Melampus, tell me when love takes least harm?
Mel. When swains' sweet pipes are puffed, and trulls are warm.
Cor. Melampus, tell me when is love best fed?
Mel. When it hath sucked the sweet that ease hath bred.   10
Cor. Melampus, when is time in love ill-spent?
Mel. When it earns meed and yet receives no rent.
Cor. Melampus, when is time well-spent in love?
Mel. When deeds win meeds, and words love's works do prove.

FROM GEORGE PEELE's *Old Wive's Tale*, 1595

Whenas the rye reach to the chin,
And chopcherry, chopcherry ripe within,
Strawberries swimming in the cream,
And schoolboys playing in the stream;
Then oh, then oh, then oh, my true love said,
Till that time come again,
She could not live a maid.

FROM GEORGE PEELE's *Love of King David and Fair Bethsabe*, 1599

Hot sun, cool fire, tempered with sweet air,
Black shade, fair nurse, shadow my white hair.
Shine, sun; burn, fire; breathe, air, and ease me;
Black shade, fair nurse, shroud me and please me;
Shadow, my sweet nurse, keep me from burning,
Make not my glad cause cause of mourning.
    Let not my beauty's fire
    Inflame unstaid desire,
    Nor pierce any bright eye
    That wand'reth lightly.   10

FROM *The Lamentable Tragedy of Locrine*, 1595

Strumbo, Dorothy, Trumpart, cobbling shoes

Trum.	We cobblers lead a merry life,
All.	Dan, dan, dan, dan;
Strum.	Void of all envy and of strife,
All.	Dan diddle dan.
Dor.	Our ease is great, our labor small,
All.	Dan, dan, dan, dan;
Strum.	And yet our gains be much withal,
All.	Dan diddle dan.
Dor.	With this art so fine and fair,
All.	Dan, dan, dan, dan,
Trum.	No occupation may compare,
All.	Dan diddle dan.
Strum.	For merry pastime and joyful glee,
	Dan, dan, dan, dan,
Dor.	Most happy men we cobblers be,
	Dan diddle dan.
Trum.	The can stands full of nappy ale,
	Dan, dan, dan, dan,
Strum.	In our shop still withouten fail,
	Dan diddle dan.
Dor.	This is our meat, this is our food,
	Dan, dan, dan, dan;
Trum.	This brings us to a merry mood,
	Dan diddle dan;
Strum.	This makes us work for company,
	Dan, dan, dan, dan,
Dor.	To pull the tankards cheerfully,
	Dan diddle dan.
Trum.	Drink to thy husband, Dorothy,
	Dan, dan, dan, dan.
Dor.	Why, then, my Strumbo, there's to thee,
	Dan diddle dan.
Strum.	Drink thou the rest, Trumpart, amain,
	Dan, dan, dan, dan.
Dor.	When that is gone, we'll fill 't again,
	Dan diddle dan.

10

20

30

FROM *The Maid's Metamorphosis*, 1600

By the moon we sport and play,
With the night begins our day,
As we dance the dew doth fall;

Trip it, little urchins all,
Lightly as the little bee,
Two by two, and three by three;
And about go we, and about go we.

From *Wily Beguiled*, 1606

Old Tithon must forsake his dear,
The lark doth chant her cheerful lay;
Aurora smiles with merry cheer,
To welcome in a happy day.

The beasts do skip,
The sweet birds sing,
The wood nymphs dance,
The echoes ring.

The hollow caves with joy resounds,
And pleasure everywhere abounds;   10
The Graces, linking hand in hand,
In love have knit a glorious band.

From *The Thracian Wonder*, 1661

Love is a law, a discord of such force
That 'twixt our sense and reason makes divorce.
Love's a desire that to obtain betime,
We lose an age of tears plucked from our prime.
Love is a thing to which we soon consent,
As soon refuse, but sooner far repent.

Then what must women be that are the cause,
That love hath life, that lovers feel such laws?
They're like the winds upon Lapanthæ's shore,
That still are changing. Oh, then love no more.   10
A woman's love is like that Syrian flower
That buds and spreads, and withers in an hour.

From Thomas Nashe's *Summer's Last Will and Testament*, 1600

Adieu, farewell earth's bliss,
This world uncertain is;
Fond are life's lustful joys,
Death proves them all but toys,
None from his darts can fly.
I am sick, I must die.
        Lord, have mercy on us!

Rich men, trust not in wealth,
Gold cannot buy you health;
Physic himself must fade,   10
All things to end are made.
The plague full swift goes by;
I am sick, I must die.
        Lord, have mercy on us!

Beauty is but a flower
Which wrinkles will devour:
Brightness falls from the air,
Queens have died young and fair,
Dust hath closed Helen's eye.
I am sick, I must die.   20
    Lord, have mercy on us!

Strength stoops unto the grave,
Worms feed on Hector brave,
Swords may not fight with fate.
Earth still holds ope her gate;
Come! come! the bells do cry.
I am sick, I must die.
    Lord, have mercy on us!

Wit with his wantonness
Tasteth death's bitterness;   30
Hell's executioner
Hath no ears for to hear
What vain art can reply.
I am sick, I must die.
    Lord, have mercy on us!

Haste, therefore, each degree,
To welcome destiny.
Heaven is our heritage,
Earth but a player's stage;
Mount we unto the sky.   40
I am sick, I must die.
    Lord, have mercy on us!

Spring, the sweet spring, is the year's pleasant king;
Then blooms each thing, then maids dance in a ring,
Cold doth not sting, the pretty birds do sing:
    Cuckoo, jug-jug, pu-we, to-witta-woo!

The palm and may make country houses gay,
Lambs frisk and play, the shepherds pipe all day,
And we hear aye birds tune this merry lay:
    Cuckoo, jug-jug, pu-we, to-witta-woo!

The fields breathe sweet, the daisies kiss our feet,
Young lovers meet, old wives a-sunning sit,   1❡
In every street these tunes our ears do greet:
    Cuckoo, jug-jug, pu-we, to-witta-woo!
      Spring, the sweet spring!

Fair summer droops, droop men and beasts therefor;
So fair a summer look for never more.
All good things vanish less than in a day,
Peace, plenty, pleasure, suddenly decay.
    Go not yet away, bright soul of the sad year,
    The earth is hell when thou leav'st to appear.

What, shall those flowers that decked thy garland erst,
Upon thy grave be wastefully dispersed?
O trees, consume your sap in sorrow's source;
Streams, turn to tears your tributary course.   10
    Go not yet hence, bright soul of the sad year,
    The earth is hell when thou leav'st to appear.

Autumn hath all the summer's fruitful treasure;
Gone is our sport, fled is poor Croydon's pleasure.
Short days, sharp days, long nights come on apace,—
Ah, who shall hide us from the winter's face?
Cold doth increase, the sickness will not cease,
And here we lie, God knows, with little ease.
    From winter, plague, and pestilence, good Lord deliver us!

London doth mourn, Lambeth is quite forlorn;
Trades cry, Woe worth that ever they were born.
The want of term is town and city's harm;   10
Close chambers we do want to keep us warm.
Long banished must we live from our friends;
This low-built house will bring us to our ends.
    From winter, plague, and pestilence, good Lord deliver us!

From Thomas Dekker's *Shoemaker's Holiday, or the Gentle Craft,* 1600

Cold's the wind, and wet's the rain,
    Saint Hugh be our good speed;
Ill is the weather that bringeth no gain,
    Nor helps good hearts in need.

Troll the bowl, the jolly nut-brown bowl,
    And here, kind mate, to thee;
Let's sing a dirge for Saint Hugh's soul,
    And down it merrily.

Down-a-down, hey, down-a-down,
    Hey derry derry down-a-down,   10
    Close with the tenor, boy;
Ho! well done, to me let come,
    Ring compass, gentle joy.

Troll the bowl, the nut-brown bowl,
    And here, kind, &c. (*As often as there be men to drink.*)

    (*At last, when all have drunk, this verse.*)

Cold's the wind, and wet's the rain,
    Saint Hugh be our good speed;
Ill is the weather that bringeth no gain,
    Nor helps good hearts in need.   20

FROM THOMAS DEKKER'S *Pleasant Comedy of Patient Grissill*, 1603

Art thou poor, yet hast thou golden slumbers?
    Oh, sweet content!
Art thou rich, yet is thy mind perplexed?
    Oh, punishment!
Dost thou laugh to see how fools are vexed
To add to golden numbers golden numbers?
    Oh, sweet content, oh, sweet, &c.

Work apace, apace, apace, apace;
Honest labor bears a lovely face,
Then hey noney, noney, hey noney, noney.   10

Canst drink the waters of the crispëd spring?
    Oh, sweet content!
Swim'st thou in wealth, yet sink'st in thine own tears?
    Oh, punishment!
Then he that patiently want's burden bears,
No burden bears, but is a king, a king.
    Oh, sweet content, &c.
Work apace, apace, &c.

————

Golden slumbers kiss your eyes,
Smiles awake you when you rise;
Sleep, pretty wantons, do not cry,
And I will sing a lullaby,
Rock them, rock them, lullaby.

Care is heavy, therefore sleep you,
You are care, and care must keep you;
Sleep, pretty wantons, do not cry,
And I will sing a lullaby,
Rock them, rock them, lullaby.   10

————

Beauty arise, show forth thy glorious shining,
Thine eyes feed love, for them he standeth pining;
Honor and youth attend to do their duty
To thee, their only sovereign, Beauty.
Beauty arise, whilst we, thy servants, sing
Io to Hymen, wedlock's jocund king.
    Io to Hymen, Io, Io, sing;
    Of wedlock, love, and youth is Hymen king.

Beauty arise, Beauty arise, thy glorious lights display,
Whilst we sing Io, glad to see this day.   10

Io, Io, to Hymen, Io, Io, sing;
Of wedlock, love, and youth is Hymen king.

FROM THOMAS DEKKER'S *London's Tempe*, [1629]

Brave iron! brave hammer! from your sound
The art of music has her ground;
On the anvil thou keep'st time,
Thy knick-a-knock is a smith's best chime.
  Yet thwick-a-thwack,
   Thwick, thwack-a-thwack, thwack,
  Make our brawny sinews crack,
  Then pit-a-pat, pat, pit-a-pat, pat,
  Till thickest bars be beaten flat.

We shoe the horses of the sun,
Harness the dragons of the moon,
Forge Cupid's quiver, bow, and arrows,
And our dame's coach that's drawn with sparrows.
  Till thwick-a-thwack, &c.

Jove's roaring cannons, and his rammers
We beat out with our Lemnian hammers;
Mars his gauntlet, helm, and spear,
And Gorgon shield, are all made here.
  Till thwick-a-thwack, &c.

The grate which, shut, the day outbars,   20
Those golden studs which nail the stars,
The globe's case, and the axle-tree,
Who can hammer these but we?
  Till thwick-a-thwack, &c.

A warming-pan to heat earth's bed,
Lying i' th' frozen zone half-dead;
Hob-nails to serve the man i' th' moon,
And sparrowbills to clout Pan's shoon,
  Whose work but ours?
  Till thick-a-thwack, &c.   30

Venus' kettles, pots, and pans
We make, or else she brawls and bans;
Tongs, shovels, andirons have their places,
Else she scratches all our faces.
  Till thwick-a-thwack, &c.

From Thomas Dekker and John Ford's *Sun's Darling*, 1656

Cast away care, he that loves sorrow
Lengthens not a day, nor can buy to-morrow;
    Money is trash, and he that will spend it,
    Let him drink merrily, fortune will send it.
Merrily, merrily, merrily, oh, ho!
Play it off stiffly, we may not part so.

Wine is a charm, it heats the blood too,
Cowards it will arm, if the wine be good too;
    Quickens the wit, and makes the back able,
    Scorns to submit to the watch or constable.   10
Merrily, &c.

Pots fly about, give us more liquor,
Brothers of a rout, our brains will flow quicker;
    Empty the cask, score up, we care not;
    Fill all the pots again, drink on, and spare not.
Merrily, &c.

From John Webster's *White Devil*, 1612

Call for the robin redbreast and the wren,
Since o'er shady groves they hover,
And with leaves and flowers do cover
The friendless bodies of unburied men.
Call unto his funeral dole
The ant, the field-mouse, and the mole,
To rear him hillocks that shall keep him warm,
And, when gay tombs are robbed, sustain no harm;
But keep the wolf far thence, that's foe to men,
For with his nails he'll dig them up again.   10

From John Webster's *Duchess of Malfi*, 1623

Hark, now everything is still;
The screech-owl and the whistler shrill
Call upon our dame aloud,
And bid her quickly don her shroud;
Much you had of land and rent,
Your length in clay's now competent.
A long war disturbed your mind;
Here your perfect peace is signed.
Of what is 't fools make such vain keeping?
Sin their conception, their birth weeping,   10

Their life a general mist of error,
Their death a hideous storm of terror.
Strew your hair with powders sweet,
Don clean linen, bathe your feet,
And, the foul fiend more to check,
A crucifix let bless your neck;
'Tis now full tide, 'tween night and day,
End your groan and come away.

FROM FRANCIS BEAUMONT and JOHN FLETCHER'S *Knight of the*
Burning Pestle, 1613

Come, you whose loves are dead,
    And whiles I sing,
        Weep, and wring
Every hand, and every head
Bind with cypress and sad yew;
Ribands black and candles blue
For him that was of men most true.

Come with heavy mourning,
    And on his grave
        Let him have   10
Sacrifice of sighs and groaning;
Let him have fair flowers enow,
White and purple, green and yellow,
For him that was of men most true.

Better music ne'er was known
Than a choir of hearts in one.
Let each other that hath been
Troubled with the gall or spleen,
Learn of us to keep his brow
Smooth and plain as ours are now.
Sing though before the hour of dying,
He shall rise, and then be crying
Hey ho! 'Tis nought but mirth
That keeps the body from the earth.   10

FROM FRANCIS BEAUMONT and JOHN FLETCHER'S *The Maid's*
Tragedy, 1619

Cynthia, to thy power and thee
    We obey.
Joy to this great company,
    And no day
Come to steal this night away,

Till the rites of love are ended,
And the lusty bridegroom say,
Welcome, light, of all befriended.

Pace out, you watery powers below;
   Let your feet,
Like the galleys when they row,
   Even beat.
Let your unknown measures, set
To the still winds, tell to all
That gods are come, immortal, great,
To honor this great nuptïal.

FROM *The Maid's Tragedy*, 1622

Lay a garland on my hearse of the dismal yew,
Maidens, willow branches bear, say I diëd true.
My love was false, but I was firm from my hour of birth;
Upon my buried body lay lightly, gently, earth.

—————

I could never have the power
To love one above an hour,
But my head would prompt mine eye
On some other man to fly.
Venus, fix mine eyes fast,
Or, if not, give me all that I shall see at last.

FROM JOHN FLETCHER's *Faithful Shepherdess*, [*c.* 1610]

Do not fear to put thy feet
Naked in the river, sweet;
Think not leech, or newt, or toad
Will bite thy foot when thou hast trod;
Nor let the water rising high,
As thou wad'st in, make thee cry
And sob; but ever live with me,
And not a wave shall trouble thee.

FROM JOHN FLETCHER's *Bloody Brother*, 1639

The drinking song

Drink to-day, and drown all sorrow,
You shall perhaps not do it to-morrow.
Best, while you have it, use your breath;
There is no drinking after death.

Wine works the heart up, wakes the wit;
There is no cure 'gainst age but it.

It helps the headache, cough, and tisic,
And is for all diseases physic.

Then let us swill, boys, for our health;
Who drinks well, loves the commonwealth.   10
And he that will to bed go sober,
Falls with the leaf still in October.

Take, oh, take those lips away
    That so sweetly were forsworn,
And those eyes, like break of day,
    Lights that do mislead the morn;
But my kisses bring again,
    Seals of love, though sealed in vain.

Hide, oh, hide those hills of snow,
    Which thy frozen bosom bears,
On whose tops the pinks that grow
    Are of those that April wears.   10
But first set my poor heart free,
    Bound in those icy chains by thee.

From Francis Beaumont and John Fletcher's *Comedies and Tragedies*, 1647

Care-charming Sleep, thou easer of all woes,
Brother to Death, sweetly thyself dispose
On this afflicted prince; fall like a cloud
In gentle showers; give nothing that is loud
Or painful to his slumbers; easy, sweet,
And as a purling stream, thou son of Night,
Pass by his troubled senses; sing his pain,
Like hollow murmuring wind or silver rain;
Into this prince gently, oh, gently slide,
And kiss him into slumbers like a bride.   10
                        From John Fletcher's *Valentinian*

God Lyæus, ever young,
Ever honored, ever sung;
Stained with blood of lusty grapes,
In a thousand lusty shapes,
Dance upon the mazer's brim,
In the crimson liquor swim;
From thy plenteous hand divine,
Let a river run with wine.

God of youth, let this day here
Enter neither care nor fear.   10
> From John Fletcher's *Valentinian*

Cast our caps and cares away,
This is beggars' holiday.
At the crowning of our king,
Thus we ever dance and sing.
In the world look out and see,
Where so happy a prince as he?
Where the nation live so free,
And so merry as do we?
Be it peace, or be it war,
Here at liberty we are,   10
And enjoy our ease and rest;
To the field we are not pressed;
Nor are called into the town
To be troubled with the gown.
Hang all officers, we cry,
And the magistrate too, by.
When the subsidy's increased,
We are not a penny cessed;
Nor will any go to law
With the beggar for a straw.   20
All which happiness, he brags,
He doth owe unto his rags.
> From John Fletcher's *Beggars' Bush*

Hence, all you vain delights,
As short as are the nights
   Wherein you spend your folly,
There's nought in this life sweet,
If man were wise to see't,
   But only melancholy,
   Oh, sweetest melancholy.
Welcome, folded arms and fixëd eyes,
A sigh that piercing mortifies,
A look that's fastened to the ground,
A tongue chained up without a sound.   10
Fountain-heads, and pathless groves,
Places which pale passion loves,
Moonlight walks, when all the fowls
Are warmly housed, save bats and owls,
   A midnight bell, a parting groan,
   These are the sounds we feed upon;

Then stretch our bones in a still gloomy valley,
Nothing's so dainty sweet as lovely melancholy.

From John Fletcher's Nice Valor

From Francis Beaumont and John Fletcher's Fifty Comedies and Tragedies, 1679

Let the bells ring, and let the boys sing,
  The young lasses skip and play,
Let the cups go round, till round goes the ground,
  Our learned old vicar will stay.

Let the pig turn merrily, merrily, ah,
  And let the fat goose swim,
For verily, verily, verily, ah,
  Our vicar this day shall be trim.

The stewed cock shall crow, cock-a-loodle-loo,
  A loud cock-a-loodle shall he crow;
The duck and the drake shall swim in a lake
  Of onions and claret below.

Our wives shall be neat, to bring in our meat
  To thee, our most noble adviser;
Our pains shall be great, and bottles shall sweat,
  And we ourselves will be wiser.

We'll labor and swink, we'll kiss and we'll drink,
  And tithes shall come thicker and thicker;
We'll fall to our plow, and get children enow,
  And thou shalt be learned old vicar.

From John Fletcher's Spanish Curate

Weep no more, nor sigh, nor groan,
Sorrow calls no time that's gone;
Violets plucked, the sweetest rain
Makes not fresh nor grow again;
Trim thy locks, look cheerfully;
Fate's hid ends eyes cannot see.
Joys as wingëd dreams fly fast,
Why should sadness longer last?
Grief is but a wound to woe;
Gentlest fair, mourn, mourn no mo.

From John Fletcher's Queen of Corinth

From *Mr. William Shakespeare's Comedies, Histories, and Tragedies,* 1623

Orpheus with his lute made trees,
And the mountain-tops that freeze,
Bow themselves when he did sing;
To his music plants and flowers
Ever sprung, as sun and showers
There had made a lasting spring.
Everything that heard him play,
Even the billows of the sea,
Hung their heads, and then lay by.
In sweet music is such art,   10
Killing care and grief of heart
Fall asleep or, hearing, die.

From Shakespeare and Fletcher's *King Henry VIII*

From Thomas Middleton's *Chaste Maid in Cheapside,* 1630

Weep eyes, break heart!
My love and I must part.
Cruel fates true love do soonest sever;
Oh, I shall see thee never, never, never.
Oh, happy is the maid whose life takes end
Ere it knows parent's frown or loss of friend.
Weep eyes, break heart!
My love and I must part.

From Thomas Middleton's *The Widow,* 1652

Give me fortune, give me health,
Give me freedom, I'll get wealth.
Who complains his fate's amiss,
When he has the wide world his?
He that has the devil in fee,
Can have but all, and so have we.
Give us fortune, give us health,
Give us freedom, we'll get wealth.
In every hamlet, town, and city,
He has lands that was born witty.

From Thomas Middleton's *More Dissemblers Besides Women,* 1657

Captain. Come, my dainty doxies,
My dells, my dells most dear,
We have neither house nor land,
Yet never want good cheer.

All. We never want good cheer.
Captain. We take no care for candle rents.

2 Gipsy. We lie. *3 Gipsy.* We
  snort.
Captain. We sport in tents,
  Then rouse betimes and steal
    our dinners.
    Our store is never taken   10
  Without pigs, hens, or ba-
    con,
  And that's good meat for sin-
    ners.
    At wakes and fairs we cozen
    Poor country folks by dozen;
  If one have money, he disburses;
  Whilst some tell fortunes, some
    pick purses;
    Rather than be out of use,

    We'll steal garters, hose or
      shoes,
  Boots, or spurs with jingling
      rowels,
  Shirts or napkins, smocks or
      towels.   20
    Come live with us, come live
      with us,
    All you that love your eases;
      He that's a gipsy
      May be drunk or tipsy
    At any hour he pleases.
All. We laugh, we quaff, we roar,
    we scuffle,
  We cheat, we drab, we filch, we
    shuffle.

FROM PHILIP MASSINGER'S *Emperor of the East*, 1632

Why art thou slow, thou rest of trouble, Death,
  To stop a wretch's breath,
That calls on thee and offers her sad heart
  A prey unto thy dart?
I am nor young nor fair; be, therefore, bold;
  Sorrow hath made me old,
Deformed, and wrinkled; all that I can crave
  Is quiet in my grave.
Such as live happy, hold long life a jewel,
  But to me thou art cruel   10
If thou end not my tedious misery,
  And I soon cease to be.
Strike, and strike home, then; pity unto me,
  In one short hour's delay, is tyranny.

FROM NATHAN FIELD'S *Amends for Ladies*, 1618

Rise, lady mistress, rise,
The night hath tedious been;
No sleep hath fallen into my
  eyes,
Nor slumbers made me sin.
Is not she a saint, then, say,
Thought of whom keeps sin
  away?

Rise, madam, rise and give me
  light,
Whom darkness still will cover,
And ignorance darker than night,
Till thou smile on thy lover.   10
All want day till thy beauty rise,
For the grey morn breaks from
  thine eyes.

FROM BARTEN HOLIDAY's *Technogamia or the Marriage of the Arts*, 1618

Tobacco's a musician,
And in a pipe delighteth;
  It descends in a close,
  Through the organ of the nose,
With a relish that inviteth.
    This makes me sing, So ho ho,
      so ho ho, boys,
  Ho boys, sound I loudly;
    Earth ne'er did breed
    Such a jovial weed,
  Whereof to boast so proudly. 10

Tobacco is a lawyer,
His pipes do love long cases;
  When our brains it enters,
  Our feet do make indentures,
Which we seal with stamping
    paces.
  This makes me sing, So ho, &c.

Tobacco's a physician,
Good both for sound and sickly;
  'Tis a hot perfume
  That expels cold rheum,   20
And makes it flow down quickly.
  This makes me sing, &c.

Tobacco is a traveler,
Come from the Indies hither;
  It passed sea and land

Ere it came to my hand,
And scaped the wind and weather.
  This makes me sing, &c.

Tobacco is a critic,
That still old paper turneth;   30
  Whose labor and care
  Is as smoke in the air
That ascends from a rag when it
    burneth.
  This makes me sing, &c.

Tobacco's an *ignis fatuus,*
A fat and fiery vapor;
  That leads men about
  Till the fire be out,
Consuming like a taper.
  This makes me sing, &c.   40

Tobacco is a whiffler
And cries, Huff snuff, with fury;
  His pipe's his club and link,
  He's the visor that does drink,
Thus armed I fear not a jury.
    This makes me sing, So ho ho,
      so ho ho, boys,
  Ho boys, sound I loudly;
    Earth ne'er did breed
    Such a jovial weed,
  Whereof to boast so proudly. 50

FROM PETER HAUSTED's *Rival Friends,* 1632

Have pity, grief, I cannot pay
  The tribute which I owe thee, tears;
    Alas, those fountains are grown dry,
    And 'tis in vain to hope supply
  From others' eyes; for each man bears
    Enough about him of his own
    To spend his stock of tears upon.

Woo then the heavens, gentle love,
  To melt a cloud for my relief;

Or woo the deep, or woo the grave;   10
Woo what thou wilt, so I may have
Wherewith to pay my debt, for grief
    Has vowed, unless I quickly pay,
    To take both life and love away.

Have you a desire to see
The glorious heaven's epitome?
Or an abstract of the spring?
Adonis' garden? or a thing
    Fuller of wonder, nature's shop displayed,
    Hung with the choicest pieces she has made?
        Here behold it open laid.

Or else would you bless your eyes
With a type of paradise?
Or behold how poets feign   10
Jove to sit amidst his train?
    Or see what made Actæon rue,
    Diana 'mongst her virgin crew?
        Lift up your eyes and view.

FROM JOHN FORD's *The Broken Heart*, 1633

Can you paint a thought, or number
Every fancy in a slumber?
Can you count soft minutes roving
From a dial's point by moving?
Can you grasp a sigh, or lastly,
Rob a virgin's honor chastely?
    No, oh no; yet you may
        Sooner do both that and this,
        This and that, and never miss,
    Than by any praise display   10
        Beauty's beauty; such a glory
        As (beyond all fate, all story)
            All arms, all arts,
            All loves, all hearts,
    Greater than those or they,
    Do, shall, and must obey.

Oh, no more, no more, too late
Sighs are spent; the burning tapers
Of a life as chaste as fate,
Pure as are unwritten papers,
    Are burnt out; no heat, no light

Now remains, 'tis ever night.
Love is dead, let lovers' eyes,
    Locked in endless dreams,
    Th' extremes of all extremes,
Ope no more, for now love dies,   10
    Now love dies, implying
Love's martyrs must be ever, ever dying.

———————

All. Glories, pleasures, pomps, delights, and ease
            Can but please
        Outward senses, when the mind
    Is not untroubled, or by peace refined.
  1. Crowns may flourish and decay,
    Beauties shine, but fade away.
  2. Youth may revel, yet it must
    Lie down in a bed of dust.
  3. Earthly honors flow and waste,
    Time alone doth change and last.   10
All. Sorrows mingled with contents, prepare
            Rest for care;
        Love only reigns in death; though art
    Can find no comfort for a broken heart.

FROM JASPER FISHER'S *Fuimus Troes*, 1633

So the silver-feathered swan,
Both by death and color wan,
Loves to sing before she die,
Leaving life so willingly.
But how can I sing a note
When dead hoarseness stops my throat?
Or how can I play a stroke
When my heartstrings are all broke?

A morisco

The sky is glad that stars above
    Do give a brighter splendor;
The stars unfold their flaming gold
    To make the ground more tender;
The ground doth send a fragrant smell
    That air may be the sweeter;
The air doth charm the swelling seas
    With pretty chirping meter;
The sea with rivers water doth
    The plants and flowers dainty;   10
The plants do yield their fruitful seed

That beasts may live in plenty;
The beasts do give both food and cloth
That man high Jove may honor;
And so the world runs merrily round,
When peace doth smile upon her.
Oh then, then oh; oh then, then oh;
This jubilee last forever,
That foreign spite or civil fight
Our quiet trouble never!   20

FROM THOMAS GOFFE'S *Tragedy of Orestes*, 1633

Lullaby, lullaby baby,
Great Argos' joy,
The King of Greece thou art born
    to be,
In despite of Troy.
Rest ever wait upon thy head,
Sleep close thine eyes;
The blessed guard tend on thy bed
    Of deities.
Oh, how his brow will beseem a
    crown!
How these locks will shine!   10
Like the rays of the sun on the
    ground,
These locks of thine.
The nurse of heaven still send
    thee milk;
Mayst thou suck a queen.
Thy drink, Jove's nectar, and
    clothes of silk;
A god mayst thou seem.
Cupid sit on this rosean cheek,
    On these ruby lips.
May thy mind like a lamb be
    meek,
In the vale which trips.   20
Lullaby, lullaby baby.

FROM WILLIAM SAMPSON'S *Vow Breaker*, 1636

When from the wars I do return,
And at a cup of good ale mourn,

I'll tell how towns without fire
    we did burn,
    And is not that a wonder?

I'll tell how that my general
Entered the breach, and scaled the
    wall,
And made the foremost battery of
    all,
    And is not that a wonder?

How that we went to take a fort,
And took it too in warlike sort;   10
I'll swear that a lie is a true report,
    And is not that a wonder?

How that we soldiers had true pay,
And cloth, and victuals every day,
And never a captain ran away,
    And is not that a wonder?

FROM JOHN JONES'S *Adrasta*, 1635

Come, lovers, bring your cares,
Bring sigh-perfumèd sweets,
Bedew the grave with tears,
Where death and virtue meets;
Sigh for the hapless hour
That knit two hearts in one,
And only gave love power
To die when 'twas begun.

FROM THOMAS MAY'S *Tragedy of Cleopatra*, 1639

Not he that knows how to acquire,
    But to enjoy, is blest.

Nor does our happiness consist
In motion, but in rest.

The gods pass man in bliss, because
They toil not for more height;
But can enjoy, and in their own
Eternal rest delight.

Then, princes, do not toil nor care;
Enjoy what you possess.   10
Which whilst you do, you equalize
The gods in happiness.

FROM THOMAS MAY's Old Couple, 1658

Dear, do not your fair beauty wrong,
In thinking still you are too young.
The roses and lilies in your cheek
Flourish, and no more ripening seek.
Your cherry lip, red, soft, and sweet,
Proclaims such fruit for taste most meet;
Then lose no time, for love has wings,
And flies away from aged things.

FROM THOMAS NABBES's Hannibal and Scipio, 1637

Beauty no more the subject be
Of wanton art to flatter thee;
Or in dull figures call thee spring,
Lily, or rose, or other thing;
All which beneath thee are, and grow
Into contempt when thou dost show
The unmatched glory of thy brow.
Behold a sphere of virgins move,
None 'mongst them less than queen of love;
And yet their queen so far excels,   10
Beauty and she are only parallels.

FROM JAMES SHIRLEY's Changes, or Love in a Maze, 1632

Melancholy, hence! go get
Some piece of earth to be thy seat;
Here the air and nimble fire
Would shoot up to meet desire;
Sullen humor, leave her blood,
Mix not with the purer flood,
But let pleasures swelling there
Make a springtide all the year.

FROM JAMES SHIRLEY's Triumph of Peace, 1633

Come away, away, away,
See the dawning of the day,
Risen   from   the   murmuring streams;
Some stars show with sickly beams
What stock of flame they are allowed,
Each retiring to a cloud;
Bid your active sports adieu,
The morning else will blush for you.

Ye feathered-footed hours, run
To dress the chariot of the sun;   10
Harness the steeds, it quickly will
Be time to mount the eastern hill.

The lights grow pale with modest fears,
Lest you offend those sacred ears
And eyes, that lent you all this grace;
Retire, retire, to your own place.

And as you move from that blest pair,
Let each heart kneel and think a prayer,
That all, that can make up the glory,
Of good and great may fill their story.   20

FROM JAMES SHIRLEY'S *Triumph of Beauty*, 1646

Cease, warring thoughts, and let
    his brain
No more discord entertain,
But be smooth and calm again.

Ye crystal rivers that are nigh,
As your streams are passing by,
Teach your murmurs harmony.

Ye winds that wait upon the
    spring,
And perfumes to flowers do bring,
Let your amorous whispers here
Breathe soft music to his ear.   10

Ye warbling nightingales repair
From every wood to charm this
    air,
And with the wonders of your
    breast,
Each striving to excel the rest.
    When it is time to wake him,
      close your parts,
    And drop down from the trees
      with broken hearts.

FROM JAMES SHIRLEY'S *Cupid and Death*, 1653

Victorious men of earth, no more
    Proclaim how wide your em-
      pires are;
Though you bind in every shore,
    And your triumphs reach as
      far
      As night or day,
    Yet you, proud monarchs, must
      obey
And mingle with forgotten ashes
    when
Death calls ye to the crowd of
    common men.

Devouring famine, plague, and
    war,

Each able to undo mankind,   10
Death's servile emissaries are;
    Nor to these alone confined,
      He hath at will
    More quaint and subtle ways to
      kill;
A smile or kiss, as he will use the
    art,
Shall have the cunning skill to
    break a heart.

FROM JAMES SHIRLEY'S *Contention of Ajax and Ulysses*, 1659

The glories of our blood and state
    Are shadows, not substantial
      things;
There is no armor against fate;
    Death lays his icy hand on kings.
      Scepter and crown
      Must tumble down,
And in the dust be equal made
With the poor crooked scythe and
    spade.

Some men with swords may reap
    the field,
    And plant fresh laurels where
      they kill;   10
But their strong nerves at last must
    yield,
    They tame but one another still.
      Early or late,
      They stoop to fate,
And must give up their murmur-
    ing breath,
When they, pale captives, creep to
    death.

The garlands wither on your
    brow,
    Then boast no more your
      mighty deeds;
Upon death's purple altar now,
    See where the victor-victim
      bleeds.   20
    Your heads must come

To the cold tomb;
Only the actions of the just
Smell sweet and blossom in their
    dust.

FROM HENRY SHIRLEY'S *Martyred Soldier*, 1638

What are earthly honors
But sin's glorious banners?
Let not golden gifts delight
    thee,
Let not death nor torments fright
    thee,
From thy place thy captain gives
    thee;
When thou faintest, he relieves
    thee.
Hark how the lark
Is to the morning singing;
Hark how the bells are ring-
    ing;
It is for joy that thou to heaven art
    flying;   10
This is not life, true life is got by
    dying.

FROM RICHARD BROME'S *Northern Lass*, 1632

A bonny, bonny bird I had,
    A bird that was my marrow;
A bird whose pastime made me
    glad,
    And Philip, 'twas my sparrow.
A pretty play-fere, chirp it would,
    And hop, and fly to fist,
Keep cut, as 'twere a usurer's gold,
    And bill me when I list.
      Philip, Philip, Philip, it cries,
      But he is fled, and my joy
        dies.   10

But were my Philip come again,
    I would not change my love
For Juno's bird with gaudy train,
    Nor yet for Venus' dove.
Nay, would my Philip come again,
    I would not change my state,
For his great namesake's wealth of
    Spain,
    To be another's mate.
      Philip, Philip, Philip, it cries,
      But he is fled, and my joy
        dies.   20

FROM RICHARD BROME'S *Jovial Crew or the Merry Beggars*, 1652

A round, a round, a round, boys, a round,
Let mirth fly aloft and sorrow be drowned.
Old sack and old songs and a merry old crew
Can charm away cares when the ground looks blue.

FROM SIR WILLIAM BERKELEY'S *Lost Lady*, 1639

Where did you borrow that last
    sigh,
    And that relenting groan?
For those that sigh, and not for
    love,
    Usurp what's not their own.
Love's arrows sooner armor pierce
    Than your soft snowy skin;
Your eyes can only teach us love,
    But cannot take it in.

FROM ROBERT CHAMBERLAIN' *Swaggering Damsel*, 1640

Farewell this company
If you love sadness,
For melancholy is
Nothing but madness;
Hang up proud costly clothes,
Peddlers and pack-toys;
Let us make the hogs-head
    weep
Claret and sack, boys.

FROM ROBERT DAVENPORT's
King John and Matilda, 1655

Matilda, now go take thy bed
In the dark dwellings of the
    dead,

And rise in the great waking day,
Sweet as incense, fresh as May.

Rest thou, chaste soul, fixed in thy
    proper sphere,
Amongst heaven's fair ones, all are
    fair ones there.

Rest there, chaste soul, whilst
    we here troubled say,
Time gives us griefs, death takes
    our joys away.

BROADSIDE BALLADS

The Introduction and Notes are at page 976

The king's hunt is up

The hunt is up, the hunt is up,
And it is well nigh day;
And Harry our king is gone hunt-
    ing,
To bring his deer to bay.

The east is bright with morning
    light,
And darkness it is fled;
And the merry horn wakes up the
    morn
To leave his idle bed.

Behold the skies with golden dyes
Are glowing all around;   10
The grass is green, and so are the
    treen,
All laughing with the sound.

The horses snort to be at the sport,
The dogs are running free;
The woods rejoice at the merry
    noise
Of hey tantara tee ree!

The sun is glad to see us clad
All in our lusty green,
And smiles in the sky as he riseth
    high
To see and to be seen.   20

Awake all men, I say again,
Be merry as you may;

For Harry our king is gone hunt-
    ing
To bring his deer to bay.
            [*Gray of Reading*]

A song between the Queen's Majesty and England

E [*ngland*]. Come over the bourn,
    Bessy,
    Come over the bourn, Bessy,
Sweet Bessy, come over to me;
    And I shall thee take
    And my dear lady make,
Before all other that ever I see.

B[*essy*]. Methink I hear a voice
    At whom I do rejoice,
And answer thee now I shall:
    Tell me, I say,   10
    What art thou that bids me
        come away,
And so earnestly dost me call?

E.   I am thy lover fair,
    Hath chose thee to mine heir,
And my name is merry England;
    Therefore come away,
    And make no more delay,
Sweet Bessy, give me thy hand!

B.   Here is my hand,
    My dear lover, England;   20
I am thine both with mind and
    heart,

Forever to endure,
Thou mayest be sure,
Until death us two depart.

E. Lady, this long space
Have I loved thy grace,
More than I durst well say;
Hoping at the last,
When all storms were past,
For to see this joyful day.   30

B. Yet, my lover England,
Ye shall understand
How fortune on me did lour;
I was tumbled and tossed
From pillar to post,
And prisoner in the Tower.

E. Dear Lady, we do know
How tyrants, not a few,
Went about for to seek thy blood;
And contrary to right   40
They did what they might,
That now bear two faces in one
hood.

B. Then was I carried to
Woodstock,
And kept close under lock,
That no man might with me
speak;
And against all reason
They accused me of treason,
And terribly they did me threat.

E. Oh, my lover fair!
My darling and mine heir!   50
Full sore for thee I did lament;
But no man durst speak,
But they would him threat
And quickly make him repent.

B. Then was I delivered their
hands,
But was fain to put in bands
And good sureties for my forth
coming;

Not from my house to de-
part,
Nor nowhere else to start,
As though I had been away running.   60

E. Why, dear Lady, I trow,
Those madmen did not
know
That ye were daughter unto King
Harry,
And a princess of birth,
One of the noblest on earth,
And sister unto Queen Mary.

B. Yes, yet I must forgive
All such as do live,
If they will hereafter amend;   69
And for those that are gone,
God forgive them every one,
And his mercy on them extend.

E. Yet, my lover dear,
Tell me now here,
For what cause had ye this pun-
ishment?
For the commons did not
know,
Nor no man would them
show,
The chief cause of your imprison-
ment.

B. No, nor they themself,
That would have decayed my
wealth,   80
But only by power and abusion,
They could not detect me,
But that they did suspect me,
That I was not of their religion.

E. Oh, cruel tyrants,
And also monstrous giants,
That would such a sweet blossom
devour!
But the Lord, of his might,
Defended thee in right,

And shortened their arm and
    power.   90

B.   Yet, my lover dear,
    Mark me well here,
Though they were men of the
    devil,
    The Scripture plainly saith,
    All they that be of faith
Must needs do good against evil.

E.   O sweet virgin pure!
    Long may ye endure
To reign over us in this land;
    For your works do ac-
      cord,   100
    Ye are the handmaid of the
      Lord,
For he hath blessed you with his
    hand.

B.   My sweet realm, be obedient
    To God's holy command-
      ment,
And my proceedings embrace;
    And for that that is abused,
    Shall be better used,
And that within short space.

E.   Dear Lady and Queen,
    I trust it shall be seen   110
Ye shall reign quietly without
    strife;
    And if any traitors there be,
    Of any kind or degree,
I pray God send them short life.

B.   I trust all faithful hearts
    Will play true subjects' parts,
Knowing me their Queen and
    true heir by right;
    And that much the rather
    For the love of my father,
That worthy prince, King Henry
    th' Eight.   120

E.   Therefore let us pray
    To God both night and day,

Continually and never to cease,
    That he will preserve your
      grace
    To reign over us long space
In tranquility, wealth, and peace.

Both. All honor, laud, and praise
    Be to the Lord God always,
Who hath all princes' hearts in
    his hands;
    That by his power and
      might,   130
    He may guide them right,
For the wealth of all Christian
    lands.
    Finis, quod WILLIAM BIRCHE.
    God save the Queen.

*A proper song, entitled: Fain
would I have a pretty thing to
give unto my lady*

To the tune of *Lusty Gallant*

Fain would I have a pretty thing
    To give unto my lady;
I name no thing, nor I mean no
    thing,
    But as pretty a thing as may
    be.

Twenty journeys would I make,
    And twenty ways would hie
    me,
To make adventure for her sake,
    To set some matter by me.

But I would fain have a pretty
    thing, &c.,
I name no thing, nor I mean no
    thing, &c.   10

Some do long for pretty knacks,
    And some for strange devices;
God send me that my lady lacks,
    I care not what the price is.
    Thus fain, &c.

Some go here, and some go there,
  Where gazes be not geason;
And I go gaping everywhere,
  But still come out of season.
    Yet fain, &c.   20

I walk the town and tread the
    street,
  In every corner seeking
The pretty thing I cannot meet,
  That's for my lady's liking.
    Fain, &c.

The mercers pull me going by,
  The silky-wives say, What lack
    ye?
The thing you have not, then say
    I,
  Ye foolish fools, go pack ye.
    But fain, &c.   30

It is not all the silk in Cheap,
  Nor all the golden treasure,
Nor twenty bushels on a heap,
  Can do my lady pleasure.
    But fain, &c.

The gravers of the golden shows
  With jewels do beset me;
The seamsters in the shops that
    sews,
  They do nothing but let me.
    But fain, &c.   40

But were it in the wit of man
  By any means to make it,
I could for money buy it than,
  And say, Fair lady, take it.
    Thus fain, &c.

O lady, what a luck is this,
  That my good willing miss-
    eth
To find what pretty thing it is
  That my good lady wisheth.

Thus fain would I have had this
    pretty thing   50

To give unto my lady;
I said no harm, nor I meant no
    harm,
  But as pretty a thing as may
    be.

A new courtly sonnet, of the Lady Greensleeves

To the new tune of *Greensleeves*

Greensleeves was all my joy,
  Greensleeves was my delight;
Greensleeves was my heart of
    gold,
  And who but Lady Green-
    sleeves?

Alas, my love, ye do me wrong
  To cast me off discourteously;
And I have lovèd you so long,
  Delighting in your company.

Greensleeves was all my joy,
  Greensleeves was my delight;
Greensleeves was my heart of
    gold,   11
  And who but Lady Green-
    sleeves?

I have been ready at your hand
  To grant whatever you would
    crave;
I have both wagèd life and land,
  Your love and good will for
    to have.

Greensleeves was all my joy, &c.

I bought thee kerchiefs to thy
    head,
  That were wrought fine and
    gallantly;
I kept thee both at board and
    bed,   20
  Which cost my purse well
    favoredly.

Greensleeves was all my joy, &c.

I bought thee petticoats of the
best,
  The cloth so fine as fine might
  be;
I gave thee jewels for thy chest,
  And all this cost I spent on
  thee.

Greensleeves was all my joy, &c.

Thy smock of silk both fair and
white,
  With gold embroidered gor-
  geously;
Thy petticoat of sendal right, 30
  And thus I bought thee gladly.

Greensleeves was all my joy, &c.

Thy girdle of gold so red,
  With pearls bedeckëd sumptu-
  ously,
The like no other lasses had,
  And yet thou wouldst not love
  me.

Greensleeves was all my joy, &c.

Thy purse and eke thy gay gilt
knives,
  Thy pin-case, gallant to the
  eye,
No better wore the burgess'
  ' wives,   40
  And yet thou wouldst not love
  me.

Greensleeves was all my joy, &c.

Thy crimson stockings all of silk,
  With gold all wrought above
  the knee,
Thy pumps as white as was the
milk,
  And yet thou wouldst not love
  me.

Greensleeves was all my joy, &c.

Thy gown was of the grossy
green,
  Thy sleeves of satin hanging
  by,
Which made thee be our harvest
  queen,   50
  And yet thou wouldst not love
  me.

Greensleeves was all my joy, &c.

Thy garters fringëd with the
gold,
  And silver aglets hanging by,
Which made thee blithe for to behold,
  And yet thou wouldst not love
  me.

Greensleeves was all my joy, &c.

My gayest gelding I thee gave,
  To ride wherever liked thee;
No lady ever was so brave,   60
  And yet thou wouldst not love
  me.

Greensleeves was all my joy, &c.

My men were clothëd all in
green,
  And they did ever wait on
  thee;
All this was gallant to be seen,
  And yet thou wouldst not love
  me.

Greensleeves was all my joy, &c.

They set thee up, they took thee
down,
  They served thee with humility;

Thy foot might not once touch
  the ground,   70
And yet thou wouldst not love
  me.

Greensleeves was all my joy, &c.

For every morning when thou
  rose
I sent thee dainties orderly,
To cheer thy stomach from all
  woes,
And yet thou wouldst not love
  me.

Greensleeves was all my joy, &c.

Thou couldst desire no earthly
  thing,
But still thou hadst it readily;
Thy music still to play and sing, 80
And yet thou wouldst not love
  me.

Greensleeves was all my joy, &c.

And who did pay for all this gear
That thou didst spend when
  pleased thee?
Even I that am rejected here,
And thou disdain'st to love me.

Greensleeves was all my joy, &c.

Well, I will pray to God on high
That thou my constancy mayest
  see;
And that yet once before I die 90
Thou wilt vouchsafe to love
  me.

Greensleeves was all my joy, &c.

Greensleeves, now farewell, adieu,
God I pray to prosper thee;
For I am still thy lover true,
Come once again and love me.

Greensleeves was all my joy, &c.

*A proper new song made by a
student in Cambridge*

To the tune of *I wish to see those
happy days*

I which was once a happy wight
  and high in fortune's grace,
And which did spend my golden
  prime
  in running pleasure's race,
    Am now enforced of late
    contrariwise to mourn,
    Since fortune joys into an-
      noys
    my former state to turn.

The toiling ox, the horse, the ass
  have time to take their rest; 10
Yea, all things else which nature
  wrought
  sometimes have joys in breast,
    Save only I, and such
    which vexëd are with
      pain;
    For still in tears my life it
      wears,
    and so I must remain.

How oft have I in folded arms
  enjoyëd my delight!
How oft have I excuses made,
  of her to have a sight!   20
    But now to fortune's will
    I causëd am to bow,
    And for to reap a hugy heap
    which youthful years did
      sow.

Wherefore all ye which do as yet
  remain and bide behind,
Whose eyes Dame Beauty's blazing beams
  as yet did never blind,
    Example let me be
    to you and other more 30

Whose heavy heart hath felt
the smart,
subdued by Cupid's lore.

Take heed of gazing over-much
on damsels fair unknown,
For oftentimes the snake doth lie
with roses overgrown;
And under fairest flowers
do noisome adders lurk,
Of whom take heed, I thee
areed,
lest that thy cares they
work.   40

What though that she doth smile
on thee?
perchance she doth not love;
And though she smack thee once
or twice,
she thinks thee so to prove;
And when that thou dost
think
she loveth none but thee,
She hath in store perhaps
some more
which so deceivëd be.

Trust not therefore the outward
show,
beware in any case: 50
For good conditions do not lie
where is a pleasant face.
But if it be thy chance
a lover true to have,
Be sure of this, thou shalt
not miss
each thing that thou wilt
crave.

And whenas thou, good reader,
shalt
peruse this scroll of mine,
Let this a warning be to thee,
and say a friend of thine   60
Did write thee this of love
and of a zealous mind,

Because that he sufficiently
hath tried the female kind.

Here, Cambridge, now I bid farewell!
adieu to students all!
Adieu unto the colleges
and unto Gonville Hall!
And you, my fellows once,
pray unto Jove that I   70
May have relief for this my
grief,
and speedy remedy.

And that he shield you everyone
from beauty's luring looks,
Whose bait hath brought me to
my bane
and caught me from my books.
Wherefore, for you my
prayer shall be
to send you better grace,
That modesty with honesty
may guide your youthful
race.   80
Finis, quod THOMAS RICHARD-
SON, *sometime student in
Cambridge.*

As you came from the holy
land of Walsingham

As you came from the holy land
Of Walsingham,
Met you not with my true love,
By the way as you came?
How should I know your true
love,
That have met many a one,
As I came from the holy land,
That have come, that have
gone?

She is neither white nor brown,
But as the heavens fair;   10

There is none hath her form so
    divine,
  On the earth, in the air.
Such a one did I meet, good sir,
  With angel-like face,
Who like a nymph, like a queen
    did appear
  In her gait, in her grace.

She hath left me here alone,
  All alone unknown,
Who sometime loved me as her
    life,
  And callèd me her own.   20
What is the cause she hath left
    thee alone,
  And a new way doth take,
That sometime did thee love as
    herself,
  And her joy did thee make?

I have loved her all my youth,
  But now am old as you see;

Love liketh not the falling fruit,
  Nor the withered tree.
For love is a careless child,
  And forgets promise past;   30
He is blind, he is deaf, when he
    list,
  And in faith never fast.

His desire is fickle found,
  And a trustless joy;
He is won with a world of de-
    spair,
  And is lost with a toy.
Such is the love of women-kind,
  Or the word, love, abused,
Under which many childish de-
    sires
  And conceits are excused.   40

But love, it is a durable fire
  In the mind ever burning,
Never sick, never dead, never
    cold,
  From itself never turning.

*The valorous acts performed at Gaunt by the brave bonny lass,
Mary Ambree, who in revenge of her lover's death,
did play her part most gallantly*

The tune is *The blind beggar*

When Captain Courageous, whom death could not daunt,
Had roundly besiegèd the city of Gaunt,
And manly they marched by two and by three,
And foremost in battle was Mary Ambree.

Thus being enforced to fight with her foes,
On each side most fiercely they seemed to close;
Each one sought for honor in every degree,
But none so much won it as Mary Ambree.

When brave Sergeant Major was slain in the fight,
Who was her own true love, her joy and delight,   10
She swore unrevenged his blood should not be;
Was not this a brave bonny lass, Mary Ambree?

She clothed herself from the top to the toe
With buff of the bravest and seemly to show;
A fair shirt of mail over that striped she;
Was not this a brave bonny lass, Mary Ambree?

A helmet of proof she put on her head,
A strong armed sword she girt on her side,
A fair goodly gauntlet on her hand wore she;
Was not this a brave bonny lass, Mary Ambree?   20

Then took she her sword and her target in hand,
And called all those that would be of her band,—
To wait on her person there came thousands three;
Was not this a brave bonny lass, Mary Ambree?

Before you shall perish, the worst of you all,
Or come to any danger of enemy's thrall,
This hand and this life of mine shall set you free;
Was not this a brave bonny lass, Mary Ambree?

The drums and the trumpets did sound out alarm,
And many a hundred did lose leg and arm,   30
And many a thousand she brought on their knee;
Was not this a brave bonny lass, Mary Ambree?

The sky then she filled with smoke of her shot,
And her enemies' bodies with bullets so hot,
For one of her own men, a score killed she;
Was not this a brave bonny lass, Mary Ambree?

And then her false gunner did spoil her intent,
Her powder and bullets away he had spent,
And then with her weapon she slashed them in three;
Was not this a brave bonny lass, Mary Ambree?   40

Then took she her castle where she did abide,
Her enemies besieged her on every side;
To beat down her castle walls they did agree,
And all for to overcome Mary Ambree.

Then took she her sword and her target in hand,
And on her castle walls stoutly did stand,
So daring the captains to match any three;
Oh, what a brave captain was Mary Ambree!

At her then they smiled, not thinking in heart
That she could have performed so valorous a part;   50
The one said to the other, we shortly shall see
This gallant brave captain before us to flee.

Why, what do you think or take me to be?
Unto these brave soldiers so valiant spoke she.
A knight, sir, of England, and captain, quoth they,
Whom shortly we mean to take prisoner away.

No captain of England behold in your sight,
Two breasts in my bosom, and therefore no knight;
No knight, sir, of England, nor captain, quoth she,   60
But even a poor bonny lass, Mary Ambree.

But art thou a woman as thou dost declare,
That hath made us thus spend our armor in war?
The like in our lives we never did see,
And therefore we'll honor brave Mary Ambree.

The Prince of great Parma heard of her renown,
Who long had advanced for England's fair crown;
In token he sent a glove and a ring,
And said she should be his bride at his wedding.

Why, what do you think or take me to be?
Though he be a prince of great dignity,   70
It shall never be said in England so free
That a stranger did marry with Mary Ambree.

Then unto fair England she back did return,
Still holding the foes of brave England in scorn;
In valor no man was ever like she;
Was not this a brave bonny lass, Mary Ambree?

In this woman's praises I'll here end my song,
Whose heart was approved in valor most strong;
Let all sorts of people, whatever they be,
Sing forth the brave valors of Mary Ambree.   80

Lord Willoughby

To the tune of *Lord Willoughby*

The fifteen day of July,
  With glistering spear and shield,

A famous fight in Flanders
  Was foughten in the field;
The most courageous officers
  Was English captains three,
But the bravest man in battle
  Was brave Lord Willoughby.

The next was Captain Norris,
 A valiant man was he; 10
The other, Captain Turner,
 That from field would never
  flee.
With fifteen hundred fighting
  men,
 Alas, there was no more,
They fought with forty thousand
  then,
 Upon the bloody shore.

Stand to it, noble pike-men,
 And look you round about;
And shoot you right, you bow-
  men,
 And we will keep them out; 20
You musket and caliver men,
 Do you prove true to me,
I'll be the foremost man in fight,
 Says brave Lord Willoughby.

And then the bloody enemy
 They fiercely did assail,
And fought it out most valiantly,
 Not doubting to prevail;
The wounded men on both sides
  fell,
 Most piteous for to see, 30
Yet nothing could the courage
  quell
 Of brave Lord Willoughby.

For seven hours to all men's view
 This fight endurèd sore,
Until our men so feeble grew
 That they could fight no more;
And then upon dead horses
 Full savorly they eat,
And drank the puddle water,
 For no better they could get. 40

When they had fed so freely,
 They kneelèd on the ground,
And praisèd God devoutly
 For the favor they had found;

And bearing up their colors
 The fight they did renew,
And turning toward the Spaniard,
 Five thousand more they slew.

The sharp steel-pointed arrows
 And bullets thick did fly; 50
Then did our valiant soldiers
 Charge on most furiously;
Which made the Spaniards waver,
 They thought it best to flee,
They feared the stout behavior
 Of brave Lord Willoughby.

Then quoth the Spanish general,
 Come, let us march away,
I fear we shall be spoilèd all,
 If that we longer stay; 60
For yonder comes Lord Wil-
  loughby
 With courage fierce and fell,
He will not give one inch of
  ground
 For all the devils in hell.

And then the fearful enemy
 Was quickly put to flight;
Our men pursued courageously,
 And rout their forces quite.
And at last they gave a shout,
 Which echoed through the
  sky, 70
God and Saint George for Eng-
  land!
 The conquerors did cry.

This news was brought to Eng-
  land
 With all the speed might be,
And told unto our gracious
  Queen,
 Of this same victory;
Oh, this is brave Lord Willough-
  by,
 My love hath ever won;

Of all the lords of honor,
  'Tis he great deeds hath
    done.   80

For soldiers that were maimed
  And wounded in the fray,
The Queen allowed a pension
  Of eighteen pence a day;
Besides, all costs and charges
  She quit and set them free,
And this she did all for the sake
  Of brave Lord Willoughby.

Then courage, noble Englishmen,
  And never be dismayed,   90
If that we be but one to ten,
  We will not be afraid
To fight with foreign enemies,
  And set our country free;
And thus I end this bloody bout
  Of brave Lord Willoughby.

A sonnet upon the pitiful burning of the Globe Play-house in London

Now sit thee down, Melpomene,
Wrapped in a sea-coal robe,
And tell the doleful tragedy
That late was played at Globe;
For no man that can sing and
  say
Was scared on St. Peter's Day.
Oh sorrow, pitiful sorrow, and
  yet all this is true.

All you that please to understand,
Come listen to my story,
To see Death with his raking
  brand   10
'Mongst such an auditory;
Regarding   neither   Cardinal's
  might,
Nor yet the rugged face of Henry
  the eight.—Oh sorrow, &c.

This fearful fire began above,
A wonder strange and true,
And to the stage-house did re-
  move,
As round as tailor's clew;
And burnt down both beam and
  snag,
And did not spare the silken flag.
  —Oh sorrow, &c.

Out run the knights, out run the
  lords,   20
And there was great ado;
Some lost their hats and some their
  swords,
Then out run Burbage too;
The reprobates, though drunk on
  Monday,
Prayed for the fool and Henry
  Condye.—Oh sorrow, &c.

The periwigs and drum-heads fry,
Like to a butter firkin;
A woeful burning did betide
To many a good buff jerkin.
Then with swollen eyes, like
  drunken Flemings,   30
Distressëd stood old stuttering
  Hemings.—Oh sorrow, &c.

No shower his rain did there down
  force,
In all that sunshine weather,
To save that great renownëd
  house,
Nor thou, O ale-house, neither.
Had it begun below, *sans doute,*
Their wives for fear. . . —Oh
  sorrow, &c.

Be warned, you stage strutters all,
Lest you again be catched,
And such a burning do befall 40
As to them whose house was
  thatched;

Forbear your whoring, breeding
    biles,
And lay up that expense for tiles.
—Oh sorrow, &c.

Go draw you a petition,
And do you not abhor it,
And get, with low submission,
A license to beg for it
In churches, *sans* churchwardens'
    checks,
In Surrey and in Middlesex.
Oh sorrow, pitiful sorrow, and yet
    all this is true.   50

The shepherd's wooing Dulcina

Tune is *Dulcina*

As at noon Dulcina rested
    In her sweet and shady bower,
Came a shepherd and requested
    In her arms to sleep an hour;
But from her look a wound he
    took,
So far that for a farther boon
The nymph he prays; wherefore
    she says,
    Forgo me now, come to me
        soon!

But in vain she did conjure him
    For to leave her presence so, 10
Having thousand means to allure
    him,
    And but one to let him go;
Where lips invite, and eyes de-
    light,
And cheeks as fresh as rose in
    June,
Persuade to stay, what boots to
    say,
    Forgo me now, come to me
        soon?

Words whose hopes have now
    enjoined
    Him to let Dulcina sleep,
Could a man's love be confined,
    Or a maid her promise keep? 20
No, for her waist he held as fast
As she was constant to her tune;
And still she spake, For Cupid's
    sake,
    Forgo me now, come to me
        soon!

He demands, What time or lei-
    sure
    Can there be more fit than
        now?
She says, Night gives love that
    pleasure
    That the day doth not allow.
The sun's kind light forgives de-
    light,
Quoth he, more easily than the
    moon;   30
In Venus' plays be bold. She says,
    Forgo me now, come to me
        soon!

But no promise nor profession
    From his hands could purchase
        scope;
Who would sell the sweet pos-
    session
    Of such a beauty for a hope?
Or for the sight of ling'ring night
Forgo the present joys of noon?
Though none so fair, her speeches
    were,
    Forgo me now, come to me
        soon!   40

How at last agreed these lovers?
    She was fair and he was young;
Tongue may tell what eye dis-
    covers,
    Joys unseen are never sung.
He said, My dear, my love not
    fear!

Bright Phœbus' beams outshine
　　the moon.
Dulcina prays, and to him says,
　　Forgo me now, come to me
　　　soon!

Truth's integrity; or a curious
northern ditty called, Love
will find out the way

To a pleasant new tune

Over the mountains
　　And under the waves,
Over the fountains
　　And under the graves,
Over floods which are the deep-
　　est
Which do Neptune obey,
Over rocks which are steepest,
　　Love will find out the way.

Where there is no place
　　For the glow-worm to lie; 10
Where there is no space
　　For receipt of a fly;
Where the gnat she dares not
　　venter,
　　Lest herself fast she lay;
But if Love come, he will enter,
　　And will find out the way.

You may esteem him
　　A child by his force,
Or you may deem him
　　A coward, which is worse; 20
But if he whom Love doth honor
　　Be concealed from the day,
Set a thousand guards upon him,
　　Love will find out the way.

Some think to lose him,
　　Which is too unkind;
And some do suppose him,
　　Poor heart, to be blind;
If that he were hidden,
　　Do the best that you may, 30

Blind Love, if so you call him,
　　Will find out the way.

Well may the eagle
　　Stoop down to the fist;
Or you may inveigle
　　The phœnix of the east;
With fear the tiger's movëd
　　To give over his prey,
But never stop a lover,
　　He will post on his way. 40

From Dover to Berwick,
　　And nations throughout,
Brave Guy of Warwick,
　　That champion so stout,
With his warlike behavior,
　　Through the world he did
　　　stray
To win his Phyllis' favor—
　　Love will find out the way.

In order next enters
　　Bevis so brave; 50
After adventures,
　　And policy grave,
To see whom he desired,
　　His Josian so gay,
For whom his heart was fired,
　　Love found out the way.

The Gordian knot
　　Which true lovers knit,
Undo you cannot,
　　Nor yet break it; 60
Make use of your inventions
　　Their fancies to betray,
To frustrate your intentions
　　Love will find out the way.

From court to the cottage,
　　In bower and in hall,
From the king unto the beggar,
　　Love conquers all;
Though ne'er so stout and lordly,
　　Strive, do what you may, 70

Yet, be you ne'er so hardy,
  Love will find out the way.

Love hath power over princes
  And greatest emperor;
In any provinces,
  Such is Love's power,
There is no resisting,
  But him to obey;
In spite of all contesting,
  Love will find out the way.   80

If that he were hidden,
  And all men that are,
Were strictly forbidden
  That place to declare,
Winds that have no abidings,
  Pitying their delay,
Will come and bring him tidings,
  And direct him the way.

If the earth should part him
  He would gallop it o'er;   90
If the seas should o'erthwart him,
  He would swim to the shore;
Should his love become a swallow,
  Through the air to stray,
Love would lend wings to follow,
  And will find out the way.

There is no striving
  To cross his intent,
There is no contriving
  His plots to prevent;   100
But if once the message greet
  him
That his true love doth stay,
If death should come and meet
  him,
  Love will find out the way.

The milkmaid's life

  To a curious new tune called
  The milkmaid's dumps

You rural goddesses
  That woods and fields possess,
Assist me with your skill,

That may direct my quill
  More jocundly to express
The mirth and delight,
Both morning and night,
  On mountain or in dale,
Of them who choose
This trade to use,   10
And through cold dews
Do never refuse
  To carry the milking pail.

The bravest lasses gay
  Live not so merry as they;
In honest civil sort
They make each other sport,
  As they trudge on their way;
Come fair or foul weather,
They're fearful of neither,   20
  Their courages never quail;
In wet and dry,
Though winds be high,
And dark's the sky,
They ne'er deny
  To carry the milking pail.

Their hearts are free from care,
  They never will despair
Whatever them befall;
They bravely bear out all,   30
  And fortune's frowns out-dare.
They pleasantly sing
To welcome the spring,
  'Gainst heaven they never rail.
If grass well grow,
Their thanks they show;
And, frost or snow,
They merrily go
  Along with the milking pail.

Base idleness they do scorn;   40
  They rise very early i' th'
  morn,
And walk into the field,
Where pretty birds do yield
  Brave music on every thorn;
The linnet and thrush

Do sing on each bush,
  And the dulcet nightingale
Her note doth strain
In a jocund vein,
To entertain   50
That worthy train
  Which carry the milking pail.

Their labor doth health preserve;
  No doctors' rules they observe,
While others, too nice
In taking their advice,
  Look always as though they
    would starve.
Their meat is digested,
They ne'er are molested,
  No sickness doth them assail; 60
Their time is spent
In merriment;
While limbs are lent,
They are content
  To carry the milking pail.

Those lasses, nice and strange,
  That keep shops in the ex-
    change,
Sit pricking of clouts
And giving of flouts,
  They seldom abroad do range;
Then comes the green sickness 71
And changeth their likeness,
  All this is for want of good
    sale;
But 'tis not so,
As proof doth show,
By them that go
In frost and snow
  To carry the milking pail.

If they any sweethearts have,
  That do their affections crave,
Their privilege is this,   81
Which many others miss,
  They can give them welcome
    brave.
With them they may walk,

And pleasantly talk,
  With a bottle of wine or ale;
The gentle cow
Doth them allow,
As they know how.
God speed the plow,   90
  And bless the milking pail!

Upon the first of May,
  With garlands fresh and gay,
With mirth and music sweet,
For such a season meet,
  They pass their time away;
They dance away sorrow,
And all the day thorough
  Their legs do never fail;
They nimbly   100
Their feet do ply,
And bravely try
The victory,
  In honor o' th' milking pail.

If any think that I
  Do practise flattery,
In seeking thus to raise
The merry milkmaids' praise,
  I'll to them thus reply:
It is their desert   110
Inviteth my art
  To study this pleasant tale
In their defence,
Whose innocence
And providence
Gets honest pence
  Out of the milking pail.
          [Martin Parker]

The four wonders

The four wonders of this land,
  Which unto you we will de-
    clare.
The Lord's great mercy, it is
    great;
  God give us grace to stand in
    fear,

*And watch and pray both night
    and day
    That God may give us all his
    grace,
To repent our sins then every
    one,—
    Our time is going on apace.*

Tune of *Dear love, regard my
    grief*

Sweet England, call for grace!
    With speed leave off thy sin,
And with a contrite heart
    To prayers now begin.

For sure the time is come
    That Christ our Savior told;
Towards the latter day
    We wonders shall behold.

And now strange wonders rare
    The Lord from heaven doth
    send,   10
In earth and in the air,
    Because we should amend.

Great lights within the sky
    Hath oft been seen, we hear,
To many people's view,
    In countries far and near.

But what it doth presage
    No man on earth does know;
None but the living God
    Such wonders strange can
    show.   20

But to the subject now
    Which I do mean to write,
The strangest news I'll tell
    Which time has brought to
    light.

In London now doth live
    One Mr. Clark by name,

A tailor by his trade,
    Of good report and fame.

His wife, being with child,
    Unto her grief and woe   30
She with a neighbor's wife
    Fell out,—the truth is so.

And after many words,
    To fighting then they go;
This woman, being with child,
    Received a grievous blow

Upon her belly; then,
    Which makes my heart to
    bleed,
That she went home and sent 39
    For midwife's help, with speed.

In haste the midwife came,
    And other women store,
When, by the help of God,
    She seven children bore!

Seven dainty boys she had,
    All which were born in sight,
All framed with perfect shape,
    With joints and limbs aright.

But they were all still-born,
    Which grieved their parents
    sore;   50
But of the works of God
    In this they do deplore.

The woman now doth mend,
    Whereby God's works are
    known;
And now this wondrous news
    Both far and near is shown.

The second news I tell
    Comes from brave Yorkshire;
A monster there was born,
    The like you ne'er did hear. 60

Three miles from Pomfret lived
  A woman of great worth,
In travail fell, and brought
  To light a monstrous birth,

Just the shape of a colt,
  To all the people's sight;
Which bred amazement great,
  With tears and with fright,

To see this woman's grief,
  And trouble of her mind,   70
In bringing forth a colt,
  Contrary unto kind.

Long legs, round feet, long nose,
  And headed like a horse;
Which filled these women's
    hearts
  With pity and remorse.

This woman now doth mend,
  Whereby God's works are
    known;
And now this wondrous news
  Both far and near is shown. 80

And the third news most rare,
  The which I have to tell,
London can witness true
  That there a monster fell.

In Christ-Church parish lived
  A woman known full well,
Of honest carriage, which
  Her neighbors all can tell.

This woman being with child,
  Which grief and sorrow bred, 90
Into the world she bore
  A child without a head!

The face was in the breast,
  To all the people's view;
But it died suddenly,
  This is approvëd true.

It is for certain true,
  And is approvëd plain;
From earth, I say, it came,
  And to earth it turned again. 100

These women now all three
  Are on the mending hand;
But three such monstrous births
  Was ne'er in fair England.

The fourth news most rare,
  The which I have to tell:
In famous Gloucestershire
  A wondrous shower fell.

Not far from Gloucester Town,
  A place is called Brand-
    wood;   110
Upon a hedge of cloths,
  For truth, it rainëd blood!

A maid being starching there,
  As reason doth require,
She went to fetch in wood
  Wherewith to make a fire;

And having on such cuffs
  As starchers oft do use,
Upon them fell some drops
  Of blood, which made her
    muse.   120

And holding up her head,
  Which made her wonder more,
She saw the hedge of cloths
  With blood besprinkled o'er.

Then she throwed down the
    wood,
  And, with amazement great,
She went into the house
  And this news did repeat.

The people then came forth
  And found the news was
    true,   130

They saw the hedge of cloths
    With blood besprinkled, to their
        view.

Then they took in the cloths,
    And washed them that same
        day;
But water, lees, nor soap,
    Could take the blood away.

We are so wicked grown
    The heavens do for us bleed,
And wonders strange are shown,
    All this is true indeed!   140

Sodom was warned afore,
    So was Jerusalem,
And many places more
    Whom God did plague for sin.

But we are like the Jews,
    Our hearts are now so hard
That we will not believe,
    Nor yet God's word regard.

Now think upon each sin,
    Pride, whoredom, drunken-
        ness,   150
Swearing, deceit, and lies,
    And vile covetousness.

Then we shall see our God
    Will take us for his own,
If we believe these signs
    And tokens God hath shown.

Concluding thus my news,
    The God of truth and peace
Grant that the gospel may
    Continually increase.   160

Sailors for my money

To the tune of *The jovial cobbler*

Country men of England,
    Who live at home with ease,
And little think what dangers
    Are incident o' th' seas,

Give ear unto the sailor
    Who unto you will show
His case, his case,
    Howe'er the wind doth blow.

He that is a sailor
    Must have a valiant heart,   10
For when he is upon the sea
    He is not like to start,
But must, with noble courage,
    All dangers undergo;
Resolve, resolve,
    Howe'er the wind doth blow.

Our calling is laborious
    And subject to much woe,
But we must still contented be
    With what falls to our share.   20
We must not be faint-hearted,
    Come tempest, rain, or snow,
Nor shrink, nor shrink,
    Howe'er the wind doth blow.

Sometimes on Neptune's bosom
    Our ship is tossed with waves,
And every minute we expect
    The sea must be our graves.
Sometimes on high she mounteth,
    Then falls again as low,   30
With waves, with waves,
    When stormy winds do blow.

Then with unfeignëd prayers,
    As Christian duty binds,
We turn unto the Lord of Hosts,
    With all our hearts and minds;
To him we fly for succor,
    For he, we surely know,
Can save, can save,
    Howe'er the wind doth blow.   40

Then he who breaks the rage,
    The rough and blusterous seas,
When his disciples were afraid,
    Will straight the storms ap-
        pease;

And give us cause to thank,
  On bended knees full low,
Who saves, who saves,
  Howe'er the wind doth blow.

Our enemies approaching,
  When we on sea espy,   50
We must resolve incontinent
  To fight although we die;
With noble resolution
  We must oppose our foe,
In fight, in fight,
  Howe'er the wind does blow.

And when by God's assistance
  Our foes are put to th' foil,
To animate our courages
  We all have share o' th'
    spoil.   60
Our foes into the ocean
  We back to back do throw,
To sink, or swim,
  Howe'er the wind doth blow.

Thus we gallant seamen,
  In midst of greatest dangers,
Do always prove our valor,
  We never are no changers;
But whatsoe'er betide us
  We stoutly undergo,   70
Resolved, resolved,
  Howe'er the wind doth blow.

If fortune do befriend us,
  In what we take in hand,
We prove ourselves still generous
  Whene'er we come to land;
There's few that shall out-brave
    us,
  Though ne'er so great in show,
We spend, and lend,
  Howe'er the wind doth blow.   80

We travel to the Indies,
  From them we bring some
    spice;

Here we buy rich merchandise
  At very little price.
And many wealthy prizes
  We conquer from the foe,
In fight, in fight,
  Howe'er the wind doth blow.

Into our native country
  With wealth we do return,   90
And cheer our wives and chil-
    dren,
  Who for our absence mourn.
Then do we bravely flourish,
  And wheresoe'er we go,
We roar, we roar,
  Howe'er the wind doth blow.

For when we have received
  Our wages for our pains,
The vintners and the tapsters
  By us have golden gains.   100
We call for liquor roundly,
  And pay before we go;
And sing, and drink,
  Howe'er the wind doth blow.

We bravely are respected
  When we walk up and down,
For if we meet good company
  We care not for a crown;
There's none more free than sail-
    ors,
  Where'er he come or go,   110
Though he'll roar o' th' shore,
  Howe'er the wind doth blow.

Then who would live in England
  And nourish vice with ease,
When he that is in poverty
  May riches get o' th' seas?
Let's sail unto the Indies,
  Where golden grass doth grow;
To sea, to sea,   119
  Howe'er the wind doth blow.
    [*Martin Parker*]

When the King enjoys his own again
To be joyfully sung with its own proper tune

What Booker can prognosticate
Concerning king's or kingdom's fate?
I think myself to be as wise
As he that gazeth on the skies.
My skill goes beyond the depth of a pond,
   Or rivers in the greatest rain;
Whereby I can tell, all things will be well,
   When the King enjoys his own again.

There's neither swallow, dove, nor dade,
Can soar more high, or deeper wade,   10
Nor show a reason from the stars
Which causeth peace or civil wars;
The man in the moon may wear out his shoon,
   By running after Charles his wain;
But all's to no end, for the times will not mend
   Till the King enjoys his own again.

Though for a time we see Whitehall
With cobwebs hanging on the wall,
Instead of silk and silver brave
Which formerly it used to have,   20
With rich perfume in every room,
   Delightful to that princely train;
Which again you shall see, when the time it shall be,
   That the King enjoys his own again.

Full forty years the royal crown
Hath been his father's and his own;
And is there anyone but he
That in the same should sharer be?
For who better may the scepter sway
   Than he that hath such right to reign?   30
Then let's hope for a peace, for the wars will not cease
   Till the King enjoys his own again.

Till then upon Ararat's hill
My hope shall cast her anchor still,
Until I see some peaceful dove
Bring home the branch she dearly love;

Then will I wait till the waters abate
Which now disturb my troubled brain,
Else never rejoice till I hear the voice,
That the King enjoys his own again.

40

[*Martin Parker*]

LYRICS FROM SONG-BOOKS

The Introduction and Notes are at page 980

FROM WILLIAM BYRD's *Psalms, Sonnets, and Songs of Sadness
and Piety*, 1588

Reasons briefly set down by the author to persuade everyone to
learn to sing.

*First, it is a knowledge easily taught and quickly learned, where there
is a good master and an apt scholar.*

2. *The exercise of singing is delightful to nature, and good to preserve
the health of man.*

3. *It doth strengthen all the parts of the breast, and doth open the
pipes.*

4. *It is a singular good remedy for a stutting and stammering in the
speech.*

5. *It is the best means to procure a perfect pronunciation, and to make
a good orator.*

6. *It is the only way to know where nature hath bestowed the benefit of
a good voice; which gift is so rare as there is not one among a thousand that hath it, and in many that excellent gift is lost because they
want art to express nature.*

7. *There is not any music of instruments whatsoever comparable to that
which is made of the voices of men, where the voices are good, and
the same well sorted and ordered.*

8. *The better the voice is, the meeter it is to honor and serve God
therewith; and the voice of man is chiefly to be employed to that end.*

Omnis spiritus laudet Dominum.

*Since singing is so good a thing,
I wish all men would learn to sing.*

[*Lulla, my sweet little baby*]

Lulla, la lulla, lulla lullaby.
My sweet little baby, what meanest thou to cry?
Be still, my blessed babe, though cause thou hast to mourn,

Whose blood most innocent to shed the cruel king hath sworn.
And lo, alas, behold what slaughter he doth make,
Shedding the blood of infants all, sweet Savior, for thy sake.
A King is born, they say, which King this king would kill.
Oh woe, and woeful heavy day, when wretches have their will!

    Lulla, la lulla, lulla lullaby.
    My sweet little baby, what meanest thou to cry?   10
Three kings this King of kings to see are come from far,
To each unknown, with offerings great, by guiding of a star.
And shepherds heard the song which angels bright did sing,
Giving all glory unto God for coming of this King,
Which must be made away, King Herod would him kill.
Oh woe, and woeful heavy day, when wretches have their will!

    Lulla, la lulla, lulla lullaby.
    My sweet little baby, what meanest thou to cry?
Lo, my little babe, be still, lament no more;
From fury thou shalt step aside, help have we still in store.   20
We heavenly warning have some other soil to seek,
From death must fly the Lord of life, as lamb both mild and meek.
Thus must my babe obey the king that would him kill.
Oh woe, and woeful heavy day, when wretches have their will!

    Lulla, la lulla, lulla lullaby.
    My sweet little baby, what meanest thou to cry?
But thou shalt live and reign as Sibyls have foresaid,
As all the prophets prophesy, whose mother, yet a maid
And perfect virgin pure, with her breasts shall upbreed
Both God and man, that all hath made, the Son of heavenly seed,   30
Whom caitiffs none can 'tray, whom tyrants none can kill.
Oh joy, and joyful happy day, when wretches want their will!

From William Byrd's *Songs of Sundry Natures*, 1589

A carol for Christmas Day

    An earthly tree a heavenly fruit it bare;
      A case of clay contained a crown immortal,
    A crown of crowns, a King, whose cost and care
      Redeemed poor man—whose race before was thrall
    To death, to doom, to pains of everlasting—
    By his sweet death, scorns, stripes, and often fasting.
        Cast off all doubtful care,
          Exile and banish tears,
       To joyful news divine
          Lend us your listening ears.   10

A star above the stars, a sun of light,
   Whose blessed beams this wretched earth bespread
With hope of heaven and of God's Son the sight,
   Which in our flesh and sinful soul lay dead.
O faith, O hope, O joys renowned forever,
O lively life that deathless shall perséver!
      Cast off all our doubtful care,
       Exile and banish tears,
     To joyful news divine
     Lend us your listening ears.   20

Then let us sing the lullabies of sleep
   To this sweet babe, born to awake us all
From drowsy sin, that made old Adam weep,
   And by his fault gave to mankind the fall.
For lo, this day, the birthday, day of days,
Summons our songs to give him laud and praise.
      Cast off all doubtful care,
       Exile and banish tears,
     To joyful news divine
     Lend us your listening ears.   30

FROM THOMAS MORLEY'S *Canzonets*, 1593

[*Arise, get up, my dear love*]

Arise, get up, my dear love, rise, make haste, begone thee!
Lo, where the bride, fair Daphne bright, still stays on thee!
Hark! O hark! Yon merry wanton maidens squealing!
Spice cake, sops in wine, spice cakes, are a-dealing!
     Run then, run apace,
     Get a bride lace
And a gilt rosemary branch while yet there is catching,
   And then hold fast for fear of old snatching.
     Alas, my love, why weep ye?
     O fear not that, dear love, the next day keep we.   10
List, hark yon minstrels! How fine they firk it!
   And see how the maids jerk it!
     With Kate and Will,
     Tom and Jill,
     Hey ho brave,
     Now a skip,
     There a trip,
     Finely set aloft,
     On a fine wedding day,
All for fair Daphne's wedding day!   20

From John Mundy's *Songs and Psalms*, 1594

[*In midst of woods*]

In midst of woods or pleasant grove
  Where all sweet birds do sing,
Methought I heard so rare a sound
Which made the heavens to
    ring.
The charm was good, the noise
    full sweet,
  Each bird did play his part;
And I admired to hear the same,
  Joy sprung into my heart.

The blackbird made the sweetest
    sound,
  Whose tunes did far excel,   10
Full pleasantly and most profound
Was all things placèd well.

Thy pretty tunes, mine own sweet
    bird,
  Done with so good a grace,
Extols thy name, prefers the same
  Abroad in every place.

Thy music grave, bedeckèd well
  With sundry points of skill,
Bewrays thy knowledge excellent,
  Engrafted in thy will.   20
My tongue shall speak, my pen
    shall write,
  In praise of thee to tell.
The sweetest bird that ever was,
  In friendly sort, farewell.

From John Dowland's *Second Book of Songs or Airs*, 1600

[*Fine knacks for ladies*]

Fine knacks for ladies, cheap, choice, brave, and new!
  Good pennyworths! but money cannot move.
I keep a fair but for the fair to view;
  A beggar may be liberal of love.
Though all my wares be trash, the heart is true.

Great gifts are guiles and look for gifts again;
  My trifles come as treasures from my mind.
It is a precious jewel to be plain;
  Sometimes in shell th' orient'st pearls we find.
Of others take a sheaf, of me a grain.   10

Within this pack, pins, points, laces, and gloves,
  And divers toys fitting a country fair;
But my heart lives where duty serves and loves,
  Turtles and twins, court's brood, a heavenly pair.
Happy the heart that thinks of no removes!

[*Now cease, my wandering eyes*]

Now cease, my wandering eyes,
  Strange beauties to admire.

In change least comfort lies;
Long joys yield long desire.
One faith, one love
Makes our frail pleasures eternal, and in sweetness prove
New hopes, new joys
Are still with sorrow declining unto deep annoys.

One man hath but one soul,
Which art cannot divide;
If all one soul must love,
Two loves must be denied.
One soul, one love,
By faith and merit united, cannot remove.
Distracted sprites
Are ever changing and hapless in their delights.

Nature two eyes hath given
All beauty to impart,
As well in earth as heaven;
But she hath given one heart,
That though we see
Ten thousand beauties, yet in us one should be
One steadfast love,
Because our hearts stand fixed, although our eyes do move.

FROM JOHN DOWLAND's *Third and Last Book of Songs or Airs*, 1603

[*Weep you no more, sad fountains*]

Weep you no more, sad fountains;
  What need you flow so fast?
Look how the snowy mountains
  Heaven's sun doth gently waste.
But my sun's heavenly eyes
  View not your weeping,
  That now lie sleeping,
Softly, now softly lies
  Sleeping.

Sleep is a reconciling,
  A rest that peace begets.
Doth not the sun rise smiling
  When fair at even he sets?
Rest you then, rest, sad eyes,
  Melt not in weeping
  While she lies sleeping
Softly, now softly lies
  Sleeping.

FROM THOMAS BATESON's *First Set of English Madrigals*, 1604

[*Beauty is a lovely sweet*]

Beauty is a lovely sweet
Where pure white and crimson
  meet,
Joined with favor of the face,

Chiefest flower of female race.
But if virtue might be seen,
It would more delight the
  eyne.

[*Your shining eyes*]

Your shining eyes and golden hair,
Your lily-rosëd lips most fair,
Your other beauties that ex-
cel,
Men cannot choose but like them well;
But when for them they say they'll die,
Believe them not, they do but lie.

FROM TOBIAS HUME'S *Musical Humors. The first part of Airs,* 1605

The soldier's song

I sing the praise of honored wars,
The glory of well-gotten scars,
The bravery of glittering shields,
Of lusty hearts and famous fields;
For that is music worth the ear of Jove,
A sight for kings, and still the soldier's love.

Look! Oh, methinks I see
The grace of chivalry;
The colors are displayed,   9
The captains bright ar-
rayed.
See now the battle's ranged,
Bullets now thick are changed.
Hark! shots and wounds abound,
The drums alarum sound.
The captains cry: Za-za!
The trumpets sound ta-ra!
Oh, this is music worth the ear of Jove,
A sight for kings, and still the soldier's love.

[*Tobacco, tobacco*]

Tobacco, tobacco, sing sweetly for tobacco!
Tobacco is like love, oh love it;
For you see, I will prove it.
Love maketh lean the fat men's tumor,
So doth tobacco.
Love still dries up the wanton humor,
So doth tobacco.
Love makes men sail from shore to shore,
So doth tobacco.
'Tis fond love often makes men poor,   10
So doth tobacco.
Love makes men scorn all coward fears,
So doth tobacco.
Love often sets men by the ears,
So doth tobacco.
Tobacco, tobacco,
Sing sweetly for tobacco.
Tobacco is like love, oh love it;
For you see I have proved it.

[*Fain would I change that note*]

Fain would I change that note
  To which fond love hath
    charmed me,
Long, long to sing by rote,
  Fancying that that harmed me.
Yet when this thought doth come,
Love is the perfect sum
  Of all delight,
I have no other choice
Either for pen or voice,
  To sing or write.   10

O love, they wrong thee much
  That say thy sweet is bit-
    ter;
When thy ripe fruit is such
  As nothing can be sweeter.
Fair house of joy and bliss
Where truest pleasure is,
  I do adore thee.
I know thee what thou art,
I serve thee with my heart
  And fall before thee.   20

From Michael East's *Second Set of Madrigals*, 1606

[*O metaphysical tobacco*]

O metaphysical tobacco,
Fetched as far as from Morocco,
  Thy searching fume
  Exhales the rheum,
O metaphysical tobacco.

From John Cooper's *Funeral Tears, for the death of the Right Honorable the Earl of Devonshire,* 1606

[*Oft thou hast*]

Oft thou hast with greedy ear
  Drunk my notes and words of
    pleasure;
  In affection's equal measure
Now my songs of sorrow hear,
  Since from thee my griefs do
    grow,
Whom alive I prized so dear:
  The more my joy, the more my
    woe.

Music, though it sweetens pain,
  Yet no whit impairs lament-
    ing,
  But in passions like consenting 10
Makes them constant that com-
    plain,
  And enchants their fancies so
That all comforts they disdain,
  And fly from joy to dwell with
    woe.

From Tobias Hume's *Poetical Music,* 1607

The hunting song

Come, come my hearts, a-hunting let us wend,
That echoing cries the hills and heavens may rend
    With shouts and sounds
    Of horns and hounds.

Why then, my lads, uncouple
Kill-buck, keen Ringwood and Roler,
    Chanter and Joler,
    Trouncer and Drummer,
    Bowman and Gunner.
Actæon's hounds were ne'er like these, I ween.   10

The stag is now roused, the game is on foot.
    Hark! hark! beauty Dainty prates.
The cry is full. Hark! how they hold the cry;
    But soft, the huntsmen rates!
    Clowder hunts counter
    And so doth Mounter,
    They're all at fault.
    Hark! Ringwood spends
    And makes amends.
        List of Joler,   20
        That's he, ho! ho!
        Joler crossed it,
        Else we had lost it.
    The buck is quite spent,
    Since to soil he went.

Why, heavenlier sport than this there cannot be.
    See, Plowman hath pinched,
    And Joler ne'er flinched.
Now with full cry they all come, frowling, trowling to the fall.
    Wind the morte!   30
    O well done there, boys!
All other sports to these are but toys.

FROM ROBERT JONES'S *Ultimum Vale*, 1608

[*Think'st thou, Kate?*]

Think'st thou, Kate, to put me
    down
With a no or with a frown?
Since love holds my heart in bands,
I must do as love commands.

Love commands the hands to dare
When the tongue of speech is
    spare;
Chiefest lesson in love's school,
Put it in adventure, fool.

Fools are they that fainting flinch
For a squeak, a scratch, a pinch.   10
Women's words have double sense,
Stand away, a simple fence.

If thy mistress swears she'll cry,
Fear her not; she'll swear and lie.
Such sweet oaths no sorrow bring
Till the prick of conscience
    sting.

FROM THOMAS WEELKES'S *Airs or Fantastic Spirits*, 1608

[*Though my carriage*]

Though my carriage be but careless,
    Though my looks be of the sternest,
Yet my passions are compareless;
    When I love, I love in earnest.

No, my wits are not so wild,
    But a gentle soul may yoke me;
Nor my heart so hard compiled,
    But it melts if love provoke me.

FROM JOHN WILBYE'S *Second Set of Madrigals*, 1609

[*Ye that do live in pleasures*]

Ye that do live in pleasures plenty,
    And dwell in music's sweetest airs,
Whose eyes are quick, whose ears are dainty,
    Not clogged with earth or worldly cares,
Come sing this song made in Amphion's praise,
Who now is dead, yet you his fame can raise.

Call him again, let him not die,
    But live in music's sweetest breath.
Place him in fairest memory,
    And let him triumph over death.   10
Oh, sweetly sung! his living wish attend ye.
These were his words: The mirth of heaven God send ye.

[*Draw on, sweet night*]

Draw on, sweet night, best friend unto those cares
    That do arise from painful melancholy.
My life so ill through want of comfort fares,
    That unto thee I consecrate it wholly.

Sweet night, draw on! my griefs, when they be told
    To shades and darkness, find some ease from paining;
And while thou all in silence dost enfold,
    I then shall have best time for my complaining.

FROM ROBERT JONES'S *Muses' Garden for Delights*, 1610

[*The sea hath many thousands sands*]

The sea hath many thousands
    sands,
  The sun hath motes as many,
The sky is full of stars, and love
    As full of woes as any.
Believe me, that do know the elf,
And make no trial by thyself.

It is in truth a pretty toy
  For babes to play withal;
But oh, the honeys of our youth
  Are oft our age's gall.   10

Self proof in time will make thee
    know
He was a prophet told thee so,

A prophet that Cassandra-like
  Tells truth without belief,
For headstrong youth will run his
    race
  Although his goal be grief.
Love's martyr, when his heat is
    past,
Proves care's confessor at the last.

[*Once did my thoughts*]

Once did my thoughts both ebb
    and flow,
  As passion did them move;
Once did I hope, straight fear
    again,
  And then I was in love.

Once did I waking spend the night,
  And told how many minutes
    move,
Once did I wishing waste the day,
  And then I was in love.

Once by my carving true love's
    knot,
  The weeping trees did prove   10
That wounds and tears were both
    our lots,
  And then I was in love.

Once did I breathe another's
    breath,
  And in my mistress move;
Once was I not mine own at all,
  And then I was in love.

Once wore I bracelets made of hair,
  And collars did approve,
Once were my clothes made out of
    wax,
  And then I was in love.   20

Once did I sonnet to my saint,
  My soul in number moved,
Once did I tell a thousand lies,
  And then in truth I loved.

Once in my ear did dangling hang
  A little turtle-dove,
Once, in a word, I was a fool,
  And then I was in love.

FROM ORLANDO GIBBONS'S *First Set of Madrigals and Motets*, 1612

[*The silver swan*]

The silver swan, who living had no note,
  When death approached, unlocked her silent throat;

Leaning her breast against the reedy shore,
Thus sung her first and last, and sung no more.
Farewell, all joys; O death, come close mine eyes;
More geese than swans now live, more fools than wise.

[Dainty fine bird]

Dainty fine bird that art encagëd there,
Alas, how like thine and my fortunes are.
Both prisoners be; and both singing, thus
Strive to please her that hath imprisoned us.
Only thus we differ, thou and I:
Thou liv'st singing, but I sing and die.

[Ah, dear heart]

Ah, dear heart, why do you rise?
The light that shines comes from your eyes.
The day breaks not, it is my heart,
To think that you and I must part.
O stay, or else my joys will die
And perish in their infancy.

From John Dowland's *Pilgrim's Solace*, 1612

[In this trembling shadow]

In this trembling shadow cast
    From those boughs which thy wings shake,
Far from human troubles placed,
    Songs to the Lord would I make.
    Darkness from my mind then take;
For thy rites none may begin
Till they feel thy light within.

As I sing, sweet flowers I'll strow
    From the fruitful valleys brought;
Praising him by whom they grow,
    Him that heaven and earth hath wrought,
    Him that all things framed of nought,
Him that all for man did make,
But made man for his own sake.

Music, all thy sweetness lend
    While of his high power I speak,

On whom all powers else depend;
   But my breast is now too weak,
   Trumpets shrill the air should break.
All in vain my sounds I raise,   20
Boundless power asks boundless praise.

From Thomas Bateson's *Second Set of Madrigals*, 1618

[*I heard a noise*]

I heard a noise and wishëd for a sight;
   I looked aside and did a shadow see
Whose substance was the sum of my delight;
   It came unseen and so it went from me.
But yet conceit persuaded my intent
There was a substance where the shadow went.
I did not play Narcissus in conceit,
   I did not see my shadow in a spring;
I knew my eyes were dimmed with no deceit,
For as I saw the shadow passing by,   10
I had a glance of something in my eye.
Shadow, or she, or both, or choose you whether,
Blest be the thing that brought the shadow hither.

From Martin Peerson's *Private Music*, 1620

[*Can a maid that is well bred*]

Can a maid that is well bred,
Hath a blush so lovely red,
Modest looks, wise, mild, discreet,
And a nature passing sweet,
Break her promise, untrue prove,
On a sudden change her love,
Or be won e'er to neglect
Him to whom she vowed re-
    spect?

Such a maid, alas, I know.
Oh, that weeds 'mongst corn
   should grow,   10
Or a rose should prickles have,

Wounding where she ought to
   save!
I that did her parts extol,
Will my lavish tongue control.
Outward parts do blind the eyes,
Gall in golden pills oft lies.

Reason, wake, and sleep no more,
Land upon some safer shore;
Think on her and be afraid
Of a faithless fickle maid.   20
Of a faithless fickle maid
Thus true love is still betrayed.
Yet it is some ease to sing
That a maid is light of wing.

From Thomas Tomkins's *Songs of three, four, five, and six parts,* 1622

[*Our hasty life*]

Our hasty life away doth post
Before we know what we have lost.

Hours into days, days into years are gone,
Years make a life, which straight is none.
Thus soon is man's short story told,
We scarce are young, when we are waxëd old.

FROM JOHN ATTEY's *First Book of Airs*, 1622

[*On a time*]

On a time the amorous Silvy
Said to her shepherd, Sweet, how do you?
Kiss me this once, and then God b' wi' you,
　　　　　My sweetest dear!
Kiss me this once, and then God b' wi' you,
For now the morning draweth near.

With that, her fairest bosom showing,
Opening her lips, rich perfumes blowing,
She said, Now kiss me and be going,
　　　　　My sweetest dear!　　　　10
Kiss me this once and then be going,
For now the morning draweth near.

With that the shepherd waked from sleeping,
And spying where the day was peeping,
He said, Now take my soul in keeping,
　　　　　My sweetest dear!
Kiss me, and take my soul in keeping,
Since I must go, now day is near.

FROM *Christ Church Ms. K 3*

[*Yet if his majesty*]

Yet if his majesty, our sovereign lord,
Should of his own accord
Friendly himself invite,
And say, I'll be your guest to-morrow night,
How should we stir ourselves, call and command
All hands to work! Let no man idle stand!
Set me fine Spanish tables in the hall;
See they be fitted all;
Let there be room to eat,
And order taken that there want no meat.　　10
See every sconce and candlestick made bright,
That without tapers they may give a light.
Look to the presence; are the carpets spread,

The dais o'er the head,
The cushions in the chairs,
And all the candles lighted on the stairs?
Perfume the chambers, and in any case
Let each man give attendance in his place.
Thus if the king were coming would we do,
And 'twere good reason too;   20
For 'tis a duteous thing
To show all honor to an earthly king,
And after all our travail and our cost,
So he be pleased, to think no labor lost.
But at the coming of the King of Heaven
All's set at six and seven;
We wallow in our sin;
Christ cannot find a chamber in the inn.
We entertain him always like a stranger,
And as at first still lodge him in the manger.   30

FROM JOHN PLAYFORD'S *Select Musical Airs and Dialogues*, 1653

[*When, Celia, I intend*]

When, Celia, I intend to flatter you,
And tell you lies to make you true,
   I swear
  There's none so fair—
  And you believe it too.

Oft have I matched you with the rose, and said
No twins so like hath nature made;
   But 'tis
  Only in this—
  You prick my hand, and fade.   10

Oft have I said there is no precious stone
But may be found in you alone;
   Though I
  No stone espy—
  Unless your heart be one.

When I praise your skin, I quote the wool
That silkworms from their entrails pull,
   And show
  That new-fall'n snow
  Is not more beautiful.   20

Yet grow not proud by such hyperboles;
Were you as excellent as these,
            Whilst I
        Before you lie,
        They might be had with ease.

FROM HENRY LAWES's *Airs and Dialogues*, 1653

Love above beauty

Lovely Chloris, though thine eyes
Far outshine the jewels of the skies,
That grace which all admire in
    thee,
No, nor the beauties of thy breast,
Which far outblaze the rest,
    Might e'er comparèd be
    To my fidelity.

Those alluring smiles that place
An eternal April on thy face,
Such as no sun did ever see,   10
No, nor the treasures of thy breast,
Which far outblaze the rest,
    Might e'er comparèd be
    To my fidelity.
                    [*Henry Reynolds*]

FROM HENRY LAWES's *Airs and Dialogues*, 1655

[*Was it a form?*]

Was it a form, a gait, a grace,
    Was it their sweetness merely?
Was it the heaven of a bright face,
    That made me love so dearly?

Was it a skin of silk and snow,
    That soul and senses wounded?
Was 't any of these, or all of these,
    Whereon my faith was founded?

Ah, no! 'Twas a far deeper part
    Than all the rest that won me;   10
'Twas a fair-clothed but feigning heart
    I loved, and has undone me.

                    [*Henry Reynolds*]

FROM JOHN WILSON's *Cheerful Airs or Ballads*, 1660

[*Greedy lover, pause awhile*]

Greedy lover, pause awhile,
And remember that a smile
    Heretofore

Would have made thy hopes a
    feast;
Which is more,

Since thy diet was increased,
　Than both looks and language
　　too,
　Or the face itself can do.

Such a province is my hand
As, if thou couldst command　　10
　Heretofore,
There thy lips would seem to
　dwell;
　Which is more,
Ever since they sped so well,
　Than they can be brought to do
By my neck and bosom too.

If the center of my breast,
A dominion unpossessed
　Heretofore,
May thy wand'ring thoughts
　suffice,　　20
　Seek no more,
And my heart shall be thy prize;

So thou keep above the line,
　All the hemisphere is thine.

If the flames of love were pure,
Which by oath thou didst assure
　Heretofore,
Gold that goes into the clear
　Shines the more
When it leaves again the fire;　30
　Let not then those looks of thine
　Blemish what they should refine.

I have cast into the fire
Almost all thou couldst desire
　Heretofore,
But I see thou art to crave
　More and more.
Should I cast in all I have,
　So that were I ne'er so free,
　Thou wouldst burn, though not
　　for me.　　40

[Sir Albertus Morton]

THOMAS CAMPION

The Introduction and Notes are at page 983

FROM *A Book of Airs,* 1601

To the Reader.

What epigrams are in poetry, the same are airs in music: then in their chief perfection when they are short and well seasoned. But to clog a light song with a long præludium is to corrupt the nature of it. Many rests in music were invented either for necessity of the fugue, or granted as an harmonical license in songs of many parts; but in airs I find no use they have, unless it be to make a vulgar and trivial modulation seem to the ignorant strange, and to the judicial tedious. A naked air without guide, or prop, or color but his own, is easily censured of every ear, and requires so much the more invention to make it please. And as Martial speaks in defence of his short epigrams, so may I say in th' apology of airs, that where there is a full volume there can be no imputation of shortness. The lyric poets among the Greeks and Latins were first inventors of airs, tying themselves strictly to the number and value of their syllables, of which sort you shall find

*here only one song in Sapphic verse; the rest are after the fashion
of the time, ear-pleasing rhymes without art. The subject of them is,
for the most part, amorous; and why not amorous songs as well as
amorous attires? Or why not new airs as well as new fashions?* . . .

FROM *Two Books of Airs,* [*c.* 1613]

To the Reader.

. . . *These airs were for the most part framed at first for one voice
with the lute, or viol, but upon occasion they have since been filled
with more parts, which whoso please may use, who like not may leave.
Yet do we daily observe that when any shall sing a treble to an instrument, the standers-by will be offering at an inward part out of
their own nature; and, true or false, out it must, though to the per-
verting of the whole harmony. Also, if we consider well, the treble
tunes (which are with us commonly called airs) are but tenors mounted
eight notes higher, and therefore an inward part must needs well become them, such as may take up the whole distance of the diapason, and
fill up the gaping between the two extreme parts; whereby though they
are not three parts in perfection, yet they yield a sweetness and content both to the ear and mind, which is the aim and perfection of music.
Short airs, if they be skillfully framed and naturally expressed, are like
quick and good epigrams in poesy, many of them showing as much
artifice, and breeding as great difficulty as a larger poem. Non omnia
possumus omnes, said the Roman epic poet. But some there are who
admit only French or Italian airs, as if every country had not his
proper air, which the people thereof naturally usurp in their music.
Others taste nothing that comes forth in print, as if Catullus' or
Martial's epigrams were the worse for being published. In these English airs, I have chiefly aimed to couple my words and notes lovingly
together, which will be much for him to do that hath not power over
both. The light of this will best appear to him who hath peised our
monosyllables and syllables combined, both of which are so loaded
with consonants as that they will hardly keep company with swift notes,
or give the vowel convenient liberty. To conclude; mine own opinion
of these songs I deliver thus:*

Omnia nec nostris bona sunt, sed nec mala libris;
Si placet hac cantes, hac quoque lege legas.

Farewell.

FROM ROBERT JONES'S *Second Book of Songs and Airs,* 1601

[*My love bound me*]

My love bound me with a kiss
   That I should no longer stay;
When I felt so sweet a bliss

I had less power to pass away.
Alas! that women do not know
Kisses make men loath to go.

Yet she knows it but too well,
 For I heard when Venus' dove
In her ear did softly tell
 That kisses were the seals of
  love.   10
Oh, muse not then though it be so,
Kisses make men loath to go.

Wherefore did she thus inflame
 My desires, heat my blood,
Instantly to quench the same
 And starve whom she had given
  food?

I the common sense can show:
Kisses make men loath to go.

Had she bid me go at first
 It would ne'er have grieved my
  heart;   20
Hope delayed had been the worst.
 But ah! to kiss and then to
  part!
How deep it struck; speak, gods,
 you know
Kisses make men loath to go.

FROM RICHARD ALISON'S *An Hour's Recreation in Music*, 1606

[*What if a day*]

What if a day, or a month, or a year
Crown thy delights with a thousand sweet contentings?
Cannot a chance of a night or an hour
Cross thy desires with as many sad tormentings?
 Fortune, honor, beauty, youth
 Are but blossoms dying;
 Wanton pleasure, doting love
 Are but shadows flying.
 All our joys are but toys,
 Idle thoughts deceiving;   10
 None have power of an hour
 In their lives' bereaving.

Earth's but a point to the world, and a man
Is but a point to the world's comparëd centure;
Shall then the point of a point be so vain
As to triumph in a seely point's adventure?
 All is hazard that we have,
 There is nothing biding;
 Days of pleasure are like streams
 Through fair meadows gliding.   20
 Weal and woe, time doth go,
 Time is never turning;
 Secret fates guide our states,
 Both in mirth and mourning.

FROM *A Book of Airs*, 1601

[*My sweetest Lesbia*]

My sweetest Lesbia, let us live and love,
And though the sager sort our deeds reprove,
Let us not weigh them. Heav'n's great lamps do dive
Into their west, and straight again revive,
But soon as once set is our little light,
Then must we sleep one ever-during night.

If all would lead their lives in love like me,
Then bloody swords and armor should not be;
No drum nor trumpet peaceful sleeps should move,
Unless alarm came from the camp of love.   10
But fools do live, and waste their little light,
And seek with pain their ever-during night.

When timely death my life and fortune ends,
Let not my hearse be vexed with mourning friends,
But let all lovers, rich in triumph, come
And with sweet pastimes grace my happy tomb;
And Lesbia, close up thou my little light,
And crown with love my ever-during night.

[*When to her lute Corinna sings*]

When to her lute Corinna sings,
Her voice revives the leaden strings,
And doth in highest notes appear
As any challenged echo clear;
But when she doth of mourning speak,
Ev'n with her sighs the strings do break.

And as her lute doth live or die,
Led by her passion, so must I:
For when of pleasure she doth sing,
My thoughts enjoy a sudden spring,   10
But if she doth of sorrow speak,
Ev'n from my heart the strings do break.

[*Follow your saint*]

Follow your saint, follow with accents sweet;
Haste you, sad notes, fall at her flying feet.
There, wrapped in cloud of sorrow, pity move,
And tell the ravisher of my soul I perish for her love.

But if she scorns my never-ceasing pain,
Then burst with sighing in her sight and ne'er return again.

All that I sung still to her praise did tend,
Still she was first, still she my songs did end.
Yet she my love and music both doth fly,
The music that her echo is and beauty's sympathy.   10
Then let my notes pursue her scornful flight:
It shall suffice that they were breathed and died for her delight.

[*Thou art not fair*]

Thou art not fair for all thy red and white,
    For all those rosy ornaments in thee;
Thou art not sweet, though made of mere delight,
    Nor fair nor sweet, unless you pity me.
I will not soothe thy fancies; thou shalt prove
That beauty is no beauty without love.

Yet love not me, nor seek thou to allure
    My thoughts with beauty, were it more divine;
Thy smiles and kisses I cannot endure,
    I'll not be wrapped up in those arms of thine.   10
Now show it, if thou be a woman right,—
Embrace, and kiss, and love me in despite.

[*The man of life upright*]

The man of life upright,
    Whose guiltless heart is free
From all dishonest deeds,
    Or thought of vanity;

The man whose silent days
    In harmless joys are spent,
Whom hopes cannot delude,
    Nor sorrow discontent;

That man needs neither towers
    Nor armor for defence,   10
Nor secret vaults to fly
    From thunder's violence.

He only can behold
    With unaffrighted eyes
The horrors of the deep
    And terrors of the skies.

Thus, scorning all the cares
    That fate or fortune brings,
He makes the heav'n his book,
    His wisdom heav'nly things,   20

Good thoughts his only friends,
    His wealth a well-spent age,
The earth his sober inn
    And quiet pilgrimage.

[*Hark, all you ladies*]

Hark, all you ladies that do sleep!
    The fairy queen Proserpina
Bids you awake and pity them that
    weep.

You may do in the dark
    What the day doth forbid;
Fear not the dogs that bark,
    Night will have all hid.

But if you let your lovers moan,
The fairy queen Proserpina
Will send abroad her fairies ev'ry
        one,   10
    That shall pinch black and blue
        Your white hands and fair
            arms
    That did not kindly rue
        Your paramours' harms.

In myrtle arbors on the downs
    The fairy queen Proserpina,
This night by moonshine leading
        merry rounds,
    Holds a watch with sweet love,
        Down the dale, up the hill;
    No plaints or groans may move
        Their holy vigil.   21

All you that will hold watch with
        love,
    The fairy queen Proserpina
Will make you fairer than Dione's
        dove;
    Roses red, lilies white,
        And the clear damask hue,
    Shall on your cheeks alight;
        Love will adorn you.

All you that love, or loved before,
    The fairy queen Proserpina   30
Bids you increase that loving
        humor more;
    They that yet have not fed
        On delight amorous,
    She vows that they shall lead
        Apes in Avernus.

[*When thou must home*]

When thou must home to shades of underground,
    And there arrived, a new admirèd guest,
The beauteous spirits do engirt thee round,
    White Iope, blithe Helen, and the rest,
To hear the stories of thy finished love
From that smooth tongue whose music hell can move,

Then wilt thou speak of banqueting delights,
    Of masks and revels which sweet youth did make,
Of tourneys and great challenges of knights,
    And all these triumphs for thy beauty's sake;   10
When thou hast told these honors done to thee,
Then tell, O tell, how thou didst murder me.

FROM *Observations in the Art of English Poesy,* 1602

[*Rose-cheeked Laura*]

Rose-cheeked Laura, come,
Sing thou smoothly with thy
        beauty's
Silent music, either other
        Sweetly gracing.

Lovely forms do flow
From concent divinely framèd;
Heav'n is music, and thy beau-
        ty's
        Birth is heavenly.

These dull notes we sing
Discords need for helps to grace
    them;   10
Only beauty purely loving
    Knows no discord,

But still moves delight,
Like clear springs renewed by
    flowing,
Ever perfect, ever in them-
    Selves eternal.

FROM *Two Books of Airs*, [*c.* 1613]

[*To music bent*]

To music bent is my retirèd mind,
    And fain would I some song of pleasure sing,
But in vain joys no comfort now I find;
    From heav'nly thoughts all true delight doth spring.
Thy power, O God, thy mercies, to record,
Will sweeten ev'ry note and ev'ry word.

All earthly pomp or beauty to express,
    Is but to carve in snow, on waves to write.
Celestial things, though men conceive them less,
    Yet fullest are they in themselves of light;   10
Such beams they yield as know no means to die,
Such heat they cast as lifts the spirit high.

[*Never weather-beaten sail*]

Never weather-beaten sail more willing bent to shore,
Never tired pilgrim's limbs affected slumber more
Than my wearied sprite now longs to fly out of my troubled breast.
O come quickly, sweetest Lord, and take my soul to rest.

Ever-blooming are the joys of heav'n's high paradise,
Cold age deafs not there our ears, nor vapor dims our eyes;
Glory there the sun outshines, whose beams the blessed only see;
O come quickly, glorious Lord, and raise my sprite to thee.

[*Jack and Joan*]

Jack and Joan they think no ill,
But loving live, and merry still;
Do their week-days' work and
    pray
Devoutly on the holy day;
Skip and trip it on the green,
And help to choose the summer
    queen;
Lash out, at a country feast,
Their silver penny with the best.

Well can they judge of nappy ale,
And tell at large a winter tale;   10
Climb up to the apple loft,
And turn the crabs till they be
    soft.
Tib is all the father's joy,
And little Tom the mother's boy.
All their pleasure is content,
And care, to pay their yearly
    rent.

Joan can call by name her cows,
And deck her windows with green
     boughs;
She can wreaths and tutties make,
And trim with plums a bridal
     cake.   20
Jack knows what brings gain or
     loss,
And his long flail can stoutly toss;
Make the hedge, which others
     break,
And ever thinks what he doth
     speak.

Now, you courtly dames and
     knights,
That study only strange de-
     lights,
Though you scorn the home-spun
     gray,
And revel in your rich array;
Though your tongues dissemble
     deep,
And can your heads from danger
     keep;   30
Yet for all your pomp and train,
Securer lives the silly swain.

[*Give beauty all her right*]

Give beauty all her right,
She's not to one form tied;
Each shape yields fair delight,
Where her perfections bide.
Helen, I grant, might pleasing
     be,
And Ros'mond was as sweet as she.

Some the quick eye commends;
Some swelling lips and red;
Pale looks have many friends,
Through   sacred   sweetness
     bred.   10

Meadows have flowers that pleas-
     ure move,
Though roses are the flowers of
     love.

Free beauty is not bound
To one unmovèd clime;
She visits ev'ry ground,
And favors ev'ry time.
Let the old loves with mine com-
     pare,
My sov'reign is as sweet and
     fair.

From *The Late Royal Entertainment . . . at Cawsome House*, 1613

[*Night as well as brightest day*]

Night as well as brightest day hath her delight.
Let us then with mirth and music deck the night;
     Never did glad day such store
          Of joy to night bequeath;
     Her stars then adore,
          Both in heav'n, and here beneath.

Love and beauty, mirth and music yield true joys,
Though the cynics in their folly count them toys;
     Raise your spirits ne'er so high,
          They will be apt to fall;   10
     None brave thoughts envý
          Who had e'er brave thought at all.

Joy is the sweet friend of life, the nurse of blood,
Patron of all health, and fountain of all good.
　　Never may joy hence depart,
　　　　But all your thoughts attend;
　　Nought can hurt the heart,
　　　　That retains so sweet a friend.

FROM *The Third and Fourth Book of Airs,* [*c.* 1617]

To the Reader.

*The apothecaries have books of gold whose leaves, being opened,
are so light as that they are subject to be shaken with the least breath,
yet rightly handled, they serve both for ornament and use; such are
light airs. But if any squeamish stomachs shall check at two or three
vain ditties in the end of this book, let them pour off the clearest and
leave those as dregs in the bottom. Howsoever, if they be but conferred
with the* Canterbury Tales *of that venerable poet, Chaucer, they will
then appear toothsome enough. Some words are in these books which
have been clothed in music by others, and I am content they then
served their turn; yet give me now leave to make use of mine own.
Likewise you may find here some three or four songs that have been
published before, but for them, I refer you to the players' bill, that is
styled,* newly revived, with additions, *for you shall find all of them reformed, either in words or notes. To be brief, all these songs are mine,
if you express them well, otherwise they are your own. Farewell.*

　　　　　　　　Yours, as you are his,
　　　　　　　　　　Thomas Campion.

[*Maids are simple*]

Maids are simple, some men say,
They, forsooth, will trust no men.
But should they men's wills obey,
Maids were very simple then.

Safer may we credit give
To a faithless wand'ring Jew, [10]
Than a young man's vows believe
When he swears his love is true.

Truth a rare flower now is grown,
Few men wear it in their hearts;
Lovers are more easily known
By their follies than deserts.

Love they make a poor blind child,
But let none trust such as he;
Rather than to be beguiled,
Ever let me simple be.

[*Now winter nights enlarge*]

Now winter nights enlarge
　The number of their hours,
And clouds their storms discharge
　Upon the airy towers.

Let now the chimneys blaze
　And cups o'erflow with wine;
Let well-tuned words amaze
　With harmony divine.

Now yellow waxen lights
  Shall wait on honey love, 10
While youthful revels, masks, and
    courtly sights
Sleep's leaden spells remove.

This time doth well dispense
  With lovers' long discourse;
Much speech hath some defence,
  Though beauty no remorse.

All do not all things well:
  Some measures comely tread;
Some knotted riddles tell;
  Some poems smoothly read. 20
The summer hath his joys,
  And winter his delights;
Though love and all his pleasures
    are but toys,
  They shorten tedious nights.

[Thrice toss these oaken ashes]

Thrice toss these oaken ashes in the air,
Thrice sit thou mute in this enchanted chair,
Then thrice three times tie up this true love's knot,
And murmur soft, She will, or she will not.

Go burn these pois'nous weeds in yon blue fire,
These screech-owl's feathers and this prickling brier,
This cypress gathered at a dead man's grave,
That all thy fears and cares an end may have.

Then come, you fairies, dance with me a round;
Melt her hard heart with your melodious sound. 10
In vain are all the charms I can devise:
She hath an art to break them with her eyes.

[Never love unless you can]

Never love unless you can
Bear with all the faults of man;
Men sometimes will jealous be,
Though but little cause they see,
  And hang the head, as discontent,
  And speak what straight they will repent.

Men that but one saint adore
Make a show of love to more;
Beauty must be scorned in none,
Though but truly served in one;
  For what is courtship but disguise? 10
  True hearts may have dissembling eyes.

Men when their affairs require
Must a while themselves retire,
Sometimes hunt, and sometimes hawk,

And not ever sit and talk.
If these and such like you can bear,
Then like, and love, and never fear.

[*Respect my faith*]

Respect my faith, regard my service past;
The hope you winged call home to you at last.
Great prize it is that I in you shall gain,
So great for you hath been my loss and pain.
    My wits I spent and time for you alone,
    Observing you and losing all for one.

Some raised to rich estates in this time are,
That held their hopes to mine inferior far;
Such, scoffing me, or pitying me, say thus,
Had he not loved, he might have lived like us.   10
    O then, dear sweet, for love and pity's sake
    My faith reward, and from me scandal take.

[*There is a garden*]

There is a garden in her face,
Where roses and white lilies grow;
    A heav'nly paradise is that place,
Wherein all pleasant fruits do flow.
    There cherries grow which none may buy
    Till cherry-ripe themselves do cry.

Those cherries fairly do enclose
Of orient pearl a double row,
    Which when her lovely laughter shows,
They look like rosebuds filled with snow.   10
    Yet them nor peer nor prince can buy,
    Till cherry-ripe themselves do cry.

Her eyes like angels watch them still;
Her brows like bended bows do stand,
    Threat'ning with piercing frowns to kill
All that attempt with eye or hand
    Those sacred cherries to come nigh,
    Till cherry-ripe themselves do cry.

[*Young and simple though I am*]

Young and simple though I am,   Men desire when they do kiss.
I have heard of Cupid's name;   Smoke can never burn, they say,
Guess I can what thing it is   But the flames that follow may.

I am not so foul or fair
To be proud, nor to despair;
Yet my lips have oft observed,
Men that kiss them press them
   hard,   10
  As glad lovers use to do
  When their new-met loves they
    woo.

Faith, 'tis but a foolish mind,
Yet methinks a heat I find,
Like thirst-longing, that doth bide
Ever on my weaker side,
  Where they say my heart doth
    move.
  Venus, grant it be not love.

If it be, alas, what then?
Were not women made for men?
As good 'twere a thing were
   past,   21
That must needs be done at last.
  Roses that are over-blown
  Grow less sweet, then fall alone.

Yet nor churl nor silken gull
Shall my maiden blossom pull;
Who shall not I soon can tell,
Who shall, would I could as
   well;
  This I know, whoe'er he be,
  Love he must, or flatter me.   30

[Fain would I wed]

Fain would I wed a fair young man that night and day could
   please me,
When my mind or body grieved that had the power to ease me.
Maids are full of longing thoughts that breed a bloodless sickness,
And that, oft I hear men say, is only cured by quickness.
Oft I have been wooed and praised, but never could be movëd;
Many for a day or so I have most dearly lovëd,
But this foolish mind of mine straight loathes the thing resolvëd;
If to love be sin in me, that sin is soon absolvëd.
Sure I think I shall at last fly to some holy order;
When I once am settled there, then can I fly no farther.   10
Yet I would not die a maid, because I had a mother,
As I was by one brought forth, I would bring forth another.

JOHN DONNE

The Introduction and Notes are at page 985

FROM *Poems*, 1633

SONGS AND SONNETS

Love's deity

I long to talk with some old lover's ghost,
  Who died before the god of love was born:
I cannot think that he, who then loved most,
  Sunk so low as to love one which did scorn.
But since this god produced a destiny,

And that vice-nature, custom, lets it be,
    I must love her that loves not me.

Sure, they which made him god meant not so much,
    Nor he in his young godhead practised it;
But when an even flame two hearts did touch,   10
    His office was indulgently to fit
Actives to passives. Correspondency
Only his subject was; it cannot be
    Love, till I love her that loves me.

But every modern god will now extend
    His vast prerogative as far as Jove.
To rage, to lust, to write to, to commend,
    All is the purlieu of the god of love.
Oh, were we wakened by this tyranny
To ungod this child again, it could not be   20
    I should love her, who loves not me.

Rebel and atheist too, why murmur I,
    As though I felt the worst that love could do?
Love may make me leave loving, or might try
    A deeper plague, to make her love me too,
Which, since she loves before, I'am loath to see;
Falsehood is worse than hate; and that must be,
    If she whom I love, should love me.

Song

Go and catch a falling star,
    Get with child a mandrake root,
Tell me where all past years are,
    Or who cleft the devil's foot,
Teach me to hear mermaids singing,
    Or to keep off envy's stinging,
            And find
            What wind
Serves to advance an honest mind.

If thou beest born to strange sights,   10
    Things invisible to see,
Ride ten thousand days and nights,
    Till age snow white hairs on thee,
Thou, when thou return'st, wilt tell me
All strange wonders that befell thee,
            And swear
            No where
Lives a woman true, and fair.

If thou find'st one, let me know,
    Such a pilgrimage were sweet;   20
Yet do not, I would not go,
    Though at next door we might meet;
Though she were true when you met her,
And last till you write your letter,
      Yet she
      Will be
False, ere I come, to two or three.

Woman's constancy

Now thou hast loved me one whole day,
To-morrow when thou leav'st, what wilt thou say?
Wilt thou then antedate some new-made vow?
    Or say that now
We are not just those persons which we were?
Or, that oaths made in reverential fear
Of love, and his wrath, any may forswear?
Or, as true deaths true marriages untie,
So lovers' contracts, images of those,
Bind but till sleep, death's image, them unloose?   10
    Or, your own end to justify,
For having purposed change and falsehood, you
Can have no way but falsehood to be true?
Vain lunatic, against these scapes I could
    Dispute and conquer, if I would;
    Which I abstain to do,
For by to-morrow, I may think so too.

The indifferent

I can love both fair and brown,
Her whom abundance melts, and her whom want betrays,
Her who loves loneness best, and her who masks and plays,
Her whom the country formed, and whom the town,
Her who believes, and her who tries,
Her who still weeps with spongy eyes,
And her who is dry cork, and never cries;
I can love her and her, and you and you,
I can love any, so she be not true.

Will no other vice content you?   10
Will it not serve your turn to do as did your mothers?
Or have you all old vices spent, and now would find out others?
Or doth a fear that men are true, torment you?
Oh, we are not, be not you so,

Let me, and do you, twenty know.
Rob me, but bind me not, and let me go.
Must I, who came to travail thorough you,
Grow your fixed subject, because you are true?

Venus heard me sigh this song,
And by love's sweetest part, variety, she swore,   20
She heard not this till now, and that it should be so no more.
She went, examined, and returned ere long,
And said, Alas, some two or three
Poor heretics in love there be,
Which think to 'stablish dangerous constancy.
But I have told them, Since you will be true,
You shall be true to them who'are false to you.

The flea

Mark but this flea, and mark in this,
How little that which thou deny'st me is;
It sucked me first, and now sucks thee,
And in this flea our two bloods mingled be;
Thou know'st that this cannot be said
A sin, nor shame, nor loss of maidenhead;
    Yet this enjoys before it woo,
    And pampered swells with one blood made of two,
    And this, alas, is more than we would do.

Oh stay, three lives in one flea spare,   10
Where we almost, yea, more than married are.
This flea is you and I, and this
Our marriage bed, and marriage temple is;
Though parents grudge, and you, w' are met,
And cloistered in these living walls of jet.
    Though use make you apt to kill me,
    Let not to that, self-murder added be,
    And sacrilege, three sins in killing three.

Cruel and sudden, hast thou since
Purpled thy nail in blood of innocence?   20
Wherein could this flea guilty be,
Except in that drop which it sucked from thee?
Yet thou triumph'st and say'st that thou
Find'st not thyself, nor me the weaker now;
    'Tis true, then learn how false fears be:
    Just so much honor, when thou yield'st to me,
    Will waste, as this flea's death took life from thee.

The message

Send home my long strayed eyes to me,
Which, oh, too long have dwelt on thee;
Yet since there they have learned such ill,
   Such forced fashions,
   And false passions,
     That they be
     Made by thee
Fit for no good sight, keep them still.

Send home my harmless heart again,
Which no unworthy thought could stain;
Which if it be taught by thine
   To make jestings
   Of protestings,
     And break both
     Word and oath,
Keep it, for then 'tis none of mine.

Yet send me back my heart and eyes
That I may know and see thy lies,
And may laugh and joy, when thou
   Art in anguish
   And dost languish
     For some one
     That will none,
Or prove as false as thou art now.

The bait

Come live with me, and be my love,
And we will some new pleasures prove,
Of golden sands, and crystal brooks,
With silken lines, and silver hooks.

There will the river whispering run,
Warmed by thy eyes more than the sun.
And there the'enamoured fish will stay,
Begging themselves they may betray.

When thou wilt swim in that live bath,
Each fish, which every channel hath,
Will amorously to thee swim,
Gladder to catch thee, than thou him.

If thou, to be so seen, beest loath,
By sun or moon, thou dark'nest both;
And if myself have leave to see,
I need not their light, having thee.

Let others freeze with angling reeds,
And cut their legs with shells and weeds,
Or treacherously poor fish beset
With strangling snare, or windowy net.   20

Let coarse bold hands from slimy nest
The bedded fish in banks out-wrest,
Or curious traitors, sleave-silk flies,
Bewitch poor fishes' wand'ring eyes.

For thee, thou need'st no such deceit,
For thou thyself art thine own bait;
That fish that is not catched thereby,
Alas, is wiser far than I.

The will

Before I sigh my last gasp, let me breathe,
Great Love, some legacies: here I bequeath
Mine eyes to Argus, if mine eyes can see;
If they be blind, then Love, I give them thee;
My tongue to Fame; to'ambassadors mine ears;
    To women or the sea, my tears.
  Thou, Love, hast taught me heretofore
By making me serve her who'had twenty more,
That I should give to none but such as had too much before.

My constancy I to the planets give;   10
My truth to them who at the court do live;
Mine ingenuity and openness
To Jesuits; to buffoons my pensiveness;
My silence to'any who abroad hath been;
    My money to a Capuchin.
  Thou, Love, taught'st me, by appointing me
To love there where no love received can be,
Only to give to such as have an incapacity.

My faith I give to Roman Catholics;
All my good works unto the schismatics   20
Of Amsterdam; my best civility
And courtship to an University;

My modesty I give to soldiers bare;
　　My patience let gamesters share.
　　Thou, Love, taught'st me, by making me
Love her that holds my love disparity,
Only to give to those that count my gifts indignity.

I give my reputation to those
Which were my friends; mine industry to foes;
To schoolmen I bequeath my doubtfulness;　　30
My sickness to physicians, or excess;
To nature, all that I in rhyme have writ;
　　And to my company my wit.
　　Thou, Love, by making me adore
Her who begot this love in me before,
Taught'st me to make as though I gave, when I did but restore.

To him for whom the passing bell next tolls,
I give my physic books; my written rolls
Of moral counsels, I to Bedlam give;
My brazen medals unto them which live　　40
In want of bread; to them which pass among
　　All foreigners, mine English tongue.
　　Thou, Love, by making me love one
Who thinks her friendship a fit portïon
For younger lovers, dost my gifts thus disproportïon.

Therefore I'll give no more, but I'll undo
The world by dying, because love dies too.
Then all your beauties will be no more worth
Than gold in mines, where none doth draw it forth;
And all your graces no more use shall have　　50
　　Than a sun-dial in a grave.
　　Thou, Love, taught'st me, by making me
Love her who doth neglect both me and thee,
To'invent, and practise this one way, to'annihilate all three.

The sun rising

　　Busy old fool, unruly sun,
　　Why dost thou thus
Through windows and through curtains call on us?
Must to thy motions lovers' seasons run?
　　Saucy pedantic wretch, go chide
　　Late schoolboys and sour prentices,
　　Go tell court-huntsmen that the King will ride,
　　Call country ants to harvest offices;

Love, all alike, no season knows, nor clime,
Nor hours, days, months, which are the rags of time.   10

Thy beams, so reverend and strong
Why shouldst thou think?
I could eclipse and cloud them with a wink,
But that I would not lose her sight so long;
If her eyes have not blinded thine,
Look, and to-morrow late tell me
Whether both the'Indias of spice and mine
Be where thou left'st them, or lie here with me.
Ask for those kings whom thou saw'st yesterday,
And thou shalt hear, all here in one bed lay.   20

She'is all states, and all princes I;
Nothing else is.
Princes do but play us; compared to this,
All honor's mimic, all wealth alchemy.
Thou, sun, art half as happy'as we,
In that the world's contracted thus;
Thine age asks ease, and since thy duties be
To warm the world, that's done in warming us.
Shine here to us, and thou art everywhere;
This bed thy center is, these walls thy sphere.   30

Break of day

'Tis true, 'tis day; what though it be?
Oh, wilt thou therefore rise from me?
Why should we rise because 'tis light?
Did we lie down because 'twas night?
Love which in spite of darkness brought us hither,
Should in despite of light keep us together.

Light hath no tongue, but is all eye;
If it could speak as well as spy,
This were the worst that it could say,
That being well I fain would stay,   10
And that I loved my heart and honor so
That I would not from him, that had them, go.

Must business thee from hence remove?
Oh, that's the worst disease of love,
The poor, the foul, the false, love can
Admit, but not the busied man.
He which hath business, and makes love, doth do
Such wrong as when a married man doth woo.

The computation

For the first twenty years, since yesterday,
I scarce believed thou couldst be gone away;
For forty more I fed on favors past,
And forty'on hopes, that thou wouldst they might last.
Tears drowned one hundred, and sighs blew out two;
A thousand, I did neither think nor do,
Or not divide, all being one thought of you;
Or in a thousand more, forgot that too.
Yet call not this long life, but think that I
Am, by being dead, immortal; can ghosts die?   10

Confined love

  Some man unworthy to be possessor
Of old or new love, himself being false or weak,
  Thought his pain and shame would be lesser
If on womankind he might his anger wreak,
      And thence a law did grow,
      One might but one man know;
      But are other creatures so?

  Are sun, moon, or stars by law forbidden
To smile where they list, or lend away their light?
  Are birds divorced, or are they chidden   10
If they leave their mate, or lie abroad a night?
      Beasts do no jointures lose
      Though they new lovers choose,
      But we are made worse than those.

  Whoe'er rigged fair ship to lie in harbors,
And not to seek new lands, or not to deal with all?
  Or built fair houses, set trees and arbors,
Only to lock up, or else to let them fall?
      Good is not good, unless   20
      A thousand it possess,
      But doth waste with greediness.

The broken heart

  He is stark mad, whoever says
    That he hath been in love an hour;
  Yet not that love so soon decays,
    But that it can ten in less space devour.
  Who will believe me if I swear

That I have had the plague a year?
   Who would not laugh at me if I should say
   I saw a flask of powder burn a day?

Ah, what a trifle is a heart,
   If once into love's hands it come!   10
All other griefs allow a part
   To other griefs, and ask themselves but some;
They come to us, but us love draws,
He swallows us, and never chaws;
   By him, as by chained shot, whole ranks do die,
   He is the tyrant pike, our hearts the fry.

If 'twere not so, what did become
   Of my heart when I first saw thee?
I brought a heart into the room,
   But from the room I carried none with me;   20
If it had gone to thee, I know
Mine would have taught thine heart to show
   More pity unto me, but love, alas,
   At one first blow did shiver it as glass.

Yet nothing can to nothing fall,
   Nor any place be empty quite;
Therefore I think my breast hath all
   Those pieces still, though they be not unite;
And now as broken glasses show
A hundred lesser faces, so   30
   My rags of heart can like, wish, and adore,
   But after one such love, can love no more.

A lecture upon the shadow

Stand still, and I will read to thee
A lecture, love, in love's philosophy.
   These three hours that we have spent
   Walking here, two shadows went
Along with us, which we ourselves produced;
   But, now the sun is just above our head,
   We do those shadows tread,
And to brave clearness all things are reduced.
   So whilst our infant loves did grow,
   Disguises did, and shadows, flow   10
   From us and our cares, but now 'tis not so.

That love hath not attained the high'st degree,
Which is still diligent lest others see.

Except our loves at this noon stay,
We shall new shadows make the other way.
   As the first were made to blind
   Others, these which come behind
Will work upon ourselves, and blind our eyes.
   If our loves faint, and westwardly decline,
   To me thou falsely thine,   20
And I to thee, mine actions shall disguise.
   The morning shadows wear away,
   But these grow longer all the day;
   But oh, love's day is short, if love decay.

Love is a growing, or full constant light,
And his short minute after noon, is night.

Love's alchemy

Some that have deeper digged love's mine than I,
Say where his centric happiness doth lie;
   I have loved, and got, and told,
   But should I love, get, tell, till I were old,
I should not find that hidden mystery.
   Oh, 'tis imposture all,
And as no chemic yet th' elixir got,
   But glorifies his pregnant pot
   If by the way to him befall
Some odoriferous thing, or medicinal,   10
   So lovers dream a rich and long delight,
   But get a winter-seeming summer's night.

Our ease, our thrift, our honor, and our day,
Shall we for this vain bubble's shadow pay?
   Ends love in this, that my man
Can be as happy'as I can, if he can
Endure the short scorn of a bridegroom's play?
   That loving wretch that swears
'Tis not the bodies marry, but the minds,
   Which he in her angelic finds,   20
   Would swear as justly that he hears,
In that day's rude hoarse minstrelsy, the spheres.
   Hope not for mind in women: at their best,
   Sweetness and wit, they'are but mummy possessed.

The ecstasy

   Where, like a pillow on a bed,
   A pregnant bank swelled up to rest

The violet's reclining head,
   Sat we two, one another's best.
Our hands were firmly cémented
   With a fast balm, which thence did spring;
Our eye-beams twisted, and did thread
   Our eyes upon one double string;
So to'entergraft our hands, as yet
   Was all the means to make us one,   10
And pictures in our eyes to get
   Was all our propagatïon.
As 'twixt two equal armies fate
   Suspends uncertain victory,
Our souls, which to advance their state
   Were gone out, hung 'twixt her and me.
And whilst our souls negotiate there,
   We like sepulchral statues lay;
All day, the same our postures were,
   And we said nothing, all the day.   20
If any, so by love refined
   That he soul's language understood,
And by good love were grown all mind,
   Within convenient distance stood,
He, though he knew not which soul spake,
   Because both meant, both spake the same,
Might thence a new concoction take
   And part far purer than he came.
This ecstasy doth unperplex,
   We said, and tell us what we love: 30
We see by this it was not sex,
   We see we saw not what did move;
But as all several souls contain
   Mixture of things, they know not what,
Love these mixed souls doth mix again
   And makes both one, each this and that.
A single violet transplant,
   The strength, the color, and the size,
All which before was poor and scant,
   Redoubles still, and multiplies.   40
When love with one another so
   Interinanimates two souls,
That abler soul, which thence doth flow,
   Defects of loneliness controls.
We then, who are this new soul, know
   Of what we are composed and made,
For th' atomies of which we grow
   Are souls, whom no change can invade.

But oh, alas, so long, so far,
    Our bodies why do we forbear?   50
They are ours, though not we; we are
    The intelligences, they the sphere.
We owe them thanks, because they thus
    Did us to us at first convey,
Yielded their forces, sense, to us,
    Nor are dross to us, but allay.
On man heaven's influence works not so,
    But that it first imprints the air;
For soul into the soul may flow,
    Though it to body first repair.   60
As our blood labors to beget
    Spirits, as like souls as it can,
Because such fingers need to knit
    That subtle knot which makes us man,
So must pure lovers' souls descend
    T' affections, and to faculties,
Which sense may reach and apprehend,
    Else a great prince in prison lies.
To'our bodies turn we then, that so
    Weak men on love revealed may look;   70
Love's mysteries in souls do grow,
    But yet the body is his book.
And if some lover, such as we,
    Have heard this dialogue of one,
Let him still mark us, he shall see
    Small change when we'are to bodies gone.

The good-morrow

I wonder by my troth, what thou and I
Did, till we loved? Were we not weaned till then,
But sucked on country pleasures, childishly?
Or snorted we in the seven sleepers' den?
'Twas so; but this, all pleasures fancies be.
If ever any beauty I did see,
Which I desired, and got, 'twas but a dream of thee.

And now good morrow to our waking souls,
Which watch not one another out of fear;
For love all love of other sights controls,   10
And makes one little room an everywhere.
Let sea-discoverers to new worlds have gone,
Let maps to other, worlds on worlds have shown;
Let us possess one world, each hath one, and is one.

My face in thine eye, thine in mine appears,
And true plain hearts do in the faces rest;
Where can we find two better hemispheres
Without sharp north, without declining west?
Whatever dies was not mixed equally;
If our two loves be one, or thou and I
Love so alike that none do slacken, none can die.

20

Air and angels

Twice or thrice had I loved thee,
Before I knew thy face or name;
So in a voice, so in a shapeless flame,
Angels affect us oft, and worshipped be;
    Still when, to where thou wert, I came,
Some lovely glorious nothing I did see.
    But since my soul, whose child love is,
Takes limbs of flesh, and else could nothing do,
    More subtle than the parent is
Love must not be, but take a body too;
    And therefore what thou wert, and who,
        I bid love ask, and now
That it assume thy body I allow,
And fix itself in thy lip, eye, and brow.

19

Whilst thus to ballast love I thought,
And so more steadily to have gone,
With wares which would sink admiration,
I saw I had love's pinnace overfraught;
    Ev'ry thy hair for love to work upon
Is much too much, some fitter must be sought;
    For, nor in nothing, nor in things
Extreme and scatt'ring bright, can love inhere;
    Then as an angel, face and wings
Of air, not pure as it, yet pure doth wear,
    So thy love may be my love's sphere;
        Just such disparity
As is 'twixt air and angels' purity,
'Twixt women's love and men's will ever be.

20

The prohibition

Take heed of loving me;
At least remember, I forbade it thee;
Not that I shall repair my'unthrifty waste
Of breath and blood, upon thy sighs and tears,
By being to thee then what to me thou wast;

But so great joy our life at once outwears;
Then, lest thy love by my death frustrate be,
If thou love me, take heed of loving me.

Take heed of hating me,
Or too much triumph in the victory.　　　　　　　10
Not that I shall be mine own officer,
And hate with hate again retaliate;
But thou wilt lose the style of conqueror,
If I, thy conquest, perish by thy hate.
Then, lest my being nothing lessen thee,
If thou hate me, take heed of hating me.

Yet love and hate me too,
So these extremes shall ne'er their office do:
Love me, that I may die the gentler way,
Hate me, because thy love is too great for me,　　　20
Or let these two, themselves not me decay;
So shall I live, thy stage not triumph be;
Lest thou thy love and hate and me undo,
To let me live, O love and hate me too.

The undertaking

I have done one braver thing
　Than all the worthies did,
And yet a braver thence doth
　　spring,
　Which is, to keep that hid.

It were but madness now t' impart
　The skill of specular stone,
When he which can have learned
　　the art
　To cut it, can find none.

So if I now should utter this,
　Others, because no more　　10
Such stuff to work upon there is,
　Would love but as before.

But he who loveliness within
　Hath found, all outward loathes,
For he who color loves, and skin,
　Loves but their oldest clothes.

If, as I have, you also do
　Virtue' attired in woman see,
And dare love that, and say so too,
　And forget the he and she;　　20

And if this love, though placèd so,
　From profane men you hide,
Which will no faith on this be-
　　stow,
　Or, if they do, deride,

Then you have done a braver thing
　Than all the worthies did;
And a braver thence will spring,
　Which is, to keep that hid.

Lovers' infiniteness

If yet I have not all thy love,
　Dear, I shall never have it all;

I cannot breathe one other sigh to move,
Nor can entreat one other tear to fall,
And all my treasure, which should purchase thee,
Sighs, tears, and oaths, and letters, I have spent.
Yet no more can be due to me
Than at the bargain made was meant;
If then thy gift of love were partïal,
That some to me, some should to others fall,
    Dear, I shall never have thee all.

10

Or if then thou gavest me all,
All was but all, which thou hadst then;
But if in thy heart since there be, or shall
New love created be, by other men
Which have their stocks entire, and can in tears,
In sighs, in oaths, and letters outbid me,
This new love may beget new fears,
For this love was not vowed by thee.
And yet it was, thy gift being general;
The ground, thy heart, is mine; whatever shall
    Grow there, dear, I should have it all.

20

Yet I would not have all yet;
He that hath all can have no more,
And since my love doth every day admit
New growth, thou shouldst have new rewards in store;
Thou canst not every day give me thy heart,
If thou canst give it, then thou never gavest it;
Love's riddles are, that though thy heart depart,
It stays at home, and thou with losing savest it;
But we will have a way more liberal
Than changing hearts to join them, so we shall
    Be one, and one another's all.

30

Love's growth

I scarce believe my love to be so pure
    As I had thought it was,
    Because it doth endure
Vicissitude, and season, as the grass;
Methinks I lied all winter, when I swore
My love was infinite, if spring make'it more.
But if this medicine, love, which cures all sorrow
With more, not only be no quintessénce,
But mixed of all stuffs, paining soul or sense,
And of the sun his working vigor borrow,

10

Love's not so pure and abstract as they use
To say, which have no mistress but their muse;
But as all else, being elemented too,
Love sometimes would contemplate, sometimes do.

And yet no greater, but more eminent,
     Love by the spring is grown;
        As in the firmament,
Stars by the sun are not enlarged, but shown.
Gentle love-deeds, as blossoms on a bough,
From love's awakened root do bud out now.   20
If, as in water stirred more circles be
Produced by one, love such additions take,
Those like so many spheres but one heaven make,
For they are all concentric unto thee.
And though each spring do add to love new heat,
As princes do in times of action get
New taxes, and remit them not in peace,
No winter shall abate the spring's increase.

The anniversary

All kings, and all their favorites,
     All glory of honors, beauties, wits,
The sun itself, which makes times as they pass,
Is elder by a year now, than it was
When thou and I first one another saw;
All other things to their destruction draw,
     Only our love hath no decay;
This no to-morrow hath, nor yesterday,
Running, it never runs from us away,
But truly keeps his first, last, everlasting day.   10

Two graves must hide thine and my corse;
     If one might, death were no divorce.
Alas, as well as other princes, we,
Who prince enough in one another be,
Must leave at last in death these eyes and ears,
Oft fed with true oaths, and with sweet salt tears;
     But souls where nothing dwells but love,
All other thoughts being inmates, then shall prove
This, or a love increasèd there above,
When bodies to their graves, souls from their graves, remove.   20

And then we shall be throughly blest,
     But we no more than all the rest;

Here upon earth we'are kings, and none but we
Can be such kings, nor of such subjects be.
Who is so safe as we, where none can do
Treason to us, except one of us two?
     True and false fears let us refrain;
Let us love nobly, and live, and add again
Years and years unto years, till we attain
To write threescore; this is the second of our reign.   30

The canonization

For God's sake hold your tongue, and let me love,
    Or chide my palsy, or my gout,
My five gray hairs, or ruined fortune flout;
     With wealth your state, your mind with arts improve,
      Take you a course, get you a place,
      Observe his honor, or his grace;
Or the king's real, or his stampèd face
    Contemplate; what you will, approve,
    So you will let me love.

Alas, alas, who's injured by my love?   10
    What merchants' ships have my sighs drowned?
Who says my tears have overflowed his ground?
     When did my colds a forward spring remove?
      When did the heats which my veins fill
      Add one more to the plaguy bill?
Soldiers find wars, and lawyers find out still
    Litigious men, which quarrels move,
    Though she and I do love.

Call us what you will, we are made such by love;
    Call her one, me another fly,   20
We'are tapers too, and at our own cost die,
     And we in us find the'eagle and the dove.
      The phœnix ridole hath more wit
      By us; we two being one, are it.
So to one neutral thing both sexes fit,
    We die and rise the same, and prove
    Mysterious by this love.

We can die by it, if not live by love,
    And if unfit for tombs and hearse
Our legend be, it will be fit for verse;   30
     And if no piece of chronicle we prove,
      We'll build in sonnets pretty rooms;

As well a well-wrought urn becomes
The greatest ashes, as half-acre tombs,
    And by these hymns, all shall approve
    Us canonized for love,

And thus invoke us: You whom reverend love
    Made one another's hermitage;
You, to whom love was peace, that now is rage;
    Who did the whole world's soul contract, and drove   40
        Into the glasses of your eyes—
        So made such mirrors and such spies
That they did all to you epitomize,—
    Countries, towns, courts; beg from above
    A pattern of your love!

A valediction of weeping

        Let me pour forth
My tears before thy face whilst I stay here,
For thy face coins them, and thy stamp they bear,
And by this mintage they are something worth,
        For thus they be
        Pregnant of thee;
Fruits of much grief they are, emblems of more—
When a tear falls, that thou fallst which it bore,
So thou and I are nothing then, when on a diverse shore.

        On a round ball   10
A workman that hath copies by, can lay
An Europe, Afric, and an Asïa,
And quickly make that which was nothing, all;
        So doth each tear
        Which thee doth wear,
A globe, yea world, by that impression grow,
Till thy tears mixed with mine do overflow
This world; by waters sent from thee, my heaven dissolvëd so.

        O more than moon,
Draw not up seas to drown me in thy sphere;   20
Weep me not dead, in thine arms, but forbear
To teach the sea what it may do too soon;
        Let not the wind
        Example find,
To do me more harm than it purposeth;
Since thou and I sigh one another's breath,
Whoe'er sighs most is cruellest, and hastes the other's death.

Song

Sweetest love, I do not go
   For weariness of thee,
Nor in hope the world can show
   A fitter love for me;
     But since that I
Must die at last, 'tis best,
To use myself in jest
   Thus by feigned deaths to die.

Yesternight the sun went hence,
   And yet is here to-day;   10
He hath no desire nor sense,
   Nor half so short a way;
     Then fear not me,
But believe that I shall make
Speedier journeys, since I take
   More wings and spurs than he.

Oh, how feeble is man's power,
   That if good fortune fall,
Cannot add another hour,
   Nor a lost hour recall!   20
     But come bad chance,

And we join to'it our strength,
And we teach it art and length,
   Itself o'er us to'advance.

When thou sigh'st, thou sigh'st not
        wind,
   But sigh'st my soul away;
When thou weep'st, unkindly kind,
   My life's blood doth decay.
     It cannot be
That thou lov'st me, as thou
        say'st,   30
If in thine my life thou waste;
   Thou art the best of me.

Let not thy divining heart
   Forethink me any ill,
Destiny may take thy part,
   And may thy fears fulfil;
     But think that we
Are but turned aside to sleep;
They who one another keep
   Alive, ne'er parted be.   40

A valediction forbidding mourning

As virtuous men pass mildly away,
   And whisper to their souls to go,
Whilst some of their sad friends do
     say,
   The breath goes now, and some
     say, No;

So let us melt, and make no noise,
   No tear-floods, nor sigh-tempests
     move;
'Twere profanation of our joys
   To tell the laity our love.

Moving of th' earth brings harms
     and fears,
   Men reckon what it did and
     meant;   10
But trepidation of the spheres,
   Though greater far, is innocent.

Dull sublunary lovers' love,
   Whose soul is sense, cannot
     admit
Absence, because it doth remove
   Those things which elemented
     it.

But we by a love so much refined
   That ourselves know not what it
     is,
Inter-assurèd of the mind,
   Care less eyes, lips, hands to
     miss.   20

Our two souls therefore, which are
     one,
   Though I must go, endure not
     yet

A breach, but an expansïon,
  Like gold to airy thinness beat.

If they be two, they are two so
  As stiff twin compasses are two;
Thy soul, the fixed foot, makes no
    show
  To move, but doth if the'other
    do.

And though it in the center sit,
  Yet when the other far doth
    roam,   30

It leans, and hearkens after it,
  And grows erect as that comes
    home.

Such wilt thou be to me who
    must,
  Like th' other foot, obliquely
    run;
Thy firmness makes my circle
    just,
  And makes me end where I be-
    gun.

The funeral

Whoever comes to shroud me, do not harm
    Nor question much
That subtile wreath of hair which crowns my arm;
  The mystery, the sign you must not touch,
      For 'tis my outward soul,
Viceroy to that, which unto heaven being gone,
      Will leave this to control
And keep these limbs, her provinces, from dissolutïon.

For if the sinewy thread my brain lets fall
    Through every part,   10
Can tie those parts, and make me one of all,
  Those hairs, which upward grew, and strength and art
      Have from a better brain,
Can better do'it; except she meant that I
      By this should know my pain,
As prisoners then are manacled, when they'are condemned to die.

Whate'er she meant by'it, bury it with me,
    For since I am
Love's martyr, it might breed idolatry
If into others' hands these relics came;   20
    As 'twas humility
To afford to it all that a soul can do,
    So 'tis some bravery,
That since you would have none of me, I bury some of you.

The relic

    When my grave is broke up again
    Some second guest to entertain,—
    For graves have learned that woman-head,

To be to more than one a bed—
      And he that digs it, spies
A bracelet of bright hair about the bone,
      Will he not let'us alone,
And think that there a loving couple lies,
Who thought that this device might be some way
To make their souls, at the last busy day,   10
Meet at this grave, and make a little stay?

     If this fall in a time or land
     Where mis-devotion doth command,
     Then he that digs us up will bring
        Us to the bishop and the king,
          To make us relics; then
Thou shalt be a Mary Magdalen, and I
        A something else thereby;
All women shall adore us, and some men;
And since at such time miracles are sought,   20
I would have that age by this paper taught
What miracles we harmless lovers wrought.

     First, we loved well and faithfully,
     Yet knew not what we loved, nor why,
     Difference of sex no more we knew
        Than our guardian angels do;
          Coming and going, we
Perchance might kiss, but not between those meals;
        Our hands ne'er touched the seals,
Which nature, injured by late law, sets free;   30
These miracles we did, but now alas,
All measure and all language I should pass,
Should I tell what a miracle she was.

Twicknam garden

Blasted with sighs, and surrounded with tears,
     Hither I come to seek the spring,
     And at mine eyes, and at mine ears,
Receive such balms as else cure everything;
     But oh, self traitor, I do bring
The spider love, which transubstantiates all,
     And can convert manna to gall;
And that this place may thoroughly be thought
     True paradise, I have the serpent brought.

'Twere wholesomer for me that winter did　　10
　　Benight the glory of this place,
　　And that a grave frost did forbid
These trees to laugh and mock me to my face;
　　But that I may not this disgrace
Endure, nor yet leave loving, Love, let me
　　Some senseless piece of this place be;
Make me a mandrake, so I may groan here,
　　Or a stone fountain weeping out my year.

Hither with crystal vials, lovers, come
　　And take my tears, which are love's wine,　　20
　　And try your mistress' tears at home,
For all are false that taste not just like mine;
　　Alas, hearts do not in eyes shine,
Nor can you more judge woman's thoughts by tears,
　　Than by her shadow what she wears.
O perverse sex, where none is true but she,
　　Who's therefore true, because her truth kills me.

A nocturnal upon Saint Lucy's Day, being the shortest day

'Tis the year's midnight, and it is the day's,
Lucy's, who scarce seven hours herself unmasks;
　　The sun is spent, and now his flasks
　　Send forth light squibs, no constant rays;
　　　　The world's whole sap is sunk;
The general balm th' hydroptic earth hath drunk,
Whither, as to the bed's feet, life is shrunk,
Dead and interred; yet all these seem to laugh,
Compared with me, who am their epitaph.

Study me then, you who shall lovers be　　10
At the next world, that is, at the next spring;
　　For I am every dead thing,
　　In whom Love wrought new alchemy.
　　　　For his art did express
A quintessence even from nothingness,
From dull privations, and lean emptiness;
He ruined me, and I am re-begot
Of absence, darkness, death—things which are not.

All others from all things draw all that's good,
Life, soul, form, spirit, whence they being have;　　20
　　I, by Love's limbec, am the grave

Of all that's nothing. Oft a flood
   Have we two wept, and so
Drowned the whole world, us two; oft did we grow
To be two chaoses, when we did show
Care to aught else; and often absences
Withdrew our souls, and made us carcasses.

But I am by her death, which word wrongs her,
Of the first nothing the elixir grown;
   Were I a man, that I were one   30
   I needs must know; I should prefer,
      If I were any beast,
Some ends, some means; yea plants, yea stones detest
And love; all, all some properties invest;
If I an ordinary nothing were,
As shadow, a light and body must be here.

But I am none; nor will my sun renew.
You lovers, for whose sake the lesser sun
   At this time to the Goat is run
   To fetch new lust, and give it you,   40
      Enjoy your summer all;
Since she enjoys her long night's festival,
Let me prepare towards her, and let me call
This hour her vigil, and her eve, since this
Both the year's and the day's deep midnight is.

ELEGIES

On his mistress

By our first strange and fatal interview,
By all desires which thereof did ensue,
By our long starving hopes, by that remorse
Which my words' masculine persuasive force
Begot in thee, and by the memory
Of hurts which spies and rivals threatened me,
I calmly beg; but by thy father's wrath,
By all pains, which want and divorcement hath,
I conjure thee; and all the oaths which I
And thou have sworn to seal joint constancy,   10
Here I unswear, and overswear them thus:
Thou shalt not love by ways so dangerous.
Temper, O fair love, love's impetuous rage,
Be my true mistress still, not my feigned page;
I'll go, and by thy kind leave, leave behind

Thee, only worthy to nurse in my mind
Thirst to come back; oh, if thou die before,
My soul from other lands to thee shall soar.
Thy else almighty beauty cannot move
Rage from the seas, nor thy love teach them love,   20
Nor tame wild Boreas' harshness; thou hast read
How roughly he in pieces shiverëd
Fair Orithea, whom he swore he loved.
Fall ill or good, 'tis madness to have proved
Dangers unurged; feed on this flattery,
That absent lovers one in th' other be.
Dissemble nothing, not a boy, nor change
Thy body's habit, nor mind's; be not strange
To thyself only; all will spy in thy face
A blushing womanly discovering grace.   30
Richly clothed apes are called apes; and as soon
Eclipsed as bright, we call the moon the moon.
Men of France, changeable chameleons,
Spitals of diseases, shops of fashions,
Love's fuellers, and the rightest company
Of players which upon the world's stage be,
Will quickly know thee, and no less, alas!
Th' indifferent Italian, as we pass
His warm land, well content to think thee page,
Will hunt thee with such lust and hideous rage   40
As Lot's fair guests were vexed. But none of these,
Nor spongy hydroptic Dutch shall thee displease,
If thou stay here. Oh, stay here! for, for thee,
England is only a worthy gallery
To walk in expectation, till from thence
Our greatest King call thee to his presénce.
When I am gone, dream me some happiness,
Nor let thy looks our long hid love confess,
Nor praise, nor dispraise me, nor bless nor curse
Openly love's force, nor in bed fright thy nurse   50
With midnight's startings, crying out, Oh, oh,
Nurse, oh, my love is slain, I saw him go
O'er the white Alps alone; I saw him, I,
Assailed, fight, taken, stabbed, bleed, fall, and die.
Augur me better chance, except dread Jove
Think it enough for me to'have had thy love.

The autumnal

No spring nor summer beauty hath such grace
As I have seen in one autumnal face.

Young beauties force our love, and that's a rape,
　　This doth but counsel, yet you cannot scape.
If 'twere a shame to love, here 'twere no shame;
　　Affection here takes reverence's name.
Were her first years the golden age? That's true,
　　But now they'are gold oft tried and ever new.
That was her torrid and inflaming time,
　　This is her tolerable tropic clime. 10
Fair eyes! who asks more heat than comes from hence,
　　He in a fever wishes pestilence.
Call not these wrinkles, graves; if graves they were,
　　They were Love's graves, for else he is no where.
Yet lies not Love dead here, but here doth sit
　　Vowed to this trench, like an anachorit;
And here till hers, which must be his death, come,
　　He doth not dig a grave, but build a tomb.
Here dwells he; though he sojourn ev'rywhere
　　In progress, yet his standing house is here— 20
Here where still evening is, not noon nor night,
　　Where no voluptuousness, yet all delight.
In all her words, unto all hearers fit,
　　You may at revels, you at council, sit.
This is Love's timber, youth his underwood;
　　There he, as wine in June, enrages blood,
Which then comes seasonabliest when our taste
　　And appetite to other things is past.
Xerxes' strange Lydian love, the platan tree,
　　Was loved for age, none being so large as she, 30
Or else because, being young, nature did bless
　　Her youth with age's glory, barrenness.
If we love things long sought, age is a thing
　　Which we are fifty years in compassing;
If transitory things, which soon decay,
　　Age must be loveliest at the latest day.
But name not winter faces, whose skin's slack,
　　Lank as an unthrift's purse, but a soul's sack;
Whose eyes seek light within, for all here's shade;
　　Whose mouths are holes, rather worn out than made; 40
Whose every tooth to a several place is gone,
　　To vex their souls at resurrection:
Name not these living death's-heads unto me,
　　For these, not ancient, but antique be.
I hate extremes, yet I had rather stay
　　With tombs than cradles, to wear out a day.
Since such love's motion natural is, may still
　　My love descend, and journey down the hill,

Not panting after growing beauties; so
I shall ebb out with them who homeward go. 50

SATIRES

Satire III

Kind pity chokes my spleen; brave scorn forbids
Those tears to issue which swell my eyelids;
I must not laugh, nor weep sins and be wise;
Can railing then cure these worn maladies?
Is not our mistress, fair religīon,
As worthy of all our souls' devotīon
As virtue was in the first blinded age?
Are not heaven's joys as valiant to assuage
Lusts as earth's honor was to them? Alas,
As we do them in means, shall they surpass 10
Us in the end? and shall thy father's spirit
Meet blind philosophers in heaven, whose merit
Of strict life may be imputed faith, and hear
Thee, whom he taught so easy ways and near
To follow, damned? Oh, if thou dar'st, fear this;
This fear great courage and high valor is.
Dar'st thou aid mutinous Dutch, and dar'st thou lay
Thee in ships, wooden sepulchers, a prey
To leaders' rage, to storms, to shot, to dearth?
Dar'st thou dive seas, and dungeons of the earth? 20
Hast thou courageous fire to thaw the ice
Of frozen North discoveries? and thrice
Colder than salamanders, like divine
Children in th' oven, fires of Spain and the Line,
Whose countries limbecs to our bodies be,
Canst thou for gain bear? and must every he
Which cries not, Goddess, to thy mistress, draw
Or eat thy poisonous words? Courage of straw!
O desperate coward, wilt thou seem bold and
To thy foes and His, who made thee to stand 30
Sentinel in his world's garrison, thus yield,
And for forbidden wars leave th' appointed field?
Know thy foes: the foul devil, whom thou
Strivest to please, for hate, not love, would allow
Thee fain his whole realm to be quit; and as
The world's all parts wither away and pass,
So the world's self, thy other loved foe, is
In her decrepit wane, and thou, loving this,
Dost love a withered and worn strumpet; last,

Flesh, itself death, and joys which flesh can taste   40
Thou lovest, and thy fair goodly soul, which doth
Give this flesh power to taste joy, thou dost loathe.
Seek true religion. Oh, where? Mirreus,
Thinking her unhoused here and fled from us,
Seeks her at Rome; there, because he doth know
That she was there a thousand years ago;
He loves her rags so, as we here obey
The statecloth where the prince sat yesterday.
Crantz to such brave loves will not be enthralled,
But loves her only, who at Geneva is called   50
Religion, plain, simple, sullen, young,
Contemptuous, yet unhandsome; as among
Lecherous humors, there is one that judges
No wenches wholesome, but coarse country drudges.
Graius stays still at home here, and because
Some preachers, vile ambitious bawds, and laws,
Still new like fashions, bid him think that she
Which dwells with us is only perfect, he
Embraceth her whom his godfathers will
Tender to him, being tender; as wards still   60
Take such wives as their guardians offer, or
Pay values. Careless Phrygius doth abhor
All, because all cannot be good; as one,
Knowing some women whores, dares marry none.
Gracchus loves all as one, and thinks that so
As women do in divers countries go
In divers habits, yet are still one kind,
So doth, so is religion; and this blind-
Ness too much light breeds; but unmovëd, thou
Of force must one, and forced but one allow,   70
And the right; ask thy father which is she,
Let him ask his; though truth and falsehood be
Near twins, yet truth a little elder is;
Be busy to seek her; believe me this,
He's not of none, nor worst, that seeks the best.
To adore, or scorn an image, or protest,
May all be bad. Doubt wisely; in strange way
To stand inquiring right, is not to stray;
To sleep, or run wrong, is. On a huge hill,
Cragged and steep, Truth stands, and he that will   80
Reach her, about must and about must go,
And what the hill's suddenness resists, win so.
Yet strive so that before age, death's twilight,
Thy soul rest, for none can work in that night.
To will implies delay, therefore now do

Hard deeds, the body's pains; hard knowledge too
The mind's endeavors reach, and mysteries
Are like the sun, dazzling, yet plain to all eyes.
Keep the truth which thou hast found; men do not stand
In so ill case, that God hath with his hand90
Signed kings blank charters to kill whom they hate;
Nor are they vicars, but hangmen, to fate.
Fool and wretch, wilt thou let thy soul be tied
To man's laws, by which she shall not be tried
At the last day? Will it then boot thee
To say a Philip or a Gregory,
A Harry or a Martin, taught thee this?
Is not this excuse for mere contraries
Equally strong? Cannot both sides say so?
That thou mayest rightly obey power, her bounds know;100
Those past, her nature and name is changed; to be
Then humble to her is idolatry.
As streams are, power is; those blest flowers that dwell
At the rough stream's calm head, thrive and do well,
But having left their roots, and themselves given
To the stream's tyrannous rage, alas, are driven
Through mills and rocks and woods, and at last, almost
Consumed in going, in the sea are lost.
So perish souls, which more choose men's unjust
Power from God claimed, than God himself to trust.110

EPIGRAMS

A lame beggar

I am unable, yonder beggar cries,
To stand or move; if he say true, he lies.

Antiquary

If in his study he hath so much care
To'hang all old strange things, let his wife beware.

Phryne

Thy flattering picture, Phryne, is like thee—
Only in this, that you both painted be.

LETTERS

The calm

[To Mr. Christopher Brooke]

Our storm is past, and that storm's tyrannous rage
A stupid calm, but nothing it, doth suage.

The fable is inverted, and far more
A block afflicts now, than a stork before.
Storms chafe, and soon wear out themselves, or us;
In calms, heaven laughs to see us languish thus.
As steady'as I can wish that my thoughts were,
Smooth as thy mistress' glass, or what shines there,
The sea is now; and as the isles which we
Seek, when we can move, our ships rooted be.   10
As water did in storms, now pitch runs out,
As lead, when a fired church becomes one spout;
And all our beauty, and our trim, decays
Like courts removing, or like ended plays.
The fighting place now seamen's rags supply,
And all the tackling is a frippery.
No use of lanthorns; and in one place lay
Feathers and dust, to-day and yesterday.
Earth's hollownesses, which the world's lungs are,
Have no more wind than the upper vault of air.   20
We can nor lost friends nor sought foes recover,
But meteor-like, save that we move not, hover.
Only the calenture together draws
Dear friends, which meet dead in great fishes' jaws;
And on the hatches, as on altars, lies
Each one, his own priest and own sacrifice;
Who live, that miracle do multiply
Where walkers in hot ovens do not die.
If in despite of these we swim, that hath
No more refreshing than our brimstone bath;   30
But from the sea into the ship we turn,
Like parboiled wretches, on the coals to burn.
Like Bajazet encaged, the shepherd's scoff,
Or like slack-sinewed Samson, his hair off,
Languish our ships. Now as a myriad
Of ants durst th' emperor's loved snake invade,
The crawling galleys, sea-gaols, finny chips,
Might brave our pinnaces, now bed-rid ships.
Whether a rotten state, and hope of gain,
Or to disuse me from the queasy pain   40
Of being beloved, and loving, or the thirst
Of honor, or fair death, out-pushed me first,
I lose my end; for here as well as I,
A desperate may live, and a coward die.
Stag, dog, and all which from or towards flies,
Is paid with life or prey, or doing, dies.
Fate grudges us all, and doth subtly lay
A scourge, 'gainst which we all forget to pray;

He that at sea prays for more wind, as well
Under the poles may beg cold, heat in hell.
What are we then? How little more, alas,
Is man now, than before he was! He was
Nothing; for us, we are for nothing fit;
Chance, or ourselves, still disproportion it.
We have no power, no will, no sense; I lie,
I should not then thus feel this misery.

50

To Sir Henry Wotton

Here's no more news than virtue:'I may as well
Tell you Cales' or Saint Michael's tale for news, as tell
That vice doth here habitually dwell.

Yet, as to'get stomachs we walk up and down,
And toil to sweeten rest, so, may God frown
If, but to loathe both, I haunt court or town.

For here no one is from the'extremity
Of vice by any other reason free,
But that the next to'him still is worse than he.

In this world's warfare, they whom rugged Fate,
God's commissary, doth so throughly hate
As in'the court's squadron to marshal their state;

10

If they stand armed with seely honesty,
With wishing prayers, and neat integrity,
Like Indians 'gainst Spanish hosts they be.

Suspicious boldness to this place belongs,
And to'have as many ears as all have tongues;
Tender to know, tough to ackowledge wrongs.

Believe me, Sir, in my youth's giddiest days,
When to be like the court was a play's praise,
Plays were not so like courts as courts'are like plays.

20

Then let us at these mimic antics jest,
Whose deepest projects and egregious gests
Are but dull morals of a game at chests.

But now 'tis incongruity to smile,
Therefore I end, and bid farewell awhile;
At court; though *From court* were the better style.

[*THE ANNIVERSARIES*]

An Anatomy of the World
The first anniversary

So did the world from the first hour decay,
That evening was beginning of the day;
And now the springs and summers which we see,
Like sons of women after fifty be.
And new philosophy calls all in doubt;
The element of fire is quite put out;
The sun is lost, and th' earth, and no man's wit
Can well direct him where to look for it.
And freely men confess that this world's spent,
When in the planets and the firmament   10
They seek so many new; they see that this
Is crumbled out again to his atomies.
'Tis all in pieces, all coherence gone,
All just supply, and all relatĭon;
Prince, subject, father, son, are things forgot,
For every man alone thinks he hath got
To be a phœnix, and that then can be
None of that kind of which he is, but he.
This is the world's condition now, and now
She that should all parts to reunion bow,   20
She that had all magnetic force alone
To draw and fasten sundered parts in one,
She whom wise nature had invented then
When she observed that every sort of men
Did in their voyage in this world's sea stray,
And needed a new compass for their way,
She that was best, and first original
Of all fair copies, and the general
Steward to fate, she whose rich eyes and breast
Gilt the West Indies, and perfumed the East,   30
Whose having breathed in this world did bestow
Spice on those isles, and bade them still smell so,
And that rich Indie which doth gold inter
Is but as single money, coined from her,
She to whom this world must itself refer
As suburbs or the microcosm of her,
She, she is dead, she's dead; when thou know'st this,
Thou know'st how lame a cripple this world is.

Of *the Progress of the Soul*
The second anniversary

. . . . . .

She of whose soul, if we may say 'twas gold,
Her body was th' electrum, and did hold
Many degrees of that; we understood
Her by her sight; her pure and eloquent blood
Spoke in her cheeks, and so distinctly wrought
That one might almost say her body thought;
She, she, thus richly and largely housed, is gone,
And chides us slow-paced snails who crawl upon
Our prison's prison, earth, nor think us well
Longer than whilst we bear our brittle shell.   10
But 'twere but little to have changed our room,
If, as we were in this our living tomb
Oppressed with ignorance, we still were so.
Poor soul, in this thy flesh what dost thou know?
Thou know'st thyself so little, as thou know'st not
How thou didst die, nor how thou wast begot.
Thou neither know'st how thou at first cam'st in,
Nor how thou took'st the poison of man's sin.
Nor dost thou, though thou know'st that thou art so,
By what way thou art made immortal, know.   20
Thou art too narrow, wretch, to comprehend
Even thyself; yea, though thou wouldst but bend
To know thy body. Have not all souls thought
For many ages that our body'is wrought
Of air, and fire, and other elements?
And now they think of new ingredients,
And one soul thinks one, and another way
Another thinks, and 'tis an even lay.
Know'st thou but how the stone doth enter in
The bladder's cave, and never break the skin?   30
Know'st thou how blood, which to the heart doth flow,
Doth from one ventricle to th' other go?
And for the putrid stuff which thou dost spit,
Know'st thou how thy lungs have attracted it?
There are no passages, so that there is,
For aught thou know'st, piercing of substances.
And of those many opinions which men raise
Of nails and hairs, dost thou know which to praise?
What hope have we to know ourselves, when we
Know not the least things which for our use be?   40
We see in authors, too stiff to recant,

A hundred controversies of an ant;
And yet one watches, starves, freezes, and sweats,
To know but catechisms and alphabets
Of unconcerning things, matters of fact—
How others on our stage their parts did act,
What Cæsar did, yea, and what Cicero said.
Why grass is green, or why our blood is red,
Are mysteries which none have reached unto.
In this low form, poor soul, what wilt thou do?   50
When wilt thou shake off this pedantery
Of being taught by sense, and fantasy?
Thou look'st through spectacles; small things seem great
Below; but up unto the watch-tower get,
And see all things despoiled of fallacies;
Thou shalt not peep through lattices of eyes,
Nor hear through labyrinths of ears, nor learn
By circuit or collections to discern.
In heaven thou straight know'st all concerning it,
And what concerns it not, shalt straight forget.   60

    .   .   .   .

DIVINE POEMS

Show me, dear Christ, thy spouse so bright and clear.
What! is it she which on the other shore
Goes richly painted? or which, robbed and tore,
Laments and mourns in Germany and here?
Sleeps she a thousand, then peeps up one year?
Is she self-truth, and errs? now new, now outwore?
Doth she, and did she, and shall she evermore
On one, on seven, or on no hill appear?
Dwells she with us, or like adventuring knights
First travel we to seek, and then make love?   10
Betray, kind husband, thy spouse to our sights,
And let mine amorous soul court thy mild dove,
Who is most true and pleasing to thee then
When she'is embraced and open to most men.

Batter my heart, three-personed God, for you
As yet but knock, breathe, shine, and seek to mend;
That I may rise and stand, o'erthrow me;'and bend
Your force to break, blow, burn, and make me new.
I, like an usurped tower to'another due,
Labor to'admit you, but oh, to no end.
Reason, your viceroy in me, me should defend,
But is captived, and proves weak or untrue.

Yet dearly'I love you,'and would be lovëd fain,
But am betrothed unto your enemy;
Divorce me,'untie or break that knot again;
Take me to you, imprison me, for I,
Except you'enthrall me, never shall be free,
Nor ever chaste, except you ravish me.

Why are we by all creatures waited on?
Why do the prodigal elements supply
Life and food to me, being more pure than I,
Simple and further from corruptïon?
Why brook'st thou, ignorant horse, subjectïon?
Why dost thou, bull and boar, so seelily
Dissemble weakness, and by'one man's stroke die,
Whose whole kind you might swallow and feed upon?
Weaker I am, woe is me, and worse than you;
You have not sinned, nor need be timorous.
But wonder at a greater wonder, for to us
Created nature doth these things subdue;
But their Creator, whom sin nor nature tied,
For us, his creatures and his foes, hath died.

If poisonous minerals, and if that tree
Whose fruit threw death on else immortal us,
If lecherous goats, if serpents envious
Cannot be damned, alas! why should I be?
Why should intent or reason, born in me,
Make sins else equal, in me more heinous?
And mercy being easy and glorious
To God, in his stern wrath why threatens he?
But who am I, that dare dispute with thee,
O God? Oh, of thine only worthy blood
And my tears, make a heavenly Lethean flood,
And drown in it my sins' black memory.
That thou remember them, some claim as debt;
I think it mercy, if thou wilt forget.

This is my play's last scene; here heavens appoint
My pilgrimage's last mile; and my race,
Idly yet quickly run, hath this last pace;
My span's last inch, my minutes' latest point;
And gluttonous death will instantly unjoint
My body and my soul, and I shall sleep a space;
But my'ever-waking part shall see that face
Whose fear already shakes my every joint.
Then as my soul to'heaven, her first seat, takes flight,

And earth-born body in the earth shall dwell,
So fall my sins, that all may have their right,
To where they'are bred, and would press me,—to hell.
Impute me righteous, thus purged of evil,
For thus I leave the world, the flesh, the devil.

What if this present were the world's last night?
Mark in my heart, O soul, where thou dost dwell,
The picture of Christ crucified, and tell
Whether his countenance can thee affright:
Tears in his eyes quench the amazing light,
Blood fills his frowns, which from his pierced head fell.
And can that tongue adjudge thee unto hell,
Which prayed forgiveness for his foes' fierce spite?
No, no; but as in my idolatry
I said to all my profane mistresses,
Beauty, of pity, foulness only is
A sign of rigor; so I say to thee:
To wicked spirits are horrid shapes assigned;
This beauteous form assumes a piteous mind.

At the round earth's imagined corners, blow
Your trumpets, angels; and arise, arise
From death, you numberless infinities
Of souls, and to your scattered bodies go;
All whom the flood did, and fire shall o'erthrow,
All whom war, dearth, age, agues, tyrannies,
Despair, law, chance hath slain, and you whose eyes
Shall behold God and never taste death's woe.
But let them sleep, Lord, and me mourn a space,
For if above all these my sins abound,
'Tis late to ask abundance of thy grace
When we are there; here on this lowly ground
Teach me how to repent; for that's as good
As if thou'hadst sealed my pardon with thy blood.

Death, be not proud, though some have callèd thee
Mighty and dreadful, for thou art not so;
For those whom thou think'st thou dost overthrow
Die not, poor Death, nor yet canst thou kill me.
From rest and sleep, which but thy pictures be,
Much pleasure; then from thee much more must flow,
And soonest our best men with thee do go,
Rest of their bones, and soul's delivery.
Thou art slave to fate, chance, kings, and desperate men,
And dost with poison, war, and sickness dwell.:

And poppy or charms can make us sleep as well
And better than thy stroke; why swell'st thou then?
One short sleep past, we wake eternally,
And death shall be no more; Death, thou shalt die.

Good Friday, 1613. Riding westward

Let man's soul be a sphere, and then in this
The intelligence that moves, devotion is;
And as the other spheres, by being grown
Subject to foreign motion, lose their own,
And being by others hurried every day
Scarce in a year their natural form obey,
Pleasure or business, so, our souls admit
For their first mover, and are whirled by it.
Hence is 't that I am carried towards the west
This day, when my soul's form bends towards the east.   10
There I should see a sun, by rising set,
And by that setting, endless day beget;
But that Christ on this cross did rise and fall,
Sin had eternally benighted all.
Yet dare I'almost be glad I do not see
That spectacle of too much weight for me.
Who sees God's face, that is self life, must die;
What a death were it then to see God die!
It made his own lieutenant, nature, shrink;
It made his footstool crack, and the sun wink.   20
Could I behold those hands which span the poles
And tune all spheres at once, pierced with those holes?
Could I behold that endless height, which is
Zenith to us and our antipodes,
Humbled below us? or that blood which is
The seat of all our souls, if not of his,
Made dirt of dust, or that flesh which was worn
By God for his apparel, ragg'd and torn?
If on these things I durst not look, durst I
Upon his miserable mother cast mine eye,   30
Who was God's partner here, and furnished thus
Half of that sacrifice which ransomed us?
Though these things, as I ride, be from mine eye,
They'are present yet unto my memory,
For that looks towards them; and thou look'st towards me,
O Savior, as thou hang'st upon the tree;
I turn my back to thee but to receive
Corrections, till thy mercies bid thee leave.
Oh, think me worth thine anger, punish me,

Burn off my rusts, and my deformity;   40
Restore thine image, so much, by thy grace,
That thou mayst know me, and I'll turn my face.

A hymn to Christ, at the author's last going into Germany

In what torn ship soever I embark,
That ship shall be my emblem of thy ark;
What sea soever swallow me, that flood
Shall be to me an emblem of thy blood;
Though thou with clouds of anger do disguise
Thy face, yet through that mask I know those eyes,
    Which, though they turn away sometimes,
        They never will despise.

I sacrifice this island unto thee,
And all whom I loved there, and who loved me;   10
When I have put our seas 'twixt them and me,
Put thou thy seas betwixt my sins and thee.
As the tree's sap doth seek the root below
In winter, in my winter now I go
    Where none but thee, th' eternal root
        Of true love, I may know.

Nor thou nor thy religion dost control
The amorousness of an harmonious soul,
But thou wouldst have that love thyself; as thou
Art jealous, Lord, so I am jealous now;   20
Thou lov'st not, till from loving more thou free
My soul; whoever gives, takes liberty;
    Oh, if thou car'st not whom I love,
        Alas, thou lov'st not me.

Seal then this bill of my divorce to all
On whom those fainter beams of love did fall;
Marry those loves, which in youth scattered be
On fame, wit, hopes (false mistresses), to thee.
Churches are best for prayer that have least light:
To see God only, I go out of sight;   30
    And to scape stormy days, I choose
        An everlasting night.

A hymn to God the Father

Wilt thou forgive that sin where I begun,
    Which was my sin, though it were done before?

Wilt thou forgive that sin through which I run,
   And do run still, though still I do deplore?
     When thou hast done, thou has not done,
       For I have more.

Wilt thou forgive that sin which I have won
   Others to sin, and made my sin their door?
Wilt thou forgive that sin which I did shun
   A year or two, but wallowed in a score?
     When thou hast done, thou hast not done,
       For I have more.

I have a sin of fear, that when I have spun
   My last thread, I shall perish on the shore;
But swear by thyself, that at my death thy Son
   Shall shine as he shines now, and heretofore;
     And having done that, thou hast done;
       I fear no more.

Hymn to God, my God, in my sickness

Since I am coming to that holy room
   Where, with thy choir of saints for evermore,
I shall be made thy music, as I come
   I tune the instrument here at the door,
   And what I must do then, think here before.

Whilst my physicians by their love are grown
   Cosmographers, and I their map, who lie
Flat on this bed, that by them may be shown
   That this is my south-west discovery,
   Per fretum febris, by these straits to die,

I joy, that in these straits I see my west;
   For though their currents yield return to none,
What shall my west hurt me? As west and east
   In all flat maps, and I am one, are one,
   So death doth touch the resurrection.

Is the Pacific sea my home? or are
   The eastern riches? is Jerusalem?
Anyan and Magellan and Gibraltar,
   All straits, and none but straits, are ways to them,
   Whether where Japhet dwelt, or Cham, or Shem.

We think that Paradise and Calvary,
   Christ's cross and Adam's tree, stood in one place;

Look, Lord, and find both Adams met in me:
  As the first Adam's sweat surrounds my face,
  May the last Adam's blood my soul embrace.

So, in his purple wrapped, receive me, Lord;
  By these, his thorns, give me his other crown;
And as to others' souls I preached thy word,
  Be this my text, my sermon to mine own:
  Therefore that he may raise, the Lord throws down.   30

BEN JONSON

The Introduction and Notes are at page 989

FROM *The Works of Benjamin Jonson*, 1616

EPIGRAMS

To the reader

Pray thee, take care, that tak'st my book in hand,
To read it well—that is, to understand.

To my book

It will be looked for, book, when some but see
  Thy title, *Epigrams*, and named of me,
Thou shouldst be bold, licentious, full of gall,
  Wormwood and sulphur, sharp, and toothed withal;
Become a petulant thing, hurl ink and wit
  As madmen stones, not caring whom they hit.
Deceive their malice, who could wish it so.
  And by thy wiser temper, let men know
Thou art not covetous of least self-fame
  Made trom the hazard of another's shame;   10
Much less, with lewd, profane, and beastly phrase,
  To catch the world's loose laughter, or vain gaze.
He that departs with his own honesty
  For vulgar praise, doth it too dearly buy.

To my bookseller

Thou that mak'st gain thy end, and wisely well
  Call'st a book good or bad as it doth sell,
Use mine so too, I give thee leave; but crave,
  For the luck's sake, it thus much favor have,

To lie upon thy stall till it be sought,
  Not offered, as it made suit to be bought;
Nor have my title-leaf on posts or walls,
  Or in cleft-sticks, advancëd to make calls
For termers, or some clerk-like servingman
  Who scarce can spell th' hard names, whose knight less can.   10
If, without these vile arts, it will not sell,
  Send it to Bucklersbury, there 'twill well.

To my mere English censurer

To thee my way in epigrams seems new,
  When both it is the old way and the true.
Thou sayst that cannot be, for thou hast seen
  Davies and Weever, and the best have been,
And mine come nothing like. I hope so; yet
  As theirs did with thee, mine might credit get,
If thou'dst but use thy faith, as thou didst then
  When thou wert wont t' admire, not censure men.
Prithee believe still, and not judge so fast,
  Thy faith is all the knowledge that thou hast.   10

On something that walks somewhere

At court I met it, in clothes brave enough
  To be a courtier, and looks grave enough
To seem a statesman; as I near it came,
  It made me a great face; I asked the name.
A Lord, it cried, buried in flesh and blood,
  And such from whom let no man hope least good,
For I will do none; and as little ill,
  For I will dare none. Good Lord, walk dead still.

To Doctor Empiric

When men a dangerous disease did 'scape
  Of old, they gave a cock to Æsculape;
Let me give two, that doubly am got free:
  From my disease's danger, and from thee.

To William Camden

Camden, most reverend head, to whom I owe
  All that I am in arts, all that I know
(How nothing's that); to whom my country owes
  The great renown and name wherewith she goes;
Than thee the age sees not that thing more grave,

More high, more holy, that she more would crave.
What name, what skill, what faith hast thou in things!
   What sight in searching the most antique springs!
What weight and what authority in thy speech!
   Man scarce can make that doubt, but thou canst teach.   10
Pardon free truth and let thy modesty,
   Which conquers all, be once overcome by thee.
Many of thine this better could than I,
   But for their powers, accept my piety.

To Francis Beaumont

How I do love thee, Beaumont, and thy muse,
   That unto me dost such religion use!
How I do fear myself, that am not worth
   The least indulgent thought thy pen drops forth!
At once thou mak'st me happy, and unmak'st;
   And giving largely to me, more thou tak'st.
What fate is mine, that so itself bereaves?
   What art is thine, that so thy friend deceives?
When even there where most thou praisest me,
   For writing better, I must envy thee.   10

To John Donne

Who shall doubt, Donne, where I a poet be,
   When I dare send my *Epigrams* to thee?
That so alone canst judge, so alone dost make;
   And, in thy censures, evenly dost take
As free simplicity to disavow
   As thou hast best authority t' allow.
Read all I send; and if I find but one
   Marked by thy hand, and with the better stone,
My title's sealed. Those that for claps do write,
   Let pui'nes', porters', players' praise delight,   10
And till they burst their backs, like asses load;
   A man should seek great glory, and not broad.

On Lucy, Countess of Bedford

This morning, timely rapt with holy fire,
   I thought to form unto my zealous muse
What kind of creature I could most desire
   To honor, serve, and love, as poets use.
I meant to make her fair, and free, and wise,
   Of greatest blood, and yet more good than great;

I meant the day-star should not brighter rise,
   Nor lend like influence from his lucent seat;
I meant she should be courteous, facile, sweet,
   Hating that solemn vice of greatness, pride;   10
I meant each softest virtue there should meet,
   Fit in that softer bosom to reside.
Only a learned, and a manly soul
   I purposed her; that should, with even powers,
The rock, the spindle, and the shears control
   Of destiny, and spin her own free hours.
Such when I meant to feign, and wished to see,
   My muse bade, Bedford write, and that was she.

To Lucy, Countess of Bedford, with Mr. Donne's satires

Lucy, you brightness of our sphere, who are
   Life of the Muses' day, their morning star!
If works, not th' author's, their own grace should look,
   Whose poems would not wish to be your book?
But these, desired by you, the maker's ends
   Crown with their own; rare poems ask rare friends.
Yet satires, since the most of mankind be
   Their unavoided subject, fewest see;
For none e'er took that pleasure in sin's sense,
   But, when they heard it taxed, took more offence.   10
They, then, that living where the matter is bred,
   Dare for these poems, yet, both ask and read
And like them too, must needfully, though few,
   Be of the best, and 'mongst those best are you,
Lucy, you brightness of our sphere, who are
   The Muses' evening, as their morning star.

Inviting a friend to supper

To-night, grave sir, both my poor house and I
   Do equally desire your company;
Not that we think us worthy such a guest,
   But that your worth will dignify our feast
With those that come, whose grace may make that seem
   Something, which else could hope for no esteem.
It is the fair acceptance, sir, creates
   The entertainment perfect, not the cates.
Yet shall you have, to rectify your palate,
   An olive, capers, or some better salad   10
Ush'ring the mutton; with a short-legged hen,
   If we can get her, full of eggs, and then

Lemons and wine for sauce; to these, a coney
    Is not to be despaired of, for our money;
And though fowl now be scarce, yet there are clerks,
    The sky not falling, think we may have larks.
I'll tell you of more, and lie, so you will come,
    Of partridge, pheasant, woodcock, of which some
May yet be there; and godwit, if we can,
    Gnat, rail, and ruff too. Howsoe'er, my man   20
Shall read a piece of Virgil, Tacitus,
    Livy, or of some better book to us,
Of which we'll speak our minds amidst our meat;
    And I'll profess no verses to repeat;
To this, if aught appear which I know not of,
    That will the pastry, not my paper, show of.
Digestive cheese, and fruit there sure will be;
    But that which most doth take my muse, and me,
Is a pure cup of rich Canary wine,
    Which is the Mermaid's now, but shall be mine;   30
Of which had Horace or Anacreon tasted,
    Their lives, as do their lines, till now had lasted.
Tobacco, nectar, or the Thespian springs
    Are all but Luther's beer to this I sing.
Of this we will sup free, but moderately,
    And we will have no polly, or parrot by;
Nor shall our cups make any guilty men,
    But at our parting we will be as when
We innocently met. No simple word
    That shall be uttered at our mirthful board
Shall make us sad next morning, or affright
    The liberty that we'll enjoy to-night.

On my first son

Farewell, thou child of my right hand, and joy;
    My sin was too much hope of thee, loved boy.
Seven years thou wert lent to me, and I thee pay,
    Exacted by thy fate, on the just day.
Oh, could I lose all father now! For why
    Will man lament the state he should envý?
To have so soon 'scaped world's and flesh's rage,
    And if no other misery, yet age!
Rest in soft peace, and asked, say, Here doth lie
    Ben Jonson his best piece of poetry.   10
For whose sake henceforth all his vows be such
    As what he loves may never like too much.

*An epitaph on S[alathiel] P[avy], a child of Q[ueen]
El[izabeth's] Chapel*

Weep with me, all you that read
   This little story;
And know, for whom a tear you shed
   Death's self is sorry.
'Twas a child that so did thrive
   In grace and feature,
As heaven and nature seemed to strive
   Which owned the creature.
Years he numbered scarce thirteen
   When fates turned cruel,   10
Yet three filled zodiacs had he been
   The stage's jewel;
And did act, what now we moan,
   Old men so duly,
As, sooth, the Parcæ thought him one,
   He played so truly.
So by error, to his fate
   They all consented;
But viewing him since, alas too late,
   They have repented,   20
And have sought, to give new birth,
   In baths to steep him;
But being so much too good for earth,
   Heaven vows to keep him.

Epitaph on Elizabeth, L. H.

Wouldst thou hear what man can say
   In a little? Reader, stay.
Underneath this stone doth lie
   As much beauty as could die;
Which in life did harbor give
   To more virtue than doth live.
If at all she had a fault,
   Leave it buried in this vault.
One name was Elizabeth,
   Th' other let it sleep with death;   10
Fitter, where it died to tell,
   Than that it lived at all. Farewell.

THE FOREST

Why I write not of Love

Some act of Love's bound to rehearse,
I thought to bind him in my verse;
Which when he felt, Away, quoth he,
Can poets hope to fetter me?
It is enough they once did get
Mars and my mother in their net;
I wear not these my wings in vain.
With which he fled me, and again
Into my rhymes could ne'er be got
By any art. Then wonder not   10
That since my numbers are so cold,
When Love is fled, and I grow old.

To Penshurst

Thou art not, Penshurst, built to envious show
    Of touch or marble, nor canst boast a row
Of polished pillars, or a roof of gold;
    Thou hast no lantern whereof tales are told,
Or stairs or courts; but stand'st an ancient pile,
    And these, grudged at, art reverenced the while.
Thou joy'st in better marks, of soil, of air,
    Of wood, of water; therein thou art fair.
Thou hast thy walks for health as well as sport;
    Thy mount, to which the Dryads do resort,   10
Where Pan and Bacchus their high feasts have made
    Beneath the broad beech, and the chestnut shade,
That taller tree, which of a nut was set
    At his great birth, where all the Muses met.
There in the writhèd bark are cut the names
    Of many a sylvan, taken with his flames;
And thence the ruddy satyrs oft provoke
    The lighter fauns to reach thy Lady's oak.
Thy copse too, named of Gamage, thou hast there,
    That never fails to serve thee seasoned deer   20
When thou wouldst feast, or exercise thy friends.
    The lower land, that to the river bends,
Thy sheep, thy bullocks, kine, and calves do feed;
    The middle grounds thy mares and horses breed.
Each bank doth yield thee conies; and the tops,
    Fertile of wood, Ashore and Sidney's copse,
To crown thy open table, doth provide

The purpled pheasant with the speckled side;
The painted partridge lies in every field,
   And, for thy mess, is willing to be killed.   30
And if the high-swollen Medway fail thy dish,
   Thou hast thy ponds that pay thee tribute fish,
Fat aged carps that run into thy net,
   And pikes, now weary their own kind to eat,
As loath the second draught or cast to stay,
   Officiously at first themselves betray;
Bright eels that emulate them, and leap on land
   Before the fisher, or into his hand.
Then hath thy orchard fruit, thy garden flowers
   Fresh as the air, and new as are the hours.   40
The early cherry, with the later plum,
   Fig, grape, and quince, each in his time doth come;
The blushing apricot and woolly peach
   Hang on thy walls, that every child may reach.
And though thy walls be of the country stone,
   They'are reared with no man's ruin, no man's groan;
There's none that dwell about them wish them down,
   But all come in, the farmer and the clown,
And no one empty handed, to salute
   Thy lord and lady, though they have no suit.   50
Some bring a capon, some a rural cake,
   Some nuts, some apples; some that think they make
The better cheeses bring 'em, or else send
   By their ripe daughters whom they would commend
This way to husbands, and whose baskets bear
   An emblem of themselves in plum or pear.
But what can this, more than express their love,
   Add to thy free provisions, far above
The need of such, whose liberal board doth flow
   With all that hospitality doth know?   60
Where comes no guest but is allowed to eat
   Without his fear, and of thy lord's own meat;
Where the same beer and bread, and self-same wine
   That is his lordship's shall be also mine.
And I not fain to sit, as some this day
   At great men's tables, and yet dine away.
Here no man tells my cups, nor, standing by,
   A waiter doth my gluttony envý,
But gives me what I call and lets me eat;
   He knows below he shall find plenty of meat.   70
Thy tables hoard not up for the next day,
   Nor when I take my lodging need I pray
For fire or lights or livery; all is there

As if thou then wert mine, or I reigned here;
There's nothing I can wish, for which I stay.
   That found King James, when hunting late this way
With his brave son, the prince, they saw thy fires
   Shine bright on every hearth as the desires
Of thy Penates had been set on flame
   To entertain them, or the country came   80
With all their zeal to warm their welcome here.
   What great I will not say, but sudden cheer
Didst thou then make 'em! and what praise was heaped
   On thy good lady then! who therein reaped
The just reward of her high huswifery;
   To have her linen, plate, and all things nigh
When she was far, and not a room but dressed
   As if it had expected such a guest!
These, Penshurst, are thy praise, and yet not all.
   Thy lady's noble, fruitful, chaste withal;   90
His children thy great lord may call his own,
   A fortune in this age but rarely known.
They are and have been taught religion; thence
   Their gentler spirits have sucked innocence.
Each morn and even they are taught to pray
   With the whole household, and may every day
Read, in their virtuous parents' noble parts,
   The mysteries of manners, arms, and arts.
Now, Penshurst, they that will proportion thee
   With other edifices when they see   100
Those proud, ambitious heaps and nothing else,
   May say, their lords have built, but thy lord dwells.

Song, to Celia [1]

Come, my Celia, let us prove
While we may the sports of love;
Time will not be ours forever,
He at length our good will sever.
Spend not then his gifts in vain;
Suns that set may rise again,
But if once we lose this light,
'Tis with us perpetual night.
Why should we defer our joys?

Fame and rumor are but toys.   10
Cannot we delude the eyes
Of a few poor household spies?
Or his easier ears beguile,
So removèd by our wile?
'Tis no sin love's fruit to steal;
But the sweet theft to reveal,
To be taken, to be seen,
These have crimes accounted been.

Song, to Celia [2]

Drink to me only with thine
   eyes,
   And I will pledge with mine;
Or leave a kiss but in the cup,

And I'll not look for wine.
The thirst that from the soul doth
   rise
   Doth ask a drink divine;

But might I of Jove's nectar sup,
  I would not change for thine.
I sent thee late a rosy wreath,
  Not so much honoring thee,   10
As giving it a hope that there
  It could not withered be.

But thou thereon didst only
    breathe,
  And sent'st it back to me,
Since when it grows and smells, I
    swear,
  Not of itself, but thee.

FROM *The Works of Benjamin Jonson*, 1641

UNDERWOODS

A celebration of Charis in ten lyric pieces

His excuse for loving

Let it not your wonder move,
Less your laughter, that I love.
Though I now write fifty years,
I have had, and have, my peers;
Poets though divine are men,
Some have loved as old again.
And it is not always face,
Clothes, or fortune, gives the grace,
Or the feature, or the youth;
But the language and the truth,   10
With the ardor and the passion,
Gives the lover weight and fash-
    ion.

If you then will read the story,
First prepare you to be sorry
That you never knew till now
Either whom to love, or how;
But be glad, as soon with me,
When you know that this is she
Of whose beauty it was sung:
She shall make the old man
    young,   20
Keep the middle age at stay,
And let nothing high decay;
Till she be the reason why
All the world for love may die.

Her triumph

See the chariot at hand here of love,
  Wherein my lady rideth!
Each that draws is a swan or a dove,
  And well the car love guideth.
As she goes all hearts do duty
    Unto her beauty,
And enamoured do wish so they might
    But enjoy such a sight,
That they still were to run by her side,
Through swords, through seas, whither she would ride.   10

Do but look on her eyes; they do light
  All that love's world compriseth!
Do but look on her hair; it is bright
  As love's star when it riseth!
Do but mark, her forehead's smoother
    Than words that soothe her:

And from her arched brows, such a grace
  Sheds itself through the face,
As alone there triumphs to the life
All the gain, all the good of the elements' strife.   20

Have you seen but a bright lily grow
  Before rude hands have touched it?
Ha'. you marked but the fall o' the snow
  Before the soil hath smutched it?
Ha' you felt the wool of beaver,
  Or swan's down ever?
Or have smelt o' the bud o' the briar?
  Or the nard in the fire?
Or have tasted the bag of the bee?
O so white! O so soft! O so sweet is she!   30

Begging another [*kiss*], *on color of mending the former*

For love's sake, kiss me once again;
I long, and should not beg in vain,
  Here's none to spy or see;
    Why do you doubt or stay?
I'll taste as lightly as the bee
That doth but touch his flower and flies away.
Once more, and faith I will be gone;
Can he that loves ask less than one?
  Nay, you may err in this
    And all your bounty wrong;   10
This could be called but half a kiss,
What we're but once to do, we should do long.
I will but mend the last, and tell
Where, how it would have relished well;
  Join lip to lip, and try,
    Each suck other's breath.
And whilst our tongues perplexëd lie,
Let who will, think us dead or wish our death.

An ode to himself

Where dost thou careless lie,
  Buried in ease and sloth?
Knowledge that sleeps doth
  die;
And this security,
  It is the common moth
That eats on wits and arts, and
  destroys them both.

Are all th' Aonian springs
  Dried up? Lies Thespia
    waste?
Doth Clarius' harp want
  strings,
That not a nymph now
  sings?   10
Or droop they as disgraced,

To see their seats and bowers by
    chatt'ring pies de-
    faced?

If hence thy silence be,
    As 'tis too just a cause,
Let this thought quicken thee:
Minds that are great and free
    Should not on fortune
    pause;
'Tis crown enough to virtue still,
    her own applause.

What though the greedy fry
    Be taken with false baits [20]
Of worded balladry,
    And think it poesy?
They die with their con-
    ceits,

And only piteous scorn upon their
    folly waits.

Then take in hand thy lyre,
    Strike in thy proper strain,
With Japhet's line aspire
Sol's chariot for new fire
    To give the world again;
Who aided him, will thee, the issue
    of Jove's brain. [30]

And since our dainty age
    Cannot endure reproof,
Make not thyself a page
To that strumpet, the stage,
    But sing high and aloof,
Safe from the wolf's black jaw,
    and the dull ass's
    hoof.

A fit of rhyme against rhyme

Rhyme, the rack of finest wits,
That expresseth but by fits
    True conceit,
Spoiling senses of their treasure,
Cozening judgment with a meas-
    ure,
    But false weight;
Wresting words from their true
    calling,
Propping verse for fear of falling
    To the ground;
Jointing syllabes, drowning let-
    ters, [10]
Fast'ning vowels as with fetters
    They were bound!
Soon as lazy thou wert known,
All good poetry hence was
    flown,
    And are banished.
For a thousand years together
All Parnassus' green did wither,
    And wit vanished.
Pegasus did fly away,
At the wells no Muse did stay, [20]
    But bewailed
So to see the fountain dry,

And Apollo's music die,
    All light failed!
Starveling rhymes did fill the
    stage;
Not a poet in an age
    Worth crowning;
Not a work deserving bays,
Not a line deserving praise,
    Pallas frowning; [30]
Greek was free from rhyme's in-
    fection,
Happy Greek by this protection
    Was not spoiled.
Whilst the Latin, queen of tongues,
Is not yet free from rhyme's
    wrongs,
    But rests foiled.
Scarce the hill again doth flourish,
Scarce the world a wit doth nourish
    To restore
Phœbus to his crown again, [40]
And the Muses to their brain,
    As before.
Vulgar languages that want
Words and sweetness, and be scant
    Of true measure,

Tyrant rhyme hath so abusëd,
That they long since have refusëd
  Other cæsure.
He that first invented thee,
May his joints tormented be,   50
  Cramped forever.
Still may syllabes jar with time,

Still may reason war with rhyme,
  Resting never.
May his sense when it would meet
The cold tumor in his feet,
  Grow unsounder;
And his title be long fool,
That in rearing such a school
  Was the founder.   60

To the immortal memory and friendship of that noble pair, Sir Lucius Cary and Sir H. Morison

THE TURN

Brave infant of Saguntum, clear
Thy coming forth in that great year
When the prodigious Hannibal did crown
His rage with razing your immortal town.
Thou, looking then about,
Ere thou wert half got out,
Wise child, didst hastily return
And mad'st thy mother's womb thine urn.
How summed a circle didst thou leave mankind,
Of deepest lore, could we the center find!   10

THE COUNTER-TURN

Did wiser nature draw thee back
From out the horror of that sack,
Where shame, faith, honor, and regard of right
Lay trampled on? The deeds of death and night
Urged, hurried forth, and hurled
Upon th' affrighted world;
Sword, fire, and famine with fell fury met,
And all on utmost ruin set;
As, could they but life's miseries foresee,
No doubt all infants would return like thee.   20

THE STAND

For what is life, if measured by the space,
Not by the act?
Or maskëd man, if valued by his face,
Above his fact?
Here's one outlived his peers,
And told forth fourscore years;
He vexëd time, and busied the whole state,
Troubled both foes and friends,

But ever to no ends;
What did this stirrer but die late?   30
How well at twenty had he fallen or stood!
For three of his fourscore he did no good.

THE TURN

He entered well, by virtuous parts
Got up, and thrived with honest arts;
He purchased friends and fame, and honors then,
And had his noble name advanced with men.
But weary of that flight,
He stooped in all men's sight
To sordid flatteries, acts of strife,
And sunk in that dead sea of life   40
So deep as he did then death's waters sup,
But that the cork of title buoyed him up.

THE COUNTER-TURN

Alas, but Morison fell young!
He never fell,—thou fall'st, my tongue.
He stood, a soldier to the last right end,
A perfect patriot and a noble friend,
But most, a virtuous son.
All offices were done
By him so ample, full, and round,
In weight, in measure, number, sound,   50
As, though his age imperfect might appear,
His life was of humanity the sphere.

THE STAND

Go now, and tell out days summed up with fears,
And make them years;
Produce thy mass of miseries on the stage,
To swell thine age;
Repeat of things a throng,
To show thou hast been long,
Not lived, for life doth her great actions spell
By what was done and wrought   60
In season, and so brought
To light; her measures are, how well
Each syllabe answered, and was formed how fair;
These make the lines of life, and that's her air.

THE TURN

It is not growing like a tree
In bulk. doth make man better be;

Or standing long an oak, three hundred year,
To fall a log at last, dry, bald, and sere;
A lily of a day
Is fairer far in May,
Although it fall and die that night,   70
It was the plant and flower of light.
In small proportions we just beauties see;
And in short measures, life may perfect be.

THE COUNTER-TURN

Call, noble Lucius, then for wine,
And let thy looks with gladness shine;
Accept this garland, plant it on thy head,
And think, nay know, thy Morison's not dead.
He leaped the present age,
Possessed with holy rage,   80
To see that bright eternal day
Of which we priests and poets say
Such truths as we expect for happy men,
And there he lives with memory, and Ben

THE STAND

Jonson, who sung this of him, ere he went
Himself to rest,
Or taste a part of that full joy he meant
To have expressed
In this bright asterism,
Where it were friendship's schism,   90
Were not his Lucius long with us to tarry,
To separate these twi-
Lights, the Dioscuri,
And keep the one half from his Harry.
But fate doth so alternate the design,
Whilst that in heav'n, this light on earth must shine.

THE TURN

And shine as you exalted are,
Two names of friendship, but one star;
Of hearts the union, and those not by chance
Made, or indenture, or leased out t' advance   100
The profits for a time.
No pleasures vain did chime
Of rhymes, or riots at your feasts,
Orgies of drink, or feigned protests;

But simple love of greatness and of good,
That knits brave minds and manners more than blood.

THE COUNTER-TURN

This made you first to know the why
You liked, then after to apply
That liking; and approach so one the t' other
Till either grew a portion of the other;   110
Each stylèd by his end
The copy of his friend.
You lived to be the great surnames
And titles by which all made claims
Unto the virtue; nothing perfect done
But as a Cary, or a Morison.

THE STAND

And such a force the fair example had,
As they that saw
The good, and durst not practise it, were glad
That such a law   120
Was left yet to mankind,
Where they might read and find
Friendship in deed was written, not in words;
And with the heart, not pen,
Of two so early men,
Whose lines her rolls were, and recórds;
Who, ere the first down bloomèd on the chin,
Had sowed these fruits, and got the harvest in.

An epistle answering to one that asked to be sealed of the
Tribe of Ben

Men that are safe and sure in all they do,
    Care not what trials they are put unto;
They meet the fire, the test, as martyrs would,
    And though opinion stamp them not, are gold.
I could say more of such, but that I fly
    To speak myself out too ambitiously,
And showing so weak an act to vulgar eyes
    Put conscience and my right to compromise.
Let those that merely talk and never think,
    That live in the wild anarchy of drink,   10
Subject to quarrel only, or else such
    As make it their proficiency how much
They've glutted in and lechered out that week,

That never yet did friend or friendship seek
But for a sealing—let these men protest.
  Or th' other on their borders, that will jest
On all souls that are absent, even the dead,
    Like flies or worms, which man's corrupt parts fed;
That to speak well, think it above all sin,
  Of any company but that they are in,
Call every night to supper in these fits
    And are received for the covey of wits;
That censure all the town and all th' affairs,
  And know whose ignorance is more than theirs,—
Let these men have their ways, and take their times
    To vent their libels and to issue rhymes;
I have no portion in them, nor their deal
  Of news they get to strew out the long meal;
I study other friendships, and more one
    Than these can ever be, or else with none.
What is 't to me whether the French design
  Be, or be not, to get the Valteline?
Or the States' ships sent forth belike to meet
    Some hopes of Spain in their West Indian fleet?
Whether the dispensation yet be sent,
  Or that the match from Spain was ever meant?
I wish all well, and pray high heaven conspire
  My prince's safety and my king's desire;
But if for honor we must draw the sword,
    And force back that which will not be restored,
I have a body yet that spirit draws
  To live, or fall a carcass, in the cause.
So far without enquiries what the States,
  Brunsfield, and Mansfield do this year, my fates
Shall carry me at call, and I'll be well,
  Though I do neither hear these news, nor tell
Of Spain or France, or were not pricked down one
  Of the late mystery of reception,
Although my fame to his not under-hears,
  That guides the motions and directs the bears.
But that's a blow by which in time I may
  Lose all my credit with my Christmas clay,
And animated porcelain of the court;
  Ay, and for this neglect, the coarser sort
Of earthen jars there may molest me too.
  Well, with mine own frail pitcher, what to do
I have decreed; keep it from waves and press,
  Lest it be jostled, cracked, made nought or less;
Live to that point I will for which I am man,

And dwell as in my center as I can,
Still looking to and ever loving heaven,
   With reverence using all the gifts then given;
'Mongst which, if I have any friendships sent
   Such as are square, well-tagged, and permanent,
Not built with canvas, paper, and false lights
   As are the glorious scenes at the great sights,
And that there be no fev'ry heats nor colds,
   Oily expansions, or shrunk dirty folds,
But all so clear, and led by reason's flame,
   As but to stumble in her sight were shame,—
These I will honor, love, embrace, and serve,
   And free it from all question to preserve.
So short you read my character, and theirs
   I would call mine, to which not many stairs
Are asked to climb. First give me faith, who know
   Myself a little; I will take you so
As you have writ yourself. Now stand; and then,
   Sir, you are sealed of the Tribe of Ben.

From *Mr. William Shakespeare's Comedies, Histories, and Tragedies*, 1623

To the memory of my beloved the author,
Mr. William Shakespeare, and what he hath left us

To draw no envy, Shakespeare, on thy name,
   Am I thus ample to thy book and fame,
While I confess thy writings to be such
   As neither man nor Muse can praise too much;
'Tis true, and all men's suffrage. But these ways
   Were not the paths I meant unto thy praise,
For seeliest ignorance on these may light,
   Which when it sounds at best but echoes right;
Or blind affection which doth ne'er advance
   The truth, but gropes and urgeth all by chance;
Or crafty malice might pretend this praise,
   And think to ruin where it seemed to raise.
These are as some infamous bawd or whore
   Should praise a matron; what could hurt her more?
But thou art proof against them, and indeed
   Above th' ill fortune of them, or the need.
I, therefore, will begin. Soul of the age!
   The applause, delight, the wonder of our stage!
My Shakespeare, rise; I will not lodge thee by

Chaucer, or Spenser, or bid Beaumont lie   20
A little further to make thee a room;
    Thou art a monument, without a tomb,
And art alive still, while thy book doth live
    And we have wits to read and praise to give.
That I not mix thee so, my brain excuses—
    I mean with great but disproportioned muses,—
For if I thought my judgment were of years
    I should commit thee surely with thy peers,
And tell how far thou didst our Lyly outshine,
    Or sporting Kyd, or Marlowe's mighty line.   30
And though thou hadst small Latin and less Greek,
    From thence to honor thee I would not seek
For names, but call forth thund'ring Æschylus,
    Euripides, and Sophocles to us,
Pacuvius, Accius, him of Cordova dead,
    To life again, to hear thy buskin tread
And shake a stage; or, when thy socks were on,
    Leave thee alone for the comparison
Of all that insolent Greece or haughty Rome
    Sent forth, or since did from their ashes come.   40
Triumph, my Britain, thou hast one to show
    To whom all scenes of Europe homage owe.
He was not of an age, but for all time!
    And all the Muses still were in their prime,
When like Apollo he came forth to warm
    Our ears, or like a Mercury to charm!
Nature herself was proud of his designs,
    And joyed to wear the dressing of his lines
Which were so richly spun, and woven so fit,
    As since, she will vouchsafe no other wit;   50
The merry Greek, tart Aristophanes,
    Neat Terence, witty Plautus, now not please,
But antiquated and deserted lie
    As they were not of nature's family.
Yet must I not give nature all; thy art,
    My gentle Shakespeare, must enjoy a part;
For though the poet's matter nature be,
    His art doth give the fashion; and that he
Who casts to write a living line, must sweat,
    Such as thine are, and strike the second heat   60
Upon the Muses' anvil, turn the same,
    And himself with it, that he thinks to frame;
Or for the laurel he may gain a scorn,
    For a good poet's made, as well as born;
And such wert thou. Look how the father's face

Lives in his issue; even so the race
Of Shakespeare's mind and manners brightly shines
   In his well-turnèd and true-filèd lines,
In each of which he seems to shake a lance,
   As brandished at the eyes of ignorance.   70
Sweet swan of Avon! what a sight it were
   To see thee in our waters yet appear,
And make those flights upon the banks of Thames
   That so did take Eliza, and our James!
But stay, I see thee in the hemisphere
   Advanced, and made a constellation there!
Shine forth, thou star of poets, and with rage
   Or influence chide or cheer the drooping stage;
Which since thy flight from hence, hath mourned like night,
   And despairs day, but for thy volume's light.   80

FROM ALEXANDER BROME'S *Songs and other Poems*, 1661

Ben Jonson's Sociable Rules for the Apollo

[A translation of Jonson's *Leges Convivales*]

Let none but guests or clubbers hither come,
Let dunces, fools, sad sordid men, keep home;
Let learned, civil, merry men b'invited,
And modest too; nor the choice ladies slighted.
Let nothing in the treat offend the guests;
More for delight than cost prepare the feasts.
The cook and purveyor must our palates know;
And none contend who shall sit high or low.
Our waiters must quick-sighted be and dumb,
And let the drawers hear and come.   10
Let not our wine be mixed, but brisk and neat,
Or else the drinkers may the vintners beat.
And let our only emulation be,
Not drinking much, but talking wittily.
Let it be voted lawful to stir up
Each other with a moderate chirping cup.
Let not our company be, or talk, too much;
On serious things or sacred let's not touch
With sated heads and bellies. Neither may
Fiddlers unasked obtrude themselves to play;   20
With laughing, leaping, dancing, jests and songs,
And whate'er else to grateful mirth belongs,
Let's celebrate our feasts; and let us see
That all our jests without reflection be.
Insipid poems let no man rehearse,

Nor any be compelled to write a verse.
All noise of vain disputes must be forborne,
And let no lover in a corner mourn.
To fight and brawl, like Hectors, let none dare,
Glasses or windows break, or hangings tear.   30
Whoe'er shall publish what's here done or said
From our society must be banishëd.
Let none by drinking do or suffer harm,
And while we stay, let us be always warm.

[SONGS FROM THE PLAYS AND MASKS]

FROM *The Works of Benjamin Jonson*, 1616

[Slow, slow, fresh fount]

Slow, slow, fresh fount, keep time with my salt tears;
    Yet slower yet, oh faintly, gentle springs;
List to the heavy part the music bears,
    Woe weeps out her division when she sings.
        Droop herbs and flowers,
        Fall grief in showers;
        Our beauties are not ours;
            Oh, I could still,
Like melting snow upon some craggy hill,
    Drop, drop, drop, drop,   10
Since nature's pride is now a withered daffodil.

                                        From *Cynthia's Revels*

[Oh, that joy so soon should waste]

Oh, that joy so soon should waste!
    Or so sweet a bliss
    As a kiss
Might not forever last!
So sugared, so melting, so soft, so delicious!
    The dew that lies on roses
When morn herself discloses,
    Is not so precious.
Oh, rather than I would it smother,
Were I to taste such another,   10
    It should be my wishing
    That I might die kissing.

                                        From *Cynthia's Revels*

[Queen and huntress]

Queen and huntress, chaste and fair,
    Now the sun is laid to sleep,

Seated in thy silver chair
State in wonted manner keep;
 Hesperus entreats thy light,
 Goddess excellently bright.

Earth, let not thy envious shade
Dare itself to interpose;
Cynthia's shining orb was made
Heaven to clear, when day did close;   10
 Bless us then with wishëd sight,
 Goddess excellently bright.

Lay thy bow of pearl apart,
And thy crystal shining quiver;
Give unto the flying hart
Space to breathe, how short soever,
 Thou that mak'st a day of night,
 Goddess excellently bright.

From Cynthia's Revels

[If I freely may discover]

If I freely may discover
What would please me in my lover:
 I would have her fair and witty,
 Savoring more of court than city;
 A little proud, but full of pity;
 Light and humorous in her toying,
 Oft building hopes and soon destroying;
 Long, but sweet, in the enjoying;
Neither too easy, nor too hard,
All extremes I would have barred.   10

She should be allowed her passions,
So they were but used as fashions;
 Sometimes froward, and then frowning,
 Sometimes sickish, and then swowning,
 Every fit with change still crowning.
 Purely jealous I would have her;
 Then only constant when I crave her,
 'Tis a virtue should not save her.
Thus, nor her delicates would cloy me,
Neither her peevishness annoy me.   20

From The Poetaster

[Swell me a bowl]

Swell me a bowl with lusty wine,
Till I may see the plump Lyæus swim
  Above the brim;
I drink as I would write,
In flowing measure, filled with flame and sprite.

From The Poetaster

[Fools]

Fools, they are the only nation
Worth men's envy or admiration,
Free from care or sorrow-taking,
Selves and others merry making;
All they speak or do is sterling.
Your fool he is your great man's darling,
And your lady's sport and pleasure;
Tongue and babble are his treasure,
E'en his face begetteth laughter,
And he speaks truth free from slaughter;   10
He's the grace of every feast,
And sometimes the chiefest guest
Hath his trencher and his stool,
When wit waits upon the fool.
  Oh, who would not be
  He, he, he?

From Volpone, or the Fox

[Still to be neat]

Still to be neat, still to be dressed
As you were going to a feast;
Still to be powdered, still perfumed:
Lady, it is to be presumed,
Though art's hid causes are not found,
All is not sweet, all is not sound.

Give me a look, give me a face
That makes simplicity a grace;
Robes loosely flowing, hair as free:
Such sweet neglect more taketh me   10
Than all th' adulteries of art;
They strike mine eyes, but not my heart.

From Epicæne, or the Silent Woman

[Had those that dwell in error foul]

Had those that dwell in error foul
And hold that women have no soul,
But seen these move, they would have then
Said, Women were the souls of men.
So they do move each heart and eye
With the world's soul, true harmony.

From *The Second Mask, which was of Beauty*

[Beauties, have ye seen]

1 Grace. Beauties, have ye seen
        this toy
Called Love, a little boy,
Almost naked, wanton, blind,
Cruel now, and then as kind?
If he be amongst ye, say;
He is Venus' runaway.

2 Grace. She that will but now
        discover
Where the wingèd wag doth
        hover,
Shall to-night receive a kiss
How or where herself would
        wish;   10
But who brings him to his
        mother,
Shall have that kiss and
        another.

3 Grace. H' hath of marks about
        him plenty;
You shall know him among
        twenty.
All his body is a fire,
And his breath a flame entire,
That being shot like light-
        ning in,
Wounds the heart, but not
        the skin.

1 Grace. At his sight the sun
        hath turned,
Neptune in the waters
        burned,   20

Hell hath felt a greater heat,
Jove himself forsook his seat;
From the center to the sky
Are his trophies rearèd high.

2 Grace. Wings he hath, which
        though ye clip,
He will leap from lip to lip,
Over liver, lights, and heart,
But not stay in any part;
And if chance his arrow
        misses,
He will shoot himself in
        kisses.   30

3 Grace. He doth bear a golden
        bow,
And a quiver, hanging low,
Full of arrows that out-brave
Dian's shafts; where if he
        have
Any head more sharp than
        other,
With that first he strikes his
        mother.

1 Grace. Still the fairest are his
        fuel.
When his days are to be cruel,
Lovers' hearts are all his food,
And his baths their warmest
        blood;   40
Nought but wounds his hand
        doth season,
And he hates none like to
        reason.

2 *Grace.* Trust him not; his
   words, though sweet,
   Seldom with his heart do
   meet.
   All his practice is deceit;
   Every gift it is a bait;
   Not a kiss but poison bears,
   And most treason in his tears.

3 *Grace.* Idle minutes are his
   reign,
   Then the straggler makes his
   gain   50
   By presenting maids with
   toys,
   And would have ye think 'em
   joys;

'Tis the ambition of the elf
To have all childish as himself.

1 *Grace.* If by these ye please to
   know him,
   Beauties, be not nice, but
   show him.

2 *Grace.* Though ye had a will
   to hide him,
   Now, we hope, ye'll not abide
   him.

3 *Grace.* Since ye hear his falser
   play,
   And that he is Venus' runaway.   60

From *The Description of the Mask . . . at
the Lord Viscount Hadington's Marriage*

[*Buz, quoth the blue fly*]

Buz, quoth the blue fly,
   Hum, quoth the bee;
Buz and hum they cry,
   And so do we.
In his ear, in his nose,
   Thus, do you see?
He eat the dormouse,
   Else it was he.

From *Oberon, the Fairy Prince*

FROM *The Works of Benjamin Jonson*, 1641

[*The fairy beam upon you*]

The fairy beam upon you,
   The stars to glister on you;
      A moon of light
      In the noon of night,
Till the fire-drake hath o'ergone you.
The wheel of fortune guide you,
   The boy with the bow beside you;
      Run aye in the way
      Till the bird of day,
And the luckier lot betide you.

From *The Gypsies Metamorphosed*

[*Thus, thus begin*]

1 Nymph.   Thus, thus begin the yearly rites
          Are due to Pan on these bright nights;
          His morn now riseth, and invites
          To sports, to dances, and delights;
             All envious and profane away,
             This is the shepherds' holy-day.

2 Nymph.   Strew, strew the glad and smiling ground
          With every flower, yet not confound
          The primrose-drop, the spring's own spouse,
          Bright daisies, and the lips of cows,   10
             The garden-star, the queen of May,
             The rose, to crown the holy-day.

3 Nymph.   Drop, drop, you violets, change your hues,
          Now red, now pale, as lovers use,
          And in your death go out as well
          As when you lived unto the smell;
             That from your odor all may say,
             This is the shepherds' holy-day.

                    From *Pan's Anniversary*

[*Here she was wont to go*]

Here she was wont to go, and here! and here!
Just where those daisies, pinks, and violets grow;
The world may find the spring by following her,
For other print her airy steps ne'er left;
Her treading would not bend a blade of grass!
Or shake the downy blow-ball from his stalk!
But like the soft west-wind she shot along,
And where she went the flowers took thickest root,
As she had sowed 'em with her odorous foot.

                    From *The Sad Shepherd*

[*Though I am young*]

Though I am young and cannot tell
    Either what death or love is well,
Yet I have heard they both bear darts,
    And both do aim at human hearts.
And then again I have been told
    Love wounds with heat, as death with cold;
So that I fear they do but bring
    Extremes to touch, and mean one thing.

As in a ruin we it call
    One thing to be blown up, or fall;
Or to our end, like way may have
    By a flash of lightning or a wave;
So love's inflaméd shaft or brand
    May kill as soon as death's cold hand;
Except love's fires the virtue have
    To fright the frost out of the grave.

From The Sad Shepherd

10

EPIGRAMS

The Introduction and Notes are at page 993

From Timothe Kendall's *Flowers of Epigrams*, 1577

To Sabidius

I love thee not, Sabidius,
    I can not tell thee why;
I can say nought but this alone,—
    I do not love thee, I.

To Fidentinus

The book which thou dost read, it is,
    Friend Fidentinus, mine;
But when thou ill dost read it, then
    Begins it to be thine.

To a married couple that could not agree

Sith that you both are like in life—
A naughty man, a wicked wife,—
I muse ye live not void of strife.

Of Fuscus, a drunkard

A certain man in physic skilled
    To F. spake in this wise:
F., drink not overmuch; take heed!
    For drink will lose your eyes.
He paused upon this sentence given,
    And pondered what was spoke,
And when he had bethought him, thus
    At last his mind he broke:
I will by drinking lose mine eyes!

Quoth he, 'tis better so
Than for to keep them for the worms
To gnaw them out below.

Of Alphus

No egg on Friday Alph will eat,
    But drunken he will be
On Friday still. Oh, what a pure
    Religious man is he!

To the reader

Take in good part these trifling toys,
    Good reader, which I write;
Whenas I was a boy with boys
    These toys I did indite.
Tush, tush, they foolish are! thou sayst.
    I grant they are indeed:
But where are thy wise wondrous works?
    Now where are they to read?

FROM SIR JOHN HARINGTON's *Elegant and Witty Epigrams,* 1618

Comparison of the sonnet and the epigram

Once by mishap two poets fell a-squaring,
The sonnet and our epigram comparing;
And Faustus, having long demurred upon it,
Yet at the last gave sentence for the sonnet.
Now for such censure this his chief defence is,
Their sugared taste best likes his lick'rous senses.
    Well, though I grant sugar may please the taste,
    Yet let my verse have salt to make it last.

Against writers that carp at other men's books

The readers and the hearers like my books,
But yet some writers cannot them digest.
But what care I? For when I make a feast,
I would my guests should praise it, not the cooks.

Of Faustus, a stealer of verses

I heard that Faustus oftentimes rehearses
To his chaste mistress certain of my verses,
In which, with use, so perfect he is grown
That she, poor fool, now thinks they are his own.

I would esteem it (trust me) grace, not shame,
If Davies, or if Daniel, did the same,—
For would I thank, or would I quarrel pick?
I, when I list, could do to them the like.
But who can wish a man a fouler spite
Than have a blind man take away his light?   10
 A begging thief is dangerous to my purse;
 A baggage poet to my verse is worse.

Of treason

Treason doth never prosper; what's the reason?
For if it prosper, none dare call it treason.

To Sextus, an ill reader

That epigram that last you did rehearse
Was sharp, and in the making neat and terse;
But thou dost read so harsh, point so perverse,
It seemed now neither witty nor a verse.
 For shame point better and pronounce it clearer,
 Or be no reader, Sextus—be a hearer.

FROM Additional Ms. 12049

Of clergymen and their livings

In ancient time old men observëd that
The clergymen were lean, their livings fat;
But in these days the case is altered clean,
The clergymen are fat, their livings lean.
 I, searching, find this cause that change to breed,—
 Now they feed fast; then they did fast and feed.

[Sir John Harington]

To Mr. John Davies

My dear friend Davies, some against us partial
Have found we steal some good conceits from Martial;
So, though they grant our verse hath some acumen,
Yet make they fools suspect we scant are true men.
But Surrey did the same, and worthy Wyatt,
And they had praise and reputation by it;
And Heywood, whom your putting down hath raised,
Did use the same, and with the same is praised.
Wherefore, if they had wit that so did trace us,
They must again for their own credits grace us;   10

Or else to our more honor, and their grieves,
Match us, at least, with honorable thieves.

[*Sir John Harington*]

From Everard Guilpin's *Skialetheia*, 1598

Of Titus

Titus oft vaunts his gentry everywhere,
Blazoning his coat, deriving's pedigree.
What needest thou daily, Titus, jade mine ear?
I will believe thy house's ancestry:
  If that be ancient which we do forget,
  Thy gentry is so—none can remember it.

Of Cornelius

See you him yonder who sits o'er the stage
With the tobacco-pipe now at his mouth?
It is Cornelius, that brave gallant youth,
Who is new printed to this fangled age.
  He wears a jerkin cudgeled with gold lace,
  A profound slop, a hat scarce pipkin-high;
  For boots a pair of dagge cases; his face
  Furred with cad's-beard, his poniard on his thigh.
He wallows in his walk, his slop to grace;
Swears by the Lord, deigns no salutation   10
But to some jade that's sick of his own fashion,
As, Farewell, sweet captain, or, Boy, come apace.
  Yet this Sir Bevis or the fairy knight
  Put up the lie because he durst not fight.

Satyra quinta

Let me alone, I prithee, in this cell;
Entice me not into the city's hell;
Tempt me not forth this Eden of content
To taste of that which I shall soon repent.
Prithee, excuse me; I am not alone,
Accompanied with meditation
And calm content, whose taste more pleaseth me
Than all the city's luscious vanity.
I had rather be encoffined in this chest
Amongst these books and papers, I protest,   10
Than free-booting abroad purchase offence,
And scandal my calm thoughts with discontents.
Here I converse with those diviner spirits

Whose knowledge and admire the world inherits:
Here doth the famous profound Stagirite
With nature's mystic harmony delight
My ravished contemplation; I here see
The now-old world's youth in an history;
Here I may be grave Plato's auditor,
And learning of that moral lecturer   20
To temper mine affections, gallantly
Get of myself a glorious victory.
And then for change, as we delight in change
(For this my study is indeed m'Exchange),
Here may I sit, yet walk to Westminster
And hear Fitzherbert, Plowden, Brooke, and Dyer
Canvass a law-case; or, if my dispose
Persuade me to a play, I'll to the Rose
Or Curtain—one of Plautus' comedies
Or the pathetic Spaniard's tragedies.   30
If my desire doth rather with the fields,
Some speaking painter, some poet, straightway yields
A flower-bespangled walk, where I may hear
Some amorous swain his passïons declare
To his sun-burnt love. Thus my books' little case,
My study, is mine all, mine every place.

.   .   .   .

From Thomas Bastard's *Chrestoleros*, 1598

Ad lectorem

How quickly doth the reader pass away
My pen's long task and travail of the day!
Four lines which hold me tug an hour or twain
He sups up with a breath, and takes no pain.
Yet use me well, reader, which to procure
Thy one short pleasure two long pains endure:
    The one of writing, when it is begun,
    Th'other of shame if't please not when 'tis done.

    The first and riper world of men and skill
    Yields to our later time for three inventions:
    Miraculously we write, we sail, we kill,
    As neither ancient scroll nor story mentions.
Print   The first hath opened learnings old concealed,
    And obscured arts restorëd to the light;
Lodestone The second hidden countries hath revealed,
    And sent Christ's gospel to each living wight.

These we commend, but oh, what needed more

Guns   To teach death more skill than it had before!   10

Lætus did in his mistress' quarrel die,
Quintus was slain defending of the lie,
Germanus in his friend's defence did fall,
Sakellus died striving for the wall,
Merus did spend his life upon a jest,
Sannius lost it at a drunken feast,
Mirus at Sunday's wake revenged the wrong
Of his bull-dog, until he lay along:
What sayst thou now, contemned religïon?
Vice hath her saints and martyrs,—thou hast none.   10

De piscatione

Fishing, if I, a fisher, may protest,
Of pleasures is the sweet'st, of sports the best,
Of exercises the most excellent,
Of recreations the most innocent.
But now the sport is marred, and wot ye why?
Fishes decrease, and fishers multiply.

FROM JOHN WEEVER'S *Epigrams in the Oldest Cut and Newest Fashion*, 1599

In Nigellum

If I should choose, yea, for my life,
To be thy hawk, Nigell, or wife,
I would the hawk choose of the one,—
She wears a hood, thy wife wears none.

De se

Some men marriage do commend
And all their life in wiving spend,
But if that I should wives have three
(God keep me from polygamy!)
   I'll give the devil two for pay
   If he will fetch the third away.

Translat. ex Martial

Sabidi, I love thee not, nor why I wot,
But this I wot, Sabidi: I love thee not.

In Rudionem

Yon goes a gallant which will get repute,
From head to heel in his carnation suit,
Slops, doublet, stockings, shoes, hat, band, and feather,
Red yard-long ribbon,—see, the youth comes hither;
Who, lest his Dutchman hose should be unseen,
Above his mid-thigh he his cloak doth pin.
Oh, that he had to his carnation hose—
I wish him well—a fair, rich, crimson nose.

In tumulum Abrahami Simple

Within this place lies Abraham the Civil,
Who never did good, who never did evil,—
Too ill then for God, too good for the devil.

Ad Io. Marston & Ben. Ionson

Marston, thy muse enharbors Horace' vein,
Then some Augustus give thee Horace' merit;
And thine, embuskined Jonson, doth retain
So rich a style and wondrous gallant spirit
That, if to praise your muses I desired,
My muse would muse. Such wits must be admired.

Ad Gulielmum Shakespeare

Honey-tongued Shakespeare, when I saw thine issue,
I swore Apollo got them, and none other;
Their rosy-tainted features, clothed in tissue,
Some heaven-born goddess said to be their mother:
Rose-cheeked Adonis, with his amber tresses,
Fair fire-hot Venus charming him to love her;
Chaste Lucretia, virgin-like her dresses,
Proud lust-stung Tarquin, seeking still to prove her;
Romeo, Richard,—more, whose names I know not—
Their sugared tongues and power-attractive beauty   10
Say they are saints, although that saints they show not,
For thousands vows to them subjective duty;
They burn in love; thy children, Shakespeare, het them.
Go, woo thy muse, more nymphish brood beget them.

FROM SAMUEL ROWLANDS's *Letting of Humor's Blood*, 1600

Severus is extreme in eloquence,
In perfumed words plunged over head and ears;

He doth create rare phrase, but rarer sense;
Fragments of Latin all about he bears.
Unto his serving-man, *alias* his boy,
He utters speech exceeding quaint and coy:
Diminutive, and my defective slave,
Reach my corps' coverture immediately.
My pleasure's pleasure is the same to have,
T'ensconce my person from frigidity.   10
His man believes all's Welsh his master spoke,
Till he rails English, Rogue, go fetch my cloak!

FROM SAMUEL ROWLANDS'S *Humor's Looking-Glass,* 1608

A scholar newly entered marriage life,
Following his studies, did offend his wife;
Because when she his company expected
By bookish business she was still neglected.
Coming unto his study, Lord (quoth she),
Can papers cause you love them more than me?
I would I were transformed into a book,
That your affection might upon me look;
But in my wish withal be it decreed
I would be such a book you love to read.   10
Husband (quoth she), which book's form should I take?
Marry (said he), t'were best an almanake.
The reason wherefore I do wish thee so
Is, every year we have a new, you know.

FROM *Chetham Ms.* 8012

An epitaph on a bellows-maker

Here lies John Goddard, maker of bellows,
His craft's master, and king of good fellows;
But for all that, he came to his death,
For he that made bellows could not make breath.

[John Hoskins]

Of a cozener

And was not death a lusty struggler
In overthrowing James the Juggler?
His life so little truth did use
That here he lies—it is no news.

[John Hoskins]

An epitaph on a man for doing nothing

> Here lies the man was born, and cried,
> Told three-score years, fell sick, and died.

[John Hoskins]

From *Reliquiæ Wottonianæ*, 1672

John Hoskins to his little child Benjamin, from the Tower

> Sweet Benjamin, since thou art young
> And hast not yet the use of tongue,
> Make it thy slave, while thou art free,—
> Imprison it, lest it do thee.

[John Hoskins]

From *Chetham Ms.* 8012

In Chus

> Chus doth so often to the doctor go,
> To know whether he be in health or no,
> That shortly if his friend chance to pass by
> And ask him how he doth, in courtesy,
> He will not answer him a point so nice
> Until he hath had his doctor's advice.

In Norgum

> Mistaking brains praise Norgus' wit for great,
> Because great store of jests he can repeat;
> When 'tis his memory deserveth most
> For hoarding up what witty men have lost.
> And who knows not that these two always hit—
> A great memory and a little wit?

From Henry Parrot's *Mouse-Trap*, 1606

> Peter hath lost his purse, but will conceal it,
> Lest she that stole it to his shame reveal it.

> Paulus a pamphlet doth in prose present
>   Unto his lord,—the fruits of idle time—
> Who, far more careless than therewith content,
>   Wishèd he would convert it into rhyme.
> Which done, and brought him at another season,
> Said, Now 'tis rhyme—before nor rhyme nor reason.

Magus would needs, forsooth, this other day
Upon an idle humor see a play;
When asking him at door that held the box,
What might you call the play? Quoth he, *The Fox.*
In goes my gen-man (who could judge of wit),
And being askëd how he likëd it,
Said, All was ill—both fox and him that played it.
But was not he, think you, a goose that said it?

FROM HENRY PARROT'S *Epigrams*, 1608

Ortus novus urbe Britannus

Who braves it now as doth young Histrio,
Walking in Paul's like to some potentate,
Richly replenished from the top to th' toe
As if he were derived from high estate?
Alas, there's not a man but may descry
His begging trade and bastard faculty.

Impar impares odit

Sotus hates wise men, for himself is none;
And fools he hates, because himself is one.

FROM HENRY PARROT'S *Laquei Ridiculosi*, 1613

Suum cuique pulchrum

Posthumus, not the last of many more,
Asks why I writ in such an idle vein,
Seeing there are of epigrams such store.
Oh, give me leave to tell thee once again
   That epigrams are fitted to the season
   Of such as best know how to make rhyme reason.

FROM HENRY PARROT'S *Mastive*, 1615

Nuptiæ post nummos

There was a time when men for love did marry
And not for lucre sake, as now we see;
Which from that former age so much doth vary
As all's for—what you'll give? or nought must be.
So that this ancient word called *matrimony*
Is wholly made *a matter now of money.*

Ebrius dissimulans

Battus, though bound from drinking wine of late,
Can thus far with his oath equivocate;
He will not drink, and yet be drunk ere noon—
His manner is to eat it with a spoon.

FROM JOHN HEATH'S *Two Centuries of Epigrams*, 1610

Ad modernos epigrammatistas

Heywood, th' old English epigrammatist,
Had wit at will, and art was all he missed;
But nowadays, we of the modern fry
Have art, and labor with wit's penury.
Wit is the substance, art the polishment;
Art does adorn, and wit it does invent;
Since, then, they are so jointly linked that neither
Can well subsist without the help of either,
I gladly could have wished, with all my heart,
That we had had his wit, or he our art.   10

Ad Zoilum

I might be better busied; I grant so.
Could I be better idle? Surely, no.
Then hold your idle chat, for I profess
These are the fruits but of my idleness.

In Porcum

Porcus, that foul unsociable hog,
Grunts me out this still: Love me, love my dog.
And reason is there why we should so do,
Since that his dog's the lovelier of the two.

Ad Tho. Bastardum epigrammatistam

Thy epigrams are of no bastard race,
For they dare gaze the world's eye in the face.

In Beatricem præpropere defunctam

In Beatrice did all perfections grow
That she could wish or nature could bestow;
When death, enamoured with that excellence,
Straight grew in love with her, and took her hence.

Ad Collegium Wintoniensem

If in this book dullness do chance to lurk,
I'll father it, 'tis mine own handiwork;
If in this book there be one witty line,
I utterly disclaim't; 'tis wholly thine.

FROM THOMAS FREEMAN'S *Rub and a Great Cast*, 1614

Me quoque vatem

Why am I not an epigrammatist?
I write in covert, and conceal their names
Whose lives I burden with some bitter jest;
Themselves I cloak, and yet uncloud their shames.
Again, methinks I am not shallow-sprited,
Nor seems my wit so insufficient;
Although not like to others, deep-conceited,
It can indite, although not excellent.
   The reader laughs, this reason he rehearses:
   The ape likes her own whelps, and I my verses.   10

To the stationer

I tell thee, stationer,—why, never fear!
They'll sell, i' faith, and 't be but for their title.
Thou canst not lose. Nay, I dare warrant clear
They'll get thee twenty nobles—not so little!
Why, read this epigram, or that, or any;
Do they not make thee itch, and move thy blood?
Of all thou hast had (and thou hast had many)
Hast e'er read better? Nay, hast read so good?
Dost laugh? They'll make the rigid'st Cato do it;
Besides, smooth verse, quaint phrase,—come, what wilt give?   10
No more but so! Ah, what shall I say to it?
   I pity poetry, but curse the time
   When none will bid us reason for our rhyme.

In epitaphium pingui minerva compositum

When Crassus died, his friends, to grace his hearse,
Requested one to make his funeral verse.
Of whom they did procure it in the end,
A ruthful one, and pitifully penned;
   That sure the man who made it made great moan—
   His epitaph was such a sorry one.

Aliud

I must needs say, were thou mine own brother,
This epitaph of thine deserveth another;
Such sorrow would make the learned to laugh,
To read: *Here lies a dead epitaph.*

In Phædram

Now, by her troth, she hath been, Phædra says,
At a play far better edified
Than at a sermon ever in her days.
Phædra, 'tis true, it cannot be denied;
     For stage-plays thou has given ear to many,
     But sermons, Phædra, never heardst thou any.

Of Spenser's Fairy Queen

Virgil from Homer, th' Italian from him,
Spenser from all; and all of these, I ween,
Were born when Helicon was full to th' brim;
Witness their works, witness our *Fairy Queen!*
     That lasting monument of Spenser's wit
     Was ne'er come near to, much less equalled, yet.

Pity, oh pity! death had power
Over Chaucer, Lydgate, Gower:
They that equalled all the sages
Of these, their own, of former ages,
And did their learned lights advance
In times of darkest ignorance;
When palpable impurity
Kept knowledge in obscurity,
And all went hood-winked in this isle,
They could see and shine the while.   10
Nor Greece nor Rome could reckon us
As then among the barbarous,
Since these three knew to turn, perdy,
The screw-pin of philosophy
As well as they; and left behind
As rich memorials of the mind;
By which they live, though they are dead;
As all may see that will but read,
And on good works will spend good hours
In Chaucers, Lydgates, and in Gowers.   20

FROM ROBERT HAYMAN's *Quodlibets*, 1628

A mad answer of a madman

One asked a madman if a wife he had.
A wife? quoth he,—I never was so mad.

An epitaph on every well-meaning man undone by his kindness

My rich heart made me poor; comforting, sad;
My helping, impotent; my goodness, bad.

Of epigrams

Short epigrams relish both sweet and sour,
Like fritters of sour apples and sweet flour.

To one of the elders of the sanctified parlor of Amsterdam

Though thou mayst call my merriments my folly,
They are my pills to purge my melancholy.
They would purge thine, too, wert not thou fool-holy.

Worse than naught

Thou art not worthy of a satire's quill;
An epigram's too short to show thine ill.

Neat, quaint, nimble pulpit wits

These nimble lads are fit for working-days—
Their witty sermons may keep some from plays.

Reasons for the taking of tobacco

Since most physicians drink tobacco still,
And they of nature have th' exactest skill,
Why should I think it for my body ill?
And since most preachers of our nation
Tobacco drink with moderation,
Why should I fear of profanation?
Yet if that I take it intemperately,
My soul and body may be hurt thereby.

FROM THOMAS BANCROFT's *Two Books of Epigrams and Epitaphs*, 1639

A drunken brabbler

Who only in his cups will fight is like
A clock, that must be oiled well ere it strike.

To Ben Jonson

As Martial's muse by Cæsar's ripening rays
Was sometimes cherished, so thy happier days
Joyed in the sunshine of thy royal James,
Whose crown shed luster on thine epigrames;
But I, remote from favor's fostering heat,
O'er snowy hills my muse's passage beat,
Where weeping rocks my harder fates lament
And shuddering woods whisper my discontent.
What wonder, then, my numbers, that have rolled
Like streams of Tigris, run so slow and cold?   10

To Shakespeare

Thy muse's sugared dainties seem to us
Like the famed apples of old Tantalus,
For we, admiring, see and hear thy strains
But none I see or hear those sweets attains.

To the same

Thou hast so used thy pen—or shook thy spear—
That poets startle, nor thy wit come near.

Peace and war

Weapons in peace grow hungry, and will eat
Themselves with rust; but war allows them meat.

JOHN DAVIES OF HEREFORD

The Introduction and Notes are at page 997

FROM *The Holy Rood*, 1609

[*Although we do not all the good*]

Although we do not all the good we love,
But still, in love, desire to do the same;
Nor leave the sins we hate, but hating move
Our soul and body's powers their powers to tame;
The good we do God takes as done aright,
That we desire to do he takes as done;
The sin we shun he will with grace requite,
And not impute the sin we seek to shun.

But good desires produce no worser deeds,
For God doth both together lightly give,   10
Because he knows a righteous man must needs
By faith, that works by love, forever live.
  Then to do nought but only in desire
  Is love that burns, but burns like painted fire.

FROM *Wit's Pilgrimage*, [1605?]

[*Some blaze the precious beauties*]

Some blaze the precious beauties of their loves
By precious stones, and other some by flowers,
Some by the planets and celestial powers,
Or by what else their fancy best approves;
Yet I by none of these will blazon mine,
But only say her self herself is like,
For those similitudes I much mislike
That are much usëd, though they be divine.
In saying she is like herself, I say
She hath no like, for she is past compare.   10
Then who aright commends this creature rare
Must say, She is; and there of force must stay,
  Because by words she cannot be expressed;
  So say, She is, and wond'ring owe the rest.

[*So shoots a star*]

So shoots a star as doth my mistress glide
At midnight through my chamber, which she makes
Bright as the sky when moon and stars are spied,
Wherewith my sleeping eyes, amazëd, wake.
Which ope no sooner than herself she shuts
Out of my sight, away so fast she flies;
Which me in mind of my slack service puts,
For which all night I wake, to plague mine eyes.
Shoot, star, once more, and if I be thy mark
Thou shalt hit me, for thee I'll meet withal.   11
Let mine eyes once more see thee in the dark,
Else they with ceaseless waking out will fall;
  And if again such time and place I lose
  To close with thee, let mine eyes never close.

FROM *The Scourge of Folly*, [c. 1611]

Of Fumosus the great tobacconist

Fumosus cannot eat a bit but he
Must drink tobacco, so to drive it down.

Without tobacco then he cannot be;
Yet drinks no ounce that costs him not a crown.
But his crown covers no empiring wit,—
To blow away his crowns at every bit;
    Yet when his crowns do fail, he pawns his cloak,
    Sith, like a chimney, he's kept sound by smoke.

To our English Terence, Mr. Will. Shakespeare

Some say, good Will, (which I in sport do sing)
    Hadst thou not played some kingly parts in sport,
Thou hadst been a companion for a king,
And been a king among the meaner sort.
Some others rail; but, rail as they think fit,
Thou hast no railing, but a reigning, wit;
    And honesty thou sow'st, which they do reap,
    So to increase their stock—which they do keep.

FROM Wit's Bedlam, 1617

Of Maurus his Orpheus-like melody

Maurus last morn at's mistress' window played
An hunt's-up on his lute. But she, it's said,
Threw stones at him; so he like Orpheus there
Made stones come flying, his sweet notes to hear!

Of the small respect had of learned men in general

Caligula, envying the bright fames
Of Homer, Virgil, and grave Livius,
O'erthrew their statues, to o'erthrow their names.
But would these times had none more barbarous!
For in this age Caligulas we find
That let them starve that shine in either kind.

JOHN TAYLOR

The Introduction and Notes are at page 997

FROM The Sculler, 1612

Epigram

The way to make a Welshman thirst for bliss
And say his prayers daily on his knees
Is to persuade him that most certain 'tis

The moon is made of nothing but green cheese,
And he'll desire of God no greater boon
But place in heaven to feed upon the moon.

Epigram

Walking along the streets the other day,
A ragged soldier crossed me on the way;
And though my purse's lining was but scant,
Yet somewhat I bestowed to ease his want.
For which he kindly thanked me, with his heart,
And took his leave, and friendly we did part.
When straight mine eyes a horse and foot-cloth spied,
Upon whose back in pompous state did ride
One whom I thought was deputy to Jove;
Yet not this soldier's wants could pity move,　　　　10
But with disdainful looks and terms of scorn
Commands him travel whither he was born.
'Twill almost make a Puritan to swear
To see an ass's horse a cloak to wear
When Christians must go naked bare, and thin,
Wanting apparel t' hide their mangled skin.
Vain world, unto thy chaos turn again,
Since brutish beasts are more esteemed than men.

From *All the Works*, 1630

*A few lines, to small purpose, against the scandalous aspersions
that are either maliciously or ignorantly cast upon
the poets and poems of these times*

There doth a strange, and true, opinion run
That poets write much worse than they have done,
And how so poor their daily writings are,
As though their best inventions were thread-bare;
And how no new things from them now do spring,
But all hath ref'rence from some other thing;
And that their daily doings do reveal
How they from one another filch and steal,
As if amongst them 'twere a statute made
That they may freely use the thieving trade.　　　　10
And some there are that will not stick to say
That many poets living at this day
Who have the Hebrew, Latin, Greek, at will,

And in th' Italian and the French have skill—
These are the greatest thieves, they say, of all
That use the trade (or art) poetical.
For ancient bards, and poets in strange tongues,
Compilëd have their verses and their songs,
And those to whom those tongues are rightly known,
Translating them, make others' verse their own,   20
As one that steals a cloak, and presently
Makes it his own by alt'ring of the dye.
So whole books and whole sentences have been
Stol'n, and the stealers great applause did win,
And by their filching thought great men of fame
By those that knew not the right author's name.
For mine own part, my conscience witness is
I ne'er was guilty of such theft as this;
Unto such robbery I could never reach
Because I understand no foreign speech.   30
To prove that I am from such filching free,
Latin and French are heathen Greek to me;
The Grecian and the Hebrew charactars
I know as well as I can reach the stars;
The sweet Italian and the chip-chop Dutch,
I know the man i' th' moon can speak as much.
Should I from English authors but purloin,
It would be soon found counterfeited coin.
Then since I cannot steal but some will spy,
I'll truly use mine own, let others' lie.   40
Yet, to excuse the writers that now write,
Because they bring no better things to light,
'Tis because bounty from the world is fled;
True liberality is almost dead.
Reward is lodged in dark oblivion deep,
Bewitched, I think, into an endless sleep;
That though a man in study take great pains,
And empt his veins, pulverize his brains,
To write a poem well, which being writ
With all his judgment, reason, art, and wit,   50
And at his own charge print and pay for all
And give away most free and liberal
Two, three, or four, or five hundred books,
For his reward he shall have nods and looks;
That all the profit a man's pains hath gat
Will not suffice one meal to feed a cat.

.   .   .   .   .   .

FRANCIS BEAUMONT
The Introduction and Notes are at page 998

FROM *Norton Ms.* 4503

Mr. Francis Beaumont's letter to Ben Jonson

The sun, which doth the greatest comfort bring
To absent friends (because the self-same thing
They know they see, however absent), is
Here our best hay-maker (forgive me this,
It is our country style); in this warm shine
I lie, and dream of your full Mermaid wine.
Oh, we have water mixed with claret-lees,
Drink apt to bring in drier heresies
Than beer, good only for a sonnet strain,
With fustian metaphors to stuff the brain;   10
So mixed that given to the thirstiest one
'Twill not prove alms unless he have the stone.
'Tis sold by Puritans, mixed with intent
To make it serve for either sacrament.
I think with one draught man's invention fades,
Two cups had quite marred Homer's *Iliads*;
'Tis liquor that will find out Sutcliffe's wit,
Lie where it will, and make him write worse yet.
Filled with such moisture, in a grievous qualm,
Did Robert Wisdom write his singing psalm;   20
And so must I do this, and yet I think
It is a potion sent us down to drink
By special providence, keeps us from fights,
Makes us not laugh when we make legs to knights;
'Tis this that keeps our minds fit for our states,
A med'cine to obey our magistrates.
For we do live more free than you; no hate,
No envy of another's happy state
Moves us, we are all equal, every whit;
Of land, that God gives men here, is their wit,   30
If we consider fully, for our best
And gravest man will, with his main house-jest,
Scarce please you; we want subtlety to do
The city tricks—lie, hate, and flatter too.
Here are none that can bear a painted show,
Strike when you wink, and then lament the blow,
Who, like mills set the right way to grind,
Can make their gains alike with every wind.
Only some fellow with the subtlest pate
Amongst us, may perchance equivocate

At selling of a horse, and that's the most.
Methinks the little wit I had is lost
Since I saw you; for wit is like a rest
Held up at tennis, which men do the best
With the best gamesters. What things have we seen
Done at the Mermaid! heard words that have been
So nimble and so full of subtle flame,
As if that everyone from whom they came
Had meant to put his whole wit in a jest,
And had resolved to live a fool the rest   50
Of his dull life; then when there has been thrown
Wit able to justify the town
For three days past, wit that might warrant be
For the whole city to talk foolishly
Till that were cancelled, and when we were gone
We left an air behind, which was alone
Able to make the two next companies
Right witty, though they were downright cockneys.
When I remember this, and see that now
The country gentlemen begin to allow   60
My wit for dry-bobs, then I needs must cry,
I see my days of ballading are nigh;
I can already riddle, and can sing
Catches, sell bargains, and I fear shall bring
Myself to speak the hardest words I find
Over as fast as any, with one wind
That takes no medicines. But one thought of thee
Makes me remember all these things to be
The wit of our young men, fellows that show
No part of good, yet utter all they know;   70
Who like trees and the guard have growing souls
Only; strong destiny, which all controls,
I hope hath left a better fate in store
For me, thy friend, than to live evermore
Banished unto this home; 'twill once again
Bring me to thee, who wilt make smooth and plain
The way of knowledge for me, and then I
Who have no good in me but simplicity,
Know that it will my greatest comfort be
To acknowledge all the rest to come from thee.   80

FROM *Poems*, 1640

[*Flattering hope*]

Flattering hope, away and leave me!
She'll not come, thou dost deceive me.

Hark, the cock crows! the envious light
Chides away the silent night.
Yet she comes not; oh, how I tire
Betwixt cold fear and hot desire!

Here alone enforced to tarry,
While the tedious minutes marry
And get hours; those, days and years,
Which I count with sighs and fears.
Yet she comes not; oh, how I tire
Betwixt cold fear and hot desire!

Restless thoughts, awhile remove
Unto the bosom of my love!
Let her languish in my pain,
Fear and hope, and fear again;
Then let her tell me, in love's fire,
What torment's like unto desire?

Endless wishing, tedious longing,
Hopes and fears together thronging,
Rich in dreams, yet poor in waking:
Let her be in such a taking,
Then let her tell me, in love's fire,
What torment's like unto desire?

Come then, love, prevent day's eying!
My desire would fain be dying;
Smother me with breathless kisses,
Let me dream no more of blisses;
But tell me, which is in love's fire
Best, to enjoy or to desire?

THOMAS HEYWOOD

The Introduction and Notes are at page 998

FROM *An Apology for Actors*, 1612

The author to his book

The world's a theater, the earth a stage,
Which God and nature doth with actors fill.
Kings have their entrance in due equipage,
And some their parts play well, and others ill.

The best no better are, in this theater,
Where every humor's fitted in his kind:
This a true subject's acts, and that a traitor,
The first applauded, and the last confined;
This plays an honest man, and that a knave,
A gentle person this, and he a clown,   10
One man is ragged, and another brave,—
All men have parts, and each man acts his own.
She a chaste lady acteth all her life;
A wanton courtesan another plays;
This covets marriage love, that nuptial strife,
Both in continual action spend their days;
Some citizens, some soldiers born to adventer,
Shepherds, and seamen. Then our play's begun
When we are born, and to the world first enter,
And all find exits when their parts are done.   20
If then the world a theater present,
As by the roundness it appears most fit,
Built with star-galleries of high ascent
In which Jehove doth as spectator sit,
And chief determiner, to applaud the best
And their endeavors crown with more than merit;
But by their evil actions dooms the rest
To end disgraced, whilst others praise inherit,—
  He that denies, then, theaters should be,
  He may as well deny a world to me.   30

From *The Silver Age*, 1613

Song

With fair Ceres, queen of grain,
The reapëd fields we roam, roam, roam;
Each country peasant, nymph, and swain
Sing their harvest home, home, home;
  Whilst the queen of plenty hallows
  Growing fields as well as fallows.

Echo, double all our lays,
Make the champians sound, sound, sound
To the queen of harvest praise,
That sows and reaps our ground, ground, ground.   10
  Ceres, queen of plenty, hallows
  Growing fields as well as fallows.

Tempests, hence; hence, winds and hails,
Tares, cockle, rotten showers, showers, showers.

Our song shall keep time with our flails,—
When Ceres sings, none lours, lours, lours.
She it is whose godhood hallows
Growing fields as well as fallows.

From *The Rape of Lucrece*, 1630

[*Come list, and hark*]

Come list, and hark!
  The bell doth toll
For some but new
  Departing soul;
And was not that
  Some ominous fowl—
The bat, the night-
  Crow, or screech-owl?
To these I hear
The wild wolf howl   10
  In this black night
That seems to scowl.
All these my black-
  Book shall enroll,
For hark! still, still
The bell doth toll
For some but now
Departing soul.

[*Pack, clouds, away*]

Pack, clouds, away! and welcome, day!
With night we banish sorrow.
Sweet air, blow soft; mount, lark, aloft
To give my love good-morrow.
Wings from the wind, to please her mind,
Notes from the lark, I'll borrow;
Bird, prune thy wing; nightingale, sing,
To give my love good-morrow.
To give my love good-morrow
Notes from them all I'll borrow.   10

Wake from thy nest, robin redbreast,
Sing, birds, in every furrow;
And from each bill let music shrill
Give my fair love good-morrow.
Blackbird and thrush in every bush,
Stare, linnet, and cock-sparrow,
You pretty elves, amongst yourselves
Sing my fair love good-morrow.
To give my love good-morrow
Sing, birds, in every furrow.   20

From *A Maidenhead Well Lost*, 1634

Song

Hence with passion, sighs, and tears,
Disasters, sorrows, cares, and fears!

See, my love, my love appears,
    That thought himself exiled.
Whence might all these loud joys grow,
Whence might mirth and banquets flow,
But that he's come, he's come, I know!
    Fair fortune, thou hast smiled!

Give to these blind windows eyes,
Daze the stars and mock the skies,   10
And let us two, us two, devise
    To lavish our best treasures;
Crown our wishes with content,
Meet our souls in sweet consent,
And let this night, this night, be spent
    In all abundant pleasures.

FROM *The Hierarchy of the blessed Angels,* 1635

[*Our modern poets*]

.   .   .   .   .

   Our modern poets to that pass are driven,
Those names are curtailed which they first had given;
And, as we wished to have their memories drowned,
We scarcely can afford them half their sound.
   Greene, who had in both academies ta'en
Degree of master, yet could never gain
To be called more than Robin; who, had he
Professed aught save the muse, served and been free
After a seven-years prenticeship, might have
(With credit too) gone Robert to his grave.   10
Marlowe, renowned for his rare art and wit,
Could ne'er attain beyond the name of Kit,
Although his *Hero and Leander* did
Merit addition rather. Famous Kyd
Was called but Tom. Tom Watson, though he wrote
Able to make Apollo's self to dote
Upon his muse, for all that he could strive,
Yet never could to his full name arrive.
Tom Nashe, in his time of no small esteem,
Could not a second syllable redeem.   20
Excellent Beaumont, in the foremost rank
Of the rar'st wits, was never more than Frank.
Mellifluous Shakespeare, whose enchanting quill
Commanded mirth or passion, was but Will.
And famous Jonson, though his learned pen
Be dipped in Castaly, is still but Ben.

Fletcher and Webster, of that learned pack
None of the mean'st, yet neither was but Jack.
Dekker's but Tom; nor May, nor Middleton;
And he's now but Jack Ford, that once were John.   30
 Nor speak I this that any here expressed
Should think themselves less worthy than the rest,
Whose names have their full syllable and sound;
Or that Frank, Kit, or Jack are the least wound
Unto their fame and merit. I for my part
(Think others what they please) accept that heart
Which courts my love in most familiar phrase,
And that it takes not from my pains or praise
If anyone to me so bluntly come,—
I hold he loves me best that calls me Tom.

. . . .

JAMES I

The Introduction and Notes are at page 999

FROM *Additional Ms.* 24195

Song

The first verses that ever the king made

Since thought is free, think what thou will,
O troubled heart, to ease thy pain;
Thought unrevealed can do no evil,
But words past out comes not again;
 Be careful aye for to invent
 The way to get thy own intent.

To please thyself with thy conceit,
And let none know what thou does mean,
Hope aye at last, though it be late,
To thy intent for to attain;   10
 Thought whiles it brake forth in effect,
 Yet aye let wit thy will correct.

Since fool-haste comes not greatest speed,
I would thou should learn for to know
How to make virtue of a need,
Since that necessity hath no law;
 With patience then see thou attend,
 And hope to vanquish in the end.

An enigma of sleep

Life is myself, I keep the life of all;
Without my help all living things they die;
Small, great, poor, rich, obey unto my call,
Fierce lions, fowls, and whales into the sea.
With meat and drink the hungry I supply;
Dead drunken, all I quicken new again;
Dearer to kings nor crowns and scepters high;
Unto the rich, nor all their wealth and gain.
I am not nice; the poor I'll not disdain,
Poor wretches more than kings may me command.   10
Where I come in, all senses man refrain;
Softer nor silk, and sadder nor the sand,
   I hurt, I help, I slay, and cure the same;
   Sleep, and advise, and pense well what I am.

An epitaph on Sir Philip Sidney

Thou mighty Mars, the god of soldiers brave,
And thou, Minerva, that does in wit excel,
And thou, Apollo, that does knowledge have
Of every art that from Parnassus fell,
With all the sisters that thereon do dwell,
Lament for him who duly served you all,
Whom-in you wisely all your arts did mell,—
Bewail, I say, his unexpected fall.
I need not in remembrance for to call
His youth, his race, the hope had of him aye,   10
Since that in him doth cruel death appal
Both manhood, wit, and learning every way.
   Now in the bed of honor doth he rest,
   And evermore of him shall live the best.

A sonnet on Sir William Alexander's harsh verses after the English fashion

Hold, hold your hand, hold; mercy, mercy, spare
Those sacred Nine that nursed you many a year.
Full oft, alas, with comfort and with care
We bathed you in Castalia's fountain clear.
Then on our wings aloft we did you bear,
And set you on our stately forkèd hill
Where you our heavenly harmonies did hear,
The rocks resounding with their echoes still.
Although your neighbors have conspired to spill

That art which did the laurel crown obtain,
And borrowing from the raven their ragg'd quill,
Bewray their harsh, hard, trotting, tumbling wain;
Such hammering hard the metals hard require;
Our songs are filed with smoothly flowing fire.

FROM *Basilikon Doron*, 1599

The argument of the book

God gives not kings the style of gods in vain,
For on his throne his scepter do they sway;
And as their subjects ought them to obey,
So kings should fear and serve their God again.
If then ye would enjoy a happy reign,
Observe the statutes of your heavenly king,
And from his law make all your laws to spring;
Since his lieutenant here ye should remain,
Reward the just, be steadfast, true, and plain,
Repress the proud, maintaining aye the right,
Walk always so, as ever in his sight
Who guards the godly, plaguing the profane;
 And so ye shall in princely virtues shine,
 Resembling right your mighty king divine.

SIR JOHN BEAUMONT

The Introduction and Notes are at page 1000

FROM *Bosworth Field, with a taste of the variety of Other Poems,* 1629

To his late Majesty, concerning the true form of English poetry

Great king, the sov'reign ruler of this land,
By whose grave care our hopes securely stand,
Since you descending from that spacious reach
Vouchsafe to be our master, and to teach
Your English poets to direct their lines,
To mix their colors, and express their signs;
Forgive my boldness that I here present
The life of muses yielding true content
In pondered numbers, which with ease I tried
When your judicious rules have been my guide.
 He makes sweet music who, in serious lines,
Light dancing tunes and heavy prose declines;

When verses like a milky torrent flow,
They equal temper in the poet show.
He paints true forms, who with a modest heart
Gives luster to his work, yet covers art.
Uneven swelling is no way to fame,
But solid joining of the perfect frame,
So that no curious finger there can find
The former chinks, or nails that fastly bind; 20
Yet most would have the knots of stitches seen,
And holes where men may thrust their hands between.
On halting feet the ragged poem goes
With accents neither fitting verse nor prose;
The style mine ear with more contentment fills
In lawyers' pleadings, or physicians' bills.
For though in terms of art their skill they close,
And joy in darksome words as well as those,
They yet have perfect sense more pure and clear
Than envious muses, which sad garlands wear 30
Of dusky clouds, their strange conceits to hide
From human eyes; and, lest they should be spied
By some sharp Œdipus, the English tongue
For this their poor ambition suffers wrong.
In ev'ry language now in Europe spoke
By nations which the Roman Empire broke,
The relish of the muse consists in rhyme;
One verse must meet another like a chime.
Our Saxon shortness hath peculiar grace
In choice of words fit for the ending place, 40
Which leave impression in the mind as well
As closing sounds of some delightful bell.
These must not be with disproportion lame,
Nor should an echo still repeat the same.
In many changes these may be expressed,
But those that join most simply run the best;
Their form, surpassing far the fettered staves,
Vain care and needless repetition saves.
These outward ashes keep those inward fires
Whose heat the Greek and Roman works inspires; 50
Pure phrase, fit epithets, a sober care
Of metaphors, descriptions clear yet rare,
Similitudes contracted smooth and round,
Not vexed by learning, but with nature crowned;
Strong figures drawn from deep invention's springs,
Consisting less in words and more in things;
A language not affecting ancient times,
Nor Latin shreds, by which the pedant climbs;

A noble subject which the mind may lift
To easy use of that peculiar gift   60
Which poets in their raptures hold most dear,
When actions by the lively sound appear:
Give me such helps, I never will despair
But that our heads which suck the freezing air,
As well as hotter brains, may verse adorn,
And be their wonder, as we were their scorn.

FRANCIS BACON, VISCOUNT ST. ALBANS

The Introduction and Notes are at page 1000

FROM *The Translation of Certain Psalms,* 1625

The translation of the 126 Psalm

When God returned us graciously
    Unto our native land,
We seemed as in a dream to be,
    And in a maze to stand.

The heathen likewise they could say,
    The God that these men serve
Hath done great things for them this day,
    Their nation to preserve.

'Tis true; God hath poured out his grace
    On us abundantly,   10

For which we yield him psalms and praise,
    And thanks with jubilee.

O Lord, turn our captivity
    As winds that blow at south
Do pour the tides with violence
    Back to the river's mouth.

Who sows in tears shall reap in joy,
    The Lord doth so ordain;
So that his seed be pure and good,
    His harvest shall be gain.   20

FROM THOMAS FARNABY's *Florilegium Epigrammatum Græcorum,* 1629

In vitam humanam

The world's a bubble, and the life of man
    Less than a span;
In his conception wretched, and from the womb
    So to the tomb;
Curst from the cradle, and brought up to years
    With cares and fears.
Who then to frail mortality shall trust
But limns the water, or but writes in dust.

Yet since with sorrow here we live oppressed,
    What life is best?   10
Courts are but only superficial schools
    To dandle fools;
The rural parts are turned into a den
    Of savage men;
And where's a city from all vice so free
But may be termed the worst of all the three?

Domestic cares afflict the husband's bed
    Or pains his head;
Those that live single take it for a curse,
    Or do things worse;   20
Some would have children; those that have them moan
    Or wish them gone;
What is it, then, to have or have no wife
But single thraldom or a double strife?

Our own affections still at home to please
    Is a disease;
To cross the sea to any foreign soil,
    Perils and toil;
Wars with their noise affright us; when they cease
    We're worse in peace.   30
What then remains, but that we still should cry
Not to be born, or being born, to die?

SIR HENRY WOTTON

The Introduction and Notes are at page 1001

FROM FRANCIS DAVISON's *Poetical Rhapsody*, 1602

An elegy

    O faithless world, and thy most faithless part,
        A woman's heart,
    The true shop of variety, where sits
        Nothing but fits
    And fevers of desire and pangs of love
        Which toys remove.
    Why was she born to please? or I to trust
        Words writ in dust,
    Suffering her eyes to govern my despair,
        My pain for air,   10

And fruit of time rewarded with untruth,
        The food of youth.
Untrue she was, yet I believed her eyes,
        Instructed spies,
Till I was taught that love was but a school
        To breed a fool.
Or sought she more than triumphs of denial,
        To see a trial
How far her smiles commanded my weakness?
        Yield and confess: 20
Excuse not now thy folly, nor her nature;
        Blush and endure
As well thy shame as passions that were vain;
        And think thy gain
To know that love lodged in a woman's breast
        Is but a guest.

FROM *Rawlinson Poetry Ms.* 212

The character of a happy life

How happy is he born or taught
    That serveth not another's
        will,
Whose armor is his honest
        thought,
    And simple truth his highest
        skill;

Whose passions not his masters
        are;
    Whose soul is still prepared for
        death,
Untied unto the world with care
    Of princes' grace or vulgar
        breath;

Who envies none whom chance
        doth raise,
    Or vice; who never under-
        stood   10
The deepest wounds are given by
        praise,
    By rule of state but not of
        good;

Who hath his life from rumors
        freed,

Whose conscience is his strong
        retreat,
Whose state can neither flatterers
        feed
    Nor ruins make accusers great;

Who God doth late and early
        pray
    More of his grace than goods
        to send,
And entertains the harmless day
    With a well-chosen book or
        friend.   20

This man is free from servile
        bands
    Of hope to rise or fear to fall,
Lord of himself, though not of
        lands,
    And having nothing, yet hath
        all.

FROM *Reliquiæ Wottonianæ*,
                1651

On his mistress, the Queen of Bohemia

You meaner beauties of the night,
    That poorly satisfy our eyes

More by your number than your
    light,
  You common people of the
    skies,—
  What are you when the sun
    shall rise?

You curious chanters of the wood
  That warble forth dame na-
    ture's lays,
Thinking your voices understood
  By your weak accents, what's
    your praise
  When Philomel her voice shall
    raise?   10

You violets that first appear,
  By your pure purple mantles
    known
Like the proud virgins of the
    year,
  As if the spring were all your
    own,—
  What are you when the rose is
    blown?

So, when my mistress shall be
    seen
  In form and beauty of her
    mind,
By virtue first, then choice, a
    queen,
  Tell me if she were not de-
    signed
  Th' eclipse and glory of her
    kind?   20

*Upon the sudden restraint of
the Earl of Somerset, then
falling from favor*

Dazzled thus with height of
    place,
  Whilst our hopes our wits be-
    guile,
No man marks the narrow space
  'Twixt a prison and a smile.

Then, since fortune's favors fade,
  You, that in her arms do sleep,
Learn to swim and not to wade,
  For the hearts of kings are
    deep.

But if greatness be so blind
  As to trust in towers of air, 10
Let it be with goodness lined,
  That at least the fall be fair.

Then, though darkened, you shall
    say,
  When friends fail and princes
    frown,
Virtue is the roughest way
  But proves at night a bed of
    down.

A description of the spring

And now all nature seemed in
    love;
The lusty sap began to move;
New juice did stir th' embracing
    vines,
And birds had drawn their valen-
    tines;
The jealous trout, that low did
    lie,
Rose at a well-dissembled fly;
There stood my friend, with pa-
    tient skill
Attending of his trembling quill.
Already were the eaves possessed
With the swift pilgrim's daubëd
    nest;   10
The groves already did rejoice
In Philomel's triumphing voice.
The showers were short, the
    weather mild,
The morning fresh, the evening
    smiled.
Joan takes her neat-rubbed pail,
    and now
She trips to milk the sand-red
    cow;

Where for some sturdy football
    swain
Joan strokes a sillabub or twain.
The fields and gardens were beset
With tulip, crocus, violet;   20
And now, though late, the mod-
    est rose
Did more than half a blush dis-
    close.
Thus all looked gay, all full of
    cheer,
To welcome the new-liveried
    year.

*A hymn to my God, in a night
    of my late sickness*

O thou great power in whom I
    move,
    For whom I live, to whom I
        die,
Behold me through thy beams of
    love
    Whilst on this couch of tears I
        lie,
And cleanse my sordid soul within
By thy Christ's blood, the bath of
    sin.

No hallowed oils, no grains I
    need,

No rags of saints, no purging
    fire;
One rosy drop from David's seed
    Was worlds of seas to quench
        thine ire.   10
O precious ransom, which once
    paid,
That *consummatum est* was said!

And said by him that said no
    more
    But sealed it with his sacred
        breath.
Thou, then, that hast dispunged
    my score,
    And dying wast the death of
        death,
Be to me now, on thee I call,
My life, my strength, my joy, my
    all!

*Upon the death of Sir Albert
    Morton's wife*

He first deceased; she for a little
    tried
To live without him, liked it not,
    and died.

EDWARD, LORD HERBERT OF CHERBURY

The Introduction and Notes are at page 1001

From *Occasional Verses*, 1665

Madrigal

How should I love my best?
What though my love unto that height be grown,
    That taking joy in you alone
    I utterly this world detest,
Should I not love it yet as th' only place
    Where beauty hath his perfect grace,
        And is possessed?

But I beauties despise;
You, universal beauty seem to me,
Giving and showing form and degree   10
To all the rest in your fair eyes,
Yet should I not love them as parts whereon
Your beauty, their perfection
And top, doth rise?

But ev'n myself I hate,
So far my love is from the least delight
That at my very self I spite,
Senseless of any happy state;
Yet may I not with justest reason fear
How, hating hers, I truly her   20
Can celebrate?

Thus unresolvëd still,
Although world, life, nay, what is fáir beside,
I cannot for your sake abide,
Methinks I love not to my fill;
Yet if a greater love you can devise,
In loving you some otherwise,
Believe 't, I will.

Another [Madrigal]

Dear, when I did from you remove,
I left my joy, but not my love—
That never can depart;
It neither higher can ascend,
Nor lower bend;
Fixed in the center of my heart,
As in his place,
And lodgëd so, how can it change,
Or you grow strange?
Those are earth's properties, and base.   10
Each where, as the bodies divine,
Heav'n's lights and you to me will shine.

Elegy over a tomb

Must I then see, alas, eternal night
Sitting upon those fairest eyes,
And closing all those beams, which once did rise
So radiant and bright
That light and heat in them to us did prove
Knowledge and love?

Oh, if you did delight no more to stay
   Upon this low and earthly stage,
But rather chose an endless heritage,
   Tell us at least, we pray,   10
Where all the beauties that those ashes owed
   Are now bestowed.

Doth the sun now his light with yours renew?
   Have waves the curling of your hair?
Did you restore unto the sky and air
   The red, and white, and blue?
Have you vouchsafed to flowers since your death
   That sweetest breath?

Had not heav'n's lights else in their houses slept,
   Or to some private life retired?   20
Must not the sky and air have else conspired,
   And in their regions wept?
Must not each flower else the earth could breed,
   Have been a weed?

But thus enriched may we not yield some cause
   Why they themselves lament no more?
That must have changed the course they held before,
   And broke their proper laws,
Had not your beauties giv'n this second birth
   To heaven and earth.   30

Tell us, for oracles must still ascend
   For those that crave them at your tomb,
Tell us where are those beauties now become,
   And what they now intend;
Tell us, alas, that cannot tell our grief,
   Or hope relief.

An ode upon a question moved, Whether love should continue forever?

Having interred her infant-birth,
   The wat'ry ground that late
   did mourn
Was strewed with flowers for
   the return
Of the wished bridegroom of the
   earth.

The well-accorded birds did sing

Their hymns unto the pleasant
   time,
And in a sweet consorted
   chime
Did welcome in the cheerful
   spring;

To which soft whistles of the
   wind,

And warbling murmurs of a
   brook,   10
And varied notes of leaves that
   shook,
An harmony of parts did bind,

While doubling joy unto each
   other
  All in so rare concent was
   shown,
  No happiness that came alone,
Nor pleasure that was not another;

When with a love none can ex-
   press,
  That mutually happy pair,
  Melander and Celinda fair,
The season with their love did
   bless.   20

Walking thus towards a pleasant
   grove,
  Which did, it seemed, in new
   delight
  The pleasures of the time
   unite,
To give a triumph to their love,

They stayed at last, and on the
   grass
  Reposèd so as o'er his breast
  She bowed her gracious head to
   rest,
Such a weight as no burden was.

While over either's compassed
   waist
  Their folded arms were so
   composed   30
  As if in straitest bonds enclosed
They suffered for joys they did
   taste.

Long their fixed eyes to heaven
   bent

Unchanged, they did never
   move,
  As if so great and pure a love
No glass but it could represent.

When with a sweet though trou-
   bled look,
  She first brake silence, saying,
   Dear friend,
  Oh, that our love might take
   no end,
Or never had beginning took!   40

I speak not this with a false heart,
  (Wherewith his hand she
   gently strained)
  Or that would change a love
   maintained
With so much faith on either
   part.

Nay, I protest, though death with
   his
  Worst counsel should divide us
   here,
  His terrors could not make me
   fear
To come where your loved presence is;

Only if love's fire with the
   breath
  Of life be kindled, I doubt   50
  With our last air 'twill be
   breathed out,
And quenchèd with the cold of
   death;

That if affection be a line
  Which is closed up in our last
   hour,
  Oh, how 'twould grieve me
   any power
Could force so dear a love as
   mine!

She scarce had done when his shut
 eyes
  An inward joy did represent,
  To hear Celinda thus intent
To a love he so much did prize. 60

Then with a look, it seemed, denied
  All earthly power but hers, yet
   so
  As if to her breath he did owe
This borrowed life, he thus replied:

O You, wherein they say souls
 rest
  Till they descend pure heavenly fires,
  Shall lustful and corrupt desires
With your immortal seed be
 blest?

And shall our love, so far beyond
  That low and dying appetite, 70
  And which so chaste desires
   unite,
Not hold in an eternal bond?

Is it because we should decline,
  And wholly from our thoughts
   exclude
  Objects that may the sense de-
   lude,
And study only the divine?

No, sure, for if none can ascend
  Ev'n to the visible degree
  Of things created, how should
   we
The invisible comprehend?   80

Or rather since that power expressed
  His greatness in his works
   alone,

B'ing here best in 's creatures
 known,
  Why is he not loved in them
   best?

But is 't not true, which you pretend,
  That since our love and knowledge here
  Only as parts of life appear,
So they with it should take their
 end.

Oh no, beloved, I am most sure
  Those virtuous habits we ac-
   quire,   90
  As being with the soul entire,
Must with it evermore endure;

For if where sins and vice reside
  We find so foul a guilt remain,
  As never dying in his stain
Still punished in the soul doth
 bide,

Much more that true and real joy
  Which in a virtuous love is
   found,
  Must be more solid in its
   ground
Than fate or death can e'er destroy;   100

Else should our souls in vain
 elect,
  And vainer yet were heaven's
   laws,
  When to an everlasting cause
They give a perishing effect.

Nor here on earth then, nor
 above,
  Our good affection can impair,
  For where God doth admit the
   fair,
Think you that he excludeth
 love?

These eyes again, then, eyes shall
    see,
  And hands again these hands
    enfold,   110
  And all chaste pleasures can be
    told
Shall with us everlasting be.

For if no use of sense remain
  When bodies once this life for-
    sake,
  Or they could no delight par-
    take,
Why should they ever rise again?

And if every imperfect mind
  Make love the end of knowl-
    edge here,
  How perfect will our love be
    where
All imperfection is refined?   120

Let then no doubt, Celinda, touch,
  Much less your fairest mind in-
    vade;
  Were not our souls immortal
    made,
Our equal loves can make them
    such;

So when one wing can make no
    way,
  Two joinëd can themselves di-
    late,
  So can two persons propagate,
When singly either would decay.

So when from hence we shall be
    gone,
  And be no more, nor you nor
    I,   130
  As one another's mystery
Each shall be both, yet both but
    one.

This said, in her uplifted face
  Her eyes, which did that
    beauty crown,
  Were like two stars, that hav-
    ing fall'n down,
Look up again to find their place;

While such a moveless silent
    peace
  Did seize on their becalmëd
    sense,
  One would have thought some
    influence
Their ravished spirits did pos-
    sess.   140

SIR ROBERT AYTOUN

The Introduction and Notes are at page 1002

FROM *Additional Ms.* 10308

Courteous Reader.

The author of these ensuing poems did not affect the name of a poet, having neither published in print nor kept copies of anything he writ, either in Latin or English, which makes this small collection the more difficult, and in many things imperfect and uncorrect, especially in the old Scots pieces which were done in his younger days. The Latin ones were published by a lover of poesy in the Delitiæ *Poetarum* Scotorum, *in his own time; and because the style of all vulgar lan-*

guages changes every age, and what may please in one doth not in others, I would not, though much importuned, expose them to the press, which he thought not worthy thereof and did only to please his own fancy upon emergent occasions, yet kept this small collection by me to let friends in after times know that though he writ carelessly, yet wittily and flowingly, without affectation or offence to any.

S. J. A.

Upon love

I loved thee once, I'll love no more,
　Thine be the grief as is the blame,
Thou art not what thou wast before,
　What reason I should be the same?
　　He that can love unloved again
　　Hath better store of love than brain;
　　God send me love my debts to pay,
　　While unthrifts fool their love away.

Nothing could have my love o'erthrown,
　If thou hadst still continued mine;
Nay, if thou hadst remained thine own,
　I might perchance have yet been thine.
　　But thou thy freedom did recall,
　　That it thou might elsewhere enthrall,
　　And then how could I but disdain
　　A captive's captive to remain?

When new desires had conquered thee,
　And changed the object of thy will,
It had been lethargy in me,
　Not constancy, to love thee still;
　　Yea, it had been a sin to go
　　And prostitute affection so,
　　Since we are taught no prayers to say
　　To such as must to others pray.

Yet do thou glory in thy choice,
　Thy choice of his good fortune boast;
I'll neither grieve, nor yet rejoice
　To see him gain what I have lost.
　　The height of my disdain shall be
　　To laugh at him, to blush for thee;
　　To love thee still, but go no more
　　A-begging at a beggar's door.

10

20

30

The answer by the author

Thou that loved once, now lov'st no more
  For fear to show more love than brain;
With heresy unhatched before,
  Apostasy thou dost maintain.
    Can he have either brain or love
    That doth inconstancy approve?
    A choice well made no change admits,
    All changes argue after-wits.

Say that she had not been the same,
  Shouldst thou therefore another be?   10
What thou in her as vice did blame,
  Can that take virtue's name in thee?
    No, thou in this her captive was,
    And made thee ready by her glass;
    Example led revenge astray,
    When true love should have kept the way.

True love hath no reflecting end,
  The object good sets it at rest,
And noble breasts will freely lend
  Without expecting interest.   20
    'Tis merchant love, 'tis trade for gain,
    To barter love for love again;
    'Tis usury, yea worse than this,
    For self-idolatry it is.

Then let her choice be what it will,
  Let constancy be thy revenge;
If thou retribute good for ill,
  Both grief and shame shall check her change.
    Thus mayst thou laugh when thou shalt see
    Remorse reclaim her home to thee,   30
    And where thou beg'st of her before,
    She now sits begging at thy door.

[When thou didst think]

When thou didst think I did not
    love,
Then thou didst dote on me;
Now when thou find'st that I do
    prove

As kind as kind can be,
  Love dies in thee.

What way to fire the mercury
  Of thy inconstant mind?

Methinks it were good policy
  For me to turn unkind,
    To make thee kind.   10

Yet I will not good nature strain,
  To buy at so great cost
That which before I do obtain,
  I make account almost
    That it is lost.

And though I might myself excuse
  By imitating thee,

Yet will I not examples use
  That may bewray in me
    Lightness to be.   20

But since I gave thee once my heart,
  My constancy shall show
That though thou play the woman's part
  And from a friend turn foe,
    Men do not so.

[*Forsaken of all comforts*]

Forsaken of all comforts but these two,
My faggot and my pipe, I sit and muse
On all my crosses, and almost accuse
The heavens for dealing with me as they do.
Then Hope steps in, and with a smiling brow
Such cheerful expectations doth infuse
As make me think ere long I cannot choose
But be some grandee, whatsoe'er I'm now.
But having spent my pipe, I then perceive
That hopes and dreams are cousins, both deceive.   10
Then make I this conclusion in my mind,
'Tis all one thing—both tend unto one scope—
To live upon tobacco and on hope,
The one's but smoke, the other is but wind.

From John Playford's *Select Airs and Dialogues*, 1659

The forsaken mistress

I do confess th' art smooth and fair,
  And I might ha' gone near to love thee,
Had I not found the slightest prayer
  That lip could move, had power to move thee;
    But I can let thee now alone,
    As worthy to be loved by none.

I do confess th' art sweet, yet find
  Thee such an unthrift of thy sweets,
Thy favors are but like the wind
  Which kisseth ev'rything it meets!   10
    And since thou canst with more than one,
    Th' art worthy to be kissed by none.

The morning rose that untouched stands,
　　Armed with her briars, how sweet she smells!
But plucked and strained through ruder hands,
　　Her sweets no longer with her dwells;
　　　　But scent and beauty both are gone,
　　　　And leaves fall from her, one by one.

Such fate, ere long, will thee betide,
　　When thou hast handled been awhile,   20
Like fair flowers to be thrown aside.
　　And I shall sigh, when some will smile,
　　　　To see thy love to ev'ryone
　　　　Hath brought thee to be loved by none.

SIR WILLIAM ALEXANDER, EARL OF STIRLING

The Introduction and Notes are at page 1002

FROM *Aurora*, 1604

Madrigal

When in her face mine eyes I fix,
A fearful boldness takes my mind;
Sweet honey love with gall doth mix,
　　And is unkindly kind.
　　　　It seems to breed,
　　　　And is indeed
A special pleasure to be pined.
No danger then I dread:
For though I went a thousand times to Styx,
I know she can revive me with her eye,   10
As many looks, as many lives to me;
　　And yet, had I a thousand hearts,
　　　　As many looks, as many darts,
　　　　Might make them all to die.

Sonnet

Let others of the world's decaying tell,
I envy not those of the golden age
That did their careless thoughts for nought engage,
But, cloyed with all delights, lived long and well.
And as for me, I mind t' applaud my fate;

Though I was long in coming to the light
Yet may I mount to fortune's highest height,
So great a good could never come too late.
I'm glad that it was not my chance to live
Till as that heavenly creature first was born,
Who as an angel doth the earth adorn
And buried virtue in the tomb revive;
 For vice overflows the world with such a flood
 That in it all, save she, there is no good.

Love resolved

Farewell, sweet fancies, and once dear delights,
The treasures of my life, which made me prove
That unaccomplished joy that charmed the sprites,
And whilst by it I only seemed to move,
 Did hold my ravished soul, big with desire,
 That, tasting those, to greater did aspire.
Farewell, free thraldom, freedom that was thrall
While as I led a solitary life,
Yet never less alone, whilst armed for all,
My thoughts were busied with an endless strife;
 For then, not having bound myself to any,
 I, being bound to none, was bound to many.
Great god that tam'st the gods' old-witted child,
Whose temples breasts, whose altars are men's hearts,
From my heart's fort thy legions are exiled,
And Hymen's torch hath burned out all thy darts;
 Since I in end have bound myself to one,
 That by this means I may be bound to none.
Thou dainty goddess with the soft white skin,
To whom so many off'rings daily smoke,
Were beauty's process yet for to begin,
That sentence I would labor to revoke,
 Which on Mount Ida, as thy smiles did charm,
 The Phrygian shepherd gave to his own harm.
And if the question were referred to me
On whom I would bestow the ball of gold,
I fear me Venus should be last of three;
For with the Thunderer's sister I would hold,
 Whose honest flames, pent in a lawful bounds,
 No fear disturbs, nor yet no shame confounds.
I mind to speak no more of beauty's dove,
The peacock is the bird whose fame I'll raise;
Not that I Argus need to watch my love,
But so his mistress Juno for to praise;

And if I wish his eyes, then it shall be
That I with many eyes my love may see.
Then farewell, crossing joys and joyful crosses!
Most bitter sweets and yet most sugared sours!
Most hurtful gains, yet most commodious losses,
That made my years to flee away like hours,   40
    And spent the springtime of mine age in vain,
    Which now my summer must redeem again.
O welcome, easy yoke! sweet bondage, come!
I seek not from thy toils for to be shielded,
But I am well content to be o'ercome,
Since that I must command when I have yielded.
    Then here I quit both Cupid and his mother,
    And do resign myself t' obtain another.

WILLIAM DRUMMOND OF HAWTHORNDEN

The Introduction and Notes are at page 1003

FROM *Poems*, 1616

SONNETS

I know that all beneath the moon decays,
And what by mortals in this world is brought
In time's great periods shall return to nought;
That fairest states have fatal nights and days.
I know how all the muses' heavenly lays,
With toil of sprite which are so dearly bought,
As idle sounds of few or none are sought,
And that nought lighter is than airy praise.
I know frail beauty, like the purple flower
To which one morn oft birth and death affords;   10
That love a jarring is of minds' accords,
Where sense and will invassal reason's power;
    Know what I list, this all can not me move,
    But that, oh me, I both must write and love!

That learned Grecian, who did so excel
In knowledge passing sense that he is named
Of all the after-worlds divine, doth tell
That at the time when first our souls are framed,
Ere in these mansions blind they come to dwell,
They live bright rays of that eternal light,

And others see, know, love, in heaven's great height;
Not toiled with aught to reason doth rebel.
Most true it is, for straight at the first sight
My mind me told that in some other place   10
It elsewhere saw the idea of that face,
And loved a love of heavenly pure delight.
   No wonder now I feel so fair a flame,
   Sith I her loved ere on this earth she came.

Sleep, silence' child, sweet father of soft rest,
Prince whose approach peace to all mortals brings,
Indifferent host to shepherds and to kings,
Sole comforter of minds with grief oppressed,
Lo, by thy charming rod all breathing things
Lie slumb'ring, with forgetfulness possessed;
And yet o'er me to spread thy drowsy wings
Thou spares, alas, who cannot be thy guest.
Since I am thine, O come, but with that face
To inward light which thou art wont to show,   10
With feignéd solace ease a true-felt woe;
Or if, deaf god, thou do deny that grace,
   Come as thou wilt, and what thou wilt bequeath;
   I long to kiss the image of my death.

Dear quirister, who from those shadows sends,
Ere that the blushing dawn dare show her light,
Such sad lamenting strains that night attends,
Become all ear, stars stay to hear thy plight:
If one whose grief even reach of thought transcends,
Who ne'er, not in a dream, did taste delight,
May thee impórtune who like case pretends,
And seems to joy in woe, in woe's despite,
Tell me (so may thou fortune milder try,
And long long sing) for what thou thus complains?   10
Sith, winter gone, the sun in dappled sky
Now smiles on meadows, mountains, woods, and plains.
   The bird, as if my questions did her move,
   With trembling wings, sobbed forth, I love, I love.

That I so slenderly set forth my mind,
Writing I wot not what in ragged rhymes,
And, charged with brass into these golden times,
When others tower so high, am left behind,
I crave not Phœbus leave his sacred cell
To bind my brows with fresh Aonian bays;
Let them have that who tuning sweetest lays

By Tempe sit, or Aganippe well.
Nor yet to Venus' tree do I aspire,
Sith she for whom I might affect that praise   10
My best attempts with cruel words gainsays;
And I seek not that others me admire.
    Of weeping myrrh the crown is which I crave,
    With a sad cypress to adorn my grave.

———————

Sound hoarse, sad lute, true witness of my woe,
And strive no more to ease self-chosen pain
With soul-enchanting sounds; your accents strain
Unto these tears uncessantly which flow;
Shrill treble, weep; and you dull basses show
Your master's sorrow in a deadly vein;
Let never joyful hand upon you go,
Nor consort keep but when you do complain;
Fly Phœbus' rays, nay, hate the irksome light—
Woods' solitary shades for thee are best,   10
Or the black horrors of the blackest night,
When all the world, save thou and I, doth rest.
    Then sound, sad lute, and bear a mourning part;
    Thou hell mayst move, though not a woman's heart.

Song

Phœbus, arise,
And paint the sable skies
With azure, white, and red;
Rouse Memnon's mother from her Tithon's bed
That she thy cáreer may with roses spread;
The nightingales thy coming each where sing;
Make an eternal spring;
Give life to this dark world which lieth dead.
Spread forth thy golden hair
In larger locks than thou wast wont before,   10
And emperor-like, decore
With diadem of pearl thy temples fair.
Chase hence the ugly night,
Which serves but to make dear thy glorious light.
This is that happy morn,
That day, long wishëd day
Of all my life so dark,
(If cruel stars have not my ruin sworn,
And fates not hope betray)
Which, only white, deserves   20
A diamond forever should it mark;
This is the morn should bring unto this grove

My love, to hear and recompense my love.
Fair king, who all preserves,
But show thy blushing beams,
And thou two sweeter eyes
Shalt see than those which by Peneus' streams
Did once thy heart surprise;
Nay, suns, which shine as clear
As thou when two thou did to Rome appear.   30
Now Flora, deck thyself in fairest guise;
If that ye, winds, would hear
A voice surpassing far Amphion's lyre,
Your stormy chiding stay;
Let Zephyr only breathe
And with her tresses play,
Kissing sometimes these purple ports of death.
The winds all silent are,
And Phœbus in his chair,
Ensaffroning sea and air,   40
Makes vanish every star;
Night like a drunkard reels
Beyond the hills to shun his flaming wheels;
The fields with flowers are decked in every hue,
The clouds bespangle with bright gold their blue;
Here is the pleasant place,
And ev'ry thing save her, who all should grace.

Alexis, here she stayed among these pines,
Sweet hermitress, she did alone repair,
Here did she spread the treasure of her hair,
More rich than that brought from the Colchian mines.
She set her by these muskëd eglantines,
The happy place the print seems yet to bear;
Her voice did sweeten here thy sugared lines,
To which winds, trees, beasts, birds did lend their ear.
Me here she first perceived, and here a morn
Of bright carnations did o'erspread her face;   10
Here did she sigh, here first my hopes were born,
And I first got a pledge of promised grace.
    But ah, what served it to be happy so,
    Sith passëd pleasures double but new woe?

Mad[rigal]

Unhappy light,
Do not approach to bring the woeful day,
When I must bid for aye

Farewell to her, and live in endless plight.
Fair moon, with gentle beams
The sight who never mars,
Long clear heaven's sable vault; and you, bright stars,
Your golden locks long glass in earth's pure streams;
Let Phœbus never rise
To dim your watchful eyes: 10
    Prolong, alas, prolong my short delight,
    And if ye can, make an eternal night.

Madrigal

This life which seems so fair
Is like a bubble blown up in the air
By sporting children's breath,
Who chase it everywhere,
And strive who can most motion it bequeath;
And though it sometime seem of its own might,
Like to an eye of gold, to be fixed there,
And firm to hover in that empty height,
That only is because it is so light;
But in that pomp it doth not long appear,   10
    For even when most admired, it in a thought
    As swelled from nothing, doth dissolve in nought.

My lute, be as thou wast when thou didst grow
With thy green mother in some shady grove,
When immelodious winds but made thee move,
And birds on thee their ramage did bestow.
Sith that dear voice which did thy sounds approve,
Which used in such harmonious strains to flow,
Is reft from earth to tune those spheres above,
What art thou but a harbinger of woe?
Thy pleasing notes, be pleasing notes no more,
But orphan wailings to the fainting ear,   10
Each stop a sigh, each sound draws forth a tear.
Be therefore silent as in woods before;
    Or if that any hand to touch thee deign,
    Like widowed turtle still her loss complain.

What doth it serve to see sun's burning face,
And skies enamelled with both the Indies' gold?
Or moon at night in jetty chariot rolled,
And all the glory of that starry place?
What doth it serve earth's beauty to behold,
The mountain's pride, the meadow's flow'ry grace,

The stately comeliness of forests old,
The sport of floods which would themselves embrace?
What doth it serve to hear the sylvans' songs,
The wanton merle, the nightingale's sad strains,   10
Which in dark shades seem to deplore my wrongs?
For what doth serve all that this world contains,
   Sith she for whom those once to me were dear,
   No part of them can have now with me here?

Mad[rigal]

My thoughts hold mortal strife,
I do detest my life,
And with lamenting cries,
Peace to my soul to bring,
Oft calls that prince which here doth monarchize;
But he, grim-grinning king,
Who caitiffs scorns and doth the blest surprise,
   Late having decked with beauty's rose his tomb,
   Disdains to crop a weed, and will not come.

URANIA, OR SPIRITUAL POEMS

Too long I followed have my fond desire,
And too long painted on the ocean streams;
Too long refreshment sought amidst the fire,
And hunted joys, which to my soul were blames.
Ah! when I had what most I did admire,
And seen of life's delights the last extremes,
I found all but a rose hedged with a briar,
A nought, a thought, a show of mocking dreams.
Henceforth on thee mine only good I'll think,
For only thou canst grant what I do crave;   10
Thy nail my pen shall be, thy blood mine ink,
Thy winding sheet my paper, study grave;
   And till that soul forth of this body fly,
   No hope I'll have but only onely Thee.

Love which is here a care
That wit and will doth mar,
Uncertain truce and a most certain war,
A shrill tempestuous wind
Which doth disturb the mind,
And like wild waves our designs all commove,—
Among those sprites above
Which see their maker's face,
It a contentment is, a quiet peace,

A pleasure void of grief, a constant rest,
Eternal joy which nothing can molest.

Thrice happy he who by some shady grove
Far from the clamorous world doth live his own;
Though solitaire, yet who is not alone,
But doth converse with that eternal love.
Oh, how more sweet is birds' harmonious moan,
Or the soft sobbings of the widowed dove,
Than those smooth whisp'rings near a prince's throne,
Which good make doubtful, do the evil approve!
Oh, how more sweet is Zephyr's wholesome breath,
And sighs perfumed, which do the flowers unfold,
Than that applause vain honor doth bequeath!
How sweet are streams to poison drunk in gold!
    The world is full of horrors, falsehoods, slights,
    Woods' silent shades have only true delights.

MADRIGALS AND EPIGRAMS

Sleeping beauty

Oh, sight too dearly bought!
She sleeps, and though those eyes
Which lighten Cupid's skies
Be closed, yet such a grace
Environeth that place
That I, through wonder, to grow faint am brought;
Suns, if eclipsed ye have such power divine,
Oh, how can I endure you when ye shine?

The quality of a kiss

The kiss with so much strife
Which I late got, sweetheart,
Was it a sign of death, or was it life?
Of life it could not be,
For I by it did sigh my soul in thee,
Nor was it death, death doth no joy impart;
Thou silent stand'st, ah! what thou didst bequeath
To me, a dying life was, living death.

The statue of Venus sleeping

Break not my sweet repose,
Thou whom free will or chance brings to this place;
Let lids these comets close;

Oh, do not seek to see their shining grace,
For when mine eyes thou seest, they thine will blind,
And thou shalt part, but leave thy heart behind.

To Chloris

See, Chloris, how the clouds
Tilt in the azure lists,
And how with Stygian mists
Each hornëd hill his giant forehead shrouds;
Jove thund'reth in the air,
The air grown great with rain,
Now seems to bring Deucalion's days again.
I see thee quake; come, let us home repair,
Come, hide thee in mine arms,
If not for love, yet to shun greater harms.

FROM *Flowers of Sion*, 1623

A good that never satisfies the mind,
A beauty fading like the April flowers,
A sweet with floods of gall that runs combined,
A pleasure passing ere in thought made ours,
A honor that more fickle is than wind,
A glory at opinion's frown that lours,
A treasury which bankrupt time devours,
A knowledge than grave ignorance more blind,
A vain delight our equals to command,
A style of greatness, in effect a dream,   10
A fabulous thought of holding sea and land,
A servile lot, decked with a pompous name,
Are the strange ends we toil for here below,
Till wisest death make us our errors know.

Look how the flower, which lingeringly doth fade,
The morning's darling late, the summer's queen,
Spoiled of that juice which kept it fresh and green,
As high as it did raise, bows low the head;
Right so my life (contentments being dead,
Or in their contraries but only seen)
With swifter speed declines than erst it spread,
And, blasted, scarce now shows what it hath been.
Therefore, as doth the pilgrim whom the night
Hastes darkly to imprison on his way,   10
Think on thy home, my soul, and think aright
Of what yet rests thee of life's wasting day.

Thy sun posts westward, passëd is thy morn,
And twice it is not given thee to be born.

O than the fairest day, thrice fairer night!
Night to best days in which a sun doth rise,
Of which that golden eye which clears the skies
Is but a sparkling ray, a shadow light;
And blessed ye, in silly pastors' sight,
Mild creatures, in whose warm crib now lies
That heaven-sent youngling, holy-maid-born wight,
Midst, end, beginning of our prophecies.
Blest cottage that hath flowers in winter spread,   10
Though withered, blessed grass, that hath the grace
To deck and be a carpet to that place.
Thus sang, unto the sounds of oaten reed,
    Before the babe, the shepherds bowed on knees,
    And springs ran nectar, honey dropped from trees.

This world a hunting is:
The prey, poor man; the Nimrod fierce is death;
His speedy greyhounds are
Lust, sickness, envy, care,
Strife that ne'er falls amiss,
With all those ills which haunt us while we breathe.
Now if, by chance, we fly
Of these the eager chase,
Old age with stealing pace   10
Casts up his nets, and there we panting die.

New doth the sun appear,
The mountain's snows decay,
Crowned with frail flowers forth comes the baby year.
My soul, time posts away,
And thou yet in that frost
Which flower and fruit hath lost,
As if all here immortal were, dost stay;
For shame, thy powers awake,
Look to that heaven which never night makes black,
And there, at that immortal sun's bright rays,   10
Deck thee with flowers which fear not rage of days.

The last and greatest herald of heaven's king,
Girt with rough skins, hies to the deserts wild,
Among that savage brood the woods forth bring,
Which he than man more harmless found and mild;
His food was locusts and what there doth spring,

With honey that from virgin hives distilled;
Parched body, hollow eyes, some uncouth thing
Made him appear, long since from earth exiled.
There burst he forth: All ye whose hopes rely
On God, with me amidst these deserts mourn,   10
Repent, repent, and from old errors turn.
Who listened to his voice? obeyed his cry?
    Only the echoes which he made relent,
    Rung from their flinty caves, Repent, repent.

From *A Cypress Grove*, 1623

To S. W. A.

Though I have twice been at the doors of death,
And twice found shut those gates which ever mourn,
This but a lightning is, truce ta'en to breath,
For late-born sorrows augur fleet return.

Amidst thy sacred cares and courtly toils,
Alexis, when thou shalt hear wand'ring fame
Tell death hath triumphed o'er my mortal spoils,
And that on earth I am but a sad name,

If thou e'er held me dear, by all our love,
By all that bliss, those joys heaven here us gave,   10
I conjure thee, and by the maids of Jove,
To grave this short remembrance on my grave:
    Here Damon lies, whose songs did sometime grace
    The murmuring Esk,—may roses shade the place!

From *Flowers of Sion*, 1630

More oft than once death whispered in mine ear:
Grave what thou hears in diamond and gold—
I am that monarch whom all monarchs fear,
Who hath in dust their far-stretched pride uprolled.
All, all is mine beneath moon's silver sphere,
And nought save virtue can my power withhold.
This, not believed, experience true thee told
By danger late when I to thee came near.
As bugbear then my visage I did show,
That of my horrors thou right use mightst make,   10
And a more sacred path of living take.
Now still walk armèd for my ruthless blow;
    Trust flattering life no more, redeem time past,
    And live each day as if it were thy last.

FROM *Poems,* 1656

No more with candied words infect mine ears,
.Tell me no more how that ye pine in anguish,
When sound ye sleep no more say that ye languish,
No more in sweet despite say you spend tears.
Who hath such hollow eyes as not to see
How those that are hare-brained boast of Apollo,
And bold give out the Muses do them follow,
Though in love's library yet no lovers be.
If we poor souls least favor but them show,
That straight in wanton lines abroad is blazed;   10
Their names doth soar on our fame's overthrow,
Marked is our lightness whilst their wits are praised.
  In silent thoughts who can no secret cover,
  He may, say we, but not well, be a lover.

FROM *Works,* 1711

When lately Pym descended into hell,
Ere he the cups of Lethe did carouse,
What place that was, he callëd loud to tell;
To whom a devil: This is the Lower House.

WILLIAM BROWNE

The Introduction and Notes are at page 1004

FROM *Britannia's Pastorals, Book Two,* 1616

Song 2

.   .   .   .

Shall I tell you whom I love?
  Harken then awhile to me,
And if such a woman move,
  As I now shall versify,
Be assured, 'tis she, or none,
That I love, and love alone.

Nature did her so much right,
  As she scorns the help of art,
In as many virtues dight
  As e'er yet embraced a heart.   10
So much good so truly tried,
Some for less were deified.

Wit she hath without desire
  To make known how much she
    hath;
And her anger flames no higher
  Than   may   fitly   sweeten
    wrath;
Full of pity as may be,
Though perhaps not so to me.

Reason masters every sense,
  And   her   virtues   grace   her
    birth;   20
Lovely as all excellence,
  Modest in her most of mirth;

Likelihood enough to prove,
Only worth could kindle love.

Such she is, and if you know
Such a one as I have sung,

Be she brown, or fair, or so,
    That she be but somewhile
        young,
Be assured, 'tis she, or none,
That I love, and love alone.   30

. . . . . .

Song 3

. . . .

                Oh! the golden age
Met all contentment in no surplusage
Of dainty viands, but as we do still,
Drank the pure water of the crystal rill,
Fed on no other meats than those they fed,
Labor the salad that their stomachs bred.
Nor sought they for the down of silver swans,
Nor those sow-thistle locks each small gale fans,
But hides of beasts, which when they lived they kept,
Served them for bed and cov'ring when they slept.   10
If any softer lay, 'twas (by the loss
Of some rock's warmth) on thick and spongy moss,
Or on the ground, some simple wall of clay
Parting their beds from where their cattle lay;
And on such pallets one man clippëd then
More golden slumbers than this age again.
That time, physicians thrived not; or if any,
I dare say all; yet then were thrice as many
As now professed, and more, for every man
Was his own patient and physicïan.   20

. . . .

        Happier those times were when the flaxen clue
By fair Arachne's hand the Lydians knew,
And sought not to the worm for silken threads
To roll their bodies in or dress their heads.
When wise Minerva did th' Athenians learn
To draw their milk-white fleeces into yarn,
And knowing not the mixtures which began,
Of colors, from the Babylonian,
Nor wool in Sardis dyed, more various known
By hues than Iris to the world hath shown;   30
The bowels of our mother were not ripped
For madder-pits, nor the sweet meadows stripped
Of their choice beauties, nor for Ceres' load
The fertile lands burdened with needless woad.
Through the wide seas no wingëd pine did go

To lands unknown for staining indigo,
Nor men in scorching climates moored their keel
To traffic for the costly cochineal.
Unknown was then the Phrygian broidery,
The Tyrian purple, and the scarlet dye, 40
Such as their sheep clad, such they wove and wore,
Russet or white, or those mixed, and no more;
Except sometimes, to bravery inclined,
They dyed them yellow caps with alder rind.
The Grecian mantle, Tuscan robes of state,
Tissue, nor cloth of gold of highest rate,
They never saw; only in pleasant woods,
Or by th' embroidered margin of the floods,
The dainty nymphs they often did behold
Clad in their light silk robes, stitched oft with gold. 50
The arras hangings round their comely halls
Wanted the cerite's web and minerals;
Green boughs of trees which fatt'ning acorns lade,
Hung full with flowers and garlands quaintly made,
Their homely cotes decked trim in low degree,
As now the court with richest tapestry.
Instead of cushions wrought in windows lain,
They picked the cockle from their fields of grain,
Sleep-bringing poppy, by the plowmen late
Not without cause to Ceres consecrate, 60
For being round and full at his half birth,
It signified the perfect orb of earth;
And by his inequalities when blown,
The earth's low vales and higher hills were shown;
By multitude of grains it held within,
Of men and beasts the number noted been;
And she, since taking care all earth to please,
Had in her Thesmophoria offered these;
Or cause that seed our elders used to eat,
With honey mixed, and was their after-meat, 70
Or since her daughter that she loved so well
By him that in th' infernal shades doth dwell
And on the Stygian banks forever reigns,
Troubled with horrid cries and noise of chains,
Fairest Proserpina was rapt away;
And she in plaints the night, in tears the day,
Had long time spent, when no high power could give her
Any redress, the poppy did relieve her,
For eating of the seeds they sleep procured,
And so beguiled those griefs she long endured; 80
Or rather since her love, then happy man,

Micon yclept, the brave Athenian,
Had been transformed into this gentle flower,
And his protection kept from Flora's power.
The daisy scattered on each mead and down,
A golden tuft within a silver crown,
(Fair fall that dainty flower, and may there be
No shepherd graced that doth not honor thee!);
The primrose, when with six leaves gotten grace, 90
Maids as a true-love in their bosoms place;
The spotless lily, by whose pure leaves be
Noted the chaste thoughts of virginity;
Carnations sweet with color like the fire,
The fit impresas for inflamed desire;
The harebell for her stainless azured hue
Claims to be worn of none but those are true;
The rose, like ready youth, enticing stands,
And would be cropped if it might choose the hands;
The yellow king-cup Flora them assigned
To be the badges of a jealous mind; 100
The orange-tawny marigold, the night
Hides not her color from a searching sight,
(To thee, then, dearest friend, my song's chief mate,
This color chiefly I appropriate,
That spite of all the mists oblivion can,
Or envious frettings of a guilty man,
Retain'st thy worth, nay, mak'st it more in price,
Like tennis balls, thrown down hard, highest rise);
The columbine in tawny often taken 110
Is then ascribed to such as are forsaken;
Flora's choice buttons of a russet dye
Is hope even in the depth of misery;
The pansy, thistle, all with prickles set,
The cowslip, honeysuckle, violet,
And many hundreds more that graced the meads,
Gardens and groves, where beauteous Flora treads,
Were by the shepherds' daughters, as yet are
Used in our cotes, brought home with special care,
For bruising them, they not alone would quell 120
But rot the rest and spoil their pleasing smell,
Much like a lad who in his tender prime
Sent from his friends to learn the use of time,
As are his mates or good or bad, so he
Thrives to the world, and such his actions be.
  As in the rainbow's many-colored hue,
Here see we watchet deepened with a blue,
There a dark tawny with a purple mixed,

Yellow and flame, with streaks of green betwixt,
A bloody stream into a blushing run,
And ends still with the color which begun, 130
Drawing the deeper to a lighter stain,
Bringing the lightest to the deep'st again,
(With such rare art each mingleth with his fellow,
The blue with watchet, green and red with yellow,
Like to the changes which we daily see
About the dove's neck, with variety,
Where none can say, though he it strict attends,
Here one begins and there the other ends),
So did the maidens with their various flowers
Deck up their windows and make neat their bowers, 140
Using such cunning as they did dispose
The ruddy piny with the lighter rose,
The monkshood with the bugloss, and entwine
The white, the blue, the flesh-like columbine
With pinks, sweet-williams, that far off the eye
Could not the manner of their mixtures spy.

Then with those flowers they most of all did prize,
With all their skill, and in most curious wise,
On tufts of herbs or rushes, would they frame
A dainty border round their shepherd's name; 150
Or posies make, so quaint, so apt, so rare,
As if the Muses only livèd there;
And that the after world should strive in vain
What they then did to counterfeit again,
Nor will the needle nor the loom e'er be
So perfect in their best embroidery,
Nor such composures make of silk and gold
As theirs, when nature all her cunning told.

The word of *mine* did no man then bewitch,
They thought none could be fortunate if rich, 160
And to the covetous did wish no wrong
But what himself desired, to live here long.

As of their songs, so of their lives they deemed,
Not of the longest, but best performed, esteemed.
They thought that heaven to him no life did give
Who only thought upon the means to live,
Nor wished they 'twere ordained to live here ever,
But as life was ordained they might persever.

O happy men! you ever did possess
No wisdom but was mixed with simpleness; 170
So wanting malice and from folly free,
Since reason went with your simplicity,
You searched yourselves if all within were fair

And did not learn of others what you were.
Your lives the patterns of those virtues gave
Which adulation tells men now they have.
     With poverty in love we only close,
Because our lovers it most truly shows,
When they who in that blessed age did move,
Knew neither poverty nor want of love.   180
     The hatred which they bore was only this,
That everyone did hate to do amiss.
Their fortune still was subject to their will;   .
Their want, oh happy, was the want of ill!
     Ye truest, fairest, loveliest nymphs that can
Out of your eyes lend fire Promethean,
All-beauteous ladies, love-alluring dames,
That on the banks of Isca, Humber, Thames,
By your encouragement can make a swain
Climb by his song where none but souls attain,   190
And by the graceful reading of our lines
Renew our heat to further brave designs;
You, by whose means my muse thus boldly says:
Though she do sing of shepherds' loves and lays,
And flagging weakly low, gets not on wing
To second that of Helen's ravishing,
Nor hath the love nor beauty of a queen
My subject graced, as other works have been;
Yet not to do their age nor ours a wrong,
Though queens, nay goddesses, famed Homer's song,   200
Mine hath been tuned and heard by beauties more
Than all the poets that have lived before,
Not 'cause it is more worth, but it doth fall
That nature now is turned a prodigal,
And on this age so much perfection spends
That to her last of treasure it extends;
For all the ages that are slid away
Had not so many beauties as this day.
     Oh, what a rapture have I gotten now!
That age of gold, this of the lovely brow,   210
Have drawn me from my song! I onward run
Clean from the end to which I first begun.
But ye, the heavenly creatures of the west,
In whom the virtues and the graces rest,
Pardon that I have run astray so long
And grown so tedious in so rude a song.
If you yourselves should come to add one grace
Unto a pleasant grove or such like place,
Where here the curious cutting of a hedge,

There by a pond the trimming of the sedge,   220
Here the fine setting of well-shading trees,
The walks there mounting up by small degrees,
The gravel and the green so equal lie,
It, with the rest, draws on your ling'ring eye;
Here the sweet smells that do perfume the air,
Arising from the infinite repair
Of odoriferous buds and herbs of price,
As if it were another paradise,
So please the smelling sense that you are fain
Where last you walked to turn and walk again;   230
There the small birds with their harmonious notes
Sing to a spring that smileth as she floats,
For in her face a many dimples show,
And often skips as it did dancing go;
Here further down an over-archëd alley,
That from a hill goes winding in a valley,
You spy at end thereof a standing lake,
Where some ingenious artist strives to make
The water, brought in turning pipes of lead
Through birds of earth most lively fashionëd,   240
To counterfeit and mock the sylvans all
In singing well their own set madrigal
(This with no small delight retains your ear,
And makes you think none blest but who live there);
Then in another place the fruits that be
In gallant clusters decking each good tree,
Invite your hand to crop some from the stem,
And liking one, taste every sort of them;
Then to the arbor's walk, then to the bowers,
Thence to the walks again, thence to the flowers,   250
Then to the birds, and to the clear spring thence,
Now pleasing one, and then another sense;
Here one walks oft, and yet anew begin'th,
As if it were some hidden labyrinth;
So loath to part and so content to stay
That when the gard'ner knocks for you away,
It grieves you so to leave the pleasures in it
That you could wish that you had never seen it:
Blame me not then, if while to you I told
The happiness our fathers clipped of old,   260
The mere imagination of their bliss
So rapt my thoughts and made me sing amiss;
And still the more they ran on those days' worth,
The more unwilling was I to come forth.

Hail, thou my native soil! thou blessed plot
Whose equal all the world affordeth not!
Show me who can so many crystal rills,
Such sweet-clothed valleys, or aspiring hills;
Such wood-ground, pastures, quarries, wealthy mines;   270
Such rocks in whom the diamond fairly shines;
And if the earth can show the like again,
Yet will she fail in her sea-ruling men.
Time never can produce men to o'ertake
The fames of Grenville, Davys, Gilbert, Drake,
Or worthy Hawkins, or of thousands more
That by their power made the Devonian shore
Mock the proud Tagus; for whose richest spoil
The boasting Spaniard left the Indian soil
Bankrupt of store, knowing it would quit cost   280
By winning this, though all the rest were lost.

· · · · · · ·

From *Lansdowne Ms.* 777

[*Poor silly fool*]

Poor silly fool, thou striv'st in vain to know
If I enjoy, or love whom thou lov'st so;
Since my affection, ever secret tried,
Blooms like the fern, and seeds still unespied.

And as the subtle flames of heaven, that wound
The inward part yet leave the outward sound,
My love wars on my heart, kills that within,
When merry are my looks and fresh my skin.

Of yellow jaundice lovers as you be,   10
Whose faces straight proclaim their malady,
Think not to find me one, who know full well
That none but French and fools love now and tell.

His griefs are sweet, his joys, oh, heavenly move,
Who from the world conceals his honest love;
Nay, lets his mistress know his passion's source
Rather by reason than by his discourse.

This is my way, and in this language new
Showing my merit, it demands my due;
And hold this maxim, spite of all dispute:
He asks enough that serves well and is mute.   20

An ode

Awake, fair Muse, for I intend
　　These everlasting lines to thee;
And, honored Drayton, come and lend
　　An ear to this sweet melody;
For on my harp's most high and silver string
To those nine sisters whom I love, I sing.

　This man through death and horror seeks
　　Honor by the victorious steel;
　Another in unmappèd creeks
　　For jewels moors his wingèd keel;
The clam'rous bar wins some, and others bite
At looks thrown from a mushroom favorite;

　But I that serve the lovely graces
　　Spurn at that dross which most adore,
And titles hate like painted faces,
　　And heart-fed care for evermore.
Those pleasures I disdain which are pursued
With praise and wishes by the multitude.

　The bays which deathless learning crowns,
　　Me of Apollo's troop installs;
The satyrs following o'er the downs
　　Fair nymphs to rustic festivals,
Make me affect, where men no traffic have,
The holy horror of a savage cave.

　Through the fair skies I thence intend,
　　With an unused and powerful wing
To bear me to my journey's end;
　　And those that taste the Muses' spring,
Too much celestial fire have at their birth
To live long time like common souls in earth.

　From fair Aurora will I rear
　　Myself unto the source of floods,
And from the Ethiopian bear
　　To him as white as snowy woods;
Nor shall I fear, from this day taking flight,
To be wound up in any veil of night.

Of death I may not fear the dart,
  As is the use of human state;
For well I know my better part
  Dreads not the hand of time or fate.   40
Tremble at death, envy, and fortune, who
Have but one life; heaven gives a poet two.

All costly obsequies away,
  Marble and painting too, as vain;
My ashes shall not meet with clay,
  As those do of the vulgar train.
And if my muse to Spenser's glory come,
No king shall own my verses for his tomb.

A round

Now that the spring hath filled our
    veins
  With kind and active fire,
And made green liv'ries for the
    plains,
  And every grove a choir,

Sing we a song of merry glee,
  And Bacchus fill the bowl.
Then here's to thee. And thou to
    me
  And every thirsty soul.

Nor care nor sorrow e'er paid debt,
  Nor never shall do mine;   10

I have no cradle going yet;
  Nor I, by this good wine.

No wife at home to send for me,
  No hogs are in my ground,
No suit in law to pay a fee,
  Then round, old Jocky, round.

Shear sheep that have them, cry we
    still,
  But see that no man 'scape
    To drink of the sherry
    That makes us so merry,   20
And plump as the lusty grape.

Cælia

Lo, I the man that whilom loved and lost,
Not dreading loss, do sing again of love,
And like a man but lately tempest-tossed,
Try if my stars still inauspicious prove;
Not to make good that poets never can
Long time without a chosen mistress be,
Do I sing thus, or my affections ran
Within the maze of mutability.
What last I loved was beauty of the mind,
And that lodged in a temple truly fair,   10
Which ruined now by death, if I can find
The saint that lived therein some otherwhere,

I may adore it there and love the cell
For entertaining what I loved so well.

Why might I not for once be of that sect
Which hold that souls, when nature hath her right,
Some other bodies to themselves elect,
And sunlike make the day and license night?
That soul whose setting in one hemisphere
Was to enlighten straight another part,
In that horizon, if I see it there,
Calls for my first respect and its desert;
Her virtue is the same and may be more,
For as the sun is distant, so his power   10
In operation differs, and the store
Of thick clouds interposed make him less our.
   And verily I think her climate such,
   Since to my former flame it adds so much.

So sat the Muses on the banks of Thames,
And pleased to sing our heavenly Spenser's wit,
Inspiring almost trees with powerful flames,
As Cælia, when she sings what I have writ;
Methinks there is a spirit more divine,
An elegance more rare when aught is sung
By her sweet voice, in every verse of mine,
Than I conceive by any other tongue;
So a musician sets what some one plays
With better relish, sweeter stroke, than he   10
That first composed; nay, oft the maker weighs
If what he hears his own or other's be.
   Such are my lines: the highest, best of choice,
   Become more gracious by her sweetest voice.

Were't not for you, here should my pen have rest
And take a long leave of sweet poesy;
Britannia's swains, and rivers far by west,
Should hear no more mine oaten melody;
Yet shall the song I sung of them awhile
Unperfect lie, and make no further known
The happy loves of this our pleasant isle,
Till I have left some record of mine own.
You are the subject now, and writing you,
I well may versify, not poetize;   10
Here needs no fiction, for the Graces true
And virtues clip not with base flatteries.

Here, could I write what you deserve of praise,
Others might wear, but I should win the bays.

[Down in a valley]

Down in a valley, by a forest's side,
Near where the crystal Thames rolls on her waves,
I saw a mushroom stand in haughty pride,
As if the lilies grew to be his slaves.
The gentle daisy, with her silver crown,
Worn in the breast of many a shepherd's lass;
The humble violet, that lowly down
Salutes the gay nymphs as they trimly pass;
These, with a many more, methought, complained
That nature should those needless things produce,   10
Which not alone the sun from others gained,
But turn it wholly to their proper use.
    I could not choose but grieve that nature made
    So glorious flowers to live in such a shade.

In obitum M. S., X Maii, 1614

May! be thou never graced with birds that sing,
            Nor Flora's pride!
In thee all flowers and roses spring,
            Mine only died.

On the Countess Dowager of Pembroke

Underneath this sable hearse
Lies the subject of all verse:
Sidney's sister, Pembroke's mother.
Death, ere thou hast slain another
Fair and learn'd and good as she,
Time shall throw a dart at thee.

Marble piles let no man raise
To her name, for after-days
Some kind woman, born as she,
Reading this, like Niobe   10
Shall turn marble, and become
Both her mourner and her tomb.

GEORGE WITHER

The Introduction and Notes are at page 1005

FROM *Juvenilia*, 1622

The Shepherd's Hunting

The fourth eclogue

To his truly beloved loving friend, Mr. William Browne, of the Inner Temple

The argument

Philarete on Willy calls
To sing out his pastorals,
Warrants fame shall grace his
    rhymes
Spite of envy and the times,
And shows how in care he uses
To take comfort from his muses.

Philarete.

Prithee, Willy, tell me this,
What new accident there is,
That thou, once the blithest lad,
Art become so wondrous sad   10
And so careless of thy quill,
As if thou hadst lost thy skill?
Thou wert wont to charm thy
    flocks,
And among the massy rocks
Hast so cheered me with thy song
That I have forgot my wrong.
Something hath thee surely
    crossed,
That thy old wont thou hast lost.
Tell me, have I aught missaid
That hath made thee ill-a-paid? 20
Hath some churl done thee a
    spite?
Dost thou miss a lamb to-night?
Frowns thy fairest shepherd's
    lass?

Or how comes this ill to pass?
Is there any discontent
Worse than this my banishment?

Willy.

Why, doth that so evil seem
That thou nothing worse dost
    deem?
Shepherd, there full many be
That will change contents with
    thee.   30
Those that choose their walks at
    will
On the valley or the hill,
Or those pleasures boast of can,
Groves or fields may yield to
    man,
Never come to know the rest
Wherewithal thy mind is blest.
Many a one that oft resorts
To make up the troop at sports,
And in company somewhere
Happens to strain forth a smile, 40
Feels more want, and outward
    smart,
And more inward grief of heart,
Than this place can bring to thee
While thy mind remaineth free.
Thou bewailst my want of mirth,
But what findst thou in this earth
Wherein aught may be believed
Worth to make me joyed or
    grieved?
And yet feel I, natheless,
Part of both, I must confess.   50
Sometime I of mirth do bor-
    row,
Otherwhile as much of sorrow;
But my present state is such
As nor joy nor grieve I much.

Philarete.

Why hath Willy then so long
Thus forborne his wonted song?
Wherefore doth he now let fall
His well-tunèd pastoral,
And my ears that music bar,
Which I more long after far   60
Than the liberty I want?

Willy.

That were very much to grant,
But doth this hold alway, lad,
Those that sing not must be sad?
Didst thou ever that bird hear
Sing well, that sings all the year?
Tom the Piper doth not play
Till he wears his pipe away;
There's a time to slack the string,
And a time to leave to sing.   70

Philarete.

Yea, but no man now is still,
That can sing or tune a quill.
Now to chant it were but reason;
Song and music are in season.
Now in this sweet jolly tide
Is the earth in all her pride;
The fair lady of the May,
Trimmed up in her best array,
Hath invited all the swains
With the lasses of the plains   80
To attend upon her sport
At the places of resort.
Corydon with his bold rout
Hath already been about
For the elder shepherds' dole,
And fetched in the summer-pole;
Whilst the rest have built a bower
To defend them from a shower,
Sealed so close with boughs all
    green
Titan cannot pry between.   90
Now the dairy-wenches dream
Of their strawberries and cream,

And each doth herself advance
To be taken in to dance;
Everyone that knows to sing
Fits him for his caroling;
So do those that hope for meed
Either by the pipe or reed,
And though I am kept away,
I do hear this very day   100
Many learned grooms do wend
For the garlands to contend,
Which a nymph that hight De-
    sart,
Long a stranger in this part,
With her own fair hand hath
    wrought—
A rare work, they say, past
    thought,
As appeareth by the name,
For she calls them wreaths of
    fame.
She hath set in their due place
Ev'ry flower that may grace,   110
And among a thousand mo,
Whereof some but serve for show,
She hath wove in Daphne's tree,
That they may not blasted be,
Which with thyme she edged
    about
Lest the work should ravel out;
And that it might wither never,
Intermixed it with live-ever.
These are to be shared among
Those that do excel for song,   120
Or their passions can rehearse
In the smooth'st and sweetest
    verse.
Then for those among the rest
That can play and pipe the best,
There's a kidling with the dam,
A fat wether and a lamb.
And for those that leapen far,
Wrestle, run, and throw the bar,
There's appointed guerdons too:
He that best the first can do   130
Shall, for his reward, be paid
With a sheep-hook, fair inlaid

With fine bone of a strange beast
That men bring out of the west;
For the next a scrip of red,
Tasselled with fine colored
    thread;
There's preparèd for their meed
That in running make most speed
Or the cunning measures foot,
Cups of turnèd maple-root,   140
Whereupon the skillful man
Hath engraved the loves of Pan;
And the last hath for his due
A fine napkin wrought with
    blue.
Then, my Willy, why art thou
Careless of thy merit now?
What dost thou here with a wight
That is shut up from delight
In a solitary den,
As not fit to live with men?   150
Go, my Willy, get thee gone,
Leave me in exile alone;
Hie thee to that merry throng,
And amaze them with thy song.
Thou art young, yet such a lay
Never graced the month of May,
As, if they provoke thy skill,
Thou canst fit unto thy quill;
I with wonder heard thee sing,
At our last year's revelling.   160
Then I with the rest was free,
When unknown I noted thee,
And perceived the ruder swains
Envy thy far sweeter strains.
Yea, I saw the lasses cling
Round about thee in a ring,
As if each one jealous were
Any but herself should hear.
And I know they yet do long
For the res'due of thy song.   170
Haste thee then to sing it forth;
Take the benefit of worth,
And Desart will sure bequeath
Fame's fair garland for thy
    wreath;
Hie, thee, Willy, hie away.

Willy.

Phila, rather let me stay,
And be desolate with thee,
Than at those their revels be;
Nought such is my skill, I wis,
As indeed thou deem'st it is,   180
But whate'er it be, I must
Be content, and shall, I trust;
For a song I do not pass
'Mongst my friends, but what,
    alas,
Should I have to do with them
That my music do contemn?
Some there are, as well I wot,
That the same yet favor not;
Yet I cannot well avow
They my carols disallow;   190
But such malice I have spied,
'Tis as much as if they did.

Philarete.

Willy, what may those men be
Are so ill to malice thee?

Willy.

Some are worthy, well-esteemed,
Some without worth are so
    deemed,
Others of so base a spirit
They have not esteem nor merit.

Philarete.

What's the wrong?

Willy.

    A slight offence,
Wherewithal I can dispense;   200
But hereafter, for their sake,
To myself I'll music make.

Philarete.

What, because some clown of-
    fends,
Wilt thou punish all thy friends?

Willy.

Do not, Phil, misunderstand me,
Those that love me may com-
    mand me;
But, thou knowst, I am but
    young,
And the pastoral I sung
Is by some supposed to be
By a strain too high for me; 210
So they kindly let me gain
Not my labor for my pain.
Trust me, I do wonder why
They should me my own deny;
Though I'm young, I scorn to flit
On the wings of borrowed wit;
I'll make my own feathers rear
    me
Whither others cannot bear me.
Yet I'll keep my skill in store
Till I've seen some winters
    more. 220

Philarete.

But, in earnest, meanst thou so?
Then thou art not wise, I trow;
Better shall advise thee Pan,
For thou dost not rightly than;
That's the ready way to blot
All the credit thou hast got.
Rather in thy age's prime
Get another start of time,
And make those that so fond be,
Spite of their own dullness see 230
That the sacred Muses can
Make a child in years a man.
It is known what thou canst do,
For it is not long ago
When that Cuddy, thou, and I,
Each the other's skill to try,
At Saint Dunstan's charmëd well,
As some present there can tell,
Sang upon a sudden theme,
Sitting by the crimson stream; 240
Where if thou didst well or no,
Yet remains the song to show.

Much experience more I've had
Of thy skill, thou happy lad,
And would make the world to
    know it,
But that time will further show
    it.
Envy makes their tongues now
    run
More than doubt of what is done;
For that needs must be thy own,
Or to be some other's known. 250
But how then will't suit unto
What thou shalt hereafter do?
Or, I wonder, where is he
Would with that song part to
    thee?
Nay, were there so mad a swain
Could such glory sell for gain,
Phœbus would not have com-
    bined
That gift with so base a mind.
Never did the Nine impart
The sweet secrets of their art 260
Unto any that did scorn
We should see their favors worn.
Therefore unto those that say,
Were they pleased to sing a lay
They could do't, and will not
    though,
This I speak, for this I know:
None e'er drunk the Thespian
    spring
And knew how, but he did sing;
For that once infused in man
Makes him show't, do what he
    can. 270
Nay, those that do only sip,
Or but ev'n their fingers dip
In that sacred fount, poor elves,
Of that brood will show them-
    selves.
Yea, in hope to get them fame
They will speak, though to their
    shame.
Let those then at thee repine
That by their wits measure thine;

Needs those songs must be thine
    own,
And that one day will be known.
That poor imputation too   281
I myself do undergo;
But it will appear ere long
That 'twas envy sought our
    wrong,
Who at twice-ten have sung
    more
Than some will do at fourscore.
Cheer thee, honest Willy, then,
And begin thy song again.

Willy.

Fain I would, but I do fear
When again my lines they
    hear,   290
If they yield they are my rhymes,
They will feign some other
    crimes,
And 'tis no safe vent'ring by
Where we see detraction lie.
For do what I can, I doubt
She will pick some quarrel out,
And I oft have heard defended,
Little said is soon amended.

Philarete.

Seest thou not in clearest days
Oft thick fogs cloud heaven's
    rays,   300
And that vapors which do breathe
From the earth's gross womb be-
    neath,
Seem not to us with black steams
To pollute the sun's bright beams,
And yet vanish into air,
Leaving it unblemished fair?
So, my Willy, shall it be
With detraction's breath on thee;
It shall never rise so high
As to stain thy poesy.   310
As that sun doth oft exhale
Vapors from each rotten vale,

Poesy so sometime drains
Gross conceits from muddy brains,
Mists of envy, fogs of spite,
'Twixt men's judgments and her
    light;
But so much her power may do
That she can dissolve them too.
If thy verse do bravely tower,
As she makes wing, she gets
    power;   320
Yet the higher she doth soar,
She's affronted still the more,
Till she to the high'st hath passed,
Then she rests with fame at last.
Let nought therefore thee af-
    fright,
But make forward in thy flight;
For if I could match thy rhyme,
To the very stars I'd climb,
There begin again and fly
Till I reached eternity.   330
But, alas, my muse is slow;
For thy pace she flags too low.
Yea, the more's her hapless fate,
Her short wings were clipped of
    late,
And poor I, her fortune rueing,
Am myself put up a-mewing.
But if I my cage can rid,
I'll fly where I never did,
And though for her sake I'm
    crossed,
Though my best hopes I have
    lost,   340
And knew she would make my
    trouble
Ten times more than ten times
    double,
I would love and keep her too
Spite of all the world could do.
For though banished from my
    flocks
And confined within these rocks,
Here I waste away the light
And consume the sullen night,
She doth for my comfort stay,

And keeps many cares away. 350
Though I miss the flow'ry fields,
With those sweets the springtide
    yields,
Though I may not see those
    groves
Where the shepherds chant their
    loves,
And the lasses more excel
Than the sweet-voiced Philomel,
Though of all those pleasures past
Nothing now remains at last,
But remembrance, poor relief,
That more makes than mends my
    grief, 360
She's my mind's companion still,
Maugre envy's evil will,
Whence she should be driven too,
Were't in mortal's power to do.
She doth tell me where to bor-
    row
Comfort in the midst of sorrow,
Makes the desolatest place
To her presence be a grace,
And the blackest discontents
To be pleasing ornaments. 370
In my former days of bliss
Her divine skill taught me this,
That from everything I saw
I could some invention draw,
And raise pleasure to her height
Through the meanest object's
    sight;
By the murmur of a spring,
Or the least bough's rusteling,
By a daisy whose leaves spread
Shut when Titan goes to bed, 380
Or a shady bush or tree,
She could more infuse in me
Than all nature's beauties can
In some other wiser man.
By her help I also now
Make this churlish place allow
Some things that may sweeten
    gladness
In the very gall of sadness.

The dull loneness, the black
    shade
That these hanging vaults have
    made, 390
The strange music of the waves
Beating on these hollow caves,
This black den which rocks em-
    boss,
Overgrown with eldest moss,
The rude portals that give light
More to terror than delight,
This my chamber of neglect,
Walled about with disrespect:
From all these and this dull air,
A fit object for despair, 400
She hath taught me by her might
To draw comfort and delight.
Therefore, thou best earthly bliss,
I will cherish thee for this.
Poesy, thou sweet'st content
That e'er heav'n to mortals lent,
Though they as a trifle leave thee,
Whose dull thoughts cannot con-
    ceive thee,
Though thou be to them a scorn
That to nought but earth are
    born, 410
Let my life no longer be
Than I am in love with thee.
Though our wise ones call thee
    madness,
Let me never taste of gladness
If I love not thy madd'st fits
More than all their greatest wits;
And though some too seeming-
    holy
Do account thy raptures folly,
Thou dost teach me to contemn
What makes knaves and fools of
    them, 420
O high power, that oft doth carry
Men above—

Willy.

Good Philarete, tarry;
I do fear thou wilt be gone

Quite above my reach anon.
The kind flames of poesy
Have now borne thy thoughts so
      high
That they up in heaven be,
And have quite forgotten me.
Call thyself to mind again;
Are these raptures for a swain   430
That attends on lowly sheep,
And with simple herds doth keep?

Philarete.

Thanks, my Willy, I had run
Till that time had lodged the sun
If thou hadst not made me stay;
But thy pardon here I pray.
Loved Apollo's sacred sire
Had raised up my spirits higher,
Through the love of poesy,
Than indeed they use to fly.   440
But as I said, I say still,
If that I had Willy's skill,
Envy nor detraction's tongue
Should e'er make me leave my
      song,
But I'd sing it every day
Till they pined themselves away.
Be thou then advised in this,

Which both just and fitting is:
Finish what thou hast begun,
Or at least still forward run.   450
Hail and thunder ill he'll bear
That a blast of wind doth fear,
And if words will thus affray
      thee,
Prithee how will deeds dismay
      thee?
Do not think so rathe a song
Can pass through the vulgar
      throng,
And escape without a touch,
Or that they can hurt it much;
Frosts we see do nip that thing
Which is forward'st in the
      spring,   460
Yet at last for all such lets
Somewhat of the rest it gets,
And I'm sure that so mayst thou.
Therefore, my kind Willy, now,
Since thy folding time draws on
And I see thou must be gone,
Thee I earnestly beseech
To remember this my speech,
And some little counsel take
For Philarete his sake;   470
And I more of this will say
If thou come next holiday.

From *Fair Virtue, the Mistress of Philarete*, 1622

Sonnet 4

Shall I wasting in despair
Die because a woman's fair?
Or make pale my cheeks with
      care
'Cause another's rosy are?
Be she fairer than the day,
Or the flow'ry meads in May,
   If she be not so to me,
   What care I how fair she be?

Shall my heart be grieved or
      pined
'Cause I see a woman kind?   10
Or a well-disposèd nature

Joinèd with a lovely feature?
Be she meeker, kinder, than
Turtle-dove or pelican,
   If she be not so to me,
   What care I how kind she be?

Shall a woman's virtues move
Me to perish for her love?
Or her well-deserving known
Make me quite forget mine
      own?   20
Be she with that goodness blest
Which may gain her name of best,
   If she be not such to me,
   What care I how good she be?

'Cause her fortune seems too high,
Shall I play the fool and die?
Those that bear a noble mind,
Where they want of riches find,
Think what with them they
    would do   ²⁹
That without them dare to woo;
    And unless that mind I see,
    What care I how great she be?

Great, or good, or kind, or fair,
I will ne'er the more despair;
If she love me, this believe,
I will die ere she shall grieve;
If she slight me when I woo,
I can scorn and let her go;
    For if she be not for me,
    What care I for whom she
    be?   ⁴⁰

Sonnet 5

I wandered out a while agone,
And went I know not whither;
But there do beauties many a one
Resort and meet together,
And Cupid's power will there be
    shown
If ever you come thither.

For like two suns, two beauties
    bright

I shining saw together,
And tempted by their double
    light
My eyes I fixed on either;   ¹⁰
Till both at once so thralled my
    sight,
I loved, and knew not whether.

Such equal sweet Venus gave,
That I preferred not either;
And when for love I thought to
    crave,
I knew not well of whether,
For one while this I wished to
    have,
And then I that had liefer.

A lover of the curious't eye
Might have been pleased in ei-
    ther;   ²⁰
And so, I must confess, might I,
Had they not been together.
Now both must love or both
    deny,
In one enjoy I neither.

But yet at last I 'scaped the smart
I feared at coming hither;
For seeing my divided heart—
I, choosing, knew not whether—
Love angry grew and did depart,
And now I care for neither.   ³⁰

A Christmas carol

So now is come our joyful'st feast,
Let every man be jolly.
Each room with ivy leaves is
    dressed,
And every post with holly.
    Though some churls at our
        mirth repine,
    Round your foreheads garlands
        twine,
    Drown sorrow in a cup of wine,
    And let us all be merry.

Now all our neighbors' chimneys
    smoke,
And Christmas blocks are burn-
    ing;   ¹⁰
Their ovens they with baked meats
    choke,
And all their spits are turning.
    Without the door let sorrow lie,
    And if for cold it hap to die,
    We'll bury 't in a Christmas pie,
    And evermore be merry.

Now every lad is wondrous trim,
And no man minds his labor;
Our lasses have provided them
A bag-pipe and a tabor.   20
   Young men and maids and girls
     and boys
    Give life to one another's joys,
    And you anon shall by their
     noise
Perceive that they are merry.

Rank misers now do sparing shun,
Their hall of music soundeth,
And dogs thence with whole
   shoulders run,
So all things there aboundeth.
   The country folk themselves
    advance,
    For crowdy-mutton's come out
     of France,   30
    And Jack shall pipe and Jill
     shall dance,
And all the town be merry.

Ned Swash hath fetched his bands
   from pawn,
And all his best apparel;
Brisk Nell hath bought a ruff of
   lawn
With droppings of the barrel;
   And those that hardly all the
    year
    Had bread to eat or rags to wear,
    Will have both clothes and
     dainty fare,
And all the day be merry.   40

Now poor men to the justices
With capons make their arrants,
And if they hap to fail of these
They plague them with their war-
   rants.
   But now they feed them with
    good cheer,
    And what they want they take
     in beer,

For Christmas comes but once
   a year,
And then they shall be merry.

Good farmers in the country nurse
The poor, that else were undone.   50
Some landlords spend their money
   worse,
On lust and pride at London.
   There the roisters they do play,
    Drab and dice their land away,
    Which may be ours another
     day;
And therefore let's be merry.

The client now his suit forbears,
The prisoner's heart is easëd,
The debtor drinks away his cares,
And for the time is pleasëd.   60
   Though others' purses be more
    fat,
    Why should we pine or grieve at
     that?
    Hang sorrow, care will kill a
     cat,
And therefore let's be merry.

Hark how the wags abroad do call
Each other forth to rambling;
Anon you'll see them in the hall
For nuts and apples scrambling.
   Hark how the roofs with laugh-
    ters sound!
    Anon they'll think the house
     goes round,   70
    For they the cellar's depth have
     found,
And there they will be merry.

The wenches with their wassail
   bowls
About the streets are singing,
The boys are come to catch the
   owls,
The wild mare in is bringing.

Our kitchen boy hath broke his
   box,
And to the dealing of the ox
Our honest neighbors come by
   flocks,
And here they will be merry.   80

Now kings and queens poor sheep-
   cotes have,
And mate with everybody;
The honest now may play the
   knave,
And wise men play at noddy.
Some youths will now a-mum-
   ming go,

Some others play at rowland-
   hoe,
And twenty other gameboys mo,
Because they will be merry.

Then wherefore in these merry
   days
Should we, I pray, be duller?   90
No, let us sing some roundelays
To make our mirth the fuller.
And, whilst thus inspired we
   sing,
Let all the streets with echoes
   ring,
Woods and hills and everything,
Bear witness we are merry.

A sonnet upon a stolen kiss

Now gentle sleep hath closèd up those eyes
Which waking kept my boldest thoughts in awe,
And free access unto that sweet lip lies,
From whence I long the rosy breath to draw;
Methinks no wrong it were if I should steal
From those two melting rubies one poor kiss;
None sees the theft that would the thief reveal,
Nor rob I her of aught which she can miss;
Nay, should I twenty kisses take away,   10
There would be little sign I had done so;
Why then should I this robbery delay?
Oh! she may wake and therewith angry grow.
   Well, if she do, I'll back restore that one,
   And twenty hundred thousand more for loan.

FROM *A Collection of Emblems*, 1635

The marigold

When with a serious musing I behold
The grateful and obsequious marigold,
How duly every morning she displays
Her open breast, when Titan spreads his rays;
How she observes him in his daily walk,
Still bending towards him her tender stalk;
How, when he down declines, she droops and mourns,
Bedewed, as 'twere, with tears, till he returns;
And how she veils her flowers when he is gone,
As if she scornèd to be lookèd on   10

By an inferior eye, or did contemn
To wait upon a meaner light than him;
When this I meditate, methinks the flowers
Have spirits far more generous than ours,
And give us fair examples to despise
The servile fawnings and idolatries
Wherewith we court these earthly things below,
Which merit not the service we bestow.
    But, O my God! though groveling I appear
Upon the ground, and have a rooting here   20
Which hales me downward, yet in my desire
To that which is above me I aspire,
And all my best affections I profess
To him that is the sun of righteousness.
Oh, keep the morning of his incarnation,
The burning noontide of his bitter passion,
The night of his descending, and the height
Of his ascension ever in my sight,
    That imitating him in that I may,
    I never follow an inferior way.   30

FROM *Halleluiah, or Britain's Second Remembrancer*, 1641

A rocking hymn

Nurses usually sing their children asleep, and through want of perti-
nent matter, they oft make use of unprofitable, if not worse, songs. This
was therefore prepared that it might help acquaint them, and their
nurse-children, with the loving care and kindness of their heavenly
Father.

    Sweet baby, sleep, what ails my dear?
    What ails my darling thus to cry?
    Be still, my child, and lend thine ear
    To hear me sing thy lullaby.
        My pretty lamb, forbear to weep,
        Be still, my dear, sweet baby, sleep.
    Thou blessed soul, what canst thou fear?
    What thing to thee can mischief do?
    Thy God is now thy father dear,
    His holy spouse thy mother too.   10
        Sweet babe, then forbear to weep;
        Be still, my babe, sweet baby, sleep.
    Though thy conception was in sin,
    A sacred bathing thou hast had;
    And though thy birth unclean hath been,
    A blameless babe thou now art made.

Sweet baby then forbear to weep;
Be still, my dear, sweet baby, sleep.
Whilst thus thy lullaby I sing,
For thee great blessings ripening be;   20
Thine eldest brother is a king,
And hath a kingdom bought for thee.
  Sweet baby then forbear to weep;
  Be still, my babe, sweet baby, sleep.
Sweet baby sleep and nothing fear,
For whosoever thee offends,
By thy protector threatened are,
And God and angels are thy friends.
  Sweet baby then forbear to weep;
  Be still, my babe, sweet baby, sleep.   30
When God with us was dwelling here,
In little babes he took delight;
Such innocents as thou, my dear,
Are ever precious in his sight.
  Sweet baby then forbear to weep;
  Be still, my babe, sweet baby, sleep.
A little infant once was he,
And strength in weakness then was laid
Upon his virgin mother's knee,
That power to thee might be conveyed.   40
  Sweet baby then forbear to weep;
  Be still, my babe, sweet baby, sleep.
In this thy frailty and thy need
He friends and helpers doth prepare,
Which thee shall cherish, clothe, and feed,
For of thy weal they tender are.
  Sweet baby then forbear to weep;
  Be still, my babe, sweet baby, sleep.
The King of kings when he was born
Had not so much for outward ease;   50
By him such dressings were not worn,
Nor such like swaddling clothes as these.
  Sweet baby then forbear to weep;
  Be still, my babe, sweet baby, sleep.
Within a manger lodged thy Lord,
Where oxen lay and asses fed;
Warm rooms we do to thee afford,
An easy cradle or a bed.
  Sweet baby then forbear to weep;
  Be still, my babe, sweet baby, sleep.   60
The wants that he did then sustain
Have purchased wealth, my babe, for thee;

And by his torments and his pain,
Thy rest and ease securëd be.
 My baby then forbear to weep;
 Be still, my babe, sweet baby, sleep.
Thou hast yet more to perfect this,
A promise and an earnest got
Of gaining everlasting bliss,
Though thou, my babe, perceiv'st it not. 70
 Sweet baby then forbear to weep;
 Be still, my babe, sweet baby, sleep.

For a poet

*Poets are prophets, not only in the vulgar acception, among human
authors, but so called also by Saint Paul, Tit. i. 12. By this hymn,
therefore, such poets as are not past grace may be remembered to exercise their faculty to that end for which it was given unto them by God.*

By art a poet is not made;
For though by art some bettered be,
Immediately his gift he had
From thee, O God, from none but
 thee.
 And fitted in the womb he was
To be, by what thou didst inspire,
In extraordinary place,
A chaplain of this lower choir.
 Most poets future things declare,
 And prophets, true or false, they
  are. 10
They who with meekness enter-
 tain,
And with a humble soul admit
Those raptures which thy grace
 doth deign,
Become for thy true service fit.
 And though the scapes which we
  condemn
In these may otherwhile be found,
Thy secrets thou revealest by them,
And mak'st their tongues thy
  praise to sound.
 Such Moses was, such David
  proved,
 Men famous, holy, and be-
  loved. 20
And such, though lower in degree,

Are some who live among us yet;
And they with truth inspirëd be,
By musing on thy holy writ.
 In ordinary, some of those
Upon thy service do attend;
Divulging forth in holy prose
The messages which thou dost
 send;
 And some of these thy truths dis-
  play,
 Not in an ordinary way. 30
But where this gift puffs up with
 pride,
The devil enters in thereby,
And through the same doth means
 provide
To raise his own inventions high;
 Blasphemous fancies are infused,
All holy new things are expelled.
He that hath most profanely mused
Is famed as having most excelled;
 And those are priests and pro-
  phets made
 To him from whom their strains
  they had. 40
Such were those poets who of old
To heathen gods their hymns did
 frame;
Or have blasphemous fables told,

To truth's abuse and virtue's
  blame.
  Such are these poets in these days
Who vent the fumes of lust and
  wine,
Then crown each others' heads
  with bays,
As if their poems were divine.
  And such, though they some
    truths foresee,
  False-hearted and false prophets
    be.   50
Therefore, since I reputed am
Among these few on whom the
  times
Imposèd have a poet's name,
Lord, give me grace to shun their
  crimes;
  My precious gift let me employ
Not, as imprudent poets use,

That grace and virtue to destroy
Which I should strengthen by my
  muse;
  But help to free them of the
    wrongs
  Sustained by drunkards' rhymes
    and songs.   60
Yea, whilst thou shalt prolong my
  days,
Lord, all the musings of my heart,
To be advancements of thy praise,
And to the public weal convert;
  That when to dust I must re-
    turn,
It may not justly be my thought
That to a blessing I was born,
Which, by abuse, a curse hath
    brought.
  But let my conscience truly say,
My soul in peace departs away.

GILES FLETCHER, THE YOUNGER

The Introduction and Notes are at page 1006

FROM *Christ's Victory and Triumph*, 1610

Christ's victory on earth

There all alone she spied (alas, the while)
In shady darkness a poor desolate
That now had measured many a weary mile,
Through a waste desert, whither heav'nly fate
And his own will him brought; he praying sate,
  And him to prey, as he to pray began,
  The citizens of the wild forest ran,
And all with open throat would swallow whole the man.

Soon did the lady to her Graces cry,
And on their wings herself did nimbly strow;   10
After her coach a thousand Loves did fly,
So down into the wilderness they throw,
Where she and all her train that with her flow
  Through the airy wave with sails so gay,
  Sinking into his breast that weary lay,
Made shipwreck of themselves and vanished quite away.

Seemëd that man had them devourëd all,
Whom to devour the beasts did make pretense;
But him their salvage thirst did nought appal,
Though weapons none he had for his defence;　　　20
What arms for innocence, but innocence?
　　For when they saw their Lord's bright cognizance
　　Shine in his face, soon did they disadvance,
And some unto him kneel, and some about him dance.

Down fell the lordly lion's angry mood,
And he himself fell down in congies low,
Bidding him welcome to his wasteful wood;
Sometime he kissed the grass where he did go,
And as to wash his feet he well did know,
　　With fawning tongue he licked away the dust;　　　30
　　And everyone would nearest to him thrust,
And everyone, with new, forgot his former lust.

Unmindful of himself, to mind his Lord,
The lamb stood gazing by the tiger's side,
As though between them they had made accord;
And on the lion's back the goat did ride,
Forgetful of the roughness of the hide;
　　If he stood still, their eyes upon him baited,
　　If walked, they all in order on him waited,
And when he slept, they as his watch themselves conceited.　　　40

Wonder doth call me up to see; oh no,
I cannot see, and therefore sink in wonder;
The man that shines as bright as God, not so,
For God he is himself, that close lies under
That man, so close that no time can dissunder
　　That band, yet not so close but from him break
　　Such beams as mortal eyes are all too weak
Such sight to see; or it, if they should see, to speak.

Upon a grassy hillock he was laid,　　　50
With woody primroses befreckelëd;
Over his head the wanton shadows played
Of a wild olive, that her boughs so spread
As with her leaves she seemed tó crown his head,
　　And her green arms to'embrace the Prince of peace;
　　The sun so near, needs must the winter cease,
The sun so near, another spring seemed to increase.

His hair was black and in small curls did twine,
As though it were the shadow of some light,

And underneath, his face as day did shine,
But sure the day shinëd not half so bright, 60
Nor the sun's shadow made so dark a night.
    Under his lovely locks her head to shroud,
    Did make Humility herself grow proud;
Hither to light their lamps did all the Graces crowd.

One of ten thousand souls I am, and more,
That of his eyes and their sweet wounds complain,
Sweet are the wounds of love, never so sore;
Ah, might he often slay me so again:
He never lives that thus is never slain.
    What boots it watch? those eyes, for all my art, 70
    Mine own eyes looking on, have stole my heart,
In them Love bends his bow and dips his burning dart.

As when the sun, caught in an adverse cloud,
Flies cross the world and there a new begets,
The wat'ry picture of his beauty proud
Throws all abroad his sparkling spangelets,
And the whole world in dire amazement sets
    To see two days abroad at once, and all
    Doubt whether now he rise or now will fall;
So flamed the godly flesh, proud of his heav'nly thrall. 80

His cheeks, as snowy apples sopped in wine,
Had their red roses quenched with lilies white,
And like to garden strawberries did shine,
Washed in a bowl of milk, or rosebuds bright
Unbosoming their breasts against the light;
    Here love-sick souls did eat, there drank, and made
    Sweet smelling posies that could never fade,
But worldly eyes him thought more like some living shade.

For laughter never looked upon his brow,
Though in his face all smiling joys did bide; 90
No silken banners did about him flow,
Fools make their fetters ensigns of their pride.
He was best clothed when naked was his side,
    A lamb he was and woolen fleece he bore,
    Wove with one thread; his feet low sandals wore,
But barëd were his legs, so went the times of yore.

As two white marble pillars that uphold
God's holy place where he in glory sets,
And rise with goodly grace and courage bold

To bear his temple on their ample jets,   100
Veined everywhere with azure rivulets,
  Whom all the people on some holy morn
  With boughs and flow'ry garlands do adorn,—
Of such, though fairer far, this temple was upborne.

Twice had Diana bent her golden bow
And shot from heav'n her silver shafts to rouse
The sluggish salvages that den below,
And all the day in lazy covert drowse;
Since him the silent wilderness did house,
  The heav'n his roof, and arbor harbor was,   110
  The ground his bed, and his moist pillow grass;
But fruit there none did grow, nor rivers none did pass.

At length an aged sire far off he saw
Come slowly footing; every step, he guessed,
One of his feet he from the grave did draw;
Three legs he had, the wooden was the best,
And all the way he went he ever blessed
  With benedicites and prayers store,
  But the bad ground was blessed ne'er the more,
And all his head with snow of age was waxen hoar.   120

A good old hermit he might seem to be,
That for devotion had the world forsaken,
And now was traveling some saint to see,
Since to his beads he had himself betaken,
Where all his former sins he might awaken
  And them might wash away with dropping brine,
  And alms, and fasts, and church's discipline,
And dead, might rest his bones under the holy shrine.

But when he nearer came, he louted low
With prone obeisance and with curt'sy kind,   130
That at his feet his head he seemed to throw;
What needs him now another saint to find?
Affections are the sails and faith the wind,
  That to this saint a thousand souls convey
  Each hour. O happy pilgrims, thither stray!
What caren they for beasts or for the weary way?

Soon the old palmer his devotions sung,
Like pleasing anthems, modulëd in time,
For well that aged sire could tip his tongue
With golden foil of eloquence and lime,   140

And lick his rugged speech with phrases prime.
   Ay me, quoth he, how many years have been
   Since these old eyes the sun of heav'n have seen!
Certes, the Son of heaven they now behold, I ween.

Ah, mote my humble cell so blessed be
As heav'n to welcome in his lowly roof,
And be the temple for thy deity!
Lo, how my cottage worships thee aloof,
That under ground hath hid his head in proof
   It doth adore thee with the feeling low;   150
   Here honey, milk, and chestnuts wild do grow,
The boughs a bed of leaves upon thee shall bestow.

But oh, he said, and therewith sighed full deep,
The heav'ns, alas, too envious are grown,
Because our fields thy presence from them keep;
For stones do grow where corn was lately sown.
So stooping down, he gathered up a stone.
   But thou with corn canst make this stone to ear;
   What needen we the angry heav'ns to fear?
Let them envy us still, so we enjoy thee here.   160

Thus on they wandered, but those holy weeds
A monstrous serpent, and no man, did cover,—
So under greenest herbs the adder feeds;
And round about that stinking corpse did hover
The dismal prince of gloomy night, and over
   His ever-damnëd head the shadows erred
   Of thousand peccant ghosts, unseen, unheard,
And all the tyrant fears, and all the tyrant feared.

He was the son of blackest Acheron,
Where many frozen souls do chatt'ring lie,   170
And ruled the burning waves of Phlegethon,
Where many more in flaming sulphur fry,
At once compelled to live and forced to die,
   Where nothing can be heard for the loud cry
   Of, Oh, and, Ah, and, Out alas that I
Or once again might live, or once at length might die.

Ere long they came near to a baleful bower,
Much like the mouth of that infernal cave
That gaping stood all comers to devour,
Dark, doleful, dreary, like a greedy grave   180
That still for carrion carcases doth crave.

The ground no herbs but venomous did bear,
Nor ragged trees did leave, but everywhere
Dead bones and skulls were cast, and bodies hangëd were.

Upon the roof the bird of sorrow sat,
Elonging joyful day with her sad note,
And through the shady air the flutt'ring bat
Did wave her leather sails and blindly float,
While with her wings the fatal screech-owl smote
   Th' unblessed house; there on a craggy stone   190
     Celeno hung, and made his direful moan,
And all about the murdered ghosts did shriek and groan.

Like cloudy moonshine in some shadowy grove,
Such was the light in which Despair did dwell,
But he himself with night for darkness strove.
His black uncombëd locks dishevelled fell
About his face, through which, as brands of hell,
   Sunk in his skull his staring eyes did glow,
     That made him deadly look; their glimpse did show
Like cockatrice's eyes, that sparks of poison throw.   200

His clothes were ragged clouts, with thorns pinned fast,
And as he musing lay, to stony fright
A thousand wild chimeras would him cast,
As when a fearful dream in midst of night
Skips to the brain, and fancies to the sight
   Some wingëd fury, straight the hasty foot,
     Eager to fly, cannot pluck up his root;
The voice dies in the tongue, and mouth gapes without boot.

Now he would dream that he from heaven fell,
And then would snatch the air, afraid to fall;   210
And now he thought he sinking was to hell,
And then would grasp the earth, and now his stall
Him seemëd hell, and then he out would crawl,
   And ever, as he crept, would squint aside
     Lest him, perhaps, some fury had espied,
And then, alas, he would in chains forever bide.

Therefore he softly shrunk, and stole away,
Ne ever durst to draw his breath for fear,
Till to the door he came, and there he lay
Panting for breath, as though he dying were,   220
And still he thought he felt their grapples tear
   Him by the heels back to his ugly den;

Out fain he would have leapt abroad, but then
The heav'n, as hell, he feared, that punish guilty men.

Within the gloomy hole of this pale wight,
The serpent wooed Him with his charms to inn;
There he might bait the day and rest the night,
But under that same bait a fearful grin
Was ready to entangle him in sin.
    But he upon ambrosia daily fed 230
      That grew in Eden, thus he answerëd;
So both away were caught, and to the temple fled.

Well knew our Savior this the serpent was,
And the old serpent knew our Savior well;
Never did any this in falsehood pass,
Never did any him in truth excel;
With him we fly to heav'n, from heav'n we fell
    With him; but now they both together met
      Upon the sacred pinnacles, that threat
With their aspiring tops Astræa's starry seat. 240

Here did Presumption her pavilion spread
Over the temple, the bright stars among
(Ah, that her foot should trample on the head
Of that most reverend place!), and a lewd throng
Of wanton boys sung her a pleasant song
    Of love, long life, of mercy, and of grace,
      And everyone her dearly did embrace;
And she herself enamoured was of her own face,

A painted face, belied with vermeil store,
Which light Euëlpis every day did trim, 250
That in one hand a gilded anchor wore,
Not fixëd on the rock, but on the brim
Of the wide air she let it loosely swim.
    Her other hand a sprinkle carriëd,
      And ever, when her lady waverëd,
Court-holy water all upon her sprinkelëd.

Poor fool, she thought herself in wondrous price
With God, as if in paradise she were;
But were she not in a fools' paradise,
She might have seen more reason to despair; 260
But Him she, like some ghastly fiend, did fear,
    And therefore as that wretch hewed out his cell
      Under the bowels, in the heart of hell,
So she above the moon, amid the stars would dwell.

Her tent with sunny clouds was sealed aloft,
And so exceeding shone with a false light
That heav'n itself to her it seemëd oft,
Heav'n without clouds to her deluded sight,
But clouds withouten heav'n it was aright;
   And as her house was built, so did her brain   270
   Build castles in the air, with idle pain,
But heart she never had in all her body vain.

Like as a ship in which no balance lies,
Without a pilot on the sleeping waves,
Fairly along with wind and water flies,
And painted masts with silken sails embraves,
That Neptune self the bragging vessel saves,
   To laugh a while at her so proud array;
   Her waving streamers loosely she lets play,
And flagging colors shine as bright as smiling day;   280

But all so soon as heav'n his brows doth bend,
She veils her banners and pulls in her beams,
The empty bark the raging billows send
Up to th' Olympic waves, and Argos seems
Again to ride upon our lower streams;
   Right so Presumption did herself behave,
   Tossëd about with every stormy wave,
And in white lawn she went, most like an angel brave.

Gently our Savior she began to shrive,
Whether he were the son of God, or no;   290
For any other she disdained to wive.
And if he were, she bid him fearless throw
Himself to ground, and therewithal did show
   A flight of little angels that did wait
   Upon their glittering wings to latch him straight,
And longëd on their backs to feel his glorious weight.

But when she saw her speech prevailëd nought,
Herself she tumbled headlong to the floor;
But him the angels on their feathers caught
And to an airy mountain nimbly bore,   300
Whose snowy shoulders, like some chalky shore,
   Restless Olympus seemed to rest upon
   With all his swimming globes; so both are gone,
The dragon with the lamb. Ah, unmeet paragon!

All suddenly the hill his snow devours,
In lieu whereof a goodly garden grew,
As if the snow had melted into flowers,
Which their sweet breath in subtile vapors threw,
That all about perfumèd spirits flew.
    For whatsoever might aggrate the sense, 310
    In all the world, or please the appetence,
Here it was poured out in lavish affluence.

Not lovely Ida might with this compare,
Though many streams his banks besilverèd,
Though Xanthus with his golden sands he bare,
Nor Hybla though his thyme depasturèd
As fast again with honey blossomèd,
    Ne Rhodope, ne Tempe's flow'ry plain;
    Adonis' garden was to this but vain,
Though Plato on his beds a flood of praise did rain. 320

For in all these some one thing most did grow,
But in this one grew all things else beside,
For sweet variety herself did throw
To every bank: here all the ground she dyed
In lily white, there pinks eblazèd wide,
    And damasked all the earth, and here she shed
    Blue violets, and there came roses red,
And every sight the yielding sense as captive led.

The garden like a lady fair was cut,
That lay as if she slumbered in delight, 330
And to the open skies her eyes did shut;
The azure fields of heav'n were sembled right
In a large round, set with the flowers of light,
    The flowers-de-luce and the round sparks of dew
    That hung upon their azure leaves did shew
Like twinkling stars that sparkle in th' evening blue.

Upon a hilly bank her head she cast,
On which the bower of Vain Delight was built,
White and red roses for her face were placed,
And for her tresses marigolds were spilt; 340
Them broadly she displayed, like flaming gilt,
    Till in the ocean the glad day were drowned,
    Then up again her yellow locks she wound,
And with green fillets in their pretty cauls them bound.

What should I here depaint her lily hand,
Her veins of violets, her ermine breast,
Which there in orient colors living stand?
Or how her gown with silken leaves is dressed?
Or how her watchmen, armed with boughy crest,
    A wall of prim hid in his bushes bears,   350
    Shaking at every wind their leafy spears,
While she supinely sleeps, ne to be wakëd fears?

Over the hedge depends the graping elm,
Whose greener head, empurpelëd in wine,
Seemëd to wonder at his bloody helm,
And half suspect the bunches of the vine,
Lest they, perhaps, his wit should undermine;
    For well he knew such fruit he never bore,
    But her weak arms embracëd him the more,
And with her ruby grapes laughed at her paramour.   360

Under the shadow of these drunken elms
A fountain rose, where Pangloretta uses,
When her some flood of fancy overwhelms
And one of all her favorites she chooses,
To bathe herself, whom she in lust abuses,
    And from his wanton body sucks his soul,
    Which, drowned in pleasure in that shaly bowl,
And swimming in delight, doth amorously roll.

The font of silver was, and so his showers
In silver fell, only the gilded bowls   370
(Like to a furnace that the min'ral pours)
Seemed to have molt it in their shining holes;
And on the water, like to burning coals
    On liquid silver, leaves of roses lay;
    But when Panglory here did list to play,
Rose-water then it ran, and milk it rained, they say.

The roof thick clouds did paint, from which three boys
Three gaping mermaids with their ewers did feed,
Whose breasts let fall the stream with sleepy noise
To lions' mouths, from whence it leapt with speed,   380
And in the rosy laver seemed to bleed.
    The naked boys, unto the waters' fall,
    Their stony nightingales had taught to call,
When Zephyr breathed into their wat'ry interal.

And all about, embayëd in soft sleep,
A herd of charmëd beasts aground were spread,
Which the fair witch in golden chains did keep,
And them in willing bondage fetterëd;
Once men they lived, but now the men were dead,
    And turned to beasts; so fabled Homer old,   390
    That Circe with her potion, charmed in gold,
Used manly souls in beastly bodies to immould.

Through this false Eden to his leman's bower,
Whom thousand souls devoutly idolize,
Our first destroyer led our Savïor.
There in the lower room, in solemn wise,
They danced a round and poured their sacrifice
    To plump Lyæus, and among the rest
    The jolly priest, in ivy garlands dressed,
Chanted wild orgials in honor of the feast.   400

Others within their arbors swilling sat,
For all the room about was arborëd,
With laughing Bacchus, that was grown so fat
That stand he could not, but was carrïed,
And every evening freshly waterëd
    To quench his fiery cheeks, and all about
    Small cocks broke through the wall, and sallied out
Flagons of wine to set on fire that spewing rout.

This their inhumëd souls esteemed their wealths,
To crown the bouzing can from day to night,   410
And sick to drink themselves with drinking healths,
Some vomiting, all drunken with delight.
Hence to a loft, carved all in ivory white,
    They came, where whiter ladies naked went,
    Melted in pleasure and soft languishment,
And sunk in beds of roses, amorous glances sent.

Fly, fly, thou holy child, that wanton room,
And thou, my chaster muse, those harlots shun,
And with him to a higher story come,
Where mounts of gold and floods of silver run,   420
The while the owners, with their wealth undone,
    Starve in their store and in their plenty pine,
    Tumbling themselves upon their heaps of mine,
Glutting their famished souls with the deceitful shine.

Ah, who was he such precious perils found?
How strongly nature did her treasures hide,
And threw upon them mountains of thick ground,
To dark their ory luster; but quaint pride
Hath taught her sons to wound their mother's side,
    And gauge the depth to search for flaring shells   430
    In whose bright bosom spumy Bacchus swells,
That neither heav'n nor earth henceforth in safety dwells.

O sacred hunger of the greedy eye,
Whose need hath end, but no end covetize,
Empty in fulness, rich in poverty,
That having all things, nothing can suffice,
How thou befanciest the men most wise!
    The poor man would be rich, the rich man great,
    The great man king, the king in God's own seat
Enthroned, with mortal arm dares flames and thunder threat. 440

Therefore above the rest Ambition sat;
His court with glitterant pearl was all enwalled,
And round about the wall in chairs of state
And most majestic splendor, were installed
A hundred kings, whose temples were impalled
    In golden diadems, set here and there
    With diamonds, and gemmëd everywhere,
And of their golden verges none disceptered were.

High over all, Panglory's blazing throne,
In her bright turret, all of crystal wrought,   450
Like Phœbus' lamp in midst of heaven, shone;
Whose starry top, with pride infernal fraught,
Self-arching columns to uphold were taught,
    In which her image still reflected was
    By the smooth crystal, that most like her glass
In beauty and in frailty, did all others pass.

A silver wand the sorceress did sway,
And for a crown of gold her hair she wore,
Only a garland of rosebuds did play
About her locks, and in her hand she bore   460
A hollow globe of glass that long before
    She full of emptiness had bladderëd,
    And all the world therein depicturëd,
Whose colors, like the rainbow, ever vanishëd.

Such wat'ry orbicles young boys do blow
Out from their soapy shells, and much admire
The swimming world, which tenderly they row
With easy breath, till it be wavèd higher;
But if they chance but roughly once aspire,
 The painted bubble instantly doth fall.   470
Here when she came she gan for music call,
And sung this wooing song to welcome him withal:

Love is the blossom where there blows
Everything that lives or grows;
Love doth make the heav'ns to move,
And the sun doth burn in love;
Love the strong and weak doth yoke,
And makes the ivy climb the oak,
Under whose shadows lions wild,
Softened by love, grow tame and mild;   480
Love no med'cine can appease,
He burns the fishes in the seas,
Not all the skill his wounds can stench,
Not all the sea his fire can quench;
Love did make the bloody spear
Once a leafy coat to wear,
While in his leaves there shrouded lay
Sweet birds, for love, that sing and play;
And of all love's joyful flame,
I the bud and blossom am.   490
 Only bend thy knee to me,
 Thy wooing shall thy winning be.

See, see the flowers that below
Now as fresh as morning blow,
And of all the virgin rose,
That as bright Aurora shows,
How they all unleavèd die,
Loosing their virginity;
Like unto a summer shade,
But now born, and now they fade.   500
Everything doth pass away,
There is danger in delay;
Come, come gather then the rose,
Gather it, or it you lose.
All the sand of Tagus' shore
Into my bosom casts his ore;
All the valley's swimming corn
To my house is yearly borne;

Every grape of every vine
Is gladly bruised to make me wine, 510
While ten thousand kings, as proud
To carry up my train, have bowed,
And a world of ladies send me,
In my chambers to attend me;
All the stars in heav'n that shine,
And ten thousand more, are mine;
 Only bend thy knee to me,
 Thy wooing shall thy winning be.

Thus sought the dire enchantress in his mind
Her guileful bait to have embosomëd, 520
But he her charms dispersëd into wind,
And her of insolence admonishëd,
And all her optic glasses shatterëd.
 So with her sire to hell she took her flight,
 The starting air flew from the damnëd sprite,
Where deeply both aggrieved, plungëd themselves in night.

But to their Lord, now musing in his thought,
A heavenly volley of light angels flew,
And from his father him a banquet brought
Through the fine element, for well they knew 530
After his lenten fast he hungry grew;
 And as he fed, the holy choirs combine
 To sing a hymn of the celestial Trine;
All thought to pass, and each was past all thought divine.

The birds' sweet notes, to sonnet out their joys,
Attempered to the lays angelical,
And to the birds the winds attune their noise,
And to the winds the waters hoarsely call,
And echo back again revoicëd all,
 That the whole valley rung with victory. 540
 But now our Lord to rest doth homewards fly;
See how the night comes stealing from the mountains high.

PHINEAS FLETCHER

The Introduction and Notes are at page 1007

From *The Locusts, or Apollyonists*, 1627

Canto I

Of men, nay beasts; worse, monsters; worst of all,
Incarnate fiends, English Italianate,

Of priests, oh no, mass-priests, priests-cannibal,
Who make their maker, chew, grind, feed, grow fat
With flesh divine; of that great city's fall,
Which born, nursed, grown with blood, th' earth's empress sat,
  Cleansed, spoused to Christ, yet back to whoredom fell,
  None can enough, something I fain would tell:
How black are quenchëd lights! Fallen heaven's a double hell!

Great Lord, who grasp'st all creatures in thy hand,   10
Who in thy lap lay'st down proud Thetis' head,
And bind'st her white curled locks in cauls of sand,
Who gather'st in thy fist and lay'st in bed
The sturdy winds, who ground'st the floating land
On fleeting seas, and over all hast spread
  Heaven's brooding wings to foster all below,
  Who mak'st the sun without all fire to glow,
The spring of heat and light, the moon to ebb and flow;

Thou, world's sole pilot, who in this poor isle
(So small a bottom) hast embarked thy light,   20
And glorious self, and steer'st it safe the while
Hoarse drumming seas and winds' loud trumpets fight,
Who causest stormy heavens here only smile,
Steer me, poor ship-boy, steer my course aright;
  Breathe, gracious spirit, breathe gently on these lays,
  Be thou my compass, needle to my ways,
Thy glorious work's my fraught, my haven is thy praise.

Thou purple whore, mounted on scarlet beast,
Gorged with the flesh, drunk with the blood of saints,
Whose amorous golden cup and charmëd feast   30
All earthly kings, all earthly men attaints;
See thy live pictures, see thine own, thy best,
Thy dearest sons, and cheer thy heart that faints.
  Hark, thou saved island, hark, and never cease
  To praise that hand which held thy head in peace,
Else hadst thou swum as deep in blood as now in seas.

The cloudy night came whirling up the sky,
And scatt'ring round the dews which first she drew
From milky poppies, loads the drowsy eye;
The wat'ry moon, cold Vesper, and his crew   40
Light up their tapers, to the sun they fly
And at his blazing flame their sparks renew.
  Oh, why should earthly lights then scorn to tine
  Their lamps alone at that first sun divine?
Hence as false falling stars, as rotten wood, they shine.

Her sable mantle was embroidered gay
With silver beams, with spangles round beset;
Four steeds her chariot drew: the first was gray,
The second blue, third brown, fourth black as jet.
The hollowing owl, her post, prepares the way,   50
And wingëd dreams, as gnat-swarms flutt'ring, let
    Sad sleep, who fain his eyes in rest would steep.
    Why then at death do weary mortals weep?
Sleep's but a shorter death, death's but a longer sleep.

And now the world, and dreams themselves, were drowned
In deadly sleep; the laborer snorteth fast,
His brawny arms unbent, his limbs unbound,
As dead, forget all toil to come, or past;
Only sad guilt and troubled greatness, crowned
With heavy gold and care, no rest can taste.   60
    Go then, vain man, go pill the live and dead,
    Buy, sell, fawn, flatter, rise, then couch thy head
In proud but dangerous gold, in silk but restless bed.

When lo, a sudden noise breaks th' empty air,
A dreadful noise which every creature daunts,
Frights home the blood, shoots up the limber hair;
For through the silent heaven hell's pursuivants,
Cutting their way, command foul spirits repair
With haste to Pluto, who their counsel wants.
    Their hoarse bass-horns like fenny bitterns sound;   70
    Th' earth shakes, dogs howl, and heaven itself, astound,
Shuts all his eyes, the stars in clouds their candles drowned.

Meantime hell's iron gates by fiends beneath
Are open flung, which framed with wondrous art
To every guilty soul yields entrance eath;
But never wight but He could thence depart,
Who, dying once, was death to endless death.
So where the liver's channel to the heart
    Pays purple tribute, with their three-forked mace
    Three Tritons stand and speed his flowing race,   80
But stop the ebbing stream, if once it back would pace.

The porter to th' infernal gate is Sin,
A shapeless shape, a foul deformëd thing,
Nor nothing, nor a substance, as those thin
And empty forms which through the air fling
Their wand'ring shapes, at length they're fastened in
The crystal sight; it serves, yet reigns as king;

It lives, yet's death; it pleases, full of pain;
  Monster! ah who, who can thy being feign?
Thou shapeless shape, live death, pain pleasing, servile reign!   90

Of that first woman and th' old serpent bred
By lust, and custom nursed, whom when her mother
Saw so deformed, how fain would she have fled
Her birth and self! But she her dam would smother,
And all her brood, had not He rescuëd,
  Who was his mother's sire, his children's brother,
    Eternity, who yet was born and died;
    His own creator, earth's scorn, heaven's pride,
Who th' deity enfleshed, and man's flesh deified.

Her former parts her mother seems resemble,   100
Yet only seems to flesh and weaker sight,
For she with art and paint could fine dissemble
Her loathsome face; her back parts, black as night,
Like to her horrid sire, would force to tremble
  The boldest heart; to th' eye that meets her right
    She seems a lovely sweet, of beauty rare,
    But at the parting, he that shall compare,
Hell will more lovely deem, the devil's self more fair.

Her rosy cheek, quick eye, her naked breast,
And whatsoe'er loose fancy might entice,   110
She bare exposed to sight, all lovely dressed
In beauty's livery and quaint device;
Thus she bewitches many a boy unblest,
  Who, drenched in hell, dreams all of paradise;
    Her breasts his spheres, her arms his circling sky,
    Her pleasures heav'n, her love eternity;
For her he longs to live, with her he longs to die.

But he that gave a stone power to descry
'Twixt natures hid, and check that metal's pride
That dares aspire to gold's fair purity,   120
Hath left a touchstone erring eyes to guide,
Which clears their sight and strips hypocrisy;
  They see, they loathe, they curse her painted hide;
    Her as a crawling carrion they esteem,
    Her worst of ills, and worse than that they deem,
Yet know her worse than they can think or she can seem.

Close by her sat Despair, sad ghastly sprite,
With staring looks, unmoved, fast nailed to Sin;

Her body all of earth, her soul of fright,
About her thousand deaths, but more within,   130
Paled, pined cheeks, black hair, torn, rudely dight,
Short breath, long nails, dull eyes, sharp-pointed chin;
   Light, life, heaven, earth, herself, and all she fled.
   Fain would she die, but could not, yet half dead,
A breathing corse she seemed, wrapped up in living lead.

In th' entrance Sickness and faint Languor dwelt,
Who with sad groans toll out their passing knell,
Late fear, fright, horror, that already felt,
The torturer's claws, preventing death and hell.
Within, loud Grief and roaring Pangs, that swelt   140
In sulphur flames, did weep and howl and yell.
   And thousand souls in endless dolors lie,
   Who burn, fry, hiss, and never cease to cry,
Oh, that I ne'er had lived; oh, that I once could die!

And now th' infernal powers through th' air driving,
For speed their leather pinions broad display;
Now at eternal death's wide gate arriving
Sin gives them passage; still they cut their way,
Till to the bottom of hell's palace diving,
They enter Dis' deep conclave; there they stay,   150
   Waiting the rest, and now they all are met,
   A full foul senate, now they all are set,
The horrid court, big swoll'n with th' hideous council sweat.

The midst but lowest (in hell's heraldry
The deepest is the highest room) in state
Sat lordly Lucifer; his fiery eye,
Much swoll'n with pride, but more with rage and hate,
As censor mustered all his company,
Who round about with awful silence sate.
   This do, this let rebellious spirits gain,   160
   Change God for Satan, heaven's for hell's sov'reign;
Oh, let him serve in hell, who scorns in heaven to reign!

Ah, wretch, who with ambitious cares oppressed,
Long'st still for future, feel'st no present good,
Despising to be better, wouldst be best,
Good never, who wilt serve thy lusting mood,
Yet all command; not he who raised his crest
But pulled it down, hath high and firmly stood.
   Fool, serve thy tow'ring lusts, grow still, still crave,
   Rule, reign, this comfort from thy greatness have,   170
Now at thy top, thou art a great commanding slave.

Thus fell this prince of darkness, once a bright
And glorious star; he willful turned away
His borrowed globe from that eternal light;
Himself he sought, so lost himself; his ray
Vanished to smoke, his morning sunk in night,
And never more shall see the springing day.
   To be in heaven the second he disdains,
    So now the first in hell and flames he reigns,   179
Crowned once with joy and light, crowned now with fire and pains.

As, where the warlike Dane the scepter sways,
They crown usurpers with a wreath of lead,
And with hot steel, while loud the traitor brays
They melt and drop it down into his head,—
Crowned he would live, and crowned he ends his days;
All so in heaven's courts this traitor sped,
   Who now, when he had overlooked his train,
    Rising upon his throne, with bitter strain
Thus gan to whet their rage and chide their frustrate pain:

See, see, you spirits, I know not whether more   190
Hated or hating heaven, ah, see the earth
Smiling in quiet peace and plenteous store.
Men fearless live in ease, in love, and mirth;
Where arms did rage, the drum and cannon roar,
Where hate, strife, envy reigned, and meagre dearth,
   Now lutes and viols charm the ravished ear;
    Men plow with swords, horse-heels their armors wear;
Ah, shortly scarce they'll know what war and armors were.

Under their sprouting vines they sporting sit.
Th' old tell of evils past; youth laugh and play,   200
And to their wanton heads sweet garlands fit,
Roses with lilies, myrtles weaved with bay;
The world's at rest; Erinnys, forced to quit
Her strongest holds, from earth is driven away.
   Even Turks forget their empire to increase;
    War's self is slain and whips of fury cease.
We, we ourselves, I fear, will shortly live in peace.

Meantime (I burn, I broil, I burst with spite)
In midst of peace that sharp two-edgèd sword
Cuts through our darkness, cleaves the misty night,   210
Discovers all our snares; that sacred word,
Locked up by Rome, breaks prison, spreads the light,
Speaks every tongue, paints, and points out the Lord,

His birth, life, death, and cross; our gilded stocks,
Our laymen's books, the boy and woman mocks;
They laugh, they fleer, and say, Blocks teach and worship blocks.

Springtides of light divine the air surround,
And bring down heaven to earth; deaf ignorance,
Vexed with the day, her head in hell hath drowned;
Fond superstition, frighted with the glance   220
Of sudden beams, in vain hath crossed her round.
Truth and religion everywhere advance
    Their conq'ring standards; error's lost and fled;
    Earth burns in love to heaven; heaven yields her bed
To earth, and common grown, smiles to be ravishèd.

That little swimming isle above the rest,
Spite of our spite and all our plots, remains
And grows in happiness; but late our nest,
Where we and Rome and blood and all our trains,
Monks, nuns, dead and live idols, safe did rest;   230
Now there (next th' oath of God) that wrestler reigns
    Who fills the land and world with peace; his spear
    Is but a pen, with which he down doth bear
Blind ignorance, false gods, and superstitious fear.

There God hath framed another paradise,
Fat olives dropping peace, victorious palms,
Nor in the midst, but everywhere doth rise
That hated tree of life, whose precious balms
Cure every sinful wound, give light to th' eyes,   240
Unlock the ear, recover fainting qualms.
    There richly grows what makes a people blest,
    A garden planted by himself and dressed,
Where he himself doth walk, where he himself doth rest.

There every star sheds his sweet influence
And radiant beams: great, little, old, and new,
Their glittering rays and frequent confluence
The milky path to God's high palace strew;
Th' unwearied pastors with steeled confidence,
Conquered and conquering fresh, their fight renew.
    Our strongest holds that thund'ring ordinance   250
    Beats down, and makes our proudest turrets dance,
Yoking men's iron necks in his sweet governance.

Nor can th' old world content ambitious light,
Virginia, our soil, our seat, and throne,

To which so long possession gives us right,
As long as hell's, Virginia's self is gone;
That stormy isle which th' Isle of Devils hight,
Peopled with faith, truth, grace, religïon.
  What's next but hell? That now alone remains,
  And that subdued, even here he rules and reigns,   150
And mortals 'gin to dream of long but endless pains.

While we, good harmless creatures, sleep or play,
Forget our former loss and following pain,
Earth sweats for heaven, but hell keeps holy-day.
Shall we repent, good souls, or shall we plain?
Shall we groan, sigh, weep, mourn, for mercy pray?
Lay down our spite, wash out our sinful stain?
  Maybe he'll yield, forget, and use us well,
  Forgive, join hands, restore us whence we fell;
Maybe he'll yield us heaven, and fall himself to hell.   270

But me, O never let me, spirits, forget
That glorious day when I your standard bore,
And scorning in the second place to sit,
With you assaulted heaven, his yoke forswore.
My dauntless heart yet longs to bleed and sweat
In such a fray; the more I burn the more
  I hate; should he yet offer grace and ease,
  If subject we our arms and spite surcease,
Such offer should I hate, and scorn so base a peace.

Where are those spirits? Where that haughty rage   280
That durst with me invade eternal light?
What? Are our hearts fallen too? Droop we with age?
Can we yet fall from hell and hellish spite?
Can smart our wrath, can grief our hate assuage?
Dare we with heaven and not with earth to fight?
  Your arms, allies, yourselves as strong as ever;
  Your foes, their weapons, numbers weaker never.
For shame, tread down this earth! What wants but your endeavor?

Now by yourselves and thunder-daunted arms,
But never-daunted hate, I you implore,   290
Command, adjure, reinforce your fierce alarms;
Kindle, I pray, who never prayed before,
Kindle your darts, treble repay our harms.
Oh, our short time, too short, stands at the door,
  Double your rage; if now we do not ply,
  We lone in hell, without due company,
And worse, without desert, without revenge shall lie.

He, spirits, (ah that, that's our main torment) he
Can feel no wounds, laughs at the sword and dart,
Himself from grief, from suff'ring wholly free;   300
His simple nature cannot taste of smart,
Yet in his members we him grievëd see,
For and in them he suffers; where his heart
   Lies bare and naked, there dart your fiery steel,
   Cut, wound, burn, sear, if not the head, the heel;
Let him in every part some pain and torment feel.

That light comes posting on, that cursëd light,
When they as he, all glorious, all divine,
Their flesh clothed with the sun, and much more bright,
Yet brighter spirits, shall in his image shine,   310
And see him as he is; there no despite,
No force, no art their state can undermine,
   Full of unmeasured bliss, yet still receiving,
   Their souls still childing joy, yet still conceiving
Delights beyond the wish, beyond quick thoughts perceiving.

But we fast pinioned with dark fiery chains
Shall suffer every ill, but do no more;
The guilty spirit there feels extremest pains,
Yet fears worse than it feels, and finding store
Of present deaths, death's absence sore complains;   320
Oceans of ills without or ebb or shore,
   A life that ever dies, a death that lives,
   And, worst of all, God's absent presence gives
A thousand living woes, a thousand dying griefs.

But when he sums his time and turns his eye
First to the past, then future pangs, past days
(And every day's an age of misery)
In torment spent by thousands down he lays,
Future by millions, yet eternity
Grows nothing less, nor past to-come allays.   330
   Through every pang and grief he wild doth run,
   And challenge coward death, doth nothing shun,
That he may nothing be, does all to be undone.

Oh, let our work equal our wages, let
Our judge fall short, and when his plagues are spent,
Owe more than he hath paid, live in our debt;
Let heaven want vengeance, hell want punishment
To give our dues; when we with flames beset
Still dying live in endless languishment,

This be our comfort, we did get and win
   The fires and tortures we are whelmëd in;
We have kept pace, outrun his justice with our sin.

And now you states of hell give your advice,
And to these ruins lend your helping hand.
This said, and ceased; straight humming murmurs rise;
Some chafe, some fret, some sad and thoughtful stand,
Some chat, and some new stratagems devise,
And everyone heaven's stronger power banned,
   And tear for madness their uncombëd snakes,
   And everyone his fiery weapon shakes,
And everyone expects who first the answer makes.

So when the falling sun hangs o'er the main,
Ready to drop into the western wave,
By yellow Cam, where all the Muses reign,
And with their towers his reedy head embrace,
The warlike gnat their flutt'ring armies train—
All have sharp spears, and all shrill trumpets have;
   Their files they double, loud their cornets sound;
   Now march at length, their troops now gather round;
The banks, the broken noise, and turrets fair rebound.

360

FROM *Piscatory Eclogues and other Poetical Miscellanies*, 1633

Eclogue VII, The prize

Thirsil, Daphnis, Thomalin.

Aurora from old Tithon's frosty bed,
Cold, wintry, withered Tithon, early creeps;
Her cheek with grief was pale, with anger red;
Out of her window close she blushing peeps;
Her weeping eyes in pearlëd dew she steeps,
Casting what sportless nights she ever led,
She dying lives to think he's living dead.
   Curst be, and cursed is that wretched sire
   That yokes green youth with age, want with desire.
Who ties the sun to snow, or marries frost to fire?

10

The morn saluting, up I quickly rise,
And to the green I post, for on this day
Shepherd and fisher boys had set a prize,
Upon the shore to meet in gentle fray,
Which of the two should sing the choicest lay:

Daphnis, the shepherd's lad, whom Mira's eyes
Had killed, yet with such wound he gladly dies;
   Thomalin, the fisher, in whose heart did reign
   Stella, whose love his life, and whose disdain
Seems worse than angry skies or never quiet main.   20

There soon I view the merry shepherd-swains
March three by three, clad all in youthful green;
And while the sad recorder sweetly plains,
Three lovely nymphs, each several row between,
More lovely nymphs could no where else be seen,
Whose faces' snow their snowy garments stains,
With sweeter voices fit their pleasing strains.
   Their flocks flock round about, the hornëd rams
   And ewes go silent by, while wanton lambs
Dancing along the plains, forget their milky dams.   30

Scarce were the shepherds set but straight in sight
The fisher-boys came driving up the stream;
Themselves in blue, and twenty sea-nymphs bright
In curious robes that well the waves might seem,
All dark below, the top like frothy cream;
Their boats and masts with flowers and garlands dight,
And round the swans guard them with armies white;
   Their skiffs by couples dance to sweetest sounds,
   Which running cornets breathe to full plain grounds,
That strikes the river's face, and thence more sweet re-
     bounds.   40

And now the nymphs and swains had took their place;
First those two boys: Thomalin, the fishers' pride,
Daphnis, the shepherds'; nymphs their right hand grace,
And choicest swains shut up the other side;
So sit they down in order fit applied,
Thirsil betwixt them both, in middle space,
Thirsil, their judge, who now's a shepherd base,
   But late a fisher-swain, till envious Came
   Had rent his nets and sunk his boat with shame;
So robbed the boys of him, and him of all his game.   50

So as they sit, thus Thirsil 'gins the lay:
Thirsil. You lovely boys, the wood's and ocean's pride,
Since I am judge of this sweet peaceful fray,
First tell us where and when your loves you spied,
And when in long discourse you well are tried,
Then in short verse by turns we'll gently play;

In love begin, in love we'll end the day.
  Daphnis, thou first; to me you both are dear,
  Ah, if I might, I would not judge, but hear;
Nought have I of a judge but an impartial ear.   60

Daph. Phœbus, if as thy words, thy oaths are true,
Give me that verse which to the honored bay,
That verse which by thy promise now is due
To honored Daphne in a sweet tuned lay,
Daphne thy changed, thy love unchangëd aye;
  Thou sangest late when she now better stayed,
  More human when a tree than when a maid,
Bending her head, thy love with gentle sign repaid.

What tongue, what thought can paint my love's perfection?
So sweet hath nature portrayed every part   70
That art will prove that artist's imperfection
Who, when no eye dare view, dares limn her face.
Phœbus, in vain I call thy help to blaze
  More light than thine, a light that never fell;
  Thou tell'st what's done in heav'n, in earth, and hell;
Her worth thou mayst admire, there are no words to tell.

She is like thee, or thou art like her, rather:
Such as her hair, thy beams; thy single light,
As her twin suns; that creature then, I gather,
Twice heav'nly is where two suns shine so bright;   80
So thou, as she, confound'st the gazing sight;
  Thy absence is my night, her absence hell.
  Since then in all thy self she doth excel,
What is beyond thyself how canst thou hope to tell?

First her I saw when, tired with hunting toil,
In shady grove spent with the weary chase,
Her naked breast lay open to the spoil,
The crystal humor trickling down apace,
Like ropes of pearl her neck and breast enlace;
  The air, my rival air, did coolly glide   90
  Through every part; such when my love I spied,
So soon I saw my love, so soon I loved, and died.

Her face two colors paint: the first a flame,
Yet she all cold, a flame in rosy dye,
Which sweetly blushes like the morning's shame;
The second snow, such as on Alps doth lie,
And safely there the sun doth bold defy;

Yet this cold snow can kindle hot desire.
Thou miracle, mar'l not if I admire
How flame should coldly freeze, and snow should burn as
    fire.   100

Her slender waist, her hand, that dainty breast,
Her cheek, her forehead, eye, and flaming hair,
And those hid beauties which must sure be best,
In vain to speak, when words will more impair;
Of all the fairs, she is the fairest fair.
    Cease then, vain words, well may you show affection,
      But not her worth; the mind her sweet perfection
Admires, how should it then give the lame tongue direction?

Thom.   Unless thy words be flitting as thy wave,
Proteus, that song into my breast inspire   110
With which the seas, when loud they roar and rave,
Thou softly charm'st, and winds' intestine ire,
When 'gainst heav'n, earth, and seas they did conspire,
    Thou quiet laid'st; Proteus, thy song to hear,
      Seas list'ning stand, and winds to whistle fear,
The lively dolphins dance, and bristly seals give ear.

Stella, my star-like love, my lovely star,
Her hair a lovely brown, her forehead high,
And lovely fair, such her cheeks' roses are,
Lovely her lip, most lovely is her eye;   120
And as in each of these all love doth lie,
    So thousand loves within her mind retiring,
      Kindle ten thousand loves with gentle firing.
Ah, let me love my love, not live in love's admiring!

At Proteus' feast where many a goodly boy
And many a lovely lass did lately meet,
There first I found, there first I lost my joy;
Her face mine eye, her voice mine ear did greet;
While ear and eye strove which should be most sweet,
    That face or voice, but when my lips at last   130
      Saluted hers, those senses strove as fast,
Which most those lips did please, the eye, ear, touch, or
    taste.

The eye swears never fairer lip was eyed,
The ear with those sweet relishes delighted,
Thinks them the spheres, the taste that nearer tried
Their relish sweet, the soul to feast invited,

The touch, with pressure soft more close united,
  Wished ever there to dwell, and never cloyed:
  While thus their joy too greedy they enjoyed,
Enjoyed not half their joy, by being overjoyed.   140

Her hair all dark more clear the white doth show,
  And with its night her face's morn commends;
  Her eyebrow black, like to an ebon bow,
  Which sporting Love upon her forehead bends,
  And thence his never-missing arrow sends.
    But most I wonder how that jetty ray,
    Which those two blackest suns do fair display,
Should shine so bright, and night should make so sweet a
      day.

So is my love an heav'n, her hair a night,
  Her shining forehead Dian's silver light,   150
  Her eyes the stars, their influence delight,
  Her voice the spheres, her cheek Aurora bright,
  Her breast the globes where heav'n's path, milky-white,
    Runs 'twixt those hills; her hand, Arion's touch,
    As much delights the eye, the ear as much.
Such is my love that, but my love, was never such.

Thirsil. The earth her robe, the sea her swelling tide,
  The trees their leaves, the moon her diverse face,
  The stars their courses, flowers their springing pride,
  Days change their length, the sun his daily race;   160
    Be constant when you love, Love loves not ranging;
    Change when you sing, Muses delight in changing.

Daph. Pan loves the pine tree, Jove the oak approves;
  High populars Alcides' temples crown;
  Phœbus, though in a tree, still Daphne loves,
  And hyacinths, though living now in ground;
    Shepherds, if you yourselves would victors see,
    Girt then this head with Phœbus' flower and tree.

Thom. Alcinous pears, Pomona apples bore;
  Bacchus the vine, the olive Pallas chose;   170
  Venus loves myrtles, myrtles love the shore;
  Venus Adonis loves, who freshly blows,
    Yet breathes no more; weave, lads, with myrtles roses,—
    And bay and hyacinth the garland loses.

Daph. Mira, thine eyes are those twin heav'nly powers
  Which to the widowed earth new offspring bring;
  No marvel then if still thy face so flowers,

And cheeks with beauteous blossoms freshly spring:
So is thy face a never fading May;
So is thine eye a never falling day.   180

Thom. Stella, thine eyes are those twin brothers fair
Which tempests slake and promise quiet seas;
No marvel then if thy brown shady hair,
Like night, portend sweet rest and gentle ease.
    Thus is thine eye an ever calming light;
    Thus is thy hair a lover's ne'er-spent night.

Daph. If sleepy poppies yield to lilies white,
If black to snowy lambs, if night to day,
If western shades to fair Aurora's light,
Stella must yield to Mira's shining ray.   190
    In day we sport, in day we shepherds toy;
    The night for wolves, the light the shepherds' joy.

Thom. Who white thorn equals with the violet?
What workman rest compares with painful light?
Who wears the glaring glass and scorns the jet?
Day, yield to her that is both day and night.
    In night the fishers thrive, the workmen play;
    Love loves the night, night's lovers' holiday.

Daph. Fly thou the seas, fly far the dangerous shore,
Mira, if thee the king of seas should spy,   200
He'll think Medusa, sweeter than before,
With fairer hair and double fairer eye,
    Is changed again, and with thee ebbing low,
    In his deep courts again will never flow.

Thom. Stella, avoid both Phœbus' ear and eye,
His music he will scorn if thee he hear;
Thee Daphne, if thy face by chance he spy,
Daphne now fairer changed he'll rashly swear,
    And viewing thee, will later rise and fall,
    Or viewing thee, will never rise at all.   210

Daph. Phœbus and Pan both strive my love to gain,
And seek by gifts to win my careless heart;
Pan vows with lambs to fill the fruitful plain;
Apollo offers skill and pleasing art;
    But Stella, if thou grant my suit, a kiss,
    Phœbus and Pan their suit, my love, shall miss.

Thom. Proteus himself and Glaucus seek unto me,
And twenty gifts to please my mind devise;
Proteus with songs, Glaucus with fish doth woo me;
Both strive to win, but I them both despise,   220
  For if my love my love will entertain,
  Proteus himself and Glaucus seek in vain.

Daph. Two twin, two spotted lambs, my song's reward,
With them a cup I got, where Jove assumed
New shapes to mock his wife's too jealous guard;
Full of Jove's fire it burns still unconsumed;
  But Mira, if thou gently deign to shine,
  Thine be the cup, the spotted lambs be thine.

Thom. A pair of swans are mine, and all their train;   230
With them a cup which Thetis' self bestowed,
As she of love did hear me sadly plain;
A pearlèd cup where nectar oft hath flowed;
  But if my love will love the gift and giver,
  Thine be the cup, thine be the swans forever.

Daph. Thrice happy swains! thrice happy shepherds' fate!
Thom. Ah, blessed life! ah, blessed fishers' state!
Your pipes assuage your love, your nets maintain you.
Daph. Your lambkins clothe you warm, your flocks sustain you;
You fear no stormy seas, nor tempests roaring.
Thom. You sit not rots or burning stars deploring;   240
In calms you fish, in roughs use songs and dances.
Daph. More do you fear your love's sweet-bitter glances,
Than certain fate, or fortune ever changing.
Thom. Ah, that the life in seas so safely ranging
Should with love's weeping eye be sunk and drowned!
Daph. The shepherd's life Phœbus, a shepherd, crowned,
His snowy flocks by stately Peneus leading.
Thom. What herb was that on which old Glaucus feeding
Grows never old, but now the gods augmenteth?
Daph. Delia herself her rigor hard relenteth;   250
To play with shepherd's boy she's not ashamed.
Thom. Venus, of frothy seas thou first wast framed;
The waves thy cradle, now love's queen art named.

Daph. Thou gentle boy, what prize may well reward thee?
So slender gift as this not half requites thee.
May prosperous stars and quiet seas regard thee,
But most that pleasing star that most delights thee;
  May Proteus still and Glaucus dearest hold thee,

But most, her influence all safe enfold thee,
May she with gentle beams from her fair sphere behold
thee.   260

Thom. As whistling winds 'gainst rocks their voices tearing,
As rivers through the valleys softly gliding,
As haven after cruel tempests fearing,
Such, fairest boy, such is thy verses' sliding.
    Thine be the prize; may Pan and Phœbus grace thee;
    Most, whom thou most admir'st, may she embrace thee,
And flaming in thy love, with snowy arms enlace thee.

Thirsil. You lovely boys, full well your art you guided,
That with your striving songs your strife is ended;
So you yourselves the cause have well decided,   270
And by no judge can your reward be mended.
Then since the prize for only one intended
    You both refuse, we justly may reserve it,
    And as your offering in Love's temple serve it;
Since none of both deserve, when both so well deserve it.

Yet, for such songs should ever be rewarded,
Daphnis, take thou this hook of ivory clearest,
Given me by Pan, when Pan my verse regarded;
This fears the wolf, when most the wolf thou fearest.
But thou, my Thomalin, my love, my dearest,   280
    Take thou this pipe, which oft proud storms restrained,
    Which spite of Camus' spite, I still retained;
Was never little pipe more soft, more sweetly plained.

And you, fair troop, if Thirsil you disdain not,
Vouchsafe with me to take some short refection;
Excess or daints my lowly roofs maintain not,
Pears, apples, plums, no sugared made confection.
So up they rose, and by love's sweet direction,
Sea-nymphs with shepherds sort; sea-boys complain not
That wood-nymphs with like love them entertain not.   290
    And all the day to songs and dances lending,
    Too swift it runs, and spends too fast in spending.
With day their sports began, with day they take their ending.

To Mr. Jo. Tomkins

Thomalin, my lief, thy music-strains to hear
More rapts my soul than when the swelling winds
On craggy rocks their whistling voices tear,

Or when the sea, if stopped his course he finds,
With broken murmurs thinks weak shores to fear,
Scorning such sandy cords his proud head binds;
   More than where rivers in the summer's ray,
   Through covert glades cutting their shady way,
Run tumbling down the lawns and with the pebbles play.

Thy strains to hear, old Camus from his cell   10
Comes guarded with an hundred nymphs around,
An hundred nymphs, that in his rivers dwell,
About him flock with water-lilies crowned;
For thee the Muses leave their silver well,
And marvel where thou all their art hast found;
   There sitting they admire thy dainty strains,
   And while thy sadder accent sweetly plains
Feel thousand sugared joys creep in their melting veins.

How oft have I, the Muses' bower frequenting,
Missed them at home and found them all with thee!   20
Whether thou sing'st sad Eupathus' lamenting,
Or tunest notes to sacred harmony,
The ravished soul with thy sweet songs consenting,
Scorning the earth, in heav'nly ecstasy
   Transcends the stars and with the angels' train
   Those courts surveys; and now, come back again,
Finds yet another heav'n in thy delightful strain.

Ah! couldst thou here thy humble mind content,
Lowly with me to live in country cell,
And learn suspect the court's proud blandishment,   30
Here might we safe, here might we sweetly dwell.
Live Pallas in her towers and marble tent,
But ah, the country bowers please me as well;
   There with my Thomalin I safe would sing,
   And frame sweet ditties to thy sweeter string;
There would we laugh at spite and fortune's thundering.

No flattery, hate, or envy lodgeth there;
There no suspicion walled in provèd steel,
Yet fearful of the arms herself doth wear;
Pride is not there, no tyrant there we feel;   40
No clamorous laws shall deaf thy music ear;
They know no change, nor wanton fortune's wheel;
   Thousand fresh sports grow in those dainty places;
   Light fawns and nymphs dance in the woody spaces,
And little Love himself plays with the naked Graces.

But seeing fate my happy wish refuses,
Let me alone enjoy my low estate.
Of all the gifts that fair Parnassus uses,
Only scorned poverty and fortune's hate
Common I find to me and to the Muses;   50
But with the Muses, welcome poorest fate.
  Safe in my humble cottage will I rest,
  And lifting up from my untainted breast
A quiet spirit to heav'n, securely live, and blest.

To thee I here bequeath the courtly joys,
Seeing to court my Thomalin is bent;
Take from thy Thirsil these his idle toys;
Here will I end my looser merriment.
And when thou sing'st them to the wanton boys
Among the courtly lasses' blandishment,   60
  Think of thy Thirsil's love that never spends,
  And softly say, His love still better mends,
Ah, too unlike the love of court or courtly friends!

Go, little pipe, for ever I must leave thee,
My little, little pipe, but sweetest ever;
Go, go, for I have vowed to see thee never,
Never, ah, never must I more receive thee;
But he in better love will still persever.
  Go, little pipe, for I must have a new;
  Farewell, ye Norfolk maids, and Ida crew;   70
Thirsil will play no more, forever now adieu.

Upon my brother, Mr. G. F. his book entitled
Christ's Victory and Triumph

Fond lads, that spend so fast your posting time,
Too posting time, that spends your time as fast,
To chant light toys or frame some wanton rhyme,
Where idle boys may glut their lustful taste,
Or else with praise to clothe some fleshly slime
With virgin roses and fair lilies chaste,
  While itching bloods and youthful ears adore it,
But wiser men, and once yourselves, will most abhor it.

But thou, most near, most dear, in this of thine
Hast proved the Muses not to Venus bound;   10
Such as thy matter, such thy muse, divine.
Or thou such grace with mercy's self hast found
That she herself deigns in thy leaves to shine,

Or stol'n from heav'n, thou brought'st this verse to ground,
  Which frights the numbëd soul with fearful thunder,
And soon with honeyed dews thaws it 'twixt joy and wonder.

Then do not thou malicious tongues esteem;
The glass through which an envious eye doth gaze
Can eas'ly make a mole-hill mountain seem,
  His praise dispraises, his dispraises praise;   20
Enough if best men best thy labors deem,
And to the highest pitch thy merit raise;
  While all the Muses to thy song decree
Victorious triumph, triumphant victory.

An hymn

Drop, drop, slow tears,
    And bathe those beauteous feet
Which brought from heav'n
    The news and prince of peace.
Cease not, wet eyes,
    His mercies to entreat;
To cry for vengeance
    Sin doth never cease;
In your deep floods
    Drown all my faults and fears,   10
Nor let his eye
    See sin but through my tears.

WILLIAM BASSE

The Introduction and Notes are at page 1008

FROM *Lansdowne Ms. 777*

On Mr. William Shakespeare

Renownëd Spenser, lie a thought more nigh
To learned Chaucer; and rare Beaumont, lie
A little nearer Spenser, to make room
For Shakespeare in your threefold, fourfold tomb.
To lodge all four in one bed make a shift
Until doomsday, for hardly will a fift
Betwixt this day and that by fate be slain,
For whom your curtains may be drawn again.
If your precedency in death doth bar
A fourth place in your sacred sepulcher,   10

Under this carvëd marble of thine own
Sleep, rare tragedian, Shakespeare, sleep alone;
Thy unmolested peace, unsharëd cave,
Possess as lord, not tenant, of thy grave,
    That unto us and others it may be
    Honor hereafter to be laid by thee.

FROM IZAAK WALTON's *Complete Angler*, 1653

The angler's song

As inward love breeds outward
    talk,
The hound some praise, and some
    the hawk;
Some better pleased with private
    sport
Use tennis, some a mistress court;
    But these delights I neither wish
    Nor envy, while I freely fish.

Who hunts doth oft in danger
    ride;
Who hawks lures oft both far and
    wide;
Who uses games may often prove
A loser, but who falls in love   10
    Is fettered in fond Cupid's
        snare;
    My angle breeds me no such
        care.

Of recreation there is none
So free as fishing is alone;
All other pastimes do no less
Than mind and body both possess;
    My hand alone my work can do,
    So I can fish and study too.

I care not, I, to fish in seas,
Fresh rivers best my mind do
    please,   20
Whose sweet calm course I con-
    template
And seek in life to imitate;
    In civil bounds I fain would
        keep,
    And for my past offences weep.

And when the timorous trout I
    wait
To take, and he devours my bait,
How poor a thing, sometimes I
    find,
Will captivate a greedy mind;
    And when none bite, I praise the
        wise
    Whom vain allurements ne'er
        surprise.   30

But yet, though while I fish I fast,
I make good fortune my repast;
And thereunto my friend invite,
In whom I more than that delight,
    Who is more welcome to my
        dish
    Than to my angle was my fish.

As well content no prize to take,
As use of taken prize to make;
For so our Lord was pleasëd when
He fishers made fishers of men;   40
    Where, which is in no other
        game,
    A man may fish and praise his
        name.

The first men that our Savior dear
Did choose to wait upon him here,
Blest fishers were, and fish the last
Food was that he on earth did
    taste;
    I therefore strive to follow those
    Whom he to follow him hath
        chose.

RICHARD CORBET, BISHOP OF OXFORD AND NORWICH

The Introduction and Notes are at page 1008

FROM *Certain Elegant Poems*, 1647

To his son, Vincent Corbet

What I shall leave thee none can tell,
But all shall say I wish thee well:
I wish thee, Vin, before all wealth,
Both bodily and ghostly health;
Nor too much wealth, nor wit, come to thee,
So much of either may undo thee.
I wish thee learning, not for show,
Enough for to instruct and know,
Not such as gentlemen require
To prate at table or at fire.   10
I wish thee all thy mother's graces,
Thy father's fortunes, and his places.
I wish thee friends, and one at court,
Not to build on, but support,
To keep thee, not in doing many
Oppressions, but from suffering any.
I wish thee peace in all thy ways,
Nor lazy nor contentious days;
And when thy soul and body part,
As innocent as now thou art.   20

A proper new ballad, intituled The fairies' farewell, or God a mercy Will

To be sung or whistled, to the tune of Meadow Brow *by the learned, by the unlearned to the tune of* Fortune

Farewell, rewards and fairies,
  Good housewives now may say,
For now foul sluts in dairies
  Do fare as well as they.
And though they sweep their hearths no less
  Than maids were wont to do,
Yet who of late for cleanliness
  Finds six-pence in her shoe?

Lament, lament, old abbeys,
  The fairies lost command;   10
They did but change priests' babies,
  But some have changed your land,
And all your children sprung from thence
  Are now grown Puritans;
Who live as changelings ever since,
  For love of your demains.

At morning and at evening both
  You merry were and glad,

So little care of sleep or sloth
  These pretty ladies had;   20
When Tom came home from la-
    bor,
Or Ciss to milking rose,
Then merrily went their tabor,
  And nimbly went their toes.

Witness those rings and rounde-
    lays
Of theirs, which yet remain,
Were footed in Queen Mary's
    days
On many a grassy plain;
But since of late, Elizabeth,
  And later James came in,   30
They never danced on any heath
  As when the time hath been.

By which we note the fairies
  Were of the old profession;
Their songs were Ave Maries,
  Their dances were procession;
But now, alas, they all are dead,
  Or gone beyond the seas,
Or further from religion fled,
  Or else they take their ease.   40

A tell-tale in their company
  They never could endure,

And whoso kept not secretly
  Their mirth was punished sure;
It was a just and Christian deed
  To pinch such black and blue;
Oh, how the commonwealth doth
    need
  Such justices as you!

Now they have left our quarters,
  A register they have,   50
Who can preserve their charters,
  A man both wise and grave;
A hundred of their merry pranks
  By one that I could name
Are kept in store; con twenty
    thanks
  To William for the same.

To William Chourne of Staf-
    fordshire
  Give laud and praises due,
Who every meal can mend your
    cheer
  With tales both old and true;   60
To William all give audience,
  And pray ye for his noddle,
For all the fairies' evidence
  Were lost, if that were addle.

WILLIAM STRODE

The Introduction and Notes are at page 1009

FROM *Harleian Ms.* 6917

The commendation of music

When whispering strains, with creeping wind,
  Distil soft passion through the heart,
And when at every touch we find
  Our pulses beat and bear a part;
    When threads can make
    A heart-string shake,
    Philosophy
    Cannot deny
  Our souls consist of harmony.

When unto heavenly joys we feign
  Whate'er the soul affecteth most,
Which only thus we can explain
  By music of the heavenly host,
     Whose lays, methinks,
     Make stars to shrink,
     Philosophy
     May judge thereby
Our souls consist of harmony.

Oh, lull me, lull me, charming air!
  My senses rock with wonder sweet;
Like snow on wool thy fallings are,
  Soft as a spirit's are thy feet;
     Grief who need fear
     That hath an ear?
     Down let him lie,
     And slumbering die,
And change his soul for harmony.

FROM *Additional Ms.* 19268

On Westwell Downs

When Westwell Downs I gan to tread,
Where cleanly winds the green do sweep,
Methought a landscape there was spread,
Here a bush and there a sheep;
    The pleated wrinkles on the face
    Of wave-swollen earth did lend such grace
    As shadows do in imagery,
    Which both deceive and please the eye.

The sheep sometimes do tread a maze
By often winding in and in,
And sometimes round about they trace
Which milkmaids call a fairy ring;
    Such semicircles they have run,
    Such lines across so lively spun,
    That shepherds term whene'er they please
    A new geometry with ease.

The slender food upon the down
Is always even, always bare,
Which neither spring nor winter's frown
Can aught improve or aught impair;

Such is the barren eunuch's chin,
Which thus doth evermore begin
With tender down to be o'ercast,
Which never comes to hair at last.

Here and there two hilly crests
Amidst them hug a pleasant green,
And these are like two swelling breasts
That close a tender fall between.
Here could I read, or sleep, or pray,
From early morn till flight of day;   30
But hark! a sheep's bell calls me up,
Like Oxford college bells, to sup.

FROM *Wit's Recreations,* 1640

On Chloris walking in the snow

I saw fair Chloris walk alone
Where feathered rain came softly down,
Then Jove descended from his tower
To court her in a silver shower;
The wanton snow flew to her breast
Like little birds into their nest,
But overcome with whiteness there
For grief it thawed into a tear,
Then falling down her garment hem
To deck her, froze into a gem.

HENRY KING, BISHOP OF CHICHESTER

The Introduction and Notes are at page 1009

FROM *Poems, Elegies, Paradoxes, and Sonnets,* 1657

The publishers to the author.

Sir,
  *It is the common fashion to make some address to the readers, but
we are bold to direct ours to you, who will look on this publication
with anger which others must welcome into the world with joy.*
  *The Lord Verulam, comparing ingenious authors to those who had
orchards ill-neighbored, advised them to publish their own labors, lest
others might steal the fruit. Had you followed his example, or liked
the advice, we had not thus trespassed against your consent, or been*

forced to an apology, which cannot but imply a fault committed. The best we can say for ourselves is, that if we have injured you, it is merely in your own defence, preventing the present attempts of others, who to their theft would, by their false copies of these poems, have added violence, and some way have wounded your reputation.

Having been long engaged on better contemplations, you may perhaps look down on these Juvenilia, *most of them the issues of your youthful muse, with some disdain; and yet the courteous reader may tell you with thanks that they are not to be despised, being far from abortive, nor to be disowned, because they are both modest and legitimate. And thus if we have offered you a view of your younger face, our hope is you will behold it with an unwrinkled brow, though we have presented the mirror against your will.*

We confess our design hath been set forward by friends that honor you, who lest the ill publishing might disfigure these things from whence you never expected addition to your credit (sundry times endeavored and by them defeated) furnished us with some papers which they thought authentic; we may not turn their favor into an accusation, and therefore give no intimation of their names, but wholly take the blame of this hasty and immethodical impression upon ourselves, being persons at a distance, who are fitter to bear it than those who are nearer related. In hope of your pardon we remain,

Your most devoted servants,
Rich. Marriot.
Hen. Herringman.

Sonnet

Tell me no more how fair she is,
    I have no mind to hear
The story of that distant bliss
    I never shall come near;
By sad experience I have found
That her perfection is my wound.

And tell me not how fond I am
    To tempt a daring fate,
From whence no triumph ever came
    But to repent too late;   10
There is some hope ere long I may
In silence dote myself away.

I ask no pity, Love, from thee,
    Nor will thy justice blame,
So that thou wilt not envy me
    The glory of my flame,

Which crowns my heart whene'er it dies,
In that it falls her sacrifice.

The retreat

Pursue no more, my thoughts, that false unkind;
You may as soon imprison the north-wind,
Or catch the lightning as it leaps, or reach
The leading billow first ran down the breach,
Or undertake the flying clouds to track
In the same path they yesterday did rack.
    Then like a torch turned downward, let the same
    Desire which nourished it, put out your flame.

Lo, thus I do divorce thee from my breast,
False to thy vow, and traitor to my rest!
Henceforth thy tears shall be, though thou repent,
Like pardons after execution sent.
Nor shalt thou ever my love's story read,
But as some epitaph of what is dead.
    So may my hope on future blessings dwell,
    As 'tis my firm resolve and last farewell.

The surrender

My once dear love, hapless that I no more
Must call thee so, the rich affection's store
That fed our hopes lies now exhaust and spent,
Like sums of treasure unto bankrupts lent.

We that did nothing study but the way
To love each other, with which thoughts the day
Rose with delight to us, and with them set,
Must learn the hateful art how to forget.

We that did nothing wish that heav'n could give
Beyond ourselves, nor did desire to live
Beyond that wish, all these now cancel must
As if not writ in faith, but words and dust.

Yet witness those clear vows which lovers make,
Witness the chaste desires that never brake
Into unruly heats; witness that breast
Which in thy bosom anchored his whole rest;
'Tis no default in us, I dare acquite
Thy maiden faith, thy purpose fair and white

As thy pure self. Cross planets did envý
Us to each other, and heaven did untie   20
Faster than vows could bind. Oh, that the stars,
When lovers meet, should stand opposed in wars!

Since, then, some higher destinies command,
Let us not strive, nor labor to withstand
What is past help. The longest date of grief
Can never yield a hope of our relief;
And though we waste ourselves in moist laments,
Tears may drown us, but not our discontents.

Fold back our arms, take home our fruitless loves,
That must new fortunes try, like turtle doves   30
Dislodgëd from their haunts. We must in tears
Unwind a love knit up in many years.
In this last kiss I here surrender thee
Back to thyself, so thou again art free;
Thou in another, sad as that, resend
The truest heart that lover e'er did lend.

Now turn from each. So fare our severed hearts
As the divorced soul from her body parts.

The exequy

Accept, thou shrine of my dead
    saint,
Instead of dirges, this complaint;
And for sweet flowers to crown thy
    hearse,
Receive a strew of weeping verse
From thy grieved friend, whom
    thou might'st see
Quite melted into tears for thee.

Dear loss! since thy untimely fate
My task hath been to meditate
On thee, on thee; thou art the book,
The library whereon I look,   10
Though almost blind. For thee,
    loved clay,
I languish out, not live, the day,
Using no other exercise
But what I practise with mine
    eyes;

By which wet glasses I find out
How lazily time creeps about
To one that mourns; this, only
    this,
My exercise and business is.
So I compute the weary hours   19
With sighs dissolvëd into showers.

Nor wonder if my time go thus
Backward and most preposterous;
Thou hast benighted me; thy set
This eve of blackness did beget,
Who wast my day, though overcast
Before thou hadst thy noon-tide
    passed;
And I remember must in tears,
Thou scarce hadst seen so many
    years
As day tells hours. By thy clear
    sun

My love and fortune first did
    run;   ³⁰
But thou wilt never more appear
Folded within my hemisphere,
Since both thy light and motion
Like a fled star is fall'n and gone;
And 'twixt me and my soul's dear
    wish
An earth now interposëd is,
Which such a strange eclipse doth
    make
As ne'er was read in almanac.

I could allow thee for a time
To darken me and my sad clime; ⁴⁰
Were it a month, a year, or ten,
I would thy exile live till then,
And all that space my mirth
    adjourn,
So thou wouldst promise to return,
And putting off thy ashy shroud,
At length disperse this sorrow's
    cloud.

But woe is me! the longest date
Too narrow is to calculate
These empty hopes; never shall I
Be so much blest as to descry   ⁵⁰
A glimpse of thee, till that day
    come
Which shall the earth to cinders
    doom,
And a fierce fever must calcine
The body of this world like thine,
My little world. That fit of fire
Once off, our bodies shall aspire
To our souls' bliss; then we shall
    rise
And view ourselves with clearer
    eyes
In that calm region where no night
Can hide us from each other's
    sight.   ⁶⁰

Meantime, thou hast her, earth;
    much good

May my harm do thee. Since it
    stood
With heaven's will I might not
    call
Her longer mine, I give thee all
My short-lived right and interest
In her whom living I loved best;
With a most free and bounteous
    grief,
I give thee what I could not keep.
Be kind to her, and prithee look
Thou write into thy doomsday
    book   ⁷⁰
Each parcel of this rarity
Which in thy casket shrined doth
    lie.
See that thou make thy reck'ning
    straight,
And yield her back again by
    weight;
For thou must audit on thy trust
Each grain and atom of this dust,
As thou wilt answer Him that lent,
Not gave thee, my dear monument.

So close the ground, and 'bout her
    shade
Black curtains draw, my bride is
    laid.   ⁸⁰
Sleep on, my love, in thy cold bed,
Never to be disquieted!
My last good-night! Thou wilt
    not wake
Till I thy fate shall overtake;
Till age, or grief, or sickness must
Marry my body to that dust
It so much loves, and fill the room
My heart keeps empty in thy tomb.
Stay for me there, I will not fail
To meet thee in that hollow vale. ⁹⁰
And think not much of my delay;
I am already on the way,
And follow thee with all the speed
Desire can make, or sorrows breed.
Each minute is a short degree,

And ev'ry hour a step towards thee.
At night when I betake to rest,
Next morn I rise nearer my west
Of life, almost by eight hours' sail,
Than when sleep breathed his
   drowsy gale. 100

Thus from the sun my bottom
   steers,
And my day's compass downward
   bears;
Nor labor I to stem the tide
Through which to thee I swiftly
   glide.

'Tis true, with shame and grief I
   yield,
Thou like the van first tookst the
   field,
And gotten hath the victory

In thus adventuring to die
Before me, whose more years
   might crave
A just precedence in the grave. 110
But hark! my pulse like a soft
   drum
Beats my approach, tells thee I
   come;
And slow howe'er my marches be,
I shall at last sit down by thee.

The thought of this bids me go
   on,
And wait my dissolution
With hope and comfort. Dear, for-
   give
The crime, I am content to live
Divided, with but half a heart,
Till we shall meet and never
   part. 120

Sic vita

Like to the falling of a star,
Or as the flights of eagles are,
Or like the fresh spring's gaudy hue,
Or silver drops of morning dew,
Or like a wind that chafes the flood,
Or bubbles which on water stood:
Even such is man, whose borrowed light
Is straight called in, and paid to night.
   The wind blows out, the bubble dies;
   The spring entombed in autumn lies; 10
   The dew dries up, the star is shot;
   The flight is past, and man forgot.

FROM *Harleian Ms.* 6917

A contemplation upon flowers

Brave flowers, that I could gallant it like you
   And be as little vain!
You come abroad and make a harmless show,
   And to your beds of earth again;
You are not proud, you know your birth,
For your embroidered garments are from earth.

You do obey your months and times, but I
Would have it ever spring;
My fate would know no winter, never die   10
Nor think of such a thing;
Oh, that I could my bed of earth but view
And smile, and look as cheerfully as you.

Oh, teach me to see death and not to fear,
But rather to take truce;
How often have I seen you at a bier,
And there look fresh and spruce;
You fragrant flowers, then teach me that my breath
Like yours may sweeten, and perfume my death.

AURELIAN TOWNSHEND

The Introduction and Notes are at page 1010

FROM JOHN PLAYFORD's *Select Musical Airs and Dialogues*, 1653

[*Victorious beauty*]

Victorious beauty, though your
         eyes
    Are able to subdue an host,
    And therefore are unlike to boast
The taking of a little prize,
Do not a single heart despise.

I came alone, but yet so armed
    With former love, I durst have
         sworn
    That as that privy coat was
         worn
With characters of beauty
         charmed,
Thereby it might have 'scaped un-
         harmed.   10

But neither steel nor stony breast

Are proofs against those looks of
         thine,
    Nor can a beauty less divine
    Of any heart be long possessed
Where you intend an interest.

The conquest in regard of me
    Alas, is small, but in respect
    Of her that did my love protect,
Were it divulged, deserved to be
Recorded for a victory.   20

And such a one, as some that view
    Her lovely face perhaps may say,
    Though you have stolen my
         heart away,
If all your servants prove not true
May steal a heart or two from you.

FROM HENRY LAWES's *Airs and Dialogues*, 1653

A dialogue betwixt Time and a Pilgrim

Pilg. . Aged man that mows these fields—
Time. Pilgrim speak, what is thy will?

Pilg. Whose soil is this that such sweet pasture yields?
Or who art thou whose foot stands never still?
Or where am I?
Time. In love.
Pilg. His lordship lies above.
Time. Yes, and below, and round about,
Wherein all sorts of flowers are growing,
Which as the early spring puts out,   10
Time falls as fast a-mowing.
Pilg. If thou art Time, these flowers have lives,
And then I fear,
Under some lily she I love
May now be growing there.
Time. And in some thistle or some spire of grass,
My scythe thy stalk, before hers come, may pass.
Pilg. Wilt thou provide it may?
Time. No.
Pilg. Allege the cause.   20
Time. Because Time cannot alter, but obey, Fate's laws.
Cho. Then happy those whom Fate, that is the stronger,
Together twist their threads, and yet draws hers the longer.

FROM JOHN COTGRAVE'S *Wit's Interpreter*, 1655

What is most to be liked in a mistress

'Tis not how witty nor how free
Nor yet how beautiful she be,
But how much kind and true to me.
Freedom and wit none can confine,
And beauty like the sun doth shine,
But kind and true are only thine.

Let others with attention sit,
To listen, and admire her wit;
That is a rock where I ne'er split.
Let others dote upon her eyes,   10
And burn their hearts for sacrifice,
Beauty's a calm where danger lies.

Yet kind and true have long been
tried,
A harbor where we may confide
And safely there at anchor ride.
From change of winds there we
are free,   18
Nor need we fear storm's tyranny,
Nor pirate, though a prince he be.

ROBERT HERRICK

The Introduction and Notes are at page 1010

FROM *Hesperides*, 1648

The argument of his book

I sing of brooks, of blossoms, birds, and bowers,
Of April, May, of June, and July flowers;

I sing of may-poles, hock-carts, wassails, wakes,
Of bridegrooms, brides, and of their bridal cakes;
I write of youth, of love, and have access
By these to sing of cleanly wantonness;
I sing of dews, of rains, and piece by piece
Of balm, of oil, of spice, and ambergris;
I sing of times trans-shifting, and I write
How roses first came red, and lilies white;   10
I write of groves, of twilights, and I sing
The court of Mab, and of the Fairy King;
I write of hell; I sing, and ever shall,
Of heaven, and hope to have it after all.

To the sour reader

If thou dislik'st the piece thou light'st on first,
Think that, of all that I have writ, the worst;
But if thou read'st my book unto the end,
And still dost this and that verse reprehend,
O perverse man! if all disgustful be,
The extreme scab take thee and thine, for me.

When he would have his verses read

In sober mornings do not thou rehearse
The holy incantation of a verse;
But when that men have both well drunk and fed,
Let my enchantments then be sung, or read.
When laurel spirts i' th' fire, and when the hearth
Smiles to itself and gilds the roof with mirth;
When up the thyrse is raised, and when the sound
Of sacred orgies flies—A round, a round!
When the rose reigns, and locks with ointments shine,
Let rigid Cato read these lines of mine.   10

His request to Julia

Julia, if I chance to die
Ere I print my poetry,
I most humbly thee desire
To commit it to the fire;
Better 'twere my book were dead,
Than to live not pérfected.

Not every day fit for verse

'Tis not ev'ry day that I
Fitted am to prophesy;
No, but when the spirit fills
The fantastic pannicles
Full of fire, then I write
As the godhead doth indite.
Thus enraged, my lines are
hurled,
Like the Sibyl's, through the
world.
Look how next the holy fire
Either slakes, or doth retire;   10
So the fancy cools, till when
That brave spirit comes again.

The departure of the good dæmon

What can I do in poetry,
Now the good spirit's gone from
    me?
Why, nothing now, but lonely sit
And over-read what I have writ.

Posting to printing

Let others to the printing press
    run fast;
Since after death comes glory, I'll
    not haste.

To live merrily, and to trust to good verses

Now is the time for mirth,
    Nor cheek or tongue be dumb;
For with the flow'ry earth
    The golden pomp is come.

The golden pomp is come;
    For now each tree does wear,
Made of her pap and gum,
    Rich beads of amber here.

Now reigns the rose, and now
    Th' Arabian dew besmears   10
My uncontrollèd brow
    And my retorted hairs.

Homer, this health to thee,
    In sack of such a kind
That it would make thee see
    Though thou wert ne'er so
        blind.

Next, Virgil I'll call forth
    To pledge this second health
In wine, whose each cup's worth
    An Indian commonwealth.   20

A goblet next I'll drink
    To Ovid, and suppose,
Made he the pledge, he'd think
    The world had all one nose.

Then this immensive cup
    Of aromatic wine,
Catullus, I quaff up
    To that terse muse of thine.

Wild I am now with heat;
    O Bacchus! cool thy rays!   30
Or frantic, I shall eat
    Thy thyrse, and bite the bays.

Round, round the roof does run;
    And being ravished thus,
Come, I will drink a tun
    To my Propertïus.

Now, to Tibullus, next,
    This flood I drink to thee;
But stay, I see a text
    That this presents to me.   40

Behold, Tibullus lies
    Here burnt, whose small re-
        turn
Of ashes scarce suffice
    To fill a little urn.

Trust to good verses then;
    They only will aspire,
When pyramids, as men,
    Are lost i' th' funeral fire.

And when all bodies meet,
    In Lethe to be drowned,   50
Then only numbers sweet
    With endless life are crowned.

His prayer to Ben Jonson

When I a verse shall make,
Know I have prayed thee,
For old religion's sake,
Saint Ben, to aid me.

Make the way smooth for me,   Candles I'll give to thee,
When I, thy Herrick,   And a new altar;   10
Honoring thee, on my knee   And thou, Saint Ben, shalt be
Offer my lyric.   Writ in my psalter.

Upon M. Ben Jonson, Epigram

After the rare arch-poet Jonson died,
The sock grew loathsome, and the buskin's pride,
Together with the stage's glory, stood
Each like a poor and pitied widowhood.
The cirque profaned was, and all postures racked,
For men did strut and stride and stare, not act.
Then temper flew from words, and men did squeak,
Look red, and blow, and bluster, but not speak;
No holy rage or frantic fires did stir
Or flash about the spacious theater.   10
No clap of hands, or shout, or praise's proof
Did crack the playhouse sides, or cleave her roof.
Artless the scene was, and that monstrous sin
Of deep and arrant ignorance came in;
Such ignorance as theirs was who once hissed
At thy unequalled play, the *Alchemist*.
Oh, fie upon 'em! Lastly too, all wit
In utter darkness did, and still will sit
Sleeping the luckless age out, till that she
Her resurrection has again with thee.   20

An ode for him

Ah Ben!
Say how, or when
Shall we thy guests
Meet at those lyric feasts
Made at the Sun,
The Dog, the Triple Tun,
Where we such clusters had
As made us nobly wild, not mad;
And yet each verse of thine
Outdid the meat, outdid the frolic wine.   10

My Ben!
Or come again,
Or send to us
Thy wit's great overplus;
But teach us yet
Wisely to husband it.

Lest we that talent spend,
And having once brought to an end
That precious stock, the store
Of such a wit the world should have no more. 20

His lachrimæ; or mirth turned to mourning

Call me no more,
As heretofore,
The music of a feast;
Since now, alas,
The mirth that was
In me is dead or ceased.

Before I went
To banishment
Into the loathèd west,
I could rehearse 10
A lyric verse,
And speak it with the best.

But time, ay me,
Has laid, I see,
My organ fast asleep;
And turned my voice
Into the noise
Of those that sit and weep.

The apparition of his mistress calling him to Elysium

Desunt nonnulla—

Come then, and like two doves with silv'ry wings,
Let our souls fly to th' shades, where ever springs
Sit smiling in the meads; where balm and oil,
Roses and cassia crown the untilled soil;
Where no disease reigns, or infection comes
To blast the air, but ambergris and gums;
This, that, and ev'ry thicket doth transpire
More sweet than storax from the hallowed fire;
Where ev'ry tree a wealthy issue bears
Of fragrant apples, blushing plums, or pears, 10
And all the shrubs, with sparkling spangles, show
Like morning sunshine tinselling the dew.
Here in green meadows sits eternal May,
Purfling the margents, while perpetual day
So double gilds the air as that no night
Can ever rust th' enamel of the light.

Here naked younglings, handsome striplings run
Their goals for virgins' kisses; which when done,
Then unto dancing forth the learned round
Commixed they meet, with endless roses crowned.   20
And here we'll sit on primrose banks, and see
Love's chorus led by Cupid; and we'll be
Two loving followers, too, unto the grove
Where poets sing the stories of our love.
There thou shalt hear divine Musæus sing
Of Hero and Leander; then I'll bring
Thee to the stand where honored Homer reads
His *Odysseys* and his high *Iliads*,
About whose throne the crowd of poets throng
To hear the incantation of his tongue;   30
To Linus, then to Pindar; and that done,
I'll bring thee, Herrick, to Anacreon,
Quaffing his full-crowned bowls of burning wine,
And in his raptures speaking lines of thine,
Like to his subject; and as his frantic
Looks show him truly Bacchanalian-like,
Besmeared with grapes, welcome he shall thee thither,
Where both may rage, both drink and dance together.
Then stately Virgil, witty Ovid, by
Whom fair Corinna sits, and doth comply   40
With ivory wrists his laureate head, and steeps
His eye in dew of kisses while he sleeps.
Then soft Catullus, sharp-fanged Martial,
And tow'ring Lucan, Horace, Juvenal,
And snaky Persius, these and those whom rage,
Dropped for the jars of heaven, filled t'engage
All times unto their frenzies; thou shalt there
Behold them in a spacious theater.
Among which glories, crowned with sacred bays
And flatt'ring ivy, two recite their plays,   50
Beaumont and Fletcher, swans to whom all ears
Listen, while they, like sirens in their spheres,
Sing their Evadne; and still more for thee
There yet remains to know, than thou canst see
By glim'ring of a fancy. Do but come,
And there I'll show thee that capacious room
In which thy father Jonson now is placed,
As in a globe of radiant fire, and graced
To be in that orb crowned, that doth include
Those prophets of the former magnitude,   60
And he one chief; but hark, I hear the cock,
The bellman of the night, proclaim the clock

Of late struck one, and now I see the prime
Of day break from the pregnant east; 'tis time
I vanish; more I had to say,
But night determines here—away.

His farewell to sack

Farewell thou thing, time-past so known, so dear
To me, as blood to life and spirit; near,
Nay, thou more near than kindred, friend, man, wife,
Male to the female, soul to body, life
To quick action, or the warm soft side
Of the resigning, yet resisting bride.
The kiss of virgins, first fruits of the bed,
Soft speech, smooth touch, the lips, the maidenhead:
These, and a thousand sweets, could never be
So near, or dear, as thou wast once to me.   10
O thou, the drink of gods and angels! wine
That scatter'st spirit and lust, whose purest shine
More radiant than the summer's sunbeams shows;
Each way illustrious, brave, and like to those
Comets we see by night, whose shagg'd portents
Foretell the coming of some dire events;
Or some full flame which with a pride aspires,
Throwing about his wild and active fires.
'Tis thou, above nectar, O divinest soul!
Eternal in thyself, that canst control   20
That which subverts whole nature, grief and care,
Vexation of the mind, and damned despair.
'Tis thou alone who, with thy mystic fan,
Work'st more than wisdom, art, or nature can
To rouse the sacred madness and awake
The frost-bound blood and spirits, and to make
Them frantic with thy raptures, flashing through
The soul like lightning, and as active too.
'Tis not Apollo can, or those thrice three
Castalian sisters, sing, if wanting thee.   30
Horace, Anacreon, both had lost their fame
Hadst thou not filled them with thy fire and flame.
Phœbean splendor! and thou Thespian spring!
Of which sweet swans must drink before they sing
Their true-paced numbers and their holy lays,
Which makes them worthy cedar and the bays.
But why, why longer do I gaze upon
Thee with the eye of admiration?
Since I must leave thee, and enforced, must say

To all thy witching beauties, Go, away! 40
But if thy whimp'ring looks do ask me why,
Then know that nature bids thee go, not I.
'Tis her erroneous self has made a brain
Uncapable of such a sovereign
As is thy powerful self. Prithee not smile,
Or smile more inly, lest thy looks beguile
My vows denounced in zeal, which thus much show thee,
That I have sworn but by thy looks to know thee.
Let others drink thee freely, and desire
Thee and their lips espoused, while I admire 50
And love thee, but not taste thee. Let my muse
Fail of thy former helps, and only use
Her inadult'rate strength; what's done by me
Hereafter, shall smell of the lamp, not thee.

The welcome to sack

So soft streams meet, so springs with gladder smiles
Meet after long divorcement by the isles,
When love, the child of likeness, urgeth on
Their crystal natures to an union;
So meet stol'n kisses, when the moony nights
Call forth fierce lovers to their wished delights;
So kings and queens meet, when desire convinces
All thoughts but such as aim at getting princes:
As I meet thee. Soul of my life and fame!
Eternal lamp of love! whose radiant flame 10
Outglares the heav'n's Osiris, and thy gleams
Outshine the splendor of his mid-day beams.
Welcome, O welcome, my illustrious spouse;
Welcome as are the ends unto my vows;
Ay! far more welcome than the happy soil
The sea-scourged merchant, after all his toil,
Salutes with tears of joy, when fires betray
The smoky chimneys of his Ithaca.
Where hast thou been so long from my embraces,
Poor pitied exile? Tell me, did thy graces 20
Fly discontented hence, and for a time
Did rather choose to bless another clime?
Or went'st thou to this end the more to move me,
By thy short absence, to desire and love thee?
Why frowns my sweet? Why won't my saint confer
Favors on me, her fierce idolater?
Why are those looks, those looks the which have been
Time-past so fragrant, sickly now drawn in

Like a dull twilight? Tell me, and the fault
I'll expiate with sulphur, hair, and salt;   30
And with the crystal humor of the spring
Purge hence the guilt, and kill this quarreling.
Wo't thou not smile, or tell me what's amiss?
Have I been cold to hug thee, too remiss,
Too temp'rate in embracing? Tell me, has desire
To thee-ward died i' th' embers, and no fire
Left in this raked-up ash-heap as a mark
To testify the glowing of a spark?
Have I divorced thee only to combine
In hot adult'ry with another wine?   40
True, I confess I left thee, and appeal
'Twas done by me more to confirm my zeal
And double my affection on thee, as do those
Whose love grows more inflamed by being foes.
But to forsake thee ever, could there be
A thought of such like possibility?
When thou thyself dar'st say, thy isles shall lack
Grapes, before Herrick leaves Canary sack.
Thou mak'st me airy, active to be borne,
Like Iphiclus, upon the tops of corn.   50
Thou mak'st me nimble, as the wingëd hours,
To dance and caper on the heads of flowers,
And ride the sunbeams. Can there be a thing
Under the heavenly Isis that can bring
More love unto my life, or can present
My genius with a fuller blandishment?
Illustrious idol! could th' Egyptians seek
Help from the garlic, onion, and the leek,
And pay no vows to thee, who wast their best
God, and far more transcendent than the rest?   60
Had Cassius, that weak water-drinker, known
Thee in thy vine, or had but tasted one
Small chalice of thy frantic liquor, he,
As the wise Cato, had approved of thee.
Had not Jove's son, that brave Tyrinthian swain,
Invited to the Thesbian banquet, ta'en
Full goblets of thy gen'rous blood, his sprite
Ne'er had kept heat for fifty maids that night.
Come, come and kiss me; love and lust commends
Thee and thy beauties; kiss, we will be friends   70
Too strong for fate to break us; look upon
Me with that full pride of complexïon,
As queens meet queens; or come thou unto me
As Cleopatra came to Antony,

When her high carriage did at once present
To the triumvir love and wonderment.
Swell up my nerves with spirit; let my blood
Run through my veins like to a hasty flood.
Fill each part full of fire, active to do
What thy commanding soul shall put it to.   80
And till I turn apostate to thy love,
Which here I vow to serve, do not remove
Thy fires from me, but Apollo's curse
Blast these-like actions; or a thing that's worse,
When these circumstants shall but live to see
The time that I prevaricate from thee,
Call me the son of beer, and then confine
Me to the tap, the toast, the turf; let wine
Ne'er shine upon me; may my numbers all
Run to a sudden death and funeral.   90
And last, when thee, dear spouse, I disavow,
Ne'er may prophetic Daphne crown my brow.

Upon love

Love scorched my finger, but did
    spare
  The burning of my heart,
To signify in love my share
  Should be a little part.

Little I love; but if that he
  Would but that heat recall,
That joint to ashes should be
  burnt
Ere I would love at all.

Delight in disorder

A sweet disorder in the dress
Kindles in clothes a wantonness;
A lawn about the shoulders thrown
Into a fine distraction,
An erring lace, which here and
  there
Enthralls the crimson stomacher,
A cuff neglectful, and thereby

Ribands to flow confusedly,
A winning wave, deserving note,
In the tempestuous petticoat,   10
A careless shoe-string, in whose tie
I see a wild civility,
Do more bewitch me than when
  art
Is too precise in every part.

To the virgins, to make much of time

Gather ye rosebuds while ye may,
  Old time is still a-flying,
And this same flower that smiles
  to-day,
  To-morrow will be dying.

The glorious lamp of heaven, the
  sun,

The higher he's a-getting,
The sooner will his race be run,
  And nearer he's to setting.

That age is best which is the
  first,
  When youth and blood are
    warmer;   10

But being spent, the worse, and
worst
Times still succeed the former.

Then be not coy, but use your time,

And while ye may, go marry;
For having lost but once your
prime,
You may for ever tarry.

To his mistress objecting to him neither toying or talking

You say I love not, 'cause I do not play
Still with your curls, and kiss the time away.
You blame me too because I can't devise
Some sport to please those babies in your eyes;
By love's religion, I must here confess it,
The most I love when I the least express it.
Small griefs find tongues; full casks are ever found
To give, if any, yet but little sound.
Deep waters noiseless are; and this we know,
That chiding streams betray small depths below.   10
So when love speechless is, she doth express
A depth in love, and that depth bottomless.
Now since my love is tongueless, know me such
Who speak but little 'cause I love so much.

The night piece, to Julia

Her eyes the glow-worm lend thee,
The shooting stars attend thee;
  And the elves also,
  Whose little eyes glow
Like the sparks of fire, befriend
  thee.

No will-o'-th'-wisp mis-light thee,
Nor snake, or slow-worm bite
  thee;
  But on, on thy way
  Not making a stay,
Since ghost there's none to affright
  thee.   10

Let not the dark thee cumber;
What though the moon does slum-
  ber?
  The stars of the night
  Will lend thee their light,
Like tapers clear without num-
  ber.

Then, Julia, let me woo thee,
Thus, thus to come unto me;
  And when I shall meet
  Thy silv'ry feet,
My soul I'll pour into thee.   20

Upon Julia's clothes

Whenas in silks my Julia goes,
Then, then, methinks, how
  sweetly flows
That liquefaction of her clothes.

Next, when I cast mine eyes and
  see
That brave vibration each way free,
Oh, how that glittering taketh me!

The rosary

One asked me where the roses
  grew;
  I bade him not go seek,

But forthwith bade my Julia
  show
  A bud in either cheek.

Cherry-ripe

Cherry-ripe, ripe, ripe, I cry,
Full and fair ones; come and buy.
If so be you ask me where
They do grow, I answer: There,

Where my Julia's lips do smile;
There's the land, or cherry-isle,
Whose plantations fully show
All the year where cherries grow.

Upon Sappho, sweetly playing and sweetly singing

When thou dost play and sweetly
  sing,
Whether it be the voice or string,
Or both of them, that do agree

Thus to entrance and ravish me,
This, this I know, I'm oft struck
  mute,
And die away upon thy lute.

To Anthea, who may command him anything

Bid me live, and I will live
  Thy protestant to be;
Or bid me love, and I will give
  A loving heart to thee.

A heart as soft, a heart as kind,
  A heart as sound and free
As in the whole world thou canst
  find,
  That heart I'll give to thee.

Bid that heart stay, and it will stay
  To honor thy decree;   10
Or bid it languish quite away,
  And 't shall do so for thee.

Bid me to weep, and I will weep
  While I have eyes to see;
And having none, yet I will keep
  A heart to weep for thee.

Bid me despair, and I'll despair
  Under that cypress tree;
Or bid me die, and I will dare
  E'en death, to die for thee. 20

Thou art my life, my love, my
  heart,
  The very eyes of me;
And hast command of every part,
  To live and die for thee.

Corinna's going a-maying

Get up, get up for shame, the blooming morn
Upon her wings presents the god unshorn.
  See how Aurora throws her fair
  Fresh-quilted colors through the air;
  Get up, sweet slug-a-bed, and see
  The dew bespangling herb and tree.
Each flower has wept and bowed toward the east

Above an hour since, yet you not dressed;
  Nay, not so much as out of bed.
  When all the birds have matins said,
  And sung their thankful hymns, 'tis sin,
  Nay, profanation to keep in,
Whenas a thousand virgins on this day
Spring, sooner than the lark, to fetch in May.

Rise and put on your foliage, and be seen
To come forth like the springtime, fresh and green,
  And sweet as Flora. Take no care
  For jewels for your gown or hair;
  Fear not, the leaves will strew
  Gems in abundance upon you;
Besides, the childhood of the day has kept,
Against you come, some orient pearls unwept;
  Come and receive them while the light
  Hangs on the dew-locks of the night,
  And Titan on the eastern hill
  Retires himself, or else stands still
Till you come forth. Wash, dress, be brief in praying:
Few beads are best when once we go a-maying.

Come, my Corinna, come; and coming, mark
How each field turns a street, each street a park
  Made green and trimmed with trees; see how
  Devotion gives each house a bough
  Or branch; each porch, each door, ere this,
  An ark, a tabernacle is,
Made up of white-thorn neatly interwove,
As if here were those cooler shades of love.
  Can such delights be in the street
  And open fields, and we not see't?
  Come, we'll abroad, and let's obey
  The proclamation made for May,
And sin no more, as we have done, by staying;
But, my Corinna, come, let's go a-maying.

There's not a budding boy or girl this day
But is got up, and gone to bring in May.
  A deal of youth, ere this, is come
  Back, and with white-thorn laden, home.
  Some have despatched their cakes and cream
  Before that we have left to dream;
And some have wept, and wooed, and plighted troth,
And chose their priest, ere we can cast off sloth;

Many a green-gown has been given,
Many a kiss, both odd and even,
Many a glance too has been sent
From out the eye, love's firmament,
Many a jest told of the keys betraying
This night, and locks picked, yet we're not a-maying.

Come, let us go while we are in our prime,
And take the harmless folly of the time.
 We shall grow old apace, and die
 Before we know our liberty.   60
 Our life is short, and our days run
 As fast away as does the sun;
And as a vapor, or a drop of rain
Once lost, can ne'er be found again,
 So when or you or I are made
 A fable, song, or fleeting shade,
 All love, all liking, all delight
 Lies drowned with us in endless night.
Then while time serves, and we are but decaying,
Come, my Corinna, come, let's go a-maying. 70

To Phyllis, to love and live with him

 Live, live with me, and thou shalt see
 The pleasures I'll prepare for thee:
 What sweets the country can afford
 Shall bless thy bed and bless thy board.
 The soft sweet moss shall be thy bed,
 With crawling woodbine overspread,
 By which the silver-shedding streams
 Shall gently melt thee into dreams.
 Thy clothing, next, shall be a gown
 Made of the fleece's purest down.   10
 The tongues of kids shall be thy meat,
 Their milk thy drink; and thou shalt eat
 The paste of filberts for thy bread
 With cream of cowslips butterëd.
 Thy feasting-tables shall be hills
 With daisies spread, and daffodils,
 Where thou shalt sit, and redbreast by,
 For meat, shall give thee melody.
 I'll give thee chains and carcanets
 Of primroses and violets.   20
 A bag and bottle thou shalt have,
 That richly wrought, and this as brave,

So that as either shall express
The wearer's no mean shepherdess.
At shearing-times, and yearly wakes,
When Themilis his pastime makes,
There thou shalt be, and be the wit,
Nay more, the feast, and grace of it.
On holy days when virgins meet
To dance the hays with nimble feet,
Thou shalt come forth, and then appear
The queen of roses for that year,
And having danced, 'bove all the best,
Carry the garland from the rest.
In wicker baskets maids shall bring
To thee, my dearest shepherdling,
The blushing apple, bashful pear,
And shame-faced plum, all simp'ring there.
Walk in the groves, and thou shalt find
The name of Phyllis in the rind
Of every straight and smooth-skin tree,
Where kissing that, I'll twice kiss thee.
To thee a sheep-hook I will send,
Bepranked with ribands, to this end,
This, this alluring hook might be
Less for to catch a sheep, than me.
Thou shalt have possets, wassails fine,
Not made of ale, but spicëd wine,
To make thy maids and self free mirth,
All sitting near the glitt'ring hearth.
Thou shalt have ribands, roses, rings,
Gloves, garters, stockings, shoes, and strings
Of winning colors, that shall move
Others to lust, but me to love.
These, nay and more, thine own shall be,
If thou wilt love and live with me.

To Perilla

Ah my Perilla! dost thou grieve to see
Me, day by day, to steal away from thee?
Age calls me hence, and my gray hairs bid come
And haste away to mine eternal home;
'Twill not be long, Perilla, after this,
That I must give thee the supremest kiss;
Dead when I am, first cast in salt, and bring
Part of the cream from that religious spring,
With which, Perilla, wash my hands and feet;

That done, then wind me in that very sheet   10
Which wrapped thy smooth limbs when thou didst implore
The gods' protection but the night before.
Follow me weeping to my turf, and there
Let fall a primrose, and with it a tear;
Then lastly, let some weekly strewings be
Devoted to the memory of me;
Then shall my ghost not walk about, but keep
Still in the cool and silent shades of sleep.

Upon the loss of his mistresses

I have lost, and lately, these
Many dainty mistresses:
Stately Julia, prime of all;
Sappho next, a principal;
Smooth Anthea, for a skin
White, and heaven-like crystal-
line;
Sweet Electra, and the choice

Myrrha, for the lute and voice;
Next, Corinna, for her wit
And the graceful use of it;   10
With Perilla, all are gone;
Only Herrick's left alone
For to number sorrow by
Their departures hence, and
die.

How roses came red [1]

Roses at first were white,
  Till they could not agree
Whether my Sappho's breast
  Or they more white should be.

But being vanquished quite,
  A blush their cheeks bespread;
Since which, believe the rest,
  The roses first came red.

How roses came red [2]

'Tis said, as Cupid danced among
The gods, he down the nectar
  flung,

Which, on the white rose being
  shed,
Made it forever after red.

How lilies came white

White though ye be, yet lilies,
  know,
From the first ye were not so;
  But I'll tell ye
  What befell ye:
Cupid and his mother lay
In a cloud, while both did play.

He with his pretty finger pressed
The ruby niplet of her breast,
Out of the which the cream of
  light,
  Like to a dew,   10
  Fell down on you,
And made ye white.

How violets came blue

Love on a day, wise poets tell,
  Some time in wrangling spent,
Whether the violets should excel,
  Or she, in sweetest scent.

But Venus having lost the day,
  Poor girls, she fell on you
And beat ye so, as some dare say,
  Her blows did make ye blue.

To daffodils

Fair daffodils, we weep to see
  You haste away so soon;
As yet the early-rising sun
  Has not attained his noon.
    Stay, stay,
  Until the hasting day
    Has run
  But to the even-song;
And, having prayed together, we
  Will go with you along. ¹⁰

We have short time to stay, as you;
  We have as short a spring,
As quick a growth to meet decay,
  As you, or anything.
    We die
  As your hours do, and dry
    Away
  Like to the summer's rain,
Or as the pearls of morning's dew,
  Ne'er to be found again. ²⁰

Discontents in Devon

More discontents I never had
  Since I was born, than here,
Where I have been, and still am
    sad,
  In this dull Devonshire;

Yet justly too I must confess,
  I ne'er invented such
Ennobled numbers for the press,
  Than where I loathed so much.

To Sir Clipsby Crew

Since to th' country first I came,
I have lost my former flame;
And, methinks, I not inherit,
As I did, my ravished spirit.
If I write a verse or two,
'Tis with very much ado,
In regard I want that wine

Which should conjure up a line.
Yet, though now of muse bereft,
I have still the manners left ¹⁰
For to thank you, noble sir,
For those gifts you do confer
Upon him, who only can
Be in prose a grateful man.

An ode to Sir Clipsby Crew

Here we securely live, and
    eat
  The cream of meat;
And keep eternal fires,
By which we sit, and do divine
  As wine
  And rage inspires.

If full we charm, then call upon
    Anacreon
  To grace the frantic thyrse;
And having drunk, we raise a
    shout   ¹⁰
  Throughout
  To praise his verse.

Then cause we Horace to be read,
    Which sung or said,
  A goblet to the brim
Of lyric wine, both swelled and
    crowned,
  A round
  We quaff to him.

Thus, thus we live and spend the
    hours
  In wine and flowers,   ²⁰
  And make the frolic year,
The month, the week, the instant
    day
  To stay
  The longer here.

Come then, brave knight, and see
the cell
Wherein I dwell,
And my enchantments too,
Which love and noble freedom is;
And this
Shall fetter you.   30

Take horse and come, or be so
kind
To send your mind,
Though but in numbers few,
And I shall think I have the heart,
Or part
Of Clipsby Crew.

His content in the country

Here, here I live with what my
board
Can with the smallest cost afford.
Though ne'er so mean the viands
be,
They well content my Prue and
me.
Or pea, or bean, or wort, or beet,
Whatever comes, content makes
sweet.
Here we rejoice because no rent
We pay for our poor tenement,
Wherein we rest, and never fear
The landlord or the usurer;   10

The quarter-day does ne'er affright
Our peaceful slumbers in the night.
We eat our own and batten more
Because we feed on no man's
score;
But pity those whose flanks grow
great,
Swelled with the lard of other's
meat.
We bless our fortunes when we see
Our own beloved privacy,
And like our living, where w'are
known
To very few, or else to none.   20

His grange, or private wealth

Though clock,
To tell how night draws hence,
I've none,
A cock
I have to sing how day draws on.
I have
A maid, my Prue, by good luck
sent
To save
That little fates me gave or lent.
A hen
I keep, which creaking day by day,
Tells when   11
She goes her long white egg to lay.
A goose
I have, which, with a jealous ear,
Lets loose
Her tongue to tell what danger's
near.

A lamb
I keep, tame, with my morsels fed,
Whose dam
An orphan left him, lately dead. 20
A cat
I keep, that plays about my house,
Grown fat
With eating many a miching
mouse.
To these
A Tracy I do keep, whereby
I please
The more my rural privacy.—
Which are
But toys to give my heart some
ease;   30
Where care
None is, slight things do lightly
please.

Content, not cates

'Tis not the food but the content
That makes the table's merriment;
Where trouble serves the board,
    we eat
The platters there as soon as meat.

A little pipkin with a bit
Of mutton or of veal in it,
Set on my table, trouble free,
More than a feast contenteth
    me.

Meat without mirth

Eaten I have, and though I had
    good cheer
I did not sup, because no friends
    were there.

Where mirth and friends are
    absent when we dine
Or sup, there wants the incense
    and the wine.

An epitaph upon a child

Virgins promised when I died
That they would each primrose-
    tide,
Duly, morn and ev'ning come,

And with flowers dress my tomb.
Having promised, pay your
    debts,
Maids, and here strew violets.

Upon a child that died

Here she lies, a pretty bud,
Lately made of flesh and blood,
Who as soon fell fast asleep

As her little eyes did peep.
Give her strewings, but not stir
The earth that lightly covers her.

Upon a maid

Here she lies in bed of spice,
Fair as Eve in Paradise,
For her beauty it was such
Poets could not praise too much.

Virgins come, and in a ring
Her supremest requiem sing;
Then depart, but see ye tread
Lightly, lightly o'er the dead.

To the reverend shade of his religious father

That for seven lusters I did never come
To do the rites to thy religious tomb;
That neither hair was cut or true tears shed
By me, o'er thee, as justments to the dead:
Forgive, forgive me, since I did not know
Whether thy bones had here their rest, or no.
But now 'tis known, behold, behold I bring
Unto thy ghost th' effusèd offering,
And look what smallage, night-shade, cypress, yew,
Unto the shades have been, or now are due,
Here I devote; and something more than so,

10

I come to pay a debt of birth I owe.
Thou gav'st me life, but mortal; for that one
Favor I'll make full satisfaction;
For my life mortal, rise from out thy hearse
And take a life immortal from my verse.

A hymn to the Lares

It was, and still my care is,
To worship ye, the Lares,
With crowns of greenest parsley
And garlic chives not scarcely;
For favors here to warm me,
And not by fire to harm me;
For gladding so my hearth here
With inoffensive mirth here;
That while the wassail bowl here
With North-down ale doth troll here,   10
No syllable doth fall here
To mar the mirth at all here.
For which, O chimney-keepers!
I dare not call ye sweepers,
So long as I am able
To keep a country table,
Great be my fare, or small cheer,
I'll eat and drink up all here.

Lar's portion, or the poet's part

At my homely country-seat
I have there a little wheat,
Which I work to meal, and make
Therewithal a holy-cake,
Part of which I give to Lar,
Part is my peculiar.

To Lar

No more shall I, since I am driven hence,
Devote to thee my grains of frankincense;
No more shall I from mantel-trees hang down,
To honor thee, my little parsley crown;
No more shall I, I fear me, to thee bring
My chives of garlic for an offering;
No more shall I, from henceforth, hear a choir
Of merry crickets by my country fire.
Go where I will, thou, lucky Lar, stay here,
Warm by a glitt'ring chimney all the year.   10

Ceremonies for Christmas

Come, bring with a noise,
My merry merry boys,
The Christmas log to the firing;
While my good dame, she
Bids ye all be free,
And drink to your heart's desiring.
With the last year's brand
Light the new block, and
For good success in his spending,
On your psaltries play,   10
That sweet luck may
Come while the log is a-teending.

Drink now the strong beer,
Cut the white loaf here;
The while the meat is a-shredding

For the rare mince-pie,
And the plums stand by
To fill the paste that's a-kneading.

Another to the maids

Wash your hands, or else the fire
Will not teend to your desire;

Unwashed hands, ye maidens know,
Dead the fire, though ye blow.

Saint Distaff's Day, or the morrow after Twelfth Day

Partly work and partly play
Ye must on Saint Distaff's day;
From the plow soon free your team,
Then come home and fother them.
If the maids a-spinning go,
Burn the flax and fire the tow;
Scorch their plackets, but beware

That ye singe no maiden hair.
Bring in pails of water then,
Let the maids bewash the men. 10
Give Saint Distaff all the right,
Then bid Christmas sport goodnight,
And next morrow, everyone
To his own vocation.

Ceremonies for Candlemas Eve

Down with the rosemary and bays,
Down with the mistletoe;
Instead of holly, now upraise
The greener box, for show.

The holly hitherto did sway;
Let box now domineer
Until the dancing Easter Day,
Or Easter's Eve appear.

Then youthful box which now hath grace
Your houses to renew, 10
Grown old, surrender must his place
Unto the crispèd yew.

When yew is out, then birch comes in,
And many flowers beside,
Both of a fresh and fragrant kin
To honor Whitsuntide.

Green rushes then, and sweetest bents,
With cooler oaken boughs,
Come in for comely ornaments,
To re-adorn the house. 20
Thus times do shift, each thing his turn does hold;
New things succeed, as former things grow old.

Charms

Bring the holy crust of bread,
Lay it underneath the head;

'Tis a certain charm to keep
Hags away while children sleep.

Another

In the morning when ye rise
Wash your hands and cleanse your eyes.
Next be sure ye have a care

To disperse the water far;
For as far as that doth light,
So far keeps the evil sprite.

Another

If ye fear to be affrighted	Carry nothing but a crust;
When ye are, by chance, benighted,	For that holy piece of bread
In your pocket, for a trust,	Charms the danger, and the dread.

Oberon's feast

> *Shapcot, to thee the fairy state*
> *I with discretion, dedicate,*
> *Because thou prizest things that are*
> *Curious and unfamiliar.*
> *Take first the feast; these dishes gone,*
> *We'll see the fairy court anon.*

A little mushroom table spread,
After short prayers, they set on bread;
A moon-parched grain of purest wheat,
With some small glitt'ring grit to eat   10
His choice bits with; then in a trice
They make a feast less great than nice.
But all this while his eye is served,
We must not think his ear was starved,
But that there was in place to stir
His spleen, the chirring grasshopper,
The merry cricket, puling fly,
The piping gnat, for minstrelsy.
And now we must imagine first,
The elves present to quench his thirst   20
A pure seed-pearl of infant dew,
Brought and besweetened in a blue
And pregnant violet; which done,
His kitling eyes begin to run
Quite through the table, where he spies
The horns of papery butterflies,
Of which he eats, and tastes a little
Of that we call the cuckoo's spittle.
A little fuzz-ball pudding stands
By, yet not blessed by his hands;   30
That was too coarse, but then forthwith
He ventures boldly on the pith
Of sugared rush, and eats the sag
And well-bestrutted bee's sweet bag,
Gladding his palate with some store
Of emmets' eggs, what would he more?

But beards of mice, a newt's stewed thigh,
A bloated earwig, and a fly,
With the red-capped worm that's shut
Within the conclave of a nut,   40
Brown as his tooth. A little moth,
Late fattened in a piece of cloth;
With withered cherries, mandrakes' ears,
Moles' eyes; to these, the slain stag's tears,
The unctuous dewlaps of a snail;
The broke-heart of a nightingale
O'ercome in music; with a wine
Ne'er ravished from the flattering vine,
But gently pressed from the soft side
Of the most sweet and dainty bride,   50
Brought in a dainty daisy, which
He fully quaffs up to bewitch
His blood to height; this done, commended
Grace by his priest; the feast is ended.

The hock-cart, or harvest home; to the Right Honorable Mildmay, Earl of Westmorland

Come, sons of summer, by whose toil
We are the lords of wine and oil;
By whose tough labors and rough hands
We rip up first, then reap our lands.
Crowned with the ears of corn, now come,
And to the pipe sing harvest home.
Come forth, my lord, and see the cart
Dressed up with all the country art.
See here a maukin, there a sheet
As spotless pure as it is sweet;   10
The horses, mares, and frisking fillies,
Clad all in linen, white as lilies;
The harvest swains and wenches bound
For joy to see the hock-cart crowned.
About the cart hear how the rout
Of rural younglings raise the shout,
Pressing before, some coming after:
Those with a shout, and these with laughter.
Some bless the cart; some kiss the sheaves;
Some prank them up with oaken leaves;   20
Some cross the fill-horse; some with great
Devotion stroke the home-borne wheat;
While other rustics, less attent
To prayers than to merriment,

Run after with their breeches rent.
Well on, brave boys, to your lord's hearth,
Glitt'ring with fire, where for your mirth
Ye shall see first the large and chief
Foundation of your feast, fat beef,
With upper stories, mutton, veal,   30
And bacon, which makes full the meal;
With sev'ral dishes standing by,
As here a custard, there a pie,
And here all-tempting frumenty.
And for to make the merry cheer,
If smirking wine be wanting here,
There's that which drowns all care, stout beer,
Which freely drink to your lord's health;
Then to the plow, the commonwealth,
Next to your flails, your fans, your fats;   40
Then to the maids with wheaten hats;
To the rough sickle and crook'd scythe,
Drink, frolic boys, till all be blithe.
Feed and grow fat, and as ye eat
Be mindful that the lab'ring neat,
As you, may have their fill of meat.
And know, besides, ye must revoke
The patient ox unto his yoke,
And all go back unto the plow
And harrow, though they're hanged up now.   50
And, you must know, your lord's word's true:
Feed him you must, whose food fills you,
And that this pleasure is like rain,
Not sent ye for to drown your pain
But for to make it spring again.

The wake

Come Anthea, let us two
Go to feast as others do;
Tarts and custards, creams and
    cakes,
Are the junkets still at wakes,
Unto which the tribes resort,
Where the business is the sport;
Morris-dancers thou shalt see,
Marian too in pageantry,
And a mimic to devise
Many grinning properties.   10
Players there will be, and those
Base in action as in clothes;
Yet with strutting they will please
The incurious villages.
Near the dying of the day
There will be a cudgel-play,
Where a coxcomb will be broke
Ere a good word can be spoke;
But the anger ends all here,
Drenched in ale, or drowned in
    beer.   20
Happy rustics, best content
With the cheapest merriment,
And possess no other fear
Than to want the wake next year.

Upon a detracter

I asked thee oft what poets thou hast read,
And lik'st the best; still thou reply'st, The dead.
I shall, ere long, with green turfs covered be;
Then sure thou't like, or thou wilt envy me.

Upon a hoarse singer

Sing me to death, for till thy voice be clear,
'Twill never please the palate of mine ear.

Upon Parson Beanes

Old Parson Beanes hunts six days of the week,
And on the seventh, he has his notes to seek.
Six days he hollows so much breath away
That on the seventh he can nor preach or pray.

To Fortune

Tumble me down, and I will sit
Upon my ruins, smiling yet;
Tear me to tatters, yet I'll be
Patient in my necessity;
Laugh at my scraps of clothes, and shun
Me as a feared infection,
Yet, scarecrow like, I'll walk as one
Neglecting thy derision.

The bad season makes the poet sad

Dull to myself and almost dead to these
My many fresh and fragrant mistresses,
Lost to all music now, since everything
Puts on the semblance here of sorrowing.
Sick is the land to th' heart, and doth endure
More dangerous faintings by her desp'rate cure.
But if that golden age would come again
And Charles here rule, as he before did reign,
If smooth and unperplexed the seasons were
As when the sweet Maria livèd here,
I should delight to have my curls half drowned
In Tyrian dews, and head with roses crowned,
And once more yet, ere I am laid out dead,
Knock at a star with my exalted head.

10

His cavalier

Give me that man that dares bestride
The active sea-horse, and with pride
Through that huge field of waters ride;
Who with his looks too can appease
The ruffling winds and raging seas
In midst of all their outrages.
This, this a virtuous man can do:
Sail against rocks and split them too;
Ay, and a world of pikes pass through.

The difference betwixt kings and subjects

'Twixt kings and subjects there's this mighty odds,
Subjects are taught by men; kings by the gods.

Kings and tyrants

'Twixt kings and tyrants there's this difference known,
Kings seek their subjects' good; tyrants their own.

Slavery

'Tis liberty to serve one lord, but he
Who many serves, serves base servility.

Ill government

Preposterous is that government, and rude,
When kings obey the wilder multitude.

Dean-bourn, a rude river in Devon, by which sometimes he lived

Dean-bourn, farewell; I never look to see
Dean, or thy warty incivility.
Thy rocky bottom that doth tear thy streams
And makes them frantic, ev'n to all extremes,
To my content I never should behold,
Were thy streams silver, or thy rocks all gold.
Rocky thou art, and rocky we discover
Thy men, and rocky are thy ways all over.
O men, O manners, now and ever known
To be a rocky generation!
A people currish, churlish as the seas,
And rude, almost, as rudest savages,
With whom I did, and may re-sojourn, when
Rocks turn to rivers, rivers turn to men.

10

His return to London

From the dull confines of the drooping west
To see the day spring from the pregnant east,
Ravished in spirit, I come, nay more, I fly
To thee, blest place of my nativity!
Thus, thus with hallowed foot I touch the ground
With thousand blessings by thy fortune crowned.
O fruitful genius! that bestowest here
An everlasting plenty, year by year.
O place! O people! Manners framed to please
All nations, customs, kindreds, languages!   10
I am a free-born Roman, suffer then
That I amongst you live a citizen.
London my home is, though by hard fate sent
Into a long and irksome banishment;
Yet since called back, henceforward let me be,
O native country, repossessed by thee!
For rather than I'll to the west return,
I'll beg of thee first here to have mine urn.
Weak I am grown, and must in short time fall;
Give thou my sacred relics burial.   20

To music, to becalm his fever

Charm me asleep, and melt me so
  With thy delicious numbers,
That being ravished, hence I go
  Away in easy slumbers.
    Ease my sick head,
    And make my bed,
Thou power that canst sever
    From me this ill,
    And quickly still,
    Though thou not kill,   10
    My fever.

Thou sweetly canst convert the same
  From a consuming fire
Into a gentle-licking flame,
  And make it thus expire.
    Then make me weep

My pains asleep,
And give me such reposes
  That I, poor I,
  May think thereby   20
  I live and die
    'Mongst roses.

Fall on me like a silent dew,
  Or like those maiden showers
Which by the peep of day do strew
  A baptime o'er the flowers.
    Melt, melt my pains
    With thy soft strains,
That having ease me given,
  With full delight   30
  I leave this light
  And take my flight
    For heaven.

Upon himself

Thou shalt not all die, for while love's fire shines
Upon his altar, men shall read thy lines,
And learn'd musicians shall to honor Herrick's
Fame, and his name, both set and sing his lyrics.

[To his book's end]

To his book's end this last line he'd have placed:
Jocund his muse was, but his life was chaste.

FROM *His Noble Numbers*, 1647, published with *Hesperides*, 1648

His prayer for absolution

For those my unbaptizëd rhymes,
Writ in my wild unhallowed times;
For every sentence, clause, and word,
That's not inlaid with thee, my Lord,
Forgive me, God, and blot each line
Out of my book, that is not thine.
But if, 'mongst all, thou find'st here one
Worthy thy benediction,
That one of all the rest shall be
The glory of my work, and me.   10

His creed

I do believe that die I must,
And be returned from out my dust;
I do believe that when I rise,
Christ I shall see with these same eyes;
I do believe that I must come
With others to the dreadful doom;
I do believe the bad must go
From thence to everlasting woe;
I do believe the good, and I,
Shall live with him eternally;   10
I do believe I shall inherit
Heaven, by Christ's mercies, not my merit;
I do believe the one in three,
And three in perfect unity;
Lastly, that Jesus is a deed
Of gift from God. And here's my creed.

What God is

God is above the sphere of our esteem,
And is the best known not defining him.

The star-song: a carol to the King, sung at Whitehall

The flourish of music; then followed the song

1. Tell us, thou clear and heavenly tongue,
   Where is the babe but lately sprung?
   Lies he the lily-banks among?

2. Or say if this new birth of ours
   Sleeps, laid within some ark of flowers,
   Spangled with dew-light; thou canst clear
   All doubts, and manifest the where.

3. Declare to us, bright star, if we shall seek
   Him in the morning's blushing cheek,
   Or search the beds of spices through   10
   To find him out.

Star. No, this ye need not do,
   But only come and see him rest,
   A princely babe in's mother's breast.

Chor. He's seen, he's seen, why then a round,
   Let's kiss the sweet and holy ground,
   And all rejoice that we have found
   A king before conception crowned.

4. Come then, come then, and let us bring
   Unto our pretty Twelfth-tide king   20
   Each one his several offering;

Chor. And when night comes, we'll give him wassailing;
   And that his treble honors may be seen,
   We'll choose him king, and make his mother queen.

His litany to the Holy Spirit

In the hour of my distress,
When temptations me oppress,
And when I my sins confess,
    Sweet Spirit, comfort me!

When I lie within my bed,
Sick in heart and sick in head,
And with doubts discomforted,
    Sweet Spirit, comfort me!

When the house doth sigh and weep,
And the world is drowned in sleep,   10
Yet mine eyes the watch do keep,
    Sweet Spirit, comfort me!

When the artless doctor sees
No one hope, but of his fees,

And his skill runs on the lees,
     Sweet Spirit, comfort me!

When his potion and his pill
Has or none or little skill,
Meet for nothing but to kill,
     Sweet Spirit, comfort me! 20

When the passing bell doth toll,
And the furies in a shoal
Come to fright a parting soul,
     Sweet Spirit, comfort me!

When the tapers now burn blue,
And the comforters are few,
And that number more than true,
     Sweet Spirit, comfort me!

When the priest his last hath
          prayed,
And I nod to what is said,   30
'Cause my speech is now decayed,
     Sweet Spirit, comfort me!

When, God knows, I'm tossed
          about,
Either with despair, or doubt,
Yet before the glass be out,
     Sweet Spirit, comfort me!

When the tempter me pursu'th
With the sins of all my youth,
And half damns me with untruth,
     Sweet Spirit, comfort me! 40

When the flames and hellish cries
Fright mine ears, and fright mine
          eyes,
And all terrors me surprise,
     Sweet Spirit, comfort me!

When the judgment is revealed,
And that opened which was sealed,
When to thee I have appealed,
     Sweet Spirit, comfort me!

A thanksgiving to God for his house

Lord, thou hast given me a cell
     Wherein to dwell,
A little house, whose humble roof
     Is weather-proof;
Under the spars of which I lie
     Both soft and dry,
Where thou my chamber for to
          ward
     Hast set a guard
Of harmless thoughts, to watch
          and keep
     Me while I sleep.   10
Low is my porch, as is my fate,
     Both void of state;
And yet the threshold of my door
     Is worn by'th' poor,
Who thither come and freely get
     Good words or meat;
Like as my parlor, so my hall
     And kitchen's small;

A little buttery, and therein
     A little bin   20
Which keeps my little loaf of
          bread
     Unchipped, unflead.
Some brittle sticks of thorn or briar
     Make me a fire,
Close by whose living coal I sit,
     And glow like it.
Lord, I confess, too, when I
          dine,
     The pulse is thine,
And all those other bits that be
     There placed by thee:
The worts, the purslain, and the
          mess   31
     Of water-cress,
Which of thy kindness thou hast
          sent;
     And my content

Makes those, and my beloved beet,
To be more sweet.
'Tis thou that crown'st my glitter-
ing hearth
With guiltless mirth;
And giv'st me wassail bowls to
drink,
Spiced to the brink.   40
Lord, 'tis thy plenty-dropping hand
That soils my land,
And giv'st me for my bushel sown
Twice ten for one.
Thou mak'st my teeming hen to
lay

Her egg each day;
Besides my healthful ewes to bear
Me twins each year,
The while the conduits of my kine
Run cream for wine.   50
All these, and better, thou dost send
Me to this end:
That I should render, for my part,
A thankful heart,
Which, fired with incense, I re-
sign
As wholly thine;
But the acceptance, that must be,
My Christ, by thee.

Another grace for a child

Here a little child I stand,
Heaving up my either hand;
Cold as paddocks though they be,

Here I lift them up to thee,
For a benison to fall
On our meat, and on us all.
Amen.

To his conscience

Can I not sin, but thou wilt be
My private protonotary?
Can I not woo thee to pass by
A short and sweet iniquity?
I'll cast a mist and cloud upon
My delicate transgression,
So utter dark as that no eye
Shall see the hugged impiety.
Gifts blind the wise, and bribes do
please
And wind all other witnesses,   10

And wilt not thou with gold be tied
To lay thy pen and ink aside,
That in the murk and tongueless
night
Wanton I may, and thou not
write?
It will not be; and therefore now,
For times to come I'll make this
vow:
From aberrations to live free,
So I'll not fear the judge, or thee.

To his angry God

Through all the night
Thou dost me fright,
And holdst mine eyes from sleep-
ing;
And day by day
My cup can say
My wine is mixed with weeping.

Thou dost my bread
With ashes knead,

Each evening and each morrow;
Mine eye and ear   10
Do see and hear
The coming in of sorrow.

Thy scourge of steel
Ay me! I feel
Upon me beating ever,
While my sick heart
With dismal smart
Is disacquainted never.

Long, long, I'm sure	My gentle God,
This can't endure, 20	To burn the rod,
But in short time 'twill please thee,	Or strike so as to ease me.

The resurrection possible and probable

For each one body that i' th' earth is sown
There's an uprising but of one for one,
But for each grain that in the ground is thrown
Threescore or fourscore spring up thence for one;
So that the wonder is not half so great
Of ours, as is the rising of the wheat.

To God

Pardon me, God, once more I thee entreat,
That I have placed thee in so mean a seat
Where round about thou seest but all things vain,
Uncircumcised, unseasoned, and profane.
But as heaven's public and immortal eye
Looks on the filth, but is not soiled thereby,
So thou, my God, mayst on this impure look,
But take no tincture from my sinful book;
Let but one beam of glory on it shine,
And that will make me, and my work divine.   10

From *Ashmole Ms.* 38

Mr. Robert Herrick, his farewell unto poetry

I have beheld two lovers, in a night
Hatched o'er with moonshine, from their stolen delight
(When this to that, and that to this, had given
A kiss to such a jewel of the heaven;
Or while that each from other's breath did drink
Healths to the rose, the violet, or pink)
Called on the sudden by the jealous mother,
Some stricter mistress or suspicious other,
Urging divorcement, worse than death to these,
By the soon jingling of some sleepy keys,—   10
Part with a hasty kiss, and in that show
How stay they would, yet forced they are to go.
Even such are we, and in our parting do

No otherwise than as those former two
Natures like ours, we who have spent our time
Both from the morning to the evening chime,
Nay, till the bellman of the night had tolled
Past noon of night, yet were the hours not old
Nor dulled with iron sleep, but have outworn
The fresh and fairest flourish of the morn
With flame and rapture, drinking to the odd
Number of nine, which makes us full with god;
And in that mystic frenzy we have hurled,
As with a tempest, nature through the world,
And in a whirlwind twirled her home, aghast
At that which in her ecstasy had passed;
Thus crowned with rosebuds, sack, thou mad'st me fly
Like fire-drakes, yet didst me no harm thereby.
O thou almighty nature, who didst give
True heat wherewith humanity doth live
Beyond its stinted circle, giving food,
White fame, and resurrection to the good,
Soaring them up, 'bove ruin, till the doom,
The general April of the world, doth come,
That makes all equal. Many thousands should,
Wert not for thee, have crumbled into mold,
And with their sereclothes rotted, not to show
Whether the world such spirits had or no,
Whereas by thee, those, and a million since,
Nor fate, nor envy, can their fames convince.
Homer, Musæus, Ovid, Maro, more
Of those godful prophets long before
Hold their eternal fires, and ours of late
Thy mercy helping, shall resist strong fate,
Nor stoop to'th' center, but survive as long
As fame or rumor hath or trump or tongue;
But unto me be only hoarse, since now,
Heaven and my soul bear record of my vow,
I my desires screw from thee, and direct
Them and my thoughts to that sublimed respect
And conscience unto priesthood. 'Tis not need,
The scarecrow unto mankind, that doth breed
Wiser conclusions in me, since I know
I've more to bear my charge than way to go,
Or had I not, I'd stop the spreading itch
Of craving more, so in conceit be rich;
But 'tis the god of nature who intends
And shapes my function for more glorious ends.

20

30

40

50

Guess, so depart; yet stay a while to see
The lines of sorrow that lie drawn in me   60
In speech, in picture; no otherwise than when,
Judgment and death denounced 'gainst guilty men,
Each takes a weeping farewell, racked in mind,
With joys before and pleasures left behind,
Shaking the head, whilst each to each doth mourn,
With thought they go whence they must ne'er return.
So with like looks as once the ministrel
Cast, leading his Eurydice through hell,
I strike thy loves and greedily pursue
Thee with mine eyes or in or out of view.   70
So looked the Grecian orator when sent
From's native country into banishment,
Throwing his eyeballs backward to survey
The smoke of his beloved Attica;
So Tully looked when from the breasts of Rome
The sad soul went, not with his love, but doom,
Shooting his eye-darts 'gainst it to surprise
It, or to draw the city to his eyes.
Such is my parting with thee, and to prove
There was not varnish only in my love,   80
But substance too, receive this pearly tear
Frozen with grief and place it in thine ear,
Then part in name of peace, and softly on
With numerous feet to hoofy Helicon,
And when thou art upon that forkèd hill
Amongst the thrice-three sacred virgins, fill
A full brimmed bowl of fury and of rage
And quaff it to the prophets of our age;
When drunk with rapture curse the blind and lame
Base ballad-mongers, who usurp thy name   90
And foul thy altar; charm some into frogs,
Some to be rats, and others to be hogs,
Into the loathsom'st shapes thou canst devise
To make fools hate them, only by disguise.
Thus with a kiss of warmth and love I part;
Not so but that some relic in my heart
Shall stand forever, though I do address
Chiefly myself to what I must profess.
Know yet, rare soul, when my diviner muse
Shall want a handmaid, as she oft will use,   100
Be ready, thou in me, to wait upon her,
Though as a servant, yet a maid of honor.
    The crown of duty is our duty; well-
    Doing's the fruit of doing well. Farewell.

THOMAS CAREW

The Introduction and Notes are at page 1013

From *Poems*, 1640

The spring

Now that the winter's gone, the earth hath lost
Her snow-white robes, and now no more the frost
Candies the grass, or casts an icy cream
Upon the silver lake or crystal stream;
But the warm sun thaws the benumbëd earth,
And makes it tender; gives a sacred birth
To the dead swallow; wakes in hollow tree
The drowsy cuckoo and the humble-bee.
Now do a choir of chirping minstrels bring
In triumph to the world the youthful spring.   10
The valleys, hills, and woods in rich array
Welcome the coming of the longed-for May.
Now all things smile, only my love doth lour;
Nor hath the scalding noonday sun the power
To melt that marble ice, which still doth hold
Her heart congealed, and makes her pity cold.
The ox, which lately did for shelter fly
Into the stall, doth now securely lie
In open fields; and love no more is made
By the fireside, but in the cooler shade   20
Amyntas now doth with his Chloris sleep
Under a sycamore, and all things keep
Time with the season; only she doth carry
June in her eyes, in her heart January.

Red and white roses

Read in these roses the sad story
Of my hard fate and your own glory.
    In the white you may discover
    The paleness of a fainting lover;
In the red the flames still feeding
On my heart, with fresh wounds bleeding.
    The white will tell you how I languish,
    And the red express my anguish;
The white my innocence displaying,
The red my martyrdom betraying.   10
    The frowns that on your brow resided

Have those roses thus divided.
Oh, let your smiles but clear the weather,
And then they both shall grow together.

Boldness in love

Mark how the bashful morn in vain
Courts the amorous marigold
With sighing blasts and weeping rain,
Yet she refuses to unfold;
But when the planet of the day
Approacheth with his powerful ray,
Then she spreads, then she receives
His warmer beams into her virgin leaves.
So shalt thou thrive in love, fond boy:
If thy tears and sighs discover   10
Thy grief, thou never shalt enjoy
The just reward of a bold lover;
But when with moving accents thou
Shalt constant faith and service vow,
Thy Celia shall receive those charms
With open ears, and with unfolded arms.

To a lady that desired I would love her

Now you have freely given me leave to love,
            What will you do?
Shall I your mirth or passion move
            When I begin to woo?
Will you torment, or scorn, or love me too?

Each petty beauty can disdain, and I,
            Spite of your hate,
Without your leave can see, and die;
            Dispense a nobler fate:
'Tis easy to destroy, you may create.   10

Then give me leave to love, and love me too;
            Not with design
To raise, as love's curst rebels do
            When puling poets whine,
Fame to their beauty from their blubbered eyne.

Grief is a puddle, and reflects not clear
            Your beauty's rays;
Joys are pure streams, your eyes appear

Sullen in sadder lays;
In cheerful numbers they shine bright with praise,   20

Which shall not mention, to express you fair,
      Wounds, flames, and darts,
Storms in your brow, nets in your hair,
      Suborning all your parts,
Or to betray, or torture captive hearts.

I'll make your eyes like morning suns appear,
      As mild and fair,
Your brow as crystal, smooth and clear,
      And your dishevelled hair
Shall flow like a calm region of the air.   30

Rich nature's store, which is the poet's treasure,
      I'll spend to dress
Your beauties, if your mine of pleasure
      In equal thankfulness
You but unlock, so we each other bless.

Celia singing

You that think love can convey
    No other way
But through the eyes into the heart
    His fatal dart,
Close up those casements, and but
    hear
    This siren sing;
    And on the wing
Of her sweet voice it shall appear
That love can enter at the ear.

Then unveil your eyes, behold   10
    The curious mould
Where that voice dwells; and as
    we know
    When the cocks crow,
    We freely may
    Gaze on the day;
So may you, when the music's
    done,
Awake and see the rising sun.

A song

Ask me no more where Jove bestows,
When June is past, the fading rose;
For in your beauty's orient deep
These flowers, as in their causes, sleep.

Ask me no more whither doth stray
The golden atoms of the day;
For in pure love heaven did prepare
Those powders to enrich your hair.

Ask me no more whither doth haste
The nightingale when May is past;   10
For in your sweet dividing throat
She winters, and keeps warm her note.

Ask me no more where those stars light
That downwards fall in dead of night;
For in your eyes they sit, and there
Fixëd become as in their sphere.

Ask me no more if east or west
The phœnix builds her spicy nest;
For unto you at last she flies,
And in your fragrant bosom dies.   20

Eternity of love protested

How ill doth he deserve a lover's name,
     Whose pale weak flame
       Cannot retain
His heat in spite of absence or disdain,
But doth at once, like paper set on fire,
     Burn and expire;
True love can never change his seat,
Nor did he ever love that could retreat.

That noble flame, which my breast keeps alive,
     Shall still survive   10
       When my soul's fled;
Nor shall my love die when my body's dead,
That shall wait on me to the lower shade,
     And never fade;
My very ashes in their urn
Shall like a hallowed lamp forever burn.

To my rival

Hence, vain intruder, haste away!
     Wash not with thy unhallowed brine
     The footsteps of my Celia's shrine;
Nor on her purer altars lay
Thy empty words, accents that may
     Some looser dame to love incline;
     She must have offerings more divine:
Such pearly drops as youthful May
Scatters before the rising day;

Such smooth soft language, as each line   10
Might stroke an angry god, or stay
    Jove's thunder, make the hearers pine
With envy; do this, thou shalt be
Servant to her, rival with me.

Mediocrity in love rejected

Give me more love or more disdain:
    The torrid or the frozen zone
Bring equal ease unto my pain,
    The temperate affords me none;
Either extreme of love or hate
Is sweeter than a calm estate.

Give me a storm; if it be love,
    Like Danaë in that golden shower,
I swim in pleasure; if it prove
    Disdain, that torrent will devour   10
My vulture-hopes; and he's possessed
Of heaven, that's but from hell released.
    Then crown my joys or cure my pain;
    Give me more love or more disdain.

A deposition from love

I was foretold your rebel sex
    Nor love nor pity knew,
And with what scorn you use to vex
    Poor hearts that humbly sue.
Yet I believed, to crown our pain,
    Could we the fortress win,
The happy lover sure should gain
    A paradise within;
I thought love's plagues like dragons sate
Only to fright us at the gate.   10

But I did enter and enjoy
    What happy lovers prove;
For I could kiss, and sport, and toy,
    And taste those sweets of love,
Which, had they but a lasting state,
    Or if in Celia's breast
The force of love might not abate,
    Jove were too mean a guest.
But now her breach of faith far more
Afflicts, than did her scorn before.   20

Hard fate! to have been once possessed,
    As victor, of a heart,
Achieved with labor and unrest,
    And then forced to depart.
If the stout foe will not resign
    When I besiege a town,
I lose but what was never mine;
    But he that is cast down
From enjoyed beauty, feels a woe
Only deposëd kings can know.   30

Ingrateful beauty threatened

Know, Celia, since thou art so proud,
    'Twas I that gave thee thy renown;
Thou hadst in the forgotten crowd
    Of common beauties lived unknown,
Had not my verse exhaled thy name,
And with it imped the wings of fame.

That killing power is none of thine,
    I gave it to thy voice and eyes;
Thy sweets, thy graces, all are mine;
    Thou art my star, shin'st in my skies;   10
Then dart not from thy borrowed sphere
Lightning on him that fixed thee there.

Tempt me with such affrights no more,
    Lest what I made I uncreate;
Let fools thy mystic forms adore,
    I'll know thee in thy mortal state;
Wise poets that wrapped truth in tales,
Knew her themselves through all her veils.

To my inconstant mistress

When thou, poor excommunicate
    From all the joys of love, shalt see
The full reward and glorious fate
    Which my strong faith shall purchase me,
Then curse thine own inconstancy.

A fairer hand than thine shall cure
    That heart which thy false oaths did wound;
And to my soul, a soul more pure
    Than thine shall by love's hand be bound,
And both with equal glory crowned.   10

Then shalt thou weep, entreat, complain
  To love, as I did once to thee;
When all thy tears shall be as vain
  As mine were then, for thou shalt be
Damned for thy false apostasy.

Disdain returned

He that loves a rosy cheek,
  Or a coral lip admires,
Or from star-like eyes doth seek
  Fuel to maintain his fires;
As old time makes these decay,
So his flames must waste away.

But a smooth and steadfast mind,
  Gentle thoughts and calm de-
    sires,
Hearts with equal love combined,
  Kindle never-dying fires.   10

Where these are not, I despise
Lovely cheeks, or lips, or eyes.

No tears, Celia, now shall win
  My resolved heart to return;
I have searched thy soul within,
  And find nought but pride and
    scorn;
I have learned thy arts, and now
Can disdain as much as thou.
  Some power, in my revenge,
    convey
That love to her I cast away. 20

Good counsel to a young maid

Gaze not on thy beauty's pride,
Tender maid, in the false tide
That from lovers' eyes doth slide.

Let thy faithful crystal show
How thy colors come and go;
Beauty takes a foil from woe.

Love, that in those smooth streams
  lies,
Under pity's fair disguise,
Will thy melting heart surprise.

Nets of passion's finest thread, 10
Snaring poems, will be spread,
All to catch thy maidenhead.

Then beware, for those that cure
Love's disease, themselves endure,
For reward, a calenture.

Rather let the lover pine,
Than his pale cheek should assign
A perpetual blush to thine.

Upon Master W. Montague his return from travel

Lead the black bull to slaughter with the boar
And lamb, then purple with their mingled gore
The ocean's curlèd brow, that so we may
The sea-gods for their careful waftage pay;
Send grateful incense up in pious smoke
To those mild spirits that cast a curbing yoke
Upon the stubborn winds that calmly blew
To the wished shore our longed-for Montague.
Then whilst the aromatic odors burn

In honor of their darling's safe return,   10
The Muses' choir shall thus with voice and hand
Bless the fair gale that drove his ship to land:
    Sweetly breathing vernal air,
    That with kind warmth dost repair
    Winter's ruins; from whose breast
    All the gums and spice of th' East
    Borrow their perfumes; whose eye
    Gilds the morn and clears the sky;
    Whose dishevelled tresses shed
    Pearls upon the violet bed;   20
    On whose brow, with calm smiles dressed,
    The halcyon sits and builds her nest;
    Beauty, youth, and endless spring
    Dwell upon thy rosy wing.
    Thou, if stormy Boreas throws
    Down whole forests when he blows,
    With a pregnant flowery birth
    Canst refresh the teeming earth;
    If he nip the early bud,
    If he blast what's fair or good,   30
    If he scatter our choice flowers,
    If he shake our hills or bowers,
    If his rude breath threaten us,
    Thou canst stroke great Æolus,
    And from him the grace obtain
    To bind him in an iron chain.
Thus, whilst you deal your body 'mongst your friends,
And fill their circling arms, my glad soul sends
This her embrace. Thus we of Delphos greet:
As laymen clasp their hands, we join our feet.   40

Epitaph on the Lady Mary Villiers

    This little vault, this narrow room,
    Of love and beauty is the tomb;
    The dawning beam that gan to clear
    Our clouded sky, lies darkened here,
    Forever set to us, by death
    Sent to inflame the world beneath.
    'Twas but a bud, yet did contain
    More sweetness than shall spring again;
    A budding star that might have grown
    Into a sun, when it had blown.   10
    This hopeful beauty did create
    New life in love's declining state;

But now his empire ends, and we
From fire and wounding darts are free;
His brand, his bow, let no man fear,—
The flames, the arrows, all lie here.

Maria Wentworth

And here the precious dust is laid,
Whose purely tempered clay was
made
So fine that it the guest betrayed.

Else the soul grew so fast within
It broke the outward shell of sin,
And so was hatched a cherubin.

In height it soared to God above;
In depth it did to knowledge move,
And spread in breadth to general
love.

Before, a pious duty shined   10
To parents, courtesy behind;
On either side an equal mind,

Good to the poor, to kindred
dear,
To servants kind, to friendship
clear,
To nothing but herself severe.

So, though a virgin, yet a bride
To every grace, she justified
A chaste polygamy, and died.

Learn from hence, reader, what
small trust
We owe this world, where virtue
must,   20
Frail as our flesh, crumble to dust.

An elegy upon the death of Doctor Donne, Dean of Paul's

Can we not force from widowed poetry,
Now thou art dead, great Donne, one elegy
To crown thy hearse? Why yet did we not trust,
Though with unkneaded dough-baked prose, thy dust,
Such as th' unscissored lect'rer from the flower
Of fading rhet'ric, short-lived as his hour,
Dry as the sand that measures it, might lay
Upon the ashes, on the funeral day?
Have we nor tune nor voice? Didst thou dispense
Through all our language both the words and sense?   10
'Tis a sad truth. The pulpit may her plain
And sober Christian precepts still retain;
Doctrines it may, and wholesome uses, frame,
Grave homilies and lectures, but the flame
Of thy brave soul, that shot such heat and light
As burnt our earth and made our darkness bright,
Committed holy rapes upon the will,
Did through the eye the melting heart distil,
And the deep knowledge of dark truths so teach
As sense might judge where fancy could not reach,   20

Must be desired forever. So the fire
That fills with spirit and heat the Delphic choir,
Which, kindled first by thy Promethean breath,
Glowed here a while, lies quenched now in thy death.
The Muses' garden, with pedantic weeds
O'erspread, was purged by thee; the lazy seeds
Of servile imitation thrown away,
And fresh invention planted; thou didst pay
The debts of our penurious bankrupt age;
Licentious thefts, that make poetic rage   30
A mimic fury, when our souls must be
Possessed, or with Anacreon's ecstasy,
Or Pindar's, not their own; the subtle cheat
Of sly exchanges, and the juggling feat
Of two-edged words, or whatsoever wrong
By ours was done the Greek or Latin tongue,
Thou hast redeemed, and opened us a mine
Of rich and pregnant fancy; drawn a line
Of masculine expression, which had good
Old Orpheus seen, or all the ancient brood   40
Our superstitious fools admire, and hold
Their lead more precious than thy burnished gold,
Thou hadst been their exchequer, and no more
They each in other's dung had searched for ore.
Thou shalt yield no precedence, but of time
And the blind fate of language, whose tuned chime
More charms the outward sense; yet thou mayst claim
From so great disadvantage greater fame,
Since to the awe of thy imperious wit
Our troublesome language bends, made only fit   50
With her tough thick-ribbed hoops to gird about
Thy giant fancy, which had proved too stout
For their soft melting phrases. As in time
They had the start, so did they cull the prime
Buds of invention many a hundred year,
And left the rifled fields, besides the fear
To touch their harvest; yet from those bare lands
Of what was only thine, thy only hands,
And that their smallest work, have gleanëd more
Than all those times and tongues could reap before.   60
    But thou art gone, and thy strict laws will be
Too hard for libertines in poetry;
They will recall the goodly exiled train
Of gods and goddesses, which in thy just reign
Was banished nobler poems; now with these,
The silenced tales i' th' *Metamorphoses*,

Shall stuff their lines, and swell the windy page,
Till verse, refined by thee in this last age,
Turn ballad-rhyme, or those old idols be
Adored again with new apostasy. 70
    Oh, pardon me, that break with untuned verse
The reverend silence that attends thy hearse,
Whose solemn awful murmurs were to thee,
More than these rude lines, a loud elegy,
That did proclaim in a dumb eloquence
The death of all the arts; whose influence,
Grown feeble, in these panting numbers lies,
Gasping short-winded accents, and so dies.
So doth the swiftly turning wheel not stand
In th' instant we withdraw the moving hand, 80
But some short time retain a faint weak course,
By virtue of the first impulsive force;
And so, whilst I cast on thy funeral pile
Thy crown of bays, oh, let it crack awhile,
And spit disdain, till the devouring flashes
Suck all the moisture up, then turn to ashes.
    I will not draw the envy to engross
All thy perfections, or weep all the loss;
Those are too numerous for one elegy,
And this too great to be expressed by me. 90
Let others carve the rest; it shall suffice
I on thy grave this epitaph incise:
    Here lies a king that ruled as he thought fit
    The universal monarchy of wit;
    Here lies two flamens, and both those the best,
    Apollo's first, at last the true God's priest.

To Ben Jonson

Upon occasion of his ode of defiance annexed to his play of The New Inn

'Tis true, dear Ben, thy just chastising hand
Hath fixed upon the sotted age a brand,
To their swollen pride and empty scribbling due;
It can nor judge nor write, and yet 'tis true
Thy comic muse, from the exalted line
Touched by thy *Alchemist*, doth since decline
From that her zenith, and foretells a red
And blushing evening, when she goes to bed;
Yet such as shall outshine the glimmering light
With which all stars shall gild the following night. 10

Nor think it much, since all thy eaglets may
Endure the sunny trial, if we say
This hath the stronger wing, or that doth shine
Tricked up in fairer plumes, since all are thine.
Who hath his flock of cackling geese compared
With thy tuned choir of swans? or else who dared
To call thy births deformed? But if thou bind
By city-custom, or by gavelkind,
In equal shares thy love on all thy race,
We may distinguish of their sex and place;   20
Though one hand form them, and though one brain strike
Souls into all, they are not all alike.
Why should the follies, then, of this dull age
Draw from thy pen such an immodest rage
As seems to blast thy else immortal bays,
When thine own tongue proclaims thy itch of praise?
Such thirst will argue drought. No, let be hurled
Upon thy works by the detracting world
What malice can suggest; let the rout say,
The running sands, that ere thou make a play   30
Count the slow minutes, might a Goodwin frame
To swallow, when th' hast done, thy shipwrecked name.
Let them the dear expense of oil upbraid,
Sucked by thy watchful lamp, that hath betrayed
To theft the blood of martyred authors, spilt
Into thy ink, whilst thou growest pale with guilt.
Repine not at the taper's thrifty waste,
That sleeks thy terser poems; nor is haste
Praise, but excuse; and if thou overcome
A knotty writer, bring the booty home;   40
Nor think it theft if the rich spoils so torn
From conquered authors be as trophies worn.
Let others glut on the extorted praise
Of vulgar breath; trust thou to after-days.
Thy labored works shall live when time devours
Th' abortive offspring of their hasty hours.
Thou art not of their rank, the quarrel lies
Within thine own verge; then let this suffice,
The wiser world doth greater thee confess
Than all men else, than thyself only less.   50

In answer of an elegiacal letter, upon the death of the King of Sweden, from Aurelian Townshend, inviting me to write on that subject

Why dost thou sound, my dear Aurelian,
In so shrill accents from thy Barbican

A loud alarum to my drowsy eyes,
Bidding them wake in tears and elegies
For mighty Sweden's fall? Alas! how may
My lyric feet, that of the smooth soft way
Of love and beauty only know the tread,
In dancing paces celebrate the dead
Victorious king, or his majestic hearse
Profane with th' humble touch of their low verse? 10
Virgil, nor Lucan, no, nor Tasso more
Than both, not Donne, worth all that went before,
With the united labor of their wit,
Could a just poem to this subject fit.
His actions were too mighty to be raised
Higher by verse; let him in prose be praised,
In modest faithful story, which his deeds
Shall turn to poems. When the next age reads
Of Frankfort, Leipzig, Würzbúrg, of the Rhine,
The Lech, the Danube, Tilly, Wallenstein, 20
Bavaria, Pappenheim, Lützen-field, where he
Gained after death a posthume victory,
They'll think his acts things rather feigned than done,
Like our romances of the Knight o' th' Sun.
Leave we him, then, to the grave chronicler,
Who, though to annals he cannot refer
His too brief story, yet his journals may
Stand by the Cæsars' years, and every day
Cut into minutes, each shall more contain
Of great designment than an emperor's reign. 30
And, since 'twas but his churchyard, let him have
For his own ashes now no narrower grave
Than the whole German continent's vast womb,
Whilst all her cities do but make his tomb.
Let us to supreme providence commit
The fate of monarchs, which first thought it fit
To rend the empire from the Austrian grasp;
And next from Sweden's, even when he did clasp
Within his dying arms the sovereignty
Of all those provinces, that men might see 40
The divine wisdom would not leave that land
Subject to any one king's sole command.
Then let the Germans fear if Cæsar shall,
Or the united princes, rise and fall;
But let us, that in myrtle bowers sit
Under secure shades, use the benefit
Of peace and plenty, which the blessed hand
Of our good king gives this obdurate land;

Let us of revels sing, and let thy breath,
Which filled fame's trumpet with Gustavus' death,   50
Blowing his name to heaven, gently inspire
Thy past'ral pipe, till all our swains admire
Thy song and subject, whilst they both comprise
The beauties of the *Shepherd's Paradise.*
For who like thee (whose loose discourse is far
More neat and polished than our poems are,
Whose very gait's more graceful than our dance)
In sweetly flowing numbers may advance
The glorious night when, not to act foul rapes
Like birds or beasts, but in their angel-shapes   60
A troop of deities came down to guide
Our steerless barks in passion's swelling tide
By virtue's card, and brought us from above
A pattern of their own celestial love?

    These harmless pastimes let my Townshend sing
To rural tunes; not that thy muse wants wing
To soar a loftier pitch, for she hath made
A noble flight, and placed th' heroic shade
Above the reach of our faint flagging rhyme,
But these are subjects proper to our clime;   70
Tourneys, masks, theaters, better become
Our halcyon days. What though the German drum
Bellow for freedom and revenge, the noise
Concerns not us, nor should divert our joys;
Nor ought the thunder of their carabines
Drown the sweet airs of our tuned violins.
Believe me, friend, if their prevailing powers
Gain them a calm security like ours,
They'll hang their arms upon the olive bough,
And dance and revel then, as we do now.   80

To my worthy friend, Master George Sandys
On his translation of the Psalms

I press not to the choir, nor dare I greet
The holy place with my unhallowed feet;
My unwashed muse pollutes not things divine,
Nor mingles her profaner notes with thine;
Here humbly at the porch she stays,
And with glad ears sucks in thy sacred lays.
So devout penitents of old were wont,
Some without door and some beneath the font,

To stand and hear the Church's liturgies,
Yet not assist the solemn exercise.   10
Sufficeth her, that she a lay-place gain,
To trim thy vestments, or but bear thy train;
Though not in tune or wing she reach thy lark,
Her lyric feet may dance before the Ark.
Who knows but that her wand'ring eyes that run
Now hunting glow-worms, may adore the sun?
A pure flame may, shot by almighty power
Into her breast, the earthy flame devour.
My eyes in penitential dew may steep
That brine, which they for sensual love did weep.   20
So, though 'gainst nature's course, fire may be quenched
With fire, and water be with water drenched,
Perhaps my restless soul, tired with pursuit
Of mortal beauty, seeking without fruit
Contentment there, which hath not, when enjoyed,
Quenched all her thirst, nor satisfied though cloyed,
Weary of her vain search below, above
In the first fair may find th' immortal love.
Prompted by thy example then, no more
In molds of clay will I my God adore;   30
But tear those idols from my heart, and write
What his blest sp'rit, not fond love, shall indite.
Then I no more shall court the verdant bay,
But the dry leafless trunk on Golgotha;
And rather strive to gain from thence one thorn,
Than all the flourishing wreaths by laureates worn.

THOMAS RANDOLPH

The Introduction and Notes are at page 1015

FROM *Poems, with The Muses' Looking-glass and Amyntas,* 1638

*A gratulatory to Mr. Ben Jonson for his adopting
of him to be his son*

I was not born to Helicon, nor dare
Presume to think myself a Muse's heir.
I have no title to Parnassus hill,
Nor any acre of it by the will
Of a dead ancestor, nor could I be
Aught but a tenant unto poetry.
But thy adoption quits me of all fear,
And makes me challenge a child's portion there.

I am akin to heroes, being thine,
And part of my alliance is divine.   10
Orpheus, Musæus, Homer too, beside
Thy brothers by the Roman mother's side,
As Ovid, Virgil, and the Latin lyre
That is so like thee, Horace,—the whole choir
Of poets are by thy adoption all
My uncles; thou hast given me power to call
Phœbus himself my grandsire; by this grant
Each sister of the Nine is made my aunt.
Go, you that reckon from a large descent
Your lineal honors, and are well content   20
To glory in the age of your great name,
Though on a herald's faith you build the same,
I do not envy you, nor think you blest
Though you may bear a gorgon on your crest
By direct line from Perseus; I will boast
No farther than my father; that's the most
I can, or should be proud of, and I were
Unworthy his adoption if that here
I should be dully modest; boast I must,
Being son of his adoption, not his lust.   30
And to say truth, that which is best in me
May call you father, 'twas begot by thee.
Have I a spark of that celestial flame
Within me, I confess I stole the same,
Prometheus-like, from thee; and may I feed
His vulture when I dare deny the deed.
Many more moons thou hast that shine by night,
All bankrupts, were 't not for a borrowed light,
Yet can forswear it; I the debt confess
And think my reputation ne'er the less.   40
For father, let me be resolved by you:
Is 't a disparagement from rich Peru
To ravish gold, or theft, for wealthy ore
To ransack Tagus', or Pactolus' shore?
Or does he wrong Alcinous, that for want
Doth take from him a sprig or two to plant
A lesser orchard? Sure it cannot be;
Nor is it theft to steal some flames from thee.
Grant this, and I'll cry, Guilty, as I am,
And pay a filial reverence to thy name.   50
For when my muse upon obedient knees
Asks not a father's blessing, let her leese
The fame of this adoption; 'tis a curse
I wish her, 'cause I cannot think a worse.

And here, as piety bids me, I entreat
Phœbus to lend thee some of his own heat
To cure thy palsy, else I will complain
He has no skill in herbs; poets in vain
Make him the god of physic. 'Twere his praise
To make thee as immortal as thy bays,   60
As his own Daphne; 'twere a shame to see
The god not love his priest more than his tree.
  But if heaven take thee, envying us thy lyre,
  'Tis to pen anthems for an angels' choir.

An ode to Mr. Anthony Stafford to hasten him into the country

   Come, spur away,
I have no patience for a longer stay,
   But must go down
And leave the chargeable noise of this great town.
   I will the country see,
   Where old simplicity
    Though hid in grey
    Doth look more gay
Than foppery in plush and scarlet clad.
   Farewell, you city wits that are   10
   Almost at civil war;
'Tis time that I grow wise, when all the world grows mad.

   More of my days
I will not spend to gain an idiot's praise,
   Or to make sport
For some slight puny of the Inns of Court.
   Then, worthy Stafford, say
   How shall we spend the day;
    With what delights
    Shorten the nights?   20
When from this tumult we are got secure
   Where mirth with all her freedom goes,
   Yet shall no finger lose,
Where every word is thought, and every thought is pure.

   There from the tree
We'll cherries pluck, and pick the strawberry.
   And every day
Go see the wholesome country girls make hay,
   Whose brown hath lovelier grace

Than any painted face   30
That I do know
Hyde Park can show;
Where I had rather gain a kiss than meet
(Though some of them in greater state
Might court my love with plate)
The beauties of the Cheap, and wives of Lombard street.

But think upon
Some other pleasures, these to me are none;
Why do I prate
Of women, that are things against my fate?   40
I never mean to wed
That torture to my bed;
My muse is she
My love shall be.
Let clowns get wealth and heirs; when I am gone,
And the great bugbear, grisly death,
Shall take this idle breath,
If I a poem leave, that poem is my son.

Of this, no more;
We'll rather taste the bright Pomona's store,—   50
No fruit shall 'scape
Our palates, from the damson to the grape.
Then full we'll seek a shade,
And hear what music's made;
How Philomel
Her tale doth tell,
And how the other birds do fill the choir;
The thrush and blackbird lend their throats,
Warbling melodious notes;
We will all sports enjoy, which others but desire.   60

Ours is the sky,
Where at what fowl we please our hawk shall fly;
Nor will we spare
To hunt the crafty fox or timorous hare;
But let our hounds run loose
In any ground they'll choose,
The buck shall fall,
The stag and all;
Our pleasures must from their own warrants be,
For to my muse, if not to me,   70
I'm sure all game is free;
Heaven, earth, are all but parts of her great royalty.

And when we mean
To taste of Bacchus' blessings now and then,
And drink by stealth
A cup or two to noble Berkeley's health,
I'll take my pipe and try
The Phrygian melody,
Which he that hears
Lets through his ears   80
A madness to distemper all the brain.
Then I another pipe will take
And Doric music make,
To civilize with graver notes our wits again.

Upon his picture

When age hath made me what I am not now,
And every wrinkle tells me where the plow
Of time hath furrowed, when an ice shall flow
Through every vein, and all my head wear snow;
When death displays his coldness in my cheek,
And I myself in my own picture seek,
Not finding what I am, but what I was,
In doubt which to believe, this or my glass:
Yet though I alter, this remains the same
As it was drawn, retains the primitive frame   10
And first complexion; here will still be seen
Blood on the cheek, and down upon the chin;
Here the smooth brow will stay, the lively eye,
The ruddy lip, and hair of youthful dye.
Behold what frailty we in man may see,
Whose shadow is less given to change than he.

On the death of a nightingale

Go, solitary wood, and henceforth be
Acquainted with no other harmony
Than the pies' chattering, or the shrieking note
Of boding owls, and fatal raven's throat.
Thy sweetest chanter's dead, that warbled forth
Lays that might tempests calm, and still the north,
And call down angels from their glorious sphere
To hear her songs, and learn new anthems there.
That soul is fled and to Elysium gone;
Thou a poor desert left; go then and run,   10
Beg there to stand a grove, and if she please

To sing again beneath thy shadowy trees,
The souls of happy lovers crowned with blisses
Shall flock about thee, and keep time with kisses.

FROM *Aristippus, or the Jovial Philosopher*, 1630

[*Slaves are they*]

Slaves are they that heap up mountains,
    Still desiring more and more;
Still let's carouse in Bacchus' fountains,
    Never dreaming to be poor.

Give us then a cup of liquor,
    Fill it up unto the brim;
For then methinks my wits grow quicker,
    When my brains in liquor swim.

WILLIAM CARTWRIGHT

The Introduction and Notes are at page 1015

FROM *Comedies, Tragi-comedies, with other poems*, 1651

A valediction

Bid me not go where neither suns nor showers
    Do make or cherish flowers,
Where discontented things in sadness lie,
    And nature grieves as I;
When I am parted from those eyes
From which my better day doth rise,
    Though some propitious power
    Should plant me in a bower,
Where amongst happy lovers I might see
    How showers and sunbeams bring   10
    One everlasting spring,
Nor would those fall, nor these shine forth to me;
    Nature herself to him is lost
    Who loseth her he honors most.
Then fairest to my parting view display
    Your graces all in one full day,
Whose blessed shapes I'll snatch and keep till when
    I do return and view again;
So by this art fancy shall fortune cross,
And lovers live by thinking on their loss.   20

To Chloe, who wished herself young enough for me

Chloe, why wish you that your years
   Would backwards run till they meet mine,
That perfect likeness, which endears
   Things unto things, might us combine?
Our ages so in date agree
That twins do differ more than we.

There are two births: the one when light
   First strikes the new awakened sense;
The other when two souls unite,
   And we must count our life from thence.   10
When you loved me and I loved you,
Then both of us were born anew.

Love then to us did new souls give,
   And in those souls did plant new powers;
Since when another life we live,
   The breath we breathe is his, not ours;
Love makes those young whom age doth chill,
And whom he finds young, keeps young still.

Love, like that angel that shall call
   Our bodies from the silent grave,   20
Unto one age doth raise us all,
   None too much, none too little have;
Nay, that the difference may be none,
He makes two not alike, but one.

And now since you and I are such,
   Tell me what's yours and what is mine?
Our eyes, our ears, our taste, smell, touch,
   Do, like our souls, in one combine;
So by this, I as well may be
Too old for you, as you for me.   30

No Platonic love

Tell me no more of minds embracing minds,
   And hearts exchanged for hearts;
That spirits spirits meet, as winds do winds,
   And mix their subtlest parts;
That two unbodied essences may kiss,
And then like angels, twist and feel one bliss.

I was that silly thing that once was wrought
   To practise this thin love;
I climbed from sex to soul, from soul to thought;
   But thinking there to move, .   10
Headlong I rolled from thought to soul, and then
From soul I lighted at the sex again.

As some strict down-looked men pretend to fast
   Who yet in closets eat,
So lovers who profess they spirits taste,
   Feed yet on grosser meat;
I know they boast they souls to souls convey,
Howe'er they meet, the body is the way.

Come, I will undeceive thee: they that tread
   Those vain aerial ways   20
Are like young heirs and alchemists, misled
   To waste their wealth and days;
For searching thus to be forever rich,
They only find a med'cine for the itch.

Love but one

See these two little brooks that slowly creep
   In snaky windings through the plains;
I knew them once one river, swift and deep,
   Blessing and blest by poets' strains.

Then, touched with awe, we thought some god did pour
   Those floods from out his sacred jar,
Transforming every weed unto a flower,
   And every flower into a star.

But since it broke itself, and double glides, .
   The naked banks no dress have worn,   10
And yon dry barren mountain now derides
   These valleys which lost glories mourn.

O Chloris! think how this presents thy love,
   Which when it ran but in one stream,
We happy shepherds thence did thrive and prove,
   And thou wast mine and all men's theme.

But since 't hath been imparted to one more,
   And in two streams doth weakly creep,
Our common muse is thence grown low and poor,
   And mine as lean as these my sheep.   20

But think withal what honor thou hast lost,
  Which we did to thy full stream pay,
Whiles now that swain that swears he loves thee most,
  Slakes but his thirst, and goes away!

Oh, in what narrow ways our minds must move!
We may not hate, nor yet diffuse our love.

[*Upon the dramatic poems of Mr. John Fletcher*]

Fletcher, though some call it thy fault that wit
So overflowed thy scenes that ere 'twas fit
To come upon the stage Beaumont was fain
To bid thee be more dull—that's write again
And bate some of thy fire, which from thee came
In a clear, bright, full, but too large a flame;
And after all, finding thy genius such
That, blunted and allayed, 'twas yet too much,
Added his sober sponge, and did contract
Thy plenty to less wit, to make 't exact;   10
Yet we through his corrections could see
Much treasure in thy superfluity,
Which was so filed away as when we do
Cut jewels, that that's lost is jewel too;
Or as men use to wash gold, which we know
By losing makes the stream thence wealthy grow.
They who do on thy works severely sit,
And call thy store the over-births of wit,
Say thy miscarriages were rare, and when
Thou wert superfluous, that thy fruitful pen 20
Had no fault but abundance, which did lay
Out in one scene what might well serve a play;
And hence do grant that what they call excess
Was to be reckoned as thy happiness,
From whom wit issued in a full spring tide:
Much did enrich the stage, much flowed beside.
For that thou couldst thine own free fancy bind
In stricter numbers, and run so confined
As to observe the rules of art, which sway
In the contrivance of a true-born play, 30
These works proclaim which thou didst write retired
From Beaumont, by none but thyself inspired;
Where we see 'twas not chance that made them hit,
Nor were thy plays the lotteries of wit,
But like to Dürer's pencil, which first knew
The laws of faces, and then faces drew,

Thou knowest the air, the color, and the place,
The symmetry, which gives the poem grace;
Parts are so fitted unto parts, as do
Show thou hadst wit and mathematics too;   40
Knewst where by line to spare, where to dispense,
And didst beget just comedies from thence;
Things unto which thou didst such life bequeath
That they, their own Blackfriars, unacted breathe.
Jonson hath writ things lasting and divine,
Yet his love-scenes, Fletcher, compared to thine,
Are cold and frosty, and expressed love so
As heat with ice, or warm fires mixed with snow;
Thou, as if struck with the same generous darts
Which burn and reign in noble lovers' hearts,   50
Hast clothed affections in such native tires,
And so described them in their own true fires,
Such moving sighs, such undissembled tears,
Such charms of language, such hopes mixed with fears,
Such grants after denials, such pursuits
After despair, such amorous recruits,
That some who sat spectators have confessed
Themselves transformed to what they saw expressed,
And felt such shafts through their captivèd sense
As made them rise parts, and go lovers thence.   60
Nor was thy style wholly composed of groves,
Or the soft strains of shepherds and their loves;
When thou wouldst comic be, each smiling birth
In that kind, came into the world all mirth,
All point, all edge, all sharpness; we did sit
Sometimes five acts out in pure sprightful wit,
Which flowed in such true salt that we did doubt
In which scene we laughed most two shillings out.
Shakespeare to thee was dull, whose best jest lies
I' th' ladies' questions and the fool's replies—   70
Old fashioned wit, which walked from town to town
In turned hose, which our fathers called the clown;
Whose wit our nice times would obsceneness call,
And which made bawdry pass for comical;
Nature was all his art, thy vein was free
As his, but without his scurrility;
From whom mirth came unforced, no jest perplexed,
But without labor, clean, chaste, and unvexed.
Thou wert not like some, our small poets, who
Could not be poets were not we poets too,   80
Whose wit is pilf'ring, and whose vein and wealth
In poetry lies merely in their stealth;

Nor didst thou feel their drought, their pangs, their qualms,
Their rack in writing, who do write for alms,
Whose wretched genius and dependent fires
But to their benefactor's dole aspires.
Nor hadst thou the sly trick, thyself to praise
Under thy friends' names, or to purchase bays
Didst write stale commendations to thy book,
Which we for Beaumont's or Ben Jonson's took;   90
That debt thou leftst to us, which none but he
Can truly pay, Fletcher, who writes like thee.

The song

Then our music is in prime,
When our teeth keep triple time;
  Hungry notes are fit for knells;
    May lankness be
    No quest to me.
The bagpipe sounds when that
  it swells.
    May lankness, &c.

A mooting-night brings whole-
  some smiles,
When John-a-Nokes and John-a-
  Stiles
Do grease the lawyer's satin. 10
  A reading day
  Frights French away,
The benchers dare speak Latin.
    A reading, &c.

He that's full doth verse com-
  pose,
Hunger deals in sullen prose;
  Take notice and discard her.
    The empty spit
    Ne'er cherished wit;
Minerva loves the larder.   20
    The empty spit, &c.

First to break fast, then to
  dine,
Is to conquer Bellarmine;
  Distinctions then are budding.
    Old Sutcliff's wit
    Did never hit
But after his bag-pudding.
    Old Sutcliff's wit, &c.

From *The Ordinary*

SIR JOHN SUCKLING

The Introduction and Notes are at page 1016

FROM *Fragmenta Aurea*, 1646

A session of the poets

A session was held the other day,
And Apollo himself was at it, they say;
The laurel that had been so long reserved
Was now to be given to him best deserved.
                                        And
Therefore the wits of the town came thither;

'Twas strange to see how they flocked together,
Each strongly confident of his own way,
Thought to gain the laurel away that day.

There was Selden, and he sat hard by the chair; 10
Wenman not far off, which was very fair;
Sandys with Townshend, for they kept no order;
Digby and Chillingworth a little further.
                                        And
There was Lucan's translator too, and he
That makes God speak so big in 's poetry;
Selwin and Waller, and Bartlets both the brothers;
Jack Vaughan and Porter, and divers others.

The first that broke silence was good old Ben,
Prepared before with Canary wine, 20
And he told them plainly he deserved the bays,
For his were called Works, where others were but Plays.
                                        And
Bid them remember how he had purged the stage
Of errors that had lasted many an age;
And he hoped they did not think the *Silent Woman*,
The *Fox*, and the *Alchemist* outdone by no man.

Apollo stopped him there, and bade him not go on,
'Twas merit, he said, and not presumption 30
Must carry 't, at which Ben turned about,
And in great choler offered to go out;
                                        But
Those that were there thought it not fit
To discontent so ancient a wit;
And therefore Apollo called him back again,
And made him mine host of his own *New Inn*.

Tom Carew was next, but he had a fault
That would not well stand with a laureate;
His muse was hard-bound, and th' issue of 's brain
Was seldom brought forth but with trouble and pain. 40
                                        And
All that were present there did agree,
A laureate muse should be easy and free;
Yet sure 'twas not that, but 'twas thought that, his grace
Considered, he was well he had a cup-bearer's place.

Will Davenant, ashamed of a foolish mischance
That he had got lately traveling in France,

Modestly hoped the handsomeness of 's muse
Might any deformity about him excuse.
                    And   50
Surely the company would have been content,
If they could have found any precedent;
But in all their records, either in verse or prose,
There was not one laureate without a nose.

To Will Bartlet sure all the wits meant well,
But first they would see how his snow would sell;
Will smiled and swore in their judgments they went less
That concluded of merit upon success.

Suddenly taking his place again,
He gave way to Selwin, who straight stepped in;   60
But alas! he had been so lately a wit
That Apollo hardly knew him yet.

Toby Mathews (pox on him, how came he there?)
Was whispering nothing in somebody's ear,
When he had the honor to be named in court;
But sir, you may thank my Lady Carlisle for 't,

For had not her care furnished you out
With something of handsome, without all doubt
You and your sorry lady muse had been
In the number of those that were not let in.   70

In haste from the court two or three came in,
And they brought letters, forsooth, from the queen;
'Twas discreetly done, too, for if th' had come
Without them, th' had scarce been let into the room.

Suckling next was called, but did not appear,
But straight one whispered Apollo i' th' ear,
That of all men living he cared not for 't;
He loved not the muses so well as his sport,

And prized black eyes, or a lucky hit
At bowls above all the trophies of wit;   80
But Apollo was angry, and publicly said,
'Twere fit that a fine were set upon 's head.

Wat Montague now stood forth to his trial,
And did not so much as suspect a denial;

But witty Apollo asked him first of all
If he understood his own pastoral.

For if he could do it, 'twould plainly appear
He understood more than any man there,
And did merit the bays above all the rest;
But the Monsieur was modest, and silence confessed. 90

During these troubles in the court was hid
One that Apollo soon missed, little Sid;
And having spied him, called him out of the throng,
And advised him in his ear not to write so strong.

Then Murray was summoned, but 'twas urged that he
Was chief already of another company.

Hales, set by himself, most gravely did smile
To see them about nothing keep such a coil;
Apollo had spied him, but knowing his mind,
Passed by, and called Falkland that sat just behind. 100

But

He was of late so gone with divinity,
That he had almost forgot his poetry;
Though to say the truth, and Apollo did know it,
He might have been both his priest and his poet.

At length who but an alderman did appear,
At which Will Davenant began to swear;
But wiser Apollo bade him draw nigher,
And when he was mounted a little higher,

He openly declared that it was the best sign 110
Of good store of wit to have good store of coin;
And without a syllable more or less said,
He put the laurel on the alderman's head.

At this all the wits were in such a maze
That for a good while they did nothing but gaze
One upon another; not a man in the place
But had discontent writ in great in his face.

Only the small poets cheered up again,
Out of hope, as 'twas thought, of borrowing;
But sure they were out, for he forfeits his crown 120
When he lends any poets about the town.

Song

Why so pale and wan, fond lover?
  Prithee, why so pale?
Will, when looking well can't
    move her,
  Looking ill prevail?
  Prithee, why so pale?

Why so dull and mute, young sin-
    ner?
  Prithee, why so mute?

Will, when speaking well can't
    win her,
  Saying nothing do 't?
  Prithee, why so mute?   10

Quit, quit, for shame, this will not
    move,
  This cannot take her.
If of herself she will not love,
  Nothing can make her.
  The devil take her!

Sonnet I

Dost see how unregarded now
  That piece of beauty passes?
There was a time when I did vow
  To that alone;
But mark the fate of faces,
That red and white works now no
    more on me
Than if it could not charm, or I
  not see.

And yet the face continues good,
  And I have still desires,
Am still the selfsame flesh and
    blood,   10
  As apt to melt

And suffer from those fires;
Oh! some kind power unriddle
  where it lies,
Whether my heart be faulty, or her
  eyes?

She every day her man does kill,
  And I as often die;
Neither her power, then, nor my
  will
  Can questioned be.
  What is the mystery?
Sure beauty's empires, like to
  greater states,   20
Have certain periods set, and hid-
  den fates.

Sonnet II

Of thee, kind boy, I ask no red and
    white,
  To make up my delight;
  No odd becoming graces,
Black eyes, or little know-not-
    whats in faces;
Make me but mad enough, give me
    good store
Of love for her I court;
  I ask no more,
'Tis love in love that makes the
    sport.

There's no such thing as that we
    beauty call,
  It is mere cozenage all;   10
For though some, long ago,
Liked certain colors mingled so
  and so,
That doth not tie me now from
    choosing new;
  If I a fancy take
  To black and blue,
That fancy doth it beauty
  make.

'Tis not the meat, but 'tis the
appetite
Makes eating a delight,
And if I like one dish
More than another, that a pheasant
is;   20

What in our watches, that in us is
found,
So to the height and nick
We up be wound,
No matter by what hand or
trick.

Sonnet III

Oh! for some honest lover's ghost,
Some kind unbodied post
Sent from the shades below!
I strangely long to know
Whether the nobler chaplets wear,
Those that their mistress' scorn did
bear,
Or those that were used kindly.

For whatsoe'er they tell us here
To make those sufferings dear,
'Twill there, I fear, be found   10
That to the being crowned
T' have loved alone will not suffice,
Unless we also have been wise
And have our loves enjoyed.

What posture can we think him in,
That here unloved again
Departs, and 's thither gone
Where each sits by his own?
Or how can that Elysium be,

Where I my mistress still must
see   20
Circled in other's arms?

For there the judges all are just,
And Sophonisba must
Be his whom she held dear,
Not his who loved her here;
The sweet Philoclea, since she died,
Lies by her Pirocles his side,
Not by Amphialus.

Some bays, perchance, or myrtle
bough,
For difference crowns the
brow   30
Of those kind souls that were
The noble martyrs here;
And if that be the only odds,
(As who can tell?) ye kinder gods,
Give me the woman here.

Song

No, no, fair heretic, it needs must
be
But an ill love in me,
And worse for thee.
For were it in my power
To love thee now this hour
More than I did the last,
I would then so fall,
I might not love at all.
Love that can flow, and can admit
increase,
Admits as well an ebb, and may
grow less.   10

True love is still the same; the tor-
rid zones,
And those more frigid ones,
It must not know;
For love, grown cold or hot,
Is lust or friendship, not
The thing we have;
For that's a flame would die,
Held down or up too high.
Then think I love more than I can
express,
And would love more, could I but
love thee less.   20

['Tis now, since I]

'Tis now, since I sat down before
  That foolish fort, a heart,
(Time strangely spent) a year
    and more,
  And still I did my part.

Made my approaches, from her
    hand
  Unto her lip did rise,
And did already understand
  The language of her eyes;

Proceeded on with no less art,
  My tongue was engineer;   10
I thought to undermine the heart
  By whispering in the ear.

When this did nothing, I brought
    down
  Great cannon-oaths, and shot
A thousand thousand to the town;
  And still it yielded not.

I then resolved to starve the place
  By cutting off all kisses,
Praising and gazing on her face,
  And all such little blisses.   20

To draw her out and from her
    strength,
  I drew all batteries in,
And brought myself to lie at
    length
  As if no siege had been.

When I had done what man
    could do,
  And thought the place mine
    own,
The enemy lay quiet too,
  And smiled at all was done.

I sent to know from whence and
    where
  These hopes and this relief;   30

A spy informed, Honor was there,
  And did command in chief.

March, march, quoth I, the word
    straight give,
  Let's lose no time, but leave
    her;
That giant upon air will live,
  And hold it out forever.

To such a place our camp remove,
  As will no siege abide;
I hate a fool that starves her love,
  Only to feed her pride.   40

A ballad upon a wedding

I tell thee, Dick, where I have
    been,
Where I the rarest things have
    seen,
  Oh, things without compare!
Such sights again cannot be found
In any place on English ground,
  Be it at wake or fair.

At Charing Cross, hard by the
    way
Where we, thou know'st, do sell
    our hay,
  There is a house with stairs;
And there did I see coming
    down   10
Such folk as are not in our town,
  Vorty at least, in pairs.

Amongst the rest, one pest'lent
    fine,
His beard no bigger though than
    thine,
  Walked on before the rest;
Our landlord looks like nothing
    to him,
The King, God bless him,
    'twould undo him
  Should he go still so dressed.

At course-a-park, without all
    doubt,
He should have first been taken
    out   20
By all the maids i' th' town;
Though lusty Roger there had
    been,
Or little George upon the Green,
    Or Vincent of the Crown.

But wot you what? the youth was
    going
To make an end of all his woo-
    ing,
The parson for him stayed;
Yet by his leave, for all his haste,
He did not so much wish all past,
    Perchance, as did the maid.   30

The maid—and thereby hangs a
    tale:
For such a maid no Whitsun ale
    Could ever yet produce;
No grape that's kindly ripe could
    be
So round, so plump, so soft as she,
    Nor half so full of juice.

Her finger was so small the ring
Would not stay on, which they
    did bring,
    It was too wide a peck;
And to say truth, for out it
    must,   40
It looked like the great collar,
    just,
    About our young colt's neck.

Her feet beneath her petticoat,
Like little mice, stole in and out,
    As if they feared the light;
But oh, she dances such a way!
No sun upon an Easter day
    Is half so fine a sight.

He would have kissed her once or
    twice,

But she would not, she was
    nice,   50
She would not do't in sight;
And then she looked as who
    should say,
I will do what I list to-day,
    And you shall do't at night.

Her cheeks so rare a white was
    on,
No daisy makes comparison,
    Who sees them is undone;
For streaks of red were mingled
    there,
Such as are on a Katherne pear,
    The side that's next the sun. 60

Her lips were red, and one was
    thin,
Compared to that was next her
    chin,
    Some bee had stung it newly;
But Dick, her eyes so guard her
    face
I durst no more upon them gaze
    Than on the sun in July.

Her mouth so small, when she
    does speak
Thou'dst swear her teeth her
    words did break,
    That they might passage get;
But she so handled still the mat-
    ter,   70
They came as good as ours, or
    better,
    And are not spent a whit.

If wishing should be any sin,
The parson himself had guilty
    been.
    She looked that day so purely;
And did the youth so oft the feat
At night, as some did in conceit,
    It would have spoiled him
    surely.

Passion o' me, how I run on!
There's that that that would be
    thought upon, 80
I trow, besides the bride.
The business of the kitchen's
    great,
For it is fit that man should eat,
    Nor was it there denied.

Just in the nick the cook knocked
    thrice,
And all the waiters in a trice
    His summons did obey;
Each serving-man, with dish in
    hand,
Marched boldly up like our
    trained band,
    Presented, and away. 90

When all the meat was on the
    table,
What man of knife or teeth was
    able
    To stay to be entreated?
And this the very reason was—
Before the parson could say
    grace,
    The company was seated.

Now hats fly off, and youths
    carouse,
Healths first go round, and then
    the house,
    The bride's came thick and
    thick;
And when 'twas named another's
    health, 100
Perhaps he made it hers by
    stealth,
    And who could help it, Dick?

O' th' sudden up they rise and
    dance,
Then sit again and sigh and
    glance,
    Then dance again, and kiss;

Thus several ways the time did
    pass,
Whilst ev'ry woman wished her
    place,
    And ev'ry man wished his.

By this time all were stolen aside
To counsel and undress the
    bride, 110
    But that he must not know;
But yet 'twas thought he guessed
    her mind,
And did not mean to stay behind
    Above an hour or so.

When in he came, Dick, there she
    lay
Like new-fallen snow melting
    away
    ('Twas time, I trow, to part);
Kisses were now the only stay,
Which soon she gave, as who
    would say,
    God b' w' ye, with all my
    heart. 120

But just as heavens would have,
    to cross it,
In came the bridesmaids with the
    posset;
    The bridegroom eat in spite,
For, had he left the women to 't,
It would have cost two hours to
    do 't,
    Which were too much that
    night.

At length the candle's out, and
    now
All that they had not done they
    do;
    What that is, who can tell?
But I believe it was no more 130
Than thou and I have done be-
    fore
    With Bridget and with Nell.

FROM *The Last Remains*, 1659

The Stationer to the Reader.

*Among the highest and most refined wits of the nation, this gentle
and princely poet took his generous rise from the court, where, having
flourished with splendor and reputation, he lived only long enough
to see the sunset of that majesty from whose auspicious beams he derived his luster, and with whose declining state his own loyal fortunes
were obscured. But after the several changes of those times, being
sequestered from the more serene contentments of his native country,
he first took care to secure the dearest and choicest of his papers in the
several cabinets of his noble and faithful friends; and among other
testimonies of his worth, these elegant and florid pieces of his fancy
were preserved in the custody of his truly honorable and virtuous sister, with whose free permission they were transcribed, and now published exactly according to the original.*

*This might be sufficient to make you acknowledge that these are the
real and genuine works of Sir John Suckling; but if you can yet doubt,
let any judicious soul seriously consider the freedom of the fancy, rich-
ness of the conceit, proper expression, with that air and spirit diffused
through every part, and he will find such a perfect resemblance with
what hath been formerly known, that he cannot with modesty doubt
them to be his.*

*I could tell you further (for I myself am the best witness of it)
what a thirst and general inquiry hath been after what I here present
you, by all that have either seen or heard of them. And by that time
you have read them, you will believe me, who have, now for many
years, annually published the productions of the best wits of our own
and foreign nations.*

H. M.

[*Out upon it! I have loved*]

Out upon it! I have loved
  Three whole days together;
And am like to love three more,
  If it prove fair weather.

Time shall moult away his wings,
  Ere he shall discover
In the whole wide world again
  Such a constant lover.

But the spite on 't is, no praise
  Is due at all to me;   10
Love with me had made no stays,
  Had it any been but she.

Had it any been but she,
  And that very face,
There had been at least ere this
  A dozen dozen in her place.

Love and debt alike troublesome

This one request I make to him that sits the clouds above,
That I were freely out of debt as I am out of love.
Then for to dance, to drink, and sing, I should be very willing,

I should not owe one lass a kiss, nor ne'er a knave a shilling.
'Tis only being in love and debt that breaks us of our rest,
And he that is quite out of both, of all the world is blest;
He sees the golden age, wherein all things were free and common;
He eats, he drinks, he takes his rest, he fears no man nor woman.
Though Crœsus compassëd great wealth, yet he still cravëd more,
He was as needy a beggar still as goes from door to door.   10
Though Ovid were a merry man, love ever kept him sad;
He was as far from happiness as one that is stark mad.
Our merchant he in goods is rich, and full of gold and treasure;
But when he thinks upon his debts, that thought destroys his pleasure.
Our courtier thinks that he's preferred, whom every man envies;
When love so rumbles in his pate, no sleep comes in his eyes.
Our gallant's case is worst of all, he lies so just betwixt them;
For he's in love and he's in debt, and knows not which most vex him.
But he that can eat beef, and feed on bread which is so brown,
May satisfy his appetite, and owe no man a crown;   20
And he that is content with lasses clothëd in plain woolen,
May cool his heat in every place; he need not to be sullen,
Nor sigh for love of lady fair, for this each wise man knows—
As good stuff under flannel lies, as under silken clothes.

Song

I prithee send me back my heart,
  Since I cannot have thine;
For if from yours you will not part,
  Why then shouldst thou have
    mine?

Yet now I think on 't, let it lie,
  To find it were in vain;
For th' hast a thief in either eye
  Would steal it back again.

Why should two hearts in one
    breast lie,
  And yet not lodge together?   10

O love, where is thy sympathy,
  If thus our breasts thou sever?

But love is such a mystery,
  I cannot find it out;
For when I think I'm best resolved,
  I then am most in doubt.

Then farewell care, and farewell
    woe,
  I will no longer pine;
For I'll believe I have her heart
  As much as she hath mine.   20

A song to a lute

Hast thou seen the down i' th' air
  When wanton blasts have
    tossed it,
Or the ship on the sea
  When ruder waves have
    crossed it?
Hast thou marked the crocodile's
    weeping,

Or the fox's sleeping?
Or hast viewed the peacock in his
    pride,
  Or the dove by his bride
When he courts for his lech-
    ery?
Oh, so fickle, oh, so vain, oh, so
    false, so false is she!   10

RICHARD LOVELACE

The Introduction and Notes are at page 1018

FROM *Lucasta*, 1649

To Althea, from prison

When Love with unconfinëd wings
  Hovers within my gates,
And my divine Althea brings
  To whisper at the grates;
When I lie tangled in her hair,
  And fettered to her eye,
The gods that wanton in the air
  Know no such liberty.

When flowing cups run swiftly round
  With no allaying Thames, 10
Our careless heads with roses bound,
  Our hearts with loyal flames;
When thirsty grief in wine we steep,
  When healths and draughts go free,
Fishes that tipple in the deep
  Know no such liberty.

When, like committed linnets, I
  With shriller throat shall sing
The sweetness, mercy, majesty,
  And glories of my King; 20
When I shall voice aloud, how good
  He is, how great should be,
Enlargëd winds that curl the flood
  Know no such liberty.

Stone walls do not a prison make,
  Nor iron bars a cage;
Minds innocent and quiet take
  That for an hermitage;

If I have freedom in my love,
  And in my soul am free, 30
Angels alone that soar above
  Enjoy such liberty.

The Vintage to the Dungeon

Sing out, pent souls, sing cheerfully!
Care shackles you in liberty,
Mirth frees you in captivity:
  Would you double fetters add?
  Else why so sad?

Chorus.

Besides your pinioned arms, you'll find
Grief too can manacle the mind.

Live then, pris'ners, uncontrolled;
Drink o' th' strong, the rich, the old,
Till wine too hath your wits in hold; 10
  Then if still your jollity
  And throats are free—

Chorus.

Triumph in your bonds and pains,
And dance to the music of your chains.

To Amarantha, that she would dishevel her hair

Amarantha sweet and fair,
Ah, braid no more that shining hair!
  As my curious hand or eye,
  Hovering round thee, let it fly.

Let it fly as unconfined
As its calm ravisher, the wind,
  Who hath left his darling, th'
    East,
  To wanton o'er that spicy nest.

Ev'ry tress must be confessed
But neatly tangled at the best, ¹⁰
  Like a clue of golden thread,
  Most excellently ravellëd.

Do not then wind up that light
In ribands, and o'er-cloud in
    night;
  Like the sun in's early ray,
  But shake your head and scatter
    day.

See, 'tis broke! Within this grove,
The bower, and the walks of
    love,
  Weary lie we down and rest,
  And fan each other's panting
    breast. ²⁰

Here we'll strip and cool our fire
In cream below, in milk-baths
    higher;
  And when all wells are drawen
    dry,
  I'll drink a tear out of thine
    eye.

Which our very joys shall leave,
That sorrows thus we can de-
    ceive;
  Or our very sorrows weep,
  That joys so ripe, so little keep.

Gratiana dancing and singing

See! with what constant motïon,
Even and glorious as the sun,
  Gratiana steers that noble
    frame,
Soft as her breast, sweet as her
    voice,

That gave each winding law and
    poise,
  And swifter than the wings of
    fame.

She beat the happy pavëment,
By such a star made firmament,
  Which now no more the roof
    envies,
But swells up high with Atlas
    ev'n, ¹⁰
Bearing the brighter, nobler
    heav'n,
  And in her all the deities.

Each step trod out a lover's
    thought
And the ambitious hopes he
    brought,
  Chained to her brave feet with
    such arts,
Such sweet command, and gentle
    awe,
As when she ceased, we sighing
    saw
  The floor lay paved with broken
    hearts.

So did she move; so did she sing
Like the harmonious spheres that
    bring ²⁰
  Unto their rounds their music's
    aid;
Which she performëd such a way
As all th' enamoured world will
    say,
  The Graces danced, and Apollo
    played.

The scrutiny

Why should you swear I am for-
    sworn,
  Since thine I vowed to be?
Lady, it is already morn,

And 'twas last night I swore to
thee
That fond impossibility.

Have I not loved thee much and
long,
  A tedious twelve hours' space?
I must all other beauties wrong,
  And rob thee of a new em-
brace,
  Could I still dote upon thy
face.   10

Not but all joy in thy brown hair
  By others may be found;
But I must search the black and
fair
  Like skillful mineralists that
sound
  For treasure in unplowed-up
ground.

Then, if when I have loved my
round,
  Thou prov'st the pleasant she,
With spoils of meaner beauties
crowned
  I laden will return to thee,
  Ev'n sated with variety.   20

To Lucasta. The rose

Sweet serene sky-like flower,
Haste to adorn her bower;
  From thy long cloudy bed,
  Shoot forth thy damask head.

New-startled blush of Flora!
The grief of pale Aurora,
  Who will contest no more,
  Haste, haste, to strew her
floor.

Vermilion ball that's given
From lip to lip in heaven,   10
  Love's couch's coverled,
  Haste, haste, to make her bed.

Dear offspring of pleased Venus
And jolly plump Silenus,
  Haste, haste, to deck the hair
  Of th' only sweetly fair.

See! rosy is her bower,
Her floor is all this flower;
  Her bed a rosy nest
  By a bed of roses pressed.   20

But early as she dresses,
Why fly you her bright tresses?
  Ah! I have found, I fear—
  Because her cheeks are near.

To Lucasta. Going to the wars

Tell me not, sweet, I am unkind,
  That from the nunnery
Of thy chaste breast and quiet
mind,
  To war and arms I fly.

True, a new mistress now I chase,
  The first foe in the field;
And with a stronger faith em-
brace
  A sword, a horse, a shield.

Yet this inconstancy is such
  As you too shall adore;   10
I could not love thee, dear, so
much,
  Loved I not honor more.

To Lucasta. Going beyond the
seas

If to be absent were to be
  Away from thee;
Or that when I am gone,
  You and I were alone;
Then, my Lucasta, might I crave
Pity from blust'ring wind, or
  swallowing wave.

But I'll not sigh one blast or gale
   To swell my sail;
Or pay a tear to suage   9
   The foaming blew-god's rage;
For whether he will let me pass
Or no, I'm still as happy as I was.

Though seas and land betwixt us
     both,
   Our faith and troth,
Like separated souls,
   All time and space controls;
Above the highest sphere we meet
Unseen, unknown, and greet as
     angels greet.

So then we do anticipate
   Our after-fate,   20
   And are alive i' th' skies,
If thus our lips and eyes
Can speak like spirits unconfined
In heav'n, their earthy bodies left
     behind.

To Lucasta, from prison

Long in thy shackles, liberty
I ask, not from these walls but
     thee
   (Left for a while another's
     bride),
To fancy all the world beside.

Yet ere I do begin to love,
See! how I all my objects prove;
   Then my free soul to that con-
     fine
   'Twere possible I might call
     mine.

First I would be in love with
     Peace,
And her rich swelling breasts' in-
     crease;   10
   But how, alas! how may that
     be,

Despising earth, she will love
     me?

Fain would I be in love with
     War,
As my dear just avenging star;
   But War is loved so ev'rywhere,
   Ev'n he disdains a lodging here.

Thee and thy wounds I would
     bemoan,
Fair thorough-shot Religïon;
   But he lives only that kills
     thee,
   And whoso binds thy hands is
     free.   20

I would love a Parliament
As a main prop from heav'n sent;
   But ah! who's he that would
     be wedded
   To the fairest body that's be-
     headed?

Next would I court my Liberty,
And then my birthright, Prop-
     erty;
   But can that be, when it is
     known
   There's nothing you can call
     your own?

A Reformation I would have,
As for our griefs a sov'reign
     salve;   30
   That is, a cleansing of each
     wheel
   Of state that yet some rust doth
     feel.

But not a Reformation so
As to reform were to o'erthrow;
   Like watches by unskillful men
   Disjointed, and set ill again.

The Public Faith I would adore,
But she is bankrupt of her store;
   Nor how to trust her can I see,

For she that cozens all, must
  me.   40

Since then none of these can be
Fit objects for my love and me,
  What then remains, but th'
    only spring
Of all our loves and joys? the
    King.

He, who being the whole ball
Of day on earth, lends it to all,
  When seeking to eclipse his
    right,
Blinded, we stand in our own
  light.

And now an universal mist
Of error is spread o'er each
    breast,   50
  With such a fury edged as is
  Not found in th' inwards of th'
    abyss.

Oh, from thy glorious starry
    wain,
Dispense on me one sacred beam
  To light me where I soon may
    see
  How to serve you, and you
    trust me.

The grasshopper

To my noble friend, Mr. Charles Cotton

O thou that swing'st upon the waving hair
  Of some well-fillèd oaten beard,
Drunk ev'ry night with a delicious tear
    Dropped thee from heav'n, where now th' art reared;

The joys of earth and air are thine entire,
    That with thy feet and wings dost hop and fly;
And when thy poppy works thou dost retire
    To thy carved acorn-bed to lie.

Up with the day, the sun thou welcom'st then,
    Sport'st in the gilt-plats of his beams,   10
And all these merry days mak'st merry, men,
    Thyself, and melancholy streams.

But ah, the sickle! Golden ears are cropped;
    Ceres and Bacchus bid good night;
Sharp frosty fingers all your flowers have topped,
    And what scythes spared, winds shave off quite.

Poor verdant fool! and now green ice! thy joys
    Large and as lasting as thy perch of grass,
Bid us lay in 'gainst winter, rain, and poise
    Their floods with an o'erflowing glass.   20

Thou best of men and friends! we will create
  A genuine summer in each other's breast,

And spite of this cold time and frozen fate,
  Thaw us a warm seat to our rest.

Our sacred hearths shall burn eternally
  As vestal flames; the North Wind, he
Shall strike his frost-stretched wings, dissolve, and fly
  This Ætna in epitome.

Dropping December shall come weeping in,
  Bewail th' usurping of his reign;   30
But when in showers of old Greek we begin,
  Shall cry, he hath his crown again!

Night as clear Hesper shall our tapers whip
  From the light casements where we play,
And the dark hag from her black mantle strip,
  And stick there everlasting day.

Thus richer than untempted kings are we,
  That asking nothing, nothing need:
Though lord of all what seas embrace, yet he
  That wants himself is poor indeed.   40

GEORGE SANDYS

The Introduction and Notes are at page 1019

FROM *A Paraphrase upon the Psalms of David,* 1636

Deo opt. max.

O thou who all things hast of nothing made,
Whose hand the radiant firmament displayed,
With such an undiscernëd swiftness hurled
About the steadfast center of the world;
Against whose rapid course the restless sun
And wand'ring flames in varied motions run,
Which heat, light, life, infuse—time, night, and day
Distinguish; in our human bodies sway!
That hung'st the solid earth in fleeting air,
Veined with clear springs which ambient seas repair.   10
In clouds the mountains wrap their hoary heads;
Luxurious valleys clothed with flow'ry meads,
Her trees yield fruit and shade; with liberal breasts
All creatures she, their common mother, feasts.

Then man thy image mad'st, in dignity,
In knowledge, and in beauty, like to thee;
Placed in a heav'n on earth, without his toil
The ever-flourishing and fruitful soil
Unpurchased food produced; all creatures were
His subjects, serving more for love than fear;　　20
He knew no lord but thee. But when he fell
From his obedience, all at once rebel
And in his ruin exercise their might;
Concurring elements against him fight;
Troops of unknown diseases, sorrow, age,
And death, assail him with successive rage.
Hell let forth all her furies; none so great
As man to man. Ambition, pride, deceit,
Wrong armed with power, lust, rapine, slaughter reigned;
And flattered vice the name of virtue gained.　　30
Then hills beneath the swelling waters stood,
And all the globe of earth was but one flood,
Yet could not cleanse their guilt; the following race
Worse than their fathers, and their sons more base,
Their godlike beauty lost, sin's wretched thrall;
No spark of their divine original
Left unextinguished, all enveloped
With darkness, in their bold transgressions dead.
When thou didst from the east a light display
Which rendered to the world a clearer day,　　40
Whose precepts from hell's jaws our steps withdraw,
And whose example was a living law;
Who purged us with his blood, the way prepared
To heaven, and those long-chained-up doors unbarred.
How infinite thy mercy! which exceeds
The world thou mad'st, as well as our misdeeds!
Which greater rev'rence than thy justice wins,
And still augments thy honor by our sins.
Oh, who hath tasted of thy clemency
In greater measure or more oft than I?　　50
My grateful verse thy goodness shall display;
O thou who went'st along in all my way
To where the morning with perfumèd wings
From the high mountains of Panchæa springs
To that new-found-out world where sober night
Takes from th' antipodes her silent flight,
To those dark seas where horrid winter reigns
And binds the stubborn floods in icy chains,
To Libyan wastes whose thirst no showers assuage,
And where swoll'n Nilus cools the lion's rage.　　60

Thy wonders in the deep have I beheld,
Yet all by those on Judah's hills excelled,
There where the virgin's son his doctrine taught,
His miracles and our redemption wrought;
Where I, by thee inspired, his praises sung,
And on his sepulcher my off'ring hung;
Which way soe'er I turn my face or feet,
I see thy glory, and thy mercy meet.
Met on the Thracian shores, when in the strife
Of frantic Simoans thou preserv'dst my life;   70
So when Arabian thieves belaid us round,
And when, by all abandoned, thee I found.
That false Sidonian wolf whose craft put on
A sheep-soft fleece, and me Bellerophon
To ruin by his cruel letter sent,
Thou didst by thy protecting hand prevent.
Thou savedst me from the bloody massacres
Of faithless Indians, from their treach'rous wars;
From raging fevers, from the sultry breath
Of tainted air, which cloyed the joys of death.   80
Preserved from swallowing seas, when tow'ring waves
Mixed with the clouds and opened their deep graves;
From barbarous pirates ransomed; by those taught,
Successfully with Salian Moors we fought;
Then broughtst me home in safety, that this earth
Might bury me, which fed me from my birth;
Blest with a healthful age, a quiet mind,
Content with little, to this work designed;
Which I, at length, have finished by thy aid,
And now my vows have at thy altar paid.   90

Iam tetigi portum,—valete.

FROM *Ovid's Metamorphosis,* 1632

The fifteenth book

. . . .

Doth not the image of our age appear
In the successive quarters of the year?
The springtide tender sucking infancy
Resembling; then the juiceful blade sprouts high,
Though tender, weak, yet hope to plowmen yields;
All things then flourish: flowers the gaudy fields
With colors paint, no virtue yet in leaves.
Then following summer greater strength receives;
A lusty youth, no age more strength acquires,

More fruitful, or more burning in desires.
Maturer autumn, heat of youth allayed,
The sober mean 'twixt youth and age, more staid
And temperate, in summer's wane repairs,
His reverend temples sprinkled with grey hairs.
Then comes old winter, void of all delight,
With trembling steps, his head or bald or white.
So change our bodies without rest or stay;
What we were yesterday, nor what to-day,
Shall be to-morrow. Once alone of men
The seeds and hope, the womb our mansion, when   20
Kind nature showed her cunning, not content
That our vexed bodies should be longer pent
In mother's stretched entrails, forthwith bare
Them from that prison to the open air.
We strengthless lie when first of light possessed;
Straight creep upon all four, much like a beast;
Then, staggering with weak nerves, stand by degrees,
And by some stay support our feeble knees;
Now lusty, swiftly run. Our youth then past
And those our middle times, we post in haste   30
To inevitable age; this last devours
The former, and demolisheth their powers.

.   .   .   .

WILLIAM HABINGTON

The Introduction and Notes are at page 1020

FROM *Castara*, 1640

The Author.

*The press hath gathered into one what fancy had scattered in many
loose papers. To write this, love stole some hours from business, and
my more serious study. For though poetry may challenge, if not priority, yet equality with the best sciences, both for antiquity and worth,
I never set so high a rate upon it as to give myself entirely up to its
devotion. It hath too much air, and (if without offence to our next
transmarine neighbor) wantons too much according to the French garb.
And when it is wholly employed in the soft strains of love, his soul
who entertains it loseth much of that strength which should confirm
him man. The nerves of judgment are weakened most by its dalliance,
and when woman (I mean only as she is externally fair) is the su-*

preme object of wit, we soon degenerate into effeminacy. For the religion of fancy declines into a mad superstition when it adores that idol which is not secure from age and sickness. Of such heathens our times afford us a pitied multitude, who can give no nobler testimony of twenty years' employment than some loose copies of lust happily expressed. Yet these the common people of wit blow up with their breath of praise and honor with the sacred name of poets; to which, as I believe they can never have any just claim, so shall I not dare by this essay to lay any title, since more sweat and oil he must spend who shall arrogate so excellent an attribute. Yet if the innocency of a chaste muse shall be more acceptable and weigh heavier in the balance of esteem than a fame begot in adultery of study, I doubt I shall leave them no hope of competition. For how unhappy soever I may be in the elocution, I am sure the theme is worthy enough. In all those flames in which I burnt, I never felt a wanton heat, nor was my invention ever sinister from the strait way of chastity. And when love builds upon that rock, it may safely contemn the battery of the waves, and threatenings of the wind. . . . And if not too indulgent to what is my own, I think even these verses will have that proportion in the world's opinion that heaven hath allotted to me in fortune—not so high as to be wondered at, nor so low as to be contemned.

To roses in the bosom of Castara

Ye blushing virgins happy are
In the chaste nunn'ry of her
  breasts,
For he'd profane so chaste a fair,
Whoe'er should call them Cupid's
  nests.

Transplanted thus how bright ye
  grow,
How rich a perfume do ye yield!
In some close garden cowslips so
Are sweeter than i' th' open field.

In those white cloisters live secure
From the rude blasts of wanton
  breath,   10
Each hour more innocent and
  pure,
Till you shall wither into death.

Then that which living gave you
  room,
Your glorious sepulcher shall be;
There wants no marble for a
  tomb,
Whose breast hath marble been
  to me.

To the World. The perfection of love

You who are earth and cannot
  rise
  Above your sense,
Boasting the envied wealth which
  lies
Bright in your mistress' lips or
  eyes,
  Betray a pitied eloquence.

That which doth join our souls,
  so light
  And quick doth move,

That like the eagle in his flight
It doth transcend all human sight.
Lost in the element of love.   10

You poets reach not this, who sing
  The praise of dust
But kneaded, when by theft you
    bring
The rose and lily from the spring
T' adorn the wrinkled face of
    lust.

When we speak love, nor art, nor
    wit
  We gloss upon;
Our souls engender and beget
Ideas, which you counterfeit
In your dull propagation.   20

While time seven ages shall dis-
    perse
  We'll talk of love,
And when our tongues hold no
    commerce
Our thoughts shall mutually con-
    verse,
And yet the blood no rebel prove.

And though we be of several kind
  Fit for offence,
Yet we are so by love refined,
From impure dross we are all
    mind;
Death could not more have con-
    quered sense.   30

How suddenly those flames ex-
    pire
  Which scorch our clay;
Prometheus-like, when we steal
    fire
From heaven, 'tis endless and en-
    tire,—
It may know age, but not decay.

The description of Castara

Like the violet which alone
Prospers in some happy shade,

My Castara lives unknown,
To no looser eye betrayed.
  For she's to herself untrue
  Who delights i' th' public view.

Such is her beauty as no arts
Have enriched with borrowed
    grace.
Her high birth no pride imparts,
For the blushes in her place;   10
  Folly boasts a glorious blood,
  She is noblest being good.

Cautious she knew never yet
What a wanton courtship meant;
Not speaks loud to boast her wit,
In her silence eloquent.
  Of herself survey she takes,
  But 'tween men no difference
    makes.

She obeys with speedy will
Her grave parents' wise com-
    mands;   20
And so innocent, that ill
She nor acts nor understands.
  Women's feet run still astray,
  If once to ill they know the
    way.

She sails by that rock, the court,
Where oft honor splits her mast;
And retiredness thinks the port
Where her fame may anchor cast.
  Virtue safely cannot fit,
  Where vice is enthroned for
    wit.   30

She holds that day's pleasure best
Where sin waits not on delight;
Without mask, or ball, or feast,
Sweetly spends a winter's night:
  O'er that darkness whence is
    thrust,
  Prayer and sleep oft governs
    lust.

She her throne makes reason
    climb,
While wild passions captive lie.
And each article of time
Her pure thoughts to heaven
    fly;   40
    All her vows religious be,
    And her love she vows to me.

To Castara, upon beauty

Castara, see that dust the sportive
    wind
So wantons with; 'tis haply all
    you'll find
Left of some beauty, and how still
    it flies
To trouble, as it did in life, our
    eyes.
Oh, empty boast of flesh! Though
    our heirs gild
The far-fetch Phrygian marble,
    which shall build
A burthen to our ashes, yet will
    deatl.
Betray them to the sport of every
    breath.
Dost thou, poor relic of our
    frailty, still
Swell up with glory? Or is it thy
    skill   10
To mock weak man, whom every
    wind of praise
Into the air doth 'bove his center
    raise?
    If so, mock on, and tell him
        that his lust
    To beauty 's madness, for it
        courts but dust.

Nox nocti indicat scientiam
David

When I survey the bright
    Celestial sphere,

So rich with jewels hung, that
    night
Doth like an Ethiop bride appear,

My soul her wings doth spread
    And heavenward flies,
Th' Almighty's mysteries to read
In the large volumes of the skies.

For the bright firmament
    Shoots forth no flame   10
So silent, but is eloquent
In speaking the Creator's name.

No unregarded star
    Contracts its light
Into so small a character,
Removed far from our human
    sight,

But if we steadfast look,
    We shall discern
In it, as in some holy book,
How man may heavenly knowl-
        edge learn.   20

It tells the conqueror
    That far stretched power
Which his proud dangers traffic
    for,
Is but the triumph of an hour.

That from the farthest north
    Some nation may,
Yet undiscovered, issue forth
And o'er his new-got conquest
    sway.

Some nation yet shut in
    With hills of ice   30
May be let out to scourge his sin
Till they shall equal him in vice.

And then they likewise shall
    Their ruin have;

For as yourselves, your empires
  fall,
And every kingdom hath a grave.

Thus those celestial fires,
  Though seeming mute,
The fallacy of our desires
And all the pride of life con-
    fute.   40

For they have watched since first
  The world had birth;
And found sin in itself accurst,
And nothing permanent on earth.

FROM *The Queen of Aragon*,
  1640

His mistress flouted

Fine young folly, though you
  were
That fair beauty I did swear,
  Yet you ne'er could reach my
    heart;
For we courtiers learn at school
Only with your sex to fool;
  Y' are not worth the serious
    part.

When I sigh and kiss your hand,
Cross my arms and wondering
  stand,

Holding parley with your eye,
Then dilate on my desires,   10
Swear the sun ne'er shot such
    fires—
  All is but a handsome lie.

When I eye your curl or lace,
Gentle soul, you think your face
    Straight some murder doth
      commit;
And your virtue both begin
To grow scrupulous of my sin,
    When I talk to show my wit.

Therefore, madam, wear no
    cloud,
Nor to check my love grow
    proud;   20
  For in sooth I much do doubt
'Tis the powder in your hair,
Not your breath, perfumes the air,
  And your clothes that set you
    out.

Yet though truth has this con-
    fessed,
And I vow I love in jest,
  When I next begin to court
And protest an amorous flame,
You will swear I in earnest am.
  Bedlam! this is pretty sport. 30

GEORGE HERBERT

The Introduction and Notes are at page 1020

FROM IZAAK WALTON'S *Life of Mr. George Herbert*, 1670

To his mother

My God, where is that ancient heat towards thee
  Wherewith whole shoals of martyrs once did burn,
    Besides their other flames? Doth poetry
Wear Venus' livery, only serve her turn?

Why are not sonnets made of thee, and lays
  Upon thine altar burnt? Cannot thy love
  Heighten a spirit to sound out thy praise
As well as any she? Cannot thy dove
Outstrip their Cupid easily in flight?
  Or, since thy ways are deep and still the same,   10
  Will not a verse run smooth that bears thy name?
Why doth that fire, which by thy power and might
  Each breast does feel, no braver fuel choose
  Than that which one day worms may chance refuse?

FROM *The Temple*, 1633

The dedication

Lord, my first fruits present themselves to thee;
Yet not mine neither, for from thee they came,
And must return. Accept of them and me,
And make us strive who shall sing best thy name.
  Turn their eyes hither who shall make a gain;
  Theirs who shall hurt themselves or me, refrain.

Jordan [*1*]

Who says that fictions only and false hair
Become a verse? Is there in truth no beauty?
Is all good structure in a winding stair?
May no lines pass except they do their duty
  Not to a true, but painted chair?

Is it no verse except enchanted groves
And sudden arbors shadow coarse-spun lines?
Must purling streams refresh a lover's loves?
Must all be veiled, while he that reads, divines,
  Catching the sense at two removes?   10

Shepherds are honest people; let them sing.
Riddle who list for me, and pull for prime;
I envy no man's nightingale or spring,
Nor let them punish me with loss of rhyme,
  Who plainly say, My God, my King.

Jordan [*2*]

When first my lines of heav'nly joys made mention,
Such was their luster, they did so excel,

That I sought out quaint words and trim invention;
My thoughts began to burnish, sprout, and swell,
Curling with metaphors a plain intention,
Decking the sense as if it were to sell.

Thousands of notions in my brain did run,
Off'ring their service, if I were not sped.
I often blotted what I had begun:
This was not quick enough, and that was dead.
Nothing could seem too rich to clothe the sun,
Much less those joys which trample on his head.

As flames do work and wind when they ascend,
So did I weave myself into the sense.
But while I bustled, I might hear a friend
Whisper, How wide is all this long pretense!
There is in love a sweetness ready penned,
Copy out only that, and save expense.

The British Church

I joy, dear mother, when I view
Thy perfect lineaments, and hue
  Both sweet and bright.
Beauty in thee takes up her place,
And dates her letters from thy face,
  When she doth write.

A fine aspect in fit array,
Neither too mean nor yet too gay,
  Shows who is best.
Outlandish looks may not compare,
For all they either painted are,
  Or else undressed.

She on the hills which wantonly
Allureth all, in hope to be
  By her preferred,
Hath kissed so long her painted shrines,
That ev'n her face by kissing shines,
  For her reward.

She in the valley is so shy
Of dressing, that her hair doth lie
  About her ears;
While she avoids her neighbor's pride,
She wholly goes on th' other side,
  And nothing wears.

But, dearest mother, what those miss,
The mean, thy praise and glory is
  And long may be.
Blessed be God, whose love it was
To double-moat thee with his grace,
  And none but thee.

The Son

Let foreign nations of their language boast,
What fine variety each tongue affords;
I like our language, as our men and coast;
Who cannot dress it well, want wit, not words.

How neatly do we give one only name
To parents' issue and the sun's bright star!
A son is light and fruit, a fruitful flame
Chasing the father's dimness, carried far
From the first man in th' East to fresh and new
Western discov'ries of posterity.
So in one word our Lord's humility
We turn upon him in a sense most true;
　　For what Christ once in humbleness began,
　　We him in glory call, The Son of Man.

The altar

A broken altar, Lord, thy servant rears,
Made of a heart and cémented with tears;
　　Whose parts are as thy hand did frame;
　　No workman's tool hath touched the same.
　　　　　A heart alone
　　　　　Is such a stone
　　　　　As nothing but
　　　　　Thy power doth cut.
　　　　　Wherefore each part
　　　　　Of my hard heart
　　　　　Meets in this frame
　　　　　To praise thy name;
　　That if I chance to hold my peace,
　　These stones to praise thee may not cease.
Oh, let thy blessed sacrifice be mine,
And sanctify this altar to be thine.

The church floor

Mark you the floor? That square and speckled stone,
　　Which looks so firm and strong,
　　　　　Is Patience;

And th' other black and grave, wherewith each one
　　Is checkered all along,
　　　　　Humility.

The gentle rising, which on either hand
　　Leads to the choir above,
　　　　　Is Confidence.

But the sweet cement, which in one sure band
　　Ties the whole frame, is Love
　　　　　And Charity.

Hither sometimes sin steals, and stains
The marble's neat and curious veins;
But all is cleansèd when the marble weeps.
Sometimes death, puffing at the door,
Blows all the dust about the floor;
But while he thinks to spoil the room, he sweeps.
Blest be the architect whose art
Could build so strong in a weak heart.   20

Easter wings

Lord, who createdst man in wealth and store,
Though foolishly he lost the same,
Decaying more and more
Till he became
Most poor;
With thee
Oh, let me rise
As larks, harmoniously,
And sing this day thy victories;
Then shall the fall further the flight in me.   10

My tender age in sorrow did begin;
And still with sicknesses and shame
Thou didst so punish sin,
That I became
Most thin.
With thee
Let me combine,
And feel this day thy victory;
For if I imp my wing on thine,
Affliction shall advance the flight in me.   20

Lent

Welcome, dear feast of Lent! Who loves not thee,
He loves not temperance or authority,
But is composed of passion.
The Scriptures bid us fast; the Church says, Now;
Give to thy mother what thou wouldst allow
To ev'ry corporation.

The humble soul, composed of love and fear,
Begins at home and lays the burden there,
When doctrines disagree.
He says, in things which use hath justly got,   10

I am a scandal to the Church, and not
   The Church is so to me.

True Christians should be glad of an occasion
To use their temperance, seeking no evasion
   When good is seasonable;
Unless authority, which should increase
The obligation in us, make it less,
   And power itself disable.

Besides the cleanness of sweet abstinence,
Quick thoughts and motions at a small expense,   20
   A face not fearing light;
Whereas in fullness there are sluttish fumes,
Sour exhalations, and dishonest rheums,
   Revenging the delight.

Then those same pendant profits, which the spring
And Easter intimate, enlarge the thing
   And goodness of the deed.
Neither ought other men's abuse of Lent
Spoil the good use, lest by that argument
   We forfeit all our creed.   30

It's true we cannot reach Christ's forti'th day;
Yet to go part of that religious way
   Is better than to rest.
We cannot reach our Savior's purity,
Yet are we bid, Be holy ev'n as he.
   In both let's do our best.

Who goeth in the way which Christ hath gone,
Is much more sure to meet with him than one
   That traveleth byways.
Perhaps my God, though he be far before,   40
May turn and take me by the hand, and more
   May strengthen my decays.

Yet, Lord, instruct us to improve our fast
By starving sin, and taking such repast
   As may our faults control;
That ev'ry man may revel at his door,
Not in his parlor; banqueting the poor,
   And among those his soul.

Sunday

O day most calm, most bright,
The fruit of this, the next world's bud,
Th' indorsement of supreme delight,
Writ by a friend, and with his blood,
The couch of time, care's balm and bay;
The week were dark but for thy light,
    Thy torch doth show the way.

The other days and thou
Make up one man, whose face thou art,
Knocking at heaven with thy brow.   10
The worky-days are the back part,
The burden of the week lies there,
Making the whole to stoop and bow
    Till thy release appear.

Man had straight forward gone
To endless death, but thou dost pull
And turn us round to look on one
Whom, if we were not very dull,
We could not choose but look on still,
Since there is no place so alone   20
    The which he doth not fill.

Sundays the pillars are
On which heav'n's palace archèd lies;
The other days fill up the spare
And hollow room with vanities.
They are the fruitful beds and borders
In God's rich garden; that is bare
    Which parts their ranks and orders.

The Sundays of man's life,
Threaded together on time's string,   30
Make bracelets to adorn the wife
Of the eternal glorious king.
On Sunday heaven's gate stands ope,
Blessings are plentiful and rife,
    More plentiful than hope.

This day my Savior rose,
And did enclose this light for his;
That, as each beast his manger knows,
Man might not of his fodder miss.

Christ hath took in this piece of ground, 40
And made a garden there for those
   Who want herbs for their wound.

   The rest of our creation
Our great Redeemer did remove
With the same shake which at his passion
Did th' earth and all things with it move.
As Samson bore the doors away,
Christ's hands, though nailed, wrought our salvation,
   And did unhinge that day.

   The brightness of that day 50
We sullied by our foul offence;
Wherefore that robe we cast away,
Having a new at his expense,
Whose drops of blood paid the full price
That was required to make us gay,
   And fit for paradise.

   Thou art a day of mirth;
And where the week-days trail on ground,
Thy flight is higher, as thy birth.
O let me take thee at the bound, 60
Leaping with thee from sev'n to sev'n,
Till that we both, being tossed from earth,
   Fly hand in hand to heav'n.

Church music

Sweetest of sweets, I thank you! when displeasure
   Did through my body wound my mind,
You took me thence, and in your house of pleasure
   A dainty lodging me assigned.

Now I in you without a body move,
   Rising and falling with your wings.
We both together sweetly live and love,
   Yet say sometimes, God help poor kings.

Comfort, I'll die; for if you post from me,
   Sure I shall do so and much more. 10
But if I travel in your company,
   You know the way to heaven's door.

To all angels and saints

O glorious spirits, who after all your bands
See the smooth face of God without a frown
    Or strict commands,
Where ev'ryone is king, and hath his crown,
If not upon his head, yet in his hands.

Not out of envy or maliciousness
Do I forbear to crave your special aid;
    I would address
My vows to thee most gladly, blessed Maid,
And Mother of my God, in my distress;   10

Thou art the holy mine whence came the gold,
The great restorative for all decay
    In young and old;
Thou art the cabinet where the jewel lay;
Chiefly to thee would I my soul unfold.

But now, alas, I dare not, for our King,
Whom we do all jointly adore and praise,
    Bids no such thing;
And where his pleasure no injunction lays,
'Tis your own case, ye never move a wing.   20

All worship is prerogative, and a flower
Of his rich crown from whom lies no appeal
    At the last hour.
Therefore we dare not from his garland steal
To make a posy for inferior power.

Although, then, others court you, if ye know
What's done on earth, we shall not fare the worse
    Who do not so;
Since we are ever ready to disburse,
If anyone our Master's hand can show.   30

Man

    My God, I heard this day
That none doth build a stately habitation
    But he that means to dwell therein.
    What house more stately hath there been,
Or can be, than is man, to whose creation
    All things are in decay?

For man is ev'rything,
And more: he is a tree, yet bears no fruit;
A beast, yet is, or should be, more;
Reason and speech we only bring;
Parrots may thank us if they are not mute,
They go upon the score.

Man is all symmetry,
Full of proportions, one limb to another,
And all to all the world besides.
Each part may call the farthest brother,
For head with foot hath private amity,
And both with moons and tides.

Nothing hath got so far
But man hath caught and kept it as his prey:
His eyes dismount the highest star;
He is in little all the sphere;
Herbs gladly cure our flesh, because that they
Find their acquaintance there.

For us the winds do blow,
The earth doth rest, heav'n move, and fountains flow.
Nothing we see but means our good,
As our delight, or as our treasure;
The whole is either our cupboard of food,
Or cabinet of pleasure.

The stars have us to bed;
Night draws the curtain, which the sun withdraws;
Music and light attend our head;
All things unto our flesh are kind
In their descent and being, to our mind
In their ascent and cause.

Each thing is full of duty:
Waters united are our navigation;
Distinguishèd, our habitation;
Below, our drink; above, our meat;
Both are our cleanliness. Hath one such beauty?
Then how are all things neat!

More servants wait on man
Than he'll take notice of; in ev'ry path
He treads down that which doth befriend him
When sickness makes him pale and wan.

Oh, mighty love! Man is one world and hath
    Another to attend him.

    Since then, my God, thou hast
So brave a palace built, O dwell in it,   50
    That it may dwell with thee at last!
    Till then afford us so much wit
That as the world serves us we may serve thee,
    And both thy servants be.

Affliction

When first thou didst entice to thee my heart,
    I thought the service brave;
So many joys I writ down for my part,
    Besides what I might have
Out of my stock of natural delights,
Augmented with thy gracious benefits.

I lookëd on thy furniture so fine,
    And made it fine to me;
Thy glorious household-stuff did me entwine,
    And 'tice me unto thee.   10
Such stars I counted mine: both heav'n and earth
Paid me my wages in a world of mirth.

What pleasures could I want whose king I served,
    Where joys my fellows were?
Thus argued into hopes, my thoughts reserved
    No place for grief or fear.
Therefore my sudden soul caught at the place,
And made her youth and fierceness seek thy face.

At first thou gav'st me milk and sweetness;
    I had my wish and way;   20
My days were strawed with flowers and happiness,
    There was no month but May.
But with my years, sorrow did twist and grow,
And made a party unawares for woe.

My flesh began unto my soul in pain:
    Sicknesses cleave my bones;
Consuming agues dwell in ev'ry vein,
    And tune my breath to groans.
Sorrow was all my soul; I scarce believed,
Till grief did tell me roundly, that I lived.   30

When I got health thou took'st away my life,
    And more, for my friends die.
My mirth and edge was lost; a blunted knife
    Was of more use than I.
Thus thin and lean, without a fence or friend,
I was blown through with ev'ry storm and wind.

Whereas my birth and spirit rather took
    The way that takes the town,
Thou didst betray me to a ling'ring book
    And wrap me in a gown.   40
I was entangled in the world of strife
Before I had the power to change my life.

Yet, for I threatened oft the siege to raise,
    Not simp'ring all mine age,
Thou often didst with academic praise
    Melt and dissolve my rage.
I took thy sweetened pill till I came near;
I could not go away, nor persevere.

Yet lest perchance I should too happy be
    In my unhappiness,   50
Turning my purge to food, thou throwest me
    Into more sicknesses.
Thus doth thy power cross-bias me, not making
Thine own gift good, yet me from my ways taking.

Now I am here, what thou wilt do with me
    None of my books will show.
I read and sigh and wish I were a tree,
    For sure then I should grow
To fruit or shade. At least some bird would trust
Her household to me, and I should be just.   60

Yet, though thou troublest me, I must be meek;
    In weakness must be stout.
Well, I will change the service and go seek
    Some other master out.
Ah, my dear God! though I am clean forgot,
Let me not love thee if I love thee not.

Frailty

Lord, in my silence how do I despise
    What upon trust

Is stylëd honor, riches, or fair eyes,
　　But is fair dust!
I surname them gilded clay,
　　Dear earth, fine grass or hay.
In all, I think my foot doth ever tread
　　Upon their head.

But when I view abroad both regiments,
　　The world's and thine,
Thine clad with simpleness and sad events,
　　The other fine,
　　Full of glory and gay weeds,
　　Brave language, braver deeds;
That which was dust before doth quickly rise,
　　And prick mine eyes.

O brook not this, lest if what even now
　　My foot did tread,
Affront those joys wherewith thou didst endow
　　And long since wed
　　My poor soul, ev'n sick of love;
　　It may a Babel prove,
Commodious to conquer heav'n and thee,
　　Planted in me.

Nature

　　Full of rebellion, I would die,
　　Or fight, or travel, or deny
　　That thou hast aught to do with me.
　　　　O tame my heart!
　　　　It is thy highest art
　　To captivate strongholds to thee.

　　If thou shalt let this venom lurk
　　And in suggestions fume and work,
　　My soul will turn to bubbles straight,
　　　　And thence by kind
　　　　Vanish into a wind,
　　Making thy workmanship deceit.

　　O smooth my rugged heart, and there
　　Engrave thy rev'rend law and fear!
　　Or make a new one, since the old
　　　　Is sapless grown,
　　　　And a much fitter stone
　　To hide my dust than thee to hold.

The pearl

Matthew xiii

I know the ways of learning: both the head
And pipes that feed the press, and make it run;
What reason hath from nature borrowëd,
Or of itself, like a good housewife, spun
In laws and policy; what the stars conspire;
What willing nature speaks, what forced by fire;
Both th'old discoveries and the new-found seas,
The stock and surplus, cause and history;
All these stand open, or I have the keys,—
   Yet I love thee.   10

I know the ways of honor: what maintains
The quick returns of courtesy and wit;
In vies of favors whether party gains
When glory swells the heart and moldeth it
To all expressions both of hand and eye,
Which on the world a true-love-knot may tie,
And bear the bundle wheresoe'er it goes;
How many drams of spirit there must be
To sell my life unto my friends or foes,—
   Yet I love thee.   20

I know the ways of pleasure: the sweet strains,
The lullings and the relishes of it;
The propositions of hot blood and brains;
What mirth and music mean; what love and wit
Have done these twenty hundred years and more;
I know the projects of unbridled store;
My stuff is flesh, not brass; my senses live,
And grumble oft that they have more in me
Than he that curbs them, being but one to five,—
   Yet I love thee.   30

I know all these and have them in my hand;
Therefore not seelëd but with open eyes
I fly to thee, and fully understand
Both the main sale and the commodities;
And at what rate and price I have thy love,
With all the circumstances that may move.
Yet through the labyrinths, not my groveling wit,
But thy silk twist let down from heav'n to me
Did both conduct and teach me how by it
   To climb to thee.   40

The pulley

When God at first made man,
Having a glass of blessings standing by,
Let us, said he, pour on him all we can.
Let the world's riches, which dispersëd lie,
    Contract into a span.

So strength first made a way,
Then beauty flowed, then wisdom, honor, pleasure.
When almost all was out, God made a stay,
Perceiving that alone of all his treasure
    Rest in the bottom lay.   10

For if I should, said he,
Bestow this jewel also on my creature,
He would adore my gifts instead of me,
And rest in nature, not the God of nature;
    So both should losers be.

Yet let him keep the rest,
But keep them with repining restlessness.
Let him be rich and weary, that at least,
If goodness lead him not, yet weariness
    May toss him to my breast.   20

Peace

Sweet Peace, where dost thou dwell? I humbly crave
    Let me once know.
  I sought thee in a secret cave,
    And asked if Peace were there.
A hollow wind did seem to answer, No,
    Go seek elsewhere.

I did, and going did a rainbow note.
    Surely, thought I,
  This is the lace of Peace's coat,
    I will search out the matter.
But while I looked, the clouds immediately   10
    Did break and scatter.

Then went I to a garden and did spy
    A gallant flower,
  The crown imperial. Sure, said I,

Peace at the root must dwell.
But when I digged, I saw a worm devour
What showed so well.

At length I met a rev'rend good old man,
Whom when for Peace
I did demand, he thus began:
There was a prince of old
At Salem dwelt, who lived with good increase
Of flock and fold.

He sweetly lived, yet sweetness did not save
His life from foes.
But after death out of his grave
There sprang twelve stalks of wheat;
Which many wond'ring at, got some of those
To plant and set.

It prospered strangely and did soon disperse
Through all the earth;
For they that taste it do rehearse
That virtue lies therein,
A secret virtue bringing peace and mirth
By flight of sin.

Take of this grain, which in my garden grows,
And grows for you;
Make bread of it, and that repose
And peace which ev'rywhere
With so much earnestness you do pursue,
Is only there.

Conscience

Peace, prattler, do not lour!
Not a fair look but thou dost call it foul.
Not a sweet dish but thou dost call it sour.
Music to thee doth howl.
By list'ning to thy chatting fears,
I have both lost mine eyes and ears.

Prattler, no more, I say!
My thoughts must work, but like a noiseless sphere;
Harmonious peace must rock them all the day,
No room for prattlers there.
If thou persistest, I will tell thee
That I have physic to expel thee.

And the receipt shall be
My Savior's blood. Whenever at his board
I do but taste it, straight it cleanseth me
    And leaves thee not a word;
      No, not a tooth or nail to scratch,
      And at my actions carp or catch.

    Yet if thou talkest still,
Besides my physic know there's some for thee;   20
Some wood and nails to make a staff or bill
    For those that trouble me.
    The bloody cross of my dear Lord
    Is both my physic and my sword.

Discipline

Throw away thy rod,
Throw away thy wrath.
    O my God,
Take the gentle path.

For my heart's desire
Unto thine is bent;
    I aspire
To a full consent.

Not a word or look
I affect to own,   10
    But by book,
And thy book alone.

Though I fail, I weep.
Though I halt in pace,
    Yet I creep
To the throne of grace.

Then let wrath remove;
Love will do the deed,
    For with love
Stony hearts will bleed.   20

Love is swift of foot.
Love's a man of war,
    And can shoot,
And can hit from far.

Who can 'scape his bow?
That which wrought on thee,
    Brought thee low,
Needs must work on me.

Throw away thy rod.
Though man frailties hath,   30
    Thou art God.
Throw away thy wrath.

Redemption

Having been tenant long to a rich Lord,
    Not thriving, I resolvëd to be bold,
    And make a suit unto him to afford
A new small-rented lease and cancel th' old.
In heaven at his manor I him sought.
    They told me there that he was lately gone
    About some land which he had dearly bought
Long since on earth, to take possessïon.
I straight returned, and knowing his great birth,

Sought him accordingly in great resorts, 10
  In cities, theaters, gardens, parks, and courts.
At length I heard a ragged noise and mirth
  Of thieves and murderers; there I him espied,
Who straight, Your suit is granted, said, and died.

Love

Love bade me welcome, yet my soul drew back,
  Guilty of dust and sin.
But quick-eyed Love, observing me grow slack
  From my first entrance in,
Drew nearer to me, sweetly questioning
  If I lacked anything.

A guest, I answered, worthy to be here.
  Love said, You shall be he.
I, the unkind, the ungrateful? ah, my dear, 10
  I cannot look on thee.
Love took my hand and smiling did reply,
  Who made the eyes but I?

Truth, Lord, but I have marred them; let my shame
  Go where it doth deserve.
And know you not, says Love, who bore the blame?
  My dear, then I will serve.
You must sit down, says Love, and taste my meat.
  So I did sit and eat.

The priesthood

Blest order, which in power doth so excel,
That with th' one hand thou liftest to the sky,
And with the other throwest down to hell
In thy just censures; fain would I draw nigh,
Fain put thee on, exchanging my lay-sword
  For that of th' holy word.

But thou art fire, sacred and hallowed fire,
And I but earth and clay. Should I presume
To wear thy habit, the severe attire,
My slender compositions might consume. 10
I am both foul and brittle, much unfit
  To deal in holy writ.

Yet have I often seen, by cunning hand
And force of fire, what curious things are made

Of wretched earth. Where once I scorned to stand,
That earth is fitted by the fire and trade
Of skillful artists for the boards of those
 Who make the bravest shows.

But since those great ones, be they ne'er so great,
Come from the earth from whence those vessels come,   20
So that at once both feeder, dish, and meat
Have one beginning and one final sum;
I do not greatly wonder at the sight,
 If earth in earth delight.

But th' holy men of God such vessels are
As serve him up who all the world commands.
When God vouchsafeth to become our fare,
Their hands convey him who conveys their hands.
Oh, what pure things, most pure, must those things be
 Who bring my God to me!   30

Wherefore I dare not, I, put forth my hand
To hold the Ark, although it seem to shake
Through th' old sins and new doctrines of our land.
Only since God doth often vessels make
Of lowly matter for high uses meet,
 I throw me at his feet.

There will I lie until my maker seek
For some mean stuff whereon to show his skill.
Then is my time. The distance of the meek
Doth flatter power. Lest good come short of ill   40
In praising might, the poor do by submission
 What pride by opposition.

Aaron

Holiness on the head,
 Light and perfections on the breast,
Harmonious bells below, raising the dead
 To lead them unto life and rest:
  Thus are true Aarons dressed.

Profaneness in my head,
 Defects and darkness in my breast,
A noise of passions ringing me for dead
 Unto a place where is no rest:
  Poor priest, thus am I dressed.   10

Only another head
I have, another heart and breast,
Another music, making live not dead,
Without whom I could have no rest:
In him I am well dressed.

Christ is my only head,
My alone only heart and breast,
My only music, striking me ev'n dead,
That to the old man I may rest,
And be in him new dressed.

So holy in my head,
Perfect and light in my dear breast,
My doctrine tuned by Christ, who is not dead,
But lives in me while I do rest,
Come people! Aaron's dressed.

The windows

Lord, how can man preach thy eternal word?
He is a brittle crazy glass,
Yet in thy temple thou dost him afford
This glorious and transcendent place
To be a window, through thy grace.

But when thou dost anneal in glass thy story,
Making thy life to shine within
The holy preacher's, then the light and glory
More rev'rend grows, and doth more win;
Which else shows wat'rish, bleak, and thin.

Doctrine and life, colors and light in one,
When they combine and mingle, bring
A strong regard and awe; but speech alone
Doth vanish like a flaring thing,
And in the ear, not conscience, ring.

The call

Come, my way, my truth, my life;
Such a way as gives us breath,
Such a truth as ends all strife,
Such a life as killeth death.

Come, my light, my feast, my strength;
Such a light as shows a feast,

Such a feast as mends in length,
Such a strength as makes his guest.

Come, my joy, my love, my heart;
Such a joy as none can move,
Such a love as none can part,
Such a heart as joys in love.

The odor

2 *Corinthians ii*

How sweetly doth My Master sound! My Master!
As ambergris leaves a rich scent
Unto the taster,
So do these words a sweet content,
An oriental fragrancy, My Master.

With these all day I do perfume my mind,
My mind ev'n thrust into them both,
That I might find
What cordials make this curious broth,
This broth of smells, that feeds and fats my mind.

My Master, shall I speak? Oh, that to thee
My servant! were a little so,
As flesh may be,
That these two words might creep and grow
To some degree of spiciness to thee!

Then should the pomander, which was before
A speaking sweet, mend by reflection
And tell me more;
For pardon of my imperfection
Would warm and work it sweeter than before.

For when My Master, which alone is sweet
And ev'n in my unworthiness pleasing,
Shall call and meet
My servant, as thee not displeasing,
That call is but the breathing of the sweet.

This breathing would with gains by sweet'ning me,
As sweet things traffic when they meet,
Return to thee;
And so this new commerce and sweet
Should all my life employ and busy me.

A true hymn

My joy, my life, my crown!
  My heart was meaning all the day
    Somewhat it fain would say;
And still it runneth mutt'ring up and down
With only this, My joy, my life, my crown.

  Yet slight not these few words.
    If truly said they may take part
      Among the best in art.
The fineness which a hymn or psalm affords
Is when the soul unto the lines accords.   10

  He who craves all the mind,
    And all the soul, and strength, and time,
      If the words only rhyme,
Justly complains that somewhat is behind
To make his verse, or write a hymn in kind.

  Whereas if th' heart be moved,
    Although the verse be somewhat scant,
      God doth supply the want,
As when th' heart says, sighing to be approved,
Oh, could I love! and stops, God writeth, Loved.   20

Dullness

Why do I languish thus, drooping and dull,
    As if I were all earth?
O give me quickness, that I may with mirth
    Praise thee brim-full!

The wanton lover in a curious strain
    Can praise his fairest fair,
And with quaint metaphors her curlèd hair
    Curl o'er again.

Thou art my loveliness, my life, my light,
    Beauty alone to me.   10
Thy bloody death and undeserved makes thee
    Pure red and white.

When all perfections as but one appear—
    That, those, thy form doth show—

The very dust where thou dost tread and go
　　Makes beauties here.

Where are my lines then, my approaches, views?
　　Where are my window-songs?
Lovers are still pretending, and ev'n wrongs
　　Sharpen their muse.　　　　　　　　　　　20

But I am lost in flesh, whose sugared lies
　　Still mock me and grow bold.
Sure thou didst put a mind there, if I could
　　Find where it lies.

Lord, clear thy gift, that with a constant wit
　　I may but look towards thee.
Look only, for to love thee, who can be,
　　What angel, fit?

The collar

I struck the board and cried, No more!
　　I will abroad.
What? Shall I ever sigh and pine?
My lines and life are free, free as the road,
　　Loose as the wind, as large as store.
　　　Shall I be still in suit?
Have I no harvest but a thorn
To let me blood, and not restore
What I have lost with cordial fruit?
　　　Sure there was wine　　　　　　　　　10
Before my sighs did dry it; there was corn
　　Before my tears did drown it.
Is the year only lost to me?
　　Have I no bays to crown it?
No flowers, no garlands gay? All blasted?
　　All wasted?
Not so, my heart! But there is fruit,
　　And thou hast hands.
Recover all thy sigh-blown age
On double pleasures. Leave thy cold dispute 　＼　20
Of what is fit and not. Forsake thy cage,
　　Thy rope of sands,
Which petty thoughts have made, and made to thee
　Good cable, to enforce and draw,
　　　And be thy law,
While thou didst wink and wouldst not see.

Away! Take heed!
I will abroad.
Call in thy death's head there. Tie up thy fears.
He that forbears   30
To suit and serve his need
Deserves his load.
But as I raved and grew more fierce and wild
At every word,
Me thoughts I heard one calling, Child!
And I replied, My Lord.

The flower

How fresh, O Lord, how sweet and clean
Are thy returns! Ev'n as the flowers in spring,
To which, besides their own demean,
The late-past frosts tributes of pleasure bring.
Grief melts away
Like snow in May,
As if there were no such cold thing.

Who would have thought my shriveled heart
Could have recovered greenness? It was gone
Quite underground, as flowers depart   10
To see their mother-root when they have blown;
Where they together
All the hard weather,
Dead to the world, keep house unknown.

These are thy wonders, Lord of power,
Killing and quick'ning, bringing down to hell
And up to heaven in an hour;
Making a chiming of a passing bell.
We say amiss
This or that is;   20
Thy word is all, if we could spell.

Oh, that I once past changing were,
Fast in thy paradise, where no flower can wither!
Many a spring I shoot up fair,
Off'ring at heav'n, growing and groaning thither;
Nor doth my flower
Want a spring shower,
My sins and I joining together.

But while I grow in a straight line,
Still upwards bent, as if heav'n were mine own,   30

Thy anger comes, and I decline.
What frost to that? What pole is not the zone
    Where all things burn,
    When thou dost turn,
And the least frown of thine is shown?

And now in age I bud again,
After so many deaths I live and write;
  I once more smell the dew and rain,
And relish versing. O my only light,
    It cannot be   40
    That I am he
On whom thy tempests fell all night.

These are thy wonders, Lord of love,
To make us see we are but flowers that glide;
  Which when we once can find and prove,
Thou hast a garden for us where to bide.
    Who would be more,
    Swelling through store,
Forfeit their paradise by their pride.

Virtue

Sweet day, so cool, so calm, so bright,
The bridal of the earth and sky;
The dew shall weep thy fall to-night,
    For thou must die.

Sweet rose, whose hue angry and brave
Bids the rash gazer wipe his eye;
Thy root is ever in its grave,
    And thou must die.

Sweet spring, full of sweet days and roses,
A box where sweets compacted lie;   10
My music shows ye have your closes,
    And all must die.

Only a sweet and virtuous soul,
Like seasoned timber, never gives;
But though the whole world turn to coal,
    Then chiefly lives.

FRANCIS QUARLES

The Introduction and Notes are at page 1022

FROM *Argalus and Parthenia*, 1629

Hos ego versiculos

Like to the damask rose you see,
Or like the blossom on the tree,
Or like the dainty flower of May,
Or like the morning to the day,
Or like the sun, or like the shade,
Or like the gourd which Jonas had:
Even such is man, whose thread is spun,
Drawn out and out, and so is done.
    The rose withers, the blossom blasteth,
    The flower fades, the morning hasteth,   10
    The sun sets, the shadow flies,
    The gourd consumes, and man he dies.

Like to the blaze of fond delight,
Or like a morning clear and bright,
Or like a frost, or like a shower,
Or like the pride of Babel's tower,
Or like the hour that guides the time,
Or like to beauty in her prime:
Even such is man, whose glory lends
His life a blaze or two, and ends.   20
    Delights vanish, the morn o'ercasteth,
    The frost breaks, the shower hasteth,
    The tower falls, the hour spends,
    The beauty fades, and man's life ends.

FROM *Divine Fancies*, 1632

A good-night

Close now thine eyes and rest secure;
Thy soul is safe enough, thy body sure;
    He that loves thee, he that keeps
And guards thee, never slumbers, never sleeps.
The smiling conscience in a sleeping breast
    Has only peace, has only rest;
    The music and the mirth of kings

Are all but very discords, when she sings;
    Then close thine eyes and rest secure;
No sleep so sweet as thine, no rest so sure.

FROM *Emblems,* 1635

[*False world, thou ly'st*]

Proverbs xxiii. 5
*Wilt thou set thine eyes upon that which is not? for riches make them-
selves wings, they fly away as an eagle.*

False world, thou ly'st; thou canst not lend
    The least delight;
Thy favors cannot gain a friend,
    They are so slight;
Thy morning pleasures make an end
    To please at night;
Poor are the wants that thou supply'st,
And yet thou vaunt'st, and yet thou vy'st
With heaven. Fond earth, thou boasts; false world, thou ly'st.

Thy babbling tongue tells golden tales   10
    Of endless treasure;
Thy bounty offers easy sales
    Of lasting pleasure;
Thou asks the conscience what she ails,
    And swear'st to ease her;
There's none can want where thou supply'st;
There's none can give where thou deny'st.
Alas, fond world, thou boasts; false world, thou ly'st.

What well-advisèd ear regards
    What earth can say?   20
Thy words are gold, but thy rewards
    Are painted clay;
Thy cunning can but pack the cards,
    Thou canst not play
Thy game at weakest, still thou vy'st;
If seen, and then revied, deny'st;
Thou art not what thou seem'st; false world, thou ly'st.

Thy tinsel bosom seems a mint
    Of new-coined treasure,
A paradise that has no stint,   30
    No change, no measure;
A painted cask, but nothing in 't,
    Nor wealth, nor pleasure;

Vain earth! that falsely thus comply'st
With man; vain man! that thus rely'st
On earth; vain man, thou dot'st, vain earth, thou ly'st.

What mean dull souls, in this high measure
    To haberdash
In earth's base wares, whose greatest treasure
    Is dross and trash?   40
The height of whose enchanting pleasure
    Is but a flash?
Are these the goods that thou supply'st
Us mortals with? are these the high'st?
Can these bring cordial peace? False world, thou ly'st.

[*Oh, whither shall I fly?*]

Job xiv. 13

Oh, that thou wouldst hide me in the grave, that thou wouldst keep me
secret until thy wrath be past!

Oh, whither shall I fly, what path untrod
Shall I seek out to 'scape the flaming rod
Of my offended, of my angry God?

Where shall I sojourn, what kind sea will hide
My head from thunder? where shall I abide
Until his flames be quenched or laid aside?

What if my feet should take their hasty flight
And seek protection in the shades of night?
Alas, no shades can blind the God of light.

What if my soul should take the wings of day   10
And find some desert? if she spring away
The wings of vengeance clip as fast as they.

What if some solid rock should entertain
My frighted soul? Can solid rocks restrain
The stroke of justice, and not cleave in twain?

Nor sea, nor shade, nor shield, nor rock, nor cave,
Nor silent deserts, nor the sullen grave,
Where flame-eyed fury means to smite, can save.

The seas will part, graves open, rocks will split,
The shield will cleave, the frighted shadows flit;   20
Where justice aims, her fiery darts must hit.

No, no, if stern-browed vengeance means to thunder,
There is no place above, beneath, nor under,
So close but will unlock, or rive in sunder.

'Tis vain to flee; 'tis neither here nor there
Can 'scape that hand until that hand forbear;
Ah me! where is he not, that's everywhere?

'Tis vain to flee; till gentle mercy show
Her better eye, the farther off we go,
The swing of justice deals the mightier blow.   30

Th' ingenious child, corrected, does not fly
His angry mother's hand, but clings more nigh,
And quenches with his tears her flaming eye.

Shadows are faithless, and the rocks are false;
No trust in brass, no trust in marble walls;
Poor cots are even as safe as princes' halls.

Great God, there is no safety here below;
Thou art my fortress, though thou seem'st my foe;
'Tis thou that strik'st the stroke must guard the blow.

Thou art my God; by thee I fall or stand;   40
Thy grace hath given me courage to withstand
All tortures, but my conscience and thy hand.

I know thy justice is thyself; I know,
Just God, thy very self is mercy too;
If not to thee, where? whither should I go?

Then work thy will; if passion bid me flee,
My reason shall obey; my wings shall be
Stretched out no further than from thee to thee.

[Oh, how my will is hurried]

Romans vii. 23
*I see another law in my members warring against the law of my mind,
and bringing me into captivity to the law of sin.*

Oh, how my will is hurried to and fro,
    And how my unresolved resolves do vary!
I know not where to fix; sometimes I go
    This way, then that, and then the quite contrary;
        I like, dislike, lament for what I could not;

I do, undo, yet still do what I should not;
And at the self-same instant will the thing I would not.

Thus are my weather-beaten thoughts oppressed
  With th' earth-bred winds of my prodigious will;
Thus am I hourly tossed from east to west   10
  Upon the rolling streams of good and ill;
    Thus am I driven upon these slipp'ry suds
    From real ills to false apparent goods;
My life's a troubled sea, composed of ebbs and floods.

The curious penman, having trimmed his page
  With the dead language of his dabbled quill,
Lets fall a heedless drop, then in a rage
  Cashiers the fruits of his unlucky skill;
    Ev'n so my pregnant soul in th' infant bud
    Of her best thoughts, showers down a coal-black flood   20
Of unadvisèd ills, and cancels all her good.

Sometimes a sudden flash of sacred heat
  Warms my chill soul, and sets my thoughts in frame;
But soon that fire is shouldered from her seat
  By lustful Cupid's much inferior flame.
    I feel two flames, and yet no flame entire;
    Thus are the mongrel thoughts of mixed desire
Consumed between that heav'nly and this earthly fire.

Sometimes my trash-disdaining thoughts outpass
  The common period of terrene conceit;   30
Oh, then methinks I scorn the thing I was,
  Whilst I stand ravished at my new estate;
    But when th' Icarian wings of my desire
    Feel but the warmth of their own native fire,
Oh, then they melt and plunge within their wonted mire.

I know the nature of my wav'ring mind;
  I know the frailty of my fleshly will;
My passion's eagle-eyed, my judgment blind;
  I know what's good, but yet make choice of ill.
    When th' ostrich wings of my desires shall be   40
    So dull, they cannot mount the least degree;
Yet grant my soul desire but of desiring thee.

[Ev'n like two little bank-dividing brooks]

Canticles ii. 16
My beloved is mine, and I am his; he feedeth among the lilies.

Ev'n like two little bank-dividing brooks
    That wash the pebbles with their wanton streams,
And having ranged and searched a thousand nooks,
    Meet both at length in silver-breasted Thames,
        Where in a greater current they conjoin,
So I my best beloved's am; so he is mine.

Ev'n so we met, and after long pursuit,
    Ev'n so we joined; we both became entire.
No need for either to renew a suit,
    For I was flax, and he was flames of fire.
        Our firm-united souls did more than twine;
So I my best beloved's am; so he is mine.

If all those glitt'ring monarchs that command
    The servile quarters of this earthly ball
Should tender, in exchange, their shares of land,
    I would not change my fortunes for them all;
        Their wealth is but a counter to my coin;
The world's but theirs; but my beloved's mine.

Nay more, if the fair Thespian ladies all
    Should heap together their diviner treasure,
That treasure should be deemed a price too small
    To buy a minute's lease of half my pleasure.
        'Tis not the sacred wealth of all the Nine
Can buy my heart from him, or his from being mine.

Nor time, nor place, nor chance, nor death can bow
    My least desires unto the least remove;
He's firmly mine by oath, I his by vow;
    He's mine by faith, and I am his by love;
        He's mine by water, I am his by wine;
Thus I my best beloved's am; thus he is mine.

He is my altar; I, his holy place;
    I am his guest, and he my living food;
I'm his by penitence, he mine by grace;
    I'm his by purchase, he is mine by blood!
        He's my supporting elm, and I his vine;
Thus I my best beloved's am; thus he is mine.

He gives me wealth, I give him all my vows;
  I give him songs, he gives me length of days;
With wreaths of grace he crowns my conq'ring brows,
  And I his temples with a crown of praise,   40
    Which he accepts as an everlasting sign
  That I my best beloved's am, that he is mine.

FROM *Hieroglyphics of the life of man*, 1638
[*Behold how short a span*]
Job xiv. 2
He cometh forth like a flower, and is cut down.

Behold
How short a span
Was long enough, of old,
To measure out the life of man!
In those well-tempered days his time was then
Surveyed, cast up, and found but threescore years and ten.

Alas,
And what is that?
They come and slide and pass,
Before my pen can tell thee what.   10
The posts of time are swift, which having run
Their seven short stages o'er, their short-lived task is done.

Our days
Begun, we lend
To sleep, to antic plays
And toys, until the first stage end;
12 waning moons, twice 5 times told, we give
To unrecovered loss; we rather breathe than live.

We spend
A ten years' breath   20
Before   we   apprehend
What is to live, or fear a death;
Our childish dreams are filled with painted joys,
Which please our sense awhile, and waking, prove but toys.

How vain,
How wretched is
Poor man, that doth remain
A slave to such a state as this!
His days are short at longest; few at most;
They are but bad at best; yet lavished out, or lost.   30

They be
The secret springs
That make our minutes flee
On wheels more swift than eagles' wings;
Our life's a clock, and every gasp of breath
Breathes forth a warning grief, till time shall strike a death.

How soon
Our new-born light
Attains to full-aged noon!
And this, how soon to grey-haired night!　　　　　　40
We spring, we bud, we blossom, and we blast
Ere we can count our days, our days they flee so fast.

They end
When scarce begun;
And ere we apprehend
That we begin to live, our life is done;
Man, count thy days, and if they flee too fast
For thy dull thoughts to count, count every day thy last.

HENRY MORE

The Introduction and Notes are at page 1023

FROM *Philosophical Poems*, 1647

Psychozoia, or the life of the soul

.　　　　.　　．　　　　　．　　．

Thus in my youth, said Mnemon, did I use
With reverend ignorance to sport and toy,
And slyly would obnoxious age abuse;
For I was a crank wit, a brisk young boy,
But naturally abhorred hypocrisy
And craft, the upshot of experienced age;
And more than life I loved my liberty,
And much suspected all that would engage
My heart to their own sect, and free-born soul encage.

For I, ev'n at those years, was well aware　　　　　10
Of man's false friendship and grown subtlety,
Which made me snuff the wind, drink the free air,
Like a young colt upon the mountains high,
And turning tail, my hunters all defy.
Ne took I any guide but th' innate light

Of my true conscience, whose voice to deny
Was the whole sting of my offended sprite;
Thus God and nature taught their rude cosmopolite.

I mean not nature's harsh obdurate light,
The shameless eyebrows of the serpent old,
That armed with custom will not stick to fight
With God, and him affront with courage bold,
But that sweet temper we may oft behold
In virgin youth as yet immaculate,
And unto drudging policy unfold,
Who do without design now love, now hate,
And freely give and take withouten price or rate.

Dear lads! how do I love your harmless years,
And melt in heart while I the morning shine
Do view of rising virtue which appears
In your sweet faces and mild modest eyne.
Adore that God that doth himself enshrine
In your untainted breasts, and give no ear
To wicked voice that may your souls incline
Unto false peace, or unto fruitless fear,
Lest, loosened from yourselves, harpies away you bear.

Abstain from censure, seek and you shall find,
Drink your own waters drawn from living well,
Mend in yourselves what ill elsewhere you mind,
Deal so with men as you would have them deal,
Honor the aged, that it may go well
With you in age, for I myself indeed
Have borne much scorn for these pranks, I you tell,
By boys oft bearded, which I deem the meed
Of my abusive youth. But now I will proceed.

. . . .

Charity and humility

Far have I clambered in my mind,
But nought so great as love I find;
Deep-searching wit, mount-moving might,
Are nought compared to that good sprite.
Life of delight and soul of bliss!
Sure source of lasting happiness!
Higher than heaven, lower than hell!
What is thy tent? Where mayst thou dwell?
My mansion hight humility,

Heaven's vastest capability;   10
The further it doth downward tend
The higher up it doth ascend;
If it go down to utmost nought,
It shall return with that it sought.
    Lord, stretch thy tent in my strait breast,
Enlarge it downward, that sure rest
May there be pight, for that pure fire
Wherewith thou wontest to inspire
All self-dead souls. My life is gone,
Sad solitude's my irksome wone.   20
Cut off from men and all this world,
In Lethe's lonesome ditch I'm hurled;
Nor might nor sight doth aught me move,
Nor do I care to be above.
O feeble rays of mental light,
That best be seen in this dark night,
What are you? What is any strength
If it be not laid in one length
With pride or love? I nought desire
But a new life, or quite t' expire.   30
Could I demolish with mine eye
Strong towers, stop the fleet stars in sky,
Bring down to earth the pale-faced moon,
Or turn black midnight to bright noon,
Though all things were put in my hand,
As parched, as dry as th' Libyan sand
Would be my life if charity
Were wanting. But humility
Is more than my poor soul durst crave,
That lies entombed in lowly grave.   40
But if 'twere lawful up to send
My voice to heaven, this should it rend:
    Lord, thrust me deeper into dust,
That thou mayst raise me with the just.

RICHARD CRASHAW

The Introduction and Notes are at page 1024

FROM *Steps to the Temple, Sacred Poems, with The Delights of the
Muses,* 1648

The Preface to the Reader.

    . . . *Here's Herbert's second, but equal, who hath retrieved poetry
of late and returned it up to its primitive use; let it bound back to*

heaven-gates whence it came. Think ye St. Augustine would have stained his graver learning with a book of poetry had he fancied its dearest end to be the vanity of love-sonnets and epithalamiums? No, no, he thought with this our poet, that every foot in a high-born verse might help to measure the soul into that better world. Divine poetry, I dare hold it in position against Suarez on the subject, to be the language of the angels; it is the quintessence of fantasy and discourse centered in heaven; 'tis the very outgoings of the soul; 'tis what alone our author is able to tell you, and that in his own verse.

It were profane but to mention here in the preface those under-headed poets, retainers to seven shares and a half, madrigal fellows, whose only business in verse is to rhyme a poor six-penny soul, a suburb sinner, into hell. May such arrogant pretenders to poetry vanish with their prodigious issue of tumorous heats and flashes of their adulterate brains, and forever after may this our poet fill up the better room of man. Oh! when the general arraignment of poets shall be, to give an account of their higher souls, with what a triumphant brow shall our divine poet sit above and look down upon poor Homer, Virgil, Horace, Claudian, &c., who had amongst them the ill luck to talk out a great part of their gallant genius upon bees, dung, frogs, and gnats, &c., and not as himself here, upon Scriptures, divine graces, martyrs, and angels.

Reader, we style his sacred poems, Steps to the Temple, and aptly, for in the temple of God, under his wing, he led his life in St. Mary's Church, near St. Peter's College. There he lodged under Tertullian's roof of angels; there he made his nest more gladly than David's swallow near the house of God; where like a primitive saint, he offered more prayers in the night than others usually offer in the day; there he penned these poems, steps for happy souls to climb heaven by.

And those other of his pieces, entitled The Delights of the Muses, though of a more humane mixture, are as sweet as they are innocent. . . .

Music's duel

Now westward Sol had spent the richest beams
Of noon's high glory, when hard by the streams
Of Tiber, on the scene of a green plat,
Under protection of an oak, there sat
A sweet lute's master, in whose gentle airs
He lost the day's heat, and his own hot cares.
    Close in the covert of the leaves there stood
A nightingale, come from the neighboring wood,
The sweet inhabitant of each glad tree,
Their muse, their siren, harmless siren she;   10
There stood she list'ning and did entertain
The music's soft report, and mold the same

In her own murmurs, that whatever mood
His curious fingers lent, her voice made good.
The man perceived his rival and her art;
Disposed to give the light-foot lady sport,
Awakes his lute, and 'gainst the fight to come
Informs it, in a sweet *præludium*
Of closer strains, and ere the war begin
He lightly skirmishes on every string,　　　　　　　20
Charged with a flying touch; and straightway she
Carves out her dainty voice as readily
Into a thousand sweet distinguished tones,
And reckons up in soft divisions
Quick volumes of wild notes, to let him know
By that shrill taste, she could do something too.

　　His nimble hands' instinct then taught each string
A cap'ring cheerfulness, and made them sing
To their own dance: now negligently rash,
He throws his arm, and with a long-drawn dash　　　30
Blends all together; then distinctly trips
From this to that; then quick returning skips
And snatches this again, and pauses there.
She measures every measure, everywhere
Meets art with art; sometimes as if in doubt
Not perfect yet, and fearing to be out,
Trails her plain ditty in one long-spun note,
Through the sleek passage of her open throat,
A clear unwrinkled song; then doth she point it
With tender accents, and severely joint it　　　　40
By short diminutives, that being reared
In controverting warbles evenly shared,
With her sweet self she wrangles. He, amazed
That from so small a channel should be raised
The torrent of a voice whose melody
Could melt into such sweet variety,
Strains higher yet, that tickled with rare art,
The tattling strings, each breathing in his part,
Most kindly do fall out: the grumbling bass
In surly groans disdains the treble's grace;　　　　50
The high-perched treble chirps at this, and chides,
Until his finger, moderator, hides
And closes the sweet quarrel, rousing all—
Hoarse, shrill, at once—as when the trumpets call
Hot Mars to th' harvest of death's field, and woo
Men's hearts into their hands. This lesson too
She gives him back; her supple breast thrills out
Sharp airs, and staggers in a warbling doubt

Of dallying sweetness, hovers o'er her skill,
And folds in waved notes with a trembling bill   60
The pliant series of her slippery song.
Then starts she suddenly into a throng
Of short thick sobs, whose thund'ring volleys float
And roll themselves over her lubric throat
In panting murmurs, stilled out of her breast,
That ever-bubbling spring, the sugared nest
Of her delicious soul, that there does lie
Bathing in streams of liquid melody;
Music's best seed-plot, whence in ripened airs
A golden-headed harvest fairly rears   70
His honey-dropping tops, plowed by her breath
Which there reciprocally laboreth
In that sweet soil. It seems a holy choir
Founded to the name of great Apollo's lyre,
Whose silver roof rings with the sprightly notes
Of sweet-lipped angel-imps that swill their throats
In cream of morning Helicon, and then
Prefer soft anthems to the ears of men,
To woo them from their beds, still murmuring
That men can sleep while they their matins sing—   80
Most divine service, whose so early lay
Prevents the eyelids of the blushing day.
There you might hear her kindle her soft voice
In the close murmur of a sparkling noise,
And lay the groundwork of her hopeful song,
Still keeping in the forward stream, so long
Till a sweet whirlwind, striving to get out,
Heaves her soft bosom, wanders round about,
And makes a pretty earthquake in her breast,
Till the fledged notes at length forsake their nest,   90
Fluttering in wanton shoals, and to the sky,
Winged with their own wild echo's prattling, fly.
She opes the floodgate and lets loose a tide
Of streaming sweetness, which in state doth ride
On the waved back of every swelling strain,
Rising and falling in a pompous train.
And while she thus discharges a shrill peal
Of flashing airs, she qualifies their zeal
With the cool epode of a graver note,
Thus high, thus low, as if her silver throat   100
Would reach the brazen voice of war's hoarse bird.
Her little soul is ravished, and so poured
Into loose ecstasies that she is placed
Above herself, music's enthusiast.

Shame now and anger mixed a double stain
In the musician's face. Yet once again,
Mistress, I come; now reach a strain, my lute,
Above her mock, or be forever mute;
Or tune a song of victory to me,
Or to thyself sing thine own obsequy.　　　　110
So said, his hands sprightly as fire he flings
And with a quavering coyness tastes the strings.
The sweet-lipped sisters, musically frighted,
Singing their fears are fearfully delighted,
Trembling as when Apollo's golden hairs
Are fanned and frizzled in the wanton airs
Of his own breath, which married to his lyre
Doth tune the spheres, and make heaven's self look higher.
From this to that, from that to this, he flies,
Feels music's pulse in all her arteries,　　　　120
Caught in a net which there Apollo spreads,
His fingers struggle with the vocal threads;
Following those little rills, he sinks into
A sea of Helicon; his hand does go
Those parts of sweetness which with nectar drop,
Softer than that which pants in Hebe's cup.
The humorous strings expound his learnèd touch
By various glosses; now they seem to grutch
And murmur in a buzzing din, then jingle
In shrill-tongued accents, striving to be single.　　　　130
Every smooth turn, every delicious stroke
Gives life to some new grace; thus doth h' invoke
Sweetness by all her names; thus, bravely thus,
Fraught with a fury so harmonious,
The lute's light genius now doth proudly rise,
Heaved on the surges of swollen rhapsodies,
Whose flourish, meteor-like, doth curl the air
With flash of high-born fancies, here and there
Dancing in lofty measures; and anon
Creeps on the soft touch of a tender tone　　　　140
Whose trembling murmurs melting in wild airs
Runs to and fro, complaining his sweet cares,
Because those precious mysteries that dwell
In music's ravished soul he dares not tell,
But whisper to the world; thus do they vary
Each string his note, as if they meant to carry
Their master's blest soul, snatched out at his ears
By a strong ecstasy, through all the spheres
Of music's heaven, and seat it there on high
In th' empyræum of pure harmony.　　　　150

At length, after so long, so loud a strife
Of all the strings, still breathing the best life
Of blest variety attending on
His fingers' fairest revolution
In many a sweet rise, many as sweet a fall,
A full-mouth diapason swallows all.
    This done, he lists what she would say to this,
And she, although her breath's late exercise
Had dealt too roughly with her tender throat,
Yet summons all her sweet powers for a note.   160
Alas, in vain! for while, sweet soul, she tries
To measure all those wild diversities
Of chatt'ring strings, by the small size of one
Poor simple voice, raised in a natural tone,
She fails, and failing grieves, and grieving dies.
She dies, and leaves her life the victor's prize,
Falling upon his lute; O fit to have,
That lived so sweetly, dead, so sweet a grave!

On marriage

I would be married, but I'd have no wife,
I would be married to a single life.

Wishes to his supposed mistress

Who e'er she be,
That not impossible she
That shall command my heart
    and me;

Where e'er she lie,
Locked up from mortal eye
In shady leaves of destiny,

Till that ripe birth
Of studied fate stand forth
And teach her fair steps to our
    earth,

Till that divine   10
Idea take a shrine
Of crystal flesh, through which to
    shine;

Meet you her, my wishes,
Bespeak her to my blisses,
And be ye called my absent kisses.

I wish her beauty
That owes not all his duty
To gaudy tire, nor glist'ring
    shoe-ty;

Something more than
Taffeta or tissue can,   20
Or rampant feather, or rich fan;

More than the spoil
Of shop, or silkworm's toil,
Or a bought blush, or a set smile.

A face that's best
By its own beauty dressed,
And can alone command the rest;

A face made up
Out of no other shop
Than what nature's white hand
    sets ope;   30

A cheek where youth,
And blood, with pen of truth
Write what the reader sweetly
    ru'th;

A cheek where grows
More than a morning rose,
Which to no box his being owes;

Lips where all day
A lover's kiss may play,
Yet carry nothing thence away;

Looks that oppress   40
Their richest tires, but dress
And clothe their simplest naked-
    ness;

Eyes that displaces
The neighbor diamond, and out-
    faces
That sunshine by their own sweet
    graces;

Tresses that wear
Jewels but to declare
How much themselves more
    precious are,

Whose native ray
Can tame the wanton day   50
Of gems, that in their bright
    shades play—

Each ruby there,
Or pearl that dare appear,
Be its own blush, be its own tear;

A well-tamed heart,
For whose more noble smart

Love may be long choosing a
    dart;

Eyes that bestow
Full quivers on Love's bow,
Yet pay less arrows than they
    owe;   60

Smiles that can warm
The blood, yet teach a charm,
That chastity shall take no harm;

Blushes that been
The burnish of no sin,
Nor flames of aught too hot with-
    in;

Joys that confess
Virtue their mistress,
And have no other head to dress;

Fears, fond and flight   70
As the coy bride's when night
First does the longing lover right;

Tears, quickly fled,
And vain, as those are shed
For a dying maidenhead;

Days that need borrow
No part of their good morrow
From a forespent night of sorrow;

Days that in spite
Of darkness, by the light   80
Of a clear mind are day all night;

Nights sweet as they,
Made short by lovers' play,
Yet long by th' absence of the
    day;

Life that dares send
A challenge to his end,
And when it comes say, Welcome
    friend;

Sidneian showers
Of sweet discourse, whose powers
Can crown old winter's head with
    flowers;   90

Soft silken hours,
Open suns, shady bowers,
'Bove all, nothing that lours:

Whate'er delight
Can make day's forehead bright,
Or give down to the wings of
    night.

In her whole frame
Have nature all the name,
Art and ornament the shame.

Her flattery,   100
Picture and poesy,
Her counsel her own virtue be.

I wish her store
Of worth may leave her poor
Of wishes, and I wish—no more.

Now if time knows
That her whose radiant brows
Weave them a garland of my
    vows,

Her whose just bays
My future hopes can raise,   110
A trophy to her present praise;

Her that dares be
What these lines wish to see:
I seek no further, it is she.

'Tis she, and here,
Lo, I unclothe and clear
My wishes' cloudy character.

May she enjoy it
Whose merit dare apply it
But modesty dares still deny it.   120

Such worth as this is
Shall fix my flying wishes,
And determine them to kisses.

Let her full glory,
My fancies, fly before ye;
Be ye my fictions, but her story.

On Mr. G. Herbert's book, entitled The Temple of Sacred Poems, sent to a gentlewoman

Know you, fair, on what you
    look:
Divinest love lies in this book,
Expecting fire from your eyes
To kindle this his sacrifice.
When your hands untie these
    strings,
Think you've an angel by the
    wings,
One that gladly will be nigh
To wait upon each morning sigh,
To flutter in the balmy air
Of your well-perfumëd prayer.   10
These white plumes of his he'll
    lend you,
Which every day to heaven will
    send you
To take acquaintance of the
    sphere
And all the smooth-faced kindred
    there.
    And though Herbert's name do
        owe
    These devotions, fairest, know
    That while I lay them on the
        shrine
    Of your white hand, they are
        mine.

On the baptized Ethiopian

Let it no longer be a forlorn
    hope

To wash an Ethiope.
He's washed: his gloomy skin a
      peaceful shade
For his white soul is made.
And now, I doubt not, the eternal
      Dove
A black-faced house will love.

To Pontius washing his hands

Thy hands are washed, but oh,
      the water's spilt
      That labored to have washed
         thy guilt;
The flood, if any can, that can
      suffice
   Must have its fountain in thine
      eyes.

On the miracle of loaves

Now Lord, or never, they'll be-
      lieve on thee,
Thou to their teeth hast proved
      thy deity.

Upon Lazarus his tears

Rich Lazarus! richer in those
      gems, thy tears,
      Than Dives in the robes he
         wears;
He scorns them now, but oh,
      they'll suit full well
   With th' purple he must wear
      in hell.

To our Lord, upon the water made wine

Thou water turn'st to wine, fair
      friend of life;
   Thy foe to cross the sweet arts
      of thy reign
Distils from thence the tears of
      wrath and strife,

And so turns wine to water
      back again.

Upon the infant martyrs

To see both blended in one flood,
The mother's milk, the children's
      blood,
Makes me doubt if heaven will
      gather
Roses hence, or lilies rather.

Mark xii
Give to Cæsar . . . and to God . . .

All we have is God's, and yet
Cæsar challenges a debt;
Nor hath God a thinner share,
Whatever Cæsar's payments are;
All is God's, and yet 'tis true
All we have is Cæsar's too;
All is Cæsar's, and what odds
So long as Cæsar's self is God's?

John iii
But men loved darkness rather than light

The world's light shines; shine as
      it will,
The world will love its darkness
      still;
I doubt though when the world's
      in hell,
It will not love its darkness half
      so well.

Samson to his Delilah

Could not once blinding me,
      cruel, suffice?
When first I looked on thee, I
      lost mine eyes.

FROM *Carmen Deo Nostro*, 1652

To the noblest and best of ladies, the Countess of Denbigh

Persuading her to resolution in religion, and to render herself without further delay into the communion of the Catholic Church

What heav'n-entreated heart is this,
Stands trembling at the gate of bliss?
Holds fast the door, yet dares not venture
Fairly to open it, and enter;
Whose definition is a doubt
'Twixt life and death, 'twixt in and out.
Say, ling'ring fair, why comes the birth
Of your brave soul so slowly forth?
Plead your pretenses, O you strong
In weakness, why you choose so long   10
In labor of yourself to lie,
Not daring quite to live nor die.
Ah linger not, loved soul! A slow
And late consent was a long no;
Who grants at last, long time tried
And did his best to have denied.
What magic bolts, what mystic bars
Maintain the will in these strange wars!
What fatal, yet fantastic, bands
Keep the free heart from its own hands!   20
So when the year takes cold, we see
Poor waters their own prisoners be;
Fettered and locked up fast they lie
In a sad self-captivity.
Th' astonished nymphs their flood's strange fate deplore,
To see themselves their own severer shore.
Thou that alone canst thaw this cold,
And fetch the heart from its stronghold,
Almighty love! end this long war,
And of a meteor make a star.   30
Oh, fix this fair indefinite,
And 'mongst thy shafts of sovereign light
Choose out that sure decisive dart
Which has the key of this close heart,
Knows all the corners of 't, and can control
The self-shut cabinet of an unsearched soul.
Oh, let it be at last love's hour;
Raise this tall trophy of thy power;
Come once the conquering way, not to confute

But kill this rebel word, irresolute,   40
That so, in spite of all this peevish strength
Of weakness, she may write, Resolved at length.
Unfold at length, unfold, fair flower,
And use the season of love's shower;
Meet his well-meaning wounds, wise heart!
And haste to drink the wholesome dart,
That healing shaft, which heav'n till now
Hath in love's quiver hid for you.
O dart of love! arrow of light!
O happy you, if it hit right;   50
It must not fall in vain, it must
Not mark the dry regardless dust.
Fair one, it is your fate, and brings
Eternal worlds upon its wings.
Meet it with wide-spread arms, and see
Its seat your soul's just center be.
Disband dull fears, give faith the day;
To save your life, kill your delay,
It is love's siege, and sure to be
Your triumph, though his victory.   60
'Tis cowardice that keeps this field,
And want of courage not to yield.
Yield then, O yield, that love may win
The fort at last and let life in;
Yield quickly, lest perhaps you prove
Death's prey, before the prize of love.
This fort of your fair self, if 't be not won,
He is repulsed indeed, but you're undone.

In the holy nativity of our Lord God, a hymn sung as by the shepherds

Chorus.   Come, we shepherds whose blest sight
               Hath met love's noon in nature's night;
               Come, lift we up our loftier song
               And wake the sun that lies too long.

               To all our world of well-stol'n joy
                   He slept, and dreamed of no such thing,
               While we found out heav'n's fairer eye,
                   And kissed the cradle of our King.
               Tell him he rises now too late
               To show us aught worth looking at.   10

Tell him we now can show him more
    Than he e'er showed to mortal sight,
Than he himself e'er saw before,
    Which to be seen needs not his light.
Tell him, Tityrus, where th' hast been;
Tell him, Thyrsis, what th' hast seen.

Tit.   Gloomy night embraced the place
        Where the noble infant lay;
    The babe looked up and showed his face:
        In spite of darkness, it was day.   20
    It was thy day, sweet, and did rise
    Not from the east, but from thine eyes.

Cho.   It was thy day, sweet, . . .

Thyr.   Winter chid aloud, and sent
        The angry north to wage his wars;
    The north forgot his fierce intent,
        And left perfume instead of scars.
    By those sweet eyes' persuasive powers,
    Where he meant frost, he scattered flowers.

Cho.   By those sweet eyes' . . .   30

Both.   We saw thee in thy balmy nest,
        Young dawn of our eternal day!
    We saw thine eyes break from their east
        And chase the trembling shades away.
    We saw thee, and we blessed the sight;
    We saw thee by thine own sweet light.

Tit.   Poor world, said I, what wilt thou do
        To entertain this starry stranger?
    Is this the best thou canst bestow,
        A cold and not too cleanly manger?   40
    Contend, ye powers of heav'n and earth,
    To fit a bed for this huge birth.

Cho.   Contend, ye powers . . .

Thyr.   Proud world, said I, cease your contest,
        And let the mighty babe alone—
    The phœnix builds the phœnix' nest,
        Love's architecture is his own;
    The babe whose birth embraves this morn,
    Made his own bed ere he was born.

Cho.   The babe whose . . .   50

Tit.   I saw the curled drops, soft and slow,
        Come hovering o'er the place's head,
    Off'ring their whitest sheets of snow
        To furnish the fair infant's bed.
    Forbear, said I, be not too bold;
    Your fleece is white, but 'tis too cold.

Cho.   Forbear, said I, . . .

Thyr.   I saw the obsequious seraphims
        Their rosy fleece of fire bestow;
    For well they now can spare their wings,   60
        Since heav'n itself lies here below.
    Well done, said I, but are you sure
    Your down so warm will pass for pure?

Cho.   Well done, said I, . . .

Tit.   No, no, your King's not yet to seek
        Where to repose his royal head;
    See, see, how soon his new-bloomed cheek
        'Twixt's mother's breasts is gone to bed.
    Sweet choice, said we! no way but so,
    Not to lie cold, yet sleep in snow.   70

Cho.   Sweet choice, said we! . . .

Both.   We saw thee in thy balmy nest,
        Bright dawn of our eternal day!
    We saw thine eyes break from their east,
        And chase the trembling shades away.
    We saw thee, and we blessed the sight;
    We saw thee by thine own sweet light.

Cho.   We saw thee, . . .

Full Chorus.   Welcome, all wonders in one sight!   80
        Eternity shut in a span,
    Summer in winter, day in night,
        Heaven in earth, and God in man.
    Great little one, whose all-embracing birth
    Lifts earth to heaven, stoops heav'n to earth.

Welcome, though not to gold nor silk,
  To more than Cæsar's birthright is,
Two sister seas of virgin-milk,
  With many a rarely tempered kiss,
That breathes at once both maid and mother,
Warms in the one, cools in the other.   90

Welcome, though not to those gay flies
  Gilded i' th' beams of earthly kings,
Slippery souls in smiling eyes;
  But to poor shepherds, homespun things,
Whose wealth's their flock, whose wit, to be
Well read in their simplicity.

Yet when young April's husband-showers
  Shall bless the fruitful Maia's bed,
We'll bring the first-born of her flowers
  To kiss thy feet and crown thy head.   100

To thee, dread lamb, whose love must keep
  The shepherds more than they the sheep;
To thee, meek majesty! soft king
  Of simple graces and sweet loves,
Each of us his lamb will bring,
  Each his pair of silver doves;
Till burnt at last in fire of thy fair eyes,
Ourselves become our own best sacrifice.

Saint Mary Magdalene, or the weeper

Hail, sister springs!
Parents of silver-footed rills!
Ever-bubbling things!
Thawing crystal! snowy hills,
Still spending, never spent! I mean
Thy fair eyes, sweet Magdalene!

Heavens thy fair eyes be,
Heavens of ever-falling stars;
'Tis seed-time still with thee,
And stars thou sow'st, whose
    harvest dares   10
Promise the earth to countershine
Whatever makes heav'n's forehead
    fine.

But we're deceivèd all.
Stars indeed they are, too true,
For they but seem to fall,
As heav'n's other spangles do.
It is not for our earth and us
To shine in things so precïous.

Upwards thou dost weep;
Heav'n's bosom drinks the gentle
    stream;   20
Where th' milky rivers creep,
Thine floats above, and is the
    cream.
Waters above th' heav'ns, what
    they be
We're best taught by thy tears and
    thee.

Every morn from hence
A brisk cherub something sips,
Whose sacred influence

Adds sweetness to his sweetest
    lips;
Then to his music, and his song
Tastes of this breakfast all day
    long.   30

Not in the evening's eyes,
    When they red with weeping
    are
For the sun that dies,
    Sits sorrow with a face so fair;
Nowhere but here did ever meet
Sweetness so sad, sadness so sweet.

When sorrow would be seen
    In her brightest majesty,
For she is a queen,
    Then is she dressed by none but
      thee;   40
Then, and only then, she wears
Her proudest pearls: I mean—thy
    tears.

The dew no more will weep
    The primrose's pale cheek to
    deck,
The dew no more will sleep,
    Nuzzled in the lily's neck;
Much rather would it be thy tear,
And leave them both to tremble
    here.

There's no need at all   49
    That the balsam-sweating bough
So coyly should let fall
    His med'cinable tears, for now
Nature hath learnt t' extract a dew
More sovereign and sweet from
    you.

Yet let the poor drops weep,
    Weeping is the ease of woe,
Softly let them creep,
    Sad that they are vanquished so;
They, though to others no relief,

Balsam may be for their own
    grief.   60

Such the maiden gem
    By the purpling vine put on,
Peeps from her parent stem
    And blushes at the bridegroom
      sun;
This wat'ry blossom of thy eyne,
Ripe, will make the richer wine.

When some new bright guest
    Takes up among the stars a
    room,
And heav'n will make a feast, 69
    Angels with crystal vials come
And draw from these full eyes of
    thine
Their master's water, their own
    wine.

Golden though he be,
    Golden Tagus murmurs
    though;
Were his way by thee,
    Content and quiet he would go;
So much more rich would he
    esteem
Thy silver, than his golden stream.

Well does the May that lies
    Smiling in thy cheeks, confess
The April in thine eyes;   81
    Mutual sweetness they express:
No April e'er lent kinder showers,
Nor May returned more faithful
    flowers.

O cheeks! beds of chaste loves
    By your own showers seasonably
    dashed;
Eyes! nests of milky doves
    In your own wells decently
    washed;
O wit of love! that thus could place
Fountain and garden in one
    face.   90

O sweet contest, of woes
With loves, of tears with smiles
   disputing!
O fair and friendly foes,
Each other kissing and confut-
   ing!
While rain and sunshine, cheeks
   and eyes,
Close in kind contrarieties.

But can these fair floods be
Friends with the bosom fires that
   fill thee?
Can so great flames agree
Eternal tears should thus distil
   thee?   100
O floods, O fires, O suns, O show-
   ers!
Mixed and made friends by love's
   sweet powers.

'Twas his well-pointed dart
That digged these wells and
   dressed this vine;
And taught the wounded heart
The way into these weeping
   eyne.
Vain loves, avaunt! bold hands,
   forbear!
The lamb hath dipped his white foot
   here.

And now where e'er he strays
Among the Galilean moun-
   tains,   110
Or more unwelcome ways,
He's followed by two faithful
   fountains,
Two walking baths, two weeping
   motions,
Portable and compendious oceans.

O thou, thy Lord's fair store!
In thy so rich and rare expenses,
Even when he showed most
   poor,

He might provoke the wealth of
   princes;
What prince's wanton'st pride e'er
   could
Wash with silver, wipe with
   gold?   120

Who is that king, but he
Who call'st his crown to be
   called thine,
That thus can boast to be
Waited on by a wand'ring mine,
A voluntary mint, that strows
Warm silver showers where e'er
   he goes?

O precious prodigal!
Fair spendthrift of thyself! thy
   measure,
Merciless love, is all,
Even to the last pearl in thy
   treasure;   130
All places, times, and objects be
Thy tears' sweet opportunity.

Does the day-star rise?
Still thy stars do fall and fall.
Does day close his eyes?
Still the fountain weeps for all.
Let night or day do what they will,
Thou hast thy task, thou weepest
   still.

Does thy song lull the air?
Thy falling tears keep faithful
   time.   140
Does thy sweet-breathed prayer
Up in clouds of incense climb?
Still at each sigh, that is, each stop,
A bead, that is, a tear, does drop.

At these thy weeping gates,
Watching their wat'ry motion,
Each wingèd moment waits,
Takes his tear and gets him
   gone;

By thine eye's tinct ennobled thus,
Time lays him up, he's precïous.

Not, So long she lived,   151
Shall thy tomb report of thee;
But, So long she grieved,
Thus must we date thy memory:
Others by moments, months, and
    years,
Measure their ages, thou by tears.

So do perfumes expire;
So sigh tormented sweets, op-
    pressed
With proud unpitying fire;
Such tears the suff'ring rose
    that's vexed   160
With ungentle flames does shed,
Sweating in a too warm bed.

Say, ye bright brothers,
The fugitive sons of those fair
    eyes,
Your fruitful mothers,
What make you here? What
    hopes can 'tice
You to be born? What cause can
    borrow

You from those nests of noble sor-
    row?

Whither away so fast?
For sure the sordid earth   170
Your sweetness cannot taste,
Nor does the dust deserve your
    birth.
Sweet, whither haste you then? O
    say
Why you trip so fast away!

We go not to seek
The darlings of Aurora's bed,
The rose's modest cheek,
Nor the violet's humble head;
Though the field's eyes, too, weep-
    ers be   179
Because they want such tears as we.

Much less mean we to trace
The fortune of inferior gems,
Preferred to some proud face,
Or perched upon feared dia-
    dems:
Crowned heads are toys. We go to
    meet
A worthy object, our Lord's feet.

A hymn to the name and honor of the admirable Saint Teresa

Foundress of the reformation of the Discalced Carmelites, both men and women. A woman for angelical height of speculation, for masculine courage of performance, more than a woman, who yet a child outran maturity, and durst plot a martyrdom.

Love, thou art absolute sole lord
Of life and death. To prove the word,
We'll now appeal to none of all
Those thy old soldiers, great and tall,
Ripe men of martyrdom, that could reach down
With strong arms their triumphant crown,
Such as could with lusty breath
Speak loud into the face of death

Their great Lord's glorious name; to none
Of those whose spacious bosoms spread a throne
For love at large to fill; spare blood and sweat,
And see him take a private seat,
Making his mansion in the mild
And milky soul of a soft child.

Scarce has she learned to lisp the name
Of martyr, yet she thinks it shame
Life should so long play with that breath
Which spent can buy so brave a death.
She never undertook to know
What death with love should have to do;
Nor has she e'er yet understood
Why to show love she should shed blood;
Yet though she cannot tell you why,
She can love and she can die.

Scarce has she blood enough to make
A guilty sword blush for her sake;
Yet has she'a heart dares hope to prove
How much less strong is death than love.

Be love but there, let poor six years
Be posed with the maturest fears
Man trembles at, you straight shall find
Love knows no nonage, nor the mind.
'Tis love, not years or limbs that can
Make the martyr or the man.

Love touched her heart, and lo it beats
High, and burns with such brave heats,
Such thirsts to die, as dares drink up
A thousand cold deaths in one cup.
Good reason, for she breathes all fire;
Her weak breast heaves with strong desire
Of what she may with fruitless wishes
Seek for amongst her mother's kisses.

Since 'tis not to be had at home,
She'll travel to a martyrdom.
No home for hers confesses she
But where she may a martyr be.
She'll to the Moors, and trade with them
For this unvalued diadem.
She'll offer them her dearest breath,
With Christ's name in 't, in change for death.
She'll bargain with them, and will give
Them God, teach them how to live
In him; or if they this deny,
For him she'll teach them how to die.

So shall she leave amongst them sown
Her Lord's blood, or at least her own.
   Farewell then, all the world, adieu!
Teresa is no more for you.
Farewell, all pleasures, sports, and joys,
Never till now esteeméd toys,
Farewell, whatever dear may be,
Mother's arms or father's knee;
Farewell house and farewell home,
She's for the Moors and martyrdom!
   Sweet, not so fast! lo, thy fair spouse
Whom thou seek'st with so swift vows
Calls thee back, and bids thee come
T' embrace a milder martyrdom.
   Blest powers forbid thy tender life
Should bleed upon a barbarous knife;
Or some base hand have power to race
Thy breast's chaste cabinet and uncase
A soul kept there so sweet; oh no,
Wise heav'n will never have it so:
Thou art love's victim, and must die
A death more mystical and high;
Into love's arms thou shalt let fall
A still surviving funeral.
His is the dart must make the death
Whose stroke shall taste thy hallowed breath;
A dart thrice dipped in that rich flame
Which writes thy spouse's radiant name
Upon the roof of heav'n, where aye
It shines, and with a sovereign ray
Beats bright upon the burning faces
Of souls, which in that name's sweet graces
Find everlasting smiles. So rare,
So spiritual, pure, and fair
Must be th' immortal instrument
Upon whose choice point shall be sent
A life so loved; and that there be
Fit executioners for thee,
The fair'st and first-born sons of fire,
Blest seraphim, shall leave their choir
And turn love's soldiers, upon thee
To exercise their archery.
   Oh, how oft shalt thou complain
Of a sweet and subtle pain,
Of intolerable joys,
Of a death in which who dies

60

70

80

90

100

Loves his death, and dies again,
And would forever so be slain,
And lives and dies, and knows not why
To live, but that he thus may never leave to die.
How kindly will thy gentle heart
Kiss the sweetly killing dart!
And close in his embraces keep
Those delicious wounds, that weep
Balsam to heal themselves with. Thus
When these thy deaths, so numerous,   110
Shall all at last die into one,
And melt thy soul's sweet mansïon
Like a soft lump of incense, hasted
By too hot a fire, and wasted
Into perfuming clouds, so fast
Shalt thou exhale to heav'n at last
In a resolving sigh; and then,
Oh, what? Ask not the tongues of men;
Angels cannot tell; suffice,
Thyself shall feel thine own full joys   120
And hold them fast forever. There
So soon as thou shalt first appear,
The moon of maiden stars, thy white
Mistress, attended by such bright
Souls as thy shining self, shall come
And in her first ranks make thee room;
Where 'mongst her snowy family
Immortal welcomes wait for thee.
Oh, what delight when revealed life shall stand
And teach thy lips heav'n with his hand,   130
On which thou now mayst to thy wishes
Heap up thy consecrated kisses.
What joys shall seize thy soul when she,
Bending her blessed eyes on thee,
Those second smiles of heaven, shall dart
Her mild rays through thy melting heart!
Angels, thy old friends, there shall greet thee,
Glad at their own home now to meet thee.
All thy good works which went before
And waited for thee at the door   140
Shall own thee there, and all in one
Weave a constellatïon
Of crowns, with which the King, thy spouse,
Shall build up thy triumphant brows.
All thy old woes shall now smile on thee,
And thy pains sit bright upon thee;

All thy sorrows here shall shine,
All thy sufferings be divine;
Tears shall take comfort and turn gems,
And wrongs repent to diadems.   150
Even thy deaths shall live, and new
Dress the soul that erst they slew;
Thy wounds shall blush to such bright scars
As keep account of the Lamb's wars.

   Those rare works where thou shalt leave writ
Love's noble history, with wit
Taught thee by none but him, while here
They feed our souls, shall clothe thine there.
Each heav'nly word by whose hid flame
Our hard hearts shall strike fire, the same   160
Shall flourish on thy brows, and be
Both fire to us and flame to thee,
Whose light shall live bright in thy face
By glory, in our hearts by grace.

   Thou shalt look round about and see
Thousands of crowned souls throng to be
Themselves thy crown; sons of thy vows,
The virgin-births with which thy sovereign spouse
Made fruitful thy fair soul, go now
And with them all about thee, bow   170
To him. Put on, he'll say, put on,
My rosy love, that thy rich zone
Sparkling with the sacred flames
Of thousand souls whose happy names
Heav'n keeps upon thy score. Thy bright
Life brought them first to kiss the light
That kindled them to stars. And so
Thou with the Lamb, thy Lord, shalt go,
And wheresoe'er he sets his white
Steps, walk with him those ways of light   180
Which who in death would live to see
Must learn in life to die like thee.

*An apology for the foregoing hymn, as having been
writ when the author was yet among the
Protestants*

Thus have I back again to thy bright name
(Fair flood of holy fires!) transfused the flame
I took from reading thee; 'tis to thy wrong,

I know, that in my weak and worthless song
Thou here art set to shine where thy full day
Scarce dawns. O pardon if I dare to say
Thine own dear books are guilty, for from thence
I learned to know that love is eloquence.
That hopeful maxim gave me heart to try
If, what to other tongues is tuned so high, 10
Thy praise might not speak English too; forbid,
By all thy mysteries that here lie hid,
Forbid it, mighty love! let no fond hate
Of names and words so far prejudicate.
Souls are not Spaniards too; one friendly flood
Of baptism blends them all into a blood.
Christ's faith makes but one body of all souls,
And love's that body's soul; no law controls
Our free traffic for heav'n; we may maintain
Peace, sure, with piety, though it come from Spain. 20
What soul soe'er, in any language, can
Speak heav'n like hers is my soul's countryman.
Oh, 'tis not Spanish, but 'tis heav'n she speaks!
'Tis heaven that lies in ambush there, and breaks
From thence into the wond'ring reader's breast,
Who feels his warm heart hatched into a nest
Of little eagles and young loves, whose high
Flights scorn the lazy dust and things that die.
   There are enow whose draughts, as deep as hell,
Drink up all Spain in sack. Let my soul swell 30
With thee, strong wine of love! Let others swim
In puddles; we will pledge this seraphim
Bowls full of richer blood than blush of grape
Was ever guilty of; change we too'our shape,
My soul: some drink from men to beasts—oh, then
Drink we till we prove more, not less, than men,
And turn not beasts but angels. Let the king
Me ever into these his cellars bring,
Where flows such wine as we can have of none
But him who trod the wine-press all alone, 40
Wine of youth, life, and the sweet deaths of love;
Wine of immortal mixture, which can prove
Its tincture from the rosy nectar; wine
That can exalt weak earth, and so refine
Our dust that at one draught mortality
May drink itself up, and forget to die.

The Flaming Heart

Upon the book and picture of the seraphical Saint Teresa,
as she is usually expressed with a seraphim beside her

O heart, the equal poise of love's both parts,
Big alike with wounds and darts,
Live in these conquering leaves; live all the same,
And walk through all tongues one triumphant flame;
Live here, great heart, and love and die and kill,
And bleed and wound, and yield and conquer still.
Let this immortal life, where'er it comes,
Walk in a crowd of loves and martyrdoms.
Let mystic deaths wait on 't, and wise souls be
The love-slain witnesses of this life of thee.   10
O sweet incendiary! show here thy art,
Upon this carcass of a hard cold heart,
Let all thy scattered shafts of light, that play
Among the leaves of thy large books of day,
Combined against this breast, at once break in
And take away from me my self and sin;
This gracious robbery shall thy bounty be,
And my best fortunes such fair spoils of me.
O thou undaunted daughter of desires!
By all thy dower of lights and fires,   20
By all the eagle in thee, all the dove,
By all thy lives and deaths of love,
By thy large draughts of intellectual day,
And by thy thirsts of love more large than they,
By all thy brim-filled bowls of fierce desire,
By thy last morning's draught of liquid fire,
By the full kingdom of that final kiss
That seized thy parting soul and sealed thee his,
By all the heav'ns thou hast in him,
Fair sister of the seraphim!   30
By all of him we have in thee,
Leave nothing of myself in me:
Let me so read thy life that I
Unto all life of mine may die.

A song

Lord, when the sense of thy sweet grace
Sends up my soul to seek thy face,
Thy blessed eyes breed such desire
I die in love's delicious fire.
O love, I am thy sacrifice.

Be still triumphant, blessed eyes;
Still shine on me, fair suns! that I
Still may behold, though still I die.

Though still I die, I live again,
Still longing so to be still slain; ¹⁰

So gainful is such loss of breath,
I die even in desire of death.

Still live in me this loving strife
Of living death and dying life;
For while thou sweetly slayest me,
Dead to myself, I live in thee.

HENRY VAUGHAN

The Introduction and Notes are at page 1025

From *Silex Scintillans, 1655*

The Author's preface to the following hymns.

That this kingdom hath abounded with those ingenious persons which in the late notion are termed wits is too well known. Many of them having cast away all their fair portion of time in no better employments than a deliberate search or excogitation of idle words, and a most vain insatiable desire to be reputed poets, leaving behind them no other monuments of those excellent abilities conferred upon them but such as they may, with a predecessor of theirs, term parricides, and a soul-killing issue; for that is the Βραβεῖον, and laureate crown, which idle poems will certainly bring to their unrelenting authors.

And well it were for them if those willingly-studied and wilfully-published vanities could defile no spirits but their own; but the case is far worse. These vipers survive their parents, and for many ages after, like epidemic diseases, infect whole generations, corrupting always and unhallowing the best-gifted souls and the most capable vessels, for whose sanctification and welfare the glorious Son of God laid down his life and suffered the precious blood of his blessed and innocent heart to be poured out. . . .

Divers persons of eminent piety and learning (I meddle not with the seditious and schismatical) have, long before my time, taken notice of this malady; for the complaint against vicious verse, even by peaceful and obedient spirits, is of some antiquity in this kingdom. And yet, as if the evil consequence attending this inveterate error were but a small thing, there is sprung very lately another prosperous device to assist it in the subversion of souls. Those that want the genius of verse fall to translating, and the people are, every term, plentifully furnished with various foreign vanities; so that the most lascivious compositions of France and Italy are here naturalized and made English; and this, as it is sadly observed, with so much favor and success that nothing takes, as they rightly phrase it, like a romance. . . .

It is a sentence of sacred authority that he that is dead is freed from sin, because he cannot in that state, which is without the body, sin any more; but he that writes idle books makes for himself another body, in which he always lives, and sins after death as fast and as foul as ever he did in his life; which very consideration deserves to be a sufficient antidote against this evil disease.

And here, because I would prevent a just censure by my free confession, I must remember that I myself have for many years together languished of this very sickness, and it is no long time since I have recovered. But, blessed be God for it, I have by his saving assistance suppressed my greatest follies, and those which escaped from me are, I think, as innoxious as most of that vein use to be; besides they are interlined with many virtuous and some pious mixtures. What I speak of them is truth; but let no man mistake it for an extenuation of faults, as if I intended an apology for them, or myself, who am conscious of so much guilt in both as can never be expiated without special sorrows, and that cleansing and precious effusion of my almighty Redeemer; and if the world will be so charitable as to grant my request, I do here must humbly and earnestly beg that none would read them. . . .

The suppression of this pleasing and prevailing evil lies not altogether in the power of the magistrate, for it will fly abroad in manuscripts when it fails of entertainment at the press. The true remedy lies wholly in their bosoms who are the gifted persons, by a wise exchange of vain and vicious subjects for divine themes and celestial praise. . . .

The first that with any effectual success attempted a diversion of this foul and overflowing stream was the blessed man, Mr. George Herbert, whose holy life and verse gained many pious converts (of whom I am the least) and gave the first check to a most flourishing and admired wit of his time. . . .

From *Poems*, 1646

To Amoret gone from him

Fancy and I last evening walked,
And, Amoret, of thee we talked;
The west just then had stolen the sun,
And his last blushes were begun.
We sat and marked how everything
Did mourn his absence: how the spring
That smiled and curled about his beams
Whilst he was here, now checked her streams;
The wanton eddies of her face
Were taught less noise and smoother grace,   10
And in a slow sad channel went
Whisp'ring the banks their discontent;
The careless ranks of flowers that spread
Their perfumed bosoms to his head,
And with an open free embrace

Did entertain his beamy face,
Like absent friends point to the west,
And on that weak reflection feast.
If creatures then that have no sense   20
But the loose tie of influence,
Though fate and time each day remove
Those things that element their love,
At such vast distance can agree,
Why, Amoret, why should not we?

From *Silex Scintillans*, 1655

The match

Dear friend! whose holy, ever-living lines
    Have done much good
To many, and have checked my blood—
My fierce, wild blood that still heaves and inclines,
    But is still tamed
By those bright fires which thee inflamed;
Here I join hands and thrust my stubborn heart
    Into thy deed,
    There from no duties to be freed,
And if hereafter youth or folly thwart   10
    And claim their share,
Here I renounce the pois'nous ware.

Idle verse

Go, go, quaint follies, sugared sin,
    Shadow no more my door;
I will no longer cobwebs spin,
    I'm too much on the score.

For since amidst my youth and
        night
    My great preserver smiles,
We'll make a match, my only light,
    And join against their wiles;

Blind, desp'rate fits, that study
        how
    To dress and trim our shame, 10
That gild rank poison, and allow
    Vice in a fairer name;

The purls of youthful blood and
        bowels,
    Lust in the robes of love,
The idle talk of fev'rish souls,
    Sick with a scarf or glove;

Let it suffice my warmer days
    Simpered and shined on you,
Twist not my cypress with your
        bays,
    Or roses with my yew;   20

Go, go, seek out some greener
        thing,
    It snows and freezeth here;
Let nightingales attend the spring,
    Winter is all my year.

Mount of Olives [1]

Sweet sacred hill! on whose fair brow
My Savior sat, shall I allow
   Language to love
And idolize some shade or grove,
Neglecting thee? Such ill-placed wit,
Conceit, or call it what you please,
   Is the brain's fit,
   And mere disease.

Cotswold and Cooper's, both have met
With learned swains, and echo yet   10
   Their pipes and wit;
But thou sleep'st in a deep neglect,
Untouched by any; and what need
The sheep bleat thee a silly lay,
   That heard'st both reed
   And sheep-ward play?

Yet if poets mind thee well,
They shall find thou art their hill
   And fountain too,
Their Lord with thee had most to do;   20
He wept once, walked whole nights on thee,
And from thence, his suff'rings ended,
   Unto glory
   Was attended.

Being there, this spacious ball
Is but his narrow footstool all,
   And what we think
Unsearchable, now with one wink
He doth comprise; but in this air
When he did stay to bear our ill
   And sin, this hill   31
   Was then his chair.

The garland

Thou who dost flow and flourish here below,
To whom a falling star and nine days' glory,
Or some frail beauty, makes the bravest show,
Hark, and make use of this ensuing story.

When first my youthful, sinful age
   Grew master of my ways,
Appointing error for my page,
   And darkness for my days,
I flung away, and with full cry
   Of wild affections, rid   10
In post for pleasures, bent to try
   All gamesters that would bid.
I played with fire, did counsel spurn,
   Made life my common stake,
But never thought that fire would burn,
   Or that a soul could ache.
Glorious deceptions, gilded mists,
   False joys, fantastic flights,
Pieces of sackcloth with silk-lists:

These were my prime delights.
I sought choice bowers, haunted the spring,
    Culled flowers and made me posies,
Gave my fond humors their full wing,
    And crowned my head with roses.
But at the height of this career
    I met with a dead man,
Who, noting well my vain abear,
    Thus unto me began:
Desist, fond fool, be not undone,
    What thou hast cut to-day
Will fade at night, and with this sun
    Quite vanish and decay.

Flowers gathered in this world die here; if thou
Wouldst have a wreath that fades not, let them grow,
And grow for thee; who spares them here shall find
A garland, where comes neither rain nor wind.

The seed growing secretly

S. Mark iv. 26

If this world's friends might see but once
What some poor man may often feel,
Glory and gold and crowns and thrones
They would soon quit, and learn to kneel.

My dew, my dew, my early love,
My soul's bright food, thy absence kills!
Hover not long, eternal Dove!
Life without thee is loose, and spills.

Something I had which long ago
Did learn to suck, and sip, and taste,
But now grown sickly, sad, and slow,
Doth fret and wrangle, pine and waste.

O spread thy sacred wings and shake
One living drop! one drop life keeps!
If pious griefs heaven's joys awake,
O fill his bottle, thy child weeps!

Slowly and sadly doth he grow,
And soon as left, shrinks back to ill;
O feed that life which makes him blow
And spread and open to thy will!

For thy eternal living wells
None stained or withered shall come near;
A fresh immortal green there dwells,
And spotless white is all the wear.

Dear, secret greenness! nursed below
Tempests and winds and winter nights,
Vex not that but one sees thee grow;
That *One* made all these lesser lights.

If those bright joys he singly sheds
On thee were all met in one crown,   30
Both sun and stars would hide their heads,
And moons, though full, would get them down.

Let glory be their bait, whose minds
Are all too high for a low cell;
Though hawks can prey through storms and winds,
The poor bee in her hive must dwell.

Glory, the crowd's cheap tinsel still
To what most takes them, is a drudge,
And they too oft take good for ill,
And thriving vice for virtue judge.   40

What needs a conscience calm and bright
Within itself an outward test?
Who breaks his glass to take more light,
Makes way for storms into his rest.

Then bless thy secret growth, nor catch
At noise, but thrive unseen and dumb;
Keep clean, bear fruit, earn life, and watch
Till the white-winged reapers come!

Quickness

False life! a foil and no more,
  when
  Wilt thou be gone?
Thou foul deception of all men
That would not have the true come
  on!

Thou art a moon-like toil, a blind
  Self-posing state,
A dark contest of waves and wind,
A mere tempestuous debate.

Life is a fixed discerning light,
  A knowing joy;   10
No chance or fit, but ever bright
And calm and full, yet doth not
  cloy.

'Tis such a blissful thing, that still
  Doth vivify
And shine and smile, and hath the
  skill
To please without eternity.

Thou art a toilsome mole, or less,
A moving mist;

But life is what none can express,
A quickness which my God hath kissed.   20

The bird

Hither thou com'st; the busy wind all night
Blew through thy lodging, where thy own warm wing
Thy pillow was. Many a sullen storm,
For which course man seems much the fitter born,
    Rained on thy bed
    And harmless head.

And now as fresh and cheerful as the light,
Thy little heart in early hymns doth sing
Unto that Providence whose unseen arm
Curbed them, and clothed thee well and warm.   10
    All things that be praise him, and had
    Their lesson taught them when first made.

So hills and valleys into singing break,
And though poor stones have neither speech nor tongue,
While active winds and streams both run and speak,
Yet stones are deep in admiration.
Thus praise and prayer here beneath the sun
Make lesser mornings, when the great are done.

For each enclosèd spirit is a star,   20
    Enlight'ning his own little sphere,
Whose light, though fetched and borrowèd from far,
    Both mornings makes and evenings there.

But as these birds of light make a land glad,
Chirping their solemn matins on each tree,
So in the shades of night some dark fowls be,
Whose heavy notes make all that hear them sad.

    The turtle then in palm trees mourns,
      While owls and satyrs howl;
    The pleasant land to brimstone turns   30
      And all her streams grow foul.

Brightness and mirth, and love and faith, all fly,
Till the day-spring breaks forth again from high.

The waterfall

With what deep murmurs through time's silent stealth
Doth thy transparent, cool, and wat'ry wealth
    Here flowing fall,
    And chide, and call,
As if his liquid, loose retínue stayed
Ling'ring, and were of this steep place afraid,
    The common pass
    Where, clear as glass,
    All must descend—
    Not to an end,   10
But quickened by this deep and rocky grave,
Rise to a longer course more bright and brave.

Dear stream! dear bank, where often I
Have sat and pleased my pensive eye,
Why, since each drop of thy quick store
Runs thither whence it flowed before,
Should poor souls fear a shade or night,
Who came, sure, from a sea of light?
Or since those drops are all sent back
So sure to thee, that none doth lack,   20
Why should frail flesh doubt any more
That what God takes he'll not restore?

O useful element and clear!
My sacred wash and cleanser here,
My first consigner unto those
Fountains of life where the Lamb goes!
What sublime truths and wholesome themes
Lodge in thy mystical deep streams!
Such as dull man can never find
Unless that spirit lead his mind   30
Which first upon thy face did move,
And hatched all with his quick'ning love.
As this loud brook's incessant fall
In streaming rings restagnates all,
Which reach by course the bank, and then
Are no more seen, just so pass men.
O my invisible estate,
My glorious liberty, still late!
Thou art the channel my soul seeks,
Not this with cataracts and creeks.   40

[*And do they so?*]

Romans viii. 19

*Etenim res creatæ exerto capite observantes expectant revelationem
Filiorum Dei.*

And do they so? Have they a sense
  Of aught but influence?
Can they their heads lift, and ex-
    pect,
  And groan too? Why th' elect
Can do no more; my volumes said
  They were all dull, and dead;
They judged them senseless, and
    their state
  Wholly inanimate.
Go, go, seal up thy looks,
  And burn thy books.   10

I would I were a stone, or tree,
  Or flower, by pedigree,
Or some poor highway herb, or
    spring
  To flow, or bird to sing!
Then should I, tied to one sure
    state,
  All day expect my date;
But I am sadly loose, and stray
  A giddy blast each way;
O let me not thus range,
  Thou canst not change!   20

Sometimes I sit with thee and tarry
  An hour or so, then vary;
Thy other creatures in this scene
  Thee only aim and mean;
Some rise to seek thee, and with
    heads
  Erect, peep from their beds;
Others, whose birth is in the tomb,
  And cannot quit the womb,
Sigh there, and groan for thee,
  Their liberty.   30

O let me not do less! shall they
  Watch, while I sleep or play?
Shall I thy mercies still abuse
  With fancies, friends, or news?
O brook it not! thy blood is
    mine,
  And my soul should be thine;
O brook it not! why wilt thou
    stop,
  After whole showers, one drop?
Sure, thou wilt joy to see
  Thy sheep with thee.   40

Man

Weighing the steadfastness and state
Of some mean things which here below reside,
Where birds like watchful clocks the noiseless date
  And intercourse of times divide,
Where bees at night get home and hive, and flowers
    Early, as well as late,
Rise with the sun, and set in the same bowers;

  I would, said I, my God would give
The staidness of these things to man! for these
To his divine appointments ever cleave,   10
  And no new business breaks their peace;

The birds nor sow nor reap, yet sup and dine,
    The flowers without clothes live,
Yet Solomon was never dressed so fine.

Man hath still either toys or care,
He hath no root, nor to one place is tied,
But ever restless and irregular
    About this earth doth run and ride;
He knows he hath a home, but scarce knows where,
    He says it is so far   20
That he hath quite forgot how to go there.

He knocks at all the doors, strays and roams,
Nay, hath not so much wit as some stones have,
Which in the darkest nights point to their homes
    By some hid sense their maker gave;
Man is the shuttle, to whose winding quest
    And passage through these looms
God ordered motion, but ordained no rest.

The night

John iii. 2

Through that pure virgin-shrine,
That sacred veil drawn o'er thy glorious noon,
That men might look and live, as glow-worms shine,
    And face the moon,
Wise Nicodemus saw such light
As made him know his God by night.

Most blest believer he!
Who in that land of darkness and blind eyes
Thy long-expected healing wings could see
    When thou didst rise,   10
And what can never more be done,
Did at midnight speak with the Sun!

Oh, who will tell me where
He found thee at that dead and silent hour!
What hallowed solitary ground did bear
    So rare a flower,
Within whose sacred leaves did lie
The fullness of the deity.

No mercy-seat of gold,
No dead and dusty cherub, nor carved stone,   20
But his own living works did my Lord hold

And lodge alone,
Where trees and herbs did watch and peep
And wonder, while the Jews did sleep.

Dear night! this world's defeat;
The stop to busy fools; care's check and curb;
The day of spirits; my soul's calm retreat
    Which none disturb;
Christ's progress, and his prayer time;
The hours to which high heaven doth chime;   30

God's silent, searching flight;
When my Lord's head is filled with dew, and all
His locks are wet with the clear drops of night;
    His still, soft call;
His knocking time; the soul's dumb watch,
When spirits their fair kindred catch.

Were all my loud, evil days
Calm and unhaunted as is thy dark tent,
Whose peace but by some angel's wing or voice
    Is seldom rent,   40
Then I in heaven all the long year
Would keep, and never wander here.

But living where the sun
Doth all things wake, and where all mix and tire
Themselves and others, I consent and run
    To ev'ry mire,
And by this world's ill-guiding light,
Err more than I can do by night.

There is in God, some say,
A deep but dazzling darkness, as men here   50
Say it is late and dusky, because they
    See not all clear;
Oh, for that night, where I in him
Might live invisible and dim!

The search

'Tis now clear day: I see a rose
Bud in the bright east, and disclose
The pilgrim-sun. All night have I
Spent in a roving ecstasy
To find my Savior; I have been
As far as Bethlem, and have seen
His inn and cradle; being there

I met the wise men, asked them where
He might be found, or what star can
Now point him out, grown up a man.
To Egypt hence I fled, ran o'er
All her parched bosom to Nile's shore,
Her yearly nurse; came back, inquired
Amongst the doctors, and desired
To see the temple, but was shown
A little dust, and for the town
A heap of ashes, where some said
A small bright sparkle was a bed
Which would one day, beneath the pole,
Awake, and then refine the whole.

   Tired here, I came to Sychar; thence
To Jacob's well, bequeathëd since
Unto his sons, where often they
In those calm golden evenings lay,
Wat'ring their flocks, and having spent
Those white days, drove home to the tent
Their well-fleeced train. And here, O fate,
I sit, where once my Savior sate;
The angry spring in bubbles swelled
Which broke in sighs still, as they filled
And whispered, Jesus had been there,
But Jacob's children would not hear.
Loath hence to part, at last I rise
But with the fountain in my eyes,
And here a fresh search is decreed,
He must be found where he did bleed;
I walk the garden, and there see
Ideas of his agony,
And moving anguishments that set
His blest face in a bloody sweat;
I climbed the hill, perused the cross
Hung with my gain and his great loss;
Never did tree bear fruit like this,
Balsam of souls, the body's bliss.
But oh, his grave! where I saw lent,
For he had none, a monument,
An undefiled and new-hewed one,
But there was not the corner-stone;
Sure, then said I, my quest is vain,
He'll not be found where he was slain;
So mild a Lamb can never be
'Midst so much blood and cruelty.
I'll to the wilderness, and can

Find beasts more merciful than man;
He lived there safe, 'twas his retreat
From the fierce Jew, and Herod's heat,
And forty days withstood the fell
And high temptations of hell;
With seraphins there talkèd he,
His father's flaming ministry;   60
He heaven'd their walks, and with his eyes
Made those wild shades a paradise,
Thus was the desert sanctified
To be the refuge of his bride;
I'll thither then; see, it is day,
The sun's broke through to guide my way.

    But as I urged thus, and writ down
What pleasures should my journey crown,
What silent paths, what shades and cells,
Fair virgin-flowers, and hallowed wells,   70
I should rove in, and rest my head
Where my dear Lord did often tread,
Sug'ring all dangers with success,
Methought I heard one singing thus:

    Leave, leave thy gadding thoughts;
        Who pores
        And spies
    Still out of doors,
        Descries
    Within them nought.   80

    The skin and shell of things,
        Though fair,
        Are not
    Thy wish nor prayer,
        But got
    By mere despair
        Of wings.

    To rack old elements,
        Or dust,
        And say   90
    Sure here he must
        Needs stay,
        Is not the way,
        Nor just.
Search well another world: who studies this,
Travels in clouds, seeks manna where none is.

Regeneration

A ward, and still in bonds, one day
　　I stole abroad;
It was high spring, and all the way
　　Primrosed and hung with shade;
　　Yet was it frost within,
　　And surly winds
Blasted my infant buds, and sin
　　Like clouds eclipsed my mind.

Stormed thus, I straight perceived
　　my spring
　　Mere stage and show, 　　10
My walk a monstrous mountained
　　thing,
　　Rough-cast with rocks and
　　　snow;
　　And as a pilgrim's eye,
　　Far from relief,
Measures the melancholy sky,
　　Then drops and rains for grief,

So sighed I upwards still; at last
　　'Twixt steps and falls
I reached the pinnacle, where
　　placed
　　I found a pair of scales; 　　20
　　I took them up and laid
　　In th' one, late pains;
The other smoke and pleasures
　　weighed,
　　But proved the heavier grains.

With that some cried, Away!
　　Straight I
　　Obeyed, and led
Full east, a fair, fresh field could
　　spy;
　　Some called it Jacob's bed,
　　A virgin soil which no
　　Rude feet ere trod, 　　30
Where, since he stepped there, only
　　go

Prophets and friends of God.

Here I reposed; but scarce well
　　set,
　　A grove descried
Of stately height, whose branches
　　met
　　And mixed on every side;
　　I entered, and once in,
　　Amazed to see't,
Found all was changed, and a new
　　spring
　　Did all my senses greet. 　　40

The unthrift sun shot vital gold,
　　A thousand pieces,
And heaven its azure did unfold,
　　Checkered with snowy fleeces;
　　The air was all in spice,
　　And every bush
A garland wore; thus fed my
　　eyes,
　　But all the ear lay hush.

Only a little fountain lent
　　Some use for ears, 　　50
And on the dumb shades language
　　spent,
　　The music of her tears;
　　I drew her near, and found
　　The cistern full
Of divers stones, some bright and
　　round,
　　Others ill-shaped and dull.

The first, pray mark, as quick as
　　light
　　Danced through the flood,
But th' last, more heavy than the
　　night,
　　Nailed to the center stood; 　　60
　　I wondered much, but tired

At last with thought,
My restless eye that still desired
As strange an object brought.

It was a bank of flowers, where I
    descried,
    Though 'twas mid-day,
Some fast asleep, others broad-
    eyed
    And taking in the ray;
Here musing long, I heard
    A rushing wind   70
Which still increased, but whence
    it stirred
No where I could not find.

I turned me round, and to each
    shade
    Dispatched an eye
To see if any leaf had made
    Least motion or reply,
    But while I list'ning sought
    My mind to ease
By knowing where 'twas, or where
    not,
    It whispered: Where I please. 80

Lord, then said I, on me one
    breath,
And let me die before my
    death!

The dwelling-place

S. John i. 38–39

What happy secret fountain,
    Fair shade or mountain,
Whose undiscovered virgin glory
Boasts it this day, though not in story,
Was then thy dwelling? Did some cloud,
Fixed to a tent, descend and shroud
My distressed Lord? Or did a star,
Beckoned by thee, though high and far,
In sparkling smiles haste gladly down
To lodge light and increase her own?   10
My dear, dear God! I do not know
What lodged thee then, nor where, nor how;
But I am sure thou dost now come
Oft to a narrow, homely room,
Where thou too hast but the least part,
My God, I mean my sinful heart.

The retreat

Happy those early days when I
Shined in my angel-infancy!
Before I understood this place
Appointed for my second race,
Or taught my soul to fancy aught
But a white celestial thought;
When yet I had not walked above

A mile or two from my first love,
And looking back at that short space,
Could see a glimpse of his bright face;   10
When on some gilded cloud or flower
My gazing soul would dwell an hour,
And in those weaker glories spy
Some shadows of eternity;
Before I taught my tongue to wound
My conscience with a sinful sound,
Or had the black art to dispense
A sev'ral sin to ev'ry sense;
But felt through all this fleshly dress
Bright shoots of everlastingness.   20
    Oh, how I long to travel back
And tread again that ancient track!
That I might once more reach that plain
Where first I left my glorious train,
From whence th' enlightened spirit sees
That shady city of palm trees.
But, ah, my soul with too much stay
Is drunk, and staggers in the way.
Some men a forward motion love,
But I by backward steps would move,   30
And when this dust falls to the urn,
In that state I came, return.

Childhood

I cannot reach it, and my striving eye
Dazzles at it, as at eternity.
    Were now that chronicle alive,
Those white designs which children drive,
And the thoughts of each harmless hour,
With their content too in my power,
Quickly would I make my path even,
And by mere playing go to heaven.

    Why should men love
A wolf more than a lamb or dove?   10
Or choose hell-fire and brimstone streams
Before bright stars and God's own beams?
Who kisseth thorns will hurt his face,
But flowers do both refresh and grace,
And sweetly living (fie on men!)
Are when dead, medicinal then.
If seeing much should make staid eyes,

And long experience should make wise,
Since all that age doth teach is ill,
Why should I not love childhood still?   20
Why if I see a rock or shelf,
Shall I from thence cast down myself,
Or by complying with the world,
From the same precipice be hurled?
Those observations are but foul
Which make me wise to lose my soul.

And yet the practice worldlings call
Business and weighty action all,
Checking the poor child for his play,
But gravely cast themselves away.   30

Dear, harmless age! the short, swift span
Where weeping virtue parts with man;
Where love without lust dwells, and bends
What way we please, without self-ends.

An age of mysteries! which he
Must live twice, that would God's face see;
Which angels guard, and with it play;
Angels, which foul men drive away!

How do I study now and scan
Thee, more than ere I studied man,   40
And only see through a long night
Thy edges, and thy bordering light!
Oh, for thy center and mid-day!
For sure that is the narrow way.

The dawning

Ah! what time wilt thou come? when shall that cry,
The bridegroom's coming, fill the sky?
Shall it in the evening run,
When our words and works are done?
Or will thy all-surprising light
     Break at midnight?
When either sleep or some dark pleasure
Possesseth mad man without measure,
Or shall these early fragrant hours
     Unlock thy bowers?   10
And with their blush of light descry
Thy locks crowned with eternity?

Indeed, it is the only time
That with thy glory doth best chime;
All now are stirring, ev'ry field
    Full hymns doth yield,
The whole creation shakes off night,
And for thy shadow looks the light;
Stars now vanish without number,
Sleepy planets set and slumber,   20
The pursy clouds disband and scatter,
All expect some sudden matter;
Not one beam triumphs, but from far
    That morning star.
Oh, at what time soever thou,
Unknown to us, the heavens wilt bow,
And with thy angels in the van
Descend to judge poor careless man,
Grant I may not like puddle lie
In a corrupt security,   30
Where, if a traveler water crave,
He finds it dead and in a grave;
But as this restless vocal spring
All day and night doth run and sing,
And though here born, yet is acquainted
Elsewhere, and flowing keeps untainted,
So let me all my busy age
In thy free services engage;
And though while here of force I must
Have commerce sometimes with poor dust,   40
And in my flesh, though vile and low,
As this doth in her channel flow,
Yet let my course, my aim, my love,
And chief acquaintance be above;
So when that day and hour shall come
In which thyself will be the sun,
Thou'lt find me dressed and on my way,
Watching the break of thy great day.

The morning watch

O joys! infinite sweetness! with
    what flowers
And shoots of glory my soul breaks
    and buds!
    All the long hours
    Of night and rest,
    Through the still shrouds
Of sleep and clouds,
    This dew fell on my breast;
    Oh, how it bloods
And spirits all my earth! Hark! in
    what rings
And hymning circulations the
    quick world   10

Awakes and sings;
The rising winds
And falling springs,
Birds, beasts, all things
Adore him in their kinds.
Thus all is hurled
In sacred hymns and order, the
    great chime
And symphony of nature. Prayer is
The world in tune,
A spirit voice,   20
And vocal joys
Whose echo is heav'n's bliss.
O let me climb

When I lie down! The pious soul
    by night
Is like a clouded star whose beams,
    though said
To shed their light
Under some cloud,
Yet are above,
And shine and move
Beyond that misty shroud.   30
So in my bed,
That curtained grave, though
    sleep like ashes hide
My lamp and life, both shall in
    thee abide.

The world

I saw eternity the other night
Like a great ring of pure and endless light,
        All calm as it was bright;
And round beneath it, time in hours, days, years,
        Driv'n by the spheres,
Like a vast shadow moved, in which the world
        And all her train were hurled:
The doting lover in his quaintest strain
        Did there complain;
Near him his lute, his fancy, and his flights,   10
        Wit's sour delights,
With gloves and knots, the silly snares of pleasure,
        Yet his dear treasure,
All scattered lay, while he his eyes did pore
        Upon a flower.

The darksome statesman, hung with weights and woe,
Like a thick midnight fog moved there so slow
        He did not stay, nor go;
Condemning thoughts, like sad eclipses, scowl
        Upon his soul,   20
And clouds of crying witnesses without
        Pursued him with one shout;
Yet digged the mole, and lest his ways be found
        Worked underground,
Where he did clutch his prey, but One did see
        That policy;
Churches and altars fed him; perjuries
        Were gnats and flies;

It rained about him blood and tears, but he
    Drank them as free.   30

The fearful miser on a heap of rust
Sat pining all his life there, did scarce trust
    His own hands with the dust,
Yet would not place one piece above, but lives
    In fear of thieves.
Thousands there were as frantic as himself,
    And hugged each one his pelf:
The downright epicure placed heav'n in sense,
    And scorned pretense;
While others, slipped into a wide excess,   40
    Said little less;
The weaker sort slight trivial wares enslave,
    Who think them brave;
And poor despisëd truth sat counting by
    Their victory.

Yet some, who all this while did weep and sing,
And sing and weep, soared up into the ring;
    But most would use no wing.
O fools, said I, thus to prefer dark night
    Before true light,   50
To live in grots and caves, and hate the day
    Because it shows the way,
The way which from this dead and dark abode
    Leads up to God,
A way where you might tread the sun, and be
    More bright than he.
But as I did their madness so discuss,
    One whispered thus:
This ring the bridegroom did for none provide
    But for his bride.   60

Ascension hymn

    Dust and clay,
  Man's ancient wear!
Here must you stay,
  But I elsewhere;
Souls sojourn here, but may not
    rest;
Who will ascend must be un-
    dressed.

    And yet some
  That know to die

    Before death come,
  Walk to the sky   10
Even in this life; but all such can
Leave behind them the old man.

    If a star
  Should leave the sphere,
She must first mar
  Her flaming wear,
And after fall, for in her dress
Of glory she cannot transgress.

Man of old
Within the line   20
Of Eden could,
Like the sun, shine
All naked, innocent and bright,
And intimate with heav'n as light;

But since he
That brightness soiled,
His garments be
All dark and spoiled,
And here are left as nothing
      worth,
Till the refiner's fire breaks
      forth.   30

Then comes he!
Whose mighty light
Made his clothes be,
Like heav'n, all bright—
The Fuller whose pure blood did
      flow
To make stained man more white
      than snow.

He alone,
And none else, can
Bring bone to bone
And rebuild man,   40
And by his all-subduing might,
Make clay ascend more quick than
      light.

[*They are all gone*]

They are all gone into the world of light!
   And I alone sit lingering here;
Their very memory is fair and bright,
   And my sad thoughts doth clear.

It glows and glitters in my cloudy breast
   Like stars upon some gloomy grove,
Or those faint beams in which this hill is dressed
   After the sun's remove.

I see them walking in an air of glory,
   Whose light doth trample on my days,   10
My days, which are at best but dull and hoary,
   Mere glimmering and decays.

O holy hope and high humility,
   High as the heavens above!
These are your walks, and you have showed them me
   To kindle my cold love.

Dear, beauteous death! the jewel of the just!
   Shining no where but in the dark;
What mysteries do lie beyond thy dust,
   Could man outlook that mark!   20

He that hath found some fledged bird's nest may know
   At first sight if the bird be flown;
But what fair well or grove he sings in now,
   That is to him unknown.

And yet, as angels in some brighter dreams
  Call to the soul when man doth sleep,
So some strange thoughts transcend our wonted themes,
  And into glory peep.

If a star were confined into a tomb,
  Her captive flames must needs burn there;   30
But when the hand that locked her up gives room,
  She'll shine through all the sphere.

O Father of eternal life, and all
  Created glories under thee,
Resume thy spirit from this world of thrall
  Into true liberty!

Either disperse these mists which blot and fill
  My perspective, still, as they pass,
Or else remove me hence unto that hill
  Where I shall need no glass.   40

Unprofitableness

How rich, O Lord, how fresh thy visits are!
'Twas but just now my bleak leaves hopeless hung,
  Sullied with dust and mud;
Each snarling blast shot through me, and did share
Their youth and beauty; cold showers nipped and wrung
  Their spiciness and blood;
But since thou didst in one sweet glance survey
Their sad decays, I flourish, and once more
  Breathe all perfumes and spice;
I smell a dew like myrrh, and all the day   10
Wear in my bosom a full sun; such store
  Hath one beam from thy eyes.
But ah, my God, what fruit hast thou of this?
What one poor leaf did ever I let fall
  To wait upon thy wreath?
Thus thou all day a thankless weed dost dress,
And when th' hast done, a stench or fog is all
  The odor I bequeath.

Mount of Olives [2]

When first I saw true beauty, and thy joys
Active as light, and calm without all noise,
Shined on my soul, I felt through all my powers

Such a rich air of sweets as evening showers,
Fanned by a gentle gale, convey and breathe
On some parched bank, crowned with a flow'ry wreath;
Odors and myrrh and balm in one rich flood
O'erran my heart and spirited my blood;
My thoughts did swim in comforts, and mine eye
Confessed, The world did only paint and lie. 10
And where before I did no safe course steer,
But wandered under tempests all the year,
Went bleak and bare in body as in mind,
And was blown through by ev'ry storm and wind;
I am so warmed now by this glance on me
That 'midst all storms I feel a ray of thee;
So have I known some beauteous paisage rise
In sudden flowers and arbors to my eyes,
And in the depth and dead of winter bring
To my cold thoughts a lively sense of spring. 20
　　Thus fed by thee, who dost all beings nourish,
My withered leaves again look green, and flourish;
I shine and shelter underneath thy wing,
Where sick with love I strive thy name to sing,
Thy glorious name! which grant I may so do
That these may be thy praise, and my joy too.

Peace

My soul, there is a country
　　Far beyond the stars,
Where stands a wingèd sentry
　　All skillful in the wars;
There above noise and danger
　　Sweet peace sits crowned with smiles,
And one born in a manger
　　Commands the beauteous files;
He is thy gracious friend,

And (O my soul, awake!)
　　Did in pure love descend 11
　　To die here for thy sake.
If thou canst get but thither,
　　There grows the flower of peace,
The rose that cannot wither,
　　Thy fortress and thy ease;
Leave then thy foolish ranges,
　　For none can thee secure
But one who never changes,
　　Thy God, thy life, thy cure.

THOMAS TRAHERNE

The Introduction and Notes are at page 1027

From *Poems of Felicity, Burney Ms.* 392

Wonder

How like an angel came I down!
How bright are all things here!

When first among his works I did appear,
　　Oh, how their glory did me crown!
The world resembled his eternity,
　　　　In which my soul did walk;
　　And ev'rything that I did see
　　　　Did with me talk.

The skies in their magnificence,
　　The lovely lively air,　　　　　　　　　　10
Oh, how divine, how soft, how sweet, how fair!
　　The stars did entertain my sense,
And all the works of God so bright and pure,
　　　　So rich and great, did seem,
　　As if they ever must endure
　　　　In my esteem.

A native health and innocence
　　Within my bones did grow,
And while my God did all his glories show,
　　I felt a vigor in my sense　　　　　　　　20
That was all spirit; I within did flow
　　　　With seas of life like wine;
　　I nothing in the world did know,
　　　　But 'twas divine.

Harsh rugged objects were concealed;
　　Oppressions, tears, and cries,
Sins, griefs, complaints, dissensions, weeping eyes,
　　Were hid, and only things revealed
Which heavenly spirits and the angels prize:
　　　　The state of innocence　　　　　　　30
　　And bliss, not trades and poverties,
　　　　Did fill my sense.

The streets seemed paved with golden stones,
　　The boys and girls all mine—
To me how did their lovely faces shine!
　　The sons of men all holy ones,
In joy and beauty then appeared to me;
　　　　And ev'rything I found,
　　While like an angel I did see,
　　　　Adorned the ground.　　　　　　　　40

Rich diamonds, and pearl, and gold
　　Might ev'rywhere be seen;
Rare colors, yellow, blue, red, white, and green,

Mine eyes on ev'ry side behold;
All that I saw a wonder did appear,
    Amazement was my bliss,
That and my wealth met ev'rywhere;
    No joy to this!

    Cursed, ill-devised proprieties,
      With envy, avarice,   50
And fraud, those fiends that spoil ev'n paradise,
    Were not the object of mine eyes;
Nor hedges, ditches, limits, narrow bounds,
    I dreamt not aught of those,
But in surveying all men's grounds
    I found repose.

    For property itself was mine,
      And hedges, ornaments,
Walls, houses, coffers, and their rich contents,   60
    To make me rich combine.
Clothes, costly jewels, laces, I esteemed
    My wealth, by others worn,
For me they all to wear them seemed,
    When I was born.

Eden

A learned and happy ignorance
    Divided me
    From all the vanity,
From all the sloth, care, sorrow, that advance
    The madness and the misery
Of men. No error, no distraction, I
Saw cloud the earth, or overcast the sky.

I knew not that there was a serpent's sting,
    Whose poison shed
    On men did overspread   10
The world, nor did I dream of such a thing
    As sin, in which mankind lay dead.
They all were brisk and living things to me,
Yea, pure and full of immortality.

Joy, pleasure, beauty, kindness, charming love,
    Sleep, life, and light,
    Peace, melody—my sight,
Mine ears, and heart did fill and freely move;

All that I saw did me delight;
The universe was then a world of treasure,   20
To me an universal world of pleasure.

Unwelcome penitence I then thought not on;
   Vain costly toys,
   Swearing and roaring boys,
Shops, markets, taverns, coaches, were unknown,
  So all things were that drown my joys;
No thorns choked up my path, nor hid the face
Of bliss and glory, nor eclipsed my place.

Only what Adam in his first estate,
   Did I behold;   30
   Hard silver and dry gold
As yet lay underground; my happy fate
  Was more acquainted with the old
And innocent delights which he did see
In his original simplicity.

Those things which first his Eden did adorn,
   My infancy
   Did crown; simplicity
Was my protection when I first was born.
  Mine eyes those treasures first did see   40
Which God first made; the first effects of love
My first enjoyments upon earth did prove,

And were so great, and so divine, so pure,
   So fair and sweet,
   So true, when I did meet
Them here at first they did my soul allure,
  And drew away mine infant feet
Quite from the works of men, that I might see
The glorious wonders of the Deity.

News

 News from a foreign country came,
As if my treasures and my joys lay there;
 So much it did my heart inflame,
'Twas wont to call my soul into mine ear,
   Which thither went to meet
   Th' approaching sweet,
   And on the threshold stood
  To entertain the secret good;

It hovered there
As if 'twould leave mine ear,
And was so eager to embrace
Th' expected tidings as they came,
That it could change its dwelling place
To meet the voice of fame;

As if new tidings were the things
Which did comprise my wishëd unknown treasure,
Or else did bear them on their wings,
With so much joy they came, with so much pleasure.
My soul stood at the gate
To recreate
Itself with bliss, and woo
Its speedier approach; a fuller view
It fain would take,
Yet journeys back would make
Unto my heart, as if 'twould fain
Go out to meet, yet stay within,
Fitting a place to entertain
And bring the tidings in.

What sacred instinct did inspire
My soul in childhood with an hope so strong?
What secret force moved my desire
T' expect my joys beyond the seas, so young?
Felicity I knew
Was out of view;
And being left alone,
I thought all happiness was gone
From earth; for this
I longed for absent bliss,
Deeming that sure beyond the seas,
Or else in something near at hand
Which I knew not, since nought did please
I knew, my bliss did stand.

But little did the infant dream
That all the treasures of the world were by,
And that himself was so the cream
And crown of all which round about did lie.
Yet thus it was! The gem,
The diadem,
The ring enclosing all
That stood upon this earthen ball,
The heav'nly eye,

Much wider than the sky,
Wherein they all included were,
The love, the soul, that was the king
Made to possess them, did appear
A very little thing.

The apostasy

One star
Is better far
Than many precious stones;
One sun, which is by its own luster seen,
Is worth ten thousand golden thrones;
A juicy herb, or spire of grass,
In useful virtue, native green,
An em'rald doth surpass,
Hath in 't more value, though less seen.   10

No wars,
Nor mortal jars,
Nor bloody feuds, nor coin,
Nor griefs which those occasion, saw I then;
Nor wicked thieves which this purloin;
I had no thoughts that were impure;
Esteeming both women and men
God's work, I was secure,
And reckoned peace my choicest gem.

As Eve,
I did believe   20
Myself in Eden set,
Affecting neither gold nor ermined crowns,
Nor aught else that I need forget;
No mud did foul my limpid streams,
No mist eclipsed my sun with frowns;
Set off with heav'nly beams,
My joys were meadows, fields, and towns.

Those things
Which cherubins
Did not at first behold   30
Among God's works, which Adam did not see—
As robes, and stones enchased in gold,
Rich cabinets, and such-like fine
Inventions—could not ravish me;
I thought not bowls of wine
Needful for my felicity.

All bliss
Consists in this,
To do as Adam did,
And not to know those superficial joys   40
Which were from him in Eden hid,
Those little new-invented things,
Fine lace and silks, such childish toys
As ribands are and rings,
Or worldly pelf that us destroys.

For God,
Both great and good,
The seeds of melancholy
Created not, but only foolish men,
Grown mad with customary folly   50
Which doth increase their wants, so dote
As when they elder grow they then
Such baubles chiefly note;
More fools at twenty years than ten.

But I,
I know not why,
Did learn among them too,
At length; and when I once with blemished eyes
Began their pence and toys to view,
Drowned in their customs, I became   60
A stranger to the shining skies,
Lost as a dying flame,
And hobby-horses brought to prize.

The sun
And moon forgone
As if unmade, appear
No more to me; to God and heaven dead
I was, as though they never were;
Upon some useless gaudy book,
When what I knew of God was fled,   70
The child being taught to look,
His soul was quickly murtherëd.

O fine!
O most divine!
O brave! they cried; and showed
Some tinsel thing whose glittering did amaze,
And to their cries its beauty owed;

Thus I on riches, by degrees,
Of a new stamp did learn to gaze,
While all the world for these   80
I lost, my joy turned to a blaze.

Poverty

As in the house I sate,
Alone and desolate,
No creature but the fire and I,
The chimney and the stool, I lift mine eye
Up to the wall,
And in the silent hall
Saw nothing mine
But some few cups and dishes shine,
The table and the wooden stools
Where people used to dine;   10
A painted cloth there was,
Wherein some ancient story wrought
A little entertained my thought,
Which light discovered through the glass.

I wondered much to see
That all my wealth should be
Confined in such a little room,
Yet hope for more I scarcely durst presume.
It grieved me sore
That such a scanty store
Should be my all;   20
For I forgot my ease and health,
Nor did I think of hands or eyes,
Nor soul nor body prize;
I neither thought the sun,
Nor moon, nor stars, nor people, mine,
Though they did round about me shine;
And therefore was I quite undone.

Some greater things, I thought,
Must needs for me be wrought,   30
Which till my craving mind could see
I ever should lament my poverty;
I fain would have
Whatever bounty gave,
Nor could there be
Without or love or deity;
For should not he be infinite

Whose hand created me?
Ten thousand absent things
Did vex my poor and wanting mind,
Which, till I be no longer blind,
Let me not see the King of kings.   40

His love must surely be
Rich, infinite, and free;
Nor can he be thought a God
Of grace and power, that fills not his abode,
His holy court,
In kind and liberal sort;
Joys and pleasures,
Plenty of jewels, goods, and treasures,   50
To enrich the poor, cheer the forlorn,
His palace must adorn,
And given all to me;
For till his works my wealth became,
No love or peace did me inflame:
But now I have a Deity.

Right apprehension

Give but to things their true esteem,
And those which now so vile and worthless seem
Will so much fill and please the mind
That we shall there the only riches find.
How wise was I
In infancy!
I then saw in the clearest light;
But corrupt custom is a second night.

Custom, that must a trophy be
When wisdom shall complete her victory;   10
For trades, opinions, errors, are
False lights, but yet received to set off ware
More false; we're sold
For worthless gold.
Diana was a goddess made
That silversmiths might have the better trade.

But give to things their true esteem,
And then what's magnified most vile will seem;
What commonly's despised will be
The truest and the greatest rarity.   20
What men should prize
They all despise:

The best enjoyments are abused;
The only wealth by madmen is refused.

A globe of earth is better far
Than if it were a globe of gold; a star
    Much brighter than a precious stone;
The sun more glorious than a costly throne—
      His warming beam,
      A living stream   30
Of liquid pearl, that from a spring
Waters the earth, is a most precious thing.

What newness once suggested to,
Now clearer reason doth improve my view;
    By novelty my soul was taught
At first, but now reality my thought
      Inspires; and I
      Perspicuously
Each way instructed am by sense,
Experience, reason, and intelligence.   40

A globe of gold must barren be,
Untilled and useless; we should neither see
    Trees, flowers, grass, or corn
Such a metalline massy globe adorn;
      As splendor blinds
      So hardness binds,
No fruitfulness it can produce;
A golden world can't be of any use.

Ah me! this world is more divine;
The wisdom of a god in this doth shine.   50
    What ails mankind to be so cross?
The useful earth they count vile dirt and dross,
      And neither prize
      Its qualities
Nor donor's love. I fain would know
How or why men God's goodness disallow.

The earth's rare ductile soil,
Which duly yields unto the plowman's toil
    Its fertile nature, gives offence,
And its improvement by the influence   60
      Of heav'n; for these
      Do not well please,
Because they do upbraid men's hardened hearts,
And each of them an evidence imparts

Against the owner; whose design
It is that nothing be reputed fine,
   Nor held for any excellence
Of which he hath not in himself the sense.
     He too well knows   70
     That no fruit grows
In him, obdurate wretch, who yields
Obedience to heav'n less than the fields.

But being, like his lovëd gold,
Stiff, barren, and impen'trable, though told
   He should be otherwise, he is
Uncapable of any heav'nly bliss.
     His gold and he
     Do well agree,
For he's a formal hypocrite,   80
Like that, unfruitful, yet on th' outside bright.

Ah, happy infant! wealthy heir!
How blessed did the heaven and earth appear
   Before thou knew'st there was a thing
Called gold! barren of good, of ill the spring
     Beyond compare!
     Most quiet were
Those infant days when I did see
Wisdom and wealth couched in simplicity.

Right apprehension II

If this I did not ev'ry moment see,
   And if my thoughts did stray
   At any time, or idly play,
  And fix on other objects, yet
    This apprehension set
     In me,
    Securëd my felicity.

The rapture

   Sweet infancy!
O heavenly fire! O sacred light!
   How fair and bright!
   How great am I,
Whom the whole world doth
    magnify!

   O heavenly joy!
O great and sacred blessedness
   Which I possess!
   So great a joy
Who did into my arms con-
    vey?   10

From God above
Being sent, the gift doth me in-
    flame
To praise his name;
The stars do move,
The sun doth shine, to show his
    love.

Oh, how divine
Am I! To all this sacred
    wealth,
This life and health,
Who raised? who mine
Did make the same? what hand
    divine?   20

Felicity

Prompted to seek my bliss above the skies,
    How often did I lift mine eyes
        Beyond the spheres!
Dame Nature told me there was endless space
Within my soul; I spied its very face.
        Sure it not for nought appears;
    What is there which a man may see
        Beyond the spheres?
        Felicity.

There in the mind of God, that sphere of love,   10
    In nature, height, extent, above
        All other spheres,
A man may see himself, the world, the bride
Of God, his church, which as they there are eyed,
        Strangely exalted each appears;
    His mind is higher than the space
        Above the spheres,
        Surmounts all place.

No empty space—it is all full of sight,
    All soul and life, an eye most bright,   20
        All light and love,
Which doth at once all things possess and give,
Heaven and earth, with all that therein live;
        It rests at quiet, and doth move;
    Eternal is, yet time includes;
        A scene above
        All interludes.

Dreams

'Tis strange! I saw the skies,
I saw the hills before mine eyes,
    The sparrow fly,
The lands that did about me lie,
The real sun, that heavenly eye!

Can closèd eyes ev'n in the darkest night
See through their lids, and be informed with sight?

    The people were to me
  As true as those by day I see,
      As true the air;   10
  The earth as sweet, as fresh, as fair,
  As that which did by day repair
Unto my waking sense! Can all the sky,
Can all the world, within my brain-pan lie?

    What sacred secret's this
  Which seems to intimate my bliss?
      What is there in
  The narrow confines of my skin
  That is alive, and feels within
When I am dead? Can magnitude possess   20
An active memory, yet not be less?

    May all that I can see
  Awake, by night within me be?
      My childhood knew
  No difference, but all was true,
  As real all as what I view;
The world itself was there; 'twas wondrous strange
That heav'n and earth should so their place exchange.

    Till that which vulgar sense
  Doth falsely call experience   30
      Distinguished things,
  The ribands, and the gaudy wings
  Of birds, the virtues and the sins,
That represented were in dreams by night,
As really my senses did delight

    Or grieve, as those I saw
  By day; things terrible did awe
      My soul with fear;
  The apparitions seemed as near
  As things could be, and things they were;   40
Yet were they all by fancy in me wrought,
And all their being founded in a thought.

    Oh, what a thing is thought!
  Which seems a dream, yea, seemeth nought,
      Yet doth the mind

Affect as much as what we find
Most near and true! Sure men are blind,
And can't the forcible reality
Of things that secret are within them see.

Thought! Surely thoughts are true;   50
They please as much as things can do;
Nay, things are dead,
And in themselves are severèd
From souls; nor can they fill the head
Without our thoughts. Thoughts are the real things
From whence all joy, from whence all sorrow springs.

Insatiableness

This busy, vast, inquiring soul
Brooks no control,
No limits will endure,
Nor any rest; it will all see,
Not time alone, but ev'n eternity.
What is it? Endless, sure.

'Tis mean ambition to desire
A single world;
To many I aspire,
Though one upon another hurled;   10
Nor will they all, if they be all confined,
Delight my mind.

This busy, vast, inquiring soul
Brooks no control;
'Tis very curious too.
Each one of all those worlds must be
Enriched with infinite variety
And worth, or 'twill not do.

'Tis nor delight nor perfect pleasure
To have a purse   20
That hath a bottom in its treasure,
Since I must thence endless expense disburse.
Sure there's a God, for else there's no delight,
One infinite.

The review

Did I grow, or did I stay?
Did I prosper or decay,
When I so
From things to thoughts did go?

Did I flourish or diminish,
When I so in thoughts did finish
What I had in things begun;
When from God's works to think upon
The thoughts of men my soul did come?
The thoughts of men, had they been wise,   10
Should more delight me than the skies;
        They mighty creatures are,
            For these the mind
Affect, afflict, do ease or grind;
        But foolish thoughts ensnare.

    Wise ones are a sacred treasure;
    True ones yield substantial pleasure;
        Compared to them,
        I things as shades esteem.
False ones are a foolish flourish,   20
Such as mortals chiefly nourish;
When I them to things compare,
Compared to things, they trifles are;
Bad thoughts do hurt, deceive, ensnare;
A good man's thoughts are of such price
That they create a paradise;
        But he that misemploys
            That faculty,
God, men, and angels doth defy,
        Robs them of all their joys.   30

FROM *Christian Ethics*, 1675

[All music, sauces, feasts]

All music, sauces, feasts, delights, and pleasures,
Games, dancing, arts, consist in governed measures;
Much more do words and passions of the mind
In temperance their sacred beauty find.

SIR FRANCIS KYNASTON

The Introduction and Notes are at page 1028

FROM *Cynthiades, or Amorous Sonnets*, published with *Leoline and
Sydanis*, 1642

On her fair eyes

Look not upon me with those lovely eyes,
    From whom there flies

So many a dart
To wound a heart
That still in vain to thee for mercy cries,
Yet dies, whether thou grantest or denies.

Of thy coy looks, know, I do not complain,
　　Nor of disdain;
　　Those sudden like
　　The lightning strike,   10
And kill me without any ling'ring pain,
And slain so once, I cannot die again.

But oh, thy sweet looks from my eyes conceal,
　　Which so oft steal
　　My soul from me,
　　And bring to thee
A wounded heart, which though it do reveal
The hurts thou giv'st it, yet thou canst not heal.

Upon those sweets I surfeit still, yet I,
　　Wretch, cannot die;   20
　　But am revived,
　　And made long-lived
By often dying, since thy gracious eye,
Like heaven, makes not a death, but ecstasy.

Then in the heaven of that beauteous face,
　　Since thou dost place
　　A martyred heart
　　Whose bliss thou art,
Since thou hast ta'en the soul, this favor do,
Into thy bosom take the body too.   30

To Cynthia

On concealment of her beauty

Do not conceal thy radiant eyes,
The starlight of serenest skies,
Lest wanting of their heavenly
　　light
They turn to chaos' endless night.

Do not conceal those tresses fair,
The silken snares of thy curled
　　hair,
Lest finding neither gold nor ore,
The curious silkworm work no
　　more.

Do not conceal those breasts of
　　thine,
More snow-white than the Apen-
　　nine,   10
Lest if there be like cold or frost,
The lily be forever lost.

Do not conceal that fragrant scent,
Thy breath, which to all flowers
　　hath lent
Perfumes, lest it being suppressed,
No spices grow in all the East.

Do not conceal thy heavenly voice,
Which makes the hearts of gods re-
    joice,
Lest music hearing no such thing,
The nightingale forget to sing. ²⁰

Do not conceal nor yet eclipse
Thy pearly teeth with coral lips,

Lest that the seas cease to bring
    forth
Gems, which from thee have all
    their worth.

Do not conceal no beauty, grace,
That's either in thy mind or face,
Lest virtue, overcome by vice,
Make men believe no paradise.

To Cynthia

On her resemblance

Forgive me, Cynthia, if as poets use
When they some divine beauty would express,
I roses, pinks, or July-flowers do choose;
It is a kind of weakness, I confess,
    To praise the great'st perfection by a less;
    And is the same as if one strove to paint
    The holiness or virtues of a saint.

Yet there is a necessity imposed,
For those bright angels, which we virtues call,
Had not been known had they not been enclosed   10
In precious stones, or things diaphanal;
    The essences and forms celestial
    Had been concealed, had not the heavenly powers
    Been stamped and printed on stones, trees, and flowers.

So thy divine pure soul and every grace
And heavenly beauty it doth comprehend,
Had not been seen, but for thy lovely face,
Which with angel-like features may contend,
Which into flesh and blood did down descend,
    That she her purest essence might disclose   20
    In it, as thy fair cheeks do in the rose.

To Cynthia

On her mother's decease

April is past, then do not shed,
    Nor do not waste in vain,
Upon thy mother's earthy bed
    Thy tears of silver rain.

Thou canst not hope that her cold
    earth

By wat'ring will bring forth
A flower like thee, or will give
    birth
To one of the like worth.

'Tis true the rain fall'n from the
    sky,

Or from the clouded air,   10
Doth make the earth to fructify,
    And makes the heaven more fair.

With thy dear face it is not so,
    Which if once overcast,
If thou rain down thy showers of
        woe,
    They, like the Sirens', blast.

Therefore when sorrow shall be-
        cloud

Thy fair serenest day,
Weep not, my sighs shall be al-
        lowed
    To chase the storm away.   20

Consider   that   the   teeming
        vine,
    If cut by chance, do weep,
Doth bear no grapes to make the
        wine,
    But feels eternal sleep.

SIDNEY GODOLPHIN

The Introduction and Notes are at page 1028

FROM *Malone Ms.* 13

Song

Or love me less, or love me more,
    And play not with my liberty,
Either take all, or all restore,
    Bind me at least, or set me free.
Let me some nobler torture find
    Than of a doubtful wavering
        mind;
Take all my peace, but you be-
        tray
    Mine honor too this cruel way.

'Tis true that I have nursed be-
        fore
    That hope of which I now
        complain;   10
And having little, sought no more,
    Fearing to meet with your dis-
        dain.
The sparks of favor you did give,
    I gently blew to make them
        live;
And yet have gained by all this
        care
    No rest in hope nor in despair.

I see you wear that pitying smile
    Which you have still vouch-
        safed my smart,
Content thus cheaply to beguile
    And   entertain   an   harmless
        heart;   20
But I no longer can give way
    To hope, which doth so little
        pay;
And yet I dare no freedom
        owe
    Whilst you are kind, though
        but in show.

Then give me more, or give me
        less,
    Do not disdain a mutual sense,
Or your unpitying beauties dress
    In their own free indiffer-
        ence;
But show not a severer eye
    Sooner to give me liberty,   30
For I shall love the very scorn
    Which for my sake you do put
        on.

[*No more unto my thoughts appear*]

No more unto my thoughts appear,
  At least appear less fair,
For crazy tempers justly fear
  The goodness of the air.

Whilst your pure image hath a place
  In my impurer mind,
Your very shadow is the glass
  Where my defects I find.

Shall I not fly that brighter light
  Which makes my fires look pale,   10
And put that virtue out of sight
  Which makes mine none at all?

No, no, your picture doth impart
  Such value, I not wish
The native worth to any heart
  That's unadorned with this.

Though poorer in desert I make
  Myself, whilst I admire,
The fuel which from hope I take
  I give to my desire.   20

If this flame lighted from your eyes
  The subject do calcine,
A heart may be your sacrifice,
  Too weak to be your shrine.

[*Chloris, it is not thy disdain*]

To the tune of, *In faith, I cannot keep my father's sheep*

Chloris, it is not thy disdain
  Can ever cover with despair
  Or in cold ashes hide that care
Which I have fed with so long pain;
I may perhaps mine eyes refrain,
And fruitless words no more impart,
But yet still serve, still serve thee in my heart.

What though I spend my hapless days
  In finding entertainments out,
  Careless of what I go about,   10
Or seek my peace in skillful ways,
Applying to my eyes new rays
Of beauty, and another flame
Unto my heart, my heart is still the same.

'Tis true that I could love no face
  Inhabited by cold disdain,
  Taking delight in other's pain.
Thy looks are full of native grace;
Since then by chance scorn there hath place,
'Tis to be hoped I may remove   20
This scorn one day, one day by endless love.

JOHN HALL

The Introduction and Notes are at page 1029

From *Poems*, 1646

The call

Romira, stay,
And run not thus like a young roe away;
    No enemy
Pursues thee, foolish girl, 'tis only I;
    I'll keep off harms,
If thou'll be pleased to garrison mine arms.
    What, dost thou fear
I'll turn a traitor? May these roses here
    To paleness shred,
And lilies stand disguisèd in new red,
    If that I lay
A snare wherein thou wouldst not gladly stay.
    See, see the sun
Does slowly to his azure lodging run;
    Come, sit but here,
And presently he'll quit our hemisphere;
    So, still among
Lovers, time is too short or else too long;
    Here will we spin
Legends for them that have love-martyrs been;   20
    Here on this plain
We'll talk Narcissus to a flower again.
    Come here and choose
On which of these proud plats thou would repose;
    Here mayst thou shame
The rusty violets, with the crimson flame
    Of either cheek,
And primroses white as thy fingers seek;
    Nay, thou mayst prove
That man's most noble passion is to love.   30

An Epicurean ode

Since that this thing we call the world
By chance on atoms is begot,
Which though in daily motions hurled
    Yet weary not,
    How doth it prove
Thou art so fair, and I in love?

Since that the soul doth only lie
Immersed in matter, chained in sense,
How can, Romira, thou and I
    With both dispense?   10
    And thus ascend
In higher flights than wings can lend.

Since man's but pasted up of earth,
And ne'er was cradled in the skies,
What *terra lemnia* gave thee birth?
    What diamond, eyes?
    Or thou alone,
To tell what others were, came down?

FROM *The Second Book of Divine Poems,* 1647, published with
Poems, 1646

[*Even as the wandering traveler*]

Ecclesiastes i. 3
What profiteth a man of all his labor, which he taketh under the sun?

Even as the wandering traveler doth stray,
    Led from his way
By a false fire, whose flame to cheated sight
    Doth lead aright,
All paths are footed over but that one
    Which should be gone;
Even so my foolish wishes are in chase
Of ev'rything but what they should embrace.

We laugh at children, that can when they please
    A bubble raise,   10
And when their fond ambition sated is,
    Again dismiss
The fleeting toy into its former air;
    What do we here
But act such tricks? Yet thus we differ: they
Destroy, so do not we; we sweat, they play.

Ambition's tow'rings do some gallants keep
    From calmer sleep;
Yet when their thoughts the most possessëd are,
    They grope but air,   20
And when they're highest, in an instant fade
    Into a shade;

Or like a stone, that more forced upwards, shall
With greater violence to 'ts center fall.

Another, whose conceptions only dream
    Monsters of fame,
The vain applause of other madmen buys
    With his own sighs,
Yet his enlargëd name shall never crawl
    Over this ball,   30
But soon consume; thus doth a trumpet's sound
Rush bravely on a little, then's not found.

But we as soon may tell how often shapes
    Are changed by apes,
As know how oft man's childish thoughts do vary,
    And still miscarry.
So a weak eye in twilight thinks it sees
    New specïes,
While it sees nought; so men in dreams conceive
Of specters, till that waking undeceive.   40

A pastoral hymn

Happy choristers of air,
Who by your nimble flight draw near
    His throne, whose wondrous story
    And unconfinëd glory
Your notes still carol, whom your sound
And whom your plumy pipes rebound.

Yet do the lazy snails no less
The greatness of our Lord confess,
    And those whom weight hath chained,
    And to the earth restrained,
Their ruder voices do as well,   10
Yea, and the speechless fishes tell.

Great Lord, from whom each tree receives,
Then pays again, as rent, his leaves,
    Thou dost in purple set
    The rose and violet,
And giv'st the sickly lily white,
Yet in them all thy name dost write.

THOMAS STANLEY

The Introduction and Notes are at page 1029

FROM *Poems and Translations,*
1647

Expectation

Chide, chide no more away
The fleeting daughters of the day,
Nor with impatient thoughts out-
    run
    The lazy sun,
Or think the hours do move too
    slow;
    Delay is kind,
And we too soon shall find
That which we seek, yet fear to
    know.

The mystic dark decrees
Unfold not of the destinies,   10
Nor boldly seek to antedate
    The laws of fate;
Thy anxious search awhile for-
    bear,
    Suppress thy haste,
And know that time at last
Will crown thy hope or fix thy
    fear.

FROM *Poems,* 1651

Changed, yet constant

Wrong me no more
    In thy complaint,
Blamed for inconstancy;
    I vowed t' adore
    The fairest saint,
Nor changed whilst thou wert
    she;
But if another thee outshine,
Th' inconstancy is only thine.

To be by such
    Blind fools admired,   10
Gives thee but small esteem,
    By whom as much
    Thou'dst be desired,
Didst thou less beauteous seem;
Sure why they love they know not
    well,
Who why they should not cannot
    tell.

Women are by
    Themselves betrayed,
And to their short joys cruel,
    Who foolishly   20
    Themselves persuade
Flames can outlast their fuel;
None, though Platonic their pre-
    tense,
With reason love unless by sense.

And he by whose
    Command to thee
I did my heart resign,
    Now bids me choose
    A deity
Diviner far than thine;   30
No power can love from beauty
    sever;
I'm still love's subject, thine was
    never.

The fairest she
    Whom none surpass
To love hath only right,
    And such to me
    Thy beauty was
Till one I found more bright;
But 'twere as impious to adore
Thee now, as not t' have done 't
    before.   40

Nor is it just
　　By rules of love
Thou shouldst deny to quit
　　A heart that must
　　Another's prove,
Ev'n in thy right to it;
Must not thy subjects captives be
To her who triumphs over thee?

Cease then in vain
　　To blot my name　　50
With forged apostasy;
　　Thine is that stain
　　Who dar'st to claim
What others ask of thee.
Of lovers they are only true
Who pay their hearts where they
　　are due.

The repulse

Not that by this disdain
　　I am released,
And freed from thy tyrannic
　　chain,
　　Do I myself think blest;

Nor that thy flame shall burn
　　No more, for know
That I shall into ashes turn
　　Before this fire doth so;

Nor yet that unconfined
　　I now may rove,　　10
And with new beauties please my
　　mind;
　　But that thou ne'er didst love.

For since thou hast no part
　　Felt of this flame,
I only from thy tyrant heart
　　Repulsed, not banished, am.

To lose what once was mine
　　Would grieve me more
Than those inconstant sweets of
　　thine
Had pleased my soul before.　20

Now I have not lost the bliss
　　I ne'er possessed;
And spite of fate am blest in this,
　　That I was never blest.

The exequies

Draw near,
　　You lovers that complain
　　Of fortune or disdain,
And to my ashes lend a tear;
Melt the hard marble with your
　　groans,
And soften the relentless stones,
Whose cold embraces the sad sub-
　　ject hide
Of all love's cruelties, and
　　beauty's pride!

No verse,
　　No epicedium bring,　　10
　　Nor peaceful requiem sing,
To charm the terrors of my
　　hearse;
No profane numbers must flow
　　near
The sacred silence that dwells
　　here.
Vast griefs are dumb; softly, oh,
　　softly mourn,
Lest you disturb the peace attends
　　my urn.

Yet strew
　　Upon my dismal grave
　　Such offerings as you have,
Forsaken cypress and sad
　　yew;　　20
For kinder flowers can take no
　　birth
Or growth from such unhappy
　　earth.
Weep only o'er my dust and say,
　　Here lies
To love and fate an equal sacri-
　　fice.

Song

I prithee let my heart alone,
    Since now 'tis raised above
        thee;
Not all the beauty thou dost own
    Again can make me love thee.

He that was shipwrecked once be-
        fore
    By such a siren's call,
And yet neglects to shun that
        shore,
    Deserves his second fall.

Each flatt'ring kiss, each tempting
        smile
    Thou dost in vain bestow,   10
Some other lovers might beguile,
    Who not thy falsehood know.

But I am proof against all art,
    No vows shall e'er persuade me
Twice to present a wounded heart
    To her that hath betrayed me.

Could I again be brought to love
    Thy form, though more divine,
I might thy scorn as justly move
    As now thou sufferest mine. 20

The relapse

Oh, turn away those cruel eyes,
    The stars of my undoing!
Or death, in such a bright dis-
        guise,
    May tempt a second wooing.

Punish their blindly impious pride,
    Who dare contemn thy glory;
It was my fall that deified
    Thy name, and sealed thy
        story.

Yet no new sufferings can pre-
        pare
    A higher praise to crown
        thee;   10
Though my first death proclaim
        thee fair,
    My second will unthrone thee.

Lovers will doubt thou canst en-
        tice
    No other for thy fuel,
And if thou burn one victim twice,
    Both think thee poor and cruel.

SIR EDWARD SHERBURNE

The Introduction and Notes are at page 1030

FROM *Salmacis . . . with several other poems and translations,* 1651

Chloris' eyes and breasts

Chloris, on thine eyes I gazed;
    When amazed
      At their brightness,
On thy breasts I cast my look;
    No less took
      With their whiteness,

Both I justly did admire—
These all snow, and those all fire.

Whilst these wonders I surveyed,
    Thus I said   10
      In suspense,
Nature could have done no less
      To express

Her providence,
Than that two such fair worlds
    might
Have two suns to give them light.

The vow

By my life I vow
That my life art thou,
By my heart and by my eyes;
    But thy faith denies
To my juster oath t' incline,
For thou sayst I swear by thine.

By this sigh I swear,
By this falling tear,
By the undeservëd pains
    My grievëd soul sustains. 10
Now thou mayst believe my moan,
These are too too much my own.

Weeping and kissing

A kiss I begged, but smiling she
    Denied it me;
When straight her cheeks with
    tears o'erflown,
    Now kinder grown,
What smiling she'd not let me
    have,
    She weeping gave.
Then you whom scornful beauties
    awe,
    Hope yet relief;
For love, who tears from smiles,
    can draw
    Pleasure from grief.

The broken faith

Lately by clear Thames his side,
Fair Lycoris I espied
With the pen of her white hand
These words printing on the sand:
None Lycoris doth approve
But Mirtillo for her love.
Ah, false nymph, those words were
    fit

In sand only to be writ;
For the quickly rising streams
Of oblivion, and the Thames, 10
In a little moment's stay
From the shore washed clean
    away
What thy hand had there im-
    pressed,
And Mirtillo from thy breast.

The happy life
To Julius Martialis

Mart. l. 10. Epig. 47

Those things which make life
    truly blest,
Sweetest Martial, hear expressed:
Wealth left, and not from labor
    growing;
A grateful soil, a hearth still
    glowing;
No strife, small business, peace of
    mind,
Quick wit, a body well inclined,
Wise innocence, friends of one
    heart,
Cheap food, a table without art;
Nights which nor cares nor sur-
    feits know, 9
No dull, yet a chaste bedfellow;
Sleeps which the tedious hours
    contract;
Be what thou mayst be, nor ex-
    act
Aught more; nor with thy last
    hour of breath
Fear, nor with wishes hasten
    death.

On Captain Ansa, a bragging
runaway

Casimir

Whilst timorous Ansa led his
    martial band

'Gainst the invaders of his native
    land,
Thus he bespake his men before
    the fight:
Courage, my mates! let's dine, for
    we to-night
Shall sup, says he, in heaven. This
    having said,
Soon as the threatening ensigns
    were displayed,
And the loud drums and trumpets
    had proclaimed
Defiance 'twixt the hosts, he, who
    ne'er shamed
At loss of honor, fairly ran away;
When being asked how chance he
    would not stay,   10

And go along with them to sup in
    heaven,
Pardon me, friends, said he, I fast
    this even.

On Bibinus, a notorious drunkard

Scaliger

The sot Loserus is drunk twice a
    day,
Bibinus only once; now of these
    say
Which may a man the greatest
    drunkard call?
Bibinus still; for he's drunk once
    for all.

ABRAHAM COWLEY

The Introduction and Notes are at page 1030

FROM *Poetical Blossoms*, 1636

To the Reader.

Reader (I know not yet whether gentle or no): Some I know have been angry (I dare not assume the honor of their envy) at my poetical boldness, and blamed in mine what commends other fruits, earliness. . . . The small fire I have is rather blown than extinguished by this wind. For the itch of poesy by being angered increaseth, by rubbing spreads farther; which appears in that I have ventured upon this second edition. . . . I would not be angry to see any one burn up Pyramus and Thisbe, nay I would do it myself, but that I hope a pardon may easily be gotten for the errors of ten years age. My Constantia and Philetus confesseth me two years older when I writ it. . . .

                                             A. C.

The vote

. . . .

This only grant me: that my means may lie
Too low for envy, for contempt too high.
    Some honor I would have,
Not from great deeds, but good alone;
Th' ignote are better than ill-known,
    Rumor can ope the grave.

Acquaintance I would hug, but when 't depends
Not from the number, but the choice of friends.

Books should, not business, entertain the light,
And sleep, as undisturbed as death, the night.   10
    My house a cottage more
Than palace, and should fitting be
For all my use, no luxury.
    My garden painted o'er
With nature's hand, not art's, and pleasures yield
Horace might envy in his Sabine field.

Thus would I double my life's fading space,
For he that runs it well twice runs his race.
    And in this true delight,
These unbought sports and happy state   20
I would not fear, nor wish my fate,
    But boldly say each night,
To-morrow let my sun his beams display,
Or in clouds hide them; I have lived to-day.

FROM *The Works of Mr. Abraham Cowley,* 1668

Ode. Of wit

Tell me, O tell, what kind of thing is wit,
    Thou who master art of it,
For the first matter loves variety less,
Less women love 't, either in love or dress.
    A thousand different shapes it bears,
    Comely in thousand shapes appears.
Yonder we saw it plain; and here 'tis now,
Like spirits in a place, we know not how.

London that vents of false ware so much store,
    In no ware deceives us more,   10
For men led by the color and the shape
Like Zeuxis' birds fly to the painted grape;
    Some things do through our judgment pass
    As through a multiplying glass,
And sometimes, if the object be too far,
We take a falling meteor for a star.

Hence 'tis a wit, that greatest word of fame,
    Grows such a common name;
And wits by our creation they become
Just so as tit'lar bishops made at Rome.   20

'Tis not a tale, 'tis not a jest
    Admired with laughter at a feast,
Nor florid talk, which can that title gain;
The proofs of wit forever must remain.

'Tis not to force some lifeless verses meet
    With their five gouty feet;
All ev'rywhere, like man's, must be the soul,
And reason the inferior powers control.
    Such were the numbers which could call
    The stones into the Theban wall;   30
Such miracles are ceased, and now we see
No towns or houses raised by poetry.

Yet 'tis not to adorn and gild each part,—
    That shows more cost than art,
(Jewels at nose and lips but ill appear);
Rather than all things wit, let none be there.
    Several lights will not be seen
    If there be nothing else between;
Men doubt, because they stand so thick i' th' sky,
If those be stars which paint the galaxy.   40

'Tis not when two like words make up one noise—
    Jests for Dutchmen and English boys—
In which who finds out wit, the same may see
In an'grams and acrostics, poetry.
    Much less can that have any place
    At which a virgin hides her face;
Such dross the fire must purge away; 'tis just
The author blush, there where the reader must.

'Tis not such lines as almost crack the stage
    When Bajazet begins to rage,   50
Nor a tall metaphor in the bombast way,
Nor the dry chips of short-lunged Seneca,
    Nor upon all things to obtrude
    And force some odd similitude;
What is it then which like the power divine
We only can by negatives define?

In a true piece of wit all things must be,
    Yet all things there agree;
As in the ark, joined without force or strife
All creatures dwelt, all creatures that had life;   60
    Or as the primitive forms of all,

If we compare great things with small,
Which without discord or confusion lie
In that strange mirror of the deity.

But love, that molds one man up out of two,
   Makes me forget and injure you;
I took you for myself sure when I thought
That you in anything were to be taught.
   Correct my error with thy pen,
   And if any ask me then   70
What thing right wit and height of genius is,
I'll only show your lines and say, 'Tis this.

On the death of Mr. Crashaw

Poet and saint! to thee alone are given
The two most sacred names of earth and heaven;
The hard and rarest union which can be,
Next that of Godhead with humanity.
Long did the Muses banished slaves abide,
And built vain pyramids to mortal pride;
Like Moses thou, though spells and charms withstand,
Hast brought them nobly home, back to their Holy Land.
   Ah, wretched we, poets of earth! but thou
Wert, living, the same poet which thou 'rt now   10
Whilst angels sing to thee their airs divine,
And joy in an applause so great as thine.
Equal society with them to hold,
Thou need'd not make new songs, but say the old,
And they, kind spirits, shall all rejoice to see
How little less than they exalted man may be.
Still the old heathen gods in numbers dwell,
The heav'nliest thing on earth still keeps up hell;
Nor have we yet quite purged the Christian land,
Still idols here, like calves at Bethel, stand,   20
And though Pan's death long since all oracles broke,
Yet still in rhyme the fiend Apollo spoke;
Nay, with the worst of heathen dotage, we,
Vain men, the monster woman deify,
Find stars and tie our fates there in a face,
And paradise in them by whom we lost it, place.
What different faults corrupt our muses thus?
Wanton as girls, as old wives fabulous!
   Thy spotless muse, like Mary, did contain

The boundless Godhead; she did well disdain 30
That her eternal verse employed should be
On a less subject than eternity,
And for a sacred mistress scorned to take
But her whom God himself scorned not his spouse to make.
It, in a kind, her miracle did do:
A fruitful mother was, and virgin too.

How well, blest swan, did fate contrive thy death,
And made thee render up thy tuneful breath
In thy great mistress' arms, thou most divine
And richest off'ring of Loretto's shrine! 40
Where like some holy sacrifice t' expire,
A fever burns thee, and love lights the fire.
Angels, they say, brought the famed chapel there,
And bore the sacred load in triumph through the air;
'Tis surer much they brought thee there, and they
And thou, their charge, went singing all the way.

Pardon, my mother church, if I consent
That angels led him when from thee he went,
For even in error sure no danger is
When joined with so much piety as his. 50
Ah, mighty God! (with shame I speak 't, and grief),
Ah, that our greatest faults were in belief!
And our weak reason were ev'n weaker yet,
Rather than thus, our wills too strong for it.
His faith perhaps in some nice tenents might
Be wrong; his life, I'm sure, was in the right.
And I myself a Catholic will be,
So far at least, great saint, to pray to thee.

Hail, bard triumphant! and some care bestow
On us, the poets militant below, 60
Opposed by our old en'my, adverse chance,
Attacked by envy and by ignorance,
Enchained by beauty, tortured by desires,
Exposed by tyrant love to savage beasts and fires.
Thou from low earth in nobler flames didst rise,
And like Elijah mount alive the skies.
Elisha-like (but with a wish much less,
More fit thy greatness and my littleness),
Lo, here I beg (I whom thou once didst prove
So humble to esteem, so good to love) 70
Not that thy spirit might on me doubled be,
I ask but half thy mighty spirit for me;
And when my muse soars with so strong a wing,
'Twill learn of things divine, and first of thee to sing.

The spring

Though you be absent here, I needs must say
The trees as beauteous are, and flowers as gay
   As ever they were wont to be;
    Nay, the birds' rural music too
   Is as melodious and free
    As if they sung to pleasure you;
I saw a rosebud ope this morn—I'll swear
The blushing morning opened not more fair.

How could it be so fair and you away?
How could the trees be beauteous, flowers so gay?   10
   Could they remember but last year
    How you did them, they you delight,
   The sprouting leaves which saw you here
    And called their fellows to the sight,
Would, looking round for the same sight in vain,
Creep back into their silent barks again.

Where'er you walked, trees were as reverend made
As when of old gods dwelt in every shade.
   Is 't possible they should not know
    What loss of honor they sustain,   20
   That thus they smile and flourish now,
    And still their former pride retain?
Dull creatures! 'tis not without cause that she
Who fled the god of wit was made a tree.

In ancient times sure they much wiser were,
When they rejoiced the Thracian verse to hear;
   In vain did nature bid them stay
    When Orpheus had his song begun;
   They called their wond'ring roots away,
    And bade them silent to him run.   30
How would those learned trees have followed you!
You would have drawn them and their poet too.

But who can blame them now? for since you're gone
They're here the only fair, and shine alone.
   You did their natural rights invade:
    Wherever you did walk or sit,
   The thickest boughs could make no shade,
    Although the sun had granted it;
The fairest flowers could please no more, near you,
Than painted flowers, set next to them, could do.   40

Whene'er then you come hither, that shall be
The time, which this to others is, to me.
    The little joys which here are now,
    The name of punishments do bear
    When by their sight they let us know
    How we deprived of greater are.
'Tis you the best of seasons with you bring;
This is for beasts, and that for men the spring.

[*Awake, awake, my lyre*]

    Awake, awake, my lyre,
And tell thy silent master's humble tale
    In sounds that may prevail,
    Sounds that gentle thoughts inspire,
        Though so exalted she
        And I so lowly be,
Tell her such different notes make all thy harmony.

    Hark how the strings awake,
And though the moving hand approach not near,
    Themselves with awful fear   10
    A kind of numerous trembling make.
        Now all thy forces try,
        Now all thy charms apply,
Revenge upon her ear the conquests of her eye.

    Weak lyre! thy virtue sure
Is useless here, since thou art only found
    To cure but not to wound,
    And she to wound but not to cure.
        Too weak, too, wilt thou prove
        My passion to remove;   20
Physic to other ills, thou'rt nourishment to love.

    Sleep, sleep again, my lyre,
For thou canst never tell my humble tale
    In sounds that will prevail,
    Nor gentle thoughts in her inspire;
        All thy vain mirth lay by,
        Bid thy strings silent lie;
Sleep, sleep again, my lyre, and let thy master die.

From Davideis, Book

JOHN CLEVELAND

The Introduction and Notes are at page 1031

FROM *Jonsonus Virbius*, 1638

An elegy on Ben Jonson

Who first reformed our stage with justest laws,
And was the first best judge in his own cause;
Who, when his actors trembled for applause,

Could with a noble confidence prefer
His own, by right, to a whole theater,
From principles which he knew could not err;

Who to his fable did his persons fit
With all the properties of art and wit,
And above all that could be acted, writ;

Who public follies did to covert drive,   10
Which he again could cunningly retrieve,
Leaving them no ground to rest on and thrive:

Here Jonson lies, whom had I named before,
In that one word alone I had paid more
Than can be now, when plenty makes me poor.

FROM *Poems*, 1653

Epitaph on the Earl of Strafford

Here lies wise and valiant dust
Huddled up 'twixt fit and just,
Strafford, who was hurried hence
'Twixt treason and convenience.
He spent his time here in a mist,
A Papist, yet a Calvinist;
His Prince's nearest joy and grief,
He had, yet wanted all relief;
The prop and ruin of the state;
The people's violent love and
hate;   10
One in extremes loved and ab-
horred.
Riddles lie here, or in a word—
Here lies blood; and let it lie
Speechless still and never cry.

FROM *Clievelandi Vindiciæ; or Clieveland's Genuine Poems*, 1677

Fuscara, or the bee errant

Nature's confectioner, the bee
(Whose suckets are moist al-
chemy,
The still of his refining mold
Minting the garden into gold),
Having rifled all the fields
Of what dainties Flora yields,
Ambitious now to take excise

Of a more fragrant paradise,
At my Fuscara's sleeve arrived,
Where all delicious sweets are
          hived.   10
The airy freebooter distrains
First on the violets of her veins,
Whose tincture, could it be more
          pure,
His ravenous kiss had made it
          bluer.
Here did he sit and essence quaff
Till her coy pulse had beat him
          off,
That pulse which he that feels
          may know
Whether the world's long-lived
          or no.
The next he preys on is her palm
(That alm'ner of transpiring
          balm),   20
So soft, 'tis air but once removed,
Tender as 'twere a jelly gloved.
Here, while his canting drone-
          pipe scanned
The mystic figures of her hand,
He tipples palmistry and dines
On all her fortune-telling lines.
He bathes in bliss and finds no
          odds
Betwixt this nectar and the gods';
He perches now upon her wrist,
A proper hawk for such a fist,   30
Making that flesh his bill of fare
Which hungry cannibals would
          spare;
Where lilies in a lovely brown
Inoculate carnation,
Her *argent* skin with *or* so
          streamed
As if the milky-way were
          creamed.
From hence he to the woodbine
          bends
That quivers at her fingers' ends,
That runs division on the tree
Like a thick-branching pedigree.

So 'tis not her the bee devours,   41
It is a pretty maze of flowers;
It is the rose that bleeds when he
Nibbles his nice phlebotomy.
About her finger he doth cling
I' th' fashion of a wedding ring,
And bids his comrades of the
          swarm
Crawl like a bracelet 'bout her
          arm.
Thus when the hovering publi-
          can
Had sucked the toll of all her
          span,   50
Tuning his draughts with drowsy
          hums
As Danes carouse by kettle-drums,
It was decreed, that posy gleaned,
The small familiar should be
          weaned.
At this the errant's courage quails,
Yet aided by his native sails
The bold Columbus still designs
To find her undiscovered mines.
To th' Indies of her arm he flies,
Fraught both with east and
          western prize;   60
Which when he had in vain es-
          sayed,
Armed like a dapper lancepresade
With Spanish pike, he broached a
          pore
And so both made and healed the
          sore;
For as in gummy trees there's
          found
A salve to issue at the wound,
Of this her breach the like was
          true,
Hence trickled out a balsam, too.
But oh, what wasp was 't that
          could prove
Ravaillac to my Queen of
          Love?   70
The King of Bees now jealo
          grown

Lest her beams should melt his
  throne,
And finding that his tribute slacks,
His burgesses and state of wax
Turned to a hospital, the combs
Built rank and file like beads-
  men's rooms,
And what they bleed but tart and
  sour
Matched with my Danaë's golden
  shower,
Live honey all,—the envious elf
Stung her, 'cause sweeter than
  himself.   80
Sweetness and she are so allied
The bee committed parricide.

*Upon Phillis walking in a
morning before sun-rising*

The sluggish morn as yet un-
  dressed,
My Phillis brake from out her
  east,
As if she'd made a match to run
With Venus, usher to the sun.
The trees, like yeomen of the
  guard,
Serving her more for pomp than
  ward,
Ranked on each side, with loyal
  duty
Weaved branches to enclose her
  beauty.
The plants, whose luxury was
  lopped,
Or age with crutches under-
  propped,   10
Whose wooden carcasses were
  grown
To be but coffins of their own,
Revive, and at her general dole
Each receives his ancient soul.
The wingëd choristers began
To chirp their matins, and the
  fan

Of whistling winds like organs
  played,
Until their voluntaries made
The weakened earth in odors rise
To be her morning sacrifice.   20
The flowers, called out of their
  beds,
Start and raise up their drowsy
  heads,
And he that for their color seeks
May see it vaulting to her cheeks,
Where roses mix—no civil war
Divides her York and Lancaster.
The marigold (whose courtier's
  face
Echoes the sun and doth unlace
Her at his rise, at his full stop
Packs and shuts up her gaudy
  shop)   30
Mistakes her cue and doth dis-
  play:
Thus Phillis antedates the day.
These miracles had cramped the
  sun,
Who, fearing that his kingdom's
  won,
Powders with light his frizzled
  locks
To see what saint his luster
  mocks.
The trembling leaves through
  which he played,
Dappling the walk with light and
  shade
Like lattice-windows, give the
  spy
Room but to peep with half an
  eye,   40
Lest her full orb his sight should
  dim
And bid us all good-night in him,
Till she should spend a gentle ray
To force us a new-fashioned day.
  But what religious palsy's this
Which makes the boughs divest
  their bliss,

And that they might her footsteps straw,
Drop their leaves with shivering awe?
Phillis perceived, and (lest her stay

Should wed October unto May, [50]
And, as her beauty caused a spring,
Devotion might an autumn bring)
Withdrew her beams, yet made no night,
But left the sun her curate-light.

Mark Antony

Whenas the nightingale chanted her vespers,
And the wild forester couched on the ground,
Venus invited me in th' evening whispers
Unto a fragrant field with roses crowned,
   Where she before had sent
   My wishes' complement;
   Unto my heart's content
   Played with me on the green.
     Never Mark Antony
     Dallied more wantonly   [10]
     With the fair Egyptian Queen.

First on her cherry cheeks I mine eyes feasted,
Thence fear of surfeiting made me retire;
Next on her warmer lips, which when I tasted,
My duller spirits made active as fire.
   Then we began to dart,
   Each at another's heart,
   Arrows that knew no smart,
   Sweet lips and smiles between.
     Never Mark, &c.   [20]

Wanting a glass to plait her amber tresses,
Which like a bracelet rich deckéd mine arm,
Gaudier than Juno wears whenas she graces
Jove with embraces more stately than warm;
   Then did she peep in mine
   Eyes' humor crystalline;
   I in her eyes was seen,
   As if we one had been.
     Never Mark, &c.

Mystical grammar of amorous glances;   [30]
Feeling of pulses, the physic of love;
Rhetorical courtings and musical dances;
Numb'ring of kisses arithmetic prove;
   Eyes like astronomy;

Straight-limbed geometry;
In her art's ingeny
Our wits were sharp and keen.
Never Mark Antony
Dallied more wantonly
With the fair Egyptian Queen.   40

SIR WILLIAM DAVENANT

The Introduction and Notes are at page 1032

FROM *Luminalia . . . a Mask at Court*, 1637

Night's first song

In wet and cloudy mists I slowly rise,
    As with mine own dull weight oppressed,
To close with sleep the jealous lover's eyes,
    And give forsaken virgins rest.

Th' advent'rous merchant and the mariner,
    Whom storms all day vex in the deep,
Begin to trust the winds when I appear,
    And lose their dangers in their sleep.

The studious that consume their brains and sight
    In search where doubtful knowledge lies,   10
Grow weary of their fruitless use of light,
    And with my shades do ease their eyes.

Th' ambitious toiling statesman that prepares
    Great mischiefs ere the day begins,
Not measures day by hours, but by his cares,
    And night must intermit his sins.

Then why, when my slow chariot used to climb,
    Did old mistaking sages weep,
As if my empire did usurp their time,
    And hours were lost when spent in sleep?   20

I come to ease their labors and prevent
    That weariness which would destroy;
The profit of their toils are still misspent
    Till rest enables to enjoy.

FROM *The Works of Sir William Davenant,* 1673

Song

The lark now leaves his wat'ry nest,
    And climbing shakes his dewy wings;
He takes this window for the east,
    And to implore your light he sings:
Awake, awake, the morn will never rise
Till she can dress her beauty at your eyes.

The merchant bows unto the seaman's star,
    The plowman from the sun his season takes;
But still the lover wonders what they are
    Who look for day before his mistress wakes.   10
Awake, awake, break through your veils of lawn!
Then draw your curtains, and begin the dawn.

To the Queen, entertained at night by the Countess of Anglesey

Fair as unshaded light, or as the day
In its first birth when all the year was May;
Sweet as the altar's smoke, or as the new
Unfolded bud, swelled by the early dew;
Smooth as the face of waters first appeared,
Ere tides began to strive or winds were heard;
Kind as the willing saints, and calmer far
Than in their sleeps forgiven hermits are;
You that are more than our discreeter fear
Dares praise with such full art, what make you here?   10
Here where the summer is so little seen,
That leaves, her cheapest wealth, scarce reach at green,
You come as if the silver planet were
Misled awhile from her much injured sphere,
And t' ease the travails of her beams to-night,
In this small lantern would contract her light.

The Countess of Anglesey led captive by the rebels at the disforesting of Pewsam

Oh, whither will you lead the fair
    And spicy daughter of the morn?
Those manacles of her soft hair,
    Princes, though free, would fain have worn.

What is her crime? what has she done?
  Did she, by breaking beauty, stay
Or from his course mislead the sun,
  So robbed your harvest of a day?

Or did her voice, divinely clear,
  Since lately in your forest bred,
Make all the trees dance after her,
  And so your woods disforested?

Run, run, pursue this Gothic rout,
  Who rudely love in bondage keep!
Sure all old lovers have the gout,
  The young are overwatched, and sleep.

Song

Endymion Porter and Olivia

Olivia.
Before we shall again behold
In his diurnal race, the world's great eye,
  We may as silent be and cold
As are the shades where buried lovers lie.

Endymion.
Olivia, 'tis no fault of love
To lose ourselves in death; but oh, I fear
  When life and knowledge is above
Restored to us, I shall not know thee there.

Olivia.
Call it not heaven, my love, where we
Ourselves shall see, and yet each other miss;
  So much of heaven I find in thee
As, thou unknown, all else privation is.

Endymion.
Why should we doubt before we go
To find the knowledge which shall ever last,
  That we may there each other know?
Can future knowledge quite destroy the past?

Olivia.
When at the bowers in the Elysian shade
I first arrive, I shall examine where

They dwell who love the highest virtue made,
For I am sure to find Endymion there.   20

Endymion.

From this vexed world when we shall both retire
Where all her lovers, and where all rejoice,
I need not seek thee in the heavenly choir,
For I shall know Olivia by her voice.

For the Lady Olivia Porter. A present upon a New Year's Day

Go! hunt the whiter ermine, and present
His wealthy skin as this day's tribute sent
To my Endymion's love; though she be far
More gently smooth, more soft, than ermines are!
Go! climb that rock, and when thou there hast found
A star, contracted in a diamond,
Give it Endymion's love, whose glorious eyes
Darken the starry jewels of the skies!
Go! dive into the Southern Sea, and when
Th'ast found, to trouble the nice sight of men,   10
A swelling pearl, and such whose single worth
Boast all the wonders which the seas bring forth,
Give it Endymion's love, whose ev'ry tear
Would more enrich the skillful jeweler.
How I command! how slowly they obey!
The churlish Tartar will not hunt to-day;
Nor will that lazy sallow Indian strive
To climb the rock, nor that dull Negro dive.
Thus poets, like to kings by trust deceived,
Give oftener what is heard of than received.   20

The philosopher and the lover
To a mistress dying

Lover.

Your beauty, ripe, and calm, and fresh
    As eastern summers are,
Must now, forsaking time and flesh,
    Add light to some small star.

Philosopher.

Whilst she yet lives, were stars decayed,
    Their light by hers relief might find;
But death will lead her to a shade
    Where love is cold, and beauty blind.

Lover.

Lovers, whose priests all poets are,
    Think ev'ry mistress when she dies 10
Is changed at least into a star;
    And who dares doubt the poets wise?

Philosopher.

But ask not bodies doomed to die
    To what abode they go;
Since knowledge is but sorrow's spy,
    It is not safe to know.

Song

O thou that sleep'st like pig in straw,
    Thou lady dear, arise;
Open, to keep the sun in awe,
    Thy pretty pinking eyes.
And having stretched each leg and arm,
    Put on your clean white smock,
And then I pray, to keep you warm,
    A petticoat on dock.
Arise, arise! why should you sleep,
    When you have slept enough? 10
Long since French boys cried, Chimney-sweep,
    And damsels, Kitchen-stuff.
The shops were opened long before,
    And youngest prentice goes
To lay at 's mistress' chamber door
    His master's shining shoes.
Arise, arise! your breakfast stays,
    Good water-gruel warm,
Or sugar-sops, which Galen says
    With mace will do no harm. 20
Arise, arise! when you are up
    You'll find more to your cost,
For morning's draught in caudle cup,
    Good nutbrown ale and toast.

From *News from Plymouth*

SIR JOHN DENHAM

The Introduction and Notes are at page 1033

FROM *Cooper's Hill . . . a corrected impression,* 1655

Cooper's Hill

My eye descending from the hill, surveys
Where Thames amongst the wanton valleys strays.

Thames, the most loved of all the ocean's sons
By his old sire, to his embraces runs,
Hasting to pay his tribute to the sea,
Like mortal life to meet eternity.
Though with those streams he no resemblance hold,
Whose foam is amber, and their gravel gold,
His genuine and less guilty wealth t' explore,
Search not his bottom, but survey his shore,
O'er which he kindly spreads his spacious wing,
And hatches plenty for th' ensuing spring;
Nor then destroys it with too fond a stay,
Like mothers which their infants overlay;
Nor with a sudden and impetuous wave,
Like profuse kings, resumes the wealth he gave.
No unexpected inundations spoil
The mower's hopes, nor mock the plowman's toil;
But godlike his unwearied bounty flows,
First loves to do, then loves the good he does.
Nor are his blessings to the banks confined,
But free and common as the sea or wind:
When he, to boast or to disperse his stores,
Full of the tributes of his grateful shores,
Visits the world, and in his flying towers
Brings home to us, and makes both Indies ours;
Finds wealth where 'tis, bestows it where it wants,
Cities in deserts, woods in cities plants;
So that to us no thing, no place is strange,
While his fair bosom is the world's exchange.
Oh, could I flow like thee, and make thy stream
My great example, as it is my theme!
Though deep, yet clear; though gentle, yet not dull;
Strong without rage, without o'erflowing full.
Here nature, whether more intent to please
Us or herself with strange varieties,
(For things of wonder give no less delight
To the wise maker's, than beholder's sight;
Though these delights from several causes move,
For so our children, thus our friends, we love)
Wisely she knew the harmony of things,
As well as that of sounds, from discord springs.
Such was the discord which did first disperse
Form, order, beauty, through the universe;
While dryness moisture, coldness heat, resists,
All that we have, and that we are, subsists;
While the steep horrid roughness of the wood
Strives with the gentle calmness of the flood;

10

20

30

40

Such huge extremes when nature doth unite,
Wonder from thence results, from thence delight. 50
The stream is so transparent, pure, and clear,
That had the self-enamoured youth gazed here,
So fatally deceived he had not been,
While he the bottom, not his face, had seen.
But his proud head the airy mountain hides
Among the clouds; his shoulders and his sides
A shady mantle clothes; his curlëd brows
Frown on the gentle stream, which calmly flows,
While winds and storms his lofty forehead beat,
The common fate of all that's high or great. 60
Low at his foot a spacious plain is placed,
Between the mountain and the stream embraced,
Which shade and shelter from the hill derives,
While the kind river wealth and beauty gives,
And in the mixture of all these appears
Variety, which all the rest endears.
This scene had some bold Greek or British bard
Beheld of old, what stories had we heard
Of fairies, satyrs, and the nymphs, their dames,
Their feasts, their revels, and their amorous flames? 70
'Tis still the same, although their airy shape
All but a quick poetic sight escape.
There Faunus and Sylvanus keep their courts,
And thither all the hornëd host resorts
To graze the ranker mead; that noble herd
On whose sublime and shady fronts is reared
Nature's great masterpiece, to show how soon
Great things are made, but sooner are undone.

. . . .

FROM *Poems and Translations,*
1668

On Mr. Abraham Cowley, his death and burial amongst the ancient poets

Old Chaucer, like the morning star,
To us discovers day from far;
His light those mists and clouds dissolved,
Which our dark nation long involved;
But he descending to the shades,
Darkness again the age invades.
Next like Aurora Spenser rose,
Whose purple blush the day foreshows;
The other three with his own fires
Phœbus, the poets' god, inspires: 10
By Shakespeare's, Jonson's, Fletcher's lines
Our stage's luster Rome's outshines.
These poets near our princes sleep,

And in one grave their mansion keep.
They lived to see so many days,
Till time had blasted all their bays;
But cursëd be the fatal hour
That plucked the fairest, sweetest flower
That in the Muses' garden grew,
And amongst withered laurels threw!   20
Time, which made them their fame outlive,
To Cowley scarce did ripeness give.
Old mother wit and nature gave
Shakespeare and Fletcher all they have;
In Spenser and in Jonson, art
Of slower nature got the start;
But both in him so equal are,
None knows which bears the happiest share;
To him no author was unknown,
Yet what he wrote was all his own.   30
He melted not the ancient gold,
Nor with Ben Jonson did make bold
To plunder all the Roman stores
Of poets and of orators;
Horace his wit and Virgil's state
He did not steal, but emulate!
And when he would like them appear,
Their garb, but not their clothes, did wear.
He not from Rome alone, but Greece,
Like Jason brought the golden fleece;   40
To him that language, though to none
Of th' others, as his own was known.
On a stiff gale, as Flaccus sings,
The Theban swan extends his wings,
When through th' ethereal clouds he flies;
To the same pitch our swan doth rise—
Old Pindar's flights by him are reached,
When on that gale his wings are stretched.
His fancy and his judgment such,
Each to the other seemed too much,   50
His severe judgment, giving law,
His modest fancy kept in awe,
As rigid husbands jealous are
When they believe their wives too fair.
His English stream so pure did flow
As all that saw and tasted know;
But for his Latin vein so clear,
Strong, full, and high, it doth appear
That were immortal Virgil here,
Him, for his judge, he would not fear;   60
Of that great portraiture, so true
A copy pencil never drew.
My muse her song had ended here,
But both their genii straight appear;
Joy and amazement her did strike,
Two twins she never saw so like.
'Twas taught by wise Pythagoras,
One soul might through more bodies pass;   68
Seeing such transmigration here,
She thought it not a fable there—
Such a resemblance of all parts,
Life, death, age, fortune, nature, arts;
Then lights her torch at theirs, to tell

And show the world this parallel.
Fixed and contemplative their
    looks
Still turning over nature's books;
Their works chaste, moral, and
    divine,
Where profit and delight com-
    bine;
They, gilding dirt, in noble verse
Rustic philosophy rehearse.   80
When heroes, gods, or god-like
    kings
They praise, on their exalted
    wings
To the celestial orbs they climb,
And with the harmonious spheres
    keep time.
Nor did their actions fall behind
Their words, but with like candor
    shined;
Each drew fair characters, yet
    none
Of these they feigned, excels their
    own.
Both by two generous princes
    loved,
Who knew and judged what they
    approved;   90
Yet having each the same desire,
Both from the busy ·throng re-
    tire.
Their bodies to their minds re-
    signed,
Cared not to propagate their kind;

Yet though both fell before their
    hour,
Time on their offspring hath no
    power;
Nor fire nor fate their bays shall
    blast,
Nor death's dark veil their day
    o'ercast.

FROM *The Sophy*, 1642

[*Somnus, the humble god*]

Somnus, the humble god that
    dwells
In cottages and smoky cells,
Hates gilded roofs and beds of
    down,
And though he fears no prince's
    frown,
Flies from the circle of a crown.

Come, I say, thou powerful god,
And thy leaden charming rod,
Dipped in the Lethean lake,
O'er his wakeful temples shake,
Lest he should sleep and never
    wake.   10

Nature, alas, why art thou so
Obligèd to thy greatest foe?
Sleep, that is thy best repast,
Yet of death it bears a taste,
And both are the same thing at
    last.

EDMUND WALLER

The Introduction and Notes are at page 1034

FROM *Poems*, 1664

At Penshurst

Had Sacharissa lived when mortals made
Choice of their deities, this sacred shade
Had held an altar to her power, that gave

The peace and glory which these alleys have;
Embroidered so with flowers where she stood,
That it became a garden of a wood.
Her presence has such more than human grace
That it can civilize the rudest place;
And beauty too, and order, can impart
Where nature ne'er intended it, nor art.   10
The plants acknowledge this, and her admire
No less than those of old did Orpheus' lyre;
If she sit down, with tops all towards her bowed,
They round about her into arbors crowd;
Or if she walk, in even ranks they stand
Like some well-marshalled and obsequious band.
Amphion so made stones and timber leap
Into fair figures from a confused heap;
And in the symmetry of her parts is found
A power like that of harmony in sound.   20
    Ye lofty beeches, tell this matchless dame
That if together ye fed all one flame
It could not equalize the hundredth part
Of what her eyes have kindled in my heart!
Go, boy, and carve this passion on the bark
Of yonder tree, which stands the sacred mark
Of noble Sidney's birth; when such benign,
Such more than mortal making stars did shine,
That there they cannot but forever prove
The monument and pledge of humble love;   30
His humble love whose hope shall ne'er rise higher
Than for a pardon that he dares admire.

The Battle of the Summer Islands

Canto I

What fruits they have, and how heaven smiles
Upon those late-discovered isles.

Aid me, Bellona, while the dreadful fight
Betwixt a nation and two whales I write.
Seas stained with gore I sing, adventurous toil,
And how these monsters did disarm an isle.
    Bermudas, walled with rocks, who does not know?
That happy island where huge lemons grow,
And orange trees, which golden fruit do bear,
Th' Hesperian garden boasts of none so fair;
Where shining pearl, coral, and many a pound,
On the rich shore, of ambergris is found.   10

The lofty cedar, which to heaven aspires,
The prince of trees, is fuel for their fires;
The smoke by which their loaded spits do turn,
For incense might on sacred altars burn;
Their private roofs on od'rous timber borne,
Such as might palaces for kings adorn.
The sweet palmettos a new Bacchus yield,
With leaves as ample as the broadest shield,
Under the shadow of whose friendly boughs
They sit, carousing where their liquor grows.   20
Figs there unplanted through the fields do grow,
Such as fierce Cato did the Romans show,
With the rare fruit inviting them to spoil
Carthage, the mistress of so rich a soil.
The naked rocks are not unfruitful there,
But at some constant seasons, every year,
Their barren tops with luscious food abound,
And with the eggs of various fowls are crowned.
Tobacco is the worst of things which they
To English landlords, as their tribute, pay;   30
Such is the mold that the blest tenant feeds
On precious fruits, and pays his rent in weeds.
With candied plantains and the juicy pine,
On choicest melons and sweet grapes they dine,
And with potatoes fat their wanton swine.
Nature these cates with such a lavish hand
Pours out among them, that our coarser land
Tastes of that bounty, and does cloth return,
Which not for warmth but ornament is worn;
For the kind spring, which but salutes us here,   40
Inhabits there, and courts them all the year.
Ripe fruits and blossoms on the same trees live;
At once they promise what at once they give.
So sweet the air, so moderate the clime,
None sickly lives, or dies before his time.
Heaven sure has kept this spot of earth uncursed,
To show how all things were created first.
The tardy plants in our cold orchards placed
Reserve their fruit for the next age's taste;
There a small grain in some few months will be   50
A firm, a lofty, and a spacious tree.
The palma-christi, and the fair papaw,
Now but a seed, preventing nature's law,
In half a circle of the hasty year
Project a shade, and lovely fruits do wear.
And as their trees, in our dull region set,

But faintly grow and no perfection get,
So in this northern tract our hoarser throats
Utter unripe and ill-constrainèd notes,
Where the supporter of the poets' style,   60
Phœbus, on them eternally does smile.
Oh! how I long my careless limbs to lay
Under the plantain's shade, and all the day
With am'rous airs my fancy entertain,
Invoke the Muses, and improve my vein!
No passion there in my free breast should move,
None but the sweet and best of passions, love.
There while I sing, if gentle love be by,
That tunes my lute and winds the strings so high,
With the sweet sound of Sacharissa's name   70
I'll make the list'ning savages grow tame.—
　　But while I do these pleasing dreams indite,
　　I am diverted from the promised fight.

On a girdle

That which her slender waist con-
　　fined
Shall now my joyful temples
　　bind;
No monarch but would give his
　　crown
His arms might do what this has
　　done.

It was my heaven's extremest
　　sphere,
The pale which held that lovely
　　deer.
My joy, my grief, my hope, my
　　love,
Did all within this circle move!

A narrow compass, and yet there
Dwelt all that's good and all
　　that's fair;   10
Give me but what this riband
　　bound,
Take all the rest the sun goes
　　round.

Song

Stay, Phœbus, stay!
The world to which you fly so
　　fast,
Conveying day
From us to them, can pay your
　　haste
With no such object, nor salute
　　your rise
With no such wonder, as De
　　Mornay's eyes.

Well does this prove
The error of those antique books,
Which made you move
About the world; her charming
　　looks   10
Would fix your beams, and make
　　it ever day,
Did not the rolling earth snatch
　　her away.

Song

Go, lovely rose!
Tell her that wastes her time and
　　me

That now she knows,
When I resemble her to thee,
How sweet and fair she seems to
be.

Tell her that's young
And shuns to have her graces
spied,
That hadst thou sprung
In deserts where no men abide,
Thou must have uncommended
died.   10

Small is the worth
Of beauty from the light retired;
Bid her come forth,
Suffer herself to be desired,
And not blush so to be admired.

Then die, that she
The common fate of all things
rare
May read in thee;
How small a part of time they
share
That are so wondrous sweet and
fair!   20

FROM *Poems*, 1668

Of English verse

Poets may boast, as safely vain,
Their work shall with the world
remain;
Both, bound together, live or die,
The verses and the prophecy.

But who can hope his lines should
long
Last in a daily changing tongue?
While they are new, envy prevails;
And as that dies, our language
fails.

When architects have done their
part,
The matter may betray their
art;   10
Time, if we use ill-chosen stone,
Soon brings a well-built palace
down.

Poets that lasting marble seek
Must carve in Latin or in Greek;
We write in sand, our language
grows
And like the tide our work o'er-
flows.

Chaucer his sense can only boast,
The glory of his numbers lost!
Years have defaced his matchless
strain,
And yet he did not sing in vain.   20

The beauties which adorned that
age,
The shining subjects of his rage,
Hoping they should immortal
prove,
Rewarded with success his love.

This was the generous poet's
scope,
And all an English pen can hope,
To make the fair approve his
flame,
That can so far extend their fame.

Verse, thus designed, has no ill
fate
If it arrive but at the date   30
Of fading beauty; if it prove
But as long-lived as present love.

FROM *Poems*, 1686

Of the last verses in the book

When we for age could neither
read nor write,

The subject made us able to indite;
The soul, with nobler resolutions decked,
The body stooping, does herself erect.
No mortal parts are requisite to raise
Her that, unbodied, can her Maker praise.
The seas are quiet when the winds give o'er;
So, calm are we when passions are no more.
For then we know how vain it was to boast
Of fleeting things, so certain to be lost. 10

Clouds of affection from our younger eyes
Conceal that emptiness which age descries.
The soul's dark cottage, battered and decayed,
Lets in new light through chinks that time has made;
Stronger by weakness, wiser, men become
As they draw near to their eternal home;
Leaving the old, both worlds at once they view,
That stand upon the threshold of the new.

ANDREW MARVELL

The Introduction and Notes are at page 1035

From *Miscellaneous Poems*, 1681

The garden

How vainly men themselves amaze
To win the palm, the oak, or bays,
And their uncessant labors see
Crowned from some single herb or tree,
Whose short and narrow vergèd shade
Does prudently their toils upbraid;
While all flowers and all trees do close
To weave the garlands of repose.

Fair quiet, have I found thee here,
And innocence, thy sister dear! 10
Mistaken long, I sought you then
In busy companies of men;
Your sacred plants, if here below,
Only among the plants will grow.
Society is all but rude,
To this delicious solitude.

No white nor red was ever seen
So am'rous as this lovely green.
Fond lovers, cruel as their flame,
Cut in these trees their mistress' name; 20
Little, alas, they know or heed
How far these beauties hers exceed!
Fair trees! wheres'e'er your barks I wound,
No name shall but your own be found.

When we have run our passion's heat,
Love hither makes his best retreat.
The gods that mortal beauty chase,
Still in a tree did end their race:
Apollo hunted Daphne so,
Only that she might laurel grow; 30

And Pan did after Syrinx speed,
Not as a nymph, but for a reed.

What wond'rous life in this I lead!
Ripe apples drop about my head;
The luscious clusters of the vine
Upon my mouth do crush their
    wine;
The nectarine and curious peach
Into my hands themselves do
    reach;
Stumbling on melons as I pass,
Ensnared with flowers, I fall on
    grass.   40

Meanwhile the mind from pleasure
    less
Withdraws into its happiness;
The mind, that ocean where each
    kind
Does straight its own resemblance
    find,
Yet it creates, transcending these,
Far other worlds and other seas,
Annihilating all that's made
To a green thought in a green
    shade.

Here at the fountain's sliding foot,
Or at some fruit tree's mossy
    root,   50
Casting the body's vest aside,

My soul into the boughs does glide;
There like a bird it sits and sings,
Then whets, then combs its silver
    wings;
And till prepared for longer flight,
Waves in its plumes the various
    light.

Such was that happy garden-state,
While man there walked without
    a mate;
After a place so pure and sweet,
What other help could yet be
    meet!   60
But 'twas beyond a mortal's share
To wander solitary there;
Two paradises 'twere, in one,
To live in paradise alone.

How well the skillful gard'ner
    drew
Of flowers and herbs this dial new,
Where, from above, the milder sun
Does through a fragrant zodiac
    run;
And as it works, th' industrious bee
Computes its time as well as we. 70
How could such sweet and whole-
    some hours
Be reckoned but with herbs and
    flowers?

On a drop of dew

See how the orient dew,
  Shed from the bosom of the morn
    Into the blowing roses,
Yet careless of its mansion new,
  For the clear region where 'twas born
    Round in itself incloses,
And in its little globe's extent
Frames as it can its native element;
How it the purple flower does slight,
  Scarce touching where it lies,   10

But gazing back upon the skies,
  Shines with a mournful light
    Like its own tear,
Because so long divided from the sphere.
  Restless it rolls and unsecure,
    Trembling lest it grow impure,
  Till the warm sun pity its pain,
And to the skies exhale it back again.
  So the soul, that drop, that ray
Of the clear fountain of eternal day,   20
Could it within the human flower be seen,
  Rememb'ring still its former height,
  Shuns the sweet leaves and blossoms green;
    And recollecting its own light,
Does, in its pure and circling thoughts, express
The greater heaven in an heaven less.
    In how coy a figure wound,
    Every way it turns away;
    So the world excluding round,
    Yet receiving in the day;   30
    Dark beneath but bright above,
    Here disdaining, there in love;
    How loose and easy hence to go,
    How girt and ready to ascend;
    Moving but on a point below,
    It all about does upwards bend.
Such did the manna's sacred dew distil,
White and entire, though congealed and chill;
Congealed on earth, but does, dissolving, run
Into the glories of th' almighty sun.   40

The mower against gardens

Luxurious man, to bring his vice in use,
  Did after him the world seduce,
And from the fields the flowers and plants allure,
  Where nature was most plain and pure.
He first enclosed within the garden's square
  A dead and standing pool of air;
And a more luscious earth for them did knead,
  Which stupefied them while it fed.
The pink grew then as double as his mind;
  The nutriment did change the kind.   10
With strange perfumes he did the roses taint;
  And flowers themselves were taught to paint.
The tulip, white, did for complexion seek,

And learned to interline its cheek;
Its onion root they then so high did hold
 That one was for a meadow sold.
Another world was searched, through oceans new,
 To find the marvel of Peru.
And yet these rarities might be allowed
 To man, that sov'reign thing and proud, 20
Had he not dealt between the bark and tree,
 Forbidden mixtures there to see.
No plant now knew the stock from which it came;
 He grafts upon the wild the tame,
That the uncertain and adult'rate fruit
 Might put the palate in dispute.
His green seraglio has its eunuchs too,
 Lest any tyrant him outdo;
And in the cherry he does nature vex,
 To procreate without a sex. 30
'Tis all enforced, the fountain and the grot,
 While the sweet fields do lie forgot,
Where willing nature does to all dispense
 A wild and fragrant innocence;
And fauns and fairies do the meadows till
 More by their presence than their skill.
Their statues, polished by some ancient hand,
 May to adorn the gardens stand;
But howsoe'er the figures do excel,
 The gods themselves with us do dwell. 40

The mower to the glow-worms

Ye living lamps, by whose dear light
The nightingale does sit so late,
And studying all the summer night,
Her matchless songs does meditate;

Ye county comets that portend
No war nor prince's funeral,
Shining unto no higher end
Than to presage the grass's fall;

Ye glow-worms, whose officious flame
To wand'ring mowers shows the way, 10
That in the night have lost their aim,
And after foolish fires do stray;

Your courteous lights in vain you waste,
Since Juliana here is come,
For she my mind hath so displaced
That I shall never find my home.

The mower's song

My mind was once the true survey
Of all these meadows fresh and gay,
And in the greenness of the grass
Did see its hopes as in a glass;
When Juliana came, and she,
What I do to the grass, does to my thoughts and me.

But these, while I with sorrow pine,
Grew more luxuriant still and fine,
That not one blade of grass you spied
But had a flower on either side;   10
When Juliana came, and she,
What I do to the grass, does to my thoughts and me.

Unthankful meadows, could you so
A fellowship so true forgo?
And in your gaudy May-games meet
While I lay trodden under feet?
When Juliana came, and she,
What I do to the grass, does to my thoughts and me.

But what you in compassion ought,
Shall now by my revenge be wrought;   20
And flowers and grass and I and all
Will in one common ruin fall.
For Juliana comes, and she,
What I do to the grass, does to my thoughts and me.

And thus, ye meadows, which have been
Companions of my thoughts more green,
Shall now the heraldry become
With which I shall adorn my tomb;
For Juliana comes, and she,
What I do to the grass, does to my thoughts and me.   30

Clorinda and Damon

C. Damon, come drive thy flocks this way.
D. No, 'tis too late, they went astray.

C. I have a grassy scutcheon spied,
    Where Flora blazons all her pride;
    The grass I aim to feast thy sheep,
    The flowers I for thy temples keep.
D. Grass withers and the flowers too fade.
C. Seize the short joys then, ere they vade.
    See'st thou that unfrequented cave?
D. That den? *C.* Love's shrine. *D.* But virtue's grave.   10
C. In whose cool bosom we may lie
    Safe from the sun. *D.* Not heaven's eye.
C. Near this a fountain's liquid bell
    Tinkles within the concave shell.
D. Might a soul bathe there and be clean,
    Or slake its drought? *C.* What is't you mean?
D. These once had been enticing things,
    Clorinda, pastures, caves, and springs.
C. And what late change? *D.* The other day
    Pan met me. *C.* What did great Pan say?   20
D. Words that transcend poor shepherd's skill,
    But he e'er since my songs does fill,
    And his name swells my slender oat.
C. Sweet must Pan sound in Damon's note.
D. Clorinda's voice might make it sweet.
C. Who would not in Pan's praises meet?

Chorus.

    Of Pan the flow'ry pastures sing,
    Caves echo, and the fountains ring;
    Sing then while he doth us inspire,
    For all the world is our Pan's choir.   30

The coronet

When for the thorns with which I long, too long,
    With many a piercing wound
    My Savior's head have crowned,
I seek with garlands to redress that wrong;
    Through every garden, every mead,
I gather flowers (my fruits are only flowers),
    Dismantling all the fragrant towers
That once adorned my shepherdess's head.
And now when I have summed up all my store,
    Thinking, so I myself deceive,   10
    So rich a chaplet thence to weave
As never yet the King of Glory wore,
    Alas, I find the serpent old
    That twining in his speckled breast

About the flowers disguised does fold
With wreaths of fame and interest.
Ah, foolish man, that wouldst debase with them
And mortal glory, heaven's diadem!
But thou who only couldst the serpent tame,
Either his slipp'ry knots at once untie   20
And disentangle all his winding snare,
Or shatter too with him my curious frame
And let these wither so that he may die,
Though set with skill and chosen out with care,
That they, while thou on both their spoils dost tread,
May crown thy feet, that could not crown thy head.

A dialogue between the resolved soul and created pleasure

Courage, my soul! now learn to wield
The weight of thine immortal shield.
Close on thy head thy helmet bright.
Balance thy sword against the fight.
See where an army, strong as fair,
With silken banners spreads the air.
Now, if thou be'st that thing divine,
In this day's combat let it shine,
And show that nature wants an art
To conquer one resolvèd heart.   10

Pleasure.
Welcome the creation's guest,
Lord of earth and heaven's heir.
Lay aside that warlike crest,
And of nature's banquet share,
Where the souls of fruits and flowers
Stand prepared to heighten yours.

Soul.
I sup above and cannot stay
To bait so long upon the way.

Pleasure.
On these downy pillows lie,   19
Whose soft plumes will thither fly;
On these roses strowed so plain
Lest one leaf thy side should strain.

Soul.
My gentler rest is on a thought,
Conscious of doing what I ought.

Pleasure.
If thou be'st with perfumes pleased,
Such as oft the gods appeased,
Thou in fragrant clouds shalt show
Like another god below.

Soul.
A soul that knows not to presume
Is heaven's and its own perfume.   30

Pleasure.
Everything does seem to vie
Which should first attract thine eye;
But since none deserves that grace,
In this crystal view thy face.

Soul.
When the creator's skill is prized,
The rest is all but earth disguised.

Pleasure.
Hark, how music then prepares
For thy stay these charming airs,
Which the posting winds recall,
And suspend the river's fall.   40

Soul.

Had I but any time to lose,
On this I would it all dispose.
Cease, tempter, none can chain a
    mind
Whom this sweet cordage cannot
    bind.

Chorus.

Earth cannot show so brave a sight
As when a single soul does fence
The batteries of alluring sense,
And heaven views it with delight.
Then persevere, for still new
    charges sound;
And if thou overcom'st, thou shalt
    be crowned.   50

Pleasure.

All this fair, and cost, and sweet,
  Which scatteringly doth shine,
Shall within one beauty meet,
  And she be only thine.

Soul.

If things of sight such heavens be,
What heavens are those we cannot
    see?

Pleasure.

Wheresoe'er thy foot shall go
  The minted gold shall lie;
Till thou purchase all below, 59
  And want new worlds to buy.

Soul.

Were 't not a price who'd value
    gold?
And that's worth nought that can
    be sold.

Pleasure.

Wilt thou all the glory have
  That war or peace commend?
Half the world shall be thy slave,
  The other half thy friend.

Soul.

What friends, if to myself untrue?
What slaves, unless I captive you?

Pleasure.

Thou shalt know each hidden
    cause,
  And see the future time;   70
Try what depth the center draws,
  And then to heaven climb.

Soul.

None thither mounts by the degree
Of knowledge, but humility.

Chorus.

Triumph, triumph, victorious soul!
The world has not one pleasure
    more.
The rest does lie beyond the pole,
And is thine everlasting store.

A dialogue between the soul and body

Soul.

Oh, who shall from this dungeon
    raise
A soul enslaved so many ways?
With bolts of bones; that fettered
    stands
In feet, and manacled in hands;

Here blinded with an eye, and
    there
Deaf with the drumming of an
    ear;
A soul hung up, as 'twere, in chains
Of nerves and arteries and veins;
Tortured, besides each other part,
In a vain head and double heart. 10

Body.

Oh, who shall me deliver whole
From bonds of this tyrannic soul?
Which, stretched upright, impales
    me so
That mine own precipice I go;
And warms and moves this need-
    less frame,
A fever could but do the same.
And, wanting where its spite to try,
Has made me live to let me die.
A body that could never rest,
Since this ill spirit it possessed.   20

Soul.

What magic could me thus confine
Within another's grief to pine?
Where whatsoever it complain,
I feel, that cannot feel, the pain.
And all my care itself employs,
That to preserve which me de-
    stroys.
Constrained not only to endure
Diseases, but, what's worse, the
    cure;

And ready oft the port to gain,
Am shipwrecked into health
    again.   30

Body.

But physic yet could never reach
The maladies thou me dost teach:
Whom first the cramp of hope does
    tear,
And then the palsy shakes of
    fear;
The pestilence of love does heat,
Or hatred's hidden ulcer eat.
Joy's cheerful madness does per-
    plex,
Or sorrow's other madness vex;
Which knowledge forces me to
    know,
And memory will not forgo.   40
What but a soul could have the
    wit
To build me up for sin so fit?
So architects do square and hew
Green trees that in the forest
    grew.

Bermudas

Where the remote Bermudas ride
In th' ocean's bosom unespied,
From a small boat that rowed along,
The list'ning winds received this song:
    What should we do but sing his praise
That led us through the wat'ry maze
Unto an isle so long unknown,
And yet far kinder than our own?
Where he the huge sea-monsters wracks,
That lift the deep upon their backs,   10
He lands us on a grassy stage,
Safe from the storms and prelates' rage.
He gave us this eternal spring
Which here enamels everything,
And sends the fowls to us in care,
On daily visits through the air.
He hangs in shades the orange bright,
Like golden lamps in a green night;
And does in the pomegranates close

Jewels more rich than Ormus shows.   20
He makes the figs our mouths to meet
And throws the melons at our feet,
But apples plants of such a price,
No tree could ever bear them twice.
With cedars, chosen by his hand,
From Lebanon, he stores the land,
And makes the hollow seas that roar
Proclaim the ambergris on shore.
He cast, of which we rather boast,
The Gospel's pearl upon our coast,   30
And in these rocks for us did frame
A temple, where to sound his name.
Oh, let our voice his praise exalt,
Till it arrive at heaven's vault;
Which thence, perhaps, rebounding, may
Echo beyond the Mexic Bay.
    Thus sung they in the English boat
An holy and a cheerful note,
And all the way, to guide their chime,
With falling oars they kept the time.   40

The nymph complaining for the death of her fawn

The wanton troopers riding by
Have shot my fawn, and it will die.
Ungentle men! they cannot thrive
To kill thee. Thou ne'er didst
    alive
Them any harm, alas, nor could
Thy death yet do them any good.
I'm sure I never wished them ill,
Nor do I for all this, nor will;
But if my simple prayers may yet
Prevail with heaven to forget   10
Thy murder, I will join my tears
Rather than fail. But oh, my fears!
It cannot die so. Heaven's King
Keeps register of everything,
And nothing may we use in vain.
Ev'n beasts must be with justice
    slain,
Else men are made their deodands;
Though they should wash their
    guilty hands
In this warm life-blood, which
    doth part

From thine, and wound me to the
    heart,   20
Yet could they not be clean, their
    stain
Is dyed in such a purple grain.
There is not such another in
The world to offer for their sin.
    Unconstant Sylvio, when yet
I had not found him counterfeit,
One morning, I remember well,
Tied in this silver chain and
    bell,
Gave it to me; nay, and I know
What he said then, I'm sure I
    do.   30
Said he, Look how your huntsman
    here
Hath taught a fawn to hunt his
    dear.
But Sylvio soon had me beguiled.
This waxëd tame, while he grew
    wild;
And quite regardless of my smart,

Left me his fawn, but took his
 heart.
 Thenceforth I set myself to play
My solitary time away,
With this, and very well content
Could so mine idle life have
 spent; 40
For it was full of sport, and light
Of foot and heart, and did invite
Me to its game; it seemed to bless
Itself in me. How could I less
Than love it? Oh, I cannot be
Unkind t' a beast that loveth me.

Had it lived long, I do not know
Whether it too might have done so
As Sylvio did; his gifts might be
Perhaps as false or more than he.
But I am sure, for aught that I 51
Could in so short a time espy,
Thy love was far more better then
The love of false and cruel men.
 With sweetest milk and sugar
 first
I it at mine own fingers nursed;
And as it grew, so every day
It waxed more white and sweet
 than they.
It had so sweet a breath! And oft
I blushed to see its foot more soft 60
And white, shall I say than my
 hand?
Nay, any lady's of the land.
 It is a wond'rous thing how fleet
'Twas on those little silver feet;
With what a pretty skipping grace
It oft would challenge me the race;
And when 't had left me far away,
'Twould stay, and run again, and
 stay,
For it was nimbler much than
 hinds,
And trod as on the foür winds. 70
 I have a garden of my own,
But so with roses overgrown
And lilies, that you would it guess
To be a little wilderness;

And all the spring time of the year
It only lovëd to be there.
Among the beds of lilies I
Have sought it oft, where it should
 lie; 78
Yet could not, till itself would rise,
Find it, although before mine eyes;
For in the flaxen lilies' shade,
It like a bank of lilies laid.
Upon the roses it would feed
Until its lips ev'n seemed to bleed,
And then to me 'twould boldly trip
And print those roses on my lip.
But all its chief delight was still
On roses thus itself to fill,
And its pure virgin limbs to fold
In whitest sheets of lilies cold. 90
Had it lived long it would have
 been
Lilies without, roses within.
 O help, O help! I see it faint
And die as calmly as a saint.
See how it weeps! The tears do
 come,
Sad, slowly dropping like a gum.
So weeps the wounded balsam, so
The holy frankincense doth flow;
The brotherless Heliades
Melt in such amber tears as these.
 I in a golden vial will 101
Keep these two crystal tears, and
 fill
It till it do o'erflow with mine,
Then place it in Diana's shrine.
 Now my sweet fawn is vanished
 to
Whither the swans and turtles go,
In fair Elysium to endure
With milk-white lambs and er-
 mines pure.
O do not run too fast, for I
Will but bespeak thy grave, and
 die. 110
 First my unhappy statue shall
Be cut in marble, and withal
Let it be weeping too; but there

Th' engraver sure his art may spare,
For I so truly thee bemoan
That I shall weep though I be stone,
Until my tears, still dropping, wear

My breast, themselves engraving there.
There at my feet shalt thou be laid,
Of purest alabaster made;   120
For I would have thine image be
White as I can, though not as thee.

The picture of little T. C. in a prospect of flowers

See with what simplicity
This nymph begins her golden days!
In the green grass she loves to lie,
And there with her fair aspect tames
The wilder flowers, and gives them names;
But only with the roses plays,
    And them does tell
What color best becomes them, and what smell.

Who can foretell for what high cause
This darling of the gods was born?   10
Yet this is she whose chaster laws
The wanton Love shall one day fear,
And under her command severe
See his bow broke and ensigns torn.
    Happy, who can
Appease this virtuous enemy of man!

Oh, then let me in time compound,
And parley with those conquering eyes,
Ere they have tried their force to wound,
Ere with their glancing wheels they drive   20
In triumph over hearts that strive,
And them that yield but more despise.
    Let me be laid
Where I may see thy glories from some shade.

Meantime, whilst every verdant thing
Itself does at thy beauty charm,
Reform the errors of the spring:
Make that the tulips may have share
Of sweetness, seeing they are fair;
And roses of their thorns disarm;   30
    But most procure
That violets may a longer age endure.

But, O young beauty of the woods,
Whom nature courts with fruits and flowers,

Gather the flowers, but spare the buds,
Lest Flora, angry at thy crime,
To kill her infants in their prime,
Do quickly make th' example yours;
  And ere we see,
Nip in the blossom all our hopes and thee.   40

The definition of love

My love is of a birth as rare
As 'tis for object strange and high;
It was begotten by despair
Upon impossibility.

Magnanimous despair alone
Could show me so divine a thing,
Where feeble hope could ne'er
 have flown,
But vainly flapped its tinsel wing.

And yet I quickly might arrive
Where my extended soul is fixed,
But fate does iron wedges drive,   11
And always crowds itself betwixt.

For fate with jealous eye does see
Two perfect loves, nor lets them
 close;
Their union would her ruin be,
And her tyrannic power depose.

And therefore her decrees of steel
Us as the distant poles have placed,

Though love's whole world on us
 doth wheel,
Not by themselves to be embraced;   20

Unless the giddy heaven fall,
And earth some new convulsion
 tear,
And, us to join, the world should
 all
Be cramped into a planisphere.

As lines, so loves, oblique may
 well
Themselves in every angle greet;
But ours so truly parallel,
Though infinite, can never meet.

Therefore the love which us doth
 bind,
But fate so enviously debars,   30
Is the conjunction of the mind,
And opposition of the stars.

The fair singer

To make a final conquest of all me,
Love did compose so sweet an enemy,
In whom both beauties to my death agree,
Joining themselves in fatal harmony;
That while she with her eyes my heart does bind,
She with her voice might captivate my mind.

I could have fled from one but singly fair;
My disentangled soul itself might save,
Breaking the curlèd trammels of her hair.
But how should I avoid to be her slave,   10

Whose subtle art invisibly can wreathe
My fetters of the very air I breathe?

It had been easy fighting in some plain,
Where victory might hang in equal choice,
But all resistance against her is vain,
Who has th' advantage both of eyes and voice;
And all my forces needs must be undone,
She having gainéd both the wind and sun.

To his coy mistress

Had we but world enough, and time,
This coyness, lady, were no crime.
We would sit down and think which way
To walk, and pass our long love's day;
Thou by the Indian Ganges' side
Shouldst rubies find; I by the tide
Of Humber would complain. I would
Love you ten years before the Flood;
And you should, if you please, refuse
Till the conversion of the Jews.   10
My vegetable love should grow
Vaster than empires, and more slow.
An hundred years should go to praise
Thine eyes, and on thy forehead gaze;
Two hundred to adore each breast,
But thirty thousand to the rest;
An age at least to every part,
And the last age should show your heart.
For, lady, you deserve this state,
Nor would I love at lower rate.   20
    But at my back I always hear
Time's wingéd chariot hurrying near;
And yonder all before us lie
Deserts of vast eternity.
Thy beauty shall no more be found,
Nor in thy marble vault shall sound
My echoing song; then worms shall try
That long preserved virginity,
And your quaint honor turn to dust,
And into ashes all my lust.   30
The grave's a fine and private place,
But none, I think, do there embrace.
    Now therefore, while the youthful hue
Sits on thy skin like morning glew,

And while thy willing soul transpires
At every pore with instant fires,
Now let us sport us while we may;
And now, like am'rous birds of prey,
Rather at once our time devour,
Than languish in his slow-chapped power.   40
Let us roll all our strength, and all
Our sweetness, up into one ball;
And tear our pleasures with rough strife
Thorough the iron gates of life.
Thus, though we cannot make our sun
Stand still, yet we will make him run.

An epitaph upon——

Enough, and leave the rest to fame,
'Tis to commend her but to name;
Courtship, which living she declined,
When dead to offer were unkind.
Where never any could speak ill,
Who would officious praises spill?
Nor can the truest wit or friend,
Without detracting, her commend.
To say she lived a virgin chaste
In this age loose and all unlaced,   10
Nor was, when vice is so allowed,
Of virtue or ashamed or proud;
That her soul was on heaven so bent
No minute but it came and went;
That ready her last debt to pay,
She summed her life up ev'ry day;
Modest as morn, as mid-day bright;
Gentle as evening, cool as night;
'Tis true, but all so weakly said,
'Twere more significant, She's dead.   20

An Horatian ode upon Cromwell's return from Ireland

The forward youth that would appear
Must now forsake his muses dear,
Nor in the shadows sing
His numbers languishing.
'Tis time to leave the books in dust,
And oil th' unusèd armor's rust,

Removing from the wall
The corslet of the hall.
So restless Cromwell could not cease
In the inglorious arts of peace,   10
But through advent'rous war
Urgèd his active star.
And like the three-forked lightning, first
Breaking the clouds where it was nursed,

Did through his own side
His fiery way divide.
For 'tis all one to courage high,
The emulous or enemy;
  And with such to enclose
  Is more than to oppose.   20
Then burning through the air he
    went,
And palaces and temples rent;
  And Cæsar's head at last
  Did through his laurels blast.
'Tis madness to resist or blame
The force of angry heaven's
    flame;
  And if we would speak true,
  Much to the man is due,
Who from his private gardens
    where
He lived reservèd and austere,   30
  As if his highest plot
  To plant the bergamot,
Could by industrious valor climb
To ruin the great work of time,
  And cast the kingdom old
  Into another mold,
Though justice against fate com-
    plain,
And plead the ancient rights in
    vain;
  But those do hold or break
  As men are strong or weak.   40
Nature that hateth emptiness
Allows of penetration less,
  And therefore must make room
  Where greater spirits come.
What field of all the civil wars
Where his were not the deepest
    scars?
  And Hampton shows what part
  He had of wiser art,
Where, twining subtile fears with
    hope,
He wove a net of such a scope   50
  That Charles himself might
    chase
  To Carisbrooke's narrow case,

That thence the royal actor borne
The tragic scaffold might adorn,
  While round the armèd bands
  Did clap their bloody hands.
He nothing common did or mean
Upon that memorable scene,
  But with his keener eye
  The axe's edge did try;   60
Nor called the gods with vulgar
    spite
To vindicate his helpless right,
  But bowed his comely head
  Down as upon a bed.
This was that memorable hour
Which first assured the forcèd
    power.
  So when they did design
  The Capitol's first line,
A bleeding head, where they be-
    gun,
Did fright the architects to run; 70
  And yet in that the state
  Foresaw its happy fate.
And now the Irish are ashamed
To see themselves in one year
    tamed;
  So much one man can do
  That does both act and know.
They can affirm his praises best,
And have, though overcome, con-
    fessed
  How good he is, how just,
  And fit for highest trust;   80
Nor yet grown stiffer with com-
    mand,
But still in the republic's hand;
  How fit he is to sway
  That can so well obey.
He to the Commons' feet pre-
    sents
A kingdom for his first year's
    rents;
  And, what he may, forbears
  His fame, to make it theirs,
And has his sword and spoils un-
    girt,

To lay them at the public's
    skirt.   90
So when the falcon high
    Falls heavy from the sky,
She, having killed, no more does
    search
But on the next green bough to
    perch,
    Where, when he first does lure,
    The falc'ner has her sure.
What may not then our isle pre-
    sume
While victory his crest does
    plume!
    What may not others fear
    If thus he crown each year! 100
A Cæsar he ere long to Gaul,
To Italy an Hannibal,
    And to all states not free,

Shall climacteric be.
The Pict no shelter now shall find
Within his parti-colored mind;
    But from this valor sad
    Shrink underneath the plaid,
Happy if in the tufted brake
The English hunter him mis-
    take,   110
    Nor lay his hounds in near
    The Caledonian deer.
But thou, the war's and fortune's
    son,
March indefatigably on;
    And for the last effect
    Still keep thy sword erect;
Besides the force it has to fright
The spirits of the shady night,
    The same arts that did gain
    A power, must it maintain. 120

KATHERINE PHILIPS

The Introduction and Notes are at page 1036

FROM *Poems*, 1667

*Friendship's mystery. To my
    dearest Lucasia*

Come, my Lucasia, since we see
    That miracles men's faith do
      move,
By wonder and by prodigy
    To the dull angry world let's
      prove
    There's a religion in our love.

For though we were designed t'
    agree,
    That fate no liberty destroys,
But our election is as free
    As angels', who with greedy
      choice
    Are yet determined to their
    joys.   10

Our hearts are doubled by the
    loss,
    Here mixture is addition
      grown;
We both diffuse and both en-
    gross,
    And we whose minds are so
      much one,
    Never, yet ever, are alone.

We court our own captivity,
    Than thrones more great and
      innocent;
'Twere banishment to be set free,
    Since we wear fetters whose
      intent
    Not bondage is, but ornament. 20

Divided joys are tedious found,
    And griefs united easier grow;
We are ourselves but by rebound,

And all our titles shuffled so,
Both princes, and both subjects
too.

Our hearts are mutual victims
laid,
While they, such power in
friendship lies,
Are altars, priests, and off'rings
made;
And each heart which thus
kindly dies
Grows deathless by the sacrifice. 30

To my excellent Lucasia, on our friendship

I did not live, until this time
Crowned my felicity,
When I could say without a
crime,
I am not thine, but thee.

This carcass breathed and walked
and slept,
So that the world believed
There was a soul the motions kept,
But they were all deceived.

For as a watch by art is wound
To motion, such was mine; 10
But never had Orinda found
A soul till she found thine;

Which now inspires, cures, and
supplies,
And guides my darkened
breast;

For thou art all that I can prize,
My joy, my life, my rest.

No bridegroom's nor crown-con-
queror's mirth
To mine compared can be;
They have but pieces of this
earth,
I've all the world in thee. 20

Then let our flames still light and
shine,
And no false fear control,
As innocent as our design,
Immortal as our soul.

Song

To the tune of *Adieu, Phillis*

'Tis true our life is but a long
disease,
Made up of real pain and seeming
ease.
You stars, who these entangled
fortunes give,
O tell me why
It is so hard to die,
Yet such a task to live?

If with some pleasure we our
griefs betray,
It costs us dearer than it can re-
pay,
For time or fortune all things so
devours,
Our hopes are crossed, 10
Or else the object lost,
Ere we can call it ours.

ALEXANDER BROME

The Introduction and Notes are at page 1037

FROM *Songs and other Poems*, 1661

The resolve

Tell me not of a face that's fair,
Nor lip and cheek that's red,

Nor of the tresses of her hair,
Nor curls in order laid,
Nor of a rare seraphic voice
That like an angel sings;

Though if I were to take my
   choice,
I would have all these things.
But if that thou wilt have me love,
   And it must be a she,   10
The only argument can move
   Is, that she will love me.

The glories of your ladies be
   But metaphors of things,
And but resemble what we see
   Each common object brings.
Roses out-red their lips and
   cheeks,
   Lilies their whiteness stain;
What fool is he that shadow seeks,
   And may the substance gain? 20
Then if thou'lt have me love a
   lass,
   Let it be one that's kind,
Else, I'm a servant to the glass
   That's with Canary lined.

The trooper

Come, come, let us drink,
'Tis in vain to think
   Like fools on grief or sadness;
Let our money fly
And our sorrows die,
   All worldly care is madness;
But sack and good cheer
Will in spite of our fear
   Inspire our souls with gladness.

Let the greedy clowns   10
That do live like hounds,
   That know neither bound nor
      measure,
Lament each loss,
For their wealth is their cross,
   Whose delight is in their treas-
      ure;
But we that have none,
Will use theirs as our own,
   And spend it at our pleasure.

Troll about the bowl,
The delight of my soul,   20
   And to my hand commend it.
A fig for chink,
'Twas made to buy drink,
   Before that we go we'll end it;
When we've spent our store,
The land will yield us more,
   And jovially we will spend it.

The riddle

Written in 1644

No more, no more,
We are already pined,
   And sore and poor
   In body and in mind;
   And yet our sufferings have
      been
   Less than our sin.
Come, long desirëd peace, we thee
   implore,
And let our pains be less, or power
   more.

Lament, lament,
And let thy tears run down   10
   To see the rent
   Between the robe and crown;
   Yet both do strive to make
      it more
   Than 'twas before.
War, like a serpent, has its head
   got in,
And will not end so soon as 't
   did begin.

One body jars,
And with itself does fight;
   War meets with wars,
   And might resisteth might; 20
    And both sides say they love
      the king,
   And peace will bring.
Yet since these fatal civil broils
   begun,

Strange riddle, both have con-
    quered, neither won.

One God, one king,
One true religion still,
    In everything
One law both should fulfil;
    All these both sides does still
        pretend
    That they defend;   30
Yet to increase the king and king-
    dom's woes,
Which side soever wins, good
    subjects lose.

The king doth swear
That he doth fight for them;
    And they declare
They do the like for him;
    Both say they wish and fight
        for peace,
    Yet wars increase.
So between both, before our wars
    be gone,
Our lives and goods are lost, and
    we're undone.   40

Since 'tis our curse
To fight we know not why,
    'Tis worse and worse
The longer thus we lie,
    For war itself is but a nurse
    To make us worse.
Come, blessed peace! we once
    again implore,
And let our pains be less, or power
    more.

The royalist

Written in 1646

Come, pass about the bowl to me,
    A health to our distressëd king!
Though we're in hold, let cups
    go free,
    Birds in a cage may freely sing.

The ground does tipple healths
    apace
    When storms do fall, and shall
        not we?
A sorrow dares not show his face
    When we are ships, and sack's
        the sea.

Pox on this grief, hang wealth,
    let's sing!
    Shall's kill ourselves for fear
        of death?   10
We'll live by th' air which songs
    do bring;
    Our sighing does but waste our
        breath.
Then let us not be discontent,
    Nor drink a glass the less of
        wine;
In vain they'll think their plagues
    are spent,
    When once they see we don't
        repine.

We do not suffer here alone;
    Though we are beggared, so's
        the king.
'Tis sin t' have wealth when he
    has none;
    Tush! poverty's a royal
        thing!   20
When we are larded well with
    drink,
    Our heads shall turn as round
        as theirs;
Our feet shall rise, our bodies
    sink
    Clean down the wind, like cav-
        aliers.

Fill this unnatural quart with
    sack,
    Nature all vacuums doth de-
        cline;
Our selves will be a zodiac,

And every mouth shall be a sign.
Methinks the travels of the glass
Are circular, like Plato's year,   30
Where everything is as it was,
Let's tipple round, and so 'tis here.

The pastoral on the King's death

Written in 1648

Where England's Damon used to keep
In peace and awe his flocks,
Who fed, not fed upon, his sheep,
There wolves and tigers now do prey,
There sheep are slain, and goats do sway;
There reigns the subtle fox,
While the poor lambkins weep.

The laureled garland which before
Circled his brows about,
The spotless coat which once he wore,   10
The sheep-hook which he used to sway,
And pipe whereon he loved to play,
Are seized on by the rout,
And must be used no more.

Poor swain, how thou lament'st to see
Thy flocks o'er-ruled by those
That serve thy cattle all like thee;
Where hateful vice usurps the crown,
And loyalty is trodden down;
Down scrip and sheep-hook goes,   20
When foxes shepherds be.

For General Monk, his entertainment at Clothworkers' Hall

Ring, bells! and let bonfires outblaze the sun!
Let echoes contribute their voice!
Since now a happy settlement's begun,
Let all things tell how all good men rejoice.
If these sad lands by this
Can but obtain the bliss
Of their desired, though abusëd peace,
We'll never, nevermore
Run mad, as we've heretofore,
To buy our ruin, but all strife shall cease.   10

The cobbler shall edify us no more,
Nor shall in divinity set any stitches;
The women we will no more hear and adore,
That preach with their husbands for the breeches.
The fanatical tribe
That will not subscribe
To the orders of church and of state,
Shall be smothered with the zeal
Of their new commonweal,
And no man will mind what they prate.   20

Chorus.

We'll eat and we'll drink, we'll dance and we'll sing,
The Roundheads and Cavs no more shall be named;

But all join together to make up
the ring,
And rejoice that the many-
headed dragon is tamed.
'Tis friendship and love that can
save us and arm us,
And while we all agree, there is
nothing can harm us.

Palinode

No more, no more of this, I vow,
'Tis time to leave this fooling
now,
Which few but fools call wit;
There was a time when I begun,
And now 'tis time I should have
done,
And meddle no more with it.
He physic's use doth quite mistake,
That physic takes for physic's sake.

My heat of youth and love and
pride
Did swell me with their strong
spring-tide,   10
Inspired my brain and blood,
And made me then converse with
toys,
Which are called Muses by the
boys,
And dabble in their flood.
I was persuaded in those days
There was no crown like love
and bays.

But now my youth and pride are
gone,
And age and cares come creeping
on,
And business checks my love;
What need I take a needless
toil,   20
To spend my labor, time, and oil,
Since no design can move?
For now the cause is ta'en away,

What reason is 't the effect should
stay?

'Tis but a folly now for me
To spend my time and industry
About such useless wit;
For when I think I have done
well,
I see men laugh, but cannot tell
Where 't be at me or it.   30
Great madness 'tis to be a drudge,
When those that cannot write
dare judge.

Besides the danger that ensu'th
To him that speaks or writes the
truth,
The premium is so small;
To be called poet and wear bays,
And factor turn of songs and
plays,
This is no wit at all.
Wit only good to sport and sing
'S a needless and an endless
thing.   40

Give me the wit that can't speak
sense,
Nor read it, but in 's own defence,
Ne'er learned but of his gran-
num;
He that can buy and sell and
cheat,
May quickly make a shift to get
His thousand pound per annum,
And purchase, without much ado,
The poems and the poet too.

FROM *Songs and other Poems*,
1664

The mad lover

I have been in love, and in debt,
and in drink,
This many and many a year;

And those three are plagues enough, one would think,
For one poor mortal to bear.
'Twas drink made me fall in love,
And love made me run into debt,
And though I have struggled and struggled and strove,
I cannot get out of them yet.

There's nothing but money can cure me,
And rid me of all my pain; 10
'Twill pay all my debts,
And remove all my lets,
And my mistress, that cannot endure me,
Will love me and love me again,—
Then I'll fall to loving and drinking amain.

STUART AND COMMONWEALTH MISCELLANIES

The Introduction and Notes are at page 1037

FROM W. B. and E. P.'s *Help to Discourse, or a Miscellany of Merriment*, 1619

A memento for mortality

Taken from the view of sepulchers of so many kings and nobles as lie interred in the Abbey of Westminster

Mortality, behold and fear!
What a change of flesh is here!
Think how many royal bones
Sleep within this heap of stones,
Hence removed from beds of ease,
Dainty fare, and what might please,
Fretted roofs, and costly shows,
To a roof that flats the nose: 8
Which proclaims all flesh is grass,
How the world's fair glories pass;
That there is no trust in health,
In youth, in age, in greatness, wealth;
For if such could have reprieved,
Those had been immortal lived.
Know from this the world a snare,
How that greatness is but care,
How all pleasures are but pain,
And how short they do remain;

For here they lie had realms and lands,
That now want strength to stir their hands; 20
Where from their pulpits ceiled with dust
They preach, In greatness is no trust.
Here's an acre sown indeed
With the richest royal'st seed
That the earth did e'er suck in
Since the first man died for sin.
Here the bones of birth have cried,
Though gods they were, as men they died.
Here are sands, ignoble things,
Dropped from the ruined sides of kings, 30
With whom the poor man's earth being shown,

The difference is not easily known.
Here's a world of pomp and state
Forgotten, dead, disconsolate.
Think then this scythe that mows
    down kings
Exempts no meaner mortal things.
Then bid the wanton lady tread
Amid these mazes of the dead,
And these, truly understood,
More shall cool and quench the
    blood   40

Than her many sports a-day
And her nightly wanton play.
Bid her paint till day of doom,
To this favor she must come.
Bid the merchant gather
    wealth,
The usurer exact by stealth,
The proud man beat it from his
    thought,
Yet to this shape all must be
    brought.

FROM *Wit's Recreations*, 1641

Interrogativa cantilena

If all the world were paper,
And all the sea were ink;
If all the trees were bread and
    cheese,
How should we do for drink?

If all the world were sand-o,
Oh, then what should we lack-o?
If as they say, there were no clay,
How should we take tobacco?

If all our vessels ran-a,
If none but had a crack-a;   10
If Spanish apes eat all the grapes,
How should we do for sack-a?

If friars had no bald pates,
Nor nuns had no dark cloisters;
If all the seas were beans and peas,
How should we do for oysters?

If there had been no projects,
Nor none that did great wrongs;
If fiddlers shall turn players all,
How should we do for songs?   20

If all things were eternal,
And nothing their end bringing;
If this should be, then how should
    we
Here make an end of singing?

FROM *Wit's Recreations*, 1645

Sighs

All night I muse, all day I cry,
    Ay me!
Yet still I wish, though still deny,
    Ay me!
I sigh, I mourn, and say that still
I only live my joys to kill,
    Ay me!

I feed the pain that on me feeds,
    Ay me!
My wound I stop not, though it
    bleeds,   10
    Ay me!

Heart, be content, it must be so,
For springs were made to overflow,
    Ay me!

Then sigh and weep, and mourn
    thy fill,
    Ay me!
Seek no redress, but languish still,
    Ay me!
Their griefs more willing they en-
    dure
That know when they are past re-
    cure,   20
    Ay me!

From *Reliquiæ Wottonianæ*, 1651

A description of the country's recreations

Quivering fears, heart-tearing cares,
Anxious sighs, untimely tears,
  Fly, fly to courts!
  Fly to fond worldlings' sports,
Where strained sardonic smiles are glozing still,
And grief is forced to laugh against her will,
  Where mirth's but mummery
  And sorrows only real be.

Fly from our country pastimes, fly,
Sad troop of human misery!   10
  Come, serene looks
  Clear as the crystal brooks
Or the pure azured heaven that smiles to see
The rich attendance of our poverty,—
  Peace, and a secure mind,
  Which all men seek, we only find.

Abusëd mortals, did you know
Where joy, heart's ease, and comforts grow,
  You'd scorn proud towers
  And seek them in these bowers   20
Where winds sometimes our woods perhaps may shake,
But blust'ring care could never tempest make,
  Nor murmurs e'er come nigh us
  Saving of fountains that glide by us.

Here's no fantastic mask, nor dance
But of our kids, that frisk and prance;
  Nor wars are seen,
  Unless upon the green
Two harmless lambs are butting one the other,
Which done, both bleating run, each to his mother; 30
  And wounds are never found
  Save what the plowshare gives the ground.

Here are no false entrapping baits
To hasten too too hasty fates,
  Unless it be
  The fond credulity
Of silly fish which worldling-like still look
Upon the bait, but never on the hook;

Nor envy, unless among
The birds, for prize of their sweet song.   40

Go, let the diving Negro seek
For gems hid in some forlorn creek;
    We all pearls scorn
    Save what the dewy morn
Congeals upon each little spire of grass,
Which careless shepherds beat down as they pass;
    And gold ne'er here appears
    Save what the yellow Ceres bears.

Blest silent groves, oh, may ye be
Forever mirth's best nursery!   50
    May pure contents
    Forever pitch their tents
Upon these downs, these meads, these rocks, these mountains,
And peace still slumber by these purling fountains,
    Which we may every year
    Find when we come a-fishing here!

FROM SIR JOHN MENNIS and JAMES SMITH'S *Musarum
Deliciæ*, 1656

The nightingale

My limbs were weary, and my head oppressed
With drowsiness, and yet I could not rest.
My bed was such as down nor feather can
Make one more soft, though Jove again turn swan;
No fear-distracted thoughts my slumbers broke,
I heard no screech-owl shriek, nor raven croak;
Sleep's foe, the flea, that proud insulting elf,
Is now at truce, and is asleep itself.
But 'twas night's darling, and the world's chief jewel,
The nightingale, that was so sweetly cruel.   10
It wooed my ears to rob my eyes of sleep,
That whilst she sung of Tereus they might weep,
And yet rejoice the tyrant did her wrong;
Her cause of woe was burthen of her song.
Which while I listened to and strove to hear,
'Twas such I could have wished myself all ear.
'Tis false that poets feign of Orpheus—he
Could neither move a beast, a stone, or tree
To follow him; but wheresoe'er she flies
The grovy satyr and the fairy hies   20

Afore her perch, to dance their roundelays,
For she sings distichs to them, while Pan plays.
Yet she sung better now, as if in me
She meant with sleep to try the mastery.
But while she chanted thus, the cock for spite,
Day's hoarser herald, chid away the night;
Thus robbed of sleep, my eyelids' nightly guest,
Methought I lay content, though not at rest.

From J. Phillips's *Sportive Wit*, 1656

[*Chloris, forbear a while*]

Chloris, forbear a while, do not o'erjoy me,
Urge not another smile lest thou destroy me;
That beauty pleaseth most and is soonest taken,
Which is soon won, soon lost, kindly forsaken.
I love a coming lady, 'faith I do,
And now and then would have her scornful too.

O cloud those eyes of thine, bo-peep thy feature,
Warmed with an April shine, scorch not thy creature;
Thus to display thy ware, thus to be fooling,
Argues how rude you are in Cupid's schooling.   10
Disdain begets a suit, scorn draws me nigh,
'Tis 'cause I would and can't, makes me try.

Chloris, I would have thee wise, when gallants woo thee,
And courtship thou despise, fly those pursue thee;
Fast moves an appetite—make hunger greater—
What's stinted oft delights, falls to the better.
Be kindly coy betimes, be smoothly rough,
And buckle now and then, and that's enough.

[*Henry Bold*]

From Abraham Wright's *Parnassus Biceps*, 1656

The liberty and requiem of an imprisoned royalist

Beat on, proud billows; Boreas, blow
Swelled curlëd waves high as Jove's roof;
Your incivility shall know
That innocence is tempest-proof.
Though surly Nereus frown, my thoughts are calm;
Then strike, afflictions, for your wounds are balm.

That which the world miscalls a jail,
A private closet is to me.

Whilst a good conscience is my bail,
And innocence my liberty.   10
Locks, bars, walls, loneness, though together met,
Make me no prisoner, but an anchoret.

I, whilst I wished to be retired,
Into this private room was turned,
As if their wisdoms had conspired
A salamander should be burned;
And like those sophies who would drown a fish,
I am condemned to suffer what I wish.

The Cynic hugs his poverty,
The pelican her wilderness,   20
And 'tis the Indian's pride to lie
Naked on frozen Caucasus.
And like to these, Stoics severe we see
Make torments easy by their apathy.

These manacles upon my arm
I as my sweetheart's favors wear,
And then to keep my ankles warm
I have some iron shackles there;
These walls are but my garrison, this cell
Which men call jail doth prove my citadel.   30

So he that struck at Jason's life,
Thinking h' had made his purpose sure,
By a malicious friendly knife
Did only wound him to a cure.
Malice I see wants wit, for what is meant
Mischief, ofttimes proves favor by th' event.

I'm in this cabinet locked up,
Like some high prizëd margarite;
Or like some great Mogul or Pope,
Am cloistered up from public sight;   40
Retiredness is a part of majesty,
And thus, proud Sultan, I'm as great as thee.

Here sin for want of food doth starve,
Where tempting objects are not seen,
And these walls do only serve
To keep vice out, not keep me in.
Malice of late's grown charitable sure,
I'm not committed, but am kept secure.

When once my prince affliction hath,
Prosperity doth treason seem,
And then to smooth so rough a path
I can learn patience too from him.
Now not to suffer shows no loyal heart,
When kings want ease, subjects must love to smart.

What though I cannot see my king,
Either in 's person or his coin,
Yet contemplation is a thing
Which renders what I have, not mine.
My king from me no adamant can part,
Whom I do wear engraven in my heart.

My soul's free as th' ambient air,
Although my baser part's immured,
Whilst loyal thoughts do still repair
T' accompany my solitude.
And though rebellion do my body bind,
My king can only captivate my mind.

Have you not seen the nightingale
When turned a pilgrim to a cage,
How she doth sing her wonted tale
In that her narrow hermitage?
Even there her chanting melody doth prove
That all her bars are trees, her cage a grove.

I am that bird, which they combine
Thus to deprive of liberty,
Who though they do my corpse confine,
Yet maugre hate, my soul is free;
And though immured, yet can I chirp and sing
Disgrace to rebels, glory to my king.

[*Sir Roger L'Estrange*]

From *Choice Drollery*, 1656

The contented prisoner, his praise of sack

How happy's that prisoner
    That conquers his fates
With silence, and ne'er
    On bad fortune complains,
But carelessly plays
    With his keys on the grates,
And makes a sweet consort

With them and his chains.
He drowns care with sack
    When his thoughts are op-
        pressed,
And makes his heart float
    Like a cork in his breast.
        Then,

The chorus.

Since we are all slaves,
     That islanders be,
And our land's a large prison
     Enclosed with the sea,
We'll drink up the ocean
To set ourselves free,
     For man is the world's epito-
          me.   20

Let pirates wear purple
     Deep dyed in the blood
Of those they have slain,
     The scepter to sway.
If our conscience be clear,
     And our title be good,
With the rags we have on us
We are richer than they.
We drink down at night
     What we beg or can bor-
          row,   30
And sleep without plotting
For more the next morrow.

The chorus. Since we, &c.

Let the usurer watch
     O'er his bags and his house;
To keep that from robbers
     He hath racked from his
          debtors,
Each midnight cries, Thieves,
     At the noise of a mouse.
Then see that his trunks   40
     Be fast bound in their fetters.
When once he's grown rich
          enough
     For a state plot,
Buff in an hour plunders
What threescore years got.

The chorus. Since we, &c.

Come, drawer, fill each man
     A peck of Canary;

This brimmer shall bid
     All our senses good-night. 50
When old Aristotle
     Was frolic and merry,
By the juice of the grape
     He turned Stagirite.
Copernicus once,
     In a drunken fit, found
By the course of his brains
     That the world turned round.

The chorus. Since we, &c.

'Tis sack makes our faces   60
     Like comets to shine,
And gives beauty beyond
     The complexïon mask.
Diogenes fell so
     In love with this wine,
That when 'twas all out,
     He dwelt in the cask.
He lived by the scent
     Of his wainscotted room,
And dying desired   70
     The tub for his tomb.

The chorus. Since we, &c.

FROM *Wit Restored,* 1658

Phillada flouts me

Oh! what a pain is love,
How shall I bear it?
She will inconstant prove,
I greatly fear it.
She so torments my mind
That my strength faileth,
And wavers with the wind
As a ship that saileth.
Please her the best I may,
She looks another way.   10
Alack and well-a-day,
     Phillada flouts me.

All the Fair yesterday,
She did pass by me;

She looked another way,
And would not spy me.
I wooed her for to dine,
But could not get her.
Will had her to the wine,
He might entreat her;   20
With Daniel she did dance,
On me she looked askance.
Oh, thrice unhappy chance,
    Phillada flouts me.

Fair maid, be not so coy,
Do not disdain me;
I am my mother's joy,
Sweet, entertain me.
She'll give me when she dies,
All that is fitting: 30
Her poultry and her bees
And her geese sitting,
A pair of mattress beds,
And a bag full of shreds;
And yet for all this goods,
    Phillada flouts me.

She hath a clout of mine,
Wrought with good Coventry,
Which she keeps for a sign
Of my fidelity.   40
But i' faith, if she flinch,
She shall not wear it;
To Tibb, my t'other wench,
I mean to bear it.
And yet it grieves my heart
So soon from her to part;
Death strikes me with his dart,
    Phillada flouts me.

Thou shalt eat curds and cream,
All the year lasting;   50
And drink the crystal stream,
Pleasant in tasting;
Wigg and whey whilst thou burst,
And ramble-berry;
Pie-lid and pasty crust,
Pears, plums, and cherry.
Thy raiment shall be thin,
Made of a weaver's skin;
Yet all's not worth a pin,
    Phillada flouts me.   60

Fair maiden, have a care,
And in time take me;
I can have those as fair,
If you forsake me.
For Doll, the dairy-maid,
Laughed on me lately,
And wanton Winifred
Favors me greatly.
One throws milk on my clothes,
T' other plays with my nose;   70
What wanton signs are those?
    Phillada flouts me.

I cannot work and sleep
All at a season;
Love wounds my heart so deep,
Without all reason.
I 'gin to pine away
With grief and sorrow,
Like to a fatted beast
Penned in a meadow.   80
I shall be dead I fear,
Within this thousand year,
And all for very fear,
    Phillada flouts me.

EXTRACTS FROM CRITICAL ESSAYS

SIR PHILIP SIDNEY

FROM *The Defence of Poesy*, 1595

. . . But since the authors of most of our sciences were the Romans, and before them the Greeks, let us a little stand upon their authorities, but even so far as to see what names they have given unto this now scorned skill. Among the Romans a poet was called *vates*, which is as much as a diviner, foreseer, or prophet, as by his conjoined words, *vaticinium* and *vaticinari*, is manifest; so heavenly a title did that excellent people bestow upon this heart-ravishing knowledge. And so far were they carried into the admiration thereof, that they thought in the chanceable hitting upon any such verses great foretokens of their following fortunes were placed; whereupon grew the word of *Sortes Virgilianæ*, when by sudden opening Virgil's book they lighted upon some verse of his making. Whereof the histories of the emperors' lives are full: as of Albinus, the governor of our island, who in his childhood met with this verse,

Arma amens capio, nec sat rationis in armis,

and in his age performed it. Although it were a very vain and godless superstition, as also it was to think that spirits were commanded by such verses —whereupon this word charms, derived of *carmina*, cometh—so yet serveth it to show the great reverence those wits were held in, and altogether not without ground, since both the oracles of Delphos and Sibylla's prophecies were wholly delivered in verses; for that same exquisite observing of number and measure in words, and that high-flying liberty of conceit proper to the poet, did seem to have some divine force in it.

And may not I presume a little further to show the reasonableness of this word *vates*, and say that the holy David's *Psalms* are a divine poem? If I do, I shall not do it without the testimony of great learned men, both ancient and modern. But even the name of psalms will speak for me, which, being interpreted, is nothing but songs; then, that it is fully written in meter, as all learned Hebricians agree, although the rules be not yet fully found; lastly and principally, his handling his prophecy, which is merely poetical. For what else is the awaking his musical instruments, the often and free changing of persons, his notable *prosopopœias*, when he maketh you, as it were, see God coming in his majesty, his telling of the beasts' joyfulness and hills' leaping, but a heavenly poesy, wherein almost he showeth himself a passionate lover of that unspeakable and everlasting beauty to be seen by the eyes of the mind only cleared by faith? But truly now having named him, I fear I seem to profane that holy name, applying it to poetry, which is among us thrown down to so ridiculous an estimation. But they that with quiet judgments will look a little deeper into it, shall find the end and working of it such as, being rightly applied, deserveth not to be scourged out of the church of God.

But now let us see how the Greeks named it and how they deemed of it. The Greeks called him ποιητήν, which name hath, as the most excellent, gone through other languages. It cometh of this word ποιεῖν, which is 'to make'; wherein I know not whether by luck or wisdom we Englishmen have met with the Greeks in calling him a maker. Which name how high and incomparable a title it is, I had rather were known by marking the scope of other sciences than by any partial allegation. There is no art delivered unto mankind that hath not the works of nature for his principal object, without which they could not consist, and on which they so depend as they become actors and players, as it were, of what nature will have set forth. So doth the astronomer look upon the stars, and, by that he seeth, set down what order nature hath taken therein. So do the geometrician and arithmetician in their divers sorts of quantities. So doth the musician in times tell you which by nature agree, which not. The natural philosopher thereon hath his name, and the moral philosopher standeth upon the natural virtues, vices, and passions of man; and 'follow nature,' saith he, 'therein, and thou shalt not err.' The lawyer saith what men have determined, the historian what men have done. The grammarian speaketh only of the rules of speech, and the rhetorician and logician, considering what in nature will soonest prove and persuade, thereon give artificial rules, which still are compassed within the circle of a question, according to the proposed matter. The physician weigheth the nature of man's body, and the nature of things helpful or hurtful unto it. And the metaphysic, though it be in the second and abstract notions, and therefore be counted supernatural, yet doth he, indeed, build upon the depth of nature.

Only the poet, disdaining to be tied to any such subjection, lifted up with the vigor of his own invention, doth grow, in effect, into another nature, in making things either better than nature bringeth forth, or, quite anew, forms such as never were in nature, as the heroes, demi-gods, cyclops, chimeras, furies, and such like; so as he goeth hand in hand with nature, not enclosed within the narrow warrant of her gifts, but freely ranging within the zodiac of his own wit. Nature never set forth the earth in so rich tapestry as divers poets have done; neither with pleasant rivers, fruitful trees, sweet-smelling flowers, nor whatsoever else may make the too-much-loved earth more lovely; her world is brazen, the poets only deliver a golden.

But let those things alone, and go to man—for whom as the other things are, so it seemeth in him her uttermost cunning is employed—and know whether she have brought forth so true a lover as Theagenes; so constant a friend as Pylades; so valiant a man as Orlando; so right a prince as Xenophon's Cyrus; so excellent a man every way as Virgil's Æneas? Neither let this be jestingly conceived, because the works of the one be essential, the other in imitation or fiction; for any understanding knoweth the skill of each artificer standeth in that idea, or fore-conceit of the work, and not in the work itself. And that the poet hath that idea is manifest, by delivering them forth in such excellency as he hath imagined them. Which delivering forth, also, is not wholly imaginative, as we are wont to say by them that build castles in the air; but so far substantially it worketh, not only to make a Cyrus, which had been but a particular excellency, as nature might have done, but to bestow a Cyrus upon the world to make many Cyruses, if they will learn aright why and how that maker made him. Neither let it be deemed too saucy a comparison to balance the highest point of man's wit with the efficacy of nature; but rather give right honor to the heavenly Maker of that maker, who, having made man to his own likeness, set him beyond and over all the works of that second nature. Which in nothing he showeth so much as in poetry, when with the force of a divine breath he bringeth things forth far surpassing her doings, with no small argument to the incredulous of that first accursed fall of Adam,— since our erected wit maketh us know what perfection is, and yet our infected will keepeth us from reaching unto it. But these arguments will by few be understood, and by fewer granted; thus much I hope will be given me, that the Greeks with some probability of reason gave him the name above all names of learning.

Now let us go to a more ordinary opening of him, that the truth may be the more palpable; and so, I hope, though we get not so unmatched a praise as the etymology of his names will grant, yet his very description, which no man will deny, shall not justly be barred from a principal commendation.

Poesy, therefore, is an art of imitation, for so Aristotle termeth it in his word μίμησις, that is to say, a representing, counterfeiting, or figuring forth; to speak metaphorically, a speaking picture, with this end,—to teach and delight.

Of this have been three general kinds. The chief, both in antiquity and excellency, were they that did imitate the inconceivable excellencies of God. Such were David in his *Psalms;* Solomon in his *Song of Songs*, in his *Ecclesiastes* and *Proverbs;* Moses and Deborah in their hymns; and the writer of *Job;* which, beside other, the learned Emanuel Tremellius and Franciscus Junius do entitle the poetical part of the Scripture. Against these none will speak that hath the Holy Ghost in due holy reverence. In this kind, though in a full wrong divinity, were Orpheus, Amphion, Homer in his hymns, and many other, both Greeks and Romans. And this poesy must be used by whosoever will follow St. James' counsel in singing psalms when they are merry; and I know is used with the fruit of comfort by some, when, in sorrowful pangs of their death-bringing sins, they find the consolation of the never-leaving goodness.

The second kind is of them that deal with matters philosophical: either moral, as Tyrtæus, Phocylides, and Cato; or natural, as Lucretius and Virgil's *Georgics;* or astronomical, as Manilius and Pontanus; or historical, as Lucan; which who mislike, the fault is in their judgment quite out of taste, and not in the sweet food of sweetly uttered knowledge.

But because this second sort is wrapped within the fold of the proposed subject, and takes not the free course of his own invention, whether they properly be poets or no let grammarians dispute; and go to the third, indeed right poets, of whom chiefly this question ariseth. Betwixt whom and these second is such a kind of difference as betwixt the meaner sort of painters, who counterfeit only such faces as are set before them, and the more excellent, who having no law but wit, bestow that in colors upon you which is fittest for the eye to see,—as the constant though lamenting look of Lucretia, when she punished in herself another's fault; wherein he painteth not Lucretia, whom he never saw, but painteth the outward beauty of such a virtue. For these third be they which most properly do imitate to teach and delight; and to imitate borrow nothing of what is, hath been, or shall be; but range, only reined with learned discretion, into the divine consideration of what may be and should be. These be they that, as the first and most noble sort may justly be termed *vates,* so these are waited on in the excellentest languages and best understandings with the foredescribed name of poets. For these, indeed, do merely make to imitate, and imitate both to delight and teach, and delight to move men to take that goodness in hand, which without delight they would fly as from a stranger; and teach to make them know that goodness whereunto they are moved; which being the noblest scope to which ever any learning was directed, yet want there not idle tongues to bark at them.

These be subdivided into sundry more special denominations. The most notable be the heroic, lyric, tragic, comic, satiric, iambic, elegiac, pastoral, and certain others, some of these being termed according to the matter they deal with, some by the sort of verse they liked best to write in,—for indeed the greatest part of poets have apparelled their poetical inventions in that numberous kind of writing which is called verse. Indeed but apparelled, verse being but an ornament and no cause to poetry, since there have been many most excellent poets that never versified, and now swarm many versifiers that need never answer to the name of poets. For Xenophon, who did imitate so excellently as to give us *effigiem justi imperii*—the portraiture of a just empire under the name of Cyrus (as Cicero saith of him)—made therein an absolute heroical poem; so did Heliodorus in his sugared invention of that picture of love in Theagenes and Chariclea; and yet both these wrote in prose. Which I speak to show that it is not rhyming and versing that maketh a poet—no more than a long gown maketh an advocate, who, though he pleaded in armor, should be an advocate and no soldier—but it is that feigning notable images of virtues, vices, or what else, with that delightful teaching, which must be the right describing note to know a poet by. Although indeed the senate of poets hath chosen verse as their fittest raiment, meaning, as in matter they passed all in all, so in manner to go beyond them; not speaking, table-talk fashion, or like men in a dream, words as they chanceably fall from the mouth, but peising each syllable of each word by just proportion, according to the dignity of the subject. . . .

The philosopher therefore and the historian are they which would win the goal, the one by precept, the other by example; but both not having both, do both halt. For the philosopher, setting down with thorny arguments the bare rule, is so hard of utterance and so misty to be conceived, that one that hath no other guide but him shall wade in him till he be old, before he shall find sufficient cause to be honest; for his knowledge standeth so upon the abstract and general that happy is that man who may understand him, and more happy that can apply what he doth understand. On the other side, the historian, wanting the precept, is so tied, not to what should be but to what is, to the particular truth of things and not to the general reason of things, that his example draweth no necessary consequence, and therefore a less fruitful doctrine.

Now doth the peerless poet perform both; for whatsoever the philosopher saith should be done, he giveth a perfect picture of it in some one by whom he presupposeth it was done, so as he coupleth the general notion with the particular example. A perfect picture, I say; for he yieldeth to the powers of the mind an image of that whereof the philosopher bestoweth but a wordish description, which doth neither strike, pierce, nor possess the sight of the soul so much as that other doth. For as in outward things, to a man that had never seen an elephant or a rhinoceros, who should tell him most exquisitely all their shapes, color, bigness, and particular marks; or of a gorgeous palace, an architector, with declaring the full beauties, might well make the hearer able to repeat, as it were by rote, all he had heard, yet should never satisfy his inward conceit with being witness to itself of a true lively knowledge; but the same man, as soon as he might see those beasts well painted, or that house well in model, should straightways grow, without need of any description, to a judicial comprehending of them: so no doubt the philosopher with his learned definitions, be it of virtues or vices, matters of public policy or private government, replenisheth the memory with many infallible grounds of wisdom, which notwithstanding lie dark before the imaginative and judging power, if they be not illuminated or figured forth by the speaking picture of poesy.

Tully taketh much pains, and many times not without poetical helps, to make us know the force love of our country hath in us: let us but hear old Anchises speaking in the midst of Troy's flames, or see Ulysses, in the fullness of all Calypso's delights, bewail his absence from barren and beggarly Ithaca. Anger, the Stoics said, was a short madness: let but Sophocles bring you Ajax on a stage, killing and whipping sheep and oxen, thinking them the army of Greeks, with their chieftains Agamemnon and Menelaus, and tell me if you have not a more familiar insight into anger, than finding in the schoolmen his genus and difference. See whether wisdom and temperance in Ulysses and Diomedes, valor in Achilles, friendship in Nisus and Euryalus, even to an ignorant man carry not an apparent shining. And, contrarily, the remorse of conscience in Œdipus; the soon-repenting pride of Agamemnon; the self-devouring cruelty in his father Atreus; the violence of ambition in the two Theban brothers; the sour sweetness of revenge in Medea; and, to fall lower, the Terentian Gnatho and our Chaucer's Pandar so expressed that we now use their names to signify their trades; and finally, all virtues, vices, and passions so in their own natural states laid to the view, that we seem not to hear of them, but clearly to see through them.

But even in the most excellent determination of goodness, what philosopher's counsel can so readily direct a prince, as the feigned Cyrus in Xenophon? Or a virtuous man in all fortunes, as Æneas in Virgil? Or a whole commonwealth, as the way of Sir Thomas More's *Utopia*? I say the way, because where Sir Thomas More erred, it was the fault of the man, and not of the poet; for that way of patterning a commonwealth was most absolute, though he, perchance, hath not so absolutely performed it. For the question is, whether the feigned image of poesy, or the regular instruction of philosophy, hath the more force in teaching. Wherein if the philosophers have more rightly showed themselves philosophers than the poets have attained to the high top of their profession,—as in truth,

> *Mediocribus esse poetis*
> *Non dii, non homines, non concessere columnæ,*—

it is, I say again, not the fault of the art, but that by few men that art can be accomplished.

Certainly, even our Savior Christ could as well have given the moral commonplaces of uncharitableness and humbleness as the divine narration of Dives and Lazarus; or of disobedience and mercy, as that heavenly discourse of the lost child and the gracious father; but that his through-searching wisdom knew the estate of Dives burning in hell, and of Lazarus in Abraham's bosom, would more constantly, as it were, inhabit both the memory and judgment. Truly, for myself, meseems I see before mine eyes the lost child's disdainful prodigality, turned to envy a swine's dinner; which by the learned divines are thought not historical acts, but instructing parables.

For conclusion, I say the philosopher teacheth but he teacheth obscurely, so as the learned only can understand him; that is to say, he teacheth them that are already taught. But the poet is the food for the tenderest stomachs; the poet is indeed the right popular philosopher. Whereof Æsop's tales give good proof; whose pretty allegories, stealing under the formal tales of beasts, make many, more beastly than beasts, begin to hear the sound of virtue from those dumb speakers.

But now may it be alleged that if this imagining of matters be so fit for the imagination, then must the historian needs surpass, who bringeth you images of true matters, such as indeed were done, and not such as fantastically or falsely may be suggested to have been done. Truly, Aristotle himself, in his discourse of poesy, plainly determineth this question, saying that poetry is φιλοσοφώτερον and σπουδαιότερον, that is to say, it is more philosophical and more studiously serious than history. His reason is, because poesy dealeth with καθόλου, that is to say with the universal consideration, and the history with καθ' ἕκαστον, the particular. 'Now,' saith he, 'the universal weighs what is fit to be said or done, either in likelihood or necessity —which the poesy considereth in his imposed names; and the particular only marketh whether Alcibiades did, or suffered, this or that.' Thus far Aristotle, which reason of his, as all his, is most full of reason. . . .

Now therein of all sciences—I speak still of human, and according to the human conceit—is our poet the monarch. For he doth not only show the way, but giveth so sweet a prospect into the way as will entice any man to enter into it. Nay, he doth, as if your journey should lie through a fair vineyard, at the very first give you a cluster of grapes, that full of that taste you may long to pass further. He beginneth not with obscure definitions, which must blur the margent with interpretations, and load the memory with doubtfulness. But he cometh to you with words set in delightful proportion, either accompanied with, or prepared for, the well-enchanting skill of music; and with a tale, forsooth, he cometh unto you with a tale which holdeth children from play, and old men from the chimney-corner, and, pretending no more, doth intend the winning of the mind from wickedness to virtue; even as the child is often brought to take most wholesome things, by hiding them in such other as have a pleasant taste,—which, if one should begin to tell them the nature of the aloes or rhubarb they should receive, would sooner take their physic at their ears than at their mouth. So is it in men, most of which are childish in the best things, till they be cradled in their graves,—glad they will be to hear the tales of Hercules, Achilles, Cyrus, Æneas; and, hearing them, must needs hear the right description of wisdom, valor, and justice; which, if they had been barely, that is to say philosophically, set out, they would swear they be brought to school again.

That imitation whereof poetry is, hath the most conveniency to nature of all other; insomuch that, as Aristotle saith, those things which in themselves are horrible, as cruel battles, unnatural monsters, are made in poetical imitation delightful. Truly, I have known men, that even with reading *Amadis de Gaule*, which, God knoweth, wanteth much of a perfect poesy, have found their hearts moved to the exercise of courtesy, liberality, and especially courage. Who readeth Æneas carrying old Anchises on his back, that wisheth not it were his fortune to perform so excellent an act? Whom do not those words of Turnus move, the tale of Turnus having planted his image in the imagination?

Fugientem hæc terra videbit?
Usque adeone mori miserum est?

Where the philosophers, as they scorn to delight, so must they be content little to move—saving wrangling whether virtue be the chief or the only good, whether the contemplative or the active life do excel—which Plato and Boethius well knew, and therefore made Mistress Philosophy very often borrow the masking raiment of Poesy. For even those hard-hearted evil men who think virtue a school-name, and know no other good but *indulgere genio*, and therefore despise the austere admonitions of the philosopher, and feel not the inward reason they stand upon, yet will be content to be delighted, which is all the good-fellow poet seemeth to promise; and so steal to see the form of goodness—which seen, they cannot but love—ere themselves be aware, as if they took a medicine of cherries. . . .

Is it the lyric that most displeaseth, who with his tuned lyre and well-accorded voice giveth praise, the reward of virtue, to virtuous acts; who giveth moral precepts and natural problems; who sometimes raiseth up his voice to the height of the heavens, in singing the lauds of the immortal God? Certainly I must confess mine own barbarousness; I never heard the old song of Percy and Douglas that I found not my heart moved more than with a trumpet; and yet it is sung but by some blind crowder, with no rougher voice than rude style; which being so evil apparelled in the dust and cobwebs of that uncivil age, what would it work, trimmed in the gorgeous eloquence of Pindar? In Hungary I have seen it the manner at all feasts, and other such meetings, to have songs of their ancestors' valor, which that right soldier-like nation think the chiefest kindlers of brave courage. The incomparable Lacedæmonians did not only carry that kind of music ever with them to the field, but even at home, as such songs were made, so were they all content to be singers of them; when the lusty men were to tell what they did, the old men what they had done, and the young men what they would do. And where a man may say that Pindar many times praiseth highly victories of small moment, matters rather of sport than virtue; as it may be answered, it was the fault of the poet, and not of the poetry, so indeed the chief fault was in the time and custom of the Greeks, who set those toys at so high a price that Philip of Macedon reckoned a horserace won at Olympus among his three fearful felicities. But as the unimitable Pindar often did, so is that kind most capable and most fit to awake the thoughts from the sleep of idleness, to embrace honorable enterprises. . . .

But I, that before ever I durst aspire unto the dignity am admitted into the company of the paper-blurrers, do find the very true cause of our wanting estimation is want of desert, taking upon us to be poets in despite of Pallas. Now wherein we want desert were a thankworthy labor to express; but if I knew, I should have mended myself. But as I never desired the title, so have I neglected the means to come by it; only, overmastered by some thoughts, I yielded an inky tribute unto them. Marry, they that delight in poesy itself should seek to know what they do and how they do; and especially look themselves in an unflattering glass of reason, if they be inclinable unto it. For poesy must not be drawn by the ears, it must be gently led, or rather it must lead; which was partly the cause that made the ancient learned affirm it was a divine gift, and no human skill, since all other knowledges lie ready for any that hath strength of wit, a poet no industry can make if his own genius be not carried into it. And therefore is it an old proverb: *orator fit, poeta nascitur*. . . .

Chaucer, undoubtedly, did excellently in his *Troilus and Cressida*; of whom, truly, I know not whether to marvel more, either that he in that misty time could see so clearly, or that we in this clear age walk so stumblingly after him. Yet had he great wants, fit to be forgiven in so reverend antiquity. I account the *Mirror of Magistrates* meetly furnished of beautiful parts; and in the Earl of Surrey's lyrics many things tasting of a noble birth, and worthy of a noble mind. *The Shepherd's Calendar* hath much poetry in his eclogues, indeed worthy the reading, if I be not deceived. That same framing of his style to an old rustic language I dare not allow, since neither Theocritus in Greek, Virgil in Latin, nor Sannazzaro in Italian did affect it. Besides these, I do not remember to have seen but few (to speak boldly) printed, that have poetical sinews in them. For proof whereof, let but most of the verses be put in prose, and then ask the meaning, and it will be found that one verse did but beget another, without ordering at the first what should be at the last; which becomes a confused mass of words, with a tinkling sound of rhyme, barely accompanied with reason.

Our tragedies and comedies not without cause cried out against, observing rules neither of honest civility nor of skillful poetry, excepting *Gorboduc* (again I say of those that I have seen), which notwithstanding as it is full of stately speeches and well-sounding phrases, climbing to the height of Seneca's style, and as full of notable morality, which it doth most delightfully teach, and so obtain the very end of poesy; yet in truth it is very defectious in the circumstances, which grieveth me, because it might not remain as an exact model of all tragedies. For it is faulty both in place and time, the two necessary companions of all corporal actions; for where the stage should always represent but one place, and the uttermost time presupposed in it should be, both by Aristotle's precept and common reason, but one day, there is both many days and many places inartificially imagined.

But if it be so in *Gorboduc*, how much more in all the rest? where you shall have Asia of the one side, and Afric of the other, and so many other under-kingdoms, that the player, when he cometh in, must ever begin with telling where he is, or else the tale will not be conceived. Now ye shall have three ladies walk to gather flowers, and then we must believe the stage to be a garden. By and by we hear news of shipwreck in the same place, and then we are to blame if we accept it not for a rock. Upon the back of that comes out a hideous monster with fire and smoke, and then the miserable beholders are bound to take it for a cave. While in the meantime two armies fly in, represented with four swords and bucklers, and then what hard heart will not receive it for a pitched field?

Now of time they are much more liberal. For ordinary it is that two young princes fall in love; after many traverses she is got with child, delivered of a fair boy, he is lost, groweth a man, falleth in love, and is ready to get another child,—and all this in two hours' space; which how absurd it is in sense even sense may imagine, and art hath taught, and all ancient examples justified, and at this day the ordinary players in Italy will not err in. Yet will some bring in an example of *Eunuchus* in Terence, that containeth matter of two days, yet far short of twenty years. True it is, and so was it to be played in two days, and so fitted to the time it set forth. And though Plautus have in one place done amiss, let us hit with him, and not miss with him. But they will say, How then shall we set forth a story which containeth both many places and many times? And do they not know that a tragedy is tied to the laws of poesy, and not of history; not bound to follow the story, but having liberty either to feign a quite new matter, or to frame the history to the most tragical conveniency? Again, many things may be told which cannot be showed,—if they know the difference betwixt reporting and representing. As for example I may speak, though I am here, of Peru, and in speech digress from that to the description of Calicut; but in action I cannot represent it without Pacolet's horse. And so was the manner the ancients took, by some *nuntius* to recount things done in former time or other place.

Lastly, if they will represent a history, they must not, as Horace saith, begin *ab ovo*, but they must come to the principal point of that one action which they will represent. By example this will be best expressed. I have a story of young Polydorus, delivered for safety's sake, with great riches, by his father Priamus to Polymnestor, King of Thrace, in the Trojan war time. He, after some years, hearing the overthrow of Priamus, for to make the treasure his own murdereth the child; the body of the child is taken up by Hecuba; she, the same day, findeth a sleight to be revenged most cruelly of the tyrant. Where now would one of our tragedy-writers begin, but with the delivery of the child? Then should he sail over into Thrace, and so spend I know not how many years, and travel numbers of places. But where doth Euripides? Even with the finding of the body, leaving the rest to be told by the spirit of Polydorus. This needs no further to be enlarged; the dullest wit may conceive it.

But, besides these gross absurdities, how all their plays be neither right tragedies nor right comedies, mingling kings and clowns, not because the matter so carrieth it, but thrust in the clown by head and shoulders to play a part in majestical matters, with neither decency nor discretion; so as neither the admiration and commiseration, nor the right sportfulness, is by their mongrel tragi-comedy obtained. I know Apuleius did somewhat so, but that is a thing recounted with space of time, not represented in one moment; and I know the ancients have one or two examples of tragi-comedies, as Plautus hath *Amphytrio*. But, if we mark them well, we shall find that they never, or very daintily, match hornpipes and funerals. So falleth it out that, having indeed no right comedy in that comical part of our tragedy, we have nothing but scurrility, unworthy of any chaste ears, or some extreme show of doltishness, indeed fit to lift up a loud laughter, and nothing else; where the whole tract of a comedy should be full of delight, as the tragedy should be still maintained in a well-raised admiration.

But our comedians think there is no delight without laughter, which is very wrong; for though laughter may come with delight, yet cometh it not of delight, as though delight should be the cause of laughter; but well may one thing breed both together. Nay, rather in themselves they have, as it were, a kind of contrariety. For delight we scarcely do but in things that have a conveniency to ourselves, or to the general nature; laughter almost ever cometh of things most disproportioned to ourselves and nature. Delight hath a joy in it either permanent or present; laughter hath only a scornful tickling. For example, we are ravished with delight to see a fair woman, and yet are far from being moved to laughter. We laugh at deformed creatures, wherein certainly we cannot delight. We delight in good chances, we laugh at mischances. We delight to hear the happiness of our friends and country, at which he were worthy to be laughed at that would laugh. We shall, contrarily, laugh sometimes to find a matter quite mistaken and go down the hill against the bias, in the mouth of some such men, as for the respect of them one shall be heartily sorry he cannot choose but laugh, and so is rather pained than delighted with laughter. Yet deny I not but that they may go well together. For as in Alexander's picture well set out we delight without laughter, and in twenty mad antics we laugh without delight; so in Hercules, painted, with his great beard and furious countenance, in woman's attire, spinning at Omphale's commandment, it breedeth both delight and laughter; for the representing of so strange a power in love procureth delight, and the scornfulness of the action stirreth laughter.

But I speak to this purpose, that all the end of the comical part be not upon such scornful matters as stir laughter only, but mixed with it that delightful teaching which is the end of poesy. And the great fault, even in that point of laughter, and forbidden plainly by Aristotle, is that they stir laughter in sinful things, which are rather execrable than ridiculous; or in miserable, which are rather to be pitied than scorned. For what is it to make folks gape at a wretched beggar or a beggarly clown, or, against law of hospitality, to jest at strangers because they speak not English so well as we do? What do we learn? since it is certain,

Nil habet infelix paupertas durius in se,
Quam quod ridiculos homines facit.

But rather a busy loving courtier; a heartless threatening Thraso; a self-wise-seeming schoolmaster; a wry-transformed traveler: these if we saw walk in stage-names, which we play naturally, therein were delightful laughter and teaching delightfulness,—as in the other, the tragedies of Buchanan do justly bring forth a divine admiration.

But I have lavished out too many words of this play-matter. I do it, because as they are excelling parts of poesy, so is there none so much used in England, and none can be more pitifully abused; which, like an unmannerly daughter, showing a bad education, causeth her mother Poesy's honesty to be called in question.

Other sorts of poetry almost have we none, but that lyrical kind of songs and sonnets, which, Lord if he gave us so good minds, how well it might be employed, and with how heavenly fruits both private and public, in singing the praises of the immortal beauty, the immortal goodness of that

God who giveth us hands to write, and wits to conceive!—of which we might well want words, but never matter; of which we could turn our eyes to nothing, but we should ever have new-budding occasions.

But truly, many of such writings as come under the banner of unresistible love, if I were a mistress would never persuade me they were in love; so coldly they apply fiery speeches, as men that had rather read lovers' writings, and so caught up certain swelling phrases—which hang together like a man which once told me the wind was at north-west and by south, because he would be sure to name winds enough—than that in truth they feel those passions, which easily, as I think, may be bewrayed by that same forcibleness, or *energia* (as the Greeks call it) of the writer. But let this be a sufficient, though short note, that we miss the right use of the material point of poesy.

Now for the outside of it, which is words, or (as I may term it) diction, it is even well worse, so is that honey-flowing matron eloquence apparelled, or rather disguised, in a courtesan-like painted affectation: one time with so far-fet words, that many seem monsters—but must seem strangers—to any poor Englishman; another time with coursing of a letter, as if they were bound to follow the method of a dictionary; another time with figures and flowers extremely winter-starved.

But I would this fault were only peculiar to versifiers, and had not as large possession among prose-printers, and, which is to be marvelled, among many scholars, and, which is to be pitied, among some preachers. Truly I could wish—if at least I might be so bold to wish in a thing beyond the reach of my capacity—the diligent imitators of Tully and Demosthenes (most worthy to be imitated) did not so much keep Nizolian paper-books of their figures and phrases, as by attentive translation, as it were, devour them whole, and make them wholly theirs. For now they cast sugar and spice upon every dish that is served to the table; like those Indians, not content to wear earrings at the fit and natural place of the ears, but they will thrust jewels through their nose and lips, because they will be sure to be fine. . . .

Now of versifying there are two sorts, the one ancient, the other modern. The ancient marked the quantity of each syllable, and according to that framed his verse; the modern observing only number, with some regard of the accent, the chief life of it standeth in that like sounding of the words, which we call rhyme. Whether of these be the more excellent would bear many speeches; the ancient no doubt more fit for music, both words and tune observing quantity; and more fit lively to express divers passions, by the low or lofty sound of the well-weighed syllable. The latter likewise with his rhyme striketh a certain music to the ear; and, in fine, since it doth delight, though by another way, it obtaineth the same purpose; there being in either, sweetness, and wanting in neither, majesty. Truly the English, before any other vulgar language I know, is fit for both sorts. For, for the ancient, the Italian is so full of vowels that it must ever be cumbered with elisions; the Dutch so, of the other side, with consonants, that they cannot yield the sweet sliding fit for a verse. The French in his whole language hath not one word that hath his accent in the last syllable saving two, called antepenultima, and little more hath the Spanish; and therefore very gracelessly may they use dactyls. The English is subject to none of these defects. Now for rhyme, though we do not observe quantity, yet we observe the accent very precisely, which other languages either cannot do, or will not do so absolutely. That cæsura, or breathing-place in the midst of the verse, neither Italian nor Spanish have, the French and we never almost fail of.

Lastly, even the very rhyme itself the Italian cannot put in the last syllable, by the French named the masculine rhyme, but still in the next to the last, which the French call the female, or the next before that, which the Italians term *sdrucciola.* The example of the former is *buono: suono;* of the *sdrucciola* is *femina: semina.* The French, of the other side, hath both the male, as *bon: son,* and the female, as *plaise: taise;* but the *sdrucciola* he hath not. Where the English hath all three, as *due: true; father: rather; motion: potion;* with much more which might be said, but that already I find the triflingness of this discourse is much too much enlarged.

So that since the ever praiseworthy poesy is full of virtue-breeding delightfulness, and void of no gift that ought to be in the noble name of learning; since the blames laid against it are either false or feeble; since the cause why it is not esteemed in England is the fault of poet-apes, not poets; since, lastly, our tongue is most fit to honor poesy, and to be honored by poesy; I conjure you all that have had the evil luck to read this ink-wasting toy of mine, even in the name of the Nine Muses, no more to scorn the sacred mysteries of poesy; no more to laugh at the name of poets, as though they were next inheritors to fools; no more to jest at the reverend title of a 'rhymer'; but to believe, with Aristotle, that they were the ancient treasurers of the Grecians' divinity; to believe, with Bembus, that they were the first bringers-in of all civility; to believe, with Scaliger, that no philosopher's precepts can sooner make you an honest man than the reading of Virgil; to believe, with Clauserus, the translator of Cornutus, that it pleased the heavenly deity by Hesiod and Homer, under the veil of fables, to give us all knowledge, logic, rhetoric, philosophy natural and moral, and *quid non;* to believe, with me, that there are many mysteries contained in poetry which of purpose were written darkly, lest by profane wits it should be abused; to believe, with Landino, that they are so beloved of the gods, that whatsoever they write proceeds of a divine fury; lastly, to believe themselves, when they tell you they will make you immortal by their verses. . . .

But if—fie of such a but!—you be born so near the dull-making cataract of Nilus, that you cannot hear the planet-like music of poetry; if you have so earth-creeping a mind that it cannot lift itself up to look to the sky of poetry, or rather, by a certain rustical disdain, will become such a mome as to be a Momus of poetry; then, though I will not wish unto you the ass's ears of Midas, nor to be driven by a poet's verses, as Bubonax was, to hang himself; nor to be rhymed to death, as is said to be done in Ireland; yet thus much curse I must send you in the behalf of all poets:

that while you live you live in love, and never get favor for lacking skill
of a sonnet; and when you die, your memory die from the earth for want
of an epitaph.

BEN JONSON

From *Advocates Ms. 33. 3. 19*, Edinburgh

*Informations by Ben Jonson to W[illiam] D[rummond] when he came to
Scotland upon foot, 1619.*

That he had an intention to perfect an epic poem entitled *Heroölogia*, of
the worthies of his country roused by fame, and was to dedicate it to his
country; it is all in couplets, for he detesteth all other rhymes. Said he had
written a discourse of poesy both against Campion and Daniel, especially this
last, where he proves couplets to be the bravest sort of verses, especially when
they are broken like hexameters, and that cross rhymes and stanzas, because
the purpose would lead him beyond eight lines to conclude, were all
forced. . . .

His censure of the English poets was this: that Sidney did not keep a de-
corum in making everyone speak as well as himself.

Spenser's stanzas pleased him not, nor his matter; the meaning of which
allegory he [Spenser] had delivered in papers to Sir Walter Ralegh.

Samuel Daniel was a good honest man, had no children, but no poet.

That Michael Drayton's *Poly-Olbion*, if [he] had performed what he
promised to write (the deeds of all the worthies) had been excellent; his
long verses pleased him not.

That Sylvester's translation of Du Bartas was not well done, and that he
wrote his verses before it, ere he understood to confer. Nor that of Fairfax
his [translation of Tasso].

That the translations of Homer and Virgil in long Alexandrines were but
prose.

That John Harington's Ariosto, under all translations, was the worst; that
when Sir John Harington desired him to tell the truth of his epigrams, he
answered him that he loved not the truth, for they were narrations, and not
epigrams.

That Warner, since the King's coming to England, [ha]d marred all his
Albion's England.

That Donne's *Anniversary* was profane and full of blasphemies; that he
told Mr. Donne if it had been written of the Virgin Mary it had been
something; to which he answered that he described the idea of a woman,
and not as she was; that Donne, for not keeping of accent, deserved hanging.

That Shakespeare wanted art.

That Sharpham, Day, Dekker, were all rogues, and that Minsheu was one.

That Abraham Fraunce, in his English hexameters, was a fool.

That next himself, only Fletcher and Chapman could make a mask. . . .

He cursed Petrarch for redacting verses to sonnets, which he said were like the tyrant's bed, where some who were too short were racked, others too long, cut short. . . .

His censure of my verses was that they were all good, especially my epitaph of the prince, save that they smelled too much of the schools and were not after the fancy of the time; for a child, says he, may write after the fashion of the Greeks and Latin verses in running; yet that he wished, to please the King, that piece of *Forth Feasting* had been his own.

He esteemeth John Donne the first poet in the world in some things; his verses of the Lost Chain he hath by heart, and that passage of the *Calm, that dust and feathers do not stir, all was so quiet*. Affirmeth Donne to have written all his best pieces ere he was 25 years old. . . .

For a heroic poem, he said there was no such ground as King Arthur's fiction, and that S. P. Sidney had an intention to have transformed all his *Arcadia* to the stories of King Arthur.

His acquaintance and behavior with poets living with him.

Daniel was at jealousies with him.

Drayton feared him, and he esteemed not of him.

That Francis Beaumont loved too much himself and his own verses. . . .

Sir W. Alexander was not half kind unto him, and neglected him because a friend to Drayton.

That Sir R. Aytoun loved him dearly.

Nid Field was his scholar, and he had read to him the Satires of Horace and some Epigrams of Martial. . . .

That Chapman and Fletcher were loved of him.

Overbury was first his friend, then turned his mortal enemy. . . .

That the Irish having robbed Spenser's goods, and burnt his house and a little child, new-born, he and his wife escaped, and after he died for lack of bread in King Street; and refused 20 pieces, sent to him by my Lord of Essex, and said he was sorry he had no time to spend them.

That in that paper S. W. Ralegh had of the Allegories of his *Fairy Queen*, by the blating [blatant] beast, the Puritans were understood; by the false Duessa, the Q. of Scots.

That Southwell was hanged, yet so he had written that piece of his, *The burning babe*, he would have been content to destroy many of his. . . .

That Donne himself, for not being understood, would perish. . . .

Shakespeare, in a play, brought in a number of men saying they had suffered shipwreck in Bohemia, where there is no sea near by some 100 miles. . . .

S. P. Sidney was no pleasant man in countenance, his face being spoiled with pimples and of high blood and long; that my Lord Lisle, now Earl of Worcester [error for Leicester], his eldest son, resembleth him. . . .

He was a minister's son; he himself was posthumous, born a month after his father's decease; brought up poorly; put to school by a friend; his master, Camden; after taken from it and put to another craft, I think was to be a wright or bricklayer, which he could not endure; then went he to the Low Countries, but returning soon, he betook himself to his wonted studies. In his service in the Low Countries, he had, in the face of both the camps, killed an enemy and taken *opima spolia* from him, and since his coming to England, being appealed to the fields, he had killed his adversary, which had hurt him in the arm, and whose sword was ten inches longer than his; for the which he was imprisoned, and almost at the gallows. Then took he his religion by trust of a priest who visited him in prison; thereafter he was 12 years a papist. He was Master of Arts in both the Universities, by their favor, not his study. He married a wife who was a shrew, yet honest. . . .

He had many quarrels with Marston, beat him and took his pistol from him, wrote his *Poetaster* on him; the beginning of them were that Marston represented him in the stage. . . .

S. W. Ralegh sent him governor with his son, *anno* 1613, to France. This youth being knavishly inclined, among other pastimes (as the setting of the favor of damosels on a cod-piece), caused him to be drunken, and dead drunk, so that he knew not where he was; thereafter laid him on a car which he made to be drawn by pioneers through the streets, at every corner showing his governor stretched out, and telling them that was a more lively image of the crucifix than any they had. At which sport young Ralegh's mother delighted much, saying his father young was so inclined, though the father abhorred it. . . .

Every first day of the new year he had 20£ sent him from the Earl of Pembroke, to buy books. . . .

He hath consumed a whole night in lying looking to his great toe, about which he hath seen Tartars and Turks, Romans and Carthaginians, fight in his imagination. . . .

Queen Elizabeth never saw herself, after she became old, in a true glass. They painted her, and sometimes would vermillion her nose. She had always about, Christmas Evens, set dice that threw sixes or five, and she knew not they were other, to make her win and esteem herself fortunate. .

His opinion of verses:

That he wrote all his first in prose, for so his master Camden had learned him. . . .

A great many epigrams were ill, because they expressed in the end what should have been understood by what was said. . . .

Some loved running verses, *plus mihi com[m]a placet*. . . .

He dissuaded me from poetry, for that she had beggared him, when he might have been a rich lawyer, physician, or merchant. . . .

He was better versed, and knew more in Greek and Latin, than all the poets in England, and quintessence their brains. . . .

He is a great lover and praiser of himself, a contemner and scorner of others, given rather to lose a friend than a jest, jealous of every word and action of those about him (especially after drink, which is one of the elements in which he liveth), a dissembler of ill parts which reign in him, a bragger of some good that he wanteth, thinketh nothing well but what either he himself, or some of his friends and countrymen, hath said or done. He is passionately kind and angry, careless either to gain or keep, vindictive, but if he be well answered, at himself. . . .

FROM *Works*, 1641

Timber, or Discoveries made upon men and matter, as they flowed out of his daily readings.

. . . I know nothing can conduce more to letters than to examine the writings of the ancients, and not to rest in their sole authority, or take all upon trust from them, provided the plagues of judging and pronouncing against them be away, such as are envy, bitterness, precipitation, impudence, and scurrile scoffing. For to all the observations of the ancients we have our own experience, which if we will use and apply, we have better means to pronounce. It is true they opened the gates, and made the way that went before us, but as guides, not commanders: *Non domini nostri, sed duces fuere.* Truth lies open to all; it is no man's several. *Patet omnibus veritas; nondum est occupata. Multum ex illa, etiam futuris relicta est.*

If in some things I dissent from others whose wit, industry, diligence, and judgment I look up at and admire, let me not therefore hear presently of ingratitude and rashness. For I thank those that have taught me, and will ever; but yet dare not think the scope of their labor and inquiry was to envy their posterity what they also could add and find out.

If I err, pardon me: *Nulla ars simul et inventa est et absoluta.* I do not desire to be equal to those that went before; but to have my reason examined with theirs, and so much faith to be given them, or me, as those shall evict. I am neither author nor fautor of any sect. I will have no man addict himself to me; but if I have anything right, defend it as truth's, not mine, save as it conduceth to a common good. It profits not me to have any man fence or fight for me, to flourish, or take a side. Stand for truth, and 'tis enough. . . .

Nothing in our age, I have observed, is more preposterous than the running judgments upon poetry and poets, when we shall hear those things commended and cried up for the best writings which a man would scarce vouchsafe to wrap any wholesome drug in; he would never light his tobacco with them. And those men almost named for miracles who yet are so vile that if a man should go about to examine and correct them, he must make all they have done but one blot. Their good is so entangled with their bad as forcibly one must draw on the other's death with it. . . . Yet their vices have not hurt them; nay, a great many they have profited, for they have been loved for nothing else. And this false opinion grows strong against the best men, if once it take root with the ignorant. Cestius, in his time, was preferred to Cicero, so far as the ignorant durst. They learned him without book, and had him often in their mouths; but a man cannot imagine that thing so foolish or rude but will find and enjoy an admirer; at least a reader or spectator. The puppets are seen now in despite of the players; Heath's epigrams and the Sculler's [Taylor, the water poet's] poems have their applause. There are never wanting that dare prefer the worst preachers, the worst pleaders, the worst poets; not that the better have left to write or speak better, but that they that hear them judge worse; *Non illi peius dicunt, sed hi corruptius judicant.* Nay, if it were put to the question of the water-rhymer's works against Spenser's, I doubt not but they would find more suffrages; because the most favor common vices, out of a prerogative the vulgar have to lose their judgments and like that which is naught.

Poetry, in this latter age, hath proved but a mean mistress to such as have wholly addicted themselves to her, or given their names up to her family. They who have but saluted her on the by, and now and then tendered their visits, she hath done much for, and advanced in the way of their own professions—both the law and the gospel—beyond all they could have hoped or done for themselves without her favor. Wherein she doth emulate the judicious but preposterous bounty of the time's grandees, who accumulate all they can upon the parasite or fresh-man in their friendship; but think an old client or honest servant bound by his place to write and starve.

Indeed, the multitude commend writers as they do fencers or wrestlers, who, if they come in robustiously, and put for it with a deal of violence, are received for the braver fellows; when many times their own rudeness is a cause of their disgrace, and a slight touch of their adversary gives all that boisterous force the foil. But in these things the unskillful are naturally deceived, and judging wholly by the bulk, think rude things greater than polished, and scattered more numerous than composed. Nor think this only to be true in the sordid multitude, but the neater sort of our gallants; for all are the multitude, only they differ in clothes, not in judgment or understanding.

I remember the players have often mentioned it as an honor to Shakespeare, that in his writing, whatsoever he penned, he never blotted out line. My answer hath been, 'Would he had blotted a thousand,' which they thought a malevolent speech. I had not told posterity this but for their ignorance, who choose that circumstance to commend their friend by wherein he most faulted; and to justify mine own candor, for I loved the man, and do honor his memory on this side idolatry as much as any. He was, indeed, honest, and of an open and free nature; had an excellent fancy, brave notions, and gentle expressions, wherein he flowed with that facility that sometime it was necessary he should be stopped. *Sufflaminandus erat,* as Augustus said of Haterius. His wit was in his own power; would the rule of it had been so too. Many times he fell into those things, could not escape laughter, as when he said in the person of Cæsar, one speaking to him: 'Cæsar, thou dost me wrong.' He replied: 'Cæsar did never wrong but with just cause'; and such like, which were ridiculous. But he redeemed his vices with his virtues. There was ever more in him to be praised than to be pardoned. . . .

. . . For a man to write well, there are required three necessaries: to read the best authors, observe the best speakers, and much exercise of his own style. In style, to consider what ought to be written, and after what manner, he must first think and excogitate his matter, then choose his words, and examine the weight of either. Then take care in placing and ranking both matter and words, that the composition be comely, and to do this with diligence and often. No matter how slow the style be at first, so it be labored and accurate; seek the best, and be not glad of the forward conceits, or first words, that offer themselves to us; but judge of what we invent, and order what we approve. Repeat often what we have formerly written; which beside that it helps the consequence, and makes the juncture better, it quickens the heat of imagination, that often cools in the time of setting down, and gives it new strength, as if it grew lustier by the going back. As we see in the contention of leaping, they jump farthest that fetch their race largest; or, as in throwing a dart or javelin, we force back our arms to make our loose the stronger. Yet if we have a fair gale of wind, I forbid not the steering out of our sail, so the favor of the gale deceive us not. For all that we invent doth please us in the conception, or birth, else we would never set it down. But the safest is to return to our judgment, and handle over again those things the easiness of which might make them justly suspected. So did the best writers in their beginnings; they imposed upon themselves care and industry; they did nothing rashly; they obtained first to write well, and then custom made it easy and a habit. By little and little their matter showed itself to 'hem more plentifully—their words answered, their composition followed—and all, as in a well-ordered family, presented itself in the place. So that the sum of all is, ready writing makes not good writing, but good writing brings on ready writing. Yet, when we think we have got the faculty, it is even then good to resist it, as to give a horse a check sometimes with bit, which doth not so much stop his course as stir his mettle. Again, whither a man's genius is best able to reach, thither it should more and more contend, lift and dilate itself; as men of low stature raise themselves on their toes, and so ofttimes get even, if not eminent. Besides, as it is fit for grown and able writers to stand of themselves, and work with their own strength, to trust and endeavor by their own faculties, so it is fit for the beginner and learner to study others and the best. For the mind and memory are more sharply exercised in comprehending another man's things than our own; and such as accustom themselves and are familiar with the best authors shall ever and anon find somewhat of them in themselves, and in the expression of their minds, even when they feel it not, be able to utter something like theirs, which hath an authority above their own. Nay, sometimes it is the reward of a man's study, the praise of quoting another man fitly; and though a man be more prone and able for one kind of writing than another, yet he must exercise all. For as in an instrument, so in style, there must be a harmony and concent of parts.

. . . And as it is fit to read the best authors to youth first, so let them be of the openest and clearest, as Livy before Sallust, Sidney before Donne. And beware of letting them taste Gower or Chaucer at first, lest, falling too much in love with antiquity, and not apprehending the weight, they grow rough and barren in language only. When their judgments are firm, and out of danger, let them read both the old and the new; but no less take heed that their new flowers and sweetness do not as much corrupt as the others' dryness and squalor, if they choose not carefully. Spenser, in affecting the ancients, writ no language; yet I would have him read for his matter, but as Virgil read Ennius. The reading of Homer and Virgil is counselled by Quintilian as the best way of informing youth and confirming man; for, besides that the mind is raised with the height and sublimity of such a verse, it takes spirit from the greatness of the matter, and is tincted with the best things. Tragic and lyric poetry is good too, and comic with the best, if the manners of the reader be once in safety. In the Greek poets, as also in Plautus, we shall see the economy and disposition of poems better observed than in Terence and the later, who thought the sole grace and virtue of their fable the sticking in of sentences, as ours do the forcing in of jests. . . .

It is not the passing through these learnings that hurts us, but the dwelling and sticking about them. To descend to those extreme anxieties and foolish cavils of grammarians is able to break a wit in pieces, being a work of manifold misery and vainness, to be *elementarii senes*. Yet even letters are, as it were, the bank of words, and restore themselves to an author as the pawns of language. But talking and eloquence are not the same: to speak, and to speak well, are two things. A fool may talk, but a wise man speaks; and out of the observation, knowledge, and use of things, many writers perplex their readers and hearers with mere nonsense. Their writings need sunshine. Pure and neat language I love, yet plain and customary. A barbarous phrase hath often made me out of love with a good sense, and doubtful writing hath wracked me beyond my patience. The reason why a poet is said that he ought to have all knowledges is that he should not be ignorant of the most, especially of those he will handle. And indeed, when the attaining of them is possible, it were a sluggish and base thing to despair; for frequent imitation of anything becomes a habit quickly. If a man should prosecute as much as could be said of everything, his work would find no end. . . .

Custom is the most certain mistress of language, as the public stamp makes the current money. But we must not be too frequent with the mint, every day coining, nor fetch words from the extreme and utmost ages; since the chief virtue of a style is perspicuity, and nothing so vicious in it as to need an interpreter. Words borrowed of antiquity do lend a kind of majesty to style, and are not without their delight sometimes; for they have the authority of years, and out of their intermission do win to themselves a kind of gracelike newness. But the eldest of the present, and newness of the past language, is the best. For what was the ancient language, which some men so dote upon, but the ancient custom? Yet when I name custom, I understand not the vulgar custom; for that were a precept no less dangerous to language than life, if we should speak or live after the manners of the vulgar; but that I call custom of speech which is the consent of the learned, as custom of life which is the consent of the good. Virgil was most loving of antiquity, yet how rarely doth he insert *aquai* and *pictai!* Lucretius is scabrous and rough in these; he seeks 'hem as some do Chaucerisms with us, which were better expunged and banished. Some words are to be culled out for ornament and color, as we gather flowers to straw houses or make garlands; but they are better when they grow to our style as in a meadow, where, though the mere grass and greenness delights, yet the variety of flowers doth heighten and beautify. Marry, we must not play or riot too much with them, as in paronomasies; nor use too swelling or ill-sounding words, *quæ per salebras, altaque saxa cadunt.* It is true there is no sound but shall find some lovers, as the bitterest confections are grateful to some palates. Our composition must be more accurate in the beginning and end than in the midst, and in the end more than in the beginning, for through the midst the stream bears us; and this is attained by custom more than care or diligence. We must express readily and fully, not profusely; there is difference between a liberal and prodigal hand. As it is a great point of art, when our matter requires it, to enlarge and veer out all sail, so to take it in and contract it is of no less praise, when the argument doth ask it. Either of them hath their fitness in the place. . . .

Nothing is more ridiculous than to make an author a dictator, as the schools have done Aristotle. The damage is infinite knowledge receives by it; for to many things a man should owe but a temporary belief, and a suspension of his own judgment, not an absolute resignation of himself, or a perpetual captivity. Let Aristotle and others have their dues; but if we can make farther discoveries of truth and fitness than they, why are we envied? Let us beware, while we strive to add, we do not diminish or deface; we may improve, but not augment. . . .

I am not of that opinion to conclude a poet's liberty within the narrow limits of laws which either the grammarians or philosophers prescribe. For before they found out those laws there were many excellent poets that fulfilled them, amongst whom none more perfect than Sophocles, who lived a little before Aristotle. Which of the Greeklings durst ever give precepts to Demosthenes? or to Pericles, whom the age surnamed Heavenly, because he seemed to thunder and lighten with his language? or to Alcibiades, who had rather nature for his guide than art for his master? But whatsoever nature at any time dictated to the most happy, or long exercise to the most laborious, that the wisdom and learning of Aristotle hath brought into an art, because he understood the causes of things; and what other men did by chance or custom he doth by reason; and not only found out the way not to err, but the short way we should take not to err. . . .

'METAPHYSICAL' POETRY

FROM *The Works of William Drummond of Hawthornden*, 1711

To his much honored friend Dr. Arthur Johnston, Physician to the King,
[*c.* 1630]

. . . In vain have some men of late, transformers of everything, consulted upon her [poetry's] reformation, and endeavored to abstract her to metaphysical ideas and scholastic quiddities, denuding her of her own habits and those ornaments with which she hath amused the world some thousand years. Poesy is not a thing that is yet in the finding and search, or which may be otherwise found out, being already condescended upon by all nations and, as it were, established *jure gentium* amongst Greeks, Romans, Italians, French, Spaniards. Neither do I think that a good piece of poesy, which Homer, Virgil, Ovid, Petrarch, Bartas, Ronsard, Boscan, Garcilasso, if they were alive and had that language, could not understand and reach the sense of the writer. Suppose these men could find out some other new idea like poesy, it should be held as if nature should bring forth some new animal, neither man, horse, lion, dog, but which had some members of all, if they had been proportionable and by right symmetry set together. What is not like the ancients and conform to those rules which hath been agreed unto by all times may, indeed, be something like unto poesy, but it is no more poesy than a monster is a man. Monsters breed admiration at the first, but have ever some strange loathsomeness in them at last. . . .

W. Drummond.

FROM SIR ASTON COCKAIN'S *Small Poems of Divers Sorts*, 1658

A funeral elegy on my dear cousin, Mistress Elizabeth Reppington

> Stifle therefore, my muse, at their first birth
> All thoughts that may reflect upon the earth;
> Be metaphysical, disdaining to
> Fix upon anything that is belôw.

FROM JOHN DRYDEN'S *Discourse concerning the Original and Progress of Satire*, 1693

[Donne] affects the metaphysics, not only in his satires, but in his amorous verses, where nature only should reign; and perplexes the minds of the fair sex with nice speculations of philosophy, when he should engage their hearts, and entertain them with the softnesses of love. . . .

INTRODUCTIONS AND NOTES

We have used the following abbreviations:

Bibl. Acc. = J. P. Collier, *Bibliographical and Critical Account of the rarest books in the English language,* two volumes, London, 1865.

D. N. B. = *Dictionary of National Biography,* sixty-three volumes, London, 1885–1900.

E. L. = Norman Ault, *Elizabethan Lyrics,* London, 1925.

J. E. G. P. = *Journal of English and Germanic Philology,* University of Illinois.

M. L. N. = *Modern Language Notes,* Johns Hopkins University.

M. L. Q. = *Modern Language Quarterly,* London.

M. L. R. = *The Modern Language Review,* Cambridge University Press.

M. P. = *Modern Philology,* University of Chicago Press.

O. E. D. = *A New English Dictionary,* ten volumes, Oxford, 1888 ff.

P. M. L. A. = *Publications* of the Modern Language Association of America.

R. E. S. = *The Review of English Studies,* London, Sidgwick and Jackson.

S. P. = *Studies in Philology,* University of North Carolina.

T. L. S. = 'Literary Supplement' of *The London Times.*

Tr. Roy. Hist. Soc. = *Transactions* of the Royal Historical Society, London.

In quoting from or referring to contemporary or early sources of information, we have economized space by giving only the author's name. The following list will identify the edition used:

Aubrey = *Brief Lives . . . by John Aubrey* (ed. by A. Clark), two volumes, Oxford, 1898.

Baker = Richard Baker, *A Chronicle of the Kings of England,* London, 1674.

Birch = Thomas Birch, *The Court and Times of James the First, containing a series of historical and confidential letters,* two volumes, London, 1849.

Chappell = W. Chappell, *Old English Popular Music* (ed. by H. E. Wooldridge), two volumes, London, 1893.

Clarendon = Edward Hyde, Earl of Clarendon, *The History of the Rebellion and Civil Wars in England* (ed. by W. D. Macray), six volumes, Oxford, 1888.

Dryden = *Essays of John Dryden* (ed. by W. P. Ker), two volumes, Oxford, 1900.

Evelyn = John Evelyn, *Diary* (ed. by A. Dobson), three volumes, London, 1906.

Fuller = Thomas Fuller, *The History of the Worthies of England,* London, 1662.

Howell = *Epistolæ Ho-Elianæ: The Familiar Letters of James Howell* (ed. by J. Jacobs), London, 1890.

Hunter = Joseph Hunter, *Chorus Vatum,* British Museum *Additional Mss.* 24487–92 (rotograph copy in the Newberry Library, Chicago).

Johnson = Samuel Johnson, *Lives of the English Poets* (ed. by G. B. Hill), three volumes, Oxford, 1905.

Langbaine = Gerard Langbaine, *An Account of the English Dramatic Poets,* Oxford, 1691.

Meres = Francis Meres, *Palladis Tamia* in G. Gregory Smith's *Elizabethan Critical Essays,* Vol. ii, Oxford, 1904.

Osborne = Francis Osborne, *Works,* London, 1682.

Phillips = Edward Phillips, *Theatrum Poetarum,* London, 1675.

Walton = Izaak Walton, *The Lives of John Donne, Sir Henry Wotton, Richard Hooker, George Herbert, and Robert Sanderson,* Oxford, 1927.

Winstanley = William Winstanley, *Lives of the most famous English poets,* London, 1687.

Wood = Anthony à Wood, *Athenæ Oxonienses* (ed. by P. Bliss), four volumes, London, 1813–20.

In the introductions to the various authors, under the heading 'Text,' we have given the location of the original copies from which our text is taken. The following list expands the abbreviated forms used.

Adams = Professor J. Q. Adams, Jr., Cornell University, Ithaca, New York.
Bodleian = The Bodleian Library, Oxford, England.
B. M. = The British Museum, London, England.
Cambridge = Cambridge University Library, Cambridge, England.
Chetham = Chetham's Library, Manchester, England.
Cornell = Cornell University Library, Ithaca, New York.
Harvard = Harvard College Library, Cambridge, Massachusetts.
Hebel = Professor J. W. Hebel, Cornell University, Ithaca, New York.
Hudson = Professor H. H. Hudson, Princeton University, Princeton, New Jersey.
Huntington = The Henry E. Huntington Library and Art Gallery, San Marino, California.
Mandel = Leon Mandel II, Chicago, Illinois.
New York = New York Public Library, New York City, New York.
Princeton = Princeton University Library, Princeton, New Jersey.
White = the late Mr. W. A. White, Brooklyn, New York.
Yale = Elizabethan Club, Yale University, New Haven, Connecticut.

In giving textual variants in the notes, we have cited the various editions by dates only. The edition may be identified by referring to the section 'Text' printed just above the notes to each author.

JOHN SKELTON

JOHN SKELTON (c. 1460–1529) stands as the most striking figure in English letters at the opening of the 16th century. He personifies the transition from the medieval England of the Plantagenets and the Wars of the Roses to the new national life which was beginning under Henry VII and Henry VIII. The poet seems to look back rather than forward, his work belonging with the tradition of Chaucer, Lydgate, Gower, and the medieval Latinists rather than with the fresh growth of poetry which, nourished by streams from Italy and the classics, came to flower and fruit in the seventy-five years after his death.

Skelton made a notable record as a student, evidently at Cambridge; by 1493 he had received from each University, and perhaps from the University of Louvain, the academic title of poet laureate. For a time he was tutor in the household of Henry VII, with the next Henry in his care. Although his temperament hardly fitted him for the duties of priesthood, he entered holy orders and became rector of Diss, a parish in Norfolk. He probably remained in residence very little, but kept up his connections with the court, where his plain speaking often made his hold upon favor a precarious one. Under Henry VIII Skelton seems at first to have flourished, receiving recognition practically equivalent to the modern laureateship. In 1522 he turned his satire upon Cardinal Wolsey, who had been to him something of a patron; the poems, *Why Come Ye Not to Court?* and *Speak, Parrot,* are the principal extant specimens of this personal satire. A few years later Wolsey's retaliatory movements forced Skelton to take sanctuary with the Abbot of Westminster; and there he remained, virtually a prisoner, until his death in 1529—four months before Wolsey's fall.

Skelton was a prolific writer, but many of the works which he lists as his own in *A Garland of Laurel* have not survived. Besides poems already mentioned or here represented, the most notable we have are *The Tunning of Elinor Rumming*, a realistic and jocular celebration of low life; *The Bowge of Court*, an allegorical satire upon life at court; *Ware the Hawk*, a diatribe against a curate who brought his hawk into the church at Diss; and *Magnificence*, the only one extant of three morality plays by the poet. Skelton's *Ballad of the Scottish King* (1513?) is usually accounted the first printed broadside. From the number of editions which appeared and from references made to him, it is plain that Skelton was considerably read throughout the 16th century; but that he was thought of as a rather crude jocular writer, admired more for his buffoonery and 'pith' than for any higher qualities. Modern readers have been attracted by his vigor and originality as well as by his occasionally eloquent lyricism. The succession of short 'breathless' lines, rhyming in no set order, which he came to adopt as his usual versification, has been termed 'Skeltonic meter' or 'Skeltoniads.' It was used by several minor satirists of the 16th century, and adapted by Drayton in his odes.

MODERN EDITIONS: *The Poetical Works* (ed. by A. Dyce), two volumes, London, 1843; *A Selection from the Poetical Works* (ed. by W. H. Williams), London, 1902; *Poems* (ed. by R. Hughes), London, 1924.

COMMENT: J. M. Berdan, *Early Tudor Poetry*, New York, 1920, Chaps. ii, iii.

TEXT: *Pithy, Pleasant, and Profitable Works of Master Skelton*, 1568 (22608), Bodleian.

3–5 *Philip Sparrow*] occasioned by the death of a pet sparrow belonging to a girl in the conventual school of the Black Nuns at Carow, near Norwich. This girl, Jane Scroupe (or Scrope), is presented as speaking throughout the poem. The passages here reprinted make up less than a fourth of the whole. *Philip Sparrow* was composed before 1508. 1 *Placebo*] the opening of the antiphon in the service of vespers for the dead. 3 *Dilexi*] another part of the same service. 12 beadrolls] prayer lists. 29 Worrowëd] worried; the original meaning of 'worry' was 'choke'; a later meaning was 'shake and tear with the teeth.' 34 stound] moment. 35 swound] 1568 reads 'sound'; but see *O.E.D.* 37 Unneth] hardly. 64 *Heu*, etc.] 'Alas, woe is me!' 66 *Ad Dominum*, etc.] Psalms cxx. 1. 69 marees] waters. 74 Alecto] with Megera (l. 78), one of the Erinyes, or Furies. 75 blo] blue-black, livid. 79 For] the reading of *c.* 1545; 1568 reads 'From'. 83 Proserpina's bower] Hades. 87 outray] vanquish. 89 From] the reading of *c.* 1545; 1568 reads 'For'. 100 keep his cut] 'A phrase of obscure origin, meaning something like: "To keep one's distance, be coy or reserved." Most of the later occurrences appear to refer to Skelton's *Phyllyp Sparrowe*, or at least, to have the same origin.' *O.E.D.* But see 'A bonny, bonny bird,' p. 407, l. 7. 109 propre] proper, handsome. prest] alert. 119 gressop] grasshopper.

123 slo] slay. 125 *Si iniquitates*] from the first antiphon in the burial service. 127 *De profundis clamavi*] Psalms cxxx. 1. 140 untwined] tore to pieces. 146 Lybany] Libya, the old name for Africa. 150 mantycors] fabled beasts having the face of a man, the body of a lion, and the tail of a scorpion. 152 Melanchates] one of Actæon's hounds. 163 Ind] India. gripes] griffins. 167 Lycaon] According to Ovid, King Lycaon of Arcadia was transformed into a wolf. 175 isles of Orchady] the Orkney islands; Skelton follows the Latin form *Orcadas*. 181 corage] heart, disposition.

5–7 *Colin Clout*] The selection here printed constitutes about one-eighth of the whole poem, supposed to contain one of Skelton's earliest attacks upon Wolsey, written about 1522. The name Colin Clout, here used to represent the speaker as a common man of the people, was adopted by Spenser for references to himself in pastoral poetry. 2 drive forth a snail] This, and making a sail of the tail of a herring, are chosen as types of futile actions. 15–37] These lines tell what people say of an author who attempts 'to teach or to preach.' 57 take] the reading of *c.* 1545; 1568 reads 'talke'. 66 blother] gabble. 69 in hudder-mudder] either in disorder or in secret. 77 seely] simple, harmless. 80 Unnethes] scarcely. 83 glomming] looking gloomy or stern mumming] disguising, playing a part; the word may also mean keeping silent, or mumbling. 89 catch] 1568 misprints 'cath'. forkèd cap] the mitre, emblem of the bishop's office. 90 lewd] base. 91 all beshrewed] altogether accursed. 98 appose] get near to. 99 crose] crozier, symbol of the bishop's office; 1568 reads 'crosse', but *c.* 1545 reads 'crose'. 103 simoniac] one who practises simony, the buying and selling of offices in the church. 104 harmoniac] a word of unknown antecedents and meaning; probably, a harmonizer. The whole expression may mean: 'One who practises simony is [to their way of thinking] merely helping maintain harmony.' 108 foresaid lay] the aforesaid laity. 110 anker] anchorite, hermit. 117 purple and pall] the rich saddle-cloth and trappings of the bishop's mule. Ostentation of wealth, throughout the 16th century, frequently took the form of luxurious trappings for the owner's mount. This passage probably pointed directly to Wolsey. 121 rotchets] a special kind of surplice. Raynes] linen manufactured at Rennes. 122 morrow's] morning's; *Harl. Ms.* reads 'marys', sometimes modernized as 'mare's.' 124 begarred] trimmed, faced; the reading of *c.* 1545; 1568 misprints 'begarded'. 128 Gil] like Jack of the Noke in the following line, a conventional name for a rustic. 136 fit] experience. Here Colin Clout turns from reporting what he has heard people say of the clergy, and addresses these directly. 142 ascry] cry out against, de-

nounce. 147 Poules] St. Paul's, the cathedral in London.

7 To Mistress Isabel Pennell] This and the following poem, *To Mistress Margaret Hussey*, are parts of the long work, *A Garland of Laurel* (in the edition of 1568 called *The Crown of Laurel*), 1600 lines in length. The whole was written in honor of the poet himself and of his works, which he lists. The two selections here given belong to a series of tributes to ladies whom Skelton presents as weaving for him a crown of laurel. 5 reflaring rosabell] fragrant fair rose. 6 flagrant] sometimes used in Skelton's time as the equivalent of 'fragrant.' camamell] camomile. 7 rosary] rose-tree. 10 nepte] mint. 11 jeloffer] gillyflower, one of the class which includes pinks and carnations. 13 Ennewèd] fresh, vivid.

7 To Mistress Margaret Hussey 3 gentil] The falcon was called 'gentil' or 'gentle' because of the careful breeding of the birds and because of the association of falconry with nobility and royalty. 4 hawk of the tower] a tower-hawk was one trained to soar and to fly high. 22 Isiphill] Hypsipyle, a beautiful woman of Lemnos, in classical legend; she appears in medieval romances. 23 Coliander] coriander, an aromatic herb. 24 pomander] a ball or bag containing perfumes, suspended from a cord about the neck or carried in the pocket. 25 Good] 1568 misprints 'Oood'. Cassaunder] Cassandra, daughter of Priam in the Trojan legend.

HENRY VIII

HENRY VIII (1491–1547) was early given a bent to letters and poetry by excellent tutors, among them John Skelton, who later boasted,

> The honor of England I learnèd to spell,
> In dignity royal that doth excel;
> Note and mark well this parcel:
> I gave him drink of the sugared well
> Of Helicon's waters crystalline,
> Acquainting him with the Muses nine.

The accession of Henry to the throne in 1509 lent encouragement to the literary men of the realm, and of all Europe; there can be no doubt that the advance of lyrical poetry in his reign received some impetus from the King himself. Henry's fondness for music led him to compose melodies and verses, all his extant poems having been written for singing. He played on the lute, the organ, and the harpsichord, and brought to court the best musicians he could find. One of his anthems, *O Lord, the Maker of all thing,* according to Pollard 'still remains a favorite in English cathedrals.'

MODERN EDITION: *Miscellaneous Writings,* Golden Cockerel Press, London, 1924.

TEXT: *Additional Ms.* 31922, B. M.

8 *Pastime with good company*] This song appears in two other mss., in one of which it is entitled *The King's ballad.* Latimer, in his second sermon preached before Edward VI, alludes to this song: 'Yet a king may take his pastime in hawking or hunting, or such like pleasures. But he must use them for recreation, when he is weary of weighty affairs, that he may return to them more lusty; and this is called *Pastime with good company.*' The music for this song is printed in Chappell, i. 42. 3 grutch] grouch, complain. lust] list. 5 pastance] pastime. 10 let] hinder.

SIR THOMAS MORE

SIR THOMAS MORE (1478–1535), humanist, statesman, and martyr, made his most important contribution to literature in his Latin *Utopia,* 1516. In common with other learned men of his time, however, he also tried his hand at verse, his best work in this kind being his large collection of Latin epigrams, in part translated from the Greek Anthology. In English verse he wrote a considerable series of poems upon Fortune and a jocular account 'how a sergeant would learn to play the friar.' His shorter English poems were written in his early youth, except for the two seven-line epigrams which he composed in prison during the last months of his life.

MODERN EDITION: *Selections from his English works* (ed. by P. S. and H. M. Allen), Oxford, 1924.

TEXT: *The Works of Sir T. More, Knight,* 1557 (18076), Cornell.

9 *Childhood*] This and the two poems following are taken from a series of nine, thus explained in *Works:* 'Master Thomas More in his youth devised in his father's house in London a goodly hanging of fine painted cloth, with nine pageants, and verses over every of those pageants; which verses expressed and declared what the images in those pageants represented.' Such poems may be classified as emblems, since they moralize a picture. 2 cockstele] a stick to throw at a cock, in the Shrovetide sport of cock-throwing. The game consisted in throwing sticks at a cock tied to a post, to try which player should succeed in knocking down or killing the fowl.

10 *Manhood* 6 swetter] sweeter.

10 *Two short ballettes . . .*] Fortune, her caprices, and the turning of her wheel, were often in More's thoughts at all periods of his life. In his youth he wrote in verse *The Book of the Fair Gentlewoman . . . Lady Fortune.*

10 *Lewis, the lost lover* 5–6] More seems to have in mind a Greek epigram which both he and his friend William Lily had translated into Latin years before. Lily's version, one that gained wide currency, follows:

Inveni portum, Spes et Fortuna valete,
Nil mihi vobiscum, ludite nunc alios.

('Hope and Fortune, farewell: I have reached the harbor. I have nothing more to do with you; sport now with others.') 7 thy] Fortune's.

JOHN HEYWOOD

JOHN HEYWOOD (*c.*1497–*c.*1580), a friend of Sir Thomas More's (whose niece he married), was a court musician and entertainer under Henry VIII, Edward VI, and Queen Mary. Because of his Catholic faith he left England after the death of Mary. In literature he is best known for his interludes, written for court performance, and for his epigrams. He also published a verse-dialogue upon marriage, containing all of the English proverbs he could collect, and a satirical poem having to do with religion, *The Spider and the Fly*, 1556. A collection of his epigrams appeared in 1550, to be followed by similar collections throughout the following decade; six hundred epigrams are included in the popular *Works* (1562, 1576, 1587, 1598). In common with most of his other writings, his epigrams are broadly humorous and thoroughly English in tone, owing little or nothing to classical models.

MODERN EDITIONS: *The Proverbs and Epigrams*, Spenser Society, 1867; *Proverbs, Epigrams, and Miscellanies* (ed. by J. S. Farmer), London, 1906.

COMMENT: R. W. Bolwell, *Life and Works of John Heywood*, New York, 1921.

TEXT: *Songs and Sonnets*, 1557 (13860), Bodleian; *Works*, 1562 (13285), Harvard.

11 *A praise of his lady*] This is a shortened version of a poem in *Harl. Ms.* 1703, headed 'A Description of a Most Noble Lady adewed [viewed?] by John Heywood, presently who advertising her years as face saith of her thus, in much eloquent phrase.' Stanzas at the end (omitted from *Songs and Sonnets*) also claim authorship for Heywood and tell that the poem was written of Princess (later Queen) Mary, when she was eighteen; hence in 1534 or 1535. 49] Ms. reads, 'How might we do to have a graff'. Bolwell suggests that the reading of *Songs and Sonnets* 'is more personal, for the anonymity of the subject and the author prevents embarrassment because of the indelicacy.'

12 *Of loving a dog*] Heywood wrote several hundred of these epigrams upon proverbs and his were imitated by some later epigrammatists, notably Davies of Hereford and Herrick. See also Sir John Harington's epigram upon treason, p. 522.

SIR THOMAS WYATT

SIR THOMAS WYATT (*c.* 1503–1542) experienced in his thirty-nine years a man's full share of adventures, of travel, of imprisonments, dangers, and escapes, of honors and disgraces, and of such pleasures as attend upon love and poetry. In the record of 16th-century literature he takes his place as a lyricist of considerable grace and strength, the first to rifle the stores of Italian poetry for the enrichment of English.

Born at his father's castle in Kent, Wyatt was at court as a boy, and entered St. John's College, Cambridge, in 1516, the year of its opening. He took the degree of M. A. about 1520; and within a year was married to Elizabeth, daughter of Lord Cobham. His abilities were soon recognized and utilized in various capacities by King Henry VIII. He went on missions to France and to Italy before he was twenty-five, and acted as Marshal of Calais from 1528 to 1532. Knighted in 1536, he was in the same year imprisoned because of a quarrel with the Duke of Suffolk at the time of the downfall of Anne Boleyn. The suspicion that he was a lover of this unfortunate lady attached to his name at the time and frequently since. Regaining favor he served as member of the Privy Council and ambassador to Spain, in which country he remained for more than a year. In 1541 he was suddenly thrown into prison, charged with dishonesty and treason during his Spanish residence; but he cleared himself by a notable speech, and was unconditionally pardoned. In 1542 he was in Parliament and was designed as Commander of the Fleet. On a hurried trip toward Falmouth to meet the Spanish ambassador, he fell ill and died at Sherborne in Dorset, where he was also buried.

Wyatt's trip to Italy, in 1527, takes on special importance because of its effects in English poetry. The young Englishman evidently was attracted by the works of Italian love-poets, especially by those of Petrarch (1304–1374) and Serafino dell' Aquila (1466–1500). Translating Petrarch, Wyatt produced the first group of sonnets in English. His *Seven Penitential Psalms* (published 1549) was written in close imitation of a work by Pietro Aretino (1492–1557). Wyatt also drew by translation upon French poetry, and wrote rondeaus, as well as other short poems imitative of the French *etrennes, huictains,* and *dizaines.* In his satires he reflects his reading of the satires of Luigi Alamanni, an exiled Florentine who was living in France.

A few of his poems were printed in a collection entitled *The Court of Venus* which survives in three fragments, each representing a different edition, the earliest of which may have been published before 1540. Ninety-seven pieces were included, with poems by Surrey and others, in Tottel's miscellany, *Songs and Sonnets,* 1557 (for which also see pages 918–919). Whoever edited the manuscript from which Wyatt's poems were printed in Tottel's collection made many changes in the poet's text; he usually modernized the older forms of third-person verb endings (e.g., *holds* for *holdeth*)—Wyatt himself may frequently have elided the suffix and pronounced such words as one syllable. Furthermore, by his alterations the editor sought to reduce Wyatt's skilfully varied rhythms to regular iambic lines. Versions much closer than Tottel's to the poet's intentions are preserved in some sixteenth-century manuscripts—especially *Egerton Ms. 2711,* in which some poems are in Wyatt's hand and others show revisions in his autograph. The reputation of no English poet, except perhaps Donne's, has undergone in the past thirty years such vigorous reappraisal as Wyatt's. No longer does one think of him as inferior to his friend and more influential successor, Surrey. The latter may be metrically smoother, but Wyatt was at once more dramatic and versatile as a poet. In the dramatic structure and conversational movement of his best verse he anticipates Donne.

MODERN EDITIONS: *The Poems* (ed. by A. K. Foxwell), two volumes, London, 1913; *The Poetry of Sir Thomas Wyatt: A Selection and a Study* (ed. by E. M. W. Tillyard), London, 1929; *Some Poems of Sir Thomas Wyatt* (ed. by Alan Swallow), New York, 1949; *The Collected Poems of Sir Thomas Wyatt* (ed. by Kenneth Muir), London, 1949.

COMMENT: A. K. Foxwell, *A Study of Sir Thomas Wyatt's Poems,* London, 1911; E. K. Chambers, *Sir Thomas Wyatt and Some Collected Studies,* London, 1933; Hallett Smith, 'The Art of Sir Thomas Wyatt,' *H. L. Q.,* ix (1946), 323–55; D. W. Harding, 'The Rhythmical Intention in Wyatt's Poetry,' *Scrutiny,* xiv (1946), 90–102; E. D. Mackerness, 'The Transitional Nature of Wyatt's Poetry,' *English,* vii (1948), 120–24; Alan Swallow, 'The Pentameter Line in Skelton and Wyatt,' *M. P.,* xlviii (1950), 1–11.

TEXT: *Songs and Sonnets,* 1557 (13860), Bodleian; *Egerton MS. 2711,* B. M.; *Additional Ms. 17492,* B. M.; *Harleian Ms. 78,* B. M.

13 *The lover compareth his state . . .*] translated from Petrarch, *Sonetto in vita* clvi. (Our numbers for Petrarch's sonnets are those of the translation in Bohn's Library.) The comparison of a lover to a storm-tossed ship became a favorite with sonneteers. See pp. 221, 222. We have inserted, for ease of reference, the titles assigned to the different poems in Tottel's *Songs and Sonnets,* even when we have taken our text from one of the manuscripts. 2 Thorrough] through; Wyatt's spelling, here and elsewhere, indicates his pronunciation of this word. 3 enemy] love,

as is also 'my lord' in the next line.

13 *The lover's life compared to the Alps*] from Sannazaro, *Rime,* Part iii, *sonetto 3.*

13–14 *Description of the contrarious passions.* . . .] from Petrarch, *In vita,* civ. In *The Art of English Poesy,* 1589, the first two lines of this sonnet are quoted as specimens of iambic verses made up of monosyllables. 4 season] seize; more strictly, of birds or beasts of prey, to 'flesh' the talons or claws. 9 eyen] eyes. 9 plain] complain.

14 *The lover for shamefastness . . .*] from Petrarch, *In vita,* cix. Compare

Surrey's translation of the same sonnet, p. 29.

14 *A renouncing of love* 3 Senec] Seneca. 8 lever] liefer, dearer.

15 *Whoso list to hunt*] from Petrarch's *In vita,* clvii. In spite of the Petrarchan source, several students of Wyatt have interpreted it as referring to Anne Boleyn; if such is the reference, l. 13 indicates that she already is queen, or at least claimed by the King. 13 *Noli me tangere*] 'Touch me not!'

15 *Divers doth use*] not printed in *Songs and Sonnets.* 3 lin] cease. 4 pease] appease. 13 of kind] natural.

15–16 *Of his return from Spain*] This and the six following poems may be classified as epigrams, though they are not so pointed as the English epigram, under Martialian influence, later became. 1 Tagus] the principal river of Spain. 4 Gainward] against. 5 Brutus] according to Geoffrey of Monmouth, London, and hence Britain, was founded by Brutus, a grandson of Æneas. 8 O mighty Jove] *Egerton MS.* 'Of mighty love the wings.'

16 *A description of such a one . . .*] The subject has not been identified; Miss Foxwell suggests Mary, Duchess of Richmond, sister of the Earl of Surrey. 7 tied] *Egerton MS.* 2711; 1557 'tried'.

16 *Description of a gun*] a riddle, translated from the Latin of Pandolphus.

16 *Wyatt being in prison, to Bryan*] addressed to Sir Francis Bryan (d. 1550), a fellow-poet; written during Wyatt's imprisonment from January 17 to March 21, 1541. Unfortunately none of Bryan's poetry can now be identified. He was among the anonymous contributors to Tottel's *Songs and Sonnets,* and for this reason was described by Meres as one of 'the most passionate among us to bewail and bemoan the perplexities of love.' 8 the scar . . . remain] Surrey quotes these words; see p. 33.

17 *Of his love called Anna*] usually supposed to have been written of Anne Boleyn.

17 *To a lady, to answer . . .*] imitated from a *douzaine* by Saint Gelais. In *Egerton Ms.* 2711 this is followed by a poem headed 'Answer,' generally ascribed to a lady. Her answer is 'Nay.' 3 bordes] jests.

17–18 *The lover to his bed . . .*] based on Petrarch's *In vita,* cxcviii, but expanded.

18–19 *Help me to seek*] In form the poem is a rondeau, an attempted reproduction in English of a pattern already long in use among French poets

5 appear] Ms. 'apere'; usually read as 'appair' (deteriorate, suffer harm). 'Appear' seems the better reading, the sense being, 'Convey my heart secretly; and to this end handle it gently or it will complain and make its presence known.' 8 lese] lose it . . . near] it concerns me deeply.

19 *And wilt thou leave me thus?* 4 grame] anger, scorn.

19–20 *Blame not my lute*] Like many of Wyatt's poems, and notably those with refrains, this was doubtless set to music and sung, with lute accompaniment. 20 quit] requite.

20–21 *Since you will needs* 7] Compare Surrey in his epitaph of Wyatt (p. 31), l. 6.

21 *Tangled I was*] imitated, but not translated, from Serafino's first *barzalleto.*

21 *Hate whom ye list*] The substitution for rhyme of repeating a single word or syllable was called 'like loose,' a term borrowed from archery. For a later example see p. 225.

21–24 *Of the mean and sure estate*] Of John Poyntz (d. 1544), to whom this and the following satire are addressed, little is known. 10 dight] decked. 53 stemming] steeming, gleaming. 64 seely] not the exact equivalent of modern 'silly.' Here the meaning is 'foolish' but usually, as in l. 27 of the next poem, 'seely' means 'simple' or 'innocent.' 81 lust] pleasure, in a general sense. 88 hay] snare. 94 affects] affections, passions; usually with an unfavorable connotation. 105 high] omitted in T.

24–26 *Of the courtier's life*] The poem follows closely the tenth satire of Luigi Alamanni, published in 1532. Tottel's text has been slightly revised by adopting a few superior readings from the MSS. 48–49] After a contest in music between Pan and Apollo, Midas awarded the prize to Pan; for his bad judgment Apollo transformed Midas' ears to those of an ass. 50–51 Sir Thopas . . . Knight told] In *Canterbury Tales,* see the *Tale of Thopas.* 67 favel] cunning, duplicity; from the favel, or fallow-colored horse, used as a type of cunning, as in the proverbial expression, 'to curry favel.' 69 change . . . place] Cruelty is often excused by the plea that in some times and places custom makes or has made it justifiable. 86 clog] Wyatt was not at perfect liberty but was confined to his father's estate. 94 Flanders' cheer] the strong liquor of Flanders. lets] prevents. 98 at Rome] Tottel alters to 'of some.'

HENRY HOWARD, EARL OF SURREY

HENRY HOWARD (1517?–1547) was of royal blood, his father having been descended from Edward the Confessor, and his mother, the daughter of Elinor Percy, from Edward III. The young Surrey received excellent schooling under his learned tutor, John Clerk; and was early grounded in Latin, Spanish, Italian, and French. When he was thirteen he became the companion of Henry Fitzroy, Duke of Richmond, the illegitimate son of Henry VIII, and with him enjoyed the advantages of that life at Windsor Palace which later he celebrated in poetry. In 1532 the two boys went to France in the train of the King, remaining there as guests of King Francis and companions of the young French princes. After the better part of a year spent in travel, the two were recalled to England that Richmond might be married to Surrey's sister, Mary Howard. Surrey had already been married to Lady Frances Vere, but because of their youth the couple did not live together until 1535.

During Surrey's brief career as a retainer of the King's, he aided his father in suppressing a rebellion, in overthrowing the power of Thomas Cromwell, and in subduing Scotland; he built a mansion, Mount Surrey, on St. Leonard's Hill near Norwich, designed to exemplify the beauties of Greek architecture; he took part in several military and naval campaigns against France, in two of which he was commander of large English forces; and he performed many other duties such as devolved upon one of the most prominent and most engaging members of the court. In December, 1546, Surrey was arrested and charged with treason. The charge grew out of the question of who should succeed Henry VIII, then in his last illness. Surrey, or his father, may have taken some steps toward promoting their family claims; at least, the quartering by young Surrey of the arms of Edward the Confessor with his own was maliciously interpreted. Several jealous noblemen brought evidence against him, with the result that on January 21, 1547, he was beheaded on Tower Hill. The King died just a week later.

That intolerable pride which seems to have been Surrey's birthright, and which was partly responsible for his death, never forsook him. In 1537 he struck a courtier who accused him of half-heartedness in suppressing the Yorkshire rebellion. Since the incident took place in the park of Hampton Court, Surrey's action incurred the penalty of loss of the right hand; but this was commuted to imprisonment at Windsor. Again, in 1542 he suffered confinement in Fleet prison for quarreling with a courtier. Early in the next year he was committed to the same prison for rioting in the streets and eating meat in Lent. In a record of 1539 he is described as 'the most foolish proud boy that is in England.'

Surrey's mother seems to have been interested in letters; it was at her house that John Skelton composed his *Garland of Laurel*. Doubtless the boy was set at tasks of making verse, either in Latin or in English translations, by his tutor, John Clerk. During his French residence he may have come into contact with polite French poets; but it is evident that acquaintance with Sir Thomas Wyatt and his imitations of Italian and French poetry strongly influenced Surrey in his writing of poems which were destined to become models for a whole school of minor English writers. Surrey's longer tribute to Wyatt (p. 31) was printed as *An Excellent Epitaph* (1542?), and in 1547 William Baldwin included his sixteen-line translation from Martial in *A Treatise of Moral Philosophy*. In 1557 Richard Tottel printed Surrey's translation of two books of Virgil's *Æneid* (an undated edition of the translation of Book Four may have appeared earlier), and also forty poems in the well-known miscellany of *Songs and Sonnets*. Surrey was the only author mentioned on the title-page of Tottel's miscellany.

He followed Wyatt in playing tunes learned from foreign poetry upon the new instrument of English; but in smoothness of versification he improved upon his older friend. His important innovation of blank verse, used in translating Virgil, was copied from similar work by Italian humanists, who seem consciously to have tried to find a rhymeless measure comparable to the classical hexameter. With less of originality and poetic energy than Wyatt, Surrey more adequately voiced for his own and the following generation the emotions proper to lyrical poetry.

MODERN EDITIONS: *The Poems* (ed. by F. M. Padelford), Seattle, 1920, and revised, 1928; *Poems* (ed. by J. Yeowell), London, 1894.

COMMENT: Edmond Bapst, *Deux gentilshommes-poètes de la cour de Henry VIII* (Surrey and Rochford), Paris, 1891; H. F. Fehse, *Henry Howard, Earl of Surrey*, Chemnitz, 1883.

TEXT: *Songs and Sonnets*, 1557 (13860), Bodleian; William Baldwin's *Treatise of Moral Philosophy*, 1547 (1253), B. M.; *Additional Ms.* 36529, B. M.; *Certain Books of Virgil's Æneis*, 1557 (24798), B. M.

27 *Description of spring . . .*] adapted from Petrarch's *Sonetto in morte* xlii. Surrey presents, by his choice of details, an English spring where Petrarch's picture was of an Italian one. 1 soote] sweet; the presence of this word in the first line of Chaucer's Prologue to the *Canterbury Tales* may have helped to keep it in use by poets. 4 make] mate. 6 pale] paling, fence; Surrey has in mind the deer kept in enclosures. 10] This line follows closely Chaucer, *Parlement of Foules*, 353. 11 mings] mingles, produces by mixing (*O.E.D.* 'meng'); 'remembers, calls to mind' is a possible meaning.

27–28 *The frailty and hurtfulness of beauty*] assigned to Lord Vaux in *Additional Ms.* 28635, though printed as Surrey's in *Songs and Sonnets*. Padelford finds that 'the alliteration is unduly studied and the imagery common, and the primitive tendency to two strong beats in each half of the verse is much less pronounced than in any of Surrey's unquestioned poems.' 4 tickle] delicate. 8 geason] rare.

28 *Description and praise of his love Geraldine*] This sonnet helped to disseminate a most interesting and persistent legend concerning Surrey, to the effect that he was long the lover of Elizabeth Fitzgerald, daughter of the Irish Earl of Kildare, and that to her he addressed all of his love-poetry. Thomas Nashe's *The Unfortunate*

Traveler, 1594, and Michael Drayton's *England's Heroical Epistles* (see p. 290) are the chief 16th-century sources for the legend. Modern scholars have pointed out that Elizabeth was nine years old when Surrey met her, his own age then being twenty, that he never was in Italy, and that the present sonnet is the only one of his poems necessarily referring to her. This poem is therefore read as a compliment turned to please a little girl who had for the moment caught the young poet's fancy. 1 Tuscan] The Fitzgeralds were supposed to be descended from the Geraldis of Florence. 3–4] Elizabeth grew up in Ireland, which faces the cliffs of Wales. 6 princes' blood] 'Geraldine's' mother was grand-daughter of Edward IV's queen. 8 With king's child] She was attached to the household of Princess Mary. 9] The meeting of Surrey and Elizabeth probably took place at Hunsdon in March, 1537, as Princess Mary is known to have been there at that time. 11 Hampton] Princess Mary, and presumably Elizabeth, were at Hampton Court in July, 1537. 12 Windsor] Surrey was confined in Windsor in July, 1537.

28 *A complaint by night . . .*] adapted from Petrarch's *In vita*, cxxxi. 4 chair] chariot.

29 *Complaint of a lover rebuked*] translated from Petrarch's *In vita*, cix; see Wyatt's translation, p. 14.

29 *Vow to love faithfully . . .*] translated from Petrarch's *In vita,* cxiii; for a later translation see p. 198.

29–30 *The lover comforteth himself . . .* 28 ure] originally, use; here, state of prevalence or existence.

31 *How no age is content . . .*] written in 'poulter's measure,' consisting of couplets made up of a line of twelve syllables followed by one of fourteen. If the lines are broken in two, each couplet yields a four-line stanza of what is known in the hymn-book as 'short measure'; see Lord Vaux's *The aged lover renounceth love,* p. 38. For a late use of poulter's measure see Fulke Greville's epitaph on Sidney, p. 125. 12 chop] trade. 16 jaws] 1557 'chewes'.

31–32 *Of the death of Sir T. W. the elder*] in 1557 headed *Of the same,* the second of two poems on the subject. Our title is that of the first. 6 Whose hammers] See Wyatt's *Since you will needs,* l. 7. 15 unparfited] unfinished. 21 affect] passion.

32–33 *Prisoned in Windsor . . .* . 6 hove] linger. 11 rue] melt, awaken pity in. 13 palm play] old form of tennis, resembling modern hand-ball. despoilëd] with impeding garments stripped off. 16 leads] either the leaden window-sills of the maidens' tower or small flat roofs whence the ladies watched the game. 21 'silver drops] probably dew, in which case 'for ruth' later in the line is figurative. 30 avaled] slackened, lowered. 46 fere] companion.

33 *Exhortation to learn . . .*] addressed to Thomas Radcliffe, third Earl of Sussex, who as a lad of eighteen was with Surrey for military operations in France in 1544. 5 Solomon said] The reference is obscure; possibly *Prov.* xii.13 or xxiv.16. 6 Wyatt said] See p. 16.

34 *The things that cause a quiet life*] This translation of an epigram of Martial's (x. 47) was probably the second specimen of Surrey's work to be printed. In Baldwin's *Treatise* of 1547 no mention is made of Surrey's authorship, though in some later editions of the work there is such mention. The epigram which Surrey chose to translate was popular throughout the 16th and 17th centuries. Versions were also made by Kendall, Jonson, Thomas Heywood, Randolph, Cowley, Sherburne, and Stanley, among authors represented in this book. It may be doubted whether Surrey's translation was ever surpassed.

See Sherburne's rendering at p. 828. 8 continuance] permanence, stability.

34–35 *London, hast thou accusëd me?*] Surrey was committed to the Fleet in April, 1543, for having gone about in the night with some companions, breaking windows with a stonebow. The younger Sir Thomas Wyatt, son of the poet, was one of his fellows in this escapade. The satire occasioned by this imprisonment is more readily understood when we remember that the city officials were drawn largely from that stricter group within the church which later became the Puritan faction. Padelford suggests these Biblical sources for various passages in the poem: *Isaiah* xlvii. 11; *Jeremiah* l and li. 48, 49; *Revelations* xviii; *Ezekiel* v. 12–17, vi. 11–14. 3–17] Padelford paraphrases these lines as follows: 'Such was my indignation at the dissolute life within the city walls that fear of retribution could not keep me from forcibly rebuking it. Mere words, as the preachers well know, are of small avail, and so I resorted to this novel method of voicing my protest. My punishment of the city under cover of the night accords with your secret sins, and should teach you that justice seeks out every fault, and that no one is secure from it.' 28 pride] This is the first to be named of the seven deadly sins, which are treated in turn. 33 shapp] Padelford's explanation of this word as 'conceive, imagine,' based upon one meaning of 'shape,' does not seem satisfactory. Of course the 'hyer' of the manuscript could be read as 'hire'; but such a reading does not explain 'shapp.' The manuscript may allow the reading 'shalbe' (shall be) instead of 'shapp'; if so, this should be preferred. 61 thy] ms. 'they'.

35 *Certain Books of Virgil's Æneis*] Surrey left a translation of the second and fourth books, published by Richard Tottel in June, 1557, two weeks after the first edition of *Songs and Sonnets.* The fourth book was published separately, and probably earlier, by John Day. Surrey is supposed to have read Italian versions by Cardinal Hippolito de Medici or his secretary Molza (1539), Nicolo Liburnio (1534), and Bartolomeo Piccolomini (1541); and to have used blank verse in imitation of the meter of these. It is evident that he also had access to the rhymed Scottish translation by Gawain Douglas (d. 1524), not published until 1553 but existing in manuscript. Padelford argues that in translating the second book Surrey had before him a French version (1529) made by Saint Gelais.

35–38 *Book II*] The passage here printed translates ll. 1–56, 199–245. 1 whisted] grew silent. 10 Dolopes] Thessalian. 29 Tenedon] Tenedos. 35 fet] fetched, in the sense of reached by sailing. 40 pight] pitched. 43 Behight] pledged. 55 Laocoon] The spelling of this name varies in 1557; sometimes three syllables were intended, and sometimes two, but never four. 94 raught] rended. 104 altar] 1557 'haltar'. 115 blive] belive, quickly.

THOMAS, LORD VAUX

THOMAS, LORD VAUX (1510–1556), without being a distinguished figure among the courtiers of Henry and Edward, has always held a place with Wyatt and Surrey as principal among the 'courtly makers.' At least two of the poems in Tottel's miscellany are Vaux's; but the greater part of his identifiable work appeared in *The Paradise of Dainty Devices*, 1576. Some of his poems gained wide currency as songs. The author of *The Art of English Poesy*, 1589, makes several references to Vaux's work, in two of which he mistakenly speaks of the poet as Sir Nicholas Vaux; Sir Nicholas was Thomas's father. For a sonnet which has been attributed to Vaux, see *The frailty and hurtfulness of beauty* (p. 27), here printed as Surrey's.

MODERN EDITION: *Poems* in *Miscellanies of the Fuller Worthies' Library* (ed. by A. B. Grosart), Vol. iv, 1872.

TEXT: *Songs and Sonnets*, 1557 (13860), Bodleian; *Paradise of Dainty Devices*, 1576 (7516), Huntington.

38 *The aged lover renounceth love*] This poem was one of the most popular of all those printed in Tottel's miscellany. In 1563 it was licensed for publication as a broadside ballad; it was set to music and other lyrics were written to be sung to the same tune. Gascoigne in a prefatory letter to his *Posies*, 1575, mentions in ridicule the legend that Vaux wrote this poem on his death-bed. It exists in several early mss.; and three stanzas, quoted with intentional inaccuracy, were used by Shakespeare as the song of the First Gravedigger in *Hamlet* (V. i. 69 ff.). 10 crutch] 1557, first edition, reads 'cowche'; 1557, second edition, and later editions read 'crowch'. The gravedigger in *Hamlet* sings 'clutch', which perhaps is the best reading of all, since it makes perfect alliteration with 'clawed.'

39 *A lover, disdained, complaineth* 4 gaze] 'At gaze' is a technical term used to describe the moment when the deer or stag hears the dogs and gazes around in apprehension.

40 *No pleasure without some pain*] This poem is another of Vaux's which caught the popular fancy. Beside appearing in the numerous editions of *The Paradise of Dainty Devices*, it was printed as a song in William Barley's *New Book of Tablature*, 1596, and in another song-book of 1626. It was imitated by George Peele in his *Sir Clyomon and Sir Clamydes*, 1599. It is extant in four early mss. The music is given in Chappell, i. 72.

40 *Of a contented mind* 2 He] 1576 'The'.

MINOR 'COURTLY MAKERS' OF HENRY VIII'S REIGN

'IN the latter end of the same king's [Henry VIII's] reign,' wrote the author of *The Art of English Poesy*, 1589, 'sprung up a new company of courtly makers, of whom Sir Thomas Wyatt the elder and Henry, Earl of Surrey, were the chieftains. . . . In the same time, or not long after, was the Lord Nicholas [*i.e.* Thomas] Vaux, a man of much facility in vulgar makings.' When we have named these three authors, however, we find it difficult, because of ignorance, to proceed with the list of noble and courtly poets of the first half of the 16th century. The Renaissance ideal demanded that one bred as a gentleman should be able to make verses; and we may be sure that a great number of Henry's courtiers fulfilled the ideal in this respect. Henry himself, as we have seen, composed verses for singing. We know that the ill-fated George Boleyn, Viscount Rochford, was a poet; but the one poem ascribed to him in modern collections is doubtfully his. Sir Francis Bryan is mentioned in early accounts as a contributor to *Songs and Sonnets,* but no one has named his contributions. Sir Anthony St. Leger (1496?–1559) was author of a brief tribute to Wyatt; Henry Parker, Lord Morley, left a number of poems and translations; Sir Thomas Chaloner (1521–1565) published verses both in Latin and in English.

If we dispense with the necessity for attributions by name, however, we find God's plenty when we turn to that great miscellany of poems largely from Henry VIII's reign, *Songs and Sonnets,* issued from the print-shop of Richard Tottel on June 5, 1557, and again, completely reset, with omissions and additions, on July 31 of the same year. Besides forty poems by Surrey, ninety-seven by Wyatt, forty by Grimald, at least two by Vaux, two by J. Canand, one by John Heywood, one by St. Leger, and one by Chaucer, these two editions preserve one hundred and twenty-six poems by 'Uncertain authors,' among these being Sir Francis Bryan and Thomas Churchyard. The three hundred and ten poems collected are for the most part lyrics (including sonnets), with a sprinkling of epigrams, epitaphs, elegies, satires, and pastoral and narrative verse. Some are translations or imitations of classical favorites, and others translate then modern French, Italian, or Latin originals. Here are the first published English sonnets and perhaps the first published English blank verse. The historical importance suggested by these facts is heightened by our knowledge of the popularity of the collection. Beside the two editions already mentioned, there are copies extant from editions of 1559, 1565, 1567, 1574, 1585, and 1587, making a total of eight within thirty years. Printers and poets used the words 'songs and sonnets' on title-pages of other books, hoping to borrow some of the interest created by the miscellany. Shakespeare alludes to the book when he makes Slender say (*Merry Wives of Windsor,* I. i): 'I had rather than forty shillings I had my book of *Songs and Sonnets* here.'

Besides *Songs and Sonnets,* the recently discovered fragment of *A Boke of Balettes* (*T. L. S.,* July 5, 1928) indicates the existence of another collection of pre-Elizabethan work; it contained poems by Wyatt and others.

In the present section we have included some of the song-lyrics written by professional musicians such as Fairfax, Cooper, and Cornish. These men were 'courtly makers' only in the sense that they were hired by the King, and their work may be said to reflect the taste of the court.

MODERN EDITIONS: *Tottel's Miscellany* (ed. by H. E. Rollins), Cambridge (Mass.), 1928–1929; *Tottel's Miscellany* (ed. by E. Arber), London, 1870; *Early 16th Century Lyrics* (ed. by F. M. Padelford), Boston, 1907; *The Surrey and Wyatt Anthology* (ed. by H. Frowde), London, 1900; *Neuenglisches Lesebuch* (ed. by E. Flügel), Halle, 1895.

COMMENT: J. M. Berdan, *Early Tudor Poetry,* New York, 1920, Chaps. iv, v, vi; H. J. Byrom, 'Richard Tottel—his Life and Work,' *The Library,* viii. 199.

TEXT: *Additional Ms.* 5465, B. M.; *Christmas Carols,* 1521 (5204), Bodleian; *XX Songs,* 1530 (22924), B. M.; *Royal Ms. Appendix* 58, B. M.; *Additional Ms.* 31922, B. M.; *Harleian Ms.* 7578, B. M.; *Additional Ms.* 26737, B. M.; *Ashmole Ms.* 48, Bodleian; *Songs and Sonnets,* 1557 (13860), Bodleian; *Songs and Sonnets,* 1557, 2nd ed. (13861), B. M.

41 *That was my woe*] Robert Fairfax (c. 1466–1521), author of this song, was a musician, a Gentleman of the Chapel Royal in 1496 or earlier. Several of his songs, with music, are preserved. 3 sikerness] sureness, safety.

41 *A carol, bringing . . .*] Only a single leaf of *Christmas Carols*, in which this song appeared, is preserved. The colophon gives the name of Wynken de Worde as printer, and the date. The form of this song suggests that it may belong to the 15th century. 1–2] 'The head of the boar I bear, giving praises to the Lord.' 2 *laudes*] 1521 'laudens'. 6] 'You who are at the feast.' 9 fand] found. 10] 'Serve with singing.'

41 *XX Songs*] This book is usually referred to as *Bassus,* the name of the only singing-part which is preserved. The title-page reads: 'In this book are contained xx songs, ix of iiii pts. and xi of three pts.,' etc.

41–42 *In youth, in age*] Robert Cooper (or Cowper), author of this poem, was a composer and court musician in the reign of Henry VIII. He was born about 1474 and died after 1529. In 1507 he was given by Cambridge University the degree of Doctor of Music. Several of his songs are preserved in manuscript, besides three in this song-book of 1530. 3, 8, 13] 'My help (cometh) from the Lord.' 12 force] care for, attach importance to.

42 *Pleasure it is*] William Cornish (d. 1524?), author of this and the following poem, was a court musician under Henry VII and Henry VIII. In 1509 he became Master of the Children of the Chapel Royal. He wrote music for several of Skelton's poems; his setting of *Woefully arrayed* is extant. *Pleasure it is* also appears in *Additional Ms.* 31922. The music is printed in Chappell, i. 35.

43 *These women all*] accompanied in ms. by a musical setting. At the beginning is a refrain, 'Hey down,' many times repeated, and another such refrain appears after l. 18. After the stanzas here reprinted is another imperfect stanza, of corrupt text, which we have omitted.

43 *O death, rock me asleep*] Ritson and others after him assign this poem to George Boleyn, Viscount Rochford, brother of Queen Anne Boleyn, and suppose it to have been written between May 1 and May 17, 1536, while Rochford was in the Tower awaiting execution. John Bale recorded that Rochford was the author of 'most elegant poems of various kinds, in the English tongue'; and Holinshed, probably following Bale, says that he 'wrote diverse songs and sonnets.' However, from Gascoigne's prefatory epistle to his *Posies,* 1575, we know that a popular poem referred to as *Soul-knell* was written by Richard Edwards, supposedly 'in extremity of sickness.' Edwards was old enough to have written the present poem in the reign of Henry VIII, from which time the ms. copy comes. Except for the reference in the third stanza, indicating that the author was imprisoned, Edwards's claim would seem to be stronger than Rochford's. Shakespeare represents Pistol (2 *Henry IV,* II. iv. 211) as saying, 'Then death, rock me asleep! Abridge my doleful days!'

44 *To his posterity*] Henry Parker, eighth Baron Morley (1476–1556), was deeply interested in literature. He published a translation of Petrarch's *Trionfi* under the title, *Triumphs of Francis Petrarch* (c. 1550). Bale mentions 'many books of comedies and tragedies' among Morley's works. 1] This line translates part of a saying quoted by Cicero (*De Officiis,* iii. 1) from Scipio Africanus, who had recorded it as a saying of Cato. The whole is: *Numquam se minus otiosum esse quam otiosus, nec minus solum quam solus esset.* 16 they] ms. 'the'.

44 *The poor estate . . .*] This poem, because the first letters of its lines, taken with the last letter of the last line, form the name 'Edwarde Somerset,' is usually supposed to have been written by Edward Seymour, Duke of Somerset, who was Protector in the early years of Edward VI's reign. The poem moralizes upon the Protector's fall, and may well have been written by some other poet concerning the unfortunate Duke. Somerset was deposed from the Protectorate in January, 1550, imprisoned in the Tower, and on January 22, 1552, beheaded as a felon.

44–45 *The lover showeth . . .* 1 marlian's] merlin's. 2 yelden] wearied, or submissive; usually 'yolden.'

45 *Upon consideration of the state . . .*] This poem exemplifies one of the figures of repetition which were especially cultivated in the period between 1550 and 1590. *The Art of English Poesy* expounds such devices as necessary to the equipment of a poet. For another specimen, see p. 73.

45 *Of a new-married student*] one of the earliest specimens in English of the true epigram.

45–47 *Harpalus' complaint . . .*] reprinted in *England's Helicon*, 1600, ascribed to Surrey; but the ascription doubtless was based only upon the association of Surrey's name with *Songs and Sonnets*. In *England's Helicon* the poem is followed by *Another on the same subject, but made as it were in answer*, by 'Shepherd Tony' or Anthony Munday. **6** yfere] in company, together. **12** forced] cared about. **68**

makes] mates; 'makes' is the reading of the second and later editions; first edition reads 'face'.
47–48 *Totus mundus in maligno positus*] 'The whole world lying in evil.' The poem, while conventional in expression, may reflect the actual feeling of many Englishmen living in the late years of Henry VIII's reign, or in the reign of Mary. **14** shent] ruined.

NICHOLAS GRIMALD

NICHOLAS GRIMALD (1519?–1562?), scholar, preacher, and author, holds his place in English literature chiefly by his forty poems which appeared in the first edition of Tottel's miscellany of *Songs and Sonnets*. All but nine of these were omitted from subsequent editions of the miscellany, a circumstance which has given rise to various conjectures; one being that Grimald was the collector and editor of the miscellany, and another, more credible, that he had fallen into bad odor because of his treachery toward the Protestant cause during the troublous reign of Queen Mary. His career as Cambridge scholar, lecturer on rhetoric at Oxford, and chaplain to Bishop Ridley, need not be detailed. He published two notable Latin plays, and made a widely circulated translation of Cicero's *De Officiis*.

A fair share of the poems by Grimald in *Songs and Sonnets* are translations from Latin, the sources having been indicated in only a few cases. Two of his translations are in blank verse; and it is not impossible that one of them was composed as early as Surrey's *Æneid*. In his use of this metrical form there is no evidence that Grimald was following an Italian model. He shows in his poems a certain ingenuity in fitting language to meter, and occasional compression and incisiveness. The rhetorical discipline in which he was trained required the composition of verses as an exercise; it was considered incumbent upon an educated man to produce epitaphs, New Year's greetings, and such occasional poems; and Grimald, in his English work at least, is versifier rather than poet.

MODERN EDITION: *The Life and Poems* (by L. R. Merrill), New Haven, 1925.
COMMENT: J. M. Berdan, *Early Tudor Poetry*, New York, 1920, Chapter iv.
TEXT: *Songs and Sonnets*, 1557 (13860), Bodleian.

49–50 *A true love* **3** Ver] spring. **9** Or] ere, before. **14** imp] child, offspring.
50 *Man's life, after Posidonius or Crates*] translation from the Greek Anthology, where the poem is ascribed to Posidippus; in the Planudean Anthology Crates is named as alternative author. It is followed in the Anthology by a reply of equal length, by Metrodorus, also translated by Grimald. These twin epigrams have been favorites with English translators. Kendall reprinted Grimald's two renderings in his *Flowers of Epigrams*, 1577; H. C. translated the first of the pair in *The Forest of Fancy*, 1579; *The Art of English Poesy*, 1589,

included translations of both; Sir John Beaumont and Philip Ayres translated both; see also Bacon's *In vitam humanam*, p. 549. **2** bate] debate.
50 *Metrodorus' mind to the contrary* **3** beek] bask.
50 *Description of virtue*] translated closely from a Latin epigram by Theodore de Beze (Beza), a French poet and religious reformer (1519–1605).
50 *To his familiar friend*] imitated from a longer Latin epigram by Marc-Antoine Muret (Muretus); this poem is a New Year's greeting sent in lieu of a gift.
51–53 *A funeral song . . .*] Merrill points out that in the parish register of

Winwick, Huntingdonshire, there is a record of the death of Agnes Grymbold in 1555. 5 disprove] disapprove. 9 Martius] Cnæus Martius, later emperor, known as Coriolanus. For the incident referred to, see Plutarch. Shakespeare and James Thomson wrote tragedies utilizing this incident. 11 Sertorius] Quintus Sertorius, a Roman general. 13 Sicil brethren] Amphinomus and Anapis, youths of Catana, who bore their parents to safety during an eruption of Ætna. Statues of them were erected in their native village. 15 Tyndar's imps] Castor and Pollux, sons of Tyndareus and Leda. 16 Arge . . . yoke] The legend of Cleobis and Biton (or Bito) who assumed the oxen's yoke and drew their mother, Cydippe of Argos, to the temple of Hera, is told by Herodotus (i. 31). 19 Caiet] Caieta, nurse of Creusa and Ascanius, in Virgil's Æneid. The town and harbor of Gaeta, in Latium, were supposed to have been named after her. fire-flame] that of burning Troy. 21-22 Acca . . . heaped] Acca was wife of the shepherd Faustulus, and nursed Romulus and Remus. Some accounts make her a prostitute, hence lupa in one sense; the other sense comes from the legend that Romulus and Remus were previously nursed by a she-wolf, lupa. The feast of Larentalia, celebrated by Romans in December, was in honor of Acca, who

had been given the addition of Larentia (mother of the Lares). 23 Capra] the nymph who fed young Jove with goat's milk; her name in the legend was Amalthea, but she was placed in the heavens under the name of Capra. 25-26 Hyades . . . face] The Hyades, nymphs who nursed the infant Bacchus, or Lyæus (here Lyai), were placed as stars in the constellation of the Bull. 26 prime-tide] springtime. 43 web] misprinted 'wed' in all editions. 47 Brownshold] probably the modern Leighton-Bromswold, in Huntingdonshire. 49 Granta] the river Cam, on which Cambridge is located. 53 fair ford] Oxford. 70 dart-thirling] piercing with a dart. 86 once appair] sometime decay. 90 Ene] Æneas.

53-54 *Marcus Tullius Cicero's death*] This poem in blank verse is closely translated from Beza's Latin *Mors Ciceronis*, which appeared in his *Juvenilia*, 1548. Grimald also made a longer blank-verse translation, *The death of Zoroas*, from Phillipus Gualtherius' *Alexandreis*. The present excerpt gives the latter half of *Marcus Tullius Cicero's death*. 2 doubt] fear. 30 Grayes] Greeks, a transliteration of Beza's *Graiæ*. 32 Pytho] the Pythian, or Delphic, Sibyl. 39 grisly sight] Popilius took the head of Cicero to Antony, to be set up at Rome.

ELIZABETH

Queen Elizabeth (1533-1603) is thus accredited as poet by the author of *The Art of English Poesy*, 1589: 'But last in recital and first in degree is the Queen, our sovereign lady, whose learned, delicate, noble muse easily surmounteth all the rest that have written before her time or since, for sense, sweetness, and subtility, be it in ode, elegy, epigram, or any other kind of poem heroic or lyric wherein it shall please her Majesty to employ her pen, even by as much odds as her own excellent estate and degree exceedeth all the rest of her most humble vassals.' Of the royal verse here alluded to, we have only a few specimens and those, for the most part, imperfectly authenticated. If the clever lyric with the refrain, 'Importune me no more,' is indeed hers, then the critic's praise is not mere flattery.

Text: *Rawlinson Poetry Ms. 85*, Bodleian; *The Art of English Poesy*, 1589 (20519), B. M.

54 *When I was fair . . .*] 'Elysabethe reginæ' is written at the end, after 'Finis.' Grosart states that in a ms. which he does not identify, this poem is attributed to the Earl of Oxford.

55 *The doubt of future foes*] This appears in *The Art of English Poesy*

(III. xx) as an example of the figure *Expolitio*, or ornamental amplification. The passage preceding the poem is as follows: 'I find none example that ever I could see so well maintaining this figure in English meter as that ditty of her Majesty's own making, passing sweet and harmonical. . . . And this was th' action: our sovereign Lady, perceiving how by the Sc[ottish] Q[ueen's] residence within this realm, at so great liberty and ease as were scarce worthy of so great and dangerous a prisoner, bred secret factions among her people and made many of her nobility incline to favor her party, . . . writeth this ditty most sweet and sententious, not hiding from all such aspiring minds the danger of their ambition and disloyalty.'

JOHN HARINGTON, THE ELDER

JOHN HARINGTON, the elder (*fl.* 1550), father of Sir John Harington (see p. 521), was a confidential servant of Henry VIII and married that king's natural daughter, Ethelreda. In the royal household Harington devoted himself especially to the service of the Princess Elizabeth. His first wife having died, he married Isabella Markham, one of Elizabeth's ladies-in-waiting; and under Queen Mary he and his wife suffered imprisonment with Elizabeth. His services to the Princess at this time won for Harington and for his son the favor of Elizabeth when she came to the throne. Several of the poems of Harington celebrate Elizabeth or her attendants. Since he copied into his manuscripts poems by other hands, some of the work ascribed to Harington in *Nugæ Antiquæ* is not his. The poem in Tottel's miscellany, *Comparison of life and death,* often ascribed to Harington upon manuscript authority, was printed in all editions of *The Paradise of Dainty Devices* as by D. S.

MODERN EDITION: *Nugæ Antiquæ* (ed. by Thomas Park), two volumes, London, 1804.

TEXT: *Nugæ Antiquæ,* 1769, Cornell.

55 *A sonnet made . . .*] The editor of *Nugæ Antiquæ* notes: 'From a Ms. of John Harington, dated 1564.' In its smoothness of versification the poem seems to show 18th-century 'improvements.'

THOMAS SACKVILLE, EARL OF DORSET

THOMAS SACKVILLE (1536–1608) as a young member of the Inner Temple showed great interest in poetry; but after a brief period of authorship he allowed professional and public duties entirely to engross him. He became one of Elizabeth's most trusted counsellors, going from a seat in Parliament to ambassadorships and the Privy Council, finally to serve as Lord Treasurer. He was also for many years Chancellor of the University of Oxford. Elizabeth honored him with the titles of Baron Buckhurst and Earl of Dorset.

In or before 1561 he wrote the last two acts of the blank-verse *Tragedy of Gorboduc* (the first three acts are by Thomas Norton), a notable landmark in English dramatic history. In the same period he, with other authors under the leadership of William Baldwin, was at work upon a poem modeled upon Lydgate's *Fall of Princes*, with the title, *A Mirror for Magistrates.* The writers attempted to tell in verse the stories of all English kings or prominent noblemen and courtiers who had suffered tragic falls from high estate. Sackville contributed the account of Henry, Duke of Buckingham; but he preceded his contribution with an induction which has proved to be the most memorable portion of the whole voluminous work. The *Mirror* was a popular success, and was issued, with successive expansions, in numerous editions dating from 1559 to 1610. Sackville's contributions appeared first in the edition of 1563. His *Induction* is usually accounted the most considerable poem written in the period between Chaucer's *Canterbury Tales* and Spenser's *Fairy Queen*.

There is evidence that Sackville wrote other poems, but none has been certainly identified. Throughout his lifetime his early work was referred to with praise by critics and fellow-poets, notably by Spenser, who acknowledged his debt to the older writer. Near the end of Sackville's life Sir Francis Bacon in a letter reminded him of his poetry, alluding to it as his 'first love.'

MODERN EDITIONS: *Mirror for Magistrates* (ed. by J. Haslewood), three volumes, London, 1815; *The Works* (ed. by R. W. Sackville-West), London, 1859.

COMMENT: J. Davies, *A Mirror for Magistrates, considered with special reference to the sources of Sackville's contributions*, Leipzig, 1906.

TEXT: *A Mirror for Magistrates*, 1563 (1248), Huntington.

56–69 *The induction*] in some copies of 1563, *Master Sackville's induction*. In this edition Baldwin sets down an account of how he brought Sackville's work before his group of collaborators. The account ends thus: ' "Hath he made a preface?" said one. "What meaneth he thereby, seeing none other hath used the like order?" "I will tell you the cause thereof," said I, "which is this: after that he understood that some of the Council would not suffer the book to be printed in such order as we had agreed and determined, he purposed to have gotten at my hands all the tragedies that were before the Duke of Buckingham's, which he would have preserved in one volume. And from that time backward, even to the time of William the Conqueror, he determined to continue and perfect the story himself. . . . And therefore to make a meet induction into the matter, he devised this poesy; which, in my judgment, is so well penned that I would not have any verse thereof left out of our volume." ' **7** tapets] figured cloths, tapestries; here figurative for foliage. **30** prest] ready. **39** Erythius] relating to the island Erythia, one of the 'happy isles' in the west (actually in the bay of Cadiz); perhaps a western star. **48** chair] chariot, car. **57** leams] gleams, lights. **97** deule] dole, lamentation. **122** shright] shrieked. **125** eft] in turn. **141** sike] sigh; 1563 misprinted 'stike' but corrected in the errata. **285** throne] 1563 'trone'. **415** Treby] Trebia, a river in upper Italy, scene of Hannibal's victory over the Romans. **441** lin] cease. **464** spercled] sparkled. **504** peased] became still.

THOMAS TUSSER

THOMAS TUSSER (*c.* 1524–1580) holds no place, or only the humblest, among English poets, but his versified advice to farmers and housewives was circulated and read throughout the realm during his own lifetime and for several generations thereafter. As a boy Tusser was trained in music and became a member of the choir of St. Paul's Cathedral. Thence he went to Eton, where he was a pupil of Nicholas Udall, author of *Ralph Roister Doister*. He also attended Cambridge for a short time. Later, unhappy as a musician at court, he retired to Suffolk, married, and became a farmer. From his farm he sent to the press of Richard Tottel in 1557 his book, *A Hundreth Good Points of Husbandry*. This was soon reprinted in several editions, and by 1570 *A Hundreth Good Points of Huswifery*, which had appeared earlier as a separate publication, was combined with the book on husbandry. In 1573 the book became *Five hundreth points of good husbandry united to as many of good huswifery*. In spite of his funds of good advice, Tusser seems never to have thrived himself; and he died while in prison for debt.

Except for being versified throughout, Tusser's book resembles the 'Farmer's Almanac' of later periods; it is a mine of lore concerning crops, tillage, weather, gardens, and household economy. In its final form it also contained a few religious poems, moral maxims, and a versified autobiography.

MODERN EDITION: *Five Hundred Points of Good Husbandrie* (ed. by W. Payne and S. J. Herrtage), English Dialect Society, London, 1878.

TEXT: *Five Hundred Points of Good Husbandry*, 1580 (24380), B. M.

70 *A preface . . .*] Saintsbury (*Manual of English Prosody*, p. 314) points out that in the history of English metrics Tusser is 'important because at the very time when men like Gascoigne were doubting whether English had any foot but the iambic, he produced lolloping but perfectly metrical continuous anapæsts, and mixed measures of various kinds.' This poem and several of those below illustrate this remark. **3**] in an earlier edition this line read, 'Of Surrey so famous that crave'.

70 *The praise of husbandry*] In 1580 this title stands in the margin; the poem is a riddle, with these words giving the answer. **9** champian] champaign, open country.

71 *A description of the properties of winds . . .* **5** noyer] annoyer. **10**] The meaning of the line is obscure; possibly 'The East is not at all a forbearer,' i. e., not at all indulgent; or, reading 'forebearer,' 'The East (in contrast with the West) is a parent of nothing.'

71 *Christmas husbandly fare* **7** shred pies] minced-meat pies.

BARNABE GOOGE

BARNABE GOOGE (1540–1594) was one of the small army of translators who made it their duty, during the early years of Elizabeth's reign, to put into English what seemed to them the treasures of other literatures. Googe chose for translation works of morality and religion that are now forgotten. His volume of original poems, *Eclogues, Epitaphs, and Sonnets*, represents the poetical exercises of a bright student who had read Tottel's miscellany with delight. In addition to the eclogues which make up the greater part of the book, there are bits of love-poetry, addresses to friends, tributes to and epitaphs upon famous men. The eclogues deserve notice as being among the early specimens of pastoral poetry in English. Googe's work is fairly representative of the verbose, conventional, highly alliterative verse which tended to prevail in the period between the passing of Surrey and the advent of Spenser. His favorite verse-form is the 'fourteener' or the poulter's measure from which it was adapted. In his book all the lines, whether of ten, twelve, or fourteen syllables, were printed in two parts, the break representing the cæsura.

MODERN EDITION: *Eglogs, Epytaphes, & Sonettes* (ed. by E. Arber), London, 1871.

TEXT: *Eclogues, Epitaphs, and Sonnets*, 1563 (12048), Huntington.

72–73 *To the right worshipful . . .*] This dedicatory letter expresses an unwillingness to appear in print often affected by poets of the 16th century. As here, the poet was likely to place upon his friends the responsibility for the publication of his work. The social feeling against exposing one's compositions to sale and to public knowledge kept the poems of many authors, particularly of noblemen, out of circulation except in manuscript. Googe had been a member of Gray's Inn. The quotation from Martial may be translated, 'You could be safer at home.'

73 *Out of sight, out of mind*] For a poem of similar schematic construction, see p. 45. **18** depart] separate; as in the marriage service of the old Prayer-book.

74 *Once musing as I sat* **25–32**] omitted in text of 1563, but printed under 'Faults escaped.'

74 *To Doctor Bale*] For John Bale, see p. 377 and note.

GEORGE TURBERVILLE

GEORGE TURBERVILLE (*c*.1540–*c*.1595) spent several years at New College, Oxford, but left in 1561 without taking a degree. He went to London and resided in one of the Inns of Court, where his ability as a versifier was appreciated and developed. By 1567 he had three books ready for the printers, two of them translations, *The Heroical Epistles of Ovid* and *Eclogues of Mantuan*, and the third a collection of original poems (interspersed, however, with translated pieces) entitled *Epitaphs, Epigrams, Songs and Sonnets*. As this title suggests, Turberville to some extent imitated Barnabe Googe. In 1568 he went to Russia as secretary to Thomas Randolph, the Queen's ambassador, and sent back to his friends verse-epistles and other poems relating to that country. His principal publication aside from those already mentioned was *Tragical Tales*, 1587, a verse-translation from Italian originals, at the end of which he added a section of 'epitaphs and sonnets.' Turberville outlived his literary fame, though to the end of his life he seems to have been held in high personal regard. Among the epigrams of Sir John Harington occurs this tribute 'in commendation of George Turberville':

> When times were yet but rude, thy pen endeavored
>   To polish barbarism with purer style;
> When times were grown most old, thy heart persévered,
>   Sincere and just, unstained with gifts or guile.

The verse of Turberville now and then rises above that facile alliterative sing-song which was the poetic vernacular of the decades in which he was writing. A certain delicacy, or fineness, of idea and sentiment (which does not, however, save him from infelicitous diction) is his principal charm. In several passages he expressed great modesty regarding his place as a poet, with more sincerity than is usually revealed in such disclaimers.

MODERN EDITIONS: *Epitaphs, Epigrams, Songs and Sonnets* (ed. by J. P. Collier), *c*. 1870, and in *English Poets* (ed. by A. Chalmers), London, 1810; *Tragical Tales*, Edinburgh, 1837; *The Heroical Epistles of Ovid* (ed. by F. S. Boas), London, 1928.

COMMENT: H. E. Rollins, 'New Facts about George Turberville,' *M.P.* xv. 129.

TEXT: *Epitaphs, Epigrams, Songs and Sonnets*, 1567 (24326), Huntington; *Tragical Tales*, 1587 (24330), Huntington.

75–76 *Verse in praise of Lord Henry Howard* 5 in mew] in keeping, a term from falconry. 15 fright] freighted. 23–24] These lines may be paraphrased: 'To do justice to the benefits he conferred and to the generosity of his mind, which duty he seems to have laid upon those who come after him, I write, etc.'

76 *Of drunkenness*] This epigram goes back to the Greek Anthology, though Turberville may have known it through Sir Thomas More's Latin version.

76 *The lover to his lady* . . .] This is the best of Turberville's several translations of epigrams from the Greek Anthology, where this poem is ascribed to Plato. See also *Sonnet*, 'Were I as base,' p. 207, and note.

76–77 *To a fair gentlewoman* . . . 2 graff] graft, tree.

77–78 *Unable by long and hard travel* . . . 11 Wight] swift. 15 Suchan] the modern Sukhona, a tributary of the Dvina.

78–79 *To his friend* . . . 10 *A per se*] 'A by itself,' first or highest of all; an expression corresponding to modern 'A number one.'

THOMAS HOWELL

THOMAS HOWELL (*fl.* 1568–1581), a member of the household of the Earl of Shrewsbury, and later of that of the Countess of Pembroke, holds his place as a minor poet, an imitator of Surrey. He published three small collections. His *Devices*, 1581, was written at Wilton and dedicated to Mary, Countess of Pembroke. One poem, *Written to a most excellent book, full of rare invention*, pays a tribute to Sidney's *Arcadia*, which Howell must have seen in manuscript in the course of its composition.

MODERN EDITIONS: *The Poems* (ed. by A. B. Grosart), Manchester, 1879; *Howell's Devises* (ed. by W. Raleigh), Oxford, 1906.

COMMENT: Sir Walter Raleigh, *Some Authors*, Oxford, 1923.

TEXT: *The Arbor of Amity*, 1568 (13874), Bodleian; *H. His Devices*, 1581 (13875), Bodleian.

79 *When he thought* . . . 15 ear'th] plows.

80 *Of misery* 5 laide] probably French *laid*, foul; if English, then 'lade,' for 'laden.' Elsewhere Howell writes, 'My limbs are lade, I cannot fly.'

80–81 *Jack shows* . . .] a dialect-song, written with scant sympathy for the rustic supposed to be the speaker. The principal characteristics of the dialect are the use of 'ich' (often shortened to ''ch') for 'I,' 'v' for 'f,' and 'z'

for 's.' 13 'chwot] ich wot, I know. 14 courtnoles] courtiers (used contemptuously); usually 'cortnolls.' 22 Dountoone's round] a country dance. 26 veow cunnigare] few cunninger. 35 bait] meal. 36 chee vore the] 'I warn you.' Cf. *Lear* IV. vi. 246. 50 red ones] gold coins. 55 friscals vet] play tricks.

81–82 *Of the golden world* 19 Irus'] proverbial name for a beggar, from that of the beggar in Ulysses' house in Ithaca, according to Homer.

THOMAS CHURCHYARD

THOMAS CHURCHYARD (*c.* 1520–1604) probably began writing in the reign of Henry VIII; his earliest publication appeared under Edward VI; he continued to publish works in verse and prose throughout the reign of Elizabeth, and issued two books after James I came to the throne. In his boyhood a page to Henry Howard, Earl of Surrey, Churchyard cherished the memory of that poet throughout his long life; nor did he materially improve upon the literary manner which he acquired in the middle decades of the century. For several years he was a soldier, serving in Ireland, Scotland, the Low Countries, and France.

According to Churchyard's account of his own writings (in *Churchyard's Challenge*, 1593), he wrote 'many things in the book of *Songs and Sonnets*,' but none of these has been identified. An extended tribute to Skelton from his pen was printed before Marsh's collected edition of Skelton's poems, 1568. Churchyard is the author of at least one poem in *The Paradise of Dainty Devices*, and one in *A Gorgeous Gallery of Gallant Inventions*. Perhaps his best work is the legend of *Shore's Wife*, contributed to the *Mirror for Magistrates* of 1563. He also wrote the story of Cardinal Wolsey for the *Mirror* of 1587. He was fond of alliterative titles, and besides *Churchyard's Challenge* he issued *Churchyard's Chips*, *Churchyard's Chance*, and *Churchyard's Charge*. Thomas Nashe in *Four Letters Confuted*, 1593, expressed admiration for Churchyard's 'aged muse, that may well be grandmother to our grandiloquentest poets at this period.' Spenser refers to Churchyard, under the name of Palemon, in *Colin Clout's Come Home Again*.

MODERN EDITIONS: *Churchyard's Good Will* (ed. by Thomas Park), in *Heliconia*, Vol. iii, 1815; *First Part of Churchyard's Chips* (ed. by J. P. Collier), 1870?; *The Worthiness of Wales*, Spenser Society, 1876; *Wished Reformation of Wicked Rebellion* and *Tragedy of Shore's Wife* in *Illustrations of Old English Literature* (ed. by J. P. Collier), 1866; *The Siege of Guisnes* in *An English Garner* (ed. by E. Arber), London, 1903.

COMMENT: H. W. Adnitt in *Transactions of the Shropshire Archæological and Natural History Society*, Vol. iii, 1880, pp. 1–68.

TEXT: *The First Part of Churchyard's Chips*, 1575 (5232), Huntington; *A Gorgeous Gallery of Gallant Inventions*, 1578 (20402), Bodleian.

84 *The lover deceived . . .*] This poem is identified as Churchyard's by the fact that the first two stanzas of it were included in *Churchyard's Charge*, 1580.

GEORGE GASCOIGNE

GEORGE GASCOIGNE (1542?–1577) seems to have been for a brief period the most considerable man of letters in England. His brilliant career as soldier, adventurer, and writer attracts increasing attention from students of Elizabeth's reign.

As a boy Gascoigne spent some time at Cambridge University; and in 1562 he married Elizabeth Breton, widow, thereby becoming step-father to Nicholas Breton (see p. 163). The circumstance that Mrs. Breton at the time was claimed as wife by another gentleman gave rise to some litigation and at least one street riot. In 1566 Gascoigne seems to have resided at Gray's Inn; for there in that year were presented the plays *Jocasta* (translated by him and his friend Kinwelmarsh) and *Supposes* (translated from Ariosto by Gascoigne). The imprudence which marked Gascoigne's career led to his being disinherited by his father, Sir John Gascoigne. In 1572 he was prevented from taking a seat in Parliament by a petition, promulgated by his creditors, charging him with slander, manslaughter, and atheism.

The plays already mentioned were printed, together with 'divers excellent devices by sundry gentlemen' and 'certain devices of Master Gascoigne,' in a book bearing the title of *A Hundreth Sundry Flowers* (1573). At the time when this book appeared Gascoigne was serving as a soldier in Holland; two years later he re-issued the collection under the title of *The Posies of George Gascoigne*, having made some changes and added editorial matter intended to make it appear that he himself was the author of all the poems included in *A Hundreth Sundry Flowers*. B. M. Ward, the modern editor of this book, is convinced that *A Hundreth Sundry Flowers* (and hence *The Posies*) contains work by the Earl of Oxford, Sir Christopher Hatton, and some others; and that Gascoigne could claim all for himself because of personal and political reasons on the part of these contributors. (For objections to this view, see articles listed under 'Comment.')

In 1575 Gascoigne also published *The Glass of Government*, 'a tragical comedy' of moralistic cast; and in 1576 he issued *The Steel Glass*, a satire, and *The Complaint of Philomene*, a long narrative poem. His series of reflective poems, or elegies, *The Grief of Joy*, he presented in manuscript to Queen Elizabeth as a New Year's gift in 1577, the year of his death. His other works, for the most part moralistic pamphlets, are in prose.

Gascoigne's writings show remarkable originality and range. *Supposes* is the first prose comedy in English; *The Steel Glass* is very nearly the first true satire and, for its time, an excellent specimen of blank verse; *Certain*

Notes of Instruction (published with Gascoigne's *Posies*) is our earliest treatise on English prosody. Thomas Nashe, writing in 1589, pays this tribute: 'Master Gascoigne is not to be abridged of his deserved esteem, who first beat the path to that perfection which our best poets have aspired to since his departure.' For two poems traditionally ascribed to Gascoigne, see those selected from *A Hundreth Sundry Flowers* in the section, 'Elizabethan Miscellanies,' pp. 187, 188.

MODERN EDITIONS: *The Complete Works* (ed. by J. W. Cunliffe), two volumes, Cambridge, 1907–1910; *A Hundreth Sundrie Flowres* (ed. by B. M. Ward), London, 1926; *Certayne notes of instruction in English verse, The steel glas, The complaynt of Philomene* (ed. by E. Arber), London, 1868; *The Complete Poems of George Gascoigne* (ed. by W. C. Hazlitt), two volumes, London, 1869–70.

COMMENT: F. E. Schelling, *The Life and Writings of George Gascoigne*, Boston, 1893; W. W. Greg, 'A Hundreth Sundry Flowers,' *The Library*, vii. 269, and corr. viii. 123; further articles in *M. L. R.* xxii. 442, and *R. E. S.* iv. 34.

TEXT: *A Hundred Sundry Flowers*, [1573] (11635), White, Huntington; *The Whole Works*, 1587 (11638), Huntington; *The Steel Glass*, [1576] (11645), White.

85–86 *Gascoigne's good morrow* 17 darksome storms] 1573; later printings alter to 'darksomeness', which satisfies the demand of rhyme. 40 than] old form of 'then.'

86–87 *Gascoigne's arraignment* 13 fitteth] 1575; 1573 'sitteth'.

87–88 *Gascoigne's lullaby* 24 eft] again.

88 *Gascoigne's De profundis*] This purports to be a preface and a proem to a translation of *Psalm* cxxx, known as *De profundis,* but the translation is not preserved. The present sonnet is interesting as being Petrarchan in rhyme-scheme; and also for its mixture of pagan with Christian terms and ideas.

88–89 *Inscription in his garden*] This is the second of a series of poems representing inscriptions in Gascoigne's garden. In 1573 it is headed, 'In that other end of his said close walk were written these toys in rhyme.'

89 *Deep Desire sung this song*] Deep Desire is a character in the allegorical mask which Gascoigne devised as part of the entertainment for Queen Elizabeth at Kenilworth in 1575. 8 counterpeise] counterbalance.

89–99 *The steel glass*] The passages here printed make up nearly one-half of the poem. 1] marginal note: 'Here the substance of the theme beginneth.' 6 surquedry] pride. 33 rue] fall. 41 at latter Lammas] at a time which will never come. 43 preach at Tyburn] beg; Tyburn Cross, in London, was a favorite stand for beggars. 60 Lucilius] a Roman satirist, d. 103 B.C. 94 Sir Simony's deceits] the practice of simony, buying and selling ecclesiastical places and honors. 100

Melchizedek] see *Hebrews* vii. 103 leese] lose. 120 pluralities] plural livings, the holding of many appointments at once. 144 beads] prayers. 218–219 some . . . in Flanders] These, and the group mentioned (l. 224) as being in Liegeland (another part of the Low Countries) are the members of the extreme Protestant and pietistic sects then flourishing on the Continent. 220 For why] because. 250 curious *quids*] subtle questions beginning with *quid.* 270 Erato] muse of love-poetry. 271 Calliope] muse of heroic poetry. 274–275] Scholars were loath to allow that English could have a grammar, since words in it are not declined, but relations are shown by prepositions and other particles—Gascoigne's *monosyllaba.* 289 Piers] This type-name for the plowman had been put into general use by the 14th-century poem, *Piers Plowman.* 306 earing up the balks] plowing up the strips of vacant land left as boundaries. 330 cockets] seals of the customs officers, indicating duty paid. 340 utt'ring] marketing. 349 firmentie] frumenty, a drink made of grain boiled in milk; Gascoigne appears to be objecting to liquor which is too weak or which is imperfectly malted. 350 Davie Diker] a type-name for a ditch-digger, or diker. 367 parchmenters] makers of parchment (*i. e., passement*) lace, or lace trimming. ferret silk] floss silk. 372 covin] deceit, collusion. 374 spy no pence] Officers searching ships were sometimes bought off. 376 strain] constrain, take up, as stray animals. 386 precious coals] an obsolete oath; sometimes 'God's precious coals!' 388 bob] either a rap or a taunt.

GEORGE WHETSTONE

GEORGE WHETSTONE (*c.* 1544–1587) was a friend of George Gascoigne and wrote his biography in verse. Usually Whetstone is named with Churchyard, as both were miscellaneous writers who lived by what they received from patrons and printers for pamphlets, translations, elegies, and other poems. Like Churchyard also he had experience as a soldier; in fact he made the acquaintance of Gascoigne and Churchyard while all three were serving in Holland. During a later term of service Whetstone was present at the battle of Zutphen, where Sir Philip Sidney was fatally wounded; and he was a member of Sir Humphrey Gilbert's expedition to Newfoundland, 1578–79.

He began publication with *The Rock of Regard*, 1576, a collection of verse-tales and miscellaneous poems. He wrote numerous encomiastic poems upon noblemen recently dead, one in 1586, for example, upon Sir Philip Sidney. His most notable production was his unacted play in two parts, *Promos and Cassandra*, 1578, in the preface to which he set down some interesting dramatic criticism. This play embodied the plot used by Shakespeare in *Measure for Measure*.

MODERN EDITIONS: *The Rock of Regard* (ed. by J. P. Collier), 1870?; *A Remembrance . . . of Sir Nicholas Bacon, A Remembrance of . . . Sir James Dyer, A Remembrance of . . . Thomas, late Earl of Sussex, Sir Philip Sidney, his Honorable Life, etc.*, in *Frondes Caducæ* (ed. by A. Boswell), Auchinleck, 1816; *A Mirror of True Honor and Christian Nobility*, in *Heliconia* (ed. by T. Park), Vol. ii, 1815; *A Remembrance of . . . George Gascoigne, Esquire*, in *English Poets* (ed. by A. Chalmers), Vol. ii, 1810.

TEXT: *The Rock of Regard*, 1576 (25348), Huntington.

99–100 *Description of cozeners*] In 1576 the title is *P. Plasino's description of cozeners.* 15 kit ne follows kind] proverbial, implying 'like breeds like.'

100 *Epilogus*] At the end of one part of the book, called 'Arbor of Virtue.'

HUMPHREY GIFFORD

HUMPHREY GIFFORD (*fl.* 1580) was the son of a gentleman of Devonshire. He evidently became an official of the Poultry Counter, a debtor's prison in London. Aside from such scanty associations with his name, we have a volume of his authorship entitled, *A Posy of Gillyflowers*, 'each differing from other in color and odor, yet all sweet,' made up of prose translations from Italian tales and a fair body of poems, imitative of Surrey and of his disciples. The titles, *A doleful dump, In praise of a contented mind*, and *Of the uncontented estate of lovers*, suggest Gifford's quality. In his poem *For soldiers* he escapes, with good effect, from the conventions within which for the most part he writes.

MODERN EDITIONS: *The Poems* in *Miscellanies of the Fuller Worthies' Library* (ed. by A. B. Grosart), 1870; *The Complete Poems and Translations in Prose* (ed. by A. B. Grosart), Occasional Issues, 1875.

TEXT: *A Posy of Gillyflowers*, 1580 (11872), B. M.

100–101 *For soldiers* 1 Brutus' land] According to legend, England had been founded by Brutus, of Trojan descent. 10 denounceth] announces.

101–102 *A delectable dream*] The selection is a song from the longer poem of this title. The author represents himself as falling asleep and hearing a harper play for dancing fairies. The harper sang the song here given, with the result that 'the fairies all on him did frown'; they called down curses on him that he might be a warning to such as would speak ill of womankind.

Although petrified by the fairies' curse, the harper by silent signs petitioned to the gods for the privilege of singing another song. Upon the granting of this permission, he sang,

Among all creatures bearing life,
A woman is the worthiest thing, etc.

The countenance of the fairies lightened; but just as the author was about to speak his own mind to the effect 'how some were good and some were bad,' a passing friend awakened him. 22 glozer's] deceiver's, flatterer's.

RICHARD STANYHURST

RICHARD STANYHURST (1547–1618) was an Irishman, born in Dublin, the son of a speaker of the Irish House of Commons. He took the degree of B.A. at Oxford in 1568 and went to study law at the Inns of Court. For Holinshed's *Chronicles* of 1577 he prepared the 'Description of Ireland' and a part of the 'History of Ireland.' After the death of his wife, in 1579, Stanyhurst went to the Low Countries, embraced the Catholic faith, and never returned to England. His sole volume of poetry, *The First Four Books of Virgil his Æneis translated into English heroical verse*, was printed in Leyden in 1582, and in London in 1583 and 1620. Besides the translation from Virgil the volume contains 'other poetical devices thereto annexed,' some of which are translations, from Sir Thomas More's Latin and other sources.

Stanyhurst continues to attract interest because of his experiments, largely unsuccessful, in reproducing classical meters in English. The use of such measures, encouraged by Ascham and attempted by Spenser, Sidney, Harvey, and others, reaches its nadir in the work of Stanyhurst. By his spelling he sought to indicate or to fix the quantities of syllables; furthermore, he employed unusual, dialectical, and unpoetical words; with the result that his verses make, for the most part, strange and difficult reading. He received few commendations for his painful poetry, but was liberally satirized. (See Hall's *Satire VI*, p. 365, and note.) For other specimens of quantitative measures see under Sidney, Greene, and Campion.

MODERN EDITION: *Translation of the First Four Books of the Æneis, etc.* (ed. by E. Arber), Westminster, 1895.

TEXT: *The First Four Books of Virgil*, 1582 (24806), Huntington.

102 *A prayer to the Trinity*] This specimen of sapphic verse is without doubt the best of Stanyhurst's quantitative poems. It was also printed in *Greene's Funerals*, 1594, as 'used by R[obert] G[reene] at the instant of his death.' An imitation appears in the same volume.

EDWARD DE VERE, EARL OF OXFORD

EDWARD DE VERE, seventeenth Earl of Oxford (1550–1604), was on his father's side nephew to Frances Vere, wife of Henry Howard, Earl of Surrey, and on his mother's side nephew to Arthur Golding, early translator of Ovid. Oxford throughout his youth and early manhood was one of Elizabeth's favorite courtiers. Usually described as capricious and foppish, he introduced novelties of toilet from Italy, and was probably the butt of Gabriel Harvey's brief satire upon the Italianate Englishman, *Speculum Tuscanismi*, though Harvey disclaimed any personal animus in the caricature and avowed a debt to Oxford's patronage. In 1579 Oxford insulted Sir Philip Sidney and was challenged; only the intervention of the Queen prevented a duel. Oxford seems to have been a generous patron of actors and of literary men. John Lyly, in the early years of his literary career, was Oxford's private secretary, and dedicated to his employer *Euphues and his England*, 1580. After running through the fortune brought him by his first wife, Anne Cecil (daughter of Lord Burghley), Oxford mended his estate by a second marriage. In 1601 he was one of the noblemen sitting on the trial of Essex for treason, and he acted as Lord Great Chamberlain (an office his by inheritance) at the coronation of James I.

Oxford may be read as the Elizabethan courtly poet *par excellence*. The judgment of contemporary critics placed him at the head of the group of noble and polite lyrists, though Sidney, Greville, and perhaps Ralegh must now be ranked above him. The conventions of the time prevented one of Oxford's rank from publishing a volume of his verse, and no one of his family or friends gave his manuscripts to printers after his death. Hence his poems must be gleaned, sometimes uncertainly, from miscellanies. B. M. Ward has made it appear that some of the poems in *A Hundreth Sundry Flowers*, 1573, are Oxford's, and is convinced that Oxford was editor of that collection. He also believes that this nobleman is the author of the songs in Lyly's plays and of some poems attributed to Watson and to other writers whom Oxford patronized. Plays by Oxford, praised by Meres, are either not extant or not identified. For another poem by Oxford, see pp. 195–196; for a poem ascribed to him by Ward, see *The lover declareth his affection*, p. 188.

MODERN EDITIONS: *Poems* in *Miscellanies of the Fuller Worthies' Library* (ed. by A. B. Grosart), 1872; *The Courtly Poets from Raleigh to Montrose* (ed. by J. Hannah), London, 1870.

COMMENT: B. M. Ward, *The Seventeenth Earl of Oxford*, London, 1928.

TEXT: *The Paradise of Dainty Devices*, 1576 (7516), Huntington; *Rawlinson Poetry Ms. 85*, Bodleian; *The Phœnix Nest*, 1593 (21516), White; *Breton's Bower of Delights*, 1591 (3633), Huntington.

102–103 *Of the mighty power of love*] 'Finis. E. O.' at the end in *P. D. D.* 4 rede] tell, relate.

103 *Who taught thee first . . .*] 'Finis Earll of Oxenforde' at the end in ms. This sonnet, slightly altered, and with the word 'love' printed at the ends of ll. 1–12, is *Sonnet 60* in Thomas Watson's *Tears of Fancy*, 1593.

103–104 *If women could be fair*] 'Finis quod Earll of Oxenforde' at the end in ms. This poem was set to music by Byrd, *Psalms, Sonnets, and Songs*, 1588.

104 *Of the birth and bringing up of Desire*] A few lines of this poem appeared, attributed to Oxford, in *The Art of English Poesy*, 1589. A lengthened version appeared in Thomas Deloney's *Garland of Goodwill*, probably first published in 1593.

104–105 *What cunning can express?*] Signed 'E. O.' in *P. N.* 1 cunning] 1593 'cunnig'.

SIR PHILIP SIDNEY

SIR PHILIP SIDNEY (1554–1586) in the scant thirty-two years of his life wrote himself high as poet, scholar, courtier, diplomat, and soldier, and highest as gentleman. He was born at Penshurst, his father's fine country place in Kent, and at the age of nine went to Shrewsbury School where on the first day of his attendance he met Fulke Greville, who became his lifelong friend and companion. From his thirteenth to his seventeenth year Sidney was in residence at Christ Church, Oxford, and briefly at Cambridge, but he took no degree. In 1572 he went to France in the train of an English ambassador. His first-hand experience of the religious dissensions which racked France at this time, culminating in the Massacre of St. Bartholomew, seems to have influenced Sidney in his later championship of the Protestant cause in Europe. On his first trip abroad he traveled in Germany, Hungary, Italy, and the Netherlands, returning to England in time to be present at the famous reception of Queen Elizabeth by the Earl of Leicester (Sidney's maternal uncle) at Kenilworth Castle, July 9–27, 1575. Sidney followed the Queen and court to Chartley Castle, the home of Lord Essex; and it is here that he is supposed to have made the acquaintance of Essex's daughter, Penelope Devereux, the Stella of *Astrophel and Stella,* then aged thirteen. The later engagement of the two young people was broken off for reasons which now are obscure, and Penelope became the wife of Lord Rich.

In 1577 Sidney went abroad a second time, as Ambassador to the Emperor of Germany and the Elector Palatine. In the following year he wrote a mask, *The Lady of May,* to be used as a part of the entertainment of the Queen and court at the Earl of Leicester's castle at Wanstead. At about this time Sidney's interest in literature seems to have been heightened by his companionship with Fulke Greville, Edward Dyer, and other congenial young men; the group, referred to by Spenser and Gabriel Harvey as the Areopagus (though not organized as a club), interested itself in the possibility of reproducing in English the quantitative meters of Greek and Latin verse. In August, 1579, a Puritanical writer named Stephen Gosson published *The School of Abuse,* attacking plays and poetry but dedicated to Sidney; Sidney's *Defence of Poesy,* though perhaps not written until 1583, replies, though not by name, to Gosson's attack. (For extracts, see p. 885.) In 1580 Sidney wrote an open letter to Queen Elizabeth, dissuading her from her projected marriage with the Duke of Anjou; and for his boldness he was practically banished from court. During his retirement, spent at Wilton House, the home of his sister who had become by marriage Countess of Pembroke, he wrote at least part of his long pastoral romance, *Arcadia.* He was knighted in 1583 and in the same year married Frances Walsingham, daughter of Sir Francis Walsingham. In 1585 he was projecting an expedition to America with Sir Francis Drake, but the Protestant cause, endangered by Spain's war with the Netherlands, and the Queen's need of his services, sent him instead to Holland as Governor of Flushing. In September of the following year Sidney was wounded in an unimportant engagement before the city of Zutphen. After twenty-six days of suffering, during which time he composed a song about his wound, entitled *La cuisse rompue,* and caused it to be sung to him, he died, to the grief of all England and a share of Europe.

None of Sidney's literary productions was printed during his lifetime. The sixth song from *Astrophel and Stella* appeared, with musical setting, in Byrd's *Psalms, Sonnets, and Songs* of 1588; and three stanzas of the tenth song were printed with music in Byrd's *Songs of Sundry Natures,* 1589. *The Countess of Pembroke's Arcadia* was published in 1590, in an incomplete form representing the revision Sidney had begun of his first draft, and again (the revision having been carried to completion by his sister) in 1593. His *Astrophel and Stella* was published in 1591 by a printer named Newman, without the consent of Sidney's family, from one of the several manuscripts then in circulation. Another printer, Lownes by name, at once reprinted Newman's edition, making slight changes. Still in 1591 Newman issued his second edition, apparently receiving in its preparation some aid from Sidney's family. Not until 1598 did the fully authorized edition appear; at that time all of Sidney's principal works were collected and printed in a folio volume, prepared for the printer by the Countess of Pembroke herself. The *Defence of Poesy* appeared in two separate editions in 1595.

The publication in 1591 of *Astrophel and Stella* had much to do with the remarkable outburst of sonnet-cycles which characterized English poetry in the 1590's. Though Sidney does not maintain that freedom from literary influences and fashions which he claims for himself in several sonnets, yet his is certainly among the most personal and least artificial of all the numerous Elizabethan cycles. In spite of borrowings from Petrarch, Ronsard, and du Bellay, *Astrophel and Stella* gives us a fairly intimate picture of Sidney's unhappy relations with Penelope Devereux. Sidney hardly won among poets a place as high as that which *The Defence of Poesy* gives him among critics and æstheticians; yet in scattered sonnets and passages he attains to a grave and musical eloquence which is the idiom only of the greatest. *The Art of English Poesy*, 1589, preserves this little song not found elsewhere in Sidney's works (though used as the basis of a sonnet in the *Arcadia*), which has become a favorite:

> My true love hath my heart and I have his,
> By just exchange one for another given;
> I hold his dear, and mine he cannot miss,
> There never was a better bargain driven.
> My true love hath my heart and I have his.
>
> My heart in me keeps him and me in one,
> My heart in him his thoughts and senses guides;
> He loves my heart, for once it was his own,
> I cherish his, because in me it bides.
> My true love hath my heart and I have his.

For other poems by Sidney, see pp. 196 and 936.

MODERN EDITIONS: *Astrophel and Stella* (ed. by A. W. Pollard), London, 1888; *The Poems* (ed. by J. Drinkwater), Muses' Library, London, 1910; *The Complete Works* (ed. by A. Feuillerat), four volumes, Cambridge, 1922–1926.

COMMENT: M. W. Wallace, *The Life of Sir Philip Sidney*, Cambridge, 1915; J. A. Symonds, *Sir Philip Sidney*, London, 1886.

TEXT: Sir P. S. His *Astrophel and Stella*, 1591 (22536), B. M.; *The Countess of Pembroke's Arcadia*, 1598 (22541), White; *The Countess of Pembroke's Arcadia*, 1593 (22540), White; *A Poetical Rhapsody*, 1602 (6373), White.

106 *To the reader*] This is an extract from the prefatory address placed before the authorized edition of Sidney's works. 'H. S.' was Henry Sandford, the Earl of Pembroke's secretary.

106–118 *Astrophel and Stella*] The present selection constitutes about one-third of this sequence, which consisted of 108 sonnets and eleven songs. The whole grew out of Sidney's love for Penelope Devereux, daughter of the first Earl of Essex. 'Astrophel' (from Greek words meaning star-lover) is Sidney; 'Stella' (Latin, star) is Penelope. She was about eight years younger than he, and was but a girl when he

first met her. From 1576 he seems to have been a serious suitor for her hand. When Essex died, in that year, he expressed the wish that Sidney might marry his daughter. The marriage of Sidney's uncle, the Earl of Leicester, to Lady Essex (Penelope's mother) in 1577 may have affected unfavorably the chances of the union. Sidney saw Penelope at various times for several years; but in 1581 she was married to Robert, Lord Rich. Sidney's love appears to have been heightened by this marriage; and while Wallace, following Pollard, believes that the first thirty-two sonnets of *Astrophel and Stella* (here the first fourteen),with the exception of 'Rich fools there be,' were written before Penelope's marriage in a spirit of friendship and 'literary courtship,' the greater part of the sequence must relate to the period when a marriage between 'Astrophel' and 'Stella' had become out of the question.

106 *Loving in truth*] This, like some other sonnets in the sequence, is written in lines of twelve syllables.

106–107 *Not at the first sight* 1 dribbed] a term from archery, describing a weak, short, or widely inaccurate shot. 3 mine] used in a military sense. 13 me] 1598; 1591 'my'.

107 *Let dainty wits* 3 Pindar's apes] imitators of Pindar. 7–8] The allusion here is to the Euphuism made popular by Lyly. B. M. Ward, following Courthope, argues that Sidney and his friends constituted a 'romantic' school definitely opposed to the Earl of Oxford and his group (which included Lyly), the 'Euphuistic' school.

108 *Alas, have I not* 5 rhubarb] bitter, tart; with the suggestion, also, of 'medicinal.'

109 *Fly, fly, my friends* 6 so fair level] so well take aim.

109–110 *Rich fools there be*] one of several sonnets playing upon the name of Penelope's husband. 4 blest] 1591 'rich'.

110 *You that with allegory's* 7 slake] slack.

110 *Whether the Turkish*] This sonnet lists the subjects of general conversation at the time of its writing, evidently late in 1580 or early in 1581. 1–2] A Turkish alliance with Persia in 1580 suggested to western Europe a Moslem attack upon Christendom. 3–4] Bathori, newly elected king of Poland, invaded Russia in 1580 and again in 1581. 5 three parts] the three religious parties in France: extreme Catholics, Politiques or moderate Catholics, and Huguenots. 6–8] Poliard says that these lines 'appear to refer to the meetings of the States on the subject of the acceptance of the sovereignty of Elizabeth's suitor, the Duke of Anjou. Though the Prince of Orange was in favor of this, the Hollanders refused any other governor than himself, and the States were thus to be divided into two friendly confederations, of one of which Anjou accepted the sovereignty in January, 1581, the month in which it is probable this sonnet was written.' 9–10] Sir Henry Sidney had three times been Lord Deputy of Ireland,

most recently from 1575 to 1578. 11] referring to the turbulent scenes preceding the Raid of Ruthven, August, 1581.

111 *Come, let me write* 4 fights] indistinct in 1598, which may read 'sights'; but we have retained 'fights' in view of this passage in Sidney's *Defence of Poesy:* 'as Aristotle saith, those things which in themselves are horrible, as cruel battles, unnatural monsters, are made in poetical imitation delightful.'

112 *My mouth doth water*] not in editions of 1591. 5 toward Aurora's court] Rich's seat was in Essex.

112 *Come sleep! O sleep* 5 prease] press.

113 *Having this day*] The reference to a tournament attended by 'some sent' from France points to a period between April 15 and August 1, 1581, when a French embassage was attempting to arrange a marriage between Anjou and Elizabeth.

114 *O grammar-rules* 12 weigh] 1591; 1598 'nay'.

115–116 *No more, my dear* 12 wish] 1591; 1598 'with'.

116–117 *Fourth song*] The first stanza was set to music by Henry Youll, *Canzonets,* 1608.

118 *Eleventh song*] The indentation of the stanzas indicates the change of speakers. 40 there] 1621; 1598 'thee'.

119–120 *Certain sonnets*] Under this title the folio of 1598 grouped twenty-seven poems from Sidney's mss. Eight of these had appeared in Henry Constable's *Diana,* 1594, and one in the *Arcadia,* but the others were printed for the first time.

119 *The nightingale*] In 1598 the heading is 'To the same tune', referring to the heading of the precedent poem, 'To the tune of *Non credo gia che piu 'infelice amante.*' 8–9 Tereus . . . Philomela] The legend of Philomela was a favorite among 16th-century poets. This lady was the dupe of the Thracian king, Tereus, who violated her and represented to her that her sister Procne, Tereus' queen, was dead. When the fraud was discovered, the sisters fled together, and were metamorphosed by the gods, one into a swallow and the other into a nightingale.

119–120 *Ring out your bells*] reprinted in *England's Helicon,* 1600, as *Astrophel's Love is dead. Additional Ms.* 28253 shows the poem to have been written by 1584.

120 *Thou blind man's mark*] This

and the sonnet following may be read as the epilogue to *Astrophel and Stella*. The ascent from carnal to spiritual love is in keeping with the Petrarchan convention; that fact, however, does not invalidate the sincerity of these poems.

120 *Splendidis longum . . .*] 'A long farewell to these glittering trifles!'

121–122 *O sweet woods*] This represents the poet's experimentation with classical meters. The particular meter here used is the asclepiad, named after its inventor, the Greek poet Asclepiades. In the *Arcadia* the poem is introduced thus: 'Dorus had long, he thought, kept silence from saying somewhat which might tend to the glory of her in whom all glory to his seeming was included, but now he brake it, singing these verses called *Asclepiadics*.' Sidney uses the lesser (or shorter) asclepiad, which scans normally as follows:

$$\_ \_ \mid \_ \cup \cup \_ \mid \_ \cup \cup \_ \mid \cup \_$$

Line 26, 'Here wrong's name is unheard, slander a monster is,' may be taken as a norm. A rhymed imitation of this poem was set to music by John Dowland, *Second Book of Songs and Airs*, 1600. 14 if 't] 1633; 1593 omits ''t'. 20 humorists'] faddists'. 34 safety] 1613; 1593 'safely'. 38 pretext] 1593 'prelext'; corrected in 1598.

122 *Two pastorals*] Only the first of the poems so headed is here reprinted. 9 prest] ready, prompt.

SIR EDWARD DYER

Sɪʀ Edward Dyer (d. 1607) is commonly named with his more famous friends, Greville and Sidney. Only a few scattered pieces of Dyer's poetry have come down to us, though a number of early references indicate that he was well known as a poet. However, both Bolton and Drummond complain, early in the 17th century, that they do not know Dyer's poetry at first-hand. Throughout most of his mature life Dyer lived in comparative obscurity, a fact which may be set down as a gloss upon his most famous poem, *My mind to me a kingdom is*.

Modern Editions: *Poems* in *Miscellanies of the Fuller Worthies' Library* (ed. by A. B. Grosart), 1872–1876; *The Courtly Poets from Raleigh to Montrose* (ed. by J. Hannah), London, 1870.

Text: Byrd's *Psalms, Sonnets, and Songs*, 1588 (4253), White; *Rawlinson Poetry Ms.* 85, Bodleian; *The Countess of Pembroke's Arcadia*, 1598 (22541), White.

123 *My mind to me a kingdom is*] This poem became popular as a song; cf. Ben Jonson, *Every Man Out of His Humor*, I. i. 11–14. John Taylor in *The Praise . . . of Beggary*, 1621, wrote:

He in his own conceit may have this
 bliss,
And sing, *My mind to me a kingdom
 is*.

Dyer's poem was also published as a broadside ballad; see *Shirburn Ballads*, p. 113. In the song-book in which the poem first was printed there appeared a song of similar sentiments in four stanzas of the same pattern. These may also be by Dyer, and may have been written as a part of the same poem. One of the stanzas follows:

I joy not in no earthly bliss,
 I force not Crœsus' wealth a straw;
For care, I know not what it is,
 I fear not Fortune's fatal law.

My mind is such as may not move
For beauty bright, nor force of love.

The version of Dyer's poem generally printed is that found in *Rawlinson Poetry Ms.* 85, which adds two stanzas to Byrd's version.

123–124 *The man whose thoughts*] 'Finis Mr. Dier' at the end in ms. 3 mishap] Grosart emends to 'desire' for the sake of rhyme. 4 pain] Grosart emends to 'plaint'.

124 *Prometheus when first*] With this poem, when first printed, appeared a reply by Sidney, as follows:

A satyr once did run away for dread
 With sound of horn which he himself did blow;
 Fearing and feared, thus from himself he fled,
Deeming strange evil in that he did
 not know.

Such causeless fears when coward minds
 do take,

It makes them fly that which they
    fain would have;
As this poor beast, who did his rest
    forsake,
Thinking not why, but how, himself
    to save.

Even thus might I, for doubts which I
    conceive
Of mine own words, my own good
    hap betray;

And thus might I, for fear of maybe,
    leave
The sweet pursuit of my desirèd prey.
Better like I thy satyr, dearest
    Dyer,
Who burnt his lips to kiss fair
    shining fire.

3 delight] Hannah gives, from *Harleian Ms.* 6910, 'the light'; Grosart defends the reading 'delight'. 6 Wood] mad.

FULKE GREVILLE

FULKE GREVILLE, Lord Brooke (1554–1628), can hardly be mentioned except in conjunction with his greater friend, Sir Philip Sidney. 'Well, my lord,' wrote Greville in a letter shortly after Sidney's death, 'divide me not from him, but love his memory, and me in it.' Born the same year as Sidney, he entered Shrewsbury School on the same day; but in 1567 the two friends were divided when Greville went to Jesus College, Cambridge, and Sidney to Oxford. By 1577 Greville had joined Sidney at court, where he enjoyed favor with the Queen, lasting, with some brief interruptions, until her death. In 1583 he was host, at his house in London, to Giordano Bruno. As a servant of the Queen and later of King James, he held many official positions, and in 1621 he was made first Baron Brooke. He acted as patron to Camden, Daniel, and Davenant. His death came as the result of a wound inflicted by a disaffected servant, who killed himself immediately after attacking his master. The epitaph Greville made for himself was: 'Servant to Queen Elizabeth, councillor to King James, and friend to Sir Philip Sidney.'

With Sidney and Dyer, Greville had undertaken the writing of poetry, probably before 1580; and he continued to write till past middle life. In 1633 appeared his collected *Works*, which did not contain his *Life of Sir Philip Sidney*, first printed in 1652. His voluminous manuscripts yielded material for another volume of verse, *Poems of Monarchy and Religion*, 1670. Greville was not a great poet, but his eager philosophical intellect shines out in many of his verses, while in his long poems he displays thoroughness and profundity of thinking which should place him among the leading speculative writers of his time. It has been suggested that under the name 'Cælica' Greville's amorous poems are addressed to Queen Elizabeth, to whom a few of them indubitably refer. It seems plain that several mistresses are celebrated in this rather miscellaneous collection.

MODERN EDITIONS: The *Works* (ed. by A. B. Grosart), four volumes, Fuller Worthies' Library, 1870; *Cælica* in *Elizabethan Sonnet-Cycles* (ed. by M. F. Crow), London, 1898.

COMMENT: M. W. Croll, *The Works of Fulke Greville*, Philadelphia, 1903; A. H. Bullen, *Elizabethans*, London, 1924.

TEXT: *The Phœnix Nest*, 1593 (21516), White; *England's Helicon*, 1600 (3191), White; *Mustapha*, 1609 (12362), White; *Certain Learned and Elegant Works*, 1633 (12361), Cornell.

125-126 *An epitaph . . .*] entitled in 1593 *Another of the same*, referring to the preceding epitaph by Ralegh (see p. 135). The ascription of this poem to Greville was first made, upon internal evidence alone, by Charles Lamb in his 'Defence of the Sonnets of Sir Philip Sidney,' *London Magazine*, 1823; the essay is reprinted in *Essays of Elia* as 'Some Sonnets of Sir Philip

Sidney.' Shortly after Sidney's death Greville wrote in a letter: 'The only question I now study is whether weeping sorrow or speaking sorrow may most honor his memory.' Cf. ll. 1–4. 9 Place] high place, rank. 25 parallels] 1593 and *Colin Clout's Come Home Again*, 1595, read 'parables'. The sense, however, demands 'parallels' and the change is one easily explained by a printer's misreading of ms.

126 *Another, of his Cynthia*] anonymous in 1600; by 'Another' the title evidently means 'another poet.' The poem had been set to music in John Dowland's *First Book of Songs and Airs*, 1597, and was taken, with two other poems, from that source by the editors of *E. H.* The presence of the poem in Greville's *Works* establishes it as his. 8 either] 1633 'causeless'.

126–127 *Chorus sacerdotum*] 'Chorus of priests.' 21 still] instil.

127 *You little stars*] set to music by Martin Peerson, *Motets*, 1630.

129 *Cælica, I overnight*] Greg suggests that in some cases Greville intended the name to be pronounced in two syllables, 'Cæl'ca,' with the accent upon the second.

129 *Under a throne*] plainly written to Queen Elizabeth; set to music by Martin Peerson, *Motets*, 1630. 6 ambition's] 1633 reads 'ambitious', but the 'u' seems to be a turned 'n.'

ROBERT DEVEREUX, EARL OF ESSEX

ROBERT DEVEREUX, second Earl of Essex (1567–1601), the brilliant favorite of Elizabeth and brother of Sidney's Stella, gave some moments from his crowded and ill-fated career to the writing of verse. Sir Henry Wotton records that it was a 'common way' with Essex 'to evaporate his thoughts in a sonnet.' Wotton preserves for us two lines of a sonnet otherwise lost, lines interesting in that, like most of his extant verse, they concern his relation with Elizabeth:

And if thou should'st by her be now forsaken,
She made thy heart too strong for to be shaken.

Essex's poems are preserved in various manuscripts and song-books. One of Campion's songs (*There is none, oh, none but you*) was attributed to Essex, on oral evidence, by Aubrey. See also *What if a day*, p. 446, and note.

MODERN EDITIONS: *Poems* in *Miscellanies of the Fuller Worthies' Library* (ed. by A. B. Grosart), 1872–1876; *Courtly Poets from Raleigh to Montrose* (ed. by J. Hannah), London, 1870.

COMMENT: Lytton Strachey, *Elizabeth and Essex*, London, 1928.

TEXT: Robert Dowland, *A Musical Banquet*, 1610 (7099), Huntington; *Chetham Ms.* 8012, Chetham.

130–131 *Change thy mind*] also in *Rawlinson Poetry Ms.* 85, with several variant readings; reprinted in *Wit's Interpreter*, 1671. In 1610 it is headed, 'The Right Honorable Robert, Earl of Essex: Earl Marshal of England'.

131–132 *To plead my faith*] headed in 1610 as the preceding poem.

132 *A passion*] 'of my Lo: of Essex' is added in ms.; also in *Ashmole Ms.* 781, headed, 'Certain verses made by Lord Essex'; said to have been sent to Elizabeth from Ireland in 1599. 1 fate] 'dayes' was first written in the ms. and crossed out. 10 robin] a play on Essex's name.

SIR WALTER RALEGH

SIR WALTER RALEGH (*c.* 1552–1618) must stand with Sidney and Oxford as a leading courtly poet of Elizabeth's reign. In his poetry as in other of his varied activities he fulfilled to a remarkable degree the pattern set for a Renaissance courtier. Most of the poetry which was connected with Ralegh's name during his lifetime was doubtless composed in the years from 1579 to

1586 when the author was a prominent courtier, winning the personal esteem of his royal mistress. The periods when he was out of favor gave rise to laments and pleas. A few pieces can be referred to bitter experiences which he underwent in the years from 1592 (when he was imprisoned for his marriage) to 1603 (when he was imprisoned, tried, and sentenced to death for complicity in plots against James I). During his lifetime a few of his poems appeared in miscellanies or as prefatory verses, but much of his poetry remained in manuscript until discovered by scholars of the eighteenth and nineteenth centuries. There can be no doubt that more of the unsigned poems in Elizabethan miscellanies, particularly in *The Phœnix Nest*, than have been ascribed to Ralegh are really his; and it is perhaps equally true that some of the ascriptions to him on the evidence of manuscripts are mistaken.

Ralegh's most ambitious poem was one entitled *The Ocean to Cynthia* (or perhaps *Cynthia, the Lady of the Sea*) in which under the name of 'the Ocean' or 'the Shepherd of the Ocean' he addressed his praise and vows to Queen Elizabeth, or 'Cynthia.' This poem, or a portion of it, he read to Spenser in Ireland, probably in 1589; and an account of the poem appears in that author's *Colin Clout's Come Home Again*, 1595. The poem as known to Spenser is lost; but we have what seems to be a first draft, in Ralegh's own hand, of the eleventh book and a part of the twelfth. From internal evidence we may judge that these belong to a later period than the portions of the poem read to Spenser, probably having been written during Ralegh's imprisonment and banishment from court, 1592–93. The material in the *Cecil Papers* containing the extant portion of *Cynthia* (including also some other poetical fragments by Ralegh) was first printed by Archdeacon Hannah in 1870.

The vigorous and eager mind which made Ralegh the associate of leading scholars and scientists of his time and country animates his poetry and sets the best of it above the level of conventional courtly verse. He seldom utilized the 'lumber' of the Petrarchan tradition. Sincerity and vigor, unhampered by superfluous ornament, characterize much of his work. For poems possibly by Ralegh see *Sought by the world*, p. 198, and *As you came from the holy land*, p. 414.

MODERN EDITIONS: *Poems by Sir Henry Wotton, Sir Walter Raleigh, and others* (ed. by J. Hannah), London, 1845; *The Courtly Poets from Raleigh to Montrose* (ed. by J. Hannah), London, 1870, reissued as *Poems of Sir Walter Raleigh . . . and other courtly poets*, 1875, 1892.

COMMENT: E. Gosse, *Raleigh*, London, 1886; W. Stebbing, *Sir Walter Raleigh*, Oxford, 1891.

TEXT: *Rawlinson Poetry Ms.* 160, Bodleian; *The Phœnix Nest*, 1593 (21516), White; *The Fairy Queen*, 1590 (23081), White; *England's Helicon*, 1600 (3191), White; *Malone Ms.* 19, Bodleian; *Harleian Ms.* 6917, B. M.; *A Poetical Rhapsody*, 1608 (6374), White; *Courtly Poets from Raleigh to Montrose*, 1870; Anthony Scoloker, *Daiphantus*, 1604 (21853), Bodleian.

132–133 *To Queen Elizabeth*] In the ms. this is headed ('absurdly,' says Hannah) 'Sir Walter Ralegh to Queen Elizabeth'. 14 access] *Rawl. Poet. Ms.*; other mss. 'excess'.

133–134 *Praised be Diana's . . .*] doubtless written of the Queen; unsigned in *P. N.*, but one of a group, some poems of which are known to be Ralegh's; reprinted in *England's Heli-* con, signed with Ralegh's initials, though in some copies a slip with the word 'Ignoto' has been pasted over the initials; marked 'W. R.' in Francis Davison's manuscript catalogue of poems in *E. H.*, *Harl. Ms.* 280.

134 *Like truthless dreams*] unsigned in *P. N.*, but certainly identified as Ralegh's by these lines in the eleventh book of *Cynthia*:

'Of all which passed the sorrow only
    stays.'
So wrote I once, and my mishap fore-
    told. . . .

The present poem was printed in *Le
Prince d'Amour*, 1660, signed 'W. R.'
4, 8, 12] With this line compare also
the passage in the Preface to Ralegh's
History of the World, where the author
says that one looking back over his life
'shall find nothing remaining but those
sorrows which grow up after our fast-
springing youth.' Cf. also the *History*,
I. ii. 5, 'We find by dear and lamentable
experience, and by the loss which can
never be repaired, that of all our vain
passions and affections past the sorrow only abideth'; and our selection
from *Cynthia*, l. 49, and note.

134 *Like to a hermit*] unsigned in
P. N., but standing just before *Like
truthless dreams;* ascribed to Ralegh in
To-day a Man, To-morrow None, a
pamphlet of 1644. There seems to be
a reference to this poem in Ralegh's
Cynthia (our selection, l. 31). The
poem appears without signature in *Harl.
Ms.* 6910 and in *Rawl. Poet. Ms.* 85.
Six lines were set to music by Alfonso Ferrabosco, *Airs*, 1609.

135 *A description of love*] unsigned
in *P. N.*; reprinted in *England's Helicon*, changed to a dialogue, signed
'S. W. R.' but with 'Ignoto' pasted
over in some copies; also in *A Poetical
Rhapsody* as *The anatomy of love*, unsigned; ascribed to 'S. W. Rawly' in
Davison's manuscript list. The poem
was set to music by Robert Jones,
Second Book of Songs and Airs, 1601.
Two stanzas, altered, were used as a
song in Thomas Heywood's *Rape of
Lucrece*. **4** sauncing-bell] saunce-bell,
or sanctus-bell.

135-137 *An epitaph upon . . . Sir
Philip Sidney*] unsigned in *P. N.*, but
ascribed to Ralegh upon evidence of
Sir John Harington's notes in his
Orlando Furioso, 1591, Book xvi, where
he speaks of Sidney as 'our English
Petrarch, or, as Sir Walter Ralegh in
his epitaph worthily calleth him, the
Scipio and the Petrarch of our time.'
This poem also appeared with Spenser's
Astrophel in *Colin Clout's Come Home
Again*, 1595. **13** princely line] Sid-
ney's great-grandfather married Anne
Brandon, whose family traced their
descent from William the Conqueror
and from Alexander, King of Scotland.
17 king . . . name] Sidney was named
after King Philip of Spain. **57** their

Hannibal] Count Hannibal Gonzago, on
the Spanish side, was mortally wounded
in the engagement at Zutphen.

137-138 *The nymph's reply . . .*]
For Marlowe's poem to which this re-
sponds, see p. 168. In *E. H.* this is
signed 'Ignoto'. Izaak Walton reprinted
it in *The Complete Angler*, 1653, as
'made by Sir Walter Ralegh in his
younger days.' In the second edition of
the *Angler* Walton inserted after the
fifth stanza the following, apparently
from a contemporary broadside (see
Roxburghe Ballads, Ballad Society, ii.
3 ff.) :

What should we talk of dainties, then,
    Or better meat than's fit for men?
These are but vain; that's only good
    Which God hath blessed and sent for
        food.

The first stanza of *The nymph's reply*
appeared in *The Passionate Pilgrim*,
1599, with the caption 'Love's answer.'
138 *To his son*] headed in the ms.
'Sir Walter Rauleigh To his sonne.'
138-139 *Nature that washed . . .*]
headed in ms. 'A poem of Sr Walter
Rawleigh's'. The Calendar assigns the
ms. to the early part of the 17th century. This poem was first printed by
A. H. Bullen in *Speculum Amantis*,
1889. **26** discolors] *Harl. Ms.* 6917
reads 'discovers'; emended from *Add.
Ms.* 25707, where the poem also
appears. **31-36**] This stanza, slightly
altered and with two lines added, was
found in the author's Bible in the Gate-
house at Westminster, whence he went
to his execution; it was printed, with
mention of this circumstance, with
Ralegh's *Prerogative of Parliaments*,
1628, in *To-day a Man, To-morrow
None*, 1644, and in *Reliquiæ Wottonianæ*, 1651, where it was given the title,
*Sir Walter Ralegh the night before his
death*. The presence of the stanza in
this lyric, where it plainly belongs,
proves that it was not written on the
eve of his execution. The added couplet, however, might have been written
at that time:

But from this earth, this grave, this
    dust,
My God shall raise me up, I trust.

139-140 *The lie*] This poem exists
in many ms. copies, several of which
ascribe it to Ralegh; at least two are
supposed to be in Ralegh's own hand.
The earliest ms. appears to date about
1593. No two of the mss. agree in text,
some giving more stanzas than were

printed in 1608. Hannah (Introduction, xxvi–xxviii) prints extracts from a number of early answers to *The lie*, several of which connect Ralegh with the poem. 2 arrant] errand. 16 affection] Some mss. read 'a faction'.

140–141 *The Ocean to Cynthia, Book XI*] The manuscript heading is 'The 11th and last book of the Ocean'. Hannah misread '21st' for '11th'. (See Agnes M. C. Latham, 'Sir Walter Ralegh's *Cynthia*,' *R. E. S.*, iv. 129; but see also J. P. Gilson, 'Sir Walter Ralegh's *Cynthia*,' *R. E. S.*, iv. 340.) The present excerpt is from the end of the book, which is about 520 lines in all. The numerous cases of incomplete stanzas and imperfect syntax indicate that the manuscript is an early draft. 31] cf. *Like to a hermit*, l. 10. brast] broken. 49] cf. with this line the refrain of *Like truthless dreams*, 'Of all which passed the sorrow only stays,' and also this line from Ralegh's *Poesy to prove affection is not love* (Hannah, p. 22): 'The life expires, the woe remains.'

142–143 *The passionate man's pilgrimage*] not ascribed to Ralegh in *Daiphantus;* in *Ashmole Ms.* 38 the poem is entitled, *Verses made by Sr. Walter Ralegh the night before he was beheaded;* printed in Ralegh's *Remains*, 1661. The poem was doubtless written after Ralegh had been tried and condemned to death in 1603. He was then expecting to be executed, but his life was spared. The passage concerning the trial (ll. 35–50) definitely glances at the unjust trial accorded him, and the denunciations of him by Sir Edward Coke, attorney-general. 1 scallop-shell] worn by pilgrims as a badge. 3 scrip] wallet. 7 balmer] embalmer. 25 suckets] candied fruits, sweetmeats. 42 angels] a pun, involving the use of the word for a gold coin, the angel-noble. 58] Some mss. and *Remains*, 1661, add the lines,

Of death and judgment, heaven and hell,
Who oft doth think must needs die well.

MARY HERBERT, COUNTESS OF PEMBROKE

MARY SIDNEY, later Mary Herbert, Countess of Pembroke (1561–1621), 'Sidney's sister, Pembroke's mother,' was a notable patron of poets, numbering among her beneficiaries Spenser, Daniel, Breton, Jonson, and Davies of Hereford. Besides editing her brother's literary remains, she completed his translation of the *Psalms*, and translated from the French of Phillipe de Mornay *A Discourse of Life and Death*, and from the French of Robert Garnier a tragedy in blank verse, *Antonius*. These two works were published together in 1592; her tragedy was given separate publication as *The Tragedy of Antony* in 1595. Daniel wrote his tragedy *Cleopatra* in 1593 as a companion-piece to *Antonius*. Her elegy upon her brother appeared with Spenser's *Astrophel*, 1595, as *The doleful lay of Clorinda*.

MODERN EDITION: *The Countess of Pembroke's Antonie* (ed. by A. Luce), Weimar, 1897.

TEXT: *Antonius*, 1592 (18138), White.

143–144 *Chorus*] This ends the third act of the tragedy; the chorus is made up of Egyptian soldiers. 20 our] 1592 'or'.

WILLIAM WARNER

WILLIAM WARNER (*c.* 1558–1609) was an attorney who won great contemporary fame by writing a versified history of England. Four books of his *Albion's England*, written in 'fourteeners,' appeared in 1586. A second edition of 1589, with two books added, brought the history down to the close of Henry VII's reign; and the third edition (1592), of nine books, concluded with the accession of Elizabeth. Later additions carried the story through Elizabeth's reign and into that of James. The early portions of

Albion's England, dealing with legend, contain some episodes of independent interest, invented or elaborated by Warner himself. Nashe in 1589 referred to Warner's poem as 'absolute' (or perfect), and the epithet was often repeated. Drayton, in his verse-epistle to Henry Reynolds (see p. 306) paid a warm tribute to his 'old friend.' The contemporary popularity of *Albion's England* must be referred to the wave of patriotic fervor which swept England throughout the period immediately before and after the defeat of the Armada.

MODERN EDITION: *Albion's England* in *English Poets* (ed. by A. Chalmers), Vol. iv, London, 1810.

TEXT: *Albion's England*, 1592 (25081), B. M.

144–146 *Chapter XXXVIII*] first printed in the edition of 1592. 7 foison] harvest. 8 Terwin . . . Tournay] Térouanne and Tournai were French cities taken by Henry's forces, 1513. 26 barded] caparisoned with plates of metal set with spikes or bosses. 53 elder daughter] Margaret, sister of Henry VII, had married James IV of Scotland. 60 coiture] union. 83 Foxe] *Acts and Monuments*, 1563, by John Foxe, usually called 'Foxe's Book of Martyrs', was the standard contemporary account of the religious troubles of Mary's reign. 84 for why] because. sexamus] not in *O.E.D.*; apparently a nonce word meaning 'one who marries six times'; perhaps made up from *sex* (L.), six, and γάμος (Gr.), marriage.

THOMAS WATSON

THOMAS WATSON (*c.* 1557–1592), although he wrote little to which succeeding ages have turned with pleasure, is a poet of considerable historical significance. Pre-eminently in his generation did he make himself the channel through which flowed strong influences from classical and continental literatures. He probably received his education at Oxford, but took no degree. His first book, published in 1581, was a Latin translation of *Antigone*. The work most often connected with his name in his own time was *Amyntas*, 1585, a poem in Latin hexameters built around Tasso's pastoral, *Aminta*. Abraham Fraunce published in 1587 an English rendering of Watson's work, without acknowledging his source; and in this form *Amyntas* enjoyed great popularity. Watson's first English book, 'Εκατομπαθία, *or a Passionate Century of Love*, 1582, helped center the attention of literary England upon the Petrarchan sonnet. After his early death appeared his *Tears of Fancy*, 1593, a conventional sonnet-cycle, containing some eight sonnets adapted from poems by Gascoigne and one sonnet by the Earl of Oxford. Scattered poems of Watson's were printed in *The Phœnix Nest*, *England's Helicon*, and other miscellanies. He was acquainted with Sir Philip Sidney and intimate with the Earl of Oxford, Lyly, Peele, Nashe, and other literary men of the 1580's, by some of whom he was highly praised.

MODERN EDITIONS: *The Poems* (ed. by E. Arber), London, 1870; *The First Set of Italian Madrigals Englished* (ed. by F. I. Carpenter), *Journal of Germanic Philology*, ii. 323 ff.

COMMENT: W. W. Greg, 'English Versions of Watson's Latin Poems,' *M. L. Q.* vi. 125.

TEXT: *Hecatompathia*, [1582] (25118a), White; *First Set of Italian Madrigals Englished*, 1590 (25119), White; *Tears of Fancy*, 1593 (25122), Huntington.

146–147 *Some that report*] Ward, following Arber, has suggested that the prose introductions above the poems were written by the Earl of Oxford, to whom the volume was dedicated.

148 *My love is past* 1–2] These lines follow closely the Italian source printed just above.

148 *The First Set of Italian Madrigals Englished*] in part translated from two books by Luca Marenzio: *Il Primo Libro de Madrigali* (Venice, 1580) and *Madrigali a Quattro Voci* (Venice, 1585).

148–149 *Vezzosi augelli*] The title, 'lovely birds,' is taken over from the Italian madrigal here translated.

149 *Questo di verde*] The title consists of the first three words of the Italian madrigal, to the tune of which Watson writes his words; he does not translate the madrigal, and the phrase is an incomplete one.

150 *In clouds she shines* 1 clouds] 1593 'clownes'. 13 clew] 1593 'cleane'; but the 'n' is probably a turned 'u' as 'cleaue', or 'clew', seems plainly intended.

ROBERT GREENE

ROBERT GREENE (1558?–1592), generally known as a writer of romances, plays, and pamphlets, takes high rank in his generation as a lyrical poet. Born at Norwich, he attended St. John's College, Cambridge, where he proceeded B. A. in 1578 and M. A. in 1583. Before taking his master's degree he had traveled on the Continent and had begun writing for the press. Established in London about 1584, he became a leader of the Bohemian literary group, turning out numerous pamphlets and romances, and involving himself scandalously with rogues and pick-purses. His long hair and beard made him a marked figure in the streets. 'His only care,' according to Thomas Nashe, 'was to have a spell in his purse to conjure up a good cup of wine at all times.' Greene's desertion of his wife and child, his excesses, his repentances, and the sordid circumstances of his death, have become familiar literary tradition; all these, with other anecdotes, were recounted in contemporary pamphlets either by Greene himself or by others writing shortly after his death. He published no book of poems, but wrote a great number of lyrics scattered through the pages of his romances. *Menaphon*, 1589, contains his best work in this kind. His verse-forms are varied and graceful; his sentiments are conventional but often far from superficial.

MODERN EDITIONS: *The Complete Works* (ed. by A. B. Grosart), Huth Library, fifteen volumes, 1881–86; *The Plays and Poems* (ed. by J. Churton Collins), two volumes, Oxford, 1902.

TEXT: *Menaphon*, 1589 (12272), White; *Greene's Mourning Garment*, 1590 (12251), Cambridge; *Greene's Never Too Late*, 1621 (12257), White; *Greene's Farewell to Folly*, 1617 (12242), White; *Philomela, the Lady Fitzwater's Nightingale*, 1592 (12296), White; *Greene's Orpharion*, 1599 (12260), Huntington.

152–153 *The shepherd's wife's song* 28 affects] passions. 42 sithe] time.

153–154 *Hexametra Alexis . . .*] 'Hexameters of Alexis in praise of Rosamund'; an experiment in English dactylic hexameters. See notes to Richard Stanyhurst.

154 *Greene's Never Too Late*] Our text follows the edition of 1621.

154 *Greene's Farewell to Folly*] Our text follows the edition of 1617.

155–156 *Cupid abroad was lated*] This version of an ode by Anacreon, usually referred to as his 'Cupid belated,' has been accounted the earliest translation into English from that poet; but a brief one in Whitney's *Emblems*, 1586, preceded it.

THOMAS LODGE

THOMAS LODGE (c. 1558–1625), son of a knight of the same name who was for a time Lord Mayor of London, received an excellent literary training at the Merchant Tailors' School, London, and Trinity College, Oxford. He was admitted B.A. in 1577, and the next year became a law student at Lincoln's Inn. Like many other law students, however, he yielded to the attractions of the growing literary and theatrical circle of the metropolis; and he entered upon authorship by answering Stephen Gosson's *School of Abuse*, 1579, with a *Defence of Plays*, 1580. Aside from some time spent as a soldier and as a member of Cavendish's expedition to South America (1591), Lodge engaged in a busy literary career lasting about fifteen years. Then he turned to the study of medicine, taking the degree of M.D. at Avignon in 1600 and at Oxford in 1602. He practised for about twenty-five years as one of the reputable physicians of London, though his clientele was limited somewhat by the fact that he had, while abroad, embraced the Roman Catholic faith.

Lodge's efforts to write for the stage seem to have been unfortunate, but in the fields of romance, lyrical poetry, and verse-satire he was more successful. He wrote several Euphuistic tales interspersed with poems, among which *Rosalind*, 1590, has become well known as the source of Shakespeare's *As You Like It*. In 1589 Lodge published *Scilla's Metamorphosis*, a mythological narrative poem (forerunner of *Venus and Adonis*), and with it a satire and a number of lyrics. Many poems of his appeared in *The Phœnix Nest*, 1593, and in the same year he issued *Phillis*, a sonnet-cycle liberally swelled out with songs and odes. He helped usher in a notable period of verse-satire by publishing *A Fig for Momus*, 1595. After he had become a physician, he made and published translations of Josephus and Seneca.

Lodge's lyrical poetry is fresh and tuneful. He leaned heavily upon French and Italian originals, but he avoided, it would seem, all the dangers inherent in translation.

MODERN EDITIONS: *Complete Works,* four volumes, Hunterian Club, 1875–1883; *Glaucus and Silla, with other . . . Poems,* Chiswick Press, 1819; *A Fig for Momus* in *Frondes Caducæ* (ed. by A. Boswell), Auchinleck, 1817.

COMMENT: E. Gosse, *Seventeenth Century Studies,* London, 1883.

TEXT: *Scilla's Metamorphosis,* 1589 (16665), B. M.; *The Life and Death of William Longbeard,* 1593 (16659), White; *The Phœnix Nest,* 1593 (21516), White; *Phillis,* 1593 (16662), Huntington, White. (16674), Huntington; *Rosalind,* 1592

156 *Sonnet*] translated from a poem by Desportes. In his *Margarite of America* Lodge wrote of this French poet: 'Few men are able to second the sweet conceits of Philip Desportes, whose poetical writings [are] for the most part englished, and ordinarily in everybody's hands.' 4 teen] trouble, or anger.

156 *Rosalind,* 1592] The edition of 1590 was inaccessible to us.

160 *O pleasing thoughts* 2 mithridates] antidotes.

161 *Love guides the roses* 11 tempt] attempt.

162–163 *An ode*] also printed in *The Phœnix Nest;* set to music by Thomas Ford, *Music of Sundry Kinds,* 1607. 33] *P. N.; Phillis* reads, 'Prime youth lusts not age still follow'.

NICHOLAS BRETON

NICHOLAS BRETON (1545?–1626?), one of the most popular and prolific of Elizabethan and Jacobean authors, was the son of an old and respectable house. The death of his father, who had built up a fortune as a London trader, in 1559, and his mother's marriage to George Gascoigne, the poet, had an unfavorable effect upon the son's worldly fortunes; but the second of these events may have turned his attention to poetry. Breton seems to have spent some time at Oxford; and in 1577 he published two books of poetry. In 1592 he again appeared as poet, under the patronage of the

Countess of Pembroke, and from this time until 1626 he issued a stream of publications both in verse and prose, about forty in all. He wrote moral and religious as well as lyrical poetry; in prose he produced the usual pamphlets, being at his best in his dialogues and characters.

The facility and haste with which Breton wrote appear to have prevented him from rising to great heights as poet. In the pastoral vein, however, he succeeded better than most of his contemporaries, and won a popularity which endured for a generation after his death. His best poems show Elizabethan lyricism in its most typical and delightful vein; they manifest a joy in the sound and repetition of well-matched words which readers still can share.

MODERN EDITIONS: *The Works in Verse and Prose* (ed. by A. B. Grosart), two volumes, Chertsey Worthies' Library, 1879; *A Bower of Delights* (selected and ed. by A. B. Grosart), London, n. d.

COMMENT: A. H. Bullen, *Elizabethans*, London, 1924.

TEXT: *The Arbor of Amorous Devices*, 1597 (3631), Huntington; *England's Helicon*, 1600 (3191), White; *Melancholic Humors*, 1600 (3666), Huntington; *The Passionate Shepherd*, 1604 (3682), White.

163 *A pastoral of Phillis and Coridon*] This poem was reprinted in *England's Helicon*, signed 'N. Breton'. 15 *ipsa quæ*] 'the very she,' or 'she herself.'

163–164 *A sweet lullaby*] doubtfully Breton's, as it was printed only in *A. A. D.*, which contained work by other poets.

164–165 *Say that I should say*] In *E. H.* this is headed *Another of the same* and is signed 'N. Breton'.

165 *Phillida and Coridon*] signed 'N. Breton'. This poem was written as a three-man's song to be sung in an entertainment given Queen Elizabeth by the Earl of Hertford at his seat in Hampshire; it was printed with the account of that entertainment, *The Honorable Entertainment . . . at Elvetham*,

1591. It was sung below the window of the Queen, to greet her on the third morning of her visit. According to the account, 'it pleased her Highness to command it again, and highly to grace it with her cheerful acceptance and commendation.' The song was printed with musical setting in Michael East's *Madrigals*, 1604, Henry Youll's *Canzonets*, 1608, and John Playford's *Select Musical Airs and Dialogues*, 1653.

165–166 *Song of Phillida and Coridon*] The full title in *E. H.* is *Astrophel's song of Phillida and Coridon;* the editor evidently was of the opinion that the poem was Sidney's and he printed 'S. Phil. Sidney' at the end, but inserted a slip correcting this to 'N. Breton'. 43 *constants*] constantest.

CHRISTOPHER MARLOWE

CHRISTOPHER MARLOWE (1564–1593) stands as a brilliant and attractive figure, one among the number of English poets whose careers were interrupted by an early death. He grew up at Canterbury, where his father was a prosperous shoe-maker; and having been granted one of the scholarships founded by Archbishop Parker, he attended Corpus Christi College, Cambridge. He was graduated B.A. in March, 1584, and M.A. in July, 1587. Between these dates he evidently spent some time abroad in government service, to the prejudice of his academic standing. An entry in the Privy Council Register (June 29, 1587) praises his 'orderly and discreet' behavior, and recommends 'that he should be furthered in the degree he was to take this next Commencement; because it was not her Majesty's pleasure that any one employed as he had been in matters touching the benefit of his country should be defamed by those that are ignorant in th' affairs he went about.' Of Marlowe's scant six years in London as a 'University wit' writing for the actors, little is known except for the plays which can be attributed to his authorship. His reputation for atheism has been much dwelt upon and made the basis for legends. He met his death at the hands of Ingram Friser, apparently in a quarrel which took place in a tavern in Deptford.

Marlowe's three or four important plays have overshadowed his non-dramatic poetry. His brief *Passionate shepherd to his love* was and remains one of the most popular of Elizabethan lyrics; and among sustained narrative poems only Shakespeare's may dispute primacy with Marlowe's *Hero and Leander*. At the time of Marlowe's death this poem, an expanded paraphrase of a Greek work by Musæus, was incomplete; George Chapman wrote the four sestiads which complete it. *Hero and Leander* belongs to a literary fashion, which it helped to set, of erotic poems upon mythological subjects, exemplified also in Lodge's *Glaucus and Scilla*, Shakespeare's *Venus and Adonis*, Drayton's *Endymion and Phœbe*, and several written later than these. Beside the poems already mentioned as his, Marlowe left verse-translations of Ovid's *Amores* and of the first book of Lucan's *Pharsalia*, the latter in blank verse. The poetic manner of Marlowe is that of the true Elizabethans, rich and exuberant. In spite of faults which derive from the influences under which it was written, *Hero and Leander* is yet a poem of great beauty, an enduring legacy left by 'that pure elemental wit' at the height of his powers.

MODERN EDITIONS: *The Works* (ed. by C. F. Tucker Brooke), Oxford, 1910; *The Works* (ed. by A. H. Bullen), three volumes, London, 1885; *Hero and Leander* (Haslewood Reprint), London, 1924.

COMMENT: U. M. Ellis-Fermor, *Christopher Marlowe*, London, 1927; J. L. Hotson, *The Death of Christopher Marlowe*, London, 1925; J. H. Ingram, *Christopher Marlowe and his Associates*, London, 1904.

TEXT: *England's Helicon*, 1600 (3191), White; *Hero and Leander . . . for E. Blunt*, 1598 (17413), White.

168 *The passionate shepherd . . .*]
For Ralegh's *Reply* see p. 137. Marlowe's poem first appeared, unsigned and with the fourth and sixth stanzas omitted, in *The Passionate Pilgrim*, a miscellany published by William Jaggard in 1599 as the work of Shakespeare. In *E. H.* it is signed 'Chr. Marlowe'. It is interesting to find in Marlowe's *Jew of Malta* (produced *c.* 1589) the lines (1815–16):

Thou in those groves, by Dis above,
Shalt live with me and be my love.

Ingram reprints Marlowe's and Ralegh's poems from a late 16th-century commonplace-book, apparently kept by Thornborough, chaplain to the Earl of Pembroke. Marlowe's was also reprinted in *Poems, written by Wil. Shakespeare*, 1640, and in Izaak Walton's *Complete Angler*, 1653. In the second edition (1655) Walton adds, evidently from a contemporary broadside (cf. *Roxburghe Ballads*, ii. 3 ff.), the following stanza after the fifth:

Thy silver dishes for thy meat,
As precious as the gods do eat,

Shall on an ivory table be
Prepared each day for thee and me.

Marlowe's popular lyric inspired many imitations; see Donne's *The bait* (p. 459) and Herrick's *To Phyllis, to love and live with him* (p. 656). 10 posies] 1600 'poesies'.

168 *To . . . Sir Thomas Walsingham*] a patron and perhaps employer of Marlowe; Chapman dedicated his portion of *Hero and Leander* to Lady Walsingham.

169 *Hero and Leander*] We have reprinted all of Marlowe's portion of the poem, as first separately published. In the same year a printer named Linley issued the whole poem, as completed by Chapman.

169–180 *First sestiad*] Blunt's edition does not divide the poem into sestiads. This division was introduced by Chapman; but it is here followed for the sake of ease in reference. 3 sea-borderers] 1629; 1598 'sea-borders'. 52 Musæus] a Greek grammarian of about the fifth century A.D., who left a poem upon Hero and Leander, consisting of 340 verses. Marlowe and his contemporaries confused him with a legendary

Greek poet of the same name, a contemporary of Orpheus. 56 Colchis] the country east of the Black Sea, legendary location of the Golden Fleece. 73–75] The reference is to Narcissus. 77 Hippolytus] son of Theseus and Hippolyte, an Amazon queen; he rejected the advances of his step-mother, Phædra. 107 pale and wat'ry star] the moon; Diana. 108 thirling] flying, whirling. 114 Ixion's shaggy-footed race] the Centaurs; so called because they were supposed to have been begotten by Ixion on a cloud. 154 lovely boy] Cyparissus; for his metamorphosis, see Ovid, *Met.* x. 121 ff. 158 turtles' blood] the blood of doves, Venus's birds. 169 course] race. 296 tralucent] clear, luminous. 336 thought] 1598 misprints 'rhought'. 388 Argus] he of the hundred eyes, set to watch Mercury. 475 Midas' brood] the phrase implies the wealthy and also those without good taste, since Midas gave the palm in singing to Pan over Apollo.

180–187 *Second sestiad* 12 train] entrain, attract. 26 affied] betrothed. 32 peised] balanced. 46 Salmacis] the nymph of a fountain which rendered effeminate all who drank of it; see

Ovid, *Met.* iv. 337, 347. 51 Æsop's cock] In the fable, the cock found a jewel in a dung-heap but did not know its use or value. 118 thrust from his sphere] out of its proper place in the Ptolemaic system of spheres. 120 Alcides like] Hercules, when raging, attacked the ocean. 123 in a diameter] with direct rays. 155 sapphire-visaged god] the blue-faced god is Neptune. 179 Helle's bracelet] Helle, after whom the Hellespont was named, had been drowned there while in flight from her step-mother. 250 swoom] swum. 279–290] In all early quartos these lines are out of their position as demanded by the story, and come between our l. 300 and l. 301; we follow the order of Tucker Brooke. 291–292 strife . . . made the world] One of the philosophical commonplaces, from Heraclitus, was that war, or contention, is the father of all things. 305 Erycine] Venus; from Eryx, a Sicilian mountain, seat of her temple. 319 hair] Bullen emends to 'air'; 1598 reads 'heare'. 320 glimpse] gleams. 326 Dis] Pluto, god of riches. 335 *Desunt nonnulla*] 'Something is lacking.'

ELIZABETHAN MISCELLANIES

The publishing of miscellanies, or anthologies, seems to have grown out of the custom of keeping commonplace-books. So long as poets did not print their collections, it behooved a lover of poetry to copy into his notebook any poems that struck his fancy, as they came under his hand in manuscript. If a printer could secure the commonplace-book of a discriminating collector, he had only to put it into type in order to publish an excellent anthology. Doubtless in the case of some miscellanies the conscious aim of collecting for the press actuated those who brought together the poems from manuscript sources; but these collectors were merely exploiting a fashion which the scores of extant commonplace-books prove to have been general. We should note also that there was at hand a classical model for the miscellany in the Greek Anthology, a favorite book with scholars and poets from the beginning of the sixteenth century; and that poetical miscellanies already had appeared in Renaissance Italy.

An account has already been given (see p. 919) of Tottel's miscellany of *Songs and Sonnets*, which gathered together the best lyrical and reflective poetry produced during the reigns of Henry VIII, Edward VI, and Queen Mary, and which kept its popularity throughout the reign of Elizabeth. Clement Robinson and Richard Edwards were the early Elizabethan collectors whose work was most fruitful. Robinson, to be sure, interested himself in broadside ballads rather than in lyrics; and his *Handful of Pleasant Delights*, 1584, scarcely belongs in the succession of true miscellanies. As Rollins shows, this book was a second and altered edition of *Pleasant Sonnets and Stories,* licensed as by Robinson in 1566, and extant only in a single leaf. While the earlier title and the running title of the *Handful,* 'Sonnets and histories,' suggest an imitation of *Songs and Sonnets,* Robinson's book merely collects broadside ballads which already had been printed separately. Extracts from it will be found under 'Broadside Ballads,' pp. 410–414.

Richard Edwards died in 1566, leaving a commonplace-book which ten years later was printed with additions as *The Paradise of Dainty Devices;* the printer Henry Disle in his dedicatory letter wrote: 'I am bold to present unto your honor this small volume, entitled *The Paradise of Dainty Devices,* being penned by divers learned gentlemen, and collected together through the travail of one of both worship and credit, for his private use.' Edwards's taste made the *Paradise* a book of graver cast than Tottel's miscellany, with a smaller proportion of love-poems. The collection was immensely popular, copies of nine editions being extant, all published within the generation from 1576 to 1606.

B. M. Ward (see under Gascoigne) has made it appear that *A Hundreth Sundry Flowers* (1573) is a miscellany, as its title-page and table of contents indicate, in spite of Gascoigne's assumption in his *Posies* of the authorship of most of its contents. What authors are represented in the collection is harder to ascertain; Ward suggests Gascoigne, Oxford, and Sir Christopher Hatton as the principal contributors.

Timothe Kendall's *Flowers of Epigrams,* 1577, is a miscellany, although the greater part of the book consists of translations made by Kendall. It is limited, though not strictly, to epigrams. Kendall reprints short pieces by Sir Thomas Eliot, Ascham, Surrey, Grimald, and Turberville. This compiler, we may be sure, had in mind to imitate the Greek Anthology.

In 1578 appeared *A Gorgeous Gallery of Gallant Inventions;* this title had been accepted by the printer, Richard Jones, in place of his earlier choices, 'A handful of hidden secrets' and 'Delicate dainties to sweeten lovers' lips withal.' Credit for the collection is given to Thomas Procter, himself then a printer's apprentice, who contributes a number of poems. Owen Roydon seems also to have had a hand in preparing the work. This miscellany falls short of the *Paradise* in quality, and it also fell short in popularity. It draws upon *Songs and Sonnets* and the *Paradise,* without introducing any new writers of consequence.

Whether *The Forest of Fancy,* 1579, is a miscellany or a collection of verse and prose by a single author has never been ascertained. No author's name appears in the book, but at the end stands the line, 'L'acquis abonde. Finis H. C.' J. P. Collier (*Bibl. Acc.,* ii. 31) says: 'Our notion is that the various poems were contributed by various hands, and that H. C. undertook the task of editorship, which may in part serve to explain the French motto.' However, the prefatory epistle seems to claim all the contents for a single author. Ault (*E. L.,* p. 78) follows Malone in assigning Henry Cheke as author of the whole book.

With *The Phœnix Nest,* 1593, a new group of lyricists enters the field; and the general advance in poetic excellence brought about by the labors of Spenser, Sidney, Watson, Breton, and Lodge, is manifest when comparison is made between this collection and any of its predecessors. 'R. S. of the Inner Temple,' who is credited with the compilation, remains unidentified. The preservation in this anthology of otherwise unprinted poems by Ralegh and Lodge, not to mention anonymous gems, more than justifies the production.

Late in the 1590's the printer William Jaggard evidently came into possession of a poetical album containing twenty choice poems, at least four of them by Shakespeare; and his volume made from these poems, *The Passionate Pilgrim*, 1599, though issued as 'By W. Shakespeare,' was really a miscellany. It contains poems by Barnfield, Marlowe, Griffin, and some other writers, besides those by Shakespeare. Comparable to this book are the two collections *Breton's Bower of Delights*, 1591 and 1597, and *The Arbor of Amorous Devices*, 1597, assigned by the printers to Nicholas Breton and containing work by him, but including poems by other poets as well. Although the printer of the *Arbor*, Richard Jones, sets the words 'By N. B. Gent.' on the title-page, his prefatory epistle describes the book as 'many men's works, excellent poets, and most not the meanest in estate and degree'; and he complains that *The Phœnix Nest* had used 'some of the best stuff' which he had hoped to include. In this miscellany appear two poems from among the anonymous contributions to the old *Songs and Sonnets*.

England's Parnassus and *Belvedere* (later called *The Garden of the Muses*), both published for the first time in 1600, were dictionaries of quotations or poetical phrase-books rather than miscellanies. The extracts included are in almost no case complete poems, and often consist of a single line. Their editors show wide reading in the poetry of the century then closed; and they have made it possible to assign authors to otherwise anonymous poems and books.

England's Helicon, also published in 1600, stands eminent among Elizabethan miscellanies, or indeed among English anthologies of any period whatever. The *Helicon* was projected, if not actually edited, by John Bodenham, who seems to have been responsible also for *Belvedere* and for two earlier quotation-books of prose. The actual editor may have been the A.B. who writes some of the prefatory notices, or Nicholas Ling, well-known as publisher. Whoever made the choices for inclusion showed wide reading and considerable taste. He went back to *Songs and Sonnets* for two selections, and to *The Phœnix Nest* for a half-dozen. He drew upon Spenser's *Shepherd's Calendar*, Watson's *Hecatompathia*, Sidney's *Astrophel and Stella*, Drayton's *Idea*, Lodge's *Phillis*, and Spenser's *Astrophel*; he recognized the exquisite lyrics that had appeared in printed plays and romances, and copied out songs from Greene's *Menaphon*, Lodge's *Rosalind*, Sidney's *Arcadia*, Peele's *Arraignment of Paris*, and Shakespeare's *Love's Labor's Lost*. He also took into account the excellent songs in the newly popular madrigal-books and song-books, and made a choice of these. Finally, he printed for the first time important poems by Henry Constable, Anthony Munday, Bartholomew Young, and others whose names we do not know.

A Poetical Rhapsody, 1602, is the last of the Elizabethan miscellanies, and the most copious. Its editor was Francis Davison, then a young man, who himself had written considerable verse but did not care to issue a volume of his work. He put with his own a number of poems written by his younger brother Walter, others by various authors, and a great many which he assigns to A. W. These initials may stand for the name of a writer yet unidentified, or they may merely mean 'Anonymous writers.' In his first preface Davison speaks of 'my dear friend *anomos*,' and in his second of 'my dear friends *Anonymoi.*' He drew upon the writings of Thomas Watson, Henry Constable, Sir Philip Sidney, Edmund Spenser, Thomas Campion, and others. The second edition of the *Rhapsody,* 1608, adds many more poems, including work by Sir John Davies, Sir Walter Ralegh, Charles Best, and others, which had not previously been printed. Third and fourth editions included more new material, but nothing of importance. *The Poetical Rhapsody* reflects the altered taste of its period in that it contains a much larger proportion of madrigals and epigrams than its predecessors. Mr. Bullen, while granting that its poetic merit falls below that of the *Helicon,* points out that the special value of Davison's work lies in the great amount of material which it published from manuscript and which otherwise might have been lost.

CROSS REFERENCES: Poems from Tottel's *Songs and Sonnets:* Heywood, p. 11; Wyatt, pp. 13–18, 21–27; Surrey, pp. 27–33; Vaux, p. 38; Minor Courtly Makers, pp. 44–49; Grimald, pp. 49–53.

Poems, not in this section, from Elizabethan miscellanies:—*Paradise of Dainty Devices:* Vaux, pp. 39–41; Oxford, p. 102.—*Gorgeous Gallery of Gallant Inventions:* Churchyard, p. 84.—*Breton's Bower of Delights,* 1591: Oxford, p. 104.—*Phœnix Nest:* Oxford, p. 104; Greville, p. 125; Ralegh, pp. 133–137; Lodge, pp. 158–160, *An ode,* p. 162.—*Passionate Pilgrim:* Marlowe, *The passionate shepherd,* p. 168; Barnfield, *Ode, The unknown shepherd's complaint,* p. 241.—*England's Helicon: Harpalus' Complaint,* p. 45; Sidney, *The nightingale, Ring out your bells,* p. 119; Greville, p. 126; Ralegh, p. 137; Greene, *Doron's description of Samela,* p. 150, *Doron's jig,* p. 151; Lodge, *Rosalind's madrigal,* p. 156, *Montanus' sonnet,* p. 157, 'My Phillis hath,' p. 161; Breton, *A pastoral of Phillis and Coridon,* p. 163, pp. 164–166; Marlowe, p. 168; Constable, pp. 232–235; Barnfield, *An ode, The unknown shepherd's complaint,* p. 241; Drayton, *The ninth eclogue,* p. 299; *Coridon and Melampus' song,* p. 386.—*Poetical Rhapsody,* 1602: Sidney, p. 122; Greene, *Cupid abroad was lated,* p. 155; Campion, *When to her lute,* p. 447; Wotton, p. 550.—*Poetical Rhapsody,* 1608: Ralegh, p. 139.

MODERN EDITIONS: *A Hundreth Sundrie Flowres* (ed. by B. M. Ward), London, 1926; *The Paradise of Dainty Devices* (ed. by H. E. Rollins), Cambridge (Mass.), 1927; *A Gorgeous Gallery of Gallant Inventions* (ed. by H. E. Rollins), Cambridge (Mass.), 1926, and in *Heliconia* (ed. by T. Park), Vol. i, London, 1815; *The Dr. Farmer Chetham Ms.* (ed. by A. B. Grosart), Chetham Society, 1873; *The Phœnix Nest* (ed. by H. Macdonald), London, 1926, and in *Heliconia* (ed. by T. Park), Vol. ii, London, 1815; *The Arbor of Amorous Devices* in *The Works of Nicholas Breton* (ed. by A. B. Grosart), Vol. i, Chertsey Worthies' Library, 1879; *The Passionate Pilgrim* in many editions of Shakespeare's complete works; *England's Helicon* (ed. by A. H. Bullen), London, 1887, and (ed. by H. Macdonald), London, 1925; *Davison's Poetical Rhapsody* (ed. by A. H. Bullen), two volumes, London, 1890–91.

COMMENT: C. Crawford, Introduction to his edition of *England's Parnassus,* Oxford, 1913.

TEXT: *A Hundreth Sundry Flowers* [1573] (11635), White; *The Paradise of Dainty Devices,* 1576 (7516), Huntington; *A Gorgeous Gallery of Gallant Inventions,* 1578 (20402), Bodleian; *The Forest of Fancy,* 1579 (4271), White; *Chetham Ms.* 8012, Chetham; *Verses of Praise and Joy,* 1586 (7605), B. M.; *The Phœnix Nest,* 1593 (21516), White; *England's Helicon,* 1600 (3191), White; *A Poetical Rhapsody,* 1602 (6373), White; *A Poetical Rhapsody,* 1608 (6374), White.

187–188 *A strange passion . . .*] This poem, like the one following, is found in the section of *A Hundreth Sundry Flowers* which is headed 'The devices of sundry gentlemen'. It has usually been ascribed to Gascoigne, as it was reprinted in his *Posies,* 1575, and *Works,* 1587.

188 *The lover declareth . . .*] Upon the evidence of the affixed motto, *Meritum petere, grave,* Ward assigns this poem to the Earl of Oxford; usually ascribed to Gascoigne. 16 So] 1575; 1573 'Go'.

188–189 *Amantium iræ . . .*] 1576 has *redintigratia* in the title; corrected in 1606. The title is translated in the refrain which ends each stanza. Rollins traces the saying to Terence, *Andria*, III. iii. 23. The poem was set to music, extant in *Add. Ms.* 30513. It is signed in *P. D. D.* For Richard Edwards, see L. Bradner, *The Life and Poems of Richard Edwards*, New Haven, 1927. For a poem possibly by Edwards, see *O death, rock me asleep*, p. 43. 3 sweet] 1578; 1576 'sore'. 8, 16, 24, 32, 40] Our reading of the refrain follows 1576; the one usually reprinted in modern times, 'The falling out of faithful friends renewing is of love,' appeared at the ends of the first three stanzas in editions of 1578 and 1580, and throughout in 1585 and later editions.

189–190 *M. Edwards' May*] signed in all editions after the first; set to music in John Forbes's *Cantus* (2nd ed., 1666). *P. D. D.* of 1578 contained *A reply to M. Edwards' May*, signed 'M. S.'; *P. D. D.* of 1585 contained *Master Edwards his I may not*, unsigned.

190–191 *Being importunate . . .*] signed in 1576, 'M. B.'; these initials represent 'Master Bew.' All editions after the first, however, give this poem to Edwards. 3 I] 1578; omitted in 1576.

191 *No pains comparable . . .*] For Hunnis see Mrs. C. C. Stopes, *William Hunnis and the Revels of the Chapel Royal*, Louvain, 1910. 9–10] 'No foot to spare' and 'No near' ('No nearer') are the answers of the man making soundings to the master's question of 'How?'

192–193 *Respice finem*] 'Consider the end.' The author of this poem and compiler of the miscellany in which it appeared, Thomas Procter, was a printer and miscellaneous author. 2 fine] end. 11 hutch] box, coffer. ruddocks] gold (red) coins.

193 *A proper sonnet . . .*] This poem stands between two signed as by Procter, but is not signed. Its poetical quality is higher than that of poems known to be by Procter.

193–194 *A true description of love*] Only two rhymes are used in this sonnet. 10 lay] law. 11 lean until our stay] 'lean' is misprinted 'leaue' in 1578; the phrase means 'lean upon our support.' Professor Kittredge (Rollins's edition, p. 173) is responsible for the improved reading. 14 denay] denial.

194 *The lover in the praise . . .* 5] Polyxena, daughter of Priam, was sacrificed at Achilles' grave by his son Pyrrhus. 7 wise] means.

194–195 *The lover exhorteth . . .*]

This is plainly a ballad. *Attend thee, go play thee* is one of the broadsides reprinted in *A Handful of Pleasant Delights*, 1584. 28 Camma] a woman who revenged the killing of her husband; the legend is told by Plutarch and by Castiglione in *The Courtier*. Rollins notes two ballads embodying the tale, registered 1569–1570.

195 *The strange pangs . . .* 11 joy] The sense seems to demand some such word as 'pain.'

195 *Chetham Ms.* 8012] This is a commonplace-book or manuscript miscellany; it contains entries of various dates and different handwritings, both in prose and poetry. Besides poems of unknown authorship, the ms. furnishes copies of works by Sir John Davies, Ralegh, Donne, Hoskins, Jonson, Dyer, and Daniel.

196 *Another of another mind* [1] 2 swad] clodhopper.

196 *Another of another mind* [2] 2 For] Grosart reads 'The'.

196 *Verses of Praise and Joy . . .*] This volume celebrates the discovery and overthrow of the Babington conspiracy against Queen Elizabeth. In September, 1586, seven of the conspirators met execution, including Chidiock Tichborne, then eighteen years of age. A letter which Tichborne wrote from the Tower to his wife is also preserved.

196–197 *Tichborne's elegy . . .*] One must admit the possibility that these verses were written by some other poet, rather than by the protagonist himself. The poem was very popular; it appears, set to music, in John Mundy's *Songs and Psalms*, 1594, Michael East's *Madrigals*, 1604, and Richard Alison's *An Hour's Recreation in Music*, 1606.

197–198 *O night, O jealous night* 1 pleasures] some editors emend to 'measures'.

198 *Set me where Phœbus' heat*] translated from Petrarch's sonnet *In vita*, cxiii; see Surrey's translation of the same sonnet, p. 29.

198–199 *Sought by the world*] The present editors suggest that upon evidence of style and content this poem might be assigned to Ralegh; in 1593 it stands with some poems known to be by Ralegh.

199 *A nymph's disdain of love*] signed 'Ignoto' in *E. H.*

199–201 *Phillida's love-call . . .*] signed 'Ignoto' in *E. H.*; set to music in *Rawlinson Poetry Ms.* 148. 28 say] silk. 42 my] The sense seems to demand 'her', *i. e.* Cynthia's. 55–60] The distribution of speeches follows 1614; 1600 gives 55–57 to Corydon and 58–60 to Phillida.

201 *The nymph Selvagia . . .*] This and the following poem, signed 'Bar. Young' in *E. H.*, were taken from Young's translation (1589) of Montemayor's *Diana*, p. 28 and p. 473.

202 *A palinode*] signed 'E. B.' in *E. H.* Three other poems in the miscellany are similarly signed, while one is signed 'Edmund Bolton'. Bolton was a Catholic poet and antiquarian, author of *Hypercritica*, an essay upon writers and literature.

202–203 *A canzon pastoral . . .*] signed 'Edmund Bolton'.

203 *To Colin Clout*] signed 'Shepherd Tony' in *E. H.*, as is one other poem. *To Colin Clout* appeared in a romance, *Primaleon of Greece*, 1619, (possibly in the newly-discovered *Second Book of Primaleon*, 1596), by Anthony Munday, who is therefore generally believed to have been 'Shepherd Tony.' Munday (1553–1633) was a voluminous author, principally of plays and pageants, but also of romances, translations, pamphlets, and ballads. Webbe's praise of Munday's pastoral poetry may well apply to the present lyric. This poem appears in three songbooks: Pilkington's *First Book of Songs or Airs*, 1605, Jones's *Ultimum Vale*, 1608, and Corkine's *Airs*, 1610. It was also reprinted in *Wit's Interpreter*, 1655.

203–204 *Ode*] Because of its presence in several mss. containing poems by Donne, and because of its character, this poem has been attributed to that poet. Grierson argues on the authority of a Hawthornden ms. (also taking into account style and sentiments) that the poem is by John Hoskins; see pp. 527, 528.

206–207 *A fiction . . .*] signed 'Anomos' in 1602; unsigned in later editions; attributed to A. W. in ms. list left by Francis Davison.

207 *Sonnet*] signed, as is another sonnet in the miscellany, 'I. S.' and upon this evidence usually ascribed to Joshua Sylvester (1563–1618), translator of Du Bartas. This sonnet is of higher poetic merit, however, than any other work by Sylvester. 5 high] 1602 reads 'hight'. 9–11] These lines translate an epigram from the Greek Anthology. See notes to Turberville.

208 *Commendation of her beauty*] This and the two poems following appear in a section of the *P. R.* headed 'Sonnets, Odes, Elegies, Madrigals, and Epigrams by Francis Davison and Walter Davison, Brethren'. The name of Francis Davison appears about halfway through the section, and the initials 'W. D.' at the end. The three poems here reprinted are from the first part.

208 *Upon the timorous silence . . .*] set to music by Robert Jones, *First set of Madrigals*, 1607.

208 *To Cupid*] first stanza set to music by Robert Jones, *First set of Madrigals*, 1607.

209 *The sound of thy sweet name*] This poem first appeared in the edition of 1608, in the section of poems evidently by Francis Davison. These stanzas were so printed as to appear to be a part of a preceding madrigal.

209 *A sonnet of the moon*] not in 1602; signed 'Ch. B.' in 1608, 'Chas. Best' in 1611. Practically nothing is known of this author. John Davies of Hereford addressed a complimentary epigram in *The Scourge of Folly* (*c.* 1611) to 'My kind friend, Mr. Charles Best.' 4 her] Ault (*E. L.*) prints, as from 1611, 'his'.

SONNET-SEQUENCES

THE EARLIEST 'true' sonnets written in English, those of Wyatt and of Surrey, remained for a considerable period without being widely imitated. Poets seized upon the word 'sonnet,' but applied it, in its etymological meaning of 'a little song,' to poems of varied lengths and measures. In Googe's *Eclogues, Epitaphs, and Sonnets*, 1563, are only two poems in sonnet-form; and these are printed in such a way as to disguise that form. In Turberville's *Epitaphs, Epigrams, Songs and Sonnets*, 1567, there are no sonnets in fourteen lines. These and other writers used the word 'sonnets' on their title-pages rather because of the popularity of the original *Songs and Sonnets*, 1557, than as an indication of the presence of a particular form of verse

An exception to this rule is Gascoigne, who wrote: 'I can best allow to call those Sonnets which are of fourteen lines, every line containing ten syllables.' In *A Hundreth Sundry Flowers* (1573) there appear thirty sonnets, of which at least eleven are by Gascoigne himself. It is notable that in one of these (see p. 88) the author seems to be attempting to follow the strict Italian rhyme-scheme and manages to avoid the final couplet. It is also notable that seven of Gascoigne's sonnets form a sequence, linked together by the author's repeating the last line of one as first line of the next; and that there are two other sequences, of three sonnets each, in *A Hundreth Sundry Flowers*. In the *Posies* (1575, 1587) all but two of the thirty sonnets were reprinted and two new ones were added. The circulation of these works, together with that of Tottel's miscellany in its successive editions, served to keep the fourteen-line sonnet before the eyes of readers.

A considerable number of sonnets, though confusingly designated, appeared in *A Theater . . . [for] Voluptuous Worldlings*, 1569, translated from the French version of a Flemish book of emblems by Van der Noodt. From later publication of some of these it seems evident that the translator was Edmund Spenser, then a school-boy. The *Theater* contained six sonnets (though five of them end at twelve lines) called 'Epigrams'; these were translated and adapted from the stanzas of a canzone by Petrarch (through the French of Marot), and were published, filled out to sonnet-length, with Spenser's *Complaints*, 1591. After the 'epigrams' in the *Theater* appeared fifteen poems in fourteen lines each, called 'Sonnets,' but written in blank verse. These were translated from du Bellay and also appeared, re-written with rhymes, in the *Complaints*. The chief significance of the *Theater* lies in the fact that what sonnets it contains came, though indirectly, from such authentic masters of this form as Petrarch and du Bellay; and in the fact that Spenser was thus early dabbling with the sonnet-form.

The prosperity of the sonnet, however, waited upon a further development—its use in an extended sequence with love as theme. Thomas Watson, whose *Hecatompathia, or Passionate Century of Love* appeared in 1582, is usually given credit for introducing into England this mode, already prevalent in Italy and France. Watson was not yet writing true sonnets, for most of the English poems in this volume are eighteen lines in length; but like Wyatt and Surrey before him he had gone to Petrarch for models and materials, as well as to minor Italian, French, and Latin authors; and his work was a forerunner of the later cycles of true sonnets. Indeed, as an apprentice task, he had translated all of Petrarch's sonnets into Latin verse; and two of these translations, one of them in fourteen lines, appear in *Hecatompathia*. Watson's only true sonnet in English in this volume is called a 'quatorzain,' a name borrowed from the French and used by many later sonneteers. With Watson we must at once name Sir Philip Sidney, who doubtless had written a large part of *Astrophel and Stella* by 1580; the circulation of this work in manuscript probably had more influence than the publication of Watson's book. Sidney also drew upon Petrarch and upon contemporary or recent French writers. Besides writing his sonnets in fourteen lines, Sidney may be said to have produced a sequence, or cycle, more truly than his contemporary. Watson's 'passionate century of love' was patched together of poems unrelated except by their general theme. *Astrophel and*

Stella, like Petrarch's work, is the lyrical reflection of a definite love story. And it was this use of the sonnet that prevailed in the hey-day of that form, following the publication of Sidney's work.

Fulke Greville, friend of Sidney, must also have written sonnets in the years about 1580; but his collection, *Cælica*, awaited publication until 1633, and then it contained a deal of later work. Nor is it a true cycle, but rather a miscellaneous gathering of various kinds of lyrics. There appeared in 1584 *Pandora*, containing some of Ronsard's sonnets translated ('with an unsurpassable crudity,' says Sidney Lee) by John Soowthern; but it seems to have been without influence. Two sonnets were printed with musical notes by Byrd in his *Psalms, Sonnets, and Songs* of 1588; and six more appeared in the same composer's *Songs of Sundry Natures*, 1589. These eight sonnets are quite in the best vein and deserve to stand with the work of minor sonneteers published in the decade following. Spenser used the sonnet for a considerable body of dedicatory material placed before the first issue of *The Fairy Queen* in 1590; and Ralegh wrote for the same publication a complimentary sonnet which is a high-water mark in its kind (see p. 137).

But the tide of sonneteering began to swell only after the publication of *Astrophel and Stella* in its three editions of 1591 and 1592. Then we find the best poets of England turning to this form and producing cycles addressed to real or imaginary mistresses. Twenty-eight sonnets by Daniel had been placed by Newman at the end of that printer's unauthorized first edition of *Astrophel and Stella*. Daniel himself issued in the next year his sonnet-cycle *Delia*, containing most of those printed by Newman and some thirty others. In *Delia and Rosamond augmented*, 1594, the cycle consists of fifty-five sonnets and an ode. Drayton published a sequence of fifty-two sonnets in 1594, under the title of *Idea's Mirror*. This sequence in its final form, the *Idea* of 1619, contained sixty-three sonnets. Spenser followed with a cycle of eighty-eight sonnets published in *Amoretti and Epithalamion*, 1595. And there is good reason to believe that the greater number of Shakespeare's sonnets, though not printed until 1609, were written in the early and middle years of the 1590's.

In the meanwhile, minor poets were also at work. Constable's *Diana* appeared in 1592, and again, 'augmented with divers quatorzains of honorable and learned persons,' in 1594. Lodge published his *Phillis* in 1593; and from the same year we have Barnabe Barnes's *Parthenophe and Parthenophil* (a title plainly imitated from Sidney's), Giles Fletcher's *Licia*, and a second cycle by Watson, *The Tears of Fancy*. In 1594, besides some cycles already mentioned, come the anonymous *Zepheria* and Percy's *Cælia*; in 1595, *Emaricdulfe* by E. C., and a short cycle addressed to a young man by Barnfield in his *Cynthia*; in 1596, *Diella* by Lynche, *Fidessa* by Griffin, and *Chloris* by Smith; and in 1597, *Laura* by Robert Tofte. The last-named sequence is made up of poems of ten and twelve lines; and if we include it with sonnet-cycles we ought also to mention the same author's *Alba* and J. C.'s *Alcilia, Philoparthen's Loving Folly*, which is a love-cycle having a six-line form as its unit. But sequences of love-poems, in miscellaneous stanza-forms, were too numerous for mention here.

As may be seen from the titles, the conventional sonnet-cycle was addressed to a lady, corresponding to Petrarch's Laura (or Sidney's Stella), who usually was given a classical name. Some of the names, as Delia, Phillis, Diana, and Idea, had already been used in titles of French cycles. In some sequences, as in Spenser's *Amoretti* and E. C.'s *Emaricdulfe*, a real woman is the subject, and details of her life and character appear. In others, as Fletcher's *Licia*, Lodge's *Phillis*, and both of Watson's collections, the reader is aware that he has only literary exercises and translations—though such might have served, to be sure, in some actual romances. The general Petrarchan conventions of the cruel mistress, golden-haired and with lilies and roses contending in her cheeks, and the faithful lover, alternately hoping and fearing, at once freezing and burning, are at the basis of most of the cycles, though transcended by the best writers. Some other specific conventional themes are: the lady walks or sits in the garden, she plays on a musical instrument, she sings, she falls sick; the lover compares himself to a ship tossed by the sea, he invokes sleep, he promises eternity of fame to the lady through his verses. There is a continual search for comparisons worthy of the lady's beauty and grace: the four seasons and the heavenly bodies are under frequent requisition; as are legendary heroes and ladies, gods and goddesses, kings and kingdoms, usages of the law court, and even the signs of the zodiac. Yet in spite of this conventional lumber, and even by the aid of it, some of the sonneteers wrote poems of exquisite grace and charm; while now and again a genuine expression of deep emotion vivifies a page in one of these collections.

The flood of sonnets met with a counter-current of satire. It must have been about 1595 that Sir John Harington wrote *A comfort for poor poets,*

> Poets henceforth for pensions need not care;
> Who call you beggars, you may call them liars:
> Verses are grown such merchantable ware
> That now for sonnets sellers are—and buyers.

John Davies at the same time was using the sonnet-form for many of his coarse and bitter epigrams; he singled out an unfortunate conceit in one of Drayton's sonnets for ridicule (*In Decium*, p. 332); and he composed for circulation among his friends a set of nine 'gulling sonnets' which parodied the passions of the sonneteers (see pp. 332–334). Shakespeare voiced his impatience with conventional notes in sonnets:

> My mistress' eyes are nothing like the sun;
> Coral is far more red than her lips' red, etc.

Again, we find Mercutio laughing at the sonnet-fashion when he says of Romeo (*R. and J.* II. iv. 40): 'Now is he for the numbers that Petrarch flowed in: Laura to his lady was but a kitchen-wench; marry, she had a better love to berhyme her.' The temper of the times about 1600, tending toward sophistication and cynicism, furthered the literary reaction against the over-sweet sonnet, and brought it about that satires and epigrams replaced sonnets in popular favor. Earlier than this, too, many readers (and writers) of love-poetry must have turned with relief from the cold ladies of the Petrarchan convention to the passionate and pursuing heroines of the Ovidian tradition as represented in *Venus and Adonis*, *Hero and Leander*, and other poems.

Religious impulses also influenced sonnet-writing, and soon after the cycles began to appear the form was turned to devotional uses. As early as 1593 the uninspired Henry Lok issued *Sundry Christian Passions contained in two hundred sonnets*. Chapman's *Coronet for his Mistress Philosophy* of

1595, while not religious, claims the sonnet for higher uses than the praise of a lady-love,—a line of thought already suggested by Giles Fletcher in his preface to *Licia*. Barnes turned from praising Parthenophe and wrote his *Divine Century of Spiritual Sonnets*, 1595, 'an hundreth quatorzains in honor of the greatest Disposer of all great honors.' Constable wrote but did not publish (doubtless because of its Catholic sentiments) a short sequence entitled *Spiritual Sonnets*. In 1597 Lok's collection, considerably augmented, saw a second printing. Some of the excellent religious sonnets of Donne will be found with the poems of that author; and it will be seen that Drummond issued both secular and religious sequences in his *Poems* of 1616, as Davies of Hereford had done in *Wit's Pilgrimage*, 1610.

Nor must it be thought that the love-cycle was extinct by 1600; besides the later works by Davies and Drummond, just mentioned, and new editions of earlier cycles, we have *Aurora*, 1604, an extended sequence by Sir William Alexander; *Amorous Songs, Sonnets, and Elegies*, 1606, by another Scottish poet, Alexander Craig; and another *Songs and Sonnets*, this time by Patrick Hannay, published with *The Nightingale*, 1622.

CROSS REFERENCES: For sonnets not in this section and not mentioned in the foregoing account, see under: Minor Courtly Makers, Oxford, Essex, Elizabethan Miscellanies, Epigrams, James I, Aytoun, Browne, Habington, and Herbert.

MODERN EDITIONS: *Elizabethan Sonnets* (ed. by S. Lee), two volumes, Westminster, 1904; *Elizabethan Sonnet-Cycles* (ed. by M. F. Crow), four volumes, London, 1896–98; *Parthenophil and Parthenophe* (ed. by A. B. Grosart), 1875; *Divine Century of Spiritual Sonnets* in *Heliconia* (ed. by T. Park), Vol. ii, London, 1815; *Emaricdulfe* in *A Lamport Garland* (ed. by C. Edmunds), The Roxburghe Club, 1881; *The Poetical Works of Alexander Craig*, Hunterian Club, 1873.

TEXT: *Licia*, [1593] (11055), Huntington; *Parthenophil and Parthenophe*, [1593], text from Sidney Lee; *Coelia*, 1594 (19618), Huntington; *Zepheria*, 1594 (26124), White; *Emaricdulfe*, 1595 (4268), Huntington; *Diella*, 1596 (17091), Huntington; *Chloris*, 1596 (22872), B. M.; *Fidessa*, 1596 (12367), Huntington; *Laura*, 1597 (24097), Huntington; *Sonnets of Christian Passions*, 1597 (16696), White; *Amorous Songs, Sonnets, and Elegies*, 1606 (5956), White.

209 *Licia*] Giles Fletcher (*c.* 1549–1611), known as 'the elder' to distinguish him from his son of the same name (see p. 599), was more famous as scholar and man of affairs than as poet. He studied at Eton and at King's College, Cambridge, where he proceeded B. A. in 1569, M. A. in 1573, and Doctor of Laws in 1581. He saw diplomatic service in Scotland, and later in Russia, where he suffered notorious illtreatment. A book about Russia which he wrote was suppressed. It seems to have been in a period of enforced idleness after this suppression (in 1591) that Fletcher turned to the new fashion of sonneteering and produced *Licia*, a sequence of fifty-two sonnets with a half-dozen of odes and elegies appended. His other works (several of them in Latin) were historical, political, and religious. The poems in *Licia* are admittedly imitative, though Fletcher turned to Neo-Latin rather than to Italian sources (cf. Janet Scott, 'The Sources of Giles Fletcher's *Licia*,' *M.L.R.* xx. 187).

211 *Seven are the lights* 14 her] Venus's.

212 *Like Memnon's rock* 3 done] 1593 'dunne'; 'dumb' seems demanded by the sense, and 'done' by the rhymescheme.

214 *Parthenophil and Parthenophe*] Barnabe Barnes (1570–1609) was at Brasenose College, Oxford, about 1586, but left without taking a degree. *Parthenophil and Parthenophe* contained one hundred and five sonnets, twenty-six madrigals, twenty-one elegies, twenty odes, five sestines, and three canzons, besides a version of the first idyl of Moschus, the story of 'runaway Cupid.' The printer's preface to *Parthenophil and Parthenophe* promises from the author 'some more excellent work hereafter'; Barnes's *Divine Century of Spiritual Sonnets* (1595) may have been printed to fulfil that promise. Aside from laying himself open to attack from Nashe, the poet seems to have had personal defects which made him fair game for ridicule, notably by Thomas Campion. Barnes drew heavily upon French poets for his inspiration; even his translation from Moschus was probably made from French rather than from Greek. A modern reader finds his work antiquated and quaint, though graceful and poetic within the conventional fashion of his decade. The unique copy of the first edition of this book is in the library of the Duke of Devonshire; our text from Lee's *Elizabethan Sonnets*.

216 *No more lewd lays* 3 sparrows' plumes] The sparrow was Venus's bird.

217 *Cælia*] William Percy (1575–1648) was a younger son of Henry Percy, eighth Earl of Northumberland. His friendship with Barnabe Barnes may have begun in Yorkshire, the home of both, whence they both went to Oxford. In writing *Sonnets to the Fairest Cælia* Percy appears to have been following the example set by Barnes. He published no other books, but left six plays in ms.

218 *Zepheria*] The author of this sequence has not been identified. That he was a member of one of the Inns of Court is suggested by the legal phraseology which he often employs and which subjected him to satirical parody by Sir John Davies (see p. 334).

218–219 *Alli veri figlioli delle Muse*] 'To the true sons of the Muse.' 10 father of delicious phrases] Petrarch (?). 15 Delian sonnetry] a term often applied to sonneteering, from Daniel's popular sequence, *Delia*. 20 Naso] Ovid. 28 Mnemosyne] The Muses were the daughters of Mnemosyne, or Memory. 31 lawful] 1594 'leyful'; 'lay' was a not uncommon form of 'law.'

219 *Proud in thy love*] lacking from the White copy; text from Lee.

220 *Emaricdulfe*] Edmunds suggests Edmund Carew as possibly author of the sequence. Lee says: ' "Emaricdulfe" is an anagram on the name of one Marie Cufeld, or Cufaud, of Cufaud Manor, near Basingstoke.' The sequence contains a number of circumstantial allusions to the lady.

220–221 *I am enchanted*] Sonnets presenting the lady as playing on a musical instrument are not uncommon in sequences; compare Shakespeare's sonnet 128.

221 *Diella*] The known publications of Lynche, or Linche, are *The Fountain of English Fiction*, 1599, and *An Historical Treatise of the Travels of Noah into Europe*, 1601, both translated from the Italian. In 1596 had appeared *Diella, certain sonnets, adjoined to the*

Amorous Poem of Dom Diego and Ginevra, the latter poem also a translation from the Italian. This work is claimed by 'R. L., Gentleman.' Most students accept Richard Lynche as the author, who may also be the R. L. to whom Richard Barnfield addressed a sonnet (see p. 239).

222 *Chloris*] Little is known of William Smith except what can be gleaned from this volume, which appeared under his name. One of the sonnets in *Chloris* had previously appeared in *The Phœnix Nest*, 1593, and a poem from the collection was reprinted in *England's Helicon*.

222–223 *To . . . Colin Clout*] addressed to Spenser, using the name which that poet adopted for himself.

224 *Fidessa*] Of this poet there remains only this volume, issued under the name B. Griffin. Grosart identified him as Bartholomew Griffin of Coventry (d. 1602). A sonnet appearing in *Fidessa*, beginning 'Venus and young Adonis sitting by her,' was printed, with alterations, in *The Passionate Pilgrim* as Shakespeare's. Griffin echoes previous English sonneteers rather than French or Italian poets.

224 *Compare me to the child* 3 foolish boy] Icarus.

225 *Fly to her heart*] an example of the form known as 'like loose'; see Wyatt's *Hate whom ye list* (p. 21) and note.

227 *Laura*] Robert Tofte (d. 1620) left two books of original poetry and several translated volumes. He is known to have traveled much in Italy; and he published versions of several works by Ariosto and of *Orlando Inamorata* by Boiardo. The lady celebrated by Tofte, if we can judge from internal evidence, was named Caryll. Tofte himself had some acquaintance among the minor writers of his time, by whom he was nick-named 'Robin Redbreast.' The poems in *Laura* are never true sonnets, but are ten or twelve lines in length.

228 *Sonnets of Christian Passions*] Lok, or Lock (c. 1553–c. 1608), most pedestrian of sonneteers, wrote little but religious poetry. In 1593 he published *Sundry Christian Passions contained in Two Hundred Sonnets*. These poems were reprinted with the author's verse-paraphrase of *Ecclesiastes* in 1597, augmented by verse-translations of some *Psalms*, 102 'Sundry affectionate sonnets of a feeling conscience' and twenty-two sonnets called 'Peculiar prayers.'

Some copies also contain sixty or more secular sonnets, addressed to notable men and women of the time.

228 *Amorous Songs, Sonnets, and Elegies*] Alexander Craig (*c.* 1567–1627) was a cultured Scotchman who came to London in the train of King James. He published *Poetical Essays* in 1604, and having received a generous pension from James, retired to Scotland to make his home. He published also his *Poetical Recreations* (1609 and 1623).

228–229 *To Pandora* 11 thame] Scottish form of 'them'. 14 saunt] Scottish variant for 'saint'; 1606 reads 'sanct'.

HENRY CONSTABLE

HENRY CONSTABLE (1562–1613), born of a good family in Warwickshire and educated at Cambridge, as a young man embraced the Catholic faith, with the result that he spent the greater part of his remaining years abroad, though in touch with English affairs and often in England. When it became apparent that James VI of Scotland was to succeed Elizabeth, Constable tried to open negotiations toward removing the disabilities of Catholics, but without avail.

A sonnet of his had appeared in King James's *Poetical Exercises* of 1591. In the next year was published his *Diana*, a sonnet-sequence of only twenty-three poems; in 1594 this was re-issued, 'augmented with divers quatorzains of honorable and learned personages.' In this second form, the sequence contains seventy-six sonnets, including eight known to be by Sir Philip Sidney. None of the others has been assigned with definiteness to any author besides Constable. In 1595 four sonnets by Constable in praise of Sidney appeared in the first edition of *An Apology for Poetry*; and four pastoral poems by him were included in *England's Helicon*, 1600. His religious sonnets, left unprinted doubtless because of their strongly Catholic sentiments, were published from manuscript early in the nineteenth century.

Constable's poetry enjoyed a deserved popularity in its generation. In *The Return from Parnassus*, the Cambridge play of 1600, one student pays this tribute:

> Sweet Constable doth take the wand'ring ear
> And lays it up in willing prisonment.

MODERN EDITIONS: *Diana: the sonnets and other poems* (ed. by T. Park), London, 1859; *Spiritual Sonnets to the honor of God and His Saints,* in *Heliconia* (ed. by T. Park), Vol. ii, London, 1815; *The Poems and Sonnets* (ed. by J. Gray), London, 1897; *Diana* in *Elizabethan Sonnet-Cycles* (ed. by M. F. Crow), London, 1896, and in *Elizabethan Sonnets* (ed. by S. Lee), Westminster, 1904.

TEXT: *Diana*, 1592 (5637), Huntington; *Diana*, [1594] (5638), Huntington; *The Harleian Miscellany*, Vol. ix, 1812; *Harleian Ms.* 7553, B. M.; *England's Helicon*, 1600 (3191), White.

230 *Whilst echo cries . . .* 5 play'st] 1594 'pay'st'.

231–232 *To his mistress . . .*] unprinted until its appearance in *The Harleian Miscellany;* unfortunately Park does not tell from what ms. he printed it, and it does not appear in the *Harleian Mss.* of Constable's authorship.

232–233 *Damelus' song . . .*] signed 'H. C.' in 1600; set to music by Francis Pilkington, *First Book of Songs or Airs,* 1605.

233–235 *The shepherd's song of Venus and Adonis*] signed 'H. C.' in 1600; the question of priority of composition between this poem and Shakespeare's on the same subject has not been settled. The legend occurs in Ovid's *Metamorphoses*, x. Both Constable and Shakespeare, however, differ from Ovid in making Adonis cold to Venus's advances. This treatment of the story is suggested in Spenser's *Fairy Queen* (III. i. xxxiv–xxxviii) and in Marlowe's *Hero and Leander* (ll. 12–14). 5 Vesta's beauty] Vesta is sometimes identified with Terra, the earth. 72 Myrrha] Adonis was the incestuous son of Myrrha and her father Cinyras, king in Assyria and Cyprus. 129 orpëd] fierce. 139 flower] the anemone, formerly called the adonium.

ROBERT SOUTHWELL

ROBERT SOUTHWELL (*c.* 1561–1595) was a Catholic poet, a member of the Society of Jesus. He was educated at Douai and Paris; and for some time was prefect of studies in the English College at Rome. In 1584, when he was ordained priest, he asked to be sent to England; although a law promulgated in the same year made it a treasonable offense for an English subject ordained as priest after 1557 to remain in England for more than forty days. Southwell returned while the Babington plot was being fomented, but he seems to have had no immediate connection with that plot. He went under the name of Cotton, and acquired a vocabulary of sporting terms (especially from falconry) in order to conceal his profession. In 1589 he became chaplain to the wife of the Earl of Arundel. A proclamation of 1591 called for a more rigorous enforcement of laws against Catholics; Southwell was arrested in 1592, and spent the remainder of his life in prison. He was thirteen times examined, several times tortured, and finally executed by hanging. There seems to have been little, if any, popular feeling against him. His books, which printers began to issue immediately after his death, were widely sold in several editions.

Besides his English poems he wrote much Latin verse and several devotional tracts in prose. His desire in writing poetry was to show that religious subjects were suitable for the poet; in two or three cases he wrote sacred redactions, or parodies, of popular love-poems.

MODERN EDITIONS: *Complete Poems* (ed. by A. B. Grosart), Fuller Worthies' Library, London, 1872; *The Book of Robert Southwell* (ed. by C. M. Hood), Oxford, 1926.

COMMENT: Mario Praz, 'St. Peter's Complaint and its Italian Source,' *M. L. R.* xix. 273; J. A. Langford, *Prison Books and their Authors*, London, 1861.

TEXT: *Mœoniæ*, 1595 (22954), White; *St. Peter's Complaint . . . for J. Wolfe*, 1595 (22957), Huntington (Chew copy); *St. Peter's Complaint, newly augmented*, [*c.* 1605] (22961), Huntington.

235 *Upon the image of death* 3 names] In Simon Wastell's *Microbiblion*, 1629, where this poem is reprinted, the reading is 'qualms'. 20 hearse] a canopy of black, to be placed over a coffin.

RICHARD BARNFIELD

RICHARD BARNFIELD (1574–1627) is remembered for three brief books of poetry published before he reached the age of twenty-five. From the age of fifteen to that of eighteen he was at Oxford, where he received the degree of B.A. in 1592. Then he spent a few years in London among the numerous young poets and poetasters of the time, and afterward retired to his country home. His publications were *The Affectionate Shepherd*, 1594, dedicated to Lady Penelope Rich (Sidney's Stella), *Cynthia*, 1595, and *The Encomion of Lady Pecunia*, 1598. Barnfield is notable for his generous tributes to contemporary authors. He seems to have been a friend of Watson, Drayton, and Meres; and his greatest admiration went out to Sidney,

Spenser, and Shakespeare. While he is distinctly a minor poet, he caught a little of the music of the great singers whom he praised. Three of the poems here reprinted, *Ode*, *To his friend Master R. L.*, and *The unknown shepherd's complaint*, were included in *The Passionate Pilgrim* of 1599 as Shakespeare's; and the first two named were generally thought to be by Shakespeare until their presence in *Poems in Divers Humors* of 1598 was pointed out; the third is ascribed to Barnfield on slighter evidence. It is possible that the R. B. who wrote and compiled the poetical pamphlet in memory of Robert Greene, *Greene's Funerals*, 1594, was Richard Barnfield.

MODERN EDITIONS: *Poems* (ed. by E. Arber), Westminster, 1895, and in *Some Longer Elizabethan Poems* (ed. by A. H. Bullen), London, n. d.; *Complete Poems*, (ed. by A. B. Grosart), The Roxburghe Club, 1876.

TEXT: *Cynthia*, 1595 (1483), Bodleian; *Poems in Divers Humors*, 1598 (1488), Bodleian.

239 *To his mistress 2 president*] probably 'presiding genius' or 'guardian'; the same form, however, frequently represents the modern 'precedent.'

239–240 *To his friend Master R. L.*] perhaps addressed to the poet Richard Lynche. 5 Dowland] see p. 981.

240 *Against the dispraisers of poetry* 13 The King of Scots] see p. 545.

240 *A remembrance of some English poets* 8 *The White Rose and the Red*] Daniel's *Civil Wars*, five books of which were published in 1595.

241 *An ode*] reprinted in a shortened version in *England's Helicon*. 23 King Pandion] in Greek legend, the father of Philomela and Procne, who were changed by the gods, in pity for their sorrows, into birds, one into a swallow and the other into a nightingale.

241–242 *The unknown shepherd's complaint*] first appeared in Thomas Weelkes's *Madrigals*, 1597, then in *The Passionate Pilgrim* of 1599, with the foregoing *Ode*. In *England's Helicon* the *Ode* follows this poem, with the heading, 'Another of the same shepherd's'; on this basis we have ascribed the present poem to Barnfield.

SAMUEL DANIEL

SAMUEL DANIEL (*c.* 1562–1619) was educated at Magdalen Hall, Oxford. After three years' residence, he left without a degree, finding himself, if we are to believe Wood, 'more prone to easier and smoother studies than in pecking and hewing at logic.' His first publication, in 1585, was a translation of *The Worthy Tract of Paulus Jovius*, an Italian work on impresas. The preface shows Daniel already a master of a remarkably clear and fluent prose style. Before 1592, he had traveled on the Continent, and while in Italy, with Sir Edward Dymmock, he had met Guarini. In England, too, he was fortunate in literary friendships; for as tutor to William Herbert he was admitted to the circle of the Countess of Pembroke at Wilton, which he spoke of as 'my best school.' Here he began to write sonnets, and twenty-eight of his composition appeared in the surreptitious edition of Sir Philip Sidney's *Astrophel and Stella* in 1591. In the next year he issued an authorized edition of his sonnets, and also published his *Complaint of Rosamond*, a tragical legend modeled on the legends of the still popular *Mirror for Magistrates*. Stimulated by the same patriotic impetus which produced the chronicle plays, he continued to write of historical subjects in his *Civil Wars*, 1595. In 1612 we have the final result of this interest in his prose *History of England*.

Daniel found it necessary to continue to earn his living by tutoring, and before 1599 he entered the service of the Countess of Cumberland as tutor to her daughter, Lady Anne Clifford. Later he lamented that he had been 'constrained to live with children' whilst he should have 'written the actions of men.' The poems he wrote during this period—*Musophilus*, and the verse epistles of dignified advice to various members of the nobility— do bear the mark of the teacher. In 1602 Campion's attack on rhyme and accentual verse stirred Daniel to write his excellent *Defence of Rhyme*, the only Elizabethan critical treatise worthy to rank with Sidney's *Defence of Poesy*.

At the accession of James, Daniel was preferred to the favor of Queen Anne by the Countess of Bedford and was commissioned to write the first mask for the new court, *The Vision of the Twelve Goddesses*, 1604. Although Jonson superseded him as the writer of masks, Daniel retained the Queen's favor and held various offices in her household. With the exception of some difficulty over his play *Philotas*, which was thought to touch too closely on the fate of the Earl of Essex, he lived quietly, in as much retirement as possible. He kept a farm at Beckington in Somerset, the county of his birth, to which he retired in 1618 when he was discharged from the Queen's service for visiting Sir Robert Floud, then in disgrace.

Daniel was commended by his contemporaries for the purity of his diction—'well-languaged Daniel' he was called by Browne. Others thought that his poetry was pitched in too low an emotional key and that his manner was 'fitter perhaps for prose,' or that he was 'too much historian in verse.' In the early 19th century, Coleridge found him an excellent example of 'that style which, as the neutral ground of prose and verse, is common to both,' and praised highly his language, 'just such as any very pure and manly writer of the present day—Wordsworth, for example—would use.' The annotations in Wordsworth's copy of Daniel, now at Dove Cottage, show that Wordsworth paid him the honor of careful study.

Daniel would undoubtedly have been pleased with the comment that he was an historian in verse, for his settled conviction was that poetic subjects should be found in true history rather than in fictitious tales. Perhaps for him this was a wise choice, for his chief merit is in his meditative reflections on life, which led Coleridge to write to Lamb, 'Thousands of educated men would become more sensible, fitter to be members of Parliament or Ministers, by reading Daniel.'

MODERN EDITIONS: *The Complete Works* (ed. by A. B. Grosart), five volumes, London, 1885–1896; *A Selection from the Poetry of Daniel and Drayton* (ed. by H. C. Beeching), London, 1899.

COMMENT: A. H. Bullen, *Elizabethans*, London, 1924; H. Sellars, 'Samuel Daniel: Additions to the Text' in *M. L. R.*, xi. 28.

TEXT: *Delia and Rosamond augmented*, 1594 (6254), Huntington; *The Whole Works*, 1623 (6238), Cornell; *Certain Small Poems*, 1605 (6239), White; *Tethys' Festival*, 1610 (13161), White.

242 *To the . . . Countess of Pembroke*] first appeared in the edition of 1594, and not reprinted in the definitive edition of 1623, from which we take the text of the other sonnets that we print. It seems possible that by 'Delia' Daniel intended his patroness, the Countess of Pembroke, to whom he is paying the conventional compliments. The intimate tone of several of the sonnets makes this ascription doubtful, but one must remember that Daniel was not attempting to give a literal account of their relations and did not wish to speak so clearly that all would recognize his Delia. The river Avon, referred to in the sonnet, 'None other fame,' is not the Warwickshire Avon, but the Wiltshire Avon, which flows near to Wilton, the seat of the Countess of Pembroke.

243 *Why should I sing* 9 If] 1594; 1623 'I'.

244 *But love whilst* 7 thy] 1623 'thy thy'.

245 *Most fair and lovely maid* 9 Stretch] 1594; 1623 'Stretcht'.

247 *An ode*] set to music in John Farmer's *First Set of English Madrigals,* 1599.

247–261 *The complaint of Rosamond*] We print 539 of the 910 lines. 4 kind] sex. 25 Shore's wife] The reference is probably to Churchyard's *Shore's Wife,* which appeared in the *Mirror for Magistrates* of 1563. In 1593, the year following the first publication of Daniel's *Rosamond,* Anthony Chute published his *Beauty Dishonored, written under the title of Shore's Wife.* 'Shore's wife' is Jane Shore, the mistress of Edward IV. 36 Although] 1623 'Although'. 43 Delia] here certainly the Countess of Pembroke. 136 woman] 1623 'women'. 249 dome] a 16th-century spelling of 'doom.' Possibly a play is intended on 'dome' and 'doom.' 305 Which] 1623 'Whih'. 382 Except] 1623 'Ecept'. 452 a-cross] Daniel probably means 'in the fashion of a cross.' 533 vanished] the reading of the two editions of 1592; 1594 reads 'vanquished', which reading is retained by 1623. It is possible that the later reading is Daniel's own change, but it seems more probable that it is a printer's error.

261–264 *To the . . . Countess of Cumberland* 8 wilds] 1623 'weilds'. 89–96] quoted by Wordsworth in *The Excursion,* bk. iv, ll. 323–331. In a note on the passage he further quotes four stanzas, ll. 33–64, which, he says, give 'an admirable picture of the state of a wise man's mind in a time of public commotion.' 90 this] 1623; 1602 'his'. 100 work] 1623 'wotke'.

264–266 *To the . . . Countess of Bedford*] next to the Countess of Pembroke, the most important patroness of poetry in late Elizabethan and in Jacobean days. Daniel, Drayton, Jonson, Donne, and many less well-known men of letters, were befriended by her.

266–280 *Musophilus*] first appeared in *Poetical Essays,* 1599, dedicated to Fulke Greville. We print the first 567 lines, and 30 lines from the closing passage, out of the total 983 lines. 43 better] 1623 'hetter'. 71 Strive] 1623 'Srive'. 118 titlers] those who pretend or assert a legal title. 231 'fords] affords, supplies from his own resources. 281 unhallowed] 1623 'unhollowed'. 329 wondrous trophy] Stonehenge. 367 became] came. 502 kay] key.

MICHAEL DRAYTON

Michael Drayton (1563–1631) is the most representative of the Elizabethan poets, and his work reflects all the changing poetical fashions of his day. In the 1590's he wrote with the fatal facility of that exuberant time, piling phrase on phrase and clause on clause. During the reign of James, he developed a neater, more concise expression, particularly in his odes; and in the reign of Charles he rivaled the younger Carolines in the lightness of his touch. He tried all the popular poetic forms—Biblical paraphrase, pastoral, legend, sonnet, mythological poem, historical narrative, verse letter, play, ode, and the mock-heroic fairy tale.

Drayton was fortunate in being brought up as a page in the house of Sir Henry Goodere at Polesworth. Here he was soon fired with enthusiasm for poetry, perhaps by the ballad singing of John Hewes,

> Which oft at Polesworth by the fire
> Hath made us gravely merry.

With youthful enthusiasm he asked his tutor to make him a poet, and diligently applied himself to study. The training at Polesworth was the whole of his formal education, for he did not attend either of the universities. Anne, the younger daughter of Sir Henry Goodere, was much in Drayton's mind when he commenced writing poetry. She is the 'Idea' of his sonnets, and the frequent occurrence of 'Idea' in his early titles seems to be a tribute to her. In 1595 she married Sir Henry Rainsford, but her friendship with Drayton continued, and each summer he spent a month at her home in the country.

Like Daniel, Drayton was moved by the patriotic enthusiasm of the 1590's to spend much energy on poems of historical narrative. He achieved his greatest success with such material in *England's Heroical Epistles*, 1597, in form modeled on Ovid's *Heroides*. In that year, lack of money forced him to become one of Henslowe's hacks, and between then and 1602 he collaborated on at least twenty-three plays. This was for him a disagreeable task, and he abandoned it as soon as he found a patron in Sir Walter Aston. With leisure he commenced work on his topographical poem, the *Poly-Olbion*, which he had already planned by 1597 as the best means of expressing adequately the glory and beauty of England. The first eighteen songs were completed and published in 1612, and in 1622 he added a second part of twelve songs. During this period, he also wrote a number of shorter poems and revised carefully his earlier ones, printing what may be regarded as a definitive edition in 1619. Then, with the long weary task of the *Poly-Olbion* completed and his early poems satisfactorily revised, his lighter muse sprang to life again in his delightful *Nymphidia* of 1627, and in his charming *Muses' Elysium* of 1630. In his later years, Drayton was looked upon as a leader by the younger Spenserians, and he numbered among his good friends Browne, Wither, Drummond, and Alexander.

Among his contemporaries, Drayton was known for his upright, respectable life. Meres says that 'among scholars, soldiers, poets, and all sorts of people, [he] is held for a man of virtues and well-governed carriage, which is almost miraculous among good wits of this declining and corrupt time.' His solidity of character is reflected in his poetry, which seems to be addressed not only to the brilliant court circle, as with so many poets then, but also to the sound, substantial citizens. Among them, if we may judge from the number of collected editions of Drayton's poetry published during his lifetime, he gained a large audience.

MODERN EDITIONS: *Poems* (ed. by J. P. Collier), London, 1856; *The Complete Works* (ed. by R. Hooper; contains only the *Poly-Olbion* and *The Harmony of the Church*), three volumes, London, 1876; *Selections from the Poems* (ed. by A. H. Bullen), Chilworth, 1883; *The Barons' Wars and other Poems* (ed. by H. Morley), London, 1887; *Poems*, Spenser Society, 1888; *Poems, Lyric and Pastoral*, Spenser Society, 1891; *The Muses' Elisium*, Spenser Society, 1892; *The Battle of Agincourt* (ed. by R. Garnett), London, 1893; *A Selection from the Poetry of Daniel and Drayton* (ed. by H. C. Beeching), London, 1899; *Minor Poems* (ed. by C. Brett), Oxford, 1907; *Endimion and Phœbe* (ed. by J. W. Hebel), Stratford-upon-Avon, 1925.

COMMENT: O. Elton, *Michael Drayton, a Critical Study*, London, 1905.

TEXT: *Idea, the Shepherd's Garland*, 1593 (7202), B. M.; *Idea's Mirror*, 1594 (7203), White; *England's Heroical Epistles*, 1599 (7195), Bodleian; *Poems*, 1619 (7222), Cornell; *Poly-Olbion*, [1612] (7226), Cornell; *The Battle of Agincourt*, 1627 (7190), Adams; *The Muses' Elysium*, 1630 (7210), Cornell.

282 *Idea, the Shepherd's Garland*] a pastoral poem in nine eclogues, inspired by Spenser's *Shepherd's Calendar*.

282–283 *The eighth eclogue* 3 Isenbras] sometimes spelled Isumbras, the hero of the medieval romance, *Sir Isumbras*. 6 Sir Thopas] the hero of a tale told by Chaucer himself in *The Canterbury Tales*. 11 yconned] taught, caused to learn. lere] lore. 15 march-

pine] marchpane, marzipan, an almond confection. 28 Lemster] Leominster. 29 Peakish hull] 1593 'peakish Hull'. It seems most probable that Drayton was thinking of a hill (obsolete spelling, 'hull') in the Peak region in Derbyshire. 33 cetywall] setwall, valerian plant. 34 harlock] unidentified flower; perhaps charlock. 43 leared] guided. 56 loke] lock of wool. 58 bauzens'] badgers'. 59 cockers] casings for the leg; high laced boots or leggings. cordiwin] cordwain, cordovan. 60 meniveere] miniver, a fur used for lining and trimming. 61 lingel] waxed thread. 62 tar-box] used by shepherds to hold tar as a salve for sheep. 63 cointrie] Coventry blue, a thread manufactured in Coventry and frequently used in embroidery. 76 a good] so well. 91 vail] lower. 110 Colin] Spenser, who had paid poetical tribute to Rosalind, as yet unidentified, in his *Shepherd's Calendar*.

284 *Idea's Mirror*] Drayton's sonnets first appeared in this volume. They were frequently reprinted, with omissions and additions, and many variant readings. We have taken his definitive edition of 1619 as the base text for his sonnets, adding from the editions of 1594 and 1599 three sonnets which he omitted in 1619.

284 *To ... Ma. Anthony Cooke*] to whom Drayton was probably preferred by the Gooderes, Cooke's daughter Margaret having married Sir Ralph Rowlet, a family connection of the Gooderes. Later, Sir John Davies dedicated his *Gulling Sonnets* to Cooke; see p. 332. 11 Portes'] Desportes, a French sonneteer, frequently paraphrased and imitated by the English poets. 14] quoted from Sidney's sonnet, 'I never drank,' p. 116.

286 *To nothing fitter* 2 penny-father] miser, niggard.

287–288. *Our floods' queen*] marginal note: 'To the river Anker'. Polesworth, the home of Anne Goodere, is on the Anker. 4 Avon's] the Avon flowing near the Countess of Pembroke's seat in Wiltshire; · frequently mentioned by Daniel.

288 *Some misbelieving* 1] 1594 has an interesting variant reading: 'Some atheist or vile infidel in love'. See Donne's *Love's deity*, l. 22, p. 456.

288–289 *Some men there be* 4 humor] disposition, mood, style.

289 *In pride of wit* 6 circuit] the playhouse, frequently referred to as round.

290 *England's Heroical Epistles*] In the first edition of 1597 there were interchanges of letters between nine pairs of famous lovers. The number was brought up to twenty-four letters between twelve pairs of lovers by additions in the 1598 and 1599 editions. This poem was reprinted thirteen times during Drayton's life and retained its popularity, probably because of the closed couplets, until the middle of the 18th century.

290–296 *Henry Howard ... to the Lady Geraldine*] This poem helped to popularize the story of Surrey's travels in Italy, first given currency by Nashe's *Unfortunate Traveler*, 1594. See notes to Surrey, p. 916. 37 flaws] sudden puffs of wind. 54 soul-reviving clime] Florence. 64 By] nearby. 84 riveled] shriveled. 96 lion] Drayton annotates: 'The blazon of the Howards' honorable armor was gules between six crosselets fitchée, a bend argent; to which afterwards was added by achievement, in the canton point of the bend an escutcheon, or within the Scottish tressure, a demi-lion rampant, gules.' 98 Flodden field] where the English, led by the Earl of Surrey (father of the poet), defeated the Scotch in 1513. 110 daded] supported when learning to walk. 145 Stanhope] Drayton annotates: 'Of the beauty of that lady, he himself testifies in an elegy which he writ of her refusing to dance with him, which he seemeth to allegorize under a lion and a wolf.' 153 Bryan] See notes to Wyatt, p. 914. 226 Æson's spring] Æson, father of Jason, was, according to Ovid, rejuvenated by Medea after the return of the Argonauts.

296 *To the Virginian voyage*] first published in 1606; probably inspired by the preparations for the voyage of 1607.

297 *The crier* 5 Oyes] 'Hear ye'; a call by the public crier or court officer, usually uttered thrice. 11 owe] own.

298–299 *To the Cambro-Britons ... his ballad of Agincourt* 8 King Harry] Henry V. 50 vaward] vanward. 51 main] main body of troops. 53 Excester] Exeter. 76 weather] atmosphere, air. 97 Gloster] Humphrey, Duke of Gloucester, brother to Henry V, but not senior to Thomas, Duke of Clarence, as Drayton's lines indicate. 113 Saint Crispin's day] October 25, 1415.

299–300 *The ninth eclogue*] Drayton's *Eclogues*, ten in number, first published in 1606, were a revision and expansion of *Idea, the Shepherd's Garland*, 1593. 6 likes] suits, becomes. 45 Batt] 1619 misprints 'Gorbo'.

300 *Poly-Olbion*] Drayton published the first eighteen songs of his 'chorographical description of tracts, rivers, mountains, forests, and other parts of this renowned isle of Great Britain' in 1612. There was a second issue bearing the date 1613. In 1622 he re-issued these eighteen songs and added twelve more.

300–304 *The thirteenth song* 5 bear] marginal note: 'The ancient coat of that kingdom.' 20 Here] 1612 'Her'. 22 gripple] greedy. 58 woosell] ouzel. 62 merle] the European blackbird; marginal note: 'Of all birds, only the blackbird whistleth.' 71 set in parts] compose part-songs. 74 nope] bullfinch. 79 tydie] tidy; possibly the wren or blue titmouse. 80 hecco] woodpecker. 82 greaves] branches. 87 thicks] thickets. 91 rascals] lean, illconditioned deer. 100 twiring] peeping, winking; perhaps the shifting play of light in the glades. 128 maund] hand basket. 150 lady's] Anne Gooderere's. 156 eleven thousand maids] St. Ursula and the 11,000 virgins were supposed to have been slain by the Huns near Cologne.

304–309 *To . . . Henry Reynolds, Of poets and poesy*] For two of Henry Reynolds's poems, see p. 443. 19 *Pueriles*] *Sententiæ Pueriles,* the Latin text used by the Elizabethan child before beginning the translation of specific authors. 20 Cato] Dionysius Cato's *Disticha de Moribus,* which had been edited by Erasmus, was almost universally used in the early training of the Elizabethan student in translating Latin. 22 Amongst] 1627 'Amonst'. 36 Mantuan] Baptista Spagnuoli Mantuanus, whose *Eclogues* were widely used as a text in the Elizabethan schools. 40 biclift] This is Drayton's form. It is impossible to tell whether he intended 'bi-cliffed' or 'bi-cleft.' Parnassus is often referred to as double-peaked. 42 Elderton] the best known ballad-writer of the 1570's and the 1580's. See p. 977. 67 Bryan] See notes to Wyatt, p. 914. 90 Lyly's writing] Euphuism. 151 Sylvester] see p. 207. His translation of Du Bartas's *Semaines,* a lengthy poem on the creation, made the poem more popular in England than it was in France. 174 Menstry] Sir William Alexander of Menstry. Hawthornden] Drummond of Hawthornden. 175 two Beaumonts] Sir John and Francis. 185 set on every post] referring to the habit of advertising books by posting

up the title-pages; cf. Jonson's *To my bookseller,* p. 494. 189 transcription] Because of the unwillingness of some men of birth to become professional writers by printing their poetry, many poems circulated for years in ms. copies, sometimes reaching the publisher only after the author's death. As a professional, Drayton was irked by these amateurs. This passage is possibly aimed at Donne. 200 circuits] playhouses.

309–321 *Nymphidia* 3 Dowsabell] Drayton is referring to his own ballad of Dowsabell in *Idea, the Shepherd's Garland,* see p. 282. 24 Jove] 1627 'Jone'. 55 Mare] a goblin, supposed to produce nightmare by sitting on the chest of the sleeper. 79 auf] oaf. 193 Tuscan poet] Ariosto, author of *Orlando Furioso.* 274 Quishott] Quixote. 276 Pancha] Panza. 305 lin] cease, leave off. 418 lubrican's] leprechaun, a pigmy sprite of Irish folk-lore.

321–323 *The Shepherd's Sirena* 137 Darwin] Derwent.

323 *The Muses' Elysium*] a pastoral poem consisting of an introductory description of Elysium and ten nymphals.

323–324 *The description of Elysium* 53 gyres] spiral turns, whirls. 69 clives] cliffs.

325–330 *The sixth nymphal* 16 tired] adorned with head-dress. 61 lyam's] leash's. 63 gaffle] a steel lever to bend the cross-bow. 70 earning] making prolonged cries. 75 sylvans] 1630 'Sylvians'. 82 matachines] matachins; sword dances in fantastic costumes. 143 weels] wicker traps for catching fish. 146 trammel] long, narrow fishing-net. 200 nine-holes] 'A game in which the players endeavor to roll small balls into nine holes made in the ground.' *O. E. D.* 201 dust-point] 'A boy's game in which "points" were laid in a heap of dust, and thrown at with a stone.' *O. E. D.* 210 chapman] merchant. 222 Whig] variously applied to sour milk, buttermilk, etc. 228 sleave] sleave-silk; silk which can be divided into smaller filaments for use in embroidery. 229 yeanëd] given birth to.

SIR JOHN DAVIES

Sir John Davies (1569–1626) was born in Wiltshire and educated at Winchester School and Queen's College, Oxford. In 1588 he became a member of the Middle Temple, London, and there he evidently took advantage of opportunities for association with authors. In 1594 his *Orchestra* was entered in the Stationers' Registers, but the earliest edition bears the date 1596. In this same year, or thereabouts, was published Davies' collection of epigrams, bound with Marlowe's translations from Ovid, under the title *Epigrams and Elegies*. All editions of this book (sometimes called *Ovid's Elegies* or *All Ovid's Elegies*) purport to have been published at Middleburgh (Holland); but this notation was doubtless a printer's ruse in the issuance of a book which quite certainly could not have been licensed. From 1598 until 1601 Davies suffered from disbarment and loss of membership in the Middle Temple, on account of an assault made upon his one-time friend, Richard Martin. During this period he published *Hymns of Astrœa*, 1599, a series of acrostic poems praising the Queen, and, in the same year, *Nosce Teipsum*, a long philosophical argument for the soul's immortality, written during retirement at Oxford. After his restoration to the bar he turned from writing poetry and began pushing himself forward in his profession. When King James made him solicitor-general for Ireland, Davies was energetic in discharging the duties of this difficult office. In 1613 he was elected speaker of the Irish Parliament, but was able to assume the chair only after a riot in which he was lifted and placed in the lap of a speaker chosen by the Catholic party. After years of public service, he was appointed Lord Chief Justice of England, but before he could assume office he died of apoplexy after a supper-party.

Besides the poems mentioned, Davies wrote a set of 'gulling sonnets' parodying the sonneteers of the '90's. These were left in manuscript until the 19th century. He also wrote a series of twelve epigrams called *Twelve Wonders of the World*, printed in Davison's *Poetical Rhapsody* of 1608 and again, set to music by John Maynard, in 1611. He is credited with the authorship of verse-translations of several *Psalms* and a number of miscellaneous poems first printed by Grosart, from an anonymous manuscript.

As suggested elsewhere (Introduction to 'Sonnet-Sequences'), Davies' work stands in opposition to the 'sugared' lyrical and erotic poetry which dominated the 1580's and 1590's. He belongs to the order represented also by Chapman, Jonson, Marston, Hall, Ralegh and Greville in their mature phase, and supremely by Donne. Energy and play of intellect, rather than grace and beauty, characterize his best work. In distinction from practically all of his contemporaries, no single lyric, in the strictest sense, is connected with his name. His short poems are epigrams or epigrammatic. Even his 'hymns' to Elizabeth proclaim, by their acrostics, the author's ingenuity. His long poems are essays or treatises in verse. *Nosce Teipsum* is one of the very few permanently readable philosophical poems in English. *Orchestra*, though unfinished, accomplishes its object of treating rhetorically and poetically the subject of dancing, and is not wholly lacking in grace and music consonant with its subject.

MODERN EDITIONS: *The Complete Poems* (ed. by A. B. Grosart), Fuller Worthies' Library, 1869; *Orchestra*, The Stanton Press, 1922; *Nosce Teipsum* and *Orchestra* in *Some Longer Elizabethan Poems* (ed. by A. H. Bullen), Westminster, 1903.

COMMENT: Margarete Seemann, *Sir John Davies, sein Leben und seine Werke*, Leipzig, 1913; E. H. Sneath, *Philosophy in Poetry*, New York, 1913; J. S. Harrison, *Platonism in English Poetry of the 16th and 17th Centuries*, New York, 1915.

TEXT: *Epigrams and Elegies* [*c.* 1595] (6350), Huntington; *Chetham Ms.* 8012, Chetham; *Orchestra*, 1596 (6360), Huntington; *Hymns of Astrœa*, 1599 (6351), Huntington; *Nosce Teipsum*, 1599 (6355), Harvard.

331 *Of a gull*] The term 'gull,' as used by Davies and some others, seems | to mean more than 'simpleton' and to refer specifically to the fop or would-

be town-gallant of the period. Dekker's *Gull's Hornbook,* 1609, is the classic treatment of this subject. Davies' character of the gull was imitated and enlarged upon by Guilpin in *Skialetheia,* 1599, and by Rowlands in *The Knave of Clubs,* 1609.

331 *In Ciprium* 1 terse] spruce. 7 lock] a love-lock, trained to fall over the temple. 10 Gascoigne's] White's copy (undated, *c.* 1621?) reads 'George Gascoigne's'.

331 *In Haywodum* 1 Heywood] John Heywood; see p. 11.

332 *In Dacum* 2 silent eloquence] supposed to refer to Daniel's *Complaint of Rosamond* (see p. 251, ll. 128–129); but Daniel was not writing of 'his love's beauty.'

332 *In Titum*] reprinted, with alterations, in almost all 17th-century and 18th-century collections of epigrams. 3 Lord Chancellor's tomb] the elaborate tomb in Westminster Abbey of Sir Christopher Hatton, erected 1592. 4 new water-work] a pumping station built in 1594–95. elephant] then being exhibited in the city as a great curiosity. 6 Counter] a debtors' prison.

332 *In Decium*] directed against Drayton; Jonson, in his conversations with Drummond, mentioned this epigram, connecting it with one of Drayton's sonnets, *To the celestial numbers* (*Amour 8* in *Idea's Mirror*) wherein Drayton adds his mistress to the nine Worthies. 4 Worthy] Huntington copy reads 'woorthly'. 6 a giant for her wit] Jonson said that this refers to a saying of Dametas in Sidney's *Arcadia,* 'For wit his mistress might be a giant.' No such saying, however, is in any printed version of the *Arcadia.*

332–333 *To . . . Sir Anthony Cooke*] This is prefatory to the *Gulling sonnets* which follow; signed 'J. D.' in the manuscript. For Cooke, see Drayton's sonnet, p. 284, and note. 3 antic] clown. 7 whisking] rapid, quickly changing.

333 *Gulling sonnets*] The entire series in the ms. consists of nine sonnets; signed 'Mr. Davyes' at the end.

333–334 *The sacred muse* 8 points] tagged laces holding together doublet and hose. 9 hose] not stockings, but breeches or trunks. codpiece] 'a bagged appendage to the front of the close-fitting hose or breeches worn by men from the 15th to the 17th century.' *O. E. D.* 12 pantofles] in view of the 'pumps' of the next line, here perhaps overshoes.

334 *My case is this*] See *Zepheria*

(p. 218) and note. 11 shrieve] sheriff; ms. reads 'sheife'. 12 esloigned] usually 'eloigned'; removed out of the jurisdiction of the court or of the sheriff. 14 withernam] legal term representing the medieval Latin *vetitum nanium,* illegal or forbidden distraint; 'in an action of replevin, the reprisal of other goods in lieu of those taken by a first distress and eloigned.' *O. E. D.*

334–356 *Orchestra*] The title-page of the collected poems of 1622 lists *Orchestra* as 'not finished'. 1–2] Jonson told Drummond that 'a gentleman reading a poem that began with,

Where is that man that never yet did hear
Of fair Penelope, Ulysses' queen,

calling his cook asked if he had ever heard of her; who, answering "no," demonstrate[d] to him,

Lo, there the man that never yet did hear
Of fair Penelope, Ulysses' queen.'

46 Tethys] sea-goddess, wife of Oceanus. 270 leman's] mistress'. 325 tralucent] transparent. 340–347] cf. Coleridge, *Rime of the Ancient Mariner,* ll. 414–421. 353–355] The doctrines of Copernicus, though advanced in 1543, had not yet gained general acceptance. 370 wringling] writhing. 394 Jump] exactly. 437 wries] twists. 491 victorious twins] Castor and Pollux. 500 imply] interweave. 530 prince of Crete] Zeus was supposed to have been hidden in a cave in Crete by his mother, to avoid the voracity of his father. 548 Linus] son of Apollo and Terpsichore, who instructed Orpheus and Hercules. 549–550 he . . . tongue] Hercules. 568 Cæneus] daughter of Elatus, turned into a boy by Neptune; Ovid, *Met.* xii. 575 Tiresias] a blind soothsayer who was metamorphosed into a woman when he killed a female snake; seven years later, upon killing a male snake, he again became a man. 635–637 wise Thessalians . . . governance] the word *coryphæus* was applied to the leader in a *choragus* (dramatic chorus) and also to a civic official. 687–693] The references in this stanza are to the classical stories of Medea and Thyestes. 698 Tereus' mad wife] Procne, sister of Philomela; the son was Itys. 703 dolphins] 1596 'Dilphins'. 883–917] omitted in 1622; new stanzas were substituted. 892 man of Mantua's] Virgil's. 894 Geoffrey's] Chaucer's. 895 Colin's] Spenser's. 896 Delia's serv-

ant's] Daniel's. 897–98] Grosart suggests Guilpin (see p. 523), but his *Skialetheia, or a Shadow of Truth* did not appear until 1599; Chapman, whose *Shadow of Night* appeared in 1594, seems better to fit Davies' description. 899 fair Salve's sad lover] not identified. 900–901] Grosart suggests Charles Best, who contributed to Davison's *Poetical Rhapsody*, 1608, *A sonnet of the sun*, 'a jewel, being a sun shining upon the marigold closed in a heart of gold, sent to his mistress named Mary.' This identification does not explain why the poet should be called 'the bay.' 904 Astrophel] Sidney. 907–910] Grosart writes: 'Perhaps a play on his (then) friend's name of Martin.' The reference to Idæas suggests Drayton, but the personal relation revealed in the next stanza strengthens Grosart's identification.

356 *Hymns of Astræa*] All of the twenty-six poems of this volume are acrostics upon the words 'Elisabetha Regina.' Astræa was the mythical goddess of justice, who wandered upon earth during the Golden Age but later returned to heaven.

357–362 *Of human knowledge*] This poem serves as an introduction or a preface to the entire work of *Nosce Teipsum*. 43 rude satyr] See Dyer's *Prometheus when first from heaven*, p. 124. 46 Jove's guest] Ixion. 50 the youth] Phaethon. 51 boy's] Icarus'. 77 wisest] Socrates. 79 mocking master] Democritus, Fragment 117. 113 lady fair] Io. 142 threat] 1608; 1599 'thereat'. 153] Davies refers to his disbarment.

362 *That the soul is immortal . . .*] one of the many sub-sections of *Nosce Teipsum*.

363 *An acclamation*] The conclusion of the work.

JOSEPH HALL

Joseph Hall (1574–1656), Bishop of Norwich, wrote the satires which give him a place in English poetry as a young man, before he had taken holy orders. He was educated at Emmanuel College, Cambridge, where he took the degree of B. A. in 1592 and that of M. A. in 1596. He added the degrees of B. D. (1603) and D. D. (1612). His satires appeared in two parts: *Virgidemiarum . . . first three books of Toothless Satires* bore the date 1597, to be augmented in the following year by *Three last books of Biting Satires*. In the Prologue to the first part Hall wrote:

> I first adventure, with foolhardy might,
> To tread the steps of perilous despite.
> I first adventure,—follow me who list
> And be the second English satirist.

His bold claim was not well founded, for Wyatt, Gascoigne, Hake, and Lodge (not to mention Barclay and Skelton) had preceded him as English satirists; and some of Donne's satires were in manuscript. Hall perhaps hoped to build up a reputation solely for satire, and to be his country's Juvenal or Persius.

Virgidemiarum, itself possibly a contribution to the Harvey-Nashe controversy, was followed by an outburst of satirical writing in verse. In an order of June 1, 1599, Archbishop Whitgift directed that all copies of Hall's and Marston's satires, and of *Epigrams and Elegies* by Marlowe and Davies, should be burned; and that no more satires or epigrams should be printed. The suppression called for by this order did not prevail, however, for long. Edward Guilpin's *Skialetheia*, 1599, contained both epigrams and satires; and the list of satirists continued to grow steadily, adding the names of Samuel Rowlands, John Weever, Henry Parrot, Robert Anton, John Taylor, Robert Braithwaite, and others.

Hall's many theological works, published from 1605 forward, need not here be dwelt upon. He became, late in life, a controversial antagonist to Milton. His satires have had readers in every generation since his time. They are spirited, concise, and witty. Among writers of satire before Dryden, Hall stands with Donne as pre-eminent in the qualities which distinguish that form.

MODERN EDITIONS: *Die Satiren Halls* (ed. by K. Schulze), Berlin, 1910; *Virgidemiarum*, Edinburgh, 1824; *Satires by Joseph Hall* (ed. by T. Warton and S. W. Singer), Chiswick, 1824.

COMMENT: R. M. Alden, *The Rise of Formal Satire*, Philadelphia, 1899; Sandford M. Salyer, 'Hall's Satires and the Harvey-Nashe Controversy,' *S. P.* xxv. 149; E. A. Beckwith, 'On the Hall-Marston Controversy,' *J. E. G. P.* xxv. 84.

TEXT: *Virgidemiarum*, 1597 (12716), Harvard.

364–365 *Satire I* 4 Mahound . . . Termagaunt] common in romances of chivalry; Termagaunt, or Trivigante, was a Saracen female divinity, sometimes represented in old religious plays as a fierce and violent character. 6 blowess] a blowzy wench. 13 trencherpoetry] poetry written in the hope of food or entertainment from a patron. 23 albe] albeit. 27–32] No Muse, he says, will stay by the Granta (or Cam) since Spenser had attracted all the Muses to the Thames and Medway by his account of the wedding of those streams (*Fairy Queen*, IV. xi).

365 *Satire VI*] attacks the English writers of hexameters. See Introduction to Richard Stanyhurst. 5 Manhood and garboils] Stanyhurst wrote (*First book*, 5) 'Manhood and *garbroyls* I chaunt'. 13 areed] divine, determine.

besets] accords with. 16 Thwick thwack, and riff raff] quoted from a translation by Stanyhurst of a passage from the eighth book of the *Æneid*, published with his completed four books, thus (modernized):

Now do they raise ghastly lightnings,
    now grisly reboundings
Of ruff raff roaring, men's hearts with
    terror agrising,
With pell mell ramping, with thwick
    thwack sturdily thund'ring.

Thomas Nashe in his preface to Greene's *Menaphon*, 1589, parodied two of these lines, as follows:

Then did he make heaven's vault to
    rebound with rounce hobble hobble
Of ruff raff roaring, with thwick thwack
    thurley bouncing.

JOHN MARSTON

JOHN MARSTON (*c.* 1575–1634), like Joseph Hall, turned to the ministry after having entered upon a career as author. Little is known of his life previous to 1598, when he seems to have been stimulated to publication by the appearance of Hall's *Virgidemiarum*. His *Pygmalion's Image* of that year is an erotic poem of the fashion set by *Venus and Adonis* and *Hero and Leander*; though in his next book Marston claimed that he intended a burlesque of the fashion. With *Pygmalion's Image* he printed five satires which seem to have been hastily written in order to take advantage of the 'rising market' for such wares. In the same year he published *The Scourge of Villainy*, more carefully (and more maliciously) written than its predecessor; in 1599 it was republished with additions. Both of Marston's books, however, fell under Archbishop Whitgift's ban upon satires (June 1, 1599), and were suppressed. The author then devoted himself to writing for the stage. His quarrel with Jonson was the basis of the *poetomachia* of 1599–1601; later he and Jonson became reconciled. Just when Marston took holy orders is not known, but he held a country living in Hampshire from 1616 to 1631.

Marston's satires are obscure to modern readers, but his crabbed and bitter spirit is always apparent. He provides an excellent criticism of his own work, in the line, 'I am myself, so is my poesy.' A long manuscript poem (B. M. *Add. Mss.* 14824, 14825, 14826), *The New Metamorphosis* by J. M., Gent., sometimes is assigned to Marston; but J. H. H. Lyon (*A Study of The Newe Metamorphosis*, 1919) assigns it to Gervase (or Jervase) Markham.

MODERN EDITIONS: *The Works* (ed. by A. H. Bullen), three volumes, London, 1887; *The Scourge of Villanie* (ed. by G. B. Harrison), London, 1925. COMMENT: Morse S. Allen, *The Satire of John Marston*, Columbus (Ohio), 1920.

TEXT: *The Scourge of Villainy*, 1598 (17485), Huntington; *The Dutch Courtezan*, 1605 (17475), White.

367-368 *Humors*] Jonson's first 'comedy of humors,' *Every Man in His Humor*, was probably the play of the moment when Marston wrote. The holding up to ridicule of humors (which may be interpreted here as more or less affected inclinations, caprices, or fads) appears both in dramatic and non-dramatic poetry for several years following the date of Marston's book. 1–8] The parallel between these lines and the opening of Milton's *L'Allegro* has been several times noted; cf. *P.M.L.A.*, xliii. 569. 24 capreal] capriole, caper. 27 *Orchestra*] the next six lines satirize Davies' poem. 31 Kemp's jig] Will Kemp, popular comedian, danced from London to Norwich in nine days. 39 H'hath] 1598 reads 'H'ath'. 41 Curtain] the Curtain theater. plaudities] appeals for applause at the end of plays; epilogues. 49 gerning] grinning. 55 engrossèd] set down and memorized.

368-369 *To everlasting Oblivion*] This poem stands at the end of the book. It is said that on Marston's tomb in the Temple Church, London, was engraved *Oblivioni sacrum*, 'Consecrated to oblivion.'

GEORGE CHAPMAN

GEORGE CHAPMAN (1559?–1634), although a writer of unusual learning, appears never to have taken a university degree. His career as poet began with Σκιὰ νυκτός, *the Shadow of Night*, 1594, to be followed by *Ovid's Banquet of Sense*, 1595, with which he included his short sonnet-sequence, *A Coronet for his Mistress Philosophy*. In 1598 was printed *Hero and Leander*, made complete by Chapman's four sestiads added to Marlowe's two. In the same year Chapman published *Seven Books of the Iliads*, the first instalment of his translation of Homer. By 1616 he had seen through the press his completed *Iliad* and *Odyssey*; and in 1624 he added the *Batrachomyomachia* and the Homeric hymns and epigrams. From about 1595 forward he wrote for the stage, with notable success; Jonson praised his masks, of which only one is extant. Tradition describes Chapman as a man of great personal dignity, temperate and religious, an account to which his works lend credence. In learning he stands next to Jonson in his poetic generation; yet neither his learning nor his continuous labors for press and stage preserved him from the bane of poets, poverty.

The tributes of Lamb and Keats have kept his *Homer* in the eye of modern readers. In this work Chapman took the liberty of adding epithets, phrases, and whole lines; and so infused the whole with the spirit of his time that Coleridge pronounced it as truly an original poem as *The Fairy Queen*. Some critics have considered the 'fourteener' couplets of his *Iliad* a better medium for Chapman's vigorous translation than the rhymed pentameters of his *Odyssey*. Schoell has shown how closely Chapman followed as a pattern the monumental edition (1583) of Homer, with Latin translation, by Jean de Sponde (Spondanus). Throughout his work, and notably in his own poems apart from translations, Chapman manifests a 'high seriousness' which commands respect even when the reader is repelled by obscure and unmusical verse.

MODERN EDITIONS: *Poems and Minor Translations* (introduction by A. C. Swinburne), London, 1875; *Homer's Iliad and Odyssey* (ed. by R. H. Shepherd), London, 1903; *The Iliads of Homer* (ed. by R. Hooper) 3rd edition, London, 1898; *The Odysseys of Homer* (ed. by R. Hooper) 2nd edition, London, 1897.

COMMENT: F. L. Schoell, *Études sur l'Humanisme Continental en Angleterre*, Paris, 1926; Alfred Lohff, *George Chapman*, Berlin, 1903.

TEXT: Σκιὰ νυκτός, *the Shadow of Night*, 1594 (4990), White; *Ovid's Banquet of Sense*, 1595 (4985), White; *The Memorable Mask of the Middle Temple and Lincoln's Inn*, 1613 (4981), White; *The Whole Works of Homer*, [1616] (13624), White; *Homer's Odysseys* [1614?] (13636), White.

369-370 *Hymnus in Noctem*] We give the ending of the poem, which with another, *Hymnus in Cynthiam*, fills the volume. 8 humor] mood, or spirit; Chapman's verb 'steeped' calls for the older meaning of this word as the fluid determining the temperament of a body. 11 glassy strumpet's] Judging from other references in Chapman (see his *Descend, fair sun*, p. 371), Tethys, wife of Oceanus, seems intended. 12 Themis' daughters] Chapman's note, 1594: 'Themis' daughters are the three hours —*viz.*, Dice, Irene, and Eunomia, begotten by Jupiter. They are said to make ready the horse and chariot of the Sun every morning. . . .' 15 bride of brides] Night. 19 Cyprian star] Venus. 21 she] Night. 25 Is] 1594 'In'. Hyperion's . . . daughter] Diana, the moon.

370 *A coronet . . .*] This is the title of a series of ten sonnets, of which the one here given is the first. 7 dying figures] material bodies.

371-374 *Iliad, Book XVIII* 1 he] Vulcan, who has consented to make a shield for Achilles, at the request of Thetis, Achilles' mother. 2 Apposed] applied. 37 queen of martials] Athena. 48 neat] cattle. 53 well-piled] well-pointed. 60 new-eared] newly plowed. 61 Larged] spacious, broad. 83 quickset] a hedge.

374 *Odyssey, Book XII* 2 spleenless] not angry, favorable.

EDWARD FAIRFAX

EDWARD FAIRFAX (d. 1635) stands in the front rank of Elizabethan translators. Little is known of his life previous to the appearance of his *magnum opus, Godfrey of Bulloigne, or the Recovery of Jerusalem*, 1600. This was the first complete translation from the Italian of Torquato Tasso's *Gerusalemme Liberata*, 1581, usually known in English as 'Jerusalem Delivered.' Fairfax also wrote twelve eclogues, most of which are lost. He spent his years largely in study and retirement in his native county of Yorkshire.

Ben Jonson stands almost alone in calling Fairfax's work 'not well done.' Henry Morley points out that Fairfax could not reproduce the simplicity of his original, but 'translated into English verse after the manner of his own vigorous time, adorning, as he went, with interwoven figures of speech and bits of classical mythology.' This license perhaps offended Jonson. But Fairfax's rich vocabulary, smooth versification, and thoroughly Elizabethan spirit united to make his work a landmark in translation. 'Many beside myself,' wrote John Dryden, 'have heard our famous Waller own that he derived the harmony of his number from *Godfrey of Bulloigne*, which was turned into English by Mr. Fairfax.' Fairfax learned much from Spenser, who had been an appreciative reader of Fairfax's original, the poem of Tasso.

MODERN EDITIONS: *Jerusalem Delivered . . . translated by Edward Fairfax* (ed. by Henry Morley), New York, 1901; 'Fairfax Eighth Eclogue' (ed. by W. W. Greg), *M. L. Q.* iv. 85.

TEXT: *Godfrey of Bulloigne*, 1600 (23698), Huntington.

375-377 *Book XVI*] Spenser drew upon this portion of Tasso's poem for a number of passages in the Second Book of *The Fairy Queen,* Canto xii; compare stanzas 59, 60, 50, 51 of that canto with ll. 1–24 of the present ex- cerpt, stanza 71 with ll. 25–32, and stanzas 74–76 with ll. 41–64. 36 leden] singing, warbling. 57 He . . . he] so in all issues of 1600, and in the second edition of 1624; the sense seems to demand 'she.'

SONGS FROM PLAYS

'THE LYRICAL tradition is an unbroken one,' writes Edward Bliss Reed of song in drama, 'from the tenth century trope, *Quem quæritis,* to the songs of Shakespeare, of Dryden, and of Sheridan.' In the amazing development of the drama in 16th-century England this kind of lyricism gained proportionately; and the more so because of the circumstances that many plays were written for presentation by choir-boys and that boy-actors who took women's parts were often trained singers. In addition to the wealth of extant songs, many others are called for by stage directions but are missing from manuscript or printed texts of the plays. From George Peele's *Famous Chronicle of King Edward I,* printed in 1593, seven songs are omitted. Thirteen songs are indicated in stage directions of John Marston's *Antonio's Revenge* and *Antonio and Mellida, Part I,* but printed versions preserve none of them. Although we usually give credit to the dramatist of the play for lyrics contained in it, known cases of interpolating another poet's song suggest that many of the songs may have been owed to others. This fact may account for the omission of song-texts from printed plays.

The number of songs, if any, in a play varied from one to a dozen. All the singing sometimes was assigned to a single character, doubtless played by an actor chosen for his voice. Seldom do we find more than three characters having songs to sing, though there are many which call for two or three voices; the song in dialogue is not uncommon.

A few excellent lyrists of our period, as Fletcher, Dekker, and Peele, wrote almost no poems except for use in dramatic performances. A golden book of songs could be compiled from Fletcher's plays alone; Nashe's best poetry lies in the one play of *Summer's Last Will and Testament;* James Shirley is now most widely known for a single song used in one of his plays; and Jonson's lyrical talent seems to have been developed in writing songs for plays and masks. Shakespeare wrote for his plays a half-dozen of the world's best lyrics.

Some of the songs given in this group are taken from masks or pageant-like entertainments given to honor royalty or nobility. The number of masks presented grew under James and Charles; and since shows of this kind depended much upon the musical element, poets were spurred to the writing of songs.

CROSS REFERENCES: For poems, not in this section, which appeared as songs in plays and masks, see: Gascoigne, *Deep Desire sung this song;* Greville, *Chorus sacerdotum;* Mary Herbert, *Chorus;* Breton, *Phillida and Coridon;* Daniel, *Love is a sickness, Are they shadows;* Marston, *O love, how strangely sweet;* Chapman, *Descend, fair sun, Now, sleep, bind fast;* Campion, *Night as well as brightest day;* Jonson, pp. 514–520; Thomas Heywood, *Song* 'With fair Ceres', *Come, list, and hark, Pack, clouds, away, Song* 'Hence with passion'; Randolph, *Slaves are they;* Cartwright, *The song;* Suckling, *Song* 'Why so pale,' *Song* 'No, no, fair heretic,' *A Song to a lute;* Habington, *His mistress flouted;* Davenant, *Night's first song, The philosopher and the lover, Song;* Denham, *Somnus, the humble God.*

MODERN EDITIONS: *Lyrics from the Dramatists of the Elizabethan Age* (ed. by A. H. Bullen), London, 1892; *Songs from the British Drama* (ed. by E. B. Reed), New Haven, 1925.

COMMENT: R. S. H. Noble, *Shakespeare's Use of Song*, London, 1923.

TEXT: *King John,* text from Bang's facsimile; *Lusty Juventus* [*c.* 1560] (25147), Huntington; *Gammer Gurton's Needle,* 1575 (23263), White; *Tom Tyler and his Wife,* 1661, text from Farmer, *Tudor Facsimile Text,* 1912; *Misogonus,* text from Bond; *Comedy of Patient and Meek Grissell,* [*c.* 1566] (19865), Yale; *Horestes,* 1567 (19917), B. M.; *Trial of Treasure,* 1567 (24271), White; *Marriage of Wit and Science,* [*c.* 1570], text from Farmer, *Tudor Facsimile Text,* 1909; *Common Conditions,* [*c.* 1576] (5592), Yale; *Fedele and Fortunio,* 1585 (19447), Huntington; *Six Court Comedies,* 1632 (17088), Harvard; *Arraignment of Paris,* 1584 (19530), Huntington; *Polyhymnia,* 1590 (19546), Huntington; *Hunting of Cupid,* not extant, text from *Collections,* Malone Society, 1911, and *England's Helicon; Old Wive's Tale,* 1595 (19545), Huntington; *Love of King David and Fair Bethsabe,* 1599 (19540), White; *Lamentable Tragedy of Locrine,* 1595, text from Farmer, *Tudor Facsimile Text,* 1911; *Maid's Metamorphosis,* 1600 (17188), White; *Wily Beguiled,* 1606 (25818), Huntington; *Thracian Wonder,* 1661, Huntington; *Summer's Last Will and Testament,* 1600 (18376), White; *Shoemaker's Holiday,* 1600 (6523), White; *Pleasant Comedy of Patient Grissil,* 1603 (6518), White; *London's Tempe,* [1629] (6509), Huntington; *Sun's Darling,* 1656, Harvard; *White Devil,* 1612 (25178), White; *Duchess of Malfi,* 1623 (25176), White; *Knight of the Burning Pestle,* 1613 (1674), White; *Maid's Tragedy,* 1619 (1676), White; *Maid's Tragedy,* 1622 (1678), White; *Faithful Shepherdess,* [*c.* 1610] (11068), White; *Bloody Brother,* 1639 (11064), Huntington; *Comedies and Tragedies,* 1647, White; *Comedies, Histories, and Tragedies,* 1623 (22273), Princeton; *Chaste Maid in Cheapside,* 1630 (17877), Huntington; *The Widow,* 1652, B. M.; *More Dissemblers Besides Women,* 1657, Harvard; *Emperor of the East,* 1632 (17636), White; *Amends for Ladies,* 1618 (10851), Huntington; *Technogamia,* 1618 (13617), White; *Rival Friends,* 1632 (12935), Adams; *Broken Heart,* 1633 (11156), Huntington; *Fuimus Troes,* 1633 (10886), Harvard; *Tragedy of Orestes,* 1633 (11982), Huntington; *Vow Breaker,* 1636 (21688), Huntington; *Adrasta,* 1635 (14721), Adams; *Tragedy of Cleopatra,* 1639 (17717), White; *Old Couple,* 1658, Harvard; *Hannibal and Scipio,* 1637 (18341), Harvard; *Triumph of Peace,* 1633 (22459), Huntington; *Triumph of Beauty,* 1646, Harvard; *Cupid and Death,* 1653, B. M.; *Contention of Ajax and Ulysses,* 1659, Harvard; *Martyred Soldier,* 1638 (22435), Huntington; *Northern Lass,* 1632 (3819), Huntington; *Jovial Crew,* 1652, White; *Lost Lady,* 1639 (1903), Harvard; *Swaggering Damsel,* 1640 (4946), Huntington; *King John and Matilda,* 1655, Harvard.

377 *King John*] John Bale (1495–1563), Bishop of Ossory, besides plays wrote *Illustrium Majoris Britanniæ Scriptorum Summarium,* 1548, the earliest history of English literature. For Googe's tribute to Bale, see p. 74.

377 *Wassail, wassail*] Text from W. Bang's facsimile of *Devonshire Ms., Materialen zur Kunde des älteren Englischen Dramas,* 1909. 4 rail] a small wading bird.

377–378 *In a herber green*] This song opens the interlude, preceded only by the prologue. 1 herber] arbor. 9 pight] determined.

378 *Gammer Gurton's Needle*] Though not published until 1575, this play was acted at Cambridge before 1560 and licensed for publication in 1563. The title-page attributes it to 'Mr. S., Mr. of Art'; modern research has practically established that the author was William Stevenson, a fellow of Christ's College 1551–54 and 1559–61, twice mentioned in the records of the college as author of a play.

378 *Back and side, go bare*] Dyce printed (in his edition of Skelton, 1843) from ms. a longer version of this song. The age of the ms., taken with the variants found therein, suggests that the author of *Gammer Gurton's Needle* may here have used a song already current. 17 nutbrown toast] Browned bread was frequently dipped or floated in beverages. 19 crab] crab-apple. 30 troll] circulate, pass around.

378 *Tom Tyler and His Wife*] An interlude of unknown authorship, referred to as about one hundred years old when printed in 1661.

379 *Misogonus*] of unknown authorship; text from R. W. Bond's *Early Plays from the Italian,* 1911.

379–380 *A song to the tune . . .* 5 snudges] sneaking fellows; sometimes, misers. 38 haking] loitering, wandering about.

380 *Comedy of Patient and Meek Grissell*] undated, but printed by Thomas Colwell whose press ran from 1562 to 1571.

380 *Lulla by baby* 5 I fancy thee, I] so in original; 'I fancy thee aye', adopted by some modern editors, seems a less likely reading.

380–381 *Farewell, adieu* 9 cheats] booty.

382 *Lustily, lustily*] preceded by the stage direction, 'here ent'reth the mariners with a song.'

383 *Fedele and Fortunio*] translated from the Italian of Luigi Pasqualigo, and doubtfully attributed to Anthony Munday.

383 *Six Court Comedies*] John Lyly (*c.* 1554–1606), popular author of *Euphues* (1578) and of court comedies, probably did not write the excellent songs printed with his plays. Twenty-one of these songs first appeared in the collected edition of 1632, having been omitted from editions published during Lyly's lifetime. One song, *What bird so sings,* was included in an altered form in Ford and Dekker's *The Sun's Darling,* and though this play was not printed until 1656, J. R. Moore ('The Songs in Lyly's Plays,' *P.M.L.A.* xlii. 623) argues that the song was 'an original part' of it when acted in 1624. *Oh, for a bowl of fat Canary* (a song in *Alexander and Campaspe*) was printed in Middleton's *A Mad World, My Masters* (1640, acted 1608). It seems quite possible that Blount, the printer of 1632, who set up his text from the songless quartos, engaged some one to write songs which he inserted as called for by stage directions. Greg ('The Authorship of the Songs in Lyly's Plays,' *M.L.R.* i. 43) would attribute some or all to Dekker. In this connection compare *A song in making of the arrows* with Dekker's 'Brave iron! brave hammer!' (p. 392). Ward, following J. T. Looney, suggests that Lyly's patron and employer, the Earl of Oxford, wrote these songs, but the suggestion hardly seems credible when they are compared with Oxford's known work. For a defence of Lyly's authorship, see W. J. Lawrence, 'The Problem of Lyly's Songs,' *T. L. S.,* December 20, 1923.

384 *A song in making . . .* 2 Lemnian] Vulcan's forge was supposed to be on the isle of Lemnos.

384 *Arraignment of Paris*] George Peele (*c.* 1558–*c.* 1597), author of six songs here given, was one of the 'University Wits,' having taken at Oxford the degree of B.A. in 1577 and that of M.A. in 1579. *The Arraignment of Paris* evidently was produced as early as 1581, played 'before the Queen's Majesty by the Children of her Chapel.'

385 *Polyhymnia*] This book consists for the most part of an account, in blank verse, of a tournament held before Queen Elizabeth; Sir Henry Lee (1530–1610) had made, in 1559, a vow of chivalry to maintain Elizabeth's honor against all challengers, and each year on her birthday he held a tournament. In 1590, finding himself too old to engage in the tilting, Sir Henry caused to be sung, at the end of the tournament, the present song, written by Peele for the occasion.

385 *The Hunting of Cupid*] This play of Peele's is lost, except for some fragments preserved by Drummond of Hawthornden in a commonplace-book. The play was licensed to be acted in 1591. Our text of the first song is from the Malone Society's *Collections, Parts IV and V,* 1911.

386 *Coridon and Melampus' song*] This song, which on the evidence of Drummond's manuscript we know to have been sung in *The Hunting of Cupid,* was printed in *England's Helicon,* 1600, whence we have reprinted it.

385 *Hot sun, cool fire*] sung by Bethsabe at the beginning of the play, as she bathes.

388 *The Thracian Wonder*] published as by John Webster and William Rowley, but their authorship has not been accepted. The story of the play follows that of Greene's *Menaphon,* 1589.

388 *Summer's Last Will and Testament*] Thomas Nashe (1567–1601) made the deepest impression upon his generation by his satirical prose pamphlets. The son of a minister, he took the degree of B.A. at Cambridge in 1586; by 1588 he was in London as one of the 'University Wits' who wrote for stage and press. His pamphlets directed against the Puritan authors of the Marprelate tracts and those against Gabriel Harvey made for him a lasting reputation. Dekker, in his *News from Hell* (1606) said that Nashe 'made the doctor [Harvey] a flat dunce, and beat him at his two sundry tall weapons, poetry and oratory.' In his picaresque tale, *The Unfortunate Traveler,* 1594, he included three poems represented as having been written by Surrey to Geraldine. He left in ms. an erotic poem, *The Choice of Valentines*.

388–389 *Adieu, farewell earth's bliss*] apparently written during a period when the plague raged; theaters were closed on account of the plague in the autumn of 1592, and again from early in 1593 until the summer of 1594.

390 *Autumn hath all* 2 Croydon's] a suburb of London. 10 want of term] Term-time, when the courts were sitting, brought throngs of people to London.

390 *Shoemaker's Holiday*] Thomas Dekker (*c.* 1570–*c.* 1632) was a prolific playwright and miscellaneous writer of the literary generation immediately following that of the 'University Wits.' He was several times imprisoned for debt, once for a term of three years. His long poem, *Canaan's Calamity, Jerusalem's Misery*, 1598, enjoyed some popularity. Some of his prose pamphlets, as *The Bellman of London*, 1608, and *The Gull's Hornbook*, 1609, are always readable; but his best works are his comedies. The songs in his plays reveal a genuine, though not rich, lyrical vein. For other songs possibly by Dekker, see those selected from Lyly's *Six Court Comedies* (pp. 383–384).

392 *Brave iron! brave hammer!* 28 sparrowbills] sparables, nails for shoes.

393 *White Devil*] John Webster (*c.* 1580–1634?), son of a London tailor and for a time himself an apprentice tailor, won a place near Shakespeare as a writer of tragedies. In non-dramatic poetry his principal compositions are a poem in honor of the accession of James and one mourning the death of Prince Henry.

394 *Knight of the Burning Pestle*] The authorship of songs in the plays written in collaboration is of course uncertain. Because of the numerous and excellent songs in plays written by Fletcher alone, readers are inclined to assign to him the songs which appear in plays written with Beaumont. For other poems by Beaumont, see p. 539.

395 *Faithful Shepherdess*] In the assigning of plays to Fletcher we follow E. H. C. Oliphant, *The Plays of Beaumont and Fletcher*, New Haven, 1927. John Fletcher (1579–1625) was a son of Richard Fletcher, Bishop of London, nephew of Giles Fletcher (the elder), and hence cousin of Phineas and Giles Fletcher. His collaboration with Beaumont began about 1607 and ceased with Beaumont's death in 1616. He also col-

laborated with Shakespeare, Massinger, and others. He was notably successful in the composition of lyrics, but appears to have written practically no poetry apart from that in his plays.

395–396 *The drinking song* 7 tisic] phthisic, consumption.

396 *Take, oh, take*] The first stanza of this song was sung in the fourth act of Shakespeare's *Measure for Measure*, and was printed as part of that play in the folio edition of 1623. There is no reason for supposing the first stanza not to be Shakespeare's, but Fletcher may have added the second stanza.

396 *Care-charming Sleep*] The text of this song, corrupt in 1647, has been corrected by the edition of 1679. 2 thyself] 1647 'thy life'. 5 his] 1647 'her'. sweet] Bullen emends to 'light' for the sake of the rhyme. 7 sing] 1647 'sings'. 9 prince] omitted in 1647.

396 *God Lyæus* 1 Lyæus] Bacchus; printed 'Lizus' in 1647, corrected in 1679.

397 *Cast our caps* 15 officers] 1679; 1647 'offices'. 16 by] of uncertain reference; perhaps 'by and by'; or the beginning of an unfinished oath, in which case it should be printed 'by—'. 18 cessed] taxed.

397 *Hence, all you vain*] supposed to have given suggestions to Milton for *Il Penseroso*.

398 *Let the bells ring* 19 enow] 1679 'enough'.

399 *Orpheus with his lute*] Because of Fletcher's large share in the writing of *King Henry VIII*, taken with the fact that in style this song does not particularly suggest Shakespeare, the poem may be doubtfully ascribed to Fletcher.

399–400 *Come, my dainty doxies* 1 doxies] wenches, sweethearts, in gipsy cant; 'dells' in the next line is an equivalent.

401 *Technogamia*] Barten Holiday became a prominent divine, and published a number of his sermons. His play was an academic allegory written for presentation by students; after it was acted at Oxford, the students insisted upon presenting it before King James when he was at Woodstock on a progress in 1618. Wood records that because it was 'too grave for the King and too scholar-like for the auditory (or, as some say, that the actors had too much wine before), his Majesty after two acts offered several times to withdraw.' He was persuaded to stay, 'much against his will.' James, an enemy of tobacco, may have been offended by the song here reprinted.

401 *Tobacco's a musician* 41 whiffler] mace-bearer, an officer who precedes a dignitary; by a derived meaning, a bully. 44 visor] Taking this word in the ordinary sense raises difficulties; perhaps it should be read as 'vizier,' i. e., 'he is the vizier that does drink [smoke], and tobacco is the whiffler that goes before him.' Nichols (*Progresses, James I,* iv. 714) reads 'wiser'.

404 *Tragedy of Orestes*] Thomas Goffe, or Gough (1591–1629), a divine with considerable reputation as scholar and orator, achieved success in his profession while a bachelor; he married a widow with several children, though warned by a friend, Thomas Thimble, that marriage would be the death of him. Within a comparatively short time he was brought to his death-bed, where he is said to have murmured, 'Oracle, oracle, Tom Thimble!'

404 *Vow Breaker*] William Sampson left a considerable body of poetry in ms. See J. F. Godfrey, *William Sampson, a Seventeenth Century Poet and Dramatist,* London, 1894.

404 *Tragedy of Cleopatra*] Thomas May (1595–1650), best known as translator and continuer of Lucan's *Pharsalia,* achieved considerable fame in his own day. Defective speech prevented his practising law, though he trained himself for that profession. He published translations of Virgil's *Georgics* and Martial's epigrams.

405 *Changes*] James Shirley (1596–1666), the last of the major dramatists who wrote before the suppression of the theater, took the degree of B.A. at Oxford about 1618. In that year he published a poem, *Echo, or the Infortunate Lovers,* closely imitating *Venus and Adonis.* He took the degree of M.A.

and entered holy orders about 1620, but after a few years became a Catholic and began teaching school. For a time he lived in Ireland, where some of his plays were written and produced. A collection of his poems appeared in 1646.

407 *Northern Lass*] Richard Brome owed his slight success as a writer for the stage to the circumstance that he was for a time servant to Ben Jonson, who gave some care to his education, and started him upon a literary career. The reference to 'my man' in l. 20 of Jonson's *Inviting a friend to supper* (p. 498) is probably to Brome.

407 *A bonny, bonny bird*] This poem owes much to Skelton's *Philip Sparrow* (p. 3), and to an intermediate poem on the same subject by Gascoigne. 7 Keep cut] see notes to *Philip Sparrow,* l. 100.

407 *Lost Lady*] Sir William Berkeley (*c.* 1605–1677) was an accomplished gentleman who in 1641 became Governor of Virginia. Although forced from this position by the Parliamentary power, he continued to reside in the colony and resumed the governorship after the Restoration. He wrote his one play before removing to America.

407 *Where did you borrow* 8] 1639 prints after this line the additional one, 'Another sigh, then, I may hope', with no punctuation after it. This may represent the first line of a second stanza, or may have been spoken by one of the characters. The scene is printed confusingly in other particulars.

407 *Swaggering Damsel*] Robert Chamberlain (1607–1660) enjoyed some vogue as a writer of epigrams and light verse. Two books of his poems are *Nocturnal Lucubrations,* 1638, and *Jocabella,* 1640. A patron sent Chamberlain to study at Oxford in 1637, when he was thirty years of age.

BROADSIDE BALLADS

THE SURVIVING broadside ballads represent the popular poetry of the street-corner in Tudor-Stuart England. The learned John Selden, an early collector of broadsides in the 17th century, justifies concisely his, and our, interest in them: 'More solid things do not show the complexion of the times so well as ballads and libels.' The traditional ballads of medieval times, composed by unknown authors and handed down by word of mouth, though sometimes printed in debased versions as broadsides, are beyond the scope of this volume. We are concerned only with broadside ballads proper, written by the 'base ballad-makers' and sold by ballad singers on the street corners. The broadside ballad was printed in blackletter on a single sheet of paper, with a rough woodcut to catch the eye of the prospective buyer and the name of the tune to which the ballad was to be sung. These broadsides were evidently regarded as decorative, for their purchasers often pasted them up on the walls of taverns and cottages.

Under the early Tudors the production of ballads was stimulated by the needs of religious propaganda, and prominent men, both Catholic and Protestant, employed ballad writers to influence public opinion. During the reign of Elizabeth, when the need for propaganda was not so great, 'ballating' fell to free-lance writers of little education. Their ballads covered a wide range of subjects—political and military events of the day, murders, executions of criminals, strange occurrences, monstrous births, together with sentimental romances, ditties of love, complaints of the married state, exhortations to repentance and godly living—thus filling for that time the place which the modern newspaper and its Sunday supplement occupies in 20th-century life. Indeed, as the news-book developed in the 17th century, some of the ballad writers became the first journalists.

About the lives of the professional ballad writers little is known, even the names of many of them being lost because of anonymous publication. The best known ones are: Gray of Reading, Protestant controversialist, patronized by Henry VIII and Protector Somerset; William Elderton of early Elizabethan days, lawyer and actor, who 'armed himself with ale when he ballated' and whose red nose was the subject of many a joke; Thomas Deloney of later Elizabethan days, 'the ballating silk-weaver' of Norwich, author also of delightful prose romances of the life of craftsmen; and Martin Parker, writer of many sentimental ballads and later during the Civil War known as the 'Prelates' Poet' from his support of the Royalist cause. By the more serious men of letters, the ballad writers were regarded with scorn and contempt. Drayton, recalling his youth, writes,

> I scorned your ballad then though it were done
> And had for finis William Elderton,

and Herrick in *His farewell unto poetry* curses

> the blind and lame
> Base ballad-mongers, who usurp thy name
> And foul thy altar.

As a class they are characterized by John Earle in his *Microcosmography* as pot-poets, inspired by thin drink to write ballads which 'go out in single sheets, and are chanted from market to market to a vile tune and a worse throat, whilst the poor country wench melts like her butter to hear them.'

The fullest account of the ballad singer is in Chettle's *Kind-heart's Dream*, 1592. The old minstrel is described as 'an odd old fellow. . . . His treble viol in his hand assured me of his profession, on which (by his continual sawing, having left but one string) after his best manner he gave me a hunt's-up.' Ben Jonson introduces in his *Bartholomew Fair* a ballad singer caroling out his wares, catching the attention of the crowd, while pick-pockets, his confederates, are at their work. Shakespeare, in *The Winter's Tale* (IV. iii), gives a more sympathetic picture of the country peddler, the rogue Autolycus, who among his wares carries ballads telling of strange wonders.

CROSS REFERENCES: Poems, not in this section, which also appeared as broadside ballads: John Heywood, *A praise of his lady;* Surrey, *The lover comforteth himself;* Vaux, *The aged lover renounceth love;* Minor Courtly Makers, *Harpalus' complaint;* Gascoigne, *Gascoigne's arraignment;* Dyer, *My mind to me a kingdom is;* Ralegh, *The nymph's reply to the shepherd;* Marlowe, *The passionate shepherd to his love;* Elizabethan Miscellanies, *The lover exhorteth his lady to be constant;* Campion, *What if a day;* Wither, *Sonnet 4;* Stuart and Commonwealth Miscellanies, *Phillada flouts me.*

MODERN EDITIONS: *Roxburghe Ballads* (ed. by W. Chappell and J. W. Ebsworth), eight volumes and supplementary volume, London, 1871–99; *Bagford Ballads* (ed. by J. W. Ebsworth), two volumes, Hertford, 1878; *Ballads from Manuscripts* (ed. by F. J. Furnivall and W. R. Morfill), two volumes, London, 1868–73; *Old English Ballads, 1553–1625* (ed. by H. E. Rollins), Cambridge, 1920; *A Pepysian Garland* (ed. by H. E. Rollins), Cambridge, 1922; *Cavalier and Puritan* (ed. by H. E. Rollins), New York, 1923; *The Pack of Autolycus* (ed. by H. E. Rollins), Cambridge (Mass.), 1927; *An American Garland* (ed. by C. H. Firth), Oxford, 1915; *Naval Songs and Ballads* (ed. by C. H. Firth), London, 1908, *Gray of Reading* (ed. by E. W. Dormer), Reading, 1923; *Songs and Ballads chiefly of the reign of Philip and Mary* (ed. by T. Wright), Roxburghe Club, 1860; *Harleian Miscellany,* vol. x. 252–78, London, 1813; *Ancient Songs and Ballads* (ed. by J. Ritson), two volumes, London, 1829; *A Collection of Seventy-nine Black-letter Ballads and Broadsides, 1559–97* (ed. by J. Lilly), London, 1867; *Ballads and Broadsides chiefly of the Elizabethan Period . . . now in the Library at Britwell Court* (ed. by H. L. Collman), Roxburghe Club, 1912; *Old Ballads from Early Printed Copies* (ed. by J. P. Collier), Percy Society, 1840; *A Collection of Songs and Ballads relating to the London Prentices and Trades* (ed. by C. Mackay), Percy Society, 1841; Clement Robinson's *Handful of Pleasant Delights* (ed. by H. E. Rollins), Cambridge (Mass.), 1924; *The Works of Thomas Deloney* (ed. by F. O. Mann), Oxford, 1912; *The Shirburn Ballads, 1585–1616* (ed. by A. Clark), Oxford, 1907; Richard Johnson's *Crown Garland of Golden Roses,* 1612 (ed. by W. Chappell), Percy Society, 1842 and 1845; *Political Ballads published in England during the Commonwealth* (ed. by T. Wright), Percy Society, 1841; *Cavalier Songs and Ballads, 1642–84* (ed. by C. Mackay), 1863; *A Century of Broadside Elegies* (ed. by J. W. Draper), London, 1928. Many of the ballad tunes are printed in W. Chappell's *Old English Popular Music* (ed. by Wooldridge), two volumes, London, 1893.

COMMENT: C. H. Firth, 'Ballads and Broadsides' in *Shakespeare's England,* vol. ii, Oxford, 1916, and articles in *Tr. Roy. Hist. Soc.,* 3rd series, ii. 21, iii. 51, v. 21, vi. 19, and *The Scottish Historical Review,* iii. 257, vi. 113, ix. 363; H. E. Rollins, articles in *S. P.* xvii. 199, and *M. P.* xvi. 449; E. v. Schaubert, 'Zur Geschichte der Black-Letter Broadside Ballad' in *Anglia,* N. F., xxxviii. 1.

TEXT: *A Handful of Pleasant Delights,* 1584 (21106), B. M.; *The Garland of Good Will,* n. d. (6554), Bodleian. The other texts are not taken from the broadsides, but from secondary sources as indicated in the notes.

408 *The king's hunt is up*] text from Dormer's *Gray of Reading,* p. 65. This ballad, written late in the reign of Henry VIII, was entered in the Stationers' Registers in 1565–6. Its popularity is spoken of in *The Art of English Poesy,* 1589: 'And one Gray, what good estimation did he grow unto with the same King Henry [VIII], and afterward with the Duke of Somerset, Protector, for making certain merry ballads, whereof one chiefly was *The Hunt is up.*' The name 'hunt's-up,' first applied to the tune played on the horn under the windows of sportsmen to awaken them, came to be extended to any tune or song intended to arouse in the morning.

408–410 *A song between the Queen's*

Majesty and England] text from *Harleian Miscellany,* x. 260; entered in the Stationers' Registers in 1558–9. The tune to which this ballad was sung is printed in Chappell, i. 121. 7 Methink] *Harl. Misc.* reads 'My think'. 24 depart] cf. *The Book of Common Prayer,* 1549, 'Matrimony': 'Till death us depart.' In 1662, 'depart' was altered to 'do part'. 48 terribly] broadside reads 'treably'. 56 bands] bonds.

410–411 *A proper song, entitled: Fain would I have a pretty thing*] text from B. M. copy of *A Handful of Pleasant Delights,* 1584. This ballad was written by 1566, for in that year a moralization, *Fain would I have a godly thing,* was entered in the Stationers' Registers. The tune, 'Lusty Gallant,' is

printed in Chappell, i. 234. 17 geason]
rare. 31 Cheap] Cheapside, the street
of fine shops in Elizabethan London.
43 than] old spelling for 'then', here
kept for the rhyme.

411–413 *A new courtly sonnet . . .*]
text from the B. M. copy of *A Handful
of Pleasant Delights,* 1584. In 1580 a
moralization of this ballad was entered
in the Stationers' Registers. *Lady Greensleeves* was twice referred to by Shakespeare in *Merry Wives of Windsor,* II.
i and V. v. Tune in Chappell, i. 239.
21 well favoredly] handsomely. 30
sendal] thin silken material. 48 grossy]
usually applied to vegetation, meaning
green and vigorous. 54 aglets] pendants
or spangles attached to a fringe.

413–414 *A proper new song . . .*]
text from the B. M. copy of *A Handful
of Pleasant Delights,* 1584. Thomas
Richardson, whose name is signed to
this ballad, was admitted to Gonville
and Caius College in 1572. 36 over-
grown] 1584 'overgrowde'. 39 areed]
advise.

414–415 *As you came . . .*] text from
the Bodleian copy of Deloney's *Garland
of Good Will,* n. d. The *Garland* was
probably first published in 1593, in
which year it was entered in the Stationers' Registers. The first stanza, with
its Catholic note, is almost certainly
traditional, but the rest of the ballad
may be by Deloney. A copy of the poem
in the Bodleian *Rawlinson Poetry Ms.*
85 is signed 'Sr. W. R.', but there is
no other evidence that it is from
Ralegh's hand. The ballad was possibly
sung to the tune printed by Chappell,
i. 69.

415–417 *The valorous acts . . . [of]
Mary Ambree*] text from *Bagford Ballads,* i. 311. *Mary Ambree* was not entered in the Stationers' Registers until
1629, but this entry must be for a re-
issue, for the ballad had been referred
to in *The Return from Parnassus, c.*
1598, and had long been a favorite with
Ben Jonson, who mentions it in *The
Silent Woman,* IV. i, and *A Tale of a
Tub,* I. ii, and quotes from it in *The
Fortunate Isles.* Rollins (*S. P.* xvii.
236) tentatively assigns the ballad to
William Elderton. Tune in Chappell,
ii. 16. 2 Gaunt] Ghent; the Spaniards
had captured Ghent in 1584, and it was
probably some assault on the city by
the Dutch, aided by English volunteers,
which gave rise to this ballad. 15
striped] Percy's *Folio Ms.* reads
'slipped'. 19 hand] Percy's *Folio Ms.;*
broadside 'side'.

417–419 *Lord Willoughby*] text from
Roxburghe Ballads, iv. 8. Lord Willoughby died in 1601. None of his recorded exploits are like those recounted
in the ballad. Firth thinks that the
ballad was written between 1624 and
1628 to aid the recruiting sergeant
(*Tr. Roy. Hist. Soc.,* 3rd series, iii.
110). Tune in Chappell, i. 152. 21
caliver] a light musket.

419–420 *A sonnet upon . . .*] text
from J. O. Halliwell-Phillips's *Outlines
of the Life of Shakespeare* (1907), i.
310, collated with E. K. Chambers's
Elizabethan Stage, ii. 420. Two ballads
on the burning of the Globe were entered in the Stationers' Registers on
June 30, 1613. Neither ballad is extant in print. This ballad, printed by
Halliwell-Phillips from an early 17th-
century ms., is probably a copy of one
of them. Chambers suggests that this is
the one written by William Parrat. The
Globe caught fire during the production of *Henry VIII* on June 29, 1613.
6 Was] Chambers conjectures 'But was'.
7 all this is true] From a letter written by Sir Henry Wotton on July 2,
1613, describing the burning of the
Globe, it seems that the play, *Henry
VIII,* was then known by a sub-title,
All is True. 17 clew] ball of thread.
18 snag] projection. 25 Condye] Con-
dell. 37] Halliwell-Phillips leaves this
line incomplete. 41 thatched] Sir
Henry Wotton wrote of the origin of
the fire: 'Certain cannon being shot off
at [Henry VIII's] entry, some of the
paper, or other stuff, wherewith one of
them was stopped, did light on the
thatch, where being thought at first an
idle smoke, and their eyes more attentive to the show, it kindled inwardly
and ran round like a train, consuming
within less than an hour the whole
house to the very ground.'

420–421 *The shepherd's wooing Dulcina*] text from *Roxburghe Ballads,* vi.
166; entered in the Stationers' Registers
in 1615, and later expanded by the addition of a second and inferior part,
here omitted. Without evidence, this ballad has been ascribed to Ralegh. In
Walton's *Complete Angler* it is among
those named by the milkmaid's mother
as she is trying to recall what song
Piscator wishes sung. Tune in Chappell, i. 160. 26–30] The text of these
lines is corrupt in the broadside ballad;
following the editor of the *Roxburghe
Ballads,* we give the reading of *The
Westminster Drollery.* 34 could] the

reading of *W. D.;* broadside reads 'to'. 41–44] the reading of *W. D.*

421–422 *Truth's integrity . . .*] text from *Roxburghe Ballads,* ii. 639; written before 1633, in which year an answer to the ballad was entered in the Stationers' Registers. Palgrave included the first five stanzas in *The Golden Treasury.* Tune in Chappell, i. 189. 43 Guy of Warwick] a legendary hero, whose marvellous adventures were recounted in the popular romance bearing his name. 50 Bevis] Sir Bevis of Hampton, another hero of medieval romance.

422–423 *The milkmaid's life*] text from *Roxburghe Ballads,* ii. 116; entered in the Stationers' Registers in 1634. Eight lines of this ballad are quoted, with some changes, by Walton in *The Complete Angler.*

423 *The four wonders*] text from *Roxburghe Ballads,* i. 354. The two surviving copies of this ballad date from the reign of Charles II. By the number of wonders packed in one ballad, it illustrates this popular type of ballad better than any of the earlier ones.

426–427 *Sailors for my money*] text from *Roxburghe Ballads,* vi. 797. There is a later altered version, called *Neptune's raging fury,* at p. 432 of the same volume. This ballad is the original of Thomas Campbell's famous song, *Ye Mariners of England.* 111 Though he'll] broadside reads 'th' eile'.

428–429 *When the King enjoys his own again*] text from *Roxburghe Ballads,* vii. 633. There is a later Restoration version at p. 682 of the same volume. Martin Parker wrote this ballad *c.* 1643–6 and it quickly became one of the most popular of the Cavalier songs. At the Restoration it was frequently reprinted, and according to Ritson survived as a Jacobite song throughout the 18th century. Tune in Chappell, i. 210. 1 Booker] John Booker (1603–1667), an astrologer and maker of almanacs. 9 dade] a wading bird.

LYRICS FROM SONG-BOOKS

SINGING SEEMS to have been almost universal in Elizabethan England. The countryside, the street corner, the cottage, and the tavern rang with ballads, rounds, catches, and three-man's songs. The craftsman's shop was 'a very bird-cage' says Dekker, and Deloney in his *Gentle Craft* writes that every journeyman shoemaker had to be able to 'sound the trumpet, or play upon the flute, and bear his part in a three-man's song, and readily reckon up his tools in rhyme.' Among the educated, singing was a necessary social accomplishment. The breeding of a man who could not join in the song after supper, reading his part at sight, was in question. This enthusiasm for singing gave English composers their opportunity. Countless lyrics, almost demanding song by their simple directness and melodic beauty, were being written, and the composers set them to madrigals and airs which are still among the chief glories of English music.

During Henry VIII's reign, ecclesiastical music dominated the efforts of the greatest composers, but in the court circle secular music was also cultivated, the King himself writing a few songs which have survived in manuscript. In 1530, the first secular English song-book was published by Wynkyn de Worde. The three-man's, corrupted into freeman's, song was the popular musical form of the day, and it continued in popularity among the lower classes long after the introduction of new forms for the fashionable. The development of secular music was interrupted by the Reformation and between 1530 and 1588 only one song-book was published, Thomas Whythorne's *Songs of three, four, and five voices,* 1571. Other music of this period of transition is preserved in various manuscripts, especially in the *Mulliner Ms.,* in which appears the famous setting of Richard Edwards's 'In going to my naked bed' (see p. 188).

With the more settled conditions of the later years of Elizabeth's reign, secular music came into its own. A new Italian form, the madrigal, pleased English singers. Nicholas Yonge, a lay-clerk of St. Paul's, imported music-books from Italy and gathered at his house 'a great number of gentlemen and merchants . . . for the exercise of music daily.' In 1588 he published *Musica Transalpina*, a collection of Italian madrigals, and in the same year, possibly a little earlier, Byrd published the first collection of English madrigals, his *Psalms, Sonnets, and Songs*. These started the great vogue of madrigal publication which lasted until about 1630. The madrigal was an unaccompanied song of from three to six voice parts, to be sung by a small group of friends sitting around a table in the home or in the tavern. It differs from our part-song, for it was polyphonic. No one voice carried the melody with the others subordinated as an accompaniment, but all parts were of equal interest, often of the same melodic material, and the voices entered successively rather than simultaneously. The poem was treated in phrases, each several times repeated, and commonly overlapping in the different voices. With this repetition the true madrigal seldom used more than one stanza of six to ten lines. Sometimes the stanzas of a longer poem were set as separate songs. To make clear the treatment of the poem, compare *Beauty is a lovely sweet*, p. 433, with these words which the Cantus, the highest voice, sang: 'Beauty is a lovely sweet, Where pure white and crimson meet, and crimson meet, where pure white and crimson meet, Joined with favor of the face, Chiefest flower of female race, chiefest flower, O chiefest flower of female race. But if virtue might be seen, but if virtue might be seen, might be seen, It would more, it would more delight the eyne, it would more, it would more delight the eyne.' The madrigals were printed in small quarto volumes, each volume containing the part for one voice only.

To supply the demand for the solo song there also developed in England the air, which although it had some precursors on the Continent, especially in Spain, was more of a native growth than the madrigal. In 1597, John Dowland, a celebrated lute player, published the first book of airs. Many composers, including Campion, followed with their books of airs, the last being published in 1622. The air was more melodic and rhythmic than the madrigal, and was harmonized on homophonic rather than polyphonic principles. It was printed so that it might be sung either as a solo by the highest voice accompanied by a lute, sometimes reinforced by a viol de gamba, or as a part song with the highest voice carrying the melody and the others accompanying. Longer poems could be set to airs as the same music was repeated for additional stanzas, a practice impossible with the madrigal.

The lyrics in the song-books were sufficiently well chosen that the volumes sometimes served the purpose of poetical miscellanies; at least so the sub-title, 'To the well-disposed to read, and to the merry disposed to sing,' of Weelkes's *Pammelia*, 1609, seems to indicate. The composers treated the lyrics kindly, striving to frame their music 'to the life of the words.' There are certain conventions in their settings, such as phrases of rapid notes for 'joy,' 'sing,' and 'fly,' and a short rest preceding 'sigh.' Most of the poems which the composers of madrigals and airs set to music remain anonymous, for the name of the poet was not given in the song-books. The only composer known to have written his own words is Campion, and although other composers may have written a few of the lyrics

which they set to music (Symonds thought it most likely that Dowland and
Jones did), their usual practice evidently was to draw on the great store of
poetry already printed or circulating in manuscript.

The composition and publication of songs fell off markedly in the
reign of Charles I, but during the Commonwealth, when ecclesiastical music
was suppressed by the Puritans, secular music flourished. Henry and William Lawes, Wilson, Gamble, and others published a number of volumes,
usually called *Airs and Dialogues*. Polyphony was abandoned and the words
were set to a succession of notes chosen to make prominent the syllables
necessary for the rhythm and sense of the poetry. It was a declamatory
style, early traces of which may be seen in Dowland's later songs. Music
suffered, but the poets were grateful to composers like Henry Lawes who

> First taught our English music how to span
> Words with just note and accent.

CROSS REFERENCES: Poems, not in this section, which also appeared set to
music in song-books or mss. (see notes for exact references to settings): Henry
VIII, all four poems; Vaux, *No pleasure without some pain;* Minor Courtly
Makers, *That was my woe, A carol, bringing in the boar's head, In youth, in
age, Pleasure it is, Ah, the sighs, Western wind, My little fool, England, be glad,
O death, rock me asleep;* Gascoigne, *Gascoigne's good morrow, Gascoigne's lullaby;*
Oxford, *If women could be fair, Epigram;* Sidney, *The nightingale, Fourth song,
O sweet woods* (a rhymed imitation); Dyer, *My mind to me a kingdom is;* Gre-
ville, *Another, of his Cynthia, You little stars, Under a throne;* Essex, *Change
thy mind, To plead my faith;* Ralegh, *Like to a hermit, A description of love;*
Watson, *Vezzosi augelli, Questo di verde;* Lodge, *An ode;* Breton, *Phillida and
Coridon;* Elizabethan Miscellanies, *Amantium iræ, M. Edwards' May, Tichborne's
Elegy, To Colin Clout, Upon his timorous silence in her presence, To Cupid;*
Constable, *Damelus' song to his Diaphenia;* Barnfield, *The unknown shepherd's
complaint;* Daniel, *An ode;* Songs from Plays, the entire section; Broadside
Ballads, the entire section; Campion, all except *Rose-cheeked Laura;* Donne,
Break of day; Jonson, *Song, to Celia* [1], *Had those that dwell in error foul,
Beauties, have ye seen, Though I am young;* Wotton, *On his mistress, the Queen
of Bohemia;* Aytoun, *The forsaken mistress;* Strode, *On Chloris walking in the
snow;* Townshend, *Victorious beauty, A dialogue betwixt Time and a Pilgrim;*
Herrick, *To the virgins, to make much of time, To Anthea, who may command
him anything, How lilies came white;* Carew, *A song, Mediocrity in love rejected,
Ingrateful beauty threatened, To my inconstant mistress, Disdain returned;*
Suckling, *Sonnet I, Sonnet II, Song* ('I prithee send'); Lovelace, *To Althea, from
prison, The Vintage to the Dungeon, To Amarantha, that she would dishevel her
hair, The scrutiny, To Lucasta. The rose, To Lucasta. Going to the wars, To
Lucasta. Going beyond the seas;* Stanley, all six poems; Davenant, *Song;* Waller,
Song ('Go, lovely rose'); Katherine Philips, *Friendship's mystery;* Stuart and
Commonwealth Miscellanies, *Chloris, forbear a while.*

MODERN EDITIONS: E. Flügel, 'Liedersammlungen des xvi. Jahrhunderts, be-
sonders aus der Zeit Heinrich's VIII' in *Anglia*, xii. 225 and 585; *Lyrics from the
Song-Books of the Elizabethan Age* (ed. by A. H. Bullen), London, 1887; *More
Lyrics from the Song-Books* (ed. by A. H. Bullen), London, 1888; *Lyrics from
the Song-Books of the Elizabethan Age,* a selection from the two previous volumes
(ed. by A. H. Bullen), London, 1913; *English Madrigal Verse* (ed. by E. H.
Fellowes), Oxford, 1920; *Lyrics from the old Song Books* (ed. by E. Duncan)
New York, 1927. The lyrics with the musical settings are being edited by E. H.
Fellowes in two series—*The English Madrigal School,* thirty-six volumes, Stainer
and Bell, London, 1913–1924, and *The English School of Lutenist Song-Writers,*
first series, fifteen volumes, and second series in progress, Stainer and Bell,
1920 ff.

COMMENT: J. A. Symonds, 'Lyrics from Elizabethan Song-Books' in *In the
Key of Blue*, London, 1896; W. Chappell, *Old English Popular Music* (ed. by
Wooldridge). two volumes, London, 1893; W. H. Grattan Flood, *Early Tudor
Composers*, Oxford, 1925; E. H. Fellowes, *The English Madrigal Composers,*

Oxford, 1921, *William Byrd,* Oxford, 1923, and *The English Madrigal,* Oxford, 1925; Peter Warlock, *The English Ayre,* Oxford, 1926; Frank Howes, *William Byrd,* London, 1928.

TEXT: *Psalms, Sonnets, and Songs,* 1588 (4253), Harvard; *Songs of Sundry Natures,* 1589 (4256), Huntington; *Canzonets,* 1593 (18121), Huntington; *Songs and Psalms,* 1594 (18284), B. M.; *Second Book of Songs or Airs,* 1600 (7095), Huntington; *Third and Last Book of Songs or Airs,* 1603 (7096), Huntington; *First Set of English Madrigals,* 1604 (1586), Harvard; *Musical Humors. The first part of Airs,* 1605 (13958), B. M.; Michael East, *Second Set of Madrigals,* 1606 (7461), Huntington; *Funeral Tears,* 1606 (5679), Huntington; *Poetical Music,* 1607 (13957), B. M.; *Ultimum Vale,* 1608, not accessible to us, text from Fellowes; *Airs or Fantastic Spirits,* 1608 (25202), Huntington; John Wilbye, *Second Set of Madrigals,* 1609 (25619a), Harvard; *Muses' Garden for Delights,* 1610 (14736), Huntington; *First Set of Madrigals and Motets,* 1612 (11826), Harvard; *A Pilgrim's Solace,* 1612 (7098), Huntington; Thomas Bateson, *Second Set of Madrigals,* 1618 (1587), B. M.; *Private Music,* 1620 (19553), Bodleian; *Songs of three, four, five, and six parts,* 1622 (24099), Huntington; *First Book of Airs,* 1622 (901), B. M.; *Christ Church Ms.* K3, not accessible to us, text from Bullen; Playford, *Select Musical Airs and Dialogues,* 1653, B. M.; Lawes, *Airs and Dialogues,* 1653, New York; Lawes, *Airs and Dialogues,* 1655, New York; Wilson, *Cheerful Airs or Ballads,* 1660, White.

429 *Reasons briefly set down* 20 *Omnis spiritus laudet Dominum*] 'Let every spirit praise the Lord.'

431 *Arise, get up, my dear* 11 firk] dance, jig, be lively.

432 *In midst of woods*] set as two songs by Mundy: the first stanza being number xxvii, and the last two stanzas number xxviii. 5 charm] singing. noise] in the obsolete meaning of melodious sound.

432 *Fine knacks for ladies* 13 lives] omitted in 1600; supplied by Fellowes.

434 *The soldier's song*] Captain Hume, a soldier by profession and an eccentric, requires of the lute the seemingly impossible task of imitating trumpets, drums, and 'great ordnance.' 13 Hark] repeated in the song; the repetition omitted here for rhythm.

435–436 *The hunting song* 10–11] Between stanzas there is the direction, 'The hounds are now a-hunting.'

436 *Think'st thou, Kate*] We have been unable to get access to a copy of *Ultimum Vale;* our text is from Fellowes's *English Madrigal Verse.*

437 *Ye that do live in pleasures* 8 breath] Cantus part reads 'birth'; other parts 'breath'.

438 *Once did my thoughts* 19 made out of wax] perfectly made; the phrase 'man of wax' was a common term of commendation.

438–439 *The silver swan* 4 her] 1612 misprints 'his'.

439 *Ah, dear heart*] This poem, with several textual variants and an additional stanza, was also set by Dowland in his *Pilgrim's Solace,* 1612. The stanza set by Gibbons is printed, with several variants, in the 1669 edition of Donne's poems as a first stanza of *Break of day.* Professor Grierson denies it to Donne and thinks it 'probably by John Dowland.' That the stanza does not really belong to Donne's poem seems clear from internal evidence, but there is no real evidence for assigning it to Dowland.

440 *I heard a noise* 9–10] Between lines 9 and 10, Fellowes has supplied a line, 'I saw the shadow of some worthy thing', not in the original. Fellowes does not give the source for this line.

441–442 *Yet if his majesty*] text from Bullen's *Lyrics from the Song-Books,* collated with Ault's *17th Century Lyrics.* 14 dais] Ault reads 'dazie'.

443 *Greedy lover, pause awhile*] Huth discovered a copy of this song in a manuscript miscellany, where it was signed 'Sir Albertus Morton' (*Inedited Poetical Miscellanies,* 1870, sig. U2 recto). Sir Albertus Morton was a nephew of Sir Henry Wotton. He spent some time in the service of Elizabeth, Queen of Bohemia. In 1624 he was appointed one of the Secretaries of State, but his death in the next year cut short his tenure of this office. For Wotton's epitaph on the death of Morton's wife, see p. 553.

THOMAS CAMPION

THOMAS CAMPION (1567–1620) was both musician and poet, a fitting combination at a time when the relation between the two arts was so close. With his heart given to music and poetry, he seems to have had difficulty in deciding on a profession, for he studied at Peterhouse, Cambridge, 1581–4, left without taking a degree, and entered Gray's Inn for the study of law, but was not called to the bar. Later, probably at a Continental university, he took a degree in medicine. He had begun writing poetry as a young legal student and five of his poems, without his signature, appeared in Newman's surreptitious edition of Sidney's *Astrophel and Stella*, 1591, while others were circulating in manuscript. In 1595, he published a volume of Latin epigrams, and in 1601, in collaboration with Philip Rosseter, a musician, he issued *A Book of Airs*, for which he wrote all of the lyrics and the musical settings for the first half. This marks Campion's appearance as a composer of airs for solo songs with a lute accompaniment. In writing of Campion as a composer, Warlock says that he was 'at his best in half serious songs' of 'deliciously pretty tunes,' distinguished by 'neatness of workmanship,' but he notes the 'absence of any deeper quality than surface charm in the music.' In 1602 Campion published a prose treatise, *Observations in the Art of English Poesy*, in which, carrying on the Cambridge tradition in the old battle between quantitative and accentual meter, he protested against the use of rhyme and accent, and wished to restore to English poetry the dignity of the classical, unrhymed, quantitative verse— a strange position for one so facile in rhyme and accent as Campion. His confusion of the two systems and his failure to understand the true nature of accent partially account for this. He was effectively answered in the next year by Daniel, and Ben Jonson said of himself that he had written 'a discourse of poesy both against Campion and Daniel,' which unfortunately has not survived. In 1607 Campion wrote his first mask, and in 1613 three others. His dramatic power is not great and the merit of his masks is their lyric beauty. Campion published two more volumes for which he composed both words and music, *Two Books of Airs*, c. 1613, and *The Third and Fourth Books of Airs*, c. 1617.

If in reading Campion the variety of rhythms, changing from line to line, is sometimes perplexing, one should remember that the poems were written to music and that Campion 'chiefly aimed to couple my words and notes lovingly together.'

MODERN EDITIONS: *Works* (ed. by P. Vivian), Oxford, 1909; *The Works* (ed. by A. H. Bullen), London, 1889; *Thomas Campion* (ed. by A. H. Bullen, omits Latin poems), London, 1903; *Poetical Works in English* (ed. by P. Vivian), Muses' Library, London, n. d. Both words and music have been reprinted by E. H. Fellowes in his series 'The English School of Lutenist Song Writers,' *Thomas Campian. Songs from Rosseter's Book of Airs, 1601*, parts 1 and 2, and *Thomas Campian. First, Second, Third, and Fourth Books of Airs*, Stainer and Bell, London, 1922 and 1925.

COMMENT: T. MacDonagh, *Thomas Campion and the Art of English Poetry*, Dublin, 1913; Peter Warlock, *The English Ayre*, Oxford, 1926.

TEXT: *A Book of Airs*, 1601 (21332), Huntington; *Two Books of Airs*, [c. 1613] (4547), Huntington; *Observations in the Art of English Poesy*, 1602 (4543), B. M.; *The Late Royal Entertainment . . . at Cawsome House*, 1613 (4545), Huntington; *The Third and Fourth Book of Airs*, [c. 1617] (4548), Huntington; Robert Jones, *Second Book of Songs and Airs*, 1601 (14733), B. M.; Richard Alison, *An Hour's Recreation in Music*, 1606 (356), Huntington.

445 *My love bound me*] The first stanza of the song appeared in Sidney's *Astrophel and Stella*, 1591. It is not signed by Campion in either printing, but internal evidence and the close similarity with one of his Latin epigrams (see ed. Vivian, p. li) makes the ascription reasonably certain.

446 *What if a day*] The authorship of this song—one of the most popular of the time, appearing in many mss., in several books of songs, and as a broadside ballad—is in dispute. It is attributed to Campion in Alison's *An Hour's Recreation in Music,* 1606, and in Alexander Gil's *Logonomia Anglica,* 1619. It had appeared in a ms. as early as 1592, and in *Rawlinson Poetry Ms.* 112 it is attributed to the E[arl] of E[ssex]. A. E. H. Swaen, in an exhaustive account of the different versions of the song (*M. P.* iv. 397 and v. 383), having misdated a manuscript (cf. ed. Vivian, p. 378), thinks it too early for Campion. There can be little doubt that the two stanzas printed by Alison in 1606 are Campion's, but the song was probably extended by other hands. A version in five stanzas may be found in the *Shirburn Ballads,* p. 238, or in the *Roxburghe Ballads,* i. 348.

448 *The man of life upright*] attributed in two mss. to Bacon, but almost certainly Campion's.

448-449 *Hark, all you ladies*] first appeared in Sidney's *Astrophel and Stella,* 1591. 24 Dione's] Venus's. 35 Apes in Avernus] The idea was common that old maids were condemned after death to lead apes in hell.

449 *When thou must home* 4 Iope] Campion is probably referring to the Iope who was the daughter of Iphicles and one of the wives of Theseus.

449-450 *Rose-cheeked Laura*] the most beautiful of the songs by which Campion illustrated his principles of quantitative versification. His comment in the *Observations* on this poem follows: 'The second kind consists of dimeter, whose first foot may either be a spondee or trochee. The two verses following are both of them trochaical and consist of four feet, the first of either of them being a spondee or trochee, the other three only trochees. The fourth and last verse is made of two trochees. The number is voluble and fit to express any amorous conceit.' 6 concent] playing or singing together in harmony.

450-451 *Jack and Joan* 7 Lash out] lavish, squander. 19 tutties] nosegays.

451 *Give beauty all her right* 8 swelling] 1613 'smelling'.

452-453 *Now winter nights enlarge* 13-14 dispense With] grant dispensation to, excuse.

454 *There is a garden* 6 cherry-ripe] the call of the London street venders.

454-455 *Young and simple though I am* 9-12] supplied from Ferrabosco's *Airs,* 1609; 1617 repeats the last four lines of the first stanza.

JOHN DONNE

JOHN DONNE (1572-1631) illustrates, in his early poetry, the diversity of the 1590's. As the Petrarchan code of love and the smooth felicities of the Spenserian manner came to their fullest development and their greatest triumph, Donne, an 'infidel in love' with an ear for rugged rhythm, steeped in medieval scholasticism rather than Renaissance humanism, broke with the tradition and, 'the lazy seeds of servile imitation thrown away,' followed the realistic bent of his 'imperious wit.' For him, thinking was a passionate experience, and it was in the play of his intellect that he found poetry— not calm, peaceful reflective poetry, but poetry intensely emotional. His striking figures of speech—drawn from the wide range of his learning rather than from his sensuous experience, intellectualized yet suffused with emotion—express aptly his mode of thought. Because of this originality, the young poets of the first half of the 17th century looked upon Donne as

> a king that ruled as he thought fit
> The universal monarchy of wit.

Naturally they imitated him, but often their thought did not fit such unusual expression and the result at times was an absurd involution of commonplace ideas. His influence did, however, help to produce in 17th-century poetry a new note of individuality, a keener intellectual activity, and a deepened passion.

To describe this manner of writing, the word 'metaphysical' came to be used, possibly first by Drummond of Hawthornden (see 'Extracts from Critical Essays,' p. 906). This term has been most clearly defined by Dr. Johnson, in his life of Cowley: 'About the beginning of the 17th century appeared a race of writers that may be termed the metaphysical poets. . . . [Their] wit . . . may be . . . considered as a kind of *discordia concors*; a combination of dissimilar images, or discovery of occult resemblances in things apparently unlike. . . . If they frequently threw away their wit upon false conceits, they likewise sometimes struck out unexpected truth; if their conceits were far-fetched, they were often worth the carriage. To write on their plan it was at least necessary to read and think.'

Donne's early education, carefully supervised by his mother (in whom flowed the blood of the Mores, the Rastells, and the Heywoods), was Catholic. In 1584 he entered Hart Hall, Oxford, and three years later transferred to Cambridge. He does not seem to have taken a degree at either University at this time, probably because as a Catholic he could not take the required oaths. A tour of the Continent possibly followed his leaving Cambridge, though the date of the tour is uncertain and is placed later by Walton and Gosse. In 1592 Donne was admitted to Lincoln's Inn for the study of law, but, as he later wrote a friend, he was 'diverted by the worst voluptuousness, which is an hydroptic, immoderate desire of humane learning and languages.' Some time went to the writing of poetry and some to a survey 'of the body of divinity as it was then controverted betwixt the Reformed and the Roman Church.' The exact history of Donne's religious change cannot be traced. Coming to the opinion that 'all churches are beams of one sun,' he was ready in 1601 to disclaim any 'love of a corrupt religion,' though it is evident from his later religious poetry that he always remained a Catholic in temperament and was at least a little uneasy within the confines of Anglicanism. Donne was a volunteer with the Earl of Essex on the expedition to Cadiz in 1596, and to the Azores in 1597. On his return he entered the service of Sir Thomas Egerton, the Lord Keeper of the Great Seal. According to Richard Baker, in his *Chronicle of the Kings of England*, Donne came to be known about London as 'not dissolute but very neat; a great visitor of ladies, a great frequenter of plays, a great writer of conceited verses.' He fell in love with Egerton's niece, Anne More, and in 1601 married her without the consent of her father, who, angry at a secret marriage, secured Donne's dismissal from his post. One observer of the time, Francis Osborne, noted that the Lord Keeper was not loath to part with a secretary so clever that he was given to 'mend the copy.' Donne, with a rapidly growing family, unable to find other employment, spent the next years in poverty and misery. He aided Morton, later Bishop of Durham, in his controversy with the Catholics, and as early as 1607 was urged by Morton to take orders in the Anglican church. Donne was unwilling, however, and continued to seek for civil preferment, even contemplating emigration in 1609, when he applied for the secretaryship of the colony of Virginia. But the King wished Donne for the Church, and all other ways of preferment were closed to him. At last sincerely convinced of his fitness for the calling and of its fitness for him, he was ordained in 1615. Then begins the period of his holy life, commemorated by his devoted parishioner, Izaak Walton. The glowing rhetoric of his sermons found him quick advancement, and in 1621 he was made Dean of St. Paul's. It was decided in 1630 to advance him to a bishopric, but his sickness and death left this plan unfulfilled.

With the exception of several occasional poems, Donne did not publish his poetry. Even the publication of his *Anniversaries* he regretted: 'The fault which I acknowledge in myself is to have descended to print anything in verse, which though it have excuse, even in our times, by example of men which one would think should as little have done it as I, yet I confess I wonder how I declined to it, and do not pardon myself.' His poems, however, circulated widely in manuscripts, the fashionable mode at court, of which Drayton complains in 1612: 'Verses are wholly deduced to chambers, and nothing esteemed in this lunatic age but what is kept in cabinets, and must only pass by transcription.' In 1614, just before entering the ministry, Donne considered publishing his poems as a public acknowledgment of them, so that the early poems might not be brought out to his scandal after he was in orders. Since no copy of such an edition survives, it is always assumed that it did not appear. His poems were published in 1633, two years after his death, and proved so popular that they went to their seventh edition in 1669.

MODERN EDITIONS: *Poetical Works* (ed. by H. J. C. Grierson), two volumes, Oxford, 1912; *Complete Poetry and Selected Prose* (ed. by J. Hayward), Bloomsbury, 1929; *The Works* (ed. by H. Alford), six volumes, London, 1839; *Poems* (ed. by E. K. Chambers), two volumes, Muses' Library, London, n. d.; *Letters to Severall Persons of Honour* (ed. by C. E. Merrill, Jr.), New York, 1910; *Sermons, Selected Passages* (ed. by L. Pearsall Smith), Oxford, 1919; *Devotions* (ed. by J. Sparrow), Cambridge, 1923; *Paradoxes and Problems* (ed. by G. Keynes), London, 1923; *Ten Sermons* (ed. by G. Keynes), London, 1923.

COMMENT: E. Gosse, *The Life and Letters of John Donne*, two volumes, London, 1899; G. Keynes, *Bibliography of the Works of Dr. John Donne*, Cambridge, 1914; M. P. Ramsay, *Les Doctrines Mediévales chez Donne*, Oxford, 1916; E. M. Simpson, *A Study of the Prose Works of John Donne*, Oxford, 1924; H. I'A. Fausset, *John Donne, A Study in Discord*, London, 1924.

TEXT: *Poems*, 1633 (7045), Harvard; *Poems*, 1635 (7046), Harvard.

455 *Songs and Sonnets*] The group headings (*Songs and Sonnets, Epigrams, Elegies, Satires, Letters, Divine Poems*) were not used in the edition of 1633, but appeared in 1635.

455-456 *Love's deity* 26 I'am] The use, by Donne, of the apostrophe with no letter omitted is probably intended to indicate a speeding up in pronunciation without a complete elision.

456 *Song* 2 mandrake root] The root of the mandrake was supposed to resemble the human shape.

458 *The flea*] This poem evidently pleased 17th-century readers. After the first edition of Donne's poems in 1633, publishers placed it first in all subsequent 17th-century editions.

459 *The message*] no title in 1633; title from 1635. 11 Which] 1633; 1635 'But'.

459-460 *The bait*] no title in 1633; title from 1635; one of the many imitations of Marlowe's *Passionate shepherd to his love*, p. 168. 18 with] 1635; 1633 'which'. 23 sleave-silk] 1635; 1633 'sleeve-sick'.

460-461 *The will* 39 Bedlam] a contraction for Bethlehem Hospital, an asylum for the insane.

461-462 *The sun rising* 24 alchemy] From its claims to transmute baser metals into gold, alchemy had the figurative meaning of 'glittering dross.'

462 *Break of day*] In 1669 this poem was printed with an additional first stanza, most probably not by Donne. For this stanza, beginning 'Ah, dear heart', see 'Lyrics from Song-Books,' p. 439, where it is printed from the version set by Orlando Gibbons. See also note, p. 983. *Break of day* was set to music by William Corkine in his *Second Book of Airs*, 1612. It is to be noted that the speaker in the poem is feminine.

463 *Confined love*] no title in 1633; title from 1635. 16 with all] 1635; 1633 reads 'withall', which reading Grierson defends.

464-465 *A lecture upon the shadow*] not in 1633; text from 1635, where the poem is headed *Song;* title from 1650. 26 short] 1635; 'first', the reading of many mss., was adopted by Grierson as the better reading.

465–467 *The ecstasy* 9 entergraft] a word of Donne's own coinage to express vividly the reciprocal nature of the grafting, entwining, of hands. 32] Grierson explains this passage: 'We see now that we did not see before the true source of our love. What we thought was due to bodily beauty, we perceive now to have its source in the soul.' 42 Interinanimates] many mss.; 1633 'Interanimates'. 52 sphere] many mss.; 1633 'spheres'. 55 forces, sense] many mss.; 1633 'senses force'.

467–468 *The good-morrow* 4 seven sleepers'] Seven Christian youths, fleeing to escape martyrdom during the Decian persecution, found refuge in a cave, where they remained asleep for 230 years. 5 but] except.

468 *Air and angels* 23–24] According to medieval belief, inherited from the Neo-Platonists, the incorporeal angels assumed bodies of air. The air was 'pure,' but not so 'pure' as the incorporeality of the angels.

468–469 *The prohibition* 5 thee then what to me] 1635; 1633 'me then that which'. 22 stage] 1635; 1633 'stay'. Grierson punctuates the line, 'So shall I, live, thy Stage, not triumph be;', and paraphrases it thus: 'Alive, I shall continue to be the stage on which your victories are daily set forth; dead, I shall be but your triumph, a thing achieved once, never to be repeated.'

469 *The undertaking*] no title in 1633; title from 1635. 6 specular stone] semi-transparent substance formerly used as window glass or for ornament; probably used here with reference to the crystal gazing of the astrologer.

469–470 *Lovers' infiniteness*] Grierson suggests that the title 'possibly should be *Love's infiniteness*.' 20 it] 1635; 1633 'is'.

470–471 *Love's growth* 18] Grierson was the first to clear up the meaning of this line: 'The stars at sunrise are not really made larger, but they are made to seem larger.'

471 *The anniversary* 22 we] many mss.; 1633 'now'.

472–473 *The canonization* 7 stampëd face] on coins. 15 plaguy bill] the weekly list of those dead from the plague. 30 legend] 1635; 1633 'legends'. 45 your] 1669; 1633 'our'.

473 *A valediction of weeping* 8–9] Grierson paraphrases, 'For, as your image perishes in each tear that falls, so shall we perish, be nothing, when

between us rolls the "salt, estranging sea." '

474–475 *A valediction forbidding mourning*] quoted by Walton in connection with his account of Donne's visit to France in 1612, probably indicating that it was written by Donne to his wife at that time. 11 trepidation] according to the Ptolemaic astronomy, a slow, swinging motion of the ninth sphere which accounted for certain phenomena really due to the motion of the earth's axis. 16 elemented] composed.

475 *The funeral*] This, and the following poem, were possibly addressed to Mrs. Magdalen Herbert, the mother of George Herbert. 17 with] 1635; 1633 'by'.

475–476 *The relic* 27–28] the kiss of salutation and of parting customary in Renaissance England.

476–477 *Twicknam garden*] Twickenham, where the Countess of Bedford had a country house, which Donne visited. 17 groan] many mss.; 1633 'grow'. The mandrake was popularly supposed to shriek when pulled from the ground. 24 woman's] many mss.; 1633 'womens'.

477–478 *A nocturnal upon Saint Lucy's Day*] According to the old style of reckoning, St. Lucy's Day, December 13, was the shortest day of the year. This poem was probably written in 1612, when Lucy, Countess of Bedford, was seriously ill. 3 flasks] powderflasks. squibs] fireworks. 21 limbec] alembic, still. 28–36] These lines play on the subtle distinction between degrees of nothingness. By her death Donne would become the quintessence of the first nothing—no longer a man, or he would be conscious of so being; nor a beast, for then (according to scholastic doctrine) he would be perceptive and moving, able to select ends and means; nor a plant or stone, for the vegetable kingdom is capable of detesting and loving; nor an ordinary nothing, such as a shadow, for to produce that a body and light are necessary. 29 elixir] quintessence. 39 Goat] the zodiacal sign, Capricorn; with reference to the supposed lust of goats.

478–479 *On his mistress*] not printed in 1633; text from 1635. 28 mind's] many mss.; 1635 'mind'. 34 spitals] hospitals, particularly for persons of low class, afflicted with foul diseases.

479–481 *The autumnal*] probably written to Mrs. Magdalen Herbert. 6

Affection . . . takes] many mss.; 1633
'Affections . . . take'. 16 anchorit]
anchorite, hermit. 20 progress] the
journey of state made by a royal per-
sonage.

481–483 *Satire III* 33 foes] 1635;
1633 'foe'. devil, whom] many mss.;
1633 'devil h'is, whom'. 44 here] 1635;
1633 'her'. 47 her] many mss.; 1633
'the'. 96 Philip . . . Gregory] Philip
II of Spain and one of the Popes
Gregory, probably XIII or XIV. 97
Harry . . . Martin] Henry VIII and
Martin Luther.

483–485 *The calm* 17 lanthorns]
lanterns; Grierson explains that 'the
reference is to the lanterns in the high
sterns of the ships, used to keep the
fleet together.' 17–18] Jonson told
Drummond that he knew these lines
by heart. 23 calenture] a delirium
said to afflict sailors in the tropics;
the victim fancies the sea to be a green
field and wishes to leap into it. 36
emperor's] Tiberius's; according to
Suetonius, as Tiberius was once about
to enter Rome, a snake, which he fed
with his own hand, was devoured by
ants. This was taken to be an omen
that Tiberius should beware the fury of
the mob, so he turned back and did
not enter the city. 37 gaols] jails;
1633 reads 'goals'. 38 pinnaces] 1635;
1633 'venices'.

485 *To Sir Henry Wotton*] In several mss., the poem is dated July 20,
1598. 2 Cales] Cadiz. St. Michael's]
a name sometimes applied to the
Azores. Donne is referring to the Cadiz
expedition of 1596 and the Island Voyage of 1597, which had become old
stories. 24 chests] chess.

486 *An Anatomy of the World. The
first anniversary*] Elizabeth, the daughter of Sir Robert Drury, died in 1610
at the age of fifteen. Donne secured
the patronage of the wealthy Sir Robert
by writing a *Funeral Elegy,* 1610, and
the two *Anniversaries,* 1611 and 1612,
which are grossly extravagant in their
eulogy of the young girl. For Ben
Jonson's comment, see 'Critical Essays,'
p. 898. We print the passages which
show Donne's bewilderment in the face

of the new science of his day, and a
few lines of the extravagant eulogy.
20 She] Elizabeth Drury. 34 single
money] small change. 37, 38 know'st]
1611; 1633 'knowest'.

487–488 *Of the Progress of the Soul.
The second anniversary* 1 She] Elizabeth Drury. 2 electrum] an alloy of
gold and silver. 11] marginal note:
'Her [*i. e.,* the soul's] ignorance in this
life and knowledge in the next.'

488 *Show me, dear Christ*] not
printed in any of the 17th-century editions. It was first printed in Gosse's
Life from the *Westmoreland Ms.* Our
text is taken from Grierson. 8 seven]
the seven hills of Rome.

490 *At the round earth's* 6 dearth]
Westmoreland Ms.; 1633 'death'.

491 *Good Friday, 1613. Riding westward*] In *Additional Ms.* 25707 this
poem is headed: 'Mr. J. Donne, going
from Sir H[enry] G[oodere] on Good
Friday sent him back this meditation
on the way.' The heading of the poem
in *Harleian Ms.* 4955 gives the objec-
tive of the ride: 'Riding to Sir Edward
Herbert in Wales.'

492 *A hymn to Christ* 12 seas] other
17th-century editions read 'blood',
which explains Donne's meaning.

492 *A hymn to God the Father*] In
speaking of this poem, Walton says
that Donne 'caused it to be set to a
most grave and solemn tune and to be
often sung to the organ by the choristers
of St. Paul's church in his own hearing,
especially at the evening service; and
at his customary devotions in that place
did occasionally say to a friend, "The
words of this hymn have restored me
to the same thoughts of joy that possessed my soul in my sickness when I
composed it. . . ." '

493–494 *Hymn to God, my God, in
my sickness*] not printed in 1633; text
from 1635. Walton, in the 1670 edition
of his *Life of Donne,* quotes part of
the poem and dates it March 23, 1631,
eight days before the death of Donne.
Walton's dating is not accepted by
all scholars. 10 *Per fretum febris*]
'Through the raging of fever.' 18
Anyan] Bering Strait.

BEN JONSON

BEN JONSON (1572–1637), the posthumous son of a minister, received his
education at Westminster School under the learned Camden, of whose
instruction he always speaks with reverent praise. He did not proceed to

a university, but worked for a time at bricklaying, the trade of his stepfather. Finding this distasteful he enlisted for a period of service in Flanders (see Jonson's own account of his adventures, 'Extracts from Critical Essays,' p. 900), and on his return from the wars he married. Not long after, he became associated with a company of actors. By 1597 he was one of Henslowe's playwrights, well enough known by 1598 to be listed by the patriotic Meres as one of 'our best for tragedy.' In that year he killed in a duel one of Henslowe's actors, Gabriel Spencer, and escaped the gallows only by claiming right of clergy. During his time in prison he was converted to Catholicism, in which religion he continued for twelve years. Jonson was the leading figure in the playwrights' quarrel, sometimes called 'the war of the theaters,' and later he was often in trouble because of his blunt speech. As his reputation increased, he became the chief writer of masks for court production, and from 1616 was granted a pension by James I, later renewed and increased by Charles I, as the 'King's poet.' In 1616 he collected his plays, masks, and poems for publication in a folio volume, called his *Works*. This choice of a dignified title occasioned many gibes at his expense, one of which appears in *Wit's Recreations*, 1640:

> Pray tell me, Ben, where doth the mystery lurk,
> What others call a play you call a work.

In his last years, he suffered greatly from illness and at times from poverty.

According to Jonson's statement to Drummond, his method of poetic composition was to write out what he had to say in prose and then to versify it. The merits and the defects of his poetry are those which one might expect from such a method. In his work, the traces of medievalism surviving in Spenser and so many Elizabethans disappear. His epigrams, his odes, his verse-letters, and his carefully fashioned songs are completely classical in form and in spirit. Like Donne he set a new manner of writing before the young poets of the 17th century, which helped to win many of them away from Petrarchism and Spenserianism.

Jonson's conversation, however, probably exercised more influence than did his poetry. He was an excellent boon companion, and young men—scholars as well as poets, for Jonson was one of the learned men of his time—loved to gather with him in the London taverns. Fortunately we have a sample of his vivid and combative conversation in the notes which Drummond of Hawthornden took of Ben's talk during his visit to Scotland. We have also his *Discoveries*, a commonplace-book largely made up of extracts and paraphrases from his reading, which indicates the tenor of his discussion of literary principles, and may have furnished the ammunition for his controversies. (For selections from the *Conversations* and the *Discoveries*, see 'Extracts from Critical Essays,' p. 898.) We may be certain that the taverns rang with Jonson's vociferous battle for 'pure and neat language,' for polished literary form, and for the use of the classics as models.

The favorite meeting place of men of letters in the first two decades of the 17th century was the Mermaid Tavern. Tom Coryate, traveling in Asia Minor in 1615, addressed a letter to 'the right worshipful fraternity of sireniacal gentlemen, that meet the first Friday of every month, at the sign of the Mermaid in Bread street.' Shakespeare at times met with this group and engaged in wit combats with Jonson, who, as described by Fuller, was 'like a Spanish great galleon . . . built far higher in learning, solid but slow in his performances,' while Shakespeare, like an 'English man-of-war, lesser in bulk but lighter in sailing, could turn with all tides, tack about, and take advantage of all winds, by the quickness of his wit and invention.' That Jonson was early recognized as a leader in these gatherings is shown by the poem which Beaumont addressed to him, about 1606, describing an evening at the Mermaid (see p. 539). By 1620, the Apollo Room of the Devil and St. Dunstan Tavern had supplanted the Mermaid in popularity, and Jonson's *Leges Convivales* were painted over its fireplace in letters of gold (see p. 513). From about this time the group was known as the Tribe of Ben, and the young poets after being 'sealed of the Tribe' became 'sons of Ben.' The esteem in which Jonson was held by these companions is shown by the volume of elegies, *Jonsonus Virbius*, published in the year following his death.

MODERN EDITIONS: *Ben Jonson* (ed. by C. H. Herford and P. Simpson), three volumes (to be completed in ten volumes), Oxford, 1925-1927; *The Works* (ed. by F. Cunningham), three volumes, London, n. d., and nine volumes, London, 1875.

COMMENT: A. C. Swinburne, *A Study of Ben Jonson,* London, 1889; M. Castelain, *Ben Jonson, L'Homme et l'Œuvre,* Paris, 1907; G. Gregory Smith, *Ben Jonson,* London, 1919.

TEXT: *Works,* 1616 (14751), Harvard; *Works,* 1641, Cornell; *Mr. William Shakespeare's Comedies, Histories, and Tragedies,* 1623 (22273), Princeton; Alexander Brome, *Songs and Other Poems,* 1661, Harvard.

494-495 *To my bookseller* 7 title-leaf] Title-pages were posted up, and, as this passage indicates, placed in cleft-sticks to advertise new books. This custom explains the full descriptions given of books on Elizabethan title-pages. 9 termers] those who came to London in term-time, the session of the law courts. 12 Bucklersbury] a street inhabited by grocers and apothecaries where the book would be used as wrapping paper, a custom commented on by Herrick in an epigram, *To his book.*

495 *To my mere English censurer* 4 Davies] Sir John Davies; see p. 331. Weever] see p. 525.

495 *On something that walks somewhere* 5 Lord] Objection was beginning to be voiced to the English nobility, because they gathered at court for amusement and neglected the old duties and kindly charities to the tenants on their country estates.

495 *To William Camden*] a renowned antiquary, and master of Westminster School when Jonson was a student there. 3-4] referring to Camden's *Britannia,* first published in 1586. The epigram was probably written too early to refer to the *Annales,* published in 1615.

496 *To Francis Beaumont*] possibly written in answer to *Mr. Francis Beaumont's letter to Ben Jonson,* p. 539.

496 *To John Donne* 1 where] whether. 10 pui'nes'] The puisne was

an inferior or junior judge in the superior courts of common law; an unskilled beginner.

496 *On Lucy, Countess of Bedford*] the favorite of Queen Anne, and next to Mary, Countess of Pembroke, the patroness most frequently celebrated by poets of the day. She acted in many of Jonson's masks. 15 rock] distaff.

497 *To Lucy, Countess of Bedford, with Mr. Donne's satires* 10 heard] 1616 reads 'hard'.

497-498 *Inviting a friend to supper* 19-20 godwit, gnat, rail] various birds. 20 ruff] perch-like fish. 36 polly] 1616 reads 'poolye'.

498 *On my first son*] born in 1596, and died during the plague in 1603. Jonson told Drummond of a vision he had at the time of the child's death: 'When the King came in England, at that time the pest was in London, he [Jonson] being in the country at Sir Robert Cotton's house with old Camden, he saw in a vision his eldest son (then a child and at London) appear unto him with the mark of a bloody cross on his forehead as if it had been cutted with a sword. At which amazed, he prayed unto God, and in the morning he came to Mr. Camden's chamber to tell him, who persuaded him it was but an apprehension of his fantasy, at which he should not be dejected. In the meantime comes there letters from his wife of the death of that boy in the plague. He appeared to him, he said, of a manly shape, and of that growth that he thinks he shall be at the resurrection.'

499 *An epitaph on Salathiel Pavy*] on one of the Children of the Chapel, who after three years of acting died in 1603, aged thirteen.

499 *Epitaph on Elizabeth, L. H.*] as yet unidentified.

500–502 *To Penshurst*] the seat of the Sidney family in Kent. 2 touch] touchstone, a fine-grained dark stone. 4 lantern] a small tower, or erection, on a roof or dome with the sides pierced to admit light. 14 his great birth] On the birth of Philip Sidney, an oak tree was planted which survived until 1768. 19 Gamage] Sir Robert Sidney, Viscount Lisle (the younger brother of Sir Philip), owner of Penshurst at the time Jonson is writing, had married Barbara Gamage. 66 yet dine away] Jonson told Drummond that 'being at the end of my Lord Salisbury's table . . . and demanded by my Lord why he was not glad: "My Lord," said he, "you promised me I should dine with you, but I do not," for he had none of his meat—he esteemed only that his meat which was of his own dish.' 69 call] 1641 'call for'.

502 *Song, to Celia* (1)] first printed in *Volpone*, 1607; set to music by Alfonso Ferrabosco in his *Airs*, 1609.

502 *Song, to Celia* (2)] paraphrased from various scattered passages in a collection of letters written by a late Greek rhetorician, Philostratus. Cf. J. A. Symonds in *The Academy*, xxvi. 377.

503 *Underwoods*] In his preface to the reader, Jonson explains that he entitles 'these lesser poems of later growth by this of Underwood, out of the analogy they hold to the Forest in my former book, and no otherwise.'

503 *A celebration of Charis*] conjectured by Simpson and Herford (i. 53) to be about the lady who played Venus in the mask usually called *The Hue and Cry after Cupid*, because the chariot of Venus described in the mask is like the chariot in *Her triumph*. If Charis is a real woman, she has the honor of inspiring Jonson's finest love poetry, written at intervals from 1608 to 1622.

503–504 *Her triumph* 11–30] These two stanzas also serve as a song in *The Devil is an Ass*.

504 *Begging another kiss . . .*] according to Drummond, Jonson frequently repeated this poem.

504–505 *An ode to himself* 6 and destroys] Various editors have inserted a monosyllable ('quite,' 'so,' or 'soon') between 'and' and 'destroys' to perfect the meter. 9 Clarius'] Apollo, so called from his temple and oracle at Clarus. 27–30] Prometheus, son of Japetus, with the aid of Minerva ('the issue of Jove's brain') stole fire from the sun and gave it to man.

505 *A fit of rhyme against rhyme* 10 syllabes] syllables.

506–509 *To the immortal memory . . .*] a Pindaric ode in which Jonson gives English names to the three divisions: the strophe is the turn, the antistrophe the counter-turn, and the epode the stand. This ode was occasioned by the death of Sir Henry Morison, about 1629. Sir Lucius Cary, better known by his later title, Lord Falkland, was the author of a few poems and a member of Ben Jonson's literary group. At his country place, Great Tew, near Oxford, he kept a hospitable home for the week-end discussions of poets, philosophers, and theologians. At the outbreak of the Civil War, he espoused, with some hesitation, the King's cause, and met an early death, desired by himself, at Newbury, 1643. The charm of his personality has been preserved in Clarendon's pages (ed. Macray, iii. 178–190). 1 Brave infant of Saguntum] After a long siege Saguntum, a Roman city in Spain, was taken by Hannibal, but the inhabitants destroyed themselves and their belongings by fire. According to Pliny, one infant about to be born returned to the mother's womb to escape the Carthaginians. 24 fact] deed. 68 bald] 1641 'bold'. 123 Friendship in deed] 1641 'Friendship, indeed'.

509–511 *An epistle answering . . .* 32 Valteline] a valley stretching from the Lake of Como to the Tyrolean mountains, which Spain had taken under her protection in 1620, for it offered the only way by which Spanish armies could pass between Italy and Germany. By 1623 France, Venice, and Savoy had formed a league for the recovery of the Valteline. 36 match from Spain] between Charles, Prince of Wales, and the Infanta of Spain. Prince Charles, impatient of diplomatic delays, had rushed off to Spain incognito, arriving on March 7, 1623, but the Pope continued to delay the dispensation. Finally the ardor of Prince Charles cooled and he sailed for England on September 18. The treaty for the marriage, which had always been unpopular in England, was then dropped. Jonson's phrase, 'My prince's safety,' indicates that the poem was written while Prince Charles was in Spain; and a reference in line 48 (see note below) shows that it could not have been written earlier than June. 40] Frederick, Elector Palatine, who had married the Princess Elizabeth (daughter of James I), had been elected King of Bohemia, but had been driven out of Bohemia and the Palatinate by the Catholic powers, headed by Spain. Many Englishmen wished to join in the war to restore him to his rights. 44 Brunsfield] Perhaps Jonson shows his lack of interest in political affairs by writing Brunsfield for Brunswick. Evidently he means to refer to Christian of Brunswick, the cousin and avowed champion of the Princess Elizabeth, now the exiled Queen of Bohemia. Mansfield] Ernest, Count of Mansfeld, in command of the army of Frederick, Elector Palatine and King of Bohemia. 48 late mystery of reception] plans being made early in June, 1623, for the reception of Prince Charles on his expected return from Spain with the Infanta as bride. Inigo Jones, with whom Jonson had earlier devised court masks but with whom he was now at odds, and Edward Alleyn, a celebrated actor, were called in to arrange the projected entertainments and masks. Evidently Jonson felt slighted that he was replaced by Alleyn and doubtless attributed it to the inimical influence of Inigo Jones. 50 guides the motions and directs the bears] Herford and Simpson (i. 90) interpret this as a reference to Inigo Jones. but Jonson must have had in mind Edward Alleyn, who was interested in bear-baiting and had from 1594 been part owner of the Bear Garden, sometimes called Paris Garden. From 1604 he was Master of the Game of Paris Garden. This identification is made more certain by a letter of June 5, 1623 (Birch, ii. 403), recounting the preparations to receive Prince Charles,

from which we learn that 'Alleyn, sometime a player, now squire of the bears, Inigo Jones, surveyor of the king's works, rode hence on Tuesday towards Winchester and Southampton, to take order for his majesty's entertainment.' 52-53] Jonson is thinking of his masks, usually produced at court during the Christmas season. 65-70] Jonson continues to draw his figures from the production of masks, and to express scorn for the flimsy, temporary scenery with which Inigo Jones decked them out.

511-513 *To . . . Shakespeare* 19-21] see Basse's *Elegy on Shakespeare*, p. 631. 35 him of Cordova dead] Seneca.

513 *Ben Jonson's Sociable Rules . . .*] On June 19, 1624, John Chamberlain wrote to Sir Dudley Carleton: 'I send here certain *leges conviviales* of Ben Jonson for a fair room or chamber, lately built at the Tavern or Sign of the Devil and St. Dunstan by Temple Bar.' The rules were engraved in Latin over the fireplace of the Apollo Room. Brome's translation is the earliest. 24 without reflection] extemporaneous.

514 *Slow, slow, fresh fount* 4 division] a rapid passage of musical notes.

514 *Queen and huntress* 1 Queen and huntress] Diana; intended as a compliment to Queen Elizabeth.

516 *Swell me a bowl* 2 Lyæus] Bacchus.

517 *Had those that dwell in error foul*] set to music by Alfonso Ferrabosco in his *Airs*, 1609. 2] marginal note: 'There hath been such a profane paradox published.' 6 world's soul, true harmony] marginal note: 'The Platonic opinion. See also Mac[robius], lib. 1 and 2, Som[nium] Scip[ionis].'

517 *Beauties, have ye seen*] set to music by Henry Lawes in *Airs and Dialogues*, 1655. The source of this poem is the first idyl of Moschus, usually called *The runaway Cupid*. Jonson's mask, from which this poem is taken, is frequently called *The Hue and Cry after Cupid*.

519 *Though I am young*] set to music by Lanier in Playford's *Select Airs*, 1653. 6 heat] 1641 'heart'.

EPIGRAMS

THE EPIGRAM ('a short poem ending in a witty or ingenious turn of thought, to which the rest of the composition is intended to lead up,' *O.E.D.*) had been written in great numbers by John Heywood in the middle decades of the 16th century. But his homespun, thoroughly English poems in this kind (see pp. 11–12) were not immediately imitated. Turberville translated epigrams from the Greek Anthology and from the Latin poet Ausonius; Kendall gathered into *Flowers of Epigrams*, 1577, a great number of translations, mostly his own, from Greek and Latin epigrams, the latter including those by classical authors and by recent writers such as Sir Thomas More.

It was not until the influence of Martial plainly manifested itself that the epigram may be said to have come into its own. Surrey had translated one of Martial's epigrams (see p. 34); Kendall had translated more than one hundred and sixty of them; but Sir John Harington and Sir John Davies first successfully reproduced in English the true Martialian satire. Many of Harington's witty trifles were written between 1580 and 1590, and Davies did his best work in the early 1590's. After Davies had published (about 1595) there came a flood of epigram-books; the form seems to have been extremely popular for some twenty years. In the period from 1598 to 1620 there were printed more than fifty collections, aside from reprints and renewed editions. Usually to these collections were joined satires or other poems to fill out the measure of a volume. Seven of the books included in our number were in Latin, but written by English authors of the time. Besides being published in collections, epigrams were scattered about as space-fillers in many volumes; they were passed from hand to hand in manuscript, and from mouth to mouth wherever gallants met.

Jonson referred to his *Epigrams* (published with his *Works* in 1616, though licensed separately in 1612) as 'the ripest of my studies.' Donne and Browne each wrote a very few excellent poems in this kind; while Herrick included in his *Hesperides*, 1648, epigrams sufficient to have formed an excellent independent collection. A choice of the best English epigrams available was made by the editors of *Wit's Recreations*, 1640, who included, without naming their authors, 660 of these short poems (in later editions increased to 900) and a great many epitaphs, both serious and jocular. The influence of the epigram upon the madrigal may be seen in such a madrigal as *The silver swan* (p. 438).

While the satirical use of the epigram predominated, there are also many of them to be classified as moralistic, encomiastic, and sepulchral. The last-named type is equivalent to the epitaph; and even these were sometimes satirical. Often a humorous anecdote was versified (see Jonson's criticism of Harington's epigrams, p. 898). Practically all of the English epigrammatists of our period drew upon Martial, many of them by direct translation.

CROSS REFERENCES: For epigrams not printed in this section, see under: Sir Thomas More, John Heywood, Wyatt, Surrey, Minor Courtly Makers, Turberville, Elizabethan Miscellanies, Sir John Davies, Donne, Jonson, Davies of Hereford, Taylor, Bacon, Wotton, Drummond, Herrick, Crashaw, and Sherburne.

MODERN EDITIONS: Kendall's *Flowers of Epigrams*, Spenser Society, 1874; *Epigrams of Sir John Harington* (ed. by N. E. McClure), Philadelphia, 1926; Guilpin's *Skialetheia* (ed. by A. B. Grosart), Manchester, 1878; Bastard's *Poems* (ed. by A. B. Grosart), Manchester, 1880, and *Chrestoleros*, Spenser Society, 1888; Weever's *Epigrammes* (ed. by R. B. McKerrow), Stratford-upon-Avon, 1922; Rowlands's *Complete Works*, Hunterian Club, 1874–1880.

COMMENT: T. K. Whipple, *Martial and the English Epigram from Sir Thomas Wyatt to Ben Jonson*, Berkeley, 1925.

TEXT: *Flowers of Epigrams*, 1577 (14927), White; *The Most Elegant and Witty Epigrams*, 1618 (12776), Harvard; *Additional Ms.* 12049, B. M.; *Skialetheia*, 1598 (12504), White; *Chrestoleros*, 1598 (1559), White; *Epigrams in the Oldest Cut and Newest Fashion*, 1599 (25224), Bodleian; *The Letting of Humor's Blood*, 1600 (21393), B. M.; *Humor's Looking-Glass*, 1608 (21386), Huntington; *Chetham*

Ms. 8012, Chetham; *Reliquiæ Wottonianæ,* 1672, Cornell; *The Mouse-Trap,* 1606 (19334), B. M.; *Epigrams,* 1608 (19329), White; *Laquei Ridiculosi,* 1613 (19332), White; *The Mastive,* 1615 (19333), White; *Two Centuries of Epigrams,* 1610 (13018), White; *Rub and a Great Cast,* 1614 (11370), White; *Quodlibets,* 1628 (12974), B. M.; *Two Books of Epigrams and Epitaphs,* 1639 (1354), White.

520 *Flowers of Epigrams*] Aside from information which can be gleaned from this book, little or nothing is known of Kendall. He was educated at Eton and Magdalen Hall, Oxford, took no degree, and became a law-student at Staple Inn. *Flowers of Epigrams* is an anthology of translations, mostly by Kendall himself. He appended to the collection a section headed *Trifles,* purporting to be made up of his own poems, but depending heavily upon the *Nugæ,* 1533, of Nicolas Bourbon. Cf. J. Hutton, 'Timothy Kendall's "Trifles" and Nicolas Bourbon's *Nugæ,'* *M.L.N.* xliv. 19.

520 *To Sabidius*] from Martial, i. 32; see Weever's version, p. 525. The most familiar English version is, of course, that beginning 'I do not like thee, Dr. Fell'.

520 *To Fidentinus*] from Martial, i. 38.

520 *To a married couple . . .*] from Martial, viii. 35.

520 *Of Fuscus, a drunkard*] from a Latin epigram by Sir Thomas More.

521 *Of Alphus*] from a Latin epigram by Bishop John Parkhurst, whose *Ludicra sive Epigrammata Juvenilia* had appeared in 1573.

521 *To the reader*] Kendall's own apology, from his *Trifles,* but imitated from Martial.

521 *Elegant and Witty Epigrams*] Sir John Harington (*c.* 1561–1612), a charming and witty member of Queen Elizabeth's entourage, amused his sovereign (who was also his godmother) by his jests, but gained little lasting emolument from his association with her. Educated at Eton and at Cambridge, Harington was a competent Latin writer, with an unusual knowledge of general literature. His principal literary achievement was his translation of Ariosto's *Orlando Furioso,* 1591; the introduction and notes which he added are still of interest. His *Metamorphosis of Ajax,* a rather scurrilous book (with the serious purpose, however, of improving domestic sanitation) caused Harington's temporary banishment from court upon its appearance, without a printer's license, in 1596. The epigrams which he had been composing from his youth onward were not printed until after his death. Harington's virtues

as a writer are a certain cleverness in rhyming and an easy, jocose urbanity such as characterizes later masters of *vers de société.* See Sir Walter Raleigh's *Some Authors,* Oxford, 1923.

521 *Against writers . . .*] from Martial, ix. 81.

522 *To Mr. John Davies*] later Sir John Davies.

523 *Skialetheia*] published anonymously with the sub-title, *A Shadow of Truth in Certain Epigrams and Satires.* Lines quoted from this book in *England's Parnassus,* 1600, are assigned to Guilpin, who may also be the E. G. whom Marston addresses as his 'very friend' in the second edition of *The Scourge of Villainy,* and the E. G. to whom Donne addresses a short verse-letter. That Everard (sometimes called Edward) Guilpin was a Cambridge man can be established both from the internal evidence of *Skialetheia* and from the records of the University. He seems to have been influenced by Davies in his epigrams and by Marston and Donne in his satires. A genuine love of letters appears to inspire the passage about books in *Satyra quinta.*

523 *Of Cornelius* 5 cudgeled] heavily trimmed. 6 slop] a pair of loose breeches. 8 cad's-beard] caddis-beard; 'caddis' was a common word for cotton wool. 13 Bevis] a hero of romances.

523–524 *Satyra quinta*] 'Fifth satire.' 26 Fitzherbert . . . Dyer] the standard writers on English law. 28–29 Rose, Curtain] two of the London playhouses. 30 pathetic Spaniard's] Seneca's.

524 *Chrestoleros*] Thomas Bastard (1566–1618) was an unfortunate country preacher, whose early promise and genial spirits were blighted by poverty and ill-fortune. In 1598 he published an extensive collection of original epigrams under the title *Chrestoleros.* The book and its author were made the butt of many jokes by rival wits; but they were defended by Harington and Heath (see p. 530).

525 *Epigrams . . .*] John Weever (1576–1632), after devoting some early years to poetry, became an antiquary and made an exhaustive study of the tombs of England. When he was twenty-three, at the end of four years spent at Cambridge, he published this volume of epigrams, which reflected wide reading both in older and in contemporary authors. He followed it with the satirical poem *Faunus and Melliflora,* 1600, and a more serious work in verse, *The Mirror of Martyrs,* 1601. In at least the first and third of these volumes Weever reveals his high regard for the works of Shakespeare by praising them outright and by echoing them in several passages. His tributes in the *Epigrams* to Spenser, Drayton, Marston, Jonson, Warner, and Daniel are fairly discerning.

525 *Translat. ex Martial*] From Martial, i. 32; see Kendall's version, p. 520.

526 *In tumulum Abrahami Simple*] 'On the tomb of Abraham Simple.'

526 *Ad Gulielmum Shakespeare*] the earliest poetic address to Shakespeare; it is the only one of Weever's epigrams in sonnet-form. **13** They] the thousands of readers mentioned in the previous line.

526 *Letting of Humor's Blood*] 'in the Head Vein' completes the title in 1600. Samuel Rowlands (*c.* 1570–*c.* 1630) was a satirist and pamphleteer who 'pestered the press' almost continuously from 1598 to 1628. In 1600 copies of his books were ordered to be burned.

527 *An epitaph on a bellows-maker*] This and the three epigrams following are by 'the facetious John Hoskins' (1566–1638), a clever lawyer who made a considerable reputation as a wit. After completing studies for the M.A. at Oxford in 1592, he taught school and began to compile a Greek lexicon, which he abandoned at the letter M. He entered the Middle Temple for training in law. After his admission to the bar he was several times in Parliament, and in 1614 he was imprisoned for making, in the House of Commons, satirical reference to the new Scottish favorites. He was a literary associate of Sir John Davies, Donne, Daniel, and others. According to Wood, Hoskins left 'a book of poems neatly written, bigger than those of Dr. Donne, which were lent by his son Sir Benedict . . . to a certain person in 1653, but he could never retrieve it.' For a poem possibly by Hoskins, see pp. 203–204. The present epitaph is signed in the manuscript, 'Mr. Hoskynes', and the two following are signed 'per eundem'.

528 *John Hoskins to his little child . . .*] His son's name is elsewhere given as Bennet or Benedict.

528 *Mouse-Trap*] Henry Parrot (*fl.* 1606–1626) left no records of his life outside the half-dozen of books which are attributed to him. He seems to have been a man of some education, perhaps a member of one of the Inns of Court. *The Mastive* contains satires as well as epigrams, and *VIII Cures for the Itch,* 1626, contains epitaphs and characters. Otherwise the books are made up entirely of epigrams, some of which, however. are not Parrot's own. His books throw considerable light on life in London as it was lived among pleasure-seekers and gallants.

528 *Paulus a pamphlet*] The incident here retold was recorded of Sir Thomas More in Harington's introduction to his translation of *Orlando Furioso,* 1591.

529 *Magus would needs* 4 *The Fox*] Jonson's *Volpone, or The Fox,* printed in 1607; this reference shows it to have been on the stage in 1606.

529 *Ortus novus urbe Britannus*] 'The new Englishman sprung up in the city.' This epigram exemplifies satire commonly directed against actors.

529 *Impar impares odit*] 'The inferior hates inferiors.'

529 *Suum cuique pulchrum*] 'To each his own is beautiful.'

529 *Nuptiæ post nummos*] 'Money, then marriage.'

530 *Ebrius dissimulans*] 'The sly sot.'

530 *Two Centuries . . .*] John Heath (*fl.* 1615), an M.A. of Oxford, is known chiefly for this book. He also translated several books from French and from Spanish, and contributed verses to memorial volumes. According to Drummond's record, Jonson classed Heath's epigrams with the works of Taylor, the water poet, as popular trash.

530 *Ad modernos epigrammatistas*] 'To modern epigrammatists.' 1 Heywood] John Heywood; see p. 11.

530 *Ad Tho. Bastardum epigrammatistam*] 'To Thomas Bastard, epigrammatist.' See p. 524.

530 *In Beatricem præpropere defunctam*] 'Upon Beatrice, too early deceased.'

531 *Ad Collegium Wintoniensem*] 'To Winchester College.'

531 *Rub and a Great Cast*] Thomas Freeman (*fl.* 1614) took the degree of B.A. at Oxford in 1611 and then went to London to try his fortune as poet. His sole publication seems to have been his volume of epigrams published in 1614 in two parts, the first entitled *Rub and a Great Cast,* and the second, *Run and a Great Cast.* These titles are taken from the sport of bowling. The book deserves reprinting.

531 *Me quoque vatem*] 'I, too, am a poet.'

531 *In epitaphium . . .*] 'On an epitaph stupidly written.'

533 *Quodlibets*] Robert Hayman as colonial governor of Harbor-Grace in Newfoundland amused himself by preparing an extensive collection of epigrams, original and translated. This he published upon his return to England, with the title *Quodlibets*. When he had gone to Newfoundland, in 1620, the popular demand for epigrams was still strong, though beginning to wane; by the time *Quodlibets* appeared, in 1628, a book of this kind was out of fashion.

533 *To one of the elders . . .*] addressed to a member of the Puritan sect.

533 *Two Books of Epigrams and Epitaphs*] Thomas Bancroft (*fl.* 1633–1658) was a poet of some pretensions in his day. In addition to the present volume, he published *The Glutton's Fever,* 1633, and *The Heroical Lover,* 1658. Sir Aston Cockain and James Shirley were his literary friends.

JOHN DAVIES OF HEREFORD

JOHN DAVIES (*c.* 1565–1618), usually designated 'of Hereford' in distinction from Sir John Davies, was a prolific writer of religious, moralistic, and occasional poetry, of which little claims the attention of posterity. By profession he was an expert penman and writing-master. He is notable for his acquaintance with the greatest writers of the time, to whom he addresses laudatory epigrams in a familiar tone. Every kind of poetry except dramatic was attempted by Davies.

MODERN EDITION: *The Complete Works* (ed. by A. B. Grosart), two volumes, Chertsey Worthies' Library, 1878.

TEXT: *The Holy Rood,* 1609 (6330), B. M.; *Wit's Pilgrimage,* [1605?] (6344), White; *The Scourge of Folly,* [*c.* 1611] (6341), White; poems from *Wit's Bedlam,* 1617, transcribed in White's copy of Parrot's *Epigrams,* 1608.

535–536 *Of Fumosus 4 ounce . . . crown*] Tobacco was expensive at the time this was written; for some varieties the buyer put a silver coin in one side of the scales and received the amount of tobacco which balanced it.

536 *Wit's Bedlam*] No copy of this book was available to Grosart. A copy was among the books of Mr. J. L. Clawson, sold in 1926. The two epigrams here printed are from ms. copies of twenty-five epigrams from *Wit's Bedlam,* written on extra pages bound with White's copy of Parrot's *Epigrams.*

536 *Of Maurus 2 hunt's-up*] see p. 978.

536 *Of the small respect . . . 6 either kind*] either in poetry or in history.

JOHN TAYLOR

JOHN TAYLOR (1580–1653), 'the water poet,' worked for about fourteen years as collector of wine-duties from ships on the Thames, and for some time as a sculler on the same river. He was an eccentric, and engaged in several journeys upon wagers; he once, with a companion, made a voyage on the Thames in a boat of brown paper, using stock-fish tied to canes as oars. From 1612 on he kept himself before the public as a pamphleteer, writing numberless works in verse and prose. In several pamphlets he laments the sad lot of watermen, whose carrying trade had been hurt by the increased use of coaches, those 'hired hackney-hell carts.' Taylor's title-pages reflect his exuberant and humorous spirit: *A Kicksey-Winsey, or a Lerry Come-Twang, A Very Merry Wherry-Ferry Voyage, The Virtue of a Jail, and Necessity of Hanging.* His works are a mine of information respecting life among London tradesmen and artisans.

MODERN EDITIONS: *Works . . . of 1630,* Spenser Society, 1869; *Works not included in the Folio Volume of 1630,* Spenser Society, 1870; *Works* (ed. by C. Hindley), London, 1872.

COMMENT: Robert Southey, 'Lives and Works of our Uneducated Poets,' in *Attempts in Verse by John Jones,* London, 1831.

TEXT: *The Sculler,* 1612 (23791), White; *All the Works,* 1630 (23725), Cornell.

536–537 *Epigram*] Jokes upon the Welshman and his cheese appear frequently in the literature of the time.

537 *A few lines to small purpose . . .*] The first half of the poem is here reprinted.

FRANCIS BEAUMONT

FRANCIS BEAUMONT (1584–1616), best known as a dramatist, is also the author of a few non-dramatic poems. He early published *Salmacis and Hermaphroditus,* 1602, a mythological poem of the type made popular by *Hero and Leander* and *Venus and Adonis.* His other poems were not collected until 1640, followed by two editions greatly enlarged in 1653. These volumes, appearing so long after his death, were in reality miscellanies, containing many poems other than his. Of the two here printed, the verse-letter to Jonson is certainly Beaumont's, appearing also in the folio editions of Beaumont and Fletcher's plays, and there is no evident reason for assigning the other poem, *Flattering hope,* to anyone else. Another poem, *On the tombs in Westminster,* included in Beaumont's volume but which is almost certainly not his, is a shortened form of *A memento for mortality* (p. 875; see note). For the lyrics from Beaumont's plays, see pp. 394–395.

MODERN EDITIONS: *The Works of Beaumont and Fletcher* (ed. by A. Dyce), Vol. xi, London, 1846; C. E. Norton, 'Francis Beaumont's letter to Ben Jonson,' in *Harvard Studies and Notes in Philology and Literature,* v. 19.

COMMENT: C. M. Gayley, *Beaumont, the Dramatist,* New York, 1914.

TEXT: *Norton Ms.* 4503, Harvard; *Poems,* 1640 (1665), Harvard.

539–540 *Mr. Francis Beaumont's letter to Ben Jonson*] no title in ms.; title supplied from *Poems,* 1653, which continues: *written before he and Mr. Fletcher came to London, with two of the precedent comedies then not finished, which deferred their merry meetings at the Mermaid.* An extract from another recently discovered verse-letter by Beaumont to Jonson was printed in *T.L.S.,* Sept. 15, 1921, p. 596. 13–14] omitted in 1653, possibly because Puritans were then in power. 17 Sutcliffe's wit] Dr. Matthew Sutcliffe published five pamphlets of theological controversy in 1606. He was described by Fuller as 'a known rigid anti-remonstrant, and when old, very morose and testy in his writings against them.' 20 Robert Wis-dom] said to have contributed the version of one psalm to the popular translation of the *Psalms* by Hopkins and Sternhold. The first complete edition was *The Whole Book of Psalms,* 1562. 35 painted] 1653; ms. 'fainted'. 43 rest] an extended exchange of strokes; a rally. 71 growing souls] vegetable souls only, not the rational soul of man. 80] 1653 adds two final lines, not in the ms.:

Ben, when these scenes are perfect, we'll taste wine; I'll drink thy muse's health, thou shalt quaff mine.

540–541 *Flattering hope* 25 prevent day's eying] forestall daybreak.

THOMAS HEYWOOD

THOMAS HEYWOOD (died *c.* 1650), dramatist and miscellaneous writer, appears to have been a Cambridge man, though records of his residence at the University are lacking. He began writing for the stage about 1595, and was a member in turn of several important companies of players. According to his own statement he had, by 1633, written or collaborated upon two hundred and twenty plays. In addition to his work for the theaters he wrote masks and Lord Mayor's pageants. His non-dramatic work comprises about a dozen published volumes, some in poetry and some in prose, including a number of translations and compilations. *Troia Britannica*, 1609, is an heroic historical poem; *The Hierarchy of the Blessed Angels*, 1635, is a didactic work, largely in verse, including many translated passages; *Pleasant Dialogues and Dramas*, 1637, is a miscellany of translations, largely from Neo-Latin sources. Except for this last, Heywood's non-dramatic writings have not been reprinted. He read widely, and loaded his works with references to writings in Latin and Greek. He twice refers to a manuscript volume he had written, *The Lives of All the Poets, Foreign and Modern*, but this is not extant.

MODERN EDITION: *Pleasant Dialogues and Dramma's* (ed. by W. Bang), Louvain, 1903.

TEXT: *An Apology for Actors*, 1612 (13309), White; *The Silver Age*, 1613 (13365), White; *The Rape of Lucrece*, 1630 (13362), Huntington; *A Maidenhead Well Lost*, 1634 (13357), Harvard; *The Hierarchy of the Blessed Angels*, 1635 (13327), Cornell.

541–542 *The author to his book*] a prefatory address; the book is in prose. 1–2] marginal note: 'So compared by the Fathers.' 29–30] marginal note: 'No theater, no world.'

543 *The Rape of Lucrece*] These two songs first appeared in the edition of 1630, though the play had been printed in 1608, 1609, and 1614.

543 *Pack, clouds, away*] appeared in the author's *Pleasant Dialogues and Dramas*, 1637, as part of an epithalamium. J. R. Moore ('Thomas Heywood's "Pack clouds away" and *The Rape of Lucrece*,' *S.P.* xxv. 171) shows that probably the poem was first written for a wedding and then inserted into the play.

554–555 *Our modern poets*] For the poets mentioned, except Shakespeare, see Index. 26 Castaly] Castalia, a fountain on Parnassus.

JAMES I

JAMES I (1566–1625) was educated by that severe tutor and scholar, George Buchanan. James's note, written in the margin of one of his Latin books, 'They would have me learn Latin before I can speak Scots,' shows that he chafed under the discipline. His love for poetry was stimulated by the Scotch poet, Alexander Montgomery, who was a member of his household. Perhaps this led to his publication in 1584 of *Essays of a Prentice in the divine art of Poesy*, to which was affixed his critical treatise 'containing some reulis and cautelis to be observit and eschewit in Scottis poesie.' In his critical principles, James is obviously indebted to Gascoigne's *Notes of Instruction*, 1575. His kingly point of view is shown in his advice to poets to avoid matters of state in their writing. As in his political principles, he is a dogmatist urging metrical propriety and definite, positive rules in technique. In 1591 he again published some of his verse, in *Poetical Exercises at vacant hours*. He seems to have written little poetry after his accession to the English throne in 1603. The English poets hailed with enthusiasm the royal poet, for they expected generous patronage, but James proved to be more interested in theological controversy, and the only English poet whom he seems personally to have aided was Ben Jonson. If James exercised any influence, as poet and critic, on the course of English poetry, it was in the direction of smoothness and formal accuracy. See Sir John Beaumont's poem, p. 547.

MODERN EDITIONS: *The Essays of a Prentice* (ed. by E. Arber), London, 1869; *A Royal Rhetorician* (ed. by R. S. Rait), Westminster, 1900; *Lusus Regius* (ed. by R. S. Rait), Westminster, 1901; *New Poems by James I* (ed. by A. F. Westcott), New York, 1911.

TEXT: *Additional Ms.* 24195, B. M.;

545 *Song*] according to the heading in the *Calderwood Ms.*, written when James was fifteen.

546 *An epitaph on Sir Philip Sidney* 7 mell] mix.

Basilikon Doron, 1599 (14348), B. M.

546 *A sonnet . . . 9* spill] destroy, waste.

547 *Basilikon Doron*] written to advise his son, Prince Henry, in matters of statecraft.

SIR JOHN BEAUMONT

SIR JOHN BEAUMONT (1583–1627), the elder brother of Francis Beaumont, published in 1602 *The Metamorphosis of Tobacco,* a mock-heroic poem dedicated to Drayton. His other poems were collected and published two years after his death by his son. The longest, *Bosworth Field,* is an historical poem in heroic couplets which, with the poem of criticism here reprinted, gives Beaumont an important place in the history of the development of the couplet in the 17th century.

MODERN EDITIONS: *The Poems* (ed. by A. B. Grosart), Fuller Worthies' Library, 1869; *The Theatre of Apollo* (ed. by W. W. Greg), London, 1926.

TEXT: *Bosworth Field,* 1629 (1694), Harvard.

547–549 *To his late Majesty . . .*] James I had published *Ane Schort Treatise* in 1584, which Beaumont refers to in l. 10, and his poem echoes its opinions. 47 fettered staves] stanzas; Beaumont is arguing for couplets. 64

freezing air] Milton also held the idea that perhaps the cold climate of England was not suited to literary production; cf. *Paradise Lost,* ix. 44–5: 'or cold Climate . . . damp my intended wing.'

FRANCIS BACON, VISCOUNT ST. ALBANS

FRANCIS BACON, Lord Verulam and Viscount St. Albans (1561–1626), gave small attention to the composition of poetry; perhaps, in view of his multifarious activities, the wonder is that he wrote any verse. All his extant remains in this kind consist of translations. It is interesting to find that after his fall from power he published, under his own name, a volume of verse-translations from the *Psalms,* written during his illness of 1624 and dedicated to George Herbert. A version of Horace's *Integer vitæ,* beginning 'The man of life upright,' though attributed to Bacon in some manuscripts, is probably Campion's (see p. 448).

MODERN EDITION: *Translations of Certain Psalms* in *The Works* (ed. by J. Spedding, R. L. Ellis, and D. D. Heath), Vol. vii, London, 1870.

TEXT: *The Translation of Certain Psalms,* 1625 (1174), White; Thomas Farnaby, *Florilegium Epigrammatum Græcorum,* 1629 (10701), Huntington.

549 *In vitam humanam*] 'Upon human life.' A Latin sub-title in 1629 ascribes this poem to Bacon and calls it a *parodia,* or imitation, of the Greek epigram by Posidippus with which it appears. It is the only English poem in Farnaby's volume. The same epigram had been translated by Grimald and others (see p. 50, and note). Professor Grierson (*M. L. R.,* vi. 145) found in a 17th-century manuscript a similar paraphrase of the complementary epigram by Metrodorus. Grierson considers that these English poems form part of a poetical debate upon the city against the country, participated in (about 1599) by Wotton, Donne, and Bacon. Thomas Bastard, who wrote an epigram upon the subject, addressed to Wotton, may have been a party to the debate. The present poem was reprinted in *Reliquiæ Wottonianæ,* 1651 and later editions, and in *Merry Drollery,* 1661.

SIR HENRY WOTTON

SIR HENRY WOTTON (1568–1639), from college days a friend of Donne, spent a large part of his life abroad, either in private travel or in diplomatic service. For a long period he was Ambassador to Venice. He was author of the famous paradox, 'An ambassador is an honest man sent to lie abroad for the good of his country,' which lost him for a time the favor of King James. From 1624 Wotton was provost of Eton. Among the friends of his later years was Izaak Walton, who first turned to the writing of biography through a desire to carry to completion a life of Donne which Wotton had commenced but did not live to finish. Wotton evidently began writing poetry in the 1590's, but most of his work awaited publication until 1651, when it was included in *Reliquiæ Wottonianæ*, a collection several times augmented before 1700.

MODERN EDITION: *The Poems of Sir Walter Raleigh . . . with those of Sir Henry Wotton and other Courtly Poets* (ed. by J. Hannah), London, 1875.

COMMENT: L. Pearsall Smith, *The Life and Letters of Sir Henry Wotton*, two volumes, Oxford, 1907.

TEXT: *A Poetical Rhapsody*, 1602 (6373), White; *Rawlinson Poetry Ms.* 212, Bodleian; *Reliquiæ Wottonianæ*, 1651, Cornell.

551 *The character of a happy life*] no title in ms.; title from 1651. Some of the changes made when the poem was printed in 1651 are interesting, as reflecting the taste of the period of the Commonwealth. 8 princes' grace] 1651 'public fame'. vulgar] 1651 'private'. 13–16] This stanza is at the end of the poem in the ms.; we follow order of 1651. 16 accusers] 1651 'oppressors'. 20 well-chosen] 1651 'religious'.

551–552 *On his mistress . . .*] one of the very popular poems of the early 17th century. It was first printed, set to music, in East's *Sixth Set of Books*, 1624. It was reprinted or paraphrased in many miscellanies and mss., often with variant debased readings and additional stanzas by other hands than Wotton's. See *T. L. S.* corr., Sept. 4, Sept. 25, Oct. 9, Oct. 30, 1924. 'The Queen of Bohemia' was Elizabeth (1596–1662), daughter of King James, who married Frederic V, Elector Palatine, in 1613; Frederic was in 1619 made King of Bohemia, but was quickly driven out by Spanish and Austrian forces. 5 sun] 1624 'moon'.

552 *Upon the sudden restraint . . .*] Robert Ker, or Carr, Earl of Somerset (d. 1645), was a favorite of James's. In 1615 he was found guilty of complicity in the poisoning of Sir Thomas Overbury, who had opposed Somerset's marriage with Lady Essex. Although both Somerset and his wife were condemned to death, neither suffered execution, but they were kept in the Tower for about seven years.

552 *A description of the spring*] composed, according to Walton, 'when he [Wotton] was beyond seventy years of age . . . as he sat quietly on a summer's evening on a bank a-fishing.'

553 *A hymn to my God* 7 grains] 'hallowed grains' were beads of the rosary; 'grains' alone sometimes meant incense.

553 *Upon the death . . .*] Sir Albertus Morton was nephew to Wotton, and his secretary at Venice. Morton died in 1625 after having been married about a year; his wife died in 1627. For a poem by Morton, see pp. 443–444.

EDWARD, LORD HERBERT OF CHERBURY

EDWARD, LORD HERBERT of Cherbury (1583–1648), married while still a student at University College, Oxford. He was highly flattered when upon his presentation at court Queen Elizabeth, 'swearing again her ordinary oath,' said, 'It is a pity he was married so young'; and he recounts as a further mark of her favor that she 'gave her hand to kiss twice, both times gently clapping me on the cheek.' He spent much time abroad, always in search of adventure, and came to be a famous duellist. He has left a vainglorious account of his adventures in his autobiography. He was, however, also a serious philosopher and wrote an able investigation of the nature of truth, *De Veritate*. It is interesting to note, since he was a brother of George Herbert, that he argued for a rational religion and distrusted the priesthood, which he thought attempted to establish its influence by upholding the claim of divine revelation. His poetry circulated only in manuscript until after his death. At times he is skillful in the metaphysical vein, though now and again he gets so entangled in its complexity that even Donne, speaking of his epitaph on Prince Henry, said that he wrote it 'to match Sir Ed. Herbert in obscureness.'

MODERN EDITIONS: *The Poems* (ed. by G. C. Moore Smith), Oxford, 1923; *The Poems* (ed. by J. Churton Collins), London, 1881; *The Autobiography* (ed. by S. Lee), London, 1886.

TEXT: *Occasional Verses*, 1665, Harvard.

554 *Elegy over a tomb*] In the original edition of 1665 this poem is dated 1617.

555–558 *An ode . . .*] an early use of the stanza of Tennyson's *In Memoriam*. 14 concent] playing or singing together in harmony. 19 Melander] a name which Herbert uses elsewhere for himself. 44 faith] 1665 'love', but corrected to 'faith' in errata. 50 doubt] fear. 85 But is 't not true] 'But it is not true'.

SIR ROBERT AYTOUN

SIR ROBERT AYTOUN (1570–1638) was one of the many Scotchmen who saw their opportunity in England when James VI of Scotland became James I of England. He had been graduated from the University of St. Andrews in 1588, and from 1590 had lived on the Continent, where he gained some reputation for Greek, Latin, and French verses. King James welcomed such a learned countryman with preferment at court. He was private secretary to Queen Anne, and later to Henrietta Maria, a position which he must have filled ably if we may judge from the courtly ease and grace of his poetry. He was the intimate friend of Ben Jonson and of Hobbes. Aubrey reports that 'Mr. John Dryden says he has seen verses of his, some of the best of that age,' a judgment which we can understand from the smoothness of Aytoun's poetry. He is thought by some to be the author of the original version of *Auld Lang Syne*, but the poem is not included in any of his manuscripts. The bulk of his English poetry was not printed in the 17th century, but survives in a manuscript carefully written by his nephew, Sir John Aytoun.

MODERN EDITIONS: *Poems* (ed. by C. Rogers), London, 1871, also included in the *Tr. Roy. Hist. Soc.*, Vol. i.

TEXT: *Additional Ms.* 10308, B. M.; Playford, *Select Airs and Dialogues*, 1659, New York.

558–559 *Courteous Reader 6 Delitiæ Poetarum Scotorum*] edited by Arthur Johnston and published at Amsterdam in 1637. 14 S. J. A.] Sir John Aytoun, Sir Robert's nephew.

561–562 *The forsaken mistress*] not included in the mss. of Aytoun's poetry; usually, though doubtfully, ascribed to him. 21 Like fair] the reading of Rogers's edition; 1659 'With fear'.

SIR WILLIAM ALEXANDER, EARL OF STIRLING

SIR WILLIAM ALEXANDER, Earl of Stirling (*c.* 1567–1640), came to England as one of 'the invading hosts of Scots' following upon the accession of

James. In Scotland he had been tutor to Prince Henry, and he continued that office in England. His friendship with Drummond (who refers to him poetically as 'Alexis') seems to date from 1613 or 1614 when that poet visited Alexander at Menstry, the seat of the Stirling manor house. Alexander wrote voluminously, among his productions in verse being *Dooms-day*, 1614, an epic poem in twelve books totalling eleven thousand lines. He lacked skill and smoothness in versification and, more than Drummond, loaded his poetry with a weight of Scotticisms.

MODERN EDITION: *The Poetical Works* (ed. by L. E. Kastner and H. B. Charlton), Vol. i, Edinburgh and London, 1921; *The Poetical Works* (ed. by R. Alison), three volumes, Glasgow, 1870–1872.

TEXT: *Aurora*, 1604 (337), White, Huntington.

562 *Madrigal* 7 pined] longed for. | child,' Love; but lines 14 and 15 refer
563–564 *Love resolved* 13–15] The | to Love. 19 dainty goddess] Venus.
construction is confusing; Hymen is the | 28 Thunderer's sister] Juno, sister as
god that tames 'the gods' old-witted | well as wife of Jove.

WILLIAM DRUMMOND OF HAWTHORNDEN

WILLIAM DRUMMOND (1585–1649), second 'laird' of Hawthornden, an estate near Edinburgh, was intended by his father for the profession of law. He took the degree of M.A. at the University of Edinburgh in 1605 and then went to France to engage in professional studies. His own bent toward literature led him, at the time of his father's death in 1610, to abandon legal pursuits, and for the rest of his life Drummond was content to remain in comparative retirement as a gentleman of letters. At the age of twenty-six he had collected a library containing two hundred and fifty works in Latin, one hundred and twenty in French, sixty-one in Italian, fifty in English, eleven in Hebrew, and eight in Spanish. He gave an excellent collection of five hundred volumes to the University of Edinburgh. Among his friends were Alexander, Drayton, and Jonson, who visited at Hawthornden in 1619. Drummond's later years were saddened by the religious and political conflicts which racked both England and Scotland. He was a staunch Royalist, and his own death is supposed to have been hastened by news of the execution of Charles I.

Drummond was a graceful translator and imitator, depending upon French and Italian originals for a large share of his sonnets and madrigals. He was most at home in the literature of sixteenth-century France, with Ronsard, Passerat, Desportes, and de Tyard as his favorite poets. He also borrowed from Neo-Latin writers, and in some isolated passages from earlier English poets. He achieved notable grace and smoothness in his verse, and struck off many passages of more than ordinary beauty. In his *Song*, 'Phœbus, arise,' we seem to have a foretaste of the early poems of Milton. The epitaph which Drummond composed for himself (see *To S. W. A.*, p. 573) suggests his poetic character.

MODERN EDITIONS: *The Poetical Works* (ed. by L. E. Kastner), two volumes, Manchester, 1913; *The Poems* (ed. by W. C. Ward), Muses' Library, London, n. d. COMMENT: D. Masson, *Drummond of Hawthornden*, London, 1873.

TEXT: *Poems*, 1616 (7255), White; *Flowers of Sion*, 1623 (7247), B. M.; *Flowers of Sion*, 1630 (7250), B. M.; *Poems*, 1656, Harvard; *Works*, 1711, Cornell.

564 *I know that all* 10 oft] 1616 | Grecian] Plato. 8] 'Not harassed with
'of,' but Kastner notes that in some | anything irrational.'
exemplars 't' has been added in ink. | 565–566 *That I so slenderly* 6 Ao-
564–565 *That learned Grecian* 1 | nian] Aonia, a part of Boetia, was the

location of Mount Helicon and the fountain Aganippe, haunted by the Muses. 9 Venus' tree] the myrtle.

566 *Sound hoarse, sad lute* 8 consort] concert, harmony.

566–567 *Song* 4 Memnon's mother] Aurora. Tithon's] Tithonus, a mortal who had been vouchsafed immortality, was the husband of Aurora. 11 decore] decorate. 26–27] The reference is to Daphne, whom Apollo met by the stream of the river-god Peneus, her father.

567 *Alexis, here she stayed* 4 Colchian] Colchis, a province east of the Black Sea, was the fabled land of the Golden Fleece, and actually one of rich gold mines.

568 *My lute, be as* 4 ramage] a general term for songs or cries of birds.

570–571 *The statue of Venus sleeping*] amplified from a four-line epigram by Tabourot, published in his *Les Touches,* 1585. Drummond had earlier

published a closer version of the epigram (Kastner, ii. 154).

571 *To Chloris* 7 Deucalion's days] Deucalion, the son of Prometheus, by means of a wooden chest saved himself and his wife Pyrrha from a flood sent by Zeus.

573 *To S. W. A.*] To Sir William Alexander. *A Cypress Grove,* a prose elegy, was published with the *Flowers,* 1623.

573 *More oft than once*] The opening line seems to refer to the serious illnesses mentioned in the sonnet above.

574 *No more with candied words*] from 'Five sonnets of Galatea.' 8 be] 1711; 1656 'he'.

574 *When lately Pym descended*] This vigorous epigram reflects Drummond's detestation of the Parliament men who caused the overthrow of Charles I. John Pym (1584–1643) was a leader of the Puritan party. 4 Lower House] a usual term for the House of Commons.

WILLIAM BROWNE

WILLIAM BROWNE (*c.* 1591–1643?) was born at Tavistock in Devonshire and much of his poetry is inspired by his love for the beauty of the River Tavy and its valley. He was in residence at Oxford, possibly at Exeter College, but left without taking a degree to enter Clifford's Inn, from which he transferred to the Inner Temple. Like many young legal students of that time he was more interested in poetry than in his studies, and found his friends among poets and aspirants to poetry. With Christopher Brooke he published *Two Elegies,* 1613, on the death of Prince Henry. In the same year appeared the first book of his *Britannia's Pastorals,* to which he added a second book in 1616. A third book remained in manuscript until printed in 1852. He also contributed to a collection of eclogues, *The Shepherd's Pipe,* 1614, which contains poems by his friends Wither, Brooke, and Davies of Hereford. In 1624 he returned to Oxford, this time certainly to Exeter College, as tutor to Robert Dormer, later Earl of Carnarvon. During the year he was granted his M.A. His capacity for friendship and enthusiasm for poetry made him many friends among the younger members of the college, who contributed a number of commendatory poems to his manuscript third book of *Britannia's Pastorals.* Browne married, possibly for a second time (see note to *In obitum M. S.,* below), in 1628. For a while he was in the service of the Herberts at Wilton.

Browne was one of the poets who continued writing in the Spenserian manner in the second and third decades of the 17th century. The freshness of his scenes and his musical, limpid lines make his pastorals a delightful field for browsing, but his lack of constructive power leaves the reader who wishes to follow the story lost in a haze. Most of his poetry was written early in life: his productivity diminished after 1616, and seems almost to have stopped after 1628. Perhaps he felt that the Jacobeans and Carolines were out of sympathy with the Spenserian pastoral and that the day belonged to the young 'metaphysicals' and 'sons of Ben.'

MODERN EDITIONS: *The Works* (ed. by W. C. Hazlitt), two volumes, London, 1868; *Poems* (ed. by G. Goodwin), two volumes, Muses' Library, London, n.d.

COMMENT: F. W. Moorman, *William Browne*, Strassburg, 1897.

TEXT: *Britannia's Pastorals*, 1616 (3915), Harvard; *Lansdowne Ms.* 777, B. M.

574 *Britannia's Pastorals*] The first two books consist of five songs, or cantos, each. Browne starts out to write of the loves of the shepherdess Marina, but the numerous digressions interrupt the story so frequently that it is really of very little consequence to the poem.

575–581 *Song 3* 1 the golden age] Moorman (p. 59) thinks this passage 'expresses more or less [Browne's] conception of an ideal life'; it is plainly based on Don Quixote's speech to the goatherds (Bk. ii, ch. iii) as translated by Shelton, 1612. 22 Arachne's] a Lydian maiden, who excelled in the art of weaving. 32 madder-pits] madder is a dye. 34 woad] herb of the mustard family, from whose leaves a blue dye was obtained. 52 cerite's] a rare mineral. 58 cockle] sometimes applied to the poppies growing in fields of grain. 67 she] Ceres. 68 Thesmophoria] marginal note, '. . . sacrifices peculiar to Ceres . . .' 103 dearest friend] probably Wither. 126 watchet]

a light blue. 188 Isca] the river Usk. 265 my native soil] Devonshire.

583 *Cælia*] Moorman dates these sonnets *c.* 1617. The references in the first sonnet to a love now dead may be to a conjectural first wife; see following note.

585 *In obitum . . .*] 'On the death of M.S., 10 May, 1614.' Bullen wished to expand the 'M.S.' to 'maritæ suæ,' making the epitaph refer to a first wife for whose existence there is not much evidence.

585 *On the Countess Dowager of Pembroke*] Mary Herbert, Countess of Pembroke, who died in 1621; see p. 143. This epitaph was formerly attributed to Jonson, but its ascription in three mss. to Browne, together with Aubrey's statement that it was written by Browne, can leave no doubt that Browne was really the author. Ault (*17th Century Lyrics*) discovered that it was first printed in the 1623 edition of Camden's *Remains concerning Britain*.

GEORGE WITHER

GEORGE WITHER (1588–1667) for the first thirty years of his life ran a career almost parallel with that of his friend and associate, William Browne. He was born in Hampshire, spent two years in residence at Magdalen College, Oxford, left without taking a degree, and entered one of the Inns of Court. Like Browne he began his literary career by publishing an elegy upon the death of Prince Henry. His next publication, a book of satires called *Abuses Stript and Whipt*, gave offense and he was for a time committed to jail, where he cultivated pastoral poetry, writing his *Shepherd's Hunting*, published in 1615. He continued in the pastoral vein with his *Fidelia*, 1615, and his *Fair Virtue*, 1622.

From about 1620 Wither grew more and more in sympathy with the Puritans. Turning his talents to the service of religion, he wrote several books of hymns and psalms, and numerous prose pamphlets of theological and political controversy. During the Civil War he was a captain in the Parliamentary army. He was captured by the Royalists and was in danger of hanging for having written severely against the King, but his life was spared on the plea of Sir John Denham who argued that 'whilst [Wither] lived, he [Denham] should not be the worst poet in England.' He continued writing until his death, his last publication bearing a date fifty-four years later than his first. In all, he issued about a hundred separate works.

Wither's early poetry achieved a considerable popularity, but the great bulk of his later controversial publication obscured his merits and his name became 'the synonym for a prosing preacher.' Lamb's enthusiasm for the 'free spirit' and the 'elasticity, like a dancing measure' of the early poetry helped to rehabilitate Wither's reputation, so that now his verve and sweetness are again appreciated. He was plagued by that facility and fluency, the bane of so many Spenserians, which kept him from knowing when to stop. At line 519 of a poem in praise of his mistress, Fair Virtue, he writes

> If I please I'll end it here
> If I list I'll sing this year.

He almost carries out his threat: the poem ends at line 4706.

MODERN EDITIONS: *Juvenilia*, three volumes, Spenser Society, 1871; *Miscellaneous Works*, eleven volumes, Spenser Society, 1872–1883; *The Poetry* (ed. by. F. Sidgwick), two volumes, London, 1902.

TEXT: *Juvenilia*, 1622 (25911), Harvard; *Fair Virtue*, 1622 (25903), Harvard; *A Collection of Emblems*, 1635 (25900a), White; *Halleluiah*, 1641, B. M.

586 *The Shepherd's Hunting*] written during Wither's imprisonment and first published in 1614; it consisted of five eclogues, in which Wither, using pastoral names, wrote of himself and his friends. Philarete, in the early editions called Roget, is Wither himself, and Wil'y is Browne.

586–592 *The fourth eclogue*] appeared before the publication of the whole poem in William Browne's *Shepherd's Pipe*, 1614. 11 quill] musical pipe made of a hollow stem. 20 ill-apaid] ill-pleased. 86 summer-pole] a May-pole. 113 Daphne's tree] laurel. 115 thyme] a pun on 'thyme' and 'time.' 212 not] not even. 235 Cuddy] Christopher Brooke. 237 Saint Dunstan's] the Devil and St. Dunstan Tavern, a favorite with the poets. See Introduction to Jonson, p. 991. 336 a-mewing] mewed up, cooped up.

592 *Fair Virtue, the mistress of Philarete*] a poem of 4160 lines, which is practically a repetitious description of his mistress. At the close one cannot be certain whether the mistress is a real or imaginary woman, or the abstraction, fair virtue. Scattered through the poem are a few separate lyrics, of which we print *Sonnets 4* and *5*. The Christmas carol is from the miscellaneous section at the close of *Fair Virtue*.

592 *Sonnet 4*. 15 to] omitted in 1622.

593 *Sonnet 5*. 13] In all early editions this line is one syllable short. Sidgwick suggests adding a second 'sweet'.

593–595 *A Christmas carol* 30 crowdy-mutton's] probably a fiddler. The crowd was an early form of the fiddle; and mutton was sometimes used as a term of contempt for a man. 76 wild mare] see-saw. 84 noddy] a card game resembling cribbage. 86 rowland-hoe] some kind of game, the details of which are unknown. 87 gameboys] not recorded in *O.E.D.*; possibly 'gambols,' which was often spelled 'gambauds,' 'gambauds,' and 'gamboldes.'

596–598 *A rocking hymn* 55–60] 1641 immediately repeats these lines.

GILES FLETCHER, THE YOUNGER

GILES FLETCHER (*c.* 1588–1623), though younger than his brother Phineas, is here placed first because his published work appeared earlier. Giles followed his father (see p. 209) and his brother Phineas to Cambridge (though to Trinity College instead of King's), where he proceeded B.A. in 1606. He remained as a minor fellow and later as reader in Greek grammar. In 1618 he became rector of Alderton, in Suffolk, but did not long survive in this uncongenial parish.

Fletcher began writing poetry while still a boy, and contributed *A Canto upon the Death of Eliza* to the Cambridge elegiac volume of 1603, *Sorrow's Joy*. He wrote his chief work, *Christ's Victory and Triumph in Heaven and*

Earth over and after Death, 1610, when about twenty years of age. He was following as poetic models the French religious poet, Du Bartas, and Edmund Spenser, using as in his juvenile *Canto* an eight-line stanza similar to Spenser's nine-line form. Milton's *Paradise Regained* owes more to *Christ's Victory and Triumph* than to any other English poem.

MODERN EDITION: *Giles and Phineas Fletcher, Poetical Works* (ed. by F. S. Boas), Vol. i, Cambridge, 1908.

TEXT: *Christ's Victory and Triumph*, 1610 (11058), Harvard.

599 *Christ's Victory and Triumph*] a poem in four books—*Christ's victory in heaven, Christ's victory on earth, Christ's triumph over death,* and *Christ's triumph after death.* We print *Christ's victory on earth,* the book of most interest to the student of Milton.

599–612 *Christ's victory on earth* 1 she] Mercy. The preceding book closes with a speech by Mercy in which she recounts briefly the life of Jesus to the time of the temptation. At the end of her speech,

> down she let her eyelids fall, to shine
> Upon the rivers of bright Palestine,

Whose woods drop honey, and her rivers skip with wine.

2 poor desolate] Jesus. 19 salvage] savage. 186 Elonging] removing far off. 191 Celeno] one of the Harpies. 221 grapples] 1610 'craples', perhaps a misprint for 'graples'. 227 bait] stop for rest and refreshment. 250 Euëlpis] a name used by Plutarch for the goddess of fortune and hope. 295 latch] catch. 334 flowers-de-luce] 1610 'flos-de-luce'. 344 cauls] netted caps or head-dresses. 350 prim] privet; a bushy evergreen shrub. 353 depends] hangs down. graping] bearing the grape-vines. 384 interal] entrail. 407 cocks] taps. 448 verges] rods, scepters. 462 bladderëd] inflated.

PHINEAS FLETCHER

PHINEAS FLETCHER (1582–1650), son of Giles Fletcher, the elder, received his education at Eton and King's College, Cambridge, taking the degrees of B.A., M.A., and B.D. While at Cambridge he wrote his 'piscatory' play, *Sicelides,* though the exact date of its production is in doubt. In 1616 he became chaplain to Sir Henry Willoughby in Derbyshire, and in 1620 rector of Hilgay in Norfolk. He occupied himself with writing a Latin poem against the Jesuits, *Locustæ,* which he published in 1627, together with an expanded English paraphrase, sub-titled *The Apollyonists,* written in a nine-line stanza adapted from Spenser's. So well had Fletcher imitated the manner of Spenser that *Britain's Ida,* now known to have been written by him, was issued in 1627 as 'by that renowned poet, Edmund Spenser.' This poem, an account of the love of Venus and Anchises, belongs in the tradition of *Venus and Adonis, Hero and Leander,* and their imitations. It is written in the eight-line stanza apparently invented by Fletcher's brother Giles.

In his own lifetime, Phineas Fletcher was known chiefly as the author of *The Purple Island,* 1633, a long allegorical presentation of man as an island. The topographical features of this island represent man physiologically, while the inhabitants and their actions symbolize man's emotions and other psychological characteristics. In the same volume appeared his *Piscatory Eclogues and other Poetical Miscellanies.*

Fletcher has the virtues and faults which arise from a close following of Spenser as a model. His diction is rich and his versification melodious, but luxuriance of detail and intricacy of allegory confuse and tire the reader. In his *Apollyonists,* perhaps his most distinctive work, he seems to approach the thought and manner of Donne as well as to copy Spenser. From this poem

Milton drew more than a hint for his account of Lucifer and the fallen angels.

MODERN EDITIONS: *Giles and Phineas Fletcher, Poetical Works* (ed. by F. S. Boas), two volumes, Cambridge, 1908–09; *Venus and Anchises and other poems* (ed. by E. Seaton), Oxford, 1926.

TEXT: *The Locusts, or Apollyonists*, 1627 (11081), Harvard; *Piscatory Eclogues, and other Poetical Miscellanies*, 1633 (11082), Hudson.

612–621 *The Locusts, or Apollyonists*] Fletcher published with this poem a Latin version, *Locustæ vel Pietas Jesuitica*, probably written first. He takes his title from *Revelations* ix. 3–11. The *Apollyonists* is a poem of five cantos, of which we print the first, the canto of most interest to students of Milton. 27 fraught] cargo, freight. 28 purple whore] the Roman Catholic Church. 75 eath] easy. 94 she] Sin. 231 wrestler] James I. 257 Isle of Devils] Bermuda. 348 banned] cursed.

621–628 *Eclogue VII* Thirsil] the poet himself. Thomalin] a name elsewhere given to John Tomkins, organ-ist of King's College Chapel, Cambridge, and later organist of St. Paul's. 48 Came] the Cam. Fletcher had been a fellow of King's College from 1603 to 1616. All of his poems which refer to his leaving Cambridge show that he felt some personal injury at the time. 99 mar'l] marvel. 164 populars] poplars. 165 Daphne] the laurel.

628–630 *To Mr. Jo. Tomkins* 2 rapts] 1633 reads 'raps'. 21 Eupathus'] possibly a coinage of Fletcher's. 56] Tomkins became organist of St. Paul's some time between 1619 and 1622. 70 Ida] probably a reference to Ide Hill, not far from Fletcher's home in Kent.

WILLIAM BASSE

WILLIAM BASSE (*c.* 1583–*c.* 1653) spent most of his life in the service of Sir Richard Wenman, later Lord Wenman, of Thame Park, to whose family he was a sort of poet laureate. In poetical manner he is a Spenserian, and his closest friend among the poets of his day seems to have been William Browne. He was also the friend of Izaak Walton. Basse published only a few of his poems, and those early in life—*Sword and Buckler*, 1602; *Three Pastoral Elegies*, 1602; and *Great Britain's Sunset*, 1613, an elegy for Prince Henry. *A Help to Discourse, or a miscellany of merriment*, 1619, has also been doubtfully attributed to him. He left much verse in manuscript, and R. W. Bond, the editor of the first collected edition of his works, thinks that at the time of his death he was preparing his poems for publication.

MODERN EDITION: *The Poetical Works* (ed. by R. W. Bond), London, 1893.

TEXT: *Lansdowne Ms.* 777, B. M.; Izaak Walton, *Complete Angler*, 1653, Harvard.

631 *On Mr. William Shakespeare*] In the *Lansdowne Ms.*, under the title is written: 'he died in April 1616.' This poem was first printed in Donne's *Poems*, 1633, but was omitted in the later editions. It appeared in the 1640 edition of Shakespeare's *Poems*, signed 'W.B.' In *Shakespeare's Century of Praise*, Miss Smith lists ten ms. and five early printed versions. The poem was in circulation before 1623, for Ben Jonson in his verses before the First Folio refers to it; see p. 511.

632 *The angler's song*] In the *Complete Angler*, the song is sung by Piscator, who introduces it thus: 'I'll promise you I'll sing a song that was lately made at my request by Mr. William Basse, one that has made the choice songs of the *Hunter in his career*, and of *Tom of Bedlam*, and many others of note; and this that I will sing is in praise of angling.'

RICHARD CORBET, BISHOP OF OXFORD AND NORWICH

RICHARD CORBET (1582–1635), the 'poetical Dean' of Christ Church, later Bishop of Oxford and Norwich, must have been a delight to generations of

Oxford undergraduates from his unceasing love of jolly pranks. When he was appointed Dean of Christ Church in 1620, 'the very school-boys stopped bowling their hoops in amazement at seeing a Dean so like themselves.' At the cross of Abingdon, on a market day, 'the jolly Doctor,' seeing a ballad-singer in distress because he could not sell his ballads, 'puts off his gown, and puts on the ballad-singer's leathern jacket, and being a handsome man, and had a rare full voice, he presently vended a great many, and had a great audience.' Aubrey tells many other amusing stories of the jovial churchman, who, as his spirited poem *Iter Boreale* (a verse account of a vacation tramp) shows, had a good bit of the vagabond in him. Corbet was one of Ben Jonson's good friends, and his ability to extemporize poetry made him popular at the Mermaid and the Devil and St. Dunstan.

MODERN EDITION: *The Poems* (ed. by O. Gilchrist), London, 1807.

COMMENT: J. E. V. Crofts, 'A Life of Bishop Corbett' in *Essays and Studies by Members of the English Association*, Vol. x, Oxford, 1924.

TEXT: *Certain Elegant Poems*, 1647, Harvard.

633-634 *A proper new ballad, intituled The fairies' farewell* 57 Wil- | liam Chourne] servant to Dr. Hutten, Corbet's father-in-law.

WILLIAM STRODE

WILLIAM STRODE (1601 or 1602-1645) was chaplain to Bishop Corbet and 'a most florid preacher in the university.' He wrote one play, *The Floating Island*, which was produced at Oxford on the visit of the King and Queen in 1636, not greatly to the pleasure of the royal guests. A few of his poems appeared unsigned in the various miscellanies of the middle decades of the 17th century, but most of his poems (popular enough with his contemporaries to be copied frequently) remained in manuscript until Bertram Dobell collected them.

MODERN EDITION: *The Poetical Works* (ed. by B. Dobell), London, 1907.

TEXT: *Harleian Ms.* 6917, B. M.; *Additional Ms.* 19268, B. M.; *Wit's Recreations*, 1640 (25870), Harvard.

636 *On Chloris walking in the snow*] set to music by Walter Porter, *Madrigals and Airs*, 1632. This was one of the most popular poems of the century. It appeared in three song-books and eleven miscellanies (see Ault, *17th Century Lyrics*, p. 478), and was copied in at least eighteen manuscripts, in six of which it is assigned to Strode. In one manuscript, it is assigned to Richard Corbet, and in two to a William Munsey. The weight of the evidence seems to be for Strode (cf. *M.L.R.*, xi. 290).

HENRY KING, BISHOP OF CHICHESTER

HENRY KING (1592-1669) was the son of a distinguished churchman and, after his education at Christ Church, Oxford, he too entered the church. He was made a prebend of St. Paul's in 1616 and was advanced, through various preferments, to the see of Chichester in 1642. He enjoyed his bishopric for only a year before he was expelled by the Puritans, not to be returned until the Restoration. Bishop King, 'noted for his obliging nature,' had many friends among men of letters. According to Walton, he was Donne's 'dearest friend' and the executor of his will. Grierson thinks it probable that he was the editor of the 1633 edition of Donne's poems. Though King's own poetry shows the influence of Donne, it is also the poetry of transition and some of the couplets already have the ring of the 18th century. James Howell, who saw a manuscript of King's poems in 1637, praises them justly for 'an exact concinnity and evenness of fancy.' It is interesting to note that when the unsold sheets of the first edition of King's poems, published in 1657, were bound up for a third issue in 1700, the book was ascribed on the new title-page to Ben Jonson.

MODERN EDITIONS: *The Poems* (ed. by J. Sparrow), London, 1925; *The English Poems* (ed. by L. Mason), New Haven, 1914; 'Henry King' in *Minor Poets of the Caroline Period* (ed. by G. Saintsbury), Vol. iii, Oxford, 1921.

COMMENT: L. Mason, 'The Life and Works of Henry King, D.D.' in the *Trans. Connecticut Academy of Arts and Sciences*, New Haven, 1913.

TEXT: *Poems, Elegies, Paradoxes, and Sonnets*, 1657, Harvard; *Harleian Ms.* 6917, B. M.

638 *The retreat* 4 first] that first. 6 rack] fly as vapor or broken clouds.

639–641 *The exequy*] The mss. supply a sub-title: 'To his matchless never to be forgotten friend.' Anne, the first wife of King, in whose memory this poem was written, died about 1624. 30 love] 1657; several mss. read 'life', which has sometimes been substituted by modern editors. 90 hollow] all mss.; 16 7 'hallow'.

641 *Sic vita*] See the original stanzas by Quarles, p. 749, and note, for the history of this poem. This stanza appeared also in Francis Beaumont's *Poems*, 1640, but it is certainly not Beaumont's, for the original poem did not begin to circulate 'until after his death.

641 *A contemplation upon flowers*] not included in 1657, but in *Harleian Ms.* 6917 signed 'H. Kinge'.

AURELIAN TOWNSHEND

AURELIAN TOWNSHEND (1583?-1651?) was a hanger-on of the court, for a time in the service of the Cecil family, then with Lord Herbert of Cherbury, and later with the Earl of Dorset. He was the friend of several men of letters, especially Carew (see p. 688). In 1632, after the quarrel between Jonson and Inigo Jones, he was employed to write two masks for the court. A manuscript note of about 1642 indicates a period of poverty: 'Mr. Aurelian Townshend, a poor and pocky poet . . . would be glad to sell an hundred verses now at sixpence apiece, fifty shillings an hundred verses.' A few of his poems appeared in the song-books and miscellanies, but there was no collected edition until that of Sir Edmund Chambers.

MODERN EDITION: *Poems and Masks* (ed. by E. K. Chambers), Oxford, 1912.

TEXT: Playford, *Select Musical Airs and Dialogues*, 1653, New York; Lawes, *Airs and Dialogues*, 1653, New York; Cotgrave, *Wit's Interpreter*, 1655, Harvard.

642 *Victorious beauty*] This poem was popular and appeared anonymously in three of Playford's song-books and in Cotgrave's *Wit's Interpreter*, 1655. It was copied in many mss., in two of which it is assigned to Townshend. In *Malone Ms.* 13, which assigns the poem to Townshend, the address 'To the Countess of Salisbury' was added. In other mss. the poem is assigned to Donne and to William Herbert, Earl of

Pembroke. 19 Were] a ms. reading; 1653 'Where'. 21 some that] a ms. reading; 1653 'chance to'.

642–643 *A dialogue betwixt Time and a Pilgrim* 1 mows] the reading of Cotgrave's *Wit's Interpreter;* 1653 'moves'.

643 *What is most . . .*] generally called *Upon kind and true love;* ascribed conjecturally to Townshend by Chambers. 14 A] 1655 'And'.

ROBERT HERRICK

ROBERT HERRICK (1591–1674) was the 'son of Ben' who profited most by the father's instruction. Like Jonson, he is free from the Petrarchan con-

ceits of the Elizabethans and the metaphysical conceits of many of the
Jacobean and Caroline poets, finding his inspiration almost wholly in the
classics, especially in Anacreon, Horace, Catullus, and Martial. But he sur-
passes Jonson in catching the true spirit of his models; for Jonson, far more
learned in classical lore, sometimes smacks of pedantry by his erudite allusions, while Herrick is a 'free-born Roman.'

After serving as an apprentice to his uncle, a successful goldsmith, Herrick entered St. John's College, Cambridge, at twenty-two, a very late age
for the 17th century. He later transferred to Trinity Hall. He was graduated B.A. in 1617, and M.A. in 1620. For the next nine years—the most
important of Herrick's life for literary history—there are no external records of him except that he served as chaplain to the Duke of Buckingham on
the expedition to the Isle of Rhé in 1627. It seems clear, from the evidence
of his poems, that he spent most of this time in London, associating with the
circle of poets and wits, by whom he was called 'the music of the feast.' By
1625 he was well enough known as a poet to have his name coupled with
Jonson and Drayton in Richard James's *Muses' Dirge*. The living of Dean
Prior in Devonshire fell vacant in 1629 and Herrick was installed as vicar.
Here he lived, sometimes content with country pleasures, at other times discontented amid his boorish parishioners, until he was ejected by the Puritans in 1647. During these years there is record of only one visit to London,
in 1640, at which time there was a project for publishing his poems. Though
entered in the Stationers' Registers on April 29, 1640, the volume did not
appear. According to a note found among Archbishop Laud's papers, Herrick was in London without leave and it is possible that he was ordered back
to his post before the details of publication could be concluded. After his
ejection from Dean Prior he went to London and, in 1648, published his
Hesperides: or the Works both human and divine of Robert Herrick, Esq.
The volume did not go to a second edition, appearing too late to attain the
popularity which it deserved, and which it might well have attained had
Herrick published ten to twenty years earlier when he was still known to the
literary group in London, and before changing fashions had made his poetry
a little out of date. Though handicapped by late publication, he did, however, get more consideration than the single edition indicates, for he was
liberally represented in the 1645, 1650, and 1654 editions of *Wit's Recreations*, a popular anthology of the day. Many of his poems, too, were set
to music and appeared in the song-books, and others were liked well enough
to be copied frequently in manuscripts. Contemporary criticism indicates that
he was quickly forgotten. Phillips (and Winstanley copies him) speaks slight-
ingly of Herrick and cites only the verses on the *errata* as an example of his
poetry. In 1662 Herrick was restored to his living at Dean Prior and there
spent his remaining years.

The seeming lack of order in the arrangement of the poems in the
Hesperides has led to the conjecture that Herrick had little to do with the
publication and that the order is the publisher's; but it is evident from the
list of *errata* that Herrick did see the volume through the press and so must
have approved the arrangement. His delight in disorder and his desire for
contrast—indeed the great number of short poems would become tedious
were they grouped—possibly determined the order in which he printed
them. We have grouped the poems in the order of Herrick's various interests.

MODERN EDITIONS: *The Poetical Works* (ed. by F. W. Moorman), Oxford,

1915; *The Hesperides and Noble Numbers* (ed. by A. W. Pollard), two volumes, Muses' Library, London, n. d.

COMMENT: F. W. Moorman, *Robert Herrick, A Biographical and Critical Study,* London, 1910; Floris Delattre, *Robert Herrick,* Paris, 1912.

TEXT: *Hesperides,* 1648, Mandel; *Ashmole Ms.* 38, Bodleian.

643–644 *The argument of his book* 3 hock-carts] the cart which carries home the last load of the harvest.

644 *When he would have his verses read* 7 thyrse] marginal note: 'A javelin twined with ivy.' 8 orgies] marginal note: 'Songs to Bacchus.' The word really has a more extensive meaning and applies to the whole of the rites or ceremonies in honor of Bacchus. round] a song by two or more persons, each taking up the strain in turn. At a time of gaiety the call, 'a round,' was used to stimulate mirth and start the singing; cf. Richard Brome, 'A round,' p. 407.

644 *Not every day fit for verse* 4 pannicles] membranes, especially of the brain.

645 *To live merrily . . .* 3 the] omitted in text of 1648, but supplied in the errata. 7 pap] pulp.

646 *An ode for him* 5–6] taverns frequented by the Tribe of Ben. The actual name of the third was, The Three Tuns. 7 clusters] of grapes, wine.

647–649 *The apparition of his mistress . . .*] This poem first appeared in a volume called *Poems, written by Wil. Shakespeare, Gent.,* published in 1640 by John Benson. *Desunt nonnulla*] 'Something is wanting.' 40 comply] enfold. 51 Beaumont and Fletcher] 1640 reads 'Shakespeare and Beaumont'. 52–53] 1640 reads:

Listen, while they call back the former year,
To teach the truth of scenes; and more for thee

53 Evadne] the heroine of *The Maid's Tragedy.*

649–650 *His farewell to sack* 23 mystic fan] symbolic emblem in festivals of Bacchus.

650–652 *The welcome to sack* 9 As] 1648 'A'. 11 Osiris] marginal note: 'The sun.' 23 went'st] 1648 'wenst'st'. 50 Iphiclus] celebrated runner, won the foot-race at the funeral games of Pelias. 54 Isis] marginal note: 'The moon.' 65 Jove's son] marginal note: 'Hercules.' 85 circumstants] by-standers.

652 *Upon love* 7 be] 1648 'he'.

652 *To the virgins . . .*] set to music by William Lawes in Playford's *Select Musical Airs and Dialogues,*

1652, 1653, and 1659. Ault, who has surveyed most carefully the miscellanies and song-books, thinks this the most popular poem of the latter half of the 17th century (*17th Century Lyrics,* p. 481). It appears in ten miscellanies and eleven song-books.

653 *To his mistress . . .* 4 babies in your eyes] pupils, from connection with the Latin 'pupilla,' a little girl. The phrase also frequently refers to the small image of oneself reflected in the pupil of another's eye; hence to look amorously.

654 *To Anthea . . .*] set to music by Henry Lawes in Playford's *Select Musical Airs and Dialogues,* 1652, 1653, and 1659.

654–656 *Corinna's going a-maying* 50 priest] 1648 'Ptiest'.

656 *To Phyllis . . .*] an imitation of Marlowe's popular poem, *The passionate shepherd to his love,* see p. 168. 18 For meat] during the meal.

658 *How lilies came white*] set to music by Nicholas Lanier in Playford's *Select Airs and Dialogues,* 1669.

659 *To Sir Clipsby Crew*] a fellow student of Herrick's at St. John's College, Cambridge, with whom Herrick remained on intimate terms. For Sir Clipsby's wedding in 1625, Herrick wrote an epithalamium.

659–660 *An ode to Sir Clipsby Crew* 7 charm] sing. 10 having] 1648 'havink', corrected in original errata. 22 instant] present.

660 *His content in the country* 4 Prue] Prudence Baldwin, Herrick's housekeeper at Dean Prior.

660 *His grange, or private wealth* 10 creaking] clucking. 24 miching] skulking, pilfering. 26 Tracy] marginal note: 'His spaniel.'

661 *To the reverend shade . . .* 1 lusters] periods of five years. 4 justments] due ceremonies. 9 smallage] wild celery or water parsley.

662 *To Lar* 3 mantel-trees] the beam across the opening of a fireplace, serving as a lintel to support the masonry above.

662–663 *Ceremonies for Christmas* 1 noise] frequently used for a band of musicians, so Herrick is probably thinking of a song, certainly of a melodious sound and not of the din that the word suggests at present. 10 psaltries] a medieval stringed instrument, with the sound-board behind and parallel with the strings, played by plucking the strings with the fingers or a plectrum. 12 teending] tindling, beginning to burn.

653 *Saint Distaff's Day*] seems to be a coinage of Herrick's for the day on which work was resumed after the Christmas holidays. 4 fother] fodder.

653 *Ceremonies for Candlemas Eve*] Candlemas is the feast of the purification of the Virgin Mary, February 2.

664–665 *Oberon's feast*] first published, with many variants from the version in the *Hesperides,* in a volume by R. S., called *A description of the King and Queen of Fairies,* 1635, thus being the first of Herrick's poems to appear in print. 1 Shapcot] Herrick addressed another poem 'To my peculiar friend Master Thomas Shapcot, Lawyer'. Shapcot was from Exeter and was admitted to the Inner Temple in 1632. the] omitted in the text of 1648, but corrected in errata. 33 sag] sagging. 34 bestrutted] swollen. 50 bride] rose.

665–666 *The hock-cart* . . . 9 mau-

kin] malkin, an untidy country wench. 45 neat] cattle.

666 *The wake*] the local annual festival in an English parish, a time for merry-making. 8 Marian] Maid Marian, a traditional figure in the folk plays of Robin Hood.

667 *The bad season* . . . 10 Maria] Henrietta Maria, the queen of Charles I.

669 *To music* . . . 26 baptime] baptism.

671–672 *His litany* . . . 18 Has] 1648 'His'.

672 *A thanksgiving* . . . 22 unflead] not flayed, not skinned; perhaps meaning 'uncut.'

673 *Another grace* . . . 3 paddocks] toads or frogs.

674–676 *Mr. Robert Herrick, his farewell unto poetry* 21 odd] ms. 'ode'. 22 nine] *Additional Ms.* 22603; *Ashmole Ms.* 38 'wine'. Cf. Horace, *Odes,* III.xix.11–15. 32 White] Hazlitt's emendation; ms. 'While'. 54 I've] Moorman's emendation; ms. 'I'am'. 71 Grecian orator] Demosthenes; Herrick's phrase is from Plutarch's *Lives.* 93 loathsom'st] ms. 'loathsoms'.

THOMAS CAREW

THOMAS CAREW (1594 or 1595–1639?), 'that excellent wit, the King's carver,' was one of the courtiers who in the 'halcyon days' of Charles I found his real profession in writing poetry. He was graduated B.A. at Oxford, having attended Merton College, and then idled through several years of supposed study of law at the Middle Temple. After this he took service under Sir Dudley Carleton, the English Ambassador at Venice, in 1613, and at the Hague in 1616, but was dismissed for slandering Sir Dudley and his wife. He made several unsuccessful attempts to secure employment in England, and finally became a member of the train of Lord Herbert of Cherbury when Herbert was sent as an ambassador to France in 1619. In 1628 an appointment as Gentleman of the Privy Chamber, and a little later as Sewer, to Charles I gave him suitable employment for the rest of his life. His tact is illustrated by an anecdote, possibly fictitious, of an evening when he was lighting the King to the Queen's chamber. Entering first, he saw the Queen somewhat compromised with Henry Jermyn, Lord St. Albans. He discreetly stumbled, putting out the light, so that the King saw nothing, and the Queen became Carew's friend for life. According to a story repeated in Hunter's *Chorus Vatum,* his 'scandalous life' was closed by a death-bed repentance.

Carew was a 'son of Ben' whose admiration for Jonson was tempered by his judgment. Howell, in his *Familiar Letters,* tells of a supper in Ben Jonson's rooms when 'Ben began to engross all the discourse, to vapor extremely of himself, and, by vilifying others, to magnify his own muse. T[om] Ca[rew] buzzed me in the ear, that though Ben has barreled up a great deal of knowledge, yet it seems he had not read the *Ethics,* which, among other precepts of morality, forbid self-commendation.' To John Donne, Carew gave unrestrained praise, and the influence of Donne, more than of Jonson, is seen in his poetry. Carew's poems, according to Clarendon, were esteemed by his contemporaries 'for the sharpness of the fancy, and the elegancy of the language in which that fancy was spread,' though some objected with Suckling that

> His muse was hard-bound, and th' issue of's brain
> Was seldom brought forth but with trouble and pain.

MODERN EDITIONS: *Poems* (ed. by A. Vincent), Muses' Library, London, n. d.; *The Poems* (ed. by W. C. Hazlitt), London, 1870; *The Poems and Masque* (ed. by J. W. Ebsworth), London, 1893.

COMMENT: C. L. Powell, 'New Material on Thomas Carew', in *M. L. R.* xi. 285.

TEXT: *Poems,* 1640 (4620), Cornell.

678 *To a lady . . .*] In his edition of the poems of Lord Herbert of Cherbury, G. C. Moore Smith has, with some doubt, claimed this poem for Herbert, on the basis of internal evidence. This ascription is possible, but since the poem appears in the 1640 edition of Carew, and not in the 1665 edition of Herbert, it is here printed as Carew's. 3 passion] the text of 1640 reads 'pastime', but the errata corrects to 'passion'.

679–680 *A song*] set to music in Wilson's *Cheerful Airs or Ballads,* 1660. *Ashmole Ms. 38* and *Egerton Ms. 2421* supply an additional stanza which may be by Carew (text from *M.L.R.,* xi. 296):

Ask me no more whether north or south
These vapors come from out thy mouth,
For unto heaven they are sent hence,
And there are made Jove's frankincense.

This popular poem inspired many imitations: cf. *Harleian Ms. 6918, Ashmole Ms. 38, Wit Restored, Merry Drollery, Rump Songs, A Royal Arbor of Loyal Poesy, Westminster Drollery;* and Kynaston's *On concealment of her beauty,* p. 818, seems to owe its origin to Carew's poem. Arthur Johnston translated the poem into Latin in 1642 (cf. *Musa Latina Aberdonensis,* 1895, ii. 202). 4 causes] the material cause of the Aristotelian philosophy; 'causes' was too difficult a reading for the editor of *Wit Restored,* who changed to 'beds'. 11 dividing] a technical term in music for the 'execution of a rapid passage, originally conceived as the dividing of each of a succession of long notes into several short ones.'

681 *Mediocrity in love rejected*] set to music by Henry Lawes in *Airs and Dialogues,* 1653.

682 *Ingrateful beauty threatened*] set to music by Henry Lawes in *Airs and Dialogues,* 1655. 6 imped] a technical term in falconry; to repair an injured wing by grafting feathers from another bird.

682 *To my inconstant mistress*] set to music by Henry Lawes in *Airs and Dialogues,* 1653.

683 *Disdain returned*] set to music by Porter in *Madrigals and Airs,* 1632, and by Henry Lawes in *Airs and Dialogues,* 1653. It also appears in Playford's *Select Airs and Dialogues,* 1659.

683 *Good counsel to a young maid* 10 passion's] 1640 'passion'.

683–684 *Upon Master W. Montague . . .*] Walter Montague returned to England in 1633, after a period of secret service and imprisonment in France. He was known as a poet (the author of *Shepherd's Paradise,* a comedy produced in 1633), and is among those mentioned by Suckling in *A session of the poets.* 22 halcyon] 1640 'halcyons'. 26 forests] 1640 'forest'. 32 he] 1640 'she'.

684 *Epitaph on the Lady Mary Villiers*] Carew has three epitaphs on Lady Mary, not yet identified but of the family of the Dukes of Buckingham.

685 *Maria Wentworth*] the second daughter of Thomas, Earl of Cleveland, who died in 1632. Carew's lines served as an epitaph on her magnificent monument.

685–687 *An elegy upon the death of Doctor Donne*] first printed in Donne's *Poems,* 1633. 5 unscissored lect'rer] lecturer with uncut hair; 1633 'uncisor'd Churchman'. 44 dung had searched] 1633 'dust had rak'd'. 87 the] Grierson, in *Metaphysical Poetry,* emends to 'thee'. 92 grave] 1633 'tomb'.

687–688 *To Ben Jonson*] *The New Inn*, produced in 1629, was hissed off the stage. When Jonson published the play in 1631, he added the *Ode to himself*, expressing 'the just indignation the author took at the vulgar censure of his play.' 18 city-custom . . . gavelkind] the custom of dividing a deceased man's property equally among his sons. 31 Goodwin] quicksands off the Kentish coast. 48 verge] jurisdiction.

688–690 *In answer of an elegiacal letter* . . . 2 Barbican] the name of a street in London where Townshend resided; used here with reference also to its original meaning of outer fortification. 5 mighty Sweden's fall] death of Gustavus Adolphus in 1632. 19–21]

places, rivers, and generals connected with the campaigns of Gustavus. 24 Knight o' th' Sun] a hero of popular romance. 26–30] Carew is comparing the deeds of Gustavus, great enough for daily recording in journals, with the deeds of the Cæsars, which could be recorded in *Annals* by *Tacitus*. 43 Cæsar] the Emperor Ferdinand II, leader of the Catholics. 44 united princes] the Protestant Union. 53 comprise] include. 54 *Shepherd's Paradise*] a pastoral comedy by Walter Montague. 58–64] In these lines, Carew is describing Townshend's mask, *Tempe Restored*. The description in detail continues for twenty-four more lines, here omitted.

690 *To my worthy friend, Master George Sandys*] see p 717.

THOMAS RANDOLPH

THOMAS RANDOLPH (1605–1635) was an infant prodigy, writing at the age of nine a 'history of our Savior's incarnation in English verse,' early evidence of the 'easy flux of language' attributed to him by his brother. After studying at Westminster School, he entered Trinity College, Cambridge, where he gained a reputation for his witty verses and for his play, *The Jealous Lovers*, presented with great success before the King and Queen on a visit to Cambridge. Randolph received a fellowship after taking his B.A., and remained for his Master's degree, which he secured in 1631. Soon after he went to London where he was known as one of the most promising of the 'sons of Ben.' His love of companionship unfortunately led to great excesses in irregular living and caused his early death. He was lamented as 'one of the most pregnant wits of his age.' Because he was so well liked for his brilliant conversation, the loss to English literature by his early death was probably exaggerated.

MODERN EDITIONS: *The Poems and Amyntas* (ed. by J. J. Parry), New Haven, 1917; *Poetical and Dramatic Works* (ed. by W. C. Hazlitt), London, 1875.

TEXT: *Poems, with The Muses' Looking-glass and Amyntas*, 1638 (20694), Harvard; *Aristippus*, 1630 (20687), White.

691–693 *A gratulatory* . . . 14 thee] the emendation of modern editors; 1638 'thy'.

695 *An ode to Mr. Anthony Stafford* 23 finger lose] In a quarrel during a drinking bout, Randolph had a finger cut off. He instantly wrote a poem on the occurrence. His friend, William Heminge, also wrote an *Elegy on Ran-*

dolph's finger, which includes the famous lines on the 'Time poets.' 36 Cheap] Cheapside, famous for its goldsmiths' shops. Lombard street] before the erection of the Royal Exchange, the meeting place of merchants and foreigners; later known for its drapers' shops. 76 Berkeley's] George, eighth Baron Berkeley.

WILLIAM CARTWRIGHT

WILLIAM CARTWRIGHT (1611–1643) attended Westminster School and then entered Christ Church, Oxford, where he spent the rest of his life. He was known as a diligent student, 'sitting sixteen hours a day at all manner of knowledge,' and after taking his Master's degree in 1635 and entering holy orders he was made reader in metaphysics. According to his contemporaries, he was an excellent teacher: in his courses, Aristotle 'ran as smooth as Virgil,' and, more astonishing, 'the theater was thin to his school, and comedy was not half so good entertainment as his philosophy.' His plays had great success at the University. Cartwright was one of the 'sons of Ben,' and Jonson complimented him highly, 'My son Cartwright writes all like a man.'

MODERN EDITION: *The Life and Poems* TEXT: *Comedies, Tragi-comedies, with*

697 *No Platonic love*] The cult of Platonic love had been introduced into England by Queen Henrietta Maria, who had spent her youth among the *précieuse* of the Hôtel de Rambouillet. The cult had become fashionable at the court of Charles I, and was frequently commented on by the poets, some praising the spiritualizing of love and others condemning the hypocrisy of the supposed Platonic lovers. Cf. J. B. Fletcher's *Religion of Beauty in Woman*.

699-701 *Upon the dramatic poems of Mr. John Fletcher*] In the edition of 1651 this is the second of the two poems upon Fletcher and is headed, *Another on the same*. We have given it the title of the first poem. It first appeared among the commendatory poems prefixed to the Beaumont and

(ed. by R. C. Goffin), Cambridge, 1918. *other poems*, 1651, Adams.

Fletcher folio of 1647. 1–10] This expresses the usual 17th-century opinion of the collaboration of Beaumont and Fletcher. Aubrey records the gossip that Beaumont's 'main business was to correct the overflowings of Mr. Fletcher's wit.' Careful analysis by recent scholars of the collaboration makes it seem that this account of their manner of work is hardly just. 44 Blackfriars] a private playhouse of the King's Men, whose public playhouse was the Globe. 59 captivëd] 1647 and 1651 both print 'captiv'd', though the 'ed' needs to be sounded to fill out the line. 60 rise parts] enter so fully into the spirit of the performance that they imagined themselves characters in the play. 68 two shillings] the price of admission to the better seats.

SIR JOHN SUCKLING

SIR JOHN SUCKLING (1609–1642) attended Trinity College, Cambridge, and Gray's Inn, but he was so little attracted by study that on coming into his inheritance at the age of eighteen he hastened off for a tour of the Continent, from which he returned 'an extraordinary accomplished gentleman, [and] grew famous at Court for his ready, sparkling wit.' He was abroad again for service under Gustavus Adolphus in 1631–2. He was known as a great gamester, both at bowling and cards—his sisters at one time coming to the Piccadilly bowling green, crying for fear that he would lose all their portions. He produced his play, *Aglaura*, probably near the close of 1637, with great magnificence, 'no tinsel, all the lace pure gold and silver,' and with such elaborate scenery as was customary only in masks. For the Scottish expedition of 1639, he again displayed his extravagance by outfitting a troop 'in white doublets, and scarlet breeches, and scarlet coats . . . well horsed and armed.' His courage on the expedition was called into question by Sir John Mennis in a poem later published in *Musarum Deliciæ*, but the truth of this slur can be doubted; according to Aubrey it was the custom to bait Suckling, since his wit was most sparkling when he was 'set upon and provoked.' On occasion, Suckling enjoyed displaying the wisdom of the serious. He wrote a readable *Account of Religion by Reason*, and in 1640 sent to Henry Jermyn a letter of excellent advice for the King. He took part in the plot to rescue Strafford from the Tower in 1641, and after its discovery fled to France, where he died, according to different stories either a suicide or killed by a spiteful servant.

Although Suckling's debt to Donne in externals is at once obvious, his natural ease and light-hearted gaiety are far removed from the intricacy and subtlety of Donne's intense thought. His clear, crisp manner of writing seems to indicate that he had learned something from Jonson. Dryden's comment that no one else expressed so nearly 'the conversation of a gentleman' would have greatly pleased Suckling.

MODERN EDITIONS: *The Works* (ed. by A. H. Thompson), London, 1910; *The Poems, Plays, and other Remains* (ed. by W. C. Hazlitt), London, 1892.

TEXT: *Fragmenta Aurea*, 1646, Harvard; *The Last Remains*, 1659, Harvard.

701–704 *A session of the poets*] E. K. Broadus, in *The Laureateship* (p. 53), thinks this poem written to ridicule the claims which Ben Jonson was making to the title of poet laureate. At the request of Jonson, Selden had inserted in his second edition of *Titles of Honor*, 1631, a passage on the history of poets laureate ending with the compliment to Jonson, 'your singular excellency in the art most eminently deserves it.' In the three earliest editions the title is *A sessions of the poets*. 10 There was] 1648; 1646 'There'. Selden] John Selden, one of the most learned lawyers of the day, remembered for his *Table Talk*. 11 Wenman] Sir Francis Wenman, one of the 'learned gentlemen of the country,' and a member of Lord Falkland's circle. 12 Sandys] see p. 717. Townshend] see p. 642. 13 Digby] Sir Kenelm Digby, one of the most brilliant men of the day, a pseudoscientist and philosopher. His *Private Memoirs* tell the romantic story of his courtship of Venetia Stanley. Chillingworth] William Chillingworth, an able defender of Protestantism in theological controversy, and a member of Lord Falkland's circle. 15 Lucan's translator] Thomas May, see p. 405. 15–16 he That] possibly Francis Quarles. 17 Selwin . . . Bartlets] unidentified. Waller] 1648; 1646 'Walter'; see p. 848. 18 Jack Vaughan] perhaps John Vaughan of the Inner Temple, a friend of Selden. Porter] Endymion Porter, the patron of Herrick and Davenant, see p. 842. 22 called Works] a common jest at Jonson's expense, see p. 990. 26 hoped] 1648; 1646 'hopes'. 36 *New Inn*] This late play of Jonson's was unsuccessful and stirred up much literary controversy. 39 hardbound] 1646; 1648 'hide-bound'. Cf. Pope's *Ep. to Arbuthnot*, 1.182: 'The Bard . . . strains from hard-bound brains, eight lines a year.' 63 Toby Mathews] son of the Archbishop of York, and a convert to Catholicism; a

close friend to Bacon. 66 Lady Carlisle] Lucy, the Countess of Carlisle, the friend and patroness of many of the Caroline poets; also the friend of both Pym and Strafford, and a character in Browning's *Strafford*. 74–75] 1648 inserts the following stanza:

This made a dispute; for 'twas plain to be seen
Each man had a mind to gratify the Queen;
But Apollo himself could not think it fit,
There was difference, he said, betwixt fooling and wit.

83 Wat Montague] author of *The Shepherd's Paradise*; see p. 683. Cf. Thorn-Drury's *Little Ark*, p. 4 ff. 92 Sid] Sidney Godolphin, whose small stature is referred to by Clarendon; see p. 820. 95 Murray] possibly William Murray, Gentleman of his Majesty's Bedchamber, created Earl of Dysart in 1643. 97 Hales] John Hales, a fellow of Eton and frequently called the 'ever memorable'; a member of Lord Falkland's circle. 100 Falkland] Lucius Cary, Lord Falkland; see Jonson's poem, p. 506 and note. 111 wit] 1648; 1646 'wit's'. 118 cheered] 1648; 1646 'cleared'.

705 *Song* 'Why so pale'] also used as a song in his play *Aglaura*.

705 *Sonnet I*] set to music in Playford's *Select Airs and Dialogues*, 1659.

705 *Sonnet II*] set to music in Playford's *Select Musical Airs and Dialogues*, 1652 and 1659.

706 *Sonnet III* 23 Sophonisba] Her story was a favorite with Elizabethan dramatists. 26–28 Philoclea . . . Pirocles . . . Amphialus] characters in Sidney's *Arcadia*.

706 *Song* 'No, no, fair heretic'] also used as a song in his play *Aglaura*.

707–709 *A ballad upon a wedding*] written for the marriage of Roger Boyle, Baron Broghill, and Lady Margaret Howard in 1641. 1 Dick] usually identified with Richard Lovelace, but more probably used as a type name for a rustic. 12 Vorty] rustic dialect form for 'forty.' 19 course-a-park] a country game. 59 Katherne] Catherine; a small and early variety of pear. 79–84] We here follow the order of 1648; in 1646 this stanza with tercets in reverse order appears after line 96. 107 Whilst] 1648; 1646 'Till'. 120 God b' w' ye] 1648; 1646 'Good boy'. 127 now] 1648; 1646 'out'. 128 do] 1648; 1646 'do't'.

710 *The Stationer to the reader* H. M.] Humphrey Moseley.

710 *Out upon it! I have loved*] An answer to this poem by Sir Toby Mathews, included in the editions of Suckling, is worth printing here:

Say, but did you love so long?
  In troth, I needs must blame you;
Passion did your judgment wrong,
  Or want of reason shame you.

Truth, time's fair and witty daughter,
  Shortly shall discover

Y' are a subject fit for laughter,
  And more fool than lover.

But I grant you merit praise
  For your constant folly;
Since you doted three whole days,
  Were you not melancholy?

She to whom you proved so true,
  And that very, very face,
Puts each minute such as you
  A dozen dozen to disgrace.

711 *Song* 'I prithee send me back'] set to music in Playford's *Select Musical Airs and Dialogues*, 1653, and in Henry Lawes's *Airs and Dialogues*, 1658. Ault, in *17th Century Lyrics*, points out that Lawes ascribes the poem to Hughes; but the style and spirit of the poem indicate Suckling.

711 *A song to a lute*] from Suckling's unfinished play, *The Sad One*. This poem is a parody of the third stanza of Ben Jonson's *Her triumph*, p. 504.

RICHARD LOVELACE

RICHARD LOVELACE (1618–1656 or 1657) is remembered for his gallant courtesy. In the judgment of Edward Phillips he was 'an approv'd both soldier, gentleman, and lover, and a fair pretender to the title of poet,' and Winstanley likens him to Sir Philip Sidney. He was educated at Charterhouse and Gloucester Hall (now Worcester College), Oxford. In his first year at Oxford, he wrote a comedy, *The Scholar*, produced and applauded at Oxford and London, but of which only the Prologue and Epilogue were printed. In his second year, 1636, during a visit of the King and Queen Lovelace obtained the favor of a great lady in attendance on the Queen, and by her request was granted his M.A., an early instance that he was, as Wood says, 'much admired and adored by the female sex.' Aubrey gives us one of the reasons for this favor, 'one of the handsomest men of England . . . an extraordinary handsome man . . . a most beautiful gentleman.' A Master's degree in two years was such a striking indication of the possibilities of favor that Lovelace took up his residence at court. He served in Goring's regiment on the two Scotch expeditions of 1639 and 1640. In 1642, he presented to Parliament the Kentish Petition in favor of the Bishops, and of the liturgy and common prayer, for which he was imprisoned for seven weeks in the Gate House, Westminster, where he occupied a part of his leisure in writing *To Althea, from prison* and *The Vintage to the Dungeon*. During the Civil War his movements cannot be traced with exactness. He saw some service in England with the King's armies, and in Holland with the French army, receiving a wound at the siege of Dunkirk in 1646. This service occasioned the farewells to Lucasta, on 'going to the wars' and 'going beyond the seas.' The identity of Lucasta is still in doubt. Wood says that her name was Lucy Sacheverell, and the recent researches of Hartmann lend some support to Wood's statement. It has also been conjectured that she was of the family of Lucas (ed. Wilkinson, i. xliv), and that she was a creature of Lovelace's imagination (*M. P.* xxiii. 77). In 1648 Lovelace was again imprisoned for connection with the Royalist risings in Kent. As before, prison stirred him to poetry and he wrote *To Lucasta, from prison.* On his release in 1649 he collected his poems and published them in a volume called *Lucasta.* After his death, his youngest brother collected his scattered pieces, and in 1659 published *Lucasta, Posthume Poems,* a volume of much lower quality than the earlier *Lucasta.*

MODERN EDITIONS: *The Poems* (ed. by C. H. Wilkinson), Oxford, 1925; *Lucasta* (ed. by W. C. Hazlitt), London, 1864.

COMMENT: C. H. Hartmann, *The Cavalier Spirit and its Influence on the Life and Work of Richard Lovelace,* London, 1925.

TEXT: *Lucasta,* 1649, Huntington.

712 *To Althea, from prison*] set to music in Playford's *Select Airs and Dialogues,* 1659, and Wilson's *Cheerful Airs or Ballads,* 1660. 7 gods] 1649 and *Harleian Ms.* 6918; other mss., sometimes followed by modern editors, read 'birds'.

712 *The Vintage to the Dungeon*] in *Lucasta,* 1649, said to be set to music by William Lawes.

712 *To Amarantha . . .*] set to music by Henry Lawes in *Airs and Dialogues,* 1653.

713 *The scrutiny*] set to music in Playford's *Select Musical Airs and Dialogues,* 1652.

714 *To Lucasta. The rose*] in *Lucasta,* 1649, said to be set to music by John Wilson. 11 coverled] coverlid, coverlet.

714 *To Lucasta. Going to the wars*] in *Lucasta,* 1649, said to be set to music by John Lanier.

714–715 *To Lucasta. Going beyond the seas*] set to music by Henry Lawes in ms. in possession of the Rev. H. R. Cooper Smith. 10 blew-god's] Palgrave, understanding the reference to

be to Neptune, emends to 'blue-god'. It is as likely that 'blow-god,' Æolus, is meant.

715 *To Lucasta, from prison* 1–4] Lovelace does not ask liberty from the prison, but from Lucasta, so that he may turn his fancy to other things. The phrase 'another's bride' has been taken to support the identification of Lucasta with Lucy Sacheverell, who, according to Wood, married on the mistaken report that Lovelace died of wounds received at Dunkirk in 1646. Lucy Sacheverell did marry a Mr. Dannet and later her cousin, George Sacheverell, but the dates of her marriages are not known.

716–717 *The grasshopper* 10 gilt-plats] plots of ground gilded by the sun's beams. 11–12] The grasshopper makes men, himself, and melancholy streams merry. 18 perch] 1649 'Peirch'. 19 poise] balance. 31 old Greek] Lovelace is probably thinking of hippocras, a cordial made of spiced wine strained through Hippocrates' sleeve or bag, and supposed to be especially wholesome.

GEORGE SANDYS

GEORGE SANDYS (1578–1644) was one of the great band of English travelers. In 1610 he began his travels in the East, a relation of which he published in 1615. When he returned to England he began a translation of Ovid's *Metamorphoses,* which he completed during his secretaryship of the Virginia colony, whither he went in 1621. This was probably the first literary work done on the continent of America. Translation proved a congenial task, and, after his return from Virginia, he published paraphrases of the *Psalms, Job, Ecclesiastes, Lamentations,* and *The Song of Solomon.* He does not seem to have written much original poetry; at least very little has come down to us. Among his literary friends were Drayton and Lord Falkland. Sandys frequently used the decasyllabic couplet in his translations, and was undoubtedly one of those who furthered the development of the heroic couplet.

MODERN EDITION: *The Poetical Works* (ed. by R. Hooper), London, 1872.

TEXT: *A Paraphrase upon the Psalms of David*, 1636 (21724), Harvard; *Ovid's Metamorphosis*, 1632 (18966), Harvard.

717–719 *Deo opt. max.*] *Deo optimo maximo:* 'To God, greatest and best.' 52 all my way] Sandys now rehearses briefly a few of his adventures on his eastern travels, of which he had writ- ten a prose account, *A relation of a journey, begun anno dom. 1610*, published in 1615. 91 *Iam tetigi portum, —valete*] 'Now I have reached the haven,—farewell.'

WILLIAM HABINGTON

WILLIAM HABINGTON (1605–1654), a Catholic, received his education at St. Omer's and at Paris. On being strongly urged by the Jesuits to join their order, he returned to England to escape their importunity. Some time between 1630 and 1633 he married Lucy Herbert, the Castara to whom he addresses his poems. As he was out of sympathy with the lyric poetry of his time, it is fitting that he frequently wrote in the sonnet form, which had lost its popularity. He found some audience, for *Castara* went through three editions. He wrote one play, *The Queen of Aragon*, 1640, and two volumes of history.

MODERN EDITION: *Castara* (ed. by E. Arber), London, 1870.

TEXT: *Castara*, 1640 (12585), Harvard; *The Queen of Aragon*, 1640 (12587), Harvard.

723 *Nox nocti indicat scientiam*] *Psalm* xix. 2. In the Authorized Ver- sion the verse is translated, 'Night unto night showeth knowledge.'

GEORGE HERBERT

GEORGE HERBERT (1593–1633), like Donne, introduced into his religious poetry an intimate personal note that was scarcely heard among the Elizabethans, and indeed would have been of little interest in that spacious time. Perhaps it is this intimacy which has caused some critics to class Herbert with the mystical poets, but in reality he has little of the mystic about him. His spiritual conflicts, and his moods of rebellion, are far from the calm assurance of the mystic, too completely possessed by the ecstasy of communion with God to be disturbed by the call of the world. Herbert is rather the poet of the church as an institution, hymning his joy in the comeliness and order of the Anglican ritual, in the symbolic beauty of the church building, in the cleanly peace of a holy life. He gives poetic expression to Archbishop Laud's conception of the Church, as exemplifying the 'beauty of holiness.'

Herbert attended Westminster School and Trinity College, Cambridge, where he took his B.A. in 1612, and his M.A. in 1616. While still an undergraduate, he began writing religious verse, thinking that so divine an art as poetry should be turned from the service of profane love to that of heavenly love. As fellow of his college, he continued at Cambridge after taking his Master's degree, commencing a systematic study of divinity; but when the Public Oratorship of the University fell vacant in 1619, he eagerly sought the position and obtained it through the aid of influential friends. His touch with the world as Public Orator filled him with 'ambition to be something more than he then was,' and he 'seldom looked toward Cambridge unless the King were there, but then he never failed.' Thus he was distracted from his original purpose, and for a time he hoped for civil preferment; but at the death of King James—other of his influential friends having died, and himself out of favor with the Duke of Buckingham—he looked again towards the Church. He became a deacon, and in 1626 was instituted to the prebend of Leighton Ecclesia in the diocese of Lincoln. In 1627 he resigned his Oratorship, but his period of hesitancy in committing himself completely to the Church continued until his marriage with Jane Danvers in 1629. This brought a happier state of mind, and in the next year, his doubts finally settled by Bishop Laud, he was ordained priest and instituted rector at Bemerton, near Salisbury. With the distress of making the decision behind him, he entered enthusiastically on his new duties, and by the piety of his last years deserved Walton's epithet, 'holy Mr. Herbert'. At times, the desire for a more active life of worldly honors disturbed his peace, but such moods seem to have passed away as he gave them poetic expression. Music was his chief recreation, and every week he walked to Salisbury to 'sing and play his part at an appointed private music-meeting.' According to Aubrey, he 'had a very good hand on the lute' and 'set [to music] his own lyrics or sacred poems.'

At the beginning of his final illness, he thought of his poems and desired his manuscript to be delivered to Nicholas Ferrar, a successful merchant who had retired from the world and established a Protestant monastic community at Little Gidding, with the message that 'he shall find in it a picture of the many spiritual conflicts that have passed betwixt God and my soul. . . . If he can think it may turn to the advantage of any dejected poor soul, let it be made public; if not, let him burn it.' Ferrar decided at once for publication, and sent the manuscript to the Vice-Chancellor of Cambridge to be licensed for publication. The Vice-Chancellor objected to two lines in *The Church Militant*,

> Religion stands on tip-toe in our land
> Ready to pass to the American strand,

but on Ferrar's refusal to change anything Herbert had written, the Vice-Chancellor waived his objections, and *The Temple* appeared in 1633, soon after Herbert's death. The book became immediately popular and stimulated other poets, among them Crashaw and Vaughan, to write religious verse.

Herbert had the gift of metrical facility. Palmer finds that of the 169 poems of *The Temple*, '116 are written in meters which are not repeated.' Several times this facility led Herbert into the over-exercise of ingenuity, but even in the extreme instances of this one marvels at the excellent fitting of the form to the matter.

MODERN EDITIONS: *The English Works* (ed. by G. H. Palmer), three volumes, Boston, 1907; *The Poems* (ed. by A. Waugh), Oxford, 1907.

COMMENT: A. G. Hyde, *George Herbert and his Times*, London, 1906.

TEXT: Izaak Walton, *The Life of Mr. George Herbert*, 1670, Harvard; *The Temple*, 1633 (13183), Harvard.

724 *To his mother*] written when Herbert was a student at Cambridge, possibly in 1610, and sent, with another sonnet on the same subject, in a letter to his mother; not included in *The Temple*.

725 *Jordan* [1]] Herbert probably chose the name of the meandering River Jordan as title for this and the following poem to symbolize the intricate meanderings of the poetry he is describing. 12 pull for prime] draw for a winning hand in a card game.

725–725 *Jordan* [2] 16 wide] wide of the mark.

726 *The British Church* 13 She on the hills] the Roman Catholic Church. 19 She in the valley] the more extreme Protestants, the Puritans.

727 *The altar*] The Renaissance delight in ingenuity produced some poems in which the lines are arranged to form various figures—columns and pyramids were especially popular. The author of *The Art of English Poesy*, 1589, discusses at length the various patterns. In this poem, and in *Easter wings*, Herbert has exercised his ingenious metrical skill, yet he has transcended mere ingenuity in the organic union of matter and form.

728 *Easter wings* 19 imp] a term in falconry; to repair the damaged wing of a hawk by inserting feathers from another bird.

732–734 *Man* 38–40] see *Genesis*, i. 9–10.

734–735 *Affliction* 25 began] made a menacing move; Palmer notes that this is an idiom which was still in use in Scotland in the 19th century: '"You had better not begin to me," is the first address of the schoolboy, half angry, half frightened, at the bullying of a companion.'

735–736 *Frailty* 9 regiments] rules, ways of life. 22 It] refers to 'honor, riches, or fair eyes' of line 3.

737 *The pearl. Matthew xiii*] verse 45. 2 press] Beeching thinks that 'Herbert intends a quibble here between the printing press and some other, such as a wine or olive press.'

738–739 *Peace* 22 prince] Christ. 23 Salem] used, both literally and figuratively, for Jerusalem. 28 twelve stalks] the twelve Apostles.

739–740 *Conscience* 14 his board] Communion.

744 *The odor. 2 Corinthians ii*] verse 15.

747 *The flower* 3 demean] demeanor. 18 passing bell] the bell tolling to announce death.

748 *Virtue* 11 closes] a technical term for the cadence or conclusion of a musical phrase.

FRANCIS QUARLES

FRANCIS QUARLES (1592–1644), after taking his B.A. at Christ's College, Cambridge, studied law at Lincoln's Inn, 'not so much out of desire to benefit himself thereby,' his wife tells us, 'as his friends and neighbors . . . by composing suits and differences amongst them.' In 1613 he went in the train of the Princess Elizabeth to the Palatinate, and later for a few years lived in Dublin as the secretary of James Usher, Archbishop of Armagh. His *Feast for Worms*, the first of his volumes of religious poetry, appeared in 1620. He proved to be an energetic writer, often rising at three in the morning to begin his work. Of his many books, his *Emblems*—poems of pious moralizing written to accompany woodcut illustrations—achieved the greatest popularity. During the Civil War he supported the Royalists with a series of pamphlets; but because of the nature of his poetry this fact was soon forgotten, and he was called 'an old puritanical poet' by Wood. His books were widely popular among people who were not habitually readers of poetry. Phillips says that Quarles was 'the darling of our plebeian judgments, that is, such as have ingenuity enough to delight in poetry, but are not sufficiently instructed to make a right choice and distinction.' There was a difference of opinion among the critics, however, for Winstanley, who frequently merely copied the opinions of Phillips, praises 'those excellent works' of Quarles.

MODERN EDITION: *The Complete Works* (ed. by A. B. Grosart), Edinburgh, 1880.

TEXT: *Argalus and Parthenia*, 1629 (20526), B. M.; *Divine Fancies*, 1632 (20529), Harvard; *Emblems*, 1635 (20540), Harvard; *Hieroglyphics*, 1638 (20548), Huntington.

749 *Hos ego versiculos*] Quarles has the best claim to the authorship of these widely imitated stanzas. His general idea had been anticipated by Barnabe Barnes in a sonnet beginning 'A blast of wind, a momentary breath' (see p.

217), and by Edmund Bolton in *A palinode* (see p. 202). Quarles, however, gave to the idea the poetic form in which it became widely popular. In this form, the poem seems to have been first printed in the seventh edition of Michael Spark's *Crumbs of Comfort*, 1628, in a version of six stanzas, the first stanza of which is the same as that printed by Quarles. Five stanzas were reprinted by Simon Wastell in *Microbiblion*, 1629. Quarles, then in Dublin, appended his two original stanzas to his romance *Argalus and Parthenia*, 1629, and to assert his claim to the authorship he gave his stanzas the heading *Hos ego versiculos,* thus referring to the story that Virgil had claimed the authorship of a disputed poem with the phrase, *Hos ego versiculos feci* ('I made these little verses'). (For the story, see *The Art of English Poesy*, 1589, Bk. I, ch. xxvii.) To leave no doubt of his claim in the minds of those to whom the Virgilian story might be unknown, Quarles also affixed his initials to the poem. In all probability Quarles's verses had been circulating in ms., and the ease with which the rhythm and similes could be imitated led others to attempt addition al stanzas. Then, before Quarles had published his stanzas, one of these imitations found its way into print. This poetic game of writing additional stanzas continued, and among those who took part in it were William Browne, Strode, and King

(see p. 641). Several imitations appeared as broadside ballads (cf. *Roxburghe Ballads,* i. 217 and ii. 12), and parodies were printed in the miscellanies. The last stanza of the earliest printed version in *Crumbs of Comfort* is a palinode, singing of the joys of the resurrection:

Like to the seed put in earth's womb,
Or like dead Lazarus in his tomb,
Or like Tabitha, being asleep,
Or like Jonah like, within the deep,
Or like the night, or stars by day,
Which seem to vanish clean away:
Even so this death man's life bereaves,
But being dead, man death deceives.
  The seed it springeth, Lazarus standeth,
    Tabitha walks, and Jonah landeth,
    The night is past, the stars remain:
  So man that dies shall live again.

750–751 *False world, thou ly'st* 5 pleasures] 1635 'pleasure'. 25 vy'st] viest; to bid, or stake a sum on one's cards. 26 scen] meet the bid; stake an equal sum. revied] to raise the bid or stake.
751 *Oh, whither shall I fly* 12 clip] fly rapidly.
755 *Behold how short a span*] For a brief discussion of patterned verse, see the note to Herbert's *Altar*. The reader will notice that the first lines of each stanza, italicized by Quarles, make a couplet by themselves containing the central idea of the poem.

HENRY MORE

HENRY MORE (1614–1687) was the most prolific writer, both in prose and verse, of the Cambridge Platonists. As a youth his father had tuned his ears to 'Spenser's rhymes, entertaining us on winter nights with that incomparable piece of his, *The Fairy Queen*.' He was educated at Eton and Christ's College, Cambridge, where he was graduated B.A. in 1635, and M.A. in 1639. He was elected a fellow of his college and remained there throughout the rest of his life, refusing any further preferment. To his father's objections to this lack of concern for worldly advancement, he answered: 'Your early encomiums also of learning and philosophy did so fire my credulous youth with the desire of the knowledge of things, that your after-advertisements, how contemptible learning would prove without riches, and what a piece of unmannerliness and incivility it would be held to seem wiser than them that are more wealthy and powerful, could never yet restrain my mind from her first pursuit, nor quicken my attention to the affairs of the world.' In his quiet academic seclusion he devoted himself to showing how the 'Christian and philosophic genius' should 'mix together.' His poem *Psychozoia* he calls 'a Christiano-Platonical display of life.' The anthologist seeking brief passages can find many of striking beauty in More's poetry.

MODERN EDITION: *Complete Poems* (ed. by A. B. Grosart), Edinburgh, 1878.
COMMENT: J. Tulloch, *Rational Theology and Christian Philosophy in England in the 17th Century*, two volumes, Edinburgh, 1874; M. H. Nicolson, 'More's *Psychozoia*,' *M. L. N.*, xxxvii. 141.
TEXT: *Philosophical Poems*, 1647, Hebel.

756 *Psychozoia, or the life of the soul*] The passage here printed consists of stanzas 121–125 of Canto II. 1 Mnemon] represents memory and occupies a large place in the poem as a relator of the events and wisdom of the past.

757-758 *Charity and humility* 17 pight] pitched. 20 wone] dwelling. 42 rend] render, recite.

RICHARD CRASHAW

RICHARD CRASHAW (1612–1649), the son of a bitterly anti-Catholic Anglican clergyman, became a convert to Roman Catholicism. The comely restraint of the middle way of Anglicanism, so loved by Herbert, was foreign to the warmer ecstasies of Crashaw's devotions. In his poetry, too, he tumultuously sweeps aside all restraint and piles exclamation upon exclamation, and metaphor upon metaphor; the very excess sometimes obscures the high imaginative quality of many of his lines. Contemplation of the life of St. Teresa seems to have been Crashaw's ladder to mystical experience—'the mystic of flame' he has been called, to distinguish him from Vaughan, 'the mystic of light.'

Crashaw was educated at Charterhouse and at Pembroke College, Cambridge, where he took his B.A. in 1634. In the same year he published his first volume of poetry, *Epigrammatum Sacrorum Liber*. He became a fellow of Peterhouse, a college with High Church tendencies, in 1635, and during the years of his fellowship seems to have been a friendly visitor at Nicholas Ferrar's community at Little Gidding. Soon after the outbreak of the Civil War, Crashaw found that the Parliamentarian sympathies of Cambridge made it an uncomfortable place for him, and he fled to the Continent. It is possible that after a time on the Continent he returned to England, residing at Oxford, then the Royalist headquarters. He was abroad again by 1645, probably the year of his conversion to Catholicism, and in the following year, provided with a letter from Queen Henrietta Maria recommending him to the favor of the Pope, he traveled to Rome. He received no preferment from the Pope, but in 1647 was taken into the household of Cardinal Palotto. Gossip has it that the free living of the Cardinal's followers stirred Crashaw to such remonstrance that his position became untenable. Whatever the cause, he was transferred in 1649 to a 'beneficiatus' at the shrine of Loretto, which appointment he did not long survive.

MODERN EDITIONS: *The Poems* (ed. by L. C. Martin), Oxford, 1927; *Poems* (ed. by A. R. Waller), Cambridge, 1904.
TEXT: *Steps to the Temple*, 1648, Harvard; *Carmen Deo Nostro*, 1652, Harvard.

758-759 *The Preface to the Reader* 8 Suarez] denied that angels use human language. 13 seven shares and a half] shares held by members of the companies of actors, to whom some poets were under contract for a certain number of plays each year. 26 St. Peter's College] Peterhouse, Cambridge.

759-763 *Music's duel*] a free translation of a Latin poem by Famianus Strada, a Jesuit, first published in 1617.

65 stilled] distilled. 78 Prefer] offer, proffer. 82 Prevents] anticipates. 104 enthusiast] 1646; 1648 'enthusiasts'. 128 grutch] complain.

763-765 *Wishes to his supposed mistress* 18 shoe-ty] shoe-tie. 70 flight] fleeing. 88 Sidneian] the reference is probably to Sidney's *Arcadia*, a favorite book with women down to the Restoration.

765 *On Mr. G. Herbert's book* 6

you've] 1648 'y'have'. 15 owe] own.

766 *To our Lord . . .*] Perhaps Crashaw's best known epigram is his Latin one on the same subject, *Aquæ in vinum versæ* from the *Epigrammata Sacra:*

Unde rubor vestris, et non sua purpura lymphis?
Quæ rosa mirantes tam nova mutat aquas?
Numen (convivæ) præsens agnoscite ·
    Numen:
Nympha pudica Deum vidit, et erubuit.

A widely-circulated translation of the last line, sometimes attributed to Crashaw, is, 'The conscious water saw its God and blushed'.

767 *To . . . the Countess of Denbigh*] Susan, Countess of Denbigh, was First Lady of the Bedchamber to Queen Henrietta Maria. When Crashaw arrived in Paris, in 1645, he either made or renewed acquaintance with her. During her stay in Paris, she was converted to Catholicism. Prefixed to the poem is an emblem of a heart with a lock and hinge, with the following quatrain:

'Tis not the work of force but skill,
To find the way into man's will.
'Tis love alone can hearts unlock,
Who knows the Word, he needs not knock.

768–771 *In the holy nativity of our Lord God* 33 east] 1652 'Eate'. 41, 43 ye] 1648; 1652 'the'. 60 wings] 1648; 1652 'wing'. 98 Maia's] the name of the month was thought by some Latin writers to be taken from the goddess, Maia.

771–774 *Saint Mary Magdalene, or*

the weeper] The poem is preceded by the emblem of a bleeding heart with the face of a weeping woman. The following couplet accompanies the emblem:

Lo, where a wounded heart with bleeding eyes conspire,
Is she a flaming fountain, or a weeping fire?

64 bridegroom] 1648; 1652 'bridegroomes'. 71 draw] 1648; 1652 'deaw'. 141 prayer] 1648; 1652 'paire'.

774–778 *A hymn . . .*] Crashaw probably became acquainted with the life of St. Teresa through her autobiography, which had been translated into English, under the title of *The Flaming Heart, or the Life of the glorious St. Teresa*, by an 'M. T.' in 1642. 40 weak] 1648; 1652 'what'. 42 kisses] 1648; 1652 'hisles'. 61] omitted in 1652; from 1648. 71 race] cut, slash. 79 His is the dart] In a vision an angel, armed with a dart of gold, appeared to St. Teresa. He thrust the dart through her heart several times, and when he withdrew left her 'wholly inflamed with a great love of almighty God.' St. Teresa found the pain so great that she was forced to utter groans, but she had no desire to be rid of it. 122 thou shalt] 1648; 1652 'you'. 147] omitted in 1652; from 1648. 151 deaths] 1648; 1652 'death'.

778–779 *An apology for the foregoing hymn* 26 hatched] omitted in 1652; from 1648. 29 enow] 1648; 1652 'now'.

780 *The Flaming Heart*] We print the last 34 of the 108 lines.

780 *A song* 1 grace] 1652 'geace'.

HENRY VAUGHAN

HENRY VAUGHAN (1622–1695) professed himself the disciple of George Herbert, and in his poetry there are many verbal reminiscences of *The Temple*. In reality, however, the difference in spirit between the two poets is much greater than their superficial similarity. Herbert is drawn to God through the Church, and Vaughan through intimations of divinity from nature. Vaughan is a loyal Anglican, but the institution means little to him compared with his own immediate intuition of the Deity, induced by those phenomena of nature which show the quickening of life—the freshness of the early morning, 'the seed swelling and stirring in the mold, the sap rising, or the branch budding.' Sustained by his vision of eternity, 'like a great ring of pure and endless light,' he never longs for the flesh-pots of the world, to him shrouded in darkness.

Though Vaughan has some skill in the simple tetrameter line, he lacks the metrical facility of Herbert, and at times, in imitating the intricate verse forms which Herbert could use with such freedom, he attains only a rugged awkwardness; yet, in attempting to communicate the ecstasy which he has known, he achieves illuminating figures and enlightening epithets quite beyond Herbert's reach.

He was born in Brecknockshire, South Wales, and, proud of his Welsh descent, he signed himself 'Silurist,' from Siluria, the Roman name for the district. His schooling began under Reverend Matthew Herbert, to whom he felt greatly indebted for a stimulus towards literature, and was continued at Jesus College, Oxford, which he probably entered in 1638. But, as he wrote to Aubrey, he 'stayed not at Oxford to take any degree, but was sent to London, being then designed by my father for the study of law, which the sudden eruption of our late Civil Wars wholly frustrated.' At London he evidently came to know the literary group and began to write poetry. After the outbreak of the Civil War, he retired to Wales and turned to the study of medicine. The evidence of his poems is contradictory regarding service in the Civil War. He seems for a time to have been a lieutenant with the Royalist troops under Sir Herbert Price. After the Civil War, he settled down in his native shire and lived a quiet and long life as a country doctor. In 1650 he published his first volume of religious poems, *Silex Scintillans*, to which he added a second part in 1655. His poetic productivity lessened after 1655 and he wrote only a few poems, published in *Thalia Rediviva*, 1678.

MODERN EDITIONS: *The Works* (ed. by L. C. Martin), two volumes, Oxford, 1914; *The Poems* (ed. by E. K. Chambers), two volumes, Muses' Library, London, n. d.

COMMENT: H. W. Wells, *The Tercentenary of Henry Vaughan*, New York, 1922; Edmund Blunden, *On the Poems of Henry Vaughan*, London, 1927.

TEXT: *Poems*, 1646, Harvard; *Silex Scintillans*, 1655, Harvard.

781 *Silex Scintillans*] 'Sparkling Flint.'

782–783 *To Amoret gone from him* 22 element] compose.

783 *The match* 1 friend] George Herbert. This poem precedes and is evidently intended as an introduction to *Rules and Lessons,* which Vaughan is matching with Herbert's *Church Porch.*

784 *Mount of Olives* [1] 9 Cotswold and Cooper's] *Annalia Dubrensa,* a collection of poems, by various hands, celebrating Dover's annual athletic games in the Cotswold Hills, was published in 1636; Sir John Denham's *Cooper's Hill* was published in 1642.

784–785 *The garland* 19 silk-lists] silk borders. 27 abear] bearing, behavior.

785 *The seed growing secretly* 5 dew] Mystics frequently compare the rapture of communion with God, refreshing to the spirit, with the freshening dew of the early morning, and refer to a period in which they are denied this ecstasy as a 'dry period.'

789 *And do they so?* 'Etenim res' etc.] 'For the earnest expectation of the creature waiteth for the manifesta-

tion of the sons of God.' 2 influence] probably with the astrological sense of the flowing in of an ethereal fluid affecting the destiny of things; occult force.

790–791 *The night. John* iii. 2] 1655 misprints 'John ii. 3'. 12 Sun] Vaughan intends a play on the double meaning, 'sun' and 'son.' 17 leaves] 1655 'leafs'. 29 Christ's] marginal note: '*Mark* i. 35; *Luke* xxi. 37.'

791–794 *The search*] At the close of the poem, Vaughan quotes *Acts,* xvii. 27–28: 'That they should seek the Lord, if happily they might feel after him, and find him, though he be not far off from everyone of us, for in him we live, and move, and have our being.' 21 Sychar] *John* iv. 5; a city 'near to the parcel of ground that Jacob gave to his son Joseph.'

794 *Regeneration*] This difficult poem gives an imaginative record of Vaughan's turning from absorption in the things of this world to the life in the spirit with its enlivening mystical experience. Edmund Blunden, in his *Henry Vaughan,* p. 20, attempts a detailed explanation, which should be considered by the close student of the poem.

799 *The world* 11 sour] 1655 'so our'.

800–801 *Ascension hymn* 12 old man] old Adam; cf. *Romans*, vi. 6. 35 Fuller] one who treads and beats cloth for the purpose of cleansing it; here

used figuratively for Christ; cf. *Mark*, ix. 3.

801 *They are all gone* 1 They] spirits, heavenly beings. 5 It] the memory. 23 well] spring, pool.

802 *Unprofitableness* 14 let] 1655 'yet'.

802–803 *Mount of Olives* [2] 17 paisage] landscape.

THOMAS TRAHERNE

THOMAS TRAHERNE (1636–1674) remained unknown as a poet until the 20th century. In 1897, two anonymous manuscripts of poetry and prose meditations appeared on a London book-stall. They sold for a few pence and came into the hands of Grosart, who, thinking the poems from the pen of Vaughan, planned an edition to include this newly-discovered material. He did not live to complete the task, and at the dispersal of his books the manuscripts came to Bertram Dobell, who after careful research found the real author and published the first edition of Traherne's *Poems* in 1903, and of the *Centuries of Meditations* in 1908. Two years later, Mr. Bell discovered and published another manuscript of Traherne's poems, which had lain unnoticed among the *Burney Mss.* in the British Museum. These discoveries made accessible to students a poet especially important for the light which he throws on the conception of childhood common to many English poets. Certainly one understands Vaughan, Blake, and Wordsworth more clearly after reading Traherne.

Traherne, the son of a Hereford shoemaker, was educated at Brasenose College, Oxford, taking his B.A. in 1656. The next year he retired to the country rectory of Credenhill, where, in reviewing the course of study at Oxford, he noticed the lack of instruction in the most important of all subjects, the attainment of felicity. To this subject he determined to devote himself, choosing 'to live upon ten pounds a year, and to go in leather clothes, and feed upon bread and water,' so that he might have all his time free for his speculation. Finally he arrived at his solution: the key to true happiness was to be found in the untutored scale of values of the child. By instinct the child valued the common natural things (air, sunlight, water), free to all and arousing no strife among mankind. In this the child was happy, but his felicity was soon destroyed by his false education which set artificial value on ownership of gold, silver, rubies, and diamonds, in real worth not to be compared with the things which the child had instinctively valued. By the aid of right thinking man could return to the true set of values of childhood.

During this time he also continued his formal studies, and was granted his M.A. in 1661 and his B.D. in 1669. Two years earlier he had become Chaplain to Sir Orlando Bridgman, the Lord Keeper of the Seals. When Sir Orlando was deprived of the seals in 1672, Traherne followed him into retirement at Teddington. Here Traherne spent the last two years of his life, loved for his 'cheerful and sprightly temper, free from anything of the sourness and formality by which some great pretenders to piety rather disparage and misrepresent true religion than recommend it.'

Traherne seems more at his ease in writing his prose *Centuries of Medita-*

tions than in his verse, which is at times awkward, for he does not have technical facility equal to the metrical patterns which he attempts. In order to appreciate fully his merits, the reader should turn also to the *Centuries of Meditations*.

MODERN EDITIONS: *The Poetical Works* (ed. by B. Dobell), London, 1903; *Poems of Felicity* (ed. by H. I. Bell), Oxford, 1910; *Centuries of Meditations* (ed. by B. Dobell), London, 1908 and 1927.

COMMENT: G. E. Willet, *Traherne, An Essay*, Cambridge, 1919.

TEXT: *Burney Ms.* 392, B. M.; *Christian Ethics*, 1675, B. M.

803 *Poems of Felicity, Burney Ms.* 392] This ms. though not published until its discovery by Bell in 1910, seems to have been prepared for the press by Traherne's brother Philip.

803-805 *Wonder*] also appears with variant readings in Dobell's ms. Traherne used the subject-matter of this poem in one of the most beautiful passages in the *Centuries of Meditations* (The Third Century, section 3), opening, 'The corn was orient and immortal wheat, which never should be reaped, nor was ever sown.' 49 proprieties] proprietorship, ownership.

805-806 *Eden*] also appears with variant readings in Dobell's ms. 24

roaring boys] a term frequently used in the 16th and 17th centuries for noisy, blustering, disorderly gangsters.

806 *News*] also appears with variant readings in Dobell's ms.

813 *Right apprehension* II] also appears, under the title of *The Apprehension*, in Dobell's ms. 7] Dobell reads 'Was all my whole felicity.'

813 *The rapture*] also appears with variant readings in Dobell's ms.

814 *Felicity* 23 with] ms. reads 'which'.

816 *Insatiableness*] This is the second poem by this title in the ms. 15 curious] difficult to satisfy; fastidious.

SIR FRANCIS KYNASTON

SIR FRANCIS KYNASTON (1587-1642) took his B.A. at Oxford and his M.A. at Cambridge. Wood says that he was 'more addicted to the superficial parts of learning, poetry and oratory (wherein he excelled), than logic and philosophy.' In 1635 he founded an academy of learning, the Museum Minervæ, which was to provide a scientific and literary education for gentlemen before their Continental tour. He translated part of Chaucer's *Troilus and Cressida* into Latin rhyme royal, and wrote a long heroic poem, *Leoline and Sydanis*, 'a romance of the amorous adventures of princes.' His shorter poems are addressed to a Cynthia. Kynaston's acquaintance with her is amusingly described in the preface to his posthumous volume: 'It is very true that a lady's beauty, with whom he was scarcely acquainted, begot these lighter fancies in his head, with whom if he had been really in love, perhaps he would have written more and better lines.'

MODERN EDITION: 'Sir Francis Kynaston' in *Minor Poets of the Caroline Period* (ed. by G. Saintsbury), Vol. ii, Oxford, 1906.

TEXT: *Leoline and Sydanis*, 1642, B. M.

SIDNEY GODOLPHIN

SIDNEY GODOLPHIN (1610-1643) received his education at Exeter College, Oxford, at one of the Inns of Court, and in travel abroad. He early became a member of Parliament and was a zealous Royalist, meeting his death in one of the skirmishes at the beginning of the Civil War. By his friends, Hobbes, Clarendon, and Falkland, he was regarded as a young man of considerable promise. He contributed a poem to *Jonsonus Virbius* (cf. *T. L. S.*

October 25, 1923) but the majority of his poems remained in manuscript until collected by Saintsbury.

MODERN EDITION: 'The Poems' in *Minor Poets of the Caroline Period* (ed. by G. Saintsbury), Vol. ii, Oxford, 1906.

TEXT: *Malone Ms.* 13, Bodleian.

JOHN HALL

JOHN HALL (1627–1656) entered St. John's College, Cambridge, in 1646 and in the same year published *Horæ Vacivæ*, a volume of essays indebted to Bacon. These essays, because of Hall's immaturity, 'amazed not only the University, but the serious part of men in the three nations.' Later in the year, Hall published a volume of poems, greeted like the essays with great applause, even Herrick writing to 'his worthy friend' in wonder at his precocity. The following year Hall left the University, disappointed at not receiving honorary advancement, and entered Gray's Inn. In London he turned to writing political pamphlets for Cromwell, grew fat for lack of exercise, and was, according to Wood, diverted by 'debauchery and intemperance' from serious studies. Phillips remarks that on his death he left unfinished a poem which had created 'great and general expectation among his friends.' This poem has not survived. Hall was the 'I. H.' whose *Emblems with Elegant Figures* appeared in 1648.

MODERN EDITION: 'John Hall' in *Minor Poets of the Caroline Period* (ed. by G. Saintsbury), Vol. ii, Oxford, 1906.

TEXT: *Poems,* 1646, Harvard.

822–823 *An Epicurean ode* 15 *terra lemnia*] reddish earth of medicinal property.

823–824 *Even as the wandering traveler* 40 specters] Saintsbury's emendation; 1646 reads 'sceptets', a word not recorded in the *O.E.D.* 'Scepters' and 'sceptics' have also been suggested.

THOMAS STANLEY

THOMAS STANLEY (1625–1678), after his education at Pembroke Hall, Cambridge, and a period of foreign travel, settled in lodgings in the Middle Temple for the quiet pursuit of literary work. He was the kindly benefactor of many needy men of letters during the Commonwealth. Having no marked originality, he found pleasure in translating from the classics and from the Romance languages. Indeed, as the work of tracing sources continues, very few poems are left to Stanley's credit (cf. *M.L.R.* xx. 280). Phillips's statement, that he was 'particularly honored for his smooth air and genteel spirit in poetry,' defines well the merit both of his translations and his original poetry. After publishing several volumes of verse, he turned to scholarship and wrote a history of philosophy, the first in English. In 1663 he prepared an edition of Æschylus with notable emendations of the text, now generally supposed to have been plagiarized.

MODERN EDITIONS: 'Thomas Stanley' in *Minor Poets of the Caroline Period* (ed. by G. Saintsbury), Vol. iii, Oxford, 1921; *Thomas Stanley: his original lyrics, complete* (ed. by L. I. Guiney), Hull, 1907; *Anacreon: with Thomas Stanley's translation* (ed. by A. H. Bullen), London, 1893.

TEXT: *Poems and Translations,* 1647, Harvard; *Poems,* 1651, Harvard.

825 *Expectation*] All the lyrics of Stanley here included were set to music by John Gamble in *Airs and Dialogues,* 1656.

SIR EDWARD SHERBURNE

SIR EDWARD SHERBURNE (1618–1702), after service in the Civil War and the confiscation of his property and large library as a Royalist, settled at the Middle Temple, where he became the intimate friend of Thomas Stanley. All of his poems, even those thought for a time to be original, seem to be translations (cf. *M.L.R.* xx. 289). There is indication of this in a remark of Sherburne's friend Phillips, who said of him that he was 'in what he hath elegantly and judiciously translated . . . a discoverer of a more pure poetical spirit and fancy, than many others can justly pretend to in their original works.' The first four poems here included are all translated from Marino, an Italian poet widely read and often imitated in 17th-century England. Sherburne himself has indicated the source of the three epigrams.

MODERN EDITIONS: 'The Poems' in *English Poets* (ed. by A. Chalmers), Vol. vi, London, 1810; *Miscellaneous Poems* (ed. by S. Fleming), London, 1819.

TEXT: *Salmacis . . . with several other poems and translations,* 1651, Harvard.

827 *Salmacis . . . 1651*] In some copies the title-page reads: *Poems and translations,* 1651.

828 *The happy life*] see Surrey's translation of the same epigram, p. 34.

828 *On Captain Ansa . . .*] Sherburne seems to be translating from A. Wright's *Deliticæ Delitiarum,* 1637. *De timido Ansa Fulvio,* by Mat. Casimirus (a Polish poet), appears on p. 117, and two pages further on appears the original, by Julius Cæsar Scaliger, of Sherburne's *On Bibinus.*

ABRAHAM COWLEY

ABRAHAM COWLEY (1618–1667) wrote of himself that he became a poet because Spenser's *Fairy Queen,* read as a youngster at home, filled his head 'with such chimes of verse, as have never since left ringing there.' As early as 1633, Cowley published his first volume, *Poetical Blossoms.* At Westminster School he was so studious that his masters were willing to pardon his refusal 'to learn without book the common rules of grammar.' He proceeded to Trinity College, Cambridge, where his play, *The Guardian,* was produced. On the outbreak of the Civil War he was ejected from Cambridge as a Royalist, and retired to Oxford. Later he was employed in France by the Queen in her cipher correspondence with Charles. He returned to England in 1656, probably as a secret agent for the Royalists; but finding his position uncomfortable, even though he masked his designs by taking an M.D. at Oxford, he again retired to France. At the Restoration he was disappointed in not securing preferment. He received, however, a small estate at Chertsey from the Duke of Buckingham, and there he spent his last two years 'concealed in his beloved obscurity, and possessed that solitude, which from his very childhood he had always passionately desired.'

Cowley is now best known for his prose essays but to his contemporaries he was 'that incomparable poet.' His metaphysical conceits, like Cleveland's, seemed to his time to reach the very boundaries of wit. By 1700 taste had changed, and Dryden records that Cowley 'is sunk in his reputation because he could never forgive any conceit which came in his way, but swept like a drag-net great and small.' Cowley's Pindaric odes, lacking the structural correspondencies of Pindar's own odes, made popular free and irregular verse forms.

MODERN EDITIONS: *The English Writings* (ed. by A. R. Waller), two volumes, Cambridge, 1905–6; *The Mistress with other select poems* (ed. by J. Sparrow), London, 1926.

TEXT: *Poetical Blossoms*, 1636 (5907), Harvard; *The Works of Mr. Abraham Cowley*, 1668, Cornell.

829 *The vote*] We print only the last three of the eleven stanzas. Cowley himself prints these stanzas as a separate poem in his essay, *Of myself*, with the following comment: 'The beginning of it is boyish, but of this part which I here set down (if a very little corrected) I should hardly now be much ashamed.'

830–832 *Ode. Of wit*] Spingarn, in his introduction to *Critical Essays of the 17th Century* (i. xxix–xxx), defines the use of the term: 'In the Elizabethan age "wit" denoted the intellect in general, in opposition to "will," the faculty of volition. . . . From this time [*i.e.*, in Jacobean and Caroline days] "wit" became identical with the imaginative or rather fanciful element in poetry, and more or less important as this element was more or less valued by succeeding schools.' Cowley seems to be using the word somewhat as we use 'creative imagination.' In the preface to *Annus Mirabilis*, 1666, Dryden defines the term: 'Wit in the poet . . . is no other than the faculty of the imagination in the writer, which, like a nimble spaniel, beats over and ranges through the field of memory, till it springs the quarry it hunted after; or, without metaphor, which searches over all the memory for the species or ideas of those things which it designs to represent.' 2 Thou] unidentified; possibly Bishop Sprat. 3 first matter] matter in its chaotic, changing condition before the creation. 4 't] variety; even women love variety, either in love or dress, less than wit loves variety. 20 tit'lar bishops] Bishops *in partibus infidelium* (in infidel countries) without a see. 27–8] Wit must be the organic principle of a poem, its very life, not something added. 29 numbers] the music of Amphion. 50 Bajazet] the conquered

emperor in Marlowe's *Tamburlaine*.

832–833 *On the death of Mr. Crashaw*] Crashaw and Cowley were college friends at Cambridge. Martin, the most recent editor of Crashaw, thinks that Crashaw submitted to Cowley for criticism the new poems in the second edition of *Steps to the Temple*, 1648. Their friendship is witnessed by their companion poems—*Against hope* by Cowley, and *Answer for hope* by Crashaw. 30 she] Crashaw's muse. 35 It] Crashaw's muse. 37] marginal note: 'Mr. Crashaw died of a fever at Loretto, being newly chosen Canon of that Church.' 55 tenents] tenets.

834 *The spring*] from *The Mistress*, of which Cowley gives an interesting account in his preface: 'The second part is called *The Mistress, or Love-Verses;* for so it is that poets are scarce thought free men of their company without paying some duties and obliging themselves to be true to love. . . . But we must not always make a judgment of their manners from their writings of this kind. . . . It is not in this sense that poesy is said to be a kind of painting; it is not the picture of the poet, but of things and persons imagined by him. He may be in his own practice and disposition a philosopher, nay, a Stoic, and yet speak sometimes with the softness of an amorous Sappho.' 7 rosebud ope] 1668 'rose-bud morning ope'. The printer probably mistakenly picked up 'morning' from the line below.

835 *Awake, awake, my lyre*] This song is from *Davideis, a sacred poem of the troubles of David,* and is sung by David beneath Michol's window to tell her of his love. The *Davideis* is an epic poem of four books in heroic couplets. Cowley had planned for twelve on the model of the *Æneid*, but he did not complete the poem.

JOHN CLEVELAND

JOHN CLEVELAND (1613–1658), 'a notable, high soaring, witty loyalist of Cambridge,' after being at Christ's College was made fellow of St. John's. He was a reader in rhetoric and, according to Aubrey, was known at St. John's 'as disputant rather than poet.' Soon after the outbreak of the Civil War he moved to Oxford and employed his pen in verse and prose satires for the Royalist cause. He also saw some military service. In his poetry he carries the metaphysical conceit to its point of greatest extravagance, so that to us it seems needless and absurd ornamentation; but he evidently judged rightly the taste of his contemporaries, for his poems went through edition after edition. 'So great a man hath Cleveland been in the estimation of the generality,' says Phillips, evidently disapproving of their judgment, 'in regard his conceits were out of the common road and wittily far fetched, that grave men in outward appearance have not spared in my hearing to affirm him the best of English poets.' He was widely imitated by now forgotten and unknown poets who, as Fuller observes, 'Clevelandized, endeavoring to imitate his masculine style,' but fell short, 'betraying the weaker sex in their deficient conceits.' The editors of the 1677 edition question 'how many such authors must be creamed and spirited to make up his *Fuscara*?' Winstanley aptly describes Cleveland's decked-out commonplaces—'a difficult plainness, difficult in the hearing, plain at the considering thereof.'

MODERN EDITIONS: *The Poems* (ed. by J. M. Berdan), New Haven, 1911; 'John Cleveland' in *Minor Poets of the Caroline Period* (ed. by G. Saintsbury), Vol. ii, Oxford, 1921.

TEXT: *Jonsonus Virbius*, 1638 (14784), White; *Poems*, 1653, Harvard; *Clievelandi Vindiciæ*, 1677, Cornell.

836 *An elegy on Ben Jonson* 2 his] 1638 'your'.

836 *Epitaph on the Earl of Strafford*] not certainly Cleveland's. In several of the early editions, it appears under the head 'Uncertain Authors,' and it is not included in the edition of 1677, but in the majority of the editions it is ascribed to Cleveland. Strafford was one of the King's advisers just before the outbreak of the Civil War. He was greatly feared by the Puritans, and one of the early acts of the Long Parliament was his impeachment. After an exciting trial a Bill of Attainder was passed, and he was executed on May 12, 1641.

836-838 *Fuscara, or the bee errant* 34 inoculate] insert a bud in; the whole clause is Cleveland's way of saying that Fuscara was freckled. 62 lancepresade] lancepesade, a lance corporal. 70 Ravaillac] the assassin of Henry IV of France.

839-840 *Mark Antony* 36 ingeny] genius, wit.

SIR WILLIAM DAVENANT

SIR WILLIAM DAVENANT (1606–1668), the son of an Oxford tavern-keeper, began early a courtier's life with service as page to the Duchess of Richmond. Later he was in the service of Fulke Greville, Lord Brooke, and throughout his life sought a succession of patrons by extravagant poems of compliment. After Jonson's quarrel with Inigo Jones, he was one of the devisers of masks for production at court. From 1638 he received a pension, which gave rise to the statement that he succeeded Jonson as poet-laureate, but though both were so called neither received an official appointment, the first of such appointments being given to Dryden. Davenant's major effort in non-dramatic poetry was *Gondibert*, an heroic poem left unfinished. During the Commonwealth, Davenant produced at Rutland House, in 1656, musical dialogues in *stilo recitativo*, the first operas in England.

MODERN EDITION: 'The Poems' in *English Poets* (ed. by A. Chalmers), Vol. vi, London, 1810 (contains very few of Davenant's shorter poems, which are still to be found only in the folio of 1673).

TEXT: *Luminalia*, 1637 (16923), Huntington; *The Works of Sir William Davenant*, 1673, Cornell.

840 *Night's first song*] *Luminalia* was published anonymously, but it is most frequently attributed to Davenant.

841 *Song*] set to music by Wilson in *Cheerful Airs or Ballads*, 1660. 4 to] 1673 'so'.

841 *To the Queen . . .*] Queen Henrietta Maria. The Countess of Anglesey is probably Mary, wife of Charles Villiers, second Earl of Anglesey.

841–842 *The Countess of Anglesey . . . 13* Gothic] barbarous, rude.

842 *Song, Endymion Porter and Olivia*] Endymion Porter held various positions in the diplomatic service under James I and Charles I, but is principally remembered as a patron of literature and art. Davenant was greatly indebted to him, and Herrick shared in his bounty.

843 *The philosopher and the lover*] also used by Davenant, with revised second and third stanzas, as 'A Song between two Boys' in his play, *The Just Italian*.

844 *Song* 8 dock] the rump.

SIR JOHN DENHAM

Sir John Denham (1615–1669) was known at Trinity College, Oxford, as a 'slow and dreaming young man . . . given more to cards and dice than his study.' He proceeded to Lincoln's Inn, where he was still troubled enough by losses from gaming to write an essay 'to show the vanities and inconveniences of it, which he presented to his father to let him know his detestation of it.' During the Civil War he saw service with the Royalists. At the Restoration he was made Surveyor General of Works, but was thought by Evelyn to be 'a better poet than architect.' For a time he had as his assistant the young Christopher Wren. Denham was best known for his bloody tragedy, *The Sophy*, and for his descriptive and didactic poem, *Cooper's Hill*, first published in 1642. The wits of the time, in order to enjoy the embarrassment of Denham, circulated the story that he 'bought *Cooper's Hill*.' An anonymous *Session of Poets* says that the poem 'was writ by a vicar, who had forty pound for it.' Largely because of *Cooper's Hill*, Denham was ranked by the Restoration and the 18th century as 'one of the fathers of English poetry.' Dryden calls *Cooper's Hill* 'a poem which . . . for the majesty of the style is, and ever will be, the exact standard of good writing,' and Pope, admiring its 'strength', imitated it in his *Windsor Forest*. Dr. Johnson briefly expresses the opinion of his century about both Denham and Waller: 'The critical decision has given the praise of strength to Denham, and of sweetness to Waller.'

Modern Edition: *The Poetical Works* (ed. by T. H. Banks, Jr.), New Haven, 1928.

Text: *Cooper's Hill*, 1655, Harvard; *Poems and Translations*, 1668, Harvard; *The Sophy*, 1642, Harvard.

844–846 *Cooper's Hill*] We print lines 159–236 from the 342 lines of the poem. **31–34**] These famous lines first appeared in this form in the edition of 1655. The suggestion for them probably came from lines 122–124 of William Cartwright's *In Memory of the most worthy Benjamin Jonson*, first published in *Jonsonus Virbius*, 1638, and included in Cartwright's collected edition in 1651:

Low without creeping, high without loss
　of wings;
Smooth, and yet not weak, and by a
　thorough care
Big without swelling, without painting
　fair.

35] marginal note: 'The forest.' **52** self-enamoured youth] marginal note: 'Narcissus.'

846–848 *On Mr. Abraham Cowley*] This poem was written by Denham soon after his recovery from an attack of madness brought on either by his passion at his wife's infidelity, or by his own early excesses. The poem was first printed as a folio sheet in 1667. **43**] marginal note: 'His pindarics.' Flaccus] Q. Horatius Flaccus. **44** Theban swan] Pindar. **58**] marginal note: 'His last work.' **64** both their genii] Virgil's and Cowley's.

848 *Somnus, the humble god*] printed also as a separate poem in the edition of 1668, where 'Somnus' was corrected in the errata to 'Morpheus'.

EDMUND WALLER

EDMUND WALLER (1606–1687) was educated at Eton and at King's College, Cambridge. He early entered Parliament and gained a reputation for brilliant eloquence. For a time he paid poetical worship (not too deeply felt if we may judge from the poems) to Dorothy Sidney, the daughter of the Earl of Leicester, under the name of Sacharissa. At the opening of the Civil War he seemed to throw in his lot with Parliament, but in 1643 he took part in a plot to turn London over to the Royalists, for which he was fined £10,000 and banished from England. While he was abroad three editions of his poems appeared in 1645, which he disowned as faulty and unauthorized in the preface to the edition of 1664. He obtained permission to return to England during the Commonwealth and wrote a panegyric on Cromwell. At the Restoration he came into favor, for though Charles II complained that Waller's address of welcome was inferior to his panegyric on Cromwell, he was placated by Waller's famous answer, 'Sir, we poets never succeed so well in writing truth as in fiction.'

Waller's 'even, sweet, and flowing' poetry pleased the Restoration and the 18th century. They admired the smoothness for which Waller strove, and hailed him 'the parent of our verse.' Dryden expresses clearly the conception which the Restoration had of Waller's place in the development of the heroic couplet: 'But the excellence and dignity of it [rhyme] were never fully known till Mr. Waller taught it; he first made writing easily an art; first showed us to conclude the sense most commonly in distichs, which, in the verse of those before him, runs on for so many lines together, that the reader is out of breath to overtake it.' Dryden and the 18th century overlooked entirely the place of Drayton, Jonson, Sir John Beaumont, and Sandys in the development of the couplet. Waller, himself, claimed that 'he derived the harmony of his numbers' from Fairfax (see p. 375), but it is interesting to note that George Sandys presented Waller with a copy (recently sold at Sotheby's from the Britwell Court Library) of the first edition of his *Paraphrase upon the Divine Poems*.

MODERN EDITION: *The Poems* (ed. by G. Thorn Drury), Muses' Library, London, n. d.

COMMENT: Julia Cartwright, *Sacharissa*, New York, 1901.

TEXT: *Poems*, 1664, Harvard; *Poems*, 1668, B. M.; *Poems*, 1686, B. M.

848–849 *At Penshurst*] This poem is headed *Another* in the 1664 edition, where it is preceded by other poems entitled *At Penshurst*. 1 Sacharissa] 1645 reads 'Dorothea'. 26 tree] planted in honor of the birth of Sir Philip Sidney; see Jonson's *To Penshurst*, l. 13, p. 500.

849–851 *The Battle of the Summer Islands*] We print only the first of the three cantos of the poem. The last two cantos describe the battle with the whales. Aubrey, writing in 1680, tells of the composition of the poem: 'He wrote verses of the Bermudas 50 years since, upon the information of one that had been there; walking in his fine woods, the poetic spirit came upon him.' 1 Bellona] Roman goddess of war. 52 palma-christi] the castor oil plant. 62 to] 1664 'do'.

851 *Song* 'Stay, Phœbus, stay'] perhaps the earliest love poem which employs a figure of speech based on the Copernican astronomy. 6 De Mornay's] unidentified; De Mornay was probably one of the Frenchwomen in the train of Queen Henrietta Maria.

851 *Song* 'Go, lovely rose'] set to music by Henry Lawes in *Airs and Dialogues*, 1655.

ANDREW MARVELL

ANDREW MARVELL (1621–1678) was educated at the Grammar School in Hull and at Trinity College, Cambridge. Later in his life he was called, by such a severe judge as Milton, 'a scholar, and well read in the Greek and Latin classics.' At some time during his residence at Cambridge he was converted to Catholicism by Jesuits, but he was soon reconverted to Anglicanism by his father, an Anglican rector. Marvell was graduated B.A. in 1639, and remained at Cambridge for study until 1641 when his father's death by drowning made it necessary for him to begin earning his living. He held a clerkship in a business house in Hull for a time and then went abroad, possibly as a tutor, for a period of about four years. He was back in England by 1649, when he contributed prefatory verses to Lovelace's *Lucasta*. By 1651 he was tutor to Mary Fairfax, the daughter of the Lord General Fairfax. The pleasant life with the Fairfaxes, at Nun Appleton House in Yorkshire, known for its beautiful garden, probably inspired much of Marvell's garden poetry. He seems to have viewed the Civil War with detachment and not to have associated himself with either party. Later he wrote: 'I think the cause was too good to have been fought for. Men ought to have trusted God—they ought to have trusted the King with that whole matter.'

By February of 1653, Marvell had left Nun Appleton, and was recommended by Milton—then Latin Secretary to the Council of State—for the position of assistant secretary. But for some reason Marvell was not appointed at this time, and he became, in July, 1653, the tutor of William Dutton, a ward of Cromwell's, with whom he lived at Eton in the house of John Oxenbridge. Oxenbridge had made several trips to the Bermudas, and from his conversation Marvell probably received the suggestion for the poem, *Bermudas*. In 1657, Marvell was appointed Milton's assistant, and in 1659 he was elected to Richard Cromwell's Parliament. His re-election in 1660 and 1661 kept him in public service until his death. He is remarkable among members of Parliament for his regularity in writing to his constituency a faithful account of Parliamentary affairs. These new interests put an end to his writing of lyric poetry, but the events and policies of the Restoration did move him to satirical poetry, which won him the name of 'the liveliest droll of the age.'

Marvell's satirical verse is not represented in this volume, since it is of interest primarily to students of the Restoration. His high reputation as a poet rests rather upon his earlier lyrics, in which the metaphysical conceit, degenerated in the writing of his contemporaries, renews its life and vigor in a setting of lyric grace.

MODERN EDITIONS: *The Poems* (ed. by H. M. Margoliouth), two volumes, Oxford, 1927; *Miscellaneous Poems* (The Nonesuch Press), London, 1923; *Poems and Satires* (ed. by G. A. Aitken), two volumes, Muses' Library, London, n. d.

COMMENT: Augustine Birrell, *Andrew Marvell*, London, 1905; *Andrew Marvell, Tercentenary Tributes* (ed. by W. H. Bagguley), Oxford, 1922; P. Legouis, *André Marvell*, Paris, 1928.

TEXT: *Miscellaneous Poems*, 1681, White, Harvard, and B. M.

853 *The garden*] In the edition of 1681 this poem is followed by a Latin version, *Hortus*, which Marvell seems to have written first, and from which the English version is partially paraphrased.

854 *On a drop of dew*] In the edition of 1681 this poem is followed by a Latin version, *Ros,* which Marvell seems to have written first and from which the English version is paraphrased.

855–856 *The mower against gardens*
1 luxurious] voluptuous. 15 onion
root] Margoliouth annotates: 'During
the tulip mania (at its height 1634–7)
the bulbs were sold in Holland by
weight like precious stones: a bulb of
10 grammes is recorded to have fetched
5,500 florins, *i. e.,* 550 times the value of
a sheep.' 18 marvel of Peru] an ornamental herb with flowers of a great
variety of color growing in the West
Indies and Peru.

857–858 *Clorinda and Damon* 8
vade] fade, wither. 20 Pan] Christ.

858 *The coronet* 7 towers] high
head-dresses.

859–860 *A dialogue between the resolved soul and created pleasure* 51
cost] the reading of 1681, which some
editors have emended, although it does
make sense and is supported by 'shine'
of the following line. Cf. Shakespeare,
Sonnet 64:

When I have seen by Time's fell hand
   defaced
The rich proud cost of outworn buried
   age.

861–862 *Bermudas*] not in the White
copy of 1681; text from the Harvard
copy. 20 Ormus] Ormuz, a famous
mart of the Portuguese, near the entrance of the Persian Gulf; like India
frequently used to suggest gorgeous
wealth. 23 apples] pineapples.

862–864 *The nymph complaining . . .*
17 deodands] given or forfeited to
God; according to old English law,
any personal chattel that had been immediately instrumental in causing the
death of a person was forfeited to the
Crown for pious uses. 53 then] the
old spelling of 'than,' here kept for
rhyme. 99 Heliades] daughters of
Helios (the sun), and sisters of Phaethon, who bewailed so bitterly their
brother's death that they were changed
into poplars and their tears into amber.

864 *The picture of little T. C. . . .*]
'T. C.' is identified by Margoliouth as
'possibly Theophila Cornewall,' born in
1644.

865 *The definition of love* 24 plani-
sphere] a plane projection of the
sphere.

866–867 *To his coy mistress* 29
dust] 1681 'durst'. 34 glew] the reading of 1681, which may be right in the
sense of 'glow.' There is no recorded
example of the use of 'glew' in this
sense, but it is parallel with 'shew' for
'show.' The usual emendation is 'dew'.
Margoliouth emends to 'lew' (warmth)
and suggests that the printer repeated
the 'g' at the end of 'morning.'

867–869 *An Horatian ode . . .*] not
in the White or Harvard copies of 1681;
text from the British Museum copy (C.
59. i. 8), one of the two copies containing this poem, which was canceled
in all other known copies. The poem
was first reprinted by Thompson, in his
edition of 1776, possibly from a ms.
Cromwell returned from Ireland at the
close of May, 1650, to direct the cam-
paign in Scotland. Margoliouth notes
that it has been suggested that the poem
represents the attitude of Lord Fairfax,
'but evidence is lacking that the poet's
acquaintance with Fairfax had begun at
the time of the General's retirement.'
47–52 Hampton . . . Carisbrooke's]
Margoliouth quotes from Sir Charles
Firth's *Cromwell:* 'Contemporary pam-
phleteers and memoir writers often put
forward the theory that Cromwell
frightened the King into his flight from
Hampton Court [to Carisbrooke] in
order to forward his own ambitious designs. . . . There is no evidence in support of this theory. In the long run, the
King's flight was one of the causes of
his dethronement and execution, and so
of Cromwell's elevation to supreme
power. At the moment, it increased
Cromwell's difficulties, and added to the
dangers which beset the Government.'
68 Capitol's] temple of Jupiter at Rome,
said to have been called the Capitol because a human head (caput) was discovered in digging the foundations.
This discovery was interpreted as a
favorable sign. 106 parti-colored] a
pun on the derivation of Pict from
'pingere.'

KATHERINE PHILIPS

KATHERINE PHILIPS (1631–1664) was the leader of a romantically minded
coterie in Cardigan, Wales. Having 'an incorrigible inclination to that
folly of rhyming,' she has perpetuated some memory of the group. Fictitious
names were taken by its members: Mrs. Philips was Orinda, always 'the
matchless Orinda' to her friends; her husband was Antenor; her principal

friend, Miss Anne Owen, was Lucasia. From the circulation of her poems in manuscript, she attained a wide reputation. On a visit to Dublin she was encouraged to translate Corneille's *Pompey*, and the Earl of Orrery had it produced with great success. In the last year of her life appeared an unauthorized edition of her poems, to which she objected in many verbose letters to her literary friends. An authorized edition was published in 1667, edited by 'Poliarchus', Sir Charles Cotterel, with an imposing list of prefatory verses.

MODERN EDITION: 'Katherine Philips' in *Minor Poets of the Caroline Period* (ed. by G. Saintsbury), Vol. i, Oxford, 1905.

COMMENT: E. W. Gosse, 'The Matchless Orinda' in *17th Century Studies*, London, 1883.

TEXT: *Poems*, 1667, Harvard.

869 *Friendship's mystery*] This poem was set to music by Henry Lawes in his *Airs and Dialogues* of 1655.

ALEXANDER BROME

ALEXANDER BROME (1620–1666) was a London attorney who, at the time of the Civil War, became a dashing Royalist trooper and a writer of Bacchanalian poems which stirred the hearts of the Cavaliers in their campaigns and cheered them during their dull days of poverty under the Commonwealth. Phillips styles him 'the English Anacreon' because his poetry was of 'so jovial a strain, that among the sons of mirth and Bacchus, to whom his sack-inspired songs have been so often sung to the sprightly violin, his name cannot choose but be immortal.' Brome wrote one play, *The Cunning Lovers*, and edited the plays of Richard Brome, to whom it seems he was not related. He also edited a variorum translation of Horace. It is thought that he was the editor of *Rump Songs*, a collection of Royalist songs and poems relating to the Civil War and the Commonwealth, published anonymously in 1662. Many of Brome's poems appeared in the drolleries, so popular just before and after the Restoration. For Brome's translation of Jonson's *Leges Convivales* see p. 513.

MODERN EDITIONS: 'Poems' in *English Poets* (ed. by A. Chalmers), Vol. vi, London, 1810; *Songs and Poems*, Louisville, 1924.

TEXT: *Songs and other Poems*, 1661, Harvard; *Songs and other Poems*, 1664, Harvard.

872–873 *The royalist* 30 circular] 1661 'circlar', but it seems evident that the 'u' was dropped out.

873 *The pastoral on the King's death. Written in 1648*] Charles I was beheaded on January 30, 1649, which according to the old calendar, then in use in England, was 1648.

873 *For General Monk, his entertainment at Clothworkers' Hall*] on March 13, 1660.

874 *Palinode* 30 Where] Whether.

STUART AND COMMONWEALTH MISCELLANIES

THE SERIES of Elizabethan miscellanies came to an end with Davison's *Poetical Rhapsody*, 1602. From that date until the publication of *Wit's Recreations* in 1640, no miscellany appeared which has attracted much attention. Commonplace-books were kept by lovers of poetry even more assiduously than during the reign of Elizabeth, but not one of excellence came into the hands of a printer. Perhaps the song-books, in which so many lyrics suitable for publication in miscellanies were appearing, took the place of the earlier miscellanies. During these years a few volumes carried on the miscellany tradition: Camden's *Remains concerning Britain*, 1605, in which a few scattered pieces of poetry, principally epigrams and epitaphs, were published; Richard Johnson's *Crown Garland of Golden Roses*, 1612, a miscellaneous collection of ballads, largely historical; W. B. and E. P.'s *Help to Discourse*, 1619, which (though largely made up of prose questions and answers, riddles, and jests) contained sections of epigrams and epitaphs; Weever's *Ancient Funeral Monuments*, 1631, containing many elegies and epitaphs; R. S.'s *Description of the King and Queen of Fairies*, 1635, noteworthy for containing the first of Herrick's poems to appear in print; and Samuel Pick's *Festum Voluptatis*, 1639, a miscellany of 'divers choice love-posies, songs, etc.'

A new series, reflecting the increased interest in cleverness, begins with *Wit's Recreations* in 1640. This volume of epigrams, epitaphs, anagrams, and lyrics proved exceptionally popular, and was reprinted with additional poems in 1641, 1645, 1650, 1654, 1663, and 1667. 'Wit' was needed to attract readers during the nervous tension of the Civil War and the Commonwealth, and the editors of many of the succeeding miscellanies used the term in their titles: John Cotgrave's *Wit's Interpreter*, 1655; J. Phillips's *Sportive Wit*, 1656; *Wit and Drollery*, 1656; Henry Bold's *Wit a-Sporting*, 1657; and James Smith's *Wit Restored*, 1658. In the titles of the more scoffing, vulgar miscellanies, the term 'drollery' came to be used, first in *Songs and Poems of Love and Drollery*, 1654, followed by *Wit and Drollery*, listed above, and *Choice Drollery*, 1656. In addition to these, two other well-known miscellanies must be named: *Musarum Deliciæ*, published in 1656 by Sir John Mennis and James Smith, a volume which depended on a coarse vulgarity to win readers; and Abraham Wright's *Parnassus Biceps*, 1656, which gathered up poems 'written by the best wits that were in both the Universities before their dissolution.'

These miscellanies were the work of Cavaliers, relieving the tedium of their life during the Commonwealth. They contain earlier as well as contemporary poems. The poetry usually has a spirited movement, and occasionally the sparkle of real wit or the gleam of beauty. But some of the volumes are marred by gross vulgarity and by indecent satirizing of the Puritans, who retaliated by suppressing the most objectionable.

During these years there were, also, several volumes appearing as the work of individual authors which were in reality miscellanies. The two editions of the poems of Francis Beeaumont, in 1640 and in 1653, contain a few of his poems and many by other hands, and in the numerous editions of John Cleveland there are many metaphysical atrocities which are not his. The *Reliquiæ Wottonianæ* has a closing section of poems, by various authors, found among Wotton's papers; and a volume of 1660, which pretends to print the poems of William Herbert, Earl of Pembroke, and Sir Benjamin Rudyerd, is largely made up of poems by others.

CROSS REFERENCES: Poems, not in this section, which also appeared in late miscellanies: Elizabethan Miscellanies, *To Colin Clout*, Ode 'Absence, hear thou'; Daniel, *Love is a sickness;* Drayton, *The crier;* Songs from Plays, 'Back and side go bare,' 'Hence all you vain delights,' 'Let the bells ring'; Campion, *Young and simple though I am;* Donne, *Break of day, The autumnal;* Jonson, *Epitaph on Elizabeth, L. H., A fit of rhyme against rhyme, Still to be neat, Beauties, have ye seen;* Bacon, *In vitam humanam;* Wotton, *On his mistress, the Queen of Bohemia;* Browne, *On the Countess Dowager of Pembroke;* Basse, *On Mr. William Shakespeare;* Strode, *The commendation of music, On Chloris walking in the snow;* Townshend, *Victorious beauty, What is most to be liked in a mistress;* Herrick, *His farewell to sack, The welcome to sack, Upon love, To the virgins, to make much of time, How violets came blue, Oberon's feast, The wake;* Carew, *A song* 'Ask me no more,' *Disdain returned;* Suckling, *Song* 'Why so pale,' *Sonnet II, A ballad upon a wedding, Out upon it!, Song* 'I prithee send me back'; Lovelace, *To Amarantha;* Quarles, *Hos ego versiculos;* Crashaw, *Wishes to his supposed mistress;* John Hall, *The call;* Sherburne, *Chloris' eyes and breasts;* Davenant, *Song* 'O thou that sleep'st'; Waller, *Song* 'Go, lovely rose.'

MODERN EDITIONS: *Musarum Deliciæ,* with *Wit Restored* and *Wit's Recreations,* two volumes, London, n. d.; *Choyce Drollery* (ed. by J. W. Ebsworth), Boston, Lincolnshire, 1876; *Parnassus Biceps* (ed. by G. Thorn-Drury), London, 1927.

TEXT: *A Help to Discourse,* 1619 (1547), Bodleian; *Wit's Recreations,* 1641, B. M.; *Wit's Recreations,* 1645, B. M.; *Reliquiæ Wottonianæ,* 1651, Cornell; *Musarum Deliciæ,* 1656, Huntington; *Sportive Wit,* 1656, Bodleian; *Parnassus Biceps,* 1656, Harvard; *Choice Drollery,* 1656, Bodleian; *Wit Restored,* 1658, Harvard.

875–876 *A memento for mortality*] This earliest printed version of the poem usually called *On the tombs in Westminster* was discovered by Ault, *17th Century Lyrics,* p. 524. The volume in which it appears is sometimes, but very doubtfully, attributed to William Basse. The poem was next printed in John Weever's *Ancient Funeral Monuments,* 1631, in a text offering only three minor variants from the earlier text here printed. As a rule, Weever is scrupulous in giving his sources, but unfortunately no author's name is given for this poem. In *Wit's Recreations,* 1640, a shorter version of eighteen lines, with the title, *In monumenta Westminsteriensia,* was printed. This shorter version was again printed in the 1653 edition of Beaumont's *Poems,* with the title, *On the tombs in Westminster,* where it followed elegies on Spenser, Shakespeare, Drayton, and Jonson. The appearance in Beaumont's *Poems* cannot be taken as evidence of his authorship, for many of the poems in the volume are not from his pen. The better known and shortened version of the poem as printed in *Wit's Recreations,* 1640, consists of our ll. 1–4, 19–30, 33, and a new line, 'Buried in dust, once dead by fate.' 21 ceiled] canopied; 1619 'seal'd'. 42 nightly] 1619 'nighty'. 43–44] cf. *Hamlet,* V. i: 'let her paint an inch thick, to this favor she must come.'

876 *Interrogativa cantilena*] 'An interrogative songlet.'

877–878 *A description . . .*] This poem, signed 'Ignoto', appears in a short section of miscellaneous poems, headed 'Poems found among the papers of S[ir] H. Wotton,' at the end of *Re-*

liquiæ Wottonianæ. 52 pitch] 1651 'picth'.

878 *The nightingale*] The first two lines suggest at once the mood of Keats in his famous ode.

879 *Chloris, forbear a while*] later reprinted with variant readings in Henry Bold's *Poems, lyric, macaronic, heroic,* 1664. The poem was set to music by John Gamble in his *Airs and Dialogues,* 1659. 8 shine] 1664; 1656 'slime'. 11 suit] 1664; 1656 'shent'. 12 makes] 1664; 1656 'make'.

879–880 *The liberty and requiem . . .*] In *Harleian Ms.* 3511, this poem is headed: 'Mr. Le Strange his verses in the prison at Linn.' 17 sophies] wise men, sages; here used in a disparaging, sarcastic sense. 31 Jason's] a tyrant of Pheræ, whose life was despaired of by his physicians because of an imposthume in his chest. An assassin, with intent to murder, stabbed him in the chest, thereby opening the imposthume and saving his life. 38 margarite] pearl.

881–882 *The contented prisoner . . .* 44 Buff] one who wears a buff-coat, a soldier. 57 course] 1656 'coruse'.

882–883 *Phillada flouts me*] referred to as a new tune in Richard Johnson's *Crown Garland of Golden Roses,* 1612. This poem appeared several times as a broadside ballad, and is printed in *Shirburn Ballads,* p. 296, and *Roxburghe Ballads,* vi. 461. 22 askance] 1658 'a sconce'. 38 Coventry] a blue thread used for embroidery, manufactured at Coventry. 53 Wigg] a kind of raised seed-cake, or currant bun; but it should be noted that the word intended here by 'wigg' may be 'whig,' variously used for 'sour milk' or 'buttermilk.'

INDEX

*Authors' names are printed in small capitals, titles of poems in italics, and
first lines of poems in roman.*